Advances in Sport

AND

Exercise Psychology Measurement

Joan L. Duda, Ph.D.
Purdue University
Editor

Fitness Information Technology, Inc.

P.O. Box 4425, University Avenue
Morgantown, WV 26504-4425 USA

Loughborough
College

Library of Congress Card Catalog Number: 97-77311

ISBN 1-885693-11-7

Cover Design: Pegasus
Copyeditor: Sandra R. Woods
Production Editor: Craig Hines
Printed by: BookCrafters

Printed in the United States of America
10 9 8 7 6 5 4 3 2

Fitness Information Technology, Inc.
P.O. Box 4425, University Ave.
Morgantown, WV 26504-4425 USA
(800) 477–4348
(304) 599–3482 (phone/fax)
E-mail: fit@fitinfotech.com
Website: www.fitinfotech.com

DEDICATION

This book is dedicated to the loving memory of my Aunt Margie

... and to the memory of two people
who have been influential in my life
and were taken from all of us much too soon,
John G. Nicholls, and, in particular, my father, Joseph Duda,

... and in honor of my family and dearest friends.
Your love and support inspires me each day.

ABOUT THE EDITOR

Joan L. Duda

Dr. Joan L. Duda is a full professor in the Department of Health, Kinesiology, and Leisure Studies and Adjunct Professor in the Department of Psychological Sciences at Purdue University. She received her Ph.D. in sport and exercise psychology in 1981 from the University of Illinois at Urbana-Champaign. Dr. Duda has been a member of the executive boards of the North American Society for the Psychology of Sport and Physical Activity, the Sport Psychology Academy, the International Society of Sport Psychology, and is a Fellow of the American Academy of Kinesiology and Physical Education. She is a past editor of the *Journal of Applied Sport Psychology* and remains on the editorial board of this journal as well as the *Journal of Sport and Exercise Psychology*. Dr. Duda has over 80 scholarly publications focused on sport and motivation and the psychological dimensions of sport and exercise behavior. She has been an invited speaker in 15 countries around the world. For over 10 years, Dr. Duda has been involved in applied work with athletes and coaches in a variety of sports at all competitive levels. She is a Certified Consultant of AAASP and is listed on the U.S. Olympic Committee's Sport Psychology Registry. Since 1992, Dr. Duda has been the consultant for the USA Gymnastics Women's Artistic Program. Her hobbies include music, traveling, and playing tennis.

TABLE OF CONTENTS

Part V   Aggression and Morality in Sport

Part VI   Self Concept and Body Image

Part VII   Exercise-Related Cognitions, Affect, and Motivation

Part VIII   Special Considerations and Alternative Approaches

CONTRIBUTORS

Bruce Abernethy

Dr. Bruce Abernethy is a professor and Head of the Department of Human Movement Studies at the University of Queensland, Australia. He is an international Fellow of the American Academy of Kinesiology and Physical Education and a Fellow of Sports Medicine Australia. Dr. Abernethy's main research interests are on the nature of expert performance in motor skills, with particular emphasis on the coupling of perception and action.

Anthony J. Amorose

Mr. Anthony J. Amorose received a M.S. degree in health and sport studies from Miami University. He is currently working towards a Ph.D. in sport and exercise psychology at the University of Virginia. His research interests include the examination of factors that influence the psychosocial development of athletes across the lifespan, with a particular emphasis on how coaching behaviors influence athletes' self-perceptions and motivation.

Susan M. Bane

Dr. Susan M. Bane received her Ph.D. in Kinesiology and her M.D. from the University of Illinois. She is currently completing her residency in obstetrics and gynecology at East Carolina University. Dr. Bane's research efforts have been directed largely at the examination of physical activity influence on body image and the role played by social cognitive factors in this relationship. She also has a strong interest in women's health.

Stuart Biddle

Dr. Stuart Biddle is a reader in exercise and sport psychology in the School of Health Sciences, University of Exeter, UK. He is director of the master's degree in exercise and sport psychology at this university, the first of its kind in the UK, and he coordinated the European master's programme in this field from 1993 to 1997. Dr. Biddle is President of the European Federation of Sport Psychology. He has published widely on aspects of motivation and emotion, including attributions, goals, climate, attitudes, and affect.

Bryan Blissmer

Mr. Bryan Blissmer completed his M.S. degree at Miami University with a focus on health appraisal and enhancement. He is presently a doctoral student in sport and exercise psychology at the University of Illinois.

Lawrence R. Brawley

Dr. Lawrence R. Brawley (Ph.D., The Pennsylvania State University) is a professor and Associate Chair, Graduate Studies, in the Department of Kinesiology, and cross-appointed professor in the Department of Health Studies and Gerontology, University of Waterloo, Canada. He is also an adjunct research professor, Department of Health and Exercise Science, Wake Forest University. Dr. Brawley is on the Editorial Board of the *Journal of Sport and Exercise Psychology* and the *Journal of Applied Sport Psychology*. He has published extensively on group cohesion in exercise and sport and on research applications of social psychology in health and exercise, particularly social factors influencing adherence and compliance behavior. Dr. Brawley is a Past President and Fellow in the Association for the Advancement of Applied Sport Psychology.

Brenda L. Bredemeier

Dr. Brenda Light Bredemeier is a sport psychology professor affiliated with the School of Education and a Dean in the College of Letters and Science at the University of California at Berkeley. Her research program focuses on moral development and action in physical education and sport contexts, with a special emphasis on the experiences of at-risk children, youth sport participants, and female athletes.

Robert J. Brustad

Dr. Robert Brustad is an associate professor at the University of Northern Colorado in the School of Kinesiology and Physical Education. His research focuses on socialization influences upon children's motivational processes in sport and physical activity settings. A particular area of focus is upon parental values and belief systems as they affect children's cognitive and affective outcomes in these contexts. He is currently the chair of the social psychology section of the Association for the Advancement of Applied Sport Psychology and an Associate Editor of the *Journal of Sport and Exercise Psychology*.

Damon Burton

Dr. Damon Burton is a professor of sport psychology in the Division of HPERD at the University of Idaho. Competitive anxiety is one of his major research interests, and he has co-authored a popular anxiety text, *Competitive Anxiety in Sport*, with University of Illinois colleagues Rainer Martens and Robin Vealey, as well as collaborated in the development of two popular measures of state anxiety, the CSAI-1 and CSAI-2. Dr. Burton has also authored numerous journal articles and three book chapters on competitive anxiety. His current research is focused on using Lazarus' model of emotion to better understand the antecedents of competitive anxiety. Dr. Burton enjoys spending time in the Idaho outdoors camping, backpacking, rafting, mountain biking, playing softball, golfing, coaching his three sons in various sports, and working as a sport psychologist with various high school, college, and Olympic athletes.

Albert Carron

Dr. Albert V. Carron (Ed.D., California) is a professor of kinesiology, cross-appointed in the Department of Psychology at the University of Western Ontario in London, Ontario. Currently, he is the Editor of the *Journal of Applied Sport Psychology* and a member of the Editorial Board of the *Journal of Sport and Exercise Psychology*. Dr. Carron is a Fellow of the Association for the Advancement of Applied Sport Psychology and the Canadian Psychomotor Learning and Sport Psychology Society and Past President of the Canadian Association of Sport Sciences. Over the past 20 years, his research has focused on group dynamics in sport and exercise. Dr. Carron is the author of five books, including *Social psychology of sport*, *Motivation: Implications for coaching and teaching*, and *Group dynamics: Theoretical and practical issues*.

Melissa A. Chase

Dr. Melissa Chase is currently with the Department of Physical Education, Health, and Sport Studies at Miami University. Her graduate work was completed at Michigan State University in the areas of sport psychology and psychosocial aspects of teaching and learning. Dr. Chase's research interests are in the area of self-efficacy and the relationship to motivation, sources of self-efficacy, and development in children, teachers, and coaches. She is a certified AAASP consultant who has worked with athletes and coaches at a variety of competitive levels in the areas of team building and individual confidence.

Packianathan Chelladurai

Dr. Packianathan Chelladurai received his Ph.D. at the University of Waterloo and is currently a professor of sport management at The Ohio State University. He has published over 70 articles, two books, and two monographs and serves on the Editorial Board of the *Journal of Sport Management* and *European Journal of Sport Management*. Dr. Chelladurai is a frequent reviewer for the *Journal of Sport and Exercise Psychology* and the *Journal of Applied Sport Psychology*.

Peter Crocker

Dr. Peter Crocker received his Ph.D. from the University of Alberta after receiving a B.A. (psychology) and a M.Sc. (kinesiology) from Simon Fraser University. He is a professor in the College of Physical Education at the University of Saskatchewan. A past president of the Canadian Society of Psychomotor Learning and Sport Psychology, he is currently the Editor of *The Sport Psychologist*. His research focuses on stress, coping, and emotion, as well as the measurement of activity in school-age children. He has coached both university level and provincial all-star youth women's soccer teams.

Edward Etzel

Dr. Edward Etzel is an associate professor in the Sport Behavior Program within the School of Physical Education and a psychologist for intercollegiate athletics at West Virginia University. At WVU, he teaches a variety of applied sport psychology courses such as psychological aspects of sport performance, psychological aspects of sport injury, and counseling athletes. Dr. Etzel is a licensed psychologist who is listed on the U.S. Olympic Committee's Sport Psychology Registry, and he has been a member of the AAASP Ethics Committee since 1993. He was a Gold Medalist in shooting at the 1984 Olympics.

Deborah L. Feltz

Dr. Deborah Feltz is a professor and Chairperson of the Department of Physical Education and Exercise Science at Michigan State University. She received her Ph.D. in physical education in 1980 from The Pennsylvania State University. Her research interests have focused on the interrelationships among self-efficacy, anxiety, and sport performance among youth, women, and athletic teams. Dr. Feltz is a Fellow of the American Academy of Kinesiology and Physical Education and the American Psychological Association. She served on the sport psychology advisory committee to the U.S. Olympic Committee and currently serves on the editorial boards of the *Journal of Sport and Exercise Psychology* and *Quest*.

Gerard Fogarty

Dr. Gerry Fogarty is Head of the Department of Psychology at the University of Southern Queensland. He completed his Ph.D. at the University of Sydney, in psychometrics and individual differences. He is a member of the College of Sport Psychology in Australia. His teaching and research interests center on the theme of psychological measurement.

Stephen Ford

Mr. Stephen Ford is completing his Ph.D. in psychology at the University of Melbourne, Australia. His research has addressed the issue of attention in sport, with particular reference to its theoretical construction and measurement. He has a broad interest in sport psychology issues, with a special interest in research methodology.

Michelle Fortier

Dr. Michelle Fortier is an assistant professor at the School of Human Kinetics at the University of Ottawa. She earned her Ph.D. in social psychology from the University of Quebec in Montreal in 1994. Her research areas of interest include the social psychology of exercise and health with an emphasis on motivation, self-perceptions, and gender differences. Dr. Fortier is a member of the Association for the Advancement of Applied Sport Psychology and the American Psychological Association and is a guest reviewer for the *Journal of Sport and Exercise Psychology*.

Kenneth Fox

Dr. Kenneth Fox is a reader in exercise and public health at the University of Exeter in the United Kingdom. He is the author of the Physical Self-Perception Profile and editor of a recently published book entitled *The Physical Self: From Motivation to Well-Being*. Dr. Fox has over 100 research and professional publications, including 28 book chapters. His research areas of interest include physical self-perceptions, exercise and sport motivation, and the relationship between exercise and public health.

Megan Garner-Holman

Ms. Megan Garner-Holman is the Assistant Director of High Performance for USA Field Hockey in Colorado Springs. She completed a M.S. degree in sport psychology at Miami University. Her research and consulting interests focus on the impact of coaching efficacy and behaviors on athletes as well as sources of confidence in athletic participants.

Lise Gauvin

Dr. Lise Gauvin is an associate professor in the Department of Exercise Science at Concordia University in Montreal, Canada. Her research focuses on the psychological outcomes and determinants of acute and chronic physical activity. Dr. Gauvin's work has been funded by national and provincial granting agencies, and the results of her research have been published in several scientific journals including *Health Psychology*, *Nutrition Reviews*, the *Journal of Drug Education*, and the *Journal of Sport and Exercise Psychology*.

Thomas Graham

Mr. Thomas Graham is a Ph.D. student in the College of Physical Education at the University of Saskatchewan. He received his undergraduate degree in psychology from the University of Manitoba and a masters degree from the University of Idaho. His dissertation is examining the influence of goal importance, goal discrepancy, and attributions on discrete emotion in adolescent sport settings. He was a member of Canada's 1976 Olympic volleyball team, he coached the University of Saskatchewan team to the National Championship, and he was recognized by his coaching peers as the coach of the year.

Nancy C. Gyurcsik

Ms. Nancy Gyurcsik is currently a doctoral student in the Department of Kinesiology at the University of Waterloo. She recently received a 2-year doctoral fellowship award from the Social Sciences and Humanities Research Council of Canada for academic scholarship. Her specific research is in the area of perceived control and its relationship to motivation. Her general interests concern the application of social psychology to problems in health, exercise, and sport domains. She has presented this work (with Drs. Brawley and Martin) at several scientific meetings, including the Society for Behavioral Medicine, the North American Society for the Psychology of Sport and Physical Activity, and the Association for the Advancement of Applied Sport Psychology.

Craig Hall

Dr. Craig Hall is a professor at the University of Western Ontario who has been investigating the role of imagery in motor skill performance and learning for the past 20 years. Two of his primary interests have been the measurement of movement imagery abilities, and the assessment of the cognitive and motivational uses of imagery by athletes. He has recently begun to examine the use of imagery by exercise participants.

Stephanie Hanrahan

Dr. Stephanie Hanrahan completed her doctorate at The University of Western Australia. She is currently a senior lecturer in the Department of Human Movement Studies and the School of Psychology at The University of Queensland. Dr. Hanrahan's main research interests include mental skills training, attributional style, and pedagogy in sport psychology. She works as a sport psychology consultant with athletes and coaches from a variety of sports and competitive levels.

Carl T. Hayashi

Dr. Carl Hayashi is an assistant professor in the Department of Health, Physical Education and Recreation at Texas Tech University. His areas of specialization within the social psychology of sport and exercise are cross-cultural differences, motivation, and developmental differences. Dr. Hayashi's comparative research experiences include the examination of Japanese and Hawaiian cultural perspectives in physical activity settings.

Thelma Horn

Dr. Thelma Horn is an associate professor in the Department of Physical Education, Health, and Sport Studies at Miami University. She is the current editor of the *Journal of Sport and Exercise Psychology* and has also edited a sport psychology textbook entitled *Advances in Sport Psychology*. Dr. Horn's primary research interests center on the study of children's self-perceptions in sport and physical activity contexts. In particular, she is interested in examining how children's self-perceptions are affected by the behavior of the significant adults in their life.

Jay Kimiecik

Dr. Jay Kimiecik is an associate professor in the Department of Physical Education, Health, and Sport Studies at Miami University. His current research interests focus on optimal experience states (e.g., flow) and their role in people's motivation to participate in exercise. Dr. Kimiecik also studies the psychosocial aspects of parental influence on children's physical activity, but because he is a father of two young children, he is becoming increasingly interested in the influence of children's physical activity on parental well-being.

Kent Kowalski

Mr. Kent Kowalski is a Ph.D. student in the College of Physical Education at the University of Saskatchewan. He received his undergraduate degree in psychology and completed his masters degree in physical education, both at the University of Saskatchewan. His dissertation focuses on coping and emotion. Mr. Kowalski has an extensive background in soccer, playing several years of professional soccer after a stellar university career that saw him receive All-Canadian recognition.

Kathleen A. Martin

Dr. Kathleen Martin is currently at Wake Forest University where she is completing a 2-year Social Sciences and Humanities Research Council of Canada postdoctoral fellowship. After receiving her Ph.D. from the Department of Kinesiology, University of Waterloo (with Dr. L. Brawley), Dr. Martin chose to conduct her postdoctoral work with Drs. Mark Leary (psychology) and Jack Rejeski (health and exercise science) at Wake Forest. Her interests and publications concern self-presentation, its relationship to health and aging, and the application of social psychology to health, exercise, and sport contexts. Dr. Martin was the recipient of the 1997 Dissertation Award for Division 47 of the American Psychological Association.

Edward McAuley

Dr. Edward McAuley received his Ph.D. from the University of Iowa and is currently a professor with the Department of Kinesiology at the University of Illinois. He has published widely in the area of physical activity, aging, and psychological health. He is particularly interested in the role played by self-efficacy in acute and chronic effects of exercise on various aspects of psychological function. He serves on the editorial boards of several journals and has been named a University Scholar at Illinois.

Penny McCullagh

Dr. Penny McCullagh is an associate professor in the Department of Kinesiology at the University of Colorado at Boulder. Her primary research interests include the influence of modeling or observational learning on both physical and psychological skills across exercise, rehabilitation, and sport settings. She has conducted research with both children and adults on motivation for participation in physical activity. Dr. McCullagh has been president of the Association for the Advancement of Applied Sport Psychology.

Shannon L. Mihalko

Dr. Shannon L. Mihalko received her Ph.D. in kinesiology from the University of Illinois and is currently an assistant professor in the Department of Kinesiology at Pennsylvania State University specializing in exercise psychology. Her research interests focus upon the role of social cognitive factors in physical activity effects on the physical and psychological health of older adults. She also has a strong interest in epidemiology and received a master of science degree in this field of study from the University of Illinois.

Shane Murphy

Dr. Shane Murphy received his doctorate in clinical psychology from Rutgers University. He was sport psychologist to the USA Olympic Team at the 1988 Summer Games in Seoul and the 1992 Winter Games in Albertville, and he worked for the United States Olympic Committee (USOC) for 7 years as Head of the Sport Psychology Department. From 1992 to 1994, he was also

Associate Director of the USOC's Division of Sport Science and Technology. Dr. Murphy co-founded Gold Medal Psychological Consultants to teach sport and business organizations the competitive skills which lead to success, and he currently consults with organizations including Pepsi, Siemens-Rolm, Paine-Webber, and Bristol-Myers Squibb. He is presently the President of Division 47 of the American Psychological Association.

Bruce Noble

Dr. Bruce Noble is professor emeritus from Purdue University and co-author of the recently published book entitled *Perceived Exertion*. He invited Professor Gunnar Borg to the University of Pittsburgh in 1967 during which time the Borg Scale was introduced, and a long-time research collaboration was initiated.

John Noble

Mr. John Noble recently completed doctoral study at the University of Colorado and is currently an assistant professor of Health, Physical Education, and Recreation at the University of Nebraska-Omaha.

Frank Perna

Dr. Frank Perna serves as an assistant professor in the sport behavior program within the School of Physical Education at West Virginia University. Dr. Perna is a licensed psychologist and an AAASP Certified Consultant. He also is listed on the U.S. Olympic Committee Sport Psychology Registry.

Harold Riemer

Dr. Harold A. Riemer is an assistant professor of sport management in the Department of Kinesiology and Health Education at the University of Texas at Austin where he teaches the graduate and undergraduate sport marketing and management theory courses. He has previously taught at Bowling Green State University. He received his B.Ed. from the University of Alberta, his M.Ed. from Eastern Washington University, and his Ph.D. from the Ohio State University. His sport psychology-related research has focused on the areas of leadership behavior, athlete satisfaction, and commitment. Beyond that, his research includes the areas of organizational effectiveness and administrative support for coaches.

Robert Schutz

Dr. Robert Schutz is a professor, and past Director, of the School of Human Kinetics at the University of British Columbia. He has served as President of the NASPSPA and of the Canadian Association of Sport Sciences. His publications deal with statistical and measurement issues in human kinetics research, with a specific focus on the measurement and analysis of change, and have in appeared in such journals as *Chance*, *Developmental Psychology*, *Educational and Psychological Measurement*, *Journal of Exercise and Sport Psychology*, *Journal of the Operational Research Society*, and *Research Quarterly for Exercise and Sport*.

David L. Shields

Dr. David Light Shields has been conducting research for more than 15 years in the area of moral development in sport. He has taught at the University of California at Berkeley, John F. Kennedy University, Pacific School of Religion, and other San Francisco Bay Area schools. Currently, he is the Education Manager with the ANR Foundation in Berkeley, California.

Ronald Smith

Dr. Ronald E. Smith is professor of psychology at the University of Washington. His major interests center on the study of stress and coping, cognitive-behavioral approaches to performance enhancement, and youth sports. He has helped develop the Sport Anxiety Scale and the Athletic Coping Skills Inventory-28, both of which are described in this volume. Dr. Smith is a past president of the Association for the Advancement of Applied Sport Psychology, and he has served as Director of Clinical Psychology Training, Head of the Social Psychology and Personality program, and co-director of the sport psychology doctoral program at Washington.

Frank Smoll

Dr. Frank L. Smoll is professor of psychology and Director of Graduate Studies in Psychology at the University of Washington, where he also serves as co-director of the sport psychology doctoral program. His major interests are in the area of youth sports research and intervention. He has helped to develop and evaluate Coach Effectiveness Training, an intervention that is designed to improve the quality of coach-athlete relationships. He also is co-director of Husky Sport Psychology Services, which provides performance-enhancement interventions to athletes and coaches at Washington.

John C. Spence

Mr. John Spence holds the position of Research Coordinator at the Alberta Center for Well-Being (University of Alberta) in Edmonton, Alberta, and he is currently completing his doctoral dissertation through Concordia University, Montreal, Canada. His doctoral research consists of an extensive meta-analysis of the literature dealing with the health and performance outcomes of androgenic-anabolic steroid use. Mr. Spence's work has been published in scientific journals including the *Journal of Drug Education*, *Nutrition Reviews*, and the *Review of Educational Research*.

Dawn Stephens

Dr. Dawn Stephens is an assistant professor in the Department of Sport, Health, Leisure, and Physical Studies at the University of Iowa. Since completing her doctorate degree at the University of California at Berkeley, her research continues to focus on the aggressive and cheating tendencies of sport participants, particularly as these tendencies relate to moral and motivational factors. She is currently involved in research examining the moral atmosphere of youth sport contexts. Her recreational pursuits include woodworking, badminton, squash, and walking her Welsh corgi.

Jeffery Summers

Dr. Jeffery Summers is Foundation Professor of Psychology at the University of Southern Queensland, Australia. He has published extensively in human motor control and learning, particularly in issues relating to coordination of movement. In the sport psychology field, his research interests include attentional mechanisms in sport, the stress-performance relationship, predisposition to injury, and exercise addiction.

Vance Tammen

Dr. Vance Tammen is a lecturer in sport psychology at Victoria University of Technology in Melbourne, Australia. He teaches undergraduate and graduate classes in current issues in sport psychology, applied sport psychology, and group processes in sport and exercise. His research focuses on issues in the social psychology of sport, particularly achievement goal orientations, motivational climate, athlete career transitions, and measurement issues with psychological testing. He is a registered sport psychologist and consults with local, national, international, and professional athletes and umpires.

Gershon Tenenbaum

Dr. Gershon Tenenbaum is an associate professor and graduate program coordinator at the University of Southern Queensland in Australia. He is the President of the International Society of Sport Psychology and the former director of the Department of Research and Sport Medicine at the Wingate Institute in Israel. He graduated from Tel Aviv University and the University of Chicago in measurement, evaluation, and statistical analysis. His main areas of teaching and research are in psychometrics and sport-related cognition.

Robert J. Vallerand

Dr. Robert Vallerand is a full professor in the Department of Psychology and Director of the Research Laboratory on Social Behavior at the University of Quebec at Montreal. He earned his doctoral degree from the University of Montreal and pursued post-doctoral studies in experimental social psychology at the University of Waterloo. Dr. Vallerand has been President of the Quebec Society for Research in Psychology, President of the Social Psychology section of the Canadian Psychological Association, and Associate Editor of the Canadian Journal of Behavioral Sciences. He is a Fellow of the Canadian Psychological Association and, in 1995, received the Sport Science Award from the International Olympic Committee. Dr. Vallerand has published three books and more than 100 articles and book chapters mainly in the area of human motivation.

Robin S. Vealey

Dr. Robin S. Vealey is a professor in the Department of Physical Education, Health, and Sport Studies at Miami University in Ohio. Dr. Vealey's research interests include competitive stress, anxiety and burnout, self-confidence in sport, coaching behavior, and psychological skills training. She has served as a sport psychology consultant for the U.S. Nordic Ski Team, U.S. Field Hockey, elite golfers, and athletes and teams at Miami University and in the Cincinnati area. Dr. Vealey is a Fellow and Certified Consultant of AAASP, past editor of *The Sport Psychologist*, and a national instructor for the American Sport Education Program.

W. Neil Widmeyer

Dr. W. Neil Widmeyer (Ph.D., Illinois) is a professor in the Department of Kinesiology at the University of Waterloo. He has just completed a 3-year term as Chair of The Social Psychology Area for the Association for the Advancement of Applied Sport Psychology. Dr. Widmeyer has published widely on the dynamics of sport teams and exercise groups and has conducted considerable research in the area of aggression in sport. He also has received considerable recognition for excellence in teaching. Most recently, Dr. Widmeyer has spent a considerable amount of time in the application of sport psychology with Major Junior A hockey players.

Shelly Wiechman

Ms. Shelley A. Wiechman is a doctoral student in the clinical sport psychology program at the University of Washington, where she provides services to athletes and coaches through the Husky Sport Psychology Program. Her major interests are in athletic identity, psychosocial factors in injuries, performance-enhancement methods, neuropsychological assessment, and health psychology. She has served as a student representative on the Executive Board of the Association for the Advancement of Applied Sport Psychology.

Jean Whitehead

Dr. Jean Whitehead received her Ph.D. from the University of Oregon and a M.Ed. and D.A.S.E. from Manchester University. Her research has focused on motivation in youth sport, and she is currently developing this work in the Chelsea School at the University of Brighton and with the Institute for the Study of Children in Sport, Eastbourne.

Michael Yura

Dr. Michael Yura is a professor in the Department of Counseling Psychology and Rehabilitation Psychology at West Virginia University. Dr. Yura is a licensed psychologist and licensed professional counselor.

FOREWORD

Herbert W. Marsh
University of Western Sydney, Macarthur

As a relative newcomer to the sport and exercise measurement area, I have been impressed with the level of progress in the last decade or so — progress that has been well documented in this monograph. This advancement is the result of more carefully developed instruments, better articulation of the links between instrument design, theory, and practice, and improved application of methodological and statistical techniques. Each of these important components of good measurement is described in chapters throughout the text (e.g., the chapters by Schutz and Tenenbaum and Fogarty discuss statistical advancements in measure development and refinement). Thankfully, the hey day of the "one shot" instrument seems to have ended. As reflected in the critiques of past measurement included in many of this book's chapters, no longer can sport/exercise psychology researchers simply pull together an ad hoc set of items that are more or less related to the construct of interest and claim — with any credibility — that they are utilizing a valid and reliable instrument.

Let me summarize my own idiosyncratic perspectives on this development. Despite recognition of the importance of psychometrically sound measures to research and practice, it is evident that the quality of assessments in early sport/exercise work was weak. Exemplifying the state of the field a number of years ago, Andrew Ostrow (1990) published the *Directory of Psychological Tests in the Sport and Exercise Sciences* in a monumental effort to catalogue sport/exercise measures used over a 25-year period. This volume included all instruments from the published sport/exercise literature with reliability or validity information. In addition to providing the reader with a summary of evidence concerning the psychometric attributes of the instruments, The Directory also provided a barometer for evaluating the quality of measurement in the field. Indeed, one of the expressed intents of the Directory was to force researchers, test authors, reviewers, journal editors, publishers, and test consumers to embrace more stringent criteria concerning the adequacy of the measures employed. However, of the 175 instruments listed in the Directory, only 1/3 of these assessments had items based on a conceptual framework, less than 1/4 reported factor analyses, and less than 10% showed evidence of extensive reference support.

For some time, there seems to have been general agreement among sport/exercise psychology researchers for the need to develop sport-specific instruments and to evaluate them within a construct validity framework. Nelson (1989), summarizing research in a special issue of the *Journal of Physical Education, Recreation, and Dance*, pointed to the need for sport-specific psychological measures and expressed wide-spread concerns about their evaluation. Vealey (1986, p. 222) claimed that significant advances in sport/exercise psychology research "await sport-specific conceptualization and measurement instrumentation." Gill, Dzewaltowski, and Deeter (1988, p. 139-140) concluded that "within sport psychology, the most promising work on individual differences involves the development and use of sport-specific constructs and measures" and argued for the construction of multidimensional instruments based on theory, followed by item and reliability analysis, exploratory and confirmatory factor analysis, tests of convergent and divergent validity, validation in relation to external criteria, and application in research and practice.

With these aims in mind, the present monograph should do much to foster the breadth and depth of measurement in sport/exercise psychology research providing concrete examples of "best practice" in our field and also reviewing weaknesses in current efforts that need to be addressed in future research. For these efforts, the editor, Joan Duda, and her publisher are to be congratulated for bringing together such a broad representation of the best measurement work in sport/exercise psychology.

A Construct Validation Approach

It can be argued that all constructs in sport and exercise psychology are hypothetical and so must be validated using a construct validity approach. However, many of our constructs suffer in that "everybody knows what this is," so that many researchers have not felt compelled to provide appropriate theoretical definition of what they are measuring or to fully evaluate the psychometric properties of responses to their measures. Although the construct validity approach is most typically applied to measures described as psychological tests, it is important to note that the logic of construct validation also applies to other measurement techniques such as interviews, surveys, behavioral observations, and physiological assessments (see Chapter 26 by Vealey and Garner-Holman). For example, even a construct as apparently tangible as "body fat" is a hypothetical construct, as can be readily seen in the diverse and only partly consistent ways that this construct is inferred.

Let me sketch my interpretation of a construct validity approach (Marsh, 1997). This perspective holds that theory, measurement, empirical research, and practice are inexorably intertwined so that the neglect of one will undermine the others. Validation from this perspective seeks to assess the usefulness of interpretations based on responses to the measure, not to establish their absolute truth or reality (see Vealey and Garner-Holman, this volume). Ideally, validation is an on-going process in which theory and practice are used to develop a measure, empirical research is used to test the theory and the measure, both the theory and the measure are revised in relation to research, new research is conducted to test these refinements, and theory and research are used to inform practice. As thoroughly described in many of the chapters in this book, reality seldom matches this ideal. All too often in the not so distant past, measures in the sports sciences (Ostrow, 1990) and other social sciences were largely ad hoc endeavors that were not soundly based on theory, not systematically evaluated, and not refined on the basis of subsequent theoretical or substantive developments. Unfortunately, weak measures undermine research and theory evaluation, thereby limiting their contribution to practice. Adding to these concerns (see Chapter 27 by Kimiecik & Blissmer), it has been suggested that some of our most rigorously researched measures have limited potential for use in applied settings. That is, more work is warranted on the validity and reliability of sport and exercise psychology measurement in practice.

Construct validity investigations can be classified as within-network or between-network studies (see chapter by Fox for a more extensive discussion of this classification). Within-network studies explore the internal structure of a construct. They test, for example, the dimensionality of the construct and may seek to show that the construct has consistent, distinct multidimensional components. Even if a construct is hypothesized to be unidimensional, however, it is important to test empirically this within-network assertion as part of the construct validation process (see Chapter 24 by Tenenbaum & Fogarty). Within-network studies typically employ empirical techniques such as factor analysis or multitrait-multimethod (MTMM) analysis.

Between-network studies attempt to establish a logical, theoretically consistent pattern of relations between measures of a construct and other constructs. The resolution of at least some within-construct issues should be a logical pre-requisite to conducting between-construct research, but researchers are often seduced into pursuing between-network research before they have done the hard work of developing an appropriate measure, evaluating the psychometric properties of responses validating the structure (using item, internal reliability, stability and factor analyses), and revising their measure appropriately. The construct validity approach should incorporate logical, correlational, and experimental approaches to evaluating the validity of a construct:

1. Logical analysis examines the logical consistency of the construct definition, the construction of items based on this definition, the acceptability of the measure's instructions, item format, scoring procedures, etc., the developmental appropriateness of the instrument to the age and maturational levels of the respondents (see Chapter 28 by Brustad), the cross-cultural equivalence of the assessment (see Chapter 29 by Duda & Hayashi), and ethical considerations that may be idiosyncratic to a particular application of the measure (see discussion by Etzel, Yura, & Perna in Chapter 25). Logical analysis is also used to generate a priori predictions to be pursued in research studies as well as to generate counter hypotheses of the interpretation of test scores that are empirically testable.

2. Correlational techniques can be used to investigate the within-network structure of a construct and the between-network relations between the construct and other constructs. Ideally, construct validation research involves relating multiple indicators of the same construct. At the individual item level, multiple indicators of each scale are used to infer internal consistency reliability and evaluate the factor structure underlying items. At the scale level, two measures of the same construct should be substantially correlated with each other (evidence for convergent validity) and less correlated with measures of different constructs (evidence for divergent validity). Responses by one group of respondents (e.g., self-report responses) should be compared to responses by another group (e.g., coaches, external observers) or "objective" measures. Competing interpretations of the same data should be compared to each other. Results from different research methodologies (e.g., qualitative and quantitative) should be compared as should the result from different studies to test the same hypothesis (see Chapter 2 by Duda and Whitehead for a nice illustration of this strategy in regard to the assessment of goal orientations). At each level, the agreement or lack of agreement between multiple indicators should be related back to the construct as a basis of support for the construct validity of interpretations based on the measure. Three correlational techniques that are particularly useful in construct validation are factor analysis, multitrait-multimethod analysis, and path analysis (or structural equation modeling).

3. Experimental techniques are also useful in testing the validity of interpretations of responses to a particular measure. Thus, for example, theory may suggest that a certain intervention should lead to a change in a researcher's selected construct. To the extent that the intervention leads to predicted changes, then there is support for the theory, the measurement instrument, and the intervention. A potentially useful test of a multidimensionality construct is to test whether the intervention influences those dimensions of the construct most relevant to the intervention, but also to ascertain that the intervention does not influence, or has substantially less influence on, those dimensions that it is not intended to influence (e.g., Burton chapter, this volume; Marsh & Peart, 1988). Not only is this approach likely to identify unintended outcomes — good or bad, but it is also likely to provide researchers with a much better understanding of their intervention and the causal processes that it is invoking. Alternatively, it may be important to include multiple outcome measures to establish that there is a consistent pattern of relations among them. For example, Kimiecik and Blissmer (Chapter 27) note that gains in self-reported exercise behavior in exercise intervention studies are rarely validated in relation to other (particularly non self-report) measures, calling into question the construct validity of interpretations of the measures (and the intervention).

The Role of Factor Analysis

The juxtaposition between approaches to factor analysis and instrument construction in sport and exercise psychology provides a useful perspective. Historically, instruments typically consisted of a collection of items designed to broadly cover the domain of interest. Although factor analysis was used widely, the intent of such factor analyses was often to discover the important dimensions of an instrument ex-post facto. A long history of factor analytic techniques demonstrated that this purely exploratory approach to factor analysis is typically ineffective. More recently (see examples provided in the chapters by Carron, Brawley, & Widmeyer; Duda & Whitehead; Smith, Smoll & Wiechman; Vallerand & Fortier), researchers have developed instruments to measure specific, a priori factors — often derived from an explicit theoretical basis. Here it is possible to use factor analysis as a hypothesis testing tool by evaluating the compatibility between the predicted and obtained factors. These two approaches to factor analysis correspond more or less to what is typically referred to as exploratory factor analysis (e.g., the principal components or principal axis factor analysis) and confirmatory factor analysis using statistical packages such as LISREL, EQS, AMOS, etc.

In exploratory factor analysis, the researcher has limited control over the factors which emerge other than specifying the number of factors and, to a limited extent, the size of relations among the factors. In confirmatory factor analysis, the researcher has considerable freedom in specifying the model to be tested and then evaluates the ability of the a priori model to fit the data. Although there are many examples of the use of exploratory factor analysis to confirm a priori factors, the use of factor analysis as a hypothesis testing tool is greatly facilitated by recent advances in the application of CFA. The usefulness of CFA for purposes of construct validation (via factor analysis, multitrait-multimethod analysis, and/or structural equation modeling) is widely endorsed, but as recently as 1993, Schutz and Gessaroli lamented a relative scarcity of good introductory demonstrations in the sport sciences. Judging from the content of chapters in this monograph, factor analysis is now a standard tool in evaluating sport and exercise psychology measures and it appears that confirmatory factor analysis has rapidly replaced the older exploratory approaches.

It is important to emphasize, however, that factor analysis does not provide a test of the construct validity of the verbal label that researchers may choose to put on the factors. Much emphasis in the construct validity of responses to a measure — particularly the within-network components — is at a micro level. However, to borrow a possibly overused metaphor, there is also a danger of loosing sight of the forest if one concentrates exclusively on the trees. Part of the role of construct validation — particularly the between-network components — is to establish the relations between a particular construct and other constructs to which it is logically related. In my days as a graduate student, I came across the concept of "jingle-jangle fallacies" which I had the opportunity to test in research on sport motivational orientations (Marsh, 1994). As described in detail in the Duda & Whitehead chapter, motivation researchers have recently placed considerable emphasis on the task and ego goal distinctions (Duda, 1993; Roberts, 1993). Although this assumption was originally challenged both empirically and conceptually by Duda (1992), Gill (1993) has suggested that her work on competitiveness reflected a similar and overlapping perspective on motivational differences. I tested Gill's suggestion by comparing responses to the Perceptions of Success Questionnaire (POSQ; Roberts, 1993), which assesses individual pronenesses for task and ego goal involvement, and the Sports Orientation Questionnaire (SOQ; Gill, 1993) and related them to external criteria. Whereas the POSQ Mastery and SOQ Goal scales were highly related and reflected a task orientation, the SOQ Competitiveness scale was more highly correlated with the POSQ Mastery and SOQ Goal scales than the POSQ Competitiveness scale. Apparently, competitiveness assessed by the SOQ reflects competition with internal standards/goals (a task perspective) more than competition with other individuals (an ego perspective), whereas the POSQ Competitiveness scale was deemed to reflect an ego orientation. The pattern of relations with other criteria (i.e., age, gender, and multiple dimensions of physical self-concept) and a careful examination of the item content supported these interpretations.

With particular reference to the assessment of motivational orientations, Duda and Whitehead (this volume) extend my arguments (Marsh, 1994) and provide additional illustrations of construct mislabeling and conceptual ambiguities and misunderstandings. In terms of other constructs considered in this monograph, a number of authors (e.g., see chapters by Brawley, Martin & Gyurcsik; Gauvin & Spence; Murphy & Tammen) have indicated their awareness of the jingle fallacy (that scales with the same label may not reflect the same construct) and the jangle fallacy (scales with different labels may not reflect different constructs). Consequently, throughout this text we repeatedly see calls for pursuing validity studies more vigorously to test the interpretations of existing measures in sport and exercise psychology. I wholeheartedly agree with this recommendation.

There are many outstanding examples of the construct validation approach in sport and exercise psychology (e.g., Chapter 16 by Fox provides a detailed overview of how such an approach has laid the groundwork in the development of physical self-concept measures specifically). To varying extents, all the authors of the substantively oriented chapters have adopted some if not all facets of the construct validation approach to evaluate the quality of measurement in their area of research. Moreover, the authors of the methodologically oriented chapters (e.g., see Schutz, Tenenbaum & Fogarty) have explicated tools to better pursue these aims. Not surprisingly then, the contributors are nearly unanimous in concluding that there has been sufficient advance in the quality of sport and exercise measurement to justify the title of the monograph. I concur with their appraisal of this contemporary review of the status of sport and exercise psychology assessment. Further, I would suggest that the publication of this important and much needed book will surely push this level of advancement considerably higher in the years to come.

References

Duda, J.L. (1992). Motivation in sport settings: A goal perspective analysis. In G. Roberts (Ed.), *Motivation in sport and exercise* (pp. 93-106). Champaign, IL: Human Kinetics.

Duda, J.L. (1993). Goals: A social-cognitive approach to the study of achievement motivation in sport. In R. N. Singer, M. Murphey, & L.K. Tennant (Eds.), *Handbook of research on sport psychology* (pp. 421-436). New York: Macmillan.

Gill, D.L. (1993). Competitiveness and competitive orientation in sport. In R. N. Singer, M. Murphey, & L.K. Tennant (Eds.), *Handbook of research on sport psychology* (pp. 314-327). New York: Macmillan.

Gill, D.L., Dzewaltowski, D.A., & Deeter, T.E. (1988). The relationship of competitiveness and achievement orientation to participation in sport and nonsport activities. *Journal of Sport and Exercise Psychology, 7,* 139-150.

Marsh, H.W. (1994). Sport motivation orientations: Beware of the jingle-jangle fallacies. *Journal of Sport and Exercise Psychology, 16,* 365-380.

Marsh, H.W. (1997). The measurement of physical self-concept: A construct validation approach. In K. Fox (Ed.), The physical self: From motivation to well-being. Champaign, IL: Human Kinetics.

Marsh, H.W., & Peart, N. (1988). Competitive and cooperative physical fitness training programs for girls: Effects on physical fitness and on multidimensional self-concepts. *Journal of Sport and Exercise Psychology,* 10.

Nelson, J.K. (1989). Measurement methodology for affective tests. In M.J. Safrit & T.M. Wood (Eds.), *Measurement concepts in physical education* (pp. 271-295). Champaign, IL: Human Kinetics.

Ostrow, A.C. (1990). *Directory of psychological tests in the sport and exercise sciences.* Morgantown, WV: Fitness Information Technology.

Roberts, G.C. (1993). Motivation in sport: Understanding and enhancing the motivation and achievement of children. In R.N. Singer, M. Murphey, & L.K. Tennant (Eds.), *Handbook of research on sport psychology* (pp. 405-420). New York: Macmillan.

Schutz, R.W., & Gessaroli, M.E. (1993). Use, misuse, and disuse of psychometrics in sport psychology research. In R.N. Singer, M. Murphey, L.K. Tennant (Eds.), *Handbook of research on sport psychology* (pp. 901-917). New York: Macmillan.

Vealey, R.S. (1986). Conceptualization of sport confidence and competitive orientation: Preliminary investigation and instrument development. *Journal of Sport Psychology, 8,* 221-246.

INTRODUCTION

When Andy Ostrow, the publisher of this book, contacted me two years ago in regard to editing a text on psychological measurement in sport and exercise settings, I did not immediately foresee the scale of such a project. I agreed with Andy that there was a striking void in the literature concerning a comprehensive and critical look at our assessment tools. I also saw the relevance of this topic to both the science and practice of sport and exercise psychology. Thus, I accepted the challenge that Andy laid before me — not as an expert in measurement theory and test development — but as someone who strongly believes that the evolution of knowledge in any field is intimately linked to the quality of the field's measures.

After I outlined the areas deemed appropriate for coverage in such a book, my next task was to target those individuals whose work has contributed to the pool of measures and/or measurement-related issues found in sport and exercise psychology. I learned that others also felt that such a text was long overdue. Among the colleagues contacted, there was almost unanimous acceptance of my invitation to prepare a chapter for a book on *Advances in Sport and Exercise Psychology Measurement*.

For those contributors reviewing existent measures of a particular construct (like leadership behavior or competitive state anxiety), I asked them to evaluate current assessment tools in regard to each instrument's theoretical foundation and evidence concerning validity and reliability. These authors were also requested to speculate on future directions in the measurement of the constructs in question.

The present book contains a review of assessments of major constructs in sport and exercise psychology — and addresses almost all of the topic areas included in the most recent edition of the *Directory of Psychological Tests in the Sport and Exercise Sciences* (Ostrow, 1996). That is, there are chapters focused on the assessment of achievement or goal orientations, aggression, anxiety, attention, attitudes toward and perceptions concerning exercise and physical activity, attributions, body image, cognitive strategies and psychological skills, cohesion, confidence in exercise and sport, imagery, leadership, and motives and affect in exercise and sport. Although this is an extensive collection of topics, the constructs selected certainly do not form an exhaustive list. It should be acknowledged that researchers and practitioners in sport and exercise psychology are concerned with the measurement of other variables not considered here (e.g., the assessment of self-reported levels of physical activity; Kriska & Casperson, 1997). Another limitation of the current text is that the assessments reviewed primarily stem from the North American sport and exercise psychology literature. This was not due to any ethnocentric bias on the part of the editor; I was unfortunately confined to the literature I am most familiar with (and material that is written in my native language). A small first step toward a text on sport and exercise psychology measures from an international perspective was made with the inclusion of authors from Great Britain and Australia.

The chapters concerning the assessment of central constructs in the field present a rich variety of measurement approaches. Quantitative and qualitative self-report, behavioral and physiological/biological measures are described and critiqued throughout the pages of this text. Importantly, the reader will find discussions of the assessment of newer concepts in sport and exercise psychology as well as newer procedures (such as confirmatory factor analysis) applied to previously established assessment tools.

In general, the contents of the first seven sections of this book provide examples of current sport and exercise psychology measures that seem sound (in terms of their psychometric attributes and theoretical underpinnings) and those that appear most questionable. Many of the contributors to this book point out critical conceptual issues regarding available assessment tools, such as the inclusion of both the hypothesized antecedents and consequences of a construct in its operational definition (e.g., see the chapters on the assessment of cohesion, intrinsic motivation, and goal perspectives in sport). Several of the authors present useful taxonomies for organizing and discriminating between existing measures of a particular construct (e.g., see the chapters on the measurement of body image, aggression, and exercise-induced feeling, states, affect, and mood). Moreover, new methods of assessment are suggested that have been employed in general psychology but have not yet been used to address important theoretical and practical questions in sport and exercise (e.g., see the chapter on the assessment of attention).

It is my wish that this text provide a fairly complete reference for contemporary psychometric information on the majority of measures in the field. The development and psychometric features of most of the assessments described here have not been previously summarized in manual or book form. Thus, prior to this edited book, someone interested in garnering details on the norms, reliability, and validity of such instruments would have needed to contact the measure's author(s) and/or search through research articles describing the employment of these measures.

With an eye toward the advancement of sport and exercise psychology measurement, it became apparent to me that a final section was needed (i.e., Part VIII). It would be remiss to not include some treatment of the measurement issues evolved when we attempt to apply or develop assessments that are appropriate for specific populations within sport and physical activity settings. Thus, separate chapters on developmental considerations and cross-cultural measurement were added. Further, as there is a practice component to the disciplines of sport and exercise psychology, I felt that discussions were warranted on the adequacy of current measures when the focus is on application and intervention in real-life sport and exercise environments.

Measurement is typically defined as the process of assigning numbers to objects according to agreed upon rules (Meier, 1994). The "objects" we study in sport and exercise psychology are typically introspective and/or abstractions of theoretical concepts; they are not usually physical and/or directly observable. Focusing on such objects raises particular concerns and difficulties in regard to the search for consistency and validity in measurement. New techniques and associated computer programs have been generated to assess the stability and reliability of psychological characteristics and their measures. Two chapters in Part VIII illustrate such developments as they may be applied to sport and exercise psychology assessment.

It is important to keep in mind that "psychological tests are tools….Any tool can be an instrument of good or harm, depending on how it is used" (Anastasi & Urbina, 1997, p. 2). Tests are less likely to be misused if there is psychometric rigor, a theoretical grounding as well as professional scruples in how they are developed, administered, and interpreted. Pertinent to this issue, a chapter on the ethics of testing and measurement was incorporated in the final section of the book.

The status of and approach often taken in measurement within sport and exercise psychology have been criticized in the past (e.g., Schutz, 1994). We are not alone in terms of such negative commentary. For example, it has been said that "psychologists seem to take great pleasure in developing new scales...but little interest in determining what scores on them mean" (Epstein, 1979, p. 381). When examining the state of measurement in the counseling psychology literature, Meier and Davis (1990) noted that most of the assessments found are investigator developed for the study and/or investigator modified. They also observed that typically, no validity and reliability information on these new or adaptive measures is provided.

The 80% increase in the number of tests contained in the second edition of the *Directory of Psychological Tests in the Sport and Exercise Sciences* when compared to the first (i.e., from 175 to 314 instruments over 7 years; Ostrow, 1988, 1996) documents sport and exercise psychology's love affair with questionnaire generation. However, many of the instruments chronicled in the latest *Directory* have at least some associated psychometric information. When we also take into account many of the measures delineated in this text, it seems that we have come a long way and are moving in the right direction.

I think all the contributors to this book will be pleased if their careful evaluations of and comments on measurement are taken very seriously by researchers and practitioners in future work. As in all the applied and basic sciences, the reckless use and production of assessments in the field need to stop. We need to "reconnect measurement with substantive theory to create better, richer, thicker descriptions from which to generate deeper conceptions and, most importantly, better questions" (Meier, 1994, p. xii). It is paramount that we go beyond face validity and thoroughly examine the psychometric features of new and former measures utilizing the most contemporary techniques. Without solid measurement, it is difficult to challenge, disconfirm, and/or extend psychological theory in sport and exercise psychology. Given the absence of meaningful, valid, and reliable assessments, our pre-assessments and post-assessments in the applied realm lack integrity and are of little value.

I hope the contents of this book allows the reader to more ably and efficiently sift through the plethora of measures in the field and make more informed decisions about which instruments are best suited for the purpose at hand. It is also my hope that this publication will foster subsequent measurement development in sport and exercise psychology that is conceptually based and meets the highest standards in terms of psychometric properties.

My thanks to Andy Ostrow for providing the impetus leading to the creation of this edited text — and for the freedom and support provided as the book evolved. My appreciation too is extended to all those friends and colleagues who listened to the editor's lament when the scope of this project seemed overwhelming and closure seemed so far away.

References

Anastasi, A., & Urbina, S. (1997). *Psychological testing* (7th ed.) Upper Saddle River, NJ: Simon & Schuster.

Epstein, M. (1979). The stability of behavior: I. On predicting most of the people much of the time. *Journal of Personality and Social Psychology, 37*, 1097-1126.

Kriska, A.M., & Casperson, C.J. (Eds.). (1997). A collection of physical activity questionnaires for health-related research. *Medicine and Science in Sports and Exercise, 29*(6).

Meier, S.T. (1994). *The chronic crisis in psychological measurement and assessment: A historical survey.* New York: Academic Press.

Meier, S.T., & Davis, J. (1990). Trends in reporting psychometric properties of scales used in counseling psychology research. *Journal of Counseling Psychology, 37*, 113-115.

Ostrow, A.C. (1988). *Directory of psychological tests in the sport and exercise sciences.* Morgantown, WV: Fitness Information Technology.

Ostrow, A.C. (1996). *Directory of psychological tests in the sport and exercise sciences* (2nd ed.). Morgantown, WV: Fitness Information Technology.

Schutz, R.W. (1994). Methodological issues and measurement problems in sport psychology. In S. Serpa, J. Alues, & V. Pataco (Eds.), *International perspectives on sport and exercise psychology* (pp. 35-56). Morgantown, WV: Fitness Information Technology.

Part I

Sport Motivation and Perceived Competence

PART I

"Motivation is one of the central aspects of human affairs" and has been assumed to provide the energy and direction to people's behaviors (Roberts, 1993, p. 405). The topic of motivation reflects a central issue for researchers and practitioners interested in understanding behavioral variability in achievement and/or intrinsically interesting activities, such as sport. In Part I, assessments of a number of major motivation-related constructs are reviewed. These measures stem from the predominant theoretical frameworks that have guided sport psychology research; i.e., attribution theory (Weiner, 1985), Bandura's (1977, 1986) self-efficacy and social cognitive theories, Harter's (1978) model of competence motivation, the cognitive evaluation and self-determination theories of intrinsic motivation (Deci & Ryan, 1985), and the achievement goal or goal perspective approaches (Ames, 1992; Dweck, 1986; Nicholls, 1984, 1989). Rather than focusing on psychological drives, personality traits, and/or motives, these theoretical models epitomize a cognitive perspective approach. That is, in regard to potential determinants of achievement patterns, they place an emphasis on how people think within a particular situation. Further, these most popular theories of sport motivation all consider the impact and determinants of perceptions of ability.

References

Ames, C. (1992). Achievement goals, motivational climate, and motivational processes. In G.C. Roberts (Ed.), *Motivation in sport and exercise* (pp. 161-176). Champaign, IL: Human Kinetics.

Bandura, A. (1977). Self-efficacy: Toward a unifying theory of behavioral change. *Psychological Review, 84*, 191-215.

Bandura, A. (1986). *Social foundations of thought and actions: A social cognitive theory*. Englewood Cliffs, NJ: Prentice Hall.

Deci, E.L., & Ryan, R.M. (1985). *Intrinsic motivation and self-determination in human behavior*. New York: Plenum.

Dweck, C.S. (1986). Motivational processes affecting learning. *American Psychologist, 41*, 1040-1048.

Harter, S. (1978). Effectance motivation reconsidered: Toward a developmental model. *Human Development, 21*, 34-64.

Nicholls, J.G. (1984). Achievement motivation: Conceptions of ability, subjective experience, task choice, and performance. *Psychological Review, 91*, 328-346.

Nicholls, J.G. (1989). *The competitive ethos and democratic education*. Cambridge, MA: Harvard University Press.

Roberts, G.C. (1993). Motivation in sport: Understanding and enhancing the motivation and achievement of children. In R. N. Singer, M. Murphey, and L.K. Tennant (Eds.), *Handbook on research on sport psychology* (pp. 405-420). New York: Macmillan.

Weiner, B. (1985). An attribution theory of achievement motivation and emotion. *Psychological Review, 92*, 548-573.

Chapter 1

ATTRIBUTIONS AND ATTRIBUTIONAL STYLE

Stuart Biddle
University of Exeter
and
Stephanie Hanrahan
The University of Queensland

Attributions are perceived causes or reasons that people give for an event related either to themselves or others. Although a great deal has been said about attributions in achievement settings, including sport, the study of attributions has been diverse and included applications in areas such as health, the law, family therapy, social affiliation, and clinical psychology settings (Weary, Stanley, & Harvey, 1989). Similarly, attributional analyses have been used to examine and explain behaviors at intrapersonal, interpersonal, intergroup, and societal levels of analysis (Hewstone, 1989).

The study of attributions in many areas of psychology, including sport and exercise psychology, has been popular since the early 1970s. Entire books have been devoted to attribution theories (e.g., Hewstone, 1989; Weiner, 1986), and substantial sections of books have appeared, including chapters in sport/exercise books reflecting Australian (Hanrahan, 1995), European (Willimczik & Rethorst, 1995), and North American (McAuley, 1992) perspectives, as well as in an international text (Biddle, 1993). Similarly, the seminal book on social cognition by Fiske and Taylor (1991) includes two chapters and over 13% of the total text on attributions. In an analysis of all motivation papers published in the *International Journal of Sport Psychology* (IJSP) and *Journal of Sport (and Exercise) Psychology* (JSEP) between 1979 and 1991, Biddle (1994) found that attribution papers were the most popular, accounting for 12.9% of 224 motivation publications.

Thus, attribution is a popular topic in sport and exercise psychology. However, much of the attribution research in sport and exercise has been narrow if one compares it with the many approaches used in other domains of psychology, and thus the full scope of attribution theory has not been exploited (Biddle, 1993). Further, we concur with Weary et al. (1989) when they state in their preface, "to us, the attributional approach is not a sacrosanct school of thought on the human condition. It is,

rather, a body of ideas and findings that we find to be highly useful in our work ..." (p. vii).

The purpose of this chapter is to review the measurement of attributions and attributional style in sport and exercise. Specifically, we shall

- provide a brief overview of attribution theory.
- summarize some key issues in sport and exercise attribution research.
- discuss important methodological issues associated with attribution research that impact on the measurement of attributions.
- critically review measures of attributions that have been used in sport and exercise psychology.
- propose other approaches to attribution measurement that, as yet, have not appeared in sport and exercise studies.

AN OVERVIEW OF APPROACHES TO THE STUDY OF ATTRIBUTIONS

The history of the systematic study of attributional processes can be traced to Heider's seminal work on interpersonal perception (Heider, 1944, 1958). From this, several variations in approach can be identified, including Jones and Davis' (1965) "correspondent inference" model, Kelley's (1967) "covariation" model, and Weiner's theory of attributions and emotion (see Weiner, 1986, 1992). These are briefly summarized elsewhere (see Biddle, 1993; Hewstone, 1989; Weary et al., 1989). Fiske and Taylor (1991) also pointed to Schachter's (1964) theory of emotion and Bem's (1967) self-perception theory as other theoretical perspectives forming, in addition to the approaches just mentioned, "the backbone of what is now called attribution theory" (p. 24).

The approach that has had most influence on attribution research in sport and exercise psychology is that of Weiner. The other perspectives have largely been neglected and will not be discussed further. However, we believe that future attribution research in sport and exercise should look to some of these different approaches (see Biddle, 1993).

Weiner's Attributional Theory of Motivation and Emotion

Starting with investigations into the attributions given for college examination success and failure, Weiner (1986) developed a comprehensive theory of attributions and emotions (see Figure 1). This theory shows that an outcome may generate positive or negative emotion (attribution-independent affect) and, especially in the case of negative, unexpected or important outcomes, a search for the reasons for the outcome. Various antecedent factors will affect the nature of these attributions. The attributions themselves are thought to be organized into key dimensions that, in turn, influence the psychological consequences of the attributions, such as expectancy change or emotional feeling (attribution-dependent affect). Finally, these consequences may affect behaviors.

Aspects of Weiner's model have been tested in many different contexts, including achievement and affiliation settings. Central to the model is the belief that people organize their attributional thinking around three main dimensions: locus of causality, stability, and controllability. These are particularly important in the context of attribution measurement, as we discuss later. However, prior to the three-dimensional approach, Weiner et al. (1972) proposed that two main clusters of attributions could be identified. These were based on prior theorizing in achievement motivation and social learning theory. The two dimensions were "locus of control" (internal/external attributions) and stability (stable/unstable attributions), the latter referring to whether the attribution was variable over time or not. Typically, attributions such as ability were labelled "internal/stable" whereas effort was "internal/unstable."

However, Weiner (1979) then proposed a third dimension, that of "controllability." At the same time he relabelled the locus dimension "locus of causality." The differentiation between locus and controllability can best be illustrated by reference to ability and effort attributions. Ability, at least in the stable sense

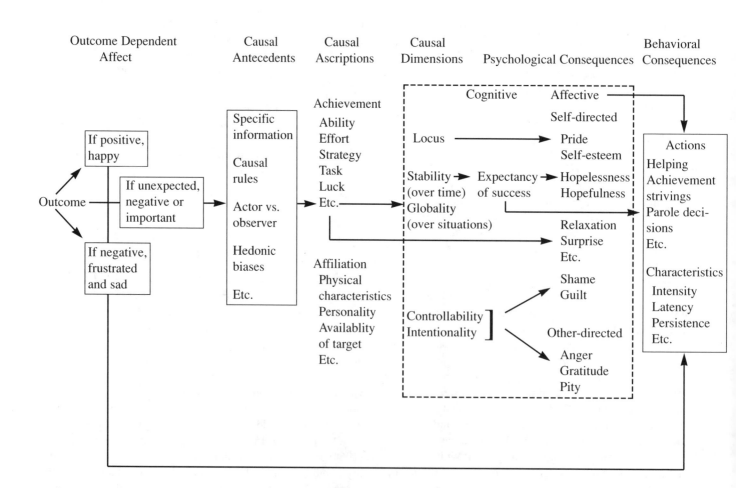

Figure 1. Weiner's (1986) attributional theory of motivation and emotion.
Note: From B. Weiner (1986) *An attributional theory of motivation and emotion.* New York: Springer-Verlag. Reprinted by permission of the author and Springer-Verlag, Inc.

of "giftedness," is likely to be seen as internal yet largely uncontrollable. Effort, on the other hand, although also internal is under volitional control as, indeed, might be ability in the sense of learned skills (see Sarrazin et al., 1996). The old locus of control dimension, therefore, was insufficient for this distinction.

Attribution Research in Sport and Exercise

As already stated, much of the research in sport and exercise psychology has been based on Weiner's theorizing. That is to say that the initial work investigated differences in attributions between winners and losers (e.g., Bukowski & Moore, 1980), or successful and unsuccessful performers (e.g., Spink & Roberts, 1980), and later some investigators researched the links between attributions and emotional reactions (e.g., Biddle & Hill, 1992; McAuley & Duncan, 1989; Rethorst, 1992).

Typically, research has confirmed that winners or successful performers attribute their outcome more to internal and controllable factors than do losers or unsuccessful players. This "self-serving bias" has been confirmed through meta-analysis (Mullen & Riordan, 1988). However, relative differences between groups do not always reflect large or 'real' differences, such that both successful and unsuccessful athletes often use internal, controllable and unstable attributions, even though they may differ from each other by degree.

Research has also confirmed that attributions are associated with emotional feelings after a sports event, although typically attributions merely augment the emotions generated by the outcome or performance itself (the "intuitive appraisal"; see Vallerand, 1987) and that the variance in emotions accounted for by attributions is usually quite low (Vlachopoulos, Biddle & Fox, 1996; Willimczik & Rethorst, 1995).

METHODOLOGICAL ISSUES IN ATTRIBUTION MEASUREMENT

In almost all attribution research, the events about which attributions are made are either positive or negative. It is false to assume that the attributions someone makes for a positive event would be the same as those made for a negative event although, as stated above, often the differences between successful and unsuccessful performers can be quite small. Separate measurement of attributions about positive and negative events has been proposed (Ickes, 1980; Tenenbaum, Furst, & Weingarten, 1984).

The positive and negative events frequently used in attribution studies in sport concern success and failure. It should be noted, however, that a person's perceptions of success and failure are distinct from objective outcomes of winning and losing. A loss will not always be considered by individuals to be a failure, and a win will not always be thought of as a success. Success and failure are psychological states based on an individual's subjective perception of the implications of the outcome on desirable personal qualities (Maehr & Nicholls, 1980). Therefore, subjective interpretations of success and failure should be used when measuring attributions (Bird, Foster, & Maruyama, 1980; Ickes, 1980; Tenenbaum & Furst, 1985).

Elements and Dimensions of Attributions

When investigating attributions, researchers can use the participants' actual responses or the attributional dimensions that the responses may represent. The actual responses, sometimes referred to as factors or elements, are the specific reasons that people give for an event. Qualitative researchers may gain insight into responses to specific situations by content analyzing the raw attributions given by participants. For example, it may be useful for coaches to understand the reasons officials give for making certain calls in specific situations. In-depth qualitative data may be more useful in this circumstance than ratings along attributional dimensions, such as locus of causality, stability, or globality.

Many studies in both sport (e.g., Iso-Ahola, 1977; Scanlan & Passer, 1980) and nonsport settings (e.g., Fielstein et al., 1985; Fontaine, 1975; Gollwitzer, Earle, & Stephan, 1982) have avoided the use of dimensions, and instead asked participants to rate the importance of four basic attributions: ability, effort, task difficulty, and luck. Qualitative analyses, however, have not been used in such research, and it has been assumed that these four factors sufficiently represent the attributions respondents would make.

Using an open-ended questionnaire, Roberts and Pascuzzi (1979) determined that the four traditional elements of ability, effort, task difficulty, and luck were used only 45% of the time in sporting situations. Similarly, Yamamoto (1983) extracted 13 attributional factors from winners and 14 attributional factors from losers. To expand participants' choices, additional factors, such as amount of practice, mood, interest in competing, and quality of officiating, have been added to some rating scales (Bukowski & Moore, 1980; Iso-Ahola & Roberts, 1977).

Problems can arise when researchers try to summarize attributions along dimensions or otherwise assume the dimensional categories of attributions (Russell, 1982). Weiner (1986) stated that ability, effort, and task difficulty can all be perceived as stable and unstable, and that luck can be considered as both internal and external to the person. Therefore, if a participant states that the cause of an event was due to lack of effort, there is no way for the researcher to know whether the individual perceives that cause to be stable or unstable. Similarly, if a participant indicates that the cause of a poor performance was that "the opposition played better defence than we did," it cannot be known whether this is perceived to be an internal or external cause.

The researcher and the attributer may not agree on the meaning of an attribution. McAuley and Gross (1983) found that two independent judges' classifications of open-ended attributions into causal dimensions differed markedly from the respondents' classifications. Many other studies have also found that outsiders' interpretations of individuals' attributions are inaccurate (e.g., Mark, Mutrie, Brooks, & Harris, 1984; Russell, McAuley, & Tarico, 1987; Watkins, 1986a). Because of these potential problems, it has been argued that research on attributions should focus on causal dimensions rather than the specific responses (Gill, Ruder, & Gross, 1982). Having participants rate their own attributions along causal dimensions avoids interpretation problems (Russell, 1982).

The main question then becomes, along which causal dimensions should individuals rate their attributions? Weiner's (1979) model involving the three attributional dimensions of locus of causality, stability, and controllability was mentioned earlier. In a wide assortment of attribution studies, the additional dimensions of globality, intentionality, and chosen or not chosen have been proposed.

Globality

Whether the cause of an event is perceived to influence just that particular event (a specific attribution) or many different events (a global attribution) is the distinction represented by the globality dimension. Globality has been considered, along with locus of causality and stability, one of the important attributional dimensions when studying "depressive attributional style" (Seligman, Abramson, Semmel, & vonBaeyer, 1979). This attributional style involves attributing uncontrollable negative events to internal, stable, and global causes.

In a study examining attributions for a single, objectively defined loss in tennis, Prapavessis and Carron (1988) found that globality was a useful dimension when studying attributions in sport. Findings suggested that players who exhibited symptoms of learned helplessness attributed losses to internal, stable, and global factors to a greater extent than did players not exhibiting these symptoms.

Intentionality

Intentionality has been used as a causal dimension by a number of researchers. There is little agreement, however, on the meaning of intentionality. Elig and Frieze (1975) included the intentionality dimension in a coding scheme of causality they created. For this coding scheme, intentional causes were defined as those that are under conscious control of the person. In this case, intentionality appears to be equivalent to controllability. Similarly, in Russell's (1982) original version of the Causal Dimension Scale (CDS; to be discussed in detail later), intentionality was one of the rating scales used to measure controllability, once again suggesting that controllability and intentionality are synonymous.

Carron (1984) also used an intentionality dimension in conjunction with the locus of causality and stability dimensions in his research. Defining external factors as those that the individual has no control over and intentional factors as those that the individual has control over, Carron appears to have confounded the intentionality and locus of causality dimensions as well as alluded to controllability to define intention.

The theoretical interpretations of the intentionality dimension have been noted as being unclear (Kelley & Michela,1980) and questionable (Weiner, 1986). Support for distinguishing between controllability and intentionality has also been provided by Hanrahan, Grove, and Hattie (1989). A confirmatory factor analysis of the Sport Attributional Style Scale (SASS; to be discussed later) allowed reasonable confidence in using these two dimensions.

Confusion about the independence of controllability and intentionality is probably accentuated when attributions about positive events are considered. Attributions perceived to be controllable will likely be perceived to be intentional as well. Hanrahan et al. (1988) found a correlation of .67 between these two dimensions when attributions were made for positive events. On the other hand, when attributions were made for negative events, the correlation between the two dimensions

fell to .38. Therefore, it may be for negative events that the distinction between intentionality and controllability is most important. This is logical, as few athletes would tend to indicate that a poor performance was intentional. However, attributing a poor performance to a controllable factor would suggest that future improvement is possible. Attributing a poor performance to the distracting behavior of spectators or other competitors is an example of an attribution that could be perceived as unintentional yet controllable.

Chosen or Not Chosen

A replacement for the locus of causality dimension was also proposed by Miller, Smith, and Uleman (1981). A "chosen or not chosen" distinction was suggested to replace the locus of causality dimension because of problems they felt were inherent with classifying attributions as internal or external. Miller et al. suggested that the diversity of causes within each existing category was too broad and that numerous closed-ended attribution measures had low convergent validity. They also indicated that the distinction between internal and external can rest on arbitrary phrasing of sentences. Their final argument against locus of causality was that it is incorrect to assume that internality and externality are inversely linked.

Miller et al. (1981) stated that participants define internal causality as denoting acts chosen freely by the actor and external causality as denoting acts for which choice and responsibility are limited. They, therefore, suggested that in future investigations of attributions, researchers should consider explicitly measuring the degree to which acts are deliberately chosen by the actor rather than the degree of internality or externality. Although other researchers have failed to act on this suggestion, including the dimension of intentionality may serve the same purpose. The chosen or not chosen distinction would appear to measure the same dimension as the intentional or unintentional distinction. If an act was unintentional, it would not have been chosen. Similarly, if an act was intentional, it would have to have been chosen.

States and Traits

State measures of attributions record the attributions individuals make about a specific situation at a specific point in time. State attribution measures can be useful when investigating emotional or behavioral responses to specific situations because they reflect beliefs about the "here and now." Indeed, the context is likely to be an important moderator of the attributional response. For example, a sport or exercise task, such as an endurance run, may be dependent on high levels of effort for success, whereas another activity, such as golf, may be related to motor skill. The context, therefore, becomes an important variable for state attributions.

Trait measures of attribution register the generally consistent manner in which people tend to account for events. People have well-established patterns of making causal attributions in familiar situations so that extensive information processing is not required (Frieze, McHugh, & Duquin, 1976). Abramson and Martin (1981) have concluded that individual differences do exist in attributional style. If measuring traits rather than states, a multi-item questionnaire must be used in order to capture different situations (Peterson & Seligman, 1984). This will ensure that a more representative measure of attributional style is achieved. If only a single-item/situation questionnaire is used, there may be something about that situation that would falsely represent the individual's typical attributional style.

When measuring attributional style, in addition to gathering attributions about both positive and negative events, it is important to balance the content of the positive and negative events about which attributions are made (Feather & Tiggeman, 1984). If, for example, an athlete attributes poor social relationships with teammates to external causes and good competitive performance to internal causes, we will not know if the attributional differences are due to dissimilar domains or to whether the event is positive or negative.

Although attributional style is a trait measure, it requires domain-specific assessment. Cutrona, Russell, and Jones (1985) found only weak evidence of a cross-situationally consistent attributional style. Anderson, Jennings, and Arnoult (1988) stated that research on social behavior has demonstrated some situational specificity suggestive of the importance of distinguishing among different types of situations. When studying sport-related attributional style, therefore, it is appropriate to use a sport-specific measure of attributional style rather than a more general measure. It could similarly be argued that as exercise environments may lack elements that exist in sport, such as competition, spectators, and obvious extrinsic rewards, sport attributional style measures may be inappropriate when researching exercise situations. However, research is required to verify this.

MEASUREMENT OF ATTRIBUTIONS IN SPORT AND EXERCISE

Assessing attributions in sport and exercise has been almost exclusively through self-report questionnaire. In this section of the chapter, we shall review both state and trait self-report measures that have been used in sport and exercise, as well as other attribution-related measures, such as learned helplessness, that are less common.

Few sport/exercise-specific inventories assess attributions. Those reported in the literature include the Sport Attributional Style Scale (SASS; Hanrahan et al., 1989) and the Wingate Sport Achievement Responsibility Scale (WSARS; Tenenbaum et al., 1984), both trait attribution measures that are reviewed later. In addition, the Performance Outcome Survey (POS; Leith & Prapavessis, 1989) — a sport-specific version of the Causal Dimension Scale — has been developed. Prapavessis and Carron (1988) have developed a sport-specific version of the Attributional Style Questionnaire.

Measurement of Self-Reported Attribution States

Prior to the development of a psychometrically standardized scale, sport attribution researchers relied on a checklist approach for assessing individual attributions (e.g., Vallerand, 1987). These were then analyzed as individual attributions (e.g., Biddle & Hill, 1988) or coded into dimensions either by the researcher or through data-reduction procedures. Some of the problems with this type of approach have already been discussed. In particular, the coding of attributions into dimensions may create the "fundamental attribution researcher error" (Russell, 1982) whereby the researcher assumes a particular dimensional property for an attribution that is not perceived in the same way by the participant.

One way around this problem is to use factor analysis to create dimensions from the individual attribution data. Surprisingly, this has not been adopted very often in the sport literature. We attempted this because, at the time, we were unhappy with alternative standardized scales (Biddle & Hill, 1992). We found three clear factors derived from both individual outcome (win or loss) and performance attributions given after competitive squash matches (see Table 1). These results suggest that

Table 1

Attribution Factors Derived From Outcome and Performance Attribution Ratings Made by Competitive Squash Players (loadings above .5), as reported by Biddle & Hill (1992).

OUTCOME ATTRIBUTIONS & FACTORS			PERFORMANCE ATTRIBUTIONS AND FACTORS		
Personal Sport Ability	*Unstable*	*Opponent*	*Personal Sport Ability*	*Unstable*	*Opponent*
ability	luck	opponent factors	ability	luck	opponent's ability
previous experience	mood	opponent's effort	previous experience	mood	opponent factors
fitness	form	opponent's ability	fitness	form	opponent's effort
motivation					motivation (-)
personality					
effort					

athletes may perceive the dimensional properties of attributions slightly differently than do attribution theorists. Although there is some commonality with theory, such as the (in)stability factor, differences are also clearly seen.

Two main disadvantages are evident with this factor analytic approach. First, it is unlikely that results will generalize across studies, thus making it difficult to compare results. Second, it is logical to expect some cross-loadings in the factor analysis because some attributions, by definition according to theory, could load on at least two factors. Biddle and Hill (1992) found some evidence for this with effort attributions for performance loading .47 on "personal sport ability" and .48 on "unstable". In response to many of these kinds of inadequacies, Russell (1982) developed the Causal Dimension Scale (CDS) based on Weiner's (1979) three-dimensional model of attributions.

The Causal Dimension Scale

The CDS and its successor the CDSII (McAuley, Duncan, & Russell, 1992), have been the most widely used state attribution measures in the past decade. The CDS was developed on the basis of two premises:

1. The measurement method should reduce or eliminate the possibility of making the fundamental attribution researcher error because the participant, not the researcher, decides on the dimensional properties of the attribution elements.
2. Attributions can be classified into the three dimensions of locus of causality, stability, and controllability.

In the first of two studies, Russell (1982) developed three semantic differential scale items to reflect the locus dimension, three items for stability, and six for controllability. U.S. undergraduate students (N=189) then rated the scales in response to eight different hypothetical achievement scenarios. The participants were given a scenario and an associated attribution for the outcome. The attributions were stable effort, unstable effort, ability, mood, other's stable effort, other's unstable effort, task difficulty, and luck. Each scenario attribution was then rated on each of the 12 scales. For example, one of the locus items was anchored by *outside of you* and *inside of you*, one stability item was anchored by *permanent* and *temporary*, and one controllability item was anchored by *someone else is responsible* and *no one else is responsible*. All items were worded to reflect Weiner's (1979) three dimensions, although the controllability dimension was modified to include both internal and external causal factors. In other words, controllability could be reflected in control by the actor or control by others (e.g., athletic opponent).

Initial psychometric analyses provided evidence for discriminant validity for the locus and stability subscales. This was done by demonstrating, through ANOVA procedures, that items designed to assess one attribution dimension did not differentiate causes on another dimension. Both the locus and stability subscales were internally consistent (Cronbach alpha for each subscale was 0.88).

The discriminant validity of the controllability subscale, however, was not confirmed because overlap with the locus scale was found. Only the "intentional or unintentional" item "was found to adequately measure controllability" (Russell,

1982, p. 1140). However, no test of factorial structure was undertaken in this first study.

In his second study, Russell (1982) kept the six locus and stability items from Study I and added two new controllability items to the "intentionality" item mentioned above. This produced a nine-item scale with three items for each attribution dimension. The scale is shown in Table 2.

Russell's second study used an identical method to his first, but this time administered the new nine-item CDS to a separate sample of 99 U.S. undergraduate students. Initially, psychometric evaluation showed that for each item the largest effect was for the dimension the item was meant to assess, a test of discriminant validity. This confirmed the results for locus and stability from Study I and provided better evidence for the psychometric properties of the controllability subscale. All three subscales were internally consistent (locus α=.87; stability α=.84; controllability α=.73). Exploratory factor analysis, using varimax rotation, identified three factors correlating between .19 and .28. The three items from each subscale loaded with its intended factor and did not load on either of the other two factors. Loadings ranged from .53 to .62 for locus, from .53 to .60 for stability, and from .55 to .59 for controllability.

Russell et al. (1987) provided further support for the CDS, although not from the physical domain. They concluded:

> we now have evidence to support the construct validity of all three causal dimension subscales. ... the following predictions ... have been supported: (a) Locus of causality scores are determined by achievement outcome, (b) violations of expectations are related to the stability of causal attributions, (c) locus of causality and controllability scores are related to affective reactions to success and failure, and (d) the controllability of attributions ... influence how ... performance is evaluated by others. (p. 1255)

In addition, Russell et al. (1987) raise doubts about the internal consistency of the controllability subscale and the high intercorrelation between locus and controllability subscales. The interrelationship between these two scales, however, has been inconsistent and may reflect their sensitivity to situational influences which, in attribution research, may not be a methodological flaw.

The CDS in Sport and Exercise Psychology

The use of the CDS has been prominent in sport and exercise psychology as a research tool but has not been subjected to rigorous psychometric scrutiny in the physical domain. Indeed, some confusion surrounds the first report of the CDS in sport. McAuley and Gross (1983) reported its use by U.S. undergraduate students enrolled in physical education classes. Using the CDS, the students rated their attributions for winning or losing a table tennis match. McAuley and Gross reported a maximum possible score of 21 for each subscale, suggesting that they used only 7-point scales instead of the original 9-point scales used by Russell (1982). Their conclusion that attributions were internal, unstable, and controllable for both winners and losers is true if indeed they used 7-point scales, but not if the 9-point scales were used. Again, the controllability subscale was found to have low internal consistency (α=.52), whereas locus (α=.76) and stability (α=.88) subscales were adequate in this respect. Unfortunately, the sample size was not large enough for a factor analysis to be computed.

Other studies in sport and exercise have assessed attributions using the CDS. For example, Van Raalte (1994) reported internal consistency coefficients for the CDS subscales with 96 U.S. undergraduate students of locus (α=.63), stability (α=.73), and controllability (α=-.03), yet continued to report results from the controllability subscale. Grove, Hanrahan, and McInman (1991), although not testing the psychometric properties of the CDS, report the use of the CDS across players, officials, and spectators, suggesting that it is suitable to use across different sport settings.

Finally, Morgan, Griffin, and Haywood (1996) report adequate psychometric properties for the CDS for a large, diverse ethnic sample (N=755) of track and field athletes. They report confirmation of a three-factor structure for the CDS, and adequate internal consistency for locus (α=.87), stability (α=.84), and controllability (α=.73) subscales. Interestingly, although no effects on attribution dimensions were found for gender or sport experience, significant effects were reported for ethnicity, suggesting that this factor may need to be accounted for in future studies of measurement.

A Sport-Specific Modification of the CDS

Leith and Prapavessis (1989) studied attributional differences between successful and unsuccessful events in both objectively and subjectively evaluated sports. Their measurement of attributions was through the Performance Outcome Survey (POS), which, they claim, was a sport-specific adaptation of the CDS. Psychometric integrity for the instrument was supported only through adequate internal consistency coefficients for two of the three subscales (locus α=.74; stability α=.83). The controllability subscale had low internal consistency (α=.63). Satisfactory face validity was established through expert ratings. Leith and Prapavessis did not state how the scale was a sport-specific adaptation. It is difficult to see how the CDS could be adapted when the attributions themselves are given in an open-ended format first. The rating scales are then context free for attribution dimension assessment.

A Critique of the CDS

The development of the CDS was certainly a breakthrough in terms of assessing dimensions of attributions from the point of view of the participant. However, a number of potential problems were evident at the time of Russell's (1982) publication.

Hypothetical contexts. The CDS was developed using only hypothetical achievement situations, and yet the assumption was that it could be used in real situations as well, although Russell (1982) did acknowledge this problem. Whether hypothetical events adequately mirror real events for the assessment of attributions remains to be seen.

Supplied attributions. The 1982 paper by Russell provided psychometric evidence for the CDS based on supplied attributions only. The CDS, as shown in Table 2, allows for individuals to write their own attributions for the outcome and then to

---

Table 2
The Causal Dimension Scale (CDS)

Instructions: Think about the reason or reasons you have written above. The items below concern your impressions or opinions of this cause or causes of your outcome. Circle one number for each of the following scales.

1. Is the cause(s) something that:
   Reflects an aspect of yourself   9 8 7 6 5 4 3 2 1   Reflects an aspect of the situation
2. Is the cause(s):
   Controllable by you or other people   9 8 7 6 5 4 3 2 1   Uncontrollable by you or other people
3. Is the cause(s) something that is:
   Permanent   9 8 7 6 5 4 3 2 1   Temporary
4. Is the cause(s) something that is:
   Intended by you or other people   9 8 7 6 5 4 3 2 1   Unintended by you or other people
5. Is the cause(s) something that is:
   Outside of you   1 2 3 4 5 6 7 8 9   Inside of you
6. Is the cause(s) something that is:
   Variable over time   1 2 3 4 5 6 7 8 9   Stable over time
7. Is the cause(s)
   Something about you   9 8 7 6 5 4 3 2 1   Something about others
8. Is the cause(s) something that is:
   Changeable   1 2 3 4 5 6 7 8 9   Unchanging
9. Is the cause(s) something for which:
   No one is responsible   1 2 3 4 5 6 7 8 9   Someone is responsible

Note: Russell, D. (1982). The Causal Dimension Scale: A measure of how individuals perceive causes. *Journal of Personality and Social Psychology, 42,* 1137-1145. Copyright ©1982 by the American Psychological Association. Reprinted by permission of the author.

A total score for each of the three subscales is arrived at by summing the responses to the individual items as follows: (1) locus of causality - items 1, 5, and 7; (2) stability - items 3, 6, and 8; controllability - items 2, 4, and 9. High scores on these subscales indicate that the cause is perceived as internal, stable, and controllable.

rate them on the nine items. However, no test was performed, and none has been done since to our knowledge, where the psychometric properties of the scale have been tested where free-response attributions are compared to supplied attributions.

How many attributions? The instructions for the CDS, as shown in Table 2, request that the individual "think about the reason or reasons you have written above." (Russell, 1982). This can be problematic if more than one attribution is given or if the reason is not clear (see Leith & Prapavessis, 1989). The following two examples illustrate our point:

1. Reasons: "I felt pretty good today and so really went for it, as usual."
2. Reason: "It went well".

For reason 1 there are three possible attributions given:

1. "I felt pretty good today": attributions to mood/psychological state
2. "really went for it": attributions to effort/motivation
3. "as usual": attributions to stable effort/personality.

How the participant then rates these attributions in terms of the three dimensions appears to be a problem. They may make an overall average rating, or just take the most salient one, if there is one. For example, Tenenbaum and Furst (1986) found that theoretical predictions were confirmed when athletes were assessed on their first attribution rated with the CDS. However, the athletes were also requested to rate their second and third attributions, also using the CDS. Significant differences between the first and third attributions were found. For instance, winners reported more internal, stable, and controllable attributions than did losers for their first attribution, thus supporting prior research. When the third attribution was analyzed, however, losers gave more internal reasons and winners reported fewer internal and controllable factors.

Returning to our example attributional statements, for reason 2 it does not appear to be very clear what the attribution is, although the participant may know and yet have decided to write only a brief statement. Indeed, this raises the additional issue of whether some people are able to accurately write down their causal thoughts at all or, indeed, whether they have given much thought to attributions! Such meta cognitive conundrums are threats to validity and reliability of all attribution measures.

Conceptual clarity of the items. The first of Russell's (1982) studies highlighted some problems with the items assessing controllability. In the final nine-item scale, the three controllability items refer to "controllability" (Item 2), "intentionality" (Item 4), and "responsibility" (Item 9). Criticism of this approach can be made on conceptual and empirical grounds. First, it is not at all clear whether intentionality and responsibility are conceptually related to controllability; and second, evidence exists for the separation of these constructs (Biddle, 1988). This has been alluded to earlier in our discussion on attribution dimensions (see also Forsterling, 1988; Weiner, 1986).

Situational relevance of dimensions. Russell's (1982) CDS was developed by having students respond to hypothetical achievement situations. It is not known whether the dimensions proposed, or the item wording, is appropriate across all settings or just achievement contexts. In addition, the interrelationship

between dimensions, such as locus and controllability, may vary between situations.

Confounding internal and external control. Russell (1982) modified Weiner's (1979) definition of controllability to include both internal and external sources of control. This resulted in the three controllability items in the CDS (Table 2) including potentially confounding statements. Items 2 (controllability) and 4 (intentionality) refer to "... you or other people," and item 9 refers to "no one" and "someone" being responsible. Rating the attribution as being controllable by "you" may be quite different from being controlled "by others". Similarly, "someone" being responsible may mean that I am responsible or my opponent is responsible, again quite different from each other.

Controllable or controlled? Item 2 refers to whether the cause or reason is perceived to be controllable. This may be different from believing that the cause was actually controlled. For example, attributing my poor performance in the local half-marathon to "laziness" may be perceived as "uncontrolled" on the day ("I couldn't get myself going"), but generally speaking, running effort should be "controllable." Alternatively, I may think that my success in a game of golf was due to a weak opponent. I rate this as relatively "uncontrollable" because I have little control over my opponent in this type of game. In this case, the attribution is both "uncontrollable" and "uncontrolled."

The issues raised above may explain why Vallerand and Richer (1988) had difficulty in confirming the hypothesized three-factor structure of the CDS for both success and failure conditions. Using confirmatory factor analysis to analyze the attributional ratings for responses to examination success and failure of undergraduate students, Vallerand and Richer (1988) found low goodness-of-fit indexes and a number of cross-loadings for items. In addition, the internal consistency of the controllability dimension was low in conditions of success (α=.53), failure (α=.42), and for the whole sample combined (α=.50). This is in contrast to the values reported for locus (α=.77-.85) and stability (α=.73-.78).

CDS: Summary and conclusions

The development of the CDS was an important step forward in assessing causal dimensions from the viewpoint of the attributer and is seen as reducing the chance of making the fundamental attribution researcher error. However, a number of methodological issues remain, particularly concerning the structure of the CDS and the nature of controllability (Biddle, 1988; Biddle & Jamieson, 1988; Vallerand & Richer, 1988). This latter point led to the development of the CDSII (McAuley et al., 1992), and this instrument has now been adopted in sport and exercise research.

The Causal Dimension Scale II

McAuley et al. (1992) developed the CDSII through four studies, three of which involved sport and exercise contexts (see McAuley & Duncan, 1989, 1990; McAuley & Tammen, 1989). The revision of the CDS focused on changes to the controllability items, with all six of the items from the locus and stability subscales left unaltered.

In Study I, 144 U.S. undergraduate students responded to the CDS after receiving their results of a psychology examination. The original CDS was used, plus an additional 10 items. These new items were developed to reflect personal control and external control, with five items each. Using item analysis and confirmatory factor analysis, 3 items were retained to represent the personal control subscale and 3 for external control. Of interest was the fact that all 3 of the original CDS controllability items were rejected. This process meant that the CDSII comprised four subscales of 3 items each, as shown in Table 3.

Internal consistency of the four subscales was confirmed across all studies, with the average Cronbach alpha values being .67 for both locus and stability, .79 for personal control, and .82 for external control. To test for factorial validity of the CDSII, confirmatory factor analysis was used by collapsing data across all studies, giving a sample size of 380. The Goodness of Fit Index (GFI) from LISREL was .958, with a chi-square/df ratio of 2.0, showing an excellent fit of the data to the hypothesized four-factor oblique model. In addition, tests of alternative two- and three-factor models showed them to fit the data less well than the four-factor model. Finally, some of the four dimensions were shown to be intercorrelated, as predicted. The main associations were between locus and personal control (.711), locus and external control (-.646), and between personal and external control (-.558). However, no distinction was made between successful and unsuccessful outcomes in analysis 1414 of the psychometric properties of the CDSII by McAuley et al. (1992).

The CDSII in Sport and Exercise Psychology

Given that three of the four studies used in the development of the CDSII by McAuley et al. (1992) were in the physical domain, the psychometric evidence in favor of the instrument in sport and exercise settings is quite strong. In addition, adequate internal consistency has been reported for all four scales by McAuley (1991) in a study of adult exercisers (α range =.70-.92).

We have developed a modification of the CDSII for children aged 10-16 years (Vlachopoulos et al., 1996) and have labelled this scale the CDSII-C. A four-factor eight-item scale was used in a study of attributions, goal orientations, and emotional reactions following an endurance run in a school physical education lesson, and the scale showed reasonably sound psychometric properties. Confirmatory factor analysis supported a four-factor oblique structure (Comparative Fit Index = .99; GFI = .98; Root Mean Squared Residual = .06). All items had statistically significant factor loadings on their appropriate factors, but inter-item correlations for the two items within each subscale were only small to moderate (range = .32-.59, all $p<.01$).

CDS and CDSII Compared

To consider the improvement of the CDSII over the original CDS, we shall revisit the points of critique made in respect to the CDS and consider them in reference to the CDSII. All four studies used in the development of the CDSII involved actual, rather than hypothetical, achievement events and allowed the participants to make their own attributions. In addition, the events included an academic examination, a laboratory physical exercise competition, a field-based gymnastics routine where individuals were observed and assessed, and one-on-one basketball competition. However, similar to the CDS, the CDSII still poses the problem of the number of attributions the individual is rating.

Our earlier concerns about conceptual clarity of items centered on the diverse constructs used to assess controllability. This has largely been eliminated with the rejection of all three controllability items from the CDS. Face validity of personal control items is higher. However, the CDSII was developed only in achievement contexts, and its applicability to other settings was not tested by McAuley et al. (1992).

Table 3
Revised Causal Dimension Scale (CDSII)

Instructions: Think about the reason or reasons you have written above. The items below concern your impressions or opinions of this cause or causes of your performance. Circle one number for each of the following questions.

Is the cause(s) something:

1. That reflects an aspect of yourself	9 8 7 6 5 4 3 2 1	Reflects an aspect of the situation
2. Manageable by you	9 8 7 6 5 4 3 2 1	Not manageable by you
3. Permanent	9 8 7 6 5 4 3 2 1	Temporary
4. You can regulate	9 8 7 6 5 4 3 2 1	You cannot regulate
5. Over which others have control	9 8 7 6 5 4 3 2 1	Over which others have no control
6. Inside of you	9 8 7 6 5 4 3 2 1	Outside of you
7. Stable over time	9 8 7 6 5 4 3 2 1	Variable over time
8. Under the power of other people	9 8 7 6 5 4 3 2 1	Not under the power of other people
9. Something about you	9 8 7 6 5 4 3 2 1	Something about others
10. Over which you have power	9 8 7 6 5 4 3 2 1	Over which you have no power
11. Unchangeable	9 8 7 6 5 4 3 2 1	Changeable
12. Other people can regulate	9 8 7 6 5 4 3 2 1	Other people cannot regulate

Note: McAuley, E., Duncan, T. & Russell, D. (1992). Measuring causal attributions: The revised Causal Dimension Scale (CDSII). *Personality and Social Psychology Bulletin, 18,* 566-573. Copyright © 1992 by Sage Publications Inc. Reprinted by permission of Sage Publications Inc.

The total scores for each dimension are obtained by summing the items as follows:
1,6,9=locus of causality; 5,8,12=external control; 3,7,11=stability; 2,4,10=personal control.

The items of the CDSII do not refer directly to control. As shown in Table 3, other words are used. However, whereas before we made the distinction between "controlled" and "controllable," the same point can be made for "manageable" (Item 2). A cause may be manageable, but on some occasions may not actually be "managed." Some confusion may arise here, although the new items do seem to be an improvement on the old ones.

CDSII: Summary and Conclusions

Although some of the points of critique remain for the CDSII, it is clear that the new scale is an improvement, at least conceptually, over the CDS. Nevertheless, there are still quite substantial points of debate and criticism that remain, such as the number of attributions being rated and the clarity of certain words (e.g., manageable). In addition, our own experience with the CDSII suggests that many people have considerable problems understanding the scale items. It is noteworthy that neither the CDS (Russell, 1982) nor the CDSII (McAuley et al., 1992) psychometric papers refer to item development through the generation and testing of item wording with diverse samples. In an effort to reflect global causal thinking through four dimensions, and to keep the semantic differential scales short, the scale anchors in the CDSII are not always clear and certainly could be open to different interpretations by different groups. Also, much of the development of the two scales involved university-level students. Whether people with lower levels of education could cope with such a scale remains to be tested thoroughly. Indeed, Smith (1995) reported that participants in a GP (physician)-referral exercise intervention study had great difficulty with the CDSII, and less than 50% of participants completed the scale.

Measurement of Attribution Traits Through Self-Report

State measures of attributions typically involve participants making attributions about a common event. Trait measures, on the other hand, need to allow participants to make attributions about multiple events. Because it cannot be assumed that respondents have had identical experiences, questionnaires that measure attributional styles (traits) usually rely on hypothetical situations.

Probably the most frequently used measure of attributional style is the Attributional Style Questionnaire (ASQ). Consisting of 12 hypothetical situations — 6 good outcomes and 6 bad outcomes — the ASQ was developed by Seligman et al. (1979) and Abramson and Martin (1981). For each situation, respondents are asked to name the one major cause of the outcome described. Each cause is then rated on a 7-point scale for the degree of internality (locus of causality), stability, and globality. Peterson et al. (1982) studied the ASQ and found it to have good construct, criterion, and content validity. However, they also found the discrimination between the individual dimensions on the ASQ to be less than precise, especially for good events.

Sport Measures of Attributional Style

Although attributional style is a trait measure, it does require domain-specific assessment (Anderson et al., 1988; Cutrona et al., 1985). When investigating sport-related attributional style, therefore, it is appropriate to use a sport-specific measure rather than a general measure.

The Wingate Sport Achievement Responsibility Scale

One of the first instruments designed to measure enduring dispositions for appraising successful and unsuccessful sport outcomes was the Wingate Sport Achievement Responsibility Scale (WSARS; Tenenbaum et al., 1984). The WSARS was designed to measure perceived responsibility for sport-related outcomes but only considers the locus of causality dimension. The WSARS is unique, however, in having separate forms for individual and team sports.

An investigation of the WSARS found it to be valid using the Rasch model (Tenenbaum et al., 1984). When comparing the results of the WSARS with Rotter's (1966) Internal-External (I-E) Locus of Control scale, however, it was found that the sport-specific scale was only weakly correlated with the I-E scale, supporting the notion that the general and sport-specific attributional styles should be assessed independently.

Modified Attributional Style Questionnaire

Prapavessis and Carron (1988) studied the responses of tennis players to failure by modifying the ASQ. Each player was requested to recall vividly a tennis match in which he or she lost or where things did not go well. Players were then allowed to select possible reasons for this failure from each of three categories: personal (e.g., return of serve), match situation (e.g., net play), and mental (e.g., concentration). The players rated these attributions along the dimensions of locus of causality, stability, and globality, as well as rating the importance of the cause of failure in the game. The same procedure was followed for all three factors, and so, according to Prapavessis and Carron, an attributional style was derived. However, their data do not truly reflect an attributional style as only a single real event was assessed. When players were classified as helpless or nonhelpless according to responses on a questionnaire assessing cognitive, motivational, and emotional responses to failure, it was found that the helpless players perceived the personal and match situation factors contributing to failure as more internal, stable, and global than did the nonhelpless group. However, no psychometric evidence is presented for the modified ASQ in the Prapavessis and Carron study.

The Sport Attributional Style Scale

The Sport Attributional Style Scale (SASS; Hanrahan et al., 1989) was developed on the basis of the following premises:

1. Subjective interpretations of success and failure should be used instead of the objective outcome of win or lose (Bird, et al., 1980; Ickes, 1980; Tenenbaum & Furst, 1985).
2. The measure should allow for a variety of causal attributions (Bukowski & Moore, 1980; Gill, et al., 1982; Yamamoto, 1983).
3. Attributions can be classified into five dimensions of locus of causality, stability, globality, controllability, and intentionality.
4. Separate attributions should be allowed for positive and

negative events, which should be matched for content.

5. It should not be assumed that researchers can accurately place causal attributions into causal dimensions.

6. A multiple-item questionnaire should be used to measure attributional style.

The SASS initially involved 12 positive and 12 negative events in sport that were matched for content. The original situations were based on modifications to items appearing in other attributional style scales (e.g., Ickes & Layden, 1978; Peterson et al., 1982; Tenenbaum et al., 1984). Respondents are asked to provide the single most likely cause of each event if it happened to them and then rate the cause on 7-point scales measuring the dimensions of locus of causality, stability, globality, controllability, and intentionality.

In the initial study of the SASS (Hanrahan et al., 1989), nearly 300 undergraduate physical education majors completed the questionnaire. Confirmatory factor analysis provided reasonable support for the five-factor model (the five attribution dimensions) for both positive and negative events. Each factor was well defined by high factor loadings, with the exception of the locus of causality dimension.

Correlations between dimensions for negative events were reasonably independent, with the strongest correlation being between locus of causality and controllability ($r=.38$). For positive events, however, a relatively high correlation ($r=.67$) was found between controllability and intentionality. The same two dimensions were relatively independent for negative events ($r=.20$), suggesting that all five dimensions may be needed for an adequate explanation of attributional style for negative events (Hanrahan et al., 1989).

Four pairs of items from the original 24-item (12 pairs) questionnaire were deleted because of low item-to-total correlations or low factor loadings across more than one dimension, or because the content of the items was inappropriate for both team and individual sports or both interactive and noninteractive sports (Hanrahan et al., 1989). The remaining 16 items were used to assess reliability and validity of the SASS. The alpha coefficients representing inter-item reliability were at respectable levels for all of the scales for both positive and negative events (mean=.71; range=.58 to .80).

Test-retest reliability was determined by readministering the SASS to 75 participants 11 weeks after initial testing (Hanrahan et al., 1989). For positive events, the test-retest correlations ranged from .45 to .71 (mean=.61). For negative events, the range was .49 to .65 (mean=.56). As with the factor loadings, the lowest test-retest correlations occurred for the locus of causality dimension, the dimension shown to be associated with inconsistent results elsewhere in the sport attribution literature (Bukowski & Moore, 1980; Gill et al., 1982; Mark et al., 1984).

Construct validity of the SASS has been demonstrated by the SASS correlating better with theoretically relevant variables than with a variable that has no theoretical relationship with attributional style (Hanrahan et al., 1989). For example, relationships between sport attributional style and resultant achievement motivation and physical self-esteem were fairly weak, but in the expected direction, whereas correlations between the SASS and measures of competitive anxiety were

close to zero. Anxiety is a variable that has no theoretical or empirical links to attributional style.

Subsequent investigation of the SASS compared it to the ASQ, a general measure of attributional style (Hanrahan & Grove, 1990a). Five of the six correlations between the ASQ and SASS subscales of locus, stability, and globality for both positive and negative events were significant (range=.34 to .61; mean=.46). The correlation between locus scores for positive events was not significant ($r=.24$). With most of the correlations being significant, but only in the moderate strength range, it can be concluded that the situation-specific SASS measures a similar construct to the more general ASQ, but without being a needless duplication.

We also examined the consistency between responses to the hypothetical events in the SASS and responses to actual sporting situations (Hanrahan & Grove, 1990a). Participants rated their attributions about real-life sporting experiences along the same dimensions as those used in the SASS and then completed the SASS. Of the 10 subscales, only ratings on the locus of causality for negative events failed to be significantly correlated. The other 9 subscales revealed significant correlations between actual sporting experiences and hypothetical situations captured in the SASS (range=.29 to .55; mean=.42). These correlations suggest that the use of hypothetical situations in the SASS is a valid method of measuring sport-related attributional style (Hanrahan & Grove, 1990a).

As the developmental studies of the SASS used university undergraduate physical education students as participants, an additional study determined the factor structure and internal consistency of the SASS when administered to athletes from outside the university environment (Hanrahan & Grove, 1990a). Confirmatory factor analysis once again supported the proposed factor structure of the SASS, with mean factor loadings actually stronger on 8 of the 10 subscales than in the original student sample. Internal consistency was stronger for the athlete sample (range=.65 to .85; mean=.77). These results indicate that the SASS is appropriate for use with non-university samples (Hanrahan & Grove, 1990a).

As the 16-item version of the SASS takes between 20 and 30 minutes to complete, we investigated the feasibility of employing a shortened 10-item version of the SASS (Hanrahan & Grove, 1990b). Using four different samples and three different versions of the 10-item form, correlations between 16-item and 10-item forms were found to be consistently high (mean=.94). Results suggest that all three versions of the short form could be used in research (see Hanrahan & Grove, 1990b).

Exercise Attributional Style?

Just as an argument was made for using a domain-specific measure of attributional style when investigating athletes, it could be argued that a domain-specific measure of attributional style should be used when investigating exercisers. Although some of the SASS items (e.g., "you have no difficulty withstanding a demanding session") may be appropriate for exercise attribution research, a measure that includes a variety of possible success and failure experiences in the exercise domain should be developed.

FUTURE DIRECTIONS IN MEASUREMENT OF ATTRIBUTIONS IN SPORT AND EXERCISE

The literature in sport and exercise psychology that has involved the assessment of attributions has been narrow (Biddle, 1993). It has been limited not only in terms of sampling and theoretical perspective, but also in terms of attribution assessment. Most studies have utilized self-report scales or checklists of state or trait attributions. In this section, therefore, we shall review other ways of assessing attributions that have either been ignored completely or have only been used rarely in sport and exercise psychology. We shall consider two broad themes of attribution assessment:

• "spontaneous" attributions and qualitative assessment
• attributional complexity.

Spontaneous Attributions

A fundamental question posed by many researchers when studying attributions is "Do people really make attributions?" This question has arisen because most research studies have used supplied attributions and have asked participants to make attributions. Even if the latter method does not involve supplied attributions, the participants may not have thought about making attributions without prompting from the researcher. As Weiner (1986) said, "... the experimental procedure was reactive; that is, the responses of the subjects were believed to be influenced by the experimenter's introducing the notion of causality" (p. 23).

To resolve this issue, Weiner (1985) located 17, and later 20 (Weiner, 1986) published studies investigating 'spontaneous' attributions. Three types of papers were located:

• Archival, including newspaper reports, corporate business reports, advice columns in newspapers, and personal journals/diaries;
• Verbalizations, including parole decisions, achievement failure, gambling outcomes, and marital events;
• "Indirect indexes," including helping behavior and social impressions (Weiner, 1986).

Weiner (1985, 1986) concluded that clear evidence was available for spontaneous attributional thinking in many areas of life. However, the data supported the view that attributions were more likely to be made when the behavior or outcome was unexpected or when a goal was not attained. It is also thought that attributions are more likely to be made after an important event, although experimental manipulations of this are rare (Weiner, 1986).

It is our belief that a great deal of richness will be achieved in the analysis of sport and exercise attributions if more studies incorporate methods of spontaneous causal thinking. However, as Weiner (1986) says, "documentation of spontaneous attributional activity is a very difficult task" (p. 23). In the sections that follow we shall attempt to illustrate a selection of these methods, some of which have been used in sport and exercise.

Qualitative Analyses

Spontaneous attributions, by definition, are made when causal thought is unprompted. This may not necessarily occur in interviews, such as when the interviewer asks the 'why?'

question, which initiates causal thinking. Spontaneous attributions may, however, occur in this context. Certainly, this ideographic form of attribution assessment is likely to yield rich data, whether truly spontaneous or not, although as with all data of this type, its generalizability is unknown.

Many different forms of qualitative data collection and analysis are available to the attribution researcher (see Silverman, 1993; Tesch, 1990). Although some form of interview is commonplace for qualitative enquiry, it has, to our knowledge, not been used in attribution research in sport or exercise contexts. This is a gap in the literature that needs to be filled.

Another form of qualitative data collection suitable for sport and exercise attribution research is that involving conversations. Silverman (1993) refers to "discourse analysis" as a "heterogeneous range of social science research based on the analysis of recorded talk" (p. 120). This may be a suitable way to proceed in the study of, say, coach-athlete interactions. Again, no such published studies could be located in the sport/exercise literature.

A form of discourse analysis, however, has been used in attribution research. For example, Diener and Dweck's (1978) study of learned helplessness in children employed the procedure of requesting the children "to think out loud" (p. 454) during participation in problem-solving tasks. These verbalizations were then coded for attributional content. We also employed this method for assessing attributions on the motor task of balancing on a balance board in a laboratory setting (Johnson & Biddle, 1988). With 29 undergraduate students as participants, we gave failure feedback to all participants after five 30sec trials of balancing. After this, they were requested to perform the task again, but this time the number of trials was left to the discretion of the participant. The number of trials was taken as the operational definition of persistence. During these trials, verbalizations concerning their performance were recorded.

Participants classified as persistent were found to make more strategy-related comments (e.g., "I think I'm not using my arms enough"). Conversely, free-response attributions (e.g., "My legs are like jelly; we had swimming this afternoon") and negative self-statements (e.g., "My balance is pretty bad") were more likely to be made by those defined as less persistent. Of the 37 statements coded as attributions, all could be classified in terms of either task difficulty, ability, or effort. Task-difficulty attributions (e.g., "I want to protest - this is an unfair test!") were made significantly more often by the less persistent participants. This was also the case for attributional statements associated with lack of ability (e.g., "So I'm no good").

The method of recording and coding free-response attributions during tasks may still possess an element of reactivity. For instance, Diener and Dweck (1978) requested the children "to think out loud", and we asked this of our participants too (Johnson & Biddle, 1988). A true spontaneous attribution, therefore, will only occur in more natural settings and without intervention from a researcher. Nevertheless, recording free-response attributions would appear to be one method suitable for development in sport and exercise psychology.

In addition to the more overt prompting of language, attribution researchers in physical activity may also wish to consider analyzing conversations and naturally occurring discourse. In family therapy sessions, conversations have been analyzed for attribution content using a specially constructed analysis system named the Leeds Attributional Coding System (LACS; Stratton et al., 1986; Stratton, Munton, Hanks, Heard, & Davidson, 1988).

Leeds Attributional Coding System

The Leeds Attributional Coding System is an example of a system developed specifically for the coding of attributions occurring in natural discourse. Such a system could be particularly valuable in sport and exercise contexts, such as the investigation of coach-athlete attributions or the analysis of attributions during performance or breaks in performance. However, we are not aware of published sport and exercise psychology research using this or a similar system.

The LACS was developed by British psychologists working primarily in family therapy settings. However, Stratton et al. (1988) stated clearly that they saw much wider application of the LACS. The coding system is based on the notion that an event is caused by a factor, but the event and cause are embedded in a set of other events and possible causes. There are three parts to this causal sequence: cause, link, and outcome. Stratton et al. (1988) said that allocating an attributional dimension to this sequence is not always easy. For example, the label of stability could be applied to the cause, the link, or the outcome. Resolving this, Stratton et al. highlight the importance of clinical usefulness: "Our overall principle has been to ask what effect the decision will have on the interpretability of the ultimate scores" (Stratton et al., 1988, pp. 28-29).

The LACS is based on classifying attributions through the following five dimensions:

1. Stable-unstable: Classification is based on probability of occurrence and is most often applied to the cause rather than the link or outcome.
2. Global-specific: This is classified in terms of the number of possible consequences stemming from the identified cause.
3. Internal-external: Classification is based on whether the outcome is seen to be due to the individual concerned and whether the speaker regards it as a characteristic of themselves or not.
4. Personal-universal: Personal attributions refer to causes that are related to the individual but not to others, whereas universal attributions are related to the individual and others.
5. Controllable-uncontrollable: This refers to the amount of influence to be had over the outcome.

Here is an example of comments from Bill, a track and field coach, that refer to Elizabeth, the athlete he is coaching. The comments in italics could be construed as attributional in nature and open to analysis, using a system such as the LACS. Possible attributional dimensions from the LACS are given in square brackets.

> "the last two months she's done really well. *I think she's begun to feel the benefit of the speedwork we've been doing* [internal; unstable; controllable?; specific?;

universal]...; *her high jump has reached a plateau - it's her layout* [internal; stable?; personal]...; *shot put has been a good event for Elizabeth - she's got quite a good throwing arm and a fair amount of speed*" [internal; stable; controllable?; global?](Sellars, 1997)

We suggest that researchers interested in furthering attribution work in sport and exercise, particularly in the important area of interpersonal relations, use a system such as the LACS to provide insight currently lacking in much of the literature. We predict this to be a trend in the coming years, particularly given the increasing interest in emerging research paradigms and qualitative approaches in sport and exercise psychology (Martens, 1987; Sparkes, 1992).

Archival Sources and Content Analysis

Another source of attributions in sport and exercise is through archival material, such as newspaper reports, yet this form of analysis remains largely untouched. Post match interviews with coaches, players, officials, and spectators are rich sources of causal statements, yet remain an underdeveloped area in research (Lau & Russell, 1980; Watkins, 1986b). The advantage of such a method lies in the relative spontaneity of the attributions, although again there is an element of prompting in the interview context.

Watkins (1986b) analyzed the New Zealand newspapers and, through content analysis, classified reasons given for sporting outcomes in terms of locus, stability, and controllability attribution dimensions. Watkins found that, regardless of the outcome of the contest, attributions tended to be internal, controllable, and unstable, although winning outcomes were more likely to be explained in these terms. These results supported the content analysis of sports reports by Lau and Russell (1980).

Attributional Complexity

When we discussed the CDS and CDSII, we raised the issue of whether some people would be able to articulate their attributions prior to rating them on the CDS(II) subscales. This may be a function of age, educational level, experience, or other factors. Similarly, social psychologists have debated for some years the issue of whether attribution theories overestimate or underestimate the complexity of cognitive activity when making attributions (Fiske & Taylor, 1991). In developing a measure of "attributional complexity" (complexity of attributional schemata), Fletcher, Danilovics, Fernandez, Peterson, and Reeder (1986) viewed cognitive complexity as domain specific, being dependent on such factors as knowledge, interest and motivation. Given that the use of attributions in sport and exercise contexts is quite likely to involve people with differential knowledge, interest, and motivation, assessing attributional complexity may be an interesting innovation for the sport and exercise psychology literature. To date, we have no knowledge of published research using the measurement of attributional complexity in sport or exercise settings.

In developing their scale of attributional complexity, Fletcher et al. (1986) postulated seven attributional constructs varying on a continuum from simple to complex:

1. Level of interest or motivation to explain and understand events and behaviors
2. Preference for complex rather than simple explanations
3. Presence of metacognition concerning explanations
4. Awareness of the extent to which other's behavior is a function of interaction with others
5. Tendency to infer abstract or causally complex internal attributions
6. Tendency to infer abstract, contemporary, external causal attributions
7. Tendency to infer external causes operating from the past.

The Attributional Complexity Scale (ACS) initially comprised 45 items, but these were reduced to 28 items representing the seven attributional constructs just outlined, with 4 items per construct. Table 4 shows sample items from each construct. The psychometric properties of the scale were supported through adequate internal consistency and test-retest reliability; verification for one factor, namely "attributional complexity;" no relationship between attributional complexity and social desirability, academic ability, and locus of control. Attributionally more complex people had a higher need for cognition; more complex subjects mentioned more causes for a close friend's personality than did those classified as less complex; attributionally complex participants displayed a stronger preference for a complex causal attribution for simple events.

The construct of attributional complexity requires testing in sport and exercise settings. We already know that the approach sport and exercise psychologists have adopted in attribution research has been narrow (Biddle, 1993), and the use of the ACS, either in the original form or modified for physical activity settings, may reduce this criticism.

SUMMARY AND CONCLUSIONS

This chapter has provided a brief overview of key attributional processes common in the study of sport and exercise causal thought. A number of methodological issues have been raised that, in addition to the discussion on actual measures used in sport/exercise attribution studies, confirm that contemporary research in our field has been overly restrictive. Reliance on self-report paper and pencil measures and a general unawareness of other approaches may be associated with the apparent decline in popularity of attribution research in sport and exercise psychology since the mid-1980s. Although some measures have been developed with a degree of rigor and success (e.g., CDSII, SASS), there remains a great deal of progress still to be made if sport and exercise attribution research is to reach the sophistication of that reported in other areas of the social psychology and social cognition literature. It is hoped that some issues raised in this chapter will assist in the process of moving sport/exercise attribution research forward.

Table 4

Example Items From Each Subscale of the Attributional Complexity Scale (Fletcher et al., 1986).

Attributional Construct	Example Item
Motivational component	I don't usually bother to analyze and explain people's behavior
Preference for complex explanations	I prefer simple rather than complex explanations for people's behavior
Metacognition	I believe it is important to analyze and understand our own thinking processes
Behavior as a function of interaction	I think very little about the different ways that people influence each other
Complex internal explanations	I tend to take people's behavior at face value and not worry about the inner causes for their behavior (e.g., attitudes, beliefs etc.)
Complex contemporary external explanations	I think a lot about the influence that society has on my behavior and personality
Use of temporal dimension	I have thought very little about my own family background and personal history in order to understand why I am the sort of person I am

References

Abramson, L.Y., & Martin, D.J. (1981). Depression and the causal inference process. In J.H. Harvey, W.J. Ickes, & R.F. Kidd (Eds.), *New directions in attribution research* (Vol. 3) (pp. 117-168). Hillsdale, NJ: Erlbaum.

Anderson, C.A., Jennings, D.L., & Arnoult, L.H. (1988). Validity and utility of the attributional style construct at a moderate level of specificity. *Journal of Personality and Social Psychology, 55,* 979-990.

Bem, D.J. (1967). Self-perception: An alternative interpretation of cognitive dissonance phenomena. *Psychological Review, 74,* 183-200.

Biddle, S.J.H. (1988). Methodological issues in the researching of attribution-emotion links in sport. *International Journal of Sport Psychology, 19,* 264-280.

Biddle, S.J.H. (1993). Attribution research and sport psychology. In R.N. Singer, M. Murphey & L.K. Tennant (Eds.), *Handbook of research on sport psychology* (pp. 437-464). New York: Macmillan.

Biddle, S.J.H. (1994). Motivation and participation in exercise and sport. In S. Serpa, J. Alves & V. Pataco, (Eds). *International perspectives on sport and exercise psychology* (pp. 103-126). Morgantown, WV: Fitness Information Technology, Inc..

Biddle, S.J.H. & Hill, A.B. (1988). Causal attributions and emotional reactions to outcome in a sporting contest. *Personality and Individual Differences, 9,* 213-223.

Biddle, S.J.H. & Hill, A.B. (1992). Attributions for objective outcome and subjective appraisal of performance: Their relationships with emotional reactions in sport. *British Journal of Social Psychology, 31,* 215-226.

Biddle, S.J.H. & Jamieson, K. (1988). Attributions dimensions: Conceptual clarification and moderator variables. *International Journal of Sport Psychology, 19,* 47-59.

Bird, A.M., Foster, C.D., & Maruyama, G. (1980).Convergent and incremental effects of cohesion on attributions for self and team. *Journal of Sport Psychology, 2,* 181-194.

Bukowski, W.M. & Moore, D. (1980). Winners' and losers' attributions for success and failure in a series of athletic events. *Journal of Sport Psychology, 2,* 195-210.

Carron, A.V. (1984). Attributing causes to success and failure. *The Australian Journal of Science and Medicine in Sport, 16(2),* 11-15.

Cutrona, C.E., Russell, D., & Jones, R.D. (1985). Cross-situational consistency in causal attributions: Does attributional style exist? *Journal of Personality and Social Psychology, 47,* 1043-1058.

Diener, C.I. & Dweck, C.S. (1978). An analysis of learned helplessness: Continuous changes in performance, strategy, and achievement cognitions following failure. *Journal of Personality and Social Psychology, 36,* 451-462.

Elig, T.W., & Frieze, I.H. (1975). A multi-dimensional scheme for coding and interpreting perceived causality for success and failure events. *CSPC Catalog of Selected Documents in Psychology, 5:313* (ms no. 1069).

Feather, N.T., & Tiggeman, M. (1984). A balanced measure of attributional style. *Australian Journal of Psychology, 36,* 267-283.

Fielstein, E., Klein, M.S., Fischer, M., Haman, C., Koburger, P., Schneider, M.J., & Leitenberg, H. (1985). Self-esteem and causal attributions for success and failure in children. *Cognitive Therapy and Research, 9,* 381-398.

Fiske, S.T. & Taylor, S.E. (1991). *Social cognition* (2nd Edn). New York: McGraw-Hill.

Fletcher, G.J.O., Danilovics, P., Fernandez, G., Peterson, D., & Reeder, G.D. (1986). Attributional complexity: An individual difference measure. *Journal of Personality and Social Psychology, 51,* 875-884.

Fontaine, G. (1975). Causal attributions in simulated versus real situations: When are people logical and when are they not? *Journal of Personality and Social Psychology, 32,* 1021-1029.

Forsterling, F. (1988). *Attribution theory in clinical psychology.* Chichester: John Wiley.

Frieze, I.H., McHugh, M., & Duquin, M. (1976). *Causal attributions for women and men and sports participation.* Paper presented at the annual meeting of the U.S. Psychological Association, Washington, D.C.

Gill, D.L., Ruder, M.K., & Gross, J.B. (1982). Open-ended attributions in team competition. *Journal of Sport Psychology, 4,* 159-169.

Gollwitzer, P.M., Earle, W.B., & Stephan, W.G. (1982).Affect as a determinant of egotism: Residual excitation and performance attributions. *Journal of Personality and Social Psychology, 43,* 702-709.

Grove, J.R., Hanrahan, S.J. & McInman, A. (1991). Success/failure bias in attributions across involvement categories in sport. *Personality and Social Psychology Bulletin, 17,* 93-97.

Hanrahan, S.J. (1995). Attribution theory. In T. Morris & J.J. Summers (Eds). *Sport psychology: Theory, applications and issues* (pp. 122-142). Brisbane: John Wiley.

Hanrahan, S.J., & Grove, J.R. (1990a). Further examination of the psychometric properties of the Sport Attribution Style Scale. *Journal of Sport Behavior, 13,* 183-193.

Hanrahan, S.J., & Grove, J.R. (1990b). A short form of the Sport Attribution Style Scale. *Australian Journal of Science and Medicine in Sport, 22(4),* 97-101.

Hanrahan, S.J., Grove, J.R., & Hattie, J.A. (1989). Development of a questionnaire measure of sport-related attributional style. *International Journal of Sport Psychology, 20,* 114-134.

Heider, F. (1944). Social perception and phenomenal causality. *Psychological Review, 51,* 358-374.

Heider, F. (1958). *The psychology of interpersonal relations.* New York: John Wiley.

Hewstone, M. (1989). *Causal attribution: From cognitive processes to collective beliefs.* Oxford: Blackwell.

Ickes, W. (1980). Attributional styles and the self-concept. In L.Y. Abramson (Ed.), *Attributional processes and clinical psychology.* New York: Guilford Press.

Ickes, W., & Layden, M.A. (1978). Attributional styles. In J.H. Harvey, W.J. Ickes, & R.F. Kidd (Eds.), *New directions in attribution research* (Vol. 2, pp. 121-152). Hillsdale, NJ: Erlbaum.

Iso-Ahola, S.E. (1977). Immediate attributional effects of success and failure in the field: Testing some laboratory hypotheses. *European Journal of Social Psychology, 7,* 275-296.

Iso-Ahola, S.E., & Roberts, G.C. (1977). Causal attributions following success and failure at an achievement motor task. *Research Quarterly, 48,* 541-549.

Johnson, L. & Biddle, S.J.H. (1988). Persistence after failure: An exploratory look at 'learned helplessness' in motor performance. *British Journal of Physical Education Research Supplement, 5,* 7-10.

Jones, E.E. & Davis, K.E. (1965). From acts to dispositions: The attribution process in person perception. In L. Berkowitz (Ed.). *Advances in experimental social psychology:* Vol. 2 (pp. 219-266). London: Academic Press.

Kelley, H.H. (1967). Attribution theory in social psychology. In D. Levine (Ed). *Nebraska symposium on motivation*: Vol. 15. (pp. 192-240). Lincoln, NE: University of Nebraska Press.

Kelley, H.H., & Michela, J.L. (1980). Attribution theory and research. *Annual Review of Psychology, 31,* 459-501.

Lau, R.R. & Russell, D. (1980). Attributions in the sports pages. *Journal of Personality and Social Psychology, 39,* 29-38.

Leith, L.M. & Prapavessis, H. (1989). Attributions of causality and dimensionality associated with sport outcomes in objectively evaluated and subjectively evaluated sports. *International Journal of Sport Psychology, 20,* 224-234.

Maehr, M.L., & Nicholls, J.G. (1980). Culture and achievement motivation: A second look. In N. Warren (Ed.), *Studies in cross-cultural psychology* (pp.221-267). New York: Academic Press.

Mark, M.M., Mutrie, N., Brooks, D.R., & Harris, D.V.(1984). Causal attributions of winners and losers in individual competitive sports: Toward a reformulation of the self-serving bias. *Journal of Sport Psychology, 6,* 184-196.

Martens, R. (1987). Science, knowledge, and sport psychology. *The Sport Psychologist, 1,* 29-55.

McAuley, E. (1991). Efficacy, attributional, and affective responses to exercise participation. *Journal of Sport and Exercise Psychology, 13,* 382-393.

McAuley, E. (1992). Self-referent thought in sport and physical activity. In T. Horn (Ed.), *Advances in sport psychology* (pp. 101-118). Champaign, IL: Human Kinetics.

McAuley, E. & Duncan, T. (1989). Causal attributions and affective reactions to disconfirming outcomes in motor performance. *Journal of Sport and Exercise Psychology, 11,* 187-200.

McAuley, E. & Duncan, T. (1990). The causal attribution process in sport and physical activity. In S. Graham & V.S. Folkes (Eds.). *Attribution theory: Applications to achievement, mental health and interpersonal conflict* (pp. 37-52). Hillsdale, NJ: Erlbaum.

McAuley, E., Duncan, T. & Russell, D. (1992). Measuring causal attributions: The revised Causal Dimension Scale (CDSII). *Personality and Social Psychology Bulletin, 18,* 566-573.

McAuley, E., & Gross, J.B. (1983). Perceptions of causality in sport: An application of the Causal Dimension Scale. *Journal of Sport Psychology, 5,* 72-76.

McAuley, E. & Tammen, V. (1989). The effects of subjective and objective competitive outcomes on intrinsic motivation. *Journal of Sport and Exercise Psychology, 11,* 84-93.

Miller, F.D., Smith, E.R., & Uleman, J. (1981).Measurement and interpretations of situational and dispositional attributions. *Journal of Experimental Social Psychology, 17,* 80-95.

Morgan, L.K., Griffin, J., & Haywood, V.H. (1996). Ethnicity, gender and experience effects on attributional dimensions. *The Sport Psychologist, 10,* 4-16.

Mullen, B. & Riordan, C.A. (1988). Self-serving attributions for performance in naturalistic settings: A meta-analytic review. *Journal of Applied Social Psychology, 18,* 3-22.

Peterson, C., & Seligman, M.E.P. (1984). Causal explanations as a risk factor for depression: Theory and evidence. *Psychological Review, 91,* 347-374.

Peterson, C., Semmel, A., von Baeyer, C., Abramson, L.Y., Metalsky, G.I., & Seligman, M.E.P. (1982). The Attributional Style Questionnaire. *Cognitive Therapy and Research, 6,* 287-299.

Prapavessis, H. & Carron, A.V. (1988). Learned helplessness in sport. *The Sport Psychologist, 2,* 189-201.

Rethorst, S. (1992). *Kognitionen und Emotionen in sportlichen Leistungssituationen: Eine Uberprufung einer attributionalen Theorie von Emotionen.* Koln, Germany: bps-Verlag.

Roberts, G.C., & Pascuzzi, D. (1979). Causal attributions in sport: Some theoretical implications. *Journal of Sport Psychology, 1,* 203-211.

Rotter, J.B. (1966). Generalized expectancies for internal versus external control of reinforcement. *Psychological Monographs, 80* (Whole No. 609), 1-28.

Russell, D. (1982). The Causal Dimension Scale: A measure of how individual perceive causes. *Journal of Personality and Social Psychology, 42,* 1137-1145.

Russell, D., McAuley, E., & Tarico, V. (1987). Measuring causal attributions for success and failure: A comparison of methodologies for assessing causal dimensions. *Journal of Personality and Social Psychology, 52,* 1248-1257.

Sarrazin, P., Biddle, S.J.H., Famose, J-P., Cury, F., Fox, K.R. &

Durand, M. (1996). Goal orientations and conceptions about the nature of sport ability in children: A social cognitive approach. *British Journal of Social Psychology, 35,* 399-414.

Scanlan, T.K., & Passer, M.W. (1980). Self-serving biases in the competitive sport setting: An attributional dilemma. *Journal of Sport Psychology, 2,* 124-136.

Schachter, S. (1964). The interaction of cognitive and physiological determinants of emotional state. In L. Berkowitz (Ed.) *Advances in experimental social psychology: Vol 1* (pp. 49-82). New York: Academic Press.

Seligman, M.E.P., Abramson, L.Y., Semmel, A., & vonBaeyer, C. (1979). Depressive attributional style. *Journal of Abnormal Psychology, 88,* 242-247.

Sellars, C. (1997). Unpublished data, School of Education, University of Exeter.

Silverman, D. (1993). *Interpreting qualitative data: Methods for analyzing talk, text and interaction.* London: Sage.

Smith, R.A. (1995). *Social psychological factors in exercise adherence in adults.* Unpublished doctoral thesis, University of Exeter.

Sparkes, A.C. (Ed) (1992). *Research in physical education and sport: Exploring alternative visions.* London: Falmer Press.

Spink, K.S. & Roberts, G.C. (1980). Ambiguity of outcome and causal attributions. *Journal of Sport Psychology, 2,* 237-244.

Stratton, P., Heard, D., Hanks, H., Munton, A., Brewin, C. & Davidson, C. (1986). Coding causal beliefs in natural discourse. *British Journal of Social Psychology, 25,* 299-313.

Stratton, P., Munton, A., Hanks, H., Heard, D., & Davidson, C. (1988). *Leeds Attributional Coding System manual.* Leeds, UK: Leeds Family Therapy and Research Centre, Department of Psychology, University of Leeds.

Tenenbaum, G., & Furst, D. (1985). The relationship between sport achievement responsibility, attribution and related situational variables. *International Journal of Sport Psychology, 16,* 254-269.

Tenenbaum, G., & Furst, D.M. (1986). Consistency of attributional responses by individuals and groups differing in gender, perceived ability, and expectations for success. *British Journal of Social Psychology, 25,* 315-321.

Tenenbaum, G., Furst, D., & Weingarten, G. (1984).Attribution of causality in sport events: Validation of the Wingate Sport Achievement Responsibility Scale. *Journal of Sport Psychology, 6,* 430-439.

Tesch, R. (1990). *Qualitative research: Analyzis types and software tools.* London: Falmer Press.

Vallerand, R.J. (1987). Antecedents of self-related affects in sport: Preliminary evidence on the intuitive-reflective appraisal model. *Journal of Sport Psychology, 9,* 161-182.

Vallerand, R.J. & Richer, F. (1988). On the use of the Causal Dimension Scale in a field setting: A test with confirmatory factor analysis in success and failure situations. *Journal of Personality and Social Psychology, 54,* 704-712.

Van Raalte, J.L. (1994). Sport performance attributions: A special case of self-serving bias? *Australian Journal of Science and Medicine in Sport, 26(3/4),* 45-48.

Vlachopoulos, S., Biddle, S.J.H. & Fox, K.R. (1996). A social-cognitive investigation into the mechanisms of affect generation in children's physical activity. *Journal of Sport and Exercise Psychology, 18,* 174-193.

Watkins, D. (1986a). Assessing causal dimensions. *Australian Psychologist, 21,* 467-472.

Watkins, D. (1986b). Attributions in the New Zealand sports pages. *The Journal of Social Psychology, 126,* 817-819.

Weary, G., Stanley, M.A. & Harvey, J.H. (1989). *Attribution.* New York: Springer-Verlag.

Weiner, B. (1979). A theory of motivation for some classroom experiences. *Journal of Educational Psychology, 71,* 3-25.

Weiner, B. (1985). 'Spontaneous' causal thinking. *Psychological Bulletin, 97,* 74-84.

Weiner, B. (1986). *An attributional theory of motivation and emotion.* New York: Springer-Verlag.

Weiner, B. (1992). *Human motivation: Metaphors, theories and research.* Newbury Park, CA: Sage.

Weiner, B., Frieze, I., Kukla, A., Reed, L., Rest, S. & Rosenbaum, R.M. (1972). Perceiving the causes of success and failure. In E.E. Jones, D. Kanouse, H.H. Kelley, R.E. Nisbett, S. Valins, & B. Weiner (Eds.), *Attribution: Perceiving the causes of behavior* (pp. 95-120). Morristown, NJ: General Learning Press.

Willimczik, K. & Rethorst, S. (1995). Cognitions and emotions in sport achievement situations. In S.J.H. Biddle (Ed.), *European perspectives on exercise and sport psychology* (pp. 218-244). Champaign, IL: Human Kinetics.

Yamamoto, Y. (1983). A study on causal attribution for coaching. *Japanese Journal of Sport Psychology, 10,* 36-42.

Acknowledgements

1. Sections of this chapter were written when Stuart Biddle was a visiting researcher in the Centre d'Optimisation de la Performance Motrice, Department of Sciences et Techniques des Activites Physiques et Sportives (STAPS), University of Montpellier I, France, while on study leave from the University of Exeter. The support and hospitality of Professor Marc Durand (Montpellier) and the financial support of the School of Education, University of Exeter, are gratefully acknowledged.

2. The assistance of Chris Sellars (National Coaching Foundation & University of Exeter) with the section on qualitative assessment of attributions is gratefully acknowledged.

Chapter 2

MEASUREMENT OF GOAL PERSPECTIVES IN THE PHYSICAL DOMAIN

Joan L. Duda
Purdue University
and
Jean Whitehead
University of Brighton

O ver the past 10 years, sport research steeped in social cognitive models of motivation that emphasize the significance of personal goals has burgeoned. Central to this growth has been the development of sport-related measures to assess the constructs critical to such theoretical frameworks. In the first part of this chapter, the major tenets of the goal perspective approach to motivation are provided and differences as well as commonalities between the positions taken by major achievement goal theorists are delineated. To foster clarity in the central concepts, the distinctions between the conceptual definitions of dispositional, situational, and state goal perspectives are presented. The chapter will then review the psychometric characteristics and conceptual underpinnings of measures of dispositional goal orientations and perceptions of situationally induced *task and ego goal perspectives* in the sport domain. Assessments of achievement goals as applied to the context of physical education will also be critically analyzed. We conclude with suggestions for future work concerning the measurement of goal perspectives and, in particular, highlight recent efforts to assess task and ego goal states in the physical domain.

THEORETICAL RATIONALE AND DEFINITION OF CONSTRUCTS
Nicholls, Maehr, Dweck, Ames: Distinctions and Similarities

Research on goal perspectives in sport and exercise settings has been grounded in the achievement goal theories proffered by Nicholls (1984, 1989, 1992), Dweck (1986; Dweck & Elliott, 1993; Dweck & Leggett, 1988), Maehr (Maehr & Braskamp, 1986; Maehr & Nicholls, 1980), and Ames (1984, 1992a, 1992b). Taken collectively, their conceptual approaches

to the study of achievement motivation hold several tenets in common. Each of these educational psychologists agrees that a major focus in achievement settings is to demonstrate competence, and thus, the salience of perceptions of ability is a central feature of achievement strivings. They concur that (at least) two major goal perspectives, one being self-referenced or mastery focused and the other comparative or normatively referenced, are operating in achievement situations. These scholars further emphasize that variations in goal perspectives are fundamental to observed differences in people's achievement-related cognitions, affect, and behavior.

The body of motivation research cultivated by Nicholls, Maehr, Dweck, and Ames can also be distinguished in a number of important ways. Maehr worked initially with Nicholls (Maehr & Nicholls, 1980) to propose that individuals differ in their personal definitions of success/failure, which are based on the perceptions that one has (or has not) demonstrated a personally meaningful attribute (such as showing that one is a hard worker or is competent). Maehr and Nicholls (1980) specifically challenged the prevailing tendency in achievement motivation research (e.g., studies testing Weiner's attributional model of achievement motvation and emotion; Weiner, 1985) to define success and failure experiences with respect to objective criteria such as winning/losing or high versus poor grades. They also suggested that three achievement orientations or perspectives on defining achievement (ability, mastery, and social approval) might be recognized worldwide, albeit with different national or ethnic group emphases.

Nicholls (1984, 1989) extended and qualified the position of Maehr and Nicholls (1980) by proposing (a) perceptions of success and failure are linked to peoples' perceptions of whether they demonstrated high or low ability; (b) variations in subjective definitions of success/failure emanate from the conception of ability that is adopted, that is, whether ability is conceived in a task- and/or ego-involved manner; (c) the conception of ability evoked is impacted by developmental change as well as dispositional and situational factors; and (d) "although there is much more to achievement-related cognition than conceptions of the nature of ability" (Nicholls, 1992), individuals' conceptions *and* perceptions of their current capacity are most relevant to the prediction of achievement patterns (p. 42).

Nicholls (1989) suggests that situations can be characterized as more or less task and/or ego involving. Environments that are marked by interpersonal competition, the public evaluation of skills, normatively based feedback, and/or the testing of an important attribute are held to be ego involving. In contrast, situations that focus on the learning process, personal improvement, and effortful involvement over outcome are considered task involving.

Most of Nicholls' (1989) work, however, examined the motivation-related correlates of orthogonal task and ego orientations (or "individual differences in proneness to the different types of involvement," p. 95). In the former case, perceived ability is self-referenced and emphasis is placed on task mastery, effort investment, and development of one's skills or increased insight. When ego orientation prevails, individuals are concerned with demonstrating normatively referenced high ability and, thus, perceive a successful event when they think that they have surpassed others or performed equally with less effort (i.e., shown that they possess superior ability).

Dweck (1986; Dweck & Leggett, 1988; Elliott & Dweck, 1988), considers goal perspectives to be bipolar and underpinned by beliefs about the flexibility or stability of intelligence (i.e., individual differences in incremental versus entity theories of intelligence). It should be emphasized that Dweck uses the term conceptions of ability (as do others who have drawn from her work; e.g., Jourden, Bandura & Banfield, 1991) with a different meaning than that held by Nicholls. In Dweck's view, people hold concepts of ability that equate ability to either an acquirable personal quality or skill *or* a fixed and inherent aptitude. On the other hand, Nicholls (1989; Nicholls & Miller, 1984) argues that a task conception of ability represents a view in which effort and ability are undifferentiated. An ego conception of ability, in contrast, indicates that ability is differentiated from effort and viewed as a capacity. Thus, Nicholls' approach to conceptions of ability does *not* specifically relate to whether individuals perceive that ability can be changed, but whether one's ability is viewed as being influenced by the degree of effort one exerts.

Typically involving an experimental laboratory paradigm, the work of Dweck and her colleagues has emphasized the effect of "learning" versus "performance" goals on motivational processes in the cognitive domain. The two goals have been found to predict two distinct behavioral patterns, particularly in response to failure. Dweck (1986) terms these respective patterns mastery oriented and helpless oriented.

Ames (1984; Ames & Archer, 1988) has focused primarily on the antecedents and motivational implications of students'

perceptions of their classroom climate. In essence, her efforts have centered on variations in situationally manifested goal perspectives (labelled mastery and ability goals) as perceived to be reflected in the behaviors and direction of teachers and the ways in which they structure their classrooms. This work has laid the basis for intervention studies designed to examine the effect of mastery-based classrooms on students' beliefs, self-perceptions and reported motivation (Ames, 1992a, 1992b).

Individual Differences, Motivational Climate and Goal States

As previously mentioned, Nicholls (1989) suggests that there are dispositional tendencies that predispose individuals to adopt one state or the other. Whether one is in a state of task or ego involvement is assumed to be also influenced by perceptions of the motivational climate (or situationally emphasized goal perspectives) and the person's stage of cognitive development.

Within the existent sport psychology research focused on achievement goals, there has been considerable confusion concerning the distinctions among individual differences in achievement goals, perceptions of the motivational climate, and goal states. In an attempt to clarify these three constructs and move toward greater consistency in the sport goal perspective literature, Duda (1992, 1996) has argued for the adoption of Nicholls' terminology. Her argument concerning the preferred employment of the terms task and ego goals as advocated by Nicholls (1984, 1989, 1992), rather than learning and performance (Dweck & Leggett, 1988) or mastery and ability (Ames, 1992a, 1992b) goals, was based on important conceptual reasons. Duda (1992, 1996) has suggested that, whether applied to goal states, dispositions, or environments, the latter terms seem more conducive to ambiguous usage and obscure definitions.

Specifically, Duda (1992, 1996) has proposed that in physical activity settings such as competitive sport, people vary in their dispositional task and ego orientations. Goal orientations and the perceived motivational climate (or degree to which the environment created by significant others such as coaches, parents, and physical education teachers is deemed task and/or ego involving) impact if an individual is task and/or ego involved while participating in practice/training, an exercise or physical education class, or a competitive event. Thus, task involvement and ego involvement are considered to be reflective of transitory goal states or distinct ways in which we process an activity at any moment of time.

Focus on Task and Ego Goal Perspectives

This chapter will focus on the assessment of task and ego goal perspectives dealing particularly with the measurement of dispositional and perceived situationally manifested goal perspectives. We first overview the available measures of individual differences in goal perspectives or dispositional goal orientations because the majority of research in the physical domain has been in this area. We then outline the developing work on the measurement of perceptions of the situational goal structure or the perceived motivational climate. In each case, the research has evolved from work in the classroom to be first applied to sport and then to the context of physical education. Therefore, our presentation follows this progression.

INDIVIDUAL DIFFERENCES IN GOAL PERSPECTIVES OR ACHIEVEMENT ORIENTATIONS

In studying individual differences in achievement motivation, Maehr and Nicholls (1980) moved from the personality-centered approach of McClelland (1961) and the interactionist approach of Atkinson (1964) to propose a cognitive approach in which motivation would be defined in terms of its purpose or meaning for people. Two complementary approaches were recommended by Maehr and Nicholls. The first approach focused on identifying diverse interpretations of achievement among different cultural groups around the world, and the possibly unique subjective meaning of achievement to individuals within these groups. This would be achieved by asking people for their own views about achievement, starting with their personal conceptions of success and failure. The second approach revolved around the identification of universal classes of achievement behavior that may be recognized worldwide, although with varying cross-cultural emphases. Maehr and Nicholls proposed that ability-oriented motivation, task-oriented motivation, and social approval-oriented motivation would be universal. Some of the early work assessing achievement goals in the athletic domain was based on their proposals for exploring diversity and universality.

Early Work in Sport

In the first study of subjective achievement goals in sport, Ewing (1981) employed the critical incident method, which asks people to provide information about self-selected meaningful personal experiences. Her Achievement Orientation Questionnaire (AOQ) requested subjects to first recall an occasion when they had felt successful in sport and then to rate, on a 5-point Likert scale anchored by Strongly Agree and Strongly Disagree, how their feelings of success corresponded with 15 statements (e.g., "I felt successful when I met the challenge"). Exploratory factor analysis of the responses provided by 452 high school students revealed ability, task, and social approval orientations and an additional intrinsic factor characterized by a feeling of adventure. Internal consistency values for the four factors ranged from .80 to .91, and in gender-specific analyses, ability and social approval factors effectively discriminated between competitors, dropouts, and nonparticipants in high school sport teams. However, as pointed out by Weiss and Chaumeton (1992),

> ... subsequent studies using the AOQ ...have resulted in different factor structures and number of factors than those found by Ewing. In addition, (research) designed specifically to assess the validity and reliability of the AOQ found little evidence of construct, factorial, and predictive validity or test-retest reliability (pp. 66-67).

In a four-phase study carried out in the United Kingdom between 1985 and 1989, Whitehead (1993a) examined the cross-cultural generalizability of the AOQ and revised it in a search for further goal orientations derived from the views of the subjects themselves. In phase I, 890 middle and upper school age adolescents completed a 17-item version of Ewing's instrument

and then added their own views of success. Exploratory factor analyses showed that Ewing's (1981) four factors were recognizable, but there were age, gender, cultural, and contextual differences in their composition and behavioral correlates (Whitehead, 1995).

In phase II, the 1,398 statements provided by the first subjects were examined for frequency and diversity of content and a 50-item multiple goals questionnaire was constructed to improve the assessment of existing goal factors and identify additional goal perspectives. This was administered to 1,159 subjects (aged 9 to 16 years), and exploratory factor analyses on age and gender-based subgroups yielded a large number (13-16) of first-order factors. This confirmed the anticipated diversity in perspectives of success and was, thus, consistent with Maehr and Nicholls' (1980) argument but the resulting factors were too varied and complex for theoretical and practical explanations. Consequently, based on the initial work, a five-factor extraction was performed on the data. This revealed the three universal orientations (labelled superiority, task, and social approval) as well as "teamwork" and "breakthrough" factors that were deemed relevant to youth sport settings. In phase III, the teamwork, superiority and breakthrough orientations discriminated between persisters and nonpersisters in a longitudinal study of track and field and rugby football athletes (Whitehead, 1990). Gender-based analyses showed two superiority factors for males.

So in phase IV (Whitehead, 1992), the multiple goals instrument was revised to comprise three pairs of first-order factors: victory and ability (focused on direct and indirect measures of superiority), mastery and breakthrough (focused on personal improvement and experiencing novelty), and social approval and teamwork (focused on pleasing or cooperating with others) and three second-order factors (namely, superiority, personal progress, and adaptation to others). Confirmatory factor analysis for the six-factor model showed an acceptable fit (GFI .94, RMSR .055), but the results indicated a need to redefine the mastery dimension and improve its reliability with younger subjects.

More Recent Sport Work Task and Ego Orientation in Sport Questionnaire (TEOSQ)

Conceptual Framework and Definition of Constructs

As Nicholls was one of the two creators of the Task and Ego Orientation in Sport Questionnaire (J. Duda being the other), it is not surprising that this instrument was designed to assess individual differences in the proneness for task and ego involvement as defined in his theory (Nicholls, 1984, 1989). In his extensive writings, Nicholls (1992) has proffered "...a framework for the study of the nature and development of achievement motivation that encompasses features that are common to academic and sport activities as well as unique to specific activities within each domain" (p. 32).

Nicholls suggests that, in each achievement activity, personal goal orientations will be operating that are equated to "habitual achievement preoccupations." These personal goals or "motivational orientations" reflect individual differences in personal criteria of success (Nicholls, 1992, p. 45). Specifically the two goal orientations, labelled task and ego orientation, relate to whether an individual is more or less likely to employ an undifferentiated or differentiated concept of ability. These dimensions of personal goals, which were discussed earlier by Asch (1952), have been found to be independent and orthogonal (Nicholls, 1989). According to Nicholls (1989), task orientation "involves the purposes of gaining skill or knowledge and performing one's best" (p. 46). Through the experience of personal improvement, learning and trying, strongly task-oriented individuals achieve a sense of competence and, consequently, feel successful. When an ego orientation prevails, people tend to be preoccupied with their ability and see the personal demonstration of superior competence as fundamental to success. The aim of the TEOSQ was to assess these goal perspectives as so defined.

Source and Selection of Items

Drawing from an existing assessment of dispositional goal perspectives in classroom settings (i.e., the Motivational Orientation Scale; Nicholls, 1989; Nicholls, Patashnick, & Nolen, 1985) and the conceptual definitions of task and ego orientation, Duda and Nicholls (in 1985) worked on the development of an instrument that would measure goal orientations in the athletic realm. The initial version of the TEOSQ had 16 items, with some taken directly from the Motivational Orientation Scale and reworded for the sport setting whereas other items were developed by the authors. The items that would constitute the first version of the TEOSQ were part of a larger collaborative study that was eventually published in 1992 by Duda and Nicholls. Duda examined the psychometric characteristics of the original 16-item questionnaire soon after the 1985 data collection and then used the instrument in subsequent projects appearing in print before the Duda and Nicholls' article (e.g., Duda, 1989).

When completing the TEOSQ, subjects are requested to think of when they felt successful in a particular sport and then indicate their agreement with items reflecting task-oriented (e.g., "I feel successful in sport when I work really hard," "I feel successful in sport when I learn something that is fun to do") or ego-oriented (e.g., "I feel successful in sport when the others can't do as well as me," "I feel successful in sport when I score the most points") criteria. Responses are indicated on a 5-point Likert-type scale with 1 = *strongly disagree* and 5 = *strongly agree*.

The results of initial factor analytic work (and examinations of internal reliabilities and item-total scale correlations) reduced the TEOSQ to its current 13-item form (Duda, 1989; Duda, Olson, & Templin, 1991). One item from the original scale that was discarded was "I feel most successful when I win" as it loaded on both the task and ego dimensions. As pointed out by Duda (1992, 1996), this finding is conceptually and practically informative as it indicates that the competitive outcome can provide information about personal improvement and mastery (which lays the basis for a task-oriented definition of success) as well as the demonstration of superiority (which is fundamental to an ego-oriented definition of success.)

Norms

As shown in Table 1, over 70 published studies have employed the TEOSQ when assessing dispositional goal perspectives. Across the samples represented in this body of research (N = 12,239), the mean for the task orientation scale is 4.08 + .57 and the average value for the ego orientation scale is 2.87 + .81. In 17 studies in which the TEOSQ scores within the same sample are analyzed separately by gender, the mean task and ego orientation scores for males (N = 1,331) are 4.11 ± .49 and 3.05 ± .80, respectively. For female subjects (N = 1,285), mean task and ego orientation values are 4.18 ± .47 and 2.82 ± .78, respectively. In eight studies in which scores have been analyzed separately for under 13 and over 13 year old subjects, means for the younger group are 4.24 ± .58 (task) and 2.65 ± .86 (ego) whereas those for the older group are 4.26 ± .53 (task) and 2.92 ± .94 (ego).

Reliability

Test-retest reliability. The task and ego orientation scales of the TEOSQ have been found to have acceptable test-retest reliability following a 3-week period (r = .68 and .75, respectively; Duda, 1992) and one soccer season (r = .71 and .72, respectively; VanYperen & Duda, 1997). Thus, the TEOSQ seems to measure a dispositional proneness in a consistent manner over time.

Internal consistency. Cronbach's alpha coefficients for a variety of samples (Table 1) have revealed mean internal reliability values over 56 studies of .79 and .81 for the task and ego orientation scales of the TEOSQ, respectively. Reflecting the robustness of the instrument, the high internal reliability of the TEOSQ scales was retained when young basketball camp participants completed the questionnaire with respect to how they think their parents operationalize athletic achievement and their parents completed the measure in terms of personal definitions and perceptions of how their children defined sport success (Duda & Hom, 1993). Thus, the TEOSQ has been found to exhibit acceptable internal consistency.

Validity

Factorial validity. Investigations employing exploratory factor analysis (with oblique and orthogonal rotations) have continuously found support for the predominant two-dimensional structure of the TEOSQ. This pattern has held across samples of youth sport, adolescent and adult sport participants, and college students from the United States (e.g., Duda, 1989; Duda, Chi, Newton, Walling, & Catley, 1994; Duda et al., 1991; White & Duda, 1994) as well as cross-cultural samples (e.g., Duda, Fox, Biddle, & Armstrong, 1992; Duda & Hayashi, this volume; Guivernau & Duda, 1994). We have noticed, however, that when the TEOSQ is employed with non-elite samples (such as recreational sport or physical education students) the task orientation dimension occasionally splits into two factors; that is, one capturing the items related to learning and the other comprised of items focused on trying hard and doing one's best. This three dimensional structure of TEOSQ is not supported when a two factor solution is called for in exploratory factor analysis or when confirmatory factor analysis is employed.

More recent work has employed structural equation modeling techniques to examine the factorial validity of the TEOSQ. Chi and Duda (1995) independently and simultane-

Table 1.
Data From Studies Using the Task and Ego Orientation in Sport Questionnaire in Ascending Order by Age

Authors	Date	Subjects	Age Mean	SD	Range	N Total	Male	Female	Task Alpha	Mean	SD	Ego Alpha	Mean	SD
Dempsey, Kimiciek, & Horn	1993	Schoolchildren			Grades 4–5	71			.52	3.46	.47	.59	3.00	.68
Duda, Fox, Biddle, & Armstrong	1992	UK schoolchildren	10.5	.8		142			.72	3.89	.41	.78	3.34	.80
Weigand & Petrie	1996	Children athletes	10.6	.8		93	43	50		4.22	.54		2.69	.83
White & Duda	1994	Youth athletes	10.8	.5		61	31	30	.86	4.32		.86	2.53	
Duda & Hom	1993	Basketball camp	11.1	2.0	8yr–15yr	77	43	34	>.78	4.36	.57		2.75	.87
Fox, Goudas, Biddle, Duda & Armstrong	1992	UK schoolchildren	11.1			231	115	116		4.16			3.45	
Boyd & Callaghan	1994	Little League baseball	11.3		10–12yr	91	91	0.0	.85	3.90	.78	.84	3.10	1.05
Stephens	1995	Coed soccer athletes	11.4	1.2	9yr–15yr	330	228	102	.80	4.24	.64	.84	2.81	1.00
Stephens & Bredemeier	1996	Female soccer athletes	11.5	1.2	9yr–14yr	212	0.0	212	.81	4.12	.64	.85	2.50	.96
Ebbeck & Becker	1994	Youth soccer players	12.0	1.3	10yr–14yr	166	75	91	.83	4.00	.63	.80	2.70	.82
Goudas, Biddle, & Fox	1994a	UK schoolchildren			12yr–15yr	255			.71	3.88	.51	.80	2.73	.77
Goudas, Biddle, & Fox	1994b	UK schoolchildren			12yr–14yr	85	39	46	.83	3.63	.69	.86	2.17	.69
Biddle & Goudas	1996	UK schoolchildren			13yr–14yr	147			.79	3.98	.72	.78	2.32	.85
Newton & Duda	1993	Elite tennis	12.7			121	80	41	.78	4.11		.81	2.88	
Williams & Gill	1995	School PE	12.7	1.1	11yr–15yr	174	71	103	.84	4.29	.54	.86	2.74	.92
Hall & Kerr	1997	UK junior fencers	12.8	1.6		111	75	36	.86	4.16	.70	.87	3.09	.96
Stephens, Janz, & Mahoney	1996	Adolescents	12.9	1.0	10yr–14yr	114	56	58	.84	4.14	.61	.82	2.94	.85
Guest & White	1996	PE and youth sport	12.9		11yr–15yr	135	63	72		4.30	.75		2.93	1.24
Tank, White, & Wingate	1996	YS leagues	13.0			200	0.0	200	.87	4.02	.74	.76	2.65	.84
Goudas, Biddle, Fox, & Underwood	1995	UK schoolgirls	13.0		12yr–13yr	24	0.0	24	.80	4.13	.49	.86	2.42	.82
Guest, White, Jones, McCaw, & Vogler	In PR	PE and youth sport	13.2	1.1	Grades 6 -9	171	71	100	.80	4.28	.53	.83	2.93	.92
Vlachopoulos Biddle, & Fox	1996	UK schoolchildren	13.2	.9	11yr–15yr	304	248	56	.82	3.7:	.64	.86	2.83	.88
Biddle, Akande, Vlachopoulos, & Fox	1996	Zimbabwe adoles.			12yr–14yr	159			.41	.70			3.70	.92
Walling, Duda, & Crawford	1992	Junior high	13.6	1.3	12yr–15yr	234	125	109	>.70	4.32		>.80	2.57	
Bock, Biddle, & Fox	1997	PE classes PE + recreation PE + competition			11yr–16yr	143 64 211			>.83	3.58 3.61 4.04	.67 .63 .58	>.83	2.42 2.57 2.70	.85 .78 .80
Morgan & Carpenter	1997	UK schoolchildren	14.0	.9	12yr–16yr	118	79	39	.81	3.70	.22	.89	2.87	.25
Andrée & Whitehead	1995	UK track and field	14.0	1.7	10yr–17yr	139	67	71	.76	4.12	.53	.80	3.21	.83
Whitehead & Andrée	1997	UK track and field	14.4	1.6	11yr–17yr	111	51	57	.81	4.32	.47	.83	2.99	.87
Lloyd & Fox	1992	UK Schoolgirls			14yr–15yr	48	0.0	48		4.17	.38		2.68	.89
Weigand & Petrie	1996	Adolescents	14.7	1.2			107	51	58	4.19	.58	2.92	.90	
White, Johnson, & Morgan	1995	Volleyball	14.7	1.4		244	0.0	244	.77	4.5:	.48	.83	2.36	.89
Swain & Harwood	1996	UK youth swimming	14.9	1.8	13yr–18yr	214	110	104		3.83	.57		3.20	.75
Duda & Nicholls	1992	High school	15.1		Grades 10–11	207	99	108	.89	4.1:	.69	.86	3.2:	.83
Walling & Duda	1995	High school PE	15.2	.8		144	66	78	.90	4.17	.68	.90	3.44	.86
White	1996a	Volleyball campers	15.4	1.1	14yr–17yr	204	0.0	204	.77	4.14	.44	.81	2.23	.78
Swain	1996	UK PE class	15.6	1.3	Grade 10	96	96	0.0	.84	3.57	.72	.83	3.12	.80

Continued on next page

Table 1 (cont)

Authors	Date	Subjects	Age			N			Task			Ego		
			Mean	SD	Range	Total	Male	Female	Alpha	Mean	SD	Alpha	Mean	SD
Harwood & Swain	1996	UK youth tennis	14.4	1.6	13yr–17yr	119	60	59		4.30	.44		3.48	.67
White & Duda	1993a	Wheelchair b/ball	15.7			59	52	7	.74	4.26	.50	.75	2.44	.81
White & Zellner	1996	High school	15.9	1.4		65	29	36		4.08	.37		3.48	.92
Williams	1994	HS athletes	15.9	1.2	14yr–18yr	162	74	78	.75	4.31	.49	.85	3.08	.90
White & Duda	1994	High school	16.3	.9		63	33	30	.77	4.24		.87	2.54	
Newton & Ddua	1994	Volleyball	16.2	1.7	14yr–18yr	385	0.0	385	.81	4.38		.86	2.66	
Newton & Duda	1996	Volley/basketball HS IC	16.4		13yr–23yr	202	0.0	202	.83	4.34		.85	2.70	
Gano-Overway & Duda	1996	Track athletes	16.5	1.3	13yr–18yr	171	83	88	.73	4.33	.46	.85	3.39	.89
Duda, Olson, & Templin	1991	Interscholastic	16.6		15yr–18yr	123	56	67	.82	4.34		.80	2.57	
Spray & Biddle	1997	UK PE classes	17.4	.7	16yr–19yr	218	115	103	.71	3.97	.44	.81	2.81	.79
Duda	1989	HS males	17.8		Grades 11–12	321	128		.82	4.28	.47	.89	2.89	.87
		HS females	17.1		Grades 11–12			193	.62	4.45	.80	.65	2.59	.96
Tank & White	1996	HS IS Rec	19.3	2.4		249	136	113	.92	4.22	.63	.86	2.54	.85
Solmon & Boone	1993	Tennis class			College	90				4.28	.45		3.05	.83
Newton & Duda	1995	Tennis class	20.2	1.7	17yr–41yr	107			.73	4.21	.43	.82	2.75	.73
Chi	1994	College skill class	20.3	1.8		270	155	115	>.70	4.43		>.80	3.25	
White & Duda	1994	Intercollegiate	20.2	1.3		62	32	30	.87	4.21		.77	3.01	
White & Zellner	1996a	Intercollegiate	20.1	1.4		91	49	42	.92	4.26	.70	.86	3.00	.76
White & Zellner	1996b	Recreational	20.6	1.1		95	60	35	.92	4.17	.92	.86	3.13	.91
Duda, Chi, Newton Walling, & Catley	1994	Volleyball/basketball skills classes	21.1	2.8		121			.83	4.13	.48	.78	2.43	.68
Duda & White	1992	Intercollegiate skier	21.4	.6		143	81	62	.79	4.13		.81	2.94	
Markland & Wilson	1997	UK weight trainers	23.4	7.0		69	69	0.0	.76	3.81	.60	.88	3.21	1.04
Weigand & Davis	1996	UK amateur soccer	24.9			115	115	0.0		3.75	.53		2.98	.75
Barnes, Page, & McKenna	1997	International. rowers UK/Canada	25.8	4.3		98	56	42	.74	4.24 / 4.22	.47 / .46	.66	3.56 / 3.38	.56 / .67
White & Duda	1994	Recreational	26.0	10.2		51	21	30	.80	4.1:		.91	2.49	
Hall & Finnie	1995	UK distance runners	34.6	12.3		246	166	80	.77	4.48	.54	.88	3.04	1.05
Hayashi & Weiss	1994	Anglo marathon	43.4		Adult	153	113	40	.80	4.05	.50	.73	2.56	.80
Newton & Fry	1996	Senior "Olympians"	65.8	7.3	50yr–80yr	60	34	23	.84	3.99	.47	.81	2.66	.76
Dempsey, Kimiciek, & Horn	1993	Parents			Adult	69			.60	3.26	.52	.64	2.87	.50
Duda & Hom	1993	Parents			Adult	76	21	55	>.78	4.31	.47	>.78	2.85	.74
TRANSLATIONS														
Balaguer, Castillo, & Tomas	1996	Spanish adolescents	13.1	1.5	11yr–17yr	283	146	13	.78	4.18	.58	.80	2.70	.82
Kim	1995	Korean school sport			12yr–18yr	334	244	90	.73	3.96	.54	.68	3.46	.63
Dorobantu & Biddle		Romanian PE	15.8	.3		145	61	84	.77	3.76	.87	.78	3.11	.99
Papaioannou & Diggelidis	1996	Greek schoolchildren			10yr–15yr	674	319	355		4.00	.69		2.91	.90
Papaioannou & Macdonald	1993	Greek PE	15.9		13yr–18yr	211	93	118	.64			.75	2.79	
Guivernau & Duda	1994	Spanish athletes	20.4	1.6	18yr–25ys	155	108	47	.75	4.36	.52	.84	3.35	.73
Li, Harmer, Acock Vongjaturapat, & Boonverabut	In PR	Thai IC athletes	21.2			421	218	203		3.00			2.96	
Hayashi & Weiss	1994	Japanese marathon	31.0		Adult	205	122	83	.80	3.74	.70	.73	2.74	.70
MEANS									.79	4.08	.57	.81	2.87	.81

ously tested the two-dimensional measurement model presumed to underlie the TEOSQ across four diverse samples (i.e., intercollegiate athletes, college students enrolled in skill classes, high school athletes, and young adolescent youth sport participants). Although somewhat weaker in the case of the college students, single-sample confirmatory factor analysis (CFA) supported the two orthogonal factor structure in each group (GFI = .89 - .91; RMSR = .06 - .09). The multisample CFA revealed that the proposed two-dimension structure of the TEOSQ was not identical across the four samples. Chi and Duda suggested that differences (due to gender, age, and/or level and type of sport involvement) between the groups tested might have contributed to this observed variance.

In their research on male and female elite Spanish athletes, Guivernau and Duda (1994) also employed CFA to examine the factorial validity of their Spanish translation of the TEOSQ. The findings provided cross-cultural support for the two-factor dimensionality of the instrument.

In a study of male and female college students, Li, Harmer, and Acock (1996) employed CFA to test for invariant measurement properties and factor structures of the TEOSQ across gender. Although there was significant variation in the latent mean structure of the ego orientation scale, Li and his colleagues found measurement invariance suggesting that the two goal orientations are similarly conceptualized by male and female students. Using a confirmatory factor analytic procedure, Li, Harmer, Chi, and Vongjaturapat (1996) also observed that the hypothesized two-factor structure of the TEOSQ provided a good fitting model for samples of male college students from the United States, Thailand, and Taiwan. Their results also supported the orthogonality of the task and ego goal dimensions, but only in the case of the U.S. and Taiwanese samples (i.e., task and ego orientations were positively correlated for the Thailand subjects). Moreover, the samples from the first two countries exhibited higher task orientation scores than the Thai college students. Li, Harmer, Chi, and Vongjaturapat (1996) indicated that it is not possible to discern whether such between country variability is due to cultural factors or competitive level differences.

Li, Harmer, Acock, Vongjaturapat and Boonverabut (in press) tested the factorial validity of the TEOSQ across male and female Thai intercollegiate athletes. CFA supported the two-factor structure in the case of both genders although a strong negative relationship between the orientations emerged. Except for the factor loadings of two items on the task scale, testings of the factor covariances across males/females supported measurement invariance.

Concurrent validity. The concurrent validity of the TEOSQ was initially examined in a study in which the task and ego orientation sport scales and the parallel measures from the classroom-based Motivation Orientation Scales were administered to a sample of 205 high school students (Duda & Nicholls, 1992). As Nicholls (1992) has suggested that the two goal orientations (task and ego) reflect individual differences in the meaning or focus of achievement activities per se, we expected considerable cross-situation generalizability. Supporting this prediction and providing evidence for the validity of the TEOSQ, strong positive correlations were found between the

sport task and ego orientation scales of the TEOSQ and their classroom counterparts (r = .67 and .62, respectively). These findings have been replicated in studies of college students (Guivernau, Thorne, & Duda, 1994) and elite Spanish student-athletes (Guivernau & Duda, 1997).

Predictive validity. Considerable work has been conducted on the relationships between task and ego orientation (as assessed by the TEOSQ) and various indices of motivation. As this research has been reviewed elsewhere (see Duda, 1992, 1993, 1994, 1996), the details of these investigations will not be described in the present chapter.

In general, the literature provides support for the predictive utility of the TEOSQ as a measure of dispositional goal perspectives in the athletic domain. For example, studies have examined the interdependencies of scores on the task and ego scores with

1. *Perceptions of the purposes of sport* (Duda, 1989; McNamara & Duda, 1997; White, Duda & Keller, 1997). Aligned with classroom-based studies and the tenets of goal perspective theory (Nicholls, 1989), scores on the task orientation scale have related to more intrinsic, prosocial views about the functions of athletic involvement. The ego orientation scale of the TEOSQ has been linked to extrinsic and self-serving perceptions concerning what the purposes of sport should be.

2. *Enjoyment, interest, satisfaction and affect/mood* (Boyd & Yin, 1996; Duda, et al., 1995; Duda, et al., 1992; Hall & Earles, 1995; Hom, Duda, & Miller, 1993; Vlachopoulos & Biddle, 1996; Vlachopoulos, Biddle, & Fox, 1996). In accord with theoretical predictions, task orientation (which entails a more process-oriented focus and the involvement in activities for their own sake rather than as a means to an end) is associated with greater enjoyment, heightened investment, and more positive affect/mood states in the physical domain.

3. *Attitudes toward intentional aggressive acts and rule violations or cheating* (Duda & Huston, 1995; Duda, et al.,1991; Stephens & Bredemeier, 1996). Because the concern is with beating others, Nicholls (1989) has suggested that an ego orientation should correspond with a "lack of concern about justice and fairness" as well as the welfare of one's opponent (p. 133). When individuals are predominantly task-oriented, sport is an end in itself. In this case, a person should be less likely to endorse cheating behaviors. The research to date employing the TEOSQ has been consonant with those predictions.

4. *Motives for participation in sport* (White & Duda, 1994). As expected based on achievement goal theory (Nicholls, 1989), scores on the task scale of the TEOSQ have been found to coincide with more intrinsic and cooperative reasons for becoming involved in sport (e.g., to develop one's skills, to be part of a team). On the other hand, ego orientation is coupled with more extrinsic motives for sport participation (e.g., to gain status and recognition).

5. *Beliefs about the causes of success* (Biddle, Akande, Vlachopoulos, & Fox, 1996; Duda, et al., 1992; Duda & Nicholls, 1992; Duda & White, 1992; Guivernau & Duda, 1994; Hom, Duda & Miller, 1993; Newton & Duda, 1993a;

Newton & Walling, 1995; Seifriz, Duda, & Chi, 1992; VanYperen & Duda, 1997; White & Duda, 1993a; White & Zellner, 1996). Because the exerting of effort is intimately tied to perceptions of competence/success when task orientation predominates, we would expect this goal orientation to positively relate to the view that hard work/training/practice are precursors to sport achievement. When ego orientation is pronounced, the focus is on the adequacy of one's ability relative to that of others. Consequently, in this case, it is predicted that the possession of superior ability would be deemed to be a central determinant of "getting ahead" in sport. Other less controllable causes of successful competitive outcomes (such as external factors or illegal practices) would also be expected to positively correlate with ego orientation. In studies employing the TEOSQ among varied groups of sport participants (e.g., youth sport athletes, older adult Master's competitors, elite athletes), this pattern of hypothesized findings has been consistently observed.

6. *Learning and competition strategies* (Lochbaum & Roberts, 1993). Achievement goal theory (Ames, 1992a; Dweck, 1986; Nicholls, 1989) suggests that the adoption of task or ego goals relates to the employment of adaptive (e.g., problem- solving) or maladaptive performance strategies, respectively. The two scales of the TEOSQ have been found to predict effective and ineffective strategy use in the expected directions.

7. *Anxiety and coping strategies* (Gano-Overway & Duda, 1996; Hall & Kerr, in press; Spink, 1995; Tank & White, 1996; White & Zellner, 1996). As the perceived demands in a competitive setting are other referenced and the probability of maintaining high perceived ability is more suspect (Duda, 1992; Nicholls, 1989), an ego orientation should be associated with higher anxiety. When athletes are experiencing stressful situations, the goal perspective literature suggests that task orientation will correspond to more effortful and problem-solving coping behaviors. The findings from studies to date utilizing the TEOSQ and examining athletes' level of state or trait anxiety and/or coping strategies are compatible with these predictions. For example, in a study of British junior fencers between 10 and 18 years of age, Hall and Kerr (in press) found ego orientation to significantly predict cognitive anxiety two and one days prior to a regional fencing tournament. Among the fencers with low perceived ability, an ego orientation was positively linked with cognitive anxiety scores whereas a negative relationship emerged between task orientation and this CSAI-2 subscale. However, Newton and Duda (1995) found goal orientations, as assessed by the TEOSQ, to predict pre-performance state confidence but not somatic and cognitive state anxiety.

8. *Sources of competence information* (Williams, 1994). As goal orientations are assumed to reflect dispositional tendencies in regard to the employment of more or less differentiated conceptions of ability, we would hypothesize that the two TEOSQ scales should differentially relate to reported sources of competence information. Specifically, it would be expected that task orientation is positively associated with more self-referenced criteria. On the other hand, we would predict that there is a positive relationship

between ego orientation and norm-referenced sources of competence. Williams (1994) administered the TEOSQ and Sport Competence Information Scale (see Horn & Amorose, this volume) to 152 high school athletes and found partial support for these predictions. A high task orientation (and low ego orientation) corresponded to such sources as goal attainment, the experience of learning and improvement, sport enjoyment, and pregame attitude as well as parental feedback. Social comparison information was the source of competence information most linked to a strong ego orientation.

9. *Perceptions of significant others' goal orientations* (Duda & Hom, 1993; Ebbeck & Becker, 1994; Kimiecik, Horn & Shurin, 1996; Weigand, 1996). It is assumed that one's goal orientation is a function of socialization processes (Duda, 1992, 1993). Thus, we would expect a correspondence between individuals' degree of task and ego orientation and the perceived goal orientations held by people important in their lives. Research to date has supported this assumption.

10. *Social loafing* (Swain, 1996). Social loafing is the term used to describe the phenomenon wherein individuals lower their exerted effort when working in a group in contrast to working by themselves on the same task. Swain argued that this process would be most pronounced among highly ego-oriented individuals if they found themselves in a group activity entailing outputs that could not be personally identified. Strongly task-oriented people (especially if their ego orientation is low) are expected to try hard regardless of whether they have an individual task or a team activity that entails identifiable or nonidentifiable personal performance. Employing the TEOSQ to assess goal orientations among a sample of 10th grade British males, Swain's findings were aligned with these suppositions, and

11. *Motivation-related behaviors.* Although the study of achievement motivation begins and ends with the study of behavior, relatively less work has been done examining the behavioral correlates of goal orientations. The studies to date have focused on self-reported behaviors rather than actual (or objective) behavioral measures. Theoretically consistent relationships have emerged between individual differences in goal perspectives, as assessed by the TEOSQ, and performance, reported effort, and task choice in sport-related settings (Chi, 1993; VanYperen & Duda, 1997). In investigations involving children, Dempsey, Kimiecik, and Horn (1993) and Kimiecik et al. (1996) have found task orientation to be positively linked with self-reported moderate-to-vigorous physical activity levels.

Summary

The TEOSQ is a conceptually driven instrument designed to assess dispositional proneness for task- and ego-involved goal states in the athletic realm. The operational definitions of task and ego orientations reflected in the TEOSQ stem specifically from the work of Nicholls (1989). This instrument has been found to possess acceptable reliability and be related to a variety of (primarily self-reported) motivation variables in a conceptually consistent manner. The factor structure of the TEOSQ has been repeatedly supported across divergent samples, although one study (Chi & Duda, 1995) has indicated that some variability between diverse groups may exist when tested simultaneously. A perusal of the mean values and standard deviations for the task and ego TEOSQ scales suggests that the task scores are typically higher and less variable than the ego scores. Thus, if the comparative evaluation of TEOSQ scores among particular individuals or subgroups is necessary in a particular study, it may be necessary to transform a very skewed task distribution prior to statistical analyses.

Perceptions of Success Questionnaire (POSQ)

Conceptual Framework and Definition of Constructs

The conceptual framework for the later development of the POSQ pulled from the work of Nicholls (1989) although different terms were first used to label the constructs. In keeping with Nicholls' (1984) focus on two major achievement goals, the POSQ was created to assess two dimensions, initially termed performance or competitiveness and mastery (Roberts & Balague, 1989, 1991) and recently renamed *ego orientation* and *task orientation* (Treasure & Roberts, 1994b).

Source and Selection of Items

Roberts and Balague (1989) created an initial pool of 48 items, drawing on the existing instruments and literature that addressed perceptions of success in sport. A panel of experts was used to identify items that best represented the constructs of mastery or competitiveness/performance (as reflected in the work of Nicholls [1989] and Dweck [1986]). Specifically, sport mastery goal orientation was defined for the experts as follows:

> This conception of ability is evident as a personal goal when a person's actions are aimed at achieving mastery, improving or perfecting a skill or task pertinent to sport performance. When effort is applied, effort is seen to lead to greater learning, mastery or personal skill. Ability is self referenced in that higher ability means the person has improved their own competence at the task.

In contrast, sport performance goal orientation was operationalized as:

> This conception of ability is evident as a personal goal when a person's actions are to compare one's own level of skill or performance with that of others. The focus of attention is on others, and one assesses the effort and ability of others in order to assess own ability and effort and judge whether own ability is greater than or less than that of others. Outcome, winning or losing is important to these people. High perceived ability means ability can be demonstrated, especially through winning, and low perceived ability means ability probably cannot be demonstrated, especially if one expects to lose. Effort is applied or not applied when it is seen to enhance demonstration of ability (e.g., winning without exerting much effort is seen as confirmation of high ability.)

Based on this rating of face validity, 29 items were retained.

The 29-item version of the POSQ was then administered to a large sample of athletes, and exploratory factor analysis

yielded two factors that accounted for 48% of the variance and were labeled "mastery" and "competitiveness" (Roberts & Balague, 1989). Three items were eliminated because they loaded on both factors or reduced alpha coefficients so the initial POSQ comprised 26 items (Roberts & Balague, 1989). Following administration to several populations the instrument was reduced to two 8-item scales, then to a short form of two 6-item scales. The short form correlated highly (Roberts & Balague, 1991) with the standard form (task orientation .98, ego orientation .97).

The POSQ uses the same stem as the TEOSQ, that is,"I feel successful in sport when...". Exemplary items from the task orientation scale include "I overcome difficulties" and "I perform to the best of my ability." Examples of items that compose the ego orientation scale include "I beat other people" and "I outperform my opponents." In contrast to the TEOSQ but not surprising given the operational definition of a sport-performance goal orientation provided above, the item "I win" also is included in the ego orientation scale. Responses to the POSQ are indicated on a 5-point Likert-type scale anchored by *strongly agree* and *strongly disagree*.

Norms

As can be seen in Table 2, the descriptive statistics for the POSQ scales follow the same pattern as for the respective scales of the TEOSQ. That is, we see a skewed distribution for the task orientation scale and a more normally distributed distribution for the ego orientation scale. For example, in the case of 96 parents of British schoolchildren, the mean for task orientation was $4.48 \pm .59$, and the mean for ego orientation was 2.82 ± 1.08 (Roberts, Treasure, & Hall, 1994). In their study of 285 male and female college students enrolled in tennis classes, Kavussanu and Roberts (1996a) report a mean task scale score of $4.37 \pm .56$ and a mean ego scale score of $3.04 \pm .90$.

Reliability

Test-retest reliability. Test-retest reliability after one week was .80 for task orientation and .78 for ego orientation as assessed via the POSQ (Roberts, Treasure, & Balague, in press).

Internal consistency. The internal consistency of the original POSQ scales (Roberts & Balague, 1989) using Cronbach's alpha was .92 for task orientation and .90 for ego orientation, whereas that of the 6-item scale was .87 for task orientation and .84 for ego orientation (Roberts, et al., in press) with values ranging from .85 to .90 for task orientation and .82 to .89 for ego orientation in different age groups (Treasure & Roberts, 1994a). Thus, the two scales of the POSQ have demonstrated acceptable internal reliability with an average alpha of .81 for the task scale and .82 for the ego scale (Table 2.)

Validity

Factorial validity. Exploratory factor analysis of the 12-item POSQ with a sample of 330 British school children (Treasure & Roberts, 1994a) yielded two factors with intercorrelations of .07 for first-year students (*M* Age = 11.3 years), .12 for 3rd-year students (*M* Age = 13.4 years), and -.27 for 5th-year students (*M* Age = 15.3 years). This two-factor structure has also emerged in the case of older adults (Roberts, et al., 1994), elite

Table 2.
Data From Studies Using the Perceptions of Success Questionnaire in Ascending Order by Age

Authors	Date	Subjects	Age			N			Task			Ego		
			Mean	SD	Range	Total	Male	Female	Alpha	Mean	SD	Alpha	Mean	SD
Treasure & Roberts	1994b	UK schoolchildren	11.3	.5	11yr - 12yr	96	53	43	.92	4.12	.82	.90	2.36	.91
Treasure & Roberts	1994a	UK schoolchildren				330								
			11.3	.5	11yr - 12yr	96	48	48	.88	4.08	.89	.82	2.56	.89
			13.4	.5	13yr-14yr	156	78	78	.85	4.12	.74	.85	2.89	.90
			15.3	.5	15yr - 16yr	78	34	44	.90	4.36	.66	.89	2.94	.27
Hall, Matthews, & Kerr	1996	UK HS runners			High school	119	45	74	.85	3.99	.71	.83	2.81	.99
									.72	3.66	.76	.76	2.66	.83
Roberts & Balague	1989	Sport participants								4.35	.60		2.43	.75
Kavussanu & Roberts	1996a	Tennis class			College	285	147	119	.88	4.37	.56	.90	3.04	.90
Kavussanu & Roberts	1996b	Activity classes	22.5	3.4	17yr - 40yr	131	103	27	.85	4.32	.49	.87	3.27	.71
Kavussanu & Roberts	1996c	Student competitors	21		18yr - 44yr	333	227	106	.80	4.63		.86	3.70	
Roberts, Treasure,& Hall	1994	Parents of UK schoolchildren			Adult	96	40	52	.90	4.46	.59	.84	2.82	1.08
TRANSLATIONS														
Gernigon & Le Bars	1995	French judo/ aikido chidren	12.1	2.0		80	47	33		4.46			2.96	
Sarrazin, Biddle, Famose, Cury, Fox, & Durand	1996	French schools	14.0	1.6	11yr - 17yr	304	184	20	.75	4.52	.50	.76	3.04	1.03
Cury, Biddle, Famose, Goudas, Sarrazin, & Durand	1996	French schoolgirls	14.5	.7	13yr - 16yr	700	0.0	700	.79	4.25	.54	.90	3.35	.99
Gernigon & Le Bars	1995	French judo/ aikido adults	28.5	10.0		84	48	36		4.33			2.54	
Roberts & Ommundsen	1996	Norwegian student athletes	21.2	1.6	19yr - 26yr	148	70	78	.81	4.69	.47	.79	3.63	.80
Brunel	1996	Graduate students			Adult	225	150	105	.81	4.43	.51	.70	2.72	.87
Pensgaard & Roberts	1995	Norwegian Winter Olympians	25.2	3.8	19yr - 35yr	69	49	20	.76	4.52	.46	.75	3.93	.67
Pensgaard, Roberts,& Ursin	1995	Norwegian Paralympic 30.4		9.4	15yr - 50yr	30	23	7	.69	4.61	.41	.78	3.99	.69
Ommundsen & Roberts	1996	Nowegian elite			Adult	230	123	107	.60	3.23	.35	.81	2.99	.77
MEANS									.81	4.27	.59	.82	3.03	.79

athletes (Roberts & Ommundsen, 1996), and cross-cultural samples (Roberts, et al., in press). Confirmatory factor analysis with a sample of 274 adolescent female basketball players (Roberts, et al., in press) yielded an acceptable fit of the data to the hypothesized two-factor model (TLI = .90; RMSR = .07).

Concurrent validity. Evidence for the validity of the POSQ scales is found in their correlation with the respective TEOSQ scales. The original version of POSQ (Roberts & Balague, 1989) had correlations of .69 for task orientation and .80 for ego orientation, and the 12-item version (Roberts & Balague, 1991) correlated .71 in the case of task orientation and .80 for ego orientation. In a recent study of Portuguese adolescent soccer players, Fonseca and Balague (1996) report correlations of .62 and .49 respectively between the task and ego scales of the latest versions of the TEOSQ and POSQ.

Construct validity. As pointed out by Roberts, et al., (in press), research providing evidence for the construct validity of the POSQ has primarily "focused on three sets of personal beliefs, namely purposes of sport, beliefs about the causes of suc-

cess and sources of satisfaction...". Given that the development of the POSQ is also steeped in Nicholls' (1989) achievement goal model of motivation, the predictions concerning the relationship of the task and ego orientation scales of the POSQ to beliefs about the determinants of achievement and views about the functions of sport are identical to what has been outlined above for the TEOSQ. Conceptually consistent findings have emerged in the case of the latter (Roberts & Ommundsen, 1996; Roberts, Hall, Jackson, Kimiecik, & Tonymon, 1995; Treasure & Roberts, 1994b) and former (Roberts, et al., in press; Treasure & Roberts, 1994b) set of variables.

Based on the conceptual definitions of task and ego goals, it would be expected that the predictors of individuals' satisfaction in sport would vary in relation to their goal orientation. Among samples ranging from children to elite adult athletes (Roberts & Ommundsen, 1996; Treasure & Roberts, 1994b), task orientation was found to correspond to reported satisfaction grounded in mastery experiences. As predicted, ego orientation was linked to the demonstration of normatively referenced ability as an important source of satisfaction.

Hall, Matthews, and Kerr (1996) examined the links between task and ego orientation scores on the POSQ and multidimensional state anxiety. The subjects were high school age runners, and the anxiety measures were obtained on four occasions before a cross-country meet. Consistent with theoretical predictions, ego orientation (assessed 30 minutes prior to performance) emerged as a positive and significant predictor of precompetition cognitive anxiety.

In their study of college students enrolled in tennis classes, Kavussanu and Roberts (1996a) examined the relationships between POSQ scale scores and the students' intrinsic motivation and self-efficacy. Compatible to results obtained with the TEOSQ, a positive association between task orientation and the composite Intrinsic Motivation Inventory score was revealed. Kavussanu and Roberts argued that "goal perspectives are expected to influence self-confidence" and regarded self-efficacy to be "a situation-specific form of self confidence" (p. 266). As perceptions of competence are self-referenced when task involved, Kavussanu and Roberts hypothesized that there would be a positive relationship between task orientation and self-efficacy. In contrast, as ego involvement entails that "perceptions of competence are inextricably linked to the performance of others...(which is a) factor over which the individual has no control," it was predicted that the "development and maintenance of confidence" would be more difficult in this case (p. 266). When perceptions of the motivational climate and perceptions of ability were entered in the regression analysis, goal orientations (as assessed by the POSQ) did not emerge as predictors of self-efficacy in this study.

Summary

The research conducted utilizing the POSQ has provided evidence for the strong psychometric attributes of this instrument. The POSQ scales exhibit acceptable internal reliability and have been found to predict motivation indices in a manner that is generally congruent with theoretical expectations. Investigations employing exploratory and confirmatory factor analysis techniques have garnered support for the factor structure of the POSQ.

Distinctions Between Measures of Goal Orientations and Other Scales (COI/ SOQ)

There are a number of distinctions between the measures of dispositional achievement goal orientations described in this chapter (i.e., the TEOSQ and POSQ) and existing assessments of other motivation-related orientations in the sport literature (i.e., the Competitive Orientation Inventory or COI) Vealey, 1986, and the Sport Orientation Questionnaire or SOQ, Gill & Deeter, 1988). Unfortunately, all of these instruments have been labelled assessments of achievement orientations specific to the realm of sport (see Gill, Kelly, Martin, & Caruso, 1991; Weiss & Chaumeton, 1994), and thus, it has been suggested that they measure similar constructs.

When compared to the TEOSQ and POSQ, the SOQ and COI have different conceptual foundations. First, although Vealey (1986) pulls from the contributions of Maehr and Nicholls (1980) in developing the COI, this instrument and the SOQ do *not* assess people's proneness for task- and ego-in-

volved goals. Moreover, the assumed underlying structures (i.e., the number of dimensions and their degree of interdependence) of the TEOSQ/POSQ, COI, and SOQ are not the same.

Vealey's (1986) Competitive Orientation Inventory was developed to assess an individual difference variable hypothesized to be impacting individuals' degree of confidence and state anxiety in competitive sport situations. In an effort to capture variability in subjective success underlying goal accomplishment, the instrument assesses one's source of satisfaction when competing, namely playing well versus winning. Emphasis on the former is assumed to reflect a "performance orientation" whereas emphasis on the latter is presumed indicative of an "outcome orientation." With an eye toward conceptual clarity, it should be noted that Vealey uses the term *performance* to reflect a perspective that could be considered more task-involved (but not equivalent to a task orientation). Dweck (1986) and Ames (1992a), on the other hand, employ the term *performance* to reflect an ego-involved goal orientation or ego-involving atmosphere, respectively. In terms of work on achievement goals, such opposing use of critical concepts leads to greater perplexity in the literature and a lack of preciseness in the definition of the concepts themselves. As stated by Nicholls (1992), the term performance goal has been used in two ways:

> to imply ego orientation (Dweck & Elliott, 1983) and something closer to task orientation (Vealey, 1986). My reading of the dictionaries suggests the latter is more consistent with established usage....(In general, however, the) use of the term performance to describe an achievement goal creates confusion because... performance has long referred to how well individuals execute tasks. Any performance (in the case of task execution) can reflect egotistic or task-intrinsic goals (p. 55).

The COI places the performance and outcome orientations in opposition to each other and, thus, requires respondents to rate their satisfaction with 16 possible combinations of outcome (e.g., close loss) and performance (e.g., above average). In Vealey's words (1986), the instrument forces "athletes to weigh the value of both goals simultaneously" (p. 225). Consequently, Vealey (1986) initially proposed scoring the COI by calculating the proportion of variance due to performance and the proportion due to outcome. These scores are negatively related. In subsequent work (Vealey, 1988), it was suggested that a composite performance-orientation be calculated by averaging the performance score and the inverse of the outcome score.

Duda (1992) presented data from a study in which the COI and TEOSQ were administered to a sample of undergraduate students enrolled in physical education classes. As shown in Table 3, ego orientation, but not task orientation, was positively and significantly related to Vealey's (1986) outcome orientation scale. This finding makes conceptual sense as a successful outcome would be more salient to someone who is concerned about demonstrating superior ability than to a person focused on personal mastery. However, it should be noted that the shared variance between the ego orientation and outcome orientation scales was very low ($R^2 = .04$) and indicates that these two scales assess different constructs. Given the theoretically

Table 3.
Correlates of the TEOSQ and POSQ Inventories With Other Scales:
TEOSQ data from Duda (1992); POSQ data from Marsh (1994)

	TEOSQ		POSQ	
	Task	Ego	Task	Ego
Competitive Orientation Inventory (Vealey, 1986)				
Performance orientation	.04	-.18		
Outcome orientation	-.04	.21*		
Sport Orientation Questionnaire (Gill & Deeter, 1988)				
Competitiveness	.25*	.53**	.56**	.50**
Goal orientation	.56**	.37**	.78**	.35**
Win orientation	.14	.61**	.07	.58**

$* p < .05$, $** p < .01$
TEOSQ=Task and Ego Orientation in Sport Questionnaire
POSQ=Perceptions of Success Questionnaire

based definition of ego orientation, this result was also expected as an individual needs to take into account the outcome as well as the difficulty of the opponent/task, amount of effort one and one's opponent exerted, etc. when judging one's level of normative ability.

Duda (1992) reported that, as hypothesized, neither ego nor task orientation was associated with scores on the COI's performance orientation scale. As she pointed out, the concept of "playing well" is ambiguous when examined from the standpoint of variations in dispositional goal perspectives. Both a person who is strongly task oriented and an individual who is markedly ego oriented want to play well. The meaning of quality play would vary, however, depending on whether the athlete was in a state of task or ego involvement.

Gill and Deeter's (1988) Sport Orientation Questionnaire was developed to measure individual differences in approaches to sport competition. In contrast to the TEOSQ, POSQ, and COI, the SOQ evolved from the multidimensional model of achievement motivation as proposed by Spence and Helmreich (1983). The instrument comprised factor analytically derived scales labeled Competitiveness (which is conceptualized as a desire to enter and strive for success in sport achievement situations) and two scales focused on major types of sport outcomes, namely to win (Win Orientation) or reach personal goals (Goal Orientation). In contrast to the TEOSQ/POSQ scales, the three dimensions of the SOQ are not orthogonal.

Research has examined the associations between scores on the TEOSQ and SOQ scales (Duda, 1992) and the POSQ and SOQ scales (Marsh, 1994). Table 3 demonstrates that, in both studies, the SOQ Competitiveness scale was ambiguous in goal perspective terms as the task and ego scales of the TEOSQ and POSQ correlated with it. This pattern of results is not surprising because we would theoretically expect both strongly task- or ego-oriented individuals to be competitive and attracted to

competition. As argued by Duda (1992, 1996), one can demonstrate both self-referenced and normative ability via the competitive process. In general, these findings exemplify the problem associated with equating an ego orientation scale to competitiveness or a desire to compete (as was the case in the original labeling of the POSQ ego scale). With respect to this point, Nicholls (1992) has argued that "competition is a defining feature of many sports....Thus speaking of competitive goals as similar to egotism is problematic" (p. 55). He suggests that the motivationally insightful issue is *why* an individual wants to compete and the answer to that question can reflect task- and/or ego-involved reasons.

Similarly all the TEOSQ/POSQ scales were significantly correlated with the SOQ Goal Orientation scale, although the relationship was higher with the task scales than with the measures of ego orientation. A person who is highly task oriented or ego oriented is *goal* oriented; such individuals vary with respect to the criteria underlying subjective goal accomplishment. The shared variance ($R^2 = .12 - .31$) between the Goal Orientation scale and the ego scales of the TEOSQ and POSQ and the task scale of the TEOSQ indicates, though, that these assessments are not redundant. In contrast, the task scale of the POSQ shared 61% of the variance with the SOQ's Goal Orientation Scale. This finding, along with the observed correlations between the POSQ and TEOSQ task scales (e.g., Roberts & Balague, 1989, 1991) suggests that the former scales are assessing a somewhat different conception of task orientation.

As would be expected based on the conceptual definition of an ego orientation, the ego goal scales of the TEOSQ and POSQ correlated significantly with the SOQ Win Orientation. However, once again the observed shared variance indicated that the constructs were not synonymous. We assume that those who are strongly ego oriented would be concerned with beating others in a competitive contest. Highly task-oriented individuals, in contrast, want to win (as they can receive information concerning personal improvement and exerted effort through winning), but this is not their motivational focus when competing.

In sum, the evidence to date demonstrates that the COI and SOQ, when compared with the TEOSQ and POSQ, do not assess the same constructs. The conceptual underpinnings of the former measures are also not aligned with the assessment of goal orientations as grounded in goal perspective theory (Dweck, 1986; Nicholls, 1984, 1989). Research that has examined the interrelationships between scores on the TEOSQ or POSQ scales and the COI and SOQ scales reinforces the distinctions between the measures and provides more insight into the nature and characteristics of task and ego orientations.

Research in Physical Education

Because physical education is also a salient achievement domain in which the demonstration of ability is important, scholars have advocated the application of goal perspective theory to frame investigations of motivation in this setting (Duda, 1996;

Papaioannou, 1995a; Treasure & Roberts, 1995). The TEOSQ has been adapted for the context of physical education by changing the stem to read "I feel most successful in PE class when...". Research based on U.S. (Solmon & Boone, 1993; Walling & Duda, 1995), British (Goudas, Biddle, & Fox, 1994a,b; Hall & Earles, 1995; Linford & Fazey, 1994) and Greek (Papaioannou, 1990; Papaioannou & Macdonald, 1993) adolescent students has provided evidence for the factorial validity, predictive validity, and internal reliability of the TEOSQ in this setting.

For example, in their study of students enrolled in college-level tennis classes, Solmon and Boone (1993) examined the relationships between goal orientations (as assessed by the TEOSQ) and students' reported class-related thoughts and behaviors. Aligned with theoretical tenets, researchers found that task orientation positively predicted students' preference for optimally challenging tasks and cognitive learning processes (e.g., the reported use of effective learning strategies). These latter variables were positively related to tennis skill attainment, which was operationalized as residual gain scores on a tennis skill test.

Some Concluding and Critical Thoughts

The two well-established measures of dispositional task and ego orientations, namely the TEOSQ and POSQ, differ conceptually and methodologically from the early assessments of achievement goal orientations such as the AOQ and the MGPQ. First, the TEOSQ and POSQ do not employ the critical incident method and request subjects to recall and record a successful personal experience. Therefore, the TEOSQ and POSQ take less time to administer. However, in some cases, the use of a critical incident when employing these two instruments may improve their validity and reliability. This method would provide a frame of reference for young subjects whose conceptions of task and, in particular, ego goals are just becoming established.

Second, the TEOSQ and POSQ (as presently structured) are designed to exclusively tap the dispositional tendency to emphasize task- and ego-involved goals. Other goal orientations, such as social approval as assessed by the AOQ and MGPQ, are not considered in the former instruments.

Third, as discussed above, it is important to note that existing measures of task and ego goal orientations should not be equated to available assessments of individuals' approaches to competition or emphases on successful competitive outcomes versus playing well. In research based on Nicholls' (1989) theoretical framework particularly, the SOQ or COI should not be substituted for a determination of individual differences in achievement goal perspectives.

Finally, an examination of the items and results from studies employing these measures suggests that the TEOSQ and POSQ interpret task orientation differently from Maehr and Nicholls' (1980) initial proposal that task-oriented motivation reflects a self-referenced perception of success in which ability is not salient. Both instruments include items about succeeding by trying hard in their task orientation scales so the definition has narrowed to reflect a self-referenced view of success that is achieved in a particular manner. This is consistent with Nicholls' (1984) modification/extension of Maehr and Nicholls' (1980) work to suggest that goal orientations arise from different conceptions of ability and that task orientation is exemplified when an undifferentiated conception of ability is employed (i.e., when demonstrated effort reflects ability). Conceptually, this characteristic of the TEOSQ and POSQ measures means that a variable that was initially a potential correlate of task orientation is now included within the construct. Methodologically, the effect is that effort-related variables are likely to correlate with task orientation but not with ego orientation.

In contrast, although Nicholls (1984, 1989) also argues that success without effort will be a feature of ego orientation, neither the TEOSQ nor the POSQ includes items relating to the emphasis placed on "easy" success in their ego scales. Revising the ego orientation scales of the TEOSQ and POSQ to include items about succeeding without effort may result in negative associations between effort-related variables and ego orientation. Such a modification, however, would probably reduce the orthogonality of the TEOSQ and POSQ task and ego scales.

SITUATIONAL GOAL STRUCTURE OR PERCEIVED MOTIVATIONAL CLIMATE

The instruments developed to assess situationally emphasized goal perspectives, or the subjective motivational climate, in the sport domain have drawn on the classroom-based work of Ames and Archer (1988). These researchers operationalized mastery and performance dimensions of classrooms by first identifying theoretical distinctions between these goals in terms of classroom parameters and then developing a set of items to assess these characteristics. The items, contained in Ames and Archer's Classroom Goals Achievement Questionnaire, were preceded by the stem "In this class...." and responded to on a 5-point Likert scale anchored by *Strongly agree* and *Strongly disagree*. Exploratory factor analysis yielded a two-factor solution with the uncorrelated factors ($r = -.03$) showing good internal consistency assessed by Cronbach's alpha (Mastery .88, Performance .77) and a mean of 3.32 (SD = .61) for the mastery climate scale and 3.51 (SD = .49) for the performance climate scale.

Measurement in Sport

Perceived Motivational Climate in Sport

Questionnaire Conceptual Framework and Definition of Constructs

Although goal perspective theory (Nicholls, 1989) predicts that an individual's transitory state of task or ego involvement is dependent on both dispositional differences and situational variables, Seifriz et al. (1992) observed that athletes' perceptions of situationally emphasized goals had not yet been examined in the literature. They drew their ideas from classroom research (Ames, 1992a) which focused on the motivational implications of competitive (or ego-involving) and individualistic (task-involving) goal structures, and they argued that the situational goal structure or motivational climate in athletic settings was a function of the goals to be achieved, the evaluation and reward process, and how individuals are requested to relate to each other in a particular setting. The Perceived Motivational Climate in Sport Questionnaire or PMCSQ (and its extensions/revisions) was constructed by Duda and her students to measure task-involving and ego-involving climates deemed to be operating in sport. These were initially termed mastery and performance climates, respectively, in accordance with Ames and Archer (1988).

Source and Selection of Items

An initial pool of 106 items was drawn from the Classroom Achievement Goals Questionnaire (Ames & Archer, 1988) or generated by the investigators. When developing this pool, we (Seifriz, et al., 1992) wanted to avoid the use of items that used the word "I" (as are found in the Classroom Achievement Goals Questionnaire). We thought that this would foster ambiguity by suggesting the assessment of personal goals in contrast to athletes' views of the pervading atmosphere on their team, in their gym, etc. That is, the objective of the PMCSQ was to tap that which is perceived to be the situational emphasis, rather than the goal perspectives that athletes have internalized. Face validity of the items was judged by a panel of eight experts, and 40 items were retained. Those items kept showed 100% agreement on the dimension hypothesized to be measured by the item and a mean of 4 or more on a 5-point scale reflecting the quality of the item in capturing the construct in question. The stem "On this basketball team ..." was used for all items. As has been the recommendation when utilizing the PMCSQ (and subsequent revisions), the initial data collection of Seifriz and his colleagues (1992) entailed administering the instrument when the motivational environment had been established (in this case, midseason).

Factorial Validity

Exploratory factor analysis (principal components followed by orthogonal and oblique rotations) with 105 basketball players from nine high school teams yielded 12 factors of which 2 were predominant and consistent with theoretical constructs and previous classroom work. Twenty-one items were retained and submitted to a second factor analysis in which 2 factors emerged with an interfactor correlation of -.26. It was suggested that the low negative correlation emerged because the subjects could not simultaneously agree with items such as "On this team, mistakes are considered part of learning" and "On this team, players are punished for mistakes."

In a subsequent study with 109 young athletes, Walling, Duda, and Chi (1993) conducted a confirmatory factor analysis that produced moderate fit indices (X^2/df 2.93, GFI .77, RMSR .108) with a large number of correlated errors in the data implying the presence of minor factors within the scales. The fit was improved after using modification indices and freeing 17 pairs of theta-deltas (X^2/df 2.02, GFI .85, RMSR .091). Content of the final items forming the task-involving dimension related to an emphasis on improving skills, working hard, and having an important role on the team. Items contained in the ego-involving scale related to an emphasis on the demonstration of better performance than others (such as one's teammates) or intra-team rivalry, unequal recognition (i.e., perceiving that the coach provides the most attention to the more talented athletes) and punishment for mistakes.

Reliability

The internal consistency of the scales, using Cronbach's alpha, ranged from .73 to .84 for the 12-item ego-involving climate scale and .80 to .81 for the 9-item task-involving climate scale (Table 4; Seifriz et al., 1992; Walling et al., 1993). The test-retest reliability of the PMCSQ was .68 over a one-month period (Barnes, Page & McKenna, 1997). We would expect that the test-retest correlation for the perceived situational goal perspective would be in the moderate range for an established motivational climate, i.e., unless there had been a change in the coaching staff, team composition, level of play/competition, etc. In other words, the test-retest reliability should be lower in this case than what has generally been observed for assessments of dispositional goal orientations.

Construct Validity

Seifriz et al. (1992) reported that the nine boys basketball teams they sampled varied in perceptions of the task-involving and ego-involving facets of their motivational climate. The authors argued that task involvement (which should be promoted in a mastery or task-involving atmosphere) would foster intrinsic motivation and the belief that hard work leads to success. They also hypothesized, based on theoretical tenets and existing research, that an ego-involving climate would be associated with the view that ability is necessary for basketball success. Using median splits (i.e., perceptions of a high/low task and high/low ego climate), Seifriz et al. (1992) found the expected differences between high and low task climate groups in intrinsic motivation (assessed by the IMI), enjoyment and beliefs in effort as a cause of success. Also aligned with predictions, the high and low ego-involving climate groups differed in their beliefs that ability determines success.

In a study of adolescent athletes involved in a multisport competition, Walling et al. (1993) found the predicted positive correlation between perceptions of a task-involving climate and reported team satisfaction. Consistent with their hypothesis, a positive association between perceptions of an ego-involving climate and the athletes' degree of performance worry also emerged. In a similar vein, Pensgaard and Roberts (1996) investigated the link between perceptions of the motivational climate and sources of stress. Their sample comprised 69 Norwegian athletes who participated in the 1994 Winter Olympic Games. Athletes who perceived that the atmosphere on their team was more ego involving were higher in reported causes of stress, particularly stress due to cognitive factors and their coaches' behaviors. Overall, a perceived task-involving climate corresponded to lower scores on all the sources of stress examined in this investigation.

Boyd, Yin, Ellis, and French (1995) examined the relationship of perceptions of the motivational climate to Little League baseball players' socialization influences and affective responses. In accordance with theoretical predictions, perceptions of a task-involving environment were tied to lower perceived coaches' expectations, more positive affective reactions from coaches and parents, and greater enjoyment and satisfaction among the players. The reverse pattern of these findings was linked to perceptions of an ego-involving sport setting. Further,

Table 4.

Data From Studies Using the Perceived Motivational Climate in Sport Questionnaire in Ascending Order by Age

Authors	Date	Subjects	Age			N			Mastery (Task Involving)			Performance (Ego-Involving)		
			Mean	SD	Range	Total	Male	Female	Alpha	Mean	SD	Alpha	Mean	SD
PMCSQ-1														
Boyd, Yin, Ellis, & French	1995	Little League baseball			11yr - 12yr	104			.79	3.51	.51	.85	1.96	.63
Ebbeck & Becker	1994	Youth soccer	12.0	1.3	10yr - 14yr	166	75	91	.81	3.90	.66	.75	2.0:	.71
Walling, Duda, & Chi	1993	Athletes	14.2	1.9		169	86	83	.80	3.7:	.64	.84	2.62	.66
Seifriz, Duda, & Chi	1992	HS Basketball	16.5		14yr - 19yr	105	105	0.0	.84	3.53	.32	.80	3.0:	.37
Kavussanu & Roberts	1996a	Univ. tennis class			College	285	147	119	.74	4.13	.43	.77	2.47	.62
Kavussanu & Roberts	1996b	Activity classes	22.5	3.4	17yr - 40yr	131	103	27	.72	4.05	.44	.79	2.50	.63
Barnes, Page, & McKenna	1996	International. rowers UK/Canada	25.8	4.3		98 / 98	56	42	.79	4.01 / 4.08	.49 / .50	.76	3.42 / 3.43	.44 / .48
Weigand & Davis	1996	Amateur soccer	24.9			115	115	0.0		3.74	.49		2.83	.60
PMCSQ-2 (Second order factors only)														
Guest, White, Jones McCaw, & Vogler	In PR	Physical education Nonschool sport	13..2	1.1	Grades 6 - 9	171 / 171	71	100	.91 / .90	3.69 / 4.00	.65 / .61	.80 / .92	2.40 / 3.00	.70 / .86
Guest & White	1996	Nonschool sport Physical education	13.2		Grades 6 - 9	110 / 110	39	71	.90 / .90	4.01 / 3.62	.86 / 1.04	.93 / .85	3.02 / 2.50	1.31 / 1.06
Andrée & Whitehead	1995	UK track and field	14.0	1.1	10yr - 17yr	138	67	71	.89	4.03	.50	.88	2.33	.65
Whitehead & Andrée	1997	UK track and field	14.4	1.6	11yr- 17yr	111	57	51	.87	4.05	.48	.85	2.58	.67
Newton & Duda	1996	Volleyball Volley/basketball HS IC	16.2 / 16.4	1.7	14yr- 18yr / 13yr - 23yr	385 / 202	0.0 / 0.0	385 / 202	.87 / .87	4.12 / 3.95		.83 / .89	2.62 / 3.12	
TRANSLATIONS														
Roberts & Ommundsen	1996	Norwegian U/G team sports	21.2	1.6	19yr - 26yr	148	70	78	.86	4.15	.75	.77	2.87	.87
Pensgaard & Roberts	1996	Norwegian Winter Olympians	25.2	3.9	19yr - 35yr	49	69	20	.76	3.70	.77	.87	2.50	1.02
CLASSROOM ACHIEVEMENT QUESTIONNAIRE (Excluded from means)														
Treasure	In PR	Elementary school	10.4	0.6	10yr - 12yr	233	114	119	.76	3.78	.56	.78	3.02	.67
MEANS									.84	3.89	.60	.83	2.66	.74

players who perceived that their team atmosphere was more ego involving were more likely to report that they compared their ability to that of other players.

Means/SDs

As shown in Table 4, means for a perceived task-involving climate range from 3.51 to 4.15 with *SD*'s from .32 to 1.04. In the case of the PMCSQ's assessment of a perceived ego-involving climate, means range from 1.96 to 3.43 with *SD*'s from .37 to 1.31. Hence with perceptions of the motivational climate as with dispositional goal orientations, the values observed to date reflect a greater emphasis on task-involving goals than ego-involving goals. However, it should be noted that the existing published data on the perceived motivational climate include only two elite athlete samples (Barnes, Page, & McKenna, 1997; Pensgaard & Roberts, 1996).

Perceived Motivational Climate in Sport Questionnaire -2

Newton and Duda (1993, 1997a) revised the PMCSQ-1 and then tested a multi-subscale version of the Perceived Motivational Climate in Sport Questionnaire (or PMCSQ-2). Their

rationale was threefold. First and foremost, Ames (1992a) has suggested that task-involving as well as ego-involving environments are a composite of a number of dimensions such as the basis and type of evaluation present, the amount of social comparison present, the nature and source of rewards, and the ways in which those in the context are expected to work with and regard each other. Second, based on the empirical findings of Walling et al. (1993), it was thought that the differentiation of a subscale structure in the original measurement model underlying the assessment of the perceived motivational climate would help account for greater unexplained variance in the original model. Third, the ability to assess various components of task- and ego-involving atmospheres would enhance our theoretical and practical understanding of how, why, and when the situational goal structure impacts indices of athletes' motivation.

Drawing from these three considerations, an initial pool of 300 items was designed to emphasize the eight following goal structures: (a) emphasis on effort, (b) skill improvement as an integral element of team atmosphere, (c) a perceived contributing role for each team member, (d) mistakes are viewed as part of the learning process, (e) cooperation/cohesiveness is reinforced among players, (f) intra-team rivalry, (g) reinforcement based on high ability, thus unequal recognition of players, and (h) the view that mistakes are punished. After ratings of face validity of the 300 new items plus the 21 items found in the PMCSQ by a group of judges, 63 items were retained and administered to 225 female volleyball players from 25 teams. This pool was further reduced to 30 items by first calculating Cronbach's alpha for each subscale and eliminating 9 items with low item-total correlations. Exploratory factor analysis on the 54 remaining items yielded 11 first-order factors after which items with loadings below .4 on any factor as well as those that crossloaded were eliminated. Factor analysis of the remaining items revealed a 30-item six-factor solution. The scales for Effort and Improvement were collapsed, and the scale labelled Mistakes Are Part of Learning was deleted. Confirmatory factor analysis showed that a six-factor model (composed of these six scales) provided a better fit (X^2/df 2.25, GFI .87, RMSR .09) than a two-factor model for the task-involving and ego-involving dimensions (X^2/df 2.33, GFI .68, RMSR .31). The hierarchical model failed to converge.

In a second study, Newton and Duda (1997a) employed structural equation modeling to test the hypothesized hierarchical structure of a further revision of the PMCSQ-2 (i.e., two scale/six subscales) in comparison to a two-scale and a six-subscale measurement model. The subjects were 385 female volleyball players from 45 teams who were participants in a national junior volleyball tournament. In general, the fit indices indicated that each of three measurement models was marginally acceptable (e.g., GFI .85-.87). However, an examination of the Q-plots and root mean square residual values suggested that the hierarchical model (RMSR .07) accounted for more residual variance than did the other two models (RMSR .32-.34).

Reliability

In the first Newton and Duda (1993) investigation, the internal reliabilities for the individual subscales and overall scales ranged from .77 to .93 except in the case of the Cooperation/Cohesiveness and Intra-Team Rivalry subscales (alpha = .66). The follow-up investigation by Newton and Duda (1997a) resulted in internal consistency values ranging from .75 to .87 although the Intra-Team Rivalry subscale proved problematic once again (alpha = .54). In terms of the test-retest reliability, Whitehead and Andrée (1997) found low correlations for the two major climate dimensions (i.e., task involving .24, ego involving .36) over a year but suggested that shorter term tests are more appropriate for climate measures.

Validity

In support of the PMCSQ-2's discriminative validity, Newton and Duda (1993) found that the 25 basketball and volleyball teams they sampled varied in their degree of perceived task- and ego-involving features (i.e., in terms of both the climate scale and subscale scores). The athletes' reported pressure/tension was predicted by a high ego-involving climate and moderate task-involving climate, or by moderate perceptions of the importance of Effort/Improvement and Punishment For Mistakes but a de-emphasis on the importance of each player's role.

In their research on 45 female volleyball teams, Newton and Duda (1997a) found perceptions of a task-involving environment (and scores on the three underlying subscales) were positively associated with the belief that effort causes success, reported effort/importance and enjoyment/interest and negatively correlated with pressure/tension (as assessed via the IMI). In contrast, perceptions of an ego-involving climate (and scores on the three underlying subscales) were negatively related with enjoyment of and interest in volleyball and positively linked to tension/pressure and the belief that ability leads to success.

The Parent-Initiated Motivational Climate Questionnaire

Conceptual Framework and Definition of Constructs

White, Duda, and Hart (1992) observed that work in the classroom (Ames & Archer, 1988) and sport (e.g., Seifriz, et al., 1992) has focused on the role of the teacher or coach in establishing the motivational climate and pointed out that parents are also significant others in establishing the situational goal structure. They cited literature from the athletic domain (e.g., Scanlan & Lewthwaite, 1984) and academic context (e.g., Eccles, Midgley and Alder, 1984) to illustrate how parents' beliefs about their children's abilities and the importance of learning different skills influence children's perceptions of what they think they can do and what is salient in achievement situations. The Parent-Initiated Motivational Climate Questionnaire (PIMCQ) was developed to measure children's perceptions of what their parents view to be most critical when learning new physical activities. This context of concern contrasts with the competitive sport emphasis of the PMCSQ as it focuses more on physical education and learning. The instrument is grounded in goal perspective theory (Nicholls, 1989) and assesses the degree to which the parental environment is deemed more or less task and/or ego involving.

Source and Selection of Items

In terms of the development of the initial version of the PIMCQ, 14 items were adapted from three scales of the Learning and Performance-Oriented Physical Education Climate Questionnaire (i.e., Teacher's Promotion of Learning, Students' Worries About Mistakes, Outcome Orientation Without Effort; Papaioannou, 1994) and written with reference to fathers, and the same 14 were written with reference to mothers. The stem was "I feel that my mother (or father) ...." Responses to the PIMCQ are indicated on a 5-point Likert scale anchored by *Strongly Agree* (1) and *Strongly Disagree* (5).

Factor Structure

Exploratory factor analysis of the 28-item PIMCQ (principal components followed by orthogonal and oblique rotations) with 210 young sport participants from the United States yielded the same three factors for mothers and for fathers (i.e., the factors collapsed across parents) and explained 51.4% of the variance. One factor (Learning-Oriented Climate) reflected a task-involving situational goal structure and two factors (Worry Conducive Climate and Success Without Effort) reflected an ego-involving structure. Exemplary items include "I feel that my mother/father pays attention to whether I am improving my skills," "I feel that my mother/father makes me

Table 5.

Data From Studies Using the Learning and Performance Orientations in Physical Education Questionnare (First Order Factors Only) and the Parent-Initiated Motivational Climate Questionnaire

Authors	Date	Subjects	Age Mean	SD	Range	N Total	Male	Female	Pupils learning Alpha	Mean	SD	Teacher learning Alpha	Mean	SD	Competitive Alpha	Mean	SD	Worries Alpha	Mean	SD	Easy success Alpha	Mean	SD
LAPOPECQ																							
Papaioannou	1994	Greek PE			13yr-16yr	1393	699	694	> .83	3.37	.61	>.79	3.70	.77	>.65	2.70	.78	>.65	3.2:	.76	>.64	2.48	.85
Papaioannou & Diggelidis	1996	Greek PE			10yr-15yr	674	319	355	.83	3.5:	.55	.80	4.05	.76		3.38	.87		3.42	.86		2.95	1.08
PIMCQ											**Learning**												
White, Duda, & Hart	1992	Young athletes				210	112	98					3.81						2.29			2.15	
			12.7	.8		58	27	31				.84						.90			.86		
			14.3	.5		91	52	39				.75						.87			.87		
			16.7	.7		61	33	28				.87						.90			.92		
PIMCQ-2											**Learning/enjoyment**												
White	1996a	Volleyball camp	15.4	1.1	14yr-17yr	204	0.0	204				.89	4.08	.46				.91	1.90	.81	.87	1.77	.65
White	In PR	Nonschool sport	14.5			301	149	152	Mother's views ...			.89	3.92	.74				.85	2.05	.94	.73	2.16	.82
									Father's views .			.90	3.98	.78				.90	2.18	1.00	.82	2.31	.95
White & Duda	1993b	PE classes				301	149	152				.92						.90			.84		
		Children	11.7	.5		96	45	51				.91	4.07	.61				.89	1.78	.76	.81	2.07	.78
		Young adoles.	14.6	.5		97	47	50				.94	3.98	.69				.89	2.09	.82	.82	2.22	.83
		Older adoles.	16.7	.8		108	60	48				.92	3.83	.68				.90	2.37	.93	.86	2.36	.79
Guest & White	1996	Young athletes	13.0		11yr-15yr	135	63	72	Mother's views ...			.84	4.16					.87	2.20		.78	2.14	
									Father's views ...			.84	4.0:					.91	2.37		.85	2.18	
									Friend's views ...			.89	3.63					.91	2.24		.83	2.42	

worried about performing skills that I am not good at," and "I feel that my mother/father believes that it is important for me to win without trying," respectively.

Reliability

The internal consistency of the scales, using Cronbach's alpha, was tested separately for three age groups (mean age = 12.7 yr, 14.3 yr., 16.7 yr.) and ranged from .75 to .92 (see Table 5). The test-retest reliability of the PIMCQ has not been examined to date.

Validity

Based on previous research on gender differences in goal perspectives (e.g., Duda, et al., 1991; White & Duda, 1994), boys would be expected to perceive a more ego-involving parental climate whereas girls were predicted to perceive a more task-involved parental perspective when learning physical skills. Providing evidence for the instruments' discriminant validity, White et al. (1992) found significant gender differences for each scale. Boys perceived that their parents reinforced success without effort more than did girls. Girls, on the other hand, perceived greater parental support for learning new skills and were less likely to report that their parents made them wary of making mistakes than were boys.

Means/SDs

Information on the means and standard deviations for the subscales of the PIMCQ reflects the pattern of the other goal perspective instruments with higher scores for task-related than ego-related scales.

Revision of the PIMCQ (the PIMCQ-2)

In subsequent work on the PIMCQ (White & Duda, 1996), four items were added to examine children's perceptions of the value their parents placed on their personal experience of enjoyment while learning new physical skills. These items were constructed on the basis of Scanlan and Simon's (1992) view that sport enjoyment is a positive affective response that denotes feelings such as fun, liking, and pleasure. It was assumed that the emphasis on such feelings while learning would be indicative of a task-involving atmosphere. An example of a new item is "I feel that my mother/father supports my feelings of enjoyment during skill development."

Validity

Exploratory factor analyses of the mother-referenced items and the father-referenced items each yielded three factors, namely a Learning-Oriented/Enjoyment Climate, Worry Conducive Climate, and Success Without Effort Climate dimension. Thus, the enjoyment items did not form a separate scale but, as they were written to do, loaded on the learning-focused factor.

Discriminant or criterion validity was examined by comparing the perceived parental-created climate as a function of age group and gender (White & Duda, 1996). As expected, males perceived that their parents promoted a worry-conducive environment and encouraged achievement with low effort more than did females. Age differences also emerged with scores on task-related scales decreasing with age whereas scores on the ego-related scales increased.

The construct validity of the PIMCQ-2 was initially determined by examining the relationships of the perceived parental motivational climate to young athletes' personal goal orientations as assessed via the TEOSQ (White, 1996a; White & Duda, 1996). Conceptually consistent relationships have been revealed in this research. In subsequent work involving 301 adolescent male and female sport participants (White, in press), higher competitive trait anxiety was linked with a parental environment that de-emphasizes learning/enjoyment, promotes concern about one's performance, and values success with little effort.

Reliability

Across samples of children and younger adolescents, the scales of the PIMCQ-2 have been found to possess high internal reliability (i.e., Learn/Enjoy: .84 - .94; Easy success: .73 - .86; Worry: .85 - .91). There is no available information on the test-retest reliability of the PIMCQ-2.

Measurement in Physical Education

The Perceived Motivational Climate in Sport

The PMCSQ has been adapted for the context of physical education by changing the stem to "In this physical education class..." (Guest, White, Jones, McCaw, & Vogler, in press). The analyses employed in this work focused on the overriding climate scales rather than the hierarchical subscale model (in the case of the PMCSQ-2, specifically). Exemplary items for the task-involving and ego-involving scales are "The PE teacher makes sure students improve on skills they're not good at" and "The PE teacher yells at students for messing up.") Peiro and her colleagues (Peiro, Escarti, & Duda, 1996) translated the PMCSQ-2 into Spanish and also applied the instrument to the assessment of adolescent students' perception of the motivational climate operating in their physical education class. Kavussanu and Roberts (1996a) examined the motivation-related correlates of perceptions of the prevailing goal perspective emphasized in college-level tennis classes. Perceptions of the motivational climate operating (as assessed by the PMCSQ, which was modified for the PE class context and reduced to 17 items) were found to predict intrinsic motivation and students' tennis self-efficacy in the expected directions. Treasure's research (in press) also provides evidence for the predictive validity of the PMCSQ when applied to youth soccer classes in which the situational goal structure was manipulated.

Reliability

When adapted for the physical education setting, Guest et al. (in press) report internal reliabilities of .90 and .85 for the task- and ego-involving scales of the PMCSQ-2, respectively. Kavussanu and Roberts (1996a) observed alpha coefficients of .74 (task) and .77 (ego) for their two modified PMCSQ subscales. Treasure (in press) found the task and ego dimensions of the PMCSQ to be reliable in his work (alphas = .84 and .85, respectively).

Mean/SDs

In the Guest and White (1996) study of 110 young adolescent students (*M* Age = 13.2 years), the mean scale scores for the task- and ego-involving climate deemed to be operating in physical education classes were 3.62 (SD = 1.04) and 2.5 (SD = 1.06), respectively.

Validity

With respect to the predictive validity of the instrument when adapted for the physical education setting, the PMCSQ-2 has been found to relate to adolescent students' personal goal orientations in the expected manner (Guest & White, 1996).

Learning And Performance Oriented Physical Education Climate Questionnaire (LAPOPECQ)

Conceptual Framework and Definition of Constructs

Papaioannou (1992, 1994) observed that most of the work on goal perspective theory had focused on the classroom context and sport rather than physical education. He argued that, at least when compared to the athletic domain, the ability range of the participants is much greater in physical education. Thus, an awareness of the goal perspectives deemed to be emphasized in PE classes would be particularly important to examine if we wish to foster achievement within this setting. As a result, Papaioannou (1994) constructed an instrument to assess perceptions of "learning" and "performance" orientations in physical education classes. In his initial research, these terms (which draw from Dweck's [1986] work) are not concisely defined but introduced in terms of their correlates.

Source and Selection of Items

An initial pool of 80 items was generated by Papaioannou (1992) from questionnaires in the literature on perceptions of the classroom motivational climate (Ames & Archer, 1988) and classroom environment (Fraser, 1986). The face validity of the items was judged by four experts. Forty-five items were retained, and these were further reduced to 24 on the basis of factor analytic data from four pilot studies (Papaioannou, 1992). Two of the five factors extracted reflected a learning or task-involving environment, the first focused on the teacher's behavior and the second on the students' satisfaction with learning. The other three factors focused on a performance or ego-involving environment, one related to evaluation by normative criteria, one related to showing ability by succeeding with little effort, and the third related to worrying about mistakes. Thus, similar to the problem we identified with Ames and Archer's (1988) Classroom Achievement Goal Questionnaire, it seems that the LAPOPECQ captures what students perceive to be the goal structure operating in their PE classes as well as their personal goal orientations in that environment. In other words, the instrument (as presently constructed) appears to combine assessments of dispositional and perceived situationally emphasized goal perspectives.

Factorial Validity

Following the pilot work, exploratory factor analysis (principal components followed by orthogonal and oblique rotations) with 696 of 1,393 adolescents from 55 Greek junior and senior high schools found that these five factors explained 49.5% of variance. Correlations between learning and performance factors were low. The highest inter-factor correlations were between the two learning factors (.39) and between the teacher-initiated learning orientation and the competitive performance orientation (-.20). Confirmatory factor analyses of the responses provided by 697 subjects from the first sample and 394 subjects from 16 junior and senior high school classes confirmed the five-factor first-order model. Results also showed that a hierarchical model, in which two factors comprised a second-order learning orientation and three factors constituted a second-order performance orientation, approached the fit indices of the first-order model and hence could be regarded as a more parsimonious explanation (e.g., GFI's .915, .913; RMSR's .051, .052, respectively).

Reliability

The internal consistency of the scales, using Cronbach's alpha, ranged from .64 to .84 (see Table 5), and (EFA) multiple correlations were low. To date, information on the test-retest reliability of this instrument has not been reported.

Construct Validity

In accord with theoretical predictions, intrinsic motivation (assessed by Harter's [1981] Preference for Challenge Versus Preference for Easy Work scale), and attitude toward the PE lesson (assessed by modifications of Midgley, Feldhaufer and Eccles' [1989] scale on Interest and Perceived Usefulness of the Lesson) positively related to a perceived learning-oriented environment in physical education and were unrelated to a perceived performance-focused climate. Except for the Competitive Orientation scale, the questionnaire discriminated between students in classes taught by different teachers.

Means/SD's

The means and standard deviations for the LAPOPECQ scales have been established separately for each sample tested and are presently specific to Greek students. The observed values generally show highest scores for the "learning" scale and lowest means for the "easy success" scale.

Adaptations of LAPOPECQ Within Physical Education

Conceptual Framework and Definition of Constructs

Goudas and Biddle (1994) argued that existing conceptualizations of the classroom and physical education climate had been largely based on the way achievement was defined and how perceptions of ability were formed in the situation at hand. They suggested that other classroom features would promote a mastery or task-involving goal structure in physical education specifically. In particular, Goudas and Biddle noted that Ames (1992a) emphasized three factors that influence situationally induced goal salience (i.e., task design, evaluation and recogni-

tion, distribution of authority) but that the third component had not been examined in physical education contexts. They therefore adapted the LAPOPECQ to include scales on "perceived teacher support" and "perceived student choice." Although no rationale was provided, Goudas and Biddle also dropped the LAPOPECQ's Outcome Without Effort scale.

Source and Selection of Items

This information is not given for the new scales that were added to form the PECCS from the LAPOPECQ. The authors reference Moos and Trickett (1987) in regard to their development of the scale for perceived teacher support. For the perceived-choice scale, Goudas and Biddle (1994) simply cite sample items; for example, ["In this PE class] pupils have a choice of what activities they take part in."

Factorial Validity

Exploratory factor analysis (principal components followed by an oblique rotation) of the responses provided by 254 schoolchildren (aged 13 to 15 years from three comprehensive schools in England) revealed six factors that explained 56.8% of variance. The two LAPOPECQ learning factors (i.e., Teacher Promotion of Learning and Student Satisfaction with Learning) split to form two different learning factors. Interfactor correlations were not given. Composite scores for each scale were subjected to a second-order principal components analysis with varimax rotation. This analysis revealed two factors (explaining 63.7% of the variance), that is, a performance dimension, which comprised the Competitive and Worry scales, and a mastery dimension, which comprised the two new learning factors, and the new Teacher Support and Choice scales.

Confirmatory factor analysis was subsequently conducted (Biddle, et al., 1995) on the 26-item scale. The fit indices for a hierarchical model were moderate (χ^2/df 2.26, GFI .82, RMSR .183) but significantly better than the null model. These authors concluded that the data supported a hierarchical model underlying the PECCS; however, they did not present results regarding a first-order model.

Reliability

The internal consistency of the scales, using Cronbach's alpha, ranged from .64 to .77 after improvement of the Competitive and Choice scales by deletion of one item in each case. Test-retest reliability has not been examined.

Construct Validity

Goudas and Biddle (1994) found that the mastery (task-involving) dimension scores of the PECCS enhanced prediction of intrinsic motivation (as assessed by the Intrinsic Motivation Inventory with the exclusion of the pressure/tension scale) after perceived competence had been accounted for, whereas the performance (ego-involving) dimension scores did not. Children who perceived their physical education environment to be high in both dimensions reported greater perceived competence and enjoyment than did children with low mastery/task-involving climate perceptions. In a second study involving a sample of 85 pupils from a comprehensive school in England, Goudas and

Biddle (1994) reported that perceptions of a task-focused climate had a direct influence on intrinsic motivation and intention in gymnastics and indirect influence in football through their effect on students' goal orientations.

Biddle et al. (1995) report the translation of the 28-item PECCS for French students to form a questionnaire labelled the L'Echelle de Perception du Climat Motivational. The authors added a 4-item scale designed to assess students' perceptions of the promotion of social comparison by their teacher. No conceptual rationale was provided for extending the PECCS in this manner, but it seems to be a logical parallel to the scale assessing promotion of learning by the teacher.

Factorial Validity of the ECPM

After exploratory factor analysis (principal components but no rotation specified) on the responses provided by 311 schoolchildren (aged 13 to 16 years from four different schools in Paris), items loading below 0.4 on any factor were deleted and 3 items were dropped to improve internal consistency. Based on the remaining 19 items, an oblique rotation produced five factors that explained 71% of the variance. These factors were labelled Pursuit of Progress by Pupils, Promotion of Learning by Teacher, Pursuit of Comparison by Pupils, Promotion of Comparison by Teacher, and Worries About Mistakes. Interfactor correlations were not reported by the authors. Further, the two new scales added to the English version of the PECCS (i.e., Teacher Support and Choice) did not emerge as factors in the French study. A second-order oblique factor analysis of the two task-focused and three ego-focused scales yielded two higher order factors explaining 68.8% of the variance. Confirmatory factor analysis with a subsequent sample of 179 schoolchildren from three Paris schools produced an acceptable fit (X^2/df = 1.95, GFI .91, RMSR .066). The internal consistency of the first- and second-order scales ranged from .70 to .89. Test-retest reliability after one week with a sample of 146 pupils from four Paris schools yielded correlations of .69 to .87. The ECPM has been modified further by Cury et al. (1996) by retaining the same factors but eliminating some items. Cury and his colleagues labelled this revised instrument the Perceived Motivational Climate Scale.

Some Concluding and Critical Thoughts

The measurement of perceived situational goal structures in the physical domain is of relatively recent origin; hence, it is less well developed than the existing measures of dispositional goal orientations. Such assessments are also more diverse in scope and focus. That is, measures of perceptions of the motivational climate in physical activity settings vary in terms of the particular context (e.g., sport, physical education) and group of significant others (e.g., coaches, physical education teachers, parents) targeted. They also can be distinguished with respect to the facets or components of the motivational environment that are examined (e.g., social support provided by teacher, interteam member rivalry) although each assesses perceptions of the two major climate dimensions, namely task-involving and ego-involving goal emphases.

Perhaps due to this diversity in the underlying dimensions or characteristics of motivational environments emphasized, careful examination of the existent research on measures of the perceived situational goal structure reveals some slippage in the concept. For example, degree of worry about one's performance is used to validate the PMCSQ but is the focus of a composite scale of the LAPOPECQ and PIMCQ. This is problematic because if such affective variables are assumed to be components rather than correlates of the perceived motivational climate, we cannot then proceed to examine affective consequences of the situationally emphasized goal perspective as these have been embraced within the construct itself.

Clearly, the perceived motivational climate is multidimensional, but researchers must be clear whether their intention is (a) to tap all the variables potentially influencing the prevailing situational goal structure and hence explain a maximum proportion of the variance, (b) to identify that subset of situational mediators that most clearly relate to self- or normatively referenced goal emphases (Nicholls, 1984, 1989), or (c) to examine the antecedents or consequences of perceptions of task- and ego-involving environments. Perhaps this area of measurement would be more conceptually tidy if we restrict the assessment of the perceived climate to the elements of task versus ego involving situations identified by Nicholls (1989). For example, measures of perceptions of the ego involving features of contexts might focus on cognitions regarding the degree to which the environment reflects a testing of valued skills, interpersonal comparison, and the public evaluation of outcomes. On the other hand, we can be less conservative (and, perhaps, more ecologically relevant) and accept the direction taken by Duda and her colleagues in terms of the assessment of the perceived motivational climate. In this case (which is steeped in Nicholls' [1989] framework but draws heavily from the contributions of Ames [1992a,b]), the emphasis is on tapping any relevant dimension of the environment which should make individuals concerned with demonstrating the adequacy of their ability (i.e., ego involving features) or focused on their own performance and the task at hand (i.e., task involving features).

Finally, regardless of which strategy is adopted in the measurement of the perceived motivational climate, there is a similar need for the items employed to accurately reflect the construct being assessed; that is, to assess the climate rather than dispositions and so capture perceptions of situational emphasis rather than internalized individual goal characteristics. For example, the item "Something I learn makes me want to practice more" has been used by Papaioannou and Biddle and his colleagues to assess perceptions of the climate in physical education, although it is from the TEOSQ, a measure of dispositional goal orientations. If the same item is on both dispositional goal orientation and climate scales, it is not surprising that the two measures will correlate, but this probably is an artifact of the way the instruments have been constructed.

At this juncture, it seems prudent to consider whether a growing multiplicity of tests assessing the perceived motivational climate is desirable. A plethora of physical domain-specific measures may provide more precise information in one particular context, but there is a danger that we might end up with a dictionary of tests and an inability to compare results across studies. In other words, it may be difficult to advance our knowledge of the implications of variability in the perceived motivational climate in physical settings because the measures employed are not common. In this case, if discrepant results are found across studies, we cannot be sure if this is a function of the specific situation, significant other, and sample selected or the questionnaire utilized. Perhaps a common core of items may be developed that are generalizable across all climates (and significant others) operating in the physical domain, to which researchers may add specific items after providing a conceptual rationale.

Illustrating the use of a common core of items in goal perspective research, Peiro, Escarti and Duda (1996) have successfully adopted the TEOSQ to assess the definitions of sport and PE success deemed to be advanced by mothers, fathers, coaches and physical education teachers. The incorporation of this common core allowed for a less confounded determination of the relationship of significant others' definitions of achievement in physical activity settings to adolescents' personal goal orientations. Consistent with the arguments expressed above however, we want to emphasize that these adaptations of the TEOSQ should not be equated to measures of the perceived motivational climate created by the significant others in question. Peiro and her colleagues were specifically concerned with examining adolescents' perceptions of the definitions of sport achievement held by important people in their lives. This is not the same as the assessment of dimensions of the perceived situationally-emphasized goal perspective.

FUTURE DIRECTIONS

In general, the literature stemming from goal perspective theory is indicative of a strongly developed conceptual line of work. The validation of theoretical tenets emanates from studies conducted in both physical education and sport contexts and stems from the efforts of many independent research groups and individuals.

This chapter has provided an overview of the measurement of dispositional and perceived situational goal perspectives in the physical domain. Such assessments have contributed greatly to the testing of goal perspective theory (Ames, 1992a; Dweck, 1986; Nicholls, 1984, 1989) in sport and physical education and have been found to relate to perceptions, values, attitudes, and self-reported behavior in conceptually consistent ways. To date, limited work has been conducted utilizing the measures described in this chapter in the prediction of actual or objective behavioral indices. To further our knowledge of the intricacies and implications of achievement goals and more comprehensively examine the predictions of the goal perspective framework, we conclude this chapter with the proposal of several considerations for subsequent research.

Assessment of Goal States

Questions about the stability of goal orientations over time and over situations have been raised since the introduction of the social cognitive approach to achievement motivation (e.g., Duda & Nicholls, 1992). Just as research on stress has progressed with Spielberger's differentiation between state and trait anxiety (Spielberger, Gorsuch, and Lushene, 1970), so has Nicholls' differentiation between transitory states of task and ego involvement and the dispositional tendencies that underpin them advanced thinking about achievement motivation. How-

ever, to date, little has been done with respect to the assessment of goal states in the physical domain.

Single-item measures of situation-specific task and ego involvement have been used by Swain and Harwood (1996) and Harwood and Swain (1996) in an attempt to assess pre-competitive goal states among age-group swimmers and tennis players. These items asked how important a particular outcome was to the competitors one hour before competition and they responded on a 7-point Likert scale anchored by *Not at all important* and *Extremely important*. The task-involvement item (state task goal) developed for swimming was "To what extent is achieving a good personal time, regardless of where you finish, important to you in this next race?" whereas the ego-involvement item (state ego goal) was "To what extent is beating other swimmers, regardless of what time you achieve, important to you in this next race?" The correlation between these items was low ($r = -.05$). Single-item measures of "race" task and ego orientations (termed trait goals) were also generated and their associations with swimming-specific TEOSQ task and ego orientation scales was also low ($r = .17$ and $.21$, respectively).

Swain and Harwood (1996) also used a measure of state goal preference to identify which goal state should dominate when both goals were rated important; that is, subjects responded to the item "What is more important to you in this next race, beating the swimmers in the race or swimming a good personal time?" Responses were indicated on a continuum with a neutral point to accomodate subjects who are high or low in both orientations. Correlations between the assessment of state goal preference and the independent state goals were moderate ($r = .43, -.47$) suggesting that the item provided additional information than would be inferred from the two goal state measures.

Within their situational measures, Swain and Harwood (1996) identified a factor focused on the perceived state goal preference of significant others, including coaches, parents, and peers. One item was "To impress your clubmates and other swimmers, which do you think is more important, to beat other swimmers and win the race , regardless of the time you swim, or to swim a very good time, regardless of where you finish?"

The items were developed and pilot tested in interviews with swimmers. They were administered in event-specific questionnaires that also tapped short-term situational variables in order to examine the relative influence of dispositional and context-induced goal perspectives on goal states. Swain and Harwood's results suggested that the major predictors of task and ego goal states were short-term situational factors and dispositional tendencies measured by single race-specific items. This study is important, not only for its attempt to measure state goal perspectives of athletic participants, but also for its recognition that state goals of significant others and the temporary match conditions are important influences on athletes' degree of pre-competition task and ego involvement. We would question, however, whether Swain and Harwood's assessment of goal states truly reflected an immediate concern with demonstrating self-referenced versus normatively-based ability (or an employment of an undifferentiated or differentiated conception of ability before the competition). Rather, the single items generated seem to capture the swimmers' degree of emphasis on their own performance (as reflected in race time) versus the competitive outcome (as reflected in beating other swimmers). Although the latter goal appears rather ego involved, the former is ambiguous with respect to the state of task involvement.

Other researchers have shown an interest in state goal assessment. For example, Williams (1996) adapted the TEOSQ to measure task and ego involvement, and Hall et al. (1996) changed the stem of the POSQ to obtain runners' perceptions of how they expected to feel in an immediate race.

We would suggest that the assessment of task and ego involvement per se may very well entail the examination of a pattern of variables that represent task and ego processing and preoccupation. This approach would be much more complicated than merely assessing individuals' emphasis on beating others versus improving their own performance *at that point in time*. In our opinion, the measurement of task- and ego-involved goal states would be dynamic and multifaceted. Variations in attentional focus, concerns about what one is doing and how one is doing, the degree of self-/other awareness and task absorption, level of effort exertion, etc., might constitute the constellation of symptoms reflecting task versus ego goal states. Most likely, in contrast to measures of dispositional goal orientations, these task and ego involvement patterns would not be orthogonal. It does not seem possible that one can be truly task involved *and* ego involved at a particular moment. Moreover, we would propose that goal states are qualitatively different from dispositional goal orientations rather than simply a manifestation of those dispositions at one moment of time. Thus, when assessing goal states in sport, attempts to use the same items found on dispositional goal orientation measures (such as the TEOSQ and POSQ) with a mere change of the stem seem suspect (Hall et al., 1996; Williams, 1996).

Moreover, from a measurement standpoint, it would seem desirable for state goals to be validated differently from dispositional measures. For example, Spielberger et al. (1970) selected their state items (assessing state anxiety) from those that gave widely different results in four contrasting anxiety inducing situations. Their trait items, on the other hand, had high retest reliability across environments. Potential state goal items could similarly be tested in task and ego involving conditions of varying intensity to determine their sensitivity to change.

Other Goal Orientations

Maehr and Nicholls (1980) originally proposed multiple subjective definitions of success and included social approval as one of their universal goal orientations. The redefinition of goal perspectives by Nicholls (1984) as reflective of differences in the conceptions of ability evoked rather than as definitions of success changed the focus of research to the measurement of task and ego goals. However, it is unlikely that these two goals will explain all the variance in achievement situations. Urdan and Maehr (1995) have argued for the examination of a subset of social goals that should be relevant to variability in achievement striving. They propose that there are a number of possible social goals including social approval goals (in which the aim is to gain approval from others such as parents, teachers, and peers), social solidarity goals (reflecting a focus on bringing

honor to one's group), and social affiliation goals (which emphasize making/retaining friends).

With a particular focus on the athletic context, Duda and colleagues (e.g., Duda & Nicholls, 1992) have identified and examined the correlates of a cooperation goal. This goal dimension was also investigated by Ames and colleagues (1984, 1992a) from a situational goal approach when they explored the impact of individualistic, competitive, and cooperative goal structures.

In research centered on the identification and measurement of other goal orientations that are salient to particular subgroups of sport participants, Gano-Overway and Duda (1996) found evidence in support of an Expressive Individualism goal perspective in the case of Anglo-American and, in particular, African-American high school track and field athletes. The 10-item expressive individualism scale we developed was factor analyzed, and two dimensions resulted. The first comprised items that reflected an emphasis on being creative and original in one's performance (e.g., "I feel successful in sport when my style is unique," "I feel successful in sport when I can express myself while performing"). The second factor contained items that indicated a concern with expressing a unique image of oneself through one's appearance (e.g., "I feel successful in sport when I can be creative in my dress," "I feel successful in sport when I can express myself in what I wear"). The first factor accounted for a greater amount of the variance than the second factor (41.9% versus 13.6%, respectively) and was found to be more internally consistent (alphas = .69 and .84, respectively). Our results also showed that, in the case of the African-American and Anglo-American athletes, the first dimension of Expressive Individualism reflects both a task and ego goal emphasis (i.e., a second-order factor analysis revealed that this scale cross-loaded on both the task and ego orientation dimensions). The appearance facet of Expressive Individualism, however, was linked to ego orientation only.

Conceptions of Failure

Instruments assessing task and ego goals have focused on conceptions of ability tied to success, but a thorough understanding of achievement motivation entails that we also are aware of the determinants and repercussions of subjective failure experiences. Preliminary evidence suggests that there may be an asymmetry in success and failure perceptions. For example, Ewing (1981) administered a questionnaire assessing the antecedents and consequences of success and failure and showed that male and female adolescents perceive these constructs quite differently. Utilizing open-ended assessments, within-subject and group discrepancies in subjective definitions of success and failure have also been reported by Duda (1986) and Whitehead (1993b).

Qualitative and Quantitative Assessment

Qualitative assessment can provide a richer source of data and more sensitive indicators of individual differences in dispositional and perceived situational goal perspectives than is furnished by classic psychometric techniques that are concerned with quantitative generalizations. Neither qualitative nor quantitative analyses supersede the other as they provide complementary information. A perusal of the literature on goal perspectives in the physical domain indicates, however, that there has been a tendency to rely too heavily on the latter. The few studies that have employed qualitative methods include work by Hayashi (1996), Harwood, Swain, and Thorpe (1996) and Thorne and Duda (1995).

In a semistructured interview, Hayashi (1996) examined subjective definitions of success among Anglo-American and Hawaiian males who participated in weight lifting. He found that "all participants defined positive and negative experiences in physical activity and weight training based on task and ego orientations" (p. 202). For both groups though, successful and unsuccessful experiences also marked an "interdependent perspective of the self" that related to meeting others' expectations and affiliative concerns. Further, the Hawaiian men also defined success in regard to the "proliferation of pride and harmony within an in-group."

During the interviews, Hayashi (1996) also examined subjective perceptions of the goal/reward structure or motivational climate operating in the weight room. According to this researcher, "all Anglo-Americans and Hawaiians (defined) the weight room climate based on individualistic, competitive, and cooperative goal/reward structures" (p. 206). However, an interdependent perspective, which emphasized being part of the group and not standing out, was perceived to be part of the weight room environment among the Hawaiian respondents.

Harwood et al. (1996) recently used qualitative methodology to investigate the motivational criteria that have both developed and situationally induced achievement goal perspectives among 17 elite tennis players. Four general dimensions emerged from the inductive content analysis that captured the major motivational criteria impacting on "players' personal theories of achievement in general and within current situations." These were cognitive-developmental skills and experiences, the motivational climate conveyed by significant others, structural and social nature of the game, and match context. Development of an ego-involved/oriented approach to tennis in general and in competitive matches was reflected by such higher order themes as "outcome-based match evaluation by the coach" and "social consequences of match outcomes." In contrast, a task-involved goal perspective was linked to such themes as "coach directed performance review and assessment," "performance-related attitudes from peers and professionals," and "early task-oriented coaching behavior." Such work provides further insight into the complexity and nature of task and ego goals. This type of research also suggests ways in which we can improve available quantitative measures of dispositional and situationally induced goal perspectives in sport settings.

Employing an idiographic analysis, Thorne and Duda (1995) examined the motivation-related correlates of goal orientations in sport. This work illustrates the use of qualitative methods to test the generality of theoretical findings (from the group case to the individual case) and examine the adequacy of our measures. Ninety-four youth ice hockey players were administered the TEOSQ, and 28 were then classified in one of four groups, that is, high task/high ego, high task/low ego, low task/high ego, or low task/low ego, in terms of their dispositional goal perspec-

tives. In an attempt to replicate previous nomothetic-based findings, the players' beliefs about the causes of success and views about the functions of sport involvement were determined. When compared with previously established group-based results, consistencies and differences were observed.

Scale Norms

The findings from most studies over-viewed in this chapter show means to be higher for task in contrast to ego assessments of goal orientations and/or the perceived climate in the physical domain. It may, therefore, be quite normal for a sample to be significantly higher in task than ego orientations or perceptions of the situationally emphasized goals. Norms for all available goal perspective scales would allow researchers to determine whether the data from a particular sample are unusually high or low.

Another reason for developing test norms is that the orthogonality of the task and ego scales has led researchers to explore goal profiles using mean or median splits (e.g., Fox, Goudas, Biddle, Duda & Armstrong, 1994). These goal profiles, however, have been sample specific so a score that may be considered high in one sample is low in another one, and this makes comparision across different studies particularly difficult if not questionable. Clearly norms are necessary to facilitate quadrant selection in the formation of goal perspective profiles. However, the construction of such norms requires not only the collection of a large amount of data, but also the careful categorization of subjects by such variables as age, gender, and competitive level.

To date, sufficient work has been done with the TEOSQ to allow for the generation of such norms (based on those studies in which researchers subdivided their samples based on age, gender, and competitive level). More research on perceptions of the motivational climate in the physical domain will facilitate the development of norms related to this variable.

In Search of Conceptual Clarity and Consistency: A Final Word

In his overviews of the state of measurement in sport psychology, Schutz (Schutz, 1994; Schutz & Gessaroli, 1993) identified a number of pervasive problems. An especially pertinent concern centered on the formation and definition of constructs in the field. Schutz suggested that there are too many instances when the constructs assessed are not conceptually based, clearly defined, and/or operationalized in a way that is consonant with the conceptual definition. We would also add that difficulties arise when researchers do not distinguish between the construct to be measured and its likely correlates.

Throughout this chapter, we have attempted to point out a number of instances where the measurement of goal perspectives suffers from at least some of these maladies. We concur with Marsh (1994) who, with specific reference to achievement goals, emphasized the need to be cognizant of "jingle (scales with the same label reflect the same construct) and jangle (scales with different labels measure different constructs) fallacies, and pursue construct validity studies more vigorously to test the interpretations of measures" (p. 365). We hope the information presented and ideas discussed within this contribution will encourage forthcoming research on goal perspectives in the physical domain, work that entails careful, consistent, and creative assessments of goal orientations, situational goals, and goal states as well as a clear distinction between these constructs.

References

Ames, C. (1984). Competitive, cooperative and individualistic goal structures: A motivational analysis. In R. Ames & C. Ames (Eds.), *Research on motivation in education: Student motivation* (pp. 177-207). New York: Academic Press.

Ames, C. (1992a). Classrooms: Goals, structures, and student motivation. *Journal of Educational Psychology, 84*, 261-271.

Ames, C. (1992b). Achievement goals, motivational climate, and motivational processes. In G. Roberts (Ed.), *Motivation in sport and exercise* (pp. 161-176). Champaign, IL: Human Kinetics.

Ames, C., & Archer, J. (1988). Achievement goals in the classroom: Students' learning strategies and motivation processes. *Journal of Educational Psychology, 80*, 260-267.

Andree, K.V., & Whitehead, J. (1995). The interactive effect of perceived ability and dispositional or situational achievement goals on intrinsic motivation in young athletes. *Journal of Sport and Exercise Psychology, 17*, (Suppl.), S7.

Asch, S.E. (1952). *Social psychology.* Englewood Cliffs, NJ: Prentice-Hall.

Atkinson, J.W. (1964). *An introduction to motivation.* Princeton, NJ: Van Nostrand.

Balaguer, I., Castillo, I., & Tomas, I. (1996). Analisis de las Questionario de Orientacion al Ego y a la Tarea en el Deporte (TEOSQ) en su traduccion al castellano. *Psicologica, 17*, 71-81.

Barnes, J.K., Page, A., & McKenna, J. (1997). Goal orientation and motivational climate of international rowers during training and competition seasons. *Journal of Sport Science, 15*, 70-71.

Biddle, S., Akande, A., Vlachopoulos, S., & Fox, K. (1996). Towards an understanding of children's motivation for physical activity: Achievement goal orientations, beliefs about sport success, and sport emotion in Zimbabwean children. *Psychology and Health, 12*, 49-55.

Biddle, S., Cury, F., Goudas, M., Sarrazin, P., Famose, J-P., & Durand, M. (1995). Development of scales to measure perceived physical education class climate: A cross-national project. *British Journal of Educational Psychology, 65*, 341-358.

Biddle, S.H.J., & Goudas, M. (1996). Analysis of children's physical activity and its association with adult encouragement and social cognitive variables. *Journal of School Health, 66*(2), 75-78.

Bock, S., Biddle, S.H.J., & Fox, K.R. (1997). Intra and inter group comparisons of achievement goal profiles for children of different levels of sport. *Journal of Sports Sciences, 15*, 72.

Boyd, M., & Callaghan, J. (1994). Task and ego goal perspectives in organized youth sport. *International Journal of Sport Psychology, 22*, 411-424.

Boyd, M., & Yin, Z. (1996). Cognitive-affective sources of sport enjoyment in adolescent sport participants. *Adolescence, 31* (122), 283-295.

Boyd, M., Yin, Z., Ellis, D., & French, K. (1995). Perceived motivational climate, socialization influences, and affective responses in Little League Baseball. *Journal of Sport and Exercise Psychology, 17*, (Suppl.), S30.

Brunel, P.C. (1996). The relationship of task and ego orientation to intrinsic and extrinsic motivation. *Journal of Sport and Exercise Psychology, 18* (Suppl.), S18.

Chi, L. (1993). *The prediction of achievement-related cognitions and behaviors in the physical domain: A test of the theories of goal perspectives and self-efficacy.* Unpublished doctoral dissertation, Purdue University.

Chi, L., & Duda, J.L. (1995). Multi-sample confirmatory factor analysis of the Task and Ego Orientation in Sport Questionnaire. *Research Quarterly for Exercise and Sport, 66*, 91-98.

Cury, F., Biddle, S.H.J., Famose, J-P., Goudas, M., Sarrazin, P., & Durand, M. (1996). Personal and situational factors influencing intrinsic motivation of adolescent girls in school physical education: A structural equation modeling analysis. *Educational Psychology, 16*, 305-315.

Dempsey, J.M., Kimiecik, J.C., & Horn, T.S. (1993). Parental influence on children's moderate to vigorous physical activity participation: An expectancy-value approach. *Pediatric Exercise Science, 5*, 151-167.

Dorobantu, M., & Biddle, S.H.J. (1997). The influence of situational and individual goals on intrinsic motivation of Romanian adolescents towards physical education. *European Yearbook of Sport Psychology, 1*, 148-165

Duda, J.L. (1986). Perceptions of sport success and failure among white, black, and Hispanic adolescents. In J. Watkins, T. Reilly, & L. Burwitz (Eds.), *Sport science* (pp. 214-222). London: Spon.

Duda, J.L. (1989). Relationship between task and ego orientation and the perceived purpose of sport among high school athletes. *Journal of Sport and Exercise Psychology, 11*, 318-335.

Duda, J.L. (1992). Sport and exercise motivation: A goal perspective analysis. In G. Roberts (Ed.), *Motivation in sport and exercise* (pp. 57-91). Champaign, IL: Human Kinetics.

Duda, J.L. (1993). Goals: A social cognitive approach to the study of motivation in sport. In R.N. Singer, M. Murphey, & L.K. Tennant (Eds.), *Handbook of research in sport psychology* (pp. 421-436). NY: Macmillan.

Duda, J.L. (1994). A goal perspective theory of meaning and motivation in sport. In S. Serpa, J. Alves, & V. Pataco (Eds.), *International Perspectives on Sport and Exercise Psychology* (pp. 127-148). Morgantown: Fitness Information Technology, Inc..

Duda, J.L. (1996). Maximizing motivation in sport and physical education among children and adolescents: The case for greater task involvement. *Quest, 48*, 290-302.

Duda, J.L., Fox, K.R., Biddle, S.J.H., & Armstrong, N. (1992). Children's achievement goals and beliefs about success in sport. *British Journal of Educational Psychology, 62*, 313-323.

Duda, J.L., Chi, L., Newton, M.L., Walling, M.D., & Catley, D. (1995). Task and ego orientation and intrinsic motivation in sport. *International Journal of Sport Psychology, 26*, 40-63.

Duda, J.L., & Hom, H.L. (1993). The interdependencies between the perceived and self-reported goal orientations of young athletes and their parents. *Pediatric Exercise Science, 5*, 234-241.

Duda, J.L., & Huston, L. (1995). The relationship of goal orientation and degree of competitive sport participation to the endorsement of aggressive acts in American football. In R. Vanfraechem-Raway & Y. Vanden Auweek (Eds.), *IXth European Congress on Sport Psychology Proceedings* (pp. 655-662). Brussels, Belgium: FEPSAC.

Duda, J.L., & Nicholls, J.G. (1992). Dimensions of achievement motivation in schoolwork and sport. *Journal of Educational Psychology, 84*, 290-299.

Duda, J.L., Olson, L.K., Templin, T.J. (1991). The relationship of task and ego orientation to sportsmanship attitudes and the perceived legitimacy of injurious acts. *Research Quarterly for Exercise and Sport, 62*, 79-87.

Duda, J.L., & White, S.A. (1992). Goal orientations and beliefs about the causes of success among elite athletes. *The Sport Psychologist, 6*, 334-343.

Dweck, C.S. (1986). Motivational processes affecting learning. *American Psychologist, 41*, 1040-1048.

Dweck, C.S., & Elliott, E. (1993). Achievement motivation. In M.

Hetherington (Ed.), *Handbook of child psychology: Vol. 4: Socialization, personality and social development* (pp. 643-691). New York: Wiley.

Dweck, C.S., & Leggett, E.L. (1988). A social-cognitive approach to motivation and personality. *Psychological Review, 95*, 256-273.

Ebbeck, V., & Becker, S.L. (1994). Psychosocial predictors of goal orientations in youth soccer. *Research Quarterly for Exercise and Sport, 65*, 355-362.

Eccles, J., Midgley, C., & Adler, T.F. (1984). Grade-related changes in the school environment: Effects on achievement motivation. In J.G. Nicholls (Ed.), *The development of achievement motivation* (pp. 283-332). Greenwich, CT: JAI Press,

Elliott, E.S., & Dweck, C.S. (1988). An approach to motivation and achievement. *Journal of Personality and Social Psychology, 54*, 5-12.

Ewing, M. (1981). *Achievement motivation and sport behavior of males and females.* Unpublished doctoral dissertation, University of Illinois, Urbana-Champaign.

Fonseca, A., & Balague, G. (1996). Measuring goal orientations in youth competitive soccer: A comparison of TEOSQ and POSQ measures. *Journal of Applied Sport Psychology, 8* (Suppl.), S143.

Fox, K., Goudas, M., Biddle, S., Duda, J., & Armstrong, N. (1994). Children's task and ego goal profiles in sport. *British Journal of Educational Psychology, 64*, 253-261.

Fraser, B. (1986). *Classroom environment.* London: Croom Helm.

Gano-Overway, L.A., & Duda, J.L. (1996). Goal perspectives and their relationship to beliefs and affective responses among African and Anglo American athletes. *Journal of Applied Sport Psychology, 8*, (Suppl.), S138.

Gill, D.L., & Deeter, T.E. (1988). Development of the Sport Orientation Questionnaire. *Research Quarterly for Exercise and Sport, 59*, 191-202.

Gill, D.L., Kelley, B.C., Martin, J.J., & Caruso, C.M. (1991). A comparison of competitive-orientation measures. *Journal of Sport and Exercise Psychology, 8*, 266-280.

Goudas, M., & Biddle, S. (1994). Perceived motivational climate and intrinsic motivation in school physical education classes. *European Journal of Psychology of Education, 9*, 241-250.

Goudas, M., Biddle, S., & Fox, K. (1994a). Achievement goal orientations and intrinsic motivation in physical fitness testing with children. *Pediatric Exercise Science, 6*, 159-167.

Goudas, M., Biddle, S., & Fox, K. (1994b). Perceived locus of causality, goal orientations, and perceived competence in school physical education classes. *British Journal of Educational Psychology, 64*, 453-463.

Goudas, M., Biddle, S., Fox, K., & Underwood, M. (1995). It ain't what you do, it's the way that you do it! Teaching style affects children's motivation in track and field lessons. *The Sport Psychologist, 9*, 254-264.

Goudas, M., Biddle, S., & Underwood, M. (1995). A prospective study of the relationships between motivational orientations and perceived competence with intrinsic motivation and achievement in a teacher education course. *Educational Psychology, 15*, 89-96.

Guest, S.M., & White, S.A. (1996). Goal orientation, gender and perceptions of the motivational climate created by significant others. *Journal of Applied Sport Psychology, 8* (Suppl.), S63.

Guest, S.A., White, S.A., Jones, D.L., McCaw, S.T., & Vogler, W.E. (in press). Dispositional and situationally-induced goal perspectives in physical education and sport. *Journal of Applied Sport Psychology.*

Guivernau, M., & Duda, J.L. (1994). Psychometric properties of a Spanish version of The Task and Ego Orientation in Sport Questionnaire (TEOSQ) and Beliefs about the Causes of Success Inventory. *Revista de Psicologia del Deporte, 5*, 31-51.

Guivernau, M., & Duda, J.L. (1997). *The generality of goals, beliefs, interest and perceived ability across sport and school: The case of Spanish student-athletes.* Manuscript submitted for publication.

Guivernau, M., Thorne, K., & Duda, J.L. (1994, February). *Cross-domain generality of goals, beliefs, perceived ability and interest: A replication.* Paper presented at the 4th Annual Midwest Sport and Exercise Psychology Symposium, Michigan State University, East Lansing, MI.

Hall, H.K., & Earles, M. (1995). Motivational determinants of interest and perceptions of success in school physical education. *Journal of Sport and Exercise Psychology, 17*, (Suppl.), S57.

Hall, H.K., & Finnie, S. (1995). Goals and perfectionism as antecedents of exercise addiction. *Journal of Sport and Exercise Psychology, 17*, (Suppl.), S7.

Hall, H.K., & Kerr, A.W. (in press). Motivational antecedents of pre-competitive anxiety in youth sport. *The Sport Psychologist.*

Hall, H.K., Matthews, J., & Kerr, A. (1994). Goals, perfectionism, and competitive stress in youth sport. *Journal of Sport and Exercise Psychology, 16*, (Suppl.), S63.

Harter, S. (1981). A new self-report scale of intrinsic versus extrinsic orientation in the classroom: Motivational and informational components. *Developmental Psychology, 17*, 300-312.

Harwood, C.G., & Swain, A.J.B. (1996). An interactionist examination of the antecedents of pre-competitive achievement goals within national tennis players. *Journal of Sport Sciences, 14*, 32-33.

Harwood, C.G., Swain, A.J.B., & Thorpe, R. (1997). Influencing meanings of achievement: Motivational criteria at work within elite junior tennis players. *Journal of Sport Sciences, 15*, 85-86.

Hayashi, C.T. (1996). Achievement motivation among Anglo-American and Hawaiian male physical activity participants: Individual differences and social contextual factors. *Journal of Sport and Exercise Psychology, 18*, 194-215.

Hayashi, C.T., & Weiss, M.R. (1994). A cross-cultural analysis of achievement motivation in Anglo-American and Japanese marathon runners. *International Journal of Sport Psychology, 25*, 187-202.

Hom, H., Duda, J.L., & Miller, A. (1993). Correlates of goal orientations among young athletes. *Pediatric Exercise Science, 5*, 168-176.

Jourden, F., Bandura, A., & Banfield, J. (1991). The impact of conception of ability on self-regulatory factors and motor skill acquisition. *Journal of Sport and Exercise Psychology, 13*, 213-226.

Kavussanu, M., & Roberts, G.C. (1996a). Motivation in physical activity contexts: The relationship of perceived motivational climate to intrinsic motivation and self efficacy. *Journal of Sport and Exercise Psychology, 18*, 264-280.

Kavussanu, M., & Roberts, G.C. (1996b). The utility of dispositional versus situational factors in predicting intrinsic motivation, beliefs about the causes of success and task choice in physical activity classes. *Journal of Sport and Exercise Psychology, 18*, (Suppl.), S46.

Kim, B.J., & Gill, D.L. (1995). Psychological correlates of achievement goal orientation in Korean youth sport. *Journal of Applied Sport Psychology*, (Suppl.), S22.

Kimiecik, J., Horn, T.S., & Shurin, C.S. (1996). Relationships among children's beliefs, perceptions of their parents' beliefs and their moderate-to-vigorous physical activity. *Research Quarterly for Exercise and Sport, 67*, 324-336.

Li, F., Harmer, P., & Acock, A. (1996). The Task and Ego Orientation in Sport Questionnaire: Construct equivalence and mean differences across gender. *Research Quarterly for Exercise and Sport, 67*, 228-238.

Li, F., Harmer, P., Acock, A.C., Vongjaturapat, N., & Boonverabut, S. (in press). Testing the cross-cultural validity of the TEOSQ and its factor covariance and mean structure across gender. *International Journal of Sport Psychology.*

Li, F., Harmer, C., Chi, L., & Vongjaturapat (1996). Cross-cultural validation of the Task and Ego Orientation in Sport Questionnaire. *Journal of Sport and Exercise Psychology, 18*, 392- 407.

Linford, J., & Fazey, D. (1994). Goal orientation of physical education lessons and the perceived physical competence of young adolescents. *Journal of Sports Sciences, 12,* 199-200.

Lloyd, J., & Fox, K.R. (1992). Achievement goals and motivation to exercise in adolescent girls: A preliminary study. *British Journal of Physical Education Research Supplement, 11,* 12-16.

Lochbaum, M., & Roberts. G.C. (1993). Goal orientations and perceptions of the sport experience. *Journal of Sport and Exercise Psychology, 15,* 160-171.

Maehr, M.L., & Braskamp, L.A. (1986). *The motivation factor: A theory of personal investment.* Lexington, MA: Lexington Books.

Maehr, M.L., & Nicholls, J.G. (1980). Culture and achievement motivation: A second look. In N. Warren (Ed.), *Studies in cross-cultural psychology* (pp. 221-267). New York: Academic Press.

Markland, D., & Wilson, S. (1997). Goal orientations, perceived legitimacy of drug-taking in sport and readiness to take a performance enhancing drug. *Journal of Sport Sciences, 15,* 94-95.

Marsh, H. (1994). Sport motivation orientations: Beware of jingle-jangle fallacies. *Journal of Sport and Exercise Psychology, 16,* 365-380.

McClelland, D.C. (1961). *The achieving society.* New York: Free Press.

McNamara, W. & Duda, J.L. (1997). *Goal orientations and perceptions of the purposes of sport among young male athletes and their parents.* Manuscript submitted for publication.

Midgley, C., Feldhaufer, H., & Eccles, J. (1989). Student/teacher relations and attitudes toward mathematics before and after transition to junior high school. *Child Development, 60,* 981-992.

Moos, R.H., & Trickett, E.H. (1987). *Classroom Environment Scale Manual.* Palo Alto, CA: Consulting Psychologists Press.

Morgan, K., & Carpenter, P. (1997). Motivational climate, achievement goals, beliefs about success, task choice and affective responses in physical education classes. *Journal of Sport Sciences, 15,* 98.

Newton, M.L., & Duda, J.L. (1993a). Elite adolescent athletes' achievement goals and beliefs concerning success in tennis. *Journal of Sport and Exercise Psychology, 15,* 437-448.

Newton, M.L., & Duda, J.L. (1993b). The Perceived Motivational Climate in Sport Questionnaire-2: Construct and predictive validity. *Journal of Sport and Exercise Psychology, 15* (Suppl.) S59

Newton, M., & Duda, J.L. (1995). Relations of goal orientations and expectations on multidimensional state anxiety. *Perceptual and Motor Skills, 81,* 1107-1112.

Newton, M.L., & Duda, J.L. (1997a). *The Perceived Motivational Climate in Sport Questionnaire-2: A test of the hierarchical factor structure.* Manuscript submitted for publication.

Newton, M.L, & Duda, J.L. (1997b). *The effect of dispositional goals and perceptions of the motivational climate on beliefs and intrinsic motivation.* Manuscript submitted for publication.

Newton, M., & Walling, M.D. (1995). Goal orientations and beliefs about success among Senior Olympic Games participants. *Journal of Sport and Exercise Psychology, 16* (Suppl.), S23.

Nicholls, J.G. (1984). Conceptions of ability and achievement motivation. In R. Ames & C. Ames (Eds.), *Research on motivation in education: Vol. 1. Student motivation.* New York: Academic Press.

Nicholls, J.G. (1989). *The competitive ethos and democratic education.* Cambridge, MA: Harvard University Press.

Nicholls, J.G. (1992). The general and the specific in the development and expression of achievement motivation. In G. Roberts (Ed.), *Motivation in sport and exercise* (pp. 31-54). Champaign, IL: Human Kinetics.

Nicholls, J.G., Patashnick, M., & Nolen, S.B. (1985). Adolescents' theories of education. *Journal of Educational Psychology, 77,* 683-692.

Nicholls, J.G., & Miller, A.T. (1984). Development and its discontents: The differentiation of the concept of ability. In J. Nicholls (Ed.),

Advances in motivation and achievement: Vol. 3. The development of achievement motivation (pp. 185-218). Greenwich, CT: JAI Press.

Ommundsen, Y., & Roberts, G.C. (1996). Goal orientations and perceived purposes of training among elite athletes. *Perceptual and Motor Skills, 83,* 463-471.

Papaioannou, A. (1990). *Goal perspectives, motives for participation, and purposes of P.E. lessons in Greece as perceived by 14 and 17 year old pupils.* Unpublished master's thesis, University of Manchester, England.

Papaioannou, A. (1992). *Students' motivation in physical education classes which are perceived to have different goal perspectives.* Unpublished doctoral dissertation, University of Manchester, England.

Papaioannou, A. (1994). Development of a questionnaire to measure achievement orientations in physical education. *Research Quarterly for Exercise and Sport, 65,* 11-20.

Papaioannou, A. (1995). Differential perceptual and motivational patterns when different goals are adopted. *Journal of Sport and Exercise Psychology, 17,* 18-34.

Papaioannou, A., & Diggelidis, N. (1996). Developmental differences in students' motivation, goal orientations, perceived motivational climate and perceptions of self in Greek physical education. *Journal of Applied Sport Psychology, 8,* (Suppl.), S15.

Papaioannou, A., & Macdonald, A.I. (1993). Goal perspectives and purposes of physical education as perceived by Greek adolescents. *Physical Education Review, 16,* 41-48.

Peiro, C., Escarti, A., & Duda, J.L. (1996). The assessment of significant others' perceived goal perspectives in sport settings. *Journal of Applied Sport Psychology, 8,* (Suppl.), S138.

Pensgaard, A.M., & Roberts, G.C. (1995). Competing at the Olympics: Achievement goal orientations and coping with stress. *IXth European Congress on Sport Psychology Proceedings: Integrating Laboratory and Field Studies.* FEPSAC, Brussels, PART II, 701-708.

Pensgaard, A.M., & Roberts, G.C. (1996). Perceived motivational climate and sources of stress for winter Olympic athletes. *Journal of Applied Sport Psychology, 7,* (Suppl.), S9.

Pensgaard, A.M., Roberts, G.C., & Ursin, H. (1995). Differences and similarities between able-bodied and disabled athletes. *Journal of Applied Sport Psychology, 7* (Suppl.), S9.

Roberts, G.C., & Balague, G. (1989). *The development of a social-cognitive scale of motivation.* Paper presented at the Seventh World Congress in Sport Psychology, Singapore. Abstracts 91.

Roberts, G.C., & Balague, G. (1991). *The development and validation of the Perception of Success Questionnaire.* Paper presented to the FEPSAC Congress, Cologne, Germany.

Roberts, G.C., Hall, H.K., Jackson, S.A., Kimiecik, J.C., & Tonymon, P. (1995). Implicit theories of achievement and the sport experience: The effect of goal orientations on achievement strategies and perspectives. *Perceptual and Motor Skills, 81,* 219-224.

Roberts, G.C., & Ommundsen, Y. (1996). Effect of goal orientations on achievement beliefs, cognitions and strategies in team sport. *Scandinavian Journal of Science in Medicine and Sport, 6,* 46-56.

Roberts, G.C., & Treasure, D.C. (1995). Achievement goals, motivational climate and achievement strategies and behaviors in sport. *International Journal of Sport Psychology, 26,* 64-80.

Roberts, G.C., Treasure, D.C., & Balague, G. (in press). Achievement goals in sport: Development and validation of the Perception of Success Questionnaire. *Journal of Sport Sciences.*

Roberts, G.C., Treasure, D.C., & Hall, H.K. (1994). Parental goal orientations and beliefs about the competitive sport experience of their child. *Journal of Applied Social Psychology, 24,* 631-645.

Roberts, G.C., Treasure, D.C., & Kavussanu, M. (1996). Orthogonality of achievement goals and its relationship to beliefs about success and satisfaction in sport. *The Sport Psychologist, 10,* 398-408.

Sarrazin, P., Biddle, S.H.J., Famose, J.P., Cury, F., Fox, K., & Durand, M. (1996). Goal orientations and conceptions of the nature of sport ability in children: A social cognitive approach. *British Journal of Social Psychology, 35*, 399-414.

Scanlan, T.K., & Lewthwaite, R. (1984). Social psychological aspects of competition for male youth sport participants: I. Predictors of competitive stress. *Journal of Sport Psychology, 6*, 208-226.

Scanlan, T.K., & Simon, J.P. (1992). The construct of sport enjoyment. In G.C. Roberts (Ed.), *Motivation in sport and exercise* (pp. 199-215). Champaign, IL: Human Kinetics.

Schutz, R.W. (1994). Methodological issues and measurement problems in sport psychology. In S. Serpa, J. Alves, & V. Pataco (Eds.), *International perspectives on sport and exercise psychology* (pp. 35-55). Morgantown, WV: Fitness Information Technology.

Schutz, R.W., & Gessaroli, M.E. (1993). Use, misuse, and disuse of psychometrics in sport psychology research. In R. Singer, M. Murphey, & L.K. Tennant, (Eds.), *Handbook of research on sport psychology* (pp. 901-920). New York: Macmillan.

Seifriz, J.J., Duda, J.L., & Chi, L. (1992). The relationship of perceived motivational climate to intrinsic motivation and beliefs about success in basketball. *Journal of Sport and Exercise Psychology, 14*, 375-391.

Solmon, M.A., & Boone, J. (1993). The impact of student goal orientation in physical education classes. *Research Quarterly for Exercise and Sport, 64*, 418-424.

Spence, J.T., & Helmreich, R.L. (1983). Achievement-related motives and behaviors. In J.T. Spence (Ed.), *Achievement and achievement motives* (pp. 7-74). San Francisco: W.H. Freeman.

Spielberger, C.D., Gorsuch, R.L. & Lushene,R.F. (1970). *Manual for the state-trait anxiety inventory*. Palo Alto, CA: Consulting Psychologists Press.

Spray, C., & Biddle, S.H.J. (1997). Beliefs about the nature of athletic ability, goal orientations, perceived competence and motivation in sport and physical education. *Journal of Sport Sciences, 15*, 105-106.

Stephens, D. (1995). Judgments about lying, hurting and cheating in youth sport: Variations in patterns of predictors for female and male soccer players. *Journal of Applied Sport Psychology, 7* (Suppl.), S111.

Stephens, D., Janz C., & Mahoney, L.(1996). Goal orientation and RPE in exercise testing of young adolescents. *Journal of Applied Sport Psychology, 8* (Suppl.), S140.

Stephens, D.E., & Bredemeier, B.J.L. (1996). Moral atmosphere and judgments about aggression in girls' soccer: Relationships among moral and motivational variables. *Journal of Sport and Exercise Psychology, 18*, 174-193.

Swain, A.B.J. (1996). Social loafing and identifiability: The mediating role of achievement goal orientations. *Research Quarterly for Exercise and Sport, 67*, 337-344.

Swain, A.B.J., & Harwood, C.G. (1996). Antecedents of state goals in age-group swimmers: An interactionist perspective. *Journal of Sports Sciences, 14*, 111-124.

Tank, K. & White, S.A. (1996). Goal orientation and trait anxiety among male and female athletes at different levels of sport involvement. *Research Quarterly for Exercise and Sport, 67* (Suppl.), S123.

Tank, K., White, S.A., & Wingate, J. (1996). Personal goals and perceptions of self, mother and father beliefs about the causes of success in sport. *Journal of Applied Sport Psychology, 8* (Suppl.), S140.

Thorne, K.S., & Duda, J.L. (1995). The motivation-related correlates of goal orientations in sport: An idiographic analysis. *Journal of Sport and Exercise Psychology, 17* (Suppl.), S6.

Treasure, D.C. (in press). Relationship between task and ego perceptions of a physical education context and elementary school children's cognitive and affective responses. *Journal of Sport and Exercise Psychology*.

Treasure, D.C., & Roberts, G.C. (1994a). Perceptions of success questionnaire: Preliminary validation in an adolescent population. *Perceptual and Motor Skills, 79*, 607-610.

Treasure, D.C., & Roberts, G.C. (1994b). Cognitive and affective concomitants of task and ego goal orientations during the middle school years. *Journal of Sport and Exercise Psychology, 16*, 15-28.

Treasure, D.C., & Roberts, G.C. (1995). Applications of achievement goal theory to physical education: Implications for enhancing motivation. *Quest, 47*, 1-14.

Treasure, D.C., & Roberts, G.C. (1996). *Relationships between children's achievement goal orientations, perceptions of the motivational climate, beliefs about success and sources of satisfaction in basketball*. Manuscript submitted for publication.

Treasure, D.C., Roberts, G.C., & Hall, H.K. (1992). The relationship between children's achievement goal orientations and their beliefs about competitive sport. *Journal of Sport Sciences, 10*, 629.

Urdan, T.C., & Maehr, M.L. (1995). Beyond a two-goal theory of motivation and achievement: A case for social goals. *Review of Educational Research, 65*, 213-243.

VanYperen, N.W., & Duda, J.L. (1997). The interrelationships between goal orientations, beliefs about success,and performance improvement among young elite Dutch soccer players. International Society for Sport Psychology. *Innovations in Sport Psychology: Linking Theory and Practice, Proceedings II* (pp. 732-734). Israel: Wingate Institute.

Vealey, R.S. (1986). Conceptualization of sport-confidence and competitive orientation: Preliminary investigation and instrument development. *Journal of Sport Psychology, 8*, 221-246.

Vealey, R.S. (1988). Sport-confidence and competitive orientation: An addendum on scoring procedures and gender differences. *Journal of Sport and Exercise Psychology, 10*, 471-478.

Vlachopoulos, S., & Biddle, S. (1996). Achievement goal orientations and intrinsic motivation in a track and field event in school physical education. *European Physical Education Review, 2*, 158-164.

Vlachopoulos, S., Biddle, S., & Fox, K. (1996). A social-cognitive investigation into the mechanisms of affect generation in children's physical activity. *Journal of Sport and Exercise Psychology, 18*, 174-193.

Walling, M.D., & Duda, J.L. (1995). Goals and their associations with beliefs about success in and perceptions of the purposes of physical education. *Journal of Teaching in Physical Education, 14*, 140-156.

Walling, M., Duda, J.L., & Chi, L. (1993). The perceived motivational climate in sport questionnaire: Construct and predictive validity. *Journal of Sport and Exercise Psychology, 15*, 172-183.

Walling, M.D., Duda, J.L., & Crawford, T. (1992). *The relationship of goal orientations and competitive outcome to enjoyment in youth sport*. Unpublished manuscript.

Weigand, D.A., & Davis, D.C. (1996). The role of goal orientations and motivational climate on amateur soccer players' perceived legitimacy of aggressive acts. *Journal of Applied Sport Psychology, 8* (Suppl.), S142.

Weigand, D.A., & Petrie, T.A. (1996). Dispositional goal orientations, perceived parental goal orientations and perceived parental pressure in young athletes. *Journal of Applied Sport Psychology, 8* (Suppl.), S142.

Weiner, B. (1985). An attribution theory of achievement motivation and emotion. *Psychological Review, 92*, 548-573.

Weiss, M.R., & Chaumeton, N. (1992). Motivational orientations in sport. In T. Horn (Ed.), *Advances in sport psychology* (pp. 61-100). Champaign, IL: Human Kinetics.

White, S.A. (1996a). Goal orientation and perceptions of the motivational climate initiated by parents. *Pediatric Exercise Science, 8*, 122-129

White, S.A. (In press). Parent-initiated motivational climate and competitive trait anxiety among sport participants high in task or ego orientation. *The Sport Psychologist*.

White, S.A, & Duda, J.L. (1993a). Dimensions of goals and beliefs among athletes with physical disabilities. *Adapted Physical Activity Quarterly, 10*, 49-58.

White, S.A., & Duda, J.L. (1993b, June). *The relationship between goal orientation and parent-initiated motivational climate among children learning a physical skill.* Paper presented at the Eighth World Congress of Sport Psychology, Lisbon, Portugal.

White, S.A., & Duda, J.L. (1994). The relationship of gender, level of sport involvement, and participation motivation to task and ego orientation. *International Journal of Sport Psychology*, 25, 4-18.

White, S.A, & Duda, J.L. (1996). *The Parent-initiated Motivational Climate Questionnare-2: Construct, criterion, and predictive validity.* Manuscript submitted for publication.

White, S.A., Duda, J.L., & Hart, S. (1992). An exploratory examination of the Parent-Initiated Motivational Climate Questionnaire. *Perceptual and Motor Skills, 75*, 875-880.

White, S.A., Duda, J.L., & Keller, M.R. (In press). The relationship between goal orientation and perceived purpose of sport among youth sport participants. *Journal of Sport Behavior.*

White, S.A., & Guest, S.M. (1996). Goal orientations and perceptions of the motivational climate created by significant others. Manuscript submitted for publication.

White, S.A., Johnson, L.A., & Morgan, J.Q. (1995). Dimensions of goals and sport commitment among female volleyball players. *Journal of Applied Sport Psychology, 7* (Suppl.), S124.

White, S.A., & Zellner, S.R. (1996). The relationship between goal orientation, beliefs about the causes of sport success, and trait anxiety among high school, intercollegiate, and recreational sport participants. *The Sport Psychologist, 10*, 58-72.

Whitehead, J. (1990). Achievement orientations and persistence in adolescent sport. *Journal of Sport Sciences, 8*, 87-88.

Whitehead, J. (1992). Toward the assessment of multiple goal perspectives in children's sport. *Olympic Scientific Congress, Malaga, Spain, Abstracts Vol. 2, PSY14.*

Whitehead, J. (1993a). Multiple goal perspectives and persistence in children's sport. Movement and Sport. *Psychological Foundations and Effects, Vol. 1: Motivation, Emotion and Stress, 51-56. Proceedings of the VIII European Congress of Sport Psychology, 1991.* Koln, Germany.

Whitehead, J. (1993b, June). *The generalizability of achievement orientations across young people's success and failure experiences in sport.* Paper presented at the VIIIth World Congress of Sport Psychology, Lisbon, Portugal.

Whitehead, J. (1995). Multiple achievement orientations and participation in youth sport: A cultural and developmental perspective. *International Journal of Sport Psychology, 26*, 431- 452.

Whitehead, J., & Andrée, K.V. (1997). Interactive effects of dispositional and situational goals and perceived ability on intrinsic motivation in young athletes. *Journal of Sport Sciences, 15*, 110-111.

Williams, L. (1994). Goal orientations and athlete's preferences for competence information sources. *Journal of Sport and Exercise Psychology, 16*, 416-430.

Williams, L. (1996). Situational influences on goal involvement. *Journal of Applied Sport Psychology, 8* (Suppl.), S17.

Williams, L., & Gill, D.L. (1995). The role of perceived competence in the motivation of physical activity. *Journal of Sport and Exercise Psychology, 17*, 363-378.

Chapter 3

SOURCES OF COMPETENCE INFORMATION

Thelma S. Horn
Miami University
and
Anthony J. Amorose
University of Virginia

Over the past couple of decades, a number of theoretical models have been developed in an effort to understand and explain differences between individuals in their motivation, performance, and behavior in achievement contexts (e.g., Deci & Ryan, 1985; Dweck & Leggett, 1988; J. S. Eccles & Harold, 1991; Harter, 1981). Although these theories certainly differ from each other in a number of important ways, there is one construct that is common to all of them. Each of the models includes the construct of perceived competence or perceived ability as a central correlate or antecedent of achievement motivation and behavior. Specifically, each of these theories suggests that individuals who have high perceptions of their ability in a particular achievement domain will be more motivated to participate in activities in that domain, will work hard to achieve competence, and will enjoy their participation. In contrast, individuals who have low perceptions of their ability will exhibit low motivation, lack of persistence, and considerably lower enjoyment when working in such a domain.

In support of these theoretical models, the research conducted to date indicates that perceived competence does serve as a mediator of individuals' achievement performance and behavior (e.g., Harter, 1992). In the physical activity setting as well, there is a considerable bank of research to show that individuals' perceptions of their competence or ability in sport or physical activity contexts have a significant effect on their performance, behavior, cognitions, and affective reactions in that context (e.g.,

Weiss & Chaumeton, 1992; Weiss & Ebbeck, 1996).

Given the importance of perceived competence as a factor affecting individuals' behavior in achievement contexts, a number of researchers have recently begun examining the processes individuals use to evaluate their competence. That is, these researchers have been interested in studying how individuals evaluate or judge their personal competence or ability in achievement contexts. Some of this process-oriented work has focused on the information individuals use to form judgments concerning their competence or ability. Although much of this research has been conducted to examine individuals' perceptions of their competence in academic or cognitive achievement contexts (e.g., Ruble, Grosovsky, Frey, & Cohen, 1992; D. Stipek & Mac Iver, 1989), a few researchers have also examined these issues in the physical activity domain (e.g., Ebbeck, 1990; Horn, Glenn, & Wentzell, 1993; Horn & Hasbrook, 1986, 1987; Horn & Weiss, 1991; Weiss, Ebbeck, & Horn, in press; Williams, 1994).

The primary purpose of this chapter is to critically examine the methodological procedures that have been used to assess the sources of competence information that individuals use in sport and physical activity contexts. To provide a conceptual basis for this analysis, the current chapter begins with an overview of the theoretical and conceptual models that have served as a basis for the current work on sources of competence information in the physical activity domain. The second section of this chapter then focuses on the assessment or measurement of individuals' preferences for and/or use of the various sources of competence information. The chapter concludes with a discussion concerning alternative ways to measure this construct.

Sources of Competence Information: Theoretical and Conceptual Frameworks

The theoretical model that has served as the basis for the sport research on sources of competence information is that formulated by Harter. Her original model (1978, 1981) was developed in an effort to explain variability among children in their motivation to achieve mastery within selected achievement contexts. In particular, Harter identified three achievement domains: the cognitive (academic), the physical (sports and outdoor games), and the social (peer relationships).

According to Harter's (1978, 1981) model, children whose initial mastery attempts at an optimally challenging task result in success and who are given positive feedback from significant socializing agents for that success will develop a positive perception of their personal competence and an internal perception of performance control. Such positive self-perceptions will cause these children to experience positive affect (e.g., pleasure, satisfaction, pride) that, in turn, results in an increase in, or at least a maintenance of, an intrinsic motivational orientation. In contrast to such a positive scenario, children whose initial mastery attempts result in failure and/or who receive either no, or negatively oriented, feedback from significant adults will perceive a lack of personal competence and will develop an external perception of performance control within that achievement context. Such negative self-perceptions cause these children to experience negative affective reactions (e.g., anxiety) and subsequently to experience a decrease in intrinsic motivation.

Based on a cognitive-developmental perspective, Harter has also incorporated a developmental component into her model (1978, 1981). Specifically, she suggests that young children whose mastery attempts in particular achievement contexts are consistently met with positive reinforcement by significant adults and who receive support and approval from these adults for independence in task-mastery attempts will (with time and cognitive maturation) develop two critical internalization systems. First, they will internalize a self-reward system (i.e., the ability to judge own performance and to praise or reinforce one's self for mastery attempts and successes). Second, they will internalize a system of performance standards or mastery goals (i.e., a set of achievement goals to which child will strive). As a result of this internalization process, older children become less dependent on external sources of competence information. That is, they become capable of making independent judgments concerning the quality of their performance attempts within a particular task domain and of determining whether they have reached the level of performance for which they have striven. Thus, these children's perceptions or judgments of their performance in a particular domain are based on a system of previously determined and internalized performance goals.

In contrast, again, to such a positive scenario, children whose initial mastery attempts in a particular achievement context are met with noncontingent performance feedback from significant adults *and* who receive disapproval from adults for their independence (or approval for dependence) will not internalize a positively based self-reward or achievement goal system. Thus, these children will continue, into adolescence and beyond, to be dependent on external sources of competence information both to determine whether they have been successful or unsuccessful in a particular task attempt and to determine the level of performance for which they should strive in any achievement context. In addition, as Harter (1978, 1981) points out, these children are likely to internalize a self-punishing system (e.g., "I am never good enough") that causes them to develop an external perception of performance control, a low perception of personal competence, and increased anxiety in that achievement context.

Although Harter's original model (1978, 1981) clearly focused on the children's success/failure experiences in combination with feedback from significant adults (primarily parents) as the primary sources of competence information and self-worth, her later writings (e.g., Harter, 1990) expand on these sources to include feedback and social support from teachers, classmates, close friends, coworkers, and life partners/spouses. In doing so, Harter also expands her theoretical model on perceived competence and self-worth to include individuals throughout the lifespan.

Furthermore, in a more recent article, Harter (1992) also incorporates a socioenvironmental perspective into her theoretical formulations as she analyzes the changes that occur in children's self-perceptions and intrinsic motivation as they progress from elementary to junior high and then to high school. In particular, she relates these changes in children's perceptions of themselves to corresponding changes that occur in the school environment. Using her own school-based research, as well as that of other researchers (e.g., J. Eccles, Midgley, & Adler, 1984), Harter documents the changes that occur from early elementary to high school classes in the processes used by school personnel to evaluate children's academic competence. Specifically, she notes an increasing use of (a) objective test scores (classroom tests as well as standardized academic achievement tests), (b) social comparison processes (e.g., grading "on the curve"), and (c) evaluatively based teacher feedback. Such age-related changes in the ways in which children's academic competence is determined are correlated with decreases in children's perceptions of academic competence and in their intrinsic motivation for school activities. Although a direct causal relationship between these two phenomena has not yet been convincingly established in actual classroom settings, Harter cites a number of experimental studies (e.g., Harter, 1978; Harter & Guzman, 1986; Lepper & Gilovich, 1981) that have shown that the type of competence information children are given following performance on an academic task does have a direct effect on their perceptions of competence and their intrinsic motivation. Specifically, an emphasis on the use of external rewards, social comparison processes, and/or evaluatively based and publicly given feedback from adults resulted in an attenuation of children's intrinsic motivation and enjoyment of that task. Thus, there is direct evidence to show that the type of information that is used to evaluate children's performance can have a causal effect on their self-perceptions and their level of intrinsic motivation.

Interestingly, as Harter (1992) notes, not all children show a decline in perceptions of personal competence and intrinsic motivation as they progress from the elementary to the junior high and high school years. Thus, it seems likely that some children are not socialized into using the sources of information (e.g., peer comparison, standardized test scores, teacher feedback) that are emphasized within the school environment. Rather, these children may be evaluating their personal competence on the basis of other sources of information that are available in the academic achievement environment but that may not be as strongly emphasized by teachers and other school personnel. Such sources could include (a) amount of personal improvement over time (i.e., how much the child has learned or improved over the instructional unit); (b) amount of effort exerted in the mastery of the task (i.e., how hard the student had to work to learn the task); (c) achievement of self-set goals (i.e., attainment of an internalized and personalized set of performance goals); (d) degree of personal enjoyment of academic material; and (e) parental approval and reinforcement. The use of such "alternative" sources of information on which to base judgments of personal competence may explain why selected children are resistant to the commonly observed decrease in perceived competence and intrinsic motivation as they progress through the school system.

In general, then, Harter's original model (1978, 1981) as well as her subsequent adaptations of it (1990, 1992) emphasizes the importance of high perceptions of personal competence, as such perceptions lead to a number of positive behavioral and affective outcomes. In addition, Harter's theoretical formulations suggest that individuals' perceptions of personal competence will vary as a function of the type of information that they either choose to use or are forced to use in judging their performance within any particular achievement context. Thus, depending on the specific source(s) of information used, the individual's perception of competence can either be high or low.

The notion that individuals' perceptions of competence or ability within any particular domain may vary as a function of the type of information they use to judge their performance ability is also inherent in several other conceptual models. The social-cognitive theoretical models developed by Nicholls (1984, 1989), Ames (1984), and Dweck (e.g., Dweck & Elliott, 1983; Dweck & Leggett, 1988) suggest that individuals in achievement contexts vary in the degree to which their perceptions of personal ability are framed in terms of a self-referenced perspective (demonstration of task mastery or personal improvement) or an other-referenced perspective (peer comparison). Furthermore, these theorists and their colleagues have provided support for the idea that individuals who adhere to a self-referenced perspective (identified by Nicholls as task involved) will differ in their behavior, cognitions, and affective reactions in achievement contexts from individuals who are other referenced (identified by Nicholls as ego involved). Specifically, task-involved individuals have been found to exhibit high levels of intrinsic motivation and persistence in working within that achievement domain. In addition, they generally experience positive affect and choose to engage in moderately challenging tasks. In contrast, ego-involved individuals, who perceive low levels of personal competence within a particular achievement context, exhibit a more maladaptive pattern of behavior (i.e., they exhibit low effort, low persistence following failure, and low intrinsic motivation toward the achievement domain). Considerable support for the applicability of this goal perspective approach to the study of individuals' behavior in sport and physical activity contexts has also been demonstrated (cf. Duda, 1993).

In addition to the theoretical models described in the previous paragraphs, a review of the empirical literature on children's competence judgments in the academic domain also provides support for the notion that there exists a wide variety of information sources that are available in the academic achievement context and that children could use to evaluate or judge their competence. These sources have been categorized or grouped (using either theoretically or empirically based categorization systems) in several different ways. D. Stipek and Mac Iver (1989), for example, in their developmentally based review of the research on children's assessments of their intellectual competence, distinguish between intra-individual comparison sources (e.g., improvement in personal performance over time, comparison of personal performance in one subject area with that in other subjects) from interindividual comparison sources (comparison of own performance with that of relevant others). They also identify a variety of other sources that are available in the academic classroom. These other sources include (a) mastery information (whether or not child completes the task or achieves some sort of goal or performance standard); (b) "objective" feedback (e.g., grades, test scores, or other symbols, such as stickers or stars); (c) social feedback (evaluation from teachers or relevant other adults in the academic context); (d) effort (how hard child perceives he or she has to or did work to accomplish academic tasks); and (e) teacher behavior (e.g., how much attention child perceives she or he receives from teacher).

As the research and theory cited in this section would suggest, there are indeed a wide range of sources of information available in any particular achievement context that individuals could use to judge their performance and/or their competence in that context. Furthermore, the particular sources of information that individuals either choose to use or are forced to use in evaluating their ability may have a significant effect on their perceptions of competence and their subsequent behavior in that achievement context. Thus, two individuals whose performance in a particular achievement context is the same may arrive at two different estimates of their ability depending on the sources of information they use to make that judgment. Based, again, on the research that shows the importance of high perceptions of competence as a factor affecting individuals' performance and behavior in achievement contexts, it would seem important to conduct research investigating the sources of information individuals use to evaluate their competence.

Of course, the value of such research is, to a great extent, dependent on the quality of the procedures or instrumentation that are used to measure individuals' preferences for, or use of, the various sources of information that are available within any particular achievement context. In the next section, issues pertaining to the assessment or measurement of the sources of information individuals use in physical contexts are discussed.

Sources of Competence Information: Assessment and Measurement

Given the plethora of information sources that may be available in any particular achievement context and that could be used by individuals within that context, it is understandable that it would be difficult to assess with a reasonable degree of accuracy which sources a particular individual might choose to use. In this section of the chapter, the instrumentation that is currently available to assess this construct is described and critiqued. In addition, alternative measurement procedures are described.

Current Instrumentation

The majority of the research conducted to date to examine interindividual variation in individuals' use of and/or preference for the various sources of information available in the physical domain has been based on a self-report questionnaire originally developed by Horn and Hasbrook (1986) for use with children in a competitive sport setting. The original instrument has subsequently been refined through a series of studies conducted with different samples of children, adolescents, and young adults (e.g., Horn et al., 1993; Horn & Weiss, 1991; Phelps & Horn, 1992).

The most current version of the questionnaire, which has been titled the Sport (or Physical) Competence Information Scale (SCIS or PCIS), consists of 39 items that represent the 13 sources of competence information presented in Table 1. The scale format consists of three scenarios, each of which describes competence judgments that athletes might make in regard to their performance in that sport context. An example of one of these scenarios for use with high school athletes is presented in Figure 1. As shown in this example, the competence judgment situation or context is briefly described. Then, the individual respondent is asked to indicate, on a specified scale, how important each of the 13 sources of information is in helping her or him to make that competence judgment. A 5-point Likert-type response format is used with verbal anchors ranging from *Extremely important* to *Not at all important*. As noted before, the SCIS contains three of these scenarios. Thus, the individual respondent rates the importance of each of the 13 sources of information in three different competence judgment contexts. The three competence scenarios were developed to correspond with three of the items composing Harter's Perceived Competence Scale (Harter, 1982). Although the current version of the SCIS is designed for use with athletes from a variety of sports (i.e., it is not specific to one sport), other researchers have modified the SCIS for use with athletes or individuals from a particular sport or physical activity (e.g., Ebbeck, 1990).

Development of the SCIS

The individual items constituting the current version of the SCIS were identified and/or selected based on a series of steps. To begin with, a content review of the theoretical and empirical literature on children's competence judgments was conducted. This literature review resulted in the identification of a number of possible sources of competence information (see previous section of this chapter concerning theoretical and conceptual frameworks). In addition, an existing inventory, developed by Minton (1979) and titled the Competence Information Scale, was found. Minton's inventory was developed on the basis of interviews with children in grades four to six to identify the dimensions of information underlying their judgments of their own competence in three different achievement domains (academic, physical, social). Minton used the responses from this sample of children to develop her Competence Information Scale. For the physical domain, Minton identified three major sources of information: feedback from significant adults (teachers, coaches, parents); peer comparison and evaluation (e.g., being picked first for teams); and task mastery/sport attraction (e.g., speed of learning, liking for new skill activities).

Horn and Hasbrook (1986) used the format of Minton's (1979) scale to develop their first version of the SCIS, which contained 12 sources of competence information. These sources were identified based on the theoretical models discussed in the previous section of this chapter and on the empirically based educational and developmental psychology literature that has been conducted to investigate children's self-assessments in the academic domain (cf. D. Stipek & Mac Iver, 1989). The 12 sources included in the original version of the SCIS included feedback from four categories of individuals (coaches, teammates, parents, and spectators); two sources related to the use of peer comparison (teammates and opponents); five internal sources of information (personal attraction toward sport, degree of perceived effort in practices, self-ratings of game performance, degree of skill improvement over time, and speed or ease in learning new skills); and one measure of game outcome (win/loss record). This initial version of the SCIS was subsequently administered to a pilot sample of 121 children ranging in age from 8 to 12 years. In addition, a modified version was administered to a pilot sample of 100 high school athletes. In both cases, study participants were asked to respond to the 12 sources of information included in the original version of the SCIS, but were also asked, via an open-ended question, to identify any additional information sources they might use in a competitive sport setting. Based on these pilot results, the initial version of the SCIS was revised. Specifically, the format of the scale was changed to make it easier to administer. In addition, the two sources of peer comparison (teammates and opponents) were combined into one category labeled "peer comparison," and a second measure of game outcome (game performance statistics) was added. Also, the source of internal information originally labeled as "self-rating of game performance" was changed to "achievement of self-set goals." Finally, a new source of internal information was identified by participants in the high school sample. This source of information included feelings and reactions experienced by athletes both pre- and postgame (e.g., "how good I feel after the game," "how nervous I am before the game"). These revisions then resulted in the 13 sources of information that are presented in Table 1. Subsequent use of this version of the SCIS in a series of data-collection projects (Horn et al., 1993; Phelps & Horn, 1992; Williams, 1994) has resulted in the continuous refinement of the questionnaire in order to increase its readability and reliability.

Table 1
Sources of Competence Information in Competitive Sport Contexts.

Source	Descriptor Items
1. Parental feedback	What my parents say to me after games/matches What my parents think about my skill or ability
2. Coach feedback	How my coach evaluates my performance The kind of praise/criticism I get from my coach
3. Peer evaluation	What my teammates/friends think about my performance How my teammates evaluate me as a player
4. Peer comparison	How my performance compares with that of my teammates How well I perform in practice activities compared to my teammates
5. Speed or ease of learning	How quickly/slowly I learn new skills or plays How easy it is for me to learn a new skill or play
6. Amount of effort exerted	How hard I have to work to learn and perform skills How much effort I have to exert to keep up my skill
7. Attraction toward sport	How much I enjoy this sport How much I like participating in this sport
8. Game performance statistics	How well or poorly I play in games or matches What my performance statistics are in games/matches
9. Game outcome	What my (or my team's) win/loss record is Whether or not I (or my team) win important games/matches
10. Internal information	How I feel before/after games or matches How good I feel about myself after practice and games/matches
11. Skill improvement	How much/little I improve in my sport over time How much/little my performance has improved from last season
12. Spectator feedback	What the spectators at games/matches think about me How the crowd reacts to my performance
13. Achievement of self-set goals	Whether or not I meet the goals I set for myself Whether or not I am playing the way I expected myself to play

Scoring Procedures for the SCIS

As noted in an earlier section of this chapter, the current version of the SCIS consists of 39 items that represent 13 sources of competence information. Thus, there are three items to represent each competence information source. Obviously, the easiest way to score the SCIS is to sum each participant's scores on the individual subscales (sources of information). These procedures will result in 13 subscale scores, each representing the extent to which individual participants use that source of information in evaluating their competence in the sport domain of interest.

Horn and her colleagues (Horn et al., 1993; Horn & Hasbrook, 1986,1987; Horn & Weiss, 1991; Weiss et al., in press), however, have chosen to conduct a factor analysis of the obtained scores and then to construct factor scores for each study participant for use in subsequent statistical analyses. Their rationale for the use of factor analysis is based on three arguments.

First, from a methodological and statistical perspective, a factor analysis typically results in the reduction of the sources of information from a total of 13 to a more manageable number. Obviously, this facilitates the use of these data in subsequent statistical analyses.

Second, from a conceptual perspective, it might be anticipated that individuals' use of, or preference for, the various

sources of information in the physical domain would not be independent of each other. That is, there may be a relatively high level of correlation between the 13 subscales (sources of information) that compose the SCIS. A factor analysis, then, allows the researcher to determine if the 13 different information sources assessed by the SCIS would actually be representative of a smaller set of more general latent constructs. The value of this approach may be particularly evident in regard to developmentally based research. As Harter and her colleagues (summarized in Harter, 1990) have found, individuals' perceptions of themselves and their self-worth tend to become more differentiated with age. Thus, the factor structure underlying younger children's conceptions or perceptions of their abilities or competencies has been found to be less diverse (i.e., fewer factors) than is the factor structure underlying the self-perceptions of older children, adolescents, and adults. In fact, during the childhood and adolescent years, age is positively correlated with number of factors. Along the same lines, several sets of researchers have found that younger children's explanations for their and their classmates' "success" in academic contexts are less differentiated or less diverse than are the explanations of older children (Blumenfeld, Pintrich, Meece, & Wessels, 1982; D. J. Stipek, 1981; D. J. Stipek & Tannatt, 1984; Yussen & Kane, 1985).

Sources of Competence Information

Some high school athletes really believe that they have all or most of the physical abilities needed to be a good athlete. Other players think they may not have all of these physical abilities.

Listed below are a series of items which represent some sources of information that a high school athlete might use in judging how good an athlete she or he is. You should rate each source of information as to how important it is in helping you know whether or not you have strong physical abilities for your sport.

Source	Extremely important		Somewhat important		Not at all important
1. How easy it is for me to learn a new skill or play	5	4	3	2	1
2. The praise/criticism I get from my coach	5	4	3	2	1
3. How confident or unsure I am before and during games or matches	5	4	3	2	1
4. Whether or not I am performing the way I expected myself to perform	5	4	3	2	1
5. What my parents say to me after my games or matches	5	4	3	2	1

Figure 1: Example narrative and selected items from the Sport Competence Information Scale (SCIS)

In their research using the SCIS, Horn and her colleagues (Horn et al., 1993; Horn & Hasbrook, 1986; Horn & Weiss, 1991; Weiss et al., in press) have also found some evidence that the factor structure underlying children's and adolescents' sources of information varies with age. In three different studies with children between the ages of 8 and 14 years, Horn and her colleagues (Horn & Hasbrook, 1986; Horn & Weiss, 1991; Weiss et al., in press) have conducted factor analyses with the SCIS that resulted in the identification of four to six conceptually distinct factors. However, with a sample of high school athletes who completed a similar version of the SCIS, Horn et al.'s (1993) factor analysis resulted in the identification of 10 conceptually distinct factors. Furthermore, Phelps and Horn (1992) also found 10 factors in their analysis of SCIS data obtained from college-aged athletes. These results, then, suggest that

adolescents and young adults may perceive the sources of information underlying their competency judgments to be more diverse or more differentiated than do younger children. As an example of this type of differentiation based on age, the factor structures from two different age groups taken from a similar sport context (i.e., children/adolescents who were current participants in a competitive sport program) are presented in Table 2. The first factor structure was found by Horn and Hasbrook (1986) in their research with 273 young athletes who ranged in age from 8 to 14 years. The second factor structure was found by Horn et al. (1993) in their research with 435 high school athletes (ages 14 to 18 years). As can be seen in Table 2, factor analysis of the SCIS with the younger sample of athletes resulted in 6 factors whereas the factor structure for the high school sample contained 10 factors. These differing results sug-

Table 2
SCIS Factor Structure for Two Different Age Groups.

Younger Age Group: 8-14 Years
(Horn & Hasbrook, 1986)

Factor 1: Peer Comparison
        (Comparison with teammates and opponents;
        Game performance statistics)
Factor 2: Evaluative Feedback
        (Coaches, Peers, Spectators)
Factor 3: Internal Information
        (Perceived Effort; Skill Improvement;
        Speed/Ease of Learning)
Factor 4: Evaluative Feedback (Parents)
Factor 5: Game Outcome (winning/losing)
Factor 6: Attraction Toward Sport

Older Age Group: 14-18 Years
(Horn et al., 1993)

Factor 1: Internal Information
        (Skill Improvement/Perceived Effort;
        Pre-/Postgame Feelings)
Factor 2: Competitive Outcomes
        (Game Outcome; Game Perf. Statistics)
Factor 3: Evaluative Feedback (Parents)
Factor 4: Peer Comparison
        (Comp. With Teammates and Opponents)
Factor 5: Eval. Feedback (Spectators)
Factor 6: Eval. Feedback (Coach)
Factor 7: Speed/Ease of Learning
Factor 8: Eval. Feedback (Peers)
Factor 9: Achievement of Self-Set Goals
Factor 10: Attraction Toward Sport

gest that the younger children's perceptions of the sources of competence information available in the athletic environment are less differentiated or diverse. Factor 2, for example, includes feedback from three categories of individuals who are typically in the sport environment (coaches, peers, and spectators). In contrast, for the older sample of athletes, these three sources of social evaluation each load on a separate factor. This indicates that adolescents may perceive the information from these three sources to be different or unique from each other whereas the younger children may perceive the information from these three sources to be similar. Along the same lines, for the younger sample of athletes, the internal information factor comprises three sources of information (amount of effort exerted in practice, skill improvement, and speed/ease of learning new skills). For the older sample, speed/ease of learning new skills loads on a separate factor from skill improvement and effort. This, again, may suggest that that older individuals perceive the sources of information available to them to be more diverse and differentiated from each other than do the younger athletes. Given the developmentally based research (e.g., Barker & Graham, 1987; Dweck & Leggett, 1988; Fry & Duda, in press; Nicholls, 1984, 1989) that suggests that children's and adolescents' perceptions regarding the relationship between effort and ability change with age (i.e., the distinction between the two constructs increases with age), it may not be surprising that these three sources of competence information may also separate with age.

As noted before, this increased differentiation with age in regard to children's and adolescents' perceptions concerning the sources of competence information available in the sport environment is consistent with developmental theory (see similar arguments presented by Harter, 1990, and D. Stipek and Mac Iver, 1989). Werner (1957) claims, for example, that "whenever development occurs, it proceeds from a state of relative globality and lack of differentiation, articulation, and hierarchic integration" (p. 126). Therefore, the use of factor analysis by researchers using the SCIS with individuals of different ages and/or at different levels of maturation may be of particular value in helping to identify possible developmental trends in individuals' judgments of themselves and their physical competencies. That is, over time and with repeated use of the SCIS with different groups of individuals, we may begin to uncover not only age-related differences in children's, adolescents', and adults' *use* of the various sources of information but also age-related differences in the way in which individuals *perceive* the sources of information that are available in the sport and physical activity domain.

In support of this notion, Butler's (1989b) research indicates that there are age-related differences in the way in which social comparison information is perceived and used by children. Specifically, younger children (5 years) used peer comparison for personal mastery reasons (i.e., to learn how to improve their own performance) whereas older children (10 years) used peer comparison information in order to assess relative ability (i.e., how my performance compares with that of peers). Given this information, it would not be surprising if the factor structure underlying younger children's (i.e., below the age of 8 years) SCIS scores would show a correlation between peer

comparison and self-comparison (i.e., items representing these sources would fall on the same factor) whereas the factor structure for older children would be more apt to show a separation of these two competence information sources (i.e., items representing the two sources of information loading on separate factors). Thus, again, continued use of factor analysis with different sets of study samples may provide information relating to the way in which children perceive and/or process sources of competence information in the physical domain.

A third and final rationale for the continued use of factor analysis with the SCIS is based on the argument that the instrument is still really in its formative stages of development. Thus, the use of exploratory and confirmatory factor analytic techniques may help to refine and revise the instrument in a positive way.

Psychometric Properties of the SCIS

In regard to psychometric properties, the SCIS has been at least initially tested for reliability and validity. To begin with, its content validity is based on an extensive review of the literature in areas relating to children's and adolescents' judgments of personal competence. Second, the internal consistency of the items constituting each of the individual source subscales and/or the identified factor subscales has been tested in several studies (Ebbeck, 1990; Horn et al., 1993; Horn & Weiss, 1991; Weiss et al., in press; Williams, 1994). Generally, obtained alpha coefficients have been found to meet or exceed the .70 level recommended by Nunnally (1978). Third, some evidence for the construct validity of selected of the subscales has been demonstrated through a variety of research studies. The results of these studies are described in the following paragraphs.

Horn and her colleagues (Horn et al., 1993; Horn & Hasbrook, 1986; Horn & Weiss, 1991; Weiss et al., in press) have used the SCIS to investigate possible developmental changes in children's and adolescents' use of the various sources of competence information that are available in the physical or sport domain. Citing developmental research and theory that suggest that the competence judgments of younger children would be based more on evaluative feedback from significant adults whereas older children would show greater dependence on peer comparison and evaluation as a means to judge their sport competence (e.g., Aboud, 1985; Boggiano & Ruble, 1979; Cook & Stingle, 1974; Feldlaufer, Midgley, & Eccles, 1988; Harter, 1978, 1981; D. Stipek & Mac Iver, 1989), Horn and her colleagues (Horn & Hasbrook, 1986; Horn & Weiss, 1991; Weiss et al., in press) hypothesized that the same age-related trends would occur in the sport setting. Support was found for these hypotheses. Specifically, these researchers found that children between the ages of 8 and 14 years show a relative decline in the use of evaluative feedback from significant adults, especially parents, and an increase in the use of peer comparison and peer evaluation.

Using an older sample of study participants (14-18 years), Horn et al. (1993) again tested age-related predictions concerning changes in adolescents' use of the various sources of information contained in the SCIS. Based on research and theory from the developmental psychology literature (e.g., Adams, 1980; Harter, 1978, 1981; Veroff, 1969), which suggests that children over the adolescent years develop or internalize a set of personal standards and/or values that can then be used to evaluate their own performance and behavior in subsequent achievement situations, Horn et al. hypothesized that the younger adolescents in their sample would indicate greater use of peer comparison, peer evaluation, and game outcome (more externally based and concrete sources of competence information) whereas older adolescents would be more apt to use such internally based information as achievement of self-set goals and skill improvement. Support was found for most of these hypotheses. Specifically, the younger adolescents did show greater use of peer evaluation whereas older adolescents reported more use of internalized information systems (achievement of self-set goals and skill improvement).

The studies cited in the previous paragraphs provide some support for the construct validity of the SCIS in that they show that some of the subscales conform with research and theory from the developmental literature concerning age-related changes in children's and adolescents' judgments of personal competence. In addition to this age-related research work, other investigators have provided support for the construct validity of the SCIS by demonstrating correlation of scores from selected subscales with relevant other psychological characteristics of individual study participants. These studies are described in the following paragraphs.

Horn and Hasbrook (1987) used the SCIS to test predictions from Harter's model (1978, 1981) concerning variability between children in the extent to which they would internalize a positive or negative self-assessment system. As noted in an earlier section of this chapter, Harter (1978, 1981) proposes that children who experience success at optimally challenging tasks and who are given positive feedback from significant adults both for task-mastery and for independence in task mastery attempts will (with time and cognitive maturation) internalize both a positive self-reward system and a system of standards or mastery goals. These children, then, will no longer be dependent on external sources of competence information and will also have high perceptions of competence and an internal perception of performance control. In contrast, children who do not experience success in task mastery and/or who receive negative feedback from significant adults accompanied by disapproval for independence in task-mastery attempts will not internalize such a positively based self-reward or achievement goal system. Thus, these children will continue to be dependent on external sources of competence information. In addition, these children will develop an external perception of performance control, a low perception of personal competence, and increased anxiety in that athletic context.

In testing these hypotheses, Horn and Hasbrook (1987) administered the SCIS, as well as perceived competence and control scales, to a sample of 229 young athletes ranging in age from 8 to 14 years. Multivariate correlational analyses revealed support for Harter's model (1978, 1981) in that children in the two older age categories (10 - 14 years) who had higher perceptions of competence and an internal perception of control did indicate greater orientation toward the use of internal standards (skill improvement, perceived effort, speed/ease of learning new skills) whereas children with an external perception of control indicated greater use of game outcome and parental and specta-

tor feedback as important sources of competence information.

From a somewhat different theoretical perspective, Williams (1994) examined the potential relationship between high school athletes' goal orientation and their preferences for particular sources of competence information (as measured by the SCIS). The results of her multivariate analyses provided some support for her hypotheses. Specifically, athletes who scored higher on task goal orientation also tended to score higher on competence information sources that were aligned with personal mastery (e.g., goal attainment, skill improvement and learning) whereas athletes who scored high on ego orientation showed a tendency to score higher on social comparison. However, Williams also noted that a relatively small amount of the variance in the competence information sources was explained by athletes' goal orientation scores (8.4%). In addition, gender differences were found in athletes' use of or preference for particular competence information sources. Such gender differences may interact with athletes' goal orientation scores to impact on their preferences for particular sources of competence information. Due to the relatively small sample size, possible gender differences in the relationship between these two data sets could not be clearly ascertained.

In general, then, the results of the studies cited in this section do provide some support for the reliability and validity of the SCIS. However, continued psychometric testing of the SCIS is very obviously needed. Given the number and diversity of the sources of information that are represented in the SCIS, it would take considerable psychometric work to test the reliability and validity of all of the subscales. In addition, in contrast to many other scales used in the field of sport psychology, the SCIS was initially developed with the notion that children's perceptions regarding the sources of competence information would change with age. Thus, a complete examination of the psychometric properties of the SCIS is complicated by the need to consider age in regard to the interpretation of the data. Recommendations and/or suggestions for future psychometric work are provided in the next section.

Recommendations for Future Psychometric Work

The SCIS-based research that has been published to date has been conducted with somewhat different versions of the SCIS and with fairly diverse subject samples. Specifically, Horn and Hasbrook (1986) used an early version of the SCIS with 273 age-group soccer athletes ranging in age from 8 to 14 years. In contrast, Horn and Weiss (1991) and Weiss et al. (in press) administered an adapted version of the SCIS that was more appropriate for assessing the competence judgments of children (ages 8 to 14) who were participants in a summer motor skill instructional program. In regard to adolescent subject samples, Horn et al. (1993) administered the most current version of the SCIS to a group of 435 high school athletes who participated in a variety of predominantly team-oriented sports (e.g., basketball, volleyball, soccer, ice hockey). Williams (1994) again modified the SCIS for use with a sample of 152 high school athletes from a mostly different set of sports (e.g., baseball, softball, track, and golf). Given such diversity in the subject samples and in the form of the SCIS used across studies, it is not surprising that factor analyses of the data from these different samples have resulted in similar, but not identical, factor structures. Thus, at this point, it is certainly essential to conduct psychometric research that would ultimately result in the identification of a stable factor structure for the SCIS. Given the argument that the factor structure underlying the SCIS may change with age, the psychometric work in this area would have to be developmentally based. This would require collection of data from multiple samples of athletes at each of several age levels and then analysis of those data using both exploratory and confirmatory factor analyses. Such work has not been completed to date but certainly is necessary in order to develop and/or demonstrate the stability of a subscale structure for individuals within *each* developmental level.

Secondly, although there is some evidence for the validity of the SCIS, considerably more work in this area is necessary. To begin with, the validity studies described in the previous section have each provided support for selected information sources represented in the SCIS. Continued research would be necessary to provide support for the validity of *all* of the subscales. Again, given the number and the diversity of the subscales (sources of information) contained within the SCIS, this would require multiple data-collection projects. At least some of these projects could be similar to that described in the previous section. For example, based on Harter's (1978, 1981) model, it could be hypothesized that athletes who are high anxious in competitive sport contexts would show greater dependence on such external sources of information as coach, peer, and parent feedback as well as performance outcomes (e.g., win/loss records, game performance statistics) than would athletes who are lower in competitive sport anxiety. Similar hypotheses concerning the relationship between selected other psychological characteristics (e.g., level of intrinsic motivation) and athletes' preference for particular sources of competence information could be generated and tested. Such procedures would contribute additional evidence for the validity of the SCIS.

In addition to the construct validity procedures described in the previous paragraph, predictive validity procedures could also be employed to test the psychometric properties of the SCIS. A good area in which to apply these procedures may be in relation to the sport environment. It has, for example, been speculated (e.g., Horn & Harris, 1996; Lee, Carter, & Xiang, 1995; Weiss et al., in press; Williams, 1994) not only that a variety of socioenvironmental factors may be associated with individuals' preferences for or use of particular sources of competence information but also that such factors may actually cause children and adults to become dependent upon particular information sources. The socioenvironmental factors that have been mentioned to date include parental behaviors, coach (or other physical activity leader) behaviors, program philosophy, and program structure. In regard to coaching behavior, for example, it could be hypothesized that coaches whose feedback is predominantly based on performance outcome (e.g., whether or not player's performance results in a successful outcome) will actually cause their athletes to become more dependent on winning/losing as a source of personal competence information (e.g., I am good only if I score a lot of goals or win a lot of games). In contrast, coaches whose feedback is predominantly based on skill technique (i.e., whether or not athlete has per-

formed the skill correctly) may facilitate their athletes' use of self-comparison or mastery sources of competence information (e.g., I am good at this sport because I am getting better at the skills). Similarly, it could be hypothesized that youth sport programs that predominantly use peer comparison as the basis for the reward structure (i.e., awards given for "Most Goals Scored" or "Highest Free Throw Shooting Percentage") will encourage young athletes to judge their competence through use of social comparison whereas programs that base the reward structure on attaining personal goals (i.e., "Did you attain the goal you set for yourself this week," or "have you improved your ball handling skills this week?") will encourage participants to use skill improvement and/or achievement of self-set goals as a means to evaluate their competence at that sport. In addition, based on research conducted in the academic domain (e.g., Mac Iver, 1988; Reuman, 1989; D. J. Stipek & Daniels, 1988), it could be hypothesized that the way in which physical education classes are structured (e.g., whether children are grouped by ability within or across classes, whether skill tasks are structured and conducted on an individualized or whole-group basis) may affect not only students' perceptions of competence but also the way in which they assess their competence on individual skills or activities.

Although these relationships between socioenvironmental factors and individuals' use of particular sources of competence information have been proposed, little research to date has been conducted in the physical domain to test for such links. However, related research in the developmental and social psychology literatures has demonstrated support for such hypothesized relationships (see, for example, Ames & Ames, 1984; Butler, 1989b; Mac Iver, 1987; Phillips, 1987). Thus, studies such as those described in the previous paragraph would not only provide useful information concerning the effects of selected aspects of the sport environment on children's psychosocial growth but could also provide evidence in support of the psychometric properties of the SCIS.

As a final note regarding future psychometric research needs, it should be pointed out that the current version of the SCIS is based on self-report. Therefore, it would be necessary to determine whether or not individuals' scores on the various subscales of the SCIS are directly reflective of their actual behavior in physical activity contexts. If an individual child, for example, scores high on the Peer Comparison subscale and low on the Parent Feedback subscale, does he or she actually show those same preferences in a behavioral way? That is, in an actual sport context, do that child's judgments of her or his competence actually reflect a preferential use of one source of information at the expense of the other? Research studies that are designed to investigate these particular links would be particularly helpful in establishing the validity of the SCIS as an accurate measure of individuals' use of, or preference for, particular competence information sources. In summary, then, continued research to examine the psychometric properties of the SCIS is certainly needed.

Conceptual Limitations of the SCIS

The previous discussion concerning the psychometric properties of the SCIS does not take into account other limitations of the instrument. That is, we cannot leave this topic until we identify other conceptual issues that may limit the current version of the SCIS in its ability to measure individuals' preference for, or use of, particular sources of competence information in the physical domain. At this point, there are three conceptual limitations that may be the most critical.

Broadness of individual subscales. Based on a review of the more current empirical and theoretical literature on self-perceptions and self-appraisal, it appears likely that some of the sources of information identified in the SCIS may be too broad to capture, with a high degree of sensitivity, the processes individuals use to judge their competence in physical activity achievement contexts. Two examples of this limitation are described in the following paragraphs.

The first example applies to the source of competence information that has been identified on the SCIS as social (or peer) comparison. High scores on this source of information imply that the individual judges her or his competence in a particular physical achievement domain by comparing her or his performance with that of peers. Although this seems a rather straightforward way to judge personal competence, research and theory in other domains (e.g., Reuman, 1989) would suggest that the type of peers one chooses for comparison may be really important and may have very differential effects on the individual's judgment of personal competence. A 16-year-old high school athlete, for example, who uses the peer comparison process to judge her competence in basketball may choose to use either "near" peers (e.g., her own teammates) or a more "extended" peer group (e.g., all basketball players in her league, in the state, or even in the nation). Depending on which peer group she uses, her assessment of her competence may be either high or low. That is, although she may perceive herself to be the best player on her school team, she may not be able to see herself as one of the best players in the league, the state, or the nation (i.e., she does not make All-League or All-State teams, and/or she is not being recruited at the Division I level of collegiate play). Thus, if she uses near peers to assess her competence, she might feel very good about herself. In contrast, if she uses extended peers to evaluate her ability, she may no longer have such positive judgments of her competence in basketball. Such differences in her perceptions of competence can affect her subsequent enjoyment of, and intrinsic motivation toward, continued participation in her sport. Similarly, a 50-year-old male who is a competitive runner may judge his ability at this activity by using such near peers as the other runners in his age group or even his sedentary friends. Alternatively, this individual can judge his running competence by comparing himself to an extended peer group (e.g., all participants in a citywide, all-age-group race). Again, that runner's ultimate judgment of his competence may certainly vary depending on which particular peer group he selects for comparison.

From a developmental perspective, it has been hypothesized (Horn & Harris, 1996) that younger children (i.e., those below 10 years), who tend to be very concrete thinkers, may be limited to the use of a near-peer comparison group only (e.g., "I know that I am good at running because I am the fastest runner in Ms. Smith's third grade class"). However, with cognitive maturation, which includes the ability to think in more abstract ways, older children and adolescents may have the option or the ability to use either a near- or an extended-peer comparison group.

As of this date, the SCIS and its adaptations do not allow for any differentiation in terms of the type of peer group an individual respondent might select to use for comparison purposes. Given the arguments cited in the previous paragraphs, however, this might be an important conceptual limitation of the SCIS.

A second example of the lack of specificity in regard to the individual sources of competence information contained in the SCIS is that illustrated by the adult feedback sources (e.g., parent, coach). Although coach feedback, for example, is clearly a source of competence information for athletes, not all of the coach's provision of competence information comes through feedback. In the teacher-behavior literature, observational and interview studies have shown that students receive information about their academic competence not only from direct teacher comments but also from observation of the teacher's behavior toward them and their classmates (Brophy, 1985; J.S. Eccles & Wigfield, 1985; Lord, Umezaki, & Darley, 1990). This includes the relative amount of attention students obtain from the teacher, the amount of time the teacher spends in helping them improve their performance, and the amount of social support the teacher provides them both in and out of the classroom. Again, the impact of adults as a source of competence information is limited in the SCIS to the provision of feedback.

Along the same lines, social feedback (as received from any significant other, including peers, parents, coaches) may vary in regard to the type of competence information given (see, for example, Chaumeton & Duda, 1988). Some coaches, for example, may base their feedback to athletes on peer comparison or performance outcomes (i.e., praise and criticism given contingent on whether or not athlete "beats" peers or "wins" a particular event) whereas other coaches may give feedback to athletes based on skill improvement or attainment of personal goals (i.e., praise and criticism given contingent on improvement or attainment of individual goals). At this point, the SCIS does not differentiate between the type of feedback that individuals in sport contexts might provide. Obviously, however, the various types of feedback that significant others give may provide the performer with considerably different information about her or his competence.

In summary, although the current version of the SCIS might be complete in identifying or measuring, in a *broad* way, the sources of competence information that a particular individual might use in a sport achievement situation, it does not necessarily provide a very sensitive measure of the particular types of information that may be contained within each source. This limitation does not negate the use of the SCIS by researchers who wish to obtain a rather generalized or broad-based measure of the sources of competence information an individual uses in a particular physical activity situation (i.e., whether he or she prefers to use peer comparison more than self-comparison). However, more specific information concerning that individual's use of the identified sources of information (e.g., whether she or he uses near or extended peers) is not accessible with the current version of the SCIS.

Relative weighting of individual sources of information. A second issue with regard to the conceptual limitations of the SCIS relates to variations in the way in which individuals might choose to *combine* the sources of information in an actual achievement context to arrive at a judgment of their ability. Specifically, although the SCIS is multidimensional in that it allows the respondent to indicate her or his use of, or preference for, *multiple* sources of information, the current format of the SCIS does not provide information regarding how individuals may combine or weight sources of information to come up with an estimate of their competence. An individual respondent, for example, might indicate that both peer comparison and adult feedback are important sources of information. However, there are times in the physical domain when these sources of information may provide conflicting information. Which particular source an individual would choose to use in times like this or how he or she might combine the two sources of information to reduce the conflict would not be well reflected in her or his scores on the SCIS. Such weighting information is of interest, however, given its ultimate effect on the individual's assessment of her or his competence.

From a developmental perspective, several sets of researchers (Barker & Graham, 1987; Lord et al., 1990; Meyer et al., 1979) have found that children's perceptions or interpretations of teachers' (or other adults') feedback vary with age. Specifically, it appears as if younger children take adult feedback at face value even when other information in the achievement context (e.g., peer comparison, performance outcomes) provides conflicting information. For older children and adults, however, adult feedback is evaluated relative to the other information, and this *combination* of information is used to make personal judgments of competence. As a specific example of this phenomenon, we can take an adolescent whose performance is not as good as that of his peers. If he receives positive reinforcement (praise) from an adult for his performance whereas his peers receive either no feedback or even critical feedback, the first adolescent may actually combine these diverse pieces of information in such a way that he arrives at a low perception of personal competence. That is, he reasons that the adult, who gave him positive feedback, must believe that this level of performance is the "best" that he can do. Because his "best" level of performance is lower than that of his peers, the adolescent concludes that he has low ability at this task. As this example shows, the personal competence judgments of older children, adolescents, and adults are likely based on information that is obtained from multiple sources and that is combined to form an integrated assessment of task competence.

Similarly, research investigating Nicholls' (1984) developmentally based achievement goal theory clearly shows that there are maturational changes in children's and adolescents' use of ability, effort, and performance outcomes to determine personal competence (Fry & Duda, in press; Nicholls, 1984, 1989; Nicholls & Miller, 1984). Specifically, children at younger age levels (or lower cognitive-reasoning levels) do not distinguish between effort, ability, and performance outcomes. At older age (or reasoning) levels, however, ability, effort, and performance outcomes are clearly differentiated. Furthermore, personal ability is inferred from the combination of the three

sources of information (i.e., if higher effort is needed to achieve a particular outcome, then this implies lower ability).

As the results of the research described in the preceding paragraphs suggest, although individuals may indicate on the SCIS (and on similar instrumentation) that several of the informational sources are useful for them, we cannot, at this point, assume that the information they derive in achievement contexts from these different sources is additive. In fact, the research by Meyer et al. (1979), Barker and Graham (1987) and Nicholls (1984; Nicholls & Miller, 1984) would indicate that the information individuals acquire from different sources may actually interact to provide the performer with an estimate of her or his competence. Thus, although individuals' scores on the current version of the SCIS may tell us *what* sources of information individual performers choose to use, such scores do not tell us *how* the information from these sources may be combined to affect individuals' judgments of personal competence. This, again, serves as a conceptual limitation of the SCIS.

Generalizability of SCIS across physical activity contexts. A third and final issue with regard to the conceptual limitations inherent in the SCIS concerns the use of the instrument across a variety of physical activity achievement contexts. As noted earlier, the SCIS was developed specifically for use with children and adolescents in the competitive sport domain, and the majority of the research conducted to date has been limited to that domain. Thus, the sources of information identified in Table 1 may be very specific to that context. One exception to the previous research work is a study conducted by Ebbeck (1990), who employed a modified version of the SCIS to measure the sources of information used by college students to judge their performance in a university weight-training program. Ebbeck's version of the scale included 48 items representing 12 competence information sources. Her assessment of the internal consistency of the 12 subscales provided support for 11 of the 12. One subscale (Performance in Workouts) was deleted from further analyses due to low internal consistency. In addition to the 12 sources of information Ebbeck included in her scale, she also allowed her respondents the opportunity (via open-ended questions) to identify other sources of information they might use in addition to the ones in the adapted SCIS. Analyses of these responses resulted in the identification of two additional sources of information that may be very specific to the exercise domain. These two sources included physical and psychological health and self-image.

Although the open-ended procedures employed by Ebbeck (1990) are certainly useful and definitely advisable for researchers who intend to use the SCIS in contexts other than the competitive sport setting, we must also keep in mind that the underlying structure of the SCIS may not be appropriate for all physical activity contexts. Thus, continued research to validate the use of the SCIS (and similar instrumentation) across a variety of physical activity achievement contexts should be conducted.

Alternative Measurement Procedures

As noted throughout this chapter, the use of the SCIS (or its adaptations) in a series of research projects has provided some useful and interesting information concerning the way in which individuals evaluate and/or judge their competence in particular physical activity contexts. However, the SCIS also has some limitations in regard to the measurement of individuals' preferences for, or use of, the sources of competence information available in the physical domain. Thus, alternative measurement systems or procedures should be explored.

Within the physical activity domain, a few other researchers have begun investigating the sources of information that might underlie other aspects of individuals' self-perceptions. Vealey and her colleagues, for example, are exploring the sources of self-confidence for individuals in sport contexts and have developed a questionnaire corresponding to this research (Vealey, Walter, Garner-Holman, & Giacobbi, 1996). The 43 items included in their Sources of Sport-Confidence Questionnaire (SSCQ) were selected based on a review of the relevant theoretical and empirical research. The 43 items represent nine sources of sport confidence, including coaches' leadership, vicarious experience, social support, mastery, physical/mental preparation, demonstration of ability, environmental comfort, situational favorableness, and physical self-presentation. In support of the psychometric properties of their scale, Vealey et al. demonstrated acceptable levels of internal consistency for all subscales. In addition, a confirmatory factor analysis provided support for the nine-subscale factor structure.

From a somewhat different perspective, Feltz and Riessinger (1990) used an open-ended questionnaire format to determine the sources of self-efficacy for college students engaged in an endurance task. Their analysis of the obtained responses resulted in a four-category classification system that reflected Bandura's (1986) primary sources of self-efficacy (performance accomplishments, physiological states, verbal persuasion, and vicarious experiences).

Although the results of the Vealey et al. (1996) and Feltz and Riessinger (1990) research studies provide some interesting information concerning the sources of information that underlie individuals' levels of confidence and self-efficacy in sport and physical activity contexts, the results of such studies may not be directly comparable to the sources of information that underlie individuals' perceptions of competence. Specifically, the constructs of perceived competence, sport-confidence, and self-efficacy are not identical to each other. Perceptions of competence represent relatively stable beliefs by individuals concerning their competence or ability in particular domains (e.g., academics, sports) or subdomains (e.g., math, swimming, basketball). In contrast, self-efficacy and self-confidence represent individuals' level of certainty regarding their ability to achieve success or to successfully perform a task or tasks within a particular situation or context. Such differences between the constructs are reflected in the instructions contained in the SCIS and the SSCQ. In the SSCQ, respondents are asked to think about a time when they felt very confident when competing in their sport and then to think about what types of things made them feel confident in those situations. In contrast, the instructions contained in the SCIS ask respondents to rate each of the presented sources of information in relation to a more broad-based judgment of competence (i.e., "in helping you know over the season whether you are good or not so good in your sport"). These differential instructions are reflected in some of the more situationally based sources of information

contained in the SSCQ (e.g., environmental comfort, situational favorableness). Thus, although the constructs of perceived competence, self-efficacy, and sport-confidence are interrelated, they do not necessarily measure the same aspects of an individual's self-perceptions. Therefore, it would also be expected that the sources of information that underlie the three constructs may overlap to a certain extent but also differ in significant ways. Thus, the continued development and use of both the SCIS and the SSCQ should contribute valuable and unique information concerning the processes individuals use to evaluate themselves and their personal abilities.

In addition to the sport research described in the previous paragraphs, a review of the literature on competency judgments in other domains does show that a variety of other measurement procedures have been used to study individuals' use of particular sources of competence information. Some of these procedures were developed for use in experimentally based research projects whereas others were employed to assess individuals' competence judgments in more naturalistic or field-based research projects. These alternative procedures are briefly described in the following paragraphs.

Experimentally Based Research Procedures

A number of researchers have examined individuals' use of selected competence information sources by placing study participants in an achievement performance situation. That is, participants are instructed to work on an achievement task either by themselves, with a partner/competitor, or in a small group. The experimenters then use one or more of the following procedures in their efforts to examine the processes individuals use to evaluate or judge their performance on the achievement task:

1. Performer is provided with competence information that comes from a particular source or sources (e.g., peer or social comparison, task mastery, skill improvement). Experimenter then observes the effect such information has on performer's perceptions of competence, affective reactions, intrinsic motivation, and/or task-persistence behavior (see, for example, studies by Keil, McClintock, Kramer, & Platow, 1990; Ruble, Boggiano, Feldman, & Loebl, 1980; D. Stipek, Recchia, & McClintic, 1992; Yee & Brown, 1992).

2. Performer is provided with two or more pieces of competence information (e.g., peer comparison and task mastery). Experimenter then observes or measures which particular source of information the performer *chooses* to use to evaluate her or his competence at the task (see, for example, studies by Butler, 1990; Ruble & Flett, 1988).

3. Performer's behavior during a structured achievement task is observed to determine how he or she chooses to evaluate personal competence (i.e., experimenter measures how many times performer glances at peers' work, the performance standard, and/or the experimenter for performance feedback) (see, for example, studies by Butler, 1989a; 1989b; D. Stipek et al., 1992).

A variation of the protocol described in the previous paragraphs involves the use of imagined scenarios where the individual participant does not actually engage in a performance situation. Rather he or she is shown a videotape or read a scenario that shows an individual in a performance situation. Similar to the preceding example situations, various or selected types of information concerning the performer's competence (e.g., peer comparison, adult feedback, task mastery) are provided. The study participant (i.e., the subject) is then asked to imagine him- or herself as the performer and to rate or judge how competent he or she would feel in that situation (see, for example, studies by Jagacinski & Nicholls, 1987; Meyer et al., 1979).

As these examples clearly show, such protocols involve experimental procedures in order to assess what type of competence information individuals choose to use in performance situations and/or how various pieces of competence information may affect the performer's perception of competence, intrinsic motivation, or affective reactions. Thus, the results of these studies have contributed valuable information concerning the ways in which individuals make judgments about their competence in specific achievement contexts.

Naturalistic or Field-Based Research Procedures

In contrast to experimentally based research procedures, other researchers have studied individuals' use of different types of competence information in more naturalistic achievement contexts. In the educational psychology literature, for example, researchers have examined the effects of different types of classroom evaluation environments on children's perceptions of their academic competence and their expectancy for future success. D. J. Stipek and Daniels (1988) compared the self-perceptions of kindergarten children who were enrolled in "high normative evaluation" classrooms (i.e., classrooms where a high emphasis is placed on peer comparison and grades are given in a highly public manner) with those of children in "low normative evaluation" classrooms (i.e., emphasis is placed on individual progress within the curriculum, and more of the work is done in small-group format). These researchers found significant differences in the perceived competence levels of the two groups of children, with those in the high normative evaluation classes scoring lower in perceived competence. Similarly, Mac Iver (1988) and Reuman (1989) found significant differences in the self-perceptions of children who were enrolled in classrooms that differed in selected structural ways (e.g., within-class ability grouping vs. between-class ability grouping, individualized task structure vs. whole-class task structure). Furthermore, Reuman's research suggests that the differences in the self-perceptions of children across the various classroom environments are due to, or may be mediated by, the type of peers children choose to use for social comparison purposes.

Although the studies described in this section are predominantly descriptive in research design and thus cannot provide us with cause-effect information, the obtained results do show a correlational association between particular types of competence information and children's subsequent judgments of their ability. Moreover, these research procedures do provide some information regarding children's susceptibility to, and use of, particular sources of competence information.

In a more direct examination of children's competence information behavior, Frey and Ruble (1985) observed children working in their classroom on independent work assignments.

Although each child was expected to complete the assigned task on her or his own, he or she was free to interact with other children as he or she chose. Trained research assistants observed and coded children's verbal and visual behavior in an effort to identify how individual children attempted to determine the quality of their work. Thus, the researchers coded such behaviors as glancing at a peer's work, making comments about a peer's work in reference to own performance, and asking for help and/or feedback from a peer. Analyses of these data resulted in some interesting information concerning developmental differences in children's performance evaluations. In addition, this type of research protocol was unique in that it provided the researcher with a more spontaneous measure of children's competence judgment behavior.

Finally, some researchers have used in-depth, individualized interview methods to study what information individuals use to assess their competence. Most of these interviews have been conducted within specific achievement contexts. Lee et al. (1995), for example, interviewed children within a physical education class to determine how they assessed their own and their classmates' ability. Similarly, Stipek and her colleagues (D. J. Stipek, 1981; D. J. Stipek & Tannatt, 1984) have interviewed young children in the context of an academic classroom to assess children's perceptions regarding their own and others' academic competence. Along the same lines, Nicholls and Miller (1984) describe their use of Piaget's method of critical exploration (Inhelder, Sinclair, & Bouvet, 1974) in which individuals are exposed to achievement-related stimuli (e.g., videotapes of individuals performing an achievement task) and are then questioned concerning their perceptions of the achievement context and the individual's performance within that context. Such procedures have been successfully used not only in academic situations but also with children in physical activity contexts (see, for example, Fry & Duda, in press).

As the research cited shows, there are a variety of ways to assess individuals' use of, or preference for, particular sources of competence information. Furthermore, each of these procedures has its own strengths and weaknesses. Many of these procedures (especially the laboratory-based protocols) are limited in that they examine or compare individuals' use of, or preference for, only two or three types of competence information. Thus, unlike the SCIS, they do not provide a broad-based examination of individuals' use of, or preference for, the wide variety of information sources that may be available within a particular achievement context. Of course, as noted earlier, the SCIS is also limited to providing relatively general information concerning the sources of information individuals choose to use or do use. In summary, then, researchers who are interested in assessing or measuring the informational sources underlying their study participants' competency judgments should carefully consider the variety of assessment procedures that are currently available and select the one or ones most appropriate for their specific study purpose.

Chapter Conclusions

We have acquired a considerable amount of information regarding the processes individuals use to evaluate or judge their competence in physical activity contexts. However, much more knowledge remains to be unearthed in this area, and continued research is certainly warranted.

The quality of our research work in this, as in any other, area of study is very much dependent on the quality of our instrumentation. Although we have developed some reasonably valid and reliable procedures to use in assessing individuals' use of, or preference for, particular sources of competence information, certain limitations to these procedures must be noted and considered. Furthermore, continued efforts to revise, refine, and/or redesign our current instrumentation and/or to select or design alternative measurement procedures should be considered an important goal for researchers in our field of study.

References

Aboud, F. (1985). The development of a social comparison process in children. *Child Development, 56*, 682-688.

Adams, J. F. (1980). Understanding adolescents. In J. F. Adams (Ed.), *Understanding adolescence: Current developments in adolescent psychology* (pp. 2-20). Boston: Allyn & Bacon.

Ames, C. (1984). Competitive, cooperative, and individualistic goal structures: A motivational analysis. In R. Ames & C. Ames (Eds.), *Research on motivation in education: Student motivation* (pp. 177-207). New York: Academic Press.

Ames, C., & Ames, R. (1984). Systems of student and teacher motivation: Toward a qualitative definition. *Journal of Educational Psychology, 76*, 535-556.

Bandura, A. (1986). *Social foundations of thought and action.* Englewood Cliffs, NJ: Prentice-Hall.

Barker, G. P., & Graham, S. (1987). Developmental study of praise and blame as attributional cues. *Journal of Educational Psychology, 79*, 62-66.

Blumenfeld, P., Pintrich, P., Meece, J., & Wessels, K. (1982). The formation and role of self-perceptions of ability in elementary classrooms. *Elementary School Journal, 82*, 401-420.

Boggiano, A. K., & Ruble, D. N. (1979). Competence and the overjustification effect: A developmental study. *Journal of Personality and Social Psychology, 37*, 1462-1468.

Brophy, J. (1985). Teacher-student interactions. In J.B. Dusek (Ed.), *Teacher expectancies* (pp. 303-320). Hillsdale, NJ: Erlbaum.

Butler, R. (1989a). Interest in the task and interest in peers' work in competitive and noncompetitive conditions: A developmental study. *Child Development, 60*, 562-570.

Butler, R. (1989b). Mastery versus ability appraisal: A developmental study of children's observations of peers' work. *Child Development, 60*, 1350-1361.

Butler, R. (1990). The effects of mastery and competitive conditions on self-assessment at different ages. *Child Development, 61*, 201-210.

Chaumeton, N., & Duda, J. (1988). Is it how you play the game or whether you win or lose? The effect of competitive level and situation on coaching behaviors. *Journal of Sport Behavior, 11*, 157-174.

Cook, H., & Stingle, S. (1974). Cooperative behavior in children. *Psychological Bulletin, 81*, 918-933.

Deci, E. L., & Ryan, R. M. (1985). *Intrinsic motivation and self-determination in human behavior.* New York: Plenum.

Duda, J. (1993). Goals: A social cognitive approach to the study of achievement motivation in sport. In R. N. Singer, M. Murphey, & L. K. Tennant (Eds.), *Handbook of research on sport psychology* (pp. 421-436). New York: MacMillan.

Dweck, C. S., & Elliott, E. (1983). Achievement motivation. In E.M. Hetherington (Ed.), *Handbook of child psychology. Vol. 4: Socialization, personality, and social development* (pp. 643-691). New York: Wiley.

Dweck, C. S., & Leggett, E. L. (1988). A social-cognitive approach to motivation and personality. *Psychological Review, 95*, 256-273.

Ebbeck, V. (1990). Sources of performance information in the exercise setting. *Journal of Sport and Exercise Psychology, 12*, 56-65.

Eccles (Parsons), J., Midgley, C., & Adler, T. (1984). Grade-related changes in the school environment: Effects on achievement motivation. In J. Nicholls (Ed.), *Advances in motivation and achievement: Vol. 3. The development of achievement motivation* (pp. 283-331). Greenwich, CT: JAI.

Eccles, J. S., & Harold, R. D. (1991). Gender differences in sport involvement: Applying the Eccles' expectancy-value model. *Journal of Applied Sport Psychology, 3*, 7-35.

Eccles, J. S., & Wigfield, A. (1985). Teacher expectations and student motivations. In J. Dusek (Ed.), *Teacher expectancies* (pp. 185-226). Hillsdale, NJ: Erlbaum.

Feldlaufer, H. C., Midgley, C., & Eccles, J. (1988). Student, teacher, and observer perceptions of the classroom environment before and after the transition to junior high. *Journal of Early Adolescence, 8*, 133-156.

Feltz, D., & Riessinger, C. (1990). Effects of in vivo emotive imagery and performance feedback on self-efficacy and muscular endurance. *Journal of Sport and Exercise Psychology, 12*, 132-143.

Frey, K. S., & Ruble, D. N. (1985). What children say when the teacher is not around: Conflicting goals in social comparison and performance assessment in the classroom. *Journal of Personality and Social Psychology, 48*, 550-562.

Fry, M., & Duda, J. L. (in press). Children's understanding of effort and ability in the physical domain. *Research Quarterly for Exercise and Sport.*

Harter, S. (1978). Effectance motivation reconsidered: Toward a developmental model. *Human Development, 21*, 34-64.

Harter, S. (1981). A model of mastery motivation in children: Individual differences and developmental change. In A. Collins (Ed.), Minnesota Symposium on *Child Psychology: Vol. 14* (pp. 215-255). Hillsdale, NJ: Erlbaum.

Harter, S. (1982). The Perceived Competence Scale for Children. *Child Development, 53*, 87-97.

Harter S. (1990). Causes, correlates, and the functional role of global self-worth: A life-span perspective. In R. J. Sternberg & J. Kolligan Jr. (Eds.), *Competence considered* (pp. 67-97). New Haven, CT: Yale University Press.

Harter, S. (1992). The relationship between perceived competence, affect, and motivational orientation within the classroom: Processes and patterns of change. In A.K. Boggiano & T.S. Pittman (Eds.), *Achievement and motivation: A social-developmental perspective* (pp. 77-114). New York: Cambridge University Press.

Harter, S., & Guzman, M. E. (1986). *The effects of perceived cognitive competence and anxiety on children's problem-solving performance, difficulty level choices, and preference for challenge.* Unpublished manuscript, University of Denver.

Horn, T. S., Glenn, S. D., & Wentzell, A. B. (1993). Sources of information underlying personal ability judgments in high school athletes. *Pediatric Exercise Science, 5*, 263-274.

Horn, T. S., & Harris, A. (1996). Perceived competence in young athletes: Research findings and recommendations for coaches and parents. In F. L. Smoll & R. E. Smith (Eds.), *Children and youth in sport: A biopsychosocial perspective* (pp. 309-329). Dubuque, IA: Brown and Benchmark.

Horn, T. S., & Hasbrook, C. (1986). Informational components influencing children's perceptions of their physical competence. In M. R. Weiss & D. Gould (Eds.), *Sport for children and youths: Proceedings of the 1984 Olympic Scientific Congress* (pp. 81-88). Champaign, IL: Human Kinetics.

Horn, T. S., & Hasbrook, C. (1987). Psychological characteristics and the criteria children use for self-evaluation. *Journal of Sport Psychology, 9,* 208-221.

Horn, T. S., & Weiss, M. R. (1991). A developmental analysis of children's self-ability judgments in the physical domain. *Pediatric Exercise Science, 3,* 310-326.

Inhelder, B., Sinclair, H., & Bouvet, M. (1974). *Learning and the development of cognition* (Susan Wedgwood, Trans.). Cambridge: Harvard University Press.

Jagacinski, C. M., & Nicholls, J. G. (1987). Competence and affect in task involvement and ego involvement: The impact of social comparison information. *Journal of Educational Psychology, 79,* 107-114.

Keil, L. J., McClintock, C. G., Kramer, R., & Platow, M. J. (1990). Children's use of social comparison standards in judging performance and their effects on self-evaluation. *Contemporary Educational Psychology, 15,* 75-91.

Lee, A. M., Carter, J. A., & Xiang, P. (1995). Children's conceptions of ability in physical education. *Journal of Teaching in Physical Education, 14,* 384-393.

Lepper, M. R., & Gilovich, T. J. (1981). The multiple functions of reward: A social-developmental perspective. In S. S. Brehm, S. M. Kassin, & F. X. Gibbons (Eds.), *Developmental social psychology* (pp. 28-42). New York: Oxford University Press.

Lord, C. G., Umezaki, K., & Darley, J. M. (1990). Developmental differences in decoding the meanings of the appraisal actions of teachers. *Child Development, 61,* 191-200.

Mac Iver, D. (1987). Classroom factors and student characteristics predicting students' use of achievement standards during ability self-assessment. *Child Development, 58,* 1258-1271.

Mac Iver, D. (1988). Classroom environments and the stratification of pupils' ability perceptions. *Journal of Educational Psychology, 80,* 495-505.

Meyer, W., Bachmann, M., Biermann, U., Hempelmann, M., Ploger, F., & Spiller, H. (1979). The informational value of evaluative behavior: Influences of praise and blame on perceptions of ability. *Journal of Educational Psychology, 71,* 259-268.

Minton, B. (1979, April). *Dimensions of information underlying children's judgments of their competence.* Paper presented at the meeting of the Society for Research in Child Development, San Francisco.

Nicholls, J. G. (1984). Achievement motivation: Conceptions of ability, subjective experience, task choice, and performance. *Psychological Review, 91,* 328-346.

Nicholls, J. G. (1989). *The competitive ethos and democratic education.* Cambridge: Harvard University Press.

Nicholls, J. G., & Miller, A.T. (1984). Development and its discontents: The differentiation of the concept of ability. In J. Nicholls (Ed.), *Advances in motivation and achievement: Vol. 3* (pp. 185-218). Greenwich, CT: JAI Press.

Nunnally, J. (1978). *Psychometric theory* (2nd ed.). New York: McGraw-Hill.

Phelps, D., & Horn, T. S. (1992). *Sex and sport type as factors affecting college-aged athletes' preferences for particular sources of competence information.* Unpublished manuscript, Miami University, Oxford, OH

Phillips, D. (1987). Socialization of perceived academic competence among highly competent children. *Child Development, 58,* 1308-1320.

Reuman, D.A. (1989). How social comparison mediates the relation between ability-grouping practices and students' achievement expectancies in mathematics. *Journal of Educational Psychology, 81,* 178-189.

Ruble, D. N., Boggiano, A. K., Feldman, N. S., & Loebl, J. H. (1980). Developmental analysis of the role of social comparison in self-evaluation. *Developmental Psychology, 16,* 105-115.

Ruble, D. N., & Flett, G. L. (1988). Conflicting goals in self-evaluative information seeking: Developmental and ability level analysis. *Child Development, 59,* 97-106.

Ruble, D. N., Grosovsky, E. H., Frey, K. S., & Cohen, R. (1992). Developmental changes in competence assessment. In A. K. Boggiano & T. S. Pittman (Eds.), *Achievement and motivation: A social-developmental perspective* (pp. 138-164). New York: Cambridge University Press.

Stipek, D. J. (1981). Children's perceptions of their own and their classmates' ability. *Journal of Educational Psychology, 73,* 404-410.

Stipek, D. J., & Daniels, D. H. (1988). Declining perceptions of competence: A consequence of changes in the child or in the educational environment? *Journal of Educational Psychology, 80,* 352-356.

Stipek, D., & Mac Iver, D. (1989). Developmental change in children's assessment of intellectual competence. *Child Development, 60,* 521-538.

Stipek, D. Recchia, S., & McClintic, S. (1992). Self-evaluation in young children. *Monographs of the Society for Research in Child Development, 57* (1, Serial No. 226).

Stipek, D.J., & Tannatt, L.M. (1984). Children's judgments of their own and their peers' academic competence. *Journal of Educational Psychology, 76,* 75-84.

Vealey, R., Walter, S., Garner-Holman, M., & Giacobbi, P. (1996). *Sources of sport-confidence: Conceptualization and instrument development.* Manuscript submitted for publication, Miami University, Oxford, OH.

Veroff, J. (1969). Social comparison and the development of achievement motivation. In C. P. Smith (Ed.), *Achievement-Related motives in children* (pp. 46-101). New York: Russell Sage Foundation.

Weiss, M. R., & Chaumeton, N. (1992). Motivational orientations in sport. In T. S. Horn (Ed.), *Advances in sport psychology* (pp. 61-100). Champaign, IL: Human Kinetics.

Weiss, M. R., & Ebbeck, V. (1996). Self-esteem and perceptions of competence in youth sport: Theory, research, and enhancement strategies. In O. Bar-Or (Ed.), *The encyclopaedia of sports medicine: Vol. VI. The child and adolescent athlete* (pp. 364-382). Oxford: Blackwell Science Ltd.

Weiss, M. R., Ebbeck, V., & Horn, T. S. (in press). Children's self-perceptions and sources of physical competence information: A cluster analysis. *Journal of Sport and Exercise Psychology.*

Werner, H. (1957). The concept of development from a comparative and organismic point of view. In D. Harns (Ed.), *The concept of development* (pp. 125-148). Minneapolis: University of Minnesota Press.

Williams, L. (1994). Goal orientations and athletes' preferences for competence information sources. *Journal of Sport and Exercise Psychology, 16,* 416-430.

Yee, M. D., & Brown, R. (1992). Self-evaluations and intergroup attitudes in children aged three to nine. *Child Development, 63,* 619-629.

Yussen, S., & Kane, P. (1985). Children's conception of intelligence. In S. R. Yussen (Ed.), *The growth of reflection in children* (pp. 207-241). Orlando, FL: Academic Press.

Chapter 4

THE MEASUREMENT OF SELF-EFFICACY AND CONFIDENCE IN SPORT

Deborah L. Feltz
Michigan State University
and
Melissa A. Chase
Miami University

One's confidence or efficacy beliefs are considered one of the most influential constructs mediating achievement strivings in sport (Feltz, 1988). The terms *self-confidence* and *self-efficacy* have been used to describe a person's perceived capability to accomplish a certain level of performance. Bandura (1977, 1986a) defined self-efficacy as the belief that one can successfully execute a specific activity in order to obtain a certain outcome. Feltz (1988) considered self-efficacy to be a situationally specific self-confidence. In the remainder of this chapter, we will use the terms self-efficacy and self-confidence interchangeably, except when describing a particular construct or instrument. Whether one uses the term self-confidence or self-efficacy, the phenomenon of interest in this chapter is the cognitive process by which people make judgments about their capabilities to accomplish a particular goal in sport or physical activity. That goal might be quite narrow (e.g., bunting a ball down the third baseline) or more broadly defined (e.g., performing successfully in one's sport). According to Bandura (1992), the degree of specificity at which self-efficacy is measured should be determined by the nature of the situation and/or task at hand and the nature of the situation to which one wishes to generalize (or predict). Regardless of the breadth of the situation or goal domain that one might wish to investigate, the importance of using valid and reliable measures in the assessment of self-efficacy cannot be underestimated. The purposes of this chapter are to describe the theoretical frameworks for the measurements of self- and team efficacy constructs, describe and critique the existing assessments, discuss special considerations and issues in measuring efficacy in sport, and provide specific recommendations for the development of future self-efficacy instruments.

Theoretical Frameworks for the Measurements of Self-Efficacy and Confidence Constructs

The measures included in this chapter were chosen for their applicability to sport. They include self- and collective efficacy measures that are based on Bandura's (1977, 1986a) theory of self-efficacy; sport confidence, based on Vealey's (1986) model of sport confidence; and movement confidence measures, based on Griffin and Keogh's (1982) model of movement confidence. Common among all three conceptual frameworks is the treatment of self-confidence as a cognitive mediator of people's motivation and behavior within a goal context. Thus, all three frameworks allow for a discussion of self-confidence as it relates to a number of motivational processes, including goal setting and causal attributions. This sets self-efficacy concepts apart from other self-concepts that are not set within a goal-striving framework.

Bandura's Self-Efficacy Theory (and Collective Efficacy Extension)

Self-efficacy theory was developed within the framework of social cognitive theory (Bandura, 1977, 1986a). Originally, the theory was proposed to account for the different results achieved by diverse methods used in clinical psychology for the treatment of anxiety. It has since been expanded and applied to other domains of psychosocial functioning including career choice and development (Lent & Hackett, 1987), health and exercise behavior (McAuley, 1992; McAuley & Mihalko, this volume; O'Leary, 1985), and sport and motor performance (Feltz, 1988).

Self-efficacy beliefs are not about an individual's skills objectively speaking. Rather, they are about an individual's judgments of what he or she can accomplish with those skills (Bandura, 1986a). Thus, self-efficacy judgments are about what one thinks one can do, not what one has. These judgments are a product of a complex process of self-persuasion that relies on cognitive processing of diverse sources of confidence information (Bandura, 1990). Bandura (1977, 1986a) categorized these sources (or antecedents) as past performance accomplishments, vicarious experiences, verbal persuasion, and physiological states. Performance accomplishments are thought to provide the most dependable efficacy information because they are based on one's own mastery experiences. Vicarious sources of efficacy information are thought to be generally weaker than performance accomplishments; however, their influence on self-efficacy can be enhanced by factors such as perceived similarities to a model who performs successfully. Persuasive information includes verbal persuasion, evaluative feedback, expectations by others, self-talk, positive imagery, and other cognitive strategies. Self-efficacy beliefs based on persuasive sources are also likely to be weaker than those based on one's accomplishments, according to the theory. Physiological information includes autonomic arousal that is associated with fear and self-doubt or with being psyched up and ready for performance, as well as one's level of fitness, fatigue, and pain (in strength and endurance activities). Physiological information has been shown to be a more important source of efficacy information with respect to sport and physical activity tasks than in the case of nonphysical tasks (Chase, Feltz, Tully, & Lirgg, 1994; Feltz & Riessinger, 1990; Wilson, Feltz, & Fitzpatrick, 1996).

Bandura's four categories of efficacy information are not mutually exclusive in terms of the information they provide, though some are more influential than others. How various sources of information are weighted and processed to make judgments given different tasks, situations, and individuals' skills is as yet unknown. The consequences of these judgments, however, are hypothesized to determine people's levels of motivation, as reflected in the challenges they undertake, the effort they expend in the activity, and their perseverance in the face of difficulties. People's self-efficacy judgments are also hypothesized to influence certain thought patterns and emotional reactions (e.g., pride, shame, happiness, sadness) that also influence motivation (Bandura, 1986a). For instance, self-efficacy beliefs may influence people's success or failure images, worries, goal intentions, and causal attributions (Bandura, 1986a). Figure 1 illustrates the relationships between the major sources of efficacy information, efficacy judgments, and consequences as predicted by Bandura's theory.

Self-efficacy judgments are also modifiable. They are expected to change from experience, modeling, social persuasion, and affect or mood shifts (Zimmerman, 1996). Various interventions, based on one or more sources of efficacy information, can alter self-efficacy beliefs. Furthermore, the relationship between self-efficacy judgments and performance accomplishments is also believed to be temporally recursive: "Mastery expectations influence performance and are, in turn, altered by the cumulative effect of one's efforts" (Bandura, 1977, p. 194). Bandura (1990) has emphasized the recursive nature of the relationship between self-efficacy and thought patterns as well.

Bandura (1977) has provided some qualifiers to the predictiveness of self-efficacy judgments. Self-efficacy beliefs are a major determinant of behavior only when people have sufficient incentives to act on their self-perception of efficacy and when they possess the requisite skills. According to Bandura, discrepancies between efficacy beliefs and performance will occur when tasks or circumstances are ambiguous or when one has little information on which to base efficacy judgments, such

as when one is first learning a skill.

Self-efficacy expectations should not be confused with outcome expectations. Outcome expectations are defined as the belief that certain behaviors will lead to certain outcomes. Self-efficacy, on the other hand, is the belief in one's ability to successfully perform the behavior in question (Bandura, 1977). In essence, outcome expectations are concerned with beliefs about one's environment, and efficacy expectations are concerned with beliefs about one's competence. Both types of expectancies are hypothesized to predict behavior, but research suggests that self-efficacy beliefs are stronger predictors of behavior (Bandura, 1986a). Thus, the outcome belief that using imagery will improve one's performance should not predict one's actual use of imagery as adequately as the confidence belief that one can image effectively.

Collective efficacy. The theory of self-efficacy is easily extended to the concept of collective efficacy. Whereas self-efficacy refers to people's judgments of individual capabilities and effort, collective efficacy is defined as a group's judgment of their conjoint capabilities to organize and execute the courses of action required to produce specified levels of performance (Bandura, 1997). In sport, collective efficacy influences, according to Bandura, what people choose to do as a team, the amount of effort they put forth, and their staying power when team efforts fail to produce results. Thus, teams with high perceived collective efficacy beliefs are hypothesized to outperform and persist longer than are teams with low perceived collective efficacy (Bandura, 1986a).

Although self- and collective efficacies differ in the unit of agency, they operate through similar processes and are influenced by similar sources of efficacy information (Bandura, 1997). As with self-efficacy beliefs, performance accomplishments of the team are predicted to be the most powerful source of information for collective efficacy beliefs (Druckman & Bjork, 1994).

In terms of the assessment of perceived collective efficacy, Bandura (1986a, 1997) suggests that team or collective efficacy may be insufficiently represented as a predictor of team performance through just the sum of the perceived personal efficacies of participants on highly interactive tasks or in situations where

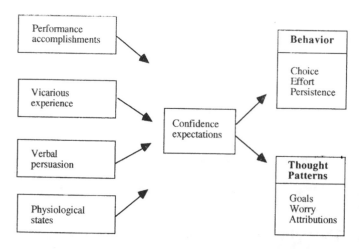

Figure 1. Relationship between sources of efficacy information, efficacy judgments, and consequences.

members must work conjointly to achieve success. On highly interactive tasks, Bandura (1997) argues that individual members' judgments about the capabilities of the group as whole are a better predictor of team performance because the "wholistic belief" encompasses the coordinative and interactive dynamics that operate within a team. Zaccaro and his colleagues (Zaccaro, Blair, Peterson, & Zazanis, 1995) go one step further in advocating that collective efficacy must directly encompass group members' judgments about their ability to coordinate, allocate, and integrate group resources in order to assess the concept adequately. Both Bandura (1997) and Zaccaro et al. agree, however, that collective efficacy is a shared belief that means that there is a significant degree of interdependence among the judgments of the group's members. Therefore, the extent to which group membership affects individual perceptions about their team's ability to execute performance skills determines whether perceptions regarding team capabilities are an individual or group phenomenon (Kenny & La Voie, 1985).

Sport Confidence

Vealey (1986) developed a model (see Figure 2) and instrumentation of sport confidence to provide an operationalization of self-confidence in sport situations that could be used across sports and sport situations. *Sport confidence* is defined as the degree of certainty individuals possess about their ability to be successful in sport and is conceptualized into trait (SC-trait) and state (SC-state) components. In addition, a competitive-orientation construct is included in her model to account for individual differences in defining success in sport. *Competitive orientation* is considered to be a dispositional construct that indicates an athlete's tendency to strive toward achieving a certain type of goal in sport (performing well or winning) that will demonstrate competence and success.[1]

The sport-confidence model was based on an interactional paradigm with SC-trait and competitive orientation (perfor-

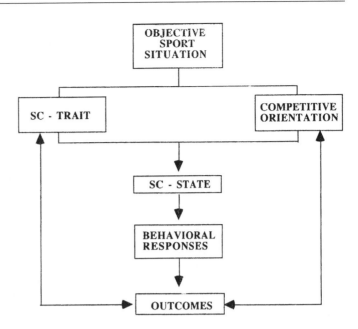

Figure 2. Conceptual model of sport confidence.
Note. From "Conceptualization of sport-confidence and competitive orientation: Preliminary investigation and instrument development," by R. S. Vealey, 1986, *Journal of Sport Psychology,* 8, p. 223. Copyright © 1986 by Human Kinetics Publishers. Reprinted with permission.

mance or outcome) predicted to interact with objective sport situations and influence SC-state. Specifically, SC-state is hypothesized to be positively related to SC-trait and performance orientation, negatively related to outcome orientation, and a critical mediator of behavior. Subjective outcomes (e.g., causal attributions, perceptions of success, and satisfaction) are predicted to have a reciprocal relationship with SC-trait and competitive orientation. Overall, the sport-confidence model and measures were developed to conceptualize self-confidence as specific and unique to the sport context.

Preliminary tests of the sport-confidence model with high school athletes found that SC-trait was positively related to precompetitive SC-state, postcompetitive SC-state, self-esteem, perceived success, and internal attributions for performance, and negatively related to competitive anxiety (Vealey, 1986). In further tests of the construct validity of her model with elite gymnasts (15 to 25 years of age), Vealey found that SC-trait and competitive orientation did predict SC-state and subjective outcomes as expected. However, precompetition SC-state did not predict performance. Her rationale for this finding was that sport performance may be too complex to be predicted by SC-state. In addition, with this particular sample of athletes, the characteristics of the athletes and importance and structure of the competition were not typical and too homogeneous.

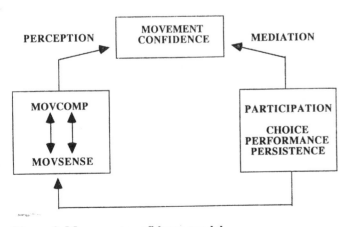

Figure 3. Movement confidence model.
Note: From *The Development of Movement Control and Coordination* (p. 214), by J.A.S. Kelson and J. Clark (Eds.), 1982, New York: Wiley. Copyright © 1982 by Wiley & Sons, Limited. Reprinted with permission.

Movement Confidence

Griffin and Keogh (1982) developed a model of movement confidence (see Figure 3) in which they define *movement con-*

1. See Duda and Whitehead, this volume, for further discussion of Vealey's assessment of competitive orientation and how this variable is distinguished from recent measures of achievement goal orientations in the sport setting.

fidence as a type of confidence that describes an individual's feeling of adequacy in performance of movement. Movement confidence encompasses not only the perception of physical competence (movement competence) but also the appraisal of sensory experiences related to movement (movement sense). Griffin and Keogh describe this sensory experience as having two components: enjoyment of expected moving sensations and perceived potential for physical harm. An individual's cognitive assessment of him- or herself in relation to the demands of the movement and in relation to his or her expectations of sensory experiences produces a sense of movement confidence. Similar to Bandura's notion of self-efficacy (1986a), Griffin and Keogh suggest that movement confidence is both a consequence and a mediator of performance. As a consequence, an individual evaluates her or his movement competence and movement sense to form a sense of movement confidence. Movement confidence, then, mediates or influences future participation (choice, performance, persistence) in movement situations. According to this model, a cycle exists in which an individual with high movement confidence will be likely to choose participation in movement situations and have enjoyable experiences, whereas an individual with low movement confidence will be less likely to choose participation, and performance will be less satisfying. The model of movement confidence is unique from other theoretical frameworks and models of self-confidence in that the sensory experiences associated with movement competence are considered.

Description and Assessment of Measures of Confidence in Sport Self-Efficacy Measures

Task-specific scales. Most researchers of self-efficacy have constructed self-efficacy measures tailored to their specific study. Bandura (1977, 1986a, 1986b) advocates using self-efficacy measures that are specific to particular domains of functioning, rather than assessing self-efficacy as a global disposition with an omnibus test. Domain-linked self-efficacy scales will be more predictive of specific behavior because of the variations in self-efficacy perceptions that occur across different activity domains, different levels of demand within activity domains, and different environmental circumstances of performance. Bandura also advocates using a microanalytic approach, which requires a detailed assessment of the level, strength, and generality of self-efficacy beliefs. *Level of self-efficacy* (or magnitude) refers to people's expected performance attainments. *Strength* refers to the certainty of people's beliefs that they can attain these different levels of performance. *Generality* indicates the number of domains of functioning in which people judge themselves to be efficacious, but is rarely used in studies on self-efficacy (Maddux, 1995; Schunk, 1995).

Self-efficacy measures are typically constructed by listing a series of tasks, usually varying in difficulty, stressfulness, or complexity. Participants are asked to designate (yes or no) the tasks they believe they can perform (efficacy level). For each task designated as "yes", they rate their degree of certainty (efficacy strength) that they can execute it on a near-continuous scale from total uncertainty to total certainty. Generally, the efficacy strength

Table 1
Illustration of Congruence Scores in Hierarchical and Nonhierarchical Scales

Performance Items	*Efficacy Scale (Level)*	*Performance Scale*	*Match*
Example 1: Hierarchical Scale Leg Endurance Time Items			
1. 15 s	yes	yes	x
2. 30 s	yes	yes	x
3. 45 s	yes	yes	x
4. 1 min	yes	yes	x
5. 1 min, 15 s	yes	no	
6. 1 min, 30 s	no	no	x
7. 1 min, 45 s	no	no	x
Score: 5		4	6
Congruence = 6/7 x 100 = 85.71%			
Example 2: Nonhierarchical Scale Wrestling Move Items			
1. Escape	yes	yes	x
2. Get reversal	yes	yes	x
3. Get back points	no	yes	
4. Not get taken down	yes	no	
5. Get take down by throw	no	no	x
6. Ride opponent	yes	yes	x
7. Pin opponent	yes	no	
Score: 5		4	4
Congruence = 4/7 x 100 = 57.14%			

scale ranges from zero to 10, in one-unit increments or from zero to 100, in 10-unit increments. However, at least one sport study (Watkins, Garcia, & Turek, 1994) reported using a visual analog scale (VAS) that was 10 centimeters in length. On a VAS scale, the participant can make a check mark or slash at any point along the line, and this is then scored in standard unit increments (e.g., centimeters for Watkins et al.). A strength measure is obtained by summing the scores across items for which subjects believe they can perform and dividing by the total number of performance items (Bandura, Adams, & Beyer, 1977). Given the specific nature of the items that constitute a self-efficacy instrument, Schunk (1995) recommends that all self-efficacy studies include their instrument as appendices to their articles.

A microanalytic approach permits an analysis of the degree of congruence between self-efficacy and action at the level of individual tasks (Bandura, 1986b). This does not mean, as some have advocated (Manzo & Silva, 1994), that self-efficacy items are constructed for minute particulars. "Rather, the items are constructed at an intermediate level of generality representing a generic level of competence at each aspect of a domain" (Bandura, 1986b, p. 372). The microanalytic approach requires that one conduct a conceptual analysis of the subskills needed to perform in a given domain and a contextual analysis of the level of situational demands. Thus, for example, the subskills needed to perform competitively in baseball could be categorized into hitting, fielding, and base running and then into generic situations within each category that vary in degree of difficulty, such as hitting a fast ball, hitting a curve ball, or hitting to the opposite field, for the hitting category.

Few researchers in the psychology or sport psychology literature have actually analyzed the degree of congruence between self-efficacy judgments and performance at the level of individual tasks (Wurtele, 1986). Analyzing the degree of congruence involves computing the percentage of items for which efficacy and performance agree. The number of congruent tasks is divided by the total number of possible tasks. This quotient is multiplied by 100 to obtain a percent congruence score (Cervone, 1985). The calculation of percentage match-scores, according to Bandura (1977), provides a more precise index of predictive accuracy than do aggregate correlations. As Bandura points out, respondents may predict and perform the same absolute number of tasks without having correspondence to the same tasks, leading to a high correlation, but a low item-by-item match. However, Cervone (1985) argues that when self-ratings and behavior are completely hierarchical (i.e., varying in difficulty, stressfulness, complexity, etc., from low to high), the level of congruence can be obtained from the aggregate scores on the efficacy and behavioral scales because there is no chance congruence. Cervone advocates a microanalytic congruence analysis when the data are not completely hierarchical.

Table 1 provides two illustrations of how congruent scores are obtained using hierarchical and nonhierarchical scales. Although the level of self-efficacy score (4) and level of performance score (5) are the same in both examples, the congruences are quite different. In the nonhierarchical example, the congruence or item-by-item match (57.14%) is little more than what would be expected by chance (at least 50%). As can be seen in the hierarchical example, there is no chance that a subject

would indicate the ability to perform at 2 minutes if he or she indicated an inability to perform at 1 minute unless the subject was confused about how to complete the scale properly.

In reporting congruence values, one needs a statistical procedure to indicate the probability of obtaining such values by chance. The above examples do not contain calculations of chance congruence. Bandura (1980) has proposed a method for computing chance congruence that is appropriate only in cases where none of the tasks are hierarchically ordered (e.g., in Kane, Marks, Zaccaro, & Blair, 1996, and Treasure, Monson, & Lox, 1996). Cervone (1985) has also outlined a procedure for computing chance congruence that is not limited to nonhierarchical tasks.

Researchers in sport psychology have typically correlated aggregate self-efficacy level or strength scores with aggregate performance scores; however, most of the scales are constructed by listing tasks in a hierarchical fashion, according to difficulty. These might include hitting a ball from 1 of 6 to 6 of 6 times, diving from increasingly difficult heights, putting with increasing accuracy or consistency, or pressing increasingly heavier weights. For instance, in the self-efficacy studies that used leg-endurance tasks (e.g., Feltz & Riessinger, 1990; George, Feltz, & Chase, 1992; Gould & Weiss, 1981), subjects were asked to indicate how confident they were that they could perform the task at each of a certain number of time designations (e.g., 15 time periods, ranging from 15 seconds to 4 minutes) that typically increased by 15-second intervals along with their certainty (efficacy strength) at each time designation.

Lee and Bobko (1994) advocated using a "composite" of self-efficacy level and strength to measure self-efficacy beliefs. A composite score is constructed by summing only the efficacy strength items for which subjects designated "yes" they could do the task. Lee and Bobko found that their composite measure of academic self-efficacy showed generally stronger predictive validity and correlations with theoretical antecedents and consequences than either level or strength measures. However, at close inspection, Lee and Bobko did not measure self-efficacy strength according to procedures recommended by Bandura (Bandura et al., 1977). Had Lee and Bobko done so, their composite measure would have been no more than a linear transformation of their strength measure. Instead, their strength measure was calculated by summing all items, regardless of whether subjects designated yes or no that they could or could not perform the tasks, and dividing by the total number of items. In other words, Lee and Bobko's strength measure was a mixture of certainty responses to yes and no items and is, therefore, of questionable utility. Lee and Bobko's composite measure was the same as the recommended efficacy strength measure. Thus, self-efficacy strength appears to show stronger predictive validity than do self-efficacy level measures.

Some studies have also been interested in competitive or comparative efficacy. These measures have typically been one-item questions in which subjects are asked to rate their percent certainty (e.g., on a 100-point probability scale) of being able to beat their opponents (Feltz & Riessinger, 1990; Weinberg, Gould, & Jackson, 1979). However, self-efficacy has been shown to have greater predictive power of performance when it is assessed using a mastery (or self-referenced) scale than when

Table 2

Correlations Between Self-Efficacy and Competitive Performance

Study	N	Sport	Performance Measure	Self-Efficacy Measure	r
Gayton et al. (1986)	33	Marathon	Finish time	PPA (Ryckman et al., 1982)	.55*
George (1994)	25	Baseball-coll.	Contact percentage	Strength of putting ball in play from zero to 4 in 4 at (Game 1)	.49*
	28	Baseball-h.s.		bats (4 items hierarchical) (Game 1)	.59*
Kane et al. (1996)	216	Wrestling	Win percentage	Strength of wrestling maneuvers (10 items)	.16*
	46		Overtime win	percentage alpha = .80	.45*
Lee (1982)	14	Gymnastics	Judges' scores	Expected score on each of 5 events (5 items)	.55*
Lee (1988)	9	Field hockey teams	Win percentage	Level of hockey skills	.08
				Strength of hockey skills No. of items not reported	.33*
Martin & Gill (1991)	73	Track	Finish time	Strength for win & place	.71*
			Finish place	(6 items - hierarchical)	.79*
			Finish time	Strength for times in	.06
			Finish place	relation to personal best (6 items - hierarchical)	.06
Martin & Gill (1995)	86	Track	Finish time	Strength for times in relation to personal best (6 items - hierarchical)	.21*
			Finish place	Strength for win & place (6 items - hierarchical)	.72*
McAuley & Gill (1983)	52	Gymnastics	Judges' scores on: vault	Strength of gymnastic maneuvers	.28*
			beam	(7 items per event -	.58*
			bars	hierarchical)	.72*
			floor		.43*
Okwumabua (1986)	90	Marathon	Finish time	Level for times in relation to personal best	.66*
				Strength for same (9 items - hierarchical)	.68*
Treasure et al. (1996)	70	Wrestling	Win/loss	Strength of wrestling	.40*
			Points scored	maneuvers (10 items)	.55*
Weiss, Wiese, & Klint (1989)	22	Gymnastics	Judges' scores on:	Expected scores 1 item per event	
			high bar		.84*
			horse		.66*
			floor		.59*
			bars		.54*
			rings		.36*
			vault		.27
			all-around		.71*

measuring perceived competence relative to others (Zimmerman, 1996). Furthermore, using one-item scales to make normative comparisons or mastery assessments also reduces self-efficacy's predictive power. Lee and Bobko (1994) found that multiple-item self-efficacy scales tailored to particular domains of functioning showed greater consistency with consequences of self-efficacy variables than did task-specific one-item scales.

In addition to the problem of reliability and validity with one-item self-efficacy scales, when these scales are used with athletes in competitive situations, they tend to have lower correlations with measures of performance outcome because of other factors beyond one's control that also influence performance (Bandura, 1990). Furthermore, one-item competitive or comparative efficacy scales have the tendency to create ceiling effects when used with athletes who may not have (or be willing to admit) much diffidence (Vealey, 1986).

An additional task-specific scale worth mentioning here is Lirgg's (1993) Self-Confidence for Learning Basketball Scale (SCLB). The SCLB was not constructed in the typical self-efficacy format, but rather used 5 positively and 5 negatively stated items with responses on a scale of 1 (*strongly disagree*) to 5 (*strongly agree*). Examples of positively and negatively stated items are "Generally, I feel confident about attempting skills in basketball," and "I'm no good in basketball." Negatively worded items were reverse scored. A subject's SCLB score was the mean of the 10 questions employed, with the higher scores indicating greater confidence. The SCLB was adapted from Fennema and Sherman's (1976) Confidence in Learning Mathematics Scale. Lirgg (1993) reported a split-half reliability of .78.

Bandura (1978) has rejected criticism that efficacy judgments should be subjected to the construct, trait, convergent, and discriminant validation of trait methodology, especially when used within a microanalytic approach. Thus, the validity of self-efficacy measures is typically inferred from how well they predict the behaviors hypothesized in the study, such as choice of task, persistence, thought patterns, and emotional responses (see also McAuley & Mihalko, this volume). Often, researchers use performance outcome scores as the measure for determining the validity of their self-efficacy measure. However, when competitive outcome scores are used to measure the effects of self-efficacy, self-efficacy will not be a strong predictor of performance because performance scores are determined by many other factors as well (Feltz, 1992). Even so, in our review of the literature for this chapter, we found that most of these studies showed a significant and moderate relationship between self-efficacy and performance scores. From the 11 studies we found that used competitive performance measures, the correlations between self-efficacy and subsequent performance ($n = 29$) ranged from .06 to .84, with a median of .55. As can be seen in Table 2, the studies that used win/loss or winning percentage as the performance measure, used level of self-efficacy, or had a low correspondence between their self-efficacy measure and performance measure had lower correlations than did studies that used points scored, used self-efficacy strength, and had greater correspondence between their measures.

In terms of internal consistency of the task-specific scales of self-efficacy, the reliabilities are consistently high when the scales are constructed in hierarchical fashion on the same task (e.g., .88 and .91 for Theodorakis, 1995). Many studies do not report the internal reliability of their scales, but for those that do, reliabilities range from .75 (Holloway, Beuter, & Duda, 1988) to .91 (Theodorakis, 1995). We recommend that internal consistency reliability be determined and reported for each study using a nonhierarchical self-efficacy scale, even if it is a scale whose psychometric properties have been previously published. The past internal reliabilities of these scales cannot be assumed to remain the same with all samples.

The Physical Self-Efficacy Scale (PSE). Although most of the self-efficacy researchers in sport and physical activity have constructed their own scales tailored to a particular study, a few have used measures with more broadly defined domains (Gayton, Matthews, & Borchstead, 1986; McAuley & Gill, 1983; Ryckman, Robbins, Thornton, & Cantrell, 1982). Ryckman and his colleagues constructed the PSE to provide a more omnibus measure of perceived physical self-efficacy. The PSE has two factors: a 10-item perceived physical ability factor and a 12-item physical self-presentation confidence factor that reflects perceived efficacy in the display of physical skills. The scales consist of 6-point Likert items, with response alternatives ranging from *strongly agree* to *strongly disagree* rather than being rated in terms of one's efficacy strength. Sample items from the perceived ability factor are "I have excellent reflexes," and "I have a strong grip." The self-presentation items include "I have physical defects that sometimes bother me," and "I am sometimes envious of those better looking than myself." The PSE was developed and tested with college students, and there has been no evaluation of whether it is appropriate with younger ages. The PSE has also been tested with older adults (e.g., Davis-Berman, 1990) and found to be a valid measure with this population.

The internal consistency and test-retest reliabilities reported for the PSE are .82 and .80, respectively. In addition to reliability indicators of the scale, Ryckman et al. (1982) found significant correlations between total PSE scores, perceived physical ability scores, and performance on a reaction time task and a motor coordination task. Gayton and his colleagues (1986) also found predictive validity for the PSE with competitive marathon runners. McAuley and Gill (1983), however, compared the PSE to a gymnastics-specific measure of self-efficacy in predicting gymnastics performance and found the task-specific measure to be a much better predictor than the PSE.

The implication of McAuley and Gill's study (1983) is that one should not replace more specific measures with omnibus ones when assessing expectations for specific tasks. However, omnibus scales are not intended to replace more specific measures but to assess generalized self-efficacy expectations when asking research questions about more general patterns of behavior, such as when assessing perceived PSE and depression (Davis-Berman, 1990), Type-A behavior (Robertson, Mellor, Hughes, Sanderson, & Reilly, 1988) or general physical fitness (Thornton et al., 1987). They may also be more appropriate when the situation is more ambiguous and less familiar to the individual (Tipton & Worthington, 1984).

The problem, we believe, with the conceptualization of the PSE is that it resembles more of a self-concept measure than a self-efficacy measure. The items on the PSE were not constructed within a goal-striving context. That is, PSE items do not focus on challenges undertaken, effort expended, or perseverance in the face of difficulties. For instance, items on the PSE reflect beliefs about one's abilities ("I have excellent reflexes"; "I have a strong grip"). For the PSE to reflect one's physical efficacy beliefs regarding strength, for example, the item should be phrased as "I can hang in a flexed-arm position for 20 seconds," or "I can hang in a flexed-arm position longer than most people my age." Maddux and Meier (1995) have similarly questioned the PSE as a self-efficacy measure. They suggested that it seems to measure physical health self-concept and self-esteem, not self-efficacy for physical activities. Thus, although there has been some predictive validity for the PSE, it may not have the construct validity as a self-efficacy measure either to mediate people's goal-striving behavior or to be modifiable through mastery experiences.

The Coaching Efficacy Scale (CES). Another self-efficacy measure that assesses efficacy in a broader domain is the CES (Feltz et al., 1994). This is an instrument that measures the extent to which coaches believe they have the capacity to affect the learning and performance of their athletes. The CES allows the researcher to collapse across sports or compare subjects from different sports without the concern for how to equate different scales for diverse athletic activities. The CES is a 24-item measure that contains four subscales: Game Strategy, Motivational, Technique, and Character-Building Efficacy. The efficacy items are rated on a 10-point Likert scale in terms of efficacy strength, ranging from *not at all confident* to *extremely confident.* All items on the CES begin with the same stem question, "How confident are you in your ability to...," and contain items such as "...detect skill errors" (technique dimension), "...motivate your athletes" (motivation dimension), "...recognize opposing team's strengths during competition" (game strategy dimension), and "...promote good sportsmanship" (character-building dimension).

Based on self-efficacy theory, hypothesized sources of CES include past coaching experience and record, perceived ability of one's athletes, and perceived community support. CES is also hypothesized to influence coaching behavior and player and team performance, efficacy, and satisfaction. The internal reliabilities for the CES subscales ranged from .87 to .90. Concurrent validity of the CES was assessed by correlating it with measures of related constructs of self-esteem, general expectancy for success, and internal locus of control. Results indicated that the CES subscales correlated moderately with self-esteem (.24 to .38), general expectancy for success (.30 to .56), and internal control (.21 to .31) as expected. Initial construct validity was assessed through canonical correlation analysis with predicted sources of the four dimensions of coaching efficacy as well as through a comparison of high- and low-efficacy coaches on predicted outcomes. Results supported the hypothesized sources and outcomes of the CES and demonstrate preliminary construct validity for the scale.

Critique. Research on self-efficacy from divergent psychosocial domains of functioning has demonstrated strong predictive and construct validity for assessments of self-efficacy (Bandura, 1986a). Lee and Bobko (1994) found convergent and predictive validity using different types of self-efficacy measures and different performance contexts. Self-efficacy is most useful in explaining motivated behavior and performance in sport and physical activity when measures have been constructed within the tenets of the theory (i.e., when proper incentives and requisite skills are present, the self-efficacy and performance measures are congruent, and a microanalytic approached is used). For instance, a number of researchers have

assumed that all subjects have the proper incentives to perform the task in question and have similar outcome expectancies. For the assessment of incentives, one method that has been used is a measure of the perceived importance to perform well on the task (George et al., 1992). George and his colleagues found that only when they used subjects who perceived the task to be at least moderately important did they find a self-efficacy/performance relationship.

In addition, when self-efficacy measures become less congruent with the performance measures used in a study, there is less predictiveness (e.g., Kane et al., 1996; Treasure et al., 1996). One can be assured of finding low correlations if there is little similarity between the efficacy measure and what people are asked to perform (Bandura, 1978; Zimmerman, 1996). Moritz, Mack, and Feltz (1996), in their meta-analysis, found that studies that were congruent in their measurement methods yielded higher correlations (Mean $r = .45$) than did studies that were not congruent (Mean $r = .25$).

For outcome expectancy, researchers should assess this variable when investigating situations where one's beliefs about outcomes may vary. For instance, subjects may vary in their beliefs about how effective karate is in deterring assaults, or they may vary in their beliefs about the situations in which karate techniques are effective or ineffective.

Another methodological issue that can weaken the predictiveness of self-efficacy beliefs is too great a time lapse between efficacy judgments and performance. If self-efficacy judgments and performance are not measured closely in time, these judgments may be altered by an intervening experience (Bandura, 1986a).

Although basing self-efficacy so heavily on self-report measures was an early criticism of the theory (Borkovec, 1978; Kazdin, 1978), Bandura (1978) argued that in situations where individuals have no reason to distort their reports, self-reports can be quite representative of cognitions. Thus, efficacy judgments are best made when evaluation apprehension has been minimized and recorded privately. Athletes, however, may still find it difficult to report that they have little confidence to perform in competitive situations in their sport (Feltz & Lirgg, 1996; George, 1994; Vealey, 1986). One way to counteract these ceiling effects is to make sure the high end of the scale is rarely reachable in actual performance. For instance, in George's hitting efficacy scale, he might have had less of a ceiling effect if the high end of his scale had been "putting the ball in play 6 times out of 6 bats" instead of 4 times out of 4 bats. Even so, when using highly skilled athletes, one may have to use a logarithmic transformation to help normalize the data.

Collective Efficacy Measures

Collective efficacy refers to people's judgments about the group's capability to execute given levels of performance (Bandura, 1986a, in press). In assessing collective efficacy, Bandura suggests that the relative predictiveness of aggregated individual and wholistic indices of collective efficacy will depend on the degree of interdependence needed among team members to achieve team success. Therefore, measurement of collective efficacy in sport should involve both types of measures. Only a few studies have examined collective efficacy in sport. The instruments used to measure collective efficacy have varied in their approach.

Feltz and Lirgg (1997) examined collective and self-efficacy in the prediction of team performance in collegiate hockey across a 32-game season. They constructed a collective efficacy measure that had athletes rate their confidence, on an 11-point Likert scale, that their team could outperform their opponent in eight dimensions of hockey play (e.g., outskate, outcheck, perform more power plays). A zero on the scale represented "cannot do at all," a 5 represented "moderately certain can do," and a 10 represented "certain can do." Reliability in terms of internal consistency for this measure was reported as .93.

Using a microanalytic approach, Chase, Lirgg, and Feltz (1996) examined the relationship between collective efficacy and the team performance of specific basketball skills across a 24-game season. Prior to each game, female collegiate athletes rated their efficacy for their team to perform well in that game generally and to perform well in that game on basketball-specific skills (e.g., rebounding, shooting, assists). Ratings were also made on an 11-point Likert scale from zero (indicating *not confident*) to 10 (indicating *very confident*). Correlations between specific efficacy judgments and performance on specific skills could be made for teams. If the scale items are used individually to correlate with specific performance skills in a microanalytic way, one need not be concerned with the internal consistency of the scale. However, if all items are summed together for a basketball efficacy measure, one would need to consider its internal consistency. Chase et al. reported a .92 for the internal consistency of this scale.

Other collective efficacy measures have used one-item questions to assess the concept (Hodges & Carron, 1992; Spink, 1990). Spink used two questions to measure team efficacy in volleyball: "What placing do you expect to attain in Supervolley?" and "How confident are you that your team will attain this placing?" The first question was intended to assess the group's team efficacy and had an open-ended response mode. The second question, using a 7-point Likert scale, assessed how confident team members were in their expectation. Reliability and validity scores were not reported for the team efficacy questions. The first question is more of an expectancy question than an efficacy one, and the second question is not valid. For instance, if Athlete A did not expect his team to do well, but rated his confidence in his expectation as only a "1", would he have less efficacy in his team or more than Athlete B who also did not expect his team to do well, but rated his confidence in his expectation of a poor placing as a "7"? Athlete A is less certain about a poor placing than Athlete B. Yet, Athlete B gets a higher efficacy score.

An experiment by Hodges and Carron (1992) examined the effects of different levels of collective efficacy on performance of a muscular endurance task. In this study, collective efficacy was measured with the questions "What do you think your group's chances are of winning?" and "How confident are you of your prediction?" Participants completed each question on a Likert scale from 0% (*definitely lose*) to 100% (*definitely win*) and 0% confident to 100% confident, respectively. The first question was intended to measure strength of efficacy expectations, and the second question measured certainty of efficacy.

However, strength and certainty are the same concept in Bandura's (1977, 1986) definitions. Reliability and validity scores were again not reported, and the measures suffer from the same problem as Spink's measure.

Paskevich, Brawley, Dorsch, and Widmeyer (1995) examined collective efficacy in sport using a group-resources approach. Their series of field investigations expanded upon the work of Zaccaro et al. (1995). Zaccaro and his colleagues emphasized that collective efficacy is "a sense of collective competence shared among members when allocating, coordinating, and integrating their resources as a successful concerted response to specific situational demands" (p. 309). Paskevich et al. have developed a multidimensional measure that reflects this complexity of shared collective efficacy beliefs (group coordination and member resources) and propose that this group-resources approach is appropriate for research questions that examine the group as a whole.

The instruments developed by Paskevich and his colleagues (1995) consisted of six scales pertaining to collective efficacy: (a) task in offense, defense, and transition; (b) communication with team members/coaches; (c) motivation and willingness to contribute knowledge/skills to collective effort; (d) confidence in the face of obstacles; (e) obstacles in general during practice/competition situations; and (f) general everyday functions within the context of a season. The scales were constructed to be sport and context specific. Thus, although the general "dimensions" of content were the same across different interactive sports, the item content differed for volleyball, basketball, and ice hockey. Participants rated their confidence for corresponding items on a scale from 0 (*no confidence at all*) to 100 (*complete confidence*). The instrument was subjected to initial content-validity tests by coaches, athletes, and other experts in the sports of volleyball, ice hockey, and basketball. Internal consistency coefficients of .86 to .91 were reported for the different aspects of the measures with studies of volleyball (Paskevich, 1995), basketball (Dorsch, Paskevich, Brawley, & Widmeyer, 1995), and ice hockey (Dorsch, Widmeyer, Paskevich, & Brawley, 1995) players. Results of these studies demonstrated that the collective efficacy measure successfully discriminated between teams that were extremely high or low in task-related cohesion and that it was significantly related to team performance. This collective efficacy measure is still in the process of validation; however, it represents a unique direction in the measurement of collective efficacy.

Critique. Collective efficacy is a fairly new concept relative to self-efficacy. Few studies and corresponding measures have been developed to investigate the concept. One issue of importance in analyzing collective efficacy data with whatever measure one uses or develops is the level of analysis to employ. Gully, Devine, and Whitney (1995) indicate that the level of analysis one uses can be different from the level of the construct of interest. For example, one can measure individual perceptions of collective efficacy (confidence in one's team) and correlate this with individual performance, which might be done if one were looking at the relationship between team efficacy and social loafing. The level of analysis in this case is the individual. If one used the mean of individual perceptions of collective efficacy to reflect "shared beliefs" and correlated this with team performance, the level of analysis would be the group. Although using aggregated individual data may be an appropriate way to assess collective efficacy, it is first necessary to examine the degree of consensus at the individual level. Gully et al. (1995) recommend that individual data be aggregated to form a group-level construct only when there exists an acceptable degree of consensus. Consensus analyses can be conducted using an index of within-group interrater agreement (James, Demaree, & Wolf, 1984) or other indices (Kozlowski & Hattrup, 1992). If individual data are aggregated as group means without ensuring homogeneity of response, then aggregation bias may result. Both Feltz and Lirgg (1997) and Paskevich et al. (1995) have demonstrated consensus for a group effect in their data. What is important in studying collective efficacy is to first consider the research question in relation to the level of analysis that should be employed. If group-level analysis is appropriate, then consensus must be demonstrated before using group as the unit of analysis.

An analysis that has yet to be used in collective efficacy (within or outside the sport domain) is microanalytic congruence. Although Chase, Lirgg, and Feltz (1996) used a microanalytic approach to measure team efficacy, they did not conduct a congruence analysis. If a group effect can be demonstrated, there should be no reason a congruence analysis at the group level cannot be conducted when examining the predictive ability of collective efficacy on team performance at the level of specific tasks.

Sport Confidence

Vealey's (1986) development of the model of sport confidence included three measures: a Trait Sport Confidence Inventory (TSCI), a State Sport Confidence Inventory (SSCI), and a Competitive Orientation Inventory (COI). The TSCI was based on one's dispositional belief about one's sport ability whereas, the SSCI was based on one's sport-ability belief in a particular situation. The COI was based on an athlete's tendency to strive toward achieving a goal in sport that will demonstrate competence and success in sport. This chapter focuses on the measurement of self-confidence and, therefore, the measurement of the COI will not be addressed.

The TSCI and SSCI each consist of 13 items in which the participants rate their sport confidence on a 9-point Likert scale (1 = low and 9 = high). Scores are obtained by summing the 13 items. The TSCI asks athletes to think about how confident they were when competing in sport and then rate their confidence for how they "generally feel" in reference to "the most confident athlete" they know. The SSCI asks athletes to think about how confident they feel "right now" about performing in an upcoming competition in reference to "the most confident athlete" they know. The 13 items address various abilities that an athlete typically displays during competition (e.g., ability to execute skills, perform under pressure, concentrate well enough). The items are the same for the TSCI and SSCI, except for the trait and state contexts.

In the preliminary development of the instruments, reliability and validity test results were reported (Vealey, 1986). A factor analysis of the scales found them to be unidimensional. Internal consistencies, as assessed by Cronbach's alpha coeffi-

cients, were .93 for the TSCI and .95 for the SSCI. Content validity, as assessed by experts in the field of sport psychology, was found to be satisfactory. Initial concurrent validity for the TSCI was supported with significant correlations with other constructs. The SSCI was found to correlate significantly and positively with TSCI, competitive state anxiety, and the physical self-presentation confidence subscale of the PSE (Ryckman et al., 1982). Later research with adolescents (mean age 15 years) found similar internal consistencies for the TSCI (.92) and SSCI (.93) (Vealey & Campbell, 1988). Construct validity was confirmed as the TSCI significantly predicted other sport cognitions and behaviors (Vealey, 1986, 1988; Vealey & Campbell, 1988).

Critique. The TSCI and SSCI were developed to measure self-confidence within the unique context of sport. The criticism of these measures has been that they should not be used when a researcher is interested in investigating self-confidence in specific sport situations because they will have lower predictive power with respect to performance (Feltz, 1988). Moritz et al. (1996) found studies using the SSCI to have lower correlations with performance (Mean $r = .31$) than those of task-specific self-efficacy measures (Mean $r = .41$). Further, the format of the TSCI and SSCI has been scrutinized because participants are instructed to rate their confidence in relation to the most confident athlete they know. This format is believed to produce unsystematic variance, depending upon whom the participants select as their standard of confidence. In addition, as Zimmerman (1996) noted, comparison-based measures show a decline over time as an individual increases in skill mastery because the individual's comparison other has also gained in skill. A mastery-based measure avoids this problem. Last, the modifiability of SC-state is uncertain. Research is needed to determine if, and under what conditions, SC-state can be altered.

Movement Confidence Measures

Movement Confidence Inventory. Movement confidence is measured with the Movement Confidence Inventory (MCI; Griffin, Keogh, & Maybee, 1984). This instrument is intended to assess an individual's feeling of adequacy in a movement situation that includes components of competence, enjoyment, and physical harm. On the MCI, respondents rate 12 movement tasks (e.g., shoot basketball free throws by yourself) on three different scales. The first scale pertains to level of experience, with items rated on a Likert scale of 1 (*I have never tried or performed the task.*) to 5 (*I have performed the task regularly on an athletic team.*). The second scale pertains to confidence in performing the skill, with items rated on a 6-point Likert scale ranging from *very non-confident* to *very confident*. The third scale consists of ratings on the extent to which 22 pairs of descriptor words (e.g., easy-difficult; safe-dangerous) contribute to an individual's level of confidence for each of the 12 tasks. The pairs of words are rated on a scale that ranged from +3 (strongly contributed) to -3 (strongly subtracted) "from my confidence in doing the task." The descriptor word pairs represent the three confidence components (competence, enjoyment, and harm).

Since the development of the MCI in 1984, very few studies have utilized it in the study of movement confidence, although two modifications of the scale —Playground Movement

Confidence Inventory (Crawford & Griffin, 1986) and Stunt Movement Confidence Inventory (Griffin & Crawford, 1989)—have been developed. The initial work by Griffin et al. (1984) to construct the MCI scale reported alpha reliability coefficients of .90. However, we should note that their factor analysis of the descriptor words failed to identify movement competence, personal enjoyment of moving sensations, and perceived physical harm as independent components of movement confidence. Instead, the items loaded on two factors, with the pairs of words loading on opposite factors. Their analysis indicated that a person's feelings of competence were the major contributor to perceived movement confidence. The MCI was developed and tested with college-aged students, and there has been no evaluation of whether this measure would be appropriate for children. The two scales, Playground Movement Confidence Inventory (Crawford & Griffin, 1986) and Stunt Movement Confidence Inventory (Griffin & Crawford, 1989), were examined with children. The study involving the PMCI employed fifth-grade students, and the investigation utilizing the SMCI reported findings with upper-elementary-age children (9 to 11 years).

Playground Movement Confidence Inventory. The Playground Movement Confidence Inventory (Crawford & Griffin, 1986) was developed to measure children's perceived competence in movement situations that involved the perception of competence in performance, potential harm, and potential enjoyment. Six playground activities were pictorially presented (e.g., a picture of a child on a merry-go-round), with questions centering on the three subscales of competence, harm, and enjoyment. Using a 4-point Likert scale similar to Harter's (1979) format in the Perceived Competence Scale for Children, children rated their perceptions for each playground activity. A sample item from Crawford and Griffin's scale is "Some kids might slip and fall off the merry-go-round while it's moving, BUT, Other kids can ride this and be safe."

The alpha reliability coefficients were .86 for competence, .87 for harm, and .84 for enjoyment. Test-retest reliability coefficients were .79 for competence, .75 for harm, and .78 for enjoyment. For the entire inventory, a reliability coefficient of .78 was reported. The authors reported support for construct validity of the PMCI by reporting that the three predicted factors (competence, harm, enjoyment) distinguished themselves in the factor analysis and accounted for 54% of the total variance. The playground inventory also discriminated high and low confidence and experience in children. The results indicated an 85% rate of correct classification accuracy with a validity coefficient for scale-classification power of .98.

How sure are you that you are good at this sport skill or activity?

Not Sure   Very Sure

Figure 4. Developmentally appropriate self-efficacy measure for children nine years and younger.

Stunt Movement Confidence Inventory. The Stunt Movement Confidence Inventory (Griffin & Crawford, 1989) was also developed to measure self-perceptions of movement confidence in children. This inventory comprises pictorial images of six movement skills involving performance demands, such as height, speed, strength, coordination, and balance (e.g., a picture of a child on a slide). Participants rated their confidence and experience, on a 4-point Likert scale with anchors of *I am very sure,* to *I know that I couldn't* for each skill. In addition, participants rated their performance perceptions on a 4-point Likert scale also in similar format to Harter's (1979) scale, for nine items representing personal perceptions of competence, perceived potential for physical harm, and perceived potential for enjoyment.

The alpha reliability coefficients were .90 for competence, .91 for harm, and .93 for enjoyment. Test-retest reliability coefficients were .82 for experience with skill, .80 for movement confidence, .88 for competence, .85 for harm, and .79 for enjoyment. The authors reported support for construct validity with the confirmation of the three model factors in the factor analysis. High-and low-confidence/experience participants were properly discriminated through multiple discriminant analysis of the Stunt Movement Confidence Inventory.

Critique. Griffin and Keogh (1982) proposed that movement confidence was unique in the conceptualization of confidence because the sensory aspect of movement was included in their model. The criticism of this literature has been the lack of research using the inventory and no evidence that movement sense is a unique component that is not accounted for in other conceptions of self-confidence (i.e., sensory experiences via physiological states in self-efficacy theory) (Feltz, 1988). Further research is needed on the Movement Confidence Inventory that examines its reliability and validity.

Special Considerations and Issues

A few special considerations should be addressed when measuring self-efficacy or self-confidence. These include developmental appropriateness of the instrument, instruments that match the research question, and ceiling problems with high-level performers.

Developmental Issues

A special consideration in measuring self-efficacy/confidence in children would be the format and appropriateness of the measures. For self-efficacy, the format of the self-efficacy measure recommended by Bandura (1986a), with measures of strength and level of self-efficacy, may be too difficult for children under nine years of age. Research with children nine years and older have incorporated this type of scale without any reported problems (Chase, Ewing, Lirgg, & George, 1994; Lirgg & Feltz, 1991). With participants under the age of nine years, some revisions to the format of the questions may be necessary. One type of adaptation would be converting the response format to a Likert scale. Instead of presenting numbers, investigators could illustrate shapes (circles or squares) increasing in size to represent the points on the Likert scale (C. A. Ames, personal communication, October 29, 1994). An example of this type of scale is presented in Figure 4. Chase (1997) conducted research with eight-to-nine-year-olds incorporating this method without problems and reported that it could be easily administered.

Self-efficacy theory does not predict that developmental differences occur in efficacy expectations as children develop and form opinions regarding their physical ability. However, research in the physical and academic domains has found consistently that as children age, they become less confident, yet more accurate, in their assessments of their ability (Benenson & Dweck, 1986; Chase, 1997; Chase, Ewing, et al., 1994; Harter, 1982; Kaley & Cloutier, 1984; Nicholls, 1978). Furthermore, research has suggested that this change in perceptions and accuracy level may be due to children's development of the capacity to differentiate between ability and effort as they grow older (Horn & Harris, 1996; Nicholls, 1989). Research conducted in the cognitive and physical domains (Fry & Duda, in press; Nicholls, 1978, 1984) indicates that children below the age of 12 are usually not able to differentiate between effort and ability. As such variation may impact the validity and reliability of self-efficacy assessment, special consideration should be given to developmental levels (e.g., whether children hold a differentiated conception of ability) prior to measurement of self-perceptions of ability in young children (see Brustad, this volume).

Appropriateness of the Instrument

As mentioned earlier in this chapter, one can be assured of finding little predictiveness of the efficacy or confidence measure employed if there is little similarity between it and the performance or behavior measure. If one is assessing self- or team efficacy at the level of individual tasks (microanalytic approach) but measuring performance in terms of wins and losses, the efficacy measure will not have much predictive power. Likewise, generalized efficacy or confidence measures should not be used when assessing performance expectations for specific tasks. However, when one is interested in research questions about more general patterns of behavior, performance across situations, or with less familiar and more ambiguous tasks, generalized efficacy or confidence scales may be more predictive.

Task-specific efficacy ratings appear to be highly dependent upon people's familiarity with the required task and the knowledge of whether the requisite skills are in their repertoire (Wang & Richarde, 1988). Wang and Richarde found that task-specific measures of self-efficacy became more realistic following performance feedback. This supports Bandura's (1986a) hypothesis that information from one's past performance is the most dependable source of efficacy information. Thus, researchers who are interested in questions regarding task-specific efficacy should make sure that subjects have had some prior experience with the research task in question. Schunk (1995) suggests that with novices, a measure of self-efficacy for learning also be included. Often self-efficacy for learning measures are more predictive of performance and motivated behavior when one is first exposed to a task because they compensate for changes in performance due to the learning (Zimmerman, 1996).

High-Level Performers

Even though high-level performers can be plagued with doubts about their self-efficacy on occasion (Bandura, 1986a), they rarely use the lower half of self- and collective efficacy scales, especially when they are measured close to competition time. It is logical that athletes would have fairly high levels of confidence going into competition. Confidence building is a part of precompetition preparation. Furthermore, unless one is investigating young or beginning level athletes, most low-confidence athletes dropped out of sport at an early age (Feltz & Petlichkoff, 1983). Therefore, scale developers need either to develop a scale that can detect subtle differences in confidence with highly skilled performers or use a logarithmic transformation to normalize the data. The VAS has not been used in sport psychology with highly experienced performers and, perhaps, could detect subtle differences if the anchors were *moderately confident and extremely confident*. This procedure would have to be tested, and reliability and validity data, collected before determining its usefulness with high-level performers. Another procedure mentioned earlier in this chapter might be to use a microanalytic assessment, selecting challenging as well as the most difficult aspects of performance that are rarely reachable in actual competition.

Future Development of Confidence Measures

Children's Measures

In the future development of self-efficacy/confidence measures for research with children, further validation of developmentally appropriate measures must be conducted. Harter's (1982) development of The Children's Perceived Competence Scale and the pictorial scale might serve as a model for the necessary steps in developing a suitable measure. This is not to suggest that future self-efficacy/confidence measures should pattern their format after Harter's scale. For example, a simple scale, as described previously, with shapes instead of numbers, increasing in size could be employed. Measurements with children should also follow recommendations by Bandura (1986a) to use a microanalytic approach in matching the efficacy measure to the corresponding task.

When measuring self-efficacy in children, researchers should also consider the children's preference and incentive to participate in the activity or sport skill. A critical aspect of self-efficacy theory proposes that self-efficacy will predict performance only when the participant has adequate skill and proper incentive is present. Therefore, before measuring self-efficacy, we recommend that a measure of importance in successfully completing the task be included. Where possible, we also recommend that participants select an activity or sport skill of their own that they enjoy and that researchers then direct the self-efficacy measurement specific to that skill.

In the development of confidence measures for children, instruments must undergo more strict reliability and validity tests. To establish reliability in self-efficacy for learning measures with children, Schunk and his colleagues (Bandura & Schunk, 1981; Schunk & Gunn, 1986; Schunk, Hanson, & Cox, 1987; Schunk & Rice, 1987) have computed test-retest reliability coefficients. This procedure involves administering the test to children not participating in the study on two occasions, with 2 to 3 days separating the testing days to preclude item recall. We acknowledge that efficacy judgments change over time as new information and experience are acquired, but there should exist some short-term reliability.

Schunk (1987) has also suggested that content, criterion-related, and construct validity can be assessed in self-efficacy measures with children. First, content validity can be established by having 50 to 70% of the self-efficacy items (format and difficulty of targeted tasks) measured correspond to tasks/activities that are typically used in their instructional program. Criterion-related validity can be assessed by relating self-efficacy to students' actual performances or relating students' posttest self-efficacy judgments to subsequent performance on a skill test. Last, construct validity could be evaluated by examining the relationship between self-efficacy and attributions for success and failure (Weiner, 1985), self-judged attitudes toward the task, and observed persistence and effort expended (Schunk, 1987).

Individualized Measures

In applied sport settings or in some individual sports where there are many levels of competition with different skills employed by different competitors (e.g., figure skating, gymnastics, diving), typical self-efficacy scales that consist of preselected items may not be completely relevant for all competitors. For instance, if a sport psychologist wants to determine the effects of a particular goal-setting program on the self-efficacy and performance of figure skaters who compete at different levels of ability and have different goals and perceived barriers to reaching their goals, one efficacy scale for all competitors will create problems of content validity across athletes. This could limit the predictive accuracy of the self-efficacy instrument. Researchers in the area of relapse prevention have effectively used an individualized assessment approach as a solution to this issue (Miller, McCrady, Abrams, & Labouvie, 1994). Miller and his colleagues constructed individualized self-efficacy scales for alcoholics by having subjects first choose the most problematic drinking antecedents from five different problem areas (e.g., work, marriage, children). The researchers then used the 3 most important items in each of the five most important areas for each subject to obtain a 15-item individualized scale on which subjects could judge their confidence to refrain from drinking. This method has also been used in the exercise-adherence literature (Dzewaltowski, Noble, & Shaw, 1990).

One application of this approach in sport was made in constructing an individualized figure-skating self-efficacy scale for skaters who varied greatly in ability (Garza & Feltz, 1996). Subjects were asked to indicate their most difficult jump, spin, and step/connecting move and then to rate their confidence in performing each skill from 1 out of 10 to 10 out of 10 times on an 11-point Likert scale. An individualized assessment approach to self-efficacy ratings may provide a promising tool for investigation of important problem areas for individual athletes or for use in clinical applications where treatment progress could be monitored with an individually tailored instrument.

Generality of Self-Efficacy Beliefs

As we noted earlier in this chapter, most investigators of the self-efficacy construct have not investigated whether self-efficacy beliefs generalize beyond a specific domain. Schunk (1995) has stated that there is an urgent need for research on generalization (or transfer) of self-efficacy and achievement outcomes. Although some evidence exists for the generalization of self-efficacy (e.g., Holloway et al., 1989), Schunk has called for research that explores the predicted causal links between self-efficacy and generalization (and maintenance) of skills and strategies. For instance, athletes who perform well in one position should have high self-efficacy for learning a new position. Of course, this generalization may depend on the extent to which the athlete believes there is positive transfer between the skills. Athletes with high self-efficacy (e.g., Michael Jordan, professional basketball player for the Chicago Bulls) may even believe they can learn a new sport if the skill builds on prior fundamentals skills, such as strength, speed, and anticipation-timing. The relationship between positive and negative transfer and generalizability of efficacy beliefs has yet to be investigated in sport and motor performance.

One's generalizability of self-efficacy beliefs may also be influenced by one's conception of ability. People who conceive ability as an acquirable skill have been shown to maintain high self-efficacy, set challenging goals, persist longer, and expend more effort in learning a skill than have those who conceive ability as a more or less inherent aptitude (Elliott & Dweck, 1998; Jourden, Bandura, & Banfield, 1991; Wood & Bandura, 1989). Thus, people who have a high self-efficacy belief in a particular domain should show greater self-efficacy transfer to new domains if they also have a conception of ability as an acquirable skill rather than as a fixed (or entity) conception. Measures of conception of ability need to be included in future research on the generality or transfer of self-efficacy beliefs.

Summary

In this chapter, we reviewed theoretical frameworks and measures for self-efficacy, team efficacy, sport confidence, and movement confidence. Most of the efficacy/confidence research in sport has occurred within the self-efficacy framework, using task-specific scales. Self-efficacy appears most useful in explaining motivated behavior and performance in sport when measures have been constructed within the tenets of the theory (i.e., when proper incentives and requisite skills are present and a microanalytic approach is used). Although there is a place for more general measures, they should not be used when assessing expectations for specific tasks.

Throughout this chapter, we have made various recommendations. We recommend that when using task-specific efficacy scales, researchers employ level and strength ratings in their analysis and include the efficacy instrument in the appendix of their paper. Researchers should also insure that subjects have proper incentives for the task and that outcome expectancies be assessed in situations where one's beliefs about outcomes may vary. Past research in sport psychology has not considered microanalytic congruence analysis in research on self-efficacy. We suggest that, at least when using nonhierarchical efficacy measures, congruence analyses be conducted because they provide a more powerful test of efficacy predictiveness. In addition, internal consistency coefficients should be reported with all nonhierarchical efficacy measures. When conducting research on teams and using team as the unit of analysis, we recommend that consensus in collective efficacy first be demonstrated. In research involving children, we recommend using pictorial scales with shapes increasing in size to represent Likert-type scales. Finally, researchers should consider developing appropriate measures for high-level performers and using individualized scales in their future work.

References

Bandura, A. (1977). Self-efficacy: Toward a unifying theory of behavioral change. *Psychological Review, 84,* 191-215.

Bandura, A. (1978). Reflections on self-efficacy. In S. Rachman (Ed.), *Advances in Behaviour Research and Therapy:* Vol. 1 (pp. 237-269). Oxford: Pergamon.

Bandura, A. (1980). Gauging the relationship between self-efficacy judgment and action. *Cognitive Therapy and Research, 4,* 263-268.

Bandura, A. (1986a). *Social foundation of thought and action: A social cognitive theory.* Englewood Cliffs, NJ: Prentice-Hall.

Bandura, A. (1986b). The explanatory and predictive scope of self-efficacy theory. *Journal of Clinical and Social Psychology, 4,* 359-373.

Bandura, A. (1990). Perceived self-efficacy in the exercise of personal agency. *Journal of Applied Sport Psychology, 2,* 128-163.

Bandura, A. (1992). On rectifying the comparative anatomy of perceived control: Comments on "Cognates of Personal Control." *Applied & Preventive Psychology, 1,* 121-126.

Bandura, A. (1997). *Self-efficacy: The exercise of control.* New York: Freeman.

Bandura, A., Adams, N.E., & Beyer, J. (1977). Cognitive processes mediating behavioral change. *Journal of Personality and Social Psychology, 35,* 125-139.

Bandura, A., & Schunk, D. H. (1981). Cultivating competence, self-efficacy, and intrinsic interest through proximal self-motivation. *Journal of Personality and Social Psychology, 41,* 586-598.

Benenson, J., & Dweck, C. (1986). The development of trait explanations and self-evaluations in the academic and social domains. *Child Development, 57,* 1179-1187.

Borkovec, T. D. (1978). Self-efficacy: Cause or reflection of behavioral change. In S. Rachman (Ed.)., *Advances in behaviour research and therapy:* Vol. 1 (pp. 163-170). Oxford: Pergamon.

Cervone, D. (1985). Randomization tests to determine significance levels for microanalytic congruences between self-efficacy and behavior. *Cognitive Therapy and Research, 9,* 357-365.

Chase, M. A. (1997). *Determinants of children's self-efficacy in physical activities and sport.* (Manuscript submitted for publication).

Chase, M. A., Ewing, M. E., Lirgg, C. D., & George, T. R. (1994). The effects of equipment modification on children's self-efficacy and basketball shooting performance. *Research Quarterly for Exercise and Sport, 65(2),* 159-168.

Chase, M. A., Feltz, D. L., Tully, D. C., & Lirgg, C. D. (1994). *Sources of collective and individual efficacy of collegiate athletes.* Paper presented at the annual meeting of North American Society for the Psychology of Sport and Physical Activity, Clearwater Beach, FL.

Chase, M. A., Lirgg, C. D., & Feltz, D. L. (1994). The relationship between individual efficacy, team efficacy, and performance: A field study. (unpublished manuscript).

Chase, M. A., Lirgg, C. D., & Feltz, D. L. (1996). *The relationship between individual efficacy, team efficacy, and performance: A field study.* (Manuscript submitted for publication).

Crawford, M. E., & Griffin, N. S. (1986). Testing the validity of the Griffin/Keogh Model for Movement Confidence by analyzing the self-report playground involvement decisions of elementary school children. *Research Quarterly for Exercise and Sport, 57,* 8-15.

Davis-Berman, J. (1990). Physical self-efficacy, perceived physical status, and depressive symptomatology in older adults. *The Journal of Psychology, 124,* 207-215.

Dorsch, K. D., Paskevich, D. M., Brawley, L. R., & Widmeyer, W. N. (1995, October) *The relationship between performance outcome, collective efficacy and cohesion as a function of group characteristics.* Paper presented at the annual meeting of the Canadian Society for Psychomotor Learning and Sport Psychology, Vancouver, British Columbia.

Dorsch, K. D., Widmeyer, W. N., Paskevich, D. M., & Brawley, L. R. (1995). Collective efficacy: [It's] measurement and relationship to cohesion in ice hockey. *Journal of Applied Sport Psychology, 7,* Supplement 56.

Druckman, D., & Bjork, R.A. (Eds.). (1994). *Learning, remembering, believing.* Washington, DC.: National Academy Press.

Dzewaltowski, D. A., Noble, J. M., & Shaw, J. M. (1990). Physical activity participation: Social cognitive theory versus the theories of reasoned action and planned behavior. *Journal of Sport and Exercise Psychology, 12,* 388-405.

Elliott, E.S., & Dweck, C.S. (1988). Goals: An approach to motivation and achievement. *Journal of Personality and Social Psychology, 54,* 5-12.

Feltz, D. L. (1988). Self-confidence and sports performance. In K. B. Pandolf (Ed.), *Exercise and Sport Sciences Reviews* (pp. 423-457). New York: MacMillan.

Feltz, D. L. (1992). Understanding motivation in sport: A self-efficacy perspective. In G. C. Roberts (Ed.), *Motivation in sport and exercise* (pp. 107-128). Champaign, IL: Human Kinetics.

Feltz, D. L., Chase, M. A., Simensky, S. G., Hodge, C. N., Jian, S., & Lee, I. (1994). Development of the multidimensional coaching efficacy scale. *Journal of Sport and Exercise Psychology, 16,* S51.

Feltz, D. L., & Lirgg, C. D. (1997). *Perceived team and player efficacy in hockey.* Unpublished manuscript, Michigan State University, East Lansing.

Feltz, D. L., & Petlichkoff, L. (1983). Perceived competence among interscholastic sport participants and dropouts. *Canadian Journal of Applied Sport Sciences, 8,* 231-235.

Feltz, D. L., & Riessinger, C. A. (1990). Effects on in vivo emotive imagery and performance feedback on self-efficacy and muscular endurance. *Journal of Sport and Exercise Psychology, 12,* 132-143.

Fennema, E., & Sherman, J. A. (1976). Fennema - Sherman Mathematics Attitude Scales: Instruments designed to measure attitudes toward the learning of mathematics by females and males. *JSAS Catalog of Selected Documents in Psychology, 6,* 31.

Fry, M. D., & Duda, J. L. (in press). A developmental examination of children's understanding of effort and ability in the physical and academic domain. *Research Quarterly for Exercise and Sport.*

Garza, D. L., & Feltz, D. L. (1996). *Effects of selected mental practice techniques on performance ratings, self-efficacy, and state anxiety, of competitive figure skaters.* Unpublished manuscript, Michigan State University, East Lansing.

Gayton, W. F., Matthews, G. R., & Borchstead, G. N. (1986). An investigation of the validity of the physical self-efficacy scale in predicting marathon performance. *Perceptual and Motor Skills, 63,* 752-754.

George, T. R. (1994). Self-confidence and baseball performance: A causal examination. *Journal of Sport and Exercise Psychology, 16,* 381-399.

George, T. R., Feltz, D. L., & Chase, M. A. (1992). The effects of model similarity on self-efficacy and muscular endurance: A second look. *Journal of Sport and Exercise Psychology, 14,* 237-248.

Gould, D., & Weiss, M. R. (1981). Effect of model similarity and model self-talk on self-efficacy in muscular endurance. *Journal of Sport Psychology, 3,* 17-29.

Griffin, N. S., & Crawford, M. E. (1989). Measurement of movement confidence with a stunt movement confidence inventory. *Journal of Sport and Exercise Psychology, 11*, 26-40.

Griffin, N. S., & Keogh, J. F. (1982). The model for movement confidence. In J. A. S. Kelso & J. E. Clark (Eds.), *The development of movement control and co-ordination* (pp. 213-236) Place: John Wiley & Sons, Ltd.

Griffin, N. S., Keogh, J. F., & Maybee, R. (1984). Performer perceptions of movement confidence. *Journal of Sport Psychology, 6*, 395-407.

Gully, S. M., Devine, D. J., & Whitney, D. J. (1995). A meta-analysis of cohesion and performance: Effects of level of analysis and task interdependence. *Small Group Research, 26*, 497-520.

Harter, S. (1979). *Perceived Competence Scale for Children Manual (Form O)*. Denver: University of Denver.

Harter, S. (1982). The Perceived Competence Scale for Children. *Child Development, 53*, 87-97.

Hodges, L., & Carron, A. (1992). Collective efficacy and group performance. *International Journal of Sport Psychology, 23*, 48-59.

Holloway, J. B., Beuter, A., & Duda, J. L. (1988). Self-efficacy and training for strength in adolescent girls. *Journal of Applied Social Psychology, 18*, 699-719.

Horn, T.S., & Harris, A. (1996). Perceived competence in young athletes: Research findings and recommendations for coaches and parents. In F.L. Smoll, & R.E. Smith (Eds.), *Children and youth in sport: A biopsychosocial perspective* (pp. 309-329). Dubuque, IA: Brown & Benchmark.

James, L.R., Demaree, R.G., & Wolf, G. (1984). Estimating within-group interrater reliability with and without response bias. *Journal of Applied Psychology, 69*, 85-98.

Jourden, F.J., Bandura, A., & Banfield, J.T. (1991). The impact of conceptions of ability on self-regulatory factors and motor skill acquisition. *Journal of Sport and Exercise Psychology, 8*, 213-216.

Kaley, R., & Cloutier, R. (1984). Developmental determinants of self-efficacy predictiveness. *Cognitive Therapy and Research, 8*, 643-656.

Kane, T. D., Marks, M. A., Zaccaro, S. J., & Blair, V. (1996). Self-efficacy, personal goals, and wrestlers' self-regulation. *Journal of Sport and Exercise Psychology, 18*, 36-48.

Kazdin, A. E. (1978). Conceptual and assessment issues raised by self-efficacy theory. In S. Rachman (Ed.), *Advances in behavior research and therapy:* Vol. 1. (pp. 177-185). Oxford: Pergamon.

Kenny, D. A., & La Voie, L. (1985). Separating individual and group effects. *Journal of Personality and Social Psychology, 48*, 339-348.

Kozlowski, S., & Hattrup, K. (1992). A disagreement about within-group agreement: Disentangling issues of consistency versus consensus. *Journal of Applied Psychology, 77*, 161-167.

Lee, C. (1982). Self-efficacy as a predictor of performance in competitive gymnastics. *Journal of Sport Psychology, 4*, 405-409.

Lee, C. (1988). The relationship between goal setting, self-efficacy, and female field hockey team performance. *International Journal of Sport Psychology, 20*, 147-161.

Lee, C., & Bobko, P. (1994). Self-efficacy beliefs: Comparison of five measures. *Journal of Applied Psychology, 79*, 364-369.

Lent, R. W., & Hackett, G. (1987). Career self-efficacy: Empirical status and future directions. *Journal of Vocational Behavior, 30*, 347-382.

Lirgg, C. D. (1993). Effects of same-sex versus coeducational physical education on the self-perceptions of middle and high school students. *Research Quarterly for Exercise and Sport, 64*, 324-334.

Lirgg, C. D., & Feltz, D. L. (1991). Teacher versus peer models revisited: Effects on motor performance and self-efficacy. *Research Quarterly for Exercise and Sport, 62*, 217-224.

Maddux, J.E. (1995). Self-efficacy theory: An introduction. In J.E. Maddux (Ed.), *Self-efficacy, adaptation, and adjustment: Theory, research, and application* (pp. 3-33). New York: Plenum.

Maddux, J.E., & Meier, L.J. (1995). Self-efficacy and depression. In J.E. Maddux (Ed.), *Self-efficacy, adaptation, and adjustment: Theory, research, and application* (pp. 143-172). New York: Plenum.

Manzo, L.G., & Silva, J.M. (1994, October). *Construction and initial validation of The Carolina Sport Confidence Inventory.* Paper presented at the Association for the Advancement of Applied Sport Psychology meeting, Lake Tahoe, NV.

Martin, J.J., & Gill, D.L. (1991). The relationships among competitive orientation, sport-confidence, self-efficacy, anxiety, and performance. *Journal of Sport and Exercise Psychology, 13*, 149-159.

Martin, J.J., & Gill, D.L. (1995). The relationships of competitive orientations and self-efficacy to goal importance, thoughts, and performance in high school distance runners. *Journal of Applied Sport Psychology, 7*, 50-62.

McAuley, E. (1992). Self-referent thought in sport and physical activity. In T. S. Horn (Ed.), *Advances in sport psychology* (pp. 101-118). Champaign, IL: Human Kinetics.

McAuley, E., & Gill, D. (1983). Reliability and validity of the physical self-efficacy in a competitive sport setting. *Journal of Sport Psychology, 5*, 185-191.

Miller, K.J., McCrady, B.S., Abrams, D.B., & Labouvie, E.W. (1994). Taking an individualized approach to the assessment of self-efficacy and the prediction of alcoholic relapse. *Journal of Psychopathology and Behavioral Assessment, 16*, 111-120.

Moritz, S. E., Mack, D. E., & Feltz, D. L. (1996). *A meta-analytic investigation of the self-efficacy and performance relationship in sport and exercise.* Unpublished manuscript, Michigan State University, East Lansing.

Nicholls, J. G. (1978). The development of the concepts of effort and ability, perception of academic attainment, and the understanding that difficult tasks require more ability. *Child Development, 49*, 800-814.

Nicholls, J. G. (1984). Achievement motivation: Conception of ability, subjective experience, task choice and performance. *Psychological Review, 91*, 328-346.

Nicholls, J.G. (1989). *The competitive ethos and democratic education.* Cambridge, MA: Harvard University Press.

Okwumabua, T.M. (1986). Psychological and physical contributions to marathon performance: An exploratory investigation. *Journal of Sport Behavior, 8*, 163-171.

O'Leary, A. (1985). Self-efficacy and health. *Behavior Therapy and Research, 23*, 437-452.

Paskevich, D. M. (1995). *Conceptual and measurement factors of collective efficacy in its relation to cohesion and performance outcome.* Unpublished doctoral dissertation, University of Waterloo, Ontario.

Paskevich, D. M., Brawley, L. R., Dorsch, K. D., & Widmeyer, W. N. (1995). Implications of individual and group level analyses applied to the study of collective efficacy and cohesion. *Journal of Applied Sport Psychology, 7*, Supplement 95.

Robertson, K., Mellor, S., Hughes, M., Sanderson, F., & Reilly, T. (1988). Psychological health and squash play. *Ergonomics, 31*, 1567-1572.

Ryckman, R., Robbins, M., Thornton, B., & Cantrell, P. (1982). Development and validation of a physical self-efficacy scale. *Journal of Personality and Social Psychology, 42*, 891-900.

Schunk, D. H. (1987, April). *Domain-specific measurement of students' self-regulated learning processes.* Paper presented at the American Educational Research Association, Washington, D.C.

Schunk, D.H. (1995). Self-efficacy and education and instruction. In J.E. Maddux (Ed.), *Self-efficacy, adaptation, and adjustment: Theory, research, and application* (pp. 281-303). New York: Plenum.

Schunk, D. H., & Gunn, T. P. (1986). Self-efficacy and skill development: Influence of task strategies and attributions. *Journal of Educational Research, 79,* 238-244.

Schunk, D. H., Hanson, A. R., & Cox, P. D. (1987) Peer model attributes and children's achievement behaviors. *Journal of Educational Psychology, 79,* 54-61.

Schunk, D. H., & Rice, J. M. (1987). Enhancing comprehension skill and self-efficacy with strategy value information. *Journal of Reading Behavior, 19,* 285-302.

Spink, K. S. (1990). Group cohesion and collective efficacy of volleyball teams. *Journal of Sport and Exercise Psychology, 12,* 301-311.

Theodorakis, Y. (1995). Effects of self-efficacy, satisfaction, and personal goals on swimming performance. *The Sport Psychologist, 9,* 245-253.

Thornton, B., Ryckman, R.M., Robbins, M.A., Donolli, J., & Biser, G. (1987). Relationship between perceived physical ability and indices of actual physical fitness. *Journal of Sport Psychology, 9,* 295-300.

Tipton, R.M., & Worthington, E.L. (1984).The measurement of generalized self-efficacy: A study of construct validity. *Journal of Personality Assessment, 48,* 545-548.

Treasure, D.C., Monson, J., & Lox, C.L. (1996). Relationship between self-efficacy, wrestling performance, and affect prior to competition. *The Sport Psychologist, 10,* 73-83.

Vealey, R. S. (1986). Conceptualization of sport-confidence and competitive orientation: Preliminary investigation and instrument development. *Journal of Sport Psychology, 10,* 471-478.

Vealey, R. S. (1988). Sport-confidence and competitive orientation: An addendum on scoring procedures and gender differences. *Journal of Sport Psychology, 10,* 471-478.

Vealey, R. S., & Campbell, J. L., (1988). Achievement goals of adolescent figure skaters: Impact on self-confidence, anxiety, and performance. *Journal of Adolescent Research, 3,* 227-243.

Wang, A. Y., & Richarde, R. S. (1988). Global versus task-specific measures of self-efficacy. *The Psychological Record, 38,* 533-541.

Watkins, B., Garcia, A.W., & Turek, E. (1994). The relation between self-efficacy and sport performance: Evidence from a sample of youth baseball players. *Journal of Applied Sport Psychology, 6,* 21-31.

Weinberg, R., Gould, D., & Jackson, A. (1979). Expectations and performance: An empirical test of Bandura's self-efficacy theory. *Journal of Sport Psychology, 1,* 320-331.

Weiner, B. (1985). An attributional theory of achievement motivation and emotion. *Psychological Review, 92,* 548-573.

Weiss, M.R., Wiese, D.M., & Klint, K.A. (1989). Head over heels with success: The relationship between self-efficacy and performance in competitive youth gymnastics. *Journal of Sport and Exercise Psychology, 11,* 444-451.

Williams, S.L., Kinney, P.J., & Falbo, J. (1989). Generalization of therapeutic changes in agoraphobia: The role of perceived self-efficacy. *Journal of Consulting and Clinical Psychology, 57,* 436-442.

Wilson, R., Feltz, D. L., & Fitzpatrick, J. M. (1996, January). *Sources of efficacy information among masters weight pentathlon champions.* Paper presented at the Midwest District of the American Alliance of Health, Physical Education, Recreation, and Dance, Dearborn, MI.

Wood, R.E., & Bandura, A. (1989). Impact of conceptions of ability on self-regulatory mechanisms and complex decision-making. *Journal of Personality and Social Psychology, 56,* 407-415.

Wurtele, S.K. (1986). Self-efficacy and athletic performance: A review. *Journal of Social and Clinical Psychology, 4,* 290-301.

Zaccaro, S. J., Blair, V., Peterson, C., & Zazanis, M. (1995). Collective efficacy. In J. E. Maddux (Ed.), *Self-efficacy, adaptation and adjustment: Theory, research and application.* (pp. 308-330) New York: Plenum.

Zimmerman, B.J. (1996, April). *Misconceptions, problems, and dimensions in measuring self-efficacy.* Paper presented at the annual meeting of the American Educational Research Association, New York.

Chapter 5

MEASURES OF INTRINSIC AND EXTRINSIC MOTIVATION IN SPORT AND PHYSICAL ACTIVITY: A REVIEW AND CRITIQUE

Robert J. Vallerand
Université du Québec à Montréal
and
Michelle S. Fortier
University of Ottawa

INTRODUCTION

Each day, countless individuals engage in different types of sport and physical activities. Such engagement is characterized by two forms of motivation. The first deals with behavior performed for itself, in order to experience pleasure and satisfaction inherent in the activity, and has been termed intrinsic motivation. This form of motivation is likely to occur when the activity is interesting, challenging, and provides people with clear feedback and freedom with which to perform the task (Deci, 1975; Deci & Ryan, 1985). These qualities clearly apply to sport and physical activity (Vallerand, Deci, & Ryan, 1987).

At the same time, any astute observer will tell you that sport and physical activity can also be engaged in for reasons that lie "outside" the activity. For instance, high school basketball players may play on a team because it brings them popularity at school or because it pleases their parents. This second type of motivation, which involves engaging in the activity in order to achieve some separable goal, such as receiving rewards or avoiding punishment, has been called extrinsic motivation.

Over the past 20 years, much research has focused on intrinsic and extrinsic motivation in sport and physical activity (see Frederick & Ryan, 1995; R.M. Ryan, Vallerand, & Deci, 1984; Vallerand et al., 1987; Vallerand & Reid, 1990 for reviews). Studying motivation in the sport context (or domain) may yield at least two benefits. First, it can lead to important tests of theoretical formulations in real-life settings and, thus, provide crucial information on the external validity of psychological theories. Second, it should contribute to a better understanding of the psychological processes underlying participation in sport and physical activity. Such knowledge can then be used to design environments that will enhance the motivation of all participants.

In order to reach the above two objectives, methodological rigor is needed. One important methodological element in any scientific endeavor deals with measurement. Over the years, different types of intrinsic and extrinsic motivation measures have been used in sport and physical activity settings. Some focus on behavioral observation, others on self-report assessments. Some deal with participants' immediate reaction to a current situation, others with their general orientation toward sport and/or physical activity. Surprisingly, to date, no comprehensive evaluation of these various measures has been performed. Such a critical review could allow us to take stock of accumulated knowledge regarding existing instruments. That is, an examination of existing measures of intrinsic and extrinsic motivation toward sport/physical activity would provide information on the level of validity and reliability of the different scales and, therefore, guide our decisions concerning which ones should be primarily used. Second, by reviewing existing measures, problems and limitations in our assessment "arsenal" would become more apparent, thereby leading to future directions in measurement advances.

In light of the above, the purpose of this chapter is to review and critique existing measures of intrinsic and extrinsic motivation in sport and physical activity. In the first section, we define intrinsic and extrinsic motivation. Then, we present and evaluate the different measures in terms of their validity and reliability. In so doing, we propose a classification that will help us clarify the different roles and functions of existing measures. Finally, in the last section, we propose future research avenues with respect to the measurement of intrinsic and extrinsic motivation in sport and physical activity settings. However, before delving into these different issues, we briefly present major theories in the area.

MAJOR THEORIES IN INTRINSIC AND EXTRINSIC MOTIVATION

A host of research has shown that various events can affect intrinsic motivation. For instance, Deci (1971) showed that extrinsic factors, such as being rewarded with money for engaging in an interesting activity, led participants to have a lower level of intrinsic motivation than did nonrewarded subjects. These findings on the negative effects of rewards and awards on intrinsic motivation have been replicated in the realm of sports in both laboratory (e.g., Orlick & Mosher, 1978) and field studies (E. D. Ryan, 1977, 1980). Other research has shown that positive performance feedback increases intrinsic motivation, whereas negative performance feedback decreases intrinsic motivation (e.g., Vallerand & Reid, 1984, 1988, Whitehead & Corbin, 1991).

Over the years, several theories have been proposed in the intrinsic and extrinsic motivation literature. These theories have tried to explain increases and decreases in intrinsic motivation following various social events (e.g., rewards, feedback, competition etc.). We will focus here only on the most important contemporary theories. The reader is referred to Deci and Ryan (1985) and Deci (1975) for a more complete treatment of theoretical formulations in the area. These theories can be mainly seen as being either cognitive or motivational in nature.

Cognitive Theories

Cognitive theories deal with people's perceptions or thoughts about a particular activity as the explanation of the effects of various variables (or determinants) on intrinsic motivation. Concepts such as expectations of reinforcements, self-efficacy perceptions, and attributions are used to this end. Self-Perception theory (e.g., Bem, 1972; Lepper, Greene, & Nisbett, 1973) proposes that people attribute internal states (e.g., intrinsic motivation) to external factors (e.g., a reward) that were present when behavior was emitted. Thus, engaging in an interesting activity when rewards are offered should be enough to lead individuals to discount (Kelley, 1972) intrinsic motivation as the cause of their behavior and attribute the latter to external causes (i.e., the reward). A loss of intrinsic motivation then follows.

Social cognitive theory (Bandura, 1986) posits that people

engage in a behavior if they expect that this behavior will lead to a valued reinforcement and that they are self-efficacious (or competent) to do the behavior. Positive performance feedback should thus increase intrinsic motivation (or free engagement in the activity) because it provides a message that the individual should be able to receive the desired reinforcement. Conversely, negative performance feedback should decrease intrinsic motivation because individuals should determine that they are not able to obtain the reinforcement (see Bandura & Schunk, 1981, on this issue).

When combined, self-perception theory and social cognitive theory can account for the increases and decreases in intrinsic motivation reported in the literature. The first theory presents a cogent interpretation of the decreases in intrinsic motivation due to the discounting of intrinsic factors in the presence of extrinsic factors (e.g., rewards), whereas the second deals with the increases in intrinsic motivation due to increases in self-efficacy expectations. We now turn to conceptual models that focus on a different set of assumptions and processes, namely motivational theories.

Motivational Theories

Motivational theories propose that the explanation of behavior has to do with an analysis of human needs. From this perspective, intrinsic motivation is seen as being energized by intrinsic needs. For instance, White (1959) proposed that the need for effectance (or competence) represents a powerful source of motivation that leads individuals to engage in activities that may satisfy their desire to be competent. Harter (1978, 1981a) later extended White's reasoning by underscoring the role of socializing agents, such as parents and teachers (or coaches), in the development of context-specific perceptions of competence (e.g., sports, music etc.). It is these perceptions of competence that will help sustain motivation in these various contexts. Similarly, deCharms (1968) posited that intrinsically motivated behaviors were engaged in out of the feeling that one is the origin of one's behavior, or out of the need for personal causation. Deci (1975) and later Deci and Ryan (1985, 1991) integrated and extended these two positions by proposing that intrinsic motivation (and, as we will see in the next section, some forms of extrinsic motivation) results from three fundamental human needs: the needs for competence, autonomy, and relatedness. These three needs represent the basis for perhaps the most influential theory in the intrinsic motivation literature, namely self-determination theory (Deci & Ryan, 1985, 1991). As Deci and Ryan (1994) put it: "People are inherently motivated to feel connected to others within a social milieu, to function effectively in that milieu, and to feel a sense of personal initiative in doing so" (p. 7).

Self-Determination theory deals with both the determinants (or causes) and the consequences (or outcomes) of intrinsic motivation. First, with respect to the determinants, the theory proposes that variables (e.g., material, social, or verbal information) that promote autonomy, competence, and relatedness will also increase intrinsic motivation, whereas variables that undermine such needs will also decrease intrinsic motivation. This is because of the functional significance of the information to the person's needs. Receiving the information that one is not competent on a given task also reveals that one is unlikely to satisfy the need for competence in this activity. Thus, intrinsic motivation toward this given activity would be reduced. Individuals would then engage in this activity only when so obliged. A similar interpretation holds for autonomy and relatedness. Thus, feeling competent, related, and autonomous on a given task is likely to increase intrinsic motivation, whereas feeling incompetent, isolated, and controlled by others should undermine one's intrinsic motivation toward the activity. Much research now supports this hypothesis (see Vallerand, 1997, for a review). For instance, research by Cadorette, Blanchard, and Vallerand (1996) revealed that the more individuals perceived themselves to be competent, autonomous, and related to others in a weight-loss exercise program, the more they reported being intrinsically motivated toward the program.

Self-Determination theory also deals with the consequences of motivation, that is, the ensuing outcomes of being motivated in a certain way (e.g., intrinsically motivated). This theory posits that because self-determination leads to enhanced functioning (Deci, 1980; R.M. Ryan, Deci, & Grolnick, 1995), self-determined forms of motivation, such as intrinsic motivation and certain forms of extrinsic motivation (i.e., integrated and identified regulation), should lead to the most positive consequences because they represent the highest forms of self-determination. On the other hand, non self-determined forms of extrinsic motivation and the absence of motivation (i.e., respectively, external regulation and amotivation) should lead to the most negative consequences. Much research now supports this position (see Vallerand, 1997, for a review). For example, athletes who were intrinsically motivated reported experiencing higher levels of concentration and positive emotions during the practice of their sport than those who were extrinsically motivated (especially externally regulated) (Blanchard & Vallerand, 1996; Brière, Vallerand, Blais, & Pelletier, 1995; Pelletier et al., 1995).

In sum, although cognitive and motivational theories lead to the same predictions with respect to the effects of determinants on intrinsic motivation, they nevertheless focus on different sets of explanations. The cognitive theories seem to remain at a superficial level in their explanation. Thus, to the question "Why was intrinsic motivation undermined by the reward? ", the cognitive theories would simply answer "because there was a reward in the environment that led individuals to reattribute their task engagement to the reward rather than to their intrinsic motivation toward the activity." However, the motivational theories (and specifically self-determination theory) would answer that "the rewards led the individuals to experience a loss in perceptions of autonomy that runs contrary to their need for autonomy. This information was then used by the individuals to turn away from this activity that is dysfunctional with respect to their needs and to engage in other activities more in line with their need for autonomy." In addition, the motivational theories go beyond the competence and autonomy aspects of motivation and include an important social need, that of relatedness. Finally, motivational theories also deal with motivational consequences. It would thus appear that motivational theories (and especially self-determination theory, Deci & Ryan, 1985, 1991) represent a rather complete account of human motivation in social settings. Not surprisingly, such theories will be useful in

our quest to better understand the validity of measures of intrinsic and extrinsic motivation in sports.

INTRINSIC AND EXTRINSIC MOTIVATION DEFINED

There are at least four issues that need to be discussed in attempting to define intrinsic and extrinsic motivation. First, we need to delineate the very nature of these two constructs and show how they can be distinguished from one another. Then, we need to address the issue of the dimensionality of the constructs. That is, are intrinsic motivation and extrinsic motivation general entities (i.e., unidimensional) or a collection of related constructs (i.e., multidimensional)? Third, it is crucial that we determine the level of generality at which motivation is assessed. That is, does intrinsic and extrinsic motivation measure an enduring quality of the person, or does it refer to the assessment of one's motivation at a given point in time? Finally, the relationship between intrinsic and extrinsic motivation deserves attention. We discuss each of these issues in turn.

The Nature of Intrinsic and Extrinsic Motivation

Intrinsic motivation generally refers to the impetus to perform an activity for itself and the pleasure and satisfaction derived from participation (Deci, 1975; Deci & Ryan, 1985). Swimmers who swim laps because they enjoy the sensation of gliding through the water are representative of individuals who are intrinsically motivated. Contrary to intrinsic motivation, extrinsic motivation refers to engaging in an activity as a means to an end and not for its own sake. Thus, when extrinsically motivated, individuals do not participate in an activity for the inherent pleasure they may experience while performing it, but rather in order to receive something positive or to avoid something negative once the activity is terminated (Deci, 1975; Kruglanski, 1978). When athletes compete in order to win trophies and medals, they represent one instance of extrinsically motivated individuals.

Based on the above, it is possible to distinguish intrinsic and extrinsic motivation on at least three counts. First, these two forms of motivation differ fundamentally from a teleological (or purposive) perspective (Bolles, 1967). Whereas for intrinsic motivation the purpose of participation lies within the process itself, that of extrinsic motivation focuses on benefits that may be obtained following participation. This distinction is often useful to better understand the motivation underlying the participation of individuals engaged in various activities, such as a fitness class. For instance, if we asked such individuals if they would pursue their engagement in the fitness class if they could take a "magic" pill that would allow them to lose weight and to be in great shape without exercising, intrinsically motivated individuals would probably say that they would still continue, whereas extrinsically motivated individuals would probably say that they would likely stop. This is because when intrinsically motivated, individuals are not involved in the activity for some external benefit, for instance, to lose weight but participate to enjoy themselves. They focus on the process, on the doing. Conversely, when extrinsically motivated, individuals engage in the activity in order to reach some end, such as losing weight and looking good. If they can achieve these ends more easily, they will gladly do it (see Vallerand, 1997, for a discussion on this issue).

A second useful distinction between intrinsic and extrinsic motivation pertains to the type of rewards that individuals seek to obtain when in these two motivational modes. When intrinsically motivated, individuals try to derive experiential rewards (e.g., enjoyment, pleasure) from their participation (Berlyne, 1971a, b). Thus, in such instances, the anticipation of positive affect would appear to represent an important motivational determinant. On the other hand, when extrinsically motivated, individuals seek to obtain social and material rewards from participation (Deci & Ryan, 1985; Harter, 1978). Approval from others (e.g., fame, recognition, popularity) would appear to loom large in the world of sports and physical activity (Vallerand et al., 1987). Subjects' perceptions as to whether or not such rewards will be forthcoming should play an important role in determining future participation in this particular activity (e.g., Bandura, 1986).

Finally, intrinsic and extrinsic motivation are also distinguished from a phenomenological perspective. Being intrinsically motivated leads individuals to experience pleasant emotions and to feel free and relaxed. They experience little pressure or tension, and they are focused on the task. Conversely, being extrinsically motivated leads individuals to feel tense and pressured. Indeed, if the goals they seek following participation of the activity are tied to their performance, they may have good reasons to be nervous. Social approval, for instance, depends on others and is, therefore, to a large extent outside of one's control. One can then understand the pressure that can be experienced when extrinsically motivated. However, as we will see below, different types of extrinsic motivation exist, some of which are self-determined and thus minimize the experience of tension and pressure.

Intrinsic and Extrinsic Motivation: One or Several Dimensions?

Although some researchers have posited the presence of a unidimensional intrinsic-motivation construct (e.g., Csikszentmihalyi & Nakamura, 1989; Lepper & Hoddell, 1989), certain theorists such as White (1959), Harter (1981a), and Deci (1975) have proposed that intrinsic motivation might be differentiated into more specific motives (a multidimensional perspective). More recently, Vallerand and his colleagues (Vallerand, 1997; Vallerand, Blais, Brière, & Pelletier, 1989; Vallerand et al., 1992, 1993) posited the existence of three types of intrinsic motivation: intrinsic motivation to know, intrinsic motivation toward accomplishments, and intrinsic motivation to experience stimulation. Because this differentiation has been used in the sport context (see Pelletier et al., 1995), we will elaborate on this tridimensional definition. The *intrinsic motivation to know* concept has a rich research tradition. It relates to constructs such as exploration (Berlyne, 1971b), learning goals (Dweck, 1985), intrinsic intellectuality (Lloyd & Barenblatt, 1984), intrinsic motivation to learn (Brophy, 1987), and intrinsic curiosity (Harter, 1981b). Thus, intrinsic motivation to know can be defined as engaging in an activity for the pleasure and the satisfaction that one experiences while learning, exploring, or trying

to understand something new. For instance, baseball players who play because they enjoy finding out more about the game display intrinsic motivation to know.

Intrinsic motivation toward accomplishments focuses on engaging in a given activity for the pleasure and satisfaction experienced while one is *attempting* to surpass oneself or to accomplish or create something. The focus is on the process of accomplishing something and not on the end result. This concept relates to constructs such as effectance motivation (White, 1959), mastery motivation (Kagan, 1972), and intrinsic challenge (Harter, 1981b). An example of this type of intrinsic motivation would be long distance runners who run for the intense pleasure they experience while trying to improve their time.

Finally, *intrinsic motivation to experience stimulation*, the third type of intrinsic motivation, is operative when one engages in an activity in order to experience pleasant sensations associated mainly with one's senses (e.g., sensory and aesthetic pleasure). This type of intrinsic motivation has been neglected in research but would appear to be related to constructs such as aesthetic experiences (Berlyne, 1971b), flow (Csikszentmihalyi, 1975, 1978, 1990; Jackson, 1995), and peak experiences (Maslow, 1970; McInman & Grove, 1991; Privette & Bundrick, 1991). Hang-gliders who engage in their activity because they enjoy the pleasant sensation they experience while their bodies soar through the air display this type of intrinsic motivation.

Research involving confirmatory factor analysis conducted in different contexts, such as education (Vallerand et al., 1989; Vallerand et al., 1992), work (Blais, Brière, Lachance, Riddle, & Vallerand, 1993), leisure (Pelletier, Vallerand, Blais, Brière, Green-Demers, 1996), and also sports (Brière et al., 1995; Pelletier et al., 1995), reveals that the three types of intrinsic motivation can be assessed separately. In addition, they have been found to lead to different consequences. For instance, it appears that individuals who favor one type of intrinsic motivation over another may prefer participating in sports activities that are congruent with such an orientation (Vallerand & Brière, 1990). Thus, someone who generally engages in sport activities out of the intrinsic motivation to experience stimulation would probably prefer parachuting to bowling.

Extrinsic motivation has also been considered from a multidimensional perspective. It was originally believed that extrinsic motivation pertained only to behaviors that were prompted by external sources of control (e.g., coaches, parents, other athletes) and were performed largely in the absence of self-determination. However, theory and research by Deci, R.M. Ryan and their colleagues (e.g., Chandler & Connell, 1987; Deci & Ryan, 1985; R.M. Ryan & Connell, 1989) have shown that different types of extrinsic motivation exist, some of which may be self-determined in nature. That is, some behaviors, although not engaged in out of pleasure (i.e., out of intrinsic motivation), may still be emitted by choice. Deci and Ryan (1985, 1991) have proposed four types of extrinsic motivation.

External regulation refers to extrinsic motivation as it generally appears in the literature. More specifically, when externally regulated, behavior is regulated through external means such as rewards and constraints. For instance, a football player might say "I'm going to tonight's practice because if I don't, the coach will be mad at me." In this case, the football player goes to practice in order to avoid punishment and is, therefore, externally regulated.

With *introjected regulation*, the individual begins to internalize the reasons for his or her actions. However, such internalization is not truly self-determined because it is limited to past external contingencies. It is as if individuals replace the external source of control by an internal one and start imposing pressure on themselves to ensure that the behavior will be emitted. For instance, tennis players who train because if they did not they would feel guilty and anxious, display introjected regulation. One can sense the self-imposed pressure that is the source of this type of motivation. Motivation is internal, but it is not self-determined.

It is only with the third type of extrinsic motivation, namely, *identified regulation*, that behavior is emitted out of choice and is thus self-determined. With this type of motivation, the behavior (e.g., participating in sport/physical activity) is highly valued and judged as important by the individual. It will thus be performed freely even if the activity is not pleasant in itself. For instance, a volleyball player might say "I want to improve my jumping ability. It is important for me. Thus, although I don't find this activity very interesting, I've decided to start training with weights." In this case, the volleyball player has freely chosen (without any external prodding —from the coach— or internal pressure — through guilt) to engage in weight training although this activity is not intrinsically motivating. It thus appears worthwhile to distinguish between these different types of motivation as they portray different realities of the world of sport, as well as lead to important differential predictions. For instance, volleyball players may not experience much fun while training with weights (at least not as much as the athlete who trains out of intrinsic motivation); however, they should feel much less pressure and tension than those who are motivated out of external and introjected regulation. We will return to this point in a later section.

Finally, the fourth and final type of extrinsic motivation, *integrated regulation*, also entails engaging in an activity out of choice. However, such choice is not simply limited at the activity level, but is now a harmonious part of the organization of the self. That is, one's choices are now made as a function of one's coherence with other aspects of the self. Thus, the integrated athlete may decide not to go for a beer after practice in order to study for tomorrow's exam.

Research has revealed that it is possible to assess these types of extrinsic motivation independently in diverse contexts, such as education, work, leisure, interpersonal relationships, and sports (Blais, Sabourin, Boucher, & Vallerand, 1990; Blais et al., 1993; Pelletier et al., 1995; Pelletier et al., 1996; R.M.

Ryan & Connell, 1989; Vallerand et al., 1989; Vallerand et al., 1992).[1] In addition, as in the case of intrinsic motivation, the different types of extrinsic motivation have been found to relate differently to determinants and consequences (see Vallerand, 1993, 1997, for reviews). For instance, research has shown that external regulation, and at times introjected regulation, have been associated with negative consequences, such as anxiety, lack of attention, and negative mood. Identified and integrated regulation, on the other hand, have been found to relate positively to cognitive, affective, and behavioral outcomes (see Deci & Ryan, 1991; Deci, Vallerand, Pelletier, & Ryan, 1991; R.M. Ryan, 1995; Vallerand, 1993, 1997, for reviews).

It should be noted that Deci and Ryan (1985) have also proposed a third construct, namely *amotivation*. This concept is similar to that of learned helplessness (Abramson, Seligman, & Teasdale, 1978) and refers to the relative absence of motivation, intrinsic or extrinsic. When amotivated, individuals do not perceive contingencies between their actions and the outcomes of their actions and no longer identify any good reasons to continue doing the activity.[2] Thus, the amotivation construct may prove helpful in predicting lack of persistence in sport and physical activity.

Thus, different types of motivation exist and are hypothesized to vary in terms of their inherent level of self-determination. As a result, it is assumed that these types of motivation can be ordered along a self-determination continuum (Deci & Ryan, 1985). From lower to higher levels of self-determination, they are: amotivation, external regulation, introjection, identification, integrated regulation, and intrinsic motivation. Research supports the validity of the self-determination continuum (e.g., Blais et al., 1990; Vallerand & Bissonnette, 1992). For instance research reveals that consequences are decreasingly positive as motivations move from intrinsic motivation to amotivation on the continuum (see Vallerand, 1997, for a review).

In sum, although some researchers assess intrinsic and extrinsic motivation as unitary constructs, recent advances have demonstrated that it is not only possible but also probably advisable to assess these in a multidimensional fashion (Vallerand, 1997). We now turn to another aspect of our discussion on the nature of intrinsic and extrinsic motivation, namely, the levels of generality of motivation.

Levels of Generality of Intrinsic and Extrinsic Motivation

It has long been recognized that there are two sides to the self: stability and change. Certain elements of the self seem stable and general in nature, whereas others appear context specific and may even vary as a function of the situation. Contem-

---

1. It should be noted that in most of our scales developed for adolescents and young adults, including the Sport Motivation Scale, we have not assessed the concept of integrated regulation. This is because results from our focus groups leading to scale development revealed that integrated reasons were not mentioned by participants. This may be due to the fact that at this age (between 16 and 20 years), the self is still developing. This may make it hard for these individuals to be motivated by integrated regulation because coherence between various evolving aspects of their self may be experienced less often than it is with older adults. In line with this reasoning, it was possible to develop an integrated regulation subscale for the Couple Motivation Scale (Blais et al., 1990) with older participants (mid 30s).

2. Pelletier and his colleagues (Stewart, Green-Demers, Pelletier, & Tuson, 1995; Tuson & Pelletier, 1992) have proposed a multidimensional taxonomy with respect to amotivation. It will not be discussed here because it has not been used in the development of sport instruments. See Vallerand (1997) for a discussion on this perspective.

porary approaches to the self have reconciled these opposing perspectives by recognizing that these different types of self-representations exist and can be integrated within hierarchical models of the self (e.g., Carver & Scheier, 1981; Harter, 1985; Kihlstrom & Cantor, 1984; McAdams, 1994). In a similar vein, Vallerand (1997) recently posited that intrinsic and extrinsic motivation exists at different levels of generality within the individual in a hierarchical fashion. More specifically, he proposes that motivation is represented at three levels of generality; these are the global, the contextual, and the situational levels (see Vallerand & Guay, 1996, for empirical support for this three-level hierarchy of intrinsic and extrinsic motivation). At the global level, motivation refers to a general motivational orientation to interact with the environment in an intrinsic and/or extrinsic way. It is akin to a personality dimension. Because this level has not been examined or applied in the sport context so far, we will not discuss it any further. However, it should be kept in mind that such a concept might be useful in future research as sport scientists focus on the determinants of contextual sport motivation (see Vallerand, 1997).

The contextual level is of particular interest for our present discussion. By context, we refer to distinct spheres of activities, such as education, work, interpersonal relationships, and the sport/physical activity setting (see Vallerand, 1997). In such life contexts, individuals have developed motivational orientations that, although still somewhat responsive to the individual's environment, are nevertheless relatively stable (Vallerand, 1997). This can be likened to a domain-specific motivational disposition. There has been extensive research in psychology at this second level of generality over the past 15 years (Deci & Ryan, 1985, 1991; Vallerand, 1997). Much of this research has assessed the relations between contextual motivation and contextual determinants and consequences. For instance, research in education (e.g., Grolnick, Deci & Ryan, 1991; Guay & Vallerand, in press; Vallerand, Fortier & Guay, 1997) has shown that contextual factors, such as the behavior of important social agents (e.g., parents, teachers, and school administrators), have an important impact on students' motivational orientation toward school. Social agents who facilitate a sense of autonomy and competence in students foster high levels of intrinsic motivation and identified regulation but low levels of external regulation and amotivation toward academic activities. Such a motivational pattern (that we call "a self-determined motivational profile"), in turn, leads to important achievement-related consequences, such as academic satisfaction (Vallerand et al., 1989; Vallerand et al., 1993), high performance (Fortier, Vallerand, & Guay, 1995; Guay & Vallerand, in press), and persistence in school (Vallerand & Bissonnette, 1992; Vallerand et al., 1997).

Similar results have been obtained in the sport and physical activity domain (see Frederick & Ryan, 1995; Vallerand & Reid, 1990, for reviews). For instance, it has been shown that the self-determined forms of motivation (intrinsic motivation and identified regulation) toward sport are positively related to autonomy-supportive behaviors from coaches (Pelletier et al., 1995) and physical education teachers (Goudas, Biddle, Fox, & Underwood, 1995), as well as to important outcomes, such as sport satisfaction, expended effort (e.g., Brière et al., 1995; Pelletier et al., 1995), and persistence (Fortier & Grenier, 1997;

Pelletier, Fortier, Vallerand, & Brière, 1997). On the other hand, non self-determined forms of motivation (i.e., amotivation and external regulation) are negatively related to such outcomes.

The situational level represents the third and last level of generality proposed by Vallerand (1997) and refers to the motivation that an individual experiences while he or she is currently engaging in an activity. This level captures the here and now or the "state" aspect of motivation. At this level, research has generally focused on the impact of situational factors such as feedback on the immediate motivation of the individual (e.g., Vallerand & Reid, 1984, 1988). Although research at this level of generality has largely been conducted in the laboratory, certain studies have been carried out in the field. Laboratory research has tended to assess situational motivation with a behavioral indicator of how much time the individual spends on the task during a subsequent free-time period (e.g., Orlick & Mosher, 1978), whereas field studies have generally used self-report questionnaires to assess intrinsic and extrinsic state motivation. For instance, using a self-report questionnaire (the Intrinsic Motivation Inventory; McAuley, Duncan, & Tammen, 1989), McAuley and Tammen (1989) have shown that physical education students who perceived that they had done well on a basketball game akin to that of the "H-O-R-S-E" game reported higher subsequent levels of situational intrinsic motivation than did those who thought that they had done poorly.

It is important to consider the level of generality of motivation measures for at least two reasons. A first reason pertains to psychometric properties of the scale to be assessed. Scales at the situational and contextual levels should not be expected to behave in the same fashion. For instance, contextual measures should display a relatively high level of temporal stability (as exemplified by high positive test-retest correlations), but this should not be the case for situational measures. This is because contextual measures reflect a relatively enduring broad motivational orientation toward sport, whereas situational measures assess state motivation that may fluctuate to a large extent as a function of situational factors.

A second reason why the level of generality is important to consider is that it may clarify our assessment of the scale's construct validity. Construct validity is typically assessed by testing relationships between the scale being assessed and various other instruments that would be predicted by theory. For instance, in light of self-determination theory (Deci & Ryan, 1985, 1991), one would expect perceptions of competence to be positively related to intrinsic motivation. Thus, the construct validity of a scale that would not show such a relationship should be questioned. However, if a researcher assessed perceived competence at the contextual level (e.g., one's general perceptions of competence toward swimming) and intrinsic motivation at the situational level (e.g., one's state motivation toward swimming) after a disastrous performance and did not obtain a significant relationship, would this entail poor construct validity for the scale? Not necessarily. Construct validity cannot be properly ascertained in such a situation because there is a confound in the level of generality of the two constructs. Thus, the level of generality must be taken into account in order to better assess the validity of existing measures.

On the Relationship Between
Intrinsic and Extrinsic Motivation

As we have seen previously, certain findings in the literature indicate that receiving extrinsic rewards to engage in interesting activities lead to a decrement of intrinsic motivation (e.g., Deci, 1971; Orlick & Mosher, 1978). According to some theorists (e.g., Harter, 1981a; Lepper & Greene, 1978), these results support the perspective that intrinsic and extrinsic motivation entertain an interactional relationship. Specifically, such a position proposes that a high level of extrinsic motivation (as produced by extrinsic factors such as rewards) is necessarily associated with a low level of intrinsic motivation and vice versa, that a high level of intrinsic motivation entails a low level of extrinsic motivation. This position therefore assumes that one is mainly intrinsically or extrinsically motivated toward a given activity; one cannot be motivated by high levels of both intrinsic and extrinsic motivation.

This assumption is in direct contrast with another position that states that intrinsic and extrinsic motivation have an additive relationship (e.g., Atkinson, 1964; Porter & Lawler, 1968). According to this position, it is proposed that intrinsic and extrinsic reasons for engaging in an activity converge in producing a higher level of motivation than any of these two types of motivation alone.

The above positions have clear implications for the assessment of intrinsic and extrinsic motivation. If one adheres to an interactional position, intrinsic and extrinsic motivation should be viewed as the two endpoints of a single continuum. Because extrinsic motivation is viewed as the mirror image of intrinsic motivation, one may simply need to assess intrinsic motivation to determine both types of motivation. Thus, according to the interactional position, if athletes report a high level of intrinsic motivation, we can infer that they also have a low level of extrinsic motivation. Knowledge of their intrinsic motivation also leads to information about their extrinsic motivation. Another assessment strategy in line with the interactional position consists in asking individuals to select between intrinsic and extrinsic alternatives to determine their level of motivation. This approach is possible because the interactional position posits that it is not possible for both intrinsic and extrinsic motivation to be high. When one is high, the other is expected to be low and vice versa. Thus, selecting one type of alternative (intrinsic or extrinsic) allows the researcher to understand the underlying motivational dynamics of sport participants.

On the other hand, proponents of the additive position posit that intrinsic and extrinsic motivation lie on two different continua. Knowledge of individuals' position on the intrinsic motivation continuum does not determine their position on the extrinsic motivation continuum. This is because an additive relationship between the two types of motivation requires independent knowledge of intrinsic and extrinsic motivation. It is thus clear, from the additive perspective, that intrinsic and extrinsic motivation need to be assessed independently with different scales.

Our own position is that the nature of the relation between intrinsic and extrinsic motivation depends on the type of extrinsic motivation involved, as well as the level of generality of the constructs. At the contextual level, athletes may indicate that they generally engage in sports for a number of reasons, including intrinsic and extrinsic ones. Thus, relationships may be additive, although this should be mostly the case for identified regulation and intrinsic motivation because these motivations involve high levels of self-determination. However, relationships between intrinsic motivation and introjected and external regulation should be orthogonal, or slightly negative (see Brière et al., 1995; Pelletier et al., 1995). The picture at the situational level (i.e., at one given point in time) is likely to be somewhat different. Here one would expect athletes to report a predominant type of motivation, especially if salient situational factors (e.g., success or failure feedback) are present. Thus, the relationships among the different types of motivation should be strengthened. Consequently, intrinsic motivation should have a strong additive relationship with identified regulation, but a strong interactional (or negative) one with external regulation. Because the relationship between intrinsic and extrinsic motivation can be both additive and interactive, it is thus essential that both types of motivation be assessed independently. As we will see below, this is the case for certain scales only.

EVALUATION OF MEASURES OF INTRINSIC AND EXTRINSIC MOTIVATION IN SPORT AND PHYSICAL ACTIVITY

In this section, a critical review of the different measures used to assess intrinsic and extrinsic motivation in sport research is conducted. The main criterion that has guided the selection of the measures presented in this section is that the measures should be fully developed instruments that have gone through validation steps. Isolated items (or ad hoc scales) dealing with enjoyment, liking, and volunteering to return on the task will not be discussed because they have not gone through validation procedures.[3] The second criterion used in the present review is that the scale must have been used in sport research, published or unpublished.

In light of our discussion on the definition of intrinsic and extrinsic motivation, it becomes possible to classify the different measures. Thus, measures can vary in terms of the construct(s) being assessed (only intrinsic motivation vs. both intrinsic motivation and extrinsic motivation); the level of generality of the measure (situational level vs. contextual level); and finally, the dimensionality aspect of the instrument (unidimensional vs. multidimensional). This classification appears in Table 1. As can be seen, eight measures will be discussed in this section: the Behavioral Measure (e.g., Deci, 1971), the Mayo Task Reaction Questionnaire (Mayo, 1977), the Intrinsic Motivation Inventory (McAuley, et al., 1989), the Situational Motivation Scale (Guay & Vallerand, 1995, 1997), the Sport Intrinsic Motivation Scale (Dwyer, 1988), the Intrinsic/Extrinsic Motivational Orientation Scale for Sports (Weiss, Bredemeier, & Shewchuk, 1985), the Sport Motivation Scale (Brière et al., 1995; Pelletier et al., 1995), and the Pictorial Mo-

---

3. See Weinberg and Ragan (1979) for an example of such items.

tivation Scale (Reid, Poulin, & Vallerand, 1994). These measures are presented in two sections. The first section reviews situational measures, whereas the second section evaluates contextual measures of intrinsic and extrinsic sport motivation. Each section will be further divided in terms of unidimensional and multidimensional measures. For each instrument, we present (a) a description of the instrument, (b) the conceptual/theoretical rationale underlying scale development, (c) the available evidence concerning its psychometric properties (i.e., validity and reliability), and finally, (d) the various problems associated with the specific measure.

Situational Measures of Intrinsic Motivation

In this section, four situational measures of intrinsic motivation will be discussed. These measures were developed to assess participants' immediate or current reactions/feelings toward an activity/sport in which they were engaged. As discussed in the preceding section, situational measures refer to a "state" measure of motivation and do not reflect in any sense a dispositional orientation of the individual, be it at the contextual or global level.

Unidimensional Measures

Measures assessed in the present section are situational measures that are unidimensional in nature. That is, they assess only one general aspect of intrinsic motivation. Two such measures are discussed: the behavioral measure (e.g., Deci, 1971) and the Task Reaction Questionnaire (Mayo, 1977).

The behavioral measure. The behavioral measure (also called the free-choice period) has been extensively used in laboratory research in psychology (e.g., Deci, 1971; Deci, Eghrari, Patrick, & Leone, 1994; Lepper et al., 1973), as well as in early

intrinsic motivation research in sport and physical activity (e.g., Orlick & Mosher, 1978; Thomas & Tennant, 1978). This measure is observational in nature and is taken once the experiment is declared "officially" over by the experimenter. More specifically, once the participant completes the task, the experimenter presents a pretext for leaving the room and leaves the participant on his or her own. The participant is then surreptitiously observed through a one-way mirror, and the time spent on the task is recorded. The more time spent on the task, the higher the inferred level of intrinsic motivation. The assumption underlying this measure is that "a person is intrinsically motivated if he (she) performs an activity for no apparent reason except the activity itself" (Deci, 1972, p. 113). Thus, if participants are intrinsically motivated toward the activity, then they should be inclined to engage in the task when they do not have to. Participants who are extrinsically motivated, on the other hand, should not return to the task because there is nothing to be gained from such a participation. Indeed, no future reward should be forthcoming following participation.

Because this measure is observational, there are few data on its psychometric properties. In terms of reliability, it has been found to exhibit high levels of interrater reliability. For instance, in a recent study wherein the task involved fine motor skills (a ball-rolling task called the labyrinth task), the free-choice behavior of 60 subjects was videotaped. It was later coded by two trained assistants. An interrater reliability (Pearson correlation) of .99 was obtained (Diblasio, Chantal, Vallerand, & Provencher, 1995). It thus appears that the behavioral measure lends itself well to reliable measurement.

However, evidence for the validity of this measure is mixed. Some studies have revealed that this measure has good construct validity. For instance, in line with self-determination

Table 1

Measures of Intrinsic and Extrinsic Motivation in Sport Research

	INTRINSIC MOTIVATION		INTRINSIC AND EXTRINSIC MOTIVATION & AMOTIVATION
	UNIDIMENSIONAL	MULTIDIMENSIONAL	MULTIDIMENSIONAL
SITUATIONAL MEASURES	The Free-Choice Period (Deci, 1971) The Task Reaction Questionnaire (Mayo, 1977)	The Intrinsic Motivation Inventory (McCauley et al., 1989)	The Situational Motivation Scale (Guay & Vallerand, 1995, 1997)
CONTEXTUAL MEASURES	The Sports Intrinsic Motivation Scale (Dwyer, 1988)	The Motivational Orientation in Sport Scale (Weiss et al., 1985)	The Sport Motivation Scale (Pelletier et al., 1995) The Pictorial Motivation Scale (Reid et al., 1994)

theory (Deci & Ryan, 1985, 1991), which posits that feelings of competence should increase intrinsic motivation, it has been found that individuals who receive indications to the effect that they are competent at the activity spend more time on the task than do individuals who experience failure (e.g., Rosenfield, Folger, & Adelman, 1980). In addition, as predicted by this theory, situations that lead individuals to feel coerced to engage in activities or to experience a lack of choice, such as being told what to do, having to compete when one does not want to, engaging in the activity in order to receive a reward, lead to less time spent on the task during a free-choice period (see Deci & Ryan, 1985, 1991).

However, certain researchers and theorists have come to question the validity of the free-choice measure from a conceptual perspective. For instance, Bandura (1977) criticizes this measure for its circularity. He argues that a given construct cannot serve as a measure of motivation as well as a motivational consequence. In the present case, time spent on the task serves as both the measure of intrinsic motivation and as the consequence of intrinsic motivation, namely, subsequent behavioral engagement (or time spent) on the activity. One can then see the circularity in this reasoning. Behavior cannot be used to assess the underlying intrinsic motivation of the individual and, at the same time, the consequence of such a motivational force. In addition, recent research suggests that the free-choice period does not always measure intrinsic motivation. For instance, it has been shown that internalized extrinsic motivation, in the form of introjected (R.M. Ryan, Koestner, & Deci , 1991) and identified regulation (Deci et al., 1994), can also lead to time spent on the task during a free-choice period. Thus, the construct validity of the behavioral measure as an indicator of intrinsic motivation needs to be reexamined.

In addition to problems of validity, the behavioral measure is plagued by other limitations. First, it represents a unidimensional measure of intrinsic motivation. Because different types of intrinsic motivation have been postulated (e.g., Harter, 1981b; Vallerand et al., 1989; Vallerand et al., 1992), this measure would not lend itself well to experiments dealing with this multidimensional perspective. Second, this measure does not assess extrinsic motivation. This represents an important consideration, especially if one is interested in determining the relation (i.e., additive vs interactive) between intrinsic and extrinsic motivation. Third, the very nature of the behavioral measure poses some methodological problems. For instance, it generally leads to skewed data and oftentimes to bimodal distributions where several participants spend a lot of time on the task, and others very little or none at all (see Farr, Vance, & McIntyre, 1977). The presence of bimodal distributions raises issues of statistical analysis as nonparametric statistics should then be used (see Siegel, 1956). It thus appears that the behavioral measure represents a gross measure of non differentiated motivation. People are either motivated (high time spent on the task) or not (no or little time on the task). Last, the behavioral measure of intrinsic motivation is not easy to employ in field settings. For example, using a free-choice period to assess intrinsic motivation after a demanding athletic event would be difficult.

In sum, the use of the behavioral measure as an indicator of situational intrinsic motivation would appear to be problematic.

Clearly more research is needed on the behavioral measure, especially as pertains to its validity. One interesting avenue for subsequent work has been suggested by Reeve and Deci (1996). In their study, these researchers had participants engage in interesting puzzles. During the free-choice period, participants had the choice of engaging in the same puzzles that they solved during the experiment or engaging in new puzzles. According to Reeve and Deci, only time spent on the new puzzles should be considered as a true index of intrinsic motivation because that choice refers to the willingness to seek out and master new challenges. Their results supported their hypothesis as time spent on the new puzzles correlated positively ($r= .32$) with a self-report measure of interest and enjoyment and negatively to a measure of frustration ($r= -.28$). On the other hand, time spent on the old puzzles correlated positively ($r= .36$) to a measure of frustration, but not with interest and enjoyment. Thus, according to Reeve and Deci, it is not just engagement on any task that is meaningful from an intrinsic motivation perspective, but only time spent on pertinent new material. Although these results provide some support for the authors' position, it should be mentioned that the correlations obtained in this study were of moderate magnitude at best. Future research is needed to further examine the Reeve and Deci position in order to determine if these results are robust.

The Mayo Task Reaction Questionnaire (1977). The Mayo Task Reaction Questionnaire (TRQ) also represents a unidimensional situational measure of intrinsic motivation. As part of his doctoral dissertation, Mayo (1977) designed a questionnaire to assess participants' immediate intrinsic motivation toward a cognitive task, namely, the soma puzzles. Since then, the TRQ has been modified to be used with different sports and physical activities, including the stabilometer (Vallerand & Reid, 1984, 1988), juggling (Anshel, Weinberg, & Jackson, 1992), and a hockey-related task (Vallerand, 1983). This scale is composed of 23 items (scored on a 7-point scale) that reflect different elements related to intrinsic motivation, such as interest and enjoyment toward the task, feelings of accomplishment, challenge, and competence. A sample item is "My feelings while improving on the stabilometer task really aroused my interest in it."

The conceptual rationale for the scale is that when intrinsically motivated, individuals are supposed to experience positive feelings of interest, enjoyment, challenge and competence, as well as a state of concentration on the task. Although such a conceptual perspective should have led to a multidimensional operational definition of intrinsic motivation, the TRQ has been constructed in a way to capture overall intrinsic motivation. Thus, only one scale has been developed.

Some support has been obtained for the psychometric properties of the TRQ. For instance, it has been shown to have high internal consistency with Cronbach alphas typically in the low .90s (Mayo, 1977; Vallerand & Reid, 1984, 1988) and high split-half reliability (.96 [Fisher, 1978]). Evidence for the construct validity of the TRQ has emerged in line with predictions stemming from self-determination theory (see Fisher, 1978; Mayo, 1977; Vallerand, 1983; Vallerand & Reid, 1984, 1988). For example, employing the TRQ, Vallerand and Reid (1984) showed that positive performance feedback increases intrinsic motivation, whereas negative feedback decreases it. Furthermore, consistent with self-determination theory, these researchers showed (through path analysis) that perceptions of competence mediated the effect of feedback on intrinsic motivation.

Although some of the psychometric properties of the TRQ would appear to be satisfactory, there are a certain number of problems related to this measure. The scale is rather long (23 items), especially if one considers that it measures only one dimension of intrinsic motivation. Furthermore, no evidence has been reported on the factor structure of the scale. It is thus difficult to determine if the scale is truly unidimensional. Similarly to the behavioral measure, it cannot be used to test hypotheses dealing with a multidimensional perspective of intrinsic motivation. Also, the TRQ does not assess extrinsic motivation,[4] thus preventing comparison with intrinsic motivation. Finally, the TRQ measures intrinsic motivation "indirectly" by assessing different affective and cognitive states that should be experienced by individuals when intrinsically motivated. In so doing, however, Mayo (1977) has incorporated in the TRQ items that refer to either determinants (variables that influence intrinsic motivation, e.g., feelings of competence and autonomy) or consequences (variables that result from motivation, e.g., concentration on the task, feelings of enjoyment) of intrinsic motivation (see Deci & Ryan, 1991; Vallerand, 1993, 1997, on this issue). Inferring motivation from motivational determinants and outcomes seriously compromises the construct validity of the TRQ (see Bandura, 1977). In addition, it leads to important confounds when attempting to relate the TRQ to determinants and consequences of intrinsic motivation. For instance, if positive relationships are obtained, is it because of correct hypotheses or simply because of shared measurement variance among the instruments assessing intrinsic motivation, determinants, and consequences? Possibly because of the above problems, the TRQ has been used much less in sport research in recent years.

Multidimensional Measures

Only one scale is known to assess situational intrinsic motivation from a multidimensional perspective. This scale is the Intrinsic Motivation Inventory (McAuley et al., 1989).

The Intrinsic Motivation Inventory (IMI; McAuley et al., 1989). The IMI represents a direct sport application of R.M. Ryan's (1982) IMI developed for laboratory tasks. In their original study, McAuley et al. (1989), applied Ryan's IMI to a basketball shooting game akin to HORSE. Since then, this adaptation of the IMI has been used in an interscholastic basketball context (Seifriz, Duda & Chi, 1992) and has been applied to other sports such as tennis (Duda, Chi, Newton, Walling, & Catley, 1995). This scale (there are 16 and 18-item versions) was designed to assess four underlying dimensions of intrinsic motivation in a specific situation: interest-enjoyment (e.g., "Playing the basketball game was fun"); perceived competence (e.g., "I am pretty skilled at basketball"); effort-importance (e.g., "I tried very hard while playing basketball"); and pressure-tension (e.g., "I felt tense while playing the basketball game"). Thus, similar to the Mayo TRQ (1977), the underlying rationale of the IMI is that when intrinsically motivated, individuals should be experiencing such affective/cognitive states and exhibiting these types of behaviors (e.g., effort). Thus, to the extent that they do report experiencing these states or exhibiting these behaviors, participants are thought to display high levels of intrinsic motivation.

Overall, results on the reliability of the scale reveal that most subscales are reliable. More specifically, internal consistency of the four subscales as assessed by Cronbach alphas has ranged from .63 (pressure/tension) to .91 (enjoyment/interest). [See Duda et al. (1995), McAuley et al. (1989); Seifriz et al. (1992).] It should be mentioned that a Cronbach alpha of .63 is considered somewhat low, although the pressure/tension subscale is made up of only 4 items. Because the alpha coefficient is biased against scales composed of a low number of items (see Smith, Schutz, Smoll, & Ptacek, 1995; Vallerand et al., 1997, on this issue), one should be careful before concluding that a scale is unreliable. Nevertheless, future research on the reliability of the pressure/tension subscale would appear in order.

There is some support for the construct validity of the scale because the IMI has yielded results in line with existing theories. For instance, it has been found that one's perceptions of having done well or poorly has a more meaningful impact on intrinsic motivation than does actually winning or losing (McAuley & Tammen, 1989). Also, as would be expected by various achievement goal theories (e.g., Dweck & Elliott, 1988; Nicholls, 1984), Duda et al. (1995) found that intrinsic motivation, as measured by the IMI, was positively related to task orientation, but negatively to ego orientation (see Duda, 1993; Duda & Whitehead, this volume).

However, data on the factorial validity (Anastasi, 1968) of the IMI are much less impressive. Using confirmatory factor analysis (CFA), McAuley et al. (1989) tested several models. The hypothesized model (a second-order factor with intrinsic motivation being subdivided into four first-order factors) was found to be the best model. Inspection of the various fit indexes reported, however, would appear to indicate that the fit for the proposed model was not adequate. First, chi-square values were all highly significant (with CFAs, nonsignificant chi-square values indicate that there is no difference between the hypothesized model and the observed data, thereby providing support for the proposed model). Second, the goodness of fit (GFI) provided by the LISREL program (Joreskog & Sorbom, 1989) was unacceptably low (.80). Generally, only GFIs above .90 are considered acceptable. Third, the delta value that compares the fit of the model to that of the null model (Bentler & Bonett, 1980) was also unacceptable (.77; whereas values of .90 are the norm). Finally, the root mean square residual was much too high (RMSR = .11). Typically, only values below .10 are seen as acceptable. Even the authors themselves concluded "...the magnitude of the RMSR and some of the residual correlations suggest that alternative models may provide a more accurate reproduction of the original correlations" (p. 54). Thus, while fit

---

4. In his dissertation, Mayo has also developed an extrinsic motivation scale. It pertains mostly to participants' motivation to do the task in order to receive social approval from the experimenter. However, this scale has not been used in sport (or any research other than that reported in Mayo's dissertation). For this reason, this scale will not be discussed.

indices from confirmatory factor analyses may be lower for situational scales, those from the IMI are surprisingly low and cast doubt on the factorial validity of this scale.

In addition to problems with the factorial validity of the scale, the IMI (McAuley et al., 1989) shows some of the limitations demonstrated by the Mayo TRQ (1977). Specifically, in addition to assessing elements closely related to intrinsic motivation (i.e., interest), it also assesses determinants (e.g., perceptions of competence) and consequences (e.g., effort) of intrinsic motivation. Using path analysis, Williams and Gill (1995) recently showed that some of the elements assessed by the IMI may influence each other. They found that perceptions of competence positively influenced interest, which in turn, determined effort. It would thus appear that the IMI includes elements that go beyond intrinsic motivation per se. As mentioned earlier, this can lead to some important problems with the interpretation of research findings involving intrinsic motivation and its determinants and outcomes. This confound in assessment may also explain why appropriate fit indexes could not be obtained in the CFA conducted by McAuley et al. (1989). Furthermore, the IMI does not assess extrinsic motivation, and this limits the type of research that can be conducted with the scale. For example, it would be impossible to use the IMI on its own to conduct research on the relationship between intrinsic and extrinsic motivation.

Although the IMI may suffer from some limitations, we would like to underscore that it is a flexible instrument. Indeed, it can be easily employed in both laboratory and field settings, where it can be readily modified for almost any type of sports or physical activities. However, future research on the reliability and validity of the IMI is warranted in order to clarify some of the issues raised above.

The Situational Motivation Scale (Guay & Vallerand, 1995, 1997). So far, we have seen that situational measures of intrinsic and extrinsic motivation show several limitations (e.g., they assess other elements than simply intrinsic motivation, they do not assess extrinsic motivation, etc.). It thus appears that a measure that does not show these limitations would represent a valuable addition to our current methodology. Recently, Guay and Vallerand (1995, 1997) have developed a situational scale of intrinsic and extrinsic motivation, the Situational Motivation Scale (SIMS). The SIMS measures extrinsic motivation multidimensionally. However, because the scale is used at the situational level and thus needs to be short, it assesses intrinsic motivation and amotivation unidimensionally. The SIMS is not sport specific but is worded such that it can be used in most situations (sport and nonsport), including laboratory and field settings. In line with some of the other scales that we have developed, such as the Sport Motivation Scale (Brière et al., 1995; Pelletier et al., 1995), the SIMS focuses on the reasons explaining why participants engage in a given activity. However, because it is a situational scale, the SIMS asks the question "Why are you *currently* engaged in this activity ?." The items represent potential reasons explaining task engagement. The SIMS is made up of 16 items and contains four subscales (of four items each), namely, intrinsic motivation (as a unidimensional construct), identified regulation, external regulation, and amotivation.

Although the SIMS is still in the process of being validated, preliminary findings reveal that it already possesses some sound psychometric properties. For instance, results from two studies dealing with educational (Study 1, Guay & Vallerand, 1995) and leisure activities (Study 2, Guay & Vallerand, 1995) revealed adequate reliability values (Cronbach alphas ranging from .76 to .91). In addition, results from exploratory (Guay & Vallerand, 1995) and confirmatory (Guay & Vallerand, 1997) factor analyses supported the four-factor structure. Finally, the different subscales have been found to be related as expected to different motivational determinants (perceived competence and autonomy) and consequences (concentration, positive affect, and behavioral intentions to engage in the activity in the future). The intrinsic motivation subscale yielded the most positive relations to the selected antecedents and consequence variables, followed by identified regulation. Amotivation revealed the most negative correlations, followed by external regulation.

The SIMS has also been used recently in sport and exercise research. In a first study (Study 2, Blanchard & Vallerand, 1996) conducted with college basketball players (*n*=181), it was found

Table 2
Correlations Between the Situational Motivation Scale and Determinants and Consequences in a Sport Situation[1]

	Determinants			*Consequences*	
	Perceptions of Relatedness	Perceptions of Competence	Perceptions of Autonomy	Concentration	Emotions
Intrinsic motivation (alpha=.87)	.53	.50	.34	.37	.74
Identified regulation (alpha=.72)	.45	.35	.31	.45	.45
External regulation (alpha=.78)	.06	.03	-.24	-.04	.07
Amotivation (alpha=.81)	-.31	-.29	-.44	-.51	-.24

1. From Blanchard and Vallerand (1996).

that the four subscales showed adequate levels of reliability, with Cronbach alpha values ranging from .72 (identified regulation) to .87 (intrinsic motivation). In addition, the four subscales were correlated as expected with variables assessing situational determinants (i.e., perceptions of competence, autonomy, and relatedness) and consequences (i.e., concentration and emotions) of motivation. Thus, the most positive correlations were obtained with the intrinsic motivation subscale, followed by the identified regulation subscale. Correlations with the external regulation subscale were either negative or close to zero. Finally, correlations with the amotivation subscale were strongly negative. These findings are reported in Table 2. Results from the Blanchard and Vallerand study were replicated in a second study with individuals (n=274) engaged in a weight-loss program based on exercise and dietary change (Cadorette et al., 1996). Similar results have been obtained by Kowal and Fortier (in press)

The findings from the above studies provide preliminary support for the construct validity of the SIMS. However, the SIMS also shows some limitations. First, we have no data on how the scale relates to actual behavior, an important outcome in sport research. Thus, future research should address this issue. In addition, the scale only assesses intrinsic motivation in a unidimensional fashion. Future research is therefore needed in order to determine if the SIMS should assess intrinsic motivation from a multidimensional perspective.

Contextual Measures of Intrinsic and Extrinsic Motivation Toward Sport

Over the past 10 years, much research (e.g., Brustad, 1988; Fortier, Vallerand, Brière, & Provencher, 1995) has examined contextual sport motivation. As indicated in our discussion on levels of generality, contextual measures assess one's usual motivational orientation toward a specific domain (e.g., sport). That is, they measure the general motivational stance that the individual adopts toward engagement in these activities. Four contextual measures of intrinsic and extrinsic motivation have been developed in the sport and exercise domain. The first one, the Sport Intrinsic Motivation Scale (Dwyer, 1988) measures motivation from a unidimensional perspective. Two others, the Motivational Orientation in Sports Scale (Weiss et al., 1985) and the Sport Motivation Scale (Brière et al., 1995; Pelletier et al., 1995) represent multidimensional measures of sport intrinsic and extrinsic motivation. Finally, the last scale has been constructed to be used with special populations and is called the Pictorial Motivation Scale (Reid, Poulin, & Vallerand, 1994). These instruments are presented below.

Unidimensional Measures

The Sport Intrinsic Motivation Scale (Dwyer, 1988). Dwyer developed this scale to assess contextual sport intrinsic motivation. It consists of 40 items, 20 positive and 20 negative, that measure one dimension of intrinsic motivation toward sport. Respondents are asked to indicate the extent to which they agree on a 5-point scale with statements such as "I like the feelings of competence the sport gives me" and "I feel good inside when I participate in sport." In terms of reliability, results from three studies (Dwyer, 1988) revealed acceptable internal consistency

values (alphas in the .90s) and acceptable temporal stability levels (a 4-week test-retest correlation of .85).

Although reliability indices for this scale appear satisfactory, results with respect to the factorial validity of the scale are less clear. More specifically, results from principal component analyses reported in Dwyer's dissertation revealed the presence of several factors (varying from study to study). Nevertheless, Dwyer (1988) decided to focus exclusively on Factor 1, which explained only approximately 30% of the variance. It should also be mentioned that no confirmatory factor analysis has been conducted on the Sport Intrinsic Motivation Scale. Nevertheless, it would be very surprising if all 40 items could load on only one factor. In addition, very little evidence exists concerning the construct validity of this scale. Although Dwyer reported a positive correlation between the scale and self-reported engagement in sport ($r = .15$), no other information pertaining to the construct validity of the scale is available.

It should be noted that in addition to the limitations just mentioned, this scale displays some of the weaknesses underscored with the other instruments. First, similarly to the TRQ (Mayo, 1977) and the IMI (McAuley et al., 1989), this scale uses motivational determinants (e.g. perceptions of competence) and motivational consequences (e.g., emotions) to infer intrinsic motivation. Second, the scale limits itself to intrinsic motivation and does not assess extrinsic motivation. Because of the above limitations, it is not surprising that the scale has not led to published research. Unless extensive validation research is done on this scale, it appears unlikely that it will be used in future investigations.

Multidimensional Measures

The Motivational Orientation in Sports Scale (MOSS - Weiss et al., 1985). The MOSS is adapted from a measure developed by Harter (1981b) to assess motivation in classroom settings. Harter's original scale, the Motivational Orientation in the Classroom Scale, is based on an interactional model of motivation which assumes that individuals having a high level of one type of motivation (i.e., extrinsic motivation) should necessarily have a low level of the other type (i.e., intrinsic motivation). Thus, for each item, participants must decide between an intrinsic or an extrinsic alternative. In addition, they must indicate if this alternative is *sort of true* or *really true* for them, thereby leading to a 4-point scale for each item.

The MOSS contains 30 items equally divided into five subscales. These scales assess five elements thought to be related to intrinsic motivation: curiosity, challenge, independent mastery, judgment, and criteria. These five dimensions are based on Harter's (1981a) motivational model and are hypothesized to form two clusters: a first cluster that deals specifically with intrinsic motivation (the curiosity, challenge, and mastery dimensions) and a second cluster that taps a cognitive-informational structure (the judgment and criteria dimensions). Harter's position (1981a) assumes that intrinsically motivated individuals display high levels of curiosity, challenge, and independent mastery in their relationships with the school environment. Weiss et al. (1985) accepted at face value that this would also apply to sport and physical settings.

Weiss et al. (1985) adapted Harter's (1981b) scale to the physical activity domain by rewording the 30 items so that they were appropriate for the sport context. In general, this entailed changing the term teacher to physical education teacher and changing the term work to skills. A sample item is "Some kids work on skills to learn how to do them" BUT "Other kids prefer easy sport skills that they are sure they can do". Participants must choose the alternative that characterizes them best as well as the extent to which it does (i.e., "sort of true" or "really true").

Since the initial study (Weiss et al., 1985), the MOSS has been used at least in two other published studies (Biddle & Brooke, 1992; Brustad, 1988). Based on the published information, it appears that the internal consistency of the different subscales is uneven. Cronbach alpha values ranging from .61 to .81 have been reported (Biddle & Brooke, 1992; Brustad, 1988; Weiss et al., 1985). It would appear that the challenge subscale consistently yields high alpha values (in the .80s), whereas the curiosity and judgment subscales display lower levels (in the .60s). These levels are slightly below what is considered acceptable (i.e., alpha = .70), especially in light of the fact that each subscale is made up of seven items. The temporal stability of the scale has not been assessed to date, but one would expect moderate to high test-retest correlations because the MOSS represents a contextual measure of intrinsic motivation.

The factorial validity of the MOSS has been examined and appears questionable. Weiss et al. (1985) reported the results of a CFA ($n = 155$) that clearly indicated that the hypothesized five-factor model did not fit the data well (highly significant chi-square values and very low goodness-and adjusted goodness-of-fit indexes, respectively .75 and .71). They subsequently conducted an exploratory factor analysis and obtained six factors. Biddle and Brooke (1992) administered the MOSS to 122 British children. They conducted an exploratory factor analysis and also did not obtain support for the Harter five-factor model. It appears that the scale as applied to sport does not possess adequate factorial validity.

There is some support for the construct validity of the scale. For example, Weiss et al. (1985) found developmental trends in some of the subscales of the MOSS similar to those reported by Harter (1981b) who found decreased intrinsic motivation toward school over time. In addition, Brustad (1988) reported that the mastery subscale positively predicted the enjoyment of boys and girls in a youth basketball league. Finally, Biddle and Brooke (1992) found that a composite measure of intrinsic motivation (challenge, curiosity, and mastery combined) was positively correlated (mean $r = .46$) with a physical performance measure (the 20-meter progressive shuttle run), whereas the cognitive-informational subscales (criteria and judgment) were not (mean $r = .32$, n.s.). All of these findings are in line with Harter's (1981a) theoretical predictions that posit that the true motivational dimension of the scale is assessed through the challenge, curiosity, and mastery subscales. The other two subscales (criteria and judgment) mainly tap participants' cognitive perspective. Thus, physical performance and enjoyment should be more strongly related to the motivational subscales than to the cognitive subscales.

In addition to the factor structure problems just mentioned, the MOSS also has a number of other weaknesses. For instance,

this scale measures only one type of extrinsic motivation, that is a specific type of external regulation: motivation for social approval (see Harter, 1981b, p. 311). As mentioned previously, different forms of extrinsic motivation exist (Deci & Ryan, 1985). In order to get a more complete picture of an individual's motivational profile, it would be important that the other types of extrinsic motivation (i.e., introjected and identified regulation) be assessed.

Furthermore, we would argue that the MOSS, as well as Harter's (1981b) Motivational Orientation in the Classroom Scale, is based on an invalid theoretical conceptualization of intrinsic and extrinsic motivation. Specifically, it is based on an interactional model of motivation that assumes that individuals who have a high level of one type of motivation (i.e., extrinsic motivation) should *necessarily* have a low level of the other type (i.e., intrinsic motivation). Much research (e.g., Amabile, Hill, Hennessey, & Tighe, 1994; Blais et al., 1990; Vallerand & Bissonnette, 1992) has proven this assumption to be incorrect. Rather, current research suggests that the relationship between intrinsic and extrinsic motivation is dependent on the type of extrinsic motivation involved. For instance, with external regulation, the two constructs (i.e., intrinsic motivation and extrinsic motivation) are sometimes negatively related, but typically, are orthogonal (Amabile et al., 1994; Pelletier et al., 1995). On the other hand, intrinsic motivation and identified regulation are positively related (e.g., Brière et al., 1995, [mean $r = .45$]; Pelletier et al., 1995 [mean $r = .40$]). Experimental research by Hennessey and her colleagues has even shown that under certain circumstances, external regulation and intrinsic motivation can combine additively and lead to higher levels of creativity than those obtained under intrinsically motivating conditions only (Hennessey, Amabile, & Martinage, 1989; Hennessey & Zbikowski, 1993). Finally, Harter herself (Harter & Jackson, 1992) has recognized the limitations of the intrinsic-extrinsic motivation bipolar continuum and has demonstrated that considering these motivations as orthogonal can lead to interesting classifications (e.g., someone can be seen as being motivated out of intrinsic or extrinsic motivation alone or by both facets of motivation; also see Amabile et al., 1994). Therefore, it appears that pitting intrinsic motivation against extrinsic motivation and forcing participants to choose between both alternatives is an inappropriate and invalid way of measuring motivation. These recent findings cast some doubts on the construct validity of the MOSS.

Finally, there are also concerns about the ecological validity of the MOSS. Harter's (1981b) scale was validated for the classroom. Weiss et al. (1985) changed a few words from the original instrument and then used it in a sport setting. Steps should have been taken (perhaps in a focus group with sport participants) to ensure that the concepts as assessed in the original instrument (dealing with education) do apply to the world of sport and physical activity. As it stands now, the findings indicate that the factorial validity of the scale is low. This could be due to at least two reasons: The items have not been properly adapted to the context of sport and physical activity, or worse, the constructs postulated by Harter (1981b) for the classroom do not generalize to the realm of sport and physical activity. Future research is needed in order to shed light on this issue.

The Sport Motivation Scale (Brière et al., 1995; Pelletier et al., 1995). In light of the fact that no existing contextual scale adequately and independently assessed intrinsic and extrinsic motivation from a multidimensional perspective (see Table 1), the Echelle de Motivation dans le Sport (EMS; Brière et al., 1995) was developed. Then, using cross-cultural validation procedures (Vallerand, 1989), Pelletier et al. (1995) validated this measure in English to make it accessible to the English-speaking scientific community. The EMS/SMS is based on the tenets of Deci and Ryan's (1985, 1991) self-determination theory. As mentioned previously, these authors postulate the existence of three main types of motivation, namely intrinsic motivation, extrinsic motivation, and amotivation. In addition, Deci and Ryan (1985, 1991) have proposed that there are, in fact, different types of extrinsic motivation, namely, external, introjected, and identified regulation. Similarly, Vallerand et al. (1989, 1992) posit the existence of three different forms of intrinsic motivation: intrinsic motivation to know, to experience stimulation, and to accomplish. Including the concept of amotivation, this makes for a total of seven different types of motivation. Thus, the EMS/SMS is composed of seven subscales that assess these different motivational constructs.

In line with the position of several theorists (e.g., Deci & Ryan, 1985; Harter, 1981a; McClelland, 1985), it was decided to operationalize motivation as the perceived reasons for participation or the "why" of behavior. For instance, intrinsic motivation is generally conceptually defined as the fact of engaging in an activity for the inherent pleasure one derives from participation (Deci, 1975). Using participants' perceived reasons for their engagement in sport would allow us to equate the operational definition of motivation with its conceptual one. In addition, focusing on the why of behavior would allow us to avoid the trap of inferring motivation from determinants (e.g., perceived competence) or consequences (e.g., feelings of enjoyment, task absorption). Therefore, it was determined that athletes would be asked the following question, "Why do you practice your sport?", at the beginning of the scale, and items would represent the perceived reasons for engaging in the activity, thus reflecting the different types of motivation. For instance, an intrinsic-motivation-to-know item is "For the pleasure of discovering new training techniques."

The second step involved generating various reasons for sport participation. First, 40 athletes from different sports were interviewed by telephone to ascertain the different reasons explaining why they engaged in their sport. These reasons were then content analyzed and categorized as fitting into one of the seven types of motivation. Subsequently, a committee of experts generated additional reasons to help create a larger pool of reasons that could serve as scale items.

In the third phase, a series of judges evaluated the content validity of the items and subsequently eliminated those that were thought to be ambiguous. This procedure left a total of 70 items (10 per subscale). This preliminary version of the EMS was then administered to 195 athletes from various sports and data were submitted to an exploratory factor analysis. Results revealed a seven-factor solution (i.e., the seven different types of motivation) that explained 69% of the variance. It was decided to keep the 4 items that had the highest factor loadings for each subscale, thus resulting in a 28 item scale.

While encouraging, results of the initial study were based on a limited number of subjects. Thus, two additional studies involving approximately 500 athletes (approximately 19 years of age) recruited from different athletic teams (basketball, volleyball, swimming, ice hockey, football, handball, soccer, and badminton) were conducted to further validate the EMS. Results from these investigations revealed that the EMS has satisfactory internal-consistency levels (alphas ranging from .71 to .92, mean alpha score = .82), as well as moderate to high indices of temporal stability (test-retest correlations ranging from .54 to .82, mean = .69) over a one-month period. Results of a confirmatory factor analysis (via LISREL) also confirmed the seven-factor structure of the EMS (GFI of .90 and a RMSR below .10). Finally, the construct validity of the scale was supported by a series of correlational analyses among the seven subscales, as well as between these scales and other psychological constructs (determinants and consequences) relevant to the sports context. More specifically, as predicted by self-determination theory (Deci & Ryan, 1985, 1991), the correlations among the different forms of motivation revealed a simplex pattern where the adjacent subscales (e.g., intrinsic motivation and identified regulation) showed high positive correlations, and the subscales at the opposite ends of the continuum (e.g., intrinsic motivation and amotivation) revealed the weakest (or even negative) correlations. In addition, correlations between the self-determined forms of sport motivation (i.e., identified regulation and the three types of intrinsic motivation) were found to be positively related to perceptions of sport competence (a motivational determinant) and to sport satisfaction and positive sport emotions (two positive motivational consequences), whereas negative correlations were obtained with non self-determined forms of motivation, especially amotivation.

Two other studies have looked at the reliability and validity of the EMS. The first study (Fortier, Vallerand, Brière, & Provencher, 1995) provided additional support for the reliability and validity of the scale. Results of internal consistency yielded scores varying from .73 (the Identified Regulation Subscale) to .90 (the Intrinsic Motivation to Know subscale). Furthermore, in line with earlier findings on the negative effects of competition on intrinsic motivation (Deci et al., 1981; Vallerand, Gauvin, & Halliwell, 1986a, 1986b), results revealed that competitive athletes reported lower levels of intrinsic motivation toward accomplishment and higher levels of amotivation than did recreational athletes. In the second study, Vallerand and Losier (1994) obtained internal consistency (alpha) values ranging from .76 to .88. In addition, they showed that a self-determined motivational profile correlated positively with a sportsmanship orientation, thereby providing support for the construct validity of the EMS. Indeed, if athletes play in order to enjoy themselves (and not to win rewards or trophies), they should be less likely to cheat and to display negative behaviors toward other participants. In sum, it appears that the French-Canadian version of the EMS is a reliable and valid measure of intrinsic and extrinsic motivation and amotivation in sport.

Because the EMS was initially validated in French, it was not available to researchers conducting research with English-speaking athletes. Therefore, it was decided to develop and validate an English-language version of the EMS, the SMS. The EMS was translated from French to English using a three-step procedure (see Vallerand, 1989). Then, two studies (Pelletier et al., 1995) involving 643 athletes who participated in nine different sports were conducted in order to assess the psychometric properties of the SMS. Results revealed satisfactory internal consistency indices (alphas ranging from .63 to .80, mean = .75). Furthermore, the temporal stability of the scale revealed acceptable levels (test-retest correlations ranging from .58 to .84, mean $r = .70$) over a 5-week period. The factorial validity of the scale (i.e., seven-factor structure) was also confirmed through a CFA that revealed acceptable fit indices [i.e., GFI = .94, AGFI = .92, RMSR = .048, Normed Fit Index (NFI) = .92].

The construct validity of the scale was assessed in two fashion. First, the pattern of correlations among the SMS subscales was assessed in order to test for the simplex pattern that was obtained with the EMS. Results provided support for the simplex pattern. Second, correlations between the various forms of motivation and their determinants and consequences were computed. As expected based on theoretical predictions originating from self-determination theory (Deci & Ryan, 1985, 1991), perceptions of competence were related positively to the most self-determined forms of motivation (i.e., the three intrinsic-motivation and the identified-regulation subscales) but negatively to the least self-determined forms of motivation (e.g., external regulation and amotivation). Similar findings were obtained with the different forms of informational as well as autonomy-supportive coaching behaviors. With regard to the motivational consequences, positive outcomes (i.e., effort and future intentions of practicing the sport) correlated positively with the more self-determined forms of motivation and correlated negatively with the amotivation subscale. The opposite pattern was observed with the negative consequence (i.e., distraction).

Recent research other than our own has also tested the construct validity of the SMS. For instance, Li and Harmer (1996) used structural equation modeling in order to test for the simplex structure of the scale. As indicated earlier, such a pattern is important because it tests for the presence of the different forms of motivation on a self-determination continuum ranging from amotivation to intrinsic motivation. A sample of 857 men and women college students engaged in various sports, including basketball, volleyball, martial arts, fencing, and weight training completed the SMS. Results using LISREL supported the simplex pattern. In addition, this pattern was found to be invariant across gender. These findings provide additional support for the construct validity of the SMS.

It should be noted that the social desirability of the SMS has not been directly assessed. However, similar motivation scales, such as the Couple Motivation Scale (Blais et al., 1990) and the Motivation Towards the Environment Scale (Pelletier et al., in press), which use the same format as the SMS, have been shown to be unrelated to social desirability. Thus, we would suggest that the SMS should be relatively free of social desirability; however, such an assumption remains to be directly tested.

Although the SMS is a useful tool to assess contextual sport intrinsic and extrinsic motivation, it also has some limitations. First, although internal-consistency levels in general were acceptable, it should be mentioned that an alpha level of .63 was

obtained with the identified-regulation subscale. This value can be considered a bit low, although it should be noted that this subscale is made up of only four items. As indicated earlier, the alpha coefficient underestimates the internal consistency of short scales (see Smith et al., 1995; Vallerand et al., 1997). Second, because the scale asks participants to assess the pertinence of different reasons for explaining their participation in sports, it necessitates a certain level of cognitive sophistication. Thus, it would be difficult to use such a scale with children younger than 10 years of age, or with intellectually challenged individuals.

Nevertheless, the SMS does seem to have some advantages relative to other contextual measures of intrinsic and extrinsic motivation. First, it is multidimensional in nature, assessing the different types of IM and EM. Second, it assesses intrinsic and extrinsic motivation independently from each other. Third, the assessment of intrinsic and extrinsic motivation is not confounded with motivational determinants and consequences. Fourth, the scale also measures amotivation, a motivational concept akin to learned helplessness, that should be of increasing interest to sport psychologists. Finally, the SMS contains 28 items in all (4 per scale) and can be applied to most sport and physical activity settings. Future research with the SMS would, therefore, appear promising.

The Pictorial Motivation Scale (Reid et al., 1994). The final scale to be discussed assesses the contextual intrinsic and extrinsic sport motivation of intellectually challenged individuals. The assessment of such populations is important for several reasons (see Vallerand & Reid, 1990, for a more elaborate discussion on this issue). First, being able to assess these individuals' intrinsic and extrinsic motivation would allow us to better understand how the current practices used in adapted physical education influence the participants' motivation. Second, such an assessment would also alert us to potential problems associated with certain practices (for instance, the overuse of rewards). Third, it may also lead to important theoretical insights. For instance, it may improve our understanding as to how individuals, who are objectively incompetent with respect to motor skills, manage to overcome feelings of incompetence and eventually come to enjoy themselves and to persevere in physical activity and sport.

The Pictorial Motivation Scale (PMS; Reid et al., 1994) assesses four constructs: intrinsic motivation (unidimensional), identified regulation, external regulation, and amotivation. The PMS contains 20 items, 5 for each of the four subscales. As in the other scales developed by our research group, we attempt to assess participants' reasons for participating in sport and physical activity. However, because of the cognitive limitations of intellectually disabled individuals, we have decided not to use the "why" question as such but to ask participants to complete the sentence: "I engage in sports..." with items such as "... because it's fun" (intrinsic motivation). In order to facilitate understanding, each item is associated with a specific picture depicting sport participants. The picture serves to underline the motivational flavor of the item. Participants are required to indicate their agreement with the item on a 4-point scale ranging from *Not like me* (1) to *Like me* (4).

The PMS was initially developed in French. Subjects were individually interviewed by a trained assistant. Initial results from pilot studies showed that participants understood the scale instructions, as well as the content of the items. The pictures were also found to be appropriate for this population. The PMS was then tested on 62 boys and girls (ranging in age from 12 to 18 years) with a mild intellectual disability. Internal consistency was found to be appropriate (average alpha value of .73) as was temporal stability involving a one-week test-retest (mean test-retest correlation of .80). Construct validity of the PMS was assessed through correlations with teachers' ratings of each student's enjoyment of physical activity, concentration, and positive emotions during physical education classes. Results were in line with predictions from self-determination theory (see Table 3) as the intrinsic motivation and identified regulation subscales were positively and significantly related to all three motivational outcomes. On the other hand, the external regulation subscale was not consistently related to the outcome measures, whereas the amotivation subscale was strongly and negatively related to the motivational consequences.

Overall, these findings provide preliminary support for the reliability and validity of the PMS. Current research is underway in order to translate the scale in English and to further test the construct and factorial validity of the PMS. The PMS could prove a very valuable tool in research, both with special and normal populations. Indeed, if one considers that the children in the Reid et al. (1994) study had a mental age of around 7 to 9 years, this opens the possibility that the scale could be used with normal children at such ages. However, further research is necessary before this hypothesis can be supported.

FUTURE RESEARCH DIRECTIONS

In closing, we would like to offer some suggestions for future research directions involving the assessment of intrinsic and extrinsic sport motivation. We see at least three types of directions worth pursuing by sport and physical activity researchers. These involve (a) refining existing instruments, (b) conducting research in uncharted areas using actual instruments, and (c) developing instruments to assess intrinsic and extrinsic motivation with new populations. These issues are addressed in turn below.

On the Refinement of Existing Instruments

In our review of the various measures of intrinsic and/or extrinsic motivation, we have identified a number of limitations. These lead logically to future research in order to rectify problems that some scales may have. A first issue deals with the factorial validity of several measures. In our review, we indicated that poor factorial validity was evidenced for the IMI (McAuley et al., 1989) as well as the MOSS (Weiss et al., 1985). In addition, no factor analysis has been conducted on the TRQ (Mayo, 1977), the Sport Intrinsic Motivation Inventory (Dwyer, 1988), and the PIMS (Reid et al., 1994). Thus, future research would do well to reassess the factor structure of these instruments, preferably through confirmatory factor analysis (with LISREL or EQS). Such research would provide us with valuable information on the validity of each scale and its usefulness for future sport research.

A second issue pertains to the reliability of existing assessments. Our review revealed that a number of scales (or subscales) show low or borderline levels of internal consistency. This is the case for the Curiosity and Judgment subscales of the MOSS (Weiss et al., 1985), the Pressure/Tension subscale of the IMI (McAuley et al., 1989), and the Identified Regulation subscale of the SMS (Pelletier et al., 1995). Thus, future research on this issue is needed. Such research would indicate if changes are in order with respect to the items of these different subscales. In addition, no data on the test-retest reliability seem to exist for the MOSS. Because the MOSS is a contextual measure, it would appear important to assess its level of temporal stability. Moderate to high correlations would be expected.

Finally, the social desirability of the scales used to assess intrinsic and extrinsic motivation should be assessed. As hard as it may be to believe, not one of the eight measures that we have reviewed has been examined in terms of its tendency to relate to social desirability concerns. One is reminded that sport is a very public arena and that one might be tempted to present answers that might look good in the eyes of others.

Research in Uncharted Areas With Existing Instruments

Using recent developments in scale measurement of intrinsic and extrinsic motivation in sport and physical activity, it is now possible to conduct research in several new directions. A first research avenue would entail determining whether the relation between intrinsic and extrinsic motivation is additive or interactional in nature. These are the two prevalent positions in the field. Proponents of the additive relationship hypothesis (e.g., Atkinson, 1964; Porter & Lawler, 1968) posit that intrinsic and extrinsic motivation combine in leading to higher levels of motivation. On the other hand, theorists who favor an interactional approach (e.g., Harter, 1981b; Lepper & Hodell, 1989) propose that both forms of motivation interact such that when one is high, the other is low.

Table 3
Correlations between the Subscales of the Pictorial Motivation Scale (PMS) and Scales Assessing Interest, Concentration, and Affect in Physical Education Classes[1]

PMS	Interest[a]	Concentration[a]	Positive Affect[a]
Intrinsic motivation	.21	.15	.22
Identified regulation	.29	.15	.24
External regulation	.18	.01[b]	.11[b]
Amotivation	-.53	-.31	-.57

1. From Reid et al. (1994).
a These scales were completed by the teacher.
b non significant, $p > .05$.

As indicated earlier, our own position is that the nature of the relation between intrinsic and extrinsic motivation depends on the type of extrinsic motivation involved, as well as the level of generality of the constructs. At the contextual level, the relationships between intrinsic motivation and self-determined forms of extrinsic motivation, such as identified regulation, may be additive because these motivations involve high levels of self-determination. On the other hand, relationships between intrinsic motivation and non self-determined forms of extrinsic motivation, such as introjected and external regulation, should be orthogonal, or slightly negative (see Brière et al., 1995; Pelletier et al., 1995). At the situational level (i.e., at one given point in time), the relationships among the different types of motivation should be strengthened because of the presence of salient situational factors (e.g., success). Thus, intrinsic motivation should have a strong additive relationship with identified regulation, but a strong interactional (or negative) one with external regulation. However, these hypotheses have never been tested in the sport context.

In order to test the above hypotheses, it is essential that the scales used assess intrinsic and extrinsic motivation independently and that they measure extrinsic motivation in a multidimensional fashion. The Sport Motivation Scale (at the contextual level) and the Situational Motivation Scale (at the situational level) use such a measurement strategy. It would be important for future research to test the above reasoning for at least two reasons. First, it would provide an answer to a key theoretical question, that of the relationship between intrinsic and extrinsic motivation. Second, and more important for our present discussion, the findings of such research would yield crucial implications for the measurement of intrinsic and extrinsic motivation. For instance, should the results of such a study provide support for the above hypotheses, this would lead to two important conclusions: (a) in line with the additive model, intrinsic and extrinsic motivation should be assessed independently in sport settings; and (b) in line with self-determination theory, extrinsic motivation should be assessed in a multidimensional fashion. Thus, research along the present lines is strongly encouraged.

A second issue deals with developmental changes in athletes' motivation. Using the MOSS, Weiss et al. (1985) showed that there seems to be a loss of contextual intrinsic motivation over time on two of the motivational subscales (curiosity and challenge). Unfortunately, there are two caveats here. First, the MOSS does not assess intrinsic and extrinsic motivation independently. Thus, we do not know if such a trend is caused by an increase in extrinsic motivation or by a decrease in intrinsic motivation. Second, the study was cross-sectional and not longitudinal in nature. Future research should attempt to resolve this issue by conducting longitudinal research using a scale, such as the Sport Motivation Scale (Brière et al., 1995; Pelletier et al., 1995), which assesses intrinsic and extrinsic motivation independently. It would then be possible to chart the developmental changes in children's contextual motivation toward sport and/or physical activity. Here again, such research would shed light on the necessity or not of assessing intrinsic and extrinsic motivation independently.

A final research area of interest pertains to athletic performance and persistence in sport. Research on these two concepts would appear important from a measurement perspective because it would allow to test the construct validity of existing scales. Indeed, if instruments such as the MOSS and the SMS are valid, they should be able to predict important types of behavioral outcomes, such as performance (Vallerand, 1997). Much research in education has shown that a contextual self-determined motivational profile (i.e., high intrinsic motivation and identified regulation, but low external regulation and amotivation) toward education leads to high academic performance (e.g., Fortier et al., 1995; Gottfried, Fleming, & Gottfried, 1994; Guay & Vallerand, in press; Lloyd & Barenblatt, 1984), even after controlling for initial performance. We believe that a similar finding should emerge in sport research. This is because athletes who are intrinsically motivated are likely to spend more time practicing their skills on their own and, consequently, should improve more than athletes who are extrinsically motivated (out of external regulation) and who play only "when it counts." In addition, by focusing on the intrinsic elements of the game, individuals with self-determined forms of motivation may be less likely to experience pressure and tension (R.M. Ryan, 1982), thereby allowing them to develop coping skills that are conducive to high performance (Smith & Christensen, 1995). We feel that the interdependencies between motivation and performance can be readily tested in sport using the SMS. In addition, by using a measure of coping strategies such as the Athletic Coping Skills Inventory-28 (Smith et al., 1995), it would be possible to test the mediational role of coping skills in the motivation-performance relationship.

On the Development of New Instruments

A final suggestion for future research pertains to the development of instruments to assess the motivation of new populations. If there is one common theme that runs through all scales discussed in this chapter, it is that they all focus on one specific population: athletes or physical activity participants. Although this population is clearly an important one, it is by far not the only one that can or should be studied. Other populations that need to be researched are those of coaches, referees, administrators, and parents.

Designing instruments assessing the intrinsic and extrinsic motivation of these individuals could lead to a host of interesting questions. For instance, what is the motivation of these social agents for participating in sports? In particular, what is the case for coaches? Do they enjoy themselves more if they are extrinsically or intrinsically motivated? Does it make a difference for children to be coached by an extrinsically motivated individual relative to an intrinsically-motivated person? Do children enjoy themselves as much? Is there a transfer effect such that children come to adopt the motivational orientation of their coach? If so, what are the psychological processes involved? Deci and Ryan (1985) reported data to the effect that teachers who had a control orientation (similar to external regulation) on the General Causality Orientations Scale (a scale that assesses motivation at the global level and is thus akin to a trait) were more likely to be controlling toward their students. Because controlling teachers have been found to undermine students' contextual academic intrinsic motivation (Deci, Nezlek, & Sheinman, 1981), one could make the prediction that coaches who are externally regulated toward sports are likely to instill a similar contextual motivational orientation in their athletes through their controlling behavior toward them. A similar analysis may apply to other social agents, especially parents. These are only some of the questions that await the development of a conceptually based and psychometrically sound scale assessing the intrinsic and extrinsic motivation of social agents in sports.

SUMMARY AND CONCLUSION

In this chapter, we have reviewed measures of intrinsic and extrinsic motivation used in the realm of sports and physical activity. We have shown that these measures are not equivalent and differ on several dimensions, including those of dimensionality and level of generality (situational vs. contextual aspects) of the constructs. We identified four situational measures: the behavioral measure, the Mayo TRQ (1977), the IMI (McAuley et al., 1989), and the SIMS (Guay & Vallerand, 1995, 1997). We showed that each measure displayed particular problems, the most important being circularity (the behavioral measure), using determinants and consequences to assess motivation (the TRQ and the IMI), and lack of factorial validity (TRQ and the IMI). Also the SIMS does not assess intrinsic motivation from a multidimensional perspective, and this may limit the type of research conducted with this scale in the future. Four contextual measures were reviewed: the MOSS (Weiss et al., 1985), the Sport Intrinsic Motivation Inventory (Dwyer, 1988), the EME/SMS (Brière et al., 1995; Pelletier et al., 1995), and the Pictorial Motivation Scale (PMS; Reid et al., 1994). Our review revealed that the Sport Intrinsic Motivation Scale lacks construct and factorial validity, whereas the MOSS displays several weaknesses such as pitting intrinsic and extrinsic motivation on a bipolar continuum and a lack of factorial validity. On the other hand, the recently developed SMS seems to be a reliable and valid multidimensional assessment of intrinsic and extrinsic motivation, as well as a unidimensional measure of amotivation. Finally, although the development process of the PMS is also very recent and all psychometric properties of the scale have not been thoroughly assessed, it would appear that this scale could be useful with special populations.

We have also proposed future research directions. We have outlined areas of needed research for existing instruments. In addition, we have suggested that by using some of the measures reviewed herein, we might be in an ideal position to research important issues such as sport performance, as well as test the construct validity of existing instruments. Finally, we have also proposed that new instruments are needed to pursue our research in novel directions. Although our attention so far has been directed at athletes and physical activity participants, it is felt that it is now time to devise instruments assessing the intrinsic and extrinsic motivation of social agents (e.g., coaches, parents, referees, etc.) whose apparent motivation should be to allow participants to maintain their own intrinsic motivation. Is it the case? It is hoped that future research will tell us.

In our introductory comments, we mentioned that measurement represents a crucial aspect of scientific inquiry. In light of new developments in the assessment of intrinsic and extrinsic motivation, we conclude that the necessary methodological tools are now present to help investigators launch new and original research programs. The future would appear to be rather promising in the intrinsic and extrinsic motivation research area.

References

Abramson, L.Y., Seligman, M.E.P., & Teasdale, J.D. (1978). Learned helplessness in humans: Critique and reformulation. *Journal of Abnormal Psychology, 87*, 49-74.

Amabile, T.M., Hill, K.G., Hennessey, B.A., & Tighe, E.M. (1994).The Work Preference Inventory: Assessing intrinsic and extrinsic motivational orientations. *Journal of Personality and Social Psychology, 66*, 950-967.

Anastasi, A. (1968). *Psychological testing*. New York: Macmillan.

Anshel, M.H., Weinberg, R.S., & Jackson, A. (1992). The effect of goal difficulty and task complexity on intrinsic motivation and motor performance. *Journal of Sport Behavior, 15*, 159-176.

Atkinson, J.W. (1964). *An introduction to motivation*. Princeton, NJ: Van Nostrand.

Bandura, A. (1977). *Social learning theory*. Englewood Cliffs, NJ: Prentice-Hall.

Bandura, A. (1986). *Social foundations of thought and action: A social cognitive theory*. Englewood Cliffs, NJ: Prentice-Hall.

Bandura, A., & Schunk, D.H. (1981). Cultivating competence, self-efficacy, and intrinsic interest through proximal self-motivation. *Journal of Personality and Social Psychology, 41*, 586-598.

Bem, D.J. (1972). Self-perception theory. In L. Berkowitz (Eds.), *Advances in experimental social psychology: Vol. 6* (pp. 1-62). New York: Academic Press.

Bentler, P.M., & Bonett, D.G. (1980). Significance tests and goodness-of-fit in covariance structures. *Psychological Bulletin, 88*, 588-606.

Berlyne, D.E. (1971a). *Aesthetics and psychobiology*. New York: Appleton-Century-Crofts.

Berlyne, D.E. (1971b). What next? Concluding summary. In H.I. Day, D.E. Berlyne, & D.E. Hunt (Eds.), *Intrinsic motivation: A new direction in education* (pp. 186-196). Toronto: Holt, Rinehart, & Winston.

Biddle, S., & Brooke, R. (1992). Intrinsic versus extrinsic motivational orientation in physical education and sport. *British Journal of Educational Psychology, 62*, 247-256.

Blais, M.R., Brière N.M., Lachance, L., Riddle, A.S., & Vallerand, R.J. (1993). L'inventaire des motivations au travail de Blais. *Revue québécoise de psychologie, 14*, 185-215.

Blais, M.R., Sabourin, S., Boucher, C., & Vallerand, R.J. (1990). Toward a motivational model of couple happiness. *Journal of Personality and Social Psychology, 59*, 1021-1031.

Blanchard, C., & Vallerand, R.J. (1996). *On the social and intrapersonal determinants of situational motivation*. Manuscript in preparation, Université du Québec à Montréal.

Bolles, R.C. (1967). *Theory of motivation*. New York: Harper & Row.

Brière, N.M., Vallerand, R.J., Blais, M.R., & Pelletier, L.G. (1995). Dévelopement et validation d'une mesure de motivation intrinsèque, extrinsèque et d'amotivation en contexte sportif: l'Échelle de Motivation dans les Sports (EMS). [Development and validation of the French form of the Sport Motivation Scale]. *International Journal of Sport Psychology, 26*, 465-489.

Brophy, J. (1987). Socializing students' motivation to learn. In M.L. Maehr & D.A. Kleiber (Eds.), *Advances in motivation and achievement: Vol 5. Enhancing motivation* (pp. 181-210). Greenwich, CT: JAI Press.

Brustad, R.J. (1988). Affective outcomes in competitive youth sport: The influence of intrapersonal and socialization factors. *Journal of Sport and Exercise Psychology, 10*, 307-321.

Cadorette, I., Blanchard, C., & Vallerand, R.J. (1996, October). *Programme d'amaigrissement: influence du centre de conditionnement physique et du style de l'entraîneur sur la motivation des participants* [On the influence of fitness centers and monitors' interactional style on participants' motivation toward a weight-loss program]. Paper presented at the annual conference of the Québec Society for Research on Psychology, Trois-Rivières, Québec, Canada.

Carver, C.S., & Scheier, M.F. (1981). *Attention and self-regulation*. New York: Springer-Verlag.

Chandler, C.L., & Connell, J.P. (1987). Children's intrinsic, extrinsic, and internalized motivation: A developmental study of children's reasons for liked and disliked behaviours. *British Journal of Developmental Psychology, 5*, 357-365.

Csikszentmihalyi, M. (1975). *Beyond boredom and anxiety*. San Francisco: Jossey-Bass.

Csikszentmihalyi, M. (1978). Intrinsic rewards and emergent motivation. In M.R. Lepper & D. Greene (Eds.), *The hidden costs of reward* (205-216). Hillsdale, NJ: Erlbaum.

Csikszentmihalyi, M. (1990). *Flow: The psychology of optimal experience*. New York: Harper Perrenial.

Csikszentmihalyi, M., & Nakamura, J. (1989). The dynamics of intrinsic motivation: A study of adolescents. In C. Ames & R. Ames (Eds.), *Motivation in education: Vol. 3. Goals and cognitions* (pp. 45-71). New York: Academic Press.

deCharms, R.C. (1968). *Personal causation: The internal affective determinants of behavior*. New York: Academic Press.

Deci, E.L. (1971). Effects of externally mediated rewards on intrinsic motivation. *Journal of Personality and Social Psychology, 18*, 105-115.

Deci, E.L. (1972). Intrinsic motivation, reinforcement, and inequity. *Journal of Personality and Social Psychology, 22*, 113-120.

Deci, E.L. (1975). *Intrinsic motivation*. New York: Plenum Press.

Deci, E.L. (1980). *The psychology of self-determination*. Lexington, MA: DC Heath.

Deci, E.L., Eghrari, H., Patrick, B.C., & Leone, D.R. (1994). Facilitating internalization: The self-determination theory perspective. *Journal of Personality, 62*, 119-142.

Deci, E.L., Nezlek, J., & Sheinman, L. (1981). Characteristics of the rewarder and intrinsic motivation of the rewardee. *Journal of Personality and Social Psychology, 40*, 1-10.

Deci, E.L., & Ryan, R.M. (1985). *Intrinsic motivation and self-determination in human behavior*. New York: Plenum Press.

Deci, E.L., & Ryan, R.M. (1991). A motivational approach to self: Integration in personality. In R. Dientsbier (Ed.), *Nebraska Symposium on Motivation: Vol. 38. Perspectives on motivation* (pp. 237-288). Lincoln: University of Nebraska Press.

Deci, E.L., & Ryan, R.M. (1994). Promoting self-determined education. *Scandinavian Journal of Educational Research, 38*, 3-14.

Deci, E.L., Vallerand, R.J., Pelletier, L.G., & Ryan, R.M. (1991). Motivation and education: The self-determination perspective. *The Educational Psychologist, 26*, 325-346.

Diblasio, L., Chantal, Y., Vallerand, R.J., & Provencher, P. (1995, October). *Effets de la récompense et de la punition sur la motivation intrinsèque* [Effects of reward and punishment on intrinsic motivation]. Paper presented at the annual conference of the Québec Society for Research on Psychology, Ottawa, Ontario, Canada.

Duda, J.L. (1993). Goals: A social cognitive approach to the study of achievement motivation in sport. In R.N. Singer, M. Murphey, & L.K. Tennant (Eds.) *Handbook on research on sport psychology* (pp. 421-436). St. Louis: Macmillan Publishing Company.

Duda, J.L., Chi, L., Newton, M., Walling, M., & Catley, D.

(1995). Task and ego orientation and intrinsic motivation in sport. *International Journal of Sport Psychology, 26*, 40-63.

Dweck, C. S. (1985). Intrinsic motivation, perceived control, and self-evaluation maintenance: An achievement goal analysis. In C. Ames & R. Ames (Eds.), *Research on motivation in education: Vol. 2. The classroom milieu* (pp. 289-305). New York: Academic Press.

Dweck, C.S., & Elliott, E.S. (1988). A social-cognitive approach to motivation and personality. *Psychological Review, 95*, 265-273.

Dwyer, J. (1988). *Development of the Sports Intrinsic Motivation Scale*. Unpublished doctoral dissertation, University of Saskatchewan.

Farr, J.L., Vance, R.J., & McIntyre, R.M. (1977). Further examination of the relationship between reward contingency and intrinsic motivation. *Organizational Behavior and Human Performance, 20*, 31-53.

Fisher, C.D. (1978). The effects of personal control, competence, and extrinsic reward systems on intrinsic motivation. *Organizational Behavior and Human Performance, 21*, 273-288.

Fortier, M.S., & Grenier, M. (1997). *Déterminants personnels et situationnels de l'adhérence à l'exercice: Une étude prospective*. [Personal and situational determinants of exercise adherence: A prospective study]. Manuscript submitted for publication.

Fortier, M.S., Vallerand, R.J., Brière, N.M., & Provencher, P.J. (1995). Competitive and recreational sport structures and gender: A test of their relationship with sport motivation. *International Journal of Sport Psychology, 26*, 24-39.

Fortier, M.S., Vallerand, R.J., & Guay, F. (1995). Academic motivation and school performance: Toward a structural model. *Contemporary Educational Psychology, 20*, 257-274.

Frederick, C.M., & Ryan, R.M. (1995). Self-determination in sport: A review using cognitive evaluation theory. *International Journal of Sport Psychology, 26*, 5-23.

Gotfried, A.E., Fleming, J.S., & Gottfried, A.W. (1994). Role of parental motivational practices in children's academic intrinsic motivation and achievement. *Journal of Educational Psychology, 86*, 104-113.

Goudas, M., Biddle, S., Fox, K., & Underwood, M. (1995). It ain't what you do, it's the way you do it! Teaching style affects children's motivation in track and field lessons. *The Sport Psychologist, 9*, 254-264.

Grolnick, W.S., Deci, E.L., & Ryan, R.M. (1991). Inner resources for school achievement: Motivational mediators of children's perceptions of their parents. *Journal of Educational Psychology, 83*, 503-518.

Guay, F., & Vallerand, R.J. (1995, June). *The Situational Motivation Scale (SMS)*. Paper presented at the annual convention of the American Psychological Society, New York.

Guay, F., & Vallerand, R.J. (1997). *On the assessment of state intrinsic and extrinsic motivation: The Situational Motivation Scale (SIMS)*. Manuscript in preparation.

Guay, F., & Vallerand, R.J. (in press). Students' motivational orientation and achievement: A process model. *Social Psychology of Education: An International Journal*.

Harter, S. (1978). Effectance motivation reconsidered. *Human Development, 21*, 34-64.

Harter, S. (1981a). A model of mastery motivation in children: Individual differences and developmental change. In A. Collins (Ed.), *Minnesota Symposium on Child Psychology: Vol. 14.* (pp. 215-255). Hillsdale, NJ: Erlbaum.

Harter, S. (1981b). A new self-report scale of intrinsic and extrinsic orientation in the classroom: Motivational and informational components. *Developmental Psychology, 17*, 300-312.

Harter, S. (1985). Competence as a dimension of self-evaluation: Toward a comprehensive model of self-worth. In R.L. Leahy (Ed.), *The development of the self* (pp. 55-121). Orlando, FL: Academic Press.

Harter, S., & Jackson, B.K. (1992). Trait vs nontrait conceptualizations of intrinsic/extrinsic motivational orientation. *Motivation and Emotion, 16*, 209-230.

Hennessey, B. A., Amabile, T. M., & Martinage, M. (1989). Immunizing children against the negative effects of reward. *Contemporary Educational Psychology, 14,* 212-227.

Hennessey, B.A., & Zbikowski, S.M. (1993). Immunizing children against the negative effects of reward: A further examination of intrinsic motivation training techniques. *Creativity Research Journal, 6,* 297-307.

Jackson, S.A. (1995). Factors influencing the occurrences of flow state in elite athletes. *Journal of Applied Sport Psychology, 7,* 138-166.

Joreskog, K.G., & Sorbom, D. (1984). *LISREL VI.* Chicago, IL: National Educational Resources.

Kagan, J. (1972). Motives and development. *Journal of Personality and Social Psychology, 22,* 51-66.

Kelley, H.H. (1972). Causal schemata and the attribution process. In E.E. Jones et al. (Eds.), *Attribution: Perceiving the causes of behavior* (pp. 151-174). Morristown, NJ: General Learning Press.

Kihlstrom, J.K., & Cantor, N. (1984). The self as a knowledge structure. In L. Berkowitz (Ed.), *Advances in experimental social psychology: Vol. 17* (pp. 1-48). New York: Academic Press.

Kowal, J., & Fortier, M.S. (in press). Motivational determinants of flow: Contributions from Self-Determination Theory. *Journal of Social Psychology.*

Kruglanski, A.W. (1978). Endogenous attribution and intrinsic motivation. In M.R. Lepper & D. Green (Eds.), *The hidden costs of reward: New perspectives on the psychology of human motivation* (pp. 85-107). Hilsdale, NJ: Erlbaum.

Lepper, M.R., Greene, D., & Nisbett, R.E. (1973). Undermining children's interest with extrinsic rewards: A test of the "overjustification effect." *Journal of Personality and Social Psychology, 28,* 129-137.

Lepper, M.R., & Hodell, M. (1989). Intrinsic motivation in the classroom. In C. Ames & R. Ames (Eds.), *Research on motivation in education: Vol. 3. Goals and cognitions* (pp. 73-105). New York: Academic Press.

Li, F., & Harmer, P. (1996). Testing the simplex assumption underlying the Sport Motivation Scale: A structural equation modeling analysis. *Research Quarterly for Exercise and Sport, 67,* 396-405.

Lloyd, J., & Barenblatt, L. (1984). Intrinsic intellectuality: Its relation to social class, intelligence, and achievement. *Journal of Personality and Social Psychology, 46,* 646-654.

Maslow, A. (1970). *Motivation and personality* (3rd ed.). New York: Harper & Row.

Mayo, R.J. (1977). The development and construct validation of a measure of intrinsic motivation (Doctoral dissertation, Purdue University, 1976). *Dissertation Abstracts International, 37,* 5417b. (University Microfilms No. 77-7491).

McAdams, D.P. (1994). Can personality change? Levels of stability and growth in personality across the life span. In T.F. Heatherton & J.L. Weinberger (Eds.), *Can personality change?* (pp. 299-314). Washington, DC: American Psychological Association.

McAuley, E., Duncan, T., & Tammen, V.V. (1989). Psychometric properties of the Intrinsic Motivation Inventory in a competitive sport setting: A confirmatory factor analysis. *Research Quarterly of Exercise and Sport , 60,* 48-58.

McAuley, E., & Tammen, V.V. (1989). The effects of subjective and objective competitive outcomes on intrinsic motivation. *Journal of Sport and Exercise Psychology, 11,* 84-93.

McClelland, D.C. (1985). *Human motivation.* London, England: Scott, Foresman, & Co.

McInman, A.D., & Grove, R.J. (1991). Peak moments in sport: A literature review. *Quest, 43,* 333-351.

Nicholls, J.G. (1984). Conceptions of ability and achievement motivation. In R. Ames & C. Ames (Eds.), *Research on motivation in education: Vol. 1* (pp. 39-73). New York: Academic Press.

Orlick, T.D., & Mosher, R. (1978). Extrinsic awards and participant motivation in a sport related task. *International Journal of Sport Psychology, 9,* 27-39.

Pelletier, L. G., Fortier, M. S., Vallerand, R. J., & Brière, N.M. (1997). *Perceived autonomy support, motivation, and persistence in physical activity: A longitudinal investigation.* Manuscript submitted for publication.

Pelletier, L.G., Fortier, M.S., Vallerand, R.J., Tuson, K.M., Brière, N.M., & Blais, M.R. (1995). Toward a new measure of intrinsic motivation, extrinsic motivation, and amotivation in sports: The Sport Motivation Scale (SMS). *Journal of Sport & Exercise Psychology, 17,* 35-53.

Pelletier, L.G., Vallerand, R.J., Blais, M.R., Brière, N.M., & Green-Demers, I. (1996). Construction et validation d'une mesure de motivation intrinsèque, de motivation extrinsèque et d'amotivation vis-à-vis des activités de loisirs: L'Échelle de Motivation vis-à-vis des Loisirs (EML) [Construction and validation of the Leisure Motivation Scale]. *Society and Leisure, 19,* 559-585.

Porter, L.W., & Lawler, E.E. (1968). *Managerial attitudes and performance.* Homewood, IL: Irwin Dorsey.

Privette, G., & Bundrick, C.M. (1991). Peak experience, peak performance, and flow: Correspondence of personal descriptions and theoretical constructs. *Journal of Social Behavior and Personality, 6,* 169-188.

Reeve, J., & Deci, E.L. (1996). Elements of the competitive situation that affect intrinsic motivation. *Personality and Social Psychology Bulletin, 22,* 24-33.

Reid, G., Poulin, C., & Vallerand, R.J. (1994, June). *A pictorial motivational scale in physical activity for people with a mental disability: Development and initial validation.* Paper presented at the annual conference of NASPSPA.

Rosenfield, D., Folger, R., & Adelman, H. (1980). When rewards reflect competence: A qualification of the overjustification effect. *Journal of Personality and Social Psychology, 39,* 368-376.

Ryan, E.D. (1977). Attribution, intrinsic motivation, and athletics. In L. Gedvillas & M. Kneer (Eds.), *Proceedings of the National College Physical Education Association for Men/National Association for Physical Education of College Women, National Conference* (pp. 346-353). Chicago: Office of Publications Services, University of Illinois.

Ryan, E.D. (1980). Attribution, intrinsic motivation, and athletics: A replication and extension. In C. Nadeau, W. Halliwell, & G. Roberts (Eds.), *Psychology of motor behavior and sport - 1979* (pp. 19-26). Champaign, IL: Human Kinetics.

Ryan, R.M. (1982). Control and information in the intrapersonal sphere: An extension of cognitive evaluation theory. *Journal of Personality and Social Psychology, 43,* 450-461.

Ryan, R.M. (1995). Psychological needs and the facilitation of the integrative processes. *Journal of Personality, 63,* 397-427.

Ryan, R.M., & Connell, J.P. (1989). Perceived locus of causality and internalization: Examining reasons for acting in two domains. *Journal of Personality and Social Psychology, 57,* 749-761.

Ryan, R.M., Deci, E.L., & Grolnick, W.S. (1995). Autonomy, relatedness, and the self: Their relation to development and psychopathology. In D. Cicchetti & D.J. Cohen (Eds.), *Developmental psychology: Vol. 1. Theory and methods* (pp. 618-655). New York: John Wiley & Sons.

Ryan, R.M., Koestner, R., & Deci, E.L. (1991). Ego-involved persistence: When free-choice behavior is not intrinsically-motivated. *Motivation and Emotion, 15,* 185-205.

Ryan, R.M., Vallerand, R.J., & Deci, E.L. (1984). Intrinsic motivation in sport: A cognitive evaluation theory interpretation. In J. Williams and W. Straub (Eds.), *Cognitive sport psychology* (pp. 231-242). Lansing, NY: Sport Science Associates.

Seifriz, J.J., Duda, J.L., & Chi, L. (1992). The relationship of perceived motivational climate to intrinsic motivation and beliefs about success in basketball. *Journal of Sport and Exercise Psychology, 14,* 375-391.

Siegel, S. (1956). *Nonparametric statistics for the behavioral sciences.* New York: McGraw-Hill.

Smith, R.E., & Christensen, D.S. (1995). Psychological skills as predictors of performance and survival in professional baseball. *Journal of Sport & Exercise Psychology, 17,* 399-415.

Smith, R.E., Schutz, R.W., Smoll, F.L., & Ptacek, J.T. (1995). Development and validation of a multidimensional measure of sport-specific psychological skills: The Athletic Coping Skills Inventory-28. *Journal of Sport & Exercise Psychology, 17,* 379-398.

Stewart, D.G., Green-Demers, I., Pelletier, L.G., & Tuson, K.M. (1995, June). *Is helplessness a dimension of environmental amotivation? New developments in the Amotivation Towards the Environment Scale (AMTES).* Paper presented at the Annual Canadian Psychological Association convention, Charlottetown, PEI.

Thomas, J.R., & Tennant, L.K. (1978). Effects of rewards on children's motivation for an athletic task. In F.L. Smoll & R.E. Smith (Eds.), *Psychological perspectives in youth sports* (pp. 123-144). Washington, DC: Hemisphere.

Tuson, K.M., & Pelletier, L.G. (1992, November). *Why do people lack motivation to help save the environment? A predictive model.* Paper presented at the annual convention of the Québec Society for Research in Psychology, Montréal.

Vallerand, R.J. (1983). The effect of differential amounts of positive verbal feedback on the intrinsic motivation of male hockey players. *Journal of Sport Psychology, 5,* 100-107.

Vallerand, R.J. (1989). Vers une méthodologie de validation trans-culturelle de questionnaires psychologiques: Implications pour la recherche en langue française. [Toward a cross-cultural methodology to validate psychological instruments: Implications for research in the French language]. *Canadian Psychology, 30,* 662-680.

Vallerand, R.J. (1993). La motivation intrinsèque et extrinsèque en contexte naturel: implications pour les secteurs de l'éducation, du travail, des relations interpersonnelles et des loisirs [Intrinsic and extrinsic motivation in natural contexts: Implications for the education, work, interpersonal relationships, and leisure contexts]. In R.J. Vallerand & E. Thill (Éds), *Introduction à la psychologie de la motivation* (pp. 533-582) Laval, Qué.: Etudes Vivantes.

Vallerand, R.J. (1997). Toward a hierarchical model of intrinsic and extrinsic motivation. In M.P. Zanna (Ed.), *Advances in experimental social psychology: Vol. 29,* (pp. 271-360). New York: Academic Press.

Vallerand, R.J., & Bissonnette, R. (1992). Intrinsic, extrinsic, and amotivational styles as predictors of behavior: A prospective study. *Journal of Personality, 60,* 599-620.

Vallerand, R.J., Blais, M.R., Brière, N.M., & Pelletier, L.G. (1989). Construction et validation de l'échelle de motivation en éducation (EME). *Revue Canadienne des Sciences du Comportement, 21,* 323-349.

Vallerand, R.J., & Brière, N.M. (1990). [On the discriminant validity of the intrinsic motivation to know, to accomplish things, and to experience stimulation]. Unpublished data, Université du Québec à Montréal.

Vallerand, R.J., Deci, E.L., & Ryan, R.M. (1987). Intrinsic motivation in sport. In K. Pandolf (Ed.), *Exercise and sport science reviews* (pp. 389-425). New York: MacMillan.

Vallerand, R.J., Fortier, M.S., & Guay, F. (1997). Self-determination and persistence in a real-life setting: Toward a motivational model of high school dropout. *Journal of Personality and Social Psychology, 72,* 1161-1176.

Vallerand, R.J., Gauvin, L., & Halliwell, W.R. (1986a). Negative effects of competition on children's intrinsic motivation. *Journal of Social Psychology, 126,* 649-657.

Vallerand, R.J., Gauvin, L., & Halliwell, W.R. (1986b). Effects of zero-sum competition on children's intrinsic motivation and perceived competence. *Journal of Social Psychology, 126,* 465-472.

Vallerand, R.J., & Guay, F. (1996). *Self-regulatory processes in human behavior: A confirmatory test of the hierarchical model of intrinsic and extrinsic motivation.* Manuscript submitted for publication.

Vallerand, R.J., & Losier, G.F. (1994). Self-determined motivation and sportsmanship orientations: An assessment of their temporal relationship. *Journal of Sport & Exercise Psychology, 16,* 229-245.

Vallerand, R.J., Pelletier, L.G., Blais, M.R., Brière, N.M., Sené-cal, C., & Vallières, E.F. (1992). The Academic Motivation Scale: A measure of intrinsic, extrinsic, and amotivation in education. *Educational and Psychological Measurement, 52,* 1003-1019.

Vallerand, R.J., Pelletier, L.G., Blais, M.R., Brière, N.M., Sénécal, C., & Vallières, E.F. (1993). On the assessment of intrinsic, extrinsic, and amotivation in education: Evidence on the concurrent and construct validity of the Academic Motivation Scale. *Educational and Psychological Measurement, 53,* 159-172.

Vallerand, R.J., & Reid, G. (1984). On the causal effects of perceived competence on intrinsic motivation: A test of cognitive evaluation theory. *Journal of Sport Psychology, 6,* 94-102.

Vallerand, R. J., & Reid, G. (1988). On the relative effects of positive and negative feedback on males' and females' intrinsic motivation. *Canadian Journal of Behavioural Science, 20,* 239-250.

Vallerand, R.J., & Reid, G. (1990). Motivation and special population: Theory, research, and implications regarding motor behavior. In G. Reid (Ed.), *Problems in movement control* (pp.159-197). New York: North Holland.

Weinberg, R.S., & Ragan, J. (1979). Effects of competition, success/failure, and sex on intrinsic motivation. *Research Quarterly, 50,* 503-510.

Weiss, M.R., Bredemeier, B.J., Shewchuk, R.M. (1985). An intrinsic/extrinsic motivation scale for the youth sport setting: A confirmatory factor analysis. *Journal of Sport Psychology, 7,* 75-91.

White, R.W. (1959). Motivation reconsidered: The concept of competence. *Psychological Review, 66,* 297-333.

Whitehead, J.R., & Corbin, C.B. (1991). Youth fitness testing: The effect of percentile-based evaluative feedback in intrinsic motivation. *Research Quarterly for Exercise and Sport, 62,* 225-231

Williams, L., & Gill, D.L. (1995). The role of perceived competence in the motivation of physical activity. *Journal of Sport & Exercise Psychology, 17,* 363-378.

Author Notes

This paper was prepared while the first author was a visiting professor in the Psychology Department at McGill University. Preparation of this paper was facilitated through grants from the Social Sciences and Humanities Research Council of Canada (SSHRC), Le Fonds pour la Formation des Chercheurs et l'Aide à la Recherche (FCAR Québec), and the Université du Québec à Montréal. We would like to thank Céline Blanchard, Yves Chantal, Frédéric Guay, Stéphane Perreault, and Pierre Provencher for their constructive feedback on an earlier version of this manuscript. Reprint requests should be addressed to Robert J. Vallerand, Laboratoire de Recherche sur le Comportement Social, Département de Psychologie, Université du Québec à Montréal, C.P. 8888, Station "Centre-Ville", Montréal, QC, Canada H3C 3P8.

Part II

Sport Anxiety and Responses to Stress

PART II

It has been said of anxiety that "everyone knows about it, until he/she is asked to explain it. No one is able to understand it, but everyone has experienced it...(and) most of us — laypersons as well as researchers — have difficulty describing it" (Hackfort & Schwenkmezger, 1993, p. 328). Given the potentially pressure-packed, performance-focused features of competitive sport, it should not be surprising that the study of anxiety in athletic settings is one of the major areas of inquiry within sport psychology. Moreover, the topic of sport competition-related stress reflects an early and outstanding example of the application of sound general psychology measures (e.g., Spielberger's State-Trait Anxiety Inventory; Spielberger, Gorsuch, & Lushene, 1970) to the sport domain *as well as* the development of sport-specific assessments (e.g., Marten's [1977] Sport Competition Anxiety Test). The latter have targeted the state (e.g., see Martens, Vealey, & Burton, 1990) and trait facets of anxiety. Other important work on stress emotions in the athletic domain has pulled from models of the stress process (Lazarus & Folkman, 1984) and concentrated on athletes' responses to anxiety in terms of their coping strategies. Critical reviews of older and more contemporary trait and state anxiety measures and self-reported coping in sport are presented in Part II.

References

Hackfort, D., & Schwenkmezger, P. (1993). Anxiety. In R.N. Singer, M. Murphey, L.K. Tennant (Eds.), *Handbook of research on sport psychology* (pp. 328-364). New York: Macmillan.

Lazarus, R.S., & Folkman, S. (1984). *Stress, appraisal, and coping*. New York: Springer.

Martens, R. (1977). Sport Competition Anxiety Test. Champaign, IL: Human Kinetics.Martens, R., Vealey, R.S., & Burton, D. (1990). *Competitive anxiety in sport*. Champaign, IL: Human Kinetics.

Spielberger, C.D., Gorsuch, R.L., & Lushene, R.E. (1970). *Manual for the State-Trait Anxiety Inventory*. Palo Alto, CA: Consulting Psychologists Press.

Chapter 6

MEASUREMENT OF TRAIT ANXIETY IN SPORT

Ronald E. Smith, Frank L. Smoll
and
Shelley A. Wiechman
University of Washington

Sport performance anxiety has been a topic of great interest to coaches, athletes, and researchers for many years. The fact that emotional and motivational factors can cause one athlete to "peak" during competition at the same time another falters or "chokes" is evident to anyone who has watched or participated in sports. Football coaches speak of "Wednesday All-Americans" who cannot perform up to their capabilities on Saturday game days because of debilitating effects of anxiety. Conversely, coaches and athletes sometimes express the view that anxiety, or certain aspects of anxiety, can facilitate performance (Jones & Swain, 1995).

Anxiety affects other outcomes as well. Some children drop out of sports because they find athletic competition to be aversive and threatening rather than enjoyable and challenging (Gould, Feltz, Horn, & Weiss, 1982; Orlick & Botterill, 1975). Trainers and sports medicine practitioners have observed that athletes who find the competitive situation to be anxiety provoking sometimes appear injury prone and/or seem to take longer to return to action following injury (Nash, 1987; Olerud, 1989).

These and other observations suggest that the role of anxiety in sport has a range of practical implications that can potentially be addressed through a greater understanding of the antecedents, dynamics, and consequences of anxiety. From a scientific perspective, sport offers a number of advantages as a setting for the study of anxiety. Here, large numbers of participants are exposed to predictable, identifiable, and repetitive situations in which anxiety can be assessed and its consequences studied within a meaningful real-life context. Performance measures having unquestioned ecological validity are readily measurable within the athletic setting (Smith & Smoll, 1990). Moreover, depending upon the sport, athletes are required to perform behaviors that vary considerably along a number of task dimensions (for example, simple vs. complex; speed vs. endurance; self-paced vs. reactive; cognitive vs. motoric), permitting researchers to assess the effects of anxiety (including its cognitive and somatic components) on various classes of behavior. Anxiety measures are also needed to assess the effects of anxiety-reduction intervention programs (Apitzsch, 1983; Crocker, 1989; Hackfort & Spielberger, 1989; Smith, 1989a).

The development of adequate measurement techniques is critical to the study of any psychological construct. In research on sport anxiety, much progress has been made in the past decade due to advances in measurement. This review will be concerned with one class of measures, namely self-report measures of trait anxiety. Before proceeding with a description of these measures, several important distinctions that have contributed to both theoretical and measurement advances in the study of anxiety should be addressed. In particular, the related concepts of arousal, stress, and anxiety need to be distinguished. These terms are often used interchangeably, resulting in no small measure of confusion within the literature.

Arousal is the most general of the three terms. Cannon (1929) used the term to refer to physiological and energy mobilization in response to situations that threatened the physical integrity of the organism. If behavior is viewed as varying along two basic dimensions of direction and intensity, then arousal is the intensity dimension. Arousal, often used interchangeably with other intensity-related terms such as tension, drive, and activation, can vary on a continuum ranging from deep sleep to peak excitement.

The term *stress* is used in two different but related ways. First, it is used in relation to situations (termed "stressors") that place significant demands on the organism. This situational definition of stress is frequently couched in terms of the balance between situational demands and the resources of the individual (e.g., Lazarus & Folkman, 1984). The second use of the term stress refers to the responses of individuals to stressors. Used in this sense, stress refers to a cognitive-affective response involving appraisal of threat and increased physiological arousal (Lazarus & Folkman, 1984; Spielberger, 1966).

Though less general than arousal, the term stress is typically used to refer to a range of aversive emotional states, such as anxiety, depression, and anger.

Anxiety is one variety of stress response, and it is a multi-faceted construct. On the one hand, it is a subjectively aversive emotional response and an avoidance motive characterized by worry and apprehension concerning the possibility of physical or psychological harm, together with increased physiological arousal resulting from the appraisal of threat. As a motivational state, anxiety is an avoidance motive that helps strengthen successful coping and/or avoidance responses through negative reinforcement (i.e., response-contingent anxiety reduction) Most athletes view anxiety as a negative influence on performance. On the other hand, for reasons to be discussed below, some participants view anxiety as a facilitator of their performance (Jones & Swain, 1995).

The concept of anxiety has undergone considerable theoretical refinement over the years, and these refinements have been reflected in the measuring instruments used to operationally define the construct. Three sets of distinctions have been particularly important. The first is the trait-state distinction. The second differentiates between general or global anxiety and situation-specific forms of anxiety. The third involves the multidimensional nature of anxiety, particularly its cognitive and somatic components.

The State-Trait Distinction

The emotional reaction of anxiety varies in intensity and fluctuates over time. Physiological and subjective calmness and serenity indicate the absence of an anxiety response. Moderate levels of anxiety involve apprehension, nervousness, worry, and tension; very high levels of anxiety may involve intense feelings of fear, catastrophic thoughts, and high levels of physiological arousal. The momentary level of anxiety experienced by an individual is termed *state anxiety*.

Spielberger (1966) highlighted the important distinction between state anxiety and trait anxiety. *Trait anxiety* refers to relatively stable individual differences in anxiety proneness that are regarded as a personality disposition or trait. That is, people who are high in trait anxiety are more anxiety prone in that they perceive or appraise a wider range of situations as threatening than do individuals who are low in trait anxiety. They are, therefore, more likely to experience state anxiety, and their anxiety responses tend to be of greater intensity and duration.

It is now generally accepted that a comprehensive theory of anxiety must distinguish between anxiety as a transitory emotional state and individual differences in the relatively stable personality trait of anxiety (see Burton, this volume). An adequate model of anxiety should also specify the nature of the cognitive processes that mediate the appraisal of threat as well as the consequences of such appraisals.

The General-Specific Anxiety Distinction

Because state anxiety is defined as a transitory emotional response, it is always measured within specific situations. Trait measures of anxiety, on the other hand, fall into two general categories. Some instruments measure anxiety as a global transitational trait, whereas others are designed to assess the tendency

of individuals to experience anxiety within particular types of situations, such as tests, social situations, or competitive sport situations. The study of situation-specific anxiety has been stimulated in part by interactional approaches to personality (e.g., Magnusson & Endler, 1977), in which behavior is assumed to be determined by the reciprocal interaction of personal traits and the characteristics of situations. If anxiety is a learned response to particular classes of situations, then we should expect that situation-specific anxiety measures would relate more strongly to behavior in the critical situations than would general transitional anxiety. An impressive array of research results supports this prediction. For example, test anxiety measures are more strongly related to test performance than are measures of general anxiety (Sarason & Sarason, 1990). Moreover, situation-specific trait anxiety measures are better predictors of elevation in state anxiety for a particular class of stress situations than are generalized trait anxiety measures (Martens, 1977; Sarason & Sarason, 1990; Spielberger, 1972).

The Multidimensional Nature of Anxiety

Recent conceptualizations of anxiety have treated it as a multidimensional construct, distinguishing between its cognitive and physiological components (e.g., Borkovec, 1976; Davidson & Schwartz, 1976; Liebert & Morris, 1967; Martens, Vealey, & Burton, 1990; Sarason, 1984; Smith, 1989a; Smith & Smoll, 1990; Smith, Smoll, & Schutz, 1990). Cognitive anxiety is characterized by negative appraisals of situation and self, worry, and aversive mental imagery, whereas somatic anxiety is reflected in increased physiological arousal as typified by rapid heart rate, shortness of breath, and increased muscle tension. Multidimensional conceptions of anxiety were stimulated in part by behavior therapy research in the 1960s and 1970s that revealed three separate and largely independent cognitive, physiological, and behavioral response dimensions (Borkovec, 1976; Lang, 1971). Measurement of anxiety responses by means of self-report, physiological, and behavioral measures of anxiety in laboratory stress studies and in behavior therapy research often indicated that these three response systems were only loosely correlated with one another.

Although they interact with one another, cognitive and somatic anxiety may at times be elicited by different classes of antecedents. In several studies, threat of electric shock had its primary impact on somatic rather than cognitive anxiety, whereas social or performance evaluation had a stronger eliciting effect upon cognitive anxiety (Morris, Harris, & Rovins, 1981; Morris & Liebert, 1973). Preperformance expectancies in evaluative situations tend to be more highly correlated with cognitive anxiety than with somatic anxiety (Liebert & Morris, 1967), and the cognitive component covaries with performance expectancy changes during subsequent performance (Morris & Engle, 1981). Cognitive and somatic anxiety also have differential effects on performance, depending upon the nature of the task. Although worry and emotionality are correlated with one another, only worry appears to be consistently related to performance decrements on cognitive tasks under evaluative stress conditions (Deffenbacher, 1980; Sarason, 1984; Tryon, 1980). On the other hand, somatic anxiety can negatively affect performance on motor tasks, particularly those requiring fine neuromuscular behaviors that might be disrupted by high arousal. Gould, Petlichkoff, Simons, and Vevera (1987) found a curvilinear (inverted U) relation between somatic state anxiety scores and pistol shooting performance, whereas cognitive anxiety was unrelated to performance. In a study of competitive swimmers, Burton (1988) reported a similar curvilinear relation between somatic state anxiety and performance, but a negative linear relation between cognitive state anxiety and performance. It thus appears that, depending upon the nature of the task, cognitive and somatic anxiety may be differentially related to performance, either in the magnitude or in the form of the relation.

Factor analytic studies of anxiety scales have likewise revealed the existence of separate cognitive (e.g., worry) and somatic (e.g., physiological response) dimensions of anxiety (Morris, Davis, & Hutchings, 1981; Sarason, 1984; Smith et al., 1990). The discovery that the cognitive and physiological dimensions of anxiety can have various degrees of statistical independence and that the components can relate differentially to other behaviors spurred the development of multidimensional anxiety scales.

The Nature of Sport Performance Anxiety

As a trait construct, sport performance anxiety may be defined as a predisposition to respond with cognitive and/or somatic state anxiety to competitive sport situations in which the adequacy of the athlete's performance can be evaluated. Although a number of specific sources of threat (including the possibility of physical harm) may reside in the sport situation, we believe that the most salient sources of threat are the possibilities of failure and of disapproval by significant others who are evaluating the athlete's performance in relation to some standard of excellence. Athletic performance anxiety is thus part of a family of performance-related fear-of-failure constructs that include test anxiety, speech anxiety, and the "stage fright" that actors, musicians, and dancers can experience within their evaluative performance situations (Kendrick, Craig, Lawson, & Davidson, 1982; Steptoe & Fidler, 1987). Like other forms of anxiety, sport performance anxiety has separate but related cognitive, affective, and behavioral components. These components can be operationally defined and measured in a variety of ways, including via self-report, informant ratings, physiological measures, and behavioral observations.

Our concern is with the most frequently employed measurement modality, namely self-report. More specifically, we will trace the development of self-report trait anxiety measures used in sport through three phases, each of which built upon the previous ones. The first phase was inspired by the trait-state distinction and is exemplified by the development of the State-Trait Anxiety Inventory (STAI; Spielberger, Gorsuch, & Lushene, 1970). The STAI consists of parallel scales to measure trait anxiety (how one generally feels) and state anxiety (how one feels at this moment). We will be concerned with only the trait version of the STAI, for state anxiety measurement is reviewed elsewhere in this text (Burton, this volume). As we shall see, the STAI has contributed importantly to research on sport anxiety, and the scale continues to be used today (see Hackfort & Spielberger, 1989).

The next phase of trait anxiety measurement in sport was

based on the global-situational distinction. Until the late 1970s, no sport-specific trait anxiety measure existed. Consequently, investigators wishing to assess individual differences in trait anxiety employed general anxiety measures such as the Manifest Anxiety Scale (Taylor, 1953), the IPAT Anxiety Scale (Cattell & Scheier, 1963), and the Trait scale from the STAI. Because general anxiety scales assess anxiety across a wide range of situations, these measures were minimally useful for assessing individual differences in sport-specific anxiety. For example, a high score on a measure of general trait anxiety does not guarantee that the person experiences high anxiety in the competitive sport situation, nor does a low score indicate that the person does not have a tendency to experience sport-specific anxiety. Thus, it is not surprising that general anxiety measures often bore little relation to performance measures in sport (Martens, 1971). The need for a sport-specific trait anxiety measure stimulated the development of the Sport Competition Anxiety Test (SCAT; Martens, 1977). The SCAT gave sport researchers an important measurement tool, and the theoretical framework upon which it was based stimulated considerable research. The impact on research made by the development of the SCAT is a prime example of how measurement helps drive research.

The most recent development in measuring sport anxiety recognizes the multidimensional nature of anxiety, particularly the distinction between cognitive and somatic anxiety components. Both the SCAT and the Competitive State Anxiety Inventory (CSAI; Martens, Burton, Rivkin, & Simon, 1980) are unidimensional anxiety measures that treat anxiety as a global phenomenon. In the late 1980s, Martens and his coworkers developed a refined measure of sport-specific state anxiety, the Competitive State Anxiety Inventory-2 (CSAI-2; Martens, Burton, Vealey, Bump, & Smith, 1990) having separate scales for somatic and cognitive state anxiety. During the same period, a multidimensional trait anxiety inventory, the Sport Anxiety Scale (SAS; Smith et al., 1990) was developed to measure cognitive and somatic trait anxiety with separate scales.

In this review, we focus on the STAI, the SCAT, and the SAS to illustrate the evolution of trait anxiety measurement in sport research. This evolution manifests itself not only in the characteristics of the measuring instruments but also in refinement of the theoretical models that underlie the measures and in the methodologies used to create them. In each instance, we describe the theoretical model underlying the instrument, the methods used in instrument development, the psychometric characteristics of the measure, and evidence relating to its validity in sport. Because the SCAT and the SAS are sport-specific and more frequently used in contemporary research, they will be reviewed in greater detail.

State-Trait Anxiety Inventory, Trait Scale (STAI-T)

Spielberger et al. (1970) developed the State-Trait Anxiety Inventory (STAI) in the late 1960s. In the 15 years to follow, the instrument was used in more than 2,500 studies (Spielberger, 1984), and it continues to be an important research tool today. The STAI comprises separate self-report scales for measuring state anxiety (A-state) and trait anxiety (A-trait). These are called the STAI-S and the STAI-T scales, respectively. This review will focus on the Trait scale of the STAI.

The STAI was originally developed as a research instrument for investigating anxiety phenomena in adults, and it has been found to be useful in the measurement of anxiety in such diverse populations as junior and senior high school students, college students, and neuropsychiatric, medical, and surgical patients.

The STAI has been used for research purposes in a variety of sports, including basketball, football, tennis, gymnastics, swimming, rowing, wrestling, and running (Spielberger, 1989). Additionally, it has been used to investigate phenomena such as respiratory distress and panic behavior in sport settings. In sport research, however, the State scale has been used far more frequently than has the Trait scale, largely because the development of the SCAT by Martens (1977) provided anxiety researchers with a sport-specific trait inventory that became the state-of-the-art measure for sport anxiety research. Nonetheless, because of the historical importance of the theoretical model underlying the STAI as well as the test-construction procedures used in its development, we will briefly discuss the STAI-T.

Theoretical Model

Spielberger's (1966) theoretical model of anxiety served as the basis for the development of the STAI. It also inspired the development of later measures, such as the SCAT, the SAS, and the CSAI and CSAI-2. As noted earlier, Spielberger's theory made the important distinction between state and trait anxiety. Spielberger et al. (1970) defined A-state as "a transitory emotional state or condition of the human organism that is characterized by subjective, consciously perceived feelings of tension and apprehension, and heightened autonomic nervous system activity. A-states may vary in intensity and fluctuate over time" (p. 2). They defined A-trait as the "relatively stable individual differences in anxiety proneness, that is...differences between people in the tendency to respond to situations perceived as threatening with elevations in A-state intensity" (p.2).

According to the trait-state model, when external stimuli are appraised as threatening, they evoke an anxiety state reaction that includes activation of the autonomic nervous system and subjective feelings of tension and anxious expectation. This in turn evokes a variety of defensive processes aimed at reducing A-state. Individual differences in A-trait determine the particular external stimuli that are cognitively appraised as threatening, the level of state anxiety experienced, and the effects of the stimuli on behavior (Spielberger, 1966).

Development of the STAI

Spielberger, Gorsuch, and Lushene began test construction in 1964 with the goal of developing a single self-report scale whose items could be used to measure both state and trait anxiety. A large number of items from existing anxiety scales were rewritten in a manner that would permit each item to be used with different instructions to measure either A-state or A-trait. However, this approach proved unsuccessful because a number of the items were inherently too "traitlike" or "statelike" to measure both constructs. Moreover, some of their best state or trait items had to be excluded because altering the instructions for these items could not overcome the strong state or trait connotations. The test construction strategy for the STAI then changed, the new goal being to generate two sets of items, one set designed to measure A-state and one set designed to measure A-trait.

Different item-selection procedures were used for the two scales. Initially, a rational-intuitive method was used to develop a large item pool on the basis of face validity. For the A-state items, the most important validational procedure was an assessment of differences in item scores obtained in imagined and actual "relaxed" or "anxious" conditions. Items having large difference scores and correlations exceeding .35 with total score (minus the item) were retained. For the A-trait items, correlations exceeding .25 with total scores on other A-trait scales, including the IPAT Anxiety Scale (Cattell & Scheier, 1963), Taylor's (1953) Manifest Anxiety Scale, and Welsh's (1956) Anxiety Scale, and subsequent item-remainder correlations exceeding .35 were required for item retention. The end result was the dual-scale STAI, Form X, which has been used in the bulk of STAI research.

The STAI consists of two 20-item scales. Five items found to be suitable for the measurement of both state and trait anxiety are included in both scales. The remaining 15 items on each scale are sufficiently different in content and/or connotation to be regarded as independent items. The A-state instructions ask examinees to report how they feel "at this moment." The A-trait instructions ask examinees to report how they "generally feel." Participants are asked to respond to each item by rating themselves on a 4-point scale. The categories for the A-trait scale are: (1) almost never, (2) sometimes , (3) often, and (4), almost always. Some items have reverse scoring to account for an acquiescence set of responses. Templates are available for scoring each subscale by hand. The range of scores can vary from a minimum score of 20 to a maximum score of 80 on both state and trait subscales. No separate norm tables have been published for athletes, though sample means and standard deviations are occasionally provided in individual studies.

Psychometric Properties

Reliability. In the STAI test manual, Spielberger et al. (1970) reported test-retest reliability on the STAI for the normative sample of college students. Subgroups of students were retested after periods of one hour, 20 days, and 104 days. The test-retest correlations for the A-trait scale were .84 (males) and .76 (females) after one hour. At 20 days the correlations were .86 (males) and .76 (females), and at 104 days the correlations were .73 (males) and .77 (females). Thus, the STAI-T appears to measure a stable personality trait in a consistent manner. Cronbach's alpha coefficients for diverse normative samples have ranged from .83 to .92, indicating good internal consistency.

Concurrent validity. Spielberger et al. (1970) reported concurrent validity correlations of the STAI trait scale with other measures of general trait anxiety, including the IPAT Anxiety Scale (Cattell & Scheier, 1963), Taylor's (1953) Manifest Anxiety Scale, and Zuckerman's (1960) Affect Adjective Checklist. The correlations between the STAI and these other anxiety measures are quite high (.75 to .80) for both college students and neuropsychiatric patients. Correlations with domain-specific measures of anxiety, such as test anxiety, social anxiety, and sport performance anxiety tend to be lower, ranging from about .25 to .50 (Martens, 1977; Smith et al., 1990; Spielberger et al., 1970). These lower correlations indicate some degree of common anxiety variance, but also a fair degree of situational specificity in characteristic anxiety reactions.

Factorial validity. The unidimensional nature of Spielberger's (1966) trait construct suggests that factorial validity would be demonstrated by the appearance of a single global factor when the scale is subjected to factor analysis. Instead, factor analytic studies of the structure of Form X have yielded inconsistent results in both the number and nature of obtained factors (Barker, Barker, & Wadsworth, 1977; Kendall, Finch, Auerbach, Hooke, & Mikulka, 1976). Because of these inconsistencies, Spielberger and his coworkers developed a revised Form Y (Spielberger, Vagg, Barker, Donham, & Westberry, 1980). However, subsequent factor analyses on the revised form have continued to show that the STAI has a multidimensional structure. Consistently, two factors termed *anxiety-present* and *anxiety-absent* have been found for the trait scale. Anxiety-present items (e.g., "Some unimportant thought runs through my mind and bothers me.") are thought to be differentially sensitive to individual differences on the high end of the anxiety scale. The anxiety-absent items (e.g. "I feel secure.") are thought to be more sensitive at measuring low levels of trait anxiety.

It is interesting to note that the multidimensional nature of the STAI-T established repeatedly by factor analytic studies has not involved separate factors for somatic and cognitive anxiety. As Spielberger et al. (1980) point out, the items of the STAI-T primarily reference cognitive aspects of anxiety, particularly worry. The minimal emphasis on the measurement of bodily symptoms of anxiety seems attributable to the underlying model, which focuses on the experiencing of threat as the chief mediational factor in anxiety arousal. It is, therefore, not surprising that the items of the STAI-T would primarily address the cognitive appraisal processes that define threat. One must conclude, therefore, that the construct being tapped by the STAI-T is primarily cognitive trait anxiety.

Predictive validity: Threat and A-state. The central tenet of the state-trait model is that A-trait is a predisposition to experience A-state under conditions of threat appraisal. Spielberger's model thus predicts that people high in A-trait will experience threat more readily. To test this hypothesis, Schwenkmezger and Laux (1986) administered a German translation of the STAI-T to elite athletes several weeks prior to important contests, then measured cognitions before and after the contests. Consistent with expectations, athletes with high A-trait scores reported significantly more worry and other interfering cognitions than did athletes with low scores. They also found that high A-trait athletes reported higher levels of A-state on the STAI-State measure than did low trait-anxious athletes. Other studies have also found significant correlations between STAI-T scores and subsequent precompetitive A-state scores in athletes, typically in the .30 range (Cooley, 1987; Martens & Simon, 1976). However, these same investigators also found that the sport-specific SCAT was a better predictor of precompetitive A-state. In contrast to these findings, other investigators have reported that a German translation of the STAI-T predicts A-state in stressful sport situations as well as the SCAT

does (Hackfort & Schwenkmezger, 1985; Singer & Ungerer-Rohrick, 1985). Despite these discrepant results, it appears that an A-trait measure specific to competitive situations is a stronger predictor of A-state than is a general A-trait measure like the STAI-T.

Task performance. Predictions derived from both drive and habit theories of anxiety and performance state that high levels of arousal will result in performance decrements on complex tasks such as those that characterize many sports. This prediction has been supported in numerous studies (see Smith & Smoll, 1990, for a review). Thus, establishing the construct validity of any anxiety scale requires studies involving linkages with performance.

In a study involving a complex laboratory task, Wankel (1977) compared the performance of high and low A-trait females on a pursuit rotor. The high STAI-T scorers performed significantly more poorly on the task, and they also reported higher levels of A-state upon completion of the task.

Other researchers have assessed relations between STAI-T scores and actual athletic performance. Schwenkmezger and Laux (1986) studied the performance of elite national-level handball players during championship games, using expert ratings of performance as the criterion variable. Significant negative correlations were found between A-trait and performance, and there was evidence that this relation was at least partially mediated by the negative influence of task-irrelevant cognitive responses. Other studies have yielded negative relations between STAI-T scores and athletic performance in both adult and child samples (Morgan, O'Connor, Ellickson, & Bradley, 1988; Porat, Lufi, & Tenenbaum, 1989).

Prediction of coaching burnout. Burnout can be regarded as a severe psychological response to chronic stress that involves negative affect, loss of meaning, negative self-evaluations, and devaluation and possible withdrawal from a previously valued activity (Smith, 1989a). Among the risk factors for burnout identified in previous research in the helping professions is A-trait. Accordingly, Vealey, Udry, Zimmerman, and Soliday (1992) administered the Maslach Burnout Inventory (Maslach & Jackson, 1981) and the STAI to 381 high school and 467 college coaches. A substantial percentage of coaches fell into the moderate to high burnout range. A-trait emerged as the strongest predictor of burnout in this athletic population.

Convergent and discriminant validity. Two important aspects of construct validity assessment are convergent and discriminant validity (Campbell & Fiske, 1959). Convergent validity requires scores on the measure to relate to other behaviors in a manner predicted by the underlying theoretical construct and model. As we have seen, there exists considerable evidence for convergent validity of the STAI-T.

Also important in evaluating construct validity is discriminant validity, that is, evidence that the scale does *not* relate to measures of presumably unrelated constructs. For scales that measure socially undesirable traits like anxiety, discriminant validity issues frequently center on relations with measures of social desirability. Where the STAI is concerned, there is little question of a substantial negative correlation with social desirability measures (Esposito, Agard, & Rosnow, 1984; Spielberger et al., 1970). These correlations frequently reach the -.60

range, depending on the sample and social desirability scale involved. There is evidence that assurances of confidentiality and anonymity can at times lower these correlations (Esposito et al., 1984), but relations between measures of negative affective states and social desirability measures seem inevitable and do not necessarily mean that the anxiety measures lack validity. The validity of anxiety measures will ultimately hinge on their ability to successfully predict extratest behaviors that are more readily interpretable in terms of anxiety than in terms of social desirability constructs.

The relation between anxiety and depression is a topic of current debate. Particularly in normal populations, consistently high correlations have been found between trait measures of anxiety and depression, causing some to suggest that there is a general factor of "negative affectivity" rather than discriminable differences between anxiety and depression (Watson & Clark, 1984). The STAI-T has been found to correlate highly with depression measures in both adolescent and adult nonclinical populations (Endler, Cox, Parker, & Bagby, 1992; Spielberger et al., 1970; Tannenbaum, Forehand, & Thomas, 1992). Whether these high correlations are due to poor discriminant validity or to the actual existence of a common negative affectivity factor is unclear. One indication that STAI measurement deficiencies may be involved is the fact that an alternate trait measure, the Endler Multidimensional Anxiety Scales, was found to have better discriminant validity than the STAI in differentiating anxiety from depression in a large nonclinical sample (Endler et al., 1992). To this point, the negative-affectivity versus separate-emotions controversy has not been studied systematically within athlete populations, but its exploration could have theoretical import as well as measurement implications.

Summary Evaluation

The STAI has contributed significantly to anxiety research since its development. The measure appears to be a reliable and valid measure of generalized A-trait. The STAI has reasonably good psychometric properties and good convergent validity. Discriminant validity remains unclear and is clouded by the current debate involving negative affectivity.

Because, as Spielberger (1984) has noted, domain-specific measures of anxiety are likely to be better predictors of behavior within the relevant domain, the STAI has been largely supplanted in sport research by sport-specific A-trait measures. It also appears that the STAI-T measures primarily cognitive anxiety, particularly worry. Sport psychologists are often interested in the distinction between cognitive and somatic anxiety because the outcomes they study frequently involve motor performance that would seem susceptible to influence by somatic anxiety. These considerations have stimulated the development of sport-specific and multidimensional measures of A-trait that should prove more useful to sport researchers.

The Sport Competition Anxiety Test (SCAT)

The need for a sport-specific A-trait measure stimulated the development and validation of the Sport Competition Anxiety Test (SCAT), which was initially published in a 150-page monograph (Martens, 1977). A revised and condensed version of the original SCAT manual was subsequently published in a book entitled *Competitive Anxiety in Sport* (Martens, Vealey, & Burton, 1990). The work contains the theoretical model on which SCAT is based and a revised presentation of the development, validation, and administration of SCAT, as well as updated normative data. Also included is a comprehensive review of SCAT research, a discussion of psychometric and theoretical issues in SCAT research, and suggestions for future research directions.

Theoretical Model

Martens' conceptualization of competitive A-trait is a situation-specific modification of the general A-trait construct developed by Spielberger (1966). Martens' approach to the phenomenon of competitive A-trait and to the development of SCAT was based on four major theoretical assumptions: (a) interactional approaches to personality, which view the person and the situation as codeterminants of behavior, result in better behavioral predictions than do pure trait or pure situational paradigms; (b) situation-specific A-trait measures are better predictors of elevation in A-state for a particular class of stress situations than are generalized A-trait measures; (c) a distinction exists between anxiety as a transitory emotional state and individual differences in anxiety proneness (i.e., the state-trait anxiety distinction); and (d) competition may be viewed as a social evaluation process.

Martens (1975) represented competition as a process consisting of four interrelated elements. The first element of the model is the *objective competitive situation* (OCS), which refers to "real factors in the physical or social environment that are arbitrarily defined as constituting a competitive situation" (p. 69). In addition to specifying the environmental or objective demand (e.g., type of task, difficulty of opponents), social evaluation is a critical component of the OCS. The second stage of the competition process is the *subjective competitive situation* (SCS), which involves how the individual perceives, appraises, and accepts the OCS. The SCS is the manner in which the individual perceives reality and is thus the base from which the individual operates. In the third stage, a *response* is emitted as a direct function of the SCS. Individuals can respond on psychological, physiological, or behavioral levels, and possible responses include the decision to compete or to avoid competition, attempts to modify the OCS, and overt competitive behavior. The final stage of the competition model involves the short- or long-term *consequences* arising from the comparison process. The perceived consequences provide important information that updates the SCS, and these consequences partly determine whether a person approaches or avoids future competitive situations.

With respect to the study of competitive anxiety, Martens (1977) adapted the competitive process model as follows: OCS —-> Perception of Threat —-> A-State Reaction. Competitive A-trait was defined as "a tendency to perceive competitive situations as threatening and to respond to these situations with feelings of apprehension or tension" (p. 23). Competitive A-trait is thus a personality variable that directly affects the perception of threat, which mediates A-state responses to the competitive situation. This sport-specific modification of the more general A-trait construct provided a theoretical basis for the development of SCAT as a measure of competitive A-trait.

Following the development of SCAT and its use in numerous research studies, Martens and his colleagues formed an expanded model of the competitive anxiety process as it occurs in sport (Martens, Vealey, & Burton, 1990). This essentially involved combining the model of the competition process (Martens, 1975) with the original competitive anxiety model (Martens, 1977). The expanded model, presented in Figure 1, consists of four links, each of which is succintly described as follows:

> The process begins in Link 1 as situational factors in the objective competitive situation (OCS) and intrapersonal factors (A-trait) interact to create a perception of threat that is part of the subjective competitive situation (SCS). This perception of threat then interacts with other intrapersonal factors to influence the individual's state responses (A-state) as well as performance (Link 2). These cognitive, somatic, and behavioral responses then interact with intrapersonal factors to create different performance outcomes, or consequences (Link 3). Link 4 completes the cycle of the model as it represents the reciprocal influence of performance outcomes on intrapersonal factors. (Martens, Vealey, & Burton, 1990, pp. 70-71)

Development of SCAT

SCAT was designed as a unidimensional measure of sport-specific A-trait. Parallel forms of the measure were eventually developed for children and for adults—SCAT-C for ages 10 through 14 years, and SCAT-A for persons 15 years of age and older. The format chosen was one adopted by Spielberger (1973) for the State-Trait Anxiety Inventory for Children (STAIC). Specifically, the inventory is self-administered, and the subject responds to each item on a 3-point Likert-type scale.

Item selection began by developing a pool of items having face validity for assessing competitive A-trait. A pool of 75 items was initially generated by modifying items from the Manifest Anxiety Scale (Taylor, 1953), the STAIC (Spielberger, 1973), and the General Anxiety Scales (Sarason, Davidson, Lighthall, Waite, & Ruebush, 1960) and by writing new items. Six expert judges then rated the 75 items on content validity and clarity of sentence structure. Based on their ratings, the pool was reduced to 21 items for inclusion in the original version of SCAT-C, along with 9 spurious items.

Version 1 was administered to a sample of male junior high school students, and the scale was subjected to three types of analyses to determine item discriminability. First, item analyses were computed using Magnusson's (1966) method for differences between extreme groups (the upper and lower 27%). Triserial correlations with total score were also computed according to Jaspen's (1946) procedures. Finally, a discriminant analysis was conducted to determine individual items that best discriminated between high and low competitive A-trait groups (i.e., participants in the upper and lower thirds of the distribution of SCAT-C scores). Based on fairly consistent patterns of results for each item, the 14 most discriminating items were retained for the second version of the scale. Version 2, consisting of 14 items and 7 spurious or "filler" items, was administered to two

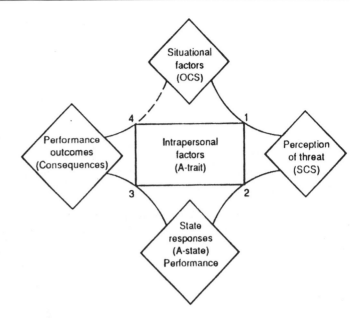

Figure 1. Martens's model of competitive anxiety.
Note: From *Competitive Anxiety in Sport* (p. 70) by R. Martens, R. S. Vealey, and D. Burton, Champaign, IL: Human Kinetics Publishers. Copyright © 1990 by Human Kinetics Publishers. Reprinted by permission.

additional samples of junior high school males. Subsequent item analyses, triserial correlations, and discriminant analyses resulted in the selection of 10 items and 5 filler items for Version 3 of SCAT-C. Version 3 was then administered to samples of male and female students (5th- and 6th-graders and junior high school students). Based on the three types of item discrimination analyses described above, it was concluded that all 10 items satisfied the acceptance criteria.

The next phase of scale development involved modification of Version 3 of SCAT-C for use with adults. After making the instructions appriopriate for adults (reading level of the average 15-year-old) and changing one word on one item, SCAT-A was given to a sample of male and female university students. Item discrimination results confirmed that all items exceeded selection criteria: mean item analysis coefficients of .61 and .67 for high and low SCAT, respectively; a mean triserial coefficient of .64; a mean discriminant function coefficient of 1.01. In a later psychometric study, Ostrow and Ziegler (1978) administered SCAT-A to male and female university students enrolled in general physical education courses. For participants whose scores fell in the upper ($n = 523$) and lower ($n = 441$) quartiles of the SCAT score distribution, the results of item analyses produced correlation coefficients ranging from .67 to .82, with a mean coefficient of .79. This indicates that participants at each extreme of the distribution answered each SCAT item consistent with their SCAT score classification. Also, the responses of all participants ($N = 1,991$) to each item were correlated with the participants' total score, yielding coefficients ranging from .60 to .82, with a mean coefficient of .71. Finally, a discriminant analysis conducted between the high and low competitive A-trait groups revealed that the SCAT items discriminated at the .001 level between participants in these extreme groups.

Table 1
The Sport Competition Anxiety Test for Adults.

Illinois Competition Questionnaire

Form A

Directions: Below are some statements about how persons feel when they compete in sports and games. Read each statement and decide if you HARDLY EVER, or SOMETIMES, or OFTEN feel this way when you compete in sports and games. If your choice is HARDLY EVER, blacken the square labeled A, if your choice is SOMETIMES, blacken the square labeled B, and if your choice is OFTEN, blacken the square labeled C. There are no right or wrong answers. Do not spend too much time on any one statement. *Remember* to choose the word that describes how you *usually* feel when competing in *sports and games*.

	Hardly Ever	Sometimes	Often
1. Competing against others is socially enjoyable.	A ☐	B ☐	C ☐
2. Before I compete I feel uneasy.	A ☐	B ☐	C ☐
3. Before I compete I worry about not performing well.	A ☐	B ☐	C ☐
4. I am a good sport when I compete.	A ☐	B ☐	C ☐
5. When I compete I worry about making mistakes.	A ☐	B ☐	C ☐
6. Before I compete I am calm.	A ☐	B ☐	C ☐
7. Setting a goal is important when competing.	A ☐	B ☐	C ☐
8. Before I compete I get a queasy feeling in my stomach.	A ☐	B ☐	C ☐
9. Just before competing I notice my heart beats faster than usual.	A ☐	B ☐	C ☐
10. I like to compete in games that demand considerable physical energy.	A ☐	B ☐	C ☐
11. Before I compete I feel relaxed.	A ☐	B ☐	C ☐
12. Before I compete I am nervous.	A ☐	B ☐	C ☐
13. Team sports are more exciting than individual sports.	A ☐	B ☐	C ☐
14. I get nervous wanting to start the game.	A ☐	B ☐	C ☐
15. Before I compete I usually get uptight.	A ☐	B ☐	C ☐

Note: From *Competitive Anxiety in Sport* (p. 70) by R. Martens, R. S. Vealey, and D. Burton, Champaign, IL: Human Kinetics Publishers. Copyright © 1990 by Human Kinetics Publishers. Reprinted by permission.

As shown in Tables 1 and 2, SCAT is a 10-item scale with items specific to sport competition. The child and adult forms are identical except for the instructions and one word on Item 8. Five additional spurious items (1, 4, 7, 10, and 13) were included in the scale in an attempt to disguise its purpose somewhat and thus reduce response bias.

Administration and Scoring

Both forms of SCAT are self-administering. They may be taken either alone or in groups, and they normally require less than 5 minutes to complete. Participants respond to each item according to how they *generally feel* in competitive sport situations, which is particularly important to emphasize if SCAT is used in conjunction with A-state scales (i.e., how respondents *feel at the moment*).

In reference to the initial planning of SCAT, Martens (1977) indicated that "no social desirability scale or lie scale were [*sic*] developed in conjunction with the test because these scales suffer from the same weakness that they supposedly detect" (p. 37). More recently, Williams and Krane (1989) found that competitive A-trait was significantly related to social desirability ($r = -.24$, $p < .05$) for a sample of 58 female collegiate golfers; and Martens, Vealey, and Burton (1990) reported that anti-social desirability instructions have proven beneficial in reducing bias to the CSAI-2, an inventory designed to measure A-state in competitive situations (Martens, Burton, et al., 1990). "Anti-social desirability" instructions were subsequently developed for use with SCAT, but their influence on test responses is unknown.

The procedure for scoring SCAT is identical for both forms. Each of the 10 items is scored on a 3-point scale labeled (1) hardly ever; (2) sometimes, and (3) often, with reverse scoring for Items 6 and 11 (i.e., (3) hardly ever, (2) sometimes, and (1) often). The spurious items are not scored. The range of possible SCAT scores thus extends from 10 to 30.

Norms

Updated SCAT norms have been developed from data on approximately 2,000 athletes (Martens, Vealey, & Burton, 1990). Over half the data used in computing the norms were obtained in numerous competitive A-trait studies involving a wide variety of sports. Composite norms (separately for males and females) are presented for youth sport athletes, high school athletes, and college athletes. Separate SCAT-A norms are also presented for baseball and basketball (pp. 60-61), football and soccer, swimming and tennis, and volleyball and wrestling (pp. 62-63).

The norms reveal a trend for competitive A-trait to increase with age through high school and then to decrease for collegiate competitors. Females were higher in competitive A-trait than were males at the youth sport level, but high school and college males demonstrated higher SCAT scores than did their female counterparts. Finally, consistent with social evaluation theory, competitive A-trait was higher for individual than for team sport athletes. (p. 56)

Table 2
The Sport Competition Anxiety Test for Children.

Illinois Competition Questionnaire

Form C

Directions: We want to know how you feel about *competition*. You know what competition is. We all compete. We try to do better than our brother or sister or friend at something. We try to score more points in a game. We try to get the best grade in class or win a prize that we want. We all compete in sports and games. Below are some sentences about how boys and girls feel when they compete in sports and games. Read each statement below and decide if *you* HARD-LY EVER, or SOMETIMES, or OFTEN feel this way when you compete in sports and games. Mark A if your choice is HARDLY EVER, mark B if you choose SOMETIMES, and mark C if you choose OFTEN. There are no right or wrong answers. Do not spend too much time on any one statement. *Remember* to choose the word which describes how you *usually* feel when competing in *sports and games.*

	Hardly Ever	Sometimes	Often
1. Competing against others is fun.	A ☐	B ☐	C ☐
2. Before I compete I feel uneasy.	A ☐	B ☐	C ☐
3. Before I compete I worry about not performing well.	A ☐	B ☐	C ☐
4. I am a good sport when I compete.	A ☐	B ☐	C ☐
5. When I compete I worry about making mistakes.	A ☐	B ☐	C ☐
6. Before I compete I am calm.	A ☐	B ☐	C ☐
7. Setting a goal is important when competing.	A ☐	B ☐	C ☐
8. Before I compete I get a funny feeling in my stomach.	A ☐	B ☐	C ☐
9. Just before competing I notice my heart beats faster than usual.	A ☐	B ☐	C ☐
10. I like rough games.	A ☐	B ☐	C ☐
11. Before I compete I feel relaxed.	A ☐	B ☐	C ☐
12. Before I compete I am nervous.	A ☐	B ☐	C ☐
13. Team sports are more exciting than individual sports.	A ☐	B ☐	C ☐
14. I get nervous wanting to start the game.	A ☐	B ☐	C ☐
15. Before I compete I usually get uptight.	A ☐	B ☐	C ☐

Note: From *Competitive Anxiety in Sport* (p. 70) by R. Martens, R. S. Vealey, and D. Burton, Champaign, IL: Human Kinetics Publishers. Copyright © 1990 by Human Kinetics Publishers. Reprinted by permission.

Reliability

Internal consistency. As indicated earlier, item analysis correlations and triserial correlations were uniformly high for both high and low SCAT participants across the various test development samples. In addition, Kuder-Richardson formula 20 (KR-20) coefficients were computed from the correlation matrices among the 10 inventory items for the four SCAT-C samples that were used to determine item discriminability of Version 3 and two SCAT-A samples of university undergraduates. The KR-20 coefficients ranged from .95 to .97 for both SCAT-C and SCAT-A, demonstrating a high degree of internal consistency. Similarly, Rupnow and Ludwig (1981) reported KR-20 coefficients of .81 and .80 for two separate samples ($n = 375$, $n = 361$) of 4th- through 6th-graders using SCAT-C; and Ostrow and Ziegler (1978) obtained internal consistency estimates of .88 for males and .89 for females. Split-half reliability coefficients of .84 (Sample 1) and .82 (Sample 2) for SCAT-C were reported by Rupnow and Ludwig (1981). Corrected odd-even reliability coefficients of .91 (males) and .92 (females) for SCAT-A were obtained by Ostrow and Ziegler (1978).

Test-retest reliability. Test-retest reliability was assessed for four samples of boys and girls (Grades 5-6 and 8-9, $N = 153$). Each sample completed SCAT-C and then was retested at one of four subsequent time intervals: 1 hour, 1 day, 1 week, and 1 month. Acceptable levels of test-retest reliability were obtained, ranging from .57 to .93, with a mean of .77 for all samples combined. ANOVA reliability estimates (Kerlinger, 1973) were also computed on responses to the initial administration of SCAT-C for the four test-retest samples. The ANOVA reliability coefficients (mean $r = .81$) for the combined samples were slightly higher than the test-retest reliability coefficients. Moreover, an even higher ANOVA reliability ($r = .85$) was obtained for SCAT-A with the participants used for item analyses.

Validity

Content and factorial validity. Inspection of SCAT items indicates that eight of them measure primarily somatic reactions, whereas Items 3 and 5 appear to tap a cognitive component of anxiety, namely, worry. Other evidence suggests that the SCAT may be tapping primarily somatic anxiety. For example, SCAT correlates more highly with the somatic anxiety subscale of the Sport Anxiety Scale (.80) than it does with the two cognitive subscales (.66 and .47, respectively; Smith et al., 1990). Similarly, in the original CSAI-2 validation studies (Martens, Burton, et al., 1990), a stronger relation was found between SCAT and the somatic component of A-state ($r = .62$) than between SCAT and cognitive competitive A-state ($r = .45$). On the other hand, four additional studies have reported equivocal findings concerning the relations between SCAT and the cognitive and somatic components of the CSAI-2 (Crocker, Alderman, & Smith, 1988; Gould, Petlichkoff, & Weinberg, 1984; Karteroliotis & Gill, 1987; Maynard & Howe, 1987).

During the initial development of SCAT, factor analytic procedures were not utilized to determine the dimensional structure of the items chosen to assess competitive A-trait. Ostrow and Ziegler (1978) did, however, conduct principal components analyses on university students' responses to SCAT-A followed by Kaiser's varimax rotation method. The single-factor structure that emerged separately for the male and female samples supported the unidimensional competitive A-trait construct for nonathletes. In contrast, recent unpublished factor analyses of SCAT-A data obtained from 120 male intercollegiate athletes resulted in the emergence of a separate cognitive factor comprised of the two worry items (Leffingwell, 1995). The present authors obtained an identical two-factor structure from a large sample of high school students (Smith & Smoll, 1995). Unfortunately, the small number of cognitive items does not provide a basis for forming separate cognitive and somatic subscales. In any event, the equivocal findings raise doubts about the unidimensional character of the SCAT construct.

Concurrent validity. The concurrent validity of SCAT was established by investigating relations between SCAT and general A-trait inventories, as well as selected personality inventories that had predictable relations with A-trait. Separate samples were used to determine SCAT-C's relation with each of three previously validated scales: the Children's Manifest Anxiety Scale Short Form (Levy, 1958), the General Anxiety Scale for Children (Sarason et al., 1960), and the Trait Anxiety Inventory for Children (Spielberger, 1973). The association between SCAT-A and the STAI-T was also assessed. Consistent with theoretical predictions, low to moderate positive correlations ranging from .28 to .46 were obtained. Consistent with these findings, Ostrow and Ziegler (1978) found low positive correlations between participants' scores on SCAT-A and the STAI-T for males ($r = .41$) and for females ($r = .42$). A similar relation between SCAT and the TAI ($r = .30$) was reported by Cooley (1987).

Additional concurrent validation studies were conducted to examine the relation between SCAT and each of five anxiety-related general personality inventories. The Junior-Senior High School Personality Questionnaire (HSPQ; Cattell & Cattell, 1969) contains a second-order anxiety factor, and 5 of its 14 primary factors (e.g., ego strength, ergic tension) are theoretically related to anxiety. SCAT-A and the HSPQ were given to 58 male and 98 female high school students. SCAT was moderately related to general anxiety scales and to those factors on the HSPQ that contain some dimension of anxiety. Watson and Friend's (1969) Social Avoidance and Distress Scale (SAD) and Fear of Negative Evaluation Scale (FNE) measure individual dispositions to becoming anxious in social situations. SCAT-C, the SAD, and the FNE were given to 50 male and 43 female junior high school students. These two scales demonstrated low to moderate positive correlations with SCAT for females, but not for males.

Additional evidence supporting SCAT's concurrent validity is provided in two other studies. Stadulis (1977) reported a low positive relation ($r = .35$, $p < .05$) between SCAT-A and the situation-specific Test Anxiety Questionnaire (Mandler & Sarason, 1952) for a sample of 74 university students. As expected, SCAT correlated highly ($r = .81$, $p < .01$) with the total score on Smith et al.'s (1990) SAS, which is another sport-specific measure of A-trait.

At this point, it should be reiterated that a high degree of correspondence was obtained between SCAT and the SAS Somatic

Anxiety subscale (Smith et al., 1990). Given that both scales were designed to measure A-trait within the context of sport, this finding is consistent with a conclusion that SCAT has especially good concurrent validity as a somatic anxiety measure.

Construct validity: Convergent and discriminant validity. Demonstration of the construct validity of SCAT was guided by a construct validation model developed by Martens (1977). The fundamental assumption of the model was that competitive A-trait, as operationalized by SCAT, is related to other constructs consistent with certain theoretical predictions.

Several of the studies conducted during the development of SCAT provided valuable information concerning its convergent and discriminant validity. Since the publication of SCAT and the wide use of the scale in sport-anxiety research, an abundance of evidence has accumulated. Our current synthesis is presented in relation to theoretical predictions that emanate from Martens, Vealey, and Burton's (1990) model of competitive anxiety (see Figure 1).

Recognizing that *intrapersonal factors* constitute the core of the conceptual model, a question of paramount importance is the following: "Does competitive A-trait fit into the constellation of other personality dispositions in a manner consistent with theoretical predictions?" In terms of *general* personality dispositions, the previous section on concurrent validity summarized considerable evidence that competitive A-trait as measured by SCAT has low to moderate correlations with general A-trait. With respect to other constructs, the correspondence between competitive A-trait and locus of control (Rotter, 1966) has been investigated. McKelvie and Huband (1980) found no relation between these two personality dispositions. In contrast, Betts (1982) reported a significant relation between competitive A-trait and external locus of control ($r = .31$, $p < .03$), and McKelvie, Valliant, and Asu (1985) also reported a significant positive relation between competitive A-trait and external locus of control ($r = .22$, $p < .05$). These findings align favorably with those obtained in the original concurrent validation research. Consistent with theoretical predictions, moderate positive correlations were found between SCAT-C and Bialer's (1961) I-EC for samples of junior high school students (r's = .32 and .37 for males and females, respectively). This suggests that individuals who do not perceive personal control over outcomes tend to become more anxious in competitive situations in which uncertainty of outcomes is high, whereas individuals perceiving high control are less anxious.

The self-worth subscale from Harter's (1979) Perceived Competence Scale for Children has been used in research concerning the relation between competitive A-trait and self-esteem. Consistent with expectations, both Passer (1983) and Brustad (1988) found that high competitive A-trait children (soccer and basketball players) were lower in self-esteem than were low competitive A-trait children. Brustad and Weiss (1987) also found this to be true for male youth baseball players, but these differences were not apparent in female youth softball players. All three studies consistently reported that self-esteem was a better predictor of competitive A-trait than was sport-specific perceived competence. This suggests that overall feelings of self-worth are more related to competitive A-trait than are the more domain-specific measures of perceived competence.

The association between competitive A-trait and another

general personality disposition deserves mention. One might expect that achievement motivation is closely related to anxiety because high achievers have a stronger motive to achieve success relative to their motive to avoid failure, whereas low achievers demonstrate the opposite tendency. Interestingly, however, the two constructs have been found to be unrelated to one another; they exist as orthogonal constructs so that individuals can be high on both, low on both, or high on one and low on the other (Atkinson & Feather, 1957). Competitive trait anxiety is best viewed as the sport-related fear-of-failure motive. In the original concurrent validation research, Mehrabian's (1968) achievement motivation scale and SCAT were administered to four samples (two each for SCAT-C and SCAT-A). Correlation coefficients ranging from .02 to .15 confirmed the hypothesis that high competitive A-trait individuals are *not* more or less motivated to achieve than are low competitive A-trait individuals. Likewise, in assessing sport-related motives, Willis (1982) reported that competitive A-trait as measured by SCAT was positively correlated with fear of failure ($r = .65$, $p < .01$), but unrelated to Willis's measure of sport-specific motive to achieve success. The independence between competitive A-trait and sport-specific achievement motives was also confirmed by Gill, Dzewaltowski, and Deeter (1988). They reported that SCAT scores were uncorrelated with the competitiveness, win orientation, and goal orientation subscales of the Sport Orientation Questionnaire (Gill & Deeter, 1988).

An interesting set of findings has been reported concerning the association between competitive A-trait and sport-specific self-confidence and perceived ability. As predicted, Vealey (1986) found that high school and college athletes' SCAT scores were negatively correlated with trait sport confidence as measured by the Trait Sport-Confidence Inventory ($r = -.28$, $p < .001$). This finding is consistent with Bandura's (1986) analysis of anxiety as comprising low self-efficacy in a situation that could produce negative outcomes. Similarly, for junior elite wrestlers, Gould, Horn, and Spreeman (1983a) found that, compared to high competitive A-trait athletes, low competitive A-trait athletes rated themselves higher in ability, predicted they would finish higher in competition, and were more confident in their performance prediction. On the other hand, neither Passer (1983) nor Brustad and Weiss (1987) found differences between high and low competitive A-trait athletes in perceived ability in younger age groups. Martens, Vealey, and Burton (1990) suggested that the equivocal findings may be attributed to the different age/experience levels of the participants. More specifically, "it may be that the relationship between competitive A-trait and other personality constructs becomes more sharply defined with age, competitive experience, or both" (p. 72).

In examining the relation between competitive A-trait and attentional focus, Albrecht and Feltz (1987) developed a baseball/softball batting version (B-TAIS) of Nideffer's (1976) Test of Attentional and Interpersonal Style. As hypothesized, competitive A-trait was found to be significantly correlated with each B-TAIS subscale measuring an ineffective deployment of attention (SCAT-overload external $r = .41$, $p < .05$; SCAT-overload internal $r = .37$, $p < .05$; SCAT-reduced attention $r = .45$, $p < .05$). It thus appears that competitive A-trait is related to the tendency to adopt an ineffective attentional focus despite the

fact that it contains no specific concentration disruption items.

Perception of threat. Construct validity ideally is based on an assessment of relations predicted by a theoretical model. It involves a nomological net involving constructs and the hypothesized relations among them (Cronbach & Meehl, 1955). The theoretical model underlying SCAT constitutes such a nonological net. Returning to the competitive anxiety model, *Link 1* predicts that *situational factors* and *intrapersonal factors* (primarily competitive A-trait) interact to create a *perception of threat*. In terms of situational factors, several researchers have identified underlying characteristics of competition that induce perceptions of threat in high A-trait individuals. Fisher and Zwart (1982) asked male college basketball players to rate the extent to which they experienced various types of anxiety responses in a variety of pregame, game, and postgame situations. A multidimensional scaling technique (INDSCAL) was applied to the matrix of responses in order to identify the anxiety dimensions underlying the athletes' ratings. Three sources of threat were revealed by the analysis. The first and most important was ego threat resulting from inadequate performance. The other two sources of threat were outcome uncertainty and expectation of losing (negative outcome certainty). Somewhat later, Passer (1983) and Rainey and Cunningham (1988) confirmed that fear of failure and fear of negative evaluation by others are sources of threat in sport competition, and that SCAT is a significant predictor of these threat perceptions. Rainey and Cunningham also reported that the perceived importance of sport was a source of threat for female athletes. Finally, Gould, Horn, and Spreeman (1983b) identified three sources of threat in junior elite wrestlers: fear of failure/feelings of inadequacy, social evaluation, and external control/guilt. High competitive A-trait was the most significant predictor of the first two sources of threat, but competitive A-trait was not related to the external control/guilt source.

With respect to the intrapersonal factors aspect of Link 1, the perception of threat in competitive situations varies from person to person, primarily as a function of competitive A-trait. Research has shown that persons with higher levels of competitive A-trait as measured by SCAT perceive a greater degree of threat in competitive situations than do persons with lower levels of competitive A-trait (e.g., Martens & Gill, 1976; Scanlan, 1977, 1978; Scanlan & Passer, 1979; Simon & Martens, 1977). To gain greater understanding of the behavioral manifestations of athletes' perceptions of threat, comparisons have been made between high *versus* low competitive A-trait individuals participating in a wide variety of sports (e.g., soccer, wrestling, basketball, gymnastics) at intramural, interscholastic, and agency-sponsored levels. The findings supported Passer's (1983) contention that perceived threat is based on performance-based worries and also worries about negative social evaluation. Specifically, high competitive A-trait individuals were found to worry more about (a) making mistakes; (b) not performing well; (c) not performing up to their level of ability; (d) improving on their last performance; (e) participating in championship competition; (f) being able to get mentally able to perform; and (g) losing (Brustad, 1988; Brustad & Weiss, 1987; Feltz & Albrecht, 1986; Passer, 1983; Pierce, 1980; Rainey, Conklin, & Rainey, 1987). High competitive A-trait individuals were also found to (a) expect to play less well in the future, (b) experience greater emotional upset, shame, and self-criticism after losing, (c) have more trouble sleeping before competition, and (d) feel that their nervousness more often hurts their performance (Gould et al., 1983a; Passer, 1983).

In accordance with the person-by-situation interaction of Link 1, empirical evidence has demonstrated the combined importance of situational factors and competitive A-trait in creating differential levels of perceived threat. Gould et al. (1983a) found that high competitive A-trait wrestlers predicted higher anxiety for themselves before and during competition than did low competitive A-trait individuals. However, these differences disappeared in situations of low potential threat, that is, for measures obtained (a) 1 week before competition, and (b) during competition against their weakest opponent. As mentioned above, Fisher and Zwart (1982) assessed basketball players' recall of sources of anxiety experienced during pregame, game, and postgame periods. Similar to the Gould et al. (1983a) findings, the athletes' anxiety responses varied with their perceptions of situational threat. Moreover, competitive A-trait as measured by SCAT accounted for almost half of the anxiety response variance. It is also worth noting that gender may play a role in the perception of threat. Feltz and Albrecht (1986) and Brustad and Weiss (1987) found that the relation between competitive A-trait and perception of threat is more pronounced for males than for females. This finding prompted Martens, Vealey, and Burton (1990) to suggest that "gender socialization may cause males to value sport success more highly and thus to perceive more threat" (p. 106).

State anxiety prediction. *Link 2* of the competitive anxiety model predicts that *perception of threat* and *intrapersonal factors* interact to influence the individual's *state responses* (particularly A-state) and *performance*. One of the most important sources of convergent validity evidence derives from a line of research in which competitive A-trait was assessed by SCAT a few weeks or months prior to a motor skill contest or an athletic event. The ability of this scale to predict *general* A-state was then examined by administering Spielberger et al.'s (1970) STAI-S or Spielberger's (1973) STAIC-S during precompetition or midcompetition periods. Laboratory research with children and adults (Gill & Martens, 1977; Martens & Gill, 1976; Murphy & Woolfolk, 1987; Poteet & Weinberg, 1980; Scanlan, 1977; Weinberg, 1978, 1979) and field research with youth sport participants, interscholastic, and intercollegiate athletes (Martens & Simon, 1976; Scanlan & Passer, 1977, 1978, 1979; Watson, 1986; Weinberg & Genuchi, 1980) consistently indicated that high competitive A-trait individuals evidenced greater A-state before and during competition than low competitive A-trait individuals. Further, Martens, Burton, Rivkin, & Simon (1980) modified the STAI and STAIC by including items that were more sensitive to A-state in competitive situations. Both adult and child forms of the new scale—the Competitive State Anxiety Inventory (CSAI)—were subsequently utilized to examine the ability of SCAT to predict *competitive* A-state in accordance with the theoretical model of competitive anxiety. The SCAT-CSAI relation was found to be stronger than the SCAT-STAI relation in laboratory experiments (Scanlan, 1978; Scanlan & Ragan, 1978) and field studies (Cooley,

1987; Huband & McKelvie, 1986; Martens & Simon, 1976; Scanlan & Lewthwaite, 1984; Simon & Martens, 1977; Sonstroem & Bernardo, 1982). True to expectations, both low and high competitive A-trait individuals increased in competitive A-state from noncompetition to competition conditions, but the increase was significantly greater for high competitive A-trait individuals.

Nine laboratory and field studies were originally conducted by Martens and his colleagues to test the predictability of A-state from SCAT scores. It was determined that high SCAT performers manifested higher A-states than did low SCAT performers in competitive situations, but not in noncompetitive situations. SCAT was also found to be a better predictor of A-state than were other person, task, and situational variables in competitive situations, but not in noncompetitive situations. Similarly, SCAT was found to correlate more strongly with A-state in competitive than in noncompetitive situations, and partial support was provided for the prediction that the correlation between SCAT and A-state would grow stronger as the level of situational threat increased (Gill & Martens, 1977; Martens & Gill, 1976; Martens & Simon, 1976; Simon & Martens, 1977).

Prediction of performance. Another critical convergent validity issue concerns the relation between competitive A-trait and motor performance. According to the theoretical model of competitive anxiety, SCAT is not predicted to influence performance directly. Rather, because state responses account for the interaction of intrapersonal and situational factors, measures of A-state should be the best predictors of performance. Consistent with this perspective, several laboratory studies have found no significant relation between competitive A-trait and performance (Broughton & Perlstrom, 1986; Martens, Gill, & Scanlan, 1976; Murphy & Woolfolk, 1987; Poteet & Weinberg, 1980). However, when performance was measured qualitatively in terms of efficiency of movement rather than quantitatively on the basis of performance outcome, SCAT emerged as a significant predictor of performance. For example, Weinberg (1978) found that, in comparison with low competitive A-trait participants, high SCAT participants used more EMG energy before, during, and after performance on a competitive throwing task. Apparently the high competitive A-trait participants' utilization of muscular energy for performance was inhibited due to their perceived threat in competitive situations.

In a field study of collegiate golfers, Weinberg and Genuchi (1980) noted that the relation between A-state and performance was stronger than was the relation between competitive A-trait and performance. Two other field studies examining the relation between competitive A-trait and motor performance found no SCAT-performance relation in rugby players (Maynard & Howe, 1987) and marathon runners (McKelvie et al., 1985). However, Sonstroem and Bernardo (1982) reported that performance prediction was enhanced by computing a composite performance score based on several types of statistics and controlling for individual differences in competitive A-state responsiveness by using intraindividual measures. Utilizing these intraindividual controls resulted in support for the inverted-U model (Yerkes & Dodson, 1908) of the arousal-performance relation, the effect being especially pronounced for high competitive A-trait athletes. The overall findings were thus in accord with theoretical predictions, providing initial support for the construct validity of SCAT.

Postperformance outcomes. *Link 3* of the competitive anxiety model concerns the influence of *performance* and *intrapersonal factors* (especially competitive A-trait) on different *performance outcomes*, that is, the thoughts, feelings, and behaviors of individuals after they perform. In the original SCAT validation studies conducted in laboratory settings (Gill & Martens, 1977; Martens & Gill, 1976; Scanlan, 1977), competitive A-trait and performance factors (success and failure) were found to be significant predictors of postcompetition A-state as measured by the STAIC (Spielberger, 1973). Performance factors accounted for more of the A-state variance, however, than did competitive A-trait. Similarly, field studies have demonstrated that, although competitive A-trait may influence postcompetition A-state, the effects are minimal when compared to the influence of competitive success/failure (Scanlan & Lewthwaite, 1984; Scanlan & Passer, 1978, 1979).

Another performance outcome with relevance to SCAT's convergent validity is postcompetition social comparison preferences. Scanlan (1977, 1978) and Scanlan and Ragan (1978) conducted a series of investigations examining how competitive A-trait affects participants' preferences for future competition and opponents after they have performed in an experimental competitive situation. Differences in competitive A-trait measured by SCAT were shown to have no effect on preferences for future opponents (level of social comparison) or competitive *versus* noncompetitive conditions. However, differences in postcompetition social comparison preferences based on competitive A-trait emerged when achievement motivation level was also considered.

Finally, Cooley (1987) examined several postcompetition performance outcomes of adult club tennis players participating in a weekend tournament. Using SCAT, the CSAI (Martens et al., 1980), and Spielberger's (1970) STAI as predictors, Cooley found that competitive A-trait was a significant predictor of perceived match outcome and perceived impact of tension on performance. Indeed, competitive A-trait accounted for 16% of the variance in each of the performance outcomes.

With respect to *Link 4*, no research has directly addressed the influence of *performance outcomes* on *intrapersonal factors*, particularly competitive A-trait. Martens, Vealey, and Burton (1990) have emphasized that "a longitudinal approach is needed to test this link by examining the influence of different performance outcomes, or consequences of sport participation, on competitive A-trait over time" (p. 100).

Intervention effects. A final construct validity issue concerns the effects of procedures intended to change the construct of interest. In other words, what is the influence of treatment programs on competitive A-trait as measured by SCAT? Several researchers have used SCAT in intervention situations with varying results. Significant reductions in athletes' competitive A-trait have been demonstrated after a seasonal psychological skills training program (Hellstedt, 1987), a 3-week physical relaxation training program (Lanning & Hisanaga, 1983), and a social support and stress-reduction training program administered to coaches (Smith, Smoll, & Barnett, 1995). Conversely, positive treatment effects were not obtained as a consequence

of implementation of Smith's (1980) stress management training program (Crocker, 1989; Crocker et al., 1988), Meichenbaum's (1985) stress inoculation training program (Kerr & Leith, 1993), or biofeedback training (Blais & Vallerand, 1986). In these cases, however, it is unclear whether negative results are attributable to SCAT insensitivity to treatment effects or to ineffective interventions.

In contrast to the rich array of evidence relating to convergent validity, relatively little work has addressed discriminant validity. As noted above, SCAT does not correlate as highly with social desirability measures as does the STAI-T. We know of no research directed at the current controversy concerning depression-anxiety relations, but this is clearly a topic that deserves empirical attention.

Summary Evaluation

Martens and his colleagues developed and validated SCAT in response to the need for a sport-specific measure of A-trait (Martens, 1977; Martens, Vealey, & Burton, 1990). Rigorous scientific methodology was systematically applied in the conceptualization of competitive anxiety and in the operationalization of SCAT. This meticulous developmental work resulted in a scale with impressive psychometric properties. Next, progressively advanced versions of child and adult forms of SCAT were developed to measure unidimensional competitive A-trait. A series of carefully controlled laboratory and field studies was then conducted, providing initial support for the concurrent and construct validity of SCAT as a measure of competitive A-trait. In addition to studies conducted during the development of SCAT, subsequent sport-anxiety research has provided abundant evidence concerning the convergent validity of the scale. In this chapter, SCAT's convergent validity was addressed by summarizing evidence that supports theoretical predictions emanating from an expanded model of competitive anxiety (Figure 1). Finally, it should also be noted that detailed guidelines for the administration of SCAT have been established, and updated norms for different populations have been developed.

During the past two decades, SCAT has been a very important research tool within sport psychology. The vast majority of studies in which individual differences in competitive A-trait have been assessed in children and adults have utilized SCAT. There is no doubt that the availability of this inventory has stimulated research that has resulted in major advances in our understanding of sport anxiety, its antecedents, and its consequences. However, because of the widespread current interest in somatic and cognitive components of anxiety, it seems likely that the SCAT will be revised to reflect this distinction or supplanted by newer multidimensional scales that measure cognitive and somatic trait anxiety more systematically.

The Sport Anxiety Scale (SAS)

The Sport Anxiety Scale (SAS; Smith et al., 1990) was developed to fill the need for a sport-specific multidimensional measure of cognitive and somatic trait anxiety. The objective was a relatively short measure having separate cognitive and somatic subscales that could be combined to yield a total anxiety score. In the course of development, however, two separate cognitive factors emerged repeatedly in exploratory factor

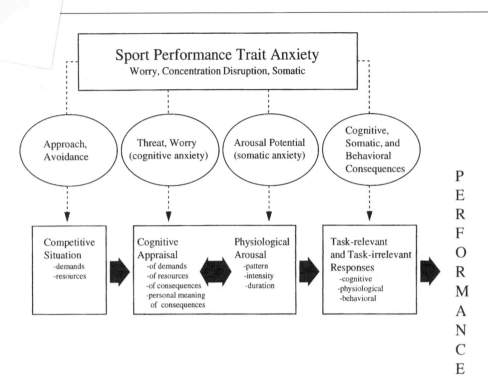

Figure 2. Conceptual model of sport performance anxiety showing the influence of cognitive and somatic trait anxiety as measured by the Sport Anxiety Scale on situational, cognitive, physiological, and behavioral variables.

analyses of data obtained from a number of different samples, so that the SAS that eventually evolved consists of subscales tapping somatic anxiety and the cognitive factors of worry and concentration disruption.

Theoretical Model

Because A-trait is defined as a predisposition to experience A-state under certain circumstances, an intimate relation exists between trait and state measures at a conceptual level. That is, the components of the trait model should relate meaningfully to the state model that represents the experiencing, expression, and consequences of A-state.

A conceptual model of athletic performance anxiety is presented in Figure 2. This model, derived from conceptions of emotionality and anxiety advanced by Arnold (1960), Ellis (1962), Lazarus and Folkman (1984), Mandler and Sarason (1952), Smith (1989a), and Spielberger (1966), includes both the trait-state distinction and the differentiation between situational, cognitive, physiological, and behavioral components of the process of anxiety. The model also accounts for the currently popular distinction between debilitative and facilitative anxiety (Jones & Swain, 1995).

The cognitive and somatic components of competitive A-state are shown within the appraisal and physiological response panels of the figure. The intensity and duration of the A-state response are assumed to be influenced by three major factors. The first of these factors is the nature of the competitive situation in which the athlete is involved. Obviously, such situations differ in the demands they place upon the athlete, as well as the degree of threat that they pose to successful performance. Such factors as strength of opponent, importance of the contest, presence of sig-

nificant others, and degree of social support received from coaches and teammates can affect the amount of threat that the situation is likely to pose for the individual. It should also be noted that A-trait influences the situations to which people will expose themselves. Thus, people with excessively high performance anxiety may choose to avoid the sport situation altogether.

A-trait is an intrapersonal individual difference variable that interacts with the situation to determine the level of A-state that is experienced. As noted above, this individual difference variable involves the individual's tendency to experience cognitive and somatic A-state reactions within competitive situations.

The objective situation and the performer's level of A-trait are assumed to influence the performer's appraisal processes. Four classes of appraisal are particularly important: appraisal of the situational demands; appraisal of the resources available to deal with them; appraisal of the nature and likelihood of potential consequences if the demands are not met (that is, the expectancies and valances relating to potential consequences); and the personal meaning that the consequences have for the individual. The meanings attached to the consequences derive from the person's belief system, and they often involve the individual's criteria for self-worth (Ellis, 1962; Rogers, 1959). Thus, an athlete who defines the present situational demands as overwhelming, who appraises his or her resources and skills as insufficient to deal with the demands, who anticipates failure and/or disapproval as a result of the demands/resources imbalance, and who defines his or her self-worth in terms of success and/or the approval of others will clearly perceive this competitive situation as threatening or dangerous. It is assumed that differences in the worry component of cognitive anxiety are especially important determinants of the kinds of appraisals that are made. Worriers perceive an unfavorable balance between demands and resources and expect the worst to occur.

Negative appraisals are likely to generate high levels of physiological arousal, and this arousal, in turn, feeds back into the ongoing process of appraisal and reappraisal. High levels of arousal may convince the athlete that he or she is "falling apart" and help generate even more negative appraisals. Athletes clearly differ in the amount of physiological arousal they report, and individual differences in the trait of somatic anxiety are likely to predispose athletes to differ in this regard. As behavior genetics research is demonstrating, some portion of the variance in somatic anxiety potential may be attributable to genetically-based constitutional factors (Buss, 1995). This is a topic that deserves empirical attention, and such research may be facilitated by the existence of a multidimensional anxiety scale that permits separate heritability indices for somatic and cognitive anxiety dimensions.

Because the relation between anxiety and performance has always been a central focus of sport anxiety research, we have included mechanisms assumed to influence performance. As Mandler and Sarason (1952) have noted, motivational and emotional states may generate two broad classes of task-related responses. Some of these responses (task-relevant responses) facilitate task performance, whereas others (task-irrelevant responses) are detrimental to performance. We suggest that the task-relevant and task-irrelevant responses may be cognitive, physiological, or behavioral in nature. Thus, cognitive responses such as concentration on the task and strategic planning may be facilitated by certain levels of A-state and would thereby contribute to performance. These responses (including the appraisal that the anxiety response will facilitate performance) are assumed to underlie some performers' reports that anxiety facilitates their performance (e.g., Jones & Swain, 1995). On the other hand, task-irrelevant cognitive responses such as worry and catastrophic thinking could readily interfere with task performance by disrupting attentional and problem-solving processes. Both the worry and concentration components of A-trait are assumed to be negative predisposing factors. Likewise, certain classes and intensities of physiological responding might facilitate task performance, whereas other types and intensities of physiological responding might interfere with task performance. Finally, behavioral responses such as persistence and smooth execution of motor responses would facilitate performance, whereas impulsive or inappropriate behaviors would interfere with it. These task-irrelevant responses contribute to debilitative anxiety effects. The balance between task-relevant and task-irrelevant responses and the manner in which they are affected by the performer's anxiety level will thus affect the adequacy of performance. It should also be noted that ongoing appraisal of performance adequacy can influence the four basic cognitive appraisal elements shown in the figure.

Development of the SAS

Three independent samples composed of 1,563 high school and college athletes participated in the scale development and factorial validation phase of the project. Sample 1 consisted of 250 male and 201 female athletes participating on 41 high school varsity teams in the sports of basketball, wrestling, and gymnastics. Sample 2 was composed of 123 college football players competing at a major university in the United States. The participants in Sample 3 were 490 male and female high school varsity athletes in the sports of football (males), soccer (females), and cross country running (males and females).

Initial item selection was carried out using a rational-intuitive, or deductive, approach in which items were selected based on their face validity as somatic and cognitive anxiety measures. Some of the initial SAS items were based on items found in existing measures of cognitive and somatic anxiety, such as Sarason's (1984) Reactions to Tests and the CSAI-2. Other items were newly written. A preliminary set of 15 cognitive items and 15 somatic items was selected for further study. This initial 30-item instrument was group administered to Samples 1 and 2 in the form of a questionnaire entitled "Reactions to Competition." The written instructions were designed to encourage accurate self-report and minimize social desirability response set and

modeled after those developed by Martens, Burton et al. (1990) for the CSAI-2. Sample 3 completed a shortened form comprising 22 of the items. Participants responded to each item on a four-point scale with the following alternatives: (1) not at all, (2) somewhat, (3) moderately so, and (4) very much so.

Exploratory Factor Analyses

To determine the dimensional structure of the items chosen to assess cognitive and somatic sport anxiety, a principal components analysis was carried out with rotation of factors to a varimax solution. A scree test resulted in the retention of three factors that accounted for 48% of the response variance. The first factor, which accounted for 22.0% of the variance, consisted of manifestations of somatic anxiety, such as muscle tension, cardiac responses, and upset stomach. The other two dimensions consisted entirely of cognitive items. The first of these factors consisted of items relating to worry and self-doubt. It accounted for 13.4% of the variance. The second cognitive factor included items dealing with intrusive thoughts and concentration disruption. It accounted for 11.1% of the variance. Supplementary principal components analyses carried out separately for males and for females yielded virtually identical factor structures and similarly high item factor loadings for both genders. This factor structure was replicated in a sample of 123 college football players.

Confirmatory Factor Analyses

The pattern of results that emerged from the exploratory factor analyses suggested that sport-specific anxiety as defined by the initial item pool comprised three independent dimensions, which were labeled Somatic Anxiety, Worry, and Concentration Disruption. Next, confirmatory factor analysis (CFA) was used to test this hypothesis, to assess the factorial validity of the measure, and to refine the item set for final scale construction. The first CFA was carried out on the readministration data provided by 384 participants from Sample 1, a different data set from that used in the initial exploratory analysis. Cross validation CFAs were performed on an independent sample of 490 high school athletes who completed a shortened 22-item version of the scale. CFAs were performed with the LISREL VI program, using the two-stage least squares followed by maximum likelihood (ML) option for parameter estimation (Jöreskog & Sörbom, 1984). The Pearson product-moment correlation matrix was the matrix analyzed, and the factors were free to correlate. In the first CFA, all 30 items were assigned to one of the three factors as identified in the earlier exploratory factor analyses. This resulted in 15 items on Factor 1 (Somatic Anxiety), 9 on Factor 2 (Worry) and 6 on Factor 3 (Concentration Disruption). In a second analysis, the originally hypothesized two-factor model was tested by combining the items from the Worry and Concentration Disruption factors into a single cognitive factor. Finally, the possibility of a unitary underlying structure was examined by testing a single-factor model.

The CFA procedures, described in greater detail in Smith et al., (1990), together with internal consistency analyses, prompted the deletion of 9 items from the original 30-item pool, resulting in a 21-item inventory with three subscales. The CFA results favored the three-factor solution over the one-factor

Table 3
The Sport Anxiety Scale.

REACTIONS TO COMPETITION

A number of statements that athletes have used to describe their thoughts and feelings before or during competition are listed below. Read each statement and then circle the number to the right of the statement that indicates how you usually feel prior to or during competition. Some athletes feel they should not admit to feelings of nervousness or worry, but such reactions are actually quite common, even among professional athletes. To help us better understand reactions to competition, we ask you to share your true reactions with us. There are, therefore, no right or wrong answers. Do not spend too much time on any one statement.

	Statement	Not At All	Some-what	Moder ately So	Very Much So
1.	I feel nervous.	1	2	3	4
2.	During competition, I find myself thinking about unrelated things.	1	2	3	4
3.	I have self-doubts.	1	2	3	4
4.	My body feels tense.	1	2	3	4
5.	I am concerned that I may not do as well in competition as I could.	1	2	3	4
6.	My mind wanders during sport competition.	1	2	3	4
7.	While performing, I often do not pay attention to what's going on.	1	2	3	4
8.	I feel tense in my stomach.	1	2	3	4
9.	Thoughts of doing poorly interfere with my concentration during competition.	1	2	3	4
10.	I am concerned about choking under pressure.	1	2	3	4
11.	My heart races.	1	2	3	4
12.	I feel my stomach sinking.	1	2	3	4
13.	I'm concerned about performing poorly.	1	2	3	4
14.	I have lapses in concentration during competition because of nervousness.	1	2	3	4
15.	I sometimes find myself trembling before or during a competitive event.	1	2	3	4
16.	I'm worried about reaching my goal.	1	2	3	4
17.	My body feels tight.	1	2	3	4
18.	I'm concerned that others will be disappointed with my performance.	1	2	3	4
19.	My stomach gets upset before or during competition.	1	2	3	4
20.	I'm concerned I won't be able to concentrate.	1	2	3	4
21.	My heart pounds before competition.	1	2	3	4

Note: Somatic Anxiety Scale: Items 1, 4, 8, 11, 12, 15, 17, 19, 21.
Worry Scale: Items 3, 5, 9, 10, 13, 16, 18.
Concentration Disruption Scale: Items 2, 6, 7, 14, 20.

(unitary underlying structure) or two-factor (somatic and one cognitive factor) models. The final 21-item scale, presented with its instructions in Table 3, had a goodness-of-fit index of .874, with a root mean square residual of .073. Item factor loadings within each of the three subscales were high, ranging from .50 to .79.

The CFA of the model proposed from the exploratory factor analyses provided reasonable support for retention of this three-factor structure. Additionally, deletion of nine of the original 30 items resulted in a more parsimonious model, without loss of internal consistency or structural reliability. The Somatic Anxiety factor seems to be the most robust, as indicated by high internal consistency indices and strong factor loadings, as well as and the amount of variance it accounts for. The splitting of the originally hypothesized cognitive factor into the two components, Worry and Concentration Disruption, is supported by the replicated CFAs involving Samples 1 and 3. Thus, the items represent three distinct factors, and all of the items on the three subscales have factor loadings exceeding .50.

Norms

Smith et al. (1990) provided normative data in the form of means and standard deviations for 489 male and 348 female high school athletes and 123 college football players. On the Somatic Anxiety scale, where scores can range from 9 to 36, the three samples had means of 19.82 (SD = 5.71), 19.97 (SD = 6.66), and 18.98 (SD = 5.48), respectively. For Worry, where scores can range from 7 to 28, the corresponding means were 15.23 (SD = 4.34), 16.21 (SD = 4.79), and 14.17 (SD = 4.47); and for Concentration Disruption, where scores can range from 5 to 20, they were 8.39 (SD = 2.91), 8.36 (SD = 2.75), and 7.71 (SD = 2.21). Total score means, which can range from 21 to 84, were 43.44 (SD = 10.81), 44.54 (SD = 12.12), and 40.86 (SD = 9.99) for the respective samples. Male-female differences were very small on all subscales, and the college football players had somewhat lower scores on the scales.

Reliability

Both internal consistency and test-retest reliability data were presented in Smith et al. (1990). Internal consistency (Cronbach's alpha) coefficients were reported for two samples. In one sample of 384 male and female high school athletes, alpha was .92 for Somatic Anxiety, .86 for Worry, and .81 for Concentration Disruption. For the total scale, alpha was .93. All item-total correlations within subscales exceeded .61. In a second sample of 490 high school athletes, alpha coefficients for the three subscales were .88 for Somatic Anxiety, .82 for Worry, and .74 for Concentration Disruption. Item-total correlations were all above .50 for the Somatic Anxiety and Worry factors, except for one item on the Worry factor, which correlated .46 with the subscale total score.

Test-retest reliability data were also reported for two samples. A sample of 77 football players was given the SAS twice over a test-retest interval of 18 days. Test-retest reliability over 18 days was .77 for the full scale. Subscale test-retest coefficients were .71, .70, and .68 for Somatic Anxiety, Worry, and Concentration Disruption, respectively. Test-retest reliability in this sample of football players was acceptable, but not as high as one would like. A plausible explanation for the attenuated test-retest reliability is that the first administration was conducted prior to the season, whereas the second occurred after the second game. Thus, the first score was likely based on past experience and the second on current reactions to competition. For this reason, another sample of 64 college athletes was assessed under more stable conditions (i.e., currently competing or not competing at both administrations). In this sample, 7-day test-retest reliabilities exceeded .85 on all scales.

Validity

Factorial validity. High factorial validity of the SAS was an expected product of the manner in which the test was constructed. Replicated factor structures based on both principal component and structural equation methods demonstrated the existence of the three factors. Structural reliability is likewise indicated by the internal consistency of its relatively brief subscales, which is quite high given the fact that coefficient alpha is heavily influenced by the number of items in the scale.

One qualification concerning the factorial validity of the SAS arose in a recent study in which the scale was administered to 9- to 11-year-old male athletes participating in a youth baseball program (Smith, Smoll, et al., 1995). A factor analysis of these data resulted in the emergence of five uninterpretable factors that contained mixtures of somatic and cognitive items, forcing the investigators to use the SAS total score (which had an acceptable alpha of .89). Whether this result is indicative of an inapplicability of the items to child populations, or whether children do not have the cognitive maturity to make the distinctions that adults do between the cognitive and somatic aspects of their affective reactions, is unclear. Clearly, the need for developmental research on the SAS is indicated, and such research may yield important information concerning emotional development.

Convergent and discriminant validity. Because the SAS is a recently developed scale, data concerning its validity are not as voluminous as in the case of the SCAT. Nonetheless, preliminary validity evidence does exist. This includes information on relations with other scales that help to establish convergent and discriminant validity, predictions of precompetitive mood states, relations with performance, and one study on its role as a predictor of injuries.

Smith et al. (1990) assessed the convergent and discriminant validity of the SAS by correlating it with other scales. One aspect of convergent validity is indicated by the concurrent validity of the scale (in this case, how it correlates with established sport anxiety measures). Concurrent validity was indicated by substantial correlations with the SCAT. In a sample of 339 high school athletes, the SAS and SCAT total scores correlated .81. As expected from the nature of the SCAT items, which are primarily somatic, the Somatic subscale of the SAS exhibited the highest correlation with the SCAT (.80). Correlations between the SCAT and the SAS cognitive subscales were lower (.66 with Worry and .47 with Concentration Disruption). The pattern of SCAT-SAS correlations indicate that the SCAT is not a sensitive measure of cognitive sport anxiety due to an insufficiently large number of cognitive items.

As expected, correlations with the general A-trait measure provided by the STAI Trait measure were lower than those exhibited with the SCAT. Correlations between the STAI-T and the subscales and total score of the SAS ranged from .38 to .49. The magnitude of these correlations with the STAI-T approximate those obtained with other situation-specific anxiety measures (typically in the .40 to .50 range). Thus, the SAS shares some degree of common variance with the general anxiety measure, but not a substantial amount. This finding, like many parallel findings with other situation-specific measures, suggests the advisability of employing scales like the SCAT and the SAS to assess situation-specific anxiety reactions.

One aspect of discriminant validity was assessed in correlations between the SAS and the Marlowe-Crowne Social Desirability Scale (M-C SDS; Crowne & Marlowe, 1960). The lat-

ter scale correlated -.35 with SAS total score and between -.23 and -.30 with the subscales. This magnitude of correlation, comparable to that found with other anxiety scales, indicates that the tendency to present oneself in a positive light is negatively related to SAS scores, particularly the full-scale score, but that the SAS total variance is not highly contaminated with extraneous social desirability variance. These data were not collected in an anonymous fashion, and we might expect correlations to be somewhat lower when data are collected anonymously.

Discriminant validity was also indicated by low correlations (ranging between -.22 and -.29) with the total score of the Mental Health Inventory, which measures general psychological adjustment (Veit & Ware, 1983). Again, we would not expect high negative correlations with general adjustment, given the domain-specific nature of the SAS.

The SAS exhibited low and nonsignificant correlations with Rosenbaum's (1980) Self-Control Schedule, indicating that anxiety is relatively independent of cognitive-behavioral coping skills. This finding suggests that it is possible to identify anxious athletes who either have or do not have such coping skills. We might hypothesize that negative relations between anxiety and outcome measures would be highest for high anxiety-low coping skills individuals.

Structural fidelity and subscale correlations. Construct validity relates to the internal structure of the scale as well as to its relations with external criterion measures. As Loevinger (1957) noted in her discussion of an aspect of construct validity that she termed structural fidelity, the components of multifaceted constructs like sport anxiety should mirror the relations posited by the underlying theory as well as those established by other sources of data. Current cognitive-affective theories of sport anxiety (e.g., Martens, Vealey, & Burton, 1990; Smith & Smoll, 1990) posit causal relations between somatic and cognitive components of the anxiety response, and such relations have been demonstrated empirically as well (e.g., Folkman & Lazarus, 1984). We should therefore expect to find significant correlations between measures of these components. This may at first glance seem incompatible with the statistical independence between the scales suggested by the factor analytic data cited above. However, despite compelling factor analytic evidence for the existence of three factors, orthogonal factor extractions do not mean that subscale scores based on summing the raw scores of the individual items will be uncorrelated (Nunnally & Bernstein, 1994; Smith, 1989b). Given the cognitive-affective relations posited by the theoretical model underlying the SAS, it is not surprising that correlations among the SAS subscales were moderately high. In a sample of 489 male and 348 female high school athletes, the Somatic Anxiety subscale correlated .62 with Worry and .50 with Concentration Disruption; the latter two subscales correlated .63. These correlations are similar to those found for A-trait measures of cognitive and somatic anxiety in other domains (e.g., Morris, Davis, et al., 1981; Sarason, 1984) and seem to reflect the characteristic correlations (real-world relations) that exist between the cognitive and somatic components of anxiety.

Mood and A-state prediction. If A-trait is defined as a predisposition to experience anxiety states under certain conditions, then an athlete who is high in sport-specific trait anxiety would be expected to experience high levels of somatic arousal, worry, and/or concentration disruption when exposed to stressful competitive conditions. To test this prediction, Smith et al. (1990) assessed the ability of SAS scores to predict anxiety reactions in such a situation, relating SAS scores obtained 2 weeks earlier to a short form of the Profile of Mood States (POMS; McNair, Lorr, & Droppleman, 1971) on the day of a very important game. The highest SAS correlations occurred with the Tension and Confusion subscales of the POMS, which would appear to be most reflective of anxiety state. On these POMS scales, Somatic Anxiety and Worry correlated most highly, whereas Concentration Disruption was minimally correlated. Although the correlations were lower, the Somatic Anxiety and Worry scales also predicted anger responses and, to a lesser extent, depression. The trait scales were not significantly related to Fatigue or Vigor on the POMS.

The results of this study provided additional evidence of convergent validity in the form of high correlations with state measures of tension and confusion, but the results were not entirely consistent with expectations. The Somatic Anxiety scale was most highly predictive of Tension, as might be expected, and Worry was also correlated with the anxiety indicators. Somewhat surprising, however, was the failure of the Concentration Disruption scale to correlate significantly with Confusion. Indeed, this SAS subscale exhibited low relations with all of the mood scales. However, it may be noteworthy that all of the items refer to concentration difficulties during competition itself, whereas the POMS was administered 3 hours before the contest. It remains for future research to assess the value of this scale for predicting cognitive and emotional reactions at various times before and during competition.

To a lesser extent, SAS scores also related to anger and depression. This was particularly true for Somatic Anxiety. Given the similarity in somatic arousal that occurs in anger and anxiety states, the relation between the Somatic scale and anger is not surprising. On the other hand, it is less clear why the Somatic Anxiety scale should relate to depressed affect more strongly than Worry did. The latter finding seems inconsistent with the discriminant validity pattern that was expected. However, as noted earlier, considerable evidence now exists that anxiety and depression frequently coexist in the form of a negative affectivity factor (Watson & Clark, 1984), and these SAS-POMS linkages may reflect a common negative affectivity factor.

Given the availability of the CSAI-2, a sport-specific measure of somatic and cognitive state anxiety, research in which the SAS scales have been used to predict these two forms of A-state is of considerable interest. Krane and Finch (1991) found evidence for predictive validity in a sample of 179 collegiate tennis and golf athletes. SAS Somatic Anxiety correlated .59 with CSAI-2 Somatic Anxiety and only .35 with CSAI-2 Cognitive Anxiety scores obtained prior to competitive events. Conversely, SAS Worry correlated .68 with CSAI-2 Cognitive Anxiety and .37 with state Somatic Anxiety. SAS Concentration Disruption's correlational pattern was less discriminable (.37 with CSAI-2 Cognitive and .25 with somatic state anxiety). This, however, may be due to the fact that the CSAI-2 does not contain a set of items that specifically address attentional difficulties.

In a more recent study by Leffingwell and Williams (1995) on prediction of A-state by the SAS and the SCAT, samples consisting of 36 college cross-country runners and 35 students in a tennis class completed the CSAI-2 before an important meet and a final tennis skill test, respectively. Among the cross-country runners, considerable discriminability was found for SAS Worry, which correlated .74 with cognitive A-state and only .24 with somatic A-state. SAS Concentration Disruption correlated significantly with cognitive A-state (.37), but not with somatic A-state (.24). Surprisingly, however, SAS Somatic anxiety also correlated more highly with cognitive A-state (.60) than it did with somatic A-state (.43). In the tennis student sample, an opposite pattern of discriminability was found. Here, SAS Somatic Anxiety predicted CSAI-2 somatic scores (.63), but was unrelated to cognitive A-state (.13). On the other hand, Worry was more strongly predictive of somatic A-state (.74) than it was of CSAI-2 cognitive scores (.47). Concentration Disruption was equally related to cognitive (.52) and somatic (.55) A-state. The SCAT also demonstrated inconsistent predictive relations, being more highly related to cognitive anxiety in the cross-country sample and more highly related to somatic anxiety in the tennis sample. How these different patterns of predictive discriminability might be related to sample differences is unclear, but Leffingwell and Williams caution that the small sample sizes preclude definitive conclusions. Clearly, more work is needed to evaluate predictive patterns of A-state in large samples of athletes who are competing in actual sporting events in order to assess this important aspect of SAS validity.

Performance. Historically, interest in sport-related anxiety has focused on associations between anxiety and performance. High levels of anxiety have consistently been related to performance decrements (Smith & Smoll, 1990). However, it is unclear whether performance decrements are caused by interfering effects of high physiological arousal, by cognitive interference, or by both factors.

Smith et al. (1990) assessed relations between the SAS and a behavioral index of task performance under competitive conditions. In this study, performance scores based on coaches' gradings of game films over the course of a college football season served as the dependent variable measure, providing a performance measure having high ecological validity. SAS scores obtained before the season were compared for high and low performers as defined during the season by the film grades they received from their coaches. A significant group difference was found for the SAS total score and for the Concentration Disruption subscale, with low performers having higher scores, but not for the Somatic or Worry scales. This pattern of results suggests that concentration disruption may be a primary factor in poor performance under stressful game conditions.

Injury prediction. In a theoretical article on psychosocial determinants of athletic injury, Andersen and Williams (1988) identified a number of individual difference variables that might be expected to moderate a relation between life stress and athletic injuries, among them A-trait. A-trait could constitute a risk factor by predisposing individuals to experience high levels of muscular tension or by disrupting attentional factors, either of which could increase injury risk. In a prospective study designed to assess anxiety as a potential moderator variable of the life stress-injury relation, Smith, Ptacek, Everett, and May (1995) administered a life stress measure and the SAS (with the word *competition* changed to *performances* in the items) to a sample of ballet dancers for whom injury data were collected on a daily basis for the next 8 months. Hierarchical regression analyses in which life stress and anxiety scores were entered first, followed by life stress and SAS subscale product scores, to test the moderator effect, revealed that neither life stress scores nor anxiety scores accounted for significant injury variance by themselves. On the other hand, the product scores used to test the life stress-anxiety interactions indicated that all three subscales of the SAS were involved in significant interactions with life stress, with high scorers on the subscales more likely to incur injury when under high levels of life stress. These findings suggest that somatic anxiety, worry, and concentration disruption may all be capable of increasing the risk of injury in highly stressed individuals, and that they may in fact predict the processes that mediate the effect.

Intervention effects. If the SAS is a valid measure of sport performance anxiety, scores should be responsive to experimental interventions designed to increase or decrease anxiety. That is, the SAS should have value as an outcome variable. Thus far, we are aware of only one investigation in which SAS was used as an outcome measure. In a study by Smith, Smoll, et al. (1995), Coach Effectiveness Training (Smith, Smoll, & Curtis, 1979), an intervention designed to train coaches to reduce the stressfulness of the athletic environment by deemphasizing winning and providing high levels of social support, resulted in a significant decrease in SAS total scores in 9-to 12-year old male baseball players. The SAS total score was used as an outcome measure when the factor structure of the SAS did not conform to the three-factor solution found in older samples (see earlier discussion). Trait anxiety reduction in the experimental group also occurred on the SCAT, which was administered only at postseason. It thus appears that the SAS is sensitive to interventions designed to decrease anxiety. As yet, we do not know if SAS scores increase when individuals are subjected to increased sport-related stress.

Summary Evaluation

Although much more research is needed to assess the validity of the SAS, the scale appears to have promise as a research tool. It appears that the scale taps three meaningful dimensions of anxiety. In addition to the somatic component, which has been customarily identified in factor analytic studies involving anxiety scales, SAS analyses indicate the viability of a distinction between the cognitive components labeled as Worry and Concentration Disruption. Both exploratory and confirmatory factor analyses indicate that these are separate aspects of the anxiety reaction. In this regard, SAS results parallel those of Sarason (1984), who found similar cognitive factors as part of the reaction pattern to another evaluative performance situation, namely academic tests. Much additional research is needed to assess relations between the subscales and various outcomes, such as performance, injuries, and the effects of various sport interventions. Because of positive correlations between the subscales when new scores are used, Smith (1989b) has recommended the use of orthogonal (varimax) factor scores to

preserve the independence of the somatic and cognitive factors when theoretical questions involving these components of A-trait are the focus of research. The availability of a multidimensional trait scale like the SAS may provide a tool for answering important theoretical questions about the dynamics of anxiety and how it affects cognition, affect, and behavior. More work is also needed on developmental issues related to the components of anxiety so as to determine the developmental course of cognitive differentiation between cognitive and somatic components of anxiety. The fact that the factor structure of the SAS, so consistently replicated in adolescent and adult samples, did not hold up in the youth baseball study may indicate either that children do not differentiate emotional components as older age groups do, or that the SAS subscales are not suitable for children and that a children's form of the SAS is needed.

Conclusion and Future Prospects

The historical development of trait measures of anxiety has proceeded from global trait measures exemplified by the STAI-T to unidimensional domain-specific measures such as the SCAT and on to the development of multidimensional measures like the SAS. Clearly, the SCAT has had the greatest impact on the field of sport psychology, providing a research tool used in more than 100 studies. Multidimensional tools like the CSAI-2 and the SAS now allow researchers to build upon the great leaps in knowledge attributable to the SCAT, refining our understanding of the somatic and cognitive components of anxiety.

Because of its centrality as a sport-related variable, anxiety will continue to be a focus of research in exercise and sport psychology. Measurement lies at the heart of all scientific activity, and advances cannot occur without adequate measures of the constructs of interest. Continued refinement of measures will both stem from and stimulate theoretical advances in understanding the complex facets of anxiety.

Advances in measurement also reflect the contribution of increasingly sophisticated test construction methods. In particular, the use of confirmatory factor analysis has not only demonstrated the psychometric inadequacies of a variety of frequently used sport psychology measures (see Chartrand, Jowdy, & Danish, 1992; Ford & Summers, 1992; and Schutz, Eom, Smoll, & Smith, 1994), but, more importantly, has provided an invaluable tool to be used in the development of measures having high factorial validity. As test construction sophistication continues to increase, we can expect progressively better measures of anxiety and other constructs to emerge.

References

Albrecht, R. R., & Feltz, D. L. (1987). Generality and specificity of attention related to competitive anxiety and sport performance. *Journal of Sport Psychology, 9,* 231-248.

Andersen, M. B., & Williams, J. (1988). A model of stress and athletic injury: Prediction and prevention. *Journal of Sport and Exercise Psychology, 10,* 294-306.

Apitzsch, E. (Ed.) (1983). *Anxiety in sport.* Magglingen, Switzerland: Guido Schilling, ETS.

Arnold, M. B. (1960). *Emotion and personality.* New York: Columbia University Press.

Atkinson, J. W., & Feather, N. T. (Eds.). *A theory of achievement motivation.* New York: Wiley.

Bandura, A. (1986). *Social foundations of thought and action: A social cognitive theory*. Englewood Cliffs, NJ: Prentice-Hall.

Barker, B.M., Barker, H.R., & Wadsworth, A.P. (1977). Factor analysis of the items of the State-Trait Anxiety Inventory. *Journal of Clinical Psychology, 33*, 450-455.

Betts, E. (1982). Relation of locus of control to aspiration level and to competitive anxiety. *Psychological Reports, 51*, 71-76.

Bialer, I. (1961). Conceptualization of success and failure in mentally retarded and normal children. *Journal of Personality, 29*, 303-320.

Blais, M. R., & Vallerand, R. J. (1986). Multimodal effects of electromyographic biofeedback: Looking at children's ability to control precompetitive anxiety. *Journal of Sport Psychology, 8*, 283-303.

Borkovec, T. D. (1976). Physiological and cognitive processes in the regulation of anxiety. In G. Schwartz & D. Shapiro (Eds.), *Conscious and self-regulation: Advances in research* (Vol. 1, pp. 261-312). New York: Plenum.

Broughton, R. S., & Perlstrom, J. R. (1986). PK experiments with a competitive computer game. *Journal of Parapsychology, 50*, 193-211.

Brustad, R. J. (1988). Affective outcomes in competitive youth sport: The influence of intrapersonal and socialization factors. *Journal of Sport and Exercise Psychology, 10*, 307-321.

Brustad, R. J., & Weiss, M. R. (1987). Competence perceptions and sources of worry in high, medium, and low competitive trait-anxious young athletes. *Journal of Sport Psychology, 9*, 97-105.

Burton, D. (1988). Do anxious swimmers swim slower? Reexamining the elusive anxiety-performance relationship. *Journal of Sport and Exercise Psychology, 10*, 45-61.

Buss, A. H. (1995). Personality: *Temperament, social behavior, and the self*. Boston: Allyn and Bacon.

Campbell, D. T., & Fiske, D. W. (1959). Convergent and discriminant validation by the multitrait-multimethod matrix. *Psychological Bulletin, 56*, 81-105.

Cannon, W. B. (1929). The mechanism of emotional disturbance of bodily functions. *New England Journal of Medicine, 198*, 877-884

Cattell, R. B., & Cattell, M. D. (1969). *Junior-senior high school personality questionnaire*. Champaign, IL: Institute for Personality and Ability Testing.

Cattell, R.B. & Scheier, I.H. (1963). *Handbook for the IPAT Anxiety Scale (2nd ed.)*. Champaign, IL: Institute for Personality and Ability Testing.

Chartrand, J., Jowdy, D. P., & Danish, S. J. (1992). The Psychological Skills Inventory for Sports: Psychometric characteristics and applied implications. *Journal of Sport and Exercise Psychology, 14*, 405-413.

Cooley, E.J. (1987). Situational and trait determinants of competitive state anxiety. *Perceptual and Motor Skills, 64*, 767-773.

Crocker, P. R. E. (1989). A follow-up of cognitive-affective stress management training. *Journal of Exercise and Sport Psychology, 11*, 236-242.

Crocker, P. R. E., Alderman, R. B., & Smith, F. M. R. (1988). Cognitive-affective stress management training with high performance youth volleyball players: Effects on affect, cognition, and performance. *Journal of Sport and Exercise Psychology, 10*, 448-460.

Cronbach, L. J., & Meehl, P. E. (1955). Construct validity in psychological tests. *Psychological Bulletin, 52*, 281-302.

Crowne, D. P., & Marlowe, D. (1960). A new scale of social desirability independent of psychopathology. *Journal of Consulting Psychology, 24*, 349-354.

Davidson, R. J., & Schwartz, G. E. (1976). The psychobiology of relaxation and related states: A multi-process theory. In D. Mostofsky (Ed.), *Behavioral control and modification of physiological activity* (pp. 399-442). Englewood Cliffs, NJ: Prentice-Hall.

Deffenbacher, J. L. (1980). Worry and emotionality in test anxiety. In I. G. Sarason (Ed.), *Test anxiety: Theory, research, and applications* (pp. 111-128). Hillsdale, NJ: Erlbaum.

Ellis, A. (1962). *Reason and emotion in psychotherapy*. New York: Lyle Stuart.

Endler, N. S., Cox, B. J., Parker, J. D., & Bagby, R. M. (1992). Self-reports of depression and state-trait anxiety: Evidence for differential assessment. *Journal of Personality and Social Psychology, 63*, 832-838.

Esposito, J. L., Agard, E., & Rosnow, R. L. (1984). Can confidentiality of data pay off? *Personality and Individual Differences, 5*, 477-480.

Feltz, D. L., & Albrecht, R. R. (1986). Psychological implications of competitive running. In M. R. Weiss & D. Gould (Eds.), *Sport for children and youths* (pp. 225-230). Champaign, IL: Human Kinetics.

Fisher, A. C., & Zwart, E. F. (1982). Psychological analysis of athletes' anxiety responses. *Journal of Sport Psychology, 4*, 139-158.

Ford, S. K., & Summers, J. J. (1992). The factorial validity of the TAIS attentional-style subscales. *Journal of Sport and Exercise Psychology, 14*, 283-297.

Gill, D. L., & Deeter, T. E. (1988). Development of the Sport Orientation Questionnaire. *Research Quarterly for Exercise and Sport, 59*, 191-202.

Gill, D. L., Dzewaltowski, D. A., & Deeter, T. E. (1988). The relationship of competitiveness and achievement orientation to participation in sport and nonsport activities. *Journal of Sport and Exercise Psychology, 10*, 139-150.

Gill, D. L., & Martens, R. (1977). The role of task type and success-failure in group competition. *International Journal of Sport Psychology, 8*, 160-177.

Gould, D., Feltz, D., Horn, T., & Weiss, M. (1982). Reasons for discontinuing involvement in competitive youth swimming. *Journal of Sport Behavior, 5*, 155-165.

Gould, D., Horn, T., & Spreeman, J. (1983a). Competitive anxiety in junior elite wrestlers. *Journal of Sport Psychology, 5*, 58-71.

Gould, D., Horn, T., & Spreeman, J. (1983b). Sources of stress in junior elite wrestlers. *Journal of Sport Psychology, 5*, 159-171.

Gould, D., Petlichkoff, L., Simons, J., & Vevera, M. (1987). The relationship between Competitive State Anxiety Inventory-2 subscale scores and pistol shooting performance. *Journal of Sport Psychology, 9*, 33-42.

Gould, D., Petlichkoff, L., & Weinberg, R. S. (1984). Antecedents of, temporal changes in, and relationships between CSAI-2 subcomponents. *Journal of Sport Psychology, 6*, 289-304.

Hackfort, D., & Schwenkmezger, P. (1985). *Angst und Angstkontrolle im Sport*. Koln: bps.

Hackfort, D., & Schwenkmezger, P. (1989). Measuring anxiety in sports: Perspectives and problems. In D. Hackfort and C. Spielberger (Eds.). *Anxiety in Sports*. New York: Hemisphere.

Hackfort, D., & Spielberger, C. D. (Eds.). (1988). *Anxiety in sports: An international perspective*. New York: Hemisphere.

Hackfort, D. & Spielberger, C.D. (1989). *Anxiety in Sports*. New York: Hemisphere Publishing.

Harter, S. (1979). *Perceived competence scale for children* (Form O) [Manual]. Denver: University of Denver.

Hellstedt, J. C. (1987). Sport psychology at a ski academy: Teaching mental skills to young athletes. *The Sport Psychologist, 1*, 56-58.

Huband, E. D., & McKelvie, J. S. (1986). Pre and post game state anxiety in team athletes high and low in competitive trait anxiety. *International Journal of Sport Psychology, 17*, 191-198.

Jaspen, N. (1946). Serial correlation. *Psychometrika, 11*, 23-30.

Jones, G., & Swain, A. (1995). Predisposition to experience debilitative and facilitative anxiety in elite and nonelite performers. *The Sport Psychologist, 9*, 201-211.

Jöreskog, K. G., & Sörbom, D. (1984). *Lisrel VI: Analysis of linear structural relationships by the method of maximum likelihood*. Mooresville, IN: Scientific Software.

Karteroliotis, C., & Gill, D. L. (1987). Temporal changes in psychological and physiological components of state anxiety. *Journal of Sport Psychology, 9,* 261-274.

Kendall, P.C., Finch, A.J., Auerbach, S.M., Hooke, J.F., & Mikulka, P.J. (1976). The State-Trait Anxiety Inventory: A systematic evaluation. *Journal of Consulting and Clinical Psychology, 44,* 406-412.

Kendrick, M. J., Craig, K. D., Lawson, D. M., & Davidson, P. O. (1982). Cognitive and behavioral therapy for musical-performance anxiety. *Journal of Consulting and Clinical Psychology, 50,* 353-362.

Kerlinger, F. N. (1973). *Foundations of behavioral research* (2nd ed.). New York: Holt, Rinehart and Winston.

Kerr, G., & Leith, L. (1993). Stress management and athletic performance. *The Sport Psychologist, 7,* 221-231.

Krane, V., & Finch, L. (1991, April). *Multidimensional trait anxiety as a predictor of multidimensional state anxiety.* Paper presented at the Annual Meeting of the American Association of Health, Physical Education, Recreation, and Dance, San Francisco, CA.

Lang, P. J. (1971). The application of psychophysiological methods to the study of psychotherapy and behavior modification. In A. E. Bergin & S. L. Garfield (Eds.), *Handbook of psychotherapy and behavior change (pp. 71-103).* New York: Wiley.

Lanning, W., & Hisanaga, B. (1983). A study of the relation between the reduction of competition anxiety and an increase in athletic performance. *International Journal of Sport Psychology, 14,* 219-227.

Lazarus, R. S., & Folkman, S. (1984). *Stress, appraisal, and coping.* New York: Springer.

Leffingwell, T. R. (1995). [Sport Competition Anxiety Test scores for a sample of male intercollegiate athletes]. Unpublished raw data.

Leffingwell, T. R., & Williams, J. M. (1995, June). *Comparison of the Sport Anxiety Scale (SAS) and the Sport Competition Anxiety Test (SCAT) at predicting multidimensional state anxiety.* Paper presented at the Meeting of the North American Society for the Psychological Study of Sport and Physical Activity, Monterey, CA.

Levy, N. A. (1958). A short form of the Children's Manifest Anxiety Scale. *Child Development, 29,* 153-154.

Liebert, R. M., & Morris, L. W. (1967). Cognitive and emotional components of test anxiety: A distinction and some initial data. *Psychological Reports, 20,* 975-978.

Loevinger, J. (1957). Objective tests as instruments of psychological theory. *Psychological Reports, 3,* 635-694.

Magnusson, D. (1966). *Test theory.* Reading, MA: Addison-Wesley.

Magnusson, D., & Endler, N. S. (Eds.). (1977). *Personality at the crossroads: Current issues in interactional psychology.* Hillsdale, NJ: Erlbaum.

Mandler, G., & Sarason, S. B. (1952). A study of anxiety and learning. *Journal of Abnormal and Social Psychology, 47,* 166-173.

Martens, R. (1971). Anxiety and motor behavior: A review. *Journal of Motor Behavior, 3,* 151-179.

Martens, R. (1975). *Social psychology and physical activity.* New York: Harper & Row.

Martens, R. (1977). *Sport competition anxiety test.* Champaign, IL: Human Kinetics.

Martens, R., Burton, D., Rivkin, F., & Simon, J. (1980). Reliability and validity of the Competitive State Anxiety Inventory (CSAI). In C. H. Nadeau, W. R. Halliwell, K. M. Newell, & G. C. Roberts (Eds.), *Psychology of motor behavior and sport - 1979* (pp. 91-99). Champaign, IL: Human Kinetics.

Martens, R., Burton, D., Vealey, R. S., Bump, L. A., & Smith, D. E. (1990). Development and validation of the Competitive State Anxiety Inventory-2. In R. Martens, R. S. Vealey, & D. Burton, *Competitive anxiety in sport* (pp. 117-190). Champaign, IL: Human Kinetics.

Martens, R., & Gill, D. L. (1976). State anxiety among successful and unsuccessful competitors who differ in competitive trait anxiety. *Research Quarterly, 47,* 698-708.

Martens, R., Gill, D. L., & Scanlan, T. K. (1976). Competitive trait anxiety, success-failure and sex as determinants of motor performance. *Perceptual and Motor Skills, 43,* 1199-1208.

Martens, R., & Simon, J. A. (1976). Comparison of three predictors of state anxiety in competitive situations. *Research Quarterly, 47,* 381-387.

Martens, R. Vealey, R. S., & Burton, D. (1990). *Competitive anxiety in sport.* Champaign, IL: Human Kinetics.

Maslach, C., & Jackson, S. (1981). The measurement of experienced burnout. *Journal of Occupational Behavior, 2,* 99-113.

Maynard, I. W., & Howe, B. L. (1987). Interrelations of trait and state anxiety with game performance of rugby players. *Perceptual and Motor Skills, 64,* 599-602.

McKelvie, S. J., & Huband, D. E. (1980). Locus of control and anxiety in college athletes and non-athletes. *Perceptual and Motor Skills, 50,* 819-822.

McKelvie, S. J., Valliant, P. M., & Asu, M. E. (1985). Physical training and personality factors as predictors of marathon time and training injury. *Perceptual and Motor Skills, 60,* 551-566.

McNair, D. M., Lorr, M., & Droppleman, L. F. (1971). *Profile of Mood States manual.* San Diego, CA: Educational and Industrial Testing Service.

Mehrabian, A. (1968). Male and female scales of the tendency to achieve. *Educational and Psychological Measurement, 28,* 493-502.

Meichenbaum, D. (1985). *Stress inoculation training.* New York: Pergamon Press.

Morgan, W.P., O'Connor, P.J., Ellickson, K.A., & Bradley, P.W. (1988). Personality, structure, mood states, and performance in elite male distance runners. *International Journal of Sport Psychology, 19(4),* 247-263.

Morris, L. W., Davis, D., & Hutchings, C. (1981). Cognitive and emotional components of anxiety: Literature review and revised worry-emotionality scale. *Journal of Educational Psychology, 73,* 541-555.

Morris, L. W., & Engle, W. B. (1981). Assessing various coping strategies and their effects on test performance and anxiety. *Journal of Clinical Psychology, 37,* 165-171.

Morris, L. W., Harris, E. W., & Rovins, D. S. (1981). Interactive effects of generalized and situational expectancies on cognitive and emotional components of social anxiety. *Journal of Research in Personality, 15,* 302-311.

Morris, L. W., & Liebert, R. M. (1973). Effects of negative feedback, threat of shock, and level of trait anxiety on the arousal of two components of anxiety. *Journal of Consulting Psychology, 20,* 321-326.

Murphy, S. M., & Woolfolk, R. L. (1987). The effects of cognitive interventions on competitive anxiety and performance on a fine motor skill accuracy task. *International Journal of Sport Psychology, 18,* 152-166.

Nash, H. L. (1987). Elite child-athletes: How much does victory cost? *The Physician and Sportsmedicine, 15,* 128-133.

Nideffer, R. M. (1976). Test of attentional and interpersonal style. *Journal of Personality and Social Psychology, 34,* 394-404.

Nunnally, J. C., & Bernstein, I. H. (1994). *Psychometric theory* (3rd ed.). New York: McGraw-Hill.

Olerud, J. E. (1989). Acne in a young athlete. In N. J. Smith (Ed.). *Common problems in pediatric sports medicine* (pp. 54-59). Chicago: Year Book Medical Publishers.

Orlick, T. D., & Botterill, C. (1975). *Every kid can win.* Chicago: Nelson-Hall.

Ostrow, A. C., & Ziegler, S. G. (1978). Psychometric properties of the Sport Competition Anxiety Test. In B. Kerr (Ed.), *Human performance and behavior* (pp. 139-142). Calgary, Alberta: University of Calgary.

Passer, M. W. (1983). Fear of failure, fear of evaluation, perceived competence, and self-esteem in competitive-trait-anxious children. *Journal of Sport Psychology, 5,* 172-188.

Pierce, W. J. (1980). *Psychological perspectives of youth sport participants and nonparticipants*. Unpublished doctoral dissertation, Virginia Polytechnic Institute and State University, Blacksburg.

Porat, Y., Lufi, D., & Tenenbaum, G. (1989). Psychological components contribute to select young female gymnasts. *International Journal of Sport Psychology, 20,* 279-286.

Poteet, D., & Weinberg, R. (1980). Competition trait anxiety, state anxiety, and performance. *Perceptual and Motor Skills, 50,* 651-654.

Rainey, D. W., Conklin, W. E., & Rainey, K. W. (1987). Competitive trait anxiety among male and female junior high school athletes. *International Journal of Sport Psychology, 18,* 171-180.

Rainey, D. W., & Cunningham, H. (1988). Competitive trait anxiety in male and female college athletes. *Research Quarterly for Exercise and Sport, 59,* 244-247.

Rogers, C. R. (1959). A theory of therapy, personality and interpersonal relationships as developed in the client-centered framework. In S. Koch (Ed.), *Psychology: A study of a science* (Vol. 3, pp. 98-197)). New York: McGraw-Hill.

Rosenbaum, M. (1980). A schedule for assessing self-control behaviors: Preliminary findings. *Behavior Therapy, 11,* 109-121.

Rotter, J. B. (1966). Generalized expectancies for internal versus external control of reinforcement. *Psychological Monographs, 80* (1, Whole No. 609).

Rupnow, A., & Ludwig, D. A. (1981). Psychometric note on the reliability of the Sport Competition Anxiety Test: Form C. *Research Quarterly for Exercise and Sport, 52,* 35-37.

Sarason, I. G. (1984). Stress, anxiety, and cognitive interference: Reactions to Tests. *Journal of Personality and Social Psychology, 46,* 929-938.

Sarason, I. G., & Sarason, B. R. (1990). Test anxiety. In H. Leitenberg (Ed.), *Handbook of social and evaluation anxiety* (pp. 475-496). New York: Plenum.

Sarason, S. B., Davidson, K. S., Lighthall, F. F., Waite, R. R., & Ruebush, B. K. (1960). *Anxiety in elementary school children.* New York: Wiley.

Scanlan, T. K. (1977). The effects of competition trait anxiety and successs-failure on the perception of threat in a competitive situation. *Research Quarterly, 48,* 144-153.

Scanlan, T. K. (1978). Perceptions and responses of high- and low-competitive trait-anxious males to competition. *Research Quarterly, 49,* 520-527.

Scanlan, T. K., & Lewthwaite, R. (1984). Social psychological aspects of competition for male youth sport participants: I. Predictors of competitive stress. *Journal of Sport Psychology, 6,* 208-226.

Scanlan, T. K., & Passer, M. W. (1977). The effects of competition trait anxiety and game win-loss perceived threat in a natural competitive setting. In D. M. Landers & R. W. Christina (Eds.), *Psychology of motor behavior and sport—1976* (pp. 157-160). Champaign, IL: Human Kinetics.

Scanlan, T. K., & Passer, M. W. (1978). Factors related to competitive stress among male youth sport participants. *Medicine and Science in Sport, 10,* 103-108.

Scanlan, T. K., & Passer, M. W. (1979). Sources of competitive stress in young female athletes. *Journal of Sport Psychology, 1,* 151-159.

Scanlan, T. K., & Ragan, J. T. (1978). Achievement motivation and competition: Perceptions and responses. *Medicine and Science in Sports, 10,* 276-281.

Schutz, R. W., Eom, H. J., Smoll, F. L., & Smith, R. E. (1994). Examination of the factorial validity of the Group Environment Questionnaire. *Research Quarterly for Exercise and Sport, 65,* 226-236.

Schwenkmezger, P., & Laux, L. (1986). Trait anxiety, worry, and emotionality in athletic competition. In C. D. Spielberger & R. Diax-Guerrero (Eds.), *Cross-cultural anxiety* (vol. 3, pp. 65-91). Washington, DC: Hemisphere Publishing Corporation.

Simon, J. A., & Martens, R. (1977). SCAT as a predictor of A-states in varying competitive situations. In D. M. Landers & R. W. Christina (Eds.), *Psychology of motor behavior and sport—1976* (pp. 146-156). Champaign, IL: Human Kinetics.

Singer, R., & Ungerer-Rohrich, U. (1985). Zum Vorhersagewert des State-Trait-Angstmodells. Eine empirische Untersuchung an Sportstudent (inn)en, Squash-und Tischtennisspielern. In G. Schilling & K. Herren (Eds.), *Proceedings of the VIth FEPSAC congress (Vol. 1, pp. 129-138).* Magglingen: ETS.

Smith, R. E. (1980). A cognitive-affective approach to stress management training for athletes. In C. H. Nadeau, W. R. Halliwell, K. M. Newell, & G. C. Roberts (Eds.), *Psychology of motor behavior and sport—1979* (pp. 54-72). Champaign, IL: Human Kinetics.

Smith, R. E. (1989a). Athletic stress and burnout: Conceptual models and intervention strategies. In D. Hackfort & C. D. Spielberger (Eds.), *Anxiety in sports: An international perspective* (pp. 183-201). New York: Hemisphere.

Smith, R. E. (1989b). Conceptual and statistical issues in research involving multidimensional anxiety scales. *Journal of Sport and Exercise Psychology, 4,* 452-457.

Smith, R. E., Ptacek, J. T., Everett, J. J., & May, E. (1995). *Cognitive and somatic sport performance anxiety as moderators of the stress-injury relation.* Unpublished manuscript, University of Washington.

Smith, R. E., & Smoll, F. L. (1990). Sport performance anxiety. In H. Leitenberg (Ed.), *Handbook of social and evaluation anxiety* (pp. 417-454). New York: Plenum.

Smith, R. E., & Smoll, F. L. (1995). [Factor analysis of the Sport Competition Anxiety Test]. Unpublished raw data.

Smith, R. E., Smoll, F. L., & Barnett, N. P. (1995). Reduction of children's sport performance anxiety through social support and stress-reduction training for coaches. *Journal of Applied Developmental Psychology, 16,* 125-142.

Smith, R. E., Smoll, F. L., & Curtis, B. (1979). Coach effectiveness training: A cognitive-behavioral approach to enhancing relationship skills in youth sport coaches. *Journal of Sport Psychology, 1,* 59-75.

Smith, R. E., Smoll, F. L., & Schutz, R. W. (1990). Measurement and correlates of sport-specific cognitive and somatic trait anxiety: The Sport Anxiety Scale. *Anxiety Research, 2,* 263-280.

Sonstroem, R. J., & Bernardo, P. (1982). Intraindividual pregame state anxiety and basketball performance: A re-examination of the inverted-U curve. *Journal of Sport Psychology, 4,* 235-245.

Spielberger, C. D. (1966). Theory and research on anxiety. In C. D. Spielberger (Ed.), *Anxiety and behavior* (pp. 1-17). New York: Academic Press.

Spielberger, C. D. (1972). Conceptual and methodological issues in anxiety research. In C. D. Spielberger (Ed.), *Anxiety: Current trends in theory and research* (Vol. 2, pp. 481-493). New York: Academic Press.

Spielberger, C. D. (1973). *Preliminary test manual for the State-Trait Anxiety Inventory for Children.* Palo Alto, CA: Consulting Psychologists.

Spielberger, C.D. (1984). *State-Trait Anxiety Inventory: A Comprehensive Bibliography.* Palo Alto, CA. Consulting Psychologists Press.

Spielberger, C.D. (1989). Stress and anxiety in sports. In D. Hackfort & C.D. Spielberger (Eds.), *Anxiety in Sports* (pp. 3-17). New York: Hemisphere Publishing.

Spielberger, C. D., Gorsuch, R. L., & Lushene, R. E. (1970). *Manual for the State-Trait Anxiety Inventory.* Palo Alto, CA: Consulting Psychologists Press.

Spielberger, C.D., Vagg, P.R. Barker, L.R., Donham, G.W. & Westberry, L.G. (1980). The factor structure of the State-Trait Anxiety Inventory. In I.G. Sarason & C.D. Spielberger (Eds.), *Stress and Anxiety* (Vol. 7, pp. 203-211). Washington, DC : Hemisphere.

Stadulis, R. E. (1977). Need achievement, competition preference and evaluation seeking. In D. M. Landers & R. W. Christina (Eds.), *Psychology of motor behavior and sport—1976* (pp. 113-122). Champaign, IL: Human Kinetics.

Steptoe, A., & Fidler, H. (1987). Stage fright in orchestral musicians: A study of cognitive and behavioural strategies in performance anxiety. *British Journal of Psychology, 78,* 241-249.

Tannenbaum, L. E., Forehand, R., & Thomas, A. M. (1992). Adolescent self-reported anxiety and depression: Separate constructs or a single entity? *Child Study Journal, 22,* 61-72.

Taylor, J. A. (1953). A personality scale of manifest anxiety. *Journal of Abnormal and Social Psychology, 48,* 285-290.

Tryon, G. S. (1980). The measurement and treatment of test anxiety. *Review of Educational Research, 50,* 343-372.

Vealey, R. S. (1986). Conceptualization of sport-confidence and competitive orientation: Preliminary investigation and instrument development. *Journal of Sport Psychology, 8,* 221-246.

Vealey, R.S., Udry, E.M., Zimmerman, V., & Soliday, J. (1992). Intrapersonal and situational predictors of coaching burnout. *Journal of Sport & Exercise Psychology, 14,* 40-58.

Veit, C. T., & Ware, J. E. (1983). The structure of psychological distress and well-being in general populations. *Journal of Consulting and Clinical Psychology, 51,* 730-742.

Wankel, L. M. (1977). Audience size and trait anxiety effects upon state anxiety and motor performance. *Research Quarterly, 48,* 181-186.

Watson, D., & Clark, L. A. (1984). Negative affectivity: The disposition to experience aversive emotional states. *Psychological Bulletin, 96,* 465-490.

Watson, D., & Friend, R. (1969). Measurement of social-evaluative anxiety. *Journal of Consulting and Clinical Psychology, 33,* 448-457.

Watson, G. G., (1986). Approach-avoidance behaviour in team sports: An application to leading Australian national hockey players. *International Journal of Sport Psychology, 17,* 136-155.

Weinberg, R. S. (1978). The effects of success and failure on the patterning of neuromuscular energy. *Journal of Motor Behavior, 10,* 53-61.

Weinberg, R. S. (1979). Anxiety and motor performance: Drive theory vs. cognitive theory. *International Journal of Sport Psychology, 10,* 112-121.

Weinberg, R. S., & Genuchi, M. (1980). Relationship between competitive trait anxiety, state anxiety, and golf performance: A field study. *Journal of Sport Psychology, 2,* 148-154.

Welch, G. S. (1956). Factor dimensions A and R. In G. S. Welsh & W. G. Dahlstrom (Eds.), *Basic readings on the MMPI in psychology and medicine* (pp. 264-281). Minneapolis: University of Minnesota Press.

Williams, J. M., & Krane, V. (1989). Response distortion on self-report questionnaires with female collegiate golfers. *The Sport Psychologist, 3,* 212-218.

Willis, J. D. (1982). Three scales to measure competition-related motives in sport. *Journal of Sport Psychology, 4,* 338-353.

Yerkes, R. M., & Dodson, J. D. (1908). The relation of strength of stimulus to rapidity of habit-formation. *Journal of Comparative Neurology and Psychology, 18,* 459-482.

Zuckerman, M. (1960). The development of an affect adjective check list for the measurement of anxiety. *Journal of Consulting Psychology, 24,* 457-462.

Chapter 7

MEASURING COMPETITIVE STATE ANXIETY

Damon Burton
University of Idaho

Competitive anxiety has long held a paradoxical fasci-
nation for sport psychologists and the coaches and athletes with whom they work (Martens, 1977; Martens, Vealey, &
Burton, 1990). Because no other single psychological attribute
can have such a debilitating effect on performance, research on
the causes and consequences of competitive anxiety as well as
on how practitioners can reduce anxiety or more effectively
cope with its effects has been one of the most heavily researched topics in sport psychology (Martens, Vealey, et al.,
1990; R.E. Smith, Smoll, & Schutz, 1990). Not surprisingly,
measurement of competitive anxiety has received more attention than perhaps any other construct in sport and exercise psychology, and several anxiety inventories have been developed
which have proved to be excellent models for the development
of psychometrically sound instruments (e.g., Martens, 1977;
Martens, Burton, Vealey, Bump & Smith, 1990; R.E. Smith et
al., 1990). However, advancement in measurement technology
is an ongoing process—a constant evolution—so the overall
objective of this chapter is to identify where we are at now in
the measurement of competitive state anxiety as well as where
we need to go with the development of future instruments.
Therefore, this chapter has three purposes: (a) to review the
evolution of state anxiety theory, (b) to summarize the development and psychometric properties of five measures of competitive state anxiety, and (c) to speculate about future directions in
state anxiety measurement and research.

Evolution of State Anxiety Theory

Anxiety is a complex negative emotion with a variety of
cognitive, physiological, and behavioral symptoms that has
often been linked with stress (Lazarus, 1991; Martens, Vealey,
et al., 1990; Spielberger, 1966). According to Spielberger
(1966), "anxiety states are characterized by subjective, consciously perceived feelings of apprehension and tension, accompanied by or associated with activation of the autonomic
nervous system" (p. 17).

In this section, the evolution of state anxiety theory will be
explored by (a) examining physiological versus self-report
measurement of state anxiety, (b) investigating Spielberger's
(1966) distinction between anxiety states and traits, (c) evaluating the value of situation-specific measurement of state anxiety,
(d) examining multidimensional conceptions of anxiety and the
benefits of this distinction for understanding the acute effects of
anxiety, and (e) investigating how incorporation of symptom
interpretation may redefine state anxiety.

Physiological Versus Self-Report
Measurement of State Anxiety

Most state anxiety research has utilized self-report questionnaires instead of physiological measures (Martens et al.,
1990). A brief review of the strengths and weaknesses of physiological measures make it apparent why self-report measures
have emerged as the strategy of choice to measure competitive
state anxiety. Psychophysiology is the study of observable
physiological arousal measures in order to better understand
underlying mental states, such as anxiety (Hatfield & Landers,
1983). Psychophysiological research on anxiety is most concerned with the body's immediate and intermediate anxiety responses. In the immediate anxiety response, the sympathetic
nervous system is stimulated by fear perceptions in the cerebral
cortex, prompting an immediate stress response that lasts from
a few seconds to several minutes in duration. This sympathetic
activation promotes stimulation of vital organ systems, such as
the cardiovascular system, that help prepare the body to respond to emergency, a phenomenon often called the *fight or
flight syndrome* (Hackfort & Schwenkmezger, 1993).

The body's intermediate anxiety response is slower because sympathetic activation also stimulates biochemical responses through the release of catecholamines into the circulatory system, a process that takes time for biochemical triggers
to reach their target sites (e.g., myocardium). This slower intermediate anxiety response has the ability to maintain anxiety responses because of the longer lifetime of catecholamines in the
bloodstream. Thus, peripheral measures of cardiovascular and

response should provide information about immedi- responses, whereas biochemical indices should be more indicative of intermediate anxiety reactions (Hackfort & Schwenkmezger, 1993).

Anxiety researchers who use psychophysiological measures of anxiety rely on three types of indicators: (a) respiratory and cardiovascular, (b) biochemical, and (c) electrophysical (Hackfort & Schwenkmezger, 1993). Specific measures typically used in anxiety assessment include cardiorespiratory indicators, such as pulse rate, blood pressure, and respiration rate; biochemical indicators, such as adrenaline and noradrenaline levels; and electrophysiological measures, such as EEG correlates, muscle potentials, and skin conductance/resistance. Hackfort and Schwenkmezger (1993) suggest that physiological indices of state anxiety have three major advantages. First, they are not tied to subjects' verbal skill and therefore not confounded by verbal expression ability. Second, they can be used with almost all types of athletes because introspection and self-analysis are not a prerequisite. Finally, the physiological parameters of state anxiety can be assessed during activity without interrupting performance.

Unfortunately, physiological measures of anxiety also have a number of disadvantages (Hackfort & Schwenkmezger, 1993). First, the relationships between many physiological indices of anxiety are quite low, suggesting that researchers may obtain different results depending on what physiological index they select. Second, stress does not always trigger similar responses across subjects (Lacey & Lacey, 1958). Lacey and Lacey discovered that individuals often differ on the physiological system that responds to stressful stimuli, a reaction termed *individual response stereotypy*. For example, physiological indices might demonstrate similar patterns for athletes who are challenged or excited to play their best and for those with extreme anxiety reactions. To date, identifying specific physiological parameters that represent solely anxiety have been difficult to quantify. Finally, physiological measures are practical only in sports in which athletes are relatively stationary because peripheral circulatory and biochemical indicators change more due to movement and physical activity than as a result of athletes' anxiety response. Thus *movement artifact* makes during-competition assessment of state anxiety practical only in such stationary sports as archery and shooting where physiological indices of anxiety are not confounded by changes due to movement (Hatfield, Landers, & Ray, 1984).

Relationships between physiological and self-report measures of state anxiety are generally weak and nonsignificant (Burton, 1989; Karteroliotis & Gill, 1987), and self-report measures of state anxiety have generally predicted performance better than do physiological indices (e.g., Burton, 1989; Yan Lan & Gill, 1984). Explanations of this finding have generally emphasized the role of perception in the anxiety experience and its measurement (Martens, 1977). That is, because anxiety is a response to a complex cognitive evaluation of mental and physiological stimuli, measures that directly tap this perceptual process should more accurately reflect the state anxiety experienced compared to direct measures of physiological response that may often be perceived inaccurately. For example, athletes may be unaware that their heart is pounding before competing,

but their low somatic anxiety level more accurately reflects their perceived normal heart rate rather than their actual cardiac reaction. This chapter will focus on self-report measures of state anxiety that trace their earliest ancestry to test anxiety pioneers such as Taylor, Cattell, and Spielberger.

State/Trait Anxiety Theory

Anxiety theory and measurement developed in the 1950s using a trait model of personality that conceptualizes behavior as largely determined by personality factors, with situational variables assumed to have little impact on how people behave (Martens, 1977). Building on this conceptual framework, researchers attempted to identify and measure important personality traits including anxiety that were thought to prompt characteristic behavior patterns (Vealey, 1992). Early anxiety researchers measured anxiety with general trait inventories, such as J.A. Taylor's (1953) Manifest Anxiety Scale, Cattell's (1957) IPAT Anxiety Scale, and Sarason, Davidson, Lighthall, Waite, and Ruebush's (1960) General Anxiety Scale, but results with these early trait instruments led Spielberger (1966) to conclude that such measures of anxiety were of little value in predicting behavior. By the 1960s, personality researchers were moving away from the trait paradigm to a more interactional perspective in which behavior was seen as the product of both personality predispositions and situational factors. This broader conception of the determinants of behavior seemed to mesh well with clinical and anecdotal evidence suggesting that anxiety was both chronic and acute, and the result was the development of a new interactional-based model of anxiety, generally credited to Spielberger (1966), which distinguished between anxiety *states* and *traits* (Vealey, 1992).

Spielberger's (1966) state/trait theory (see R.E. Smith, Smoll, & Weichman, this volume for a more complete review) conceptualized *trait anxiety* as an enduring psychological condition that represents the individual's typical or average level of anxiety, or more practically, the normal level of anxiety when situational variables have minimal impact on behavior. Thus, psychological traits represent the influence of personality on behavior when situational variables are held constant. At the same time, Spielberger identified *state anxiety* as momentary fluctuations in anxiety levels that individuals may experience in a particular situation, reflecting the influence of situational factors on anxiety response. Note that for the sake of clarity and brevity throughout the remainder of this chapter, state anxiety will be abbreviated as *A-state* and trait anxiety as *A-trait*.

Spielberger's state/trait model suggests that when state and trait anxiety levels are similar, it can be assumed that situational factors exert little impact on the anxiety experienced. However, when state and trait anxiety levels differ significantly, these fluctuations reflect situational factors that prompt individuals to become more or less anxious than usual. Perhaps the most basic prediction of state/trait theory is that state anxiety should predict behavior or performance in a particular situation more accurately than should trait anxiety. More recently, anxiety researchers (Burton, 1988; Gould, Petlichkoff, & Weinberg, 1984) have confirmed that *intraindividual* measures of anxiety, that represent the difference between anxiety in a particular situation and normal anxiety levels (i.e., acute compared to chronic), predict behavior and performance more accurately than do traditional anxiety measures (i.e., raw A-state scores). Intraindividual measures of state anxiety can be calculated two ways. First, the individual's state anxiety level can be measured in three or more competitions and an average state anxiety score calculated. The state anxiety level in each competition is then subtracted from this mean state anxiety score, with the difference representing how much more or less anxious than usual athletes are in particular situations. Second, intraindividual state anxiety can also be calculated by simply using athletes' trait anxiety score as representative of average anxiety and subtracting state anxiety scores in particular situations from athletes' trait anxiety scores, with this difference representing positive or negative fluctuations in anxiety based on the influence of situational factors. Obviously, using trait anxiety as the baseline for calculating intraindividual measures of state anxiety requires compatible state and trait instruments or norms available for both A-state and A-trait questionnaires that can permit comparison across incompatible instruments. This chapter will focus on measurement of competitive state anxiety, whereas the development of competitive trait anxiety is chronicled in a separate chapter (see R.E. Smith, Smoll, & Wiechman, this volume)

Situation-Specific Measurement of State Anxiety

At about the same time Spielberger (1966) was elucidating his state/trait conception of anxiety, a number of researchers (e.g., Mellstrom, Cicala, & Zuckerman, 1976; Sarason et al., 1960; Watson & Friend, 1969) confirmed that measures of anxiety that were situation specific predicted behavior better than did more general anxiety scales. These instruments included scales to measure test anxiety (Sarason et al., 1960), social evaluation anxiety (Watson & Friend, 1969), and anxieties about such diverse fears as snakes, heights, and darkness (Mellstrom et al., 1976). Within sport, Martens and his colleagues (Martens, 1977; Martens, Burton, Rivkin, & Simon, 1980) developed sport-specific state and trait anxiety measures, the Competitive State Anxiety Inventory -1 (CSAI-1) and the Sport Competition Anxiety Test (SCAT), and demonstrated that they measured anxiety better in sport situations than did the more general measures of A-state (i.e., SAI) and A-trait (i.e., TAI) developed by Spielberger and his colleagues (Spielberger, Gorsuch, & Lushene, 1970). This chapter will focus exclusively on state anxiety measures designed specifically for competitive situations.

Multidimensional Conceptualization of State Anxiety

Further evolution of state anxiety theory revolved around the conceptualization of anxiety as a multidimensional rather than a unidimensional construct (Davidson & Schwartz, 1976; Liebert & Morris, 1967; Martens, Burton, et al., 1990). Both clinical evidence and factor analytical studies of existing anxiety measures suggested that anxiety has separate mental and physical components.

The mental component, typically termed *cognitive anxiety*, is closely related to worry and deals with "negative expectations and cognitive concerns about oneself, the situation at hand, and potential consequences" (Morris, Davis, & Hutch-

ings, 1981, p. 541). In sport, cognitive anxiety is manifested by negative expectations of success and subsequent negative self-evaluation that can prompt one or more of four types of negative mental consequences, including (a) worry and other negative thoughts, (b) images of disaster and other disturbing evaluation-related imagery, (c) concentration problems in which distractions prevent appropriate attentional focus, and (d) control problems that vary from slight feelings of loss of control to feeling totally overwhelmed.

Conversely, *somatic anxiety* is the physical component of anxiety, reflecting perceptions about the physiological and affective elements of the anxiety reaction that develop directly from the autonomic arousal process. Somatic anxiety is manifested by how individuals perceive such responses as rapid heartbeat, shallow breathing, butterflies in the stomach, clammy hands, dry mouth, and tense muscles.

The basic premise of a multidimensional conceptualization of state anxiety is that the two components of anxiety are independent because they have different antecedents and consequences, particularly that they differentially influence behavior (Davidson & Schwartz, 1976; Liebert & Morris, 1967; Martens, Burton, et al., 1990). Thus, some individuals may respond to stress primarily with increases in cognitive anxiety, whereas other persons might react with somatic anxiety responses to similar stressors. In fact, the same individual may respond differently in different situations, eliciting primarily cognitive anxiety responses in one situation and somatic responses under different conditions. Despite this notion of conceptual independence, most multidimensional anxiety researchers (e.g., Borkovec, 1976; Morris, Davis, et al., 1981) acknowledge that most stressful situations will generally elicit both types of anxiety. Thus, athletes may initially experience somatic responses to precontest stimuli, such as game uniforms, locker-room preparation, an audience in the stands, pep band playing, and pregame warmup routines, that may prompt worry and other cognitive anxiety responses due to negative interpretation of these somatic symptoms. On the other hand, cognitive anxiety in the form of negative self-talk and imagery may also trigger specific somatic responses. Thus, a reciprocal relationship exists between these two components of anxiety, although it is difficult to specify the exact contribution of each type of anxiety in real competitive situations.

Evidence Documenting the Need for Multidimensional Measures of State Anxiety

Early multidimensional anxiety research (e.g., Liebert & Morris, 1967; Morris, Davis, & Hutchings, 1981; Morris & Liebert, 1970, 1973), conducted almost exclusively with nonsport populations, attempted to demonstrate the conceptual independence of the two components of anxiety in three general ways, thus validating the multidimensional model and justifying the separate measurement of cognitive and somatic anxiety. First, factor analytical procedures were employed to assess whether the underlying factor structure of anxiety scales is uni- or multidimensional, and correlational analyses were used to examine relationships between cognitive and somatic subscales. Second, differential antecedent patterns for the two types of anxiety were investigated by experimentally attempting to manipulate conditions designed to elicit one type of anxiety but not the other. Finally, differential consequences of cognitive versus somatic anxiety were examined, particularly their influence on performance and intervention.

Factor analytical and correlational evidence. Liebert and Morris (1967) were among the first anxiety researchers to factor analyze existing anxiety scales and find a multidimensional rather than a unidimensional factor structure. A number of other factor analytic studies of general anxiety scales (see Morris, Davis, & Hutchings, 1981, for a review of those studies) have documented a multidimensional model of anxiety, yielding two types of anxiety items that generally parallel the cognitive versus somatic distinction. The finding that factor analysis of J.A. Taylor's (1953) Manifest Anxiety Scale yielded a two-factor structure prompted Liebert and Morris (1967) to develop the first multidimensional measure of anxiety called the Worry-Emotionality Inventory (WEI). Confirmatory factor analysis of the WEI corroborated this two-factor structure that they labelled worry and emotionality (Morris & Liebert, 1970).

Early researchers also attempted to provide evidence of the multidimensional nature of A-state by demonstrating the conceptual independence of cognitive and somatic anxiety with correlational analyses designed to test the magnitude of relationships between these two anxiety types. Low to moderate correlations between these two A-state components were believed to provide positive support for this conceptual independence. Unfortunately, initial correlational data obtained from six early studies were somewhat higher than desirable, ranging from .55 to .76 (Deffenbacher, 1977, 1978, 1980; Morris & Liebert, 1970, 1973; Morris & Perez, 1972), prompting Morris, Davis, and Hutchings (1981) to revise the WEI in order to yield a more moderate relationship (i.e., $r = .48$) between the two components of anxiety. However, the WEI was not directly employed in the physical domain.

Although even these more modest correlations obtained with revised instruments are not low enough to provide strong support for the independence of these two anxiety components, researchers have generally interpreted these data to confirm the *relative* independence of cognitive and somatic anxiety because most situations that evoke stress contain anxiety-provoking stimuli that elicit and maintain both types of anxiety (Morris, Davis, & Hutchings, 1981).

Differential antecedent evidence. Even more compelling evidence of the multidimensional nature of A-state comes from construct-validation research testing theoretical predictions that the two components of anxiety have differential antecedents (Liebert & Morris, 1967; Morris, Davis, & Hutchings, 1981). Differential antecedent research has focused on two types of conceptual predictions made by multidimensional anxiety theory (Morris, Davis, & Hutchings, 1981). First, somatic anxiety should respond to antecedents that prompt changes in autonomic arousal, whereas cognitive anxiety should be elicited by changes in self-evaluation, particularly expectations of success. Second, cognitive and somatic anxiety should demonstrate differential temporal patterns as competition approaches. Somatic anxiety should increase steadily until the start of competition and then decrease somewhat, whereas cognitive anxiety should

fluctuate prior to and during competition only if expectations of success change.

Early multidimensional anxiety researchers were confronted with a paradox. Although testing the differential antecedent prediction seems straightforward conceptually, actually conducting this research is difficult because experimental conditions must be established in which high levels of one component of state anxiety are elicited without changing the other (Morris, Davis, & Hutchings, 1981). For example, if high arousal can be evoked without changing expectations of success (e.g., electric shock without performance evaluation), individuals should report high levels of somatic anxiety without accompanying elevation of cognitive anxiety. Unfortunately, in many situations cues that are salient for eliciting one component of anxiety also tend to manifest the other type of anxiety as well.

Not surprisingly, the general anxiety literature has demonstrated only moderate support for these predictions about differential antecedents for cognitive and somatic anxiety. Five studies (Liebert & Morris, 1967; Morris & Liebert, 1970, 1973; Morris, Brown, & Halbert, 1977; Morris, Harris, & Rovins, 1981) manipulated stimuli designed to elicit one type of anxiety but not the other and found expected changes in the appropriate component of anxiety, but six other studies (Deffenbacher & Dietz, 1978; Holroyd, 1978; Holroyd, Westbrook, Wolf & Badhorn, 1978; Morris & Perez, 1972; C.A. Smith & Morris, 1976, 1977) used similar manipulations without finding expected changes in cognitive and/or somatic anxiety.

However, studies testing temporal patterning of anxiety components prior to competition yielded more consistent results (Morris, Davis, & Hutchings, 1981). Four general A-state studies have confirmed steady increases of somatic anxiety until the start of competition, whereas cognitive anxiety changed only when expectations of success were modified experimentally (Doctor & Altman, 1969; Morris & Engle, 1981; Morris & Fulmer, 1976; C.A. Smith & Morris, 1976). Unfortunately, such predictions for the WEI were never tested in the physical domain.

Differential consequence evidence on performance and intervention. Conceptualizations of multidimensional anxiety predict that the two components of anxiety will demonstrate differential relationships with performance, primarily because somatic anxiety peaks at the onset of competition and then dissipates while cognitive anxiety, because of its conceptual link to expectations of success, may impact performance throughout the competition. Specifically, cues believed to arouse or maintain somatic anxiety are typically of short duration and consist primarily of conditioned responses to stimuli, such as locker-room preparation, a crowd in the stands, and precontest warmup routines, that lose their salience once the contest begins and attention is turned to the competition itself. Because these antecedents remain fairly consistent across competitive situations, somatic anxiety usually demonstrates a characteristic pattern of change prior to competition—first gradually increasing as competition draws near, reaching its peak as competition begins, and then decreasing and leveling off rapidly. Conversely, the antecedents of cognitive anxiety are hypothesized to be those factors in the competitive environment that influence athletes' expectations of success. Cognitive anxiety arises whenever expectations of success become negative, thus accounting for why athletes often begin worrying several days prior to competition. However, this type of mental worry should remain relatively constant prior to and during competition unless expectations change because of factors such as key injuries, exceptionally good or bad practices, or a game plan that works better or worse than expected.

In fact, Morris, Davis, and Hutchings (1981) term the multidimensional anxiety prediction that cognitive anxiety will be more consistently and strongly related to performance than somatic anxiety as the *anxiety-performance hypothesis*. Morris, Davis, and Hutchings (1981) reviewed the early nonsport research testing the anxiety-performance hypothesis and concluded that solid support was evident for this prediction. Moreover, Deffenbacher (1977) has concluded that the relationship between cognitive and somatic A-state may be complex such that anxiety becomes debilitating only when both components of anxiety are high.

Similarly, intervention research with the WEI provided some evidence that cognitive A-state is more debilitating to performance than is somatic A-state. In five nonsport intervention studies in which performance improved as a result of using anxiety-reduction techniques, cognitive A-state was significantly reduced in each study, but somatic A-state was significantly lowered in only four of the investigations (Deffenbacher, Mathis, & Michaels, 1979; Deffenbacher, Michaels, Michaels, & Daley, 1980; Kirkland & Hollandsworth, 1980; Osarchuk, 1976; Thompson, Griebstein, & Kuhlenschmidt, 1980). Although cognitive A-state accounted for more performance variance than did somatic A-state in each study, both anxiety components combined accounted for less than 10% of the total variance, suggesting only a modest impact on performance. In summary, although early nonsport research on multidimensional A-state was somewhat equivocal, the weight of the accumulated evidence supported the value of distinguishing between cognitive and somatic A-state.

Interpreting Symptom Effect: Toward a Redefinition of State Anxiety

Over the past decade, a number of anxiety researchers, most notably Jones and his colleagues (Burton, 1990; Edwards & Hardy, 1996; Jones, 1995; Jones & Hanton, 1996; Jones, Hanton, & Swain, 1994; Jones & Swain, 1992, 1995; Jones, Swain, & Hardy, 1993; Lewthwaite, 1990; Swain & Jones, 1993), have recognized that scores on self-report inventories such as the CSAI-2 may not accurately measure A-state because they measure only the *intensity* of symptoms and not the *direction* or meaning of those symptoms to the individual. The problem stems from the format employed by most self-report A-state questionnaires such as the CSAI-2, which are composed of a list of symptoms common to individuals with competitive state anxiety, and respondents then rate the intensity with which they experience each symptom. However, many of these symptoms are worded somewhat neutrally so that they are characteristic of not only anxiety but also more positive affective states, such as challenge or excitement. For example, a somatic A-state item such as *I feel nervous* or a cognitive A-state

item such as *I am concerned about this competition* are perceptions or cognitions that may reflect negative cognitive or somatic states and be detrimental or debilitating to performance for some athletes, but other competitors may view the same symptoms as indicative of positive excitement and effective mental preparation that may facilitate their performance. The crux of the problem is that if subjects indicate that they are experiencing these symptoms intensely, those responses will be scored as high cognitive or somatic A-state, which is assumed to be debilitating to performance, even though these responses may actually reflect that performers are experiencing positive emotional states that facilitate performance.

The notion of measuring direction as well as intensity is not new to anxiety measurement. Over three decades ago, Alpert and Haber (1960) developed the Achievement Anxiety Test to measure facilitating and debilitating types of test anxiety. Moreover, their research found that measuring both types of anxiety accounted for more variance in academic performance than did more conventional debilitating anxiety scales. Subsequent independent nonsport research (e.g., Carrrier, Higson, Klimoski, & Peterson, 1984; Couch, Garber, & Turner, 1983) has supported the value of distinguishing between facilitating and debilitating anxiety. Therefore, both conceptual and empirical arguments suggest that future A-state instruments need to employ measurement formats that allow subjects to rate both the intensity and direction of symptoms to ensure that they distinguish between effects that are facilitating versus debilitating.

Evolution of Competitive State Anxiety Measurement

Refinements in anxiety theory have logically led to advancements in state anxiety measurement. This section will discuss five instruments that have been employed to measure competitive state anxiety: (a) Spielberger et al.'s (1970) State Anxiety Inventory (SAI); (b) Martens, Burton, et al.'s (1980) Competitive State Anxiety Inventory - 1 (CSAI-1); (c) Martens, Burton, et al.'s (1990) multidimensional update of the CSAI-1, the Competitive State Anxiety Inventory -2 (CSAI-2); (d) the directional modification of the CSAI-2 (DM-CSAI-2) designed to differentiate between facilitating and debilitating A-state symptoms (Jones & Swain, 1992); and (e) field modifications of the CSAI-2 such as the Mental Readiness Form (MRF, Murphy, Greenspan, Jowdy, & Tammen, 1989) and the revised MRF (MRF-2, Krane, 1994). Description of each instrument will include two sections, with Section 1 reviewing the conceptual rationale supporting the instrument and providing a general description of the scale and how it is scored, and Section 2 summarizing the evidence of the scale's psychometric properties. Nevertheless, it must be recognized that because of the more stringent psychometric criteria placed on contemporary instruments as well as the increased volume of anxiety research during the past decade, the review of research supporting the psychometric properties of each of these five inventories will necessarily vary in both quantity and quality across instruments.

State Anxiety Inventory (SAI)

Conceptual Rationale and Description of SAI

Spielberger's (1966) state/trait anxiety theory offered the conceptual breakthrough that dramatically changed how anxiety was subsequently measured, and Spielberger and his colleagues (Spielberger, 1973; Spielberger et al., 1970) then pioneered refinements in anxiety measurement to assess both acute and chronic components of anxiety by developing the State-Trait Anxiety Inventory (STAI), comprised of two 20-item inventories to separately measure state and trait anxiety. The format of the STAI used similar items for each scale, with only slight changes in scale directions and item wording to measure state and trait forms of anxiety. In order to measure A-state, the State Anxiety Inventory (SAI) directions ask subjects to respond according to *how you feel right now at this moment*, and items deal with present-oriented concerns. Conversely, directions for the Trait Anxiety Inventory (TAI) requested subjects to rate *how you generally feel,* and individual items focus on more long-term concerns or symptoms. Each item is rated on a 4-point Likert scale, and scoring is additive across the 20 items with reverse scoring for positive items, yielding total scores that range from 20 to 80. Subsequently, Spielberger (1973) developed a children's version of the SAI for use with younger populations. The SAI represented a significant advancement in state anxiety measurement technology, and it became the anxiety instrument of choice for the next decade.

Psychometric Properties of SAI

Spielberger et al. (1970) provided strong support for the psychometric properties of the SAI with general populations, including high internal consistency reliability exceeding .85 and extensive concurrent, construct, and predictive validity evidence. Research using the SAI in competitive situations has been minimal, although the inventory has been used extensively in the physical domain to assess the anxiety-reduction effects of exercise (e.g., Long & Van Stavel, 1995; Petruzzello, Landers, Hatfield, Kubitz, & Salazar, 1991). Several researchers continue to use the SAI in competitive settings, particularly to test Hanin's Zone of Optimal Functioning theory that was originally developed using the SAI (e.g., Raglin & Morris, 1994). The use of SAI to measure the anxiety reduction effects of exercise is beyond the scope of this chapter (see Long & Van Stavel, 1995 and Petruzzello et al., 1991, for reviews). However, there has been recent evidence suggesting that anxiety reduction effects of exercise may be due more to lowering arousal than to changes in cognitive components of anxiety (Rejeski, Hardy, & Shaw, 1991). If this is true, the SAI may have outlived its usefulness in the exercise domain as well.

Competitive State Anxiety Inventory-1 (CSAI-1)

Conceptual Rationale and Description of CSAI-1

Martens' (1977) early validation research with SCAT confirmed the need to develop a sport-specific A-state measure. Martens, Burton, et al. (1980) modified Spielberger et al.'s (1970) SAI by identifying 10 items from the 20-item scale that were most sensitive at identifying competitive anxiety, labeling this new instrument the Competitive State Anxiety Inventory-1 (CSAI-1). Initial identification of items for the CSAI-1 was made based on factor analysis of precompetition A-state scores of women volleyball players and male boxers. Items were selected based on (a) factor weightings that significantly related to competitive anxiety, (b) concurrent validity with Thayer's (1967) Activation-Deactivation Adjective Checklist (AD-ACL), and (c) face validity of items for competition. Simon and Martens (1979) used similar factor analytic methods on responses of youth soccer participants to derive almost identical items for the child version. Because it was derived from the SAI, each item of the CSAI-1 is also rated on a 4-point Likert scale, with scoring totalled across the scale's 10 items. Positive items are reverse scored, yielding total scores that range from 10 to 40. Although its use was never widespread, the CSAI-1 provided a sport-specific measure of unidimensional state anxiety.

Psychometric Properties of CSAI-1

In Martens, Burton, et al.'s (1980) original validation research, alpha reliability for the CSAI-1 ranged from .94 to .97 across four studies for the adult version and .88 to .96 across three studies for the children's version. Concurrent validity research with the AD-ACL confirmed predictions that the CSAI-1 would correlate less well with the more general measure of anxiety in precompetitive compared to baseline conditions (Martens, Burton, et al., 1980). Finally, Martens, Burton, et al.'s (1980) initial construct validity research was centered on three conceptual issues. First, Martens and his colleagues summarized evidence from eight studies and found consistent support for the theoretical prediction that the relationship between the CSAI-1 and SCAT would increase from baseline to precompetitive conditions (e.g., Martens, 1977; Martens & Simon, 1976). Second, they confirmed that the CSAI-1 was a better predictor of SCAT in precompetitive compared to baseline situations (e.g., Martens, 1977; Martens, Rivkin, & Burton, 1980). Finally, they confirmed that the CSAI-1 demonstrated a stronger relationship with SCAT compared to a more general measure of A-trait (i.e., TAI) in precompetitive situations (e.g., Martens, Rivkin, et al., 1980). Thus, research with the CSAI-1 confirmed that it demonstrated solid psychometric properties and was more consistent with the conceptual predictions for the antecedent and consequent relationships in sport settings than was the more general SAI (Martens, Burton, et al., 1980). The CSAI-1 was also not used extensively in the physical domain, although several researchers employed this instrument to measure anxiety when an instrument was desired that was conceptually congruent with SCAT or greater conceptual simplicity was desired, such as Hanson and Gould's (1988) study testing coaches' ability to predict athletes' A-state levels. Moreover, the CSAI-1 remains the instrument of choice for research with children 12 years old and younger who do not seem to have the cognitive sophistication to fully comprehend the cognitive versus somatic anxiety distinction (e.g., Vealey, 1988).

Although the development of the CSAI-1 was beneficial for enhancing competitive A-state measurement, the general anxiety community had already begun to move toward multidimensional conceptualizations of anxiety and the development of instruments to measure the different components of A-state and A-trait (Liebert & Morris, 1967; Morris, Davis, et al., 1981;

Table 1

Summary of Construct Validity Evidence From Independent Research Using the CSAI-2

Study	Subjects	Alpha Reliability	Construct Validity Factors Investigated	Level of Support
Conceptual Independence of A-State Components				
Interrelationships between Cognitive and Somatic Anxiety:				
Barnes, Sime, Dienstbier, & Plake (1986)	14 M swimmers		CA/SA = .21, CA/SC = -.54, SA/SC = -.43	Moderate
Caruso, Gill, Dzewaltowski, & McElroy (1990)	24 M undergrads		CA/SA = .46, CA/SC = -.41, SA/SC = -.37	Strong
Crocker (1989)	16 M, 15 F volleyball players		mean (for women): CA/SA = .65	Strong
Crocker, Alderman, & Smith (1988)	16 M, 15 F volleyball players		CA/SA = .48, CA/SC = -.61, SA/SC = -.33	Strong
Gould, Petlichkoff, & Weinberg (1984)	Study 1 - 37 M wrestlers		CA/SA = .52, CA/SC = -.48, SA/SC = -.40	Moderate
	Study 2 - 63 F volleyball players			
Jones, Swain, & Cale (1990)	125 M distance runners		CA/SA = .51, CA/SC = -.60, SA/SC = -.39	Strong
Karteroliotis & Gill (1987)	41 M PE students		mean CA/SA = .50	Moderate
Maynard & Howe (1987)	22 M rugby players		CA/SA = .67, CA/SC = -.45, SA/SC = -.51	Strong
McAuley (1985)	7 F golfers		CA/SA = .22, CA/SC = -.54, SA/SC = -.39	Strong
Taylor (1987)	63 M, 21 F NCAA Div. 1 athletes		CA/SA = .44, CA/SC = -.39, SA/SC = -.35	Strong
Temporal Patterning Changes in State Anxiety Components:				
Caruso, Gill, Dzewaltowski, & McElroy (1990)	24 M undergrads		Pre-, Mid-, and Post-Competition	Strong
Gould, Petlichkoff, & Weinberg (1984)	Study 1 - 37 M wrestlers		Pre-Competition - 10 min prior to 2 matches	Moderate
	Study 2 - 63 F volleyball players		Pre-Competition - 1wk, 48hr, 24hr, 2hr, 20min	
Jones & Cale (1989)	20 M, 20 F collegiate athletes		Pre-Competition - 2wk, 1wk, 2days, 1day, 2hr, 30min	Strong
Jones, Swain, & Cale (1991)	28 M, 28 F collegiate athletes		Pre-Competition - 1wk, 2days, 1day, 2hrs, 30min	Strong
Karteroliotis & Gill (1987)	41 M PE students		Pre-, Mid-, and Post-Competition	Moderate
Krane & Williams (1987)	36 F HS gymnasts, 44 F collegiate golfers		Pre-Competition - 24hrs, 1hr, 10min	Moderate
Parfitt & Hardy (1987)	34 athltes - various sports		Pre-Competition (2day, 1hr), Post-Competition (2day)	Strong
Swain & Jones (1992)	60 M track and field athletes		Pre-Competition - 7days, 48hr, 24hrs, 2hrs, 30min	Strong
Swain & Jones (1993)	27 M, 22 F track and field athletes		Pre-Competition - 2days, 1day, 2 hrs, 30min	Strong
Evidence for Differential Antecedents of A-State				
Personal Antecedent Research:				
Crocker, Alderman, & Smith (1988)	16 M, 15 F volleyball players		Trait Anxiety	Strong
Gould, Petlichkoff, & Weinberg (1984)	Study 1 - 37 M wrestlers		Trait Anxiety	Moderate
	Study 2 - 63 F volleyball players			
Hammermeister & Burton (1995)	181 M, 112 F endurance athletes	CA = .79, SA = .86	Age, Experience, Competitive Level	Strong
Jones & Cale (1989)	20 M, 20 F collegiate athletes		Gender	Strong
Jones & Hanton (1996)	45 M, 46 F swimmers	CA = .89, SA = .81	Goal Attainment Expectancy	Strong
Jones, Hanton, & Swain (1994)	97 elite, 114 non-elite swimmers		Intensity, Interpretation of Anxiety	Strong
Jones & Swain (1992)	69 M IM sport performers		Achievement Orientation	Strong
Jones, Swain, & Cale (1990)	125 M distance runners		Readiness, Attitude	Strong
Jones, Swain, & Cale (1991)	28 M, 28 F collegiate athletes		Gender	Strong
Karteroliotis & Gill (1987)	41 M PE students		Trait Anxiety	Moderate
Krane & Williams (1994)	82 M, 139 F track and field athletes		Gender, Competitive Level	Strong
Krane, Williams, & Feltz (1992)	100 F golfers		Performance Expectations	Strong
Lane, Terry, & Karageorghis (1995)	122 M duathletes		Goals, Readiness, Attitude	Strong
Martin & Gill (1991)	73 M runners		Competitive Orientation, Confidence	Strong
Matheson & Mathes (1991)	50 F gymnasts		Competitive Environment, Experience	Moderate
Maynard & Howe (1987)	22 M rugby players		Trait Anxiety	Strong
Swain & Jones (1992)	60 M track and field athletes		Achievement Orientation	Strong
Yan Lan & Gill (1984)	32 F undergrads		Self-Efficacy	Strong
Situational Antecedent Research:				
Hammermeister & Burton (1995)	181 M, 112 F endurance athletes	CA = .79, SA = .86	Sport Type	Strong
Krane & Williams (1987)	36 F HS gymnasts, 44 F collegiate golfers		Subjective vs. Objective Scoring	Moderate
Krane & Williams (1994)	82 M, 139 F track and field athletes		Task Complexity	Strong
Matheson & Mathes (1991)	50 F gymnasts		Task Complexity	Moderate
Evidence for Differential Consequences of A-State				
Relationships between A-State and Motor Performance:				
Barnes, Sime, Dienstbier, & Plake (1986)	14 M swimmers		CSAI-2 and Performance	Moderate
Burton (1988)	Sample 1 - 15 M, 13 F swimmers		CSAI-2 and Performance	
	Sample 2 - 31 M, 39 F swimmers			
Caruso, Gill, Dzewaltowski, & McElroy (1990)	24 M undergrads		CSAI-2 and Performance	Weak
Edwards & Hardy (1996)	45 F netball players		Catastrophe Model	Strong
Gould, Petlichkoff, Simons, & Vevera (1987)	35 M, 4 F pistol shooters		CSAI-2 and Performance	Moderate
Gould, Petlichkoff, & Weinberg (1984)	Study 1 - 37 M wrestlers		CSAI-2 and Performance	Weak
	Study 2 - 63 F volleyball players			
Gould, Tuffey, Hardy, & Lochbaum (1993)	6 M, 5 F runners		ZOF Hypothesis	Strong
Hammermeister & Burton (1995)	181 M, 112 F endurance athletes	CA = .79, SA = .86	CSAI-2 and Performance	Weak
Hardy & Parfitt (1991)	8 F basketball players		Catastrophe Model	Strong
Jones, Swain, & Hardy (1993)	48 F gymnasts		CSAI-2 Intensity/Direction and Performance	Strong
Karteroliotis & Gill (1987)	41 M PE students		CSAI-2 and Performance	Weak
Krane (1993)	16 F soccer players	CA = .88, SA = .83	ZOF Hypothesis	Strong
Krane & Williams (1987)	36 F HS gymnasts, 44 F collegiate golfers		CSAI-2 and Performance	Moderate
Krane, Williams, & Feltz (1992)	100 F golfers		CSAI-2 and Performance	Moderate
Martin & Gill (1991)	73 M runners		CSAI-2 and Performance	Weak
Maynard & Cotton (1993)	20 M field hockey players		CSAI-2 and Performance	Moderate
Maynard & Howe (1987)	22 M rugby players		CSAI-2 and Performance	Weak
Maynard, Smith, & Warwick-Evans (1995)	24 M soccer players		CSAI-2 and Performance	Weak
McAuley (1985)	7 F golfers		CSAI-2 and Performance	Weak
Taylor (1987)	63 M, 21 F NCAA Div. 1 athletes		CSAI-2 and Performance	Strong
Williams & Krane (1992)	83 F golfers		CSAI-2 and Performance	Moderate
Relationship Between A-State and Other Psychological Variables:				
Bird & Horn (1990)	202 F softball players		Mental Errors	Strong
Kenow & Williams (1992)	11 F basketball players	CA = .79, SA = .70, SC = .80	Evaluation of Coaching Behaviors	Strong
Prapavessis & Carron (1996)	68 M, 42 F athletes - various sports	CA = .75, SA = .79, SC = .80	Cohesion	Strong
Impact of Anxiety Reduction Interventions on A-State				
Burton (1989)	17 M, 13 F swimmers		Goal-Setting Intervention	Strong
Crocker (1989)	16 M, 15 F volleyball players		SMT Intervention	Strong
Crocker, Alderman, & Smith (1988)	16 M, 15 F volleyball players		SMT Intervention	Strong
Elko & Ostrow (1991)	6 F gymnasts		RET Intervention	Strong
Maynard & Cotton (1993)	20 M field hockey players		SMT Intervention	Strong
Maynard, Hemmings, & Warwick-Evans (1995)	17 M soccer players		Somatic Intervention	Strong
Maynard, Smith, & Warwick-Evans (1995)	24 M soccer players		Cognitive Intervention	Strong
Prapavessis, Grove, McNair, & Cable (1992)	1 M rifle shooter		Self-Regulation Training Intervention	Strong

Schwartz, Davidson, & Goleman, 1978), prompting Martens and his colleagues to attempt to revise the CSAI-1 to make it multidimensional.

Competitive State Anxiety Inventory-2 (CSAI-2)
Conceptual Rationale and Description of CSAI-2

As researchers (Liebert & Morris, 1967; Davidson & Schwartz, 1976) began to find compelling evidence of the multidimensional nature of anxiety, the development of instruments to measure these multiple components became the next logical step. The first major multidimensional measure of anxiety was Liebert and Morris' Worry-Emotionality Inventory (WEI), a measure of cognitive and somatic A-state that was later revised by Morris, Davis, et al. (1981). In sport, Martens, Burton, et al. (1990) became convinced of the conceptual validity of the multidimensional anxiety model and the need to revise the CSAI-1 to measure cognitive, somatic, and perhaps other components of A-state. Through a systematic development process, Martens and his colleagues conceptualized, constructed, and validated a multidimensional version of the CSAI-1 that they labelled the CSAI-2. The CSAI-2 has three nine-item subscales measuring cognitive state anxiety, somatic state anxiety, and state self confidence. Individual items are rated on a 4-point Likert scale from 1=*not at all* to 4=*very much so*. Subscale scoring is additive although one somatic item has reverse scoring, yielding subscale totals ranging from 9 to 36. Additionally, Martens, Burton, et al. have developed special administration instructions designed to reduce the effects of social desirability.

Development of the CSAI-2. Based on previous research and theory (Deffenbacher, 1980; Endler, 1978; Liebert & Morris, 1967; Schwartz et al., 1978), the CSAI-2 was originally constructed to include items designed to measure not only cognitive and somatic A-state but also fear of physical harm and generalized anxiety. The initial item pool for the CSAI-2 included 102 items generated in three ways: (a) items borrowed from the original CSAI-1, (b) items modified from other cognitive-somatic A-state scales (e.g., Liebert & Morris, 1967; Schwartz et al., 1978) to make them sport specific, and (c) items composed specifically for the new inventory. Three judges then rated each item on syntax, clarity, and face validity based on the test construction protocol originally used in the development of SCAT (Martens, 1977). Five subsequent versions of the CSAI-2 were developed before the scale was pared down to its final 27 items. At each step, that version of the instrument was given to a large sample of subjects whose responses were then subjected to a series of statistical analyses to confirm the scale's psychometric properties, including item analysis, item-to-subscale correlations, factor analysis, and discriminant analysis. A composite of these criteria was employed to select more appropriate items for retention in the item pool based on standard test-construction evaluation criteria (Magnusson, 1966). An interesting finding emerged during factor analysis of Form A. Under iterative factor analytic procedures, the cognitive A-state subscale split into two components, with one factor comprised of positively worded items being labeled self-confidence, whereas the other factor retained all the negatively worded items, prompting retention of the cognitive-anxiety label for this subscale. This serendipitous finding was considered noteworthy, and the self-confidence subscale retained after similar analyses with subsequent samples yielded similar results. Eventually, the factor structure of Form E was deemed sufficiently consistent to warrant investigation of the CSAI-2's reliability and validity.

Psychometric Properties of CSAI-2

Reliability. Martens, Burton, et al.'s (1990) initial psychometric research on the CSAI-2 confirmed that all three CSAI-2 subscales had solid internal consistency, with alpha reliability coefficients ranging from .79 to .90 across three samples of athletes. Although many of the 49 subsequent studies using the CSAI-2 have not reported scale reliability values, studies reporting internal consistency values have documented alpha reliability coefficients ranging from .76 to .91, confirming the internal consistency of this multidimensional measure of state anxiety.

Initial validity. Martens, Burton, et al.'s (1990) initial *concurrent validity* research demonstrated reasonably consistent relationships with eight previously validated state and trait inventories, although some of the relationships with other state scales were stronger than expected (see Martens, Burton, et al., 1990, for more complete details).

Martens, Burton, et al.'s (1990) *construct validation* research was guided by a validation model modified from the model used by Martens (1977) in validating SCAT. Four studies were conducted to investigate the construct validity of the CSAI-2 by testing conceptual predictions about the antecedents and consequences of multidimensional state anxiety, including (a) variables influencing competitive A-state, (b) changes in competitive A-state as time to compete nears, and (c) relationships between CSAI-2 subscales and performance.

Study 1 was designed to examine key antecedent variables of competitive state anxiety, including the situational factor of sport type and individual difference variables of competitive A-trait, skill level, and gender. Consistent with previous research and anxiety theory, athletes in individual, subjectively scored and contact sports who were lower in skill and higher in trait anxiety reported higher levels of cognitive A-state and lower levels of state self-confidence than did team, objectively scored and noncontact performers with higher skill levels and lower levels of trait anxiety. No differences were predicted for somatic A-state between these comparisons, although somatic anxiety results were congruent with those for cognitive anxiety (see Martens, Burton, et al., 1990, for more complete results).

The purpose of Study 2 was to further investigate the independence of cognitive and somatic A-state by testing predictions that these two components of A-state will manifest differential patterns of change prior to competition. Two studies were conducted to test these temporal patterning predictions, one with 45 high school wrestlers at their league championships and the other with 40 elite gymnasts competing at the National Sports Festival. For the wrestling sample, the CSAI-2 was administered to each wrestler five times prior to competition, including (a) 48 to 64 hours, (b) 20 to 24 hours, (c) 2 hours, (d) 1hour, and (e) 15 to 20 minutes prior to competition. For the gymnastics sample, the precompetitive testing intervals included (a) 4 days, (b) 24 hours, (c) 2 hours, and (d) 5 minutes before athletes competed. Results for both samples confirmed predictions by revealing a significant change across testing periods for somatic A-state but not for cognitive A-state or state self-confidence. Thus, results from these two samples were remarkably similar and supported temporal patterning predictions of multidimensional anxiety theory that somatic A-state would be lower than cognitive A-state several days prior to competition but increase significantly as competition approached (see Martens, Burton, et al., 1990, for more complete results).

The primary purpose of Study 3 was to test the *anxiety-performance hypothesis* that cognitive anxiety should be more consistently and strongly related to performance than would somatic anxiety. Subjects for Study 3 were 49 male golfers who competed in the Western Junior National Golf Tournament. All subjects completed the CSAI-2 three times: (a) *noncompetition,* taken 1 to 2 days before the tournament began; (b) *precompetition,* within one hour of teeing off; and (c) *midcompetition,* immediately following their first 18-hole round but retrospectively responding according to how they felt after completing their first 9 holes. Consistent with multidimensional anxiety theory, results from this study confirmed that cognitive A-state did not change significantly from noncompetition to precompetition, but once golfers had played the first nine holes, cognitive A-state increased significantly. A similar but opposite pattern was evident for state self-confidence, which decreased significantly from precompetition to midcompetition after remaining unchanged from noncompetition to precompetition. However, correlational data examining the relationship between CSAI-2 components and performance at the three time periods were not consistent with predictions. The noncompetition and precompetition CSAI-2 subscale scores were not significantly correlated with performance for the first nine holes, but noncompetition and precompetition cognitive and somatic A-state scores were significantly correlated with performance for the second nine holes. Midcompetition scores for all CSAI-2 subscales were significantly correlated with performance on both the front and back nine holes. Moreover, regression analysis confirmed that midcompetition CSAI-2 subscale scores predicted performance on the first nine holes better than performance on the final nine holes (see Martens, Burton, et al., 1990, for more complete results). However, several concerns about the measurement of both anxiety and performance in this study prompted Study 4 to better evaluate the construct validity of the CSAI-2 by more explicit testing of the anxiety-performance hypothesis.

Study 4 (published separately as Burton, 1988) was designed to better address concerns about whether the real impact of CSAI-2 components on performance was tested in Study 3. Study 4 utilized more sophisticated measurement techniques that employed intraindividual measures of both state anxiety and performance to test three significant issues about the relationship between multidimensional anxiety and performance: (a) the anxiety-performance hypothesis, (b) the inverted-U relationship, and (c) the impact of task variables on the relationship between somatic A-state and performance.

Correlational data for two different samples of swimmers supported the anxiety-performance hypothesis prediction that cognitive A-state would be more consistently and strongly related to performance than would somatic A-state. For Sample 1, CSAI-cog demonstrated a higher correlation with performance than did CSAI-som for each of the three meets, and in Sample 2, the anxiety-performance hypothesis was supported for all events and for 7 of 8 individual events highlighted, with the only exception being technical events where the correlations with performance were quite small (i.e., -.04 to .05).

Linear trend analysis was conducted to test predictions about the relationships between CSAI-2 components and performance using procedures advocated by Sonstroem and Bernardo (1982). Employing intraindividual measures of anxiety and performance, results confirmed theoretical predictions by demonstrating a negative linear trend between CSAI-cog and performance, a positive linear trend between CSAI-sc and performance, and a curvilinear trend between CSAI-som and performance

Finally, correlational data partially supported predictions about the impact of task characteristics on relationships between CSAI-som and performance. Task duration results were equivocal. As predicted, somatic A-state seemed to be an important mediator of sprint performance, with correlations between CSAI-som and performance significant for the 50-yard freestyle and still approaching significance when data from the 100-yard freestyle were added. Moreover, consistent with predictions, the relationship between CSAI-som and performance decreased sharply as distance increased, but only up to a point. Surprisingly, for events 400 yards and over, particularly 800 yards and longer, the strength of the relationship increased again, approaching significance for the two longest distance events. Interestingly, the direction of the relationship differed for sprint and distance freestyle events, with sprinters performing better when they kept somatic A-state under control and distance performers swimming faster when they got themselves more physiologically aroused. Task complexity findings failed to support theoretical predictions. Results revealed no differences in CSAI-som means between high-complexity events, such as breaststroke, and low-complexity events, such as sprints and distance freestyle races (see Martens, Burton, et al., 1990 for more complete details). In summary, construct validity evidence from Martens, Burton, et al.'s (1990) initial validation research provided solid support for the psychometric properties of the CSAI-2.

Norms. Established psychological instruments often develop norms so that researchers have some basis for comparison of data they collect with typical scores for similar populations. Martens, Vealey, et al. (1990) have computed norms for CSAI-2 subscales in a number of categories, including male and female high school, college, and elite athletes as well as for the sports of basketball, cycling, golf, swimming, track and field, and wrestling, with over half of the data for norm computation provided by colleagues conducting independent research using the CSAI-2. A percentile rank and standard score are provided for each raw score for each normative sample in order to provide a quick reference for the meaning of a particular score in terms of athletes' state anxiety and state confidence levels (see Martens, Vealey, et al., 1990 for norm tables).

Independent Construct Validity Evidence for CSAI-2

In addition to the 17 studies Martens, Burton, et al. (1990) conducted to develop and confirm the initial psychometric properties of the CSAI-2, 49 published studies have used the

CSAI-2 to assess A-state with competitive populations. Because of the volume of independent research and the importance of the CSAI-2 to contemporary A-state measurement, this section will briefly review this independent research and summarize its support for the psychometric properties of the CSAI-2 under four major headings: (a) evidence of the conceptual independence of A-state components, (b) support for differential antecedents of cognitive and somatic A-state, (c) evidence of differential consequences of A-state subcomponents, and (d) support for the impact of anxiety-reduction interventions on cognitive and somatic A-state.

Evidence of the Conceptual Independence of A-State Components

The conceptual independence of multidimensional components of A-state has been documented in two primary ways: (a) through assessment of interrelationships between cognitive and somatic state anxiety and (b) through examination of temporal patterning changes in A-state components.

Interrelationships between cognitive and somatic state anxiety. Martens, Vealey, et al. (1990) reviewed five independent studies (Barnes, Sime, Dienstbier, & Plake, 1986; Gould et al., 1984; Maynard & Howe, 1987; McAuley, 1985; J. Taylor, 1987) examining relationships between CSAI-2 components and found relationships comparable to those identified in the original validation research but with even greater variability. A meta-analysis was conducted using the eight original CSAI-2 validation studies plus the five subsequent independent CSAI-2 investigations and yielded mean true correlations between CSAI-2 components of (a) .63 between cognitive and somatic A-state, (b) -.64 between cognitive A-state and state self-confidence, and (c) -.51 between somatic A-state and state self-confidence. Five more recent studies (Caruso, Gill, Dzewaltowski, & McElroy, 1990; Crocker, 1989; Crocker, Alderman, & Smith, 1988; Jones, Swain, & Cale, 1990; Karteroliotis & Gill, 1987) have yielded correlations between cognitive and somatic A-state that ranged between .03 and .77, with most of the relationships in the moderate range found in previous research.

Temporal patterning changes in state anxiety components. A review of seven studies examining temporal patterning of A-state responses (Caruso et al., 1990; Gould et al., 1984; Jones & Cale, 1989; Jones, Swain, & Cale, 1991; Karteroliotis & Gill, 1987; Krane & Williams, 1987; Swain & Jones, 1992) provides partial support for the theoretical predictions that cognitive A-state and state self-confidence should remain relatively unchanged prior to competition, whereas somatic A-state should increase rapidly as competition nears. All seven studies demonstrated differences in temporal patterning of CSAI-2 subcomponents, although several studies revealed patterns that were not consistent with conceptual predictions. Nevertheless, because few of these studies also concurrently measured expectations of success, it was impossible to determine whether differences in temporal patterns simply reflect changing expectations of success that could alter cognitive A-state and state self-confidence. Research also confirmed that intrapersonal and situational factors such as sport type (Krane & Williams, 1987), gender (Jones & Cale, 1989; Jones et al., 1991), and competitiveness (Swain & Jones, 1992) influenced changes in compo-

nents across time, whereas experience did not (Gould et al., 1984). Moreover, research corroborated initial validation results that concluded that concurrent measurement of expectations of success and A-state is needed in order to adequately test predictions that changes in cognitive A-state and state self-confidence occur when expectations of success fluctuate.

Evidence for Differential Antecedents of Cognitive and Somatic State Anxiety

The evidence for differential antecedents of cognitive and somatic A-state has been demonstrated by assessing congruency with conceptual predictions for the relationships with key (a) personal variables and (b) situational factors.

Personal antecedent research. A significant amount of A-state research has attempted to confirm the prediction that cognitive and somatic A-state should have differential antecedents, and this research can be summarize in six general antecedent categories including (a) trait anxiety, (b) self-confidence/self-efficacy, (c) goal orientation, (d) goals/expectancies, (e) age/experience/skill level, and (f) gender.

Two of the most interesting intrapersonal variables, competitive A-trait and self-confidence, generally have related to CSAI-2 components in predicted ways. Antecedent research (Crocker et al., 1988; Gould et al., 1984; Karteroliotis & Gill, 1987; Maynard & Howe, 1987) has confirmed the predicted significant relationship between competitive A-trait and A-state components. However, research is equivocal on whether A-trait as measured by SCAT is related more strongly to cognitive or somatic A-state. For example, Crocker et al. (1988) supported predictions that SCAT would be more strongly related to somatic than cognitive A-state, but several other researchers (Yan Lan & Gill, 1984; Gould et al., 1984) found cognitive A-state-SCAT relationships to be more robust.

For self-confidence, research has been moderately supportive of predicted antecedent links. Vealey (1986) demonstrated strong support for predicted relationships between her measures of state and trait sport confidence and A-state components, whereas Yan Lan and Gill (1984) revealed only minimal relationships between self-efficacy and A-state components. Similarly, research has generated equivocal findings about what role sport orientation plays as an antecedent of A-state. Martin and Gill (1991) found that sport orientation failed to predict cognitive and somatic A-state, but Swain and Jones (1992) found that A-state varied as a function of track performers' level of competitiveness.

Recent research has partially confirmed the role of goals/expectancies as antecedents of competitive A-state (Jones & Hanton, 1996; Jones et al., 1990; Krane, Williams, & Feltz, 1992; Lane, Terry, & Karageoghis, 1995). Three studies (Jones et al., 1990; Krane et al., 1992; Lane et al., 1995) revealed that goals or expectations were significant predictors of A-state, and consistent with conceptual predictions, goals/expectancies were better predictors of cognitive than somatic state anxiety. On the other hand, Jones and Hanton (1996) found no differences in A-state based on swimmers' expectancies of reaching their goals.

Predictions about the role of age/experience/skill level as antecedents of competitive A-state have received solid support from recent independent research (Gould et al., 1984; Hammermeister & Burton, 1995; Jones & Swain, 1995; Krane & Williams, 1994; Matheson & Mathes, 1991). Three studies (Gould et al., 1984; Hammermeister & Burton, 1995; Krane & Williams, 1994) found differences in A-state levels due to differences in age, experience, or skill level, although the remaining two studies found no significant differences comparing elite and nonelite cricketeers (Jones & Swain, 1995) and more versus less experienced high school gymnasts (Matheson & Mathes, 1991). On the positive side, Gould et al. (1984) found experience was the best predictor of cognitive A-state. Hammermeister and Burton (1995) also found that older endurance athletes had lower cognitive A-state than did younger performers, whereas Krane and Williams (1994) found high school athletes were higher in both cognitive and somatic A-state than were collegiate athletes.

Finally, three studies have provided solid support for the role of gender as an antecedent of competitive A-state (Jones & Cale, 1989a; Jones, Swain, & Cale, 1991; Krane & Williams, 1994). Krane and Williams revealed that female high school track and field performers reported higher somatic anxiety than did their male teammates. Similarly, Jones and Cale (1989a) found temporal A-state patterning differed based on gender, with male results generally conforming to conceptual predictions whereas female patterns reflected more gradual increases in both cognitive and somatic A-state as competition approached.

Situational antecedents research. Several recent independent studies have investigated the situational antecedents of cognitive and somatic A-state, and this situational antecedent research will be summarize under two general categories including (a) sport type and (b) task complexity.

Recent research has provided solid support for the role of sport type as an situational antecedent of competitive A-state. Hammermeister and Burton (1995) found that triathletes reported higher levels of cognitive A-state than did marathoners or cyclists, and Krane and Williams (1987) found collegiate golfers had lower cognitive and somatic A-state and demonstrated different temporal patterning of A-state components compared to high school gymnasts.

Antecedent results assessing the role of task complexity in competitive A-state levels are equivocal. Krane and Williams (1994) revealed that track and field performers competing in highly complex events experienced greater cognitive anxiety than did teammates in lower complexity events. Conversely, Matheson and Mathes (1991) found that difficulty of routines had no impact on A-state levels of high school gymnasts.

Evidence of Differential Consequences for Cognitive and Somatic State Anxiety

The evidence for differential consequences of cognitive and somatic A-state has been demonstrated by testing conceptual predictions for relationships (a) between A-state subcomponents and performance and (b) between cognitive and somatic A-state and other psychological variables.

Relationships between A-state subcomponents and motor performance. Overall results assessing relationships between cognitive and somatic A-state and performance have been somewhat equivocal. Several studies (Gould, Tuffey, Hardy, & Lochbaum, 1993; Krane, 1993) testing zone of optimal function-

ing predictions have confirmed that performance is significantly related to cognitive and somatic A-state levels that are within optimal ranges. Two additional studies (Edwards & Hardy, 1996; Hardy, Parfitt, & Pates, 1994) testing catastrophe theory predictions have generally confirmed predicted relationships between A-state components and performance. Five studies (Barnes et al., 1986; Gould, Petlichkoff, Simons, & Vevera, 1987; Jones & Cale, 1989b; Krane et al., 1992; Maynard & Cotton, 1993; Williams & Krane, 1992) employing intraindividual measures of performance have partially confirmed predicted relationships between A-state subcomponents and performance, although contrary to anxiety-performance hypothesis predictions, all of these studies found that somatic state anxiety predicted performance better than did cognitive A-state. Finally, nine other studies (Caruso et al., 1990; Gould et al., 1984; Hammermeister & Burton, 1995; Karteroliotis & Gill, 1987; Krane & Williams, 1987; Martin & Gill, 1991; Maynard & Howe, 1987; Maynard, Smith & Warwick-Evans, 1995; McAuley, 1985), most of which failed to use intraindividual measures of anxiety and/or performance, were unable to demonstrate significant anxiety-performance relationships. Although these results concerning the exact nature of the anxiety-performance relationship are equivocal, and even contradictory, evidence does suggest that A-state components can predict performance. Perhaps the most critical finding to date has been that prediction is enhanced when researchers employ intraindividual measures of anxiety and performance as well as the need to explore more fully the complex interrelationships between state anxiety components.

Relationships between cognitive and somatic A-state and other psychological varibles. Three other studies have assessed the consequences of A-state subcomponents on other psychological variables of interest, including mental errors, cohesion, and leadership behaviors. Bird and Horn (1990) found that cognitive but not somatic A-state was signficantly related to mental errors committed by high school softball players. Similarly, Prapavessis and Carron (1996) also found that cohesion was related to cognitive but not somatic anxiety. Specifically, they found that individuals reporting high task cohesion indicated they were less cognitively anxious compared to performers lower in task cohesion. Finally, in a case study of the leadership behavior of a female collegiate basketball coach, Kenow and Williams (1992) found that players high in cognitive A-state who perceived the coach as high in cognitive state anxiety evaluated coaching behaviors more negatively than did teammates lower in cognitive A-state.

Impact of Anxiety-Reduction Interventions on Cognitive and Somatic State Anxiety

Results testing the impact of anxiety-reduction interventions on cognitive and somatic A-state and performance have been limited to eight studies, with six studies revealing generally positive results and two studies finding no change in A-state levels following treatment. Burton (1989) conducted a season-long goal-setting training (GST) intervention with collegiate swimmers and found a corresponding difference in cognitive A-state and performance but not somatic A-state for GST versus non-GST swimmers from another conference team. Similarly, Elko and Ostrow (1991) conducted a rational-emotive education program with a collegiate gymnastics team and found five of six gymnasts significantly lowered their cognitive A-state levels, even though the program had no significant impact on somatic A-state or performance. Prapavessis, Grove, McNair, and Cable (1992) conducted a 6-week intervention on a competitive rifle shooter and found significant decreases in both cognitive and somatic A-state and increases in performance compared to baseline. Finally, Maynard and his colleagues (Maynard & Cotton, 1993; Maynard, Hemmings, & Warwick-Evans, 1995; Maynard, Smith, et al., 1995) have conducted a series of intervention studies to test the compatibility notion that treatments are more effective when they are implemented with individuals who suffer from a compatible type of anxiety. For example, somatic treatments should be more effective with individuals who suffer from predominantly somatic types of anxiety, whereas cognitively anxious performers should most benefit from cognitive-based treatments. In all three studies, the compatibility notion was supported as the greatest anxiety reduction was evident for compatible versus incompatible treatments.

Only two studies failed to demonstrate anxiety reduction as a result of stress management intervention (Crocker, 1989; Crocker et al., 1988). Crocker et al. investigated the effects of an 8-week cognitive-affective stress management training (SMT) program on CSAI-2 components and performance for elite junior volleyball players. Despite a decrease in negative thoughts and better performance in a controlled setting, no changes were evident in CSAI-2 scores. Similarly, Crocker (1989) conducted a SMT program with a similar sample of junior volleyball players and paradoxically found that controls reported significantly lower levels of cognitive A-state than did players receiving the SMT treatment.

In summary, this section summarizing independent research using the CSAI-2 demonstrates reasonably solid support for the construct validity of the CSAI-2, even though numerous individual difference and situational factors have been identified that can impact predicted relationships.

Directional Modification of the Competitive State Anxiety Inventory-2 (DM-CSAI-2)

Conceptual Rationale and Description of DM-CSAI-2

As awareness has increased about the need to assess the direction as well as the intensity of A-state symptoms, Jones and Swain (1992) modified the CSAI-2 to add a *direction* scale. First, respondents complete the normal CSAI-2 to assess the intensity with which they experience each of the 27 symptoms. Next, participants rate the degree to which the experienced intensity of each symptom was either facilitative or debilitative to subsequent performance on a 7-point Likert scale from *-3 = very debilitative* to *+3 = very facilitative*, with *0* representing *unimportant*. Thus, direction scores for each subscale range from -27 to +27.

Psychometric Properties of DM-CSAI-2

Although eight published studies have been identified using the DM-CSAI-2, only Jones and Hanton (1996) have reported internal consistency reliability, which for a sample of 91

swimmers was .89 for cognitive A-state direction and .81 for somatic A-state direction.

Moreover, seven of the eight studies demonstrated support for predictions that the direction dimension of A-state should be more directly related to performance than should the intensity dimension. In five of the studies, Jones and his colleagues (Jones & Hanton, 1996; Jones et al., 1994; Jones & Swain, 1992; Jones et al., 1993) have tested a number of theoretical predictions about the direction component of A-state. First, Jones and Swain (1992) divided 69 intramural athletes into high and low competitiveness groups and found that highly competitive performers perceived their anxiety symptoms as more facilitating and less debilitating than did less competitive participants. Second, Jones et al. (1993) compared good and poor performance groups of gymnasts and found no differences on intensity or somatic A-state direction, but they did reveal that the good performers reported cognitive anxiety as more facilitating and less debilitating than did poor performers. Third, Jones et al. (1994) compared elite and nonelite swimmers and discovered that elite performers reported that both cognitive and somatic A-state were more facilitative than did nonelite competitors. Moreover, nonelite swimmers had a higher incidence of debilitating anxiety than did their more elite counterparts. Finally, Jones and Hanton (1996) divided 91 swimmers into positive and negative/uncertain goal expectancy groups and demonstrated no differences in cognitive A-state intensity, but swimmers with positive goal expectancies reported symptoms as significantly more facilitating than did swimmers with negative or uncertain expectancies.

In two intervention studies, Maynard and his colleagues (Maynard, Hemmings, & Warwick-Evans, 1995; Maynard, Smith, & Warwick-Evans, 1995) generally supported the conceptual prediction that compatibility between treatment focus and dominant type of anxiety should enhance treatment effectiveness. Moreover, they partially supported predictions that interventions should lower anxiety intensity, which should, in turn, increase perceptions that anxiety is more facilitating and less debilitating.

Edwards and Hardy (1996) provide the only contradictory findings among published research using the DM-CSAI-2. In their study with netball players, they reported three interesting findings. First, somatic anxiety predicted performance better than did cognitive anxiety. Second, the intensity dimension of cognitive and somatic A-state contributed more to performance variance than did the direction dimension. Finally, combined intensity X direction scores accounted for less variance than each score separately and the combination did not significantly enhance prediction efficiency.

Therefore, the limited initial research employing the DM-CSAI-2 suggests that future A-state instruments need to employ measurement formats that include some combination of intensity and direction dimensions.

Mental Readiness Form (MRF): A Field Measure of the CSAI-2

Conceptual Rationale and Description of MRF

As sport psychology research began to move from the lab to

the field in the 1980s, anxiety researchers (Krane, 1994; Martens, Burton, et al., 1990; Murphy et al., 1989) found that the CSAI-2 was too long to be utilized in some field-testing situations. These field-related time constraints prompted Murphy et al. to develop a three-item version of the CSAI-2 that employed single items to measure cognitive A-state, somatic A-state, and state self-confidence. This short form was labeled the Mental Readiness Form (MRF) and asked subjects to mark a spot on a 10-cm line bounded by descriptors representing high and low levels of cognitive A-state, somatic A-state, and state self-confidence. Cognitive state anxiety was anchored by the descriptors *calm* and *worried*, somatic A-state used the endpoints *relaxed* to *tense*, whereas self confidence employed the descriptors *confident* to *scared*. The MRF proved to be quicker and easier to use in field research that had time constraints preventing use of the entire CSAI-2, and correlations were moderate with components of the original CSAI-2. Subsequently, Krane refined the MRF to include a Likert-scale format and revised endpoint descriptors so they were more conceptually opposite. In the revised version of the MRF (MRF-2), Krane added an 11-point Likert scale, and the third version (MRF-3) employed slightly modified anchor terms, including (a) *worried-not worried* for cognitive anxiety, (b) *tense-not tense* for somatic anxiety, and *confident-not confident* for self-confidence.

Psychometric Properties of MRF

Unfortunately, it is not possible to calculate a reliability coefficient on a single-item measure of A-state. Nevertheless, Krane's (1994) validation research with the revised versions of the MRF not only demonstrated moderate correlations between MRF, MRF-2, and MRF-3 items and CSAI-2 subscale scores, but it also revealed that the MRF-2 and MRF-3 demonstrated somewhat higher correlations with CSAI-2 subscale scores than did the original MRF, although the correlations between the CSAI-2 and the MRF-2 and MRF-3 were very similar. Moreover, Krane, Joyce, and Rayfield (1994) provided initial construct validity for the MRF-2 by demonstrating support for the predicted relationships between situation criticality, MRF-2 subscale scores, and intraindividual performance.

Future Directions
in State Anxiety Measurement

The future of state anxiety measurement must address five major problems inherent in contemporary A-state assessment. First, state anxiety inventories must be developed that distinguish between anxiety and other more positive emotional states with similar symptoms. Second, measurement techniques or strategies must be found that allow assessment of A-state during competition and not just before or after athletes compete. Third, statistical techniques must be routinely employed that minimize multicollinearity problems due to the moderate correlations between cognitive and somatic A-state measures. Fourth, the influence of social desirability must be reduced, eliminated, or at least measured consistently with A-state in order that its effects can be statistically evaluated and removed if necessary. Finally, measurement techniques must be developed that better assess the interactive effects of A-state subcomponents.

Measuring Direction Revisited:
Separating Anxiety From Positive Emotions

Although most anxiety researchers agree with the necessity of measuring the direction of anxiety symptoms, four compelling questions need to be asked about the approach that Jones and his colleagues have taken to this problem and their focus on facilitating and debilitating dimensions of anxiety. First, is anxiety really facilitative, or are researchers simply mislabelling other more positive emotions such as challenge, excitement, or self confidence, as facilitative anxiety? Second, does Jones and Swain's (1992) method of rating the direction of current symptoms experienced potentially confound the measurement of the direction component because subjects are evaluating symptoms of varying intensity levels? Third, do methods need to be found to combine the intensity and direction components into some compositive measure of cognitive and somatic A-state? Fourth, how can A-state measures account for highly anxious performers who experience only a few anxiety symptoms but at an extremely high intensity level?

Is A-state really facilitative? Jones's (1995) recent model of facilitative/debilitative competitive state anxiety is based on Carver and Scheier's (1988) control theory approach to anxiety. The model focuses on perceived control over coping and goal attainment, with positive expectations of control leading to facilitating anxiety and negative expectations leading to debilitating anxiety. Interestingly, this model is closely related to the Lazarus' (1991) model of stress with one interesting difference. Lazarus suggests that positive expectations of goal attainment and coping should lead to more positive emotions, such as challenge, excitement, and self-confidence.

Consistent with Spielberger's (1972) original theoretical conception of anxiety as a response to stress, modern conceptions of stress (Lazarus, 1991; Lazarus & Folkman, 1984) still view A-state as a consequence of stress perceptions. Lazarus and his colleagues (Lazarus, 1991; Lazarus & Folkman, 1984) have conceptualized stress as a complex cognitive evaluation in which individuals weigh at least three types of information in order to determine the amount and quality of stress experienced, including primary appraisal, secondary appraisal, and coping resources. *Primary appraisal* is the initial assessment made about a transaction in which individuals evaluate the personal significance of the encounter for them (Folkman, 1992). During this phase, individuals ask themselves, "What do I have at stake in this encounter?" and try to identify the potential impact of the environment on their personal well-being. Lazarus suggests that there are three types of primary appraisals, threat, challenge, and harm/loss, and contends that primary appraisal is influenced by three constructs: (a) goal relevance or the extent to which the encounter impacts valued personal goals; (b) ego involvement, the diverse aspects of ego identity or personal commitment, that are at stake; and (c) goal congruency, the degree to which the transaction facilitates or impairs goal attainment. Lazarus postulates that the three components of primary appraisal impact the cognitive evaluation of the transaction, prompting the development of certain discrete emotions. For example, Lazarus suggests that the primary appraisal antecedents of anxiety are goal relevance, goal incongruity, and danger to identity structures that individuals use to define themselves, particularly personal meaning and ego identity. Similarly, he would contend that goal relevance, goal congruity, and modest ego threat should lead to more positive emotions, such as challenge or self-confidence.

Once individuals determine what is at stake for them in an encounter, *secondary appraisal* focuses on assessing how well they can handle or manage the encounter (Folkman, 1992). At this stage, individuals ask themselves, "What can I do?" Thus, during secondary appraisal, individuals evaluate how much *control* they have over (a) preventing or overcoming harm or (b) improving their prospects for receiving positive benefits from the transaction. Coping potential is conceptualized as a key dimension of secondary appraisal, and it impacts stress by providing an evaluation of prospects of doing something that will change the person-environment relationship (Lazarus, 1991). Thus, stress will be high when environmental demands are thought to exceed coping capabilities, a problem that might occur for several reasons, including environmental demands perceived as uncontrollable or perceived lack of coping resources to eliminate or manage demands. Thus, similar to Carver and Scheier (1988), Lazarus believes that perceived control is a major mediator of A-state reactions.

The third component of the stress model is *coping resources*. Coping strategies are the actual cognitive and behavioral techniques that individuals have at their disposal to deal with problems and improve emotional well-being. Coping is a dynamic process of continuous appraisal and reappraisal (Folkman, 1992). Although there are hundreds of coping strategies that can be employed, Lazarus and Folkman (1984) defined two major categories of coping strategies that they termed *problem-focused coping (PFC)* and *emotion-focused coping (EFC)*. Problem-focused coping strategies are cognitive and/or behavioral efforts to reduce or eliminate the sources of stress (e.g., planning, problem solving, and increasing effort), whereas EFC strategies are cognitive/behavioral ploys to decrease emotional distress and increase well-being, even if the source of threat remains unchanged (e.g., emotional social support, positive reinterpretation, and denial, Lazarus & Folkman, 1984). Lazarus (1991) emphasizes that individuals need to have requisite coping skills and the ability to use them when needed.

Lazarus (1991) believes that stress is a complex cognitive evaluation that prompts the elicitation of anxiety responses when primary appraisal is threatening and coping resources seem insufficient to effectively deal with the threat. He also suggests that challenge appraisal should lead to other more positive emotions. Thus, the model suggests that factors that raise the perceived threat during primary appraisal, decrease perceived control during secondary appraisal, or reduce perceived coping capabilities should increase A-state, particularly cognitive A-state, whereas primary appraisal factors that increase perceived challenge, secondary appraisal factors that increase perceived control, and general enhancement of perceived coping resources should prompt more positive emotions such as excitement and self-confidence.

Lazarus' (1991) model argues against an approach such as employed by Jones and Swain (1992) of using a single construct to define two or more discrete emotions that clearly have different antecedents and consequences. Just as anxiety theorists differentiated between cognitive and somatic components of anxiety because they have different antecedents and consequences, it would seem more conceptually explicit to separate negative affective states, such as anxiety, that typically have debilitating effects on performance from positive affective states, such as challenge or excitement, that facilitate performance. Moreover, anecdotal evidence suggests that preparatory worry or concern (i.e., CSAI-2 uses the term *concern* in its cognitive subscale) is often interpreted in a challenging way and facilitates subsequent performance. However, worry during competition when coping options are more limited is much more likely to be interpreted as anxiety that is debilitating to performance. Future A-state measurement needs to wrestle with this difficult question and probably needs to differentiate between these discrete emotions and the different types of appraisal processes that promote their development.

Does rating differential intensity levels allow accurate assessment of A-state direction? Jones and Swain's (1992) MD-CSAI-2 seems to have a major measurement confound because individuals rate the facilitative or debilitative nature of their current anxiety symptoms, despite widely varying levels of A-state intensity. That means that individuals with a wide range of cognitive or somatic A-state levels, from low to high intensity, may find that particular intensity level to be equally facilitating or debilitating. Thus, because the stimuli being rated are variable rather than standard across subjects, this approach violates the tenets of nomothetic research in which individuals receive a standard prompt to which they must respond. The result should be dramatic increases in error variance that cast serious doubt on the validity of the scale. Future A-state instruments need to provide standard rather than variable stimuli for subjects to respond to in order to validly measure the nature of the symptoms experienced.

Shouldn't intensity and direction components be combined into a composite A-state measure? It is certainly easier to deal with the intensity and direction components of anxiety separately. However, if these measures represent separate emotions, then intensity and direction measures need to be combined in order to accurately describe the nature of the emotion as well as the intensity with which it is felt.

Can A-state instruments account for differences in the number of symptoms experienced versus the intensity of the emotional response? Physiological research on A-state suggests that for some individuals only several response systems respond to A-state, but these select systems are activated intensely (Lacey & Lacey, 1958), whereas other performers may experience many more symptoms, although each at a somewhat less intense level. Currently, anxiety scales rate state anxiety as higher for respondents who have a lot of symptoms, even if only experiencing moderate symptom intensity, compared to participants who experience only a few symptoms but with great intensity. In reality, these two individuals may have similar overall levels of A-state which impact behavior in a virtually identical fashion. Thus, future A-state instruments need to develop strategies that accurately assess cognitive and somatic A-state for both types of individuals, particularly only a few symptoms at a high intensity level.

Measuring State Anxiety During Competition

Martens, Vealey, and Burton (1990) have suggested that a major problem with current A-state research is when anxiety is measured. Most current anxiety-measurement protocols assess A-state prior to or following competition in order to make inferences about its impact on performance and other cognitive and affective consequences during competition, even though researchers realize that cognitive and somatic A-state levels fluctuate significantly during competition in response to performance that is better or worse than expected. Martens, Vealey, and Burton concluded that the only way to overcome this problem is to employ measurement instruments, techniques, and/or strategies that allow A-state assessment during competition and not just pre- and postcompetition. Two predominantly idiographic methods of measuring during-competition A-state are currently feasible, even though neither has been utilized a great deal by anxiety researchers to date. First, subjects can be trained to become aware of fluctuations in cognitive and somatic A-state, and then the MRF-2 can be employed to assess A-state levels during short breaks in competition. Second, videotapes of recent competitions can be used to stimulate recall of changes in A-state levels during critical competitive situations. Regretably, the tradeoff for moving to these more time-intensive idiographic approaches for studying during-competition A-state is that sample sizes of such studies must necessarily be significantly reduced. Nevertheless, in order to answer many of the interesting questions that remain unanswered about A-state, this tradeoff seems necessary.

Using MRF During Breaks in Competition

In order to collect A-state data during competition, anxiety researchers must develop a collaborative relationship with subjects that allows athletes to enhance their awareness of differences between subtle fluctuations in cognitive and somatic A-state levels. Then, in addition to using the CSAI-2 to assess A-state prior to and following competition, a field measure of multidimensional A-state such as the MRF-2 could be used during short breaks in the action to assess changes in cognitive and somatic anxiety levels. For example, Krane, Joyce, and Rafeld (1994) investigated the impact of situation criticality on softball players' cognitive and somatic A-state levels and performance over a five-game tournament. First, players were trained in the use of the MRF-2 at a practice session in which each type of anxiety was described, that subscale of the CSAI-2 was completed, and finally the corresponding MRF-2 subscale was rated under three types of conditions: (a) how players felt at the moment, (b) how they felt during a recent successful softball performance, and (c) how they felt during a recent unsuccessful softball performance. During each tournament game, players responded to the three questions of the MRF-2 in the on-deck circle before each at bat, and situation criticality and performance were rated for each at bat by trained observers. Obviously this type of protocol has a number of advantages. It not only allows researchers to capture the ebb and flow of A-state levels during competition more accurately, but it would also provide a means for better assessing the antecedents and consequences of such A-state fluctuations.

Stimulated Videotape Recall

The second method of collecting during-competition A-state data involves using videotapes of recent competitions to stimulate recall of A-state levels at critical points while competing. Although stimulated videotape recall has the obvious advantage of being less invasive to the competing athlete, it has the disadvantage of suffering from memory biases that are inherent in any retrospective technique (Runkel & McGrath, 1972). Nevertheless, stimulated videotape recall procedures do provide a mechanism for investigating changes in during-competition A-state levels, and the more relaxed time constraints of this technique provide a good opportunity to explore antecedents and consequences of A-state changes. For example, in a recent study, Burton, Hansen, Hammermeister, and Gaskill (1994) used videotape-stimulated recall to investigate A-state and goal orientation changes during positive and negative critical incidents within 12 matches for a collegiate volleyball team. In this study, three positive and negative critical incidents (i.e., operationalized as a run of three or more straight points by the experimental team or their opponent) were selected for each match. Within 3 days following the match, the head coach and each player who was on the floor during one or more of these critical incidents went through the stimulated recall procedure of viewing the video of each incident, answering open-ended interview questions, completing a 7-item questionnaire about changes in A-state and goal orientation levels, and then discussing key antecedents and consequences of any identified changes. Results demonstrated that consistent change in A-state and goal orientation accompanied both positive and negative critical incidents. Interestingly, individual differences were evident in perceptions of the antecedents and consequences of A-state changes, although findings demonstrated consistency in individual perceptions across negative critical incidents and to a lesser degree across positive critical incidents. Overall, more creative methods are needed to assess variations in during-competition A-state and the antecedents and consequences of those changes.

Employing Statistical Procedures to Reduce Multicollinearity

R. E. Smith (1989) cogently identified an important statistical problem for multidimensional anxiety scales known as multicollinearity, or the statistical problems created when variables are too highly correlated. Although multicollinearity is normally defined as variables correlating .90 or greater (Tabachnick & Fidell, 1989), it may cause problems even for more moderately correlated variables, such as multidimensional anxiety components, making it difficult to accurately assess the unique contribution of cognitive and somatic A-state in analyses such as regression or separate t tests or correlations. The problem is that the significant bivariate correlation between anxiety components may result in underrepresenting the impact of the component with the weaker relationship with the criterion measure. Thus, in regression analysis, the contribution of the second variable to enter the regression equation is artificially reduced because its shared variance with the other component has already been accounted for. Similarly, when A-state components are analyzed separately in relation to a criterion measure, such as with t tests or correlations, significant relationships may be identified based predominantly, or even solely, on the redundant variance shared by the correlated subscales (Tabachnick & Fidell, 1989).

R.E. Smith (1989) recommends using factor scores to overcome these multicollinearity problems. That is, factor analysis should be conducted on the CSAI-2 for each sample and factor scores calculated through orthogonal rotation procedures. Subscale scores then would be computed by summing factor scores rather than using raw scores, with the resulting benefit that factor score-based subscale totals will be highly correlated with raw scores but be uncorrelated with each other. Although this procedure can help reduce multicollinearity concerns, it does require a sufficiently large enough sample in order to conduct valid factor analysis, usually at least 100 subjects so that there is at least a 5 to 1 subject to variable ratio. Nevertheless, this methodological precaution should help alleviate some of the statistical problems that may have plagued previous multidimensional A-state research, thus masking the true relationship of cognitive and somatic A-state with criterion variables of interest, such as performance.

Impact of Social Desirability on State Anxiety Measurement

As discussed earlier, social desirability is the major validity problem with self-report instruments (Runkel & McGrath, 1972). Social desirability has been defined by Crowne and Marlowe (1960) as "the need for subjects to obtain approval by responding in a culturally appropriate and acceptable manner" (p. 353). This tendency, for subjects to consciously or unconsciously distort their responses to psychological questionnaires to make themselves look better any time that it seems in their best interest to do so, is a major problem for anxiety measurement. The primary concern for measuring A-state is the presence of individuals called *repressors* (Weinberger, Schwartz & Davidson, 1979), who report both low A-state and high social desirability. Repressors are performers who are really high in cognitive and somatic A-state but respond in a socially desirable way by reporting low A-state scores. Obviously, the presence of repressors in A-state samples has the potential to dramatically impact measurement validity. In fact, Williams and Krane (1992) found that CSAI-2 subscales could account for over twice as much variance in golfers' performance with repressors eliminated from the sample than with all golfers included.

Just as Martens, Burton, et al. (1990) did in the development of the CSAI-2, instrument developers have attempted to minimize social desirability problems by (a) ensuring anonymity and confidentiality of responses, (b) wording items to reduce reactivity that may trigger significant social desirability problems and (c) utilizing anti-social desirability instructions. Regrettably, even these precautions can not guarantee elimination of social desirability problems with every population or in all situations. Therefore, Williams and Krane (1989) suggest that anxiety researchers should routinely measure social desirability along with A-state and report relationships between cognitive and somatic A-state and social desirability. When social desirability problems are identified, several strategies can be employed. First, statistical procedures such as AN-

COVA can be used to minimize the impact of social desirability on A-state scores and subsequent relationships with other variables of interest. Second, repressors can be identified and eliminated from the sample if their data significantly distort results.

Measurement of the Interactive Effects of Cognitive and Somatic State Anxiety

Future A-state measurement needs to focus less on the independent assessment of cognitive and somatic A-state and more on how these two A-state components interact to impact performance. Two newer conceptual models, catastrophe theory and reversal theory, make specific predictions for the more sophisticated interactions between anxiety components and performance. Anxiety measurement needs to study these new conceptual models and let their predictions provide guidelines for how to develop instruments that better assess the complex interrelationships between A-state components. Let us look at the predictions that each model makes for the anxiety-performance relationship and try to identify its implications for future A-state measurement.

Catastrophe Theory

Although catastrophe theory was developed by Thom (1975) to explain discontinuities in mathematical functions that are normally continuous, Zeeman (1976) popularized the theory and showed how it might have application to the behavioral sciences. In sport, Hardy (1990) has pioneered work on catastrophe theory, and he suggests that the anxiety-performance relationship will differ significantly depending on the interaction between cognitive and somatic A-state. Specifically, catastrophe theory makes two major predictions. First, it hypothesizes that when cognitive A-state is low, somatic A-state and performance should demonstrate a classic inverted-U relationship. Second, when cognitive A-state is high, somatic A-state and performance are hypothesized to demonstrate an inverted-U relationship up to a point, beyond which athletes should demonstrate a catastrophic dropoff in performance, a drop of such magnitude that they will probably not be able to recover during that competition. Although testing catastrophe theory is extremely demanding because of the sophisticated statistical procedures required to evaluate model predictions, catastrophe theory remains a promising area of future research for how cognitive and somatic A-state interact to impact performance. More importantly, catastrophe theory suggests that future measurement of A-state must try to more directly assess interrelationships between cognitive and somatic state anxiety.

Reversal Theory

Reversal theory was developed by Apter (1982) and adapted to sport by Kerr (1993) to explain how differential levels of arousal are experienced. Reversal theory posits that motivation is characterized by regular and frequent movement or *reversals* between paired opposite mental states (Kerr, 1993). Most reversal research has concentrated on the telic/paratelic metamotivational states. The theory hypothesizes that high arousal in a *telic* or evaluative state will typically be experienced as unpleasant and labeled as *anxiety*, whereas the same high level of arousal experienced in a *paratelic* or nonevaluative state will normally be interpreted positively as *excitement*. Conversely, under evaluative conditions athletes will experience low arousal positively as *relaxation*, whereas underarousal under nonevaluative conditions will be interpreted negatively as *boredom*. Reversal theory would seem to suggest that the interaction of high cognitive and somatic anxiety leads to poor performance, but low cognitive and high somatic anxiety promotes good performance. Moreover, Kerr (1993) suggests that intervention can focus on decreasing arousal to achieve relaxation, but a more effective strategy may be to change the interpretation of the situation by inducing a reversal so cognitive A-state is reduced, thus allowing arousal to be experienced positively as excitement rather than negatively as somatic anxiety. The telic/paratelic metamotivational states seem to be conceptually quite close to goal perspective theory, conceptualized by Nicholls (1992) and applied to sport by Duda (1992), which distinguishes the differential motivational impact of task versus ego involvement (see Duda & Whitehead, this volume). Thus, future research may focus on how the interaction of goal orientation and A-state interrelationships directly influences affect and performance as well as how intervention designed to change goal perspectives may influence A-state and performance relationships.

In summary, five issues related to future directions in state anxiety measurement were discussed. First, although it is clear that A-state instruments need to take direction as well as intensity into consideration, future research may be better served by trying to distinguish accurately between anxiety and positive emotions with similar symptoms. Second, measurement strategies need to be utilized to assess during-competition A-state such as using abbreviated A-state measures during short breaks in competition or employing stimulated videotape recall to better identify the quantity and quality of A-state experienced at key points during competition. Third, statistical procedures such as using factor scores need to be routinely used to reduce multicollinearity problems due to moderately correlated CSAI-2 components. Fourth, social desirability problems must be addressed, not only by reducing or eliminating social desirability as much as possible but also by measuring social desirability routinely so effects can be removed statistically if needed. Finally, future A-state measurement must focus on interrelationships between A-state components and find better ways to measure this interaction.

Summary and Conclusions

This chapter has attempted to examine the current status of state anxiety measurement. First, the evolution of state anxiety was chronicled, starting with Spielberger's state/trait theory and progressing to multidimensional theories of A-state that now dominate contemporary research. Next, refinements in state anxiety measurement technology were highlighted, including both the development and description of the instrument and a summary of the scale's psychometric properties, from Spielberger and colleagues' SAI, to the sport-specific CSAI (Martens, Burton, et al., 1980), to the multidimensional CSAI-2 (Martens, Burton, et al., 1990), to the directional modification of the CSAI-2 (Jones & Swain, 1992), and finally to field modifications of the CSAI-2 such as the MRF-2 (Krane, 1994). Fi-

nally, despite the impressive support for the psychometric properties of the CSAI-2, the last section identified five measurement problems that are currently limiting A-state research and provided guidelines for the development and use of future generation A-state instruments.

References

Alpert, R., & Haber, R.N. (1960). Anxiety in academic achievement situations. *Journal of Abnormal and Social Psychology, 61*, 207-215.

Apter, M.J. (1982). *The experience of motivation: The theory of psychological reversals.* New York: Academic Press.

Barnes, M.W., Sime, W., Dienstbier, R., & Plake, B. (1986). A test of construct validity of the CSAI-2 questionnaire on male elite college swimmers. *International Journal of Sport Psychology, 17*, 364-374.

Bird, A.M., & Horn, M.A. (1990). Cognitive anxiety and mental errors in sport. *Journal of Sport and Exercise Psychology, 12*, 217-222.

Borkovec, T.D. (1976). Physiological and cognitive processes in the regulation of anxiety. In G. Schwartz & D. Shapiro (Eds.), *Consciousness and self-regulation: Advances in research* (Vol 1, pp. 261-312). New York: Plemen Press.

Burton, D. (1988). Do anxious swimmers swim slower? Reexamining the elusive anxiety-performance relationship. *Journal of Sport and Exercise Psychology, 10*, 45-61.

Burton, D. (1989). Winning isn't everything: Examining the impact of performance goals on collegiate swimmers' cognitions and performance. *The Sport Psychologist, 3*, 105-132.

Burton, D. (1990). Multimodal stress management in sport: Current status and future directions. In J.G. Jones & L. Hardy (Eds.), *Stress and performance in sport* (pp. 171-201). Chichester, UK: John Wiley and Sons.

Burton, D., Hansen, K., Hammermeister, J., & Gaskill, S. (1994). *Changes in state anxiety and motivational style during critical incidents in collegiate volleyball matches: A team case study.* Manuscript in preparation.

Carrier, C., Higson, V., Klimoski, V., & Peterson, E. (1984). The effects of facilitative and debilitative achievement anxiety on notetaking. *Journal of Education Research, 77*, 133-138.

Caruso, C.M., Gill, D.L., Dzewaltowski, D.A., & McElroy, M.A. (1990). Psychological and physiological changes in competitive state anxiety during noncompetition and competitive success and failure. *Journal of Sport and Exercise Psychology, 12*, 6-20.

Carver, C.S., & Scheier, M.F. (1988). A control-process perspective on anxiety. *Anxiety Research, 1*, 17-22.

Cattell, R.B. (1957). *The IPAT Anxiety Scale.* Champaign, IL: Instititute for Personality and Ability Testing.

Couch, J.V., Garber, T.B., & Turner, W.E. (1983). Facilitating and debilitating test anxiety in academic achievement. *Psychological Record, 33*, 237-244.

Crocker, P.R.E. (1989). Evaluating stress management training under competitive conditions. *International Journal of Sport Psychology, 20*, 191-204.

Crocker, P.R.E., Alderman, R.B., & Smith, F.M.R. (1988). Cognitive-affective stress management training with high performance youth volleyball players: Effects on affect, cognition and performance. *Journal of Sport and Exercise Psychology, 10*, 448-460.

Crowne, D.P., & Marlowe, D. (1960). A new scale of social desirability independent of psychopathology. *Journal of Consulting Psychology, 24*, 349-354.

Davidson, R.J., & Schwartz, G.E. (1976). The psychobiology of relaxation and related states: A multi-process theory. In D. Mostofsky (Ed.), *Behavioral control and modification of physiological activity* (pp. 399-442). Englewood Cliffs, NJ: Prentice-Hall.

Deffenbacher, J.L. (1977). Relationship of worry and emotionality to performance on the Miller Analogies Test. *Journal of Educational Psychology, 69,* 191-195.

Deffenbacher, J.L. (1978). Worry, emotionality, and task-generated interference in test anxiety: An empirical test of attentional theory. *Journal of Educational Psychology, 70,* 248-254.

Deffenbacher, J.L. (1980). Worry and emotionality in test anxiety. In I.G. Sarason (Ed.), *Test anxiety: Theory, research and applications* (pp. 111-128). Hillsdale, NJ: Erlbaum.

Deffenbacher, J.L., & Dietz, S.R. (1978). Effects of test anxiety on performance, worry, and emotionality in naturally occurring exams. *Psychology in the Schools, 15,* 446-450.

Deffenbacher, J.L., Mathis, H., & Michaels, A.C. (1979). Two self-control procedures in the reduction of targeted and nontargeted anxieties. *Journal of Counseling Psychology, 26,* 120-127.

Deffenbacher, J.L., Michaels, A.C., Michaels, T., & Daley, P.C. (1980). Comparison of anxiety management training and self-control desensitization. *Journal of Counseling Psychology, 27,* 232-239.

Doctor, R.M., & Altman, F. (1969). Worry and emotionality as components of test anxiety: Replication and further data. *Psychological Reports, 24,* 563-568.

Duda, J.L. (1992). Motivation in sport settings: A goal perspective approach. In G.C. Roberts (Ed.), *Motivation in sport and exercise* (pp. 57-91). Champaign, IL: Human Kinetics.

Edwards, T., & Hardy, L. (1996). The interactive effects of intensity and direction of cognitive and somatic anxiety and self-confidence upon performance. *Journal of Sport and Exercise Psychology, 18,* 296-312.

Elko, P.K., & Ostrow, A.C. (1991). Effects of a rational-emotive education program on heightened anxiety levels of female collegiate gymnasts. *The Sport Psychologist, 5,* 235-255.

Endler, N.S. (1978). The interactional model of anxiety: Some possible implications. In R.W. Christina & D.M. Landers (Eds.), *Psychology of motor behavior and sport — 1977* (pp. 332-351). Champaign, IL: Human Kinetics.

Fenz, W.D. (1975). Coping mechanisms and performance under stress. In D.M. Landers (Ed.), *Psychology of sport and motor behavior - 2* (pp. 3-24). University Park: Pennsylvania State University, College of Health, Physical Education & Recreation.

Folkman, S. (1992). Making a case for coping. In B.N. Carpenter (Ed.), *Personal coping: Theory, research and application* (pp. 31-46). Westport, CT: Praeger.

Gould, D., Petlichkoff, L., Simons, J., & Vevera, M. (1987). Relationship between Competitive State Anxiety Inventory - 2 subscale scores and pistol shooting performance. *Journal of Sport Psychology, 9,* 33-42.

Gould, D., Petlichkoff, L., & Weinberg, R.S. (1984). Antecedents of, temporal changes in, and relationships between CSAI-2 subcomponents. *Journal of Sport Psychology, 6,* 289-304.

Gould, D., Tuffey, S., Hardy, L., & Lochbaum, M (1993). Multidimensional state anxiety and middle distance running performance: An exploratory examination of Hanin's (1980) zones of optimal functioning hypothesis. *Journal of Applied Sport Psychology, 5,* 85-95.

Hackfort, D., & Schwenkmezger, P. (1993). Anxiety. In R.N. Singer, M. Murphey, & L.K. Tennant (Eds.), *Handbook of research on sport psychology* (pp. 328-364). New York: MacMillan.

Hammermeister, J., & Burton, D. (1995). Anxiety and the Ironman: Investigating the antecedents and consequences of endurance athletes' state anxiety. *The Sport Psychologist, 9,* 29-40.

Hanson, T.W., & Gould, D. (1988). Factors affecting the ability of coaches to estimate their athletes' trait and state anxiety levels. *The Sport Psychologist, 2,* 298-313.

Hardy, L. (1990). A catastrophe model of performance in sport. In J.G. Jones & L. Hardy (Eds.), *Stress and performance in sport* (pp. 81-106). Chichester, UK: John Wiley & Sons.

Hardy, L., & Parfitt, G. (1991). A catastrophe model of anxiety and performance. *British Journal of Psychology, 82,* 163-178.

Hardy, L., Parfitt, G., & Pates, J. (1994). Performance catastrophes in sport: A test of the hysteresis hypothesis. *Journal of Sport Sciences, 12,* 327-334.

Hatfield, B.D. & Landers, D.M. (1983). Psychophysiology—A new direction for sport psychology. *Journal of Sport Psychology, 5,* 243-259.

Hatfield, B.D., Landers, D.M., & Ray, W.J. (1984). Cognitive processes during self-paced motor performance: An electroencephalographic profile of skilled marksmen. *Journal of Sport Psychology, 6,* 42-59.

Holroyd, K.A. (1978). Effectiveness of an "attribution therapy" manipulation with test anxiety. *Behavior Therapy, 9,* 526-534.

Holroyd, K.A., Westbrook, T., Wolf, M., & Badhorn, E. (1978). Performance, cognition and physiological responding in test anxiety. *Journal of Abnormal Psychology, 87,* 442-451.

Jones, J.G. (1995). More than just a game: Research developments and issues in competitive anxiety in sport. *British Journal of Psychology, 86,* 449-478.

Jones, J.G., & Cale, A. (1989a). Precompetition temporal patterning of anxiety and self-confidence in males and females. *Journal of Sport Behavior, 12,* 183-195.

Jones, J.G., & Cale, A. (1989b). Relationships between multidimensional competitive state anxiety and cognitive and motor subcomponents of performance. *Journal of Sport Sciences, 7,* 163-173.

Jones, J.G., & Hanton, S. (1996). Interpretation of competitive anxiety symptoms and goal attainment expectancies. *Journal of Sport and Exercise Psychology, 18,* 144-157.

Jones, J.G., Hanton, S., & Swain, A. (1994). Intensity and interpretation of anxiety symptoms in elite and non-elite sports performers. *Personality and Individual Differences, 17,* 657-663.

Jones, J.G., & Swain, A. (1992). Intensity and direction as dimensions of competitive state anxiety and relationships with competitiveness. *Perceptual and Motor Skills, 74,* 467-472.

Jones, J.G., & Swain, A. (1995). Predispositions to experience debilitative and facilitative anxiety in elite and non-elite performers. *The Sport Psychologist, 9,* 201-211.

Jones, J.G., Swain, A., & Cale, A. (1990). Antecedents of multidimensional competitive state anxiety and self-confidence in elite intercollegiate middle-distance runners. *The Sport Psychologist, 4,* 107-118.

Jones, J.G., Swain, A., & Cale, A. (1991). Gender differences in precompetition temporal patterning and antecedents of anxiety and self-confidence. *Journal of Sport and Exercise Psychology, 13,* 1-15.

Jones, J.G., Swain, A. & Hardy, L. (1993). Intensity and direction dimensions of competitive state anxiety and relationships with performance. *Journal of Sport Sciences, 11,* 525-532.

Karteroliotis, C., & Gill, D.L. (1987). Temporal changes in psychological and physiological components of state anxiety. *Journal of Sport Psychology, 9,* 261-274.

Kenow, L.J., & Williams, J.M. (1992). Relationship between anxiety, self-confidence, and evaluation of coaching behaviors. *The Sport Psychologist, 6,* 344-357.

Kerr, J.H. (1993). An eclectic approach to psychological interventions in sport: Reversal theory. *The Sport Psychologist, 7,* 400-418.

Kirkland, K., & Hollandsworth, J.G. (1980). Effective test taking: Skills-acquisition versus anxiety-reduction techniques. *Journal of Consulting and Clinical Psychology, 48,* 431-439.

Krane, V. (1993). A practical application of the anxiety-athletic performance relationship: The zone of optimal functioning hypothesis. *The Sport Psychologist, 7,* 113-126.

Krane, V. (1994). The mental readiness form as a measure of competitive state anxiety. *The Sport Psychologist, 8,* 189-202.

Krane, V., Joyce, D., & Rafeld, J. (1994). Anxiety, situation criticality, and collegiate softball performance. *The Sport Psychologist, 8,* 58-72.

Krane, V., & Williams, J.M. (1987). Performance and somatic anxiety, cognitive anxiety, and confidence changes prior to competition. *Journal of Sport Behavior, 10,* 47-56.

Krane, V., & Williams, J. (1994). Cognitive anxiety, somatic anxiety, and confidence in track and field athletes: The impact of gender, competitive level and task characteristics. *International Journal of Sport Psychology, 25,* 205-217.

Krane, V., Williams, J., & Feltz, D. (1992). Path analysis examining relationships among cognitive anxiety, somatic anxiety, state confidence, performance expectations, and golf performance. *Journal of Sport Behavior, 15,* 279-295.

Lacey, J.I., & Lacey, B.C. (1958). Verification and extension of the principle of autonomic response stereotypy. *American Psychologist, 71,* 51-73.

Lane, A., Terry, P., & Karageorghis, C. (1995). Antecedents of multidimensional competitive state anxiety and self-confidence in duathletes. *Perceptual and Motor Skills, 80,* 911-919.

Lazarus, R. (1991). *Emotion and adaptation.* New York: Oxford University Press.

Lazarus, R., & Folkman, S. (1984). *Stress, appraisal and coping.* New York: Springer.

Lewthwaite, R. (1990). Threat perception in competitive trait anxiety: The endangerment of important goals. *Journal of Sport and Exercise Psychology, 12,* 280-300.

Liebert, R.M., & Morris, L.W. (1967). Cognitive and emotional components of test anxiety: A distinction and some initial data. *Psychological Reports, 20,* 975-978.

Long, B.C., & Van Stavel, R. (1995). Effects of exercise training on anxiety: A meta-analysis. *Journal of Applied Sport Psychology, 7,* 167-189.

Magnusson, D. (1966). *Test theory.* Reading, MA: Addison-Wesley.

Martens, R. (1977). *Sport Competition Anxiety Test.* Champaign, IL: Human Kinetics.

Martens, R., Burton, D., Rivkin, F., & Simon, J. (1980). Reliability and validity of the Competitive State Anxiety Inventory (CSAI). In C.H. Nadeau, W.C. Halliwell, K.M. Newell, & G.C. Roberts (Eds.), *Psychology of motor behavior and sport—1979* (pp. 91-99). Champaign, IL: Human Kinetics.

Martens, R., Burton, D., Vealey, R.S., Bump, L.A., & Smith, D.E. (1990). Development and validation of the Competitive State Anxiety Inventory - 2 (CSAI-2). In R. Martens, R.S. Vealey, & D. Burton, *Competitive anxiety in sport* (pp. 117-190). Champaign, IL: Human Kinetics.

Martens, R., Rivkin, F., & Burton, D. (1980). Who predicts anxiety better: Coaches or athletes? In C.H. Nadeau, W.C. Halliwell, K.M. Newell, & G.C. Roberts (Eds.), *Psychology of motor behavior and sport—1979* (pp.100-108). Champaign, IL: Human Kinetics.

Martens, R., & Simon, J. (1976). Comparison of three predictors of state anxiety when competing. *Research Quarterly, 47,* 381-387.

Martens, R., Vealey, R.S., & Burton, D. (1990). *Competitive anxiety in sport.* Champaign, IL: Human Kinetics.

Martin, J.J., & Gill, D.L. (1991). The relationships among competitive orientation, sport-confidence, self-efficacy, anxiety and performance. *Journal of Sport and Exercise Psychology, 13,* 149-159.

Matheson, H., & Mathes, S. (1991). Influence of performance setting, experience and difficulty of routine on precompetition anxiety and self-confidence of high school female gymnasts. *Perceptual and Motor Skills, 72,* 1099-1105.

Maynard, I.W., & Cotton, P.C.J. (1993). An investigation of two stress-management techniques in a field setting. *The Sport Psychologist, 7,* 375-387.

Maynard, I.W., Hemmings, B., & Warwick-Evans, L. (1995). The effects of a somatic intervention strategy on competitive state anxiety and performance in semiprofessional soccer players. *The Sport Psychologist, 9,* 51-64.

Maynard, I.W., & Howe, B.L. (1987). Interrelations of trait and state anxiety with game performance of rugby players. *Perceptual and Motor Skills, 64,* 599-602.

Maynard, I.W., Smith, M.J., & Warwick-Evans, L. (1995). The effects of a cognitive intervention strategy on competitive state anxiety and performance in semiprofessional soccer players. *Journal of Sport and Exercise Psychology, 17,* 428-446.

McAuley, E. (1985). State anxiety: Antecedent or result of sport performance. *Journal of Sport Behavior, 8,* 71-77.

Mellstrom, M., Jr., Cicala, G.A., & Zuckerman, M. (1976). General versus specific trait anxiety measures in the prediction of fear of snakes, heights, and darkness. *Journal of Consulting and Clinical Psychology, 44,* 83-91.

Morris, L.W., Brown, N.R., & Halbert, B. (1977). Effects of symbolic modeling on the arousal of cognitive and affective components of anxiety in preschool children. In C.D. Spielberger & I.G. Sarason (Eds.), *Stress and anxiety* (Vol. 4, pp. 153-170). Washington, DC: Hemisphere.

Morris, L.W., Davis, D., & Hutchings, C. (1981). Cognitive and emotional components of anxiety: Literature review and revised worry-emotionality scale. *Journal of Educational Psychology, 73,* 541-555.

Morris, L.W., & Engle, W.B. (1981). Assessing various coping strategies and their effects on test performance and anxiety. *Journal of Clinical Psychology, 37,* 165-171.

Morris, L.W., & Fulmer, R.S. (1976). Test anxiety (worry and emotionality) changes during academic testing as a function of feedback and test importance. *Journal of Educational Psychology, 68,* 817-824.

Morris, L.W., Harris, E.W., & Rovins, D.S. (1981). Interactive effects of generalized and situational expectancies on cognitive and emotional components of social anxiety. *Research in Personality, 15,* 302-311.

Morris, L.W., & Liebert, R.M. (1970). The relationship of cognitive and emotional components of test anxiety to physiological arousal and academic performance. *Journal of Consulting and Clinical Psychology, 35,* 332-337.

Morris, L.W., & Liebert, R.M. (1973). Effects of negative feedback, threat of shock and level of trait anxiety on the arousal of two components of anxiety. *Journal of Counseling Psychology, 20,* 321-326.

Morris, L.W., & Perez, T.J. (1972). Effects of interruption on emotional expression and performance in a testing situation. *Psychological Reports, 31,* 559-564.

Murphy, S.M., Greenspan, M., Jowdy, D., & Tammen, V. (1989, September). *Development of a brief rating instrument of competitive anxiety: Comparison with the Competitive State Anxiety Inventory - 2 (CSAI-2).* Paper presented at the meeting of the Association for the Advancement of Applied Sport Psychology, Seattle, WA.

Nicholls, J.G. (1992). The general and the specific in the development and expression of achievement motivation. In G.C. Roberts (Ed.), *Motivation in sport and exercise* (pp. 31-56). Champaign, IL: Human Kinetics.

Osarchuk, M.M. (1976). A comparison of a cognitive, a behavior therapy and a cognitive-and-behavior therapy treatment of test anxious college students. (Doctoral dissertation, Adelphi University, 1974). *Dissertation Abstracts International, 36,* 3619B. (University Microfilms No. 76-14, 25.)

Parfitt, C.G., & Hardy, L. (1987). Further evidence for the differential effects of competitive anxiety upon a number of cognitive and motor sub-systems. *Journal of Sport Sciences, 5,* 62-63.

Parfitt, C.G., & Hardy, L. (1993). The effects of competitive anxiety on memory span and rebound shooting tasks in basketball players. *Journal of Sport Sciences, 11,* 517-524.

Petruzzello, S.J., Landers, D.M., Hatfield, B.D., Kubitz, K.A., & Salazar, W. (1991). A meta-analysis on the anxiety-reducing effects of acute and chronic exercise: Outcomes and mechanisms. *Sports Medicine, 11,* 143-182.

Prapavessis, H., & Carron, A.V. (1996). The effect of group cohesion on competitive state anxiety. *Journal of Sport and Exercise Psychology, 18,* 64-74.

Prapavessis, H., Grove, J.R., McNair, P.J., & Cable, N.T. (1992). Self-regulation training, state anxiety, and sport performance: A psychophysiological case study. *The Sport Psychologist, 6,* 213-229.

Raglin, J.S., & Morris, M.J. (1994). Precompetition anxiety in women volleyball players: A test of ZOF theory in a team sport. *British Journal of Sports Medicine, 28,* 47-51.

Rejeski, W.J., Hardy, C., & Shaw, J. (1991). Psychometric confounds of assessing state anxiety in conjunction with acute bouts of vigorous exercise. *Journal of Sport and Exercise Psychology, 13,* 65-74.

Runkel, P.J., & McGrath, J.E. (1972). *Research on human behavior: A systematic guide to method.* New York: Holt, Rinehart & Winston.

Sarason, S.B., Davidson, K.S., Lighthall, F.F., Waite, R.R., & Ruebush, B.K. (1960). *Anxiety in elementary school children.* New York: Wiley.

Schwartz, G.E., Davidson, R.J., & Goleman, D.J. (1978). Patterning of cognitive and somatic processes in the self-regulation of anxiety: Effects of meditation versus exercise. *Psychosomatic Medicine, 40,* 321-328.

Simon, J.A., & Martens, R. (1979). Children's anxiety in sport and nonsport evaluative activities. *Journal of Sport Psychology, 1,* 160-169.

Smith, C.A., & Morris, L.W. (1976). Effects of stimulative and sedative music on two components of test anxiety. *Psychological Reports, 38,* 1187-1193.

Smith, C.A., & Morris, L.W. (1977). Differential effects of stimulative and sedative music on anxiety, concentration and performance. *Psychological Reports, 41,* 1047-1053.

Smith, R.E. (1989). Conceptual and statistical issues in research involving multidimensional anxiety scales. *Journal of Sport and Exercise Psychology, 11,* 452-457.

Smith, R.E., Smoll, F.L., & Schutz, R.W. (1990). Measurement correlates of sport-specific cognitive and somatic trait anxiety: The Sport Anxiety Scale. *Anxiety Research, 2,* 263-280.

Sonstroem, R.J., & Bernardo, P. (1982). Intraindividual pregame state anxiety and basketball performance: A re-examination of the inverted-U curve. *Journal of Sport Psychology, 4,* 235-245.

Spielberger, C.D. (1966). Theory and research on anxiety. In C.D. Spielberger (Ed.), *Anxiety and behavior* (pp. 3-20) . New York: Academic Press.

Spielberger, C.D. (1972). Conceptual and methodological issues in anxiety research. In C.D. Spielberger (Ed.), *Anxiety: Current trends in theory and research* (Vol. 2, pp. 481-493). New York: Academic Press.

Spielberger, C.D. (1973). *Preliminary test manual for the State-Trait Anxiety Inventory for Children.* Palo Alto, CA: Consulting Psychologists.

Spielberger, C.D., Gorsuch, R.I., & Lushene, R.L. (1970). *Manual for the State-Trait Anxiety Inventory.* Palo Alto, CA: Consulting Psychologists.

Swain, A., & Jones, J.G. (1992). Relationships between sport achievement orientation and competitive state anxiety. *The Sport Psychologist, 6,* 42-54.

Swain, A., & Jones, J.G. (1993). Intensity and frequency dimensions of competitive state anxiety. *Journal of Sport Sciences, 11,* 533-542.

Tabachnick, B.G., & Fidell, L.S. (1989). *Using multivariate statistics* (2nd Ed.). New York: Harper-Collins.

Taylor, J. (1987). Predicting athletic performance with self-confidence and somatic and cognitive anxiety as a function of motor and physiological requirements in six sports. *Journal of Personality, 55,* 139-153.

Taylor, J.A. (1953). A personality scale of manifest anxiety. *Journal of Abnormal and Social Psychology, 48,* 285-290.

Thayer, R. (1967). Measurement of activation through self-report. *Psychological Reports, 20,* 663-678.

Thom, R. (1975). *Structural stability and morphogenesis* (D.H. Fowler, Trans.). New York: Benjamin-Addison Wesley.

Thompson, J.G., Griebstein, M.G., & Kuhlenschmidt, S.L. (1980). Effects of EMG biofeedback and relaxation training in the prevention of academic underachievement. *Journal of Counseling Psychology, 27,* 97-106.

Vealey, R.S. (1986). Conceptualization of sport-confidence and competitive orientation: Preliminary investigation and instrument development. *Journal of Sport Psychology, 8,* 221-246.

Vealey, R.S. (1988). Achievement goals of adolescent figure skaters: Impact on self-confidence, anxiety and performance. *Journal of Adolescent Research, 3,* 227-243.

Vealey, R.S. (1992). Personality and sport: A comprehensive view. In T. Horn (Ed.), *Advances in sport psychology* (pp. 25-59). Champaign, IL: Human Kinetics.

Watson, D., & Friend, R. (1969). Measurement of social-evaluative anxiety. *Journal of Consulting and Clinical Psychology, 33,* 448-457.

Weinberger, D.A., Schwartz, G.E., & Davidson, R.J. (1979). Low-anxious, high-anxious, and repressive coping styles: Psychometric patterns and behavioral and physiological responses to stress. *Journal of Abnormal Psychology, 88,* 369-380.

Williams, J.M., & Krane, V. (1989). Response distortion on self-report questionnaires with female collegiate golfers. *The Sport Psychologist, 3,* 212-218.

Williams, J.M., & Krane, V. (1992). Coping styles and self-reported measures of state anxiety and self confidence. *Journal of Applied Sport Psychology, 4,* 134-143.

Yan Lan, L., & Gill, D.L. (1984). The relationship among self-efficacy, stress responses and a cognitive feedback manipulation. *Journal of Sport Psychology, 6,* 227-238.

Zeeman, E. C. (1976). Catastrophe theory. *Scientific American, 234,* 65-82.

Chapter 8

MEASUREMENT OF COPING STRATEGIES IN SPORT

Peter R.E. Crocker
Kent C. Kowalski
Thomas R. Graham
University of Saskatchewan

Introduction

Participating in competitive sport places athletes under intense physical and psychological demands. These rigorous challenges require athletes not only to use automated technical and tactical skills but also to develop and employ an arsenal of cognitive and behavioral coping skills to achieve performance success and satisfaction (Crocker, Alderman, & Smith, 1988; Gould, Eklund, & Jackson, 1993; Gould, Finch, & Jackson, 1993). The investigation of how athletes cope with sport-related stress has been recognized for both its practical and theoretical importance (Crocker & Graham, 1995; Gould, 1996; Smith, 1986).

Sport researchers have begun to identify how athletes cope, or believe they would cope, under varying sport-related conditions (Crocker, 1992; Crocker & Graham, 1995; Gould, Eklund, et al., 1993; Madden, Summers, & Brown, 1990). These studies have reported how athletes cope with not only game- or match-related demands, but also the requirements of managing time, interpersonal relationships, media, injury, and finances. Many studies have provided general descriptive information on the types and amount of coping used by athletes (Crocker & Graham, 1995; Gould, Finch, et al., 1993). Some research has raised significant conceptual and measurement questions, such as those involving the stability of coping over time as well as the factor stability of scales (Crocker, 1992; Crocker & Isaak, in press). Although conceptual issues are becoming more pronounced, sport coping research is limited by a number of methodological and measurement problems.

The purpose of this chapter is to review issues related to the measurement of coping strategies in the physical activity and sport field. It will provide a comprehensive review of the various coping instruments that have been utilized. Both quantitative and qualitative assessment of coping strategies will be discussed. We will also provide some background information on conceptual and theoretical issues because measurement approaches are rooted in theoretical orientation (Aldwin, 1994; Lazarus, 1990). It should be noted that coping and stress reflect a complex field and there exists a huge literature in the general psychology domain. To cover all the issues that may be pertinent to understanding the measurement of coping is far beyond the scope of this chapter. Readers are referred to the work of Carpenter (1992), Lazarus (1991), and Aldwin (1994) concerning related issues in the general coping field.

Conceptual and Theoretical Issues

Coping defined. As noted by Compas and Epping (1993), the construct of coping has proven difficult to define and operationalize. The history of coping research has been plagued by differences in conceptualizations. Early work (e.g., Freud, 1936) focused on unconscious processes whereas more recent inquiry has concentrated on conscious cognitive processes (Endler & Parker, 1989; Lazarus & Folkman, 1984; Miller, 1980). Despite differences in recent theoretical orientations in the coping literature, there is a growing consensus that coping can be characterized as cognitive, affective, and behavioral efforts to manage specific external and/or internal demands (Endler, Parker, & Summerfeldt, 1993; Lazarus, 1991). As such, coping is seen as a critical mediator between stressful events and subsequent reactions, such as emotion and performance.

Although coping models feature diversity at the microlevel, most models feature two basic types of coping distinctions based on the intention and function of coping efforts (Compas & Epping, 1993). Macrolevel analyses have suggested that coping strategies could be categorized into two broad functional dimensions: (a) problem focused and (b) emotion focused (Compas, Malcarne, & Banez, 1992; Lazarus &

Folkman, 1984), although other general dimensions, such as emotion oriented and task oriented, have been proposed (e.g., Endler, Parker, & Summerfeldt, 1993). Problem-focused coping refers to cognitive and behavioral efforts used to change the problem or challenge causing the distress. Emotion-focused coping involves strategies that help control emotional arousal and distress that are caused by the stressor.

Microlevel analyses have suggested that the two basic coping dimensions can be further divided based on the specific functions of coping (Carver, Scheier, & Weintraub, 1989; Compas et al., 1992; Folkman & Lazarus, 1985). These analyses have produced numerous specific categories. Problem-focused coping can be separated into distinct categories, such as problem-solving, planning, information seeking, suppression of competing behaviour, and increasing efforts. Emotion-focused coping can be delineated as mental and behavioral withdrawal, denial, relaxation, self-blame, avoidance, acceptance, and wishful thinking. Many of the subtypes of coping are present in the sport coping literature. Compas and his colleagues (1992) argued that the number and structure of specific categories will vary as a function of the problem being investigated and the sample characteristics. Therefore, sport researchers may use different coping scales depending on the type of problem and target population being studied.

Coping and outcome. There is a consensus among stress and coping researchers that coping should not be confused and confounded with outcome. If an athlete is failing, it does not follow that he or she is not coping. The athlete may be attempting to cope with a demanding sporting situation, but the selected coping strategies may be ineffective, inefficient, or inappropriate for that specific situation. Performance problems may be due to poor technical skills, coaching, and physiological factors as well as maladaptive coping. It must be emphasized that coping involves both behaviours and thoughts that require effort to manage demanding person-environment transactions (Aldwin, 1994; Lazarus, 1991). The use of any particular coping strategy, whether problem- or emotion-focused, may not be successful depending upon the particular type and level of stressor.

Trait and process conceptualizations of coping. The measurement of coping will be heavily influenced by the particular coping model the researcher adopts. Models vary in terms of how much emphasis is placed on person characteristics or situational characteristics (Compas & Epping, 1993). Trait models place more emphasis on personal characteristics and assume cross-situational and temporal consistency. Process models, on the other hand, place more emphasis on situational factors and assume coping may change not only across situations but also over the course of a stressor (e.g., Lazarus, 1991; Lazarus & Folkman, 1984). The importance of these assumptions cannot be underestimated as they will shape basic research factors, such as the wording of instructions, wording of coping items, the selection of independent and dependent variables, and the analysis of data.

The trait model holds that individuals have a disposition to think or act in a stable manner. Specific to coping responses, it is assumed that "people do not approach each coping context anew, but rather bring to bear a preferred set of coping strategies that remains relatively fixed across time and circum-

stances" (Carver et al., 1989, p. 270). Although not explicitly stated in all cases, many researchers have assumed such a consistent coping style in investigating relationships between coping and other variables in sport (e.g., Grove, 1995; Madden, Kirkby, & McDonald, 1989; Madden et al., 1990; Prapavessis & Grove, 1995). From a measurement perspective, the trait approach is reflected by instructions that ask the person to indicate what an individual usually does to handle a problem (Aldwin, 1994). For example, in a study of basketball players, Madden et al. (1990) asked players to what extent coping strategies were used on and off the court to deal with performance slumps. The instructions never made any reference to a specific slump or a phase of a particular slump.

Although athletes may have a preferred coping style to deal with sport-related stress, none of the sport studies has provided direct evidence of such stability. Indeed, there is little data on the coping pattern of athletes across situations or over time in the same situation. Such an analysis would require researchers to use measures that ask athletes to report how they coped with a particular situation or at a particular time. This data could then be analyzed by intraclass correlational techniques to determine situational or temporal consistency in coping. This issue will be discussed later in a section on future research issues.

In contrast to the trait model of coping, the contextual approach holds that athletes will use different coping strategies across situations and even within a stressful incident depending on the demands of the problem. Aldwin (1994) argued that an assumption of the contextual approach is that how an individual copes is dependent on the cognitive evaluation of the situation. Consistent with the transactional view of stress, different coping strategies will be applied dependent on the appraisal of key factors, such as the meaning of the situation in terms of personal well-being and coping options (Lazarus, 1991; C.A. Smith, 1993), perceptions of control and personal competence (Compas & Oroson, 1993). For example, if an athlete perceives she has control over a stressful situation, then she is more likely to use problem-focused coping. In contrast, low perceptions of control would lead to distress and lead the athlete to use more emotion-focused coping in an effort to reduce the distress.

Overemphasizing either person or environmental characteristics may lead to a distorted understanding of the role of coping in the stress process. Many theorists are recognizing that person and situational attributes transact in the unfolding of stress. The transactional view is that stress occurs as the result of an ongoing dynamic relationship between the person and environment (Lazarus & Folkman, 1984). This latter conceptualization is the most widely adopted view of stress today and has been a driving force in stress and coping sport research (Gould, 1996). The transactional view of stress would imply that person factors (stable and unstable processes) and environment factors need to be considered when defining coping. Yet it is clear, that when coping research from sport is examined, that this is not the case. In many cases, researchers have focused on either person or environment factors in terms of the coping process.

Quantitative Assessment of Coping

When one attempts to make judgments regarding the use of any test instrument in the behavioral sciences, reliability and validity issues are always a key concern. The evaluation of reliability and validity is based on different criteria depending on whether the measure is norm referenced or criterion referenced. At this time the coping measures that are used in sport research have been norm referenced (based on individual differences) where test scores are compared to other scores in the distribution, as opposed to the criterion referenced measurement approach, which emphasizes the proportion of the domain mastered (Safrit, 1989).

One approach to assess the reliability of a norm referenced instrument is to look at the consistency of scores for an individual over time, which can be estimated using an intraclass correlation coefficient (Baumgartner, 1989). Such an approach toward reliability may be problematic with coping instruments because the use of coping strategies over time may not be consistent. Ghiselli, Campbell, and Zedeck (1981) suggested that such systematic variation should not be regarded as unreliability, making it inappropriate to use test-retest reliability for a dynamic construct such as coping. If coping is assumed to be stable across time and situations, then test-retest reliability would be appropriate. The more appropriate method of assessing the reliability for dynamic constructs is internal consistency analysis, which takes into account the intercorrelations among items.

Wood (1989) provided an overview of how to provide validation support for norm-referenced measurements, but this has been difficult thus far for coping instruments. Content-related evidence supports the extent to which test items accurately reflect the defined domain of a construct. Coping instruments have been primarily developed for nonsport populations, and content-related evidence of the instruments for a sporting population needs to be established. Criterion-related evidence is demonstrated by showing that the test scores are related to scores on another test measuring the same construct. This type of validation assumes that there is an appropriate criterion with which to compare the test scores, but to date there is no well-established criterion measure of coping available; therefore, validity evidence for coping instruments may need to be established by other means. The final method of validation proposed by Wood is construct validity. Construct validity involves developing a hypothesized network of interrelationships among measures that can then be tested to provide convergent or divergent support. This type of validity evidence has also been difficult to establish because little is known about the relationships between coping and other constructs, thereby making interpretation of significant or nonsignificant relationships difficult. Unexpected relationships between coping and other constructs may reflect either a lack of validity of the instrument or contradictory evidence against the theoretically proposed model. Also, as part of establishing construct validity it is important to establish stability of factor structures for coping measures. Factor structures represent underlying constructs for a set of variables, and these types of latent variables should remain stable over time and across samples.

Sport Modifications of the Ways of Coping Checklist

Madden and his colleagues (1989, 1990), Crocker (1992), and Haney and Long (1995) have reported coping instruments that are sport modifications of Folkman and Lazarus's (1985) Ways of Coping Checklist (WWC). Folkman and Lazarus used the two general dimensions of problem-focused and emotion-focused coping as a conceptual guide to develop the Ways of Coping Checklist. The WCC consisted of 66 items, each describing a cognitive or behavioral action. Based on exploratory alpha factor analysis, Folkman and Lazarus (1985) identified several general types of coping. These included wishful thinking, detachment, self-blame, tension reduction, keeping to self, emphasizing the positive, problem focused, and seeking social support. Subsequent research by Folkman, Lazarus, Dunkel-Schetter, Delongis, and Gruen (1986) found eight coping factors, but the factors had slightly different clustering of items. The internal consistency values for each of the 8 factors were as follows: confrontive coping (α =.70), distancing (α =.61), self-controlling (α =.70), seeking social support (α =.76), accepting responsibility (α =.66), escape-avoidance (α =.72), planful problem solving (α =.68), positive reappraisal (α =.79). Since each of the sport modifications of the WCC was developed independently and consist of different items, they will be discussed in turn.

Ways of Coping Checklist for Sport (WOCS)

Madden and colleagues (1989, 1990) reported the factor structure of a sport modification of the WCC that was initially presented in an unpublished manuscript. The instrument, called the Ways of Coping Checklist for Sport (WOCS), contained eight different scales. It appears that the original WOCS contained 66 items but that only 54 items loaded over .4 on the eight factors developed through principal component analysis with varimax rotation. The eight scales in the WOCS were problem-focused coping, seeking social support, general emotionality, increased effort and resolve, detachment, denial, wishful thinking, and emphasizing the positive. The number of items per scale range from seven (problem-focused coping) to three (emphasizing the positive). Madden et al. (1989, 1990) reported the internal consistency to be α =.91 for the full 54-item WOCS, but no internal consistency values for each of the scales were reported. Internal consistency data for each of the subscales are needed to properly assess the reliability of the scale, because a high internal consistency value for a composite may be due to the large number of items compared to the subscales. Also, if the subscales are proposed to measure conceptually distinct coping strategies, then internal consistency needs to be established for the subscales rather than for the heterogenous composite.

Support for the validity of the WOCS has been limited, but there has been some evidence for construct validity of the scale. In a 1989 study involving 21 distance runners, Madden et al. reported that the strategies of seeking social support, increased effort, and problem-focused coping were consistently used by runners when experiencing performance slumps, which, as the authors suggest, may be due to these strategies being the most appropriate and available resources for middle-distance runners. Based on the notion that coping would be implemented in response to perceived stress, Madden and colleagues (1990) found that basketball players who reported high levels of competitive stress used increased effort, problem-focused coping, seeking social support, and wishful thinking more frequently than did low stress basketball players. The results of these two studies do suggest initial support for construct validity of the WOCS, but this conclusion is not based on studies designed to assess the validity of the measure. Little other validity evidence for the WOCS has been provided, and it would be especially useful to examine the stability of its factor structure with various sport populations.

Modified Ways of Coping Checklist

Crocker (1992) modified the Ways of Coping Checklist to measure coping based on a recent stressful athletic situation. The modified WCC was developed through a multifaceted process. Based on athletes written responses and interviews, six new items were added to the original WCC, four items were deleted, and several items were reworded to make the scale more sport relevant. Thus, the modified WCC began with 68 items. Athletes were required to rate the extent to which they used each coping strategy during a stressful sporting situation. The items were scored on a 4-point scale labelled 1 (not used), 2 (used somewhat), 3 (used much), and 4 (used very much). Twelve items were deleted due to excessive positive skewness, and another 18 items for not fitting the eight factors that were asked for in principal axis factor analysis with varimax rotation. Thus, the final form of the modified WCC included the following eight scales: active coping, problem focused, social support, positive reappraisal, wishful thinking, self-control, detachment, and self-blame. The number of items per scale ranged from seven (active coping) to two (self-blame).

The data of 237 competitive athletes, ranging from 16 to 32 years of age involved in various sports and levels of sport, were used to examine the psychometric properties of the modified WCC (Crocker, 1992). Cronbach's alpha was used to examine the reliability of the modified WCC. The internal consistency values for the subscales were as follows: active coping (α=.78), problem focused (α =.77), social support (α =.70), positive reappraisal (α =.68), wishful thinking (α =.73), self-control (α =.60), detachment (α =.58), and self-blame (α =.68). Several of the alpha coefficients were below .70 suggesting reliability problems for some of the subscales, especially self-control and detachment. Similar reliability problems occurred for the Distancing subscale on the original WCC (Folkman et al., 1986), which appears to coincide in content with Detachment on Crocker's (1992) modified WCC. Further work appears to be warranted to increase the reliability of at least some of the subscales on the modified WCC.

The modifications made to the original WCC, which were designed to make the WCC applicable to sport, appear to have provided the scale with acceptable content validity. Preliminary construct-validity evidence for the modified WCC was demonstrated by the emergence of a wide range of cognitive and behavioral coping strategies being selected by athletes to manage sport-related stress, which would be expected given that athletes were asked to recall individual stressful situations.

The unstable factor structure of the modified WCC (Crocker, 1992) appears to be an obvious weakness of the measure. There was a lack of consistency of items within scales when the modified WCC was compared to the original WCC (Folkman et al., 1986). Not only did the factor structure reported by Crocker differ from the original WCC, but also from

the WOCS as reported by Madden and colleagues (1989, 1990). For example, the item "I knew what I had to do, so I doubled my efforts to make things work" loaded on the problem-focused coping factor for Crocker, but on the increased effort dimension in the Madden et al. (1990) study. This difference cannot be accounted for solely by different labels being assigned to item groupings because Madden et al. had a separate problem-focused coping factor that was composed of some of the other problem-focused coping items found by Crocker. Thus, even among sport applications of the WCC, the items do not load consistently on the same factors. It should be noted that Madden and colleagues used principal component analysis, which has a number of weaknesses, including assuming there is no measurement error. Confirmatory factor analysis needs to be done on both the WOCS and modified WCC in order to properly assess the factorial validity of each measure.

The measurement problem in the WOCS and WCC was addressed by Aldwin (1994), who suggested factor instability in the WCC may reflect changes in the coping process or result from application across situations. She stated that process instruments like the WCC are meant to tap variability and thus are likely to be unstable. We would disagree with this logic in that the factors such as active coping represent latent variables, with the corresponding items of each factor tapping that latent coping dimension. Although the use of specific coping dimensions may change across time (a central feature of the process of coping in which an individual may select a variety of strategies), the items should not move between factors when used in a different context. This item movement suggests that the same item is measuring more than one latent coping variable. Item-factor instability can happen if coping dimensions are moderately or highly correlated and the wording of a coping item is vague. Such instability also is more likely to occur when the scales are developed primarily on the basis of specific strategies reported by individuals (strategies that also vary in level of abstractness) and the factors are formed by exploratory factor analysis. Whatever the reason for the factor instability, the sport modifications of the WCC suffer from psychometric weaknesses that need to be resolved. Thus, factorial validity of the modified WCC needs to be further established before the instrument is widely used in sport coping research.

Further limitations of the modified WCC (Crocker, 1992) and WOCS (Madden et al., 1989, 1990) can also be found in criticisms of the original WCC made by Stone, Greenberg, Kennedy-Moore, and Newman (1991). They suggested that the WCC has a number of deficiencies including (a) the applicability of its coping items to different situations, (b) the lack of a well-defined coping period, and (c) problems with a multiple definition response key. First, some of the items included on the modified WCC may not be appropriate for some sporting situations. For example, the coping strategy assessed by the item "I yelled at or expressed anger to the person(s) who caused the problem" may not be appropriate in some individual sporting events. This type of problem has the potential of preventing accurate comparison of scale values among sporting contexts (Stone et al., 1991). Second, in assessing the coping process in sporting settings, there is also possible variability in the time period in question for which coping is assessed. This presents a problem if athletes are reporting on very different stress stages such as anticipation, confrontation, or being overwhelmed, or dealing with the aftermath (Meichenbaum, 1985). Finally, as mentioned by Stone et al., the extent to which athletes rate use of coping strategies may mean they used the strategies often, used them for a long period of time, or used a great deal of effort in trying to implement the strategy. One athlete's interpretation of what is meant by extent can vary across items and differ from that of other athletes, making interpretation of scale scores and comparisons among athletes difficult because of the uncertainties as to what the differences reflect.

Higher Order Ways of Coping Modifications: Engagement-Disengagement

Haney and Long (1995) have modified the WCC to assess higher-order coping in a physical activity context. The higher-order factor structure was developed to provide a more global assessment of coping than problem- and emotion-focused coping. The modified WCC includes engagement and disengagement coping dimensions, which were previously identified by Tobin, Holroyd, Reynolds, and Wigal (1989). *Engagement coping* refers to managing a situation through engaging in active coping, whereas *disengagement coping* involves distancing or detaching oneself from the task.

The engagement-disengagement checklist was revised from a 46-item version of the Ways of Coping Checklist (WCC; Folkman et al., 1986) and 4 additional items that were deemed relevant for sport situations from Carver et al. (1989) "suppression of competing activities" scale. The final 18-item version of the WCC resulted from a series of confirmatory factor analyses using LISREL VI to represent the theoretically proposed two-factor structure. This involved a series of steps after the original analysis of the 50-item two-factor model indicated a poor fit between the model and the data. Subsequent 35-item, 29-item, 24-item, 22-item, 20-item, and 18-item two-factor models were examined. Attempts to reduce the model below 18 items resulted in nonsignificant model change. The final 18-item two-factor model resulted in a goodness-of-fit index of .84 and root mean square residual of .08. Eleven items measured on a 4-point Likert scale make up the engagement coping factor, and seven items make up the assessment of disengagement coping. Higher scores on the engagement (0 to 33) and disengagement (0 to 21) scales reflect higher levels of this type of coping. Reliability analysis using Cronbach's alpha indicated moderate internal consistency for the engagement (α =.82) and disengagement (α =.75) factors. Although the reliability of the scale is acceptable, the indices of model fit are not very good for a simple two-factor model.

There is some preliminary construct-validation evidence for the modified WCC developed by Haney and Long (1995). The checklist was used to examine the relationship between coping and several other variables (self-efficacy, control appraisals, performance satisfaction, and performance) in female athletes during controlled competition situations. Individuals were asked to "think about the shots you just performed" and then to "indicate the extent to which you used each of the following strategies during the activity just performed." Path analysis was used to test the predicted relationships among measures. It was expected that the engagement and disengagement factors would be related to sport performance (basketball free-throws and field hockey/soccer penalty shots) over two rounds. Disengagement was expected to be negatively related to performance because this type of strategy distracts an individual from the task at hand. Engagement coping by definition is attempts to manage the stressful event; therefore, it was expected to be positively related to shooting performance. The path coefficients for the model indicated that engagement coping was positively related to performance (Round 1, b=.25; Round 2, b=.29), and disengagement coping was negatively related to performance (Round 1, b=-.34; Round 2, b=-.21). Further, control appraisals (ability to control emotions) were associated (b=-.30) with disengagement coping in the first round.

The strength of the revised engagement-disengagement checklist is that it assesses higher order coping strategies in athletes. The engagement and disengagement dimensions of coping may provide a basis for helping to understand the coping process as it relates to sport. The reduced number of items also reduces measurement burden, which is important when other psychological constructs are being assessed.

There are, however, some limitations with the engagement-disengagement checklist. Although most of the items on the checklist appear to be appropriate for sport-related coping strategies, the assessment of engagement or disengagement coping may not include items that are general enough to assess such broad dimensions. The engagement and disengagement items were originally designed to assess coping at a more specific level, and may be inappropriate for more global coping strategy factors. Thus, it is not surprising that the two-factor model fit indices were less than optimal. Also, the mean values on the disengagement scale for both performance rounds in the Haney and Long (1995) study were .6 with a standard deviation of .5 on the seven item (0 to 3) scale. These means for disengagement indicate there is little variability in the disengagement scale, with most athletes scoring at the low end of the scale.

The criticisms made by Stone et al. (1991) of the original WCC also apply to Haney and Long's (1995) modified WCC. There may be a problem with some items on the engagement-disengagement checklist being applicable to sporting situations. For example, the disengagement coping item "I avoided being with people in general" may not be a choice in some sporting situations. This may be especially true in team sporting events where the option to be alone often does not exist. This is important given the broad level of coping that the modified WCC by Haney and Long attempts to assess.

Despite these limitations, Haney and Long's (1995) work on forming higher order coping scales is an important development in the sport psychology field. Several coping researchers (e.g., Billings & Moos, 1984; Endler & Parker, 1989) have attempted to develop such higher order scales in the general coping literature. What is required, however, is a carefully consideration of what higher order coping dimensions need to be assessed in sport and the development of appropriate higher order items to tap these constructs. Also, scales should be developed on conceptual not just empirical grounds with items developed and evaluated for each coping dimension.

Modified COPE

Carver et al. (1989), citing concerns with the WCC, developed the original COPE instrument. They felt the two-dimension structure (problem- and emotion-focused coping) on the WCC was too simplistic and noted that research with the WCC usually resulted in more than just the two factors. Carver et al. also reported that the meaning of some items on the WCC were ambiguous and difficult to interpret and that the WCC was developed primarily from an empirical rather than a theoretical base. The COPE contained 13 conceptually distinct scales based primarily on theoretical and functional considerations, including the transactional model of coping, the model of behavioral self-regulation, preexisting measures of coping, and potential adaptive value of specific strategies (Carver et al., 1989). The COPE instrument contained five scales to measure distinct aspects of problem-focused coping (active coping, planning, suppression of competing activities, restraint coping, seeking instrumental social support), five scales of emotion-focused coping (seeking emotional social support, positive reinterpretation and growth, acceptance, denial, turning to religion), and three other scales (focus on and venting of emotions, behavioral disengagement, mental disengagement). Two exploratory scales (humour and drug/alcohol use) had also been developed.

Crocker and his colleagues (Bouffard & Crocker, 1992; Crocker & Graham, 1995; Crocker & Isaak, in press) have modified the Carver et al. (1989) COPE instrument to study situational-based coping in physical activity. Recently, Grove (1995) has applied modifications of the COPE using trait-like instructions. Situation-based coping refers to attempts to manage a specific environmental situations, whereas trait-like coping refers to a coping style across situations and time. These studies have provided information regarding reliability and validity of the modified COPE.

Crocker and Graham (1995) used a modified form of the COPE instrument to assess coping in recent stressful performance situations. The coping instrument employed consisted of nine original COPE scales and three additional sport relevant scales (based on previous coping research; Crocker, 1992; Madden et al., 1990). Some items in the COPE scales were slightly modified to provide greater sport relevance. For example, references to *problem* on original COPE items were replaced with *performance,* and items were modified to be worded at a grade 5 education level. The modified COPE scales were active coping, seeking social support for instrumental reasons, planning, seeking social support for emotional reasons, denial, humour, behavioral disengagement, venting of emotion, suppression of competing activities, self-blame, wishful thinking, and increasing effort. Each scale consisted of four items, with each item scored on a 5-point scale ranging from *used not at all/very little* to *used very much.* Item scores are summed for each scale with the composite reflecting greater use of a particular coping strategy. In the Crocker and Graham study, athletes were asked to indicate how much they had used each strategy during a stressful performance situation.

Reliability of the COPE scales has been assessed using standardized alpha coefficients. The internal consistency values found for a sample of 235 competitive athletes were as follows: active coping (α =.64), seeking social support for instru-

mental reasons (α =.79), planning (α =.82), seeking social support for emotional reasons (α =.81), denial (α =.42), humour (α =.92), behavioral disengagement (α =.63), venting of emotion (α =.87), suppression of competing activities (α =.73), self-blame (α =.76), wishful thinking (α =.62), and increasing effort (α =.80) (Crocker & Graham, 1995). Because of the low coefficient alpha found for the denial scale, it was dropped from the modified COPE in any further analysis assessing the relationships of coping strategies to affect.

Reliability analysis in a study by Crocker and Isaak (in press) with 25 male and female youth swimmers resulted in internal consistency values for the modified COPE scales as follows: active coping (α =.74), seeking social support for instrumental reasons (α =.85), planning (α =.80), seeking social support for emotional reasons (α =.88), humour (α =.94), venting of emotion (α =.85), suppression of competing activities (α =.81), self-blame (α =.80), wishful thinking (α =.61), and increasing effort (α =.75). Crocker and Isaak also included positive reinterpretation and growth (α =.83) and acceptance (α =.75) as additional factors, but dropped both the denial and behavioral disengagement scales from further analysis for having internal consistency values below .50.

Bouffard and Crocker (1992) looked at coping with challenging situations for a group of 30 athletes with physical disabilities. They found that active coping, venting of emotions, planning, religion, and seeking social support for both emotional and instrumental reasons were the only COPE scales to have internal consistency values (averaged over three time periods) greater than .70.

Grove (1995) has provided data from 622 Australian athletes (recreational to international level) using the same instrument as Crocker and Graham (1995) but utilizing trait-like instructions. Athletes were asked how often they had used each strategy when experiencing a performance slump. Grove's descriptive results were very similar to those reported by Crocker and Graham. He found that scale means were highest for effort (17.0), active coping (15.4), self-blame (14.3), and planning (14.1). The lowest means were reported for behavioral disengagement (7.7) and denial (9.4). The three highest means found by Crocker and Graham (1995) were for increasing effort (16.3), self-blame (14.5), and active coping (14.1). The lowest mean value was behavioral disengagement (5.7). These results demonstrate some consistency in the reporting of coping strategies on the modified COPE scale across samples. Reliability of the modified COPE scales used by Grove, assessed using standardized alpha coefficients, was also similar to that of Crocker and Graham. The internal consistency values were as follows: active coping (α =.63), seeking social support for instrumental reasons (α =.83), planning (α =.80), seeking social support for emotional reasons (α =.81), humour (α =.88), behavioral disengagement (α =.77), venting of emotion (α =.80), suppression of competing activities (α =.72), self-blame (α =.68), wishful thinking (α =.71), and increasing effort (α =.74). Both the behavioral disengagement and wishful thinking scales were found to have better scale reliability in Grove's study than in the Crocker and Graham investigation. Most notable among Grove's findings was that the denial scale had acceptable internal reliability (α =.75).

Taken together, these four studies provide support for the reliability of some subscales of the modified COPE. The denial subscale seems the most problematic, demonstrating acceptable internal reliability in only the Grove study (1995). Other subscales have also had reliabilities <.70 in at least one of the four studies, indicating that more work needs to be done to improve the reliability of the modified COPE as a whole.

Despite the abundance of information on reliability of the modified COPE scales, relatively little work has been done to directly test the validity of the instrument. Initial support for factor stability of the modified COPE (Crocker & Graham, 1995) was shown by the clustering of types of coping being similar to clustering found in nonsport populations using the original COPE (Carver et al., 1989). Construct validity appeared to be supported by showing that athletes used primarily problem-focused coping strategies, because problem-focused strategies were expected to be a way for competitive athletes to manage performance challenges (Crocker & Graham, 1995). Problem-focused coping variables were positively related to positive affect; emotion-focused and social support variables were associated with negative affect. These results were expected since in community populations it has been shown that problem-focused coping is associated with challenge and benefit emotions whereas emotion-focused coping is related to threat and harm emotions (Folkman & Lazarus, 1985, 1988). Women's socialization to use primarily emotion-focused coping strategies and seek social support was the hypothesized reason for the expected result that females used more emotion-focused coping strategies (Crocker & Graham, 1995). Bouffard and Crocker (1992) suggested that use of varied coping strategies across situations may be of adaptive value, and their results showed that physically disabled athletes tended to be inconsistent in choice of coping strategies on the modified COPE across situations. Although the Bouffard and Crocker study does seem to provide construct validity evidence, the results of the Crocker and Isaak study (in press) are less clear. They found that for youth swimmers, only active coping demonstrated consistency for competitive swim races, which would support the theory, but there was much more consistency in reporting of coping strategies across practices. Although the coping consistency across practices was unexpected, the possibility of athletes aggregating coping responses over time for the training data (indicating what they usually do as opposed to what they actually did) seems to be a plausible explanation (Crocker & Isaak, in press). Thus, the theoretically proposed relationships between coping strategies and other variables were detected by the instrument and seem to provide support for the modified COPE, but it should again be noted that no study was designed to specifically assess the validity of the scale.

A strength of the modified COPE instrument is that there appears to be a more consistent factor structure with the original measure than was demonstrated by sport modifications of the Ways of Coping Checklist (i.e., Crocker, 1992). Also, the scales on the COPE were originally designed to be conceptually distinct and based primarily on theory, as opposed to the modified WCC, which was developed more from an empirical base. It seems probable that the modified COPE provides a stronger factor structure than do other multidimensional measures of the coping process in athletics, but factorial validity still needs to be systematically established. Procedures such as confirmatory factor analysis need to be utilized to identify potential factor instability.

Another potential limitation of the modified COPE is that it may be subject to some of the same criticisms that were made previously of the WCC (Stone et al., 1991). The modified COPE contains items assessing coping strategies that would be appropriate to most stressful sporting situations, but the problems of what coping periods are actually being recalled by the athletes and whether reporting of a strategy reflects frequency, duration, or effort has not yet been addressed. The modified COPE asks athletes to indicate "how much" they use a particular strategy, but similar to the "extent" rating on the WCC, this may mean that they used the strategy often, for a long duration, or with great effort. Also, as with the WCC, various stages of a stressful problem are potentially being recalled by different athletes on the modified COPE. These types of questions need to be addressed in order to help eliminate sources of variability in the assessment of the coping process.

Athletic Coping Skills Inventory-28

R.E. Smith, Schutz, Smoll, and Ptacek (1995) developed the Athletic Coping Skills Inventory-28 (ACSI-28) which is designed to assess psychological coping skills within a sport context (see also Murphy & Tammen, this volume, for a review of this instrument). The ACSI-28 was revised and shortened from the 42-item Athletic Coping Skills Inventory developed by R.E. Smith, Smoll, and Schutz (1988). The development of the ACSI-28 raises conceptual issues that have measurement implications. These issues include measurement of stressor reactively (coping choice and coping effectiveness) and conscious and subconscious coping skills. These issues are best discussed, however, after a description of the ASCI-28 and its measurement properties.

The ACSI-28 provides a trait-like measure of psychological coping skills thought to be instrumental to improve performance. It is composed of seven underlying psychological skill factors with subscales measuring coping with adversity, peaking under pressure, goal setting/mental preparation, concentration, freedom from worry, confidence and achievement motivation, and coachability. The seven subscales on the ACSI-28 can be summed to yield a general measure of psychological coping skills (Personal Coping Resources). It is suggested, however, that the ACSI-28 measures a multifaceted construct and that each subscale can be used as a specific measure.

Athletes are asked to read statements on the ACSI-28 that describe experiences of other athletes and to recall how often they experience the same thing. Each subscale is composed of four items measured on a 4-point scale labelled 0 (almost never), 1 (sometimes), 2 (often), and 3 (almost always). Thus, each of the seven subscale scores can range from 0 to 12, and the composite Personal Coping Resources score can range from 0 to 84, with higher scores reflecting higher levels of psychological skill.

Test-retest reliability of the Personal Coping Resources score on the ACSI-28 was found to be .87 over a one-week period for a sample of 97 male and female college athletes. Internal consistency reliability of the ACSI-28 total score was .86 for a sample of 594 male and 433 female high school athletes. One-week test-retest reliability coefficients and alpha coefficients for the subscales were as follows: Coping with Adversity (r=.63, α =.66); Peaking Under Pressure (r=.87, α =.78); Goal Setting/Mental Preparation (r=.82, α =.71); Concentration (r=.72, α =.62); Freedom From Worry (r=.77, α =.76); Confidence and Achievement Motivation (r=.83, α =.66); and Coachability (r=.47, α =.72).

Smith and his colleagues (1995) have provided preliminary convergent validity evidence supporting the ACSI-28. The ACSI-28 total score has been shown to be related to the Self-Control Schedule (Rosenbaum, 1980), which measures cognitive-behavioral coping skills, the Problem Focused Coping subscale on the Ways of Coping Checklist (Vitalino, Russo, Carr, Maiuro, & Becker, 1985), and the Sport Anxiety Scale (Smith, Smoll, & Schutz, 1990), as well as measures of generalized self-efficacy (Coppel, 1980) and general self-esteem (Smoll, Smith, Barnett, & Everett, 1993). Support for the subscales on the ACSI-28 was mixed. The Freedom From Worry subscale on the ACSI-28 has been related to the Sport Anxiety Scale worry factor, but the Concentration subscale did not correlate highly with the concentration disruption scale on the Sport Anxiety Scale.

The ACSI-28 has also been shown to be related to performance, supporting the construct validity of the instrument. Overachievers in high school athletics had higher psychological skills scores than did normal achievers and underachievers. In a study of professional baseball players, psychological and physical skills accounted for approximately equal amounts of explained variance in hitters' batting average, and psychological skills accounted for most of the explained variance in pitchers' earned run average at the end of the season (Smith & Christensen, 1995).

One strength of the ACSI-28 is that it was designed specifically for sporting research and asks sport related questions, reflecting psychological skills in athletics as being multifaceted. Also, the ACSI-28 has been validated using confirmatory factor analysis to test the specific hypothesized factor structure that resulted from the initial exploratory factor analysis procedure. The convergence of ACSI-28 scores with related scales and its relationship to performance measures appear to indicate preliminary support for the ACSI-28 as a measure of psychological skills in sporting research.

There are a number of limitations to using the ACSI-28, some of which have been noted by Smith et al. (1995). The ACSI-28 has limited validity at the present time. More work needs to assess the construct validity, predictive ability, and stability of the factor structure on the ACSI-28. Also, the convergent validity of the ACSI-28 should involve other measures of coping and psychological skills that are not self-report, because all self-report measures may present the same types of method-variance problems, such as cognitive distortions, memory limitations, and social desirability.

One of the problems encountered when using the ACSI-28 in coping research may be that the measure was not developed based on any theory of the coping process. Although the ACSI-28 was designed as a multidimensional measure of coping skills, the factors emerged from a range of psychological skills items, not from explicit theory, as the authors themselves state (Smith et al., 1995). Not only may this present problems in as-

sessing the larger domain of coping as it relates to performance, but it also neglects the possible person-environment transaction that may be very important to the coping process. For example, the questions on the ACSI-28 may also be too general to assess coping in specific situations or coping as it relates to specific performance outcomes. The ACSI-28 items may be too general to capture the dynamic nature of coping, and thus the scale may assess general levels of psychological skills, but not necessarily coping itself. Different situations may require various coping strategies, which may not be most effectively assessed by items measured at very general levels. Smith and his colleagues (1995) have acknowledged that their work does not assume that the ACSI-28 samples the universe of functionally significant coping responses.

The ACSI-28 raises two conceptual issues that have significant implications for the measurement of coping in sport. First, it is important to distinguish between choice of coping strategy and the effectiveness of the strategy (Bolger & Zuckerman, 1995; R.E. Smith, personal communication). Choice measures reflect what strategies were selected by participants to deal with a particular stressful situation. Instruments such as sport modifications of the Ways of Coping Checklist and COPE instruments can be considered choice measures. The ASCI-28, on the other hand, is an effectiveness measure designed to assess the extent to which an athlete uses psychological skills functionally linked to improved performance (R.E. Smith, personal communication). As Bolger and Zuckerman (1995) argued, how individuals manage stress may reflect differences in the choice of coping strategies, the effectiveness of those strategies in particular contexts, or the combination of choice and effectiveness.

A second issue concerns whether psychological skills as measured by the ASCI-28 are equivalent to coping skills. Some theorists have argued that coping skills involve effort and that automated skills should be considered management skills and not coping skills (Aldwin, 1994; Lazarus & Folkman, 1984). Aldwin has stated, however, that coping strategies and emotional responses may not be fully conscious. In this sense, any cognition and behaviour that are used to manage threatening or challenging person-situation transaction may be considered a coping skill. R.E. Smith (personal communication) suggested that researchers may need to discriminate between automatic and controlled (conscious) application of psychological skills. The inclusion of automated skills as part of the coping definition raises additional measurement challenges. If coping skills can be both automated and conscious, then the accurate assessment of coping becomes a problem using self-report methods. Because automatic processing is rapid and not readily available to conscious awareness, athletes may not be able to recall the use of these skills. Clearly, this issue of identifying all psychological skills involved in the adaptive (and maladaptive) process as coping skills needs further thought and elaboration.

There is no doubt that the ACSI-28 scales are an important step in assessing psychological skills in sporting situations. The work of R.E. Smith and colleagues (1995) provides sound direction for future research in this area, especially in the development of sport-specific measures. We believe the ACSI-28 represents a good measure of specific coping resources that athletes can call upon when appraising the potential threat or challenge of a sport situation, determining various coping options, and managing potentially troubled person-environment conditions.

Qualitative Analysis of Coping in Sport

Increasingly, qualitative assessment has been used to examine stress and coping in the physical activity domain (Gould, Eklund, et al., 1993; Gould, Finch, et al., 1993; Scanlan, Stein, & Ravizza, 1991). This approach to research has several characteristics that distinguish it from quantitative methodology. First, it is inductive in nature. No a priori hypotheses are made. Rather, variables and processes gradually emerge as the analysis proceeds. For this reason, qualitative research can be discovery oriented and especially useful when little is known about a phenomenon beforehand. Second, subjects respond to interview questions in an open-ended manner and determine the parameters of the data. This results in rich information that is not limited by response categories. Although quantitative methods focus on the influence of a limited number of variables, contextual information is actively sought in qualitative investigations. Third, the researchers interact with the data. At some point, responses by the subjects must be classified into more general themes by the investigators. Qualitative methodology assumes that the perceptions of the investigators affect the data. Finally, the small sample sizes, case-study format, and nuances of the researchers make results less generalizable to other groups or settings. Thus, limited generalizability is the price to be paid for the depth of information that is gathered.

The selection of a research design should be determined by the problem under investigation and the questions it raises. To date, the limited research on coping in physical activity has been primarily quantitative. One of the concerns arising from these studies is how to adequately assess coping. Typically, questionnaires have been used to identify coping strategies that were employed to manage stressful performance situations (Crocker, 1992; Crocker & Graham, 1995; Haney & Long, 1995). A limitation of studying coping in this fashion is that contextual variables influencing appraisal and the choice of coping strategies can be overlooked. According to Locke (1989), qualitative methods are superior for understanding personal and situational variables whose influences are embedded in a larger context. Given this characteristic, a qualitative design seems well suited to the description and understanding of the complex issues associated with coping in sport.

The purpose of this section is to demonstrate how qualitative research might contribute to a better understanding of the coping process. The findings of Gould, Finch, et al. (1993) will provide a basis for this discussion. These researchers examined relationships between stress sources and coping strategies in U.S. national champion figure skaters. A structured interview guide was developed that contained sections on the sources of stress experienced as a national champion and the coping strategies used to manage the stress. Stress was conceptualized as negative emotions, feelings, and thoughts that the athletes had with respect to their skating experience. Coping was defined as "constantly changing cognitive and behavioral efforts to manage specific demands that are appraised as taxing or exceeding the resources of the person" (Lazarus & Folkman, 1984, p.141).

Gould, Finch, et al. (1993) identified six major stress di-

mensions. Expectations and pressure to perform consisted of others' expectations and the pressure to perform up to national champion standards. Relationship issues reflected relationships with significant others, coaches, and skating partners. Environmental demands on skater resources included media demands and effects, excessive time demands (trying to balance skating and other interests), and lack of finances. Psychological demands on skater resources consisted of self-doubts and competitive stress or anxiety. Physical demands on skater resources were reflected in the higher order themes of physical demands on the body (such as fatigue), maintenance of low body weight, and injury. Finally, life-direction concerns were reported by some athletes.

At this point, the skaters were asked how they coped with each source of stress. When faced with expectations and pressure to perform, strategies such as positive focus, hard training, smart and rational thinking, and self-talk were used. Challenging relationship issues were most often addressed through positive focus and social support. The coping strategies of time management and isolation and deflection were employed to manage environmental demands on skater resources. Psychological demands were generally handled through precompetitive mental preparation and anxiety management as well as positive focus. When skaters faced physical demands, rational thinking and self-talk and precompetitive mental preparation and anxiety management were used most often.

Two important general conclusions emerged from this study. First, athletes clearly implemented different coping strategies in response to the stressors encountered. This finding is consistent with Folkman and Lazarus' (1990) claim that coping effectiveness appears to depend on whether the strategies available to the individual fit the suitable options in that situation. Second, this study failed to support the a priori assignment of particular coping strategies to specific higher order dimensions like problem-focused and emotion-focused coping. Clearly, strategies such as physical relaxation were used to cope with emotional responses. Other strategies, such as time management and training hard and smart, were aimed at changing the stressful situation. The distinction between methods, however, was not always clear. In some cases, a coping strategy (i.e., social support) was used to regulate emotion (be around people who made them feel better) or to manage the environment (seek advice from others). It is important, therefore, that researchers classify coping according to purpose instead of assigning strategies automatically to predetermined problem-focused and emotion-focused categories.

Although qualitative analysis was used by Gould, Finch, et al. (1993) to pair coping strategies with sources of stress, this method can be applied to more complex coping questions. A limitation of this study is that the transactional nature of the coping process is not addressed. The relationship between appraisal and coping has been described as recursive with each affecting the other (Folkman & Lazarus, 1990). Emotion begins with a situation that is appraised in terms of potential harm or benefit. Initial appraisal generates emotions that influence the coping process. Coping, in turn, may modify the troubled relationship between the person and the environment. The altered situation is then reappraised and may lead to a different emotional state. In a process such as this, unidirectional methods may have limited effectiveness. The strength of qualitative designs, on the other hand, is the depiction of detail and the portrayal of process (Patton, 1980). As a result, these methods can help clarify the mutually dependent relationships between appraisal and coping.

Recently, system theories have been developed (Hobfoll, 1989; Lazarus, 1991) to address the coping process. Such theories assume that a majority of variables in the process are interdependent. As a result, research parameters in the coping area have been expanded from small groups of independent variables to larger chains of nested variables. Specifically, coping research requires measurement of personal variables as well as environmental demands, constraints, opportunities, and resources that might be excluded from quantitative studies in the interest of error reduction (Lazarus, 1991). Recent advocation of joint theory use (Brawley, 1993; Crocker & Graham, 1995) is consistent with the position that larger combinations of predictor variables are necessary to understand the coping process. It is expected that variables from related theories will explain more about the phenomena under investigation than will a single conceptual framework. As theory is integrated, a methodology that assesses the growing number of coping variables and interrelationships will become a more important consideration.

Qualitative methods and system theory have much to offer each other. First, theory can be developed inductively or modified using in-depth qualitative designs. Although quantitative studies have linked stress sources with coping strategies (e.g., Crocker, 1992), the reader can only infer from the questionnaire items why specific strategies were selected. In contrast, answers to well conceived interview questions can clarify the personal and situational considerations that influence the choice of coping methods. If the goal of theory development is to understand the complex person X situation interactions associated with coping behavior, qualitative methods can provide the depth of information needed. Second, theory can help frame qualitative inquiry. A good theory of stress and coping should clearly define the critical psychological constructs and their relationship to each other in an integrated structure. As a result, theory can lend initial direction to a qualitative study by providing the basis for comprehensive coping interviews. Although guided by theory, such interviews are also flexible enough to follow the athlete into unexplored areas that can add to the existing model.

In any research endeavor, collecting and analyzing data in a credible way is critical. Although quantitative research seeks to explain coping behavior through objective measurement, qualitative research is more concerned with understanding the process from the athletes' perspective. As such, the methods and interpretations of the investigator are the primary threats to the integrity of qualitative findings. Two of the more important procedures for collecting and interpreting qualitative data (gaining entry and external auditing of results) address this concern. First, gaining entry involves both the access to a sample and the development of trust with those participants. Locke (1989) has suggested that social desirability, the tendency to give outsiders a difficult time, the need to protect sensitive information, and the inclination to be guarded around strangers

may compromise qualitative data. According to Lincoln and Guba (1985), prolonged engagement is an important method of establishing trust and collecting valid information. Ideally, researchers and athletes should be familiar with each other before any data are gathered. Eklund (personal communication, October 23, 1994) has noted that this period of association can be especially beneficial when the interviewer has a working knowledge of the sport setting. A coping study by Gould, Eklund, et al. (1993) in which wrestlers were interviewed by a former elite wrestler is a good example of using affiliation. Despite the advantages of cultivating rapport, however, several qualitative studies have used structured mail or telephone interviews in which little contact was possible beforehand (Gould, Eklund, et al., 1993; Prapavessis & Grove, 1995).

Second, the external auditing of results is used as a control for researcher bias. Qualitative researchers have been urged to actively seek both confirming and disconfirming explanations to a variety of phenomena (Campbell, 1979). This would seem especially important when theory is used to frame qualitative research. To further reduce partiality, however, qualitative results must be reproducible by other competent individuals. According to Lincoln and Guba (1985), auditing is a process that must be carried out by people external to the research team. Indications are that this was not done in the Gould, Finch, et al. (1993) study. Instead, a deductive analysis was conducted by the investigators in which higher order themes were checked against original interview transcripts. Researcher bias is possible when investigators verify their own decisions and may affect the results of qualitative studies.

The Gould, Finch, et al. (1993) study was among the first to use qualitative methods to examine coping in sport. The interviews and inductive analysis produced in-depth information on the relationships between stress appraisals and coping strategies. In addition, the research indicated that single coping options may serve a variety of purposes. Although these results indicate the importance of assessing cognitive appraisal, a limitation of the study was its unidirectional focus. Coping strategies followed sources of stress in the temporal sequence. As a next step, qualitative research must address the transactional process of coping in which appraisal and coping affect each other. Because little is known about the coping process, it is necessary to identify direct and indirect influences and understand the relationships involved. Methodologically sound qualitative methods are well suited to this purpose.

Future research directions

Coping research in the sporting domain is still in its infancy. Given this state, several fundamental conceptual and measurement issues await clarification. Burton and Crocker (1995) identified several future research issues that need to be resolved including determining (a) whether coping strategies change at different points of a competitive transaction, (b) whether athletes cope in a similar or varied ways to different types of stressors or with the same sport stressor (temporal and situation consistency), (c) gender differences, and (d) the development of sport-specific coping instruments. These issues have important implications for the measurement of coping.

The majority of athlete coping studies have examined the

competitive encounter at a single point in time. Gould (1996) advocates a transactional view of stress and coping, and thus, argues that it is critical to assess multiple points during a stress encounter. This is consistent with process models of coping that hold that assessment of coping must be capable of determining situational and temporal changes (Compas & Epping, 1993). Trait models, on the other hand, assume coping is relatively consistent across situations and/or time. A fundamental issue in theory development and the measurement of coping concerns whether athletes cope in a consistent way. Researchers like Madden et al. (1990) and Grove (1995) assume temporal consistency. This is evident in their methodology which requires subjects to report what they usually do when under stress. A weakness of this procedure is that it may produce spurious results because an athlete may aggregate coping responses utilized across many slumps.

Research in the physical domain that has directly examined the question of coping consistency suggests participants do not cope in an invariable manner. Bouffard and Crocker (1992) and Crocker and Isaak (in press) used a similar methodology and data analysis procedure to examine coping consistency. In both studies, coping patterns across three temporal, distinct events were examined by generalizability theory (Morrow, 1989), an extension of intraclass correlational techniques. By examining variance components (person, situation, person X situation), the relative stability of coping could be determined. The interpretation of the interaction component, over and above the main effects of person and situation, is that consistent coping across situations would be reflected by a low interaction component. It is important, however, to examine each study separately because there are methodological and statistical factors that may have biased their findings.

Bouffard and Crocker (1992) found that individuals with physical disabilities did not use a consistent style of coping across three challenging physical activity settings. Using a modification of the COPE scales, participants were assessed three times over a 6-month period. The analysis found that all scales had relatively high interaction components, suggesting a lack of situational consistency in coping. These findings, however, could have been produced by differences in the types of physical activities reported by an individual across the three assessments. These different activities may require different coping strategies for effective resolution. If a single type of sport or physical activity was assessed, then researchers may find that athletes do cope in a consistent fashion. For example, athletes competing in closed sports like swimming, bowling, and archery face similar demands across competition. A relatively constant environment may allow the athlete to apply a consistent pattern of coping strategies to regulate his or her race or training behavior over time. This latter view is consistent with that of Compas and colleagues (1992), who argued that people may have preferred coping patterns for specific classes of situations.

Following this argument, Crocker and Isaak (in press) examined the coping patterns of age-class swimmers in competition and training situations. Their findings revealed the complexity of measuring coping. Using a sport modification of the COPE instrument, they assessed coping during competition races and in the one-week training period following a race.

Coping during a race was assessed immediately following a race in three different swim meets. One week later, coping in training was assessed. Findings from the competition swim races provided evidence against the notion of a coping style in swimming, with the exception that swimmers did consistently use active coping across races. In contrast, the training session findings provided evidence of consistent coping. Coping that would have positive adaptive value in swimming, such as active coping, planning, suppression of competing activities, positive reinterpretation and growth, seeking social support, and increased training effort, all showed evidence of relative stability across the three training sessions. Crocker and Isaak (in press) suggested differences in coping patterns in competition and training may have been due to variations in ego-involvement across swim meets and the differences across training and race contexts.

There are some other methodological and statistical weaknesses that may cloud the coping consistency research of Crocker and his colleagues (1992, in press). First, in both studies, coping scales were examined independently. When examining coping patterns, it would be beneficial to examine the multivariate pattern of coping. Although the degree of a problem-focused strategy like planning may vary across situations, its relative use compared to emotion-focused coping may remain constant. A useful strategy may be to compare the ratio of problem-focused to emotion focused strategies across time and situations (Aldwin, 1994). Second, a statistical dilemma in interpreting the interaction variance component is that it is confounded by measurement error. Lack of reliability in a coping scale will inflate the interaction term. Because both studies by Crocker and his colleagues had relatively small samples, trying to correct for the reliability problem would produce large standard errors of estimates. Given the methodological and statistical challenges, the issue of coping consistency requires future research.

Another important research question concerns gender differences. Gender differences in coping with athletic stress has implications at both the conceptual and measurement level. Studies from community populations indicate that women are more likely to seek social support and to use more emotion-focused coping than are men (Carver et al., 1989: Ptacek, Smith, & Zanas, 1992). Madden, et al. (1989) found evidence that female cross-country runners use more emotional responses in reaction to injury than do their male counterparts. Crocker and Graham (1995) found females reported using higher levels of seeking social support for emotional reasons than did males, although the findings indicated that females reported statistically higher levels of increasing effort to deal with performance-related stress. Gender differences in coping may exist for two reasons. First, men and women may experience types and level of stressors that require different coping strategies for successful resolution (structural hypothesis). A second reason for gender differences has been termed the socialization hypothesis. Sex-role stereotyping and role expectations may lead men and women to use different coping strategies to the same type of stressor. Retrospective methodologies, such as that employed by Crocker and his colleagues (1992, in press), make analysis of gender differences difficult. It is not possible to draw strong conclusions from the data when males and females may be recalling different types of stressors (see Ptacek et al., 1992). Without a common performance stressor, which is often not possible in naturalistic settings, it is difficult to ascertain if gender differences in coping found in any study are due to true gender differences or due to differences in types of reported stressors.

The possibility of gender differences also cast reservations about the measurement properties of coping instruments. Due to structural and socialization differences, items that describe specific coping responses may be irrelevant for particular sport stressors. The intercorrelations among items to capture a definite coping dimension (e.g., wishful thinking) may be different across male and female samples. Combining distinct homogeneous groups using correlational or factor analytic techniques to form scales may produce less than optimal instruments. Clearly, researchers need to provide evidence that the measurement properties of instruments are stable across the genders.

The resolution of critical conceptual issues, such as the situational and temporal stability of coping, cognitive appraisal-coping relations, and gender differences, will all hinge on the development of valid coping scales for sport and physical activity settings. All of the quantitative coping instruments reviewed in this article have fundamental weaknesses when applied in sport settings. With the exception of the ASCI-28, the instruments were not originally developed for sporting populations. The application of sophisticated statistical tools, such as structural equation modelling, cannot overcome measurement weaknesses such as poor reliability and validity (Endler et al., 1993).

The development of an instrument to assess coping should involve a multistep process that includes generating an item pool, determining measurement format, having item pool reviewed by experts, and evaluating items based on administration to a development sample (see DeVellis, 1991). Before any item generation and evaluation can occur, however, the coping constructs must be clearly specified. The resulting scales then need to be evaluated for criterion and construct validity. Scale development needs to be integrated with conceptual and theoretical developments concerning the coping process in sport. This will be a major challenge to coping researchers in the sporting domain.

In conclusion, our knowledge of coping in sport and physical activity is clearly in the genesis stage. There is a need to resolve conceptual and measurement issues before any significant growth can transpire. Sport researchers have used various instruments and methodologies to gain some glimmer of understanding of the complexity of coping processes. All existing coping measures and methodologies suffer from a variety of psychometric weaknesses. A more thorough comprehension will necessitate ingenious thought and painstaking research capitalizing on various methodologies.

References

Aldwin, C.M. (1994). *Stress, coping, and development: An integrative perspective.* New York: Guildford Press.

Baumgartner, T. A. (1989). Norm-referenced measurement: Reliability. In M. J. Safrit & T. M. Wood (Eds.), *Measurement concepts in physical education and exercise science.* (pp. 45-72). Champaign, IL: Human Kinetics.

Billings, A.G., & Moos, R.H. (1984). Coping, stress, and social resources among adults with unipolar depression. *Journal of Personality and Social Psychology, 46,* 877-891.

Bolger, N. & Zuckerman, A. (1995). A framework for studying personality in the stress process. *Journal of Personality and Social Psychology, 69,* 890-902.

Bouffard, M. & Crocker, P.R.E. (1992). Coping by individuals with physical disabilities with perceived challenge in physical activity: Are people consistent? *Research Quarterly for Exercise and Sport, 63,* 410-417.

Brawley, L.R. (1993). Introduction to the special issue: Application of social psychological theories to health and exercise behaviour. *Journal of Applied Sport Psychology, 5,* 95-98.

Burton, D., & Crocker, P.R.E. (1995). *Coping in sport: Research issues and future directions.* Paper presented at the meeting of the Canadian Society for Psychomotor Learning and Sport Psychology, Vancouver, B.C.

Campbell, D.T. (1979). "Degrees of freedom" and the case study. In T.D. Cook & C.S. Reichardt (Eds.), *Qualitative and quantitative methods in evaluation research* (pp. 49-67). Beverly Hills, CA: Sage Publications.

Carpenter, B.N. (1992). *Personal coping: Theory, research, and application.* London: Praeger.

Carver, C.S., Scheier, M.F., & Weintraub, J.K. (1989). Assessing coping strategies: A theoretically based approach. *Journal of Personality and Social Psychology, 56,* 267-283.

Compas, B.E., & Epping, J.E. (1993). Stress and coping in children and families. In C.F. Saylor (Ed.), *Children and disasters* (pp. 11-28). New York: Plenum Press.

Compas, B.E., Malcarne, V.L., & Banez, G.A. (1992). Coping with psychosocial stress: A developmental perspective. In B.N. Carpenter (Ed.), *Personal coping: Theory, research, and application* (pp. 47-63). London: Praeger.

Compas, B.E., & Orosan, P.G. (1993). Cognitive appraisal and coping with stress. In B.C. Long & S.E. Kahn (Eds.), *Women, work, and coping: A multidisciplinary approach to workplace stress* (pp. 219-237). Montreal: McGill-Queens's University Press.

Coppel, D.B. (1980). *The relationship of perceived social support and self-efficacy to major and minor stressors.* Unpublished doctoral dissertation. University of Washington.

Crocker, P.R.E. (1992). Managing stress by competitive athletes: Ways of coping. *International Journal of Sport Psychology, 23,* 161-175.

Crocker, P.R.E., Alderman, R.B., & Smith, F.M.R. (1988). Cognitive affective stress management training with high performance youth volleyball players: Effects on affect, cognition, and performance. *Journal of Sport and Exercise Psychology, 10,* 448-460.

Crocker, P.R.E., & Graham, T.R. (1995). Coping by competitive athletes with performance stress: Gender differences and relationships with affect. *The Sport Psychologist, 9,* 325-338.

Crocker, P.R.E., & Isaak, K. (in press). Coping during competitions and training sessions: Are youth swimmers consistent? *International Journal of Sport Psychology.*

DeVellis, R.F. (1991). *Scale development: Theory and application.* London: Sage Publications.

Endler, N.S., & Parker, J.A. (1989). Multidimensional assessment of coping: A critical evaluation. *Journal of Personality and Social Psychology, 58,* 844-854.

Endler, N.S., Parker, J.A., & Summerfeldt, L.J. (1993). Coping with health problems: Conceptual and methodological issues. *Canadian Journal of Behavioural Sciences, 40,* 384-399.

Folkman, S., & Lazarus, R.S. (1985). If it changes it must be a process: Study of emotion and coping during three stages of a college examination. *Journal of Personality and Social Psychology, 48,* 150-170.

Folkman, S., & Lazarus, R.S. (1988). Coping as a mediator of emotion. *Journal of Personality and Social Psychology, 54,* 466-475.

Folkman, S., & Lazarus, R.S. (1990). Coping and emotion. In N. Stein, B. Leventhal & T. Trabasso (Eds.), *Psychological and biological approaches to emotion* (pp. 313-332). Hillsdale, NJ: Erlbaum.

Folkman, S., Lazarus, R.S., Dunkel-Schetter, C., Delongis, A., & Gruen, R.J. (1986). Dynamics of a stressful encounter: Cognitive appraisal, coping, and encounter outcomes. *Journal of Personality and Social Psychology, 50,* 992-1003.

Freud, S. (1936). *Inhibitions, symptoms and anxiety.* London: Hogarth.

Ghiselli, E. E., Campbell, J. P., & Zedeck, S. (1981). *Measurement theory for the behavioral sciences.* New York: W. H. Freeman and Company.

Gould, D. (1996). Coping with adversity and stress. In L. Hardy, G. Jones, & D. Gould (Eds.), *The psychological preparation of elite sport performers: Theory and practice.* Chichester: Wiley.

Gould, D., Eklund, R.C., & Jackson, S.A. (1993) Coping strategies used by more or less successful U.S. Olympic wrestlers. *Research Quarterly for Exercise and Sport, 64,* 83-93.

Gould, D., Finch, L., & Jackson, S. (1993). Coping strategies utilized by national championship figure skaters. *Research Quarterly for Exercise and Sport, 64,* 453-468.

Grove, R.J. (1995). *Summary data for the athlete coping inventory in a sample of Australian sport performers.* Unpublished manuscript.

Haney, C.J., & Long, B.C. (1995). Coping effectiveness: A path analysis of self-efficacy, control, coping, and performance in sport situations. *Journal of Applied Social Psychology, 25,* 1726-1746.

Hobfoll, S.E. (1989). Conservation of resources: A new attempt at conceptualizing stress. *American Psychologist, 44,* 513-524.

Lazarus, R.S. (1990). Theory-based stress measurement. *Psychological Inquiry, 1,* 3-13.

Lazarus, R.S. (1991). *Emotion and adaptation.* New York: Oxford University Press.

Lazarus, R.S., & Folkman, S. (1984). *Stress, appraisal, and coping.* New York: Springer.

Lincoln, Y. & Guba, E. (1985). *Naturalistic inquiry.* Beverly Hills, CA: Sage.

Locke, L.F. (1989). Qualitative research as a form of scientific inquiry in sport and physical education. *Research Quarterly for Exercise and Sport, 60,* 1-20.

Madden, C.C., Kirkby, R.J., & McDonald, D. (1989). Coping styles of competitive middle distance runners. *International Journal of Sport Psychology, 20,* 287-296.

Madden, C.C., Summers, J.J., & Brown, D.F. (1990). The influence of perceived stress on coping with competitive basketball. *International Journal of Sport Psychology, 21,* 21-35.

Meichenbaum, D. (1985). *Stress inoculation training.* New York: Pergamon Press.

Miller, S.M. (1980). When is a little information a dangerous thing? Coping with stressful life-events by monitoring and blunting. In S. Levine & H. Ursin (Eds.), *Coping and health* (pp. 145-169). New York: Plenum.

Morrow, J. R. (1989). Generalizability theory. In M.J. Safrit & T.M. Woods (Eds.), *Measurement concepts in physical education and exercise science* (pp. 73-96). Champaign, IL: Human Kinetics.

Patton, M.Q. (1980). *Qualitative evaluation methods.* Newbury Park, CA: Sage Publications.

Prapavessis, H., & Grove, R.J. (1995). Ending slumps in baseball: A qualitative investigation. *The Australian Journal of Science and Medicine in Sport, 27,* 14-19.

Ptacek, J.T., Smith, R.E., & Zanas, J. (1992). Gender, appraisal, and coping: A longitudinal analysis. *Journal of Personality, 60,* 747-770.

Rosenbaum, M. (1980). A schedule for assessing self-control behaviours: Preliminary findings. *Behaviour Therapy, 11,* 109-121.

Safrit, M. J. (1989). Criterion-referenced measurement: Validity. In M. J. Safrit & T. M. Wood (Eds.), *Measurement concepts in physical education and exercise science.* (pp. 119-135). Champaign, IL: Human Kinetics.

Scanlan, T.K., Stein, G.L. and Ravizza, K. (1991) An in-depth study of former elite figure skaters: III. Sources of stress. *Journal of Sport and Exercise Psychology, 13,* 103-120.

Smith, C.A. (1993). Evaluation of what's at stake and what I can do? In B.C. Long & S.E. Kahn (Eds.), *Women, work, and coping: A multidisciplinary approach to workplace stress* (pp. 238-265). Montreal: McGill-Queens's University Press.

Smith, R.E. (1986). Towards a cognitive-affective model of athletic burn-out. *Journal of Sport Psychology, 8,* 36-50.

Smith, R.E., & Christensen, D.S. (1995). Psychological skills as predictors of performance and survival in professional baseball. *Journal of Sport and Exercise Psychology, 17,* 399-415.

Smith, R.E., Schutz, R.W., Smoll, F.L. & Ptacek, J.T. (1995). Development and validation of a multidimensional measure of sport-specific psychological skills: The Athletic Coping Skills Inventory-28. *Journal of Sport and Exercise Psychology, 17,* 379-399.

Smith, R.E., Smoll, F.L. & Schutz, R.W. (1988). *The Athletic Coping Skills Inventory: Psychometric properties, correlates and confirmatory factor analysis.* Unpublished manuscript.

Smith, R.E., Smoll, F.L. & Schutz, R.W. (1990). Measurement and correlates of sport-specific cognitive and somatic trait anxiety: The Sport Anxiety Scale. *Anxiety Research, 2,* 263-280.

Smoll, F.L., Smith, R.E., Barnett, N.P., & Everett, J.J. (1993). Enhancement of children's self-esteem through social support training for youth sport coaches. *Journal of Applied Psychology, 78,* 602-610.

Stone, A.A., Greenberg, M.A., Kennedy-Moore, E., & Newman, M.G. (1991). Self-report, situation-specific coping questionnaires: What are they measuring? *Journal of Personality and Social Psychology, 61,* 648-658.

Tobin, D.L., Holroyd, K.A., Reynolds, R.V., & Wigal, J.K. (1989). The hierarchical factor structure of the coping strategies inventory. *Cognitive Therapy and Research, 13,* 343-361.

Vitalino, P.P., Russo, J., Carr, J.E., Maiuro, R.D., & Becker, J. (1985). The Ways of Coping Checklist: Revision and psychometric properties. *Multivariate Behavioral Research, 20,* 3-26.

Wood, T. M. (1989). The changing nature of norm-referenced validity. In M. J. Safrit & T. M. Wood (Eds.), *Measurement concepts in physical education and exercise science.* (pp. 23-44). Champaign, IL: Human Kinetics.

Acknowledgements

We would like to thank Dr. Ronald Smith, Dr. Dan Gould, Dr. Colleen Haney, and Dr. Robert Grove for providing recent research that was not yet published at the initial stages of writing this chapter. We would also like to thank Drs. Smith and Grove, along with an anonymous reviewer and Dr. Duda, for providing feedback on an earlier draft of this chapter.

This chapter was supported by a grant from the University of Saskatchewan President's SSHRC fund.

Part III

Imagery, Attention, and Psychological Skills

PART III

A perusal of the sport psychology literature indicates that imagery is used often by high-level and successful athletes (Hall, Rodgers, & Barr, 1990) and is a component of many mental skills training programs (e.g., Kendall, Hrycaiko, Martin, & Kendall, 1990). In Part III, efforts to assess the frequency and quality of imagery rehearsal and individual differences in the ability to image are examined.

Concentration training is another consistent and important component of most sport psychology intervention programs. Variations in attention have been implicated as a contributor to sport performance variability as well as a potential mechanism by which we may have anxiety reduction via exercise. To date in sport psychology research and practice, Nideffer's Test of Attentional and Interpersonal Style (1976, 1990) and sport-specific modifications have dominated. These self-report assessments of individual differences in attentional abilities are critiqued in the following pages, and alternative methods of assessing attention in sport settings are proposed.

With respect to mental skills training in general, Vealey (1988) has pointed out conceptual and practical distinctions between psychological skills and methods. It appears that subsequent work on the assessment of psychological skills needs to further clarify the differences between this construct and measures of coping skills. Such issues and the status of current psychological skills inventories are also addressed in this third section.

References

Hall, C.R., Rodgers, W.M., & Barr, K.A. (1990). The use of imagery by athletes in selected sports. *The Sport Psychologist*, *4*, 1-10.

Kendall, G., Hrycaiko, D., Martin, G.L., & Kendall, T. (1990). The effects of imagery rehearsal, relaxation, and self-talk package on basketball game performance. *Journal of Sport and Exercise Psychology*, *12*, 157-166.

Nideffer, R.M. (1976). The Test of Attentional and Interpersonal Style. *Journal of Personality and Social Psychology*, *34*, 394-404.

Nideffer, R.M. (1990). Use of the Test of Attentional and Interpersonal Style (TAIS) in sport. *The Sport Psychologist*, *4*, 285-300.

Vealey, R.S. (1988). Future directions in psychological skills training. *The Sport Psychologist*, *2*, 318-336.

Chapter 9

MEASURING IMAGERY ABILITIES AND IMAGERY USE

Craig R. Hall
University of Western Ontario

Athletes, coaches, and sport psychologists all realize mental imagery is a valuable technique for improving performance and competing more effectively. Denis (1985) defined imagery as a psychological activity that evokes the physical characteristics of an object, person, or place that is either permanently or temporarily absent from our perception. Images are not exclusively passive reproductions but can be active and dynamic (Paivio, 1986). Athletes report using imagery in their daily training; however, they use it most in conjunction with competition (Hall, Rodgers, & Barr, 1990). Coaches often encourage their athletes to use imagery to help them learn new skills and to improve skills they already possess (Hall & Rodgers, 1989). Furthermore, imagery is often a key component in the mental training programs developed and implemented by sport psychologists (Daw & Burton, 1994; Fenker & Lambiotte, 1987; Hughes, 1990). Given the recognized value and widespread use of imagery, it is not surprising that researchers have been interested in investigating why imagery works and how to use it effectively.

Imagery can be empirically examined using one or more of three general classes of operational procedures [as in imagery research on memory and other cognitive phenomena], namely, (a) using experimental procedures, such as instructions to image in particular ways; (b) manipulating such relevant item attributes as the image-evoking value of movements or other materials to which subjects attend; and (c) assessing individual differences in imagery abilities or modes of thought (see Paivio, 1971). Although imagery research specific to motor skill acquisition and performance has taken all three forms, the present chapter focuses on individual differences as measured by questionnaires. The measurement of movement imagery abilities will be addressed, followed by a discussion of various methods of measuring the use of imagery by athletes and exercisers.

The Measurement of Imagery Abilities

There has been interest in identifying and measuring the abilities or traits that underlie motor task performance. For ex-

ample, Fleishman (Fleishman, 1972; Fleishman & Quaintance, 1984) has proposed 11 identifiable and measurable perceptual-motor abilities (e.g., multilimb coordination, reaction time) and 9 physical proficiency abilities (e.g., static strength, dynamic flexibility). Several researchers (Hall, Pongrac, & Buckolz, 1985; Isaac, Marks, & Russell, 1986) have proposed that another group of abilities that are important to consider are movement imagery abilities. One reason for this proposal is that virtually everyone seems to have the ability to generate and use images, but not to the same degree. Another reason is the reported widespread use of imagery in sport and physical activity (Hall et al., 1990; Hausenblas & Hall, 1996).

Paivio (1986) argues that individual differences in imagery are a product of experience interacting with genetic variability. The main interest of researchers has been to try to determine whether it is possible to predict motor task performance and learning from variations in imagery ability. It seems reasonable to assume that if individuals are instructed to use imagery to help perform or learn a task and they are low in imagery ability (i.e., poor imagers), it is likely that imagery will have little or no effect. High imagers, by contrast, should be able to use imagery very effectively. Thus, the primary question being asked by imagery researchers is, do high imagers have an advantage in the performance and learning of motor skills?

To investigate individual differences in imagery, an appropriate test instrument is required. The two types of tests that have been employed in cognitive psychology can be classified as being a) subjective, self-report or b) objective, behavioral in nature (Katz, 1983). One example of the former is the Vividness of Visual Imagery Questionnaire (VVIQ) developed by Marks (1973), which requires people to rate the vividness of their imagery according to four aspects of four familiar scenes. Other subjective tests ask people to report on certain aspects of their images, such as manipulability (e.g., Gordon, 1949), or tap imaginal habits and preferences (e.g., Paivio & Harshman, 1983).

In objective tests, people are presented stimulus objects and are asked to mentally perform some spatial manipulations of these objects. They are then asked to choose, from a set of alternatives, the object that would be in the correct orientation following manipulation. Imagery is assumed to be an important component in the solution of these tests (Barratt, 1953), which include the Minnesota Paper Form Board (Likert & Quasha, 1941) and the Space Relations Test (Bennett, Seashore, & Wesman, 1947).

Do subjective and objective tests measure the same abilities? The answer appears to be no. Subjective and objective measures tend to be uncorrelated or show only a weak positive correlation (see Ernest, 1977, for a review). The question then is, which type of test should be used? Katz (1983) argues in favor of subjective tests because he believes they are more directly linked to the construct of imagery than are the objective ones. Certainly within the motor domain, subjective tests appear to be favored, the two most popular ones being the Vividness of Movement Imagery Questionnaire (VMIQ; Isaac et al., 1986) and the Movement Imagery Questionnaire (MIQ; Hall & Pongrac, 1983).

The Vividness of Movement Imagery Questionnaire

The VMIQ consists of 24 items, each item being a different movement or action to be imagined (e.g., kicking a stone, riding a bike). Subjects rate the vividness of these actions in two ways: when "watching somebody else" and when "doing it yourself." The ratings are done using a 5-point scale where 1 = *perfectly clear and as vivid as normal vision*, and 5 = *no image at all, you only "know" that you are thinking of the movement*. Atienza, Balaguer, and Garcia-Merita (1994) reported that the VMIQ is a reliable instrument with acceptable temporal stability (e.g., a test-retest correlation of .76 over a 3-week period) and convergent validity (e.g., a correlation of .81 has been found between the scores of the VMIQ and the VVIQ). An analysis of the factor structure of the VMIQ (Campos & Perez, 1990) produced one underlying factor that was defined as vividness of visual images.

A study by Isaac (1992) suggests the VMIQ is a useful measure of imagery ability. Novice and skilled trampolinists were divided into two groups, an imagery practice group and a control (no imagery) group. Both groups attempted to learn or improve three trampoline skills over each of three 6-week training periods. These subjects were also assigned to either a high or low imagery-ability group depending on their VMIQ scores. Subjects in the imagery practice group, regardless of skill level, showed significantly more improvement over the training periods than did subjects in the control group. With respect to imagery ability, high imagers improved significantly more than low imagers. Isaac concluded that high imagery ability combined with mental imagery practice is a significant factor in the improvement of motor skills.

The Movement Imagery Questionnaire

The MIQ was constructed by Hall and Pongrac (1983) to assess both visual and kinesthetic imagery. It consists of 18 items, 9 visual and 9 kinesthetic. Each item involves an arm, leg, or whole body movement. Completing each item entails four steps. First, the starting position for a movement is described, and the subject is required to assume this position. Second, the movement is described, and the subject is asked to perform it. Third, the subject is asked to reassume the starting position and then to imagine making the movement (no actual movement is made). Finally, the subject is required to rate the ease/difficulty with which he or she imagined the movement on a 7-point scale, where 1 = *very easy to picture/feel* and 7 = *very difficult to picture/feel*. This procedure was developed to ensure that all subjects completing the questionnaire would be imagining and rating exactly the same movement.

The reliability of the MIQ is acceptable. Hall et al. (1985) reported a test-retest coefficient of .83 for a 1-week interval. In addition, they found internal consistency coefficients of .87 for the visual subscale and .91 for the kinesthetic subscale. Atienza et al. (1994) have found similar internal consistencies for the MIQ (visual subscale = .89; kinesthetic subscale = .88). These same authors also provided support for the bifactorial structure of the MIQ, finding all of the visual items loading on one factor and all of the kinesthetic items loading on a second factor.

Several studies indicate that the MIQ, like the VMIQ, is a useful measure of imagery ability. Goss, Hall, Buckolz, and Fishburne (1986) employed the MIQ to compare three different imagery ability groups on their learning, retention, and reacquisition of movements. The groups were classified based on their MIQ scores as low visual/low kinesthetic (LL), high visual/low kinesthetic (HL), and high visual/high kinesthetic (HH). They were then required to learn simple movements to a set criterion performance level. Their retention and reacquisition of these movements were tested one week later. The results indicated that imagery ability is related to acquiring motor skills. The LL group required the most trials to acquire the movements, the HL group required an intermediate number of trials, and the HH group learned the movements in the least number of trials. A similar trend was found for the reacquisition of these movements, but only weak support was found for a relationship between imagery ability and retention.

In a later study, Hall, Buckolz, and Fishburne (1989) also classified subjects as high and low imagers based on their MIQ scores. These subjects were then examined on their ability to remember simple movements using standard recall and recognition tests. There were no performance differences between the two groups of imagers on either type of test. However, when the physical accuracy with which the movements were reproduced was assessed, high imagers were more accurate than low imagers. The authors concluded that individual differences in imagery ability can influence some aspects of motor task performance (e.g., movement accuracy).

The MIQ, like any test instrument, has certain weaknesses. One weakness is that some subjects refuse to physically perform all of the items on the questionnaire. This is because these items (e.g., a front roll, a 360-degree turn) are perceived as being too difficult. Another weakness is that the MIQ takes more time to complete (normally more than 20 minutes) than do many other sport psychology questionnaires because each movement (item) on the MIQ is physically performed before it is imagined and rated. These weaknesses prompted Hall and Martin (1997) to revise the original questionnaire. The length was reduced by removing the items that subjects often failed to answer and by eliminating items that provided redundant information (e.g., if two items on the MIQ involved strictly arm movements, one was deleted). In addition, the rating scale was reversed (i.e., 1 = *very hard to see/feel* and 7 = *very easy to see/feel*) so the resulting MIQ scores would be easier to interpret, and some of the items were re-worded to enhance clarity.

The revised MIQ (MIQ-R) comprises eight items, four visual and four kinesthetic. The same four steps required to answer each item on the MIQ are required to complete each item on the MIQ-R. Hall and Martin (1997) conclude the MIQ-R is an acceptable revision of the MIQ because the corresponding subscales on the two questionnaires are highly correlated ($r = .77$, $p < .001$ for both visual and kinesthetic subscales). It should be noted, however, that the psychometric properties of the MIQ-R have yet to be determined.

Comparing the VMIQ and the MIQ

Do the VMIQ and the MIQ measure the same thing? The answer appears to be no. Hall and Martin (1997) found a correlation of .65 between the visual MIQ subscale and the VMIQ, and a correlation of .49 between the kinesthetic MIQ subscale and the VMIQ. These results are to be expected given that the VMIQ measures a very specific dimension of imagery ability, vividness, whereas the MIQ requires a more general rating (i.e., ease/difficulty of imagining a movement). Therefore, in addition to vividness, the MIQ ratings are likely reflecting other dimensions of imagery such as accuracy, manipulability, and even unvividness (i.e., images that become vague and dim in certain situations) (see Ahsen, 1990, for a detailed discussion of unvividness). Furthermore, the MIQ measures both visual and kinesthetic imagery whereas the VMIQ measures only vividness of visual imagery (Atienza et al., 1994).

Given that the VMIQ, MIQ, and MIQ-R can all be employed to measure movement imagery abilities, Hall and Martin (1997) have suggested in what situations each instrument might be most useful. When working with individuals or small groups, the MIQ-R is probably the instrument of choice because it is easily administered and measures both visual and kinesthetic imagery. With large groups, especially when space is limited, the VMIQ could be used because no actual physical movements are required (i.e., it is a "pencil and paper test"). The MIQ-R and MIQ, by contrast, require the actual production of movements in order for each questionnaire item to be completed, and this requires a certain amount of space. The MIQ should probably be employed if (a) young, fit individuals are being assessed because they are more likely to complete all the items, and (b) the time necessary to answer the questionnaire is not limited. Of course, the VMIQ can be used in combination with the MIQ or MIQ-R to provide a more complete assessment of imagery abilities. This is important to consider because any single questionnaire score of imagery is obviously an oversimplification of a highly complex set of underlying processes (Ahsen, 1990).

It must be stressed that all three imagery questionnaires were designed primarily for research purposes and not for sport, clinical, or therapeutic application. Janssen and Sheikh (1994) believe, however, that the assessment of an athlete's imagery ability is a key component of developing and implementing an effective imagery training program. If the VMIQ, MIQ, or MIQ-R is to be used for such a purpose, it should be used with caution. These questionnaires provide a very general measure of how good an individual is at imaging specific movements, but they give no indication of how good an individual might be at using imagery for other purposes that are equally, or even more, important in physical activity and sport. How people use imagery in sport is addressed in detail in the next section.

Measuring the Use of Imagery by Athletes

One of the first systematic studies on imagery use was undertaken by Betts (1909). He investigated the spontaneous use of imagery in a variety of tasks such as simple association, logical thinking, mental multiplications, and discrimination judgments. He concluded that although imagery is often employed in doing these tasks, it is more helpful in certain tasks than others and is probably not employed as much as might be expected. Although Betts did not investigate the use of imagery in performing motor tasks, there is considerable evidence stemming from athlete interviews and anecdotal reports that elite athletes make extensive use of imagery. For example, Orlick and Partington (1986) interviewed 165 Canadian Olympians following the 1984 games. The athletes' reports were so detailed and convincing that Orlick and Partington concluded that "the extent to which the athletes could control their mental imagery and feel performance images from the inside, as if doing it, was directly related to performance outcomes at the Olympic Games" (p. 5). Both Suinn (1983) and Paivio (1985) have noted that top athletes like Chris Evert Lloyd, Jean Claude Killy, and Jack Nicklaus allude to using imagery for both strategy and skill rehearsal.

More recently, imagery use by athletes has been examined through the administration of questionnaires. These instruments take two forms. They can be general in nature with imagery as one of a number of psychological skills assessed, or they can be specifically designed to measure just imagery use.

The Psychological Skills Inventory for Sports

Probably the best known and most widely used of the general instruments is the Psychological Skills Inventory for Sports (PSIS; Mahoney, Gabriel, & Perkins, 1987). The original PSIS consisted of 51 items. Each item was responded to as "true" or "false," and the instrument was intended to measure five broad psychological areas: anxiety, concentration, self-confidence, team emphasis, and mental preparation. Five of the mental preparation items dealt specifically with mental imagery. One of the primary objectives of the Mahoney et al. (1987) study was the identification of skills that differentiate elite and nonelite athletes. With respect to mental preparation, it was found that elite athletes rely more on internally referenced and kinesthetic preparation than do their nonelite peers. This supported previous research (Mahoney & Avener, 1977; Rotella, Gansneder, Ojala, & Billing, 1980) that has shown that more elite athletes seem to favor an internal imagery perspective (i.e., athletes see themselves performing as if they were physically doing the skill) whereas less exceptional athletes tend to use an external imagery perspective (i.e., athletes take a third-person perspective and view themselves as though they were watching a film).

The PSIS was modified to have athletes respond on a 5-point Likert-type scale (0 = *strongly disagree* to 4 = *strongly agree*) and to contain 45 items designed to measure six psychological areas: anxiety control, concentration, confidence, motivation, team focus, and mental preparation. The revised instrument, the PSIS R-5, has been employed in a number of studies (e.g., Mahoney, 1989; White, 1993); however, the value of this instrument for research or applied purposes has been questioned. Originally, internal consistency and split-half reliability estimates were reported only for the total scale and were quite low (i.e., split-half = .567 and coefficient alpha = .636; Mahoney, 1989). The validity of the PSIS R-5 was also suspect because nonelite athletes sometimes scored higher on the scales than did elite athletes (Mahoney, 1989), yet the instrument was designed to measure psychological skills relevant to superior athletic performance. Due to these findings, Chartrand, Jowdy, and Danish (1992) decided to examine the psychometric characteristics of the PSIS R-5 by administering it to 340 intercollegiate athletes participating in a variety of sports. Internal consistency estimates were computed for each of the scales; interscale correlations were calculated to investigate the relationships between the scales; and construct validity was examined by conducting a confirmatory factor analysis.

The findings of Chartrand et al. (1992) verified concerns about the PSIS R-5 were justified. First, the internal consistency estimates (coefficient alpha) for each scale were quite low, and more important to the present discussion, the Mental Preparation scale had a value of only -.34. This is well below the acceptable level for applied instruments (Nunnally, 1978). Some items in the Mental Preparation scale were negatively correlated with each other, leading Chartrand et al. (1992) to conclude that this scale is conceptually ambiguous. Second, the confirmatory factor analysis indicated that the predicted six-factor model did not fit the data. Even when model modifications were examined, there failed to be an adequate fit. Based on these results, Chartrand et al. (1992) recommended that more psychometric research should be conducted on the PSIS R-5 before it was used for research or applied purposes.

The Imagery Use Questionnaire

Hall et al. (1990) developed an instrument specifically to investigate the use of imagery by athletes in numerous sports and at all skill levels. These researchers were interested in determining when, where, and how athletes incorporate imagery into their training and competitions. The Imagery Use Questionnaire (IUQ) was administered to 381 male and female athletes competing in football, ice hockey, soccer, squash, gymnastics, and figure skating. The IUQ consists of 37 items, and athletes respond on a 7-point Likert scale for all but two items, which require yes/no responses. The anchor points on the rating scales take two forms, either 1 = *never* and 7 = *always* or 1 = *very difficult* and 7 = *very easy*. No psychometric evaluation of the IUQ has been undertaken.

Hall et al. (1990) found that athletes use imagery more in conjunction with competition than with training. In fact, athletes reported using imagery most just prior to competing. Several other general trends were noted. Athletes often see themselves winning and receiving an award for their accomplishments. Athletes indicate that when they engage in imagery, their imagery sessions are not very structured (i.e., they do not plan in advance what they are going to imagine and for how long) and not very regular (i.e., at a specific time each

day). In addition, athletes seem to use an internal visual perspective and an external visual perspective with about equal frequency. Hall et al. (1990) also found that imagery use varies across sports and that competitive level (i.e., house league, local, provincial, and national/international) influences imagery use. The higher the competitive level, the more often the athletes report using imagery in practice, in competition, and before an event.

Two sport-specific versions of the IUQ have been developed, the IUQ for Rowing (Barr & Hall, 1992) and the IUQ for Figure Skating (Rodgers, Hall, & Buckolz, 1991). These instruments were developed with the help of athletes and coaches in the two respective sports to ensure the questionnaire items were pertinent and in no way ambiguous. Both instruments seem to elicit reliable (i.e., test-retest) self-evaluations on imagery use (r values have ranged from .65 to .95), but other psychometric information on these instruments is not available.

There were three main purposes for developing and administering the IUQ for Rowing. One purpose was to confirm some of the general trends on imagery use reported by Hall et al. (1990) through examining a large number of athletes in a single sport. Another purpose was to determine if imagery use varied with age or gender. The third purpose was to investigate differences in imagery use between elite and nonelite rowers. The instrument was completed by 211 male and 137 female rowers ranging in age from 15 to 54 years and ranging in skill level from novice (i.e., just started rowing) to expert (i.e., finished top three in the world).

Most of the general trends in imagery use observed by Hall et al. (1990) were evident in the rowers' use of imagery. The rowers used imagery most just before a race, often imagined themselves winning and receiving a gold medal, and did not have very structured or regular imagery sessions. One difference was that the rowers used an internal visual perspective more than an external one, and this may be due to the nature of the sport. Rowing takes place in a relatively stable environment, and rowers do not even face in the direction in which they are going. Thus, it seems most appropriate to imagine rowing as if doing it through your own eyes. Rowers also indicated a greater use of kinesthetic imagery than visual imagery, and again this likely is due to rowing being a closed skill.

The age of the rowers generally did not affect how imagery was used. Furthermore, males and females responded similarly. It was possible, however, to differentiate elite and nonelite rowers by their use of imagery. Elite rowers had significantly more structure and regularity to their imagery sessions than did nonelites. Elite rowers more often imagined themselves executing a prerace routine and reported using more kinesthetic imagery. As would be expected, nonelite rowers were more likely to imagine themselves rowing incorrectly.

The main reason for developing the IUQ for Figure Skating was to investigate how skaters changed their use of imagery when participating in an imagery-training program. Fourteen skaters were administered the instrument prior to and following a 16-week imagery-training program. For 12 of the weeks, each skater attended two 15-minute individual sessions per week. Each skater was also encouraged to do imagery practice (e.g., imagine doing jumps, spins and programs) daily on his or her own for the entire length of the training program. During this 16-week period the skaters were physically practicing about 2 hours per day. The significant changes in imagery use following the training were related to the nature of the training given the skaters. The skaters increased their use of kinesthetic imagery and felt they could control their images better. They were more likely to imagine themselves being successful (e.g., winning). They increased their use of imagery before and after physical practices and had more structure in their daily imagery sessions (i.e., they planned what they were going to imagine ahead of time).

The Imagery Use Questionnaire for Soccer Players

Paivio (1985) suggested that imagery plays both cognitive and motivational roles in mediating behavior, each capable of being targeted toward either general or specific behavioral goals. The relations can be represented as a 2 X 2 model with the cognitive-motivational contrast as one dimension and the general-specific contrast as the other (Figure 1). The functional distinctions are reflected in differences in imagery content. On the cognitive side, imagery involves the rehearsal of general strategies of play or specific skills. On the motivational side, imagery can represent emotion-arousing situations as well as specific goals and goal-oriented behaviors.

The four classes of imagery can be summarized and illustrated as follows. *Cognitive general* (CG) refers especially to imagery related to strategies for a competitive event. Sporting legends like Chris Evert Lloyd report imagery rehearsal of strategies geared to the style of a particular tennis opponent. *Cognitive specific* (CS) refers to imagery directed at improving skills. This has commonly been researched under the heading of mental practice (see Hall, Buckolz, & Fishburne, 1992). *Motivational general* (MG) refers to images related to general physiological and emotional arousal (e.g., "parking" the excitement or psyching up) and to images of mastery of a given situation (e.g., being focused and in control at a competition). Finally, *motivational specific* (MS) refers to goal-oriented imagery, such as imagining oneself winning an event or standing on a podium receiving a medal.

Sport imagery research has focused primarily on the cognitive function of imagery. The IUQ addressed the motivational function of imagery to a limited extent (e.g., athletes reported how often they imagined themselves winning), but it is only recently that this dimension of imagery has received any detailed examination. Salmon, Hall, and Haslam (1994) employed the Imagery Use Questionnaire for Soccer Players (IUQ-SP) in an attempt to investigate both functions of imagery in the sport of soccer. This instrument has four sections. The first section contains demographic questions (e.g., age, experience), and the second section considers the general use of imagery similar to what is examined, at least in part, by the IUQ (e.g., use of imagery in practice versus competition, use of different imagery perspectives, and coaches encouragement of the use of imagery). The third section deals specifically with the four cells of Paivio's model (i.e., CG, CS, MG, and MS). The final section contains questions concerning auditory imagery (i.e., "When you are imagining, to what extent do you hear the opposition players"). This section was included because verbal communication among players during practices and competitions is important in soccer.

Goal-oriented Responses (MS)	Skill Rehearsal (CS)
Arousal (MG-A) & Mastery (MG-M)	Strategy Rehearsal (CG)

Figure 1. The functions of imagery in sport.

cation among players during practices and competitions is important in soccer.

The psychometric qualities of the IUQ-SP indicate that it can be employed with some confidence for research and applied purposes. Salmon et al. (1994) reported test-retest r values for the items ranging from .55 to .92, and internal consistency coefficients (alpha) of CG = .75, CS = .85, MS = .82, and MG = .76. Using a corrected item-total correlation (CIT) minimum of .40, they found only 2 of 34 coefficients failed this standard. When a more lenient minimum CIT of .20 was used, as recommended by Kline (1980), all items met the standard. A principle-components factor analysis assuming a four-factor solution was conducted. An orthogonal (varimax) rotation was employed to simplify the interpretation of each factor. It was found that the items in the questionnaire were quite well-defined by the four-factor solution. With a cut-off of .40 for inclusion of an item in the interpretation of a factor, the MG and MS cells of the model were captured by Factors 1 and 2, respectively. The distinction between the CG and CS cells was less well-defined. Some items loaded on both CG (Factor 3) and CS (Factor 4).

Salmon et al. (1994) administered the IUQ-SP to 90 national level players, 112 provincial level players, and 161 regional level (nonelite) players. There were 201 males and 160 females, and the players ranged in age from 15 to 30 years. The general trends of how athletes use imagery (e.g., more in conjunction with competition than training) were again confirmed in this study. As reported by Barr and Hall (1992), there were only minor differences found between how males and females use imagery. Another finding consistent with previous IUQ studies (Barr & Hall, 1992; Hall et al., 1990) was that elite and nonelite players could be distinguished by how they used imagery. The most important finding from this research was that the players used imagery more for motivational purposes than cognitive ones. Regardless of skill level, players responded with the highest ratings for the MG cell.

The Sport Imagery Questionnaire

The IUQ-SP has one major limitation. It is soccer specific and can not be readily adapted for use in other sports. To overcome this problem, Hall, Mack, Paivio, and Hausenblas (in press) have recently developed a new instrument to examine the cognitive and motivational functions of imagery. The Sport Imagery Questionnaire (SIQ) was developed under the assumption that the four imagery categories proposed by Paivio (1985) are orthogonal. That is, all possible combinations would emerge when individual differences are measured. For example, an athlete might report frequent use of general motivational imagery (MG) as well as specific goal-oriented imagery (MS), infrequent use of both, or frequent use of one and not the other, along with any frequency of CS and CG imagery. Over subjects, the four functional categories would emerge as independent factors.

The SIQ was developed over a series of three studies. The purpose of the first study was to assess the motivational and cognitive functions of imagery through the development of the questionnaire. To achieve this purpose, the SIQ was administered to 113 athletes competing in 10 different sports and the psychometric properties of the items developed for the SIQ were examined through the use of various analytic procedures (i.e., individual-item and internal consistency measures, and factor analysis). The purpose of the second study was to obtain an independent evaluation of the SIQ using a sorting task. The participants were 161 kinesiology students, and their task was to group the SIQ items into similar categories. The result of these two studies was the finalization of a 30-item instrument with 6 items representing each of 5 subscales, namely, CS, CG, MS, and two forms of MG, which were labelled MG-Arousal (MG-A) and MG-Mastery (MG-M). The MG-A items examine athletes' imagery of the excitement and anxiety associated with competition whereas the MG-M items tap athletes' imagery of being in control and coping with difficult situations. The internal consistency estimates for each subscale are acceptable (above alpha coefficient of .70), and all items load on their appropriate factor above the criterion level (.40).

In the third study the SIQ was administered to 271 athletes in track and field and 91 ice hockey players. The track and field athletes competed at either the high school ($n = 94$), varsity ($n = 27$), or national ($n = 59$) level; whereas 53% of the hockey players were varsity athletes, and the remainder played in regional competitive leagues. The factor structure of the SIQ was confirmed, and it was shown that imagery use by athletes can predict their performance success in certain situations. The motivational functions of imagery (i.e., goal-oriented imagery and arousal control) predicted performance for elite athletes (i.e., national level), and the cognitive functions of imagery predicted performance for athletes at lower competitive levels (e.g., high school). Based on the findings of these three studies, Hall et al. (1996) concluded that the SIQ is a useful instrument for further systematic investigations of how athletes use imagery.

Some evidence indicating that the SIQ may indeed prove to be a valuable instrument comes from a recent study by Moritz, Hall, Martin, and Vadocz (1996). They attempted to identify the specific image content of confident athletes by administering the SIQ and the State Sport Confidence Inventory (SSCI; Vealey, 1986) to 57 elite competitive roller skaters. High sport-confident athletes were found to use more MG-M imagery than did low sport-confident athletes. A hierarchical multiple regression analysis was conducted to determine if SIQ variables (MG-M, MG-A, and CS) and MIQ-R visual and kinesthetic scores could predict a significant proportion of the variance in SSCI scores. This proved to be the case, with the five variables predicting 37% of the variance in SSCI scores. An examination of the unique contribution of the variables to the total variance accounted for by the model indicated that the SIQ subscales accounted for the majority of the explained vari-

ance (27%), with MG-M accounting for 20%. Moritz et al. (1996) suggested, based on these findings, that if athletes want to develop, maintain, or regain sport confidence via mental imagery, they would be advised to use MG-M imagery rather than other forms of imagery (e.g., CS imagery).

The Exercise Imagery Questionnaire

The use of imagery by athletes has been a subject of interest to researchers for some years and is becoming relatively well documented (e.g., Hall et al., 1990; Salmon et al., 1994). Sport, however, is only one form of physical activity, and recently Hausenblas and Hall (1996) asked the question, "do exercisers use imagery?" They conducted three studies and in the first one had 144 aerobic participants respond to open-ended questions regarding their imagery use. It was found that 75.7% of the participants reported imagining themselves exercising for a variety of purposes including losing weight, getting and keeping fit, reducing stress, learning exercise patterns and steps, and motivating and energizing themselves.

The purpose of Studies 2 and 3 was to develop a questionnaire designed to measure imagery use by exercisers. Based on the open-ended results from Study 1, the Exercise Imagery Questionnaire (EIQ) was developed. The initial version of the EIQ contained 23 items presented on a 9-point scale anchored at the extremes by 1 = *never* and 9 = *always*. This version was administered to 307 aerobic exercisers in Study 2, and a principal component factor analysis with varimax rotation was conducted on the resulting data. From this analysis, a three-factor structure emerged accounting for 63.8% of the variance. The first factor incorporated five items reflecting mood enhancement (e.g., when I imagine exercising it relieves my stress), the second factor comprised five items related to health and physical appearance (e.g., I imagine losing weight by exercising), and the third factor consisted of four items representing cognitive functions (e.g., I imagine doing the pattern/steps).

In Study 3, the 14-item version of EIQ was administered to 171 aerobic participants. The results of a principal component factor analysis with varimax rotation confirmed the three-factor solution found in Study 2. All items loaded at .50 or above, except for one item from Factor 3, which was subsequently discarded. The Health and Physical Appearance scale accounted for 44.6% of the variance; the Mood Enhancement scale accounted for 13.3% of the variance; and the Cognitive Function scale accounted for 9.7% of the variance. Internal consistencies were determined by calculating alpha and all three scales were highly reliable (Health and Physical Appearance = .84, Mood Enhancement = .85, Cognitive Functions = .84).

To examine the construct validity of the EIQ, differences in frequency of exercise and imagery use were investigated in Study 3. Researchers have found that elite athletes use imagery more than do nonelites (e.g., Hall et al., 1990), so it was hypothesized that more avid exercisers would use imagery more than less avid exercisers. The participants were subdivided into two extreme groups on the basis of the number of hours they exercised per week (3 hours or less, $n = 38$; 8 hours or more, $n = 35$). A MANOVA was performed in which hours exercised served as the independent variable and the EIQ scale scores served as dependent variables. There was a significant multivariate main effect for frequency of exercise, and univariate ANOVAs revealed high-frequency exercisers used all three types of imagery (i.e., health and physical appearance, mood enhancement, and cognitive functions) more than did low-frequency exercisers. The authors concluded that exercisers use imagery, the EIQ possesses favorable psychometric properties, and the EIQ may be useful in examining if imagery use by exercisers is related to such variables as adherence and addiction.

Some Final Thoughts

Imagery has been and will continue to be one of the primary psychological techniques used to enhance motor performance. There are various factors that can influence how effective imagery will be, two of the most important being imagery ability and imagery instructions (Hall, Schmidt, Durand, & Buckolz, 1994). The latter, of course, will be partly determined by the type of imagery (i.e., cognitive or motivational) to be used by the participants. Consequently, there is a need to be able to measure both imagery ability and imagery use, and researchers have developed various appropriate tests (Table 1).

An interest in measuring imagery abilities has existed for many years (e.g., Betts, 1909), and more recently there have been attempts to measure visual and kinesthetic movement imagery abilities. The instruments commonly employed, the MIQ and VMIQ, have proven to be useful both for examining

whether high imagers have an advantage in the acquisition of motor skills and for controlling the potential effects of individual differences in imagery research. These instruments are general in nature (i.e., they pertain to a variety of movements), and in many research and applied situations, it would be preferable to have more specific instruments. These instruments could assess categories of actions like throws or jumps, or they could be sport specific. No such instruments seem to be currently available, and their development would be worthwhile.

Athletes use imagery for more than just rehearsing movements or skills. They use imagery to motivate themselves and to rehearse strategies. Unfortunately, the MIQ and VMIQ measure imagery abilities only for movements and do not take into account these other possible uses. Just because athletes might be able to easily and vividly imagine themselves performing a skill (e.g., throwing a ball), does not mean they can just as easily and vividly imagine themselves receiving a medal or being in control in a difficult situation. If we are going to fully measure the imagery abilities of athletes, then we need to develop additional instruments that consider athletes' abilities to imagine these other situations.

The use of imagery by athletes can be effectively measured by the IUQ and the SIQ. These instruments, however, can be further refined. For example, there are some aspects of motivational imagery that the SIQ does not address, such as the possible use of imagery for distraction control at a competition. With respect to possible directions for research on imagery use, we need to better understand how imagery use varies with the type of sport (e.g., individual vs. team) and the time of year (e.g., preseason vs. regular season vs. playoffs). We also need to understand how imagery use is related to other variables (e.g., competitive anxiety) that influence practice behavior and competition performance.

The MIQ-R and EIQ are new instruments, but both seem to be promising. The psychometric characteristics of the MIQ-R still need to be determined, and a more general version of the EIQ should be developed. The present version of the EIQ applies to only one form of physical exercise, namely, aerobics. How other exercisers (e.g., joggers, roller skaters, and mountain climbers) use imagery, and the valid and reliable assessment of such usage, still needs to be investigated.

Table 1
Tests of Imagery Ability and Imagery Use

Test Type	Name	Test-Retest Reliability	Subscales	Cronbach's Alpha
Ability	VMIQ	.76	Visual	NA
Ability	MIQ	.83	Visual	.87 - .89
			Kinesthetic	.88 - .91
Use	PSIS R-5	.57 *	Anxiety Control	.59
			Concentration	.52
			Confidence	.85
			Motivation	.62
			Team Emphasis	.53
			Mental Preparation	-.34
Use	IUQ-SP	.55 - .92	Cognitive Specific	.85
			Cognitive General	.75
			Motivational Specific	.82
			Motivational General	.76
Use	SIQ	NA	Cognitive Specific	.85
			Cognitive General	.75
			Motivational Specific	.88
			Motivational General-arousal	.70
			Motivational General-mastery	.83
Use	EIQ	NA	Health and Physical Appearance	.84
			Mood Enhancement	.85
			Cognitive Function	.84

NA = not available
* split-half reliability
The MIQ-R and the IUQ are not included because psychometric information is not available for these tests.

References

Ahsen, A. (1990). AA-VVIQ and imagery paradigm: Vividness and unvividness issue in VVIQ research programs. *Journal of Mental Imagery*, *14*, 1-58.

Atienza, F., Balaguer, I., & Garcia-Merita, M.A. (1994). Factor analysis and reliability of the Movement Imagery Questionnaire. *Perceptual and Motor Skills*, *78*, 1323-1328.

Barr, K., & Hall, C. (1992). The use of imagery by rowers. *International Journal of Sport Psychology*, *23*, 243-261.

Barratt, P.E. (1953). Imagery and thinking. *Australian Journal of Psychology*, *5*, 154-164.

Bennett, G.K., Seashore, M.G., & Wesman, A.G. (1947). *Differential aptitude tests*. New York: Psychological Corporation.

Betts, G.H. (1909). *The distribution and functions of mental imagery*. New York: Teachers College, Columbia University.

Campos, A., & Perez, M.J. (1990). A factor analytic study of two measures of mental imagery. *Perceptual and Motor Skills*, *71*, 995-1001.

Chartrand, J.M., Jowdy, D.P., & Danish, S.J. (1992). The Psychological Skills Inventory for Sports: Psychometric characteristics and applied implications. *Journal of Sport & Exercise Psychology*, *14*, 405-413.

Daw J., & Burton, D. (1994). Evaluation of a comprehensive psychological skills training program for collegiate tennis players. *The Sport Psychologist*, *1*, 37-57.

Denis, M. (1985). Visual imagery and the use of mental practice in the development of motor skills. *Canadian Journal of Applied Sport Sciences*, *10*, 4S-16S.

Ernest, C.H. (1977). Imagery ability and cognition: A critical review. *Journal of Mental Imagery*, *2*, 181-216.

Fenker, R.M., & Lambiotte, J.G. (1987). A performance enhancement program for a college football team: One incredible season. *The Sport Psychologist*, *1*, 224-236.

Fleishman, E.A. (1972). On the relationship between abilities, learning, and human performance. *American Psychologist*, *27*, 1017- 1032.

Fleishman, E.A., & Quaintance, M.K. (1984). *Taxonomies of human performance*. Orlando, FL: Academic Press.

Gordon, R. (1949). An investigation into some of the factors that favour the formation of stereotyped images. *British Journal of Psychology*, *40*, 156-167.

Goss, S. Hall, C., Buckolz, E., & Fishburne, G. (1986). Imagery ability and the acquisition and retention of movements. *Memory & Cognition*, *14*, 469-477.

Hall, C., Buckolz, E., & Fishburne, G. (1989). Searching for a relationship between imagery ability and memory of movements. *Journal of Human Movement Studies*, *17*, 89-100.

Hall, C., Buckolz, E., & Fishburne, G.J. (1992). Imagery and the acquisition of motor skills. *Canadian Journal of Sport Sciences*, *17*, 19-27.

Hall, C., Mack, D., Paivio, A., & Hasenblas, H. (in press). Imagery use by athletes: Development of the Sport Imagery Questionnaire. *International Journal of Sport Psychology*.

Hall, C., & Martin, K. (1997). Measuring movement imagery abilities: A revision of the Movement Imagery Questionnaire. *Journal of Mental Imagery, 21*, 143-154.

Hall, C., & Pongrac, J. (1983). *Movement Imagery Questionnaire*. London, Ontario: University of Western Ontario.

Hall, C., Pongrac, J., & Buckolz, E. (1985). The measurement of imagery ability. *Human Movement Science*, *4*, 107-118.

Hall, C.R., & Rodgers, W.M. (1989). Enhancing coaching effectiveness in figure skating through a mental skills training program. *The Sport Psychologist*, *3*, 142-154.

Hall, C., Rodgers, W., & Barr, K. (1990). The use of imagery by athletes in selected sports. *The Sport Psychologist*, *4*, 1-10.

Hall, C., Schmidt, D., Durand, M., & Buckolz, E. (1994). Imagery and motor skills acquisition. In A.A. Sheikh & E.R. Korn (Eds.), *Imagery in sports and physical performance* (pp. 121-134). Amityville, NY: Baywood Publishing Company.

Hausenblas, H.A., & Hall, C.R. (1996). *Do exercisers use imagery?: An exploratory study*. Paper submitted for publication.

Hughes, S. (1990). Implementing a psychological skills training program in high school athletes. *Journal of Sport Behavior*, *13*, 15-22.

Isaac, A. (1992). Mental practice - does it work in the field? *The Sport Psychologist*, *6*, 192-198.

Isaac, A., Marks, D., & Russell, E. (1986). An instrument for assessing imagery of movement: The Vividness of Movement Imagery Questionnaire (VMIQ). *Journal of Mental Imagery*, *10*, 23-30.

Janssen, J.J., & Sheikh, A.A. (1994). Enhancing athletic performance through imagery: An overview. In A.A. Sheikh & E.R. Korn (Eds.), *Imagery in sports and physical performance* (pp. 1-22). Amityville, NY: Baywood Publishing Company.

Katz, A.N. (1983). What does it mean to be a high imager? In J.C. Yuille (Ed.), *Imagery, memory and cognition* (pp. 39-63). Hillsdale, NJ: Lawrence Erlbaum.

Kline, P. (1980). *The construction of psychological tests*. London: Batsford.

Likert, R., & Quasha, W. (1941). *Revised Minnesota Paper Form Board Test*. New York: Psychological Corporation.

Mahoney, M.J. (1989). Psychological predictors of elite and non-elite performance on Olympic weightlifting. *International Journal of Sport Psychology*, *20*, 1-20.

Mahoney, M.J., & Avener, M. (1977). Psychology of the elite athlete: An exploratory study. *Cognitive Therapy and Research*, *1*, 135-141.

Mahoney, M.J., Gabriel, T.J., & Perkins, T.S. (1987). Psychological skills and exceptional athletic performance. *The Sport Psychologist*, *1*, 181-199.

Marks, D.F. (1973). Visual imagery differences in the recall of pictures. *British Journal of Psychology*, *64*, 17-24.

Moritz, S.E., Hall, C.R., Martin, K.A., & Vadocz, E. (1996). What are confident athletes imaging?: An examination of image content. *The Sport Psychologist*, *10*, 171-179.

Nunnally, J.C. (1978). *Psychometric theory*. New York: McGraw-Hill.

Orlick, T., & Partington, J. (1986). *Psyched*. Ottawa: Coaching Association of Canada.

Paivio, A. (1971). *Imagery and verbal processes*. New York: Holt, Rinehart & Winston.

Paivio, A. (1985). Cognitive and motivational functions of imagery in human performance. *Canadian Journal of Applied Sport Sciences*, *10*, 22S-28S.

Paivio, A. (1986). *Mental representations*. New York: Oxford University Press.

Paivio, A., & Harshman, R. (1983). Factor analysis of a questionnaire on imaginal and verbal habits and skills. *Canadian Journal of Psychology*, *37*, 461-483.

Rodgers, W., Hall, C., & Buckolz, E. (1991). The effect of an imagery training program on imagery ability, imagery use, and figure skating performance. *Journal of Applied Sport Psychology*, *3*, 109-125.

Rotella, R.J., Gansneder, B., Ojala, D., & Billing, J. (1980). Cognitions and coping strategies of elite skiers: An exploratory study of young developing athletes. *Journal of Sport Psychology*, *2*, 350-354.

Salmon, J., Hall, C., & Haslam, I. (1994). The use of imagery by soccer players. *Journal of Applied Sport Psychology*, *6*, 116-133.

Suinn, R.M. (1983). Imagery and sport. In A.A. Sheikh (Ed.), *Imagery: Current theory, research, and application* (pp. 507-534). New York: John Wiley & Sons, Inc.

Vealey, R.S. (1986). Conceptualization of sport confidence and competitive orientation: Preliminary investigation and instrument development. *Journal of Sport Psychology*, *8*, 221-246.

White, S.A. (1993). The relationship between psychological skills, experience, and practice commitment among collegiate male and female skiers. *The Sport Psychologist*, *7*, 49-57.

Chapter 10

Issues in the Measurement of Attention

Bruce Abernethy
The University of Queensland
Jeffery J. Summers
University of Southern Queensland
and
Stephen Ford
The University of Melbourne

Performance of movement skills in both sport and exercise settings appears, intuitively at least, to be inextricably linked to the act of paying attention to the task at hand. In sport settings, coaches constantly remind athletes to maintain attention (or concentration) by applying all their available mental capacities to the task being undertaking and by optimizing the effectiveness of such application of mental effort through attending to only the most relevant sources of information. Poor performance is frequently attributed to either loss of sustained attention to the task or failure to attend to the correct, most appropriate, or most informative features of the task. Conversely, in noncompetitive exercise settings, participants frequently report on the value of the physical activity in acting as a distractor (i.e., in taking attention away) from other daily life stressors. Whether it be in the context of a selective focussing of available mental capacities or in the context of mental distraction, attention as a concept appears centrally within the consideration of virtually all behaviors and cognitions within sport and exercise. The broad-ranging nature of attention and its frequent appearance in intuitions, anecdotes, and reflections by performers and coaches alike highlight the importance of subjecting the phenomenon of attention to systematic study in order not only to describe but also explain and understand it.

Defining Attention

Although the broad, omnipresent nature of attention makes it a critical concept for sport and exercise psychologists to understand, it is these very same characteristics that also generate the major problem in its accurate, reproducible, and objective measurement. Accurate measurement of any construct is dependent upon the unambiguous definition of the construct. In the case of attention this has proven problematic because attention as a concept has been operationalized in many different ways, the term meaning many different things to different people.

Moray (1969, 1970) noted that the term *attention* has been applied imprecisely to a range of processes and behaviors including *mental concentration, vigilance, selectivity, visual search, mental set, activation* and *information processing*. Both cognitive psychologists (e.g, Eysenck, 1984) and biological psychologists (e.g., Näätänen, 1992) have warned that attention as a concept is relatively meaningless when applied so broadly and defined so loosely. Enhancement of the explanatory power of attention as a construct is dependent on removing the ambiguity from its definition and focussing more clearly on narrower aspects of human information processing and behavior for which definitional agreement can be obtained.

Attention and Consciousness

The early phenomenologists, such as Hamilton (1859), James (1890), and Titchener (1908), defined attention in terms of consciousness, but this approach has not gained universal acceptance. Particular difficulties for this approach have been the demonstrations that significant selective processing of information can occur without conscious awareness and therefore without subjects being able to reliably report on such processing. A substantial body of evidence now exists showing the central role that so-called automatic (nonconscious) forms of information processing play in cognition and action (Shiffrin & Schneider, 1977; Underwood, 1982), the fallible, unreliable nature of introspective reports on conscious mental processes (Nisbett & Wilson, 1977; Posner, 1973), and the frequent discrepancy between explicit verbalizable knowledge and performance (Berry & Broadbent, 1984; Reber, 1989).

While James's (1890) assertion that "everyone knows what attention is..." remains one of the most cited quotes in all of psychology, it is clear that we do *not* know what attention is or, at least, cannot reach agreement as to what it is (Stelmach & Hughes, 1983). The term attention is now used in a variety of ways in the experimental psychology literature (and, in turn, in the sport and exercise psychology literature), each with important but nevertheless different meanings. Focusing upon and defining more clearly these different subclasses of attention offer one way forward to improving definitional clarity.

Attention as a Multidimensional Construct

Posner and Boies (1971) identified three major uses of (or dimensions within) the term attention. Although the three areas identified by Posner and Boies are by no means completely independent, their categorization nevertheless provides a useful heuristic for clustering both empirical studies and methodological approaches to attention. All three areas of attention identified are equally relevant to the motor domain as to the cognitive (Näätänen, 1992) and are of direct pertinence to the development of both theory and practice in sport and exercise psychology.

The first use of the term attention identified by Posner and Boies (1971) is of attention in the context of *alertness or arousal* with particular focus upon the development and maintenance of optimal sensitivity and readiness for responding. Central to this usage are studies of vigilance performance and studies of the effects upon performance of arousal, activation, and related constructs, such as stress and anxiety. Measurement issues with respect to attention in the other context of alertness, arousal and anxiety are sufficiently central to sport and exercise psychology to be devoted separate chapters elsewhere in this book (See Smith, Smoll, & Wiechman; Burton, this volume) and hence will not be given further treatment in this chapter. Two of us [Abernethy, 1993; Morris & Summers, 1995] have also written separately on this aspect of attention and its measurement elsewhere.

A second use of the term attention identified by Posner and Boies (1971) is of attention as a *limited capacity or resource*. Studies examining mental workload or effort, capacity and/or resource limitations in information processing, and the notion of automaticity have been to the foreground in this context. Attention in the context of limited information-processing space (Keele, 1973), capacity (Moray, 1967) or resources (Wickens, 1984) refers directly to the demonstrable individual differences in the mental workload posed by different tasks and the known limitations humans have in performing two or more tasks simultaneously. Such notions are particularly important in many

sports where the concurrent performance of multiple tasks (such as controlling a ball while monitoring the position of teammates and opponents) is an integral part of routine performance. Skilled players appear capable of meeting these concurrent processing demands with a minimum of effort whereas less skilled performers inevitably either produce errors in one or both tasks or are forced to slow down to the point of being ineffective.

A third use of attention is in the context of *selectivity*, with particular reference to the phenomena and processes of selective attention. Selective attention refers to the processes by which certain information is preferentially selected for detailed processing whereas other information is ignored. Such a process of selection is absolutely essential given the inconceivably large amounts of information from both external and internal sources that reach the nervous system every millisecond of our lives. In sport tasks selective attention to only the most pertinent of information and, equally, the active avoidance of the processing of irrelevant or distracting information (be it from external or internal sources) is central to successful performance. As we have noted elsewhere (Abernethy, 1993),

> the success of the boxer trying to anticipate his opponent's punches, the baseball batter trying to predict the forthcoming pitch, the pole-vaulter or golfer trying to avoid distraction from crowd noise, or the rugby player trying to field a high kick while being stormed by opposing tacklers all depend on the extent to which they can attend to only relevant information and exclude attending to irrelevant or distracting events. (p. 152)

The Place of Attention Within Theories of Psychology

The way in which any construct is defined reflects strongly the prevailing theoretical and paradigmatic orientation of the era as well as that of the individual researcher. It is appropriate therefore in considering and delimiting the operational definition(s) of attention to also consider the place of the concept of attention within the major theoretical schools in psychology. Such considerations are central to any attempt not only to understand how contemporary approaches to the measurement of attention have arisen but also to make some principled projections as to the future of attentional measurement.

Attention, albeit in somewhat different forms, has featured prominently as a construct in all but one of the major schools and periods of psychological theorizing. Interest in the concept of attention is as old as the field of experimental psychology itself (Boring, 1970), dating back at least to the early phenomenologists who, through the use of introspective reports, linked the concept of attention directly to the experienced phenomenon of consciousness. The subjective nature of phenomenology led ultimately to its demise and its replacement throughout the first half of this century by behaviorism as the dominant school of psychological theory. Behaviorism focused on measurable aspects of stimuli and responses and explicitly disregarded the study of internal processes that could not be subjected to direct measurement. This led to a dramatic waning of experimental interest in a whole range of mental constructs, including attention. Attention did not then reappear on the research agenda until the emergence of cognitive psychology in the 1950s. This emergence of cognitive psychology flowed from the development of mathematical models of information (Wiener, 1948) and conceptions of perception, cognition and action in information processing terms (Craik, 1947, 1948; Welford, 1952).

Understanding attention in its many contexts has been one of, if not *the*, central research issue within cognitive psychology. With its emphasis upon computation, processing capacities and limitations, and the nature of underlying neural 'software', the information-processing models of cognitive psychology have provided the major theoretical framework for research on attention not only as it operates within cognitive skills but also as it functions in and constrains performance of motor skills. From the very beginnings of information-processing/computational models, emphasis has been given to the question of overall processing capacities and putative bottlenecks in information processing (e.g., Broadbent, 1958; Keele, 1973; Welford, 1952, 1967) and to the issue of how and why some types of stimuli (input information) are given preferential processing over others (e.g., Cherry, 1953; Moray, 1959; Treisman, 1964, 1969). These two key issues provide the forerunners to the two major attentional contexts of mental workload/capacities and selectivity that we examine in this chapter.

Although information-processing/computational approaches remain the dominant theoretical position within experimental psychology, there have, over recent years, being growing identification and concern over a number of inherent assumptions within these approaches. In particular there have been concerns over (a) the assumption of symbolic representation within these models and the arbitrary nature of the description of such representations (Carello, Turvey, Kugler, & Shaw, 1984), (b) the reductionist approach to processing elements that differentiates and separates processing stages such as those involved in perception and action rather than recognizing the essential interconnectedness of these processes (Fitch & Turvey, 1978; Turvey & Carello, 1986), and (c), in the case of movement control, an (over)emphasis on top-down, centralized control overlooking the high degree of control inherent within the natural dynamics and intrinsic biomechanics of the musculoskeletal system (Kelso, 1986; Turvey, Fitch, & Tuller, 1982).

As a consequence of these concerns, there has been the clear development over the past decade and a half of an alternative school of psychological theorizing that might best be termed ecological psychology. This school of theorizing draws heavily on the work of J.J. Gibson on perception (e.g., J.J. Gibson, 1979) and Bernstein on movement control or action (Bernstein, 1967) and is based on a quite different set of philosophical assumptions to that underpinning traditional cognitive psychology (Burgess-Limerick, Abernethy, & Limerick, 1994; Lombardo, 1987). Central to ecological psychology are notions of animal-environment reciprocity and direct perception-action coupling. These notions portray all animals, including humans, as actively interacting rather than passively engaging with their environment to the extent that movement through the environment in order to enrich perception is viewed as equally important to the animal as the act of perception is to movement. Notions implicit in cognitive psychology that mind and body (or person and environment) can be meaningfully separated, and that perception and cognition for action are reliant upon mental

representations of the "outside" world, are rejected. These differences in philosophy lead to the posing of different research questions and the adoption of different research methodologies. (For an example of how these different theoretical orientations impact upon the study of sport and motor expertise, see Williams, Davids, Burwitz, & Williams, 1992 or Abernethy, Burgess-Limerick, & Parks, 1994.)

The notion of attention, especially within the context of selectivity, maintains an important place in ecological psychology (E.J. Gibson, 1969; Turvey, 1990), with the orientation being now very much one of attempting to isolate, for natural tasks, those perceptual variables that directly and lawfully specify control variables in the action system (Flach, Lintern, & Larish, 1990; Fowler & Turvey, 1978; Turvey, Carello, & Kim, 1990). Intention, rather than being linked to a mental notion of consciousness, is now being examined in natural physical terms as an additional nonlinear dynamic imposed upon the natural dynamics of the human motor system (Kugler, Shaw, Vicente, & Kinsella-Shaw, 1990; Shaw & Kinsella-Shaw, 1988). It remains to be seen whether the new orientations provided by ecological psychology will succeed in driving understanding of attention and other key concepts beyond the level reached through information-processing perspectives (Michaels & Beek, in press).

In this chapter we attempt to critically review issues in the measurement of attention, with particular reference to the use of concepts of attention in sport and exercise psychology. We do so by first examining the different levels of analysis from which attention can, and has, been observed, described, and measured, giving particular focus to attention within the contexts of *mental workload* and *selectivity*. Behavioral, cognitive, and physiological/biological measures of attention are then discussed with respect to what information they have revealed to date, their current and prospective uses in sport and exercise psychology, their underlying rationales and assumptions, their known psychometric characteristics, and their overall strengths and weaknesses as measures. We conclude with some observations on the importance of multilevel, integrative models of attentional concepts not only as a means of enhancing confidence in the psychometric properties of attentional measurement but also as a means of addressing a number of key but largely ignored theoretical questions about the interplay between neural biology, thoughts, and actions.

Levels of Analysis for the Measurement of Attentional Constructs

Levels of analysis in psychology refer to the different scales (from microscopic to macroscopic) at which either brain or behavior can be represented (Cacioppo & Berntson, 1992). At least three levels of analysis (what we might somewhat arbitrarily label as the behavioral, cognitive, and physiological/biological) are frequently used in sport and exercise psychology in an attempt to understand more about attentional phenomena.

The *behavioral level of analysis* involves measurement of directly observable behaviors, as manifestations of underlying cognitive and neurophysiological processes. Behavioral measures of attention include measures of attentional capacity and workload based on concurrent performance of multiple tasks and measures of attentional selectivity based on the performance of subjects under experimental conditions of reduced or manipulated information. The *cognitive level of analysis* is concerned with measurement of underlying information processes (i.e., thought processes broadly defined), inclusive of both conscious and nonconscious processes. Cognitive measures of attention include a range of self-report instruments designed to ascertain both mental workload and attentional selectivity. The *physiological/biological level of analysis* involves measurement of a host of largely physiological parameters, changes that have been associated with the more traditional psychological phenomena of attention. Currently favored physiological measures of attentional workload and selectivity include electroencephalographic and magnetoencephalographic measures of brain activity, measures of cerebral blood flow and metabolism, cardiovascular measures related to cardiac deceleration and variability, and measures of visual activity related to ocular fixations and pupil diameter. Such parameters are typically viewed as markers of attention.

All three levels of analysis are clearly related, with the distinction between levels of analysis often blurred. The relationships between levels of analysis are not necessarily simple ones, and, although different levels of analysis of attentional phenomena may arrive at compatible conclusions, a quite high degree of nonconcordance between measures derived from different levels is frequently observed. Researchers studying attentional phenomena are therefore regularly confronted with the decision of whether to select the single level of analysis most directly appropriate to the construct and context of interest (e.g., the physiological level for arousal, the cognitive level for anxiety, and the behavioral level for performance) or rather to use multiple levels of analysis in order to measure constructs which are manifest and expressed at a number of different levels. This selection inevitably depends on the specific nature of the questions being asked: The first approach, through being more focused, may produce the best psychometrics, at least with respect to reliability and repeatability, but the second approach may be more valuable in understanding the ultimately more important questions about links (such as brain-behavior links) between different levels of the system.

In the sections that follow we will briefly review some of the major behavioral, cognitive, and biological/physiological approaches to the measurement of attentional phenomena, in each case examining what is known of the psychometrics and conceptual underpinnings of these measures as they apply to the capacity (workload) and selectivity dimensions of the attention construct. Emphasis is given throughout these sections to a working assessment of the assumptions, strengths, and weaknesses of each approach.

Behavioral Measures of Attention
Dual-Task Measures of Attentional Capacity and Workload

As we noted earlier, many sport tasks require the concurrent performance of multiple tasks. The dual-task method provides for direct behavioral tests of the attention demand differences within and between different tasks and between different people performing the same tasks. From performance on concurrent tasks, inferences can be, and have been, made as to the

extent of the mental/processing workloads imposed by the task and to the automatic (or otherwise) nature of the information processing being undertaken.

Applications within sport and exercise psychology. Although dual-task methods have played a central role in theory testing in cognitive psychology (e.g., Logan, 1985; Neumann, 1987; Schneider, 1985) and in applied assessment in ergonomics (e.g, Brown, 1978; Ogden, Levine & Eisner, 1979; Wickens, 1992), the use of dual-task approaches in sport and exercise psychology has been surprisingly limited. Applications in sport and exercise psychology have been of two main types, namely, (a) applications that use dual-task methods to examine the nature of expert-novice differences in attention demand (e.g., Leavitt, 1979; Parker, 1981) and (b) applications, following the leads presented in studies of simple limb-positioning movements (e.g., Posner & Keele, 1969; Zelaznik, Shapiro, & McClosky, 1981), which seek to determine fluctuations in attention demand or mental workload throughout the time course of activities such as catching (Populin, Rose, & Heath, 1990; Starkes, 1986), shooting (Landers, Wang, & Courtet, 1985; Rose & Christina, 1990), and playing a racquet sport (Abernethy, 1988a). The studies of expert-novice differences have consistently demonstrated superior secondary task performance, and hence generally more automatic control of the primary task, by expert performers, even in cases where an expert advantage is not observable on the primary task alone. Studies using dual-task methods in an attempt to map attentional fluctuations across the time course of a sport skill have been less systematic in their findings, most likely because such applications push the limits of the temporal resolution capabilities of the method itself.

The dual-task method has also been used extensively in ergonomics to assess the relative workloads presented by different tasks (Wickens, 1992). Although such uses are not yet apparent in sport and exercise psychology, the method would at least appear to have potential to also be applied in these settings to examine the appropriate sequencing of practice activities (in terms of their attention demand) and the effectiveness of laboratory simulations in simulating the attentional demands of natural tasks (Abernethy, 1988a, 1993).

Basic rationale and assumptions. As the name implies, the dual-task method is based around having subjects perform two tasks simultaneously: a *primary task*, about which understanding of attention demand is sought, and a *secondary task*, generally selected to require different sensory and response systems to that of the primary task. In sport studies the primary task is usually a fundamental skill required in the sport. The secondary task is often a discrete reaction time task (termed in this context *probe reaction time*) although a large range of secondary tasks have been used (Ogden et al., 1979). The usual instruction given to subjects in dual-task studies is to assign priority to the performance of the primary task (so as to maintain performance at the same level as when the primary task is performed alone) although inevitably some decrements in primary task performance are observed in the dual setting as time and attention are switched by subjects between the processing demands of the concurrent tasks.

The basic rationale underlying the dual-task method is that secondary task performance will be a direct reflection of the information-processing capacity that remains after the demands of the primary task have been met. If the primary task demands much (or even all) of the available processing capacity, then secondary task performance will be poor; conversely if secondary task performance is unchanged between the dual-task conditions and its performance as a single task, then it will be concluded that the primary task demands no processing capacity. Under such conditions the task is considered to be controlled automatically (Shiffrin & Schneider, 1977). Fluctuations in secondary task performance across the time course of the primary task are generally considered to be indicative of fluctuations in the processing (attentional) demands at corresponding points throughout the primary task.

The dual-task method is based on a number of assumptions, the tenability of which can be assessed (see Brown, 1978; McLeod, 1980, and Abernethy, 1988a, for more detailed considerations). The first assumption is that total information-processing capacity is finite and fixed. Although there is no doubt that our information-processing capacity has finite limits, the assumption that this capacity is fixed is less convincing. In particular, fluctuations in levels of activation or arousal may effectively modify the total available processing capacity, leading to functional reductions in overall processing capacity under situations of non-optimal arousal (Glencross, 1978; Kahneman, 1973). Any such fluctuations may impact on the validity of comparisons of attention across individuals and across time for the same individual.

A second key assumption is that processing priority is given exclusively to the primary task such that secondary task performance is based only on "spare" capacity. In reality, most subjects, however rigorously they attempt to follow the instructional set, engage to some degree or other in time (and attention) sharing between the two tasks such that primary task performance under the dual conditions is invariably poorer than when it is performed alone. Although such attentional sharing may not be a concern if the researcher's interest is in understanding either how well subjects can cope with two concurrent tasks (as might be the case if both tasks were simulations of dual demands present within the actual sport setting) or the nature of interference between different types of tasks, it presents major interpretative problems if the issue of interest is determining the genuine attentional requirements of the primary task and/or comparing this demand between different individuals.

A third assumption is that the limiting factor to dual-task performance is the cumulative attentional demands the two tasks place on the total available processing capacity rather than very specific demands the two tasks may have for common input or output processes, such as might occur if both tasks demand the use of the same sensory system (e.g, two concurrent visual tasks) or the same response system (e.g, two concurrent manual responses). The decrements in performance evident in the first situation have been labelled *capacity interference*, those in the latter situation, *structural interference* (Kahneman, 1973). The practical difficulty for the experimentalist is separating these two effects as structural interference may arise in unexpected ways, such as in the case of tasks sharing a common timing structure (McLeod, 1978). Of concern is that different secondary tasks may result in different conclusions being

reached about the attentional demand of any particular primary task. It is precisely such concerns that have resulted in the development of models of attention based more on notions of special-purpose resource pools than general, undifferentiated processing capacity (Allport, 1980; Navon & Gopher, 1979). Identification of the nature and composition of the special-purpose resource pools remains difficult.

A fourth assumption, which is of significance when the measurement of attentional fluctuations across the time course of a particular primary task is of paramount concern, is that attentional peaks and troughs can be localized with accuracy from probe reaction time data. The traditional approach has been to use probe reaction time as a measure of the attention demand of the primary task at the time the probe (secondary task stimulus) is presented. The inaccuracy in this approach is that attention demand may remain elevated throughout the duration of the secondary task response. Plotting attention demand more appropriately from the time of presentation of the secondary task stimulus through to the completion of the response to that stimulus invariably leads to a more conservative localization of the time of peak attentional demands (Girouard, Laurencelle, & Proteau, 1984; McLeod, 1980) and, for primary tasks of relatively short duration, may render the dual-task approach of limited utility.

Strengths and weaknesses. Sheridan and Stassan (1979) and Wickens (1984) have proposed that there are five key criteria determining the suitability of different measures of mental workload, namely, the measure's *sensitivity* to alterations in workload demand, its *selective* influence by only those factors affecting resource demand, its *diagnostic* capability to identify the specific resources being taxed by a given task, its *unobtrusiveness* to natural performance of the task of interest, and its *reliability*. The dual-task method satisfies each of these to some degree but within the constraints of the assumptions identified in the previous section.

The dual-task method has a number of strengths, the most obvious of which is its capability to provide comparative data on the "spare capacity" for individuals and the demands of different tasks. Importantly, these are data that may reveal differences between individuals and tasks not apparent from simple observation of performance of the primary task and not easily obtained through any other method. The dual-task approach has a high degree of face and ecological validity with respect to actual performance with the opportunity existing, through careful primary and secondary task selection, to simulate quite precisely the processing requirements of the actual performance setting. An additional strength of the approach is the capability of extracting useful and objective information about attention without the necessity to unnecessarily constrain the task or require sophisticated and expensive techniques.

The biggest drawback in the use of dual-task methods is that the veracity of the data obtained is so dependent upon decisions made with respect to the selection of the secondary task. Selection of a single secondary task from amongst the nearly endless range of possible tasks (Ogden et al., 1979; Wickens, 1984) depends, among other things, on consideration of whether the secondary task should be discrete or temporally coexistent (Heuer & Wing, 1984), whether structural interference is to be sought or avoided (Kahneman, 1973), and knowledge of the measurement grain or sensitivity of the particular secondary task. The nature of the control conditions used (i.e., the primary-task-alone condition and the secondary-task-alone condition) is also pivotal to the veracity of the dual-task data, and any inadequacies in this area can dramatically limit the value of the collected data. These control conditions must match precisely the dual-task condition on not only superficial features, such as the task objective and general setup, but also more subtle features, such as the timing and relative frequency of stimulus presentation. For example, measuring reaction time (in cases where the secondary task is probe reaction time) over a shorter test period or with higher relative stimulus frequency in the control condition than the dual condition can result in artificially inflated single-task performance and, in turn, inflated estimates of the actual level of attention demand of the primary task.

The time and effort required to both design and collect dual-task data are significant operational weaknesses in the dual-task method. Three test conditions must be administered on all occasions, namely, the dual condition and two single-task control conditions. Not only does this requirement create the potential for subject fatigue/boredom effects, but it also acts as an impediment for researchers doing applied work who may have only limited time access to their subject group. The latter practicality may well be an important force in directing most sport and exercise psychologists to rely to a much greater extent on the more readily administered cognitive measures of mental workload (see next major section) even though the dual-task approach may well satisfy more of the essential criteria for mental workload assessment. An additional concern, which may ultimately drive sport and exercise psychologists more in the direction of physiological measures of mental workload, is that the dual-task method provides only a discrete or discontinuous measure of attentional demand. These limitations aside, it is nevertheless true that there exists considerable scope for greater use of dual-task methods in sport and exercise psychology.

Occlusion Measures of Attentional Selectivity

Key issues within the study of selective attention include determining (a) the specific stimulus events that are relevant and warranting of our attention and equally the stimulus events that are irrelevant and, if attended, potentially counterproductive; (b) the nature of the mechanism through which the selective allocation of processing resources occurs; and (c) the means by which attentional selectivity can be modified with practice and experience. Auditory (Cherry, 1953) and visual (Neisser & Becklen, 1975) tasks providing multiple competing sources of information have been used in the laboratory to examine the second of these issues. The first and third issues, which are arguably of more practical significance to sport and exercise psychologists, have been addressed using behavioral measures of subject performance under conditions where access to normal display information is selectively masked or occluded. These approaches involve selective occlusion of either specific time periods (*temporal occlusion*) or specific regions (*spatial occlusion*) of the visual display typically available to sports performers. The visual display is either viewed directly or provided through a film, video or computer-generated simulation, and the subject's task is to execute his or her normal ac-

tion, or make a perceptual judgment (e.g., "What direction is the ball going in?"), or a response selection decision (e.g., "Where should you move next?").

Applications within sport and exercise psychology. Both the temporal and, to a lesser extent, the spatial occlusion methods have been applied to sport tasks with the intention of identifying the relevant information sources for skilled perception and decision-making. In many cases this has involved comparison of the relative use of different sources of information by expert and less skilled performers.

Methods of temporal occlusion were first used by Whiting and his associates in the 1970s in a series of studies that attempted to determine the time period for key pickup of information for catching (e.g, Sharp & Whiting, 1974; Whiting, Alderson, & Sanderson, 1973; Whiting & Sharp, 1974), and interest in this issue has persisted (e.g, Fischman & Schneider, 1985; Savelsbergh & Bootsma, 1994; Savelsbergh, Whiting, & Pijpers, 1992; see Williams et al., 1992 for a critique). In these studies, subjects were required to perform one-handed catching under conditions where the time to view the approaching ball was varied through control of the room lighting conditions. More recent applications of the temporal occlusion technique have involved simulation of the perceptual display available to defensive players in a range of ball sports with different temporal occlusion conditions being used to demonstrate expert-novice differences in anticipation of the opponent's actions and in the time course of their information pickup (Abernethy, 1990a; Abernethy & Russell, 1987a; Helsen & Pauwels, 1993). Although historically such approaches have typically used display simulations, the technology now exists in the form of electronically controlled goggles to permit the same manipulations to be performed in the natural setting (Milgram, 1987). Spatial occlusion methods have been used less frequently, but where they have been used, they have provided more direct evidence than is provided from the temporal occlusion method of the differential pickup of information from different regions of the display by expert and novice athletes (Abernethy & Russell, 1987a). Occlusion studies in sport have provided objective evidence of the earlier pickup of advance information about their opponent's action by expert players and, through strategic selection of the specific temporal and spatial occlusion conditions, have enabled the major cues for advance information used by different players to be identified in terms of their time of appearance and location.

Basic rationale and assumptions. In the temporal occlusion method subjects are typically presented, throughout the course of an experiment, with repeat viewings of the same perceptual event but under different degrees of temporal occlusion. These temporal occlusion conditions range incrementally from conditions in which only early viewing of the developing event (such as the service action of an opposing tennis player) is provided through to (control) conditions in which the full event is available for viewing. Improvements in the subject's performance in predicting the ultimate event outcome (or production of a successful action in the case of natural task settings) from one temporal occlusion period to the next is used to make inferences about the availability and pickup of key information throughout the time period (or time window) bounded by the

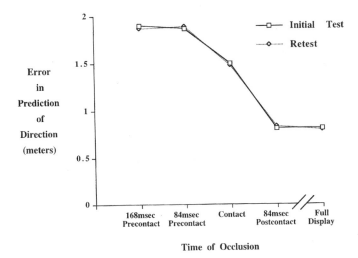

Figure 1. Test-retest performance of eight novice subjects on the temporal occlusion task of Abernethy & Russell (1987a). The time between the first and second administration of the test was 4 weeks.

two occlusion conditions. The emphasis within the temporal occlusion approach is therefore upon discovery of those time periods in which task performance improves rapidly with these periods being taken as indicative of active information pickup. By then examining the key events occurring within the perceptual display during that time period, inference can be made as to the location of the likely sources of information upon which the improved performance is based. The spatial occlusion technique follows a similar logic with the importance of different regions of the display being inferred from the response decrements occurring when visibility to particular sources of information is masked (Abernethy, 1985).

The occlusion techniques, or at least some of their variants, are based on a number of assumptions. The first, pertinent in the case of simulations, is that the display presented contains all the sources of information as are needed and selectively attended to in the natural setting. Most simulations either do not provide all of the sources of information available in the natural setting (e.g., almost all nonvisual sources of information are typically not provided) or provide display information degraded from that available in the natural setting (e.g., narrow two-dimensional presentations of the natural visual field). To what extent this alters the selective attention of the athlete in the laboratory from that in the natural setting has not been well established although the advent of improved technologies should enable this issue to be more actively addressed in the future.

A second assumption, present in the case of the temporal occlusion approach, is that the improvements in prediction performance that one inevitably sees when progressively more information is provided are a direct consequence of the availability of new information within later time windows rather than an effect that arises simply as a consequence of a total increase in available viewing (and processing) time. Although studies keeping the available viewing time constant but varying when in the event sequence this viewing is provided have been undertaken on ball catching, these important studies have not, as

yet, been undertaken to verify the conclusion currently made with respect to expert-novice differences in advance information pickup in ball sports.

A parallel assumption, present in the spatial occlusion approach, is that the decrements in performance observed when some specific regions of the display are masked are a direct consequence of subjects' being denied vision of a critical cue normally used rather than a consequence of distraction brought about by the masking procedure itself. Control conditions in which irrelevant background features of the display are occluded can be used to test this assumption (Abernethy & Russell, 1987a).

With respect to psychometric properties, laboratory-based applications of the temporal occlusion method have been shown to capture comparable attention-demands to actual playing (Abernethy, 1988a) and to be robust to changes in the dependent measures used to assess performance (Abernethy, 1989). Both the temporal occlusion (Figure 1) and spatial occlusion methods (Figure 2) have good test-retest reliability with comparable conclusions being achievable from test administrations spaced 4 weeks apart.

Strengths and weaknesses. The major advantage of the occlusion approaches is that they provide a reasonably direct indication of the information sources able to be used by athletes to make sport-specific perceptual judgments and, in turn, to guide the selection and execution of action. The major limitation, which arises because they are behavioral measures using task performance to make inference about underlying cognitive processes, is that they reveal only information that is attended to *and able to be used to improve task performance*; the occlusion methods cannot, by their very nature, measure selective attention to stimulus features/events that do not translate into in-

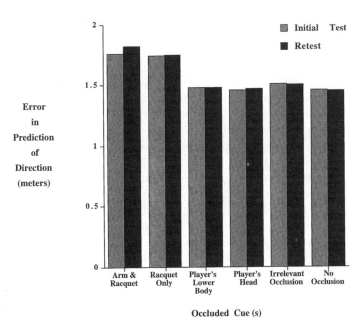

Figure 2. Test-retest performance of eight novice subjects on the spatial occlusion task of Abernethy & Russell (1987a). The time between the first and second administration of the test was 4 weeks.

formation pickup. The temporal occlusion method is quite easily developed and administered, especially now given the ready access of researchers to basic video recording and editing equipment. The spatial occlusion method, although it provides a more direct method of determining cue usage, has been used much less often than has the temporal occlusion approach. This is because the former method is much more difficult technically, requiring the frame-by-frame masking of the region of interest. Recent advancements in computer-generated graphics and video interfacing enhance the viability of both occlusion methods, especially the spatial one.

Cognitive Measures of Attention

A problem with behavioral (and physiological) measures of attention is that they are unable to access directly an athlete's thoughts, experiences, and insights about his or her own attentional processes. That is, such objective techniques cannot tell us directly how athletes differ from one another in attentional skills and strategies (Moran, 1996). Self-report measures, in contrast, are based on the assumption that people are able to accurately reflect on their own attentional functioning. Self-rating is being increasingly used by applied sport psychologists in evaluating an athlete's attentional strengths and weaknesses and as a basis for intervention strategies to improve attentional efficiency.

Self-Report Measures of Attentional Capacity and Workload

Subjective measures of attentional capacity or mental workload have been very popular in cognitive and applied psychology. This is partly due to the intuitive appeal of the concept of mental workload. In the sporting arena, for example, we can all cite instances where two athletes, although achieving the same objectively measured performance level, appear to do so with differing degrees of mental effort. Furthermore, subjective estimates of the effort required to perform a task are easy to obtain and enjoy high face validity. It is commonly believed that people are able to accurately report the mental effort needed to meet particular task demands. As a group of experts on the measurement of workload concluded: "If the person tells you that he is loaded and effortful, he is loaded and effortful whatever the behavioral and performance measures may show" (Moray et. al., 1979, p.105).

Applications within sport and exercise psychology. The measurement of mental workload has been of particular concern in the field of engineering psychology, where it is important for designers of systems to consider the workload imposed by that system on the operator. For example, measurements of mental workload may be used to compare and choose between two different pieces of equipment that give comparable performance. Although subjective workload measures have been little used in the sport domain, they are potentially useful in determining the level of skill or automaticity achieved by the performer and in determining the demands posed by specific situations within particular sports.

Basic rationale and assumptions. A variety of techniques have been developed for the subjective rating of the mental effort required to perform a task. Although some techniques use a structured rating scale requiring a single dimensional rating (Casali & Wierwille, 1983), the most widely used are multidimensional assessment techniques. Two such techniques are the NASA Task Load Index (TLX) and the Subjective Workload Assessment Technique (SWAT).

The NASA TLX (Hart & Staveland, 1988) provides an overall workload score based on a weighted average of ratings on six bipolar dimensions of mental demands, physical demands, temporal demands, performance, effort, and frustration level (Table 1). These dimensions were derived from extensive research and psychometric analyses in a variety of environments including laboratory experiments and simulations. Implementation of the TLX involves a two-part process: (a) scale development and (b) event scoring. During the scale-development phase, a set of weights or importance estimates is obtained for the six dimensions. This process involves presenting all 15 possible paired comparisons of the six dimensions and asking respondents to indicate the member of each pair that contributed more to the workload of the task(s) they have completed. Thus a relative rank ordering of the importance associated with each dimension for the task is produced. In the event-scoring phase, respondents assign individual numerical ratings to six 21-point bipolar subscales, resulting in scores ranging from 0 to 100 for each dimension. These scores are then weighted by the values derived from the paired comparison procedure. The weighted values are then combined to obtain an overall workload index.

The SWAT (Reid & Nygren, 1988) is based on an additive three-dimensional model of mental workload. These dimensions are defined as time load, mental effort load, and psychological stress load (see Table 1), with each dimension represented by a 3-point rating scale. Like the TLX, implementation of the SWAT involves two phases. During scale development, subjects rank order the 27 rating-scale combinations in terms of perceived workload. The rank-ordered data set is then used to construct a single interval workload scale with a range from 0 to 100 using conjoint scaling procedures. In the event-scoring phase, the subject performs some task and then simply indicates the perceived workload for each of the three dimensions using the 3-point rating scale. The event scores can then be translated into an overall workload score using the values derived from the scale-development phase.

Both the TLX and SWAT scales tend to produce similar outcomes when applied to the same data set (Vidulich & Tsang, 1986). The advantage of the SWAT is that it is based on a testable psychological model of subjective judgment, the three-dimensional additive model. On the other hand, the TLX has a greater number of scales and greater resolution per scale, making it potentially a much more sensitive scale than the SWAT (Wickens, 1992).

Strengths and Weaknesses. There are a number of reasons why subjective techniques are among the most frequently employed mental workload measures. In addition to enjoying high face validity, subjective measures are more direct than many other measures and can easily be obtained in a variety of operating environments without disrupting primary-task perfor-

Table 1
Multidimensional Mental Workload Rating Scale
(Adapted From Wickens, 1992)

NASA TLX Scale:
Rating Scale Definitions

Title	Endpoints	Description
Mental demand	*Low/High*	How much mental and perceptual activity was required (e.g., thinking, deciding, calculating, remembering, looking, searching)? Was the task easy or demanding, simple or complex, exacting or forgiving?
Physical demand	*Low/High*	How much physical activity was required (e.g., pushing, pulling, turning, controlling, activating)? Was the task easy or demanding, slow or brisk, slack or strenuous, restful or laborious?
Temporal demand	*Low/High*	How much time pressure did you feel due to the rate or pace at which the tasks or task elements occurred? Was the pace slow and leisurely or rapid and frantic?
Performance	*Good/Poor*	How successful do you think you were in accomplishing the goals of the task set by the experimenter (or yourself)? How satisfied were you with your performance in accomplishing these goals?
Effort	*Low/High*	How hard did you have to work (mentally and physically) to accomplish your level of performance?
Frustration level	*Low/High*	How insecure, discouraged, irritated, stressed, and annoyed versus secure, gratified, content, relaxed, and complacent did you feel during the task?

SWAT Scale

Time Load	Mental Effort Load	Stress Load
1. Participant often has spare time. Interruptions or overlap among activities occur infrequently or not at all.	1. Very little conscious mental effort or concentration is required. Activity is almost automatic, requiring little or no attention.	1. Little confusion, risk, frustration, or anxiety exists and can be easily accommodated.
2. Participant occasionally has spare time. Interruptions or overlap among activities occur frequently.	2. Moderate conscious mental effort or concentration is required. Complexity of activity is moderately high due to uncertainty, unpredictability, or unfamiliarity. Considerable attention is required.	2. Moderate stress due to confusion, frustration, or anxiety noticeably adds to workload. Significant compensation is required to maintain adequate performance.
3. Participant never has spare time. Interruptions or overlap among activities are very frequent or occur all the time.	3. Extensive mental effort and concentration are necessary. Very complex activity requires total attention.	3. High to very intense stress exists due to confusion, frustration, or anxiety. High to extreme determination and self-control are required.

mance. They can also be used to cross-validate more objective measures of workload.

There are, however, several problems with the use of subjective techniques to obtain accurate evaluations of workload. The first relates to the degree an individual's subjective judgment truly reflects the availability of, or demand for, processing resources. Subjective judgments, by definition, reflect the content of consciousness, and there is continuing debate as to what aspects of processing are available to consciousness. Furthermore, as subjective measures are obtained retrospectively, it is likely that some of the information available to the subject during task performance has been lost or distorted by the time workload estimates are sought. These problems, of course, are common to most self-report measures. Second, workload measures have been developed more on pragmatic than theoretical grounds. As a consequence, there is a lack of theoretical consistency in the analysis of the workload concept and a lack of clarity regarding the relationship between subjective measures and psychological processes and the behavioral phenomena of which they are supposed to be a manifestation (Gopher & Donchin, 1986). Without an understanding of the aspects of mental workload being assessed by subjective measures, comparison of workload estimates between tasks is meaningless.

Finally, there has been little attempt to examine the psychometric properties of subjective workload measurement techniques. Advocates of subjective techniques have relied almost exclusively on face validity in evaluating workload measurement. In fact, Nygren (1991) was unable to locate any studies assessing predictive, concurrent, or construct validity of subjective measures. Overall, subjective measures of mental workload appear of limited utility, and at this stage, their import and application to the sport and exercise psychology field does not seem warranted.

Self-Report Measures of Attentional Selectivity

In the sport psychology field, the subjective assessment of attentional selectivity has been dominated by the Test of Attentional and Interpersonal Style (TAIS) developed by Robert Nideffer in 1976.

Applications within sport and exercise psychology. During the period 1974 to 1992, attentional style was the third most researched topic in sport psychology (Fogarty, 1995). The TAIS and sport-specific versions of the instrument have been used extensively in examining the attentional styles of athletes in a variety of sports (e.g., Albrecht & Feltz, 1987; Maynard & Howe, 1989; Nideffer, 1987; Summers & Maddocks, 1986; Summers, Miller, & Ford, 1991; Vallerand, 1983; Van Schoyck & Grasha, 1981). Although the TAIS was designed as both a research tool and feedback device, there is little strong empirical support for its use as a research instrument to examine the relationship between attentional abilities and sport performance (See Cox, 1994; Moran, 1996; Summers & Ford, 1995). There is, however, some support for its use as a diagnostic tool for helping athletes to identify attentional problems that may be affecting performance. For example, the TAIS has been used for over 15 years in conjunction with other measures (e.g., coach reports, interviews, structured observations performance statistics) at the Australian Institute of Sport "to assess and educate athletes and coaches" and as "an important precursor for attentional training" (Bond & Sargent, 1995, p. 415). Thus, although the TAIS may lack construct validity, it does appear to enjoy substantial face validity (Moran, 1996).

Basic rationale and assumptions. The TAIS was developed on the basis of two main theoretical assumptions about the relationship between attentional processes and performance (Nideffer, 1981). The first, derived from the work of Easterbrook (1959) and Watchel (1967), is that three dimensions of attention are essential for effective performance: the width of attention, the direction of attentional focus, and the flexibility to alter attentional width and direction. Width and direction were

A Model of Attentional Style

BROAD

Broad–External

Awareness of environment needed in order to read and react to changing situations (e.g., negotiation sessions, sales).

Sport:
Optimal for reading complex sport situations. For assessing the environment. Used in team sports. (Athletes with this ability have great anticipation).

Broad–Internal

Used for long-range planning and integration. Anticipation of consequences, development of complex-flexible programs.

Sport:
Optimal for analyzing sport. Used by coaches to make game plans, to anticipate the future, and to recall past information. (Quick learners have this ability).

EXTERNAL ———————————————————————————— **INTERNAL**

Narrow–External

Focused nondistractible attention, necessary for being able to perform a specific task (converse with one person, hit a ball, repair watches, perform delicate surgery).

Sport:
Required at the moment a response is given. Attention narrowed and focused externally in order to hit a ball, react to an individual opponent.

Narrow–Internal

Necessary for intellectual tasks demanding focused concentration (e.g., computer programming, mathematical computation, mediation, and mental rehearsal).

Sport:
Optimal for learning to become sensitive to one's own body. Type of attention required in order to center and calm oneself, to rehearse a particular skill, or move mentally.

NARROW

Figure 3. TAIS Attentional Style dimensions and characterizations of the four attentional styles. (Adapted from Nideffer, 1981)

conceived as independent, continuous dimensions with width (broad-narrow) referring to the number of cues that receive attention at any one time and direction (internal-external) referring to the source of the cues that receive attention. These dimensions form a two-dimensional matrix representing four attentional styles (see Figure 3). At any time a person's attention can be described by its width and direction. Similarly, the attention requirements of most situations and tasks can be easily translated in terms of these two dimensions. For example, a free throw in basketball would require a narrow external form of attention at the moment of execution. In contrast, analyzing the patterns of play of the opposition would require a broad, internal focus. Effective attention, therefore, results from adopting the appropriate attentional style to match the task requirements. There is some evidence that athletes engaged in closed-skill sports (e.g., diving, gymnastics, shooting) tend to have a narrower focus of attention than do athletes involved in open (e.g., judo, wrestling, fencing) and team sports (Nideffer, 1990). To maintain appropriate attention, a person must adapt his or her attention to the situational requirements as they

Table 2
TAIS Attention-Related SubScales (Adapted from Nideffer, 1981)

Subscale	Abbreviation	Description
Overloaded by external stimuli	OET	The higher the score, the more mistakes are due to being confused and overloaded with external stimuli.
Overloaded by internal stimuli	OIT	The higher the score, the more mistakes individuals make because they confuse themselves by thinking about too many things at once.
Broad external attentional focus	BET	High scores on this subscale are obtained by individuals who describe themselves as able to effectively integrate many external stimuli at one time.
Broad internal attentional focus	BIT	High scorers see themselves as effectively integrating ideas and information from several different areas and as being analytical.
Narrow attentional focus	NAR	The higher the score, the more effectively individuals see themselves with respect to being able to narrow their attention when they need to.
Reduced attentional focus	RED	High scores indicate that individuals make mistakes because they narrow their attention too much, failing to include all task–related information.

change; attention must therefore be flexible. Flexible attention is conceived as moving among the four attentional styles as the situation demands. Thus, an individual needs to be able to adopt all attentional styles to function effectively.

The second major assumption of Nideffer's model (1990) is that individuals tend to have preferred attentional styles. Furthermore, there are individual differences in attentional abilities so that each person has attentional strengths and weaknesses. For example, some athletes are too analytical and make mistakes because they pay insufficient attention to the environment. In contrast, some athletes are dominated by an external attentional focus and, therefore, tend to be reactive, failing to think before acting because they are not sufficiently analytical. Increases in arousal are associated with a breakdown in the ability to shift attentional focus when appropriate, a reliance on one's preferred attentional style, a general narrowing of attention, and a tendency for individuals to become more internally focused.

The TAIS consists of 17 subscales, 6 specifically devoted to measuring attentional style whereas the remaining 11 measure behavioral or interpersonal styles. Typically, researchers examining attentional style involved in athletic performance have used only the 6 subscales relating to attentional abilities. Of the 6 attention-related subscales, 3 relate to effective attentional style: Broad-External (BET), Broad-Internal (BIT), and Narrow Focus (NAR), and 3 refer to ineffective attentional

styles: Internal Overload (OIT), External Overload (OET), and Reduced Focus (RED). The 6 subscales and their descriptions are summarized in Table 2.

The test consists of items that are behaviorally anchored (situationally specific) with content that relates to general activities in life (e.g., making choices at the supermarket, driving a car, cooking, conducting a conversation). A rational-intuitive approach to personality-test construction was used during test development. An item analysis was then conducted on a sample of 302 college undergraduates to validate the structural content of the scales and develop norms. The effects of item-scale overlap were also examined during test development because (a) the attentional subscales were considered independent, and (b) it was important to demonstrate that the subscales measure different aspects of attentional style (i.e., have discriminant validity). Two methods were used to check scale independence. The first was interscale correlations, which ranged from 0.07 to 0.80 for the 6 attention-related scales and suggested that "questions can be raised about independence" of the subscales (Nideffer, 1976, p. 398). The second method compared the mean corrected item-total correlation for each subscale with the item-total correlation of the remainder of nonsubscale items to determine the percentage of items with a score as high as, or higher than, the mean of the subscale items. The highest percentage overlap for all 17 subscales was 2.2% (or three items). These results were interpreted as demonstrating subscale independence.

Strengths and weaknesses. The model of attentional style has considerable intuitive appeal and provides a useful heuristic for understanding attention in sport. It also has more practical implications than do many other models of attention. The operationalization of the model in the form of the TAIS has also been beneficial in that it has been used as a scientific instrument as well as a tool in applied settings to assess athlete's attentional strengths and weaknesses.

A number of researchers, however, have raised some serious concerns about the psychometric properties of the TAIS. Of particular concern has been the assumption of subscale independence. Van Schoyck and Grasha (1981), for example, examined the number of items that correlated better with irrelevant subscales than with their own. They found, considering only the attention-related subscales, that 46% of the TAIS items correlated better with other subscales. Similarly, Albrecht and Feltz (1987) and Ford and Summers (1992), using the same method, reported that 48% and 44%, respectively, of the TAIS attentional subscale items correlate better with an irrelevant sub-

Table 3
Summary of Subscale Analyses

Subscale	Internal consistency (alpha)		MCFA factor loadings <0.3		Correlation greater with irrelevant scale		Corrected item–total coeff. <0.245	
OET	.72	(.67)	33	(25)	33	(50)	8	(17)
OIT	.69	(.67)	44	(22)	56	(67)	33	(22)
BET	.61	(.67)	0	(0)	0	(0)	0	(0)
BIT	.62	(.67)	37	(12)	37	(13)	13	(25)
NAR	.66	(.60)	33	(33)	33	(42)	33	(50)
RED	.57	(.59)	47	(40)	73	(60)	53	(47)
Total	--		35	(26)	44	(44)	27	(31)

Note: Results from cross–validation samples are in parentheses. Factor loadings, correlations, and coefficients are given in percentages of the subscales.

scale. These results cast doubt on the independence and construct validity of the subscales. Some studies have also computed internal consistency coefficients for each subscale to determine their internal validity or reliability (Albrecht & Feltz, 1987; Bergandi, Shryock, & Titus, 1990; Ford & Summers, 1992; Summers, et al., 1991; Van Schoyck & Grasha, 1981). Overall, the only scale that consistently reached the minimum acceptable magnitude of 0.7 (Nunnally, 1978) was OET.

More recently, Ford and Summers (1992) examined the factorial validity of the TAIS using a variety of analytical approaches. A summary of subscale analyses is presented in Table 3. A multidimensional confirmatory factor analysis (MCFA) was conducted to assess the overall validity of the measurement model. The adjusted goodness-of-fit index (AGFI), which is independent of sample size, was 0.65 and 0.66 respectively, for two samples of 210 subjects. It is generally accepted that models with AGFIs below 0.8 are inadequate (Bentler & Bonnett, 1980; Cuttance, 1987).

Overall, there is mounting evidence that the TAIS attention-related subscales lack construct validity. Although there are many forms of validity for tests (e.g., content, concurrent, face, predictive, construct), only construct validity is sufficient if a test is designed to be a measure of "real" traits. The evidence also strongly suggests that fewer than six factors are measured by the attention-related subscales, and the direction dimension, in particular, is inadequately measured in the current version of the test. In a recent study (Ford, 1996), exploratory factor analysis was used to restructure the TAIS to determine the constructs adequately measured by the attentional style items. Only a three-factor model met the criteria for item

fit. Factor 1 appeared to relate to the inability to focus attention (poor focus): Factor 2 related to the ability to focus narrowly without distraction (focused attention); and Factor 3 related to broad attention encompassing both internal and external stimuli and scanning (broad attention).

The inadequacies of the general TAIS in predicting sport performance has led researchers to develop sport-specific versions of the test. Sport-specific versions include a baseball/softball version (BB-TAIS; Albrecht & Feltz, 1987), a basketball version (B-TAIS; Summers, et al., 1991); a tennis version (T-TAIS; Van Schyock & Grasha, 1981); and a diving version (Nideffer, 1987). Although these versions of the TAIS do show superior psychometric properties, in terms of test-retest reliability and internal consistency, they have only marginally improved the measurement of attentional styles in sport. This is not surprising given that sport-specific versions of the TAIS have been constructed as parallel versions of the parent instrument. Therefore, the measurement problems evident in the general TAIS will be inherited by sport-specific versions of the instrument.

Finally, there are a number of aspects of attention neglected by the TAIS that may be important in sport performance. These dimensions include attentional flexibility, alertness, intensity, maintenance, and capacity (e.g., Etzel, 1979; Summers & Ford, 1990).

Although attentional style theory has contributed much to the understanding of the role of attention in sport, criticisms of the psychometric properties of the TAIS suggest that the instrument may have limited value in assessing attentional processes in athletes (Boutcher, 1992; Summers & Ford, 1995). It is clear that the model of attentional style requires revision and, perhaps, the incorporation of dimensions of attention neglected by the TAIS. One of us (Ford, 1996) has attempted to develop a new self-report instrument to measure attentional processes in sport. The Attention and Concentration Tendencies Survey (ACTS) is a 73-item pencil-and-paper test designed to measure seven attentional dimensions: broad attention, focused attention, flexibility, alertness, internal distraction, external distraction, and distractibility. The seven subscales and their descriptions are summarized in Table 4. The overall goodness-of-fit statistics from MCFA are only moderate (e.g., Comparative Fit Index = 0.66). Parameter fit, however, is very good, and internal consistency reliabilities are excellent (0.87 - 0.94). Despite the high parameter discriminant validity, some high latent interscale correlations (0.60 - 0.72) are evident. Preliminary external validation of the test with competitive trait anxiety, attentional style, performance level, and social desirability provided some evidence for convergent and discriminant validity. Overall the

Table 4
ACTS Subscales

Subscale	Description
Internal distraction	High scores on this subscale indicate the tendency to be cognitively distracted by negative and irrational thoughts and to be overanalytical.
External distraction	High scores indicate susceptibility to external distractions, particularly from spectators, loud noises (such as yelling), and movements.
Broad attention	High scorers see themselves as able to deal with a lot of information at one time, distribute attention over multiple tasks, and use their peripheral vision.
Focused attention	A high score indicates the ability to focus attention on the immediate task and screen out irrelevant stimuli.
Flexibility	A high score indicates the ability to alter the width of attention, anticipate events, maintain attention on task–relevant cues, and alter the intensity of attention when necessary.
Alertness	High scores indicate poor alertness in the form of mental fatigue, low arousal, confusion, overload, and difficulty regaining concentration.
Distractibility	High scorers see themselves as generally distractible, and having difficulty maintaining concentration.

test is a promising instrument, although considerable additional validation is required.

Perhaps, the most important issue that future research needs to resolve is the adequacy of the self-rating approach to attentional functioning. Two underlying assumptions of this approach are that (a) people are able to accurately report their attentional focus across varying situations, and (b) attentional processes can be described accurately through self-analysis and language (Boutcher, 1992). Nisbett and Wilson (1977), for example, have argued that there may be little or no direct introspective access to higher order processes. They argue that people's report of cognitive processes is based on a priori implicit causal theories or judgments rather than accurate descriptions of events. A further problem for the use of retrospective-recall measures to assess attention in sport relates to the view that, in expert sports performers, much processing has become automatized and not accessible to self-report. It is possible, therefore, that the failure of self-report instruments such as the TAIS to demonstrate construct validity may be more a reflection of inadequacy in the methodological approach than in the structure of the measuring instrument. Boutcher has suggested that the use of thought-sampling techniques, in which an athlete's thoughts are tape-recorded during an actual performance, may

provide a more valid way of examining attentional processes in certain sports, such as running (Schomer, 1986) and golf (Boutcher & Rotella, 1987).

Physiological/Biological Measures of Attention

Although attention is a psychological construct, it nevertheless follows that it must have biological, especially neurophysiological, underpinnings. To ignore such underpinnings or to fail to address the essential biological nature of all psychological phenomena would be a major inadequacy in theory and method development. Nevertheless, this is an inadequacy that has been identified within sport and exercise psychology (e.g., Dishman, 1991). A considerable literature now exists on the psychobiology of attention (see Näätänen, 1992, for an excellent recent review), yet the methods used to develop this knowledge base have, disappointingly, had only limited impact on research within sport and exercise psychology.

Physiological Measures of Attentional Capacity and Workload

A wide variety of psychophysiological measures have been used to examine the overall mental workload of cognitive tasks plus fluctuations in attentional demand across the time course of such tasks. Pupil diameter, cardiac acceleration/deceleration and variability, and event-related potential measures from the electroencephalogram (EEG) and the magnetoencephalogram (MEG) have all been used on different occasions to measure the overall magnitude of, and temporal variations in, attentional workload.

Applications within sport and exercise psychology. Although psychophysiological measures of attentional workload have been widely used in the study of cognitive tasks, these methods have been applied much less broadly to the study of sport and exercise. The principal reason for this is the confounding effects of physical activity on many of the physiological parameters used to assess attention. Further, the constraining nature of much of the physiological recording apparatus restricts application to only that limited subset of sport tasks that involve a minimum of gross motor activity. As a consequence, the existing sport studies of attention using psychophysiological measures are effectively restricted to description of the attentional changes that occur throughout the preparatory phases of primarily static activities, such as rifle shooting (e.g., Hatfield, Landers, & Ray, 1984, 1987), archery (e.g., Salazar, Landers, Petruzzello, Crews, & Kubitz, 1988; Salazar et al., 1990), and golf putting (e.g., Boutcher & Zinsser,

1990; Crews, 1989; Molander & Backman, 1989). These studies have revealed identifiable patterns of heart rate deceleration and suppression of left hemisphere activity in the last few seconds preceding self-initiated movement, with such patterns apparently being modifiable with training.

Basic rationale and assumptions. An individual's level of activation or arousal is directly determined by the balance of sympathetic and parasympathetic activity within the autonomic nervous system. Sympathetic activity acts to increase arousal or activation and does so by inducing a host of measurable physiological changes, including pupil dilation; heart rate, blood pressure, and respiratory rate elevation; and increased sweat production and cortical activity. Parasympathetic activity reverses these effects. As activation levels either locally or more globally may be indicative of elevated workload demands, the measurement of the state of the various physiological systems affected by the autonomic nervous system provides one means of attempting to determine in continuous, quantitative terms the extent and timing of underlying attentional activity. The common assumption for this family of psychophysiological measures is that these peripheral measurements of physiological state are reliably indicative of central attentional processes. As a general rule, this assumption appears reasonable with respect to overall measures of attentional workload but, given the variable time periods taken for peripheral systems to respond to autonomic stimulation, more tenuous with respect to evaluating the time course of any changes in attentional demand (Näätänen, 1992).

Pupil dilation occurs in response to sympathetic stimulation; consequently, the measurement of pupil diameter has been a popular psychophysiological method to investigate attentional changes throughout a variety of cognitive tasks. In such tasks, pupil diameter appears to be quite linearly related to task difficulty and therefore presumably total information-processing load (Beatty & Wagoner, 1978; Kahneman & Beatty, 1967). Less is known about the latencies between central attentional demands and the appearance of concomitant pupillary responses. Pupillometry has been used little, if at all, in studies attempting to examine attentional processes in sport.

Changes in heart rate, as opposed to absolute heart rates, have been suggested by some (e.g., J. I. Lacey, 1967) as being informative with respect to attentional processes. Jennings, Lawrence, and Kasper (1978) have suggested that cardiac acceleration/deceleration, assessed from relative changes in interbeat interval, is systematically related to available processing capacity (as determined from dual-task methods). Heart rate acceleration is prevalent in situations where task requirements exceed available processing capacity whereas heart rate deceleration accompanies situations in which there is spare attentional capacity. Heart rate *variability* appears to decrease as the attentional demands of a task are increased (Mulder & Mulder, 1981; Vincente, Thornton, & Moray, 1987) making it an increasingly popular tool for the measurement of mental workload in ergonomic settings (Meshkati, 1988). The measure appears to reflect total processing load, yet like many of the other measures, it has yet to be applied to the measurement of attention in sport or exercise situations.

The electroencephalogram (EEG) provides a measure of the electrical activity of the brain; an attempt is then made to match identifiable and repeatable characteristics within the pattern of electrical activity to underlying brain activity and information processing. EEG recordings over the scalp reveal spontaneous patterns of electrical activity consisting of signals of a range of different frequencies, each associated with a different behavioral state. Suppression of electrical signals in the 8 to 13 Hz range (the so-called *alpha waves*) is reliably indicative of increased levels of activation; comparison of alpha wave suppression between the two cerebral hemispheres provides a measure of relative involvement of each hemisphere in the processing demands posed by any particular task (Collins, Powell, & Davies, 1990; Hatfield, et al., 1984). In a range of sport tasks, activation of the left hemisphere appears to decrease whereas right hemisphere activity remains unchanged in the period immediately preceding movement execution, possibly suggesting a preferential use of the superior visual-spatial processing capabilities of the right hemisphere for response preparation (Hatfield et al., 1984, 1987; Salazar et al., 1988; Salazar et al., 1990). Both the hemispheric asymmetries and the associated cardiac deceleration that accompany movement preparation appear to be learned psychophysiological patterns, being modifiable with practice (Landers et al., 1994).

In addition to the spontaneous waveforms evident within the EEG patterns, there is also considerable interest in isolating other, smaller voltage, changes in the EEG, the appearance of which are directly related to the presence (or absence) of specific sensory events. These so-called *event-related potentials* (or ERPs) are small in amplitude, and their presence is revealed only through sophisticated averaging techniques that remove the background spontaneous EEG activity. The amplitude and time of occurrence of some of the identifiable positive peaks or negative troughs within particular ERPs have been linked to various aspects of attention (see Donchin, 1979, 1984; Hillyard, 1984; or Näätänen, 1988a for reviews). Of particular interest has been the P300 component, a positive polarity component of ERPs occurring around 300 msec following stimulus onset. The precise latency of the P300 component appears to be related to memory load imposed by the primary task whereas its amplitude appears indicative of overall processing demand. The P300 amplitude is inversely proportional to secondary task demand in dual-task settings (Israel, Wickens, Chesney, & Donchin, 1980; Kramer & Strayer, 1988).

A relatively recent improvement to psychophysiological measurement of brain activity has occurred with the development of the magnetoencephalogram (MEG). The MEG, through recording magnetic fields rather than electric fields, provides for a more accurate localization of the source of particular signals and for greater disambiguation of signals arising from the cerebral cortices from those arising from other sources. The data derived from the MEG are complementary to those derived from the study of ERPs within the EEG (Kaufman & Williamson, 1982), and the two methods collectively have the potential to further advance understanding of brain mechanisms of attention. The MEG technique is quite new and yet to be used to any extent to examine attentional issues in sport and exercise despite potential for eventual use in this field.

Strengths and weaknesses. The peripheral physiological measures of nervous system activity, such as pupillometry and the cardiovascular measures, have a number of shortcomings that limit their direct individual utility as measures of attentional workload. The major shortcomings of such measures of attention are, according to Näätänen (1992, pp. 74-75), that the responses recorded are:

1. Too slow or late

    The variable time delay between central attentional peaks and the appearance of associated change in the peripheral indicators makes the precise temporal mapping of attentional variations across the duration of a task problematic.

2. Too remote from the processes that are of primary interest

    Attentional processes are presumably central whereas these measures are peripheral.

3. Too stimulus- and task-nonspecific, at least when a single measure is concerned

4. Too nonspecific with regard to different processing stages, and

5. Too closely associated with activational or energetical (energy mobilization) bodily events and emotions.

This is a particular concern where physical activity is an integral part of the attentional task under examination.

There is also a nontrivial difficulty associated with the low levels of concordance between the different peripheral physiological measures of attention, posing the researcher with the issue of which measure or combination of measures to select to extract a valid, reliable, and objective indication of attentional workload.

Some of the difficulties with peripheral psychophysiological measures can be alleviated, at least partially, through the use of more direct measures of brain activity, such as the EEG and MEG. Although such approaches still present difficulties with respect to precise localization of the neural origins of specific EEG and MEG patterns, measures such as the P300 have important advantages over most others in being sensitively graded to perceptual and cognitive load and being of potential diagnostic value in the identification of specific resource limitations (Wickens, 1984). The use of these methods by sport and exercise psychologists is nevertheless likely to remain limited because of the cost and physical constraints imposed by the recording apparatus and, particularly, by the inability to use and interpret such measures unambiguously when there is any significant movement component within the task.

Physiological Measures of Attentional Selectivity

In addition to the cardiac acceleration/deceleration, ERP, and MEG measures already discussed with respect to attentional capacity and workload, selective attention has also been examined through the recording of eye movements and measurement of regional cerebral blood flow and metabolism.

Areas of application within sport and exercise psychology. The recording of the eye movements of sports performers has been an increasingly common pursuit by sport and exercise psychologists for the past two decades (since Bard & Fleury, 1976). Analyses of visual search patterns (the patterns of ocular fixations on objects or features within the surrounding display) have been used in sport tasks in an attempt both to determine the location of critical sources of visual information in specific sports and to examine the nature of expert-novice differences in visual search behavior and strategy. Arguments have been presented for differences in the location, sequence, and rate of visual fixations of expert performers compared to those of novices, but the evidence is far from compelling (Abernethy, 1988b). Although expert-novice differences are often reported in visual search (e.g., Ripoll, Papin, Guezennec, Verdy, & Philip, 1985; Vickers, 1992; Williams, Davids, Burwitz, & Williams, 1994), such differences are neither necessary nor sufficient for expert-novice differences in information pickup (Abernethy, 1990b; Abernethy & Russell, 1987b; Helsen & Pauwels, 1993). Other potential psychophysiological/biological indicators of selective attention, such as cardiac deceleration/acceleration, ERPs, and MEG, and the various measures of regional blood flow and metabolism have, thus far, been restricted almost entirely in their application to cognitive tasks with only minimal physical activity components.

Basic rationale and assumptions. The recording of eye movements is intuitively appealing as a means of extracting some information, albeit indirect, of visual selective attention. As the direction of gaze is constantly changed in order to permit reflected light from objects of interest to be focussed upon the fovea (optimizing visual resolution of the object being viewed) and as the active pickup of information is primarily restricted to *fixations* (periods when the eye is essentially stationary and the direction of gaze is unchanged), measurement of the location, order, and sequence of ocular fixations has been assumed to provide meaningful information regarding the attentional selectivity of subjects. It is commonly assumed that those items assigned greatest importance for selective attention attract the greatest number of fixations or the longest period of fixation whereas unattended items attract few, if any, fixations. Similarly, for static displays, areas of greatest pertinence are assumed to attract more fixations early in the search sequence whereas for dynamic displays the sequence of fixations is assumed to reflect meaningfully the changing patterns of information availability as it emerges throughout the stimulus sequence. As fixations are primarily active periods available for information pickup and saccades (the typical movement carrying the eye from one fixation to another) are not, an assumption is also occasionally made that lower search rates (i.e., fewer fixations per unit time) are indicative of more efficient information processing. All of these assumptions may hold under some conditions but equally are demonstrably untenable in other circumstances (Abernethy, 1985, 1988b).

Cardiac acceleration/deceleration measures, as was noted earlier, provide one possible measure of attentional workload. These same measures may also reflect, to some degree, on attentional selectivity. Heart rate deceleration, unrelated to respiration, is systematically present in the last 2 to 7 seconds of preparation prior to stimulus onset in reaction time tasks (B.C. Lacey & Lacey, 1970; Stern, 1976) or movement initiation in self-paced activities such as golf putting (Boutcher & Zinsser, 1990; Molander & Backman, 1989). The intake-rejection hypothesis of J.I. Lacey (1967) proposes that deceleration accompanies the intake of environmental information whereas acceleration occurs where the focus is more on internal processes.

Even if such an assumption holds true, this measure is restricted to simply differentiating internal from external attentional foci and is of limited assistance in determining, within these broad orientations, the specific stimuli to which the subject is attending. The repeated and controlled presentation of specific visual stimuli may allow determination of whether or not attention is being selectively allocated to the stimulus feature if EEG recordings are taken. Both the P1 and N1 components of the visual ERPs appear to be enhanced if attention is provided to the viewed pattern or feature (Hillyard, Münte, & Neville, 1985), although these stimuli are typically much less complex and dynamic than are those encountered in sport settings. Distinct MEG effects of visual attention to spatially separated targets have also been reported at latencies comparable to these ERP effects (Aine, George, Oakley, Medvick, & Flynn, 1990).

Neural activity in the brain can be indirectly measured by monitoring changes in cerebral metabolic rate and blood flow (Näätänen, 1992), the assumption being that blood flow per unit time increases to meet the metabolic requirements of neurally active tissues involved in information processing. Importantly, changes in cerebral blood flow occur with short latency following neural activity and are spatially confined to only the local region of the neural activity. Regional blood flow and metabolism can be measured through a number of different measures. Cerebral blood flow can be measured invasively through the use of intracarotid monitors of the clearance rates of radioactive tracer substances (e.g., Roland, 1982) or indirectly through the inhalation of small amounts of 133-Xenon (e.g., Obrist, Thompson, Wang, & Wilkinson, 1975). Such methods provide good spatial resolution of cortical activity but poor temporal resolution. They may provide a valuable complement to ERP and MEG methodologies (Näätänen, 1988b).

The advent of advanced imaging techniques such as PET (Positron Emission Tomography) has made it possible to now perform direct, high spatial resolution measurements of blood flow and metabolism from all regions of the brain regardless of their distance from the cortical surface (Roland & Widen, 1988) although the cost of such methodology still remains prohibitive. Another relatively new technique, functional magnetic resonance imaging (MRI), offers the potential to enhance not only the spatial but also the temporal resolution of brain imaging, providing an even more direct indicator of brain activity (Belliveau et al., 1991). Collectively these advanced techniques for the measurement of regional blood flow and metabolism have already proven valuable in understanding more about the task-dependent brain activity accompanying conscious attention to different types of stimuli (Näätänen, 1992); they will likely provide far less, however, in terms of determining where or to what a subject's limited attentional capacity is selectively directed within a complex stimulus set of the type typically encountered in sport settings.

Strengths and weaknesses. The great strength of eye-movement recording is that it provides a very tangible means of observing changes in the visual orientation of subjects to different features or events within the display. The major drawback with such approaches is that although visual orientation may in some cases be indicative of selective attention, the two are by no means synonymous. It is possible, for instance, to move at-

tention around the visual field without making any eye movements (Posner, 1980; Remington, 1980; Shulman, Remington, & McLean, 1979) whereas, equally, visual orientation to a particular region of the visual field in no way guarantees information pickup from that area (Stager & Angus, 1978). A particularly important limitation of eye-movement-recording measures in this regard is that they only provide information about the direction of central visual gaze and reveal nothing about the concurrent attentional processes and information pickup occurring in peripheral vision. Information pickup through peripheral vision has long been proposed to play an integral part in skilled sports performance (Holson & Henderson, 1941), but valid and reliable means of measuring peripheral information processing are not yet available. An additional difficulty with the use of eye movement data is that visual search patterns typically show not only tremendous individual differences (even between athletes of comparable skill level) but also substantial trial-to-trial variability even for the same individual. This makes generalizable, repeatable conclusions about selective attention very difficult (Abernethy, 1988b).

The other psychophysiological/biological approaches to the measurement of attentional selectivity described in the preceding section are mainly relatively new technologies and have received little or no application to attentional issues in sport and exercise. Although it is therefore difficult at this time to make definitive judgements on the respective strengths of these measures, the principal weaknesses of these approaches are the same major weaknesses as were observed for many of the psychophysiological/biological measures of attentional capacity and workload, namely, (a) cost and access to the recording and analytical technology, (b) the limitations on subject movement imposed by both the physical structure and requirements of the recording apparatus, and (c) the potential confounds created by physical exertion interacting with the variables of interest.

Concluding Remarks

To date, the predominant approach to the measurement of attention in sport and exercise psychology has been the use of unitary measures drawn from a single level of analysis. In the majority of cases, these measures have been drawn from the cognitive level of analysis and are primarily self-report in nature. Sport and exercise psychologists studying the complex, multidimensional phenomena of attention have arguably been shackled for too long to an unnecessarily narrow range of measures. It would appear, in reviewing our state of understanding of attentional phenomena in sport, that measures of attention have often been chosen more in terms of their availability, ease of administration, and prior use by other researchers, than for their compatibility to the phenomena. Sport and exercise psychologists, like all other scientists, must select and use methods that fit the question of importance rather than find questions to suit the methods available.

As we have seen in the preceding sections, there is now a range of measures drawn from different levels of analysis that are available to measure aspects of attention although each, taken in isolation, has significant limitations. These limitations are maximal when measures are drawn from a single level of analysis but may be reduced considerably when measures from one level of analysis are combined with and/or complemented by concurrent measures drawn from other levels of analysis. In this regard, there is a clear need for sport and exercise psychologists to follow the approach increasingly adopted both by other subdisciplines of sport and exercise science (Dishman, 1991; Stelmach, 1987) and by those psychologists studying attentional phenomena in purely cognitive tasks (e.g., Cowen, 1995; McLeod & Driver, 1993) and use multiple levels of analysis (behavioral and physiological as well as cognitive) to study and develop multilevel models of attentional phenomena in sport and exercise. The use of multiple levels of analysis is not just to improve measurement accuracy but to push theorizing toward the critical, but largely ignored and certainly unresolved, issues about the interplay between neural biology, thoughts (cognition), and actions (behavior).

It is increasingly apparent from the study of other psychological phenomena, both intrapersonal (e.g., Marr, 1982) and extrapersonal (e.g., Cacioppo, Berntson, & Crites, 1996), that reductionism and the use of single levels of analysis are inadequate for developing comprehensive understanding of complex psychological phenomena. As Cacioppo et al. (1996) note:

> The predictable yield from isolated research on discrete determinants of multiply determined ... psychological phenomena is a portfolio of fact lists and disparate microtheories. These microtheories each provide a limited account of the phenomenon of interest and are at best pieces of a larger conceptual puzzle. (p. 74)

This synopsis is certainly apt with respect to the phenomena of attention, and a strong case can be built for the necessity of multilevel analyses to overcome the constraints imposed by single-level analyses in psychological research.

To this end Cacioppo and Berntson (1992) have proposed a doctrine of multilevel analysis for the study of complex psychological phenomena. Their doctrine is based on three principles, all of which ring true for the study of attention. The first of these (*the principle of multiple determinism*) posits that a target event (such as selective attention to a particular stimulus event) may have multiple antecedents within or across levels of organization. A corollary to this (*the corollary of proximity*) is that the mapping between elements across different levels of organization becomes more complex as the number of intervening levels increases. The second principle (that of *nonadditive determinism*) is that properties of the collective whole are not always predictable from the properties of the component parts, at least until the properties of the whole have been clearly documented and studied across levels. This is arguably the strongest reason for studying systemwide collective behavior in favour of component reductionism. The third principle (*the principle of reciprocal determinism*) is that there can be mutual influences between microscopic and macroscopic factors in determining brain and behavioral processes. Although unitary levels of analysis still clearly have an important role to play in providing detail, consideration of all of these principles leads to the inevitable conclusion that comprehensive understanding of attentional phenomena will require integrative, multilevel measurement approaches.

Whatever level or levels of analysis are ultimately chosen to measure and study attention, it is imperative that researchers clearly consider what is known of the strengths and weaknesses and basic rationale and assumptions of the measure(s) they use. Only through such consideration will it be possible to extract meaningful data and advance both theoretical and practical understanding of the many aspects of attention of central significance to sport and exercise psychology.

References

Abernethy, B. (1985). Cue usage in 'open' motor skills: A review of the available procedures. In D.G. Russell & B. Abernethy (Eds.), *Motor memory and control: The Otago symposium* (pp. 110-122). Dunedin, New Zealand: Human Performance Associates.

Abernethy, B. (1988a). Dual-task methodology and motor skills research: Some applications and methodological constraints. *Journal of Human Movement Studies, 14*, 101-132.

Abernethy, B. (1988b). Visual search in sport and ergonomics: Its relationship to selective attention and performer expertise. *Human Performance, 1*, 205-235.

Abernethy, B. (1989). Expert-novice differences in perception: How expert does the expert have to be? *Canadian Journal of Sport Sciences, 14*, 27-30.

Abernethy, B. (1990a). Anticipation in squash: Differences in advance cue utilisation between expert and novice players. *Journal of Sport Sciences, 8*, 17-34.

Abernethy, B. (1990b). Expertise, visual search, and information pick-up in squash. *Perception, 19*, 63-77.

Abernethy, B. (1993). Attention. In R.N. Singer, M. Murphey, & L.K. Tennant (Eds.) *Handbook of research on sport psychology* (pp. 127-170). New York: Macmillan.

Abernethy, B., Burgess-Limerick, R., & Parks, S. (1994). Contrasting approaches to the study of motor expertise. *Quest, 46*, 186-198.

Abernethy, B., & Russell, D.G. (1987a). Expert-novice differences in an applied selective attention task. *Journal of Sport Psychology, 9*, 326-345.

Abernethy, B., & Russell, D.G. (1987b). The relationship between expertise and visual search strategy in a racquet sport. *Human Movement Science, 6*, 283-319.

Aine, C.J., George, J.S., Oakley, M.T., Medvick, P.A., & Flynn, E.R. (1990). Effects of spatial attention on visual-evoked neuromagnetic responses. In C.H.M. Brunia, A.W.K. Gaillard, & A. Kok (Eds.), *Psychophysiological brain research: Vol. 1* (pp. 3-11). Tilburg, Netherlands: Tilburg University Press.

Albrecht, R.R., & Feltz, D.L. (1987). Generality and specificity of attention related to competitive anxiety and sport performance. *Journal of Sport Psychology, 9*, 231-248.

Allport, D.A. (1980). Attention and performance. In G. Claxton (Ed.), *New directions in cognitive psychology* (pp. 112-153). London: Routledge & Kegan Paul.

Bard, C., & Fleury, M. (1976). Analysis of visual search activity in sport problem situations. *Journal of Human Movement Studies, 3*, 214-222.

Beatty, J., & Wagoner, B.L. (1978). Pupillometric signs of brain activation vary with level of cognitive processing. *Science, 199*, 1216-1218.

Belliveau, J.W., Kennedy, D.N., McKinstry, R.C., Buchbinder, B.R., Weisskoff, R.M., Cohen, M.S., Vevea, J.M., Brady, T.J., & Rosen, B.R. (1991). Functional mapping of the human visual cortex by magnetic resonance imaging. *Science, 254*, 716-719.

Bentler, P.M., & Bonnett, D.G. (1980). Significance tests and goodness of fit in the analysis of covariance structures. *Psychological Bulletin, 88*, 588-606.

Bergandi, T.A., Shryock, M.G., & Titus, T.G. (1990). The Basketball Concentration Survey: Preliminary development and validation. *The Sport Psychologist, 4*, 119-129.

Bernstein, N. (1967). *The co-ordination and regulation of movements*. Oxford: Pergamon.

Berry, D.C., & Broadbent, D.E. (1984). On the relationship between task performance and associated verbalisable knowledge. *Quarterly Journal of Experimental Psychology, 36*, 209-231.

Bond, J. & Sargent, G. (1995). Concentration skills in sport: An applied perspective. In T. Morris, & J.J. Summers (Eds.), *Sport psychology: Theory, applications and issues* (pp. 386-419). Brisbane: Wiley.

Boring, E.G. (1970). Attention: Research and beliefs concerning the concept in scientific psychology before 1930. In D.I. Mostofsky (Ed.), *Attention: Contemporary theory and analysis*. New York: Appleton-Century-Crofts.

Boutcher, S.H. (1992). Attention and athletic performance: An integrated approach. In T.S. Horn (Ed.), *Advances in sport psychology* (pp. 251-265). Champaign, IL: Human Kinetics.

Boutcher, S.H., & Rotella, R.J. (1987). A psychological skills educational program for closed-skill performance enhancement. *The Sport Psychologist, 1*, 127-137.

Boutcher, S.H., & Zinsser, N.W. (1990). Cardiac deceleration of elite and beginning golfers during putting. *Journal of Sport and Exercise Psychology, 12*, 37-47.

Broadbent, D.E. (1958). *Perception and communication*. New York: Pergamon.

Brown, I.D. (1978). Dual task methods of assessing work-load. *Ergonomics, 21*, 221-224.

Burgess-Limerick, R.J., Abernethy, B., & Limerick, B. (1994). Identification of underlying assumptions is an integral part of research: An example from motor control. *Theory & Psychology, 4*, 139-146.

Cacioppo, J.T., & Berntson, G.G. (1992). Social psychological contributions to the decade of the brain: Doctrine of multilevel analysis. *American Psychologist, 47*, 1019-1028.

Cacioppo, J.T., Berntson, G.G., & Crites, S.L., Jr. (1996). Social neuroscience: Principles of psychophysiological arousal and response. In A.T. Higgins & A.W. Kruglanski (Eds.), *Social psychology: Handbook of basic principles* (pp. 72-101). New York: Guilford Press.

Carello, C., Turvey, M.T., Kugler, P.N., & Shaw, R.E. (1984) Inadequacies in the computer metaphor. In M. Gazzaniga (Ed.), *Handbook of cognitive neuroscience* (pp. 229-248). New York: Plenum.

Casali, J.G., & Wierwille, W.W. (1983). A comparison of rating scale, secondary task, physiological, and primary task workload estimation techniques in a simulated flight task emphasizing communications load. *Human Factors, 25*, 623-641.

Cherry, E.C. (1953). Some experiments on the recognition of speech, with one and with two ears. *Journal of the Acoustical Society of America, 25*, 975-979.

Collins, D., Powell, G., & Davies, I. (1990). An electroencephalographic study of hemispheric processing patterns during karate performance. *Journal of Sport and Exercise Psychology, 12*, 223-234.

Cowen, N. (1995). *Attention and memory: An integrated framework*. New York: Oxford University Press.

Cox, R.H. (1994). *Sport psychology: Concepts and applications*. Madison, WI: Brown & Benchmark.

Craik, K.J.W. (1947). Theory of the human operator in control systems I. The operator as an engineering system. *British Journal of Psychology, 38*, 56-61.

Craik, K.J.W. (1948). Theory of the human operator in control systems II. Man as an element in a control system. *British Journal of Psychology, 38*, 142-148.

Crews, D.L. (1989). *The influence of attentive states on golf putting as indicated by cardiac and electrocortical activity*. Unpublished doctoral dissertation, Arizona State University, Tempe.

Cuttance, P. (1987). Issues and problems in the application of structural equation models. In P. Cuttance & R. Ecob (Eds.), *Structural modeling by example: Applications in educational, sociological and behavioural research* (pp. 241-279). New York: Cambridge University Press.

Dishman, R.K. (1991). The failure of sport psychology in the exercise and sport sciences. In R.J. Park & H.M. Eckert (Eds.), *New possibilities, new paradigms? American Academy of Physical Education Papers, No. 24* (pp. 39-47). Champaign, IL: Human Kinetics.

Donchin, E. (1979). Event-related brain potentials: A tool in the study of human information-processing. In H. Begleiter (Ed.), *Evoked potentials and behavior* (pp. 13-75). New York: Plenum Press.

Donchin, E. (1984). Dissociation between electrophysiology and behavior - A disaster or a challenge? In E. Donchin (Ed.), *Cognitive psychophysiology: Event-related potentials and the study of cognition* (pp. 107-118). Hillsdale, NJ: Erlbaum.

Easterbrook, J.A. (1959). The effect of emotion on cue utilization and the organization of behavior. *Psychological Review, 66*, 183-201.

Etzel, E.F. (1979). Validation of a conceptual model characterising attention among international rifle shooters. *Journal of Sport Psychology, 1*, 281-290.

Eysenck, M.W. (1984). *A handbook of cognitive psychology*. London: Erlbaum.

Fischman, M., & Schneider, T. (1985). Skill level, vision and proprioception in simple catching. *Journal of Motor Behavior, 17*, 219-229.

Fitch, H.L., & Turvey, M.T. (1978). On the control of activity: Some remarks from an ecological point of view. In D.M. Landers & R.W. Christina (Eds.), *Psychology of Motor Behavior and Sport - 1977* (pp. 3-35). Champaign, IL: Human Kinetics.

Flach, J.M., Lintern, G., & Larish, J.F. (1990). Perceptual-motor skill: A theoretical framework. In R. Warren & A.H. Wertheim (Eds.), *Perception and control of self-motion* (pp. 327-355). Hillsdale, NJ: Erlbaum.

Fogarty, G.J. (1995). Some comments on the use of psychological tests in sport settings. *International Journal of Sport Psychology, 26*, 161-170.

Ford, S.K. (1996). *Measuring attention in sport*. Unpublished doctoral dissertation, University of Melbourne, Parkville, Victoria.

Ford, S.K., & Summers, J.J. (1992). The factorial validity of the TAIS attentional-style subscales. *Journal of Sport & Exercise Psychology, 14*, 283-297.

Fowler, C.A., & Turvey, M.T. (1978). Skill acquisition: An event approach with special reference to searching for the optimum of a function of several variables. In G.E. Stelmach (Ed.), *Information processing in motor control and learning* (pp.1-40). New York: Academic Press.

Gibson, E.J. (1969). *Principles of perceptual learning and development*. New York: Appleton-Century-Crofts.

Gibson, J.J. (1979). *An ecological approach to visual perception*. Boston, MA: Houghton-Mifflin.

Girouard, Y., Laurencelle, L., & Proteau, L. (1984). On the nature of the probe reaction-time to uncover the attentional demands of movement. *Journal of Motor Behavior, 16*, 442-459.

Glencross, D.J. (1978). Control and capacity in the study of skill. In D.J. Glencross (Ed.), *Psychology and sport* (pp. 72-96). Sydney: McGraw Hill.

Gopher, D., & Donchin, E. (1986). Workload: An examination of the concept. In K. Boff, L. Kauffman, & J.P. Thomas (Eds.), *Handbook of perception and human performance* (pp. 41.1 - 41.49). New York: Wiley.

Hamilton, W. (1859). *Lectures on metaphysics and logic*. Edinburgh: Blackwood.

Hart, S.G., & Staveland, L.E. (1988). Development of NASA-TLX (Task Load Index): Results of empirical and theoretical research. In P.A. Hancock & N. Meshkati (Eds.), *Human mental workload* (pp. 139-183). Amsterdam: North Holland.

Hatfield, B.D., Landers, D.M., & Ray, W.J. (1984). Cognitive processes during self-paced motor performance: An electroencephalographic profile of skilled marksmen. *Journal of Sport Psychology, 6,* 42-59.

Hatfield, B.D., Landers, D.M., & Ray, W.J. (1987). Cardiovascular-CNS interactions during a self-paced, intentional state: Elite marksmanship performance. *Psychophysiology, 24,* 542-549.

Helsen, W., & Pauwels, J.M. (1993). The relationship between expertise and visual information processing in sport. In J.L. Starkes & F. Allard (Eds.), *Cognitive issues in motor expertise* (pp. 109-134). Amsterdam: Elsevier.

Heuer, H., & Wing, A.M. (1984). Doing two things at once: Process limitations and interactions. In M.M. Smyth & A.M. Wing (Eds.), *The psychology of human movement* (pp. 183-213). London: Academic Press.

Hillyard, S.A. (1984). Event-related potentials and selective attention. In E. Donchin (Ed.), *Cognitive psychophysiology: Event-related potentials and the study of cognition* (pp. 51-72). Hillsdale, NJ: Erlbaum.

Hillyard, S.A., Münte, T.F., & Neville, H.J. (1985). Visual-spatial attention, orienting and brain physiology. In M.I. Posner & O.S.M. Marin (Eds.), *Attention and performance XI* (pp. 63-84). Hillsdale, NJ: Erlbaum.

Holson, R., & Henderson, M.T. (1941). A preliminary study of visual fields in athletes. *Iowa Academy of Science, 48,* 331-337.

Israel, J.B., Wickens, C.D., Chesney, G.L., & Donchin, E. (1980). The event-related brain potential as an index of display monitoring workload. *Human Factors, 22,* 211-224.

James, W. (1890). *Principles of psychology.* New York: Holt.

Jennings, J.R., Lawrence, B.E., & Kasper, P. (1978). Changes in alertness and processing capacity in a serial learning task. *Memory and Cognition, 6,* 43-53.

Kahneman, D. (1973). *Attention and effort.* Englewood Cliffs, NJ: Prentice-Hall.

Kahneman, D., & Beatty, J. (1967). Pupillary response in a pitch-discrimination task. *Perception and Psychophysics, 2,* 101-105.

Kaufman, L., & Williamson, S.J. (1982). Magnetic location of cortical activity. In I. Bodis-Wollner (Ed.), *Evoked potentials: Annals of the New York Academy of Sciences: Vol. 388,* (pp. 197-213). NY: The New York Academy of Sciences.

Keele, S.W. (1973). *Attention and human performance.* Pacific Palisades, CA: Goodyear Publishing.

Kelso, J.A.S. (1986). Pattern formation in multi-degree of freedom speech and limb movements. *Experimental Brain Research Supplement, 15,* 105-128.

Kramer, A.F., & Strayer, D.L. (1988). Assessing the development of automatic processing: An application of dual-task and event-related brain potential methodologies. *Biological Psychology, 26,* 231-267.

Kugler, P.N., Shaw, R.E., Vicente, K.J., & Kinsella-Shaw, J. (1990). Inquiry into intentional systems. I: Issues in ecological physics. *Report No. 30/1990, Research Group on Mind and Brain, Perspectives in Theoretical Physics and the Philosophy of Mind (ZiF),* University of Bielefeld.

Lacey, B.C., & Lacey, J.I. (1970). Some autonomic-central nervous system interrelationships. In P. Block (Ed.), *Physiological correlates of emotion* (pp. 50-83). New York: Academic Press.

Lacey, J.I. (1967). Somatic response patterning and stress: Some revision of activation theory. In M.H. Appley & R. Trumbull (Eds.), *Psychological stress: Issues in research* (pp. 170-179). New York: Appleton-Century-Crofts.

Landers, D.M., Han, N., Salazar, W., Petruzzello, S.J., Kubitz, K.A., & Gannon, T.L. (1994). Effects of learning on electroencephalographic patterns in novice archers. *International Journal of Sport Psychology, 25,* 313-330.

Landers, D.M., Wang, M.Q., & Courtet, P. (1985). Peripheral narrowing among experienced and inexperienced rifle shooters under low- and high-time stress conditions. *Research Quarterly for Exercise and Sport, 56,* 122-130.

Leavitt, J.L. (1979). Cognitive demands of skating and stick handling in ice hockey. *Canadian Journal of Applied Sport Sciences, 4,* 46-55.

Logan, G.D. (1985). Skill and automaticity: Relations, implications, and future directions. *Canadian Journal of Psychology, 39,* 367-386.

Lombardo, T.J. (1987). *The reciprocity of perceiver and environment: The evolution of James J. Gibson's ecological psychology.* Hillsdale, NJ: Erlbaum.

Marr, D. (1982). *Vision: A computational investigation into the human representation and processing of visual information.* San Francisco: Freeman.

Maynard, I.W., & Howe, B.L. (1989). Attentional style in rugby players. *Perceptual and Motor Skills, 69,* 283-289.

McLeod, P. (1978). Does probe RT measure central processing demand? *Quarterly Journal of Experimental Psychology, 30,* 83-89.

McLeod, P. (1980). What can probe RT tell us about the attentional demands of movement? In G.E. Stelmach & J. Requin (Eds.), *Tutorials in motor behavior* (pp. 579-589). Amsterdam: North-Holland.

McLeod, P., & Driver, J. (1993). Filtering and physiology in visual search: A convergence of behavioural and neurophysiological measures. In A. Baddeley & L. Weiskrantz (Eds.), *Attention: Selection, awareness, and control* (pp. 72-86). Oxford: Clarendon Press.

Meshkati, N. (1988). Heart rate variability and mental workload assessment. In P.A. Hancock & N. Meshkati (Eds.), *Human mental workload* (pp. 101-115). Amsterdam: North-Holland.

Michaels, C., & Beek, P. (in press). The state of ecological psychology. *Ecological Psychology.*

Milgram, P. (1987). A spectacle-mounted liquid-crystal tachistoscope. *Behavior Research Methods, Instruments, & Computers, 19,* 449-456.

Molander, B., & Backman, L. (1989). Age differences in heart rate patterns during concentration in a precision sport: Implications for attentional functioning. *Journal of Gerontology: Psychological Sciences, 44,* 80-87.

Moran, A.P. (1996). *The psychology of concentration in sports performers: A cognitive analysis.* Hove, East Sussex: Psychology Press.

Moray, N. (1959). Attention in dichotic listening: Affective cues and the influence of instructions. *Quarterly Journal of Experimental Psychology, 11,* 59-60.

Moray, N. (1967). Where is attention limited? A survey and a model. *Acta Psychologica, 27,* 84-92.

Moray, N. (1969). *Listening and attention.* Baltimore: Penguin.

Moray, N. (1970). *Attention: Selective processes in vision and hearing.* New York: Academic Press.

Moray, N., Johansen, J., Pew, R.W., Rasmussen, J., Sanders, A.F., & Wickens, C.D. (1979). Report of the experimental psychology group. In N. Moray (Ed.), *Mental workload: Its theory and measurement.* New York: Plenum.

Morris, T., & Summers, J.J. (Eds.). (1995). *Sport psychology: Theory, applications and current issues.* Brisbane: Wiley.

Mulder, G., & Mulder, L.J.M. (1981). Information processing and cardiovascular control. *Psychophysiology, 18,* 392-401.

Näätänen, R. (1988a). Implications of ERP data for psychological theories of attention. *Biological Psychology, 26,* 117-163.

Näätänen, R. (1988b). Regional cerebral blood-flow studies supplementing information provided by event-related potentials on the brain mechanisms of selective attention. In G. Galbraith, E. Donchin, & M. Kietzman (Eds.), *Neurophysiology and psychology: Basic mechanisms and clinical applications* (pp. 144-156). Hillsdale, NJ: Erlbaum.

Näätänen, R. (1992). *Attention and brain function*. Hillsdale, NJ: Erlbaum.

Navon, D., & Gopher, D. (1979). On the economy of the human processing system. *Psychological Review, 86*, 214-255.

Neisser, U., & Becklen, R. (1975). Selective looking: Attending to visually specified events. *Cognitive Psychology, 7*, 480-494.

Neumann, O. (1987). Beyond capacity: A functional view of attention. In H. Heuer & A.F. Sanders (Eds.), *Perspectives on perception and action* (pp. 361-394). Hillsdale, NJ: Erlbaum.

Nideffer, R.M. (1976). The Test of Attentional and Interpersonal Style. *Journal of Personality and Social Psychology, 34*, 394-404.

Nideffer, R.M. (1981). *The ethics and practice of applied sport psychology*. Ithaca, NY: Mouvement Publications.

Nideffer, R.M. (1987). Issues in the use of psychological tests in applied settings. *The Sport Psychologist, 1*, 18-28.

Nideffer, R. M. (1990). Use of the Test of Attentional and Interpersonal Style (TAIS) in sport. *The Sport Psychologist, 4*, 285-300.

Nisbett, R.E., & Wilson, T.D. (1977). Telling more than we can know: Verbal reports on mental processes. *Psychological Review, 84*, 231-259.

Nunnally, J.C. (1978). *Psychometric theory*. New York: McGraw-Hill.

Nygren, T.E. (1991). Psychometric properties of subjective workload measurement techniques: Implications for their use in the assessment of perceived mental workload. *Human Factors, 33*, 17-33.

Obrist, W.D., Thompson, H.K., Jr., Wang, H.S., & Wilkinson, W.E. (1975). Regional cerebral blood flow estimated by 133-xenon inhalation. *Stroke, 6*, 245-256.

Ogden, G.D., Levine, J.M., & Eisner, E.J. (1979). Measurement of workload by secondary tasks. *Human Factors, 21*, 529-548.

Parker, H. (1981). Visual detection and perception in netball. In I.M. Cockerill & W.W. MacGillivary (Eds.), *Vision and sport* (pp. 42-53). London: Stanley Thornes.

Populin, L., Rose, D.J., & Heath, K. (1990). The role of attention in one-handed catching. *Journal of Motor Behavior, 22*, 149-158.

Posner, M.I. (1973). *Cognition: An introduction*. Glenview, IL: Scott, Foresman.

Posner, M.I. (1980). Orienting of attention. *Quarterly Journal of Experimental Psychology, 32*, 3-25.

Posner, M.I., & Boies, S.J. (1971). Components of attention. *Psychological Review, 78*, 391-408.

Posner, M.I., & Keele, S.W. (1969). Attention demands of movements. *Proceedings of the 17th International Congress of Applied Psychology*. Amsterdam: Swets & Zeitlinger.

Reber, A.S. (1989). Implicit learning and tacit knowledge. *Journal of Experimental Psychology: General, 118*, 219-235.

Reid, G.B., & Nygren, T.E. (1988). The subjective workload assessment technique: A scaling procedure for measuring mental workload. In P.A. Hancock & N. Meshkati (Eds.), *Human mental workload* (pp. 185-218). Amsterdam: North-Holland.

Remington, R.W. (1980). Attention and saccadic eye movements. *Journal of Experimental Psychology: Human Perception and Performance, 6*, 726-744.

Ripoll, H., Papin, J-P., Guezennec, J-Y., Verdy, J-P., & Philip, M. (1985). Analysis of visual scanning patterns of pistol shooters. *Journal of Sport Sciences, 3*, 93-101.

Roland, P.E. (1982). Cortical regulation of selective attention in man: A regional cerebral blood flow study. *Journal of Neurophysiology, 48*, 1059-1077.

Roland, P.E., & Widen, L. (1988). Quantitative measurements of brain metabolism during physiological stimulation. In G. Pfurtscheller & F.H. Lopes da Silva (Eds.), *Functional brain imaging* (pp. 213-228). Toronto: Hans Huber.

Rose, D.J., & Christina, R.W. (1990). Attention demands of precision pistol- shooting as a function of skill level. *Research Quarterly for Exercise and Sport, 61*, 111-113.

Salazar, W., Landers, D.M., Petruzzello, S.J., Crews, D.J., & Kubitz, K. (1988). The effects of physical/cognitive load on electrocortical patterns preceding response execution in archery. *Psychophysiology, 25*, 478-479.

Salazar, W., Landers, D.M., Petruzzello, S.J., Crews, D.J, Kubitz, K., & Han, M.W. (1990). Hemispheric asymmetry, cardiac response, and performance in elite archers. *Research Quarterly for Exercise and Sport, 61*, 351-359.

Savelsbergh, G.J.P., & Bootsma, R.J. (1994). Perception-action coupling in hitting and catching. *International Journal of Sport Psychology, 25*, 331-343.

Savelsbergh, G.J.P., Whiting, H.T.A., & Pijpers, J.R. (1992). The control of catching. In J.J. Summers (Ed.), *Approaches to the study of motor control and learning* (pp. 313-342). Amsterdam: North-Holland.

Schneider, W. (1985). Towards a model of attention and the development of automatic processing. In M.I. Posner & O. Marin (Eds.), *Attention and performance XI* (pp.475-492). Hillsdale, NJ: Erlbaum.

Schomer, H. (1986). Mental strategies and the perception of effort of marathon runners. *International Journal of Sport Psychology, 17*, 41-59.

Sharp, R.H., & Whiting, H.T.A. (1974). Exposure and occluded duration effects in a ball-catching skill. *Journal of Motor Behavior, 6*, 139-147.

Shaw, R., & Kinsella-Shaw, J. (1988). Ecological mechanics: A physical geometry for intentional constraints. *Human Movement Science, 7*, 155-200.

Sheridan, T., & Stassen, H. (1979). Definitions, models and measures of human workload. In N. Moray (Ed.), *Mental workload: Its theory and measurement* (pp. 219- 233). New York: Plenum Press.

Shiffrin, R.M., & Schneider, W. (1977). Controlled and automatic human information processing: II. Perceptual learning, automatic attending, and a general theory. *Psychological Review, 84*, 127-190.

Shulman, G.L., Remington, R.W., & McLean, J.P. (1979). Moving attention through visual space. *Journal of Experimental Psychology: Human Perception and Performance, 5*, 522-526.

Stager, P., & Angus, R. (1978). Locating crash sites in simulated air-to-ground visual search. *Human Factors, 20*, 453-466.

Starkes, J.L. (1986). Attention demands of spatially locating the position of a ball in flight. *Perceptual and Motor Skills, 63*, 1327-1335.

Stelmach, G.E. (1987). The cutting edge of research in physical education and exercise science: The search for understanding. In M.J. Safrit & H.M. Eckert (Eds.), *The cutting edge in physical education and exercise science research* (pp. 8-25). Champaign, IL: Human Kinetics.

Stelmach, G.E., & Hughes, B. (1983). Does motor skill automation require a theory of attention? In R.A. Magill (Ed.), *Memory and control of action* (pp. 67-92). Amsterdam: North-Holland.

Stern, R.M. (1976). Reaction time and heart rate between the GET SET and GO of simulated races. *Psychophysiology, 13*, 149-154.

Summers, J.J., & Ford, S.K. (1990). The test of attentional and interpersonal style: An evaluation. *International Journal of Sport Psychology, 21*, 102-111.

Summers, J.J., & Ford, S.K. (1995). Attention in sport. In T. Morris & J.J. Summers (Eds.), *Sport psychology: Theory, applications and issues* (pp. 63-89). Brisbane: Wiley.

Summers, J.J., & Maddocks, D. (1986). Attentional style profiles and sport performance. *Behaviour Change, 3*, 105-111.

Summers, J.J., Miller, K., & Ford, S.K. (1991). Attentional style and basketball performance. *Journal of Sport & Exercise Psychology, 8*, 239-253.

Titchener, E.B. (1908). *Lectures on the elementary psychology of feeling and attention*. New York: Macmillan.

Treisman, A. (1964). Selective attention in man. *British Medical Bulletin, 20,* 12-16.

Treisman, A. (1969). Strategies and models of selective attention. *Psychological Review, 76,* 282-299.

Turvey, M.T. (1990). Coordination. *American Psychologist, 45,* 938-953.

Turvey, M.T., & Carello, C. (1986). The ecological approach to perceiving-acting: A pictorial essay. *Acta Psychologica, 63,* 133-155.

Turvey, M.T., Carello, C., & Kim, N-G. (1990). Links between active perception and action. In H. Haken & M. Stadler (Eds.), *Synergetics of cognition* (pp. 269-295). Berlin: Springer-Verlag.

Turvey, M.T., Fitch, H.L., & Tuller, B. (1982). The Berstein perspective III: The problem of degrees of freedom and context-conditioned variability. In J.A.S. Kelso (Ed.), *Human motor behavior: An introduction* (pp. 239-252). Hillsdale, NJ: Erlbaum.

Underwood, G. (1982). Attention and awareness in cognitive and motor skills. In G. Underwood (Ed.), *Aspects of consciousness. Vol. 3: Awareness and self-awareness* (pp. 111-145). London: Academic Press.

Vallerand, R.J. (1983). Attention and decision-making: A test of the predictive validity of the Test of Attentional and Interpersonal Style (TAIS) in a sport setting. *Journal of Sport Psychology, 5,* 449-459.

Van Schyock, S.R., & Grasha, A.F. (1981). Attentional style variations and athletic ability: The advantages of a sport-specific test. *Journal of Sport Psychology, 3,* 149-165.

Vickers, J.N. (1992). Gaze control in putting. *Perception, 21,* 117-132.

Vidulich, M.A., & Tsang, P.S. (1986). Techniques of subjective workload assessment: A comparison of SWAT and the NASA-bipolar methods. *Ergonomics, 29,* 1385-1398.

Vincente, K.J., Thornton, D.C., & Moray, N. (1987). Spectral analyses of sinus arrhythmia: A measure of mental effort. *Human Factors, 29,* 171-182.

Watchel, P. (1967). Conceptions of broad and narrow attention. *Psychological Bulletin, 68,* 417-429.

Welford, A.T. (1952). The psychological refractory period and the timing of high-speed performance—A review and a theory. *British Journal of Psychology, 43,* 2-19.

Welford, A.T. (1967). Single channel operation in the brain. *Acta Psychologica, 27,* 5-22.

Whiting, H.T.A., Alderson, G.J.K., & Sanderson, F.H. (1973). Critical time intervals for viewing and individual differences in performance of a ball-catching task. *International Journal of Sport Psychology, 4,* 155-164.

Whiting, H.T.A., & Sharp, R.H. (1974). Visual occlusion factors in a discrete ball catching task. *Journal of Motor Behavior, 6,* 11-16.

Wickens, C.D. (1984). *Engineering psychology and human performance.* Columbus, OH: Charles E. Merrill.

Wickens, C.D. (1992). *Engineering psychology and human performance* (2nd ed). New York: Harper Collins.

Wiener, N. (1948). *Cybernetics.* New York: Wiley.

Williams, A.M., Davids, K., Burwitz, L., & Williams, J.G. (1992). Perception and action in sport. *Journal of Human Movement Studies, 22,* 147-204.

Williams, A.M., Davids, K., Burwitz, L., & Williams, J.G. (1994). Visual search strategies in experienced and inexperienced soccer players. *Research Quarterly for Exercise and Sport, 65,* 2, 127-135.

Zelaznik, H.N., Shapiro, D.C., & McClosky, D. (1981). Effects of secondary task on the accuracy of single aiming movements. *Journal of Experimental Psychology: Human Perception and Performance, 7,* 1007-1018.

Chapter 11

IN SEARCH OF PSYCHOLOGICAL SKILLS

Shane Murphy
Gold Medal Psychological Consultants
and
Vance Tammen
Victoria University

Sport psychologists believe that psychological skills can be used to enhance athletic performance, but what are "psychological skills?" Can athletes learn and practice psychological skills in much the same way as a tennis player can work upon her kick serves or a golfer upon his high fade? If these skills exist, how can they be measured?

Such questions are important for sport psychologists as one of their major activities is the provision of psychological skills training (PST) to athletes and coaches (Sachs, 1991). The effectiveness of PST interventions and the use of performance-enhancement strategies have been the subject of much interest (Greenspan & Feltz, 1989; Swets & Bjork, 1990). For these issues to be addressed, however, we need to accurately identify and accurately assess the psychological skills and strategies used by athletes. In this chapter we look at the development of the concept of psychological skills and the research that has been done on the assessment of psychological skills, and we offer suggestions for future research directions.

Definitions

Athletic participants have always been aware of the gap between the attainment of physical skills and the ability to demonstrate those skills in competitive situations. Coaches know the frustration of working with an athlete who excels during practice sessions but fails to live up to those standards during competition. On the other hand is the "gamer," the athlete who displays lower levels of sports skills, but who excels in game situations. Athletes know the disappointment of losing to a less skilled opponent and the embarrassment of making a mistake on a simple task or skill long since mastered. What is the cause of these discrepancies in performance? Because skill level cannot explain such differential outcomes, many have assumed that psychological variables must be responsible. Sports participants at all levels have developed a lexicon to describe these variables: "Your head wasn't in the game;" "I choked;" "You didn't have the killer instinct;" "We didn't play as a team;" "I couldn't concentrate;" and so on.

Researchers in sport psychology have addressed this issue. There is sound research to show that instructing people in various approaches to thinking has a demonstrably beneficial impact on motor skill performance (see, for example, Feltz & Landers, 1983; Greenspan & Feltz, 1989; Meyers, Whelan, & Murphy, 1996). Helping athletes learn, acquire and master the self-regulatory skills needed to succeed in sports became known as *psychological skills training,* or PST (Martens, 1987). Vealey (1988) defines PST as describing the "techniques and strategies designed to teach or enhance mental skills that facilitate performance and a positive approach to sport competition" (p. 319). This enterprise goes back to at least the time of Coleman Roberts Griffith (1930). The needs of athletes and coaches to address the effects of psychological variables upon sports performance seem to have been the impetus that has spurred the growth of PST applications (Murphy, 1995).

Theoretical Foundations of Psychological Skills

Coleman Roberts Griffith was a pioneer in this, as in so many other areas. Martens (1987) quotes Griffith from a manuscript written in 1930, saying that:

> We know that some men [sic] see better than others . . . some men [sic] have a better type of attention than others . . . some men have a better imagination than others . . . if we realize that we are what we are in all of these psychological skills mostly because of the ways in which we have been trained, we shall discover that there is a great deal we can do about some of them. . . The coach who does know something about psychology can hope to train his men in psychological as well as physical skills (p. 74).

We will now examine how the theory underlying this concept of psychological skill development has changed from Griffith's time till today.

1. Trait Theory: Establishing a Relationship Between Psychological Processes and Performance

Researchers have long been interested in the psychological factors that affect human performance. Several important constructs have been identified that mediate performance, including anxiety (Spielberger, 1966), motivation (Atkinson, 1957; White, R., 1959), and confidence (Bandura, 1977). Early attempts to measure the impact of these constructs in athletic performance were based on personality trait theory, which was prevalent at that time. Individual differences were described in terms of enduring dispositions towards certain kinds of behavior. Thus, instruments such as the Athletic Motivation Inventory (AMI; Tutko & Ogilvie, 1969) were designed to measure traits such as drive, aggressiveness, and determination.

2. Social Learning Theory: Learning Self-Regulatory Skills

The rise of social cognitive theories in the 1970s and 1980s changed the way these psychological constructs were conceptualized. Instead of focusing upon enduring characteristics of the person over time, the emphasis was on situational specificity. Researchers became interested in the influence of the social environment on the behavioral differences between individuals. A key assumption of social cognitive theories was that individual differences were the result of learning experiences.

The influence of this approach in sport psychology can be seen in the type of psychological skills training conducted by applied practitioners. It was assumed that athletes could learn to reduce anxiety, increase motivation, and enhance confidence, given the proper training. Many of the training methods described in the growing PST literature were drawn from interventions developed within cognitive behavior therapy, which was based upon cognitive and social learning theory.

For example, nearly all the relaxation approaches commonly used by sport psychologists to reduce anxiety were developed by social learning proponents, the most popular being variants of Jacobson's Progressive Muscle Relaxation (PMR) approach, especially the brief version developed by Wolpe (1958) for his systematic desensitization procedure. Similarly, the most popular approaches to lowering cognitive athletic anxiety, such as self-talk and thought stopping (Bunker, Williams, & Zinsser, 1993), were developed by cognitive behavior therapists such as Beck (1976), Ellis (Ellis & Harper, 1975), and Meichenbaum (1977).

Cognitive behavior therapy was a psychological approach that grew in prominence during the 1970's. It differed from the traditional theoretical orientations of psychoanalysis, which emphasized a passive intervention approach, and humanistic psychology, which emphasized reflection and empathy, by proposing that interventions be active and goal directed. This approach to applied psychology found a naturally receptive audience among those concerned with performance issues. The emphasis on skill development and on coaching of clients was a natural fit with athletic populations. Researchers began to systematically describe the nature of cognitive skills used by athletes in competitive situations.

3. Qualitative Research:
Identifying the Nature of Psychological Skills

Initial surveys of psychological skills used by athletes by Loehr (1983) and Garfield (Garfield & Bennett, 1984) were largely anecdotal, but in the late 1980s researchers began to examine the self-reported experiences of elite athletes more systematically. The breakthrough study in the area was that of Orlick and Partington (1988). After the 1984 Summer and Winter Olympic Games, they surveyed 160 Canadian athletes and interviewed an additional 75 competitors in order to determine common elements of success. As Orlick and Partington reported, "A striking result of our study was the consistency of certain success elements for virtually all of our best performers in all sports" (p. 110). These common elements included quality training, clear daily goals, imagery training, simulation training, and thorough mental preparation for competition. This research design has since been employed in a variety of settings and across several sports such as wrestling (Eklund, Gould & Jackson, 1993) and figure skating (Gould, Jackson & Finch, 1993).

Such studies have yielded a rich understanding, not only of the types of mental processes used in the competitive process by elite athletes, but also of the ways in which these mental strategies are learned, developed and applied. They indicate an important growth in maturity of PST research.

4. The Search for Individual Differences

Psychological skills came to be viewed as the learned behaviors used by athletes to regulate their athletic performance. If such skills can be learned, it is reasonable to expect that measurable differences exist in the level of skill development displayed by experts and novices in various sports. Research into expert/novice differences and into differences between more and less successful athletes became a mainstay of PST research in the 1970s and 1980s.

An early study of this type was conducted by Mahoney and Avener (1977), who examined differences between the 6 male gymnasts who qualified for the 1976 U.S.A. Olympic team and the 6 finalists who did not. The team members reported being more self-confident, reported more gymnastics dreams, thought more about gymnastics in everyday situations, and used more self-talk in training and competition than did the unsuccessful candidates. Several studies of this type followed (Gould, Weiss & Weinberg, 1981; Highlen & Bennett, 1979; Meyers, Cooke, Cullen, & Liles, 1979; and Rotella, Gansneder, Ojala, & Billing, 1980), all finding some correlations between specific psychological approaches and level of performance. This type of research was strongly critiqued, however, by Heyman (1982) who suggested that prior experience might be responsible for the psychological patterns and cognitions seen, rather than the psychological states being the cause of performance success.

Popular books in this area also emphasized the characteristics of successful performers. Typical of such books was *Profile of a Winner* by Bennett and Pravitz (1987). Based upon their own unpublished work with athletes and upon a survey of coaches and athletes, they identified the 10 most important "traits of a winner" as: confidence, goal-setter, concentration, commitment, courage, communication, patience, intelligence, self-esteem and consistency. Similar themes reoccur in other popular books.

A variation of this approach is to consider the factors common to successful experiences, rather than to successful individuals. Researchers have sought to identify the common thoughts and feelings experienced during "peak performance"

(Garfield & Bennett, 1984), "peak experience" (Privette, 1983; Ravizza, 1984), or the "ideal performance state" (Loehr, 1983). Loehr (1986) advocated that athletic excellence is reached through training in visualization, self-motivation, muscle relaxation, management of negative energy, meditation, breath control, activation, centering, and team harmony.

Two assumptions underlie this work. First, that successful athletes achieve good results through these shared qualities, not because of other characteristics (social support, quantity of practice, competitiveness, etc.). Second, that what elite athletes do is necessarily the best way for all sports participants to achieve success. Both assumptions are open to challenge. Further, it is possible that other psychological skills exist that have yet to be discovered, by elite performers or by sport psychologists.

5. The Personal Strengths Approach

This is included as a separate influence on the development of PST because the work of practitioners such as Orlick contains a subtle difference from the previously described approach. The emphasis is not on the shared qualities of top athletes, but on discovering the personal strengths that have led the individual to be successful in the past. The "Competition Reflections" instrument of Orlick (1986) captures this approach. It asks respondents to think back to their "all-time best performances" and to "worst competitive performances" and to compare how they approached each in terms of their thinking, concentration, energy and anxiety levels. Based upon the differences between the two, the respondent is helped to identify successful approaches to performance and to eliminate nonproductive approaches.

This approach emphasizes that the psychological approaches that lead to success in sport differ between individuals and may even be idiosyncratic. As a practical matter, however, when it comes to helping athletes develop approaches to change their behaviors, Orlick and others describe the same methods identified by others, such as goal setting, consistency, confidence, team harmony, communication, relaxation and imagery (Orlick, 1980, 1986).

6. Current Assessment Issues

Clearly the concept of psychological skills has been an important one to sport psychologists since the inception of the field. There have been several different approaches to the definition of psychological skills, and there seems to be no clear agreement as to which specific skills are critical to successful sports performance. Although a consensus seems to have emerged that athletes cognitively manage their performance by the use of skills such as goal setting and concentration, a comprehensive model of psychological skill development has yet to emerge.

A thoughtful contribution to this literature was provided by Vealey (1988). In her article, she made the distinction between psychological skills and methods. She argues that skills are basic components of the mental side of sports performance and identifies the key skills as volition, self-awareness, self-esteem, and self-confidence. The methods used by athletes and sport psychologists to increase the level of these skills are the PST approaches of goal-setting, imagery, relaxation, and thought control.

Vealey makes an important point, arguing that we need to distinguish between the results to be achieved (changing psychological states) and the methods used to achieve them (psychological interventions). In a cogent critique of the PST literature, Morris and Thomas (1995) make a similar point. In their model of the performance-enhancement process, they separate the "skills/attributes" of the performer (e.g., self-awareness, motivation, leadership) from the "techniques" used to influence these skills (e.g., physical relaxation, biofeedback, therapy).

The arguments over these definitional issues are not arbitrary. Our concepts shape both the research programs we embark on and the types of interventions in which we trust. Our own evaluation of the literature on psychological skills suggests that it is useful to consider athletic performance management as a 3-step process. This process is illustrated in Figure 1.

First, the athlete must be able to identify the ideal psychological state which corresponds to high performance. As suggested by the "personal strengths" approach, this ideal state may vary from performer to performer. PST theorists suggest that there are "ideal" levels of states such as motivation, anxiety, and confidence that lead to optimal sports performance (Loehr, 1986; Ravizza, 1977). An athlete must have the self-knowledge necessary to be able to identify his or her personal ideal states. The ideal performance state will reflect the changing conditions of sporting competition and the psychological development of the athlete. For example, a skilled basketball player may need a lower tension level at the end of a match than at the beginning, knowing that he has a tendency to get tight at the conclusion of close games. A beginner tennis player may be much more adversely affected by anxiety than an expert player.

The second step in the process of performance management is for the athlete to monitor his or her psychological state in order to determine if changes are needed. For example, an athlete may monitor his anxiety and decide that he needs to lower his physical tension in order to compete at a higher level. Such self-monitoring is an important aspect of psychological skill development. An interesting aspect of this step is that some theorists argue that peak performance is often an almost unconscious process. That is, little self-evaluation is thought to occur when an athlete is in "flow" (Jackson, 1995). This implies that sometimes one consequence of self-monitoring is to decide to reduce one's level of self-monitoring!

The final step in the 3-step performance management process is to make a change in order to affect one's behavior, emotions, or cognitions. This step is usually described in terms of specific actions engaged in by athletes, for example, using deep breathing to lower anxiety, or engaging in imagery to enhance confidence. An athlete must become skilled in breathing methods, or in use of imagination, in order to successfully implement this third step in performance management. Athletes have self-employed such methods for centuries, and an important element of coaching is teaching athletes these methods of self management.

This analysis helps us understand that there are several important facets in the development of a "psychological skill". In order to achieve the first step, the athlete must be skilled in *self-analysis* in order to identify desired performance states. These states will vary from situation to situation, and will vary over

Step 3
Self-Regulation
(e.g., cognitive restructuring)

Step 2
Self-Monitoring
(e.g., recognize that anxiety is too high -
the need to decrease worry)

Step 1
Awareness of Ideal Psychological State
(e,g,. knowledge that low cognitive anxiety
is needed to pitch effectively)

**Figure 1. A 3-Step Process for the Application
of Psychological Skills for Performance Management**

time. In the second step, the athlete must be proficient in *self-monitoring* in order to recognize the need to make cognitive, emotional or physical changes as necessary. If there is no awareness of the need for change, there will be no motivation to employ psychological skills. Finally, the third phase in the process requires proficiency in *self-regulation* in order to use effective intervention methods. An athlete may be proficient in one phase of the performance management process and not another.

For example, an athlete might be very good at knowing how to relax his muscles and yet still have problems dealing with excessive tension in tournaments. Worse, athletes may sometimes hurt their own performance by the mis-application of a psychological technique, such as the weightlifter who does deep breathing before the event and then finds that she is too relaxed to lift effectively. The weightlifter can be said to be skilled in relaxation (step 3, self-regulation), but unskilled in monitoring her own anxiety level and deciding when to change (step 2, self-monitoring), or perhaps she does not know what the ideal energy level she needs is (step 1, self-analysis).

Several studies, for example, have shown that imagery use can have adverse effects on motor performance (Budney, Murphy, & Woolfolk, 1994; Budney & Woolfolk, 1990). This strongly suggests that an athlete may possess the self-regulation skill of visualization, but may be unable to use this skill to improve performance. Although the research literature has focused primarily on the question of whether athletes use self-regulation skills (i.e., step 3), the present analysis suggests that it may be even more important to determine whether athletes are skilled in steps 1 and 2 of the performance management process.

The skilled practitioner and the skilled athlete will realize that there exists another area in the use of psychological skills in sport which is not covered by this analysis of the performance management process. This area is the use of psycholog-

ical skills for problem solving. For example, the Olympic kayaker who is having trouble deciding upon the best route down the river and who uses her imagination to visualize a new approach to the obstacles she is facing is clearly using a psychological skill. She is not, however, using visualization to reach an ideal performance state. Her use of imagination is directed to solving a problem in her sports participation. There are countless such examples of the use of psychological skills in the world of sport. As we will see in the next section of this review, there has been limited assessment of the use of problem solving psychological skills in sport psychology.

Assessment of Psychological Skills

Several methods have been used in the assessment of psychological skills, including inventory development, qualitative interviews, observation, and single-subject designs. In this section, a critical review of these attempts to assess psychological skills is provided. Psychological skill inventories are critiqued first.

Psychological Skills Inventories

In this section we will examine several inventories that were designed to assess general psychological skills in sport. There are other inventories that assess specific skills, such as attention and imagery, and that are covered in other chapters (see Hall, this volume; Abernethy, Summers, & Ford, this volume). Another overlapping area of research is focused on coping skills (see Crocker, Kowalski, & Graham, this volume). Whereas psychological skills are defined as those used in the performance process, coping skills are defined as skills used to deal with stressors in the sporting environment. It is sometimes difficult to make clear distinctions between the two, especially between problem solving psychological skills and coping skills.

1. Athletic Motivation Inventory
(AMI; Tutko, Lyon, & Ogilvie, 1969)

The AMI was designed to measure some of the characteristics that today might be called psychological skills. However, the items and the interpretation referred to traits rather than skills. Eleven traits are assessed by the AMI: drive, aggressiveness, responsibility (or guilt-proneness), leadership, self-confidence, emotional control, mental toughness, coachability, conscientiousness, trust, and determination. The test consists of 190 forced-choice items.

The AMI can be viewed as a precursor to modern attempts to assess psychological skills. Few studies have been published on its validity. Hammer and Tutko (1974) gave 112 college football players both the AMI and the 16-PF personality inventory. There were low but significant correlations between scales with similar descriptions, indicating some level of construct validity.

Criterion validity was assessed by Davis (1991). In this study, 649 ice hockey players were given the AMI and were also assessed for "psychological strength" via on-ice observations by three professional hockey scouts. Less than 4% of the variance in scout ratings was accounted for by scores on the AMI.

2. Psychological Performance Inventory (PPI; Loehr, 1986)

Loehr's PPI, which appeared in *Mental Toughness Training for Sports* (1986), was perhaps the first instrument to incorporate the cognitive-behavioral approach (Meyers et al., 1996;

Perna, Neyer, Murphy, Ogilvie, & Murphy, 1995) to the assessment of what Loehr called "mental strengths and weaknesses" (p. 161). The PPI profile incorporates seven factors: self-confidence, negative energy, attention control, visual and imagery control, motivational level, positive energy, and attitude control. Some of the items ask athletes to reflect upon their behaviors, not just their attitudes and feelings. This is a key aspect of the cognitive-behavioral approach. For example "I mentally practice my physical skills," and "My self-talk during competition is negative."

Unfortunately, little research has been published with the PPI. Norms, validity, and reliability data are not available, and it does not appear to have become a widely used measure in the field. However, some more recent measures have many items that are constructed in a manner similar to the PPI items.

3. The Psychological Skills Inventory for Sport (PSIS; Mahoney, Gabriel & Perkins, 1987)

The PSIS has been the most popular instrument for the general assessment of psychological skills. Indeed, in a study of approaches to practice of 44 applied sport psychology consultants, Gould, Tammen, Murphy, and May (1989) found that the PSIS was the only general psychological skills assessment instrument mentioned by more than one respondent, and it was rated as the most useful test (mean of 8.8 on a 10-point scale).

Mahoney et al. (1987) designed the PSIS to assess psychological skills relevant to exceptional athletic performance. Items were based on the prior research of Mahoney and his colleagues with collegiate and Olympic athletes (Mahoney, 1979; Mahoney & Avener, 1977; Shelton & Mahoney, 1978). The original PSIS consisted of 51 true/false items developed to identify differences between elite, pre-elite, and collegiate-level athletes in their use of psychological skills for sport. Based on individual item, discriminant, factor, and cluster analyses of 713 athletes' responses, six subscales of the PSIS were identified. These subscales were anxiety control, concentration, confidence, mental preparation, motivation, and team emphasis. The researchers then developed a revised version of the instrument (the PSIS-R-5), shortened to 45 questions, each using a 5-point Likert-style response format.

Norms. Normative data were collected on a sample of 1,080 athletes, ranging from world-class and collegiate athletes to recreational athletes (Greenspan, Murphy, Tammen, & Jowdy, 1988). Analyses indicated that there was a significant main effect for level of competitor on all six scales. There was also a significant gender effect, with males scoring higher than females on four of the scales. S.A. White (1993) also found a significant effect for gender within a group of collegiate skiers, with females scoring higher than males on team emphasis. A significant effect for age was found on two scales by Lesser and Murphy (1988), with younger athletes scoring higher on motivation and older athletes scoring higher on anxiety control.

But Mahoney himself, in a study of weightlifters, found that non-elite athletes scored higher than elite athletes on five of the six scales (Mahoney, 1989). This finding contradicts the theoretical basis of the instrument, which is that it measures the psychological skills that lead to superior athletic performance.

Reliability. Internal cronbach alphas for the PSIS-R-5 scales were calculated on a sample of 128 collegiate skiers (S.A. White, 1993) and were found to be satisfactory on all scales (range = .71 - .92). However, in a study of 340 intercollegiate athletes, internal consistency statistics for four of the six proposed scales were low, ranging from .52 to .62 (Chartrand, Jowdy, & Danish, 1992). One scale, confidence, had a high consistency rating (.85), whereas another, mental preparation, actually had a negative internal reliability (-.34).

Test-retest reliability was calculated on a sample of 34 elite figure skaters and judo players tested three months apart (Lesser & Murphy, 1988). Significant correlations emerged on five of the scales, but not on concentration. Correlations over .60 were found on only three scales (i.e., Confidence, Mental Preparation, and Motivation).

Construct validity. Intercorrelations between the PSIS-R-5 and a well-established measure of competitive sports anxiety, the CSAI-2 (Martens, Vealey & Burton, 1990), were reported by Lesser and Murphy (1988) for a sample of 194 Olympic athletes. The Anxiety Control and Confidence scales were significantly correlated with all three CSAI-2 scales (Cognitive Anxiety, Somatic Anxiety and Self-Confidence) with correlations ranging from -.37 (Anxiety Control and Somatic Anxiety) to .60 (Confidence and Self-Confidence). Significant, but lower, correlations also emerged between PSIS-R-5 concentration and the three CSAI-2 scales (-.14 to .29)

Investigators have also reexamined the factor structure of the 45 items of the PSIS-R-5. Tammen and Murphy (1990) found that the six-factor structure suggested by Mahoney et al. (1987) was not supported by an independent factor analysis of a sample of 927 athletes. A different six-factor solution emerged, with the first factor containing 18 items from the original Anxiety Control, Confidence and Concentration scales and accounting for nearly 20% of the variance in the solution. Researchers using confirmatory factor analysis procedures on a sample of 340 intercollegiate athletes found an unacceptable goodness-of-fit index (.754) between their data and the proposed six-factor solution (Chartrand et al., 1992).

Based on this review of the research, it is not possible to recommend the PSIS-R-5 as suitable for further research in its present format. It fails to meet adequate psychometric standards for validity and reliability.

4. The Sport-Related Psychological Skills Questionnaire (SPSQ; Nelson & Hardy, 1990)

This 56-item measure of seven psychological skills grew out of a theoretical approach to sport performance that argued that athletes learn self-regulatory skills in order to manage their performance (Hardy & Nelson, 1988). Their basic premise is that competitive sport entails a high potential for stress and that successful competitors must acquire the skills necessary both to cope with stress and to enhance their performance. The overlap with the coping model is clear in this approach.

The skills hypothesized to underlie sport performance are imaginal skill, mental preparation, self-efficacy, cognitive anxiety control, concentration skill, relaxation skill, and motivation (Nelson & Hardy, 1990). Internal consistency of the factors is high, being greater than .78 for each scale. The SPSQ was successfully used to track a cognitive-behavioral intervention with an elite athlete (Jones, 1993). However, no normative data are available for the SPSQ, and at this time it is impossible to evaluate the psychometric properties of the instrument. Further research with this instrument would be necessary for development of the measure, but contact with one of the authors of the SPSQ indicated that it is not being developed due to initiation of a research program with a new measure.

5. The Golf Performance Survey (Thomas & Over, 1994)

This is a sport-specific test of psychological skills. It is instructive to examine the Golf Performance Survey in this chapter because with the increased specificity of the items, the researchers were able to discover new relationships between psychological strategies and performance.

Internal reliability. The survey comprised 95 items assessing psychological and psychomotor skills in golf, as well as level of involvement in the game. Some of the items were drawn from the PPI and the PSIS, though most were created by the authors. Exploratory factor analysis on a sample of 165 competitive club golfers yielded five psychological skills factors, three psychomotor skills factors, and one level-of-involvement factor. The psychological skills factors were negative emotions and cognitions, mental preparation, a conservative approach (a tactical factor), concentration, and driving for maximum distance. Alpha coefficients for these factors ranged from .67 to .81, and test-retest reliabilities (obtained from a sample of 40 respondents who took the test 3 months after the initial occasion) ranged from .72 to .90.

The three psychomotor skills identified were automaticity, putting skill, and seeking improvement. Alpha coefficients ranged from .67 to .80, and test-retest reliabilities from .78 to .92. Finally, one factor, commitment, emerged from the factor analysis of the level-of-involvement items, with an alpha coefficient of .67 and a test-retest reliability of .85.

Criterion validity. Because the handicaps of all players in the study were recorded, a comparison between high-handicap (20 or greater) and low-handicap (11 or less) players was possible. Significant differences between these two groups emerged on five of the factors. Skilled golfers reported greater mental preparation, a higher level of concentration when playing golf, fewer negative emotions and cognitions, greater psychomotor automaticity, and more commitment to golf.

The findings clearly suggest that investigators who study a specific sport are likely to find factors related to performance that are unique to that sport. For example, Thomas and Over (1994) found that a conservative approach to competition, putting skill and driving for maximum distance were identifiable psychological strategy factors among the 165 golfers studied. This suggests that there are benefits to assessing psychological skills within an individual sport. This sport-specific research approach has since been extended to the sport of bowling (Thomas, Schlinker, & Over, 1996) and was again found to be productive in that sport. One approach for future research might be to utilize a general sport psychological skills instrument supplemented with sport-specific items. It might also be possible to develop a general sports measure that includes definitions of sports skills relevant to the athletic population being assessed at the time.

It is not clear whether the Golf Performance Survey continues to be used in the assessment of competitive golfers. Further research with this instrument is required in order to assess other psychometric properties.

6. The Athletic Coping Skills Inventory-28 (ACSI-28; Smith, Schutz, Smoll & Ptacek, 1995)

This is a recent addition to the family of assessment instruments that grew out of the original Athletic Coping Skills Inventory, designed to measure ways in which athletes cope with the stress of competition (Smith, Smoll, & Ptacek, 1990). Although the original inventory comes from the coping model (see Crocker et al., this volume), the new instrument is conceptualized as assessing the psychological skills used by athletes to manage their sports performance, and yields a total Personal Coping Resources score, which is assumed to reflect a multi-faceted psychological skills construct. The ACSI-28, therefore, warrants inclusion in the present survey of psychological skills assessment instruments.

A principal components analysis of data from 637 high school and college athletes on an 87-item instrument called the Survey of Athletic Experiences (Smith et al., 1990) yielded eight factors. This eight-factor solution, comprising 42 items from the original survey, was then evaluated through a confirmatory factor analysis procedure (Smith et al., 1995). The eight-factor solution was not confirmed, but when two factors were combined and a number of items deleted, a revised seven-factor solution (the ACSI-28) produced a reasonable goodness-of-fit (index = .91) to the data. The final seven factors, using 28 items, accounted for slightly over 50% of the variance in the data. The seven scales of the ACSI-28 are coping with adversity, peaking under pressure, goal setting/mental preparation, concentration, freedom from worry, confidence and achievement motivation, and coachability.

Internal reliability. Internal consistency statistics (Cronbach's alphas) for the seven scales ranged from .62 (for Concentration) to .78 (Peaking). A sample of 94 intramural and club sport athletes took the test a week apart, and test-retest reliability coefficients from this sample ranged from .47 (for Coachability) to .87 (for Peaking), although five of the scales had coefficients over .70.

Construct validity. The ACSI-28 and several other instruments were administered to the same group of athletes. Several ACSI-28 scales showed meaningful correlations with the other instruments. For example, the Freedom From Worry scale correlated signficantly ($r = -.59$) with the Worry subscale from the Sport Anxiety Scale (SAS; Smith, Smoll, & Schutz, 1990). Perhaps reflecting the coping background from which the ACSI-28 originated, five of the scales displayed moderate (r's = .39 - .47) correlations with a generalized self-efficacy measure (Coppel, 1980).

Criterion validity. An initial study using the ACSI-28 to examine the relationship between psychological skills and physical skills and long-term survival in the sport of professional baseball (Smith & Christensen, 1995) indicates that the instrument is a useful predictor of which athletes remain active in professional baseball over a 3-year period. Indeed, the ACSI-28 was a much better predictor of athletic success for pitchers than was an assessment of physical skill level.

Further research on this instrument appears warranted, but several cautions are necessary. First, it appears that the confirmatory factor analysis was carried out on the same data as the original exploratory principal components analysis, a procedure that violates the inventory construction guidelines proposed by Schutz and Gessaroli (1993). Until a confirmatory factor analysis on an independent sample is conducted, the proposed factor structure of the ACSI-28 should be interpreted cautiously.

Second, it remains open to question whether the ACSI-28 accurately assesses psychological skills as they have been discussed here or is better viewed as a coping skills measure. A problem for this measure is that several scales contain items that appear to represent varied skill domains. For example, the Freedom From Worry scale contains both imagery-related items ("I think about and imagine what will happen if I fail or screw up") and cognitive items ("I worry quite a bit about what others think about my performance"); whereas the Coping With Adversity scale contains items that have face validity in terms of the measurement of relaxation skills ("When I feel myself getting too tense, I can quickly relax my body and calm myself") as well as emotional control skills ("I maintain emotional control no matter how things are going for me"). In part, this reflects a lack of use of PST theory in the development of the test. Smith et al. (1995) acknowledge this problem, noting that

> . . . we had a general idea of the range of psychological skills that we wanted to measure, but no explicit theory. We do not in any way assume that the variables that we are measuring exhaust the domain of psychological skills that may contribute to performance (p. 392).

Further research may well demonstrate that the ACSI-28 is a better measure of specific sport coping skills than it is a general measure of psychological skills used in performance management.

7. Summary: Psychological Skills Inventories

Changes in general sport psychological skill assessment instruments have reflected the theoretical changes described earlier in the chapter, moving from assessment of general traits and qualities thought to be determinants of success to assessment of specific behaviors and actions within a cognitive-behavioral perspective. However, our review of the research suggests two problems that have characterized attempts to develop general assessment instruments. First, there has been a lack of instrument development based upon follow-up research into the psychometric properties of several of the instruments reviewed. For example, the development of the PSIS-R-5 was guided by the research with the original PSIS, but subsequent concerns raised by factor analytic research with the PSIS-R-5 have not been addressed. Other instruments with promising internal reliability and containing scales based upon sound factor analytic research have not been further developed by research into their criterion and construct validity (e.g., the SPSQ and the Golf Performance Survey). The ACSI-28 is a step in the right direction in this respect. Its construction has been guided by the appropriate use of exploratory factor analysis and by attempts to establish convergent and predictive validity. Further research is warranted with this instrument.

Second, there has been a great deal of confusion in the selection of items to represent the relevant domain of psychological skills. Too often, items have been thrown together piecemeal, without regard to careful construction based upon research findings and current theory. The ACSI-28 appears to suffer from this problem, and it may be a better measure of coping skills than of psychological performance skills. Examination of the SPSQ suggests that the items were chosen carefully based upon current PST theory, but unfortunately, insufficient follow-up work has been done with this instrument to allow an adequate psychometric evaluation of its properties. We will return to the issue of integrating inventory development with theory development when we discuss possible future research directions.

Qualitative Assessment of Psychological Skills

The use of qualitative assessment methods to investigate the relationship between psychological strategies and performance was discussed earlier in this chapter. Qualitative research has made a valuable contribution by clarifying the types of strategies used by top-level performers to manage their performance and by showing how these strategies are applied in competition situations. Several studies have furthered the pioneering work of Orlick and Partington (1988) (Eklund et al., 1993; Gould, Eklund, & Jackson, 1993; Gould, Finch, & Jackson, 1993; Madden, Kirkby, & McDonald, 1989). By its very nature, however, this research method is suited for description rather for standardization purposes. Qualitative research should be used to guide the content of quantitative assessment approaches.

Individualized Assessment Methods

Several other methodologies focus on an individualized approach to the assessment of psychological skills. These methods use assessment in order to guide intervention. There is usually no attempt to generalize from the specific situation to make broad statements about the nature of psychological skills in general. Because the lack of standardization limits the utility of these approaches for research purposes, they will be dealt with only briefly in this chapter.

1. The Personal Profile

This approach to assessment is based upon the personal construct theory of Kelly (1955) and the use of repertory grid analysis (Beail, 1985) to reveal an individual's guiding theories about life. Butler and Hardy (1992) and Jones (1993) have described how a personal profile may be constructed by the athlete and the consultant to summarize an athlete's psychological strengths and weaknesses. "[I]n contrast to tests or questionnaires that plot the performer against axes chosen by the sport psychologist. . . [the personal profile] frees the performer to construct a picture of himself or herself in terms that readily make sense" (Butler & Hardy, 1992, p. 255).

Performance profiles typically include a wide variety of descriptors of an athlete's strengths and weaknesses. Some of these may fit the concept of a "psychological skill" (for example, "relaxation skill" and "concentration"), but many others describe traits or emotional qualities, such as "will to win," "good coordination," and "quick." The personal profile is usually self-referenced (against the athlete's ideal) although it can also be compared against ratings from another (e.g., a coach).

The use of this approach in a team setting has also been examined (Dale & Wrisberg, 1996).

Advantages of the personal profile approach include the emphasis on the athlete's involvement in the process, the face validity of the approach to the performer, and the ability to structure interventions based upon the profile. A major disadvantage of this approach is that important aspects of performance may be overlooked when the athlete is the sole arbiter of the self-analysis. Also, this approach is time consuming.

2. Single-Subject Method

This approach to research eschews the "group norms" approach of typical quantitative research and focuses on tracking the individual over time. It has been used in several studies to investigate the effectiveness of PST interventions (Kendall, Hrycaiko, Martin, & Kendall, 1990; Savoy, 1993; Vernacchia & Cook, 1993). Although the single-subject method can employ inventories and questionnaires to monitor psychological skill use over time, the method can also be used with self-monitoring and behavioral observation approaches in order to track these skills (Edmundson & McCann, 1994). Both self-monitoring of behaviors thought to represent psychological skill development and the behavioral observation of athletes' use of psychological skills [see Van Raalte, Brewer, Rivera, & Petitpas (1994) for an example] are approaches that have been neglected in the research literature. We especially encourage the use of such approaches in the validation of psychological skill inventories. The field could benefit from studies that correlate self-report of psychological skill use via inventory assessment with behavioral observations of the use of the same skill.

3. Individual Diagnostic Analysis

An interesting combination of personal interview, psychological testing, and situation x person grid analysis has been described in the assessment of elite athletes (Van Mele, Auweele, & Rzewnicki, 1995). The authors argue that a diagnostic procedure for use in guiding interventions should not only incorporate the athletes' personal view of their skills (Butler & Hardy, 1992), but should also be guided by a theoretical approach based on the consultant's expertise. This diagnostic procedure is really a combination of several other methods, and although its use for research is limited, it does represent a useful method of building upon the strengths of both the nomothetic and the idiographic approaches.

Commonalities in Psychological Skills Assessment

It is now time to return to the definitional issues broached earlier in the chapter. Have researchers investigating the use of psychological skills in athletes reached a consensus on the nature of these skills?

The sport psychological skill inventories offer the best chance to compare the content of the skills assessed across studies. In order to compare the findings from the inventories reviewed earlier, Table 1 shows the skills identified by each inventory. The factors/scales from the five inventories reviewed, as well as the psychological skills and methods proposed by Vealey (1988), are included.

Table 1 reveals that there is indeed some consistency in the psychological performance skills identified in the research to date. Concentration (or attention control), for example, is identified in all six studies, and five studies identify confidence, imagery (or mental practice), and motivation/commitment as critical factors in the psychology of peak performance. In four of the studies, anxiety control is identified. Relaxation is specifically identified in three studies, as is the skill of goal setting. Two studies identify thought or attitude control and the skill of coping with negative thoughts and emotions.

The labels used to identify these skills sometimes vary greatly. For example, a factor which describes the ability to deal with anxiety and remain calm was variously described as anxiety control (PSIS-R-5), cognitive anxiety skill (SPSQ), negative energy (PPI), and freedom from worry (ACSI-28). A mental preparation factor contained many goal setting items in the study by Nelson and Hardy (1990), but a factor with the same name had many visualization items in the study by Thomas and Over (1994).

An important consideration is that although a factor may have emerged in only one study, this does not reduce its potential significance for researchers. For example, the skill labelled "automaticity" emerged in only one of the studies from Table 1 (Thomas & Over, 1994). Yet this psychological aspect of performance may be critical to a complete understanding of expert performance, as has been suggested by several theorists (e.g., Ericsson & Charness, 1994). This leads to a discussion of possible directions for future research.

Future Directions in Assessment

We conclude by offering our thoughts on potentially productive avenues of research within the area of psychological skills assessment. There are five areas deserving of greater attention: First, assessment instruments should be more closely related to current theory; second, research must begin to address distinctions between psychological skills used for performance management and psychological skills used in problem solving; third, assessment should take into account the environment in which the athlete is performing; fourth, skill inventory development needs to incorporate a greater emphasis on validity; and fifth, assessment should examine how athletes develop psychological skills over time. Each issue is examined in turn.

1. The Development of Assessment Inventories Should be Based on Current PST Theory

In reviewing existing psychological skill inventories we were struck by the wide variety in the nature and structure of the items assembled for each instrument. Such heterogeneity of items makes it more difficult to understand what the inventory is actually measuring. In part, this situation reflects the lack of use of a systematic theoretical framework in the development of the inventory items, a situation acknowledged by some researchers (e.g., Smith et al., 1995).

For example, consider the following items from the PSIS-R-5: "I am very self-confident about my athletic skills" and "When I am preparing to perform, I try to imagine what it will *feel* like in my muscles." A moment's reflection will reveal that these are very different items. The first item asks the respondent to make a judgement on the current level of a psychological state (self-confidence). There is no indication that the athlete

Table 1
Comparison of Subscales/Skills Identified in PST Research

Loehr (1986, PPI)	Vealey (1988)	Nelson & Hardy (1990, SPSQ)	Mahoney et al. (1987, PSIS)
Motivational level	Volition/motivation	Motivation	Motivation
	(goal setting)	Mental preparation	
Visual & imagery control	(imagery)	Imaginal skill	Mental practice
Self-confidence	Self-confidence	Self-efficacy	Confidence
	Self-esteem		
	Self-awareness		
Attitude control	(thought control)		
Attention control	Attentional control	Concentration skill	Concentration
Positive energy	Arousal control (physical relaxation)	Relaxation skill	
Negative energy		Cognitive anxiety skill	Anxiety Control
	Interpersonal skills		
	Lifestyle management		
			Team emphasis

(Vealey's "methods" are in parentheses)

Thomas & Over (1994, GPS)	Smith et al. (1995, ACSI-28)	Commonalities	
Commitment		Motivation/Commitment	5
	Goal-setting/Preparation	Preparation/Goal setting	3
Search for improvement		Search for improvement	1
Mental preparation		Imagery/Mental practice	5
	Confidence	Confidence	5
		Self-esteem	1
		Self-awareness	1
		Attitude/Thought control	2
Concentration	Concentration	Concentration/Attention	6
		Relaxation	3
Automaticity		Automaticity	1
	Peak under pressure	Peak under pressure	1
	Freedom from worry	Anxiety control	4
Negative emotions and cognitions	Cope with adversity	Emotional control	2
		Interpersonal skills	1
		Lifestyle management	1
		Team emphasis	1
Conservative approach		Conservative approach	1
	Coachability	Coachability	1

has done anything to increase this level of confidence. The second item, on the other hand, is very specific in asking the athlete whether a certain behavior has been engaged in (kinesthetic imaginal rehearsal).

The result is that the "skills" that are measured by the inventory (in this case Confidence and Mental Preparation) are not comparable skills. The Confidence scale is really a measure of a psychological state. The Mental Preparation scale attempts to measure the frequency of use of a specific self-regulation strategy.

The PSIS-R-5 is not alone in this confusion over what is being measured. For example, Smith et al.'s (1995) ACSI-28 contained the item "I feel confident that I will play well." This is clearly a psychological state assessment item. It is interesting to note that many other items in the ACSI-28 tend to be more specific. For example, the Coping With Adversity scale contains the item "When I feel myself getting too tense, I can quickly relax my body and calm myself." This item reflects the third step in the performance management process, self-regulation. The result of this lack of theoretical clarity in inventory development is that users of the inventory are unclear whether they have measured the athlete's self-knowledge of their ideal performance state, the athlete's ability to monitor their current emotions and cognitions, or the athlete's skill in using an intervention method in order to effect a psychological change.

Future inventory development would be improved by recognizing the three-step process of psychological performance management described earlier. Items should be selected to measure a specific step in the performance management process. That is, items should be constructed to measure an awareness of ideal psychological state, or the ability to self-monitor, or the use of specific self-regulation strategies.

Our simple recommendation for researchers is that they specify which phase(s) of the performance process they wish to assess with their instrument. This is commonly done in applied work. Consultants discuss the process of helping athletes identifying the "optimal" state they require to perform well (for example, the "zone of optimal functioning" approach of Hanin [Hanin & Syrja, 1995]); they assess whether the athlete has the ability to self-monitor cognitions, emotions, and behaviors during performance; and they assess the ways in which athletes utilize psychological processes, such as imagery and relaxation (Weinberg & Williams, 1993). It is time that PST assessment methods provided information on all three phases of the performance management process.

2. Research Must Begin to Address the Use of Psychological Skills Used for Problem Solving as well as for Performance Management

This issue should see the greatest amount of attention in the near future. How do athletes use their psychological skills on a daily basis to manage their training, solve problems, and seek continuous improvement? Such skills have scarcely been examined in current assessment instruments. In her 1988 article, Vealey pinpointed this as a widespread problem in PST:

I have also noticed that athletes tend to get bogged down in learning all of the methods (imagery, relaxation, goal setting) and many times lose sight of the skills these methods are designed to facilitate. Orlick (1982) emphasizes that athletes often lose interest in PST unless the psychological training is directed specifically at meeting their individual needs. (p. 327)

At present there is no quantitative research to suggest what the domain of problem solving skills in sport might be. The following suggestions are drawn from practical experience and from the qualitative work of researchers such as Orlick and Partington (1988). Assessment of how athletes decide they have a problem, and how they try to deal with it, is likely to tell us far more about the relationship between mental preparation and performance excellence than focusing solely on competitive performance.

Creative Thinking

Items from current psychological skills inventories focus on the use of imagery in the rehearsal of motor skills, an approach commonly known as mental practice (Murphy & Jowdy, 1992). However, field studies of the actual use of imagery by athletes indicate that imagery is also used for many other performance issues, including pre-competition planning, stress management, skill acquisition and maintenance, and problem solving. These aspects of imagery are barely considered by current general inventories, although they are beginning to receive recognition in inventories designed specifically to measure imagery. The Imagery Use Questionnaire (IUQ; Hall, Rodgers, & Barr, 1990), for example, makes a useful distinction between cognitive and motivational functions of imagery (see Hall, this volume).

We propose that the general skill of using imagery to effectively enhance and manage sports training and performance is creative thinking. High levels of creative thinking should be correlated with high levels of sports performance. Research suggests that the imagery skills which form the foundation of creative thinking can be practiced and improved (George, 1986). The challenge for researchers is to generate a domain of creative thinking items which adequately samples the real world psychological skills utilized by athletes.

Staying Calm in Pressure Situations

Modern multidimensional theories of anxiety suggest that successful athletes must learn to recognize signs of impending panic and prevent it (Gould & Krane, 1992; Hardy & Parfitt, 1991). Rather than simply learning a relaxation technique, this skill might require the ability to self-monitor one's anxiety level, know one's own zone of optimal functioning (Hanin & Syrja, 1995), and have the skill to reduce anxiety in both the somatic and cognitive dimensions (Gould & Udry, 1994; Maynard, Hemmings, & Warwick-Evans, 1995). The factor labeled "freedom from worry" by Smith et al. (1995) may well be a component of this skill, although Smith et al. point out that none of the scales of the ACSI-28 correlated significantly with the somatic anxiety scale of the Sport Anxiety Scale (SAS, Smith, Smoll, & Schutz, 1990). They concluded that this suggests ". . . the need for a subscale that measures arousal-control skills, specifically relaxation, more effectively than our scale does" (pp. 393-394). This "staying calm" construct has often been subsumed under the general rubric of "arousal control," but several cogent analyses have shown that the general notion of "arousal" is a confusing oversimplification (Neiss, 1988).

Concentration

As shown in Table 1, the construct of concentration or attentional control was identified as integral to the performance management process in all the studies reviewed. Few, if any, of the items in the inventories reviewed define actual strategies to increase concentration, reflecting a difficulty in conceptualizing this complex skill. For example, an item from the ACSI-28 simply states, "When I am playing sports I can focus my attention and block out distractions" (Smith et al., 1995, p. 384).

Beyond the need to focus attention when performing, athletes face constant demands on their concentration capacities. High level problem solving skills are needed to prioritize training needs and allocate appropriate attention to each, to block out competing demands on time, to focus when training with an injury, and to concentrate upon relevant feedback from coaches and teammates.

Essential components of concentration that seem to be important to athletes include being able to shift attention when necessary, being able to maintain concentration despite distractions, recognizing relevant cues and distinguishing them from irrelevant ones (Abernethy & Russell, 1987), and being able to broaden or narrow attention to include relevant cues. Attempts to influence this skill are a mainstay of PST. Gould et al. (1989) found that 80% of the sport psychology consultants they surveyed reported conducting attention training with their clients.

Various theories within sport psychology have examined the nature of concentration (Abernethy, Summers & Ford, this volume; Boutcher, 1992; Nideffer & Sharpe, 1978). Nideffer's theory, in particular, has become influential in the field. Recent advances in the cognitive brain sciences, however, are not reflected in these theories (see, for example, the critique of Nideffer's theory in Moran [1996, pp. 142-150]). The implications of research based upon neural network theory and modern information-processing theories must be incoporated into future conceptualizations of the problem solving skill of concentration.

The work of Csikszentmihalyi (1990) suggests that intense levels of concentration are produced when an athlete's skill level is well matched with the challenge he or she faces. This analysis suggests that concentration is closely related to the task being performed, the level of competition being faced, and so on. An athlete may have good concentration skills in one sport, but not another, and, indeed, variations in concentration are probable for an athlete between different tasks within the same sport. For example, a tennis player may have good concentration on the return of serve, but poor concentration when serving. The assessment of this skill should always be closely related to a specific sport task, suggesting that sport-specific measures may be very important in the assessment of this psychological skill.

Goal Attainment

Although "motivation" has been frequently identified as a basic psychological skill, we would argue that this term refers to a psychological state. The more specific term "goal-setting" has also been used interchangeably with motivation, but merely knowing how to set goals is probably insufficient to cause performance gains. Some research, for example, has shown that setting certain types of goals and receiving positive feedback on goal attainment can lead to performance decrements (Burton, 1992; Kirschenbaum & Smith, 1983). We propose that much more research is needed to understand how successful athletes develop the ability to reach their goals consistently.

Thought Control

Constructs such as attitude control (Loehr, 1986) and thought control (Vealey, 1988) have been proposed as critical psychological skills. Research shows that people can readily identify their level and quality of self-talk. It has been hypothesized that the nature of one's self-talk is an important determinant of athletic behavior (Bunker et al., 1993; Van Raalte et al., 1994). Yet we know little about how athletes manage their self-talk on a daily basis in order to achieve their goals (Hardy, Jones, & Gould, 1996). None of the current research-based assessment inventories measures this skill.

Emotional Control

There is evidence that an ability to deal with frustration and negative emotions is important for competitive athletes. Smith et al. (1995), for example, identified coping with adversity as an important factor in successful athletic performance. Items loading on this factor included "I maintain emotional control no matter how things are going for me" (p. 384). Similarly, Thomas and Over (1994) found that handling "negative emotions and cognitions" was an integral aspect of golf performance. Their factor included items such as "I get angry and frustrated by a poor shot."

The skill of managing emotions in order to achieve high performance is one that may overlap with general coping skills (see Crocker et al., this volume). We suggest that skills that are used to manage emotions in order to reduce stress be viewed as coping skills (Crocker & Graham, 1995), whereas the management of emotions in the pursuit of high level performance be viewed as a psychological problem solving skill.

Consistency

Athletes frequently describe one of their performance goals as becoming more consistent during competition. How do athletes manage their training and preparation in order to achieve such consistency?

In the performance process, consistent performance is linked to unconscious, almost automatic skill execution. Most major theories of skill acquisition in sport posit the development of an expert stage of performance in which performance is smooth and conscious cognitive control is minimal. This stage has been called "autonomous" (Fitts & Posner, 1967), "procedural" (Anderson, 1982), and "automatic" (Schneider & Shiffrin, 1977).

However, this skill emerged uniquely in only one of the studies from Table 1 (Thomas & Over, 1994). Thomas and Over termed the factor they identified "automaticity." Items loading on this scale included "My golf swing is well grooved" and

"My swing is so automatic, I could drive blindfolded." This construct appears similar to the psychological skill identified by Moore and Stevenson (1991) as "trust." They defined trust as "the ability to free oneself from fear of mistakes in execution or outcome and to release control during motor skill execution" (Moore & Stevenson, 1994, p. 11). This skill is one that we believe has been neglected by researchers in the PST area and that deserves increased attention.

These, then, are some problem solving psychological skills we suggest should be researched more thoroughly in future assessment efforts. Other skills will likely emerge as the study of problem solving in sport develops. Note that we focused only on psychological skills that are intrapsychic in nature. Therefore, interactive or social variables, such as teamwork, coachability and interpersonal skills, were excluded from this discussion.

3. Assessment Must Take into Account the Interaction of Skill and Environment

The lack of attention to the influence of environment on assessment is most clearly seen in attempts to assess psychological skill use in practice settings. There are none. It is astonishing that all the research we reviewed has focused on psychological skills used in competition, neglecting to assess the use of psychological skills in training environments. This is particularly puzzling in view of the fact that committed athletes spend up to 99% of their time in training, rather than competition (McCann, 1995). How do athletes manage their performance in the practice environment? This issue awaits research attention.

Research that has defined the sports context and focused on a single sport environment has yielded results that are, in turn, sport-specific (Thomas & Over, 1994; Thomas et al., 1996). It is probable that every sport has unique environmental demands that are reflected in the development of psychological strategies unique to that sport. It will therefore be important to identify both the broad range of skills that generalize across sports, as well as the specific approaches inherent to each sport.

4. Skill Inventory Development Needs to Incorporate a Greater Emphasis on Validity

Our review of psychological skill inventories indicated that a major weakness of previous research efforts has been the demonstration of the validity of the instruments. It is vital to know whether an assessment instrument, as well as being reliable and internally consistent, can track meaningful athlete behaviors. Recent research shows promise in this regard. For example, Thomas and Over (1994) showed that low handicap golfers reported using some psychological skills to a greater extent than high handicap golfers. Even more impressively, Smith and Christensen (1995) found that the psychological skills they measured predicted athletes' survival in baseball over a 3-year period. Assessment of validity can include a variety of methods, including cross-validation against pre-existing instruments; comparisons with skill ratings by others, including coaches; tracking changes in psychological skill use over time, especially with the development of expertise in a sport; demonstrating changes in psychological skill use concurrently with PST programs; showing that changes in psychological skill use correspond to major environmental changes; and predicting future athlete behaviors based upon reported use of psychological skills.

5. PST Assessment Should Focus on the Development of Psychological Skills

PST theorists invariably emphasize the importance of practicing psychological skills in order to gain proficiency in their use (Vealey, 1988). Although several studies have evaluated the effectiveness of overall PST training programs for athletes (Daw & Burton, 1994; Savoy, 1993), little attention has been paid to the process by which psychological skills develop over time within individual athletes. Several important issues deserve attention here, including the issue of whether children and adolescents use different types of psychological skills than do adults; who the important sources are for athletes for learning psychological skills in sport; and how athletes can best practice psychological skill development. Research in these areas would represent a real breakthrough in the advance of understanding of psychological skills in sport.

Conclusion

This chapter is titled "In Search of Psychological Skills" because we are still searching for clear definitions and clarity of assessment in this area. The theoretical foundations of this area are strong. There is a long and vigorous history into the psychological processes that mediate athletic performance, such as motivation, confidence, and attention. The PST literature has also been strong in describing the intervention methods used by athletes and coaches to prepare for performance, such as relaxation training and mental rehearsal. What is lacking, is a comprehensive model of how athletes manage their peformance psychologically and how the psychological skills and strategies they use can be assessed. We have attempted to guide research in this area by outlining a three-step psychological model of the performance management process that takes into account identifying the ideal performance state, self-monitoring emotions and cognitions during performance, and using self-regulation strategies to gain greater self-control over psychological processes. Assessment inventory developers must be cognizant of all three steps in performance management. For progress in assessment to occur, there needs to be a long-term research effort focused on inventory development. Inventory content can be guided by good qualitative research, but development must focus on establishing reliability and validity according to sound psychometric principles.

In addition, we have proposed that the assessment of psychological skills should include more than the assessment of performance. Athletes utilize a variety of psychological strategies to solve a host of problems in their training and competition environments, and a complete understanding of the process of achievement in sport must include an assessment of these psychological problem solving skills. Future research will no doubt move beyond inventory development to multi-system approaches to the assessment of psychological skills.

References

Abernethy, B., & Russell, D. (1987). Expert-novice differences in an applied selective attention task. *Journal of Sport Psychology, 9*, 326-345.

Anderson, J.A. (1982). Acquisition of cognitive skill. *Psychological Review, 89*, 369-406.

Atkinson, J.W. (1957). Motivational determinants of risk-taking behaviors. *Psychological Review, 64*, 359-372.

Bandura, A. (1977). Self-efficacy: Toward a unifying theory of behavioral change. *Psychological Review, 84*, 191-215.

Beail, N. (Ed.) (1985). *Repertory grid technique and personal constructs.* London: Croom Helm.

Beck, A.T. (1976). *Cognitive therapy and the emotional disorders.* New York: International Universities Press.

Bennett, B. K., & Pravitz, J. E. (1987). *Profile of a winner: Advanced mental skills for athletes.* Ithaca, NY: Sport Science International.

Boutcher, S.H. (1992). Attention and athletic performance: An integrated approach. In T.S. Horn (Ed.), *Advances in sport psychology* (pp. 251-266). Champaign, IL: Human Kinetics.

Budney, A.J., Murphy, S.M., & Woolfolk, R.L. (1994). Imagery and motor performance: What do we really know? In E.R. Korn & A.A. Shiekh, Eds., *Imagery in sports and physical performance* (pp. 97-120). New York: Baywood Press.

Budney, A.J., & Woolfolk, R.L. (1990). Using the wrong image: An exploration of the adverse effects of imagery on motor performance. *Journal of Mental Imagery, 14*, 75-86.

Bunker, L., Williams, J.M., & Zinsser, N. (1993). Cognitive techniques for improving performance and building confidence. In J.M. Williams (Ed.), *Applied sport psychology* (2nd ed., pp. 225-242). Palo Alto, CA: Mayfield.

Burton, D. (1992). The Jekyll/Hyde nature of goals: Reconceptualizing goal setting in sport. In T.S. Horn (Ed.), *Advances in sport psychology* (pp. 267-297). Champaign, IL: Human Kinetics.

Butler, R.J., & Hardy, L. (1992). The Performance Profile: Theory and application. *The Sport Psychologist, 6*, 253-264.

Chartrand, J.M., Jowdy, D.P., & Danish, S.J. (1992). The Psychological Skills Inventory for Sports: Psychometric characteristics and applied implications. *Journal of Sport & Exercise Psychology, 14*, 405-413.

Coppel, D.B. (1980). The relationship of perceived social support and self-efficacy to major and minor stressors. *Unpublished doctoral dissertation*, University of Washington.

Crocker, P.E., & Graham, T.R. (1995). Coping by competitive athletes with performance stress: Gender differences and relationships with affect. *The Sport Psychologist, 9*, 325-338.

Csikszentmihalyi, M. (1990). *Flow: The psychology of optimal experience.* New York: Harper & Row.

Dale, G.A., & Wrisberg, C.A. (1996). The use of a performance profiling technique in a team setting: Getting the athletes and coach on the "same page". *The Sport Psychologist, 10*, 261-177.

Davis, H. (1991). Criterion validity of the Athletic Motivation Inventory: Issues in professional sport. *Journal of Applied Sport Psychology, 3*, 176-182.

Daw, J., & Burton, D. (1994). Evaluation of a comprehensive psychological skills training program for collegiate tennis players. *The Sport Psychologist, 8*, 37-57.

Edmundson, D., & McCann, S. (1994). *Single subject research in sport psychology: The impact of training on elite athletes use of mental skills.* Manuscript submitted for publication.

Eklund, R. C., Gould, D., & Jackson, S. A. (1993). Psychological foundations of Olympic wrestling excellence: Reconciling individual differences and nomothetic characterization. *Journal of Applied Sport Psychology, 5*, 35-47.

Ellis, A., & Harper, R.A. (1975). *A new guide to rational living.* New York: Prentice-Hall.

Ericsson, K.A., & Charness, N. (1994). Expert performance, its structure and acquisition. *American Psychologist, 49*, 725-747.

Feltz, D.L., & Landers, D.M. (1983). The effects of mental practice on motor skill learning and performance: A meta-analysis. *Journal of Sport Psychology, 5*, 25-57.

Fitts, P., & Posner, M. (1967). *Human performance.* Belmont, CA: Brooke/Cole.

Garfield, C.A., & Bennett, H.L. (1984). *Peak performance: Mental training techniques of the world's greatest athletes.* Los Angeles: Jeremy Tarcher.

George, L. (1986). Mental imagery enhancement training in behavior therapy: Current status and future prospects. *Psychotherapy, 23*, 81-92.

Gould, D., Eklund, R.C., & Jackson, S.A. (1993). Coping strategies used by more or less successful U.S. Olympic wrestlers. *Research Quarterly for Exercise and Sport, 64*, 453-468.

Gould, D., Finch, L., & Jackson, S.A. (1993). Coping strategies utilized by national chamionship figure skaters. *Research Quarterly for Exercise and Sport, 64*, 134-159.

Gould, D., Jackson, S. A., & Finch, L. M. (1993). Life at the top: The experiences of U. S. National champion figure skaters. *The Sport Psychologist, 7*, 354-374.

Gould, D., & Krane, V. (1992). The arousal-athletic performance relationship: Current status and future directions. In T. Horn (Ed.), *Advances in sport psychology* (pp. 119-142). Champaign, IL: Human Kinetics.

Gould, D., Tammen, V., Murphy, S., & May, J. (1989). An examination of U.S. Olympic sport psychology consultants and the services they provide. *The Sport Psychologist, 3*, 300-312.

Gould, D., & Udry, E. (1994). Psychological skills for enhancing performance: Arousal regulation strategies. *Medicine and Science in Sports and Exercise, 26*, 478-485.

Gould, D., Weiss, M., & Weinberg, R.S. (1981). Psychological characteristics of successful and non-successful Big Ten wrestlers. *Journal of Sport Psychology, 3*, 69-81.

Greenspan, M.J., & Feltz, D.L. (1989). Psychological interventions with athletes in competitive situations: A review. *The Sport Psychologist, 3*, 219-236.

Greenspan, M.J., Murphy, S.M., Tammen, V.V., & Jowdy, D.P. (1988, October). *Effects of athletic achievement level and test administration instructions on the Psychological Skills Inventory for Sports (PSIS).* Paper presented at the annual meeting of the Association for the Advancement of Applied Sport Psychology, Nashua, NH.

Griffith, C.R. (1930). *Psychology of football.* Unpublished manuscript cited in R. Martens (1987), *Coaches guide to sport psychology*, Chamapign, IL: Human Kinetics.

Hall, C.R., Rodgers, W.M., & Barr, K.A. (1990). The use of imagery by athletes in selected sports. *The Sport Psychologist, 4*, 1-10.

Hammer, W., & Tutko, T.A. (1974). Validation of the Athletic Motivation Inventory. *International Journal of Sport Psychology, 19*, 247-263.

Hanin, Y., & Syrja, P. (1995). Performance affect in junior ice hockey players: An application of the individual Zones of Optimal Functioning model. *The Sport Psychologist, 9*, 169-187.

Hardy, L., Jones, G., & Gould, D. (1996). *Understanding psychological preparation for performance: Theory and practice of elite performers.* Chichester, U.K.: Wiley.

Hardy, L., & Nelson, D. (1988). Self-regulation training in sport and work. *Ergonomics, 31*, 1573-1585.

Hardy, L., & Parfitt, G. (1991). A catastrophe model of anxiety and performance. *British Journal of Psychology, 82*, 163-178.

Heyman, S.R. (1982). Comparisons of successful and unsuccessful competitors: A reconsideration of methodological questions and data. *Journal of Sport Psychology, 4*, 295-300.

Highlen, P.S., & Bennett, B.B. (1979) Psychological characteristics of successful and non-successful elite wrestlers: An exploratory study. *Journal of Sport Psychology, 1*, 123-137.

Jackson, S.A. (1995). Factors influencing the occurrence of flow state in elite athletes. *Journal of Applied Sport Psychology, 7,* 138-166.

Jones, G. (1993). The role of performance profiling in cognitive-behavioral interventions in sport. *The Sport Psychologist, 7,* 160-172.

Kelly, G.A. (1955). *The psychology of personal constructs,* New York: Norton.

Kendall, G., Hrycaiko, D., Martin, G.L., & Kendall, T. (1990). The effects of an imagery rehearsal, relaxation, and self-talk package on basketball game performance. *Journal of Sport and Exercise Psychology, 12,* 157-166.

Kirschenbaum, D.S., & Smith, R. J. (1983). Sequencing effects in simulated coach feedback: Continuous criticism, or praise, can debilitate performance. *Journal of Sport Psychology, 5,* 332-342.

Lesser, M., & Murphy, S.M. (1988, August). *The Psychological Skills Inventory for Sports (PSIS): Normative and reliability data.* Paper presented at the annual meeting of the American Psychological Association, Atlanta, GA.

Loehr, J.E. (1983, January). The ideal performance state. *Science Periodical on Research and Technology in Sport.* Ottawa: Coaching Association of Canada.

Loehr, J.E. (1986). *Mental toughness training for sports: Achieving athletic excellence.* Lexington, MA: Stephen Greene Press.

Madden, C.C., Kirkby, R.J., & McDonald, D. (1989). Coping styles of competitive middle distance runners. *International Journal of Sport Psychology, 20,* 21-35.

Mahoney, M.J. (1979). Cognitive skills and athletic performance. In P.C. Kendall & S.D. Hollon (Eds.), *Cognitive-behavioral interventions: Theory, research, and procedures* (pp. 423-443). New York: Academic Press.

Mahoney, M.J. (1989). Psychological predictors of elite and non-elite performance in Olympic weightlifting. *International Journal of Sport Psychology, 20,* 1-12.

Mahoney, M.J., & Avener, M. (1977). Psychology of the elite athlete: An exploratory study. *Cognitive Therapy and Research, 1,* 135-141.

Mahoney, M.J., Gabriel, T.J., & Perkins, T.S. (1987). Psychological skills and exceptional athletic performance. *The Sport Psychologist, 1,* 181-199.

Martens, R. (1987). *Coaches guide to sport psychology.* Champaign, IL: Human Kinetics.

Martens, R., Vealey, R.S., & Burton, D. (1990). *Competitive anxiety in sport.* Champaign, IL: Human Kinetics.

Maynard, I., Hemmings, B., & Warwick-Evans, L. (1995). The effects of a somatic intervention strategy on competitive state anxiety and performance in semiprofessional soccer players. *The Sport Psychologist, 9,* 51-64.

McCann, S. (1995). Overtraining and burnout. In S.M. Murphy (Ed.), *Sport psychology interventions* (pp. 347-368). Champaign, IL: Human Kinetics.

Meichenbaum, D. (1977). *Cognitive-behavior modification* (2nd ed.). New York: Plenum Press.

Meyers, A.W., Cooke, C.J., Cullen, J., & Liles, L. (1979). Psychological aspects of athletic competitors: A replication across sports. *Cognitive Research and Therapy, 3,* 361-366.

Meyers, A.W., Whelan, J.P., & Murphy, S.M. (1996). Cognitive behavioral strategies in athletic performance enhancement. In M. Hersen, R.M. Eisler, & P.M. Miller (Eds.), *Progress in behavior modification: Volume 30* (pp. 137-164). Pacific Grove, CA: Brooks/Cole.

Moore, W.E., & Stevenson, J.R. (1991). Understanding trust in the performance of complex automatic sport skills. *The Sport Psychologist, 5,* 281-289.

Moore, W.E., & Stevenson, J.R. (1994). Training for trust in sport skills. *The Sport Psychologist, 8,* 1-12.

Moran, A.P. (1996). *The psychology of concentration in sports performers: A cognitive analysis.* East Sussex, UK: Psychology Press.

Morris, T., & Thomas, P. (1995). Approaches to applied sport psychology. In T. Morris & J. Summers (Ed.), *Sport psychology: Theories, applications and issues* (pp. 215-258). Milton, Qld: John Wiley & Sons.

Murphy, S.M. (Ed.) (1995). *Sport psychology interventions.* Champaign, IL: Human Kinetics.

Murphy, S.M., & Jowdy, D.P. (1992). Imagery and mental practice. In T.Horn (Ed.), *Advances in sport psychology* (pp. 221-250). Champaign, IL: Human Kinetics.

Neiss, R. (1988). Reconceptualizing arousal: Psychobiological states in motor performance. *Psychological Bulletin, 103,* 345-366.

Nelson, D., & Hardy, L. (1990). The development of an empirically validated tool for measuring psychological skill in sport. *Journal of Sports Sciences, 8,* 71.

Nideffer, R.M., & Sharpe, R.C. (1978). *Attention control training: How to get control of your mind through total concentration.* New York: Wideview.

Orlick, T. (1980). *In pursuit of excellence.* Champaign, IL: Human Kinetics.

Orlick, T. (1982). Beyond excellence. In T. Orlick, J.T. Partington, & J.H. Salmela (Eds.), *Mental training for coaches and athletes* (pp.1-7). Ottawa: Coaching Association of Canada.

Orlick, T. (1986). *Psyching for sport: Mental training for athletes.* Champaign, IL: Leisure Press.

Orlick, T., & Partington, J. (1988). Mental links to excellence. *The Sport Psychologist, 2,* 105-130.

Perna, F., Neyer, M., Murphy, S.M., Ogilvie, B.C., & Murphy, A. (1995). Consultation with sport organizations: A cognitive-behavioral model. In S.M. Murphy (Ed.), *Sport psychology interventions* (pp. 235-252). Champaign, IL: Human Kinetics.

Privette, G. (1983). Peak experience, peak performance, and flow: A comparative analysis of positive human experiences. *Journal of Personality and Social Psychology, 45,* 1361-1368.

Ravizza, K. (1977). Peak experiences in sport. *Journal of Humanistic Psychology, 17,* 35-40.

Ravizza, K. (1984). Peak experiences in sport. In J. M. Silva and R. S. Weinberg (Eds.), *Psychological foundations of sport.* (pp. 452-462). Champaign, IL: Human Kinetics.

Rotella, R.J., Gansneder, B., Ojala, D., & Billing, J. (1980). Cognitions and coping strategies of elite skiers: An exploratory study of young developing athletes. *Journal of Sport Psychology, 2,* 350-354.

Sachs, M.L. (1991). Reading list in applied sport psychology: Psychological skills training. *The Sport Psychologist, 5,* 88-91.

Savoy, C. (1993). A yearly mental training program for a college basketball player. *The Sport Psychologist, 7,* 173-190.

Schneider, W., & Shiffrin, R.M. (1977). Controlled and automatic human information processing: I. Detection, search, and attention. *Psychological Review, 84,* 1-66.

Schutz, R.W., & Gessaroli, M.E. (1993). Use, misuse, and disuse of psychometrics in sport psychology research. In R.N. Singer, M. Murphey, & L.K. Tennant (Eds.), *Handbook of research on sport psychology* (pp. 901-917). New York: Macmillan.

Shelton, T.O., & Mahoney, M.J. (1978). The content and effect of "psyching-up" strategies in weightlifters. *Cognitive Therapy and Research, 2,* 275-284.

Smith, R.E., & Christensen, D.S. (1995). Psychological skills as predictors of performance and survival in professional baseball. *Journal of Sport & Exercise Psychology, 17,* 399-415.

Smith, R.E., Schutz, R.W., Smoll, F.L., & Ptacek, J.T. (1995). Development and validation of a multidimensional measure of sport-specific psychological skills: The Athletic Coping Skills Inventory-28. *Journal of Sport & Exercise Psychology, 17,* 379-398.

Smith, R.E., Smoll, F.L., & Ptacek, J.T. (1990). Conjunctive moderator variables in vulnerability and resiliency research: Life stress, social support and coping skills, and adolescent sport injuries. *Journal of Personality and Social Psychology, 58,* 360-370.

Smith, R.E., Smoll, F.L., & Schutz, R.W. (1990). Measurement and correlates of sport-specific cognitive and somatic trait anxiety: The Sport Anxiety Scale. *Anxiety Research, 2,* 263-280.

Spielberger, C.D. (1966). *Anxiety and behavior.* New York, Academic.

Swets, J.A., & Bjork, R.A. (1990). Enhancing human performance: An evaluation of "New Age" techniques considered by the U.S. Army. *Psychological Science, 1,* 85-96.

Tammen, V.V., & Murphy, S.M. (1990, June). *Reevaluating the Psychological Skills Inventory for Sports: Factor analysis and implications.* Paper presented at the annual meeting of the North American Society of Psychology of Sport and Physical Activity, Asilomar, CA.

Thomas, P.R., & Over, R. (1994). Psychological and psychomotor skills associated with performance in golf. *The Sport Psychologist, 8,* 73-86.

Thomas, P.R., Schlinker, P.J., & Over, R. (1996). Psychological and psychomotor skills associated with prowess at ten-pin bowling. *Journal of Sport Sciences, 14,* 255-268.

Tutko, T.A., Lyon, L.P., & Ogilvie, B.C. (1969). *Athletic Motivation Inventory.* San Jose, CA: Institute for the Study of Athletic Motivation.

Van Mele,V., Auweele,Y.V., & Rzewnicki, R. (1995). An integrative procedure for the diagnosis of an elite athlete: A case study. *The Sport Psychologist, 9,* 130-147.

Van Raalte, J.L., Brewer, B.W., Rivera, P.M., & Petitpas, A.J. (1994). The relationship between observable self-talk and competitive junior tennis players' match performances. *Journal of Sport & Exercise Psychology, 16,* 400-415.

Vealey, R.S. (1988). Future directions in psychological skills training. *The Sport Psychologist, 2,* 318-336.

Vernacchia, R.A., & Cook, D.L. (1993, March). The influence of a mental training technique upon the performance of selected intercollegiate basketball players. *Applied Research in Coaching and Athletics Annual,* 188-200.

Weinberg, R.S., & Williams, J.M. (1993). Integrating and implementing a psychological skills training program. In J.M. Williams (Ed.), *Applied sport psychology* (2nd ed.) (pp. 274-298). Palo Alto, CA: Mayfield.

White, R. (1959). Motivation reconsidered: The concept of competence. *Psychological Review, 66,* 297-333.

White, S.A. (1993). The relationship between psychological skills, experience, and practice commitment among collegiate male and female skiers. *The Sport Psychologist, 7,* 49-57.

Wolpe, J. (1958). *Psychotherapy by reciprocal inhibition.* Stanford, CA: Stanford University Press.

Part IV

Group Dynamics
in Sport and Exercise

PART IV

The worlds of sport and exercise clubs typically entail the formation of groups. There is a need to assess group attributes before we can truly understand what influences group formation as well as the impact of group membership and group dynamics. Dating back to the seminal work of Fiedler (1954), assessments of cohesion have been developed and applied to the study of groups in the physical domain. Part IV provides a detailed account of this evolution and, with specific reference to the sport-relevant Group Environment Questionnaire (Carron, Widmeyer, & Brawley, 1985), discusses how best to measure cohesion in other settings and among various groups.

The athletic realm also involves important relationships and interactions between coaches and athletes. Of particular concern is the assessment of the attributes, antecedents, and consequences of leadership in sport. Much of the work on leadership in sport has been grounded in Chelladurai's (1978) Multidimensional Model of Leadership or Smith, Smoll, and associates' Mediational Model of Leadership (Smoll, Smith, Curtis, & Hunt, 1978). In Part IV, the reader will also find an examination of assessments of coaching behaviors (and athletes' preferences for and perceptions of their coach's behavior) that have emanated from these conceptual frameworks. Measures of decision styles in coaching are also included in this review.

References

Carron, A., Widmeyer, W.N., & Brawley, L.R. (1985). The development of an instrument to assess cohesion in sport teams: The Group Environment Questionnaire. *Journal of Sport Psychology, 7*, 244-266.

Chelladurai, P. (1990). Leadership in sports: A review. *International Journal of Sport Psychology, 21*, 328-354.

Fiedler, F.E. (1954). Assumed similarity measures as predictors of team effectiveness. *Journal of Abnormal and Social Psychology, 49*, 381-388.

Smoll, F.L., Smith, F.L., Curtis, B. & Hunt, E. (1978). Toward a mediational model of coach-player relationships. *Research Quarterly, 49*, 528-541.

Chapter 12

THE MEASUREMENT OF COHESIVENESS IN SPORT GROUPS

Albert V. Carron
University of Western Ontario
and
Lawrence R. Brawley
W. Neil Widmeyer
University of Waterloo

The terms *group* and *cohesion* are intertwined—if a group exists, it has to be cohesive to some extent. Thus, it is not surprising that when groups have been the focus, cohesion has been a preeminent topic of interest in sport psychology and other disciplines, such as sociology, social psychology, counseling psychology, military psychology, organizational psychology, and educational psychology. It is also not surprising that numerous authors in these various disciplines have attempted to define and measure cohesion.

Unfortunately, however, it is difficult to measure a theoretical construct—which is by definition an abstraction and, therefore, not directly observable. This difficulty is well illustrated with the theoretical construct of cohesion. After examining the history of research on cohesiveness, Mudrack (1989a) concluded that it "has been dominated by confusion, inconsistency, and almost inexcusable sloppiness with regard to defining the construct" (p. 45). Part of our purpose in writing this chapter is to have sport psychology researchers avoid such criticism in the future.

In the first section, we introduce our constitutive definition of cohesiveness—one that has won general acceptance from group dynamics theoreticians (cf. Cota, Evans, Dion, Kilik, & Longman, 1995; Mudrack, 1989a, 1989b). We then provide a brief history of the measurement of cohesion in sport teams. In the third section, we present our operational definition for cohesiveness in sport and exercise groups, which we refer to as the *Group Environment Questionnaire (*GEQ). In the fourth and final section, we discuss some important theoretical and practical issues related to the nature and measurement of cohesion.

The Definition of Cohesion

Cohesion can be defined as a dynamic process that is reflected in the tendency for a group to stick together and remain united in the pursuit of its instrumental objectives and/or for the satisfaction of member affective needs. This definition, which represents a slight modification of one originally introduced by Carron (1982), explicitly highlights the nature of cohesiveness as it is manifested in most groups—including, we believe, sport teams, work groups, military units, fraternity groups, and social and friendship groups.

One property of cohesion that this definition is intended to highlight is that cohesion is *multidimensional*. There are many factors that cause any group to stick together and remain united. The factor(s) that cause(s) one group to stick together may not be present in equal weight in another apparently identical group. Thus, for example, one rowing team may be highly united around its task objectives and yet be in open conflict from a social perspective. Conversely, a second apparently similar rowing team may be very cohesive socially but completely lack task unity.

A second property of cohesion that this definition emphasizes is that cohesion is *dynamic*. Cohesion is not as transitory as a state, but neither is it as stable as a trait. Cohesion in a group can (and does) change over time so that the factor(s) contributing to cohesion early in a group's history may or may not be critical when the group is well developed. Thus, for example, in the initial, forming stage of a social group, a common religious belief and/or socioeconomic status may be important for group unity. After a year of interaction and communication, however, maintaining close personal ties and/or carrying out the group's objectives may become preeminent (whereas similarity in religious beliefs and/or socioeconomic status may become unimportant—at least in matters of consequence to the group).

A third property that the above definition is intended to highlight is the *instrumental* nature of cohesion. That is, all

Table 1
Operational Differences of Cohesion in Sport Sciences

Author(s)	Cohesion Measure(s)	Characteristics
Fiedler (1954)	Assumed similarity--a measure of liking and personal warmth	Unidimensional approach Emphasis on social aspects No direct measure of task cohesion
Myers (1962)	Esteem for teammates Perceived acceptance by teammates Attribution of responsibility	Multidimensional approach Confounded task and social aspects Used consequence to represent construct
McGrath (1962)	Positive interpersonal relations --subjects rated teammates	Unidimensional approach Emphasis on social aspects No direct measure of task unity
Stogdill (1964)	Perceived group task integration on each play of a football game	Unidimensional approach Emphasis on task aspects Rating carried out by individuals outside the group Outcome considered to be synonymous with cohesion Construct treated as a state
Lenk (1969)	Sociometric social and leadership choices Participant observation of social relationships	Multidimensional approach Emphasis on social aspects No direct measure of task unity
Klein & Christiansen (1969)	Attraction to the group	Unidimensional approach Attraction (a) underrepresents cohesion, (b) cannot explain cohesion under conditions of negative affect, (c) has not been supported empirically, (d) is not necessary for group formation.
Martens et al. (1972)	Sport Cohesiveness Questionnaire: friendship, value of membership, enjoyment, influence/power, sense of belonging, closeness, teamwork	Multidimensional approach Emphasis on social aspects (but task aspects considered Single items to assess dimensions Psychometric properties untested
Gruber & Gray (1981, 1982)	Team performance satisfaction, self performance satisfaction, value of membership, task cohesion, desire for recognition, affiliation	Multidimensional approach Task & social cohesion assessed Antecedents/consequences of cohesion included in item pool
Yukelson et al. (1984)	Multidimensional Sport Cohesion Inventory: quality of teamwork, attraction to group, valued roles, unity of purpose	Multidimensional approach Task & social cohesion assessed Antecedents/consequences of cohesion included among item pool Validity untested

groups form for a purpose. Sport groups, work groups, and military units form for task-oriented reasons. Even groups that may be considered purely "social" in nature have an instrumental basis for their formation. Thus, for example, acquaintances who decide to form a social club to develop or maintain better friendships are cohering for instrumental reasons. Therefore, the instrumentality that characterizes cohesion stems from the motivational base of the group (Sherif & Sherif, 1969).

Finally, the above definition is intended to highlight the fact that cohesion has an *affective* dimension. Social relationships among group members may be present in a group initially and/or they might evolve over time. Even in highly task-oriented groups—work crews, sport teams, military units—social cohesion generally develops as a result of member instrumental and social interactions and communications.

Any constitutive (conceptual) definition of a construct has important implications for measurement. That is, the constitutive definition of cohesion influences (a) development of an operational definition, (b) hypotheses pertaining to the relative importance of the various manifestations of cohesiveness throughout the history of the group, and, finally, (c) hypotheses pertaining to the relationship of various dimensions of cohesion to other constructs. These implications are addressed in detail in the final two sections of this chapter.

Historical Developments in the Measurement of Cohesion in Sport Psychology

Early Developments From Social Psychology

The study of group cohesion in sport and its relationship to team effectiveness has had a long, rich tradition (see Table 1). In particular, the University of Illinois has played a predominant role in its development beginning with the work of Fiedler (1954),

Myers (1962), and McGrath (1962), then, later, with the contribution of Martens, Landers, and Loy (1972), and more recently with the research and writing of Martens' students, Gill (Gill, 1977; Ruder & Gill, 1982) and Widmeyer (cf. Widmeyer, Brawley, & Carron, 1985; Widmeyer & Martens, 1978).

It could be argued that neither Fiedler, Myers, nor McGrath was studying cohesion; the term is used only once in the three articles (when Myers suggested that individual adjustment to the team, the construct he examined, incorporated Gross and Martin's [1952] concept of cohesion). Nonetheless, their research is worth considering here because they were among the first to examine the relationship of team dynamics to team effectiveness.

In Fiedler's (1954) research with high school basketball teams, interpersonal relationships within the team were assessed with 100 statements formed into blocks of five statements each. The athlete was required to indicate which statement in a block was most characteristic of himself and which was least characteristic of himself. The process was repeated three times so that the athlete could describe himself, the person with whom he cooperated best, and the person with whom he cooperated most poorly. Responses from the three questionnaires were then compared to yield "assumed similarity" measures. Fiedler's work helped to highlight the importance of team dynamics for understanding team effectiveness. However, his unidimensional operational measure emphasized the social aspects that bind groups together; the task aspects were not considered (see Table 1).

In 1962, both McGrath and Myers published research undertaken with recreational rifle teams organized with the assistance of the University of Illinois ROTC unit. In the Myers study, the individual's relationship to his team was assessed using three measures: esteem for teammates (measured by having the subject rate each teammate using Fiedler's Least Preferred Coworker Scale), perceived acceptance (measured using a 5-item inventory), and attributions for failure (measured by having the subject indicate whether team failure was the product of the performance of himself, his teammates, or the other team). On the one hand, Myers did attempt to take into account the multidimensional nature of intrateam relationships (and their association with team effectiveness). On the other hand, however, esteem for teammates and perceived acceptance—two of the operational measures employed—confounded the task and social bases of group closeness. As well, attributions for failure, the third operational measure he used, reflected one of the consequences of cohesion; it is not a manifestation of cohesion itself.

In the McGrath (1962) study, rifle teams varying in positive interpersonal relationships were assembled by combining the responses from one sociometric nomination question and the sum of four behavioral description items. For the former, the subject indicated if either of his two teammates had helped him stay calm and relaxed. The four behavior description items required the subject to rate the degree to which each teammate was warm, standoffish, disruptive, and attentive. Because McGrath's interest was in a construct he called positive interpersonal relationships in the team, it may not be surprising that his operational definition relied exclusively on social factors. However, given that rifle teams and their performance effectiveness were also the focus, it could be argued that the absence of some assessment of task cohesion/unity was an unfortunate oversight.

Typically, evaluation of the degree of cohesion present in a group has been provided by its members. In 1964, Stogdill took a rather novel approach in the analysis of what he referred to as the group integration of the Ohio State football team during its six home games. Four independent judges sitting at different places in the stadium rated how integrated the team was on each play. Although the question of whether an objective outsider is in a better position to assess the integration (i.e., task cohesion) of a team than are more closely involved members of the group is interesting, it has never been examined experimentally. Further, the measure of integration used by Stogdill was probably more influenced by the observation of the outcome (i.e., number of yards gained on the play) than by group processes. Finally, another aspect of the Stogdill measure worth noting is its incorporation of the temporal nature of cohesion. Assessing cohesion on every play implicitly assumes that the construct is very transitory and can change within one or two minutes.

In a frequently cited study on team cohesion, Lenk (1969) found that teams of rowers—the 1960 German gold medalist rowing eight and the 1962 German world champion rowing eight—were highly successful despite open conflict and an apparent lack of cohesion. Lenk claim-ed that his findings refuted the invalid "thesis that seems to have been taken for granted ... namely, the proposition: only small groups, which are low in conflict, or highly integrated can produce especially high performances" (p. 393). Group unity was assessed through sociometric social and leadership choices and by participant observation of social relationships. Although a multidimensional approach was used by Lenk to represent group unity, the emphasis was on social relationships and leadership choices only; no assessment was made of task cohesion.

With the benefit of hindsight (and without assessment), it might be argued that Lenk's rowing eights were, in fact, highly integrated, but in a task cohesive sense only. It also could be argued that Lenk's study highlighted the multidimensional nature of group cohesion, and not, as he suggested, that groups high in conflict or poorly integrated can produce especially high performance. In short, the absence of social cohesion in the rowing eights did not preclude the possibility that they were highly task cohesive or that they would have had greater success if they also had been socially cohesive.

Klein and Christiansen (1969) suggested that cohesion is present in a group "when as high as possible a percentage perceives that the group is attractive" (p. 398). This did not represent a very promising start in that conceptions of cohesion based solely on interpersonal attraction are inadequate conceptually. However, Klein and Christiansen then went on to elaborate that the presence of cohesion "would indicate that there are no severe conflicts within the group or contrary opinions about the strategy to achieve goals" (p. 398). Clearly, lack of conflicts and consensus on goal strategies reflect both a social and task basis for group unity. Thus, Klein and Christiansen were among the first researchers in the sport sciences to explicitly acknowledge the task and social dimensions of cohesiveness. Unfortunately, however, their operational definition of cohesion was based on a single question in which members of 3-on-3 basketball teams rated the attractiveness of their unit prior to competition.

Early Developments From Sport Psychology

From a historical perspective, the instrument that has had the most significant impact on cohesion research in sport psychology is the Martens et al. (1972) Sport Cohesiveness Questionnaire (SCQ). It was the first inventory to have a specific sport orientation and, possibly because of this, it stimulated considerable research on issues associated with cohesion in sport teams. The 7-item SCQ assesses team cohesion through group member ratings of friendship (interpersonal attraction), personal power or influence, enjoyment, closeness, teamwork, sense of belonging, and perceived value of membership. The seven items have been considered independently (cf. Arnold & Straub, 1973) and in categories where the combinations of items were assumed to be conceptually meaningful (cf. Carron & Chelladurai, 1981). A strength of the SCQ is its multidimensional perspective (although single items are used to assess each dimension). One limitation, however, is that with the exception of the teamwork item, the task and social bases for unity are confounded. Also, as Gill (1977) noted, the SCQ may possess face validity, but published evidence for its reliability and other forms of validity is not available.

Both Gruber and Gray (1981, 1982) and Yukelson, Weinberg, and Jackson (1984) used similar data-driven approaches to develop sport cohesion instruments. That is, previous questionnaires and other similar sources were used to develop as comprehensive an item pool as possible. In the case of Gruber and Gray, for example, a factor analysis was conducted on 13 items that had appeared most frequently in previous research examining cohesion. Factor analysis revealed the presence of six scales: team performance satisfaction, self-performance satisfaction, task cohesion, affiliation cohesion, desire for recognition, and value of membership.

To develop their Multidimensional Sport Cohesion Instrument (MSCI), Yukelson et al. (1984) obtained a pool of questions from four sources: existing cohesion questionnaires, operational definitions proposed by theoreticians, research in organizational and industrial psychology, and interviews with sport scientists and coaches. They then subjected their item pool to factor analysis, and four scales were derived, each with high internal consistency: quality of teamwork reflecting how well teammates work together (alpha = .86); attraction to the group signifying attraction to and satisfaction with being a member of the group (alpha = .88); unity of purpose reflecting commitment to norms, goals, operating procedures, and group strategies (alpha = .86); and valued roles reflecting identification with group membership (alpha = .79).

Both the Gruber and Gray (1981) instrument and the MSCI represent a valuable contribution to the measurement of team cohesion because they were the first sport-related questionnaires to explicitly acknowledge that cohesion is multidimensional containing both task and social bases. However, one limitation that both measures suffer from is they were data driven in their development. A data-driven approach fails to take into account the danger of borrowing the problems of previous studies when it relies on past instruments as a major source of items. Such borrowing often results in analysis procedures that group related

items without a priori regard to whether they are antecedent or consequent to the focal variable. Such is the case for the Gruber and Gray and *MSCI* instruments. For example, both questionnaires included items to assess enjoyment and satisfaction whereas the MSCI includes items to assess various aspects of role performance including role clarity. Enjoyment, satisfaction, and/or role clarity may result from or contribute to cohesiveness, but they are not cohesiveness itself. The resulting product is based upon factor analysis of related but confounded concepts. Thus, the instrument generated is not likely to be much better than the original data (items). Problems such as these in mainstream psychology prompted Mudrack's (1989a) complaint that the history of cohesion measurement has been dominated by confusion and inconsistency. A second limitation of the Gruber and Gray instrument and the MSCI is that their validity is unknown. In the period since their introduction, neither of these instruments has been used in a program of research.

The Group Environment Questionnaire[1]

The Group Environment Questionnaire (GEQ) is distinctively different from its sport predecessors in that it is a conceptually-driven, multidimensional instrument. From 1982 to 1984, we carried out the research that led to the development of the GEQ. Subsequently, in a series of publications, we outlined the conceptual model that formed the basis for item development and test construction as well as the research undertaken by us to test the psychometric properties of the GEQ (cf. Brawley, Carron, & Widmeyer, 1987, 1988; Carron, Widmeyer, & Brawley, 1985, 1988; Widmeyer et al., 1985). We have summarized that literature here in order to provide the background that characterizes the research program undertaken with the GEQ.

Conceptual Model

A conceptual model is an organized, systematic representation of a phenomenon or construct. As Henry (1968) noted, scientific knowledge is generally viewed as a hierarchy. The foundation of this hierarchy is the hypothesis, a prediction about the relationships among a set of variables. With increasing levels of knowledge, a theory evolves—a comprehensive set of definitions and predictions that specify the relationships among a set of variables. Finally, a law, a well-defined, repeatedly verified theory, resides at the apex of the hierarchy. Within this hierarchy, a conceptual model falls midway between a hypothesis and a theory; it presents a more elaborate representation of the relationships among variables than does a hypothesis but is not as well developed and its variables not as well defined as is the case with a theory. Like a theory, however, a conceptual model "is a set of propositions consisting of defined interrelated constructs ...[it] sets out the interrelationships among a set of variables (constructs) ... [and it] explains phenomena" (Kerlinger, 1973, p. 9).

The conceptual model that forms the basis for the development of the GEQ evolves from three fundamental assumptions. The first, based on research in social cognition theory (cf. Bandura, 1986; Kenny & Lavoie, 1985; Levine & Moreland, 1991; Schlenker, 1975; Schlenker & Miller, 1977; Zander, 1971), is that cohesion—a group property—can be assessed through the per-

---

1. Much of the present discussion appeared initially in Carron et al. (1985) and Widmeyer et al. (1985).

ceptions of individual group members. In short, we believe that

1. A group has clearly observable properties, such as an organizational structure of role and status relationships.
2. Members experience the social situation of their group, are socialized into it, and develop a set of beliefs about the group.
3. These beliefs, like other social cognitions, are a product of the member's selective processing and personal integration of group-related information.
4. Perceptions about the group held by a group member are a reasonable estimate of various aspects of unity characteristic of the group.
5. The social cognitions about cohesion can be measured.

Theoreticians in the group dynamics literature have emphasized the need to distinguish between the group and the individual (cf. Cattell, 1948; Van Bergen & Koekebakker, 1959; Zander, 1971). Thus, our second assumption is that the social cognitions that each group member holds about the cohesiveness of the group are related to the group as a totality and to the manner in which the group satisfies personal needs and objectives. These social cognitions are labeled

1. Group Integration, which reflects the individual's perceptions about the closeness, similarity, and bonding within the group as a whole, as well as the degree of unification of the group field.
2. Individual Attractions to the Group, which reflects the individual's perceptions about personal motivations acting to retain him or her in the group, as well as his or her personal feelings about the group.

Theoreticians in the group dynamics literature also have emphasized the need to distinguish between the task-oriented and socially oriented concerns of groups and their members (cf. Festinger, Schachter, & Back, 1950; Fiedler, 1967; Hersey & Blanchard, 1969; Mikalachki, 1969). Thus, our third assumption is that there are two fundamental focuses to a group member's perceptions:

1. A task orientation representing a general orientation or mo-

tivation towards achieving the group's objectives.
2. A social orientation representing a general orientation or motivation toward developing and maintaining social relationships and activities within the group.

Consequently, in our conceptual model (and the resulting GEQ), four constructs are identified: Group Integration-Task (GI-T), Group Integration-Social (GI-S), Individual Attractions to the Group-Task (ATG-T), and Individual Attractions to the Group-Social (ATG-S). GI-T and GI-S are represented by "us," "our," and "we" perceptions whereas ATG-T and ATG-S are represented by "I," "my," and "me" perceptions. The constitutive definition for each of the four constructs and a sample question from the GEQ are presented in Table 2.

Validity of the GEQ

The cornerstone of any measurement instrument lies in its validity—the extent to which any instrument measures what it is supposed to measure. There are different forms of validity; confidence in an instrument increases as it meets the criteria for these different forms of validity. Table 3 provides an overview of research carried out with the GEQ in which the various types of validity have been explicitly stated and tested and the type of validity being examined was clear. Studies using the GEQ in which the type of validity being examined is not clear are not summarized here.

Content validity. The most elementary form of validity is content validity, or face validity as it is also called. Content validity is usually carried out by independent experts who assess the degree to which the items (i.e., operational definition) offer a representative estimate of the construct (this was the protocol followed in the development of the GEQ). Generally, the content-validation process occurs once (i.e., early) in instrument development. As Table 3 shows, we reported on the content validity of the GEQ in our first publications on the instrument (Carron et al., 1985; Widmeyer et al., 1985).

Concurrent validity. Concurrent validity involves the correlation of the instrument with other similar instruments. To demonstrate concurrent validity, the new instrument is expected

---

Table 2
Specific Constructs Constituting Perceived Cohesiveness in Sport Groups.

Construct	*Definition & Sample Item*
Group Integration-Task (GI-T)	Individual team member's feelings about the similarity, closeness, and bonding within the team as a whole around the group's task; for example, "Our team is united in trying to reach its goals for performance."
Group Integration-Social (GI-S)	Individual team member's feelings about the similarity, closeness, and bonding within the team as a whole around the group as a social unit; for example, "Members of our team do not stick together outside of practices and games."
Interpersonal Attractions to the Group-Task (ATG-T)	Individual team member's feelings about his or her personal involvement with the group task, productivity, and goals and objectives; for example, "I do not like the style of play on this team."
Interpersonal Attractions to the Group-Social (ATG-S)	Individual team member's feelings about his or her personal acceptance, and social interaction with the group; for example, "Some of my best friends are on this team."

Table 3
Overview of Research Pertaining to the Validity of the GEQ*.

Dependent Measure	Type of Validity	Result	Author(s)
GEQ items	Content	+	Carron et al. (1985, Phase 2)
Sport Cohesion Questionnaire	Concurrent	+	Brawley, Carron, & Widmeyer (1987, Study 1)[a]
Team Climate Questionnaire	Concurrent	+	Brawley, Carron, & Widmeyer (1987, Study 1)[b]
Bass Inventory	Concurrent	+	Brawley, Carron, & Widmeyer (1987, Study 1)[c]
Adherence Behavior in Exercise Groups:			
Drop out	Predictive	+	Carron, Widmeyer, & Brawley (1988, Study 1)
Drop out	Predictive	+	Spink & Carron (1993)
Attendance	Predictive	+	Spink & Carron (1994, Study 1)
Attendance	Predictive	+	Spink & Carron (1994, Study 2)
Absenteeism	Predictive	+	Spink & Carron (1992)
Lateness	Predictive	+	Spink & Carron (1992)
Early Exit	Predictive	-	Spink & Carron (1993)
Adherence Behavior in Sport Groups:			
Absent/Late	Predictive	+	Carron, Widmeyer, & Brawley (1988, Study 2)
Resistance to Disruption			
Sport	Predictive	+	Brawley, Carron, & Widmeyer (1988, Study 1)
Sport	Predictive	-	Brawley, Carron, & Widmeyer (1988, Study 2)[d]
Exercise	Predictive	+	Brawley, Carron, & Widmeyer (1988, Study 2)
Attributions	Predictive	+	Brawley, Carron, & Widmeyer (1987, Study 3)
Social Loafing	Predictive	+	Naylor & Brawley (1992)
	Predictive	+	McKnight, Williams, & Widmeyer (1991)
Group Size			
Exercise	Predictive	+	Carron & Spink (1995, Study 1)
Exercise	Predictive	+	Carron & Spink (1995, Study 2)
Exercise	Predictive	+	Carron & Spink (1995, Study 3)
Sport	Predictive	+	Widmeyer, Brawley, & Carron (1990, Study 1)
Leadership	Predictive	+	Westre & Weiss (1991)
	Predictive	+	Widmeyer & Williams (1991)
Team Building			
Sport	Predictive	+	McClure & Foster (1991)
Sport	Predictive	-	Prapavessis, Carron, & Spink (In press)
Exercise	Predictive	+	Carron & Spink (1993)
Exercise	Predictive	+	Spink & Carron (1993)
Role Involvement			
Clarity	Predictive	+	Dawe & Carron (1990)
Clarity	Predictive	+	Grand & Carron (1982)
Acceptance	Predictive	+	Dawe & Carron (1990)
Acceptance	Predictive	+	Grand & Carron (1982)
Collective Efficacy	Predictive	+	Paskevich (1995)
Communication	Predictive	-	Huntley & Carron (1992)
	Predictive	+	Widmeyer & Williams (1991)
	Predictive	+	Widmeyer, Carron, & Brawley (1993)
Coordination	Predictive	-	Huntley & Carron (1992)
	Predictive	-	Widmeyer, Carron, & Brawley (1993)
Team sport vs. Individual Sport	Predictive	+	Brawley, Carron, & Widmeyer (1987, Study 2)
Duration of Membership	Predictive	-	Brawley, Carron, & Widmeyer (1987, Study 2)
Group Environment Questionnaire			
	Factorial	+	Carron, Widmeyer, & Brawley (1985, Phase 4)
	Factorial	-	Schutz, Eom, Smoll, & Smith (1994)
	Factorial	-	Kozub (1993)
	Factorial	+	Li & Harmer (1996)

*The + sign indicates support from the research for the conceptual model; the - sign indicates a lack of support.
a. Six out of eight analyses supported predictions.
b. Nine out of 12 analyses supported predictions.
c. Twenty-eight out of 32 analyses supported predictions.
d. One out of two analyses supported predictions.

to correlate moderately well (i.e., $r = .35$ to $.60$) with an instrument that assesses similar or related constructs. Excessively high correlations (i.e., $r = .75$ or greater) raise doubts about the validity of the new instrument (i.e., it is redundant with existing instruments). Similarly, excessively low correlations (i.e., $r = .20$ or less) also raise doubts about the validity of the new instrument (i.e., it does not appear to measure the construct). Furthermore, the instrument should be less correlated with measures of unrelated constructs. Generally, concurrent validation also occurs early in instrument development. As Table 3 shows, we did subject the GEQ to various tests of concurrent validity (Brawley et al., 1987; Widmeyer et al., 1985); in the overwhelming majority of analyses, the GEQ was shown to possess concurrent validity.

Predictive validity. Predictive validity is considered to be present if a construct (i.e., cohesion in the present case) is empirically tied to some theoretically related variable. Thus, for example, adherence is a multidimensional construct that reflects the tendency for members to retain their participation, motivation, and contributions to the group. Consequently, it should be expected that cohesion would predict the various dimensions of nonadherence: drop-out behavior, diminished work output, absenteeism, lateness, early departure. As Table 3 shows, with only one exception, that was the case.

Gross and Martin (1952) argued that resistance to disruption is conceptually the most valid definition of cohesion. Thus, it should be expected that because the two constructs are tautological, cohesion should predict resistance to disruption. Again, with one exception, this was the case (Table 3).

The myriad of performance, leadership, and social psychological consequences associated with increasing the number of members in a group (cf. Carron, 1990) would provide support for a prediction that perceptions of cohesion would be negatively related to increasing group size. As Table 3 indicates, this prediction has been reliably supported for both sport teams and exercise groups.

Leadership in sport can be task oriented and person oriented. A task-oriented leadership style could be predicted to have a strong relationship to task cohesion whereas a person-oriented leadership style could be predicted to have a strong relationship with social cohesion. As Table 3 shows, there has been support for the predictions between leadership and cohesion as assessed by the GEQ.

Team building in sport and exercise groups would be predicted to have a positive influence on task cohesion. Although this prediction was reliably supported in exercise groups, the results from research with sport teams have been mixed (see Table 3).

The components of role involvement represent an integral part of group structure. It would be predicted that cohesion is positively related to both role clarity and role acceptance. Results from two studies have supported this prediction (see Table 3).

Cohesion is the tendency for groups to stick together and remain united in the pursuit of instrumental objectives. Thus, it would be predicted that social loafing would be negatively associated with task cohesion. Two studies supported this prediction.

Sticking together implicitly contains the assumption that individual group members will not engage in scapegoating after unsuccessful group ventures. Thus, it would be predicted that attributions of responsibility for failure would be team enhancing (i.e., the individual assumes a level of personal responsibility for the outcome that is at least equal to the average teammate) rather than self-enhancing (i.e., the individual assigns greater responsibility to teammates for the outcome). In three out of four instances, this prediction was supported.

Collective efficacy reflects a shared perception that the group has the resources to pursue its group goals. It would be predicted that task cohesion is positively related to collective efficacy. Results from studies by Paskevich (1995) supported this prediction.

The final set of studies presented in Table 3 that were concerned with predictive validity involved the relationship between cohesion and intragroup communication and coordination. The rationale was that coordination and communication are fundamental group processes that have traditionally been associated with group cohesion. Thus, it would be predicted that the three constructs would be highly related. Some support has been found for this relationship in the case of communication but none for the case of coordination.

Factorial validity. The four GEQ scales (and their items) were developed on the basis of a conceptual model. Thus, the presence of four robust factors, verified through factorial validity, would also contribute to a conclusion that the GEQ possessed this form of validity. As Table 3 shows, the four studies that have examined the factor structure of the GEQ have produced mixed results—some supporting the factor structure of the GEQ, others failing to find support. One of the studies in which the factor structure of the GEQ was not supported was conducted by Schutz, Eom, Smoll, and Smith (1994). In an attempt to put their results into perspective, Schutz et al. concluded that:

> First, other researchers are encouraged to attempt to replicate our work. Second, researchers utilizing the GEQ should confirm the factor structure inherent in their own data (assuming sufficient sample size) before computing any factor or scale scores. Third, given the lack of factorial validity of the GEQ with the ... [present] data, one would question the validity of the findings of other sport cohesion studies that have used this instrument. Specifically, sport scientists should be cautious in interpreting findings with respect to any one of the hypothesized "factors". Finally, it is surprising that in spite of the widespread use of the GEQ, its factorial validity has not been questioned by other researchers or by journal editors and reviewers. This points to the need for diligence by journal editors in assuring that any research based on inventory data can be supported by psychometric evidence, especially factorial validity. (p. 235)

These are particularly strong comments and worth examining in depth because of their general relevance to the fields of psychometrics and group dynamics as well as their specific relevance to the measurement of cohesion in sport groups and the validity of the GEQ.

The first suggestion by Schutz et al. (1994) about the need

for replication is an excellent point—replication is a corner-stone of science. We would urge researchers, however, to pro-vide a valid test of the instrument and its model. As Kerlinger (1973) noted "poor measurement can invalidate any scientific investigation" (p. 473). Poor measurement involves more than faulty data collection and/or poor test administration; it also in-cludes inappropriate analyses and/or hypothesizing. If the as-sumptions upon which the research is based are faulty, what fol-lows is invalid measurement. The work of Schutz et al. should not be replicated directly because it suffers from a lack of un-derstanding about the nature of group dynamics generally and cohesion specifically; it represents poor hypothesizing and, therefore, does not represent a valid test. These are also strong comments and require explanation.

From both a group dynamics and cohesion perspective, it is well established that groups go through dramatic changes in their history. Over 30 years ago, Bruce Tuckman (1965) re-viewed 50 studies in search of a common interpretation of how groups develop. He then proposed that there is an evolution through forming, storming, norming, and performing stages. (Tuckman & Jensen, 1977, later added an adjourning stage.) It should be emphasized that the stages identified by Tuckman are characterized by differences in cohesiveness.[2] Our constitutive definition (presented above) also highlights the fact that cohe-sion is dynamic and multidimensional, changing over the life history of a group. What all of this means is that it is important for researchers to bear in mind that

1. There are numerous dimensions accounting for the fact that groups stick together (i.e., are cohesive).
2. The predominant dimension(s) can be expected to change over the group's history.
3. All dimensions are not necessarily present at any given point in a group's history.
4. All dimensions are not necessarily present in all types of groups.

A confirmatory factor analysis conducted on a set of groups tested at one stage in the history of those groups has as its basis the implicit assumption that cohesion is a trait-like property with all factors present in an equally weighted fashion in the minds of all group members. If researchers wish to uti-lize CFA on the dynamic, multidimensional construct of cohe-sion, either of two approaches should be taken:

1. Multiple teams must be followed over an extended period of time using multiple assessments in order to detect any changes in the weighted components of cohesion.
2. A wide cross-section of teams with heterogeneous mem-bership characteristics must be used, and the cohesion in these teams must be sampled over a broad band of group development.

If only a rather narrow range of teams are tested (e.g., the six high school sports containing players with unknown charac-

teristics tested by Schutz et al., 1994), or most important, if all of the teams are tested at one point in their history (e.g., one week after the end of seasons of varying lengths in the Schutz et al. study), it is largely a question of chance whether the fac-tor structure will or will not be confirmed.

An analogy might help to illustrate the latter point. Assume for the moment that cohesion in marriages is a function of sex-ual attraction, religious similarity, commitment to child rearing, and striving for financial security and that a questionnaire exists to assess these four dimensions of marriage cohesion. A CFA undertaken on an exclusive sample of young couples married for just 2 weeks would be inappropriate. Commitment to child rearing and/or financial security could be irrelevant in the ma-jority of these groups. Consequently, the results from such a CFA might not produce a full and interpretable picture of the nature of cohesion in marriages.

Similarly, a CFA undertaken with an exclusive sample of older couples married for 50 years also would be inappropriate. Religious similarity and/or sexual attraction might be irrelevant in the majority of these groups. As was the case above, a CFA might produce an incomplete picture of the nature of all factors characteristic of cohesion in marriages. Better tests of the con-ceptual model for cohesion in marriages would be to test (a) a sample of couples over an extended period of time (i.e., honey-moon to silver anniversary) or (b) samples of couples who rep-resent the broad band of marriage history (i.e., couples married from 1 month to 75 years).

In our original factor analysis of the GEQ (Carron et al., 1985), 26 different teams from more than 12 different sports varying in level of competition (i.e., industrial league, commu-nity, intercollegiate, intramural) and group and membership char-acteristics (i.e., amount of playing experience, tenure on team, age, team size, and demographics) were tested at different stages of their competitive season. Our protocol and sampling provided conditions more closely approximating the criteria we suggest for testing our conceptual model of cohesion in sport teams.

Given the nature of group dynamics and cohesion, the sec-ond suggestion made by Schutz et al. (1994), namely that re-searchers utilizing the GEQ should confirm the factor structure inherent in their own data, may have merit but only under spe-cific circumstances. On the one hand, if the study involves a one-time testing of teams participating in the same sport early in either the season or the life of the group, the data should not nec-essarily be expected to yield the broad set of factors that charac-terizes group cohesion. If researchers hypothesized multiple fac-tors without establishing conditions to detect these, then their results should be questioned. Those results, whether they sup-ported or refuted the GEQ or its conceptual model, would have evolved from poor measurement, and poor measurement serves to invalidate any scientific investigation (Kerlinger, 1973).

On the other hand, if a test of the research question about multiple factors involved the sampling of a large number of

---

2. Tuckman's conceptualization, which can be labeled a linear model of group development, is different conceptually from the life cycle models and the pendular models of group development (cf. Carron, 1988). Essentially, in the life-cycle models, it is assumed that as groups form and evolve, members prepare psychologically for the group's dissolution. In the pendular models, it is assumed that groups undergo pendulum-like shifts in cohesiveness throughout their tenure. It is irrelevant which of the three models is endorsed; all include the premise that there are dra-matic changes in cohesion throughout the tenure of the group's existence.

teams with differing membership characteristics from different sports tested at a variety of times along the group-development continuum, the data might be expected to reflect a broader set of dimensions. The essential point here is that different a priori predictions could be advanced about the presence (or absence) of different aspects of cohesion depending upon the research question being posed and, for example, type of group, level of group development, and time of season. Confirmatory procedures could be conducted using a very specific set of predictions. To argue for a four-factor structure and then not gather data under conditions that could be expected to yield the structure amounts to designing a study that minimizes the conditions necessary to detect a hypothesized effect (cf. Fiske, 1987).

The third Schutz et al. (1994) conclusion that their results draw into "question the validity of the findings of other sport cohesion studies" (p. 235) is useful in that it provides for the opportunity to highlight three important test-construction and psychometric considerations. First, test developers (and researchers) must bear in mind that there are a number of protocols to evaluate validity, each of which requires a different methodology. To suggest that only CFA can give insight into the issue of validity brings to mind a statement by Platt (1964): "Beware of the man of one method or one instrument, either experimental or theoretical. He tends to become method-oriented rather than problem oriented; the method-oriented man is shackled" (p. 351). As Table 3 clearly indicates, the GEQ has demonstrated validity with a wide cross-section of groups (containing subjects of varying ages in groups with a breadth of development history) examined across a variety of situations using a number of validity protocols. To suggest that all of these results should be viewed as suspect because of a single study using CFA is unreasonable from both a scientific (i.e., probability) and psychometric (i.e., nature of validity) perspective.

Second, test developers must bear in mind that validation is a process, not an endpoint. The ongoing nature of validation is an elemental dictum in psychometrics. As we pointed out over 10 years ago at the conclusion of our first validation study, "Nunnally (1978) clearly emphasized the ongoing nature of validation in stating that it is an unending process, and validity is a matter of degree within the process" (Brawley et al., 1987, p. 292).

Third, test developers should take care how and when they use CFA to establish validity.[3] CFA and other confirmatory procedures have as a requirement that specific assumptions must be met before such procedures are used. One such assumption is that theory development has reached a point where a priori causal predictions can be made (cf. James & Brett, 1984).

Given the assumption pertaining to theory development, it would be premature to use CFA when developing an instrument based upon a new conceptual model. It would be questionable whether the model was sufficiently well developed to advance a priori hypotheses. Although we felt that this was the case for the conceptual model of cohesion and the GEQ instrument in 1985, it could be argued that the model and associated theoretical propositions now have reached a point where a priori hypotheses can be advanced. Therefore, what would be hypothesized about the structure of cohesion as reflected in the GEQ?

If a homogeneous sample of sport teams were the target of investigation and the most common of their characteristics was that (a) they had recently formed and, in general, all members had (b) little tenure with their team, and (c) few relationships had been developed with other members through previous interactions in another context, then the following hypothesis could be advanced. For most athletes examined early in the season, the most salient aspect of the GEQ would be attraction to the group task (ATG-T). In thinking about their team, the athletes would be evaluating the degree to which their personal task needs were being fulfilled through group membership. In order to examine this hypothesis, the teams should be assessed early in the season after some interactions had occurred but before stable patterns of team-related strategies were regularly practiced and used in competitions.

If the assessment occurred later in the early season, after team-task interaction was a regular part of practices and after two or three competitions, the hypothesis could be advanced that both ATG-T and group integration-task (GI-T) would be aspects of cohesion most likely to be salient to team members. In brief, the rationale for such predictions comes from the group dynamics literature on group development (Moreland & Levine, 1988; Sherif & Sherif, 1969). Task-oriented groups such as sport teams pursue the object of their motivational base as a primary goal; social relationships (and social cohesiveness) develop as a consequence of the task and social interactions and communications that are an integral aspect of group life. Thus, social manifestations of team cohesion might be expected to be weak and/or quite variable until the midpoint of the season. In fact, if circumstances encouraged a team to be strongly task focused and discouraged team-related social interaction, it is quite conceivable that social cohesion would have minimal salience to group members.

From this example, it is clear that the four aspects of cohesion would not be equally stable for teams in a given sample. However, when investigators are faced with assessing the multidimensional construct of cohesion, the instrument must possess multiple indicators to capture those aspects that are salient at the time of assessment. Stability can be expected among some but not all aspects of cohesion measured. There would not (should not) be an expectation of high stability in the responses to all four aspects of cohesion. Although the latter phenomenon possibly may be observed in well-developed groups of long standing tenure, the observation of stability in only some aspects of cohesion is more likely.

Researchers who use CFA to examine personality structure deal with a context in which the question to the individual pertains to whether a characteristic or adjective is "within the individual" or generally "describes the individual." Thus, all responses come from one individual about him or herself.

---

3. Schutz et al. are adamant in their belief that CFA is essential for the validation *Good Housekeeping* seal of approval. They suggested that the absence of validity in the factor structure of the GEQ found in their data "is not entirely surprising for instruments that were developed without the use of CFA and substantiates the need for utilization of theory-based confirmatory psychometric procedures for inventory development and subsequent validation" (Schutz et al., 1994, p. 233).

Accordingly, multiple dimensions of a person can be observed in factors that are strong and stable or weak and stable. In short, trait personality measurement requires individuals to focus on themselves in general without expectations for change (e.g., someone who is extroverted remains extroverted).

By contrast, group-oriented measures tie the individual to the group (ATG scales) or ask the individual about his or her group's response (GI scales). Both of these sets of group-oriented responses, by their very nature, are not trait-like. Further, both would be expected to have much greater temporal variability than would trait measures because responses are required that force the individual to take into account others in the group.

To ignore the nature of the construct and the nature of the responses required by the instrument when using a procedure like CFA ignores the nature of the phenomenon (i.e., cohesion) as well as the research question posed (i.e., When do groups exhibit specific or multiple aspects of cohesion?). As indicated above, identifying the presence of multiple dimensions of cohesion in one investigation requires a research strategy that involves the use of groups heterogeneous in a number of different dimensions tested over an extended developmental history.

Construct validity. Construct validation represents an ongoing process of verification of the instrument and the underlying theory. Instances of construct validity are demonstrated through a series of investigations in a program of research (Nunnally, 1978; Paunonen, 1984). The cumulative evidence presented in Table 3 relating to content, concurrent, predictive, and factorial validity also provides support for the presence of construct validity. The validation process must continue, however, with a variety of protocols. Well-conceived validation studies (as discussed above) will ultimately provide the most insight into the utility of the GEQ.

Reliability of the GEQ

The reliability of an instrument can be considered from two perspectives: stability over time (e.g., test-retest reliability) and equivalence (e.g., internal consistency). Measures of stability over time have been most often cited as indices of reliability. However, they suffer from response reactivity and over-time response change (Bohrnstedt, 1970). Also, changes over time should be expected conceptually in the case of cohesion (which is a dynamic, multidimensional property). The example used above to illustrate this point was a social club. In the initial, forming stage, a common religious belief could be important for group unity whereas carrying out the group's objectives of meeting new friends could be largely irrelevant. At a later stage, however, the converse could be the case. Test-retest reliability in this situation would yield meaningless information about the stability of the scales. Thus, our approach to the examination of the reliability of the GEQ has been to focus on its internal consistency.

In our initial research with the GEQ, we used 247 athletes from 26 different teams (14 female, 12 male), heterogeneous in sport type (basketball, cross-country running, cross country skiing, curling, figure skating, gymnastics, ice hockey, precision skating, ringette, speed skating, swimming, and wrestling) (Carron et al., 1985). The Cronbach alpha values for the resulting 18-item GEQ were: ATG-T (.75), ATG-S (.64), GI-T (.70), and GI-S

(.76). Similar and larger values have been reported for the GEQ in other studies (e.g., Li & Harmer, 1996; Paskevich, 1995).

Conceptual and Measurement Issues in the Measurement of Cohesion

Measurement of Cohesion in Other Contexts and Among Diverse Groups

The GEQ was specifically developed, its psychometric properties investigated, and norms established with recreational and competitive sport teams composed of North American female and male athletes between the ages of approximately 18 to 30 years. An important issue that must be addressed is whether the GEQ has validity in other contexts: teams in other cultures, high school teams, masters level teams, Special Olympics teams. In short, is there a generalizability in the GEQ across cultures and/or to other groups outside the population for which it was developed? How should cohesion be assessed in these other contexts? These questions underscore a complex issue that cannot be answered with a simple prescription.

In our own research, we have made minor changes to the wording of GEQ items to better reflect specific situations outside sport—with some success. (In every instance, the samples were composed of North American subjects similar in age to our original population.) For example, we have modified the GEQ for exercise groups in order to examine the relationship of cohesion to adherence behavior (e.g., Carron et al., 1988). Subsequently, Carron and Spink (1992) reported on the internal consistency of the exercise-group version of the GEQ and found almost identical Cronbach alpha values for two different samples (N = 290 and 198): ATG-T (.78, .75), ATG-S (.61, .62), GI-T .71, .71), and GI-S (.78, .76). These internal consistency values were very similar to the values originally reported by Carron et al. (1985) for sport teams. Also, other studies using revised exercise versions of the GEQ have reported similar and higher values (Courneya & McAuley, 1995).

As another example, in research on conformity and cohesion in university residence halls, minor changes were made in the wording of the GEQ items to better reflect that context (cf. Carron & Ramsay, 1994). Again, the resulting Cronbach alpha values for the residence-hall version of the GEQ were good (ATG-T, .78; ATG-S, .75; GI-T, .73; and GI-S, .83).

Through personal correspondence, however, we have come to the understanding that generally when the GEQ has been modified for athletes in other countries—India, Portugal, and Spain are just a few examples—Cronbach alpha coefficients have been unacceptable. Also, the factor structure of the revised GEQ generally has been examined using CFA with the results showing uninterpretable or altered cohesion scales. However, the research protocol consistently has utilized teams selected from one sport and/or examined at one point in the season. For the reasons that we have discussed above, as well as perhaps for other methodological and cultural factors (discussed subsequently), this research protocol provides an invalid test of the GEQ and its conceptual model.

What implications does this have for potential users of the GEQ from other countries or across situations inside and outside sport? First, we believe that the conceptual model that formed the basis for the development of the GEQ is sound; therefore, it could be used as the basis for any measures of cohesion developed in other countries or for other contexts. Our belief has also been echoed by other group dynamics theoreticians. For example, Dion and Evans (1992) observed:

> The cohesiveness construct has been applied to many different types of groups ...it is thus perhaps unlikely that a single "generic" measure of cohesion will likely be developed to apply without modification to all such instances. Still the two-dimensional conceptualization of cohesion ... [proposed by Carron et al., 1985] appears promising as a conceptual and methodological approach with potentially broad applicability to different types of groups. (p. 247)

> Similarly, Cota et al. (1995) suggested that cohesion be considered as a multidimensional construct with primary and secondary dimensions ... we want to underscore that we are not presenting a new model of cohesion; rather our ideas represent a heuristic of this construct ... the individual-group and task-social dimensions identified by Carron et al. (1985) are primary components of the heuristic. (pp. 576-577)

Using our conceptual framework as a guideline, researchers interested in the measurement of cohesiveness in other cultures or contexts should (a) directly use any of the original GEQ items that appear to represent cohesiveness in the group(s) under focus, (b) revise the wording on any item that appears to be useful but that contains language, terminology, or a situational reference not characteristic of the group(s) under focus, (c) delete those items that, through pilot testing, appear to be inappropriate, and (d) add new items that are more culturally meaningful or better represent the situation for any of the four scales in the conceptual model. The context-specific measure of cohesiveness can then be examined for its psychometric properties.

This is not to say that the GEQ should be rewritten for every situation on the basis of the investigator's opinion. Study-by-study revision of an instrument designed to be generic for many sport teams would void the entire purpose of attempting to measure cohesion. However, if there is any question about the appropriateness of the GEQ for a specific context, investigators should pilot test and determine if all the items are applicable to the sample and situation. If any items are found to be unsuitable, a similar sample should be used in a procedure that elicits construct-relevant words or items representing the particular GEQ dimension. These items then should be included in the revised, culturally appropriate GEQ to determine their meaningfulness to the target sample.

The Unit of Analysis in Cohesion Research

Another important question which arises in the measurement of cohesion is "What is the appropriate unit of analysis?" Three approaches have been used in the study of group dynamics issues (Cota et al., 1995). In one approach, the individual group member has been used as the unit of analysis. The Spink and Carron (1993, 1994) research examining the relationship between individual perceptions of cohesiveness and individual adherence behavior in exercise classes provides an example of this protocol.

A second approach has been to use aggregate group variables (i.e., summary statistics such as the group mean) as the unit of analysis. The Carron and Ball (1978) research examining the relationship of cohesion to team success in ice-hockey teams illustrates this protocol. That is, the group average was used to represent the cohesiveness in each team and win/loss percentage was used to represent team success.

Finally, the intact group can be used as the unit of analysis. The Widmeyer, Carron, and Brawley (1993) research focusing on communication, coordination, and cohesion in intramural basketball teams provides an example of an intact team being used as the unit of analysis. From experimenter observation of the teams, the total amount of communication and coordination among members in each team was recorded.

Which of these three approaches is best? Unfortunately, there is no simple prescription; the appropriate unit of analysis is a function of three factors. One of these factors is the nature of the research question. That is, some research questions are better answered with a specific unit of analysis. If the question of interest is centered on the relationship of cohesiveness to individual behavior—adherence, for example—then the individual's cognition about his or her group's cohesion is the critical consideration. In this case, the individual can be the unit of analysis.

A second factor associated with choosing the appropriate unit of analysis is the nature of the theory being tested (Cota et al., 1995). For example, social comparison theory is derived from the premise that individuals have a need to compare their behavior, cognitions, and attitudes with the behavior, cognitions, and attitudes of others in order to evaluate personal efficacy. In this instance, the aggregate group value can be the unit of analysis.

The third factor that influences the appropriate unit of analysis is empirical in nature. That is, in some instances, analyses at either the group level or the individual level or both the group and individual levels would provide information of interest. A statistical consideration that cannot be ignored is that individual responses are nested within groups. That is, in real groups, individual responses are interdependent and reflect group influences—a case of statistical nonindependence.

A statistical dilemma in group research is that traditionally used analysis procedures such as ANOVA proceed from the assumption that observations are independent; thus, individual effects are analyzed and group effects are ignored. The consequence of violating this assumption is that estimates of error are biased because group effects make the scores of members more similar than different if a true group effect (i.e., cohesion) is present. In the traditional ANOVA model, an individual's score is represented by systematic effects plus error. Thus, an analysis of individual scores that ignores the group effect results in correlated errors and biased estimates of error variance. In order to avoid overlooking either individual or group effects when examining group cohesion, an alternate approach to the analysis of group data should be considered.

Kenny and Lavoie (1985) have suggested a method allowing investigators the strategy of simultaneously studying the group and the individual. A situation in which the relationship between collective efficacy (cf. Bandura, 1986) and cohesion is examined provides a useful example. The Kenny and Lavoie strategy consists of first testing for statistical nonindependence (i.e., group effects) using the intraclass correlation procedure (ICC). If the ICC is not significant, there is no evidence of a group effect, and individual analysis procedures and the interpretation of results at the individual level would follow. It would make little sense to compute group means and/or use a group-as-the-unit-of-analysis interpretation. Conversely, however, if the ICC is significant and positive, there is evidence of group level variance in the collective efficacy and cohesion measures. Further, the larger the ICC, the more pronounced is the group effect. In a case where large, significant ICCs were present, the researcher would use group means in the analysis and a group-level interpretation.

A more common case, however, might be the presence of a significant and moderate-level ICC. In this case, correlations between the collective efficacy and cohesion measures should be computed and examined as follows. First, individual-level correlations should be computed—correlations calculated within groups where the group mean is partialled out and then the adjusted scores for collective efficacy and cohesion are correlated. Second, group-level correlations should be computed—adjusted for the individual-level correlations. The researcher can then compare the adjusted correlations (i.e., group and individual) to their unadjusted counterparts to examine for differences in magnitude. Also, both sets of adjusted correlations can be examined to determine if the relationship between collective efficacy and cohesion is equal or stronger at the individual level or the group level.

The comparison of relationships at the group versus individual level has important implications for theory. For example, Paskevich (1995) and Paskevich, Brawley, Dorsch, and Widmeyer (1995) used the Kenny and Lavoie (1985) procedure to demonstrate that the relationship between collective efficacy and group cohesion is due to powerful group influences and that multiple aspects of cohesion (GI-T and ATG-T) are related to multiple aspects of collective efficacy.

It is beyond the scope of this portion of the chapter to provide more than a brief summary of the Kenny and Lavoie analysis strategy. The interested reader should examine their 1985 article closely for both the procedures and limitations in their approach. In addition, it should be noted that the estimated (adjusted) correlations can be used in multivariate analyses such as multiple regression. This would offer an opportunity, for example, to examine models where group-level variables such as multiple aspects of cohesion would predict collective efficacy and determine if regression effects are of greater magnitude when adjusted group scores are predictors (cf. Paskevich, 1995). In short, investigators now have a statistical protocol for resolving the unit-of-analysis issue in cohesion (and group) research. When this strategy is coupled with a strong rationale for the research question posed, a clearer picture of the influence of group effects can be observed.

Summary

Measurement lies at the heart of science. The general purpose of this chapter was to discuss the measurement of cohe-

sion in sport and exercise groups. To that end, we provided a constitutive definition for group cohesion, charted historically the development of operational measures of cohesion in sport teams, outlined the conceptual model that provided the basis for the development of the Group Environment Questionnaire, and then provided some evidence pertaining to its validity and reliability. In addition, two other issues were discussed, that is, the measurement of cohesion in other contexts and the choice of an appropriate unit of analysis. We hope that the issues discussed here will serve as a catalyst for better measurement, design, and analysis of future research on the cohesion of sport and exercise groups. The challenge will be for investigators to attend to the suggestions and cautions raised in order to avoid a future repetition of Mudrack's (1989a) claim that the history of cohesion has been inexcusably sloppy.

References

Arnold, G., & Straub, W. (1973). Personality and group cohesiveness as determinants of success among interscholastic basketball teams. In I. Williams & L. Wankel (Eds.), *Proceedings of the Fourth Canadian Psycho-Motor Learning and Sport Psychology Symposium* (pp. 346-353). Ottawa: Department of National Health and Welfare.

Bandura, A. (1986). *Social foundations of thought and action: A social cognitive theory*. Englewood Cliffs, NJ: Prentice-Hall.

Bohrnstedt, G. W. (1970). Reliability and validity assessment in attitude measurement. In G. F. Summers (Ed.), *Attitude measurement* (pp. 80-99). Chicago: Rand-McNally.

Brawley, L. R., Carron, A. V., & Widmeyer, W. N. (1987). Assessing the cohesion of teams: Validity of the Group Environment Questionnaire. *Journal of Sport Psychology, 9*, 275-294.

Brawley, L. R., Carron, A. V., & Widmeyer, W. N. (1988). Exploring the relationship between cohesion and group resistance to disruption. *Journal of Sport Psychology, 10*, 199-213.

Carron, A. V. (1982). Cohesiveness in sport groups: Interpretations and considerations. *Journal of Sport Psychology, 4*, 123-138.

Carron, A.V. (1988). *Group dynamics in sport: Theoretical and practical issues*. London, Ontario: Sports Dynamics.

Carron, A. V. (1990). Group size in sport and physical activity: Social psychological and performance consequences. *International Journal of Sport Psychology, 21*, 286-304.

Carron, A. V., & Ball, J. R. (1978). Cause-effect characteristics of cohesiveness and participation motivation in intercollegiate hockey. *International Review of Sport Sociology, 12*, 49-60.

Carron, A. V., Brawley, L. R. & Widmeyer, W. N. (1990). The impact of group size in an exercise setting. *Journal of Sport and Exercise Psychology, 12*, 376-387.

Carron, A. V., & Chelladurai, P. (1981). The dynamics of group cohesion in sport. *Journal of Sport Psychology, 3*, 123-129.

Carron, A.V., & Ramsay, M.C. (1994). Internal consistency of the Group Environment Questionnaire modified for university residence settings. *Perceptual and Motor Skills, 79*, 141-142.

Carron, A. V., & Spink, K. S. (1992). Internal consistency of the Group Environment Questionnaire modified for an exercise setting. *Perceptual and Motor Skills, 74*, 1-3.

Carron, A. V., & Spink, K. S. (1993). Team building in an exercise setting. *The Sport Psychologist, 7*, 8-18.

Carron, A. V., & Spink, K. S. (1995). The group-size cohesion relationship in minimal groups. *Small Group Research, 26*, 86-105.

Carron, A. V., Widmeyer, W. N., & Brawley, L. R. (1985). The development of an instrument to assess cohesion in sport teams: The Group Environment Questionnaire. *Journal of Sport Psychology, 7*, 244-266.

Carron, A. V., Widmeyer, W. N., & Brawley, L. R. (1988). Group cohesion and individual adherence to physical activity. *Journal of Sport Psychology, 10*, 119-126.

Cattell, R. B. (1948). Concepts and methods in the measurement of group syntality. *Psychological Review, 55*, 48-63.

Cota, A. A., Evans, C. R., Dion, K. L., Kilik, L., & Longman, R. S. (1995). The structure of group cohesion. *Personality and Social Psychology Bulletin, 21*, 572-580.

Courneya, K.S., & McAuley, E. (1995). Cognitive mediators of the social influence-exercise adherence relationship: A test of the theory of planned behavior. *Journal of Behavioral Medicine, 18*, 499-515.

Dawe, S.W.L., & Carron, A.V. (1990). Interrelationships among role acceptance, role clarity, task cohesion, and social cohesion. *Canadian Psychomotor Learning and Sport Psychology 21st Annual Conference Abstracts* (p. 22). Canadian Psychomotor Learning and sport Psychology Association: Windsor, Ontario

Dion, K. L., & Evans, C. R. (1992). On cohesiveness: Reply to Keyton and other critics of the construct. *Small Group Research, 23*, 242-250.

Festinger, L., Schachter, S., & Back, K. (1950). *Social pressure in informal groups*. New York: Harper & Row.

Fiedler, F. E. (1954). Assumed similarity measures as predictors of team effectiveness. *Journal of Abnormal and Social Psychology, 49*, 381-388.

Fiedler, F. E. (1967). A theory of leadership effectiveness. New York: McGraw-Hill.

Fiske, D.W. (1987). Construct invalidity comes from method effects. *Educational and Psychological Measurement, 47*, 285-307.

Gill. D. L. (1977). Cohesiveness and performance in sport groups. In R. S. Hutton (Ed.), *Exercise and sport science reviews* (Vol. 5, pp. 131-155). Santa Barbara: Journal Publishing Affiliates.

Grand, R.R., & Carron, A.V. (1982). Development of a team climate questionnaire. In L.M. Wankel & R.B. Wilberg (Eds.), *Psychology of sport and motor behaviour: Research and practice* (pp. 217-229). Edmonton, Alberta: Department of Recreation and Leisure Studies, University of Alberta.

Gross, N., & Martin, W. (1952). On group cohesiveness. *American Journal of Sociology, 57*, 533-546.

Gruber, J. J., & Gray, G. R. (1981). Factor patterns of variables influencing cohesiveness at various levels of basketball competition. *Research Quarterly for Exercise and Sport, 52*, 19-30.

Gruber, J. J., & Gray, G. R. (1982). Responses to forces influencing cohesion as a function of player status and level of male varsity basketball competition. *Research Quarterly for Exercise and Sport, 53*, 27-36.

Henry, F. M. (1968). *The physiology of work*. Unpublished manuscript, University of California, Berkeley.

Hersey, P., & Blanchard, K. H. (1969). *Management and organizational behavior*. Englewood Cliffs, NJ: Prentice-Hall.

Huntley, M., & Carron, A.V. (1992). The behaviour-cohesion relationship in sport teams. *The child in sport and physical activity: Joint CASS/SCAPPs Conference Programmes & Abstracts*, (p. 104). University of Saskatchewan: Saskatoon, Saskatchewan.

James, L. R., & Brett, J. M. (1984). Mediators, moderators, and tests for mediation. *Journal of Applied Psychology, 69*, 307-321.

Kenny, D. A., & Lavoie, L. (1985). Separating individual and group effects.
Journal of Personality and Social Psychology, 48, 339-348.

Kerlinger, F. N. (1973). *Foundations of behavioral research*. New York: Holt, Rinehart, & Winston.

Klein, M., & Christiansen, G. (1969). Group composition, group structure, and group effectiveness of basketball teams. In J. W. Loy & G. S. Kenyon (Eds.), *Sport, culture, and society: A reader on the sociology of sport* (pp. 397-408). Toronto: Collier-Macmillan.

Kozub, S. A. (1993). *Exploring the relationships among coaching behavior, team cohesion, and player leadership*. Unpublished doctoral dissertation, University of Houston, Houston, TX.

Lenk, H. (1969). Top performance despite internal conflict: An antithesis to a functionalistic proposition. In J. W. Loy & G. S. Kenyon (Eds.), *Sport, culture, and society: A reader on the sociology of sport* (pp. 393-396). Toronto: Collier-Macmillan.

Levine, J. M., & Moreland, R. L. (1991). Culture and socialization in work groups. In L. B. Resnick, J. M. Levine, & S. D. Teasley (Eds.), *Perspectives on socially shared cognition*. Washington, DC: American Psychological Association.

Li, F., & Harmer, P. (1996). Confirmatory factor analysis of the Group Environment Questionnaire with an intercollegiate sample. *Journal of Sport and Exercise Psychology, 18*, 49-63.

Martens, R., Landers, D. M., & Loy, J. W. (1972). *Sport cohesiveness questionnaire*. Unpublished manuscript, University of Illinois: Champaign, IL.

McClure, B.A., & Foster, C.D. (1991). Group work as a method of promoting cohesiveness within a women's gymnastics team. *Perceptual and Motor Skills, 73*, 307-313.

McGrath, J. (1962). The influence of positive interpersonal relations on adjustment and effectiveness in rifle teams. *Journal of Abnormal and Social Psychology, 65*, 365-375.

McKnight, T., Williams, J.M., & Widmeyer, W.N. (1991, October). *Effects of cohesion and identifiably on reducing the likelihood of social loafing*. Paper presented at the meeting of the Association for the Advancement of Applied Sport Psychology, Savannah, GA.

Mikalachki, A. (1969). *Group cohesion revisited*. London, Ontario: School of Business Administration, University of Western Ontario.

Moreland, R.L., & Levine, J.M. (1988). Group dynamics over time: Development and socialization in small groups. In J.E. McGrath (Ed.), *The social psychology of time: New perspectives* (pp. 151-181). Newbury Park, CA: Sage.

Mudrack, P. E. (1989a). Defining group cohesiveness: A legacy of confusion. *Small Group Behavior, 20*, 37-49.

Mudrack, P. E. (1989b). Group cohesiveness and productivity: A closer look. *Human Relations, 42*, 771-785.

Myers, A. (1962). Team competition, success, and the adjustment of team members. *Journal of Abnormal and Social Psychology, 65*, 325-332.

Naylor, K., & Brawley, L.R. (1992, October). *Social loafing: Perceptions and implications*. Paper presented at the joint meeting of the Canadian Association of Sport Sciences and the Canadian Society for Psychomotor Learning and Sport Psychology, Saskatoon, Saskatchewan.

Nunnally, J. C. (1978). *Psychometric theory*. New York: McGraw-Hill.

Paskevich, D.M. (1995). *Conceptual and measurement factors of collective efficacy in its relationship to cohesion and performance outcome*. Unpublished doctoral dissertation, University of Waterloo, Ontario.

Paskevich, D. M., Brawley, L. R., Dorsch, K. D., & Widmeyer, W. N. (1995). Implications of individual and group level analyses applied to the study of collective efficacy and cohesion. *Journal of Applied Sport Psychology, 7*, S95.

Paunonen, S. V. (1984). Optimizing the validity of personality assessments: The importance of aggregation and item content. *Journal of Research in Personality, 18*, 411-431.

Platt, J. R. (1964). Strong inference. *Science, 146*, 347-352.

Prapavessis, H., Carron, A.V., & Spink, K.S. (In press). Team building in sport. *International Journal of Sport Psychology*.

Ruder, M. K., & Gill, D. L. (1982). Immediate effects of win-loss on perceptions of cohesion in intramural and intercollegiate volleyball teams. *Journal of Sport Psychology, 4*, 227-234.

Schlenker, B. R. (1975). Group members' attributions of responsibility for prior performance. *Representative Research in Social Psychology, 6*, 96-108.

Schlenker, B. R., & Miller, R. S. (1977). Group cohesiveness as a determinant of egocentric perceptions in cooperative groups. *Human Relations, 11*, 1039-1055.

Schutz, R. W., Eom, H. J., Smoll, F. L., & Smith, R. E. (1994). Examination of the factorial validity of the Group Environment Questionnaire. *Research Quarterly for Exercise and Sport, 65*, 226-236.

Sherif, M., & Sherif, C. (1969). Social psychology (Rev. ed.). New York: Harper & Row.

Spink, K. S., & Carron, A. V. (1992). Group cohesion and adherence in exercise classes. *Journal of Sport and Exercise Psychology, 14*, 78-86.

Spink, K. S., & Carron, A. V. (1993). The effects of team building on the adherence patterns of female exercise participants. *Journal of Sport and Exercise Psychology, 15*, 39-49.

Spink, K. S., & Carron, A. V. (1994). Group cohesion effects in exercise classes. *Small Group Research, 25*, 26-42.

Stogdill, R. M. (1964). *Team achievement under high motivation.* Columbus, OH: Bureau of Business Research, Ohio State University.

Tuckman, B. W. (1965). Developmental sequence in small groups. *Psychological Bulletin, 63*, 384-399.

Tuckman, B. W., & Jensen, M. A. C. (1977). Stages of small group development revisited. *Group and Organizational Studies, 2*, 419-427.

Van Bergen, A., & Koekebakker, J. (1959). Group cohesiveness in laboratory experiments. *Acta Psychologica, 16*, 81-98.

Westre, K.R., & Weiss, M.R. (1991). The relationship between perceived coaching behavior and group cohesion in high school football teams. *The Sport Psychologist, 5*, 41-54.

Widmeyer, W. N., Brawley, L. R., & Carron, A. V. (1985). *The measurement of cohesion in sport teams: The Group Environment Questionnaire.* London, Ontario: Sports Dynamics.

Widmeyer, W. N., Brawley, L. R., & Carron, A. V. (1990). The effects of group size in sport. *Journal of Sport and Exercise Psychology, 12*, 177-190.

Widmeyer, W.N., Carron, A.V., & Brawley, L.R. (1993). The cohesion-performance outcome relationship with teams as the unit of analysis. *Journal of Sport and Exercise Psychology, 1993, 15*, p. S90.

Widmeyer, W. N., & Martens, R. (1978). When cohesion predicts performance outcome in sport. *Research Quarterly, 49*, 372-380.

Williams, J.M., & Widmeyer, W.N. (1991). The cohesion-performance outcome relationship in coacting teams. *The Journal of Sport & Exercise Psychology, 13*, 364-371.

Yukelson, D., Weinberg, R., & Jackson, A. (1984). A multidimensional group cohesion instrument for intercollegiate basketball teams. *Journal of Sport Psychology, 6*, 103-117.

Zander, A. (1971). Motives and goals in groups. New York: Academic Press.

Author Note

The authors would like to thank Peter Terry for his comments on an earlier draft of this chapter. Correspondence concerning this chapter should be addressed to Albert V. Carron, who is in the Faculty of Kinesiology at the University of Western Ontario, London, Ontario, N6A 3K7, CANADA, email: bcarron@julian.uwo.ca

Chapter 13

MEASUREMENT OF LEADERSHIP IN SPORT

Packianathan Chelladurai
The Ohio State University
and
Harold A. Riemer
The University of Texas at Austin

Leadership may be defined as "the behavioral process of influencing individuals and groups toward set goals" (Barrow, 1977, p. 232). In sport, this process of leadership has historically been assigned great value by participants and spectators alike. Victorious athletes often cite the vital role the coach played in their achievement (e.g., George, 1993), whereas fans may even deify coaches who have brought a measure of success to a particular athletic organization (e.g., Woody Hayes at Ohio State University, Daryl Royal at University of Texas). However, the efforts to understand leadership have been sparse and sporadic; that is, there has been a lack of sustained research in the area (Riemer & Chelladurai, 1995).

One of the most critical issues relating to research in a given domain is how the variables, important to a particular theory, have been operationalized and/or measured. The measurement of these variables is the foundation upon which theories and models rest. It is incumbent upon scientists to evaluate the relative stability of that foundation. The purpose of this chapter is to examine how the critical variables have been and/or are currently measured in three major contemporary approaches to the study of leadership in sports: (a) Smith, Smoll, and associates'[1] (Smith, Smoll, & Curtis, 1978; Smoll & Smith, 1989; Smoll, Smith, Curtis, & Hunt, 1978) media-

tional model of leadership; (b) Chelladurai's (1978; 1993a) multidimensional model of leadership; and (c) Chelladurai and Haggerty's (1978) normative model of decision styles in coaching.

Mediational Model of Leadership

Theoretical Overview

The focus of the mediational model of leadership (Smoll & Smith, 1989; Smoll, Smith, Curtis, & Hunt, 1978) is on those

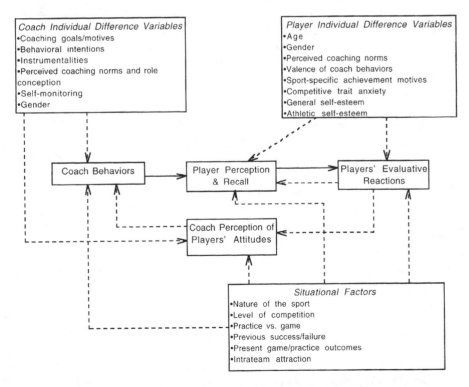

Figure 1. Mediational model of leadership (Smoll & Smith, 1989).
Note: From Smoll & Smith (1989). Reprinted with permission from *Journal of Applied Social Psychology,* Vol. 19, No.18, pp. 1522-1551. © V.H. Winston & Son, Inc., 360 South Ocean Boulevard, Palm Beach, FL. 33480. All rights reserved.

---

1. The only difference between the two models as presented in 1978 and 1989 is in the variables/factors proposed as antecedents. The latter version is more specific.

cognitive and affective processes and individual difference variables that mediate the relationships between leader behavior and its antecedents and consequences. Smoll and Smith argue that such variables are equally important to understanding the processes of leadership as are overt behaviors and situational factors. Their model (Smoll & Smith, 1989; Smoll et al., 1978) consisted of three basic elements: coach behaviors, player perception and recall, and players' evaluative reactions. It was proposed that players' reactions to a coach's behaviors are mediated by their perception and recall of those behaviors; that is, the outcome of a particular coaching behavior is mediated by the meaning a player attributes to it (Smoll & Smith, 1989; Smoll et al., 1978). Smoll and Smith note that "cognitive and affective processes serve as filters between overt coaching behaviors and youngsters' attitudes toward their coach and their sport experience" (p. 1527). Moreover, a coach's perception of a player's attitudes is thought to mediate the relationship between a coach's behaviors and a player's evaluative reaction to those behaviors. The model also stipulates categories of antecedents (i.e., coach's individual difference variables, situational factors, player's individual difference variables) and their relationship to the primary variables. It is important to note that the model also allows for reciprocal interactions among appropriate variables in addition to the one-way causal or moderator relationships (Smoll & Smith, 1989). The model is presented in Figure 1.

Coach's Individual Difference Variables

Smoll and Smith (1989) suggest that differences in coaching behavior are a reflection of an individual's coaching *goals* and his or her *behavioral intentions*. Goals are defined as "an anticipated positive outcome of an act" (p. 1533) whereas behavioral intentions are those cognitive decisions an individual makes to behave in a particular manner that precede the behavior. Behavioral intentions (and goals) are said to be influenced by *instrumentalities* (i.e., the product of the perceived probability that an outcome will occur as a consequence of one's behavior and the value a person assigns to that particular outcome). Specifically, the model suggests that "the predictive utility of instrumentalities for behavioral intentions will be highest when the specific coaching behavior is consistently correlated with consequences and when these consequences have high positive or negative valence for the coach" (p. 1535). Smoll and Smith also argue that social factors affect one's behavioral intentions and, therefore, suggest that the *conceptions* a coach has of his or her role and his or her perceptions of the *norms* associated with that particular role will influence a coach's behaviors, attitudes, and values. A coach's *beliefs regarding athlete motivation* are also thought to influence expectations of potential responses to a given behavior and, therefore, may affect how the coach structures the situation and responds to the athlete. Suggesting that effective behavior requires awareness of one's behavior and its consequences, Smoll and Smith hypothesize that differences in *self-monitoring* (i.e., "willingness or ability to modify behavior in accordance with the norms of situational appropriateness" [Miller & Thayer, 1988, p. 545]) would be an important antecedent. Finally, given the expansion of female athletic programs and the increasing number of women coaches, the coach's gender was deemed to be a potentially salient variable.

Player's Individual Difference Variables

According to the model, these variables are assumed to influence a player's perception of, and response to a coach's behavior. Smoll and Smith (1989) argue that the *age* of an athlete influences his or her perceptions and attitudes. They note that their previous research (i.e., Smith et al., 1979) demonstrated that younger players typically perceived differences in coaches based on punitive behaviors, preadolescents differentiated among coaches on the basis of positive and encouraging behaviors, and adolescents focused on the quality and quantity of the technical instruction. Citing the increasing participation of females in organized sport, Smoll and Smith suggest that the player's *gender* may influence his or her perceptions and preference for a coach's behaviors. Smith and Smoll (1989) note that girls perceived and preferred some behaviors (e.g., reinforcement, encouragement) more than did boys. The athlete's *normative beliefs* regarding appropriate coaching behaviors which may vary by sport and may be influenced by traditional sex-role expectations are hypothesized to influence the athlete's reactions toward specific coaching behavior. Specifically, Smoll and Smith suggest "that athletes who expect coaches to be 'tough' may respond less negatively to punitive behaviors than those who believe that coaches are 'warm and caring'" (p. 1538). The *valence* (i.e., value) players assign to specific behaviors can also be expected to affect perceptions and responses and is thought to vary as a function of other individual difference variables, situational factors (e.g., team size, type of sport), and experiential factors (e.g., maturity of athlete, level of competition). Given that sport is an achievement setting, another important variable suggested by Smoll and Smith is the player's *achievement-related motivation(s)* for performing well. They argue that both a person's desire to succeed and his or her fear of failure need to be considered as potential variables. Finally, a number of personality variables were proposed as moderators. The first of these is *competitive trait anxiety* (i.e., a person's predisposition to perceive objectively nondangerous situations as threatening [Spielberger, 1966]). Smoll and Smith hypothesize that given their proclivity to attend to threatening stimuli, children who are more trait anxious children would perceive their coaches as less reinforcing and encouraging, and as more punitive. Second, an individual's evaluation of his or her *general self-worth* and *athletic self-esteem* are proposed as important moderators of perceptions and evaluative responses. The hypothesis was based on earlier research (e.g., Smith, Smoll, & Curtis, 1978) that indicated differences in behavioral responses for children low in self-esteem compared to those high in self-esteem.

Situational Factors

A primary situational factor that is said to affect coaches' behavior, players' perceptions of those behaviors, and players' reactions to coaches' behavior is the nature of the sport. Smoll and Smith (1989) suggest that a comparison of some of their earlier work in baseball and basketball seemed to indicate potential sport-related differences. Other researchers have also found that task variability and task dependency influence an athlete's perceptions and preferences for various coaching behaviors (e.g., Chelladurai, 1978; Riemer & Chelladurai, 1995). Other potentially viable situational factors include *practice ses-*

sions versus games, previous team success/failure, current game/practice developments (e.g., is the team behind, has it lost its lead, etc.), the level of competition (i.e., recreational versus competitive), and intrateam attraction.

This latest version of the mediational model of leadership has not yet been adequately tested. Many of the complex relationships suggested by the model have yet to be verified. Smoll and Smith (1989) have indicated that the use of structural equation modeling to empirically test the myriad of hypotheses the model advances would be beneficial.

Measures

A fundamental tenet of theory construction is that the theory must be testable (Bacharach, 1989). Thus, a proposal of a theory or model should be accompanied by suggestions concerning measurement of the model's variables. Accordingly, Smith, Smoll, and their associates have developed a set of measures related to their mediational model of leadership. To measure actual leader behavior, an observational method was developed. The athlete's perceptions and recall of leader behavior, as well as the athlete's affective reactions to the sport experience, are typically assessed through the use of structured interviews. Finally, the coach's perceptions of his or her own behavior are operationalized through the use of a paper and pencil questionnaire.

In developing these various measures, Smith, Smoll, and their colleagues initially identified and described 12 categories of leader behavior in sport. This initial step was driven by social learning theory and other schema proposed in the context of small groups (Parsons & Bales, 1955), classroom management (White, 1975), and managerial behavior (Komaki, 1986).

Actual Leader Behavior (Observational Method)

The Coaching Behavior Assessment System (CBAS) was developed over several years by observing and recording behaviors of youth soccer coaches during practice and game sessions. Transcriptions of the behavior descriptions were then content analyzed, and an initial set of scoring categories was developed. Subsequently, the system was used to observe the behaviors of basketball, baseball, and football coaches. Results indicated that the scoring system was sufficiently comprehensive to incorporate the vast majority of coaching behaviors, that individual differences in behavioral patterns can be discerned, and that the coding system can be used easily in field settings (Smith, Smoll, & Hunt, 1977, p. 402).

Coaching behaviors are categorized into 12 behavioral dimensions (Table 1) and classified as either reactive (i.e., responses to an immediately preceding player/team behavior) or spontaneous (i.e., initiated by the coach and not a response to an immediately preceding event) (Smith et al., 1977a). Reactive behaviors include (a) responses to desirable performances, (b) reactions to mistakes, or (c) responses to misbehaviors, whereas spontaneous behaviors are either (a) game related or (b) game irrelevant.

The actual leader behavior is a measure of the frequencies with which the coach exhibits each of the 12 categories of leader behaviors. Typically, one or more individuals observe

---

Table 1.
Behavioral Dimensions of the Coaching Behavior Assessment System (Smith et al., 1977a)

Reactive Behaviors

Responses to desirable performances
Reinforcement	A positive, rewarding reaction, verbal or nonverbal, to a good play or good effort
Nonreinforcement	Failure to respond to good performance

Responses to mistakes
Mistake-contingent encouragement	Encouragement given to a player following a mistake
Mistake-contingent technical instruction	Instructing or demonstrating to a player how to correct a mistake
Punishment	A negative reaction, verbal or nonverbal, following a mistake
Punitive technical instruction	Technical instruction which is given in a punitive or hostile manner following a mistake
Ignoring mistakes	Failure to respond to a player mistake

Responses to misbehavior
Keeping control	Reactions intended to restore or maintain order among team members

Spontaneous Behaviors

Game related
General technical instruction	Spontaneous instruction in the techniques and strategies of the sport (not following a mistake)
General encouragement	Spontaneous encouragement which does not follow a mistake
Organization	Administrative behavior which sets the stage for play by assigning duties, responsibilities, positions, etc.

Game irrelevant
General communication	Interactions with players unrelated to the game

Note: Modified from Smith, Smoll, & E.B. Hunt, 1977. With permission from *Research Quarterly for Exercise and Sport,* Vol. 48, No. 2, 401-407. Copyright © 1977 by the American Alliance for Health, Physical Education, Recreation and Dance, 1900 Association Drive, Reston, VA 20191.

the coach during practice or game or both, and record the observed behavior(s) into one of the 12 categories.

Reliability. Given the naturalistic perspective of the scoring system, considerable effort has been made to examine and improve the reliability of the coding system. First, its authors devised an intensive training program to prepare observers to record coaching behaviors. It generally includes (a) extended study of a training manual (Smith et al., 1977a), (b) group instruction in the use of the scoring system using a training videotape (Smith, Smoll, Hunt, & Clarke, 1976), (c) written tests that require defining of the 12 categories and scoring of behavioral examples, (d) scoring of videotaped sequences, and (e) extensive practice and reliability checks in actual field settings (Smith, Smoll, & Hunt, 1977b; Smith, Zane, Smoll, & Coppel, 1983).

Second, several attempts were made to assess the reliability of the coding system. Specifically the extent of agreement between two individuals coding the leader behaviors and/or between two time-lagged coding sessions by the same individual was determined, and the correlations between the category frequencies reported by any two observers. Smith et al. (1977a) reported that 31 trainees, who coded 48 randomly ordered videotape sequences of discrete coaching behaviors, had an agreement rate of 97.8% with the codings of two of the authors. Further, the mean number of scoring errors was only 1.06 (range = 0-5). In order to assess the consistency of coding over time, 24 trainees, with no knowledge about the results of their initial coding, were asked to code the same 48 behaviors one week later. The percentage of behaviors that were scored identically ranged from 87.5% to 100% (mean = 96.4%). Later, Smith et al. (1983) found that the scoring of videotape sequences by 17 trainees agreed with those of the experts over 90% of the time.

Smith et al. (1977b) also reported results of two field studies in which interrater reliability was operationalized as the correlation of the coding frequencies between a pair of observers across the 12 categories. In the first study, five trainees observed the coaching behavior of a female little league baseball coach during the course of six innings. Interrater reliability ranged from .77 to .99 (mean = .88). In the second study, 19 trainees coded the behaviors of a male Little League baseball coach. Interrater reliability ranged from .50 to .99 (mean = .88). Reliability coefficients were also computed between the 19 trainees and criterion codings of the authors and ranged from .62 to .98 (mean = .86).

In a later study, Smith et al. (1983) reported that the correlations of the frequencies of observed leader behaviors in a field setting by an observer and an expert ranged from .85 to .98 (median = .96) across 10 behavioral dimensions. Two of the categories (i.e., nonreinforcement, ignoring mistakes) were omitted because of the difficulty associated with scoring them in the sport of basketball. As Smith et al. explained, these "nonbehavior" categories were difficult to score reliably because they require the assumption that the coach has observed the desired or undesired behavior, an assumption not always justified during the diffused and semi-organized mayhem that often characterize youth basketball games. (p. 209)

Other authors have also provided evidence of high degrees of agreement between raters. For example, Chaumeton and Duda (1988) reported that application of Cohen's (1960) Mea-

sure of Interjudge Agreement to a somewhat revised version of the scale (i.e., two of the dimensions were subdivided to reflect punishment or positive reinforcement based on the process or outcome) resulted in a median reliability coefficient of .90 (range = .68 to .96) across the behavioral categories. In a study of junior high softball teams, Horn (1984) obtained interrater reliability coefficients ranging from .78 to .92 across all categories. Unfortunately, not all those who have made use of this observational methodology have reported reliability estimates (e.g., Rejeski, Darracott, & Hutslar, 1979; Wandzilak, Ansorge, & Potter, 1988).

Another concern regarding reliability is that the protocol associated with the model has not been consistently followed. For example, the criterion for acceptance as a coder has varied considerably. Although some researchers have been quite strict (e.g., must score at least 95% accuracy on the written and proficiency training tests; Horn, 1984), others have not (e.g., score of 80% accuracy was considered acceptable in Sherman & Hassan, 1986). Moreover, the coder training periods have varied considerably (e.g., 4 hours in Wandzilak et al., 1988 to one month in Horn, 1984; Rejeski et al., 1979; Smith et al., 1979). Still others failed to report any details concerning coder training procedures (e.g., Chaumeton & Duda, 1988; Krane, Ecklund, & McDermott, 1991).

Smith and Smoll have also maintained that it is important that the coach not realize he or she is being observed (i.e., not know who the coders are and when they are coming; coders should appear as normal interested observers) and that observers be unobtrusive (Smith et al., 1978, 1979). These guidelines are logical because coaches may alter their behavior if they realize an observation is taking place. However, not all researchers have adhered to this guideline (e.g., Chaumeton & Duda, 1988; Horn, 1984; Krane et al., 1991; Rejeski et al., 1979; Sherman & Hassan, 1986; Wandzilak et al., 1988). Certainly the possibility of behaviors being altered as a result of knowledge of evaluation affects not only reliability but also the validity of the data.

Validity. The Coaching Behavioral Assessment System (CBAS) relies on qualitative procedures. That is, the 12 behavioral categories that are the hallmark of the system were derived from observational data (Smith et al., 1977a). The details provided regarding the data collection and analyses that led to the derivation of the 12 categories are meager, a lack that makes it difficult to evaluate not only the methodology and procedures employed but also the validity of the system. According to Patton (1990), persons undertaking qualitative inquiry have the "obligation to be methodical in reporting sufficient details of data collection and the processes of analysis to permit others to judge the quality of the resulting product" (p. 462). Unfortunately, the original record of the development of the CBAS (i.e., Smith et al., 1977a) provides only a brief description. For example, there is no mention of the number of soccer coaches observed, the number of games and practices observed, or the nature of the time-sampling procedure employed (e.g., Did they make observations of 5 minutes in length every 60 minutes, or observations of 10 minutes in duration every 30 minutes?).

Nevertheless, there is content validity in that these 12 categories tap behaviors that have been shown to affect children and adults in nonathletic settings (Smith & Smoll, 1990; Smoll &

Smith, 1989; Smoll et al., 1978). Bales and Slater (1955) proposed that two general categories of acts of communication that may take place in small group settings are positive and negative reactions. A number of CBAS behaviors are positive or negative responses. White (1975) examined teacher verbal approval (i.e., praise and encouragement) and disapproval (i.e., criticism, reproach, corrective statement) for instructional and classroom management activities. These are analogous to the CBAS behaviors of (a) keeping control, (b) punitive technical instruction, (c) reinforcement, (d) mistake-contingent instruction, and (e) general encouragement. Komaki (1986) examined the effect of supervisory behaviors on managerial performance. The Operant Supervisory Taxonomy and Index (OSTI)(Komaki, Zlotnick, & Jensen, 1986) used in that research also has categories of leader behavior similar to those found in the CBAS. Specifically, *performance expectations* (OSTI dimension) are often conveyed during general technical instruction; *work- but not performance-related communications* (OSTI dimension) could be equated with the CBAS category of organization; and the OSTI subscale of *non-work-related behavior* is analogous to the CBAS category of general communication.

Additionally, the CBAS taps all of the behavioral categories included in Chelladurai and Saleh's (1980) Leadership Scale for Sports (LSS), which is discussed later. In fact as Chelladurai (1993a) noted, the CBAS is much more comprehensive than the LSS and permits a more thorough analysis of leadership in youth sports. From the foregoing, it appears that the CBAS is content valid in the sense that it is measuring the entirety of the construct. However, as Smith and Smoll (1990) have noted, "the CBAS is a broad -banded coding system that does not presently make distinction between other potentially important aspects of coaching behaviors, such as verbal and nonverbal responses, magnitude of reinforcement, quality and duration of instruction, and so forth" (p. 991).

The validity of the qualitative procedures for collecting data was enhanced through multiple analyst triangulation (Patton, 1990). That is, the use of several observers (although Smith et al., 1977a, fail to indicate how many) reduced the potential bias that may arise when only one person collects all the data. However, this approach also suggests the resulting data be content analyzed independently by two or more individuals with results being compared later. Unfortunately, Smith et. al. (1977a) do not indicate the specific procedures associated with content analysis. Another approach would be to "have those who were studied review the findings" (Patton, 1990, p. 468) to learn about the accuracy, fairness, and validity of the data analysis.

One method of assessing construct validity is to use factor analysis techniques to evaluate the factor structure underlying a given set of data. If the emergent structure is conceptually meaningful and/or is consistent with an existing theoretical framework (exploratory techniques), then it can be said to be construct valid. Similarly, if a hypothesized structure is supported in a given data set (confirmatory techniques), construct validity is demonstrated. A hallmark of a good scale is that it

Table 2
Component Structure of the CBAS Observed Behavior Categories (Based on PCA With Varimax Rotation)

	Component Loadings										
	Smith et al., 1983			Smoll et al. 1978[a]				Smith & Smoll, 1990[a]			
Dimension	1	2	3	1[b]	2[c]	3[d]	4[e]	1[e]	2[b]	3[d]	4[c]
Reinforcement	.00	.64	.03	*	.85	*	*	-.18	-.14	-.07	.86
Nonreinforcement	n/a	n/a	n/a	*	*	*	-.88	.86	-.02	.05	-.13
Mistake-Contingent Encouragement	.08	.78	.07	*	.73	*	*	-.08	.00	-.10	.72
Mistake-Contingent Technical Instruction	.73	.21	.06	*	*	.64	*	.03	.14	.64	-.20
Punishment	.83	.08	.11	.74	*	*	*	.10	.74	.18	-.24
Punitive Technical Instruction	.86	-.09	.47	.62	*	*	*	-.07	.62	.26	-.41
Ignoring Mistakes	n/a	n/a	n/a	*	*	*	-.90	.85	.04	-.06	-.10
Keeping Control	.05	-.03	.62	-.58	*	*	*	-.26	-.59	-.10	-.37
General Technical Instruction	.66	.50	.04	*	*	.72	*	-.29	-.13	.73	-.38
General Encouragement	.29	.81	.02	.60	*	-.58	*	-.29	.58	-.59	-.15
Organization	.30	.35	.26	-.78	*	*	*	.24	-.77	.20	-.03
General Communication	.11	-.01	.93	*	*	-.76	*	-.01	-.14	-.76	-.40

[a] Smoll et al. (1978) and Smith & Smoll (1990) results are based on the same data set. Equivalent factors are indicated by the same superscript letter.
n/a = this dimension was not included in the analysis
* = loadings not presented in original manuscript

would yield the same factor structure (i.e., subscale structure) from different data sets.

The principal components analysis of one data set (Smoll et al, 1978; Smith & Smoll, 1990) examined the structure related to the 12 original categories of the CBAS, whereas with another data set (Smith et al., 1983) only ten categories were analyzed. The principal components analysis of the first data set yielded four orthogonal components: (a) punitiveness (positive loadings of punishment, punitive technical instruction, and giving general encouragement versus negative loadings of keeping control and organization), (b) supportiveness (positive loadings of reinforcement and mistake-contingent encouragement), (c) instructiveness (positive loadings of mistake-contingent technical instruction and general technical instruction, and negative loadings of general encouragement and general communication), and (d) responsiveness (negative loadings of nonreinforcement and ignoring mistakes), which accounted for a total of 69% of the variance. One concern here relates to the simple structure of the final solution. Specifically, the category of general encouragement loaded highly on two of the components.

In the second data set (Smith et al., 1983), the behavioral categories of nonreinforcement and ignoring mistakes were eliminated from the analysis. In the previously discussed data set (i.e. Smoll et al, 1978; Smith & Smoll, 1990), these two categories of behaviors both loaded on the component named "responsiveness." Therefore, one would expect three components, similar to "punitiveness," "supportiveness," and "instructiveness" (previously described), to be extracted.

The first orthogonally extracted component in this second data set included general technical instruction, general mistake-contingent instruction, general punitive technical instruction, and punishment. The second consisted of reinforcement, mistake-contingent encouragement, general encouragement, and general technical instruction. The third component included

general communication and keeping control. A total of 72.5% of the variance was accounted for. It must be noted that general technical instruction loaded highly on two components, and organization loaded equally on all three components. More importantly, the component structure and item loadings were not similar in the two data sets (Table 2). These results do not permit us to make a definitive statement regarding the construct validity of the CBAS.

Player Perceptions of Coach's Behavior

With respect to players' perceptions of their coaches' behaviors, these are generally derived through structured interviews that are based on a carefully prepared set of questions. An investigator provides each player with a verbal description and example of each of the 12 behavioral dimensions of the CBAS. The examples are essentially identical to those contained in the manual to train observers. The player is then asked to indicate, on a 7-point scale (1 for almost never to 7 for almost always), how frequently his or her own coach engaged in each of the twelve behaviors.

Reliability. Because these are single-item scales, they cannot be subjected to rigorous psychometric assessments (e.g., internal consistency). However, it is possible to assess stability of the scales (i.e., test-retest reliability) by administering the scale at two different points in time to a randomly selected subsample. There is no report of any such efforts being undertaken.

Validity. It might be argued that this particular measure is face valid because, intuitively it would seem that each item is a direct measure of its corresponding leadership behavior. However, it is desirable to have evidence of other types of validity prior to passing judgments on the measurement instrument itself. Again, extraction of the same underlying factor structure in two data sets would provide some evidence of construct validity. When all 12 categories were included in a principle compo-

Table 3
Component Structure of the Player Perceived Behavior Categories (Based on PCA With Varimax Rotation)

	Smoll et al. 1978			*Smoll et al. 1993*	
Dimension	1	2	3	1	2
Reinforcement	.56	*	*	.77	.06
Nonreinforcement	*	.53	*	-.72	-.15
Mistake-Contingent Encouragement	*	*	*	n/a	n/a
Mistake-Contingent Technical Instruction	*	*	.57	.44	.54
Punishment	*	.76	*	-.68	.38
Punitive Technical Instruction	*	.80	*	-.69	-.01
Ignoring Mistakes	*	*	-.87	n/a	n/a
Keeping Control	.56	*	*	-.11	.77
General Technical Instruction	.61	*	*	.72#	.18#
General Encouragement	.68	*	*	.58#	-.22#
Organization	*	*	*	n/a	n/a
General Communication	*	*	*	n/a	n/a

n/a = this dimension was not included in the analysis

* = loadings not presented in original manuscript

= The assumption is made that terms *encouragement* and *technical instruction* used by Smoll et al. (1993) refer to the more commonly used *general encouragement* and *general technical instruction,* respectively.

nents analysis (Smoll et al., 1978), three orthogonal components were extracted to explain 45.6% of the variance in the data. These components were (a) supportiveness and spontaneity (positive loadings of reinforcement, keeping control, general technical information, and general encouragement), (b) punitiveness (positive loadings of nonreinforcement, punishment, and punitive technical instruction), and (c) correctiveness (positive loading of mistake-contingent technical instruction and negative loading of ignoring mistakes).

Recently, Smoll, Smith, Barnett, and Everett (1993) reported the extraction of only two components that accounted for 53.1% of the variance. The first orthogonally rotated component had positive loadings of the categories of reinforcement, encouragement, and technical instruction, and negative loadings of nonreinforcement, punishment, and punitive instruction. The second component consisted only of two categories: keeping control and corrective instruction. However, corrective instruction also loaded strongly (.44) on the first component. It is not clear why only eight categories were listed in the component structure. At any rate, the emerging factor structure and item loadings from the two exercises were dissimilar. Table 3 presents the component structures and item loadings from the different data sets. Again, these results do not allow any conclusions to be made regarding construct validity of the scale.

Coaches' Perceptions of Their Own Behavior

Similar to the player version, in the assessment of coaches' perceptions of their own behavior, coaches are also provided with a description and example of each of the 12 CBAS dimensions. They are asked to indicate, on 7-point scales (1 for almost never to 7 for almost always), the extent to which they engage in each of the behaviors. No published evidence has been provided for this scale's reliability or validity although, as was the case for the player perceptions measure, one might argue that this particular measure is intuitively face valid because it would seem that each item is a direct measure of its corresponding leadership behavior.

Issues

Factor structures of leadership behavior categories. The 12 leadership behavior categories form the basis for the measures of actual coach behavior, player perception of coach behavior, and coach perception of self-behavior. Because the conceptual foundation for each measure is the same, one would expect that the underlying factor structure for all of the scales to be essentially similar. However, when the solutions from different data sets are compared (Tables 2 & 3), it becomes evident that the structure of the rotated components is not similar; that is, although certain categories load together in one case, they do not necessarily do so in the others. A possible explanation for this discrepancy may be found in the use of an orthogonal rotation. Such a rotation forces the components (or factors in factor analysis) to be uncorrelated. However, this restriction may be unreasonable because various forms of coaching behaviors are likely to be correlated. Raymond Cattell has noted "there are no orthogonal factors in Nature" (quoted in Nesselroade, 1994, p. 150). It is possible that, if the components were allowed to rotate obliquely, the structure of the components in the data sets

may have been more similar. Further, as the purpose of principal components analysis (and exploratory factor analysis) is to condense data into fewer and fewer components (factors), such analysis is likely to yield different component (factor) structures with different data sets because of some minor differences in such data. One concern with using exploratory techniques in such instances is that the analysis is data driven. Because measurement is, by and large, a conceptual exercise, hypotheses regarding underlying structures should be tested, rather than explored. A more useful approach would be to employ confirmatory procedures, such as confirmatory factor analysis, to verify the conceptually based hypothesized factor structures.

Discrepancies among measures of coaching behavior. The three different measures of coaching behavior (i.e., actual, player perceptions, self-perceptions) are secured from three different sources. The actual behavior is assessed by third-party observers. The players provide the scores for the player-perception scores, and the coaches are the source of self-reports of the extent to which they engage in specific categories of leader behavior. As all three measures are supposed to reflect an objective reality of coaching behavior, they are expected to be highly related to each other. Yet the results do not provide strong support for this premise.

Player perceptions and observed behavior. In one of the earlier studies, Smoll et al. (1978) reported that the rank order correlation between player perceptions of coaching behaviors and observed frequencies of coaching behaviors was .58. However, the category of keeping control was found to be responsible for most of the discrepancy between observations and perceptions. With this category removed, the correlation increased to .78. The authors concluded that "aside from keeping control (or maintaining order) which was reported to occur more frequently by the players than it actually did, the relative frequencies of occurrence of behaviors corresponded rather closely with player's perceptions" (p. 534). In contrast, Smith et al. (1979) reported that player perception and CBAS measures correlated significantly only in 4 of the 12 behavioral categories: punishment (r=.54), punitive technical instruction (r=.37), mistake-contingent technical instruction (r=.31), and general communication (r=.26). With respect to the other 8 categories, the correlations were not significant.

Moreover, Smoll et al. (1978) employed canonical correlational analysis of the observed and player-perception scores and extracted two canonical variates. They also examined the percentage of variance in player perceptions and CBAS scores accounted for by the two canonical variates (i.e., the variance in each of the 12 player-perception behavioral categories accounted for by the two canonical variates of observed scores). They found that substantial agreement between players and observers existed only with respect to punitive-type behaviors. In 4 instances the variance accounted for was equal to or less than 10%; in 4 other categories variances ranged between 14% and 19%; and in another 4 cases the variance ranged between 21% and 30%.

Additionally, as noted previously, the factor structures of the CBAS and player-perception versions were different from each other. Smoll et al. (1978) acknowledged that despite correspondence in some areas, "the factor analytic data indicate that the pattern of overt behaviors is different from the organization of perceived behaviors" (p. 538). They go on to recommend that both behavioral and perceptual data be collected when assessing leader behavior.

Coaches' self-reports and observed behavior. With respect to the relationship between coaches' self-reports of their behaviors and scores obtained via the CBAS, Smith et al. (1978) reported that correlations were generally low. Only the correlation between self-perceptions and the CBAS measure of punishment was significant ($r=.45$). Wandzilak et al. (1988) conducted separate t-tests concerning the percentage of observed behaviors and coaches' self reports of percentage of behaviors during games and practice sessions. Although only four behavioral categories were included, coaches perceptions were significantly different from observed frequencies in encouraging remarks, and instructional/organizational comments. Coaches perceived they were providing more encouragement and less instruction/organizational comment than was observed. Wandzilak et al. (1988) also reported generally low correlations between observed behaviors and coach perceptions of those same behaviors (only one was greater than .40). Generally, the results indicated that the coaches had different perceptions of the extent to which they engaged in various categories of behavior; the self-reports did not bear much resemblance to assessments made by observers or players.

Goals and perceived behaviors. Smith et al. (1978) found that coaches tended to perceive themselves as behaving in a manner that would facilitate attainment of their coaching objectives. After indicating the importance of eight different goals, coaches were asked to indicate the extent to which each of the 12 coaching behaviors was instrumental to each of the eight goals. An instrumentality measure was attained for each of the 12 behaviors by multiplying the "coach's importance scores of each of the eight coaching goals (Value) and the coach's rating of the instrumentality of each behavior in attaining that goal (Expectancy)" (p. 187). This measure correlated significantly with the coaches' perceptions of their own behaviors (mean $r=.42$). The authors concluded:

> It appears that the perceived instrumentality of behavior as measured in this study is related only to the coaches' cognitive representations of their own behavior. Coaches believe that they are behaving in a way that will be instrumental in achieving their goals, but this rationality is not reflected in the eyes of other beholders. (p. 187)

It is not clear whether the instrumentality measure was correlated with observed behaviors. It is conceivable that the observed behaviors may indeed reflect coaches' goals that may be distinct from those of the observers and those of the players. This begs the question whether every measure is influenced by the goals of those who are the source of the data (e.g., the observer for the measure of actual behavior, the athlete for the measure of player perceptions). For instance, the players may have their own goals for their participation. If coaches' goals influence their perceptions of their own behaviors, we can also expect that the players' goals will influence their perceptions of the coach's behaviors. For example, one important reason children have for participating in sport is to have fun (Ewing &

Seefeldt, 1989). They may perceive more of a particular behavior (e.g., punishment) than the actual frequencies because they do not see it as instrumental to the goal of having fun.

By the same token, if perceptions are influenced by instrumentalities for coaches, and athletes, it would certainly be possible that they might also affect neutral observers (i.e., raters employing the CBAS). A useful avenue of research in this regard would be to assess the goal orientations and associated instrumentalities of specific behaviors held by participants and observers, as well as coaches, and investigate the extent to which these orientations and instrumentalities are related to the perceptions of coaching behavior of players, observers, and coaches.

Discrepancies and Mediation.

It must be noted that the three central features of the mediational model are (a) the actual leader behavior as tabulated by external observers, (b) players' perceptions of those leader behaviors, and (c) players' affective and evaluative reactions to those leader behaviors and their sport experiences. Coaches' self-perceptions of their own behavior are not central to the model. In fact, coaches' self-perceptions do not find a place in the model as depicted in Figure 1. Therefore, the discrepancies between coaches' self-reports and observed behavior do not negate the tenets of the mediational model of leadership. However, this does not minimize the importance of the measure of coaches' self-perceptions. Smith, Smoll, and associates (e.g., Smith et al., 1979) have used that measure for a very worthy reason: coach education. That is, after identifying the discrepancies between observed behaviors and coach's self-reports, these authors were able to train and develop coaches.

In contrast, the discrepancies between observed and player-perceived behaviors are more germane to testing the mediating effects of player-perceived behaviors. The model's major tenet is that players' reactions to coach's behaviors are mediated by players' perception and recall of those behaviors. In other words, player's perception is the mediator that "represents the generative mechanism through which the focal independent variable is able to influence the dependent variable of interest" (Baron & Kenny, 1986; p. 1173). In the present case, the dependent variable(s) is(are) the affective response(s) of the subject(s); the focal independent variables are the actual (observed) coaching behaviors; and as suggested by the model, the mediator/third variable would be perceptions of coaching behavior.

In order to function as a mediator, a variable (i.e., player perception in our case) must meet the following criteria:

> (a) variations in the levels of the independent variable [observed behavior] significantly account for variations in the presumed mediator [player-perceived behaviors], (b) variations in the mediator significantly account for variations in the dependent variable [player's evaluative reactions], and (c) when controlling for the two previously described relationships (i.e., conditions a and b), the relationship between the independent and dependent variables should no longer be significant. (Baron & Kenny, 1986, p. 1176).

The closer to zero this final relationship is, the stronger the effect of the mediator.

In testing the above conditions of mediation, regression analyses are typically employed. Three regression equations are called for: (a) mediator on independent variable, (b) dependent variable on independent variable, and (c) dependent variable on independent variable and the mediator. If mediation exists, the following conditions must be observed:

1. In the first equation, the independent variable must affect the mediator.
2. In the second equation, the independent variable must affect the dependent variable.
3. In the third equation, the mediator alone must affect the dependent variable.

"If these conditions all hold in the predicted direction, then the effect of the independent variable on the dependent variable must be less in the third equation than in the second" (Baron & Kenny, 1986, p. 1177).

The results to date associated with the mediational model do support the first two conditions (although evidence for the first condition is somewhat mixed; refer to section *Discrepancies Among Measures of Coaching Behavior*). However, the third condition is not supported. Even though they are derived from the 12-category CBAS, Smoll et al. (1978) showed that the two types of data (observed and perceptual) provide different types of information. In their study, the CBAS observation scores and player-perception scores explained 21% and 24% of the variance, respectively, in the player's attraction to the coach. However, the cumulative variance explained was 42%, almost the sum of the independent effects. These results clearly showed that the observed and player-perceived leader behaviors had substantial and independent effects on players' evaluative reactions. Thus, these results negate the mediating effects of player perception and recall between actual leader behavior and players' evaluative reactions as suggested by the mediational model (see Figure 1). If these results were to be replicated in future studies, it may be necessary to reformulate the model to emphasize the independent effects of observed and player-perceived leader behaviors and to remove the suggestion of a mediational effect.

A more appropriate statistical methodology for assessing the mediation hypothesis proposed by the model is structural equation modeling. Models are used to specify the relationships thought to exist between the various constructs. Essentially, structural equation modeling is used to specify these relationships in mathematical form; specifically, it is a "simultaneous system of highly restrictive linear regression equations" (Bentler, 1980, p. 420). A variety of computer programs (e.g., LISREL, RAMONA) are available to estimate the parameters suggested by the model and determine the goodness of fit between the model and the sample data on the measured variables. If the model does not fit the data well, then it is generally rejected as a plausible explanation of the relationships between the latent variables. Although the goal of structural equation modeling techniques is typically one of theory/model testing, Bentler (1980) notes that an "appropriate interplay between theory and data surely involves exploration as well as confirmation" (p. 421). That is, the results of such investigations may also provide insights into possible appropriate revisions for the

theory or model under consideration. Given the accessibility to structural equation modeling computer software (e.g., LISREL, RAMONA) it would seem appropriate to examine the mediation hypothesis using such techniques.

Use of Single Item Measures

It is noteworthy that the scales of perception (both player and coach) are essentially single item indicants of a given dimension. This is problematic because it is impossible to evaluate the reliability (other than test-retest). The practice of operationalizing constructs as single item measures (e.g., Barnett, Smoll, & Smith, 1992; Smith et al., 1979), is not recommended. For instance, Zeller and Carmines (1980) say that

> many studies in the social sciences use a single indicant to approximate a theoretical concept. From a measurement perspective, this approach is highly undesirable, for unless there is a priori information available (and such information is not usually available), it is impossible to estimate the reliability of a single indicant. Moreover, even if the reliability of single indicants can be obtained, it is usually inferior to combined multiple indicants (that is, a composite) because it is more affected by random error. (p. 48)

Moreover, because scale reliability is a necessary condition for scale validity, the importance of this concern should not be taken lightly (particularly given the lack of evidence for the validity of the measures). Thus, future research may be focused on reconstructing the items into specific subscales and empirically confirming the subscale structure. Such efforts would lead to verification of reliability and validity of the scales.

Validity

Establishing the validity of a given scale/measure is a laborious process. In fact, it is a process that is never ending; one can never "prove" a measure is valid, only provide for ever-increasing evidence of its validity or confirm that it is not valid. Certainly, measurement in the field of sport psychology (with certain exceptions) has generally avoided this issue by not addressing the validity of the multitude of measures that have been developed. If there is doubt regarding what is being measured (as must be the case when validity, and even reliability, have not been established), then results of research employing such measures should be viewed with caution.

Players' Evaluative Reactions

In assessing players' evaluative reactions, children have been asked to respond to written questions about various aspects of their participation in sport. The number of items asked varied from 6 (Smith, Zane, Smoll & Coppel, 1983), to 8 (Barnett et al., 1992; Smoll et al 1993), to 10 (Smith & Smoll, 1990; Smoll et al., 1978), and finally to 11 items (Smith et al., 1979) . Players were generally requested to read each of the items (along with the interviewer or on their own) and then record their response privately. Again, items were scored on a 7-point Likert type scale (Table 4).

Some observations are relevant. First, there has not been a

Table 4
Items From Scale Measuring Player Evaluative Reactions

	Dislike a lot					Like a lot	
How much do you like baseball?	1	2	3	4	5	6	7
How much do you like playing for your coach?	1	2	3	4	5	6	7
How much would you like to have the same coach again next year?	1	2	3	4	5	6	7
How much do you like your coach?	1	2	3	4	5	6	7
How much do your parents like your coach?	1	2	3	4	5	6	7
How much does your coach like you?	1	2	3	4	5	6	7
	Much less					Much more	
Do you like baseball more or less than you did at the beginning of the season?	1	2	3	4	5	6	7
	Almost nothing					Almost everything	
How much does your coach know about baseball?	1	2	3	4	5	6	7
	Very poorly					Very well	
How well did the players on your team get along?	1	2	3	4	5	6	7
How well did you like the other players on your team?	1	2	3	4	5	6	7

Note: From Smoll, Smith, Curtis, & Hunt, 1978. With permission from *Research Quarterly for Exercise and Sport*, Vol. 48, No. 2, 401-407. Copyright © 1977 by the American Alliance for Health, Physical Education, Recreation and Dance, 1900 Association Drive, Reston, VA 20191

consistent set of items used to assess player attitudes. Second, the change in the wording of items has resulted in different meanings regarding the constructs being measured. For example, the question "How do you like baseball?" posed by Smith et al. (1979) was reworded as "How do you like *playing* baseball?" by Barnett et al. (1992) (emphasis added). Third, the items were sometimes combined to form composite scales (e.g., Smith & Smoll, 1990; Smoll et al., 1978), and treated as separate dependent variables at other times (e.g., Barnett et al., 1992; Smith et al., 1979).

There is empirical evidence to suggest that the items appear to be linked to some general underlying construct. For example, Smoll et al. (1978) and Smith and Smoll (1990) were able to extract two principal components (varimax rotation) based on 10 attitude items: attraction to the coach and attraction to the sport or the team. The two components accounted for over 62% of the variance in the items. They went on to use the component scores in subsequent analyses. The sets of items loading highly on each component were also combined to assess internal consistency. Cronbach's alpha for attraction to the coach was .87, whereas attraction to the sport or team was .81 (Smith & Smoll, 1990). In another study, Smith et al. (1983) combined four of their six attitude items together to form a subscale measuring a player's evaluation of the coach. Reported inter-item correlations were all above .75. These results clearly show that many of the items employed as attitude measures relate to the player's attraction/evaluation of the coach. Although there appeared to be two strong and conceptually meaningful dimensions of player reactions, they have not been emphasized in subsequent research, and no further steps were taken to develop the seemingly logical subscales. It is an area worthy of future research.

Summary

In summary, Smith, Smoll, and their associates have provided us with a good description of leader/coach behaviors in youth sports. Their 12 dimensional scheme is broad enough to encompass most of the meaningful coaching behaviors. It is also noteworthy that they have developed measures to assess the variables of their study. One possible drawback in this regard is the use of single item measures. However, it must be noted that the use of single item measures is not uncommon in social psychology research. These scholars have also demonstrated the importance of measuring leadership from three perspectives: observers, coaches themselves, and the players. Their research highlights the difficulty arising out of the differences among observed behaviors, coaches' perceptions, and players' perceptions. They also point out that coaches' behaviors are consistent with their goals and perceived instrumentalities of specific forms of coaching behavior. This is an important finding because it identifies the points of intervention for coach development: goals of coaching and instrumentalities of coaching behaviors. Finally, that the hypothesis of mediation is not supported does not take anything away from the authors' contributions to and extensions of theory and research in youth sport.

Multidimensional Model of Leadership

Theoretical Overview

The multidimensional model of leadership (Chelladurai, 1978, 1993a; Chelladurai & Carron, 1978) synthesized and extended to the athletic context (a) Fiedler's (1967) contingency model of leadership effectiveness, (b) Evan's (1970) and House's (1971; House & Dressler, 1974) path-goal theory of leadership, (c) Osborne and Hunt's (1975) adaptive-reactive theory of leadership, and (d) Yukl's (1971) discrepancy model

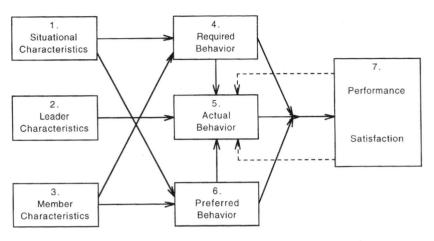

Figure 2. Multidimensional model of leadership (Chelladurai, 1991).
Note: From P. Chelladurai, "Leadership." Reprinted with permission of MacMillan Reference USA, a Simon & Schuster MacMillan Company, from Singer, R.N., Murphy, M., & Tennant, L.K. (Eds.). *Handbook of Research on Sport Psychology*. Copyright © 1993 by The International Society of Sport Psychology.

of leadership. Whereas these earlier theories generally focused on only one aspect of leadership as the crucial dimension (i.e., the leader, the member, or the situational context), the multidimensional model brought these elements together and placed equal emphasis on each. The latest version of the model (Chelladurai, 1993a) is diagrammed in Figure 2.

The multidimensional model proposes that group performance and member satisfaction are functions of the congruence among three states of leader behavior: required, preferred, and actual leader behavior. Characteristics of the situation, the leader, and the members are considered antecedents to these three facets of leader behavior. The demands and constraints created by situational characteristics (i.e., parameters of the organization and/or its environment, such as the goals of the team, the formal organizational structure of the team, the group task and associated technology, social norms, cultural values, and government regulations) would require that the leader behave in certain ways (from Box 1 to Box 4). In addition, characteristics of the groups defined by such factors as gender, age, ability would also influence the required behavior (Box 3 to Box 4). The preferences members have for specific leader behaviors are considered a function of the individual difference factors, such as ability, traits, and needs (Box 3 to Box 6). Further, to the extent individual members are aware of the situational demands and constraints, their preferences are likely to be influenced by the situation (from Box 1 to Box 6). Finally, a leader's actual behavior (Box 5) is said to be influenced by (a) his or her personal characteristics of personality, ability, experience, etc. (Box 2); (b) the required behavior (Box 4); and (c) preferences of members (Box 6). The degree of congruence among the required, actual, and preferred leadership behavior (Boxes 4, 5, and 6) is said to determine the levels of performance and satisfaction (Box 7). The final element in the model is the feedback loop that implies that actual leader behavior may also be influenced by group performance and satisfaction.

Much of the research regarding the multidimensional model of leadership has been descriptive. One line of inquiry has been to assess the influence of selected antecedent variables on preferred

and/or perceived leadership. Such antecedent variables included gender (Chelladurai & Saleh, 1978; Erle, 1981; Liukkonen & Salminen, 1990; Salminen, Liukkonen, Telama, 1990; Serpa, Pataco, & Santos, 1991), personality (Chelladurai & Carron, 1981b; Erle, 1981), age, experience, and maturity (Chelladurai & Carron, 1983; Erle, 1981; Serpa, 1990), and ability (Liukkonen & Salminen, 1990; Garland & Barry, 1988). The situational characteristics studied in relation to preferred and/or perceived leadership included organizational goals (Erle, 1981), task type (Chelladurai, 1978; Kim, Lee, & Lee, 1990; Liukkonen & Salminen, 1990; Serpa, 1990), culture (Chelladurai, Imamura, Yamaguchi, Oinuma, & Miyauchi, 1988; Chelladurai, Malloy, Imamura, & Yamaguchi, 1987; Terry, 1984), and the distinction between offensive and defensive squads in football (Riemer & Chelladurai, 1995).

A second and more complex approach has been to study the congruence between the perceived and preferred leadership in relation to one of the consequences specified in the model, such as satisfaction with leadership, team performance, and/or individual performance (Chelladurai, 1978, 1984; Chelladurai et al. 1988; McMillin, 1990; Riemer & Chelladurai, 1995; Schliesman, 1987; Summers, 1983; Weiss & Friedrichs, 1986). The general conclusion emerging from these studies is that

> athletes are satisfied with leadership to the extent that the coach emphasizes (a) training and instruction that enhances the ability and co-ordinated effort by members, which in turn contributes to task accomplishment; and (b) positive feedback that recognizes and rewards good performance. (Chelladurai, 1993a, p. 654)

Few studies have also attempted to relate leadership to performance (e.g., Chelladurai, 1978; Gordon, 1986; Serpa et al., 1991; Weiss & Friedrichs, 1986). Only one study included required leader behavior along with actual and preferred leader behaviors in relation to performance. Chelladurai (1978) operationalized required behavior as the mean preferences of all basketball players included in the study and the actual behavior as the mean of the perceptions of players of a particular team. Chelladurai's hypothesis that congruence between required behavior and actual behavior would be related to performance was not supported. This finding could have been a function of the low number of teams (n=10) he studied.

Measurement and Operationalization of the Model's Constructs

Preferred and Perceived Leader Behavior — Leadership Scale for Sports (LSS)

The Leadership Scale for Sports, developed in conjunction with the MML, consists of 40 items representing five dimensions of leader behavior: training and instruction (13 items), democratic behavior (9 items), autocratic behavior (5 items), social support (8 items), and positive feedback/rewarding behavior (5 items). These dimensions of leader behavior are described in

Table 5
Dimensions of the Leadership Scale for Sports

Dimension	*Description*
Training and instruction	Coaching behavior aimed at improving the athletes' performance by emphasizing and facilitating hard and strenuous training; instructing them in the skills, techniques and tactics of the sport; clarifying the relationship among the members; and structuring and coordinating the members' activities
Democratic behavior	Coaching behavior that allows greater participation by the athletes in decisions pertaining to group goals, practice methods, and game tactics and strategies
Autocratic behavior	Coaching behavior that involves independence in decision making and which stresses personal authority
Social support	Coaching behavior characterized by a concern for the welfare of individual athletes, positive group atmosphere, and warm interpersonal relations with member
Positive feedback	Coaching behavior that reinforces an athlete by recognizing and rewarding good (proficient/quality) performance

Source: Chelladurai (1989)

Table 5. Response categories are quantified as: (a) always, (b) often - 75% of the time, (c) occasionally - 50% of the time, (d) seldom - 25% of the time, and (e) never. The scale has been used to measure (a) athletes' preferences for specific leader behaviors, (b) athletes' perceptions of their coaches' leader behaviors, and/or (c) coaches' perceptions of their own behavior (e.g., Chelladurai, 1984; Chelladurai & Carron, 1983; Chelladurai et al., 1988; Chelladurai et al., 1987; Dwyer & Fischer, 1988b; Garland & Barry, 1988; Gordon, 1986; Horne & Carron, 1985; Liukkonen & Salminen, 1989; Riemer & Chelladurai, 1995; Robinson & Carron, 1982; Schliesman, 1987; Schliesman, Beitel, & DeSensi (in press); Summers, 1983; Terry, 1984; Terry & Howe, 1984; Weiss & Friedrichs, 1986).

The LSS was developed in two stages. The first stage (Chelladurai & Saleh, 1978) consisted of a principal components analysis with varimax (orthogonal) rotation of 99 items, most of which were chosen and modified from existing leadership scales (i.e., LBDQ, Halpin & Winer, 1957; SBDQ, Fleishman, 1957a; LOQ, Fleishman, 1957b; LBDQ Form XII, Stogdill, 1963). The items, which were preceded with the phrase "The coach should..." (preferences), had response categories of always, often, occasionally, seldom, and never. Questionnaires were completed by 160 Canadian university physical education students (equal number of males and females). A five-component solution (Training, Autocratic, Democratic, Social Support, and Rewarding Behaviors) was reported to be the most meaningful. Only those items (*n*=37) that (a) loaded high on one component (i.e., >.40) and loaded low on every other component (i.e., <.30) were selected to represent the five-component solution. It should be noted that using the data of only 160 subjects to conduct a principal components analysis of 99 items is not very appropriate. Many authors have suggested the ratio of items to subjects be, at the very least, 1:5 (e.g., Tabachnik & Fidell, 1989).

It was noted that none of the items in the original item pool referred to the coaching behavior of teaching skills and strategies. Therefore, seven items reflecting this behavior were added in the second stage (Chelladurai & Saleh, 1980), and six more social support items were included to better capture the leader's interpersonal orientation. The authors also quantified the re-

sponse categories (noted previously) during this phase of development. The questionnaire was then administered to samples of 102 physical education students (45 males and 57 females) and 223 male varsity athletes. The students and athletes completed the preference version with the stem "I prefer my coach to... ." In addition, the athletes completed the perception version with the stem "My coach... ."

Principal components analysis with varimax rotation was employed to analyze each of the three data sets. However, the number of factors to extract (i.e., 5) was determined a priori. As was the case previously, items were selected to constitute each of the components based on the criteria that an item (a) had its highest loading on the same factor for all three solutions and (b) loaded at least .30 in two of the solutions. The 40 retained items make up the current version of the scale.

Reliability. The test-retest reliability estimates derived from the data of 53 physical education students who responded to the questionnaire after a lapse of 4 weeks were .72 for Training and Instruction, .82 for Democratic Behavior, .76 for Autocratic Behavior, .71 for Social Support, and .79 for Positive Feedback (Chelladurai, 1993a). These values are considered adequate during initial stages of social science instrument development (Nunnally & Bernstein, 1994).

Of greater interest for this chapter are the internal consistency estimates reported by various authors (Table 6). It must first be noted that the alpha values are relatively higher for the perception version than for the preference version although the items are identical with only a change in the stem. This is consistent with the notion that when the same subjects report both their preferences and perceptions, perceptions are likely to dominate (White, Crino, & Hatfield, 1985). If perceptions dominate, then the expression of those perceptions is likely to be more consistent across the various items of a subscale than would be the case in the expression of preferences.

Second, the internal consistency estimates for the autocratic behavior subscale were low across the included studies. Cronbach's alpha, an index of internal consistency of a scale, is the estimated average correlation among items of a scale and, thus, is a function of the number of items in that scale (Nunnally &

Table 6
Internal Consistency Estimates for the LSS Dimensions

| | Dimensions | | | | | | | | | |
| | Preferences | | | | | Perceptions | | | | |
Source	TI	DB	AB	SS	PF	TI	DB	AB	SS	PF
Chelladurai (1986):										
Indian athletes	.76	.71	.56	.51	.57	.87	.78	.49	.70	.61
Chelladurai et al. (1988):										
Japanese athletes	.81	.72	.55	.72	.73	.89	.81	.57	.84	.81
Canadian athletes	.77	.67	.55	.78	.77	.88	.75	.59	.84	.91
Chelladurai & Saleh (1980):										
Canadian Athletes	.83	.75	.45	.70	.82	.93	.87	.79	.86	.92
Dwyer & Fischer (1988b):										
Canadian wrestlers						.86	.81	.52	.77	.82
Iordanoglou (1990):										
Greek soccer players						.86	.73	.11	.59	.60
Isberg & Chelladurai (1990)										
Swedish athletes	.78	.77	.44	.60	.57	.88	.72	.54	.86	.77
Keehner (1988):										
American fitness club members						.99	.97	.93	.97	.98
Kim et al. (1990)										
Korean athletes	.81	.74	.61	.76	.66	.86	.83	.64	.80	.72
Riemer & Chelladurai (1995)										
American college football athletes	.83	.79	.57	.72	.80	.89	.85	.61	.83	.84
Toon (1996)										
American college tennis athletes	.86	.82	.67	.80	.81	.88	.86	.59	.78	.87

Bernstein, 1994). Estimates lower than .70 suggest that the items may not be measuring the same construct (i.e., the items are not from the same sampling domain). Further, although Nunnally and Bernstein have suggested that modest reliability of .70 is adequate during the early stages of measurement development, reliability of .80 or greater is certainly more appropriate because the amount of measurement error is then being reduced.

With reference to autocratic behavior measured by the LSS, two of the items refer to the aloofness of the coach (i.e., the coach works relatively independent of the athletes; the coach keeps to him- or herself), two refer to how he or she handles issues/decisions (i.e., the coach does not explain his/her action; the coach refuses to compromise a point), and one seems to capture how the coach addresses players (i.e., the coach speaks in a manner not to be questioned). Although all the items in democratic behavior clearly revolve around decision making, the items in autocratic behavior reflect two to three distinct facets of leadership behavior and, hence, may be one reason for the low internal consistency scores.

The items in autocratic behavior do not reflect autocratic behavior in the traditional sense (i.e., the opposite end of the continuum from democratic behavior). It must be noted that the derivation of these two dimensions was based on orthogonal rotation of the components, and therefore, they are deemed to be uncorrelated. That is, these two sets of behaviors are purported to constitute two unipolar dimensions, and not the opposite ends of the same continuum. Thus, the scale might need to be renamed as, for example, aloof behavior, authoritarian behav-

ior, or inflexible behavior. However, renaming the dimension does not minimize the problem of low internal consistency.

What is intriguing is that the autocratic behavior subscale items all loaded highly on the same factor and/or component in four different data sets. Also, the subscale has been found to be meaningfully associated with player preferences and their reactions. Therefore, we would argue that it would be unwise to discard the dimension. Instead, future revisions of the LSS may attempt to strengthen the scale by adding more homogeneous items from the same sampling domain and/or splitting the dimensions into more specific forms of autocratic behavior, such as aloofness and inflexibility.

Validity. With respect to validity of the LSS, Chelladurai and Saleh (1980) claimed content validity for the scale because each of the components extracted was meaningful. In a subsequent paper, Chelladurai (1981) explained that the LSS dimensions of training and instruction, positive feedback, and social support could be placed in juxtaposition with Porter and Lawler's (1968) model of individual motivation. This model of motivation envisages that an individual's expenditure of effort in an activity results in a certain level of performance. This level of performance in turn leads to certain rewards with which the individual would be differentially satisfied. According to Chelladurai (1981), training and instruction contributes to enhancement of ability and clearer role perceptions, which are instrumental to improved performance. Positive feedback ensures the equitable distribution of rewards based on performance, which is fundamental to feelings of equity and satisfaction. Social support becomes critical to the effort phase, which is much more prolonged and agonistic in athletics than in other spheres.

Chelladurai (1993a) suggested that criterion-related validity could be inferred from the empirical support for theoretical relationships between selected criterion variables and the dimensions of leader behavior. These included (a) athletes' satisfaction (Chelladurai, 1984; Chelladurai et al., 1988; Riemer & Chelladurai, 1995; Schliesman, 1987; Schliesman et al., in press; Weiss & Friedrichs, 1986), (b) the performance level of athletes (Garland & Barry, 1988), (c) performance (Gordon, 1986; Summers, 1983; Weiss & Friedrichs, 1986); (d) drop-out behavior or turn-over in athletics (Robinson & Carron, 1982); and (e) coach-athlete compatibility (Horne & Carron, 1985).

Chelladurai and Saleh (1980) also claimed factorial validity (i.e., construct validity) for the scale because (a) a similar five-factor principal component solution was extracted in three different samples and was similar to those extracted in a previous study (i.e., Chelladurai & Saleh, 1978), and (b) the scree plots were essentially the same for each of the three solutions. However, several concerns should be raised. First, as Chelladurai (1993a) noted, the relatively low percentage of variance explained by the original five factors (41.2%, 39.3%, and 55.8% in three different samples, respectively) is a source of concern. Second, an examination of the scree plots reported by Chelladurai and Saleh (1980) suggests that a two- or three-factor solution (rather than a five-factor solution) could have been accepted in each case (provided those factors were interpretable). Third, because Chelladurai and Saleh (1980) selected only the highest loading items ($n=40$ out of 50) to represent a given factor, the orthogonality of the factors was lost. That is, the factors could be expected to be correlated. In Riemer and Chelladurai's (1995) study, the correlations among the dimensions of LSS ranged from -.01 to .66 for a mean of .33 in the preferred version and from -.03 to .74 for a mean of .35 in the perceived version. With significant intercorrelations among the dimensions, we can also expect some items to correlate higher with the irrelevant dimensions than with their own respective dimensions.

Finally, Summers (1983) and Gordon (1986) reported that they were unable to replicate the subscale structure of the LSS using exploratory techniques. However, the dimensional substructure of the LSS cannot be adequately tested using conventional exploratory factor analysis techniques because their purpose is to condense the information of a given data set (Hair, Anderson, Tatham, & Black, 1992). Therefore, it is possible the analysis would likely yield different factor structures with different data sets because minor (or major) variations in the data may ultimately influence the number of factors extracted and the subsequent factor loadings.

Chelladurai and his associates, and other scholars, have verified the subscale structure of the LSS through item-to-total correlations, a less rigorous method of confirmation (e.g., Chelladurai, 1986; Chelladurai & Carron, 1981a; Chelladurai, Imamura, & Yamaguchi, 1986; Chelladurai et al., 1988; Dwyer & Fischer, 1988a; Iordanoglou, 1990; Isberg & Chelladurai, 1990; Keehner, 1988; Kim et al., 1990; Lacoste & Laurencelle, 1989). In this particular procedure, the subscale structure is verified by correlating each item with the sum of all the other items from the same subscale, and with the sum of the items from the other subscales. A good item should correlate higher with its own subscale total than with other subscale totals. It is understandable that researchers in the past might have been constrained to employ such procedures because of the lack of computing facilities. However, with easy access to more sophisticated and powerful programs, such as LISREL, it is appropriate and necessary to employ the more rigorous confirmatory factor analysis to verify the hypothesized factor structure of the LSS and assess the extent to which it fits the data set.

With the foregoing in mind, a preliminary examination of the construct validity of both versions of the LSS using confirmatory factor analysis techniques (LISREL) was carried out for inclusion in this chapter (the Riemer & Chelladurai, 1995, data set was used). Such procedures allow for an evaluation of the overall fit of the model in a given data set (i.e., whether the hypothesized subscale structure is actually supported by the data)

Table 7
Goodness-of-Fit Results of LSS Confirmatory Factor Analysis

	X^2	df	q	$c2/df$	TLI	D^2	RMSEA	RMSEA (90% CI)	$H_0 = EF$	$H_0 = CF$**
Pref. ($n=247$)	1376.39	730	90	1.89	.77	.78	.060	.055-.065	.000	.000
Pref. Null	3728.28	780	40	4.77	n/a	n/a	.124	.120-.128	.000	.000
Perc. ($n=180$)	1228.36	730	90	1.68	.83	.85	.062	.056-.068	.000	.001
Perc. Null	3971.90	780	40	5.09	n/a	n/a	.151	.147-.156	.000	.000

Null = null model
df = degrees of freedom
q = parameters
TLI = Tucker Lewis Index
D^2 = Bollen's (1989) Delta 2 Index
RMSEA = Root Mean Square Error of Approximation
* Exact Fit = Probability that the model holds exactly in the population
** Close Fit = Probability that the model holds closely in the population (i.e., RMSEA < .05)

and an examination of the relationships between individual items and their respective subscales. Thedata set used consisted of collegiate football players (n=217 for the perception version, and n=317 for the preference version).

As noted in Table 7, the overall fit of the preference and perception models could be considered adequate. First, although the chi-square values are quite large, their ratio to the degrees of freedom is at acceptable levels (< 2). Also, the Root Mean Square Error of Approximation (RMSEA) was .06 and .062, respectively for the preferred and perceived versions of the LSS. These values fall within the range of .05 to .08 suggesting a fair fit of the model in the data set (Steiger & Lind, 1980). Considering that a good fit is indicated by a value less than .05, there is room for improvement of the LSS. The need to revisit the LSS is further shown by the low values of Bollen's (1989) fit index values of .78 and .85 which were lower than .90, a value said to be indicative of a good fit (Bollen, 1989). Further, the values of .77 and .83 for the Tucker-Lewis Index were also considerably lower than the minimum .90 value considered indicative of a good model.

Although the appropriateness of the model to the data (i.e., model fit) is an important evaluative consideration, Browne and DuToit (1991) note that a second vital requirement is that the fitted model makes sense. That is, "the values of the model's parameters should convey meaningful information. This requirement cannot be formulated in objective terms; it can only be assessed subjectively" (p. 50). From this perspective, the five-dimensional scheme of the LSS can be deemed to be conceptually appropriate. Overall, there is enough evidence to suggest that the psychometric properties are adequate, and at the same time, there is evidence for the need to revise the scale in terms of its subscale structure. For example, many of the parameter estimates in the confirmatory factor analysis (e.g., Lambda matrix) went beyond the normal logical bounds (i.e., > 1.0), and many of the estimates of error variance in an item (i.e., delta matrix elements) were quite large. At the least, it is necessary to verify the subscale structure of the LSS through confirmatory analyses in other sets of data.

Issues. Although the foregoing critique of the LSS was based on empirical examination of the LSS and its constructs, there is also the conceptual concern of whether the LSS captures all the relevant coaching behaviors. The original 99 items from which the LSS dimensions were derived (Chelladurai, 1978) were largely drawn from existing scales in business and industry. Insofar as the athletic context is quite different from those of business and industry, the five dimensions of the LSS may not tap all of the dimensions of critical coaching behavior. That the LSS dimensions are not comprehensive is shown by a comparison with Smith and Smoll's CBAS (Smith et al., 1977a) which allows for a more thorough analysis of leadership behavior.

Another concern within the LSS dimensions is that they do not encompass those behaviors associated with the emerging conceptualization of transformational leadership. Earlier approaches to leadership, such as House's (1971) path-goal theory, Osborn and Hunt's (1975) adaptive-reactive theory, and Graen and Cashman's (1975) role-making model of leadership, are deemed to be transactional in nature. That is, these models assume that the leader extends his or her support and rewards to

members in exchange for members' compliance to organizational requirements and/or leader's directives. Transformational leadership views the leader as engaging in behavior that incites the higher order needs of members, motivates them to perform beyond expectations, expresses confidence in members, and empowers them (e.g., Bass, 1985; Conger & Kanungo, 1988). In addition, transformational leaders may also be charismatic (i.e., members believe in the extraordinary qualities of their leader and are committed to upholding his or her values), and engage in unconventional behaviors to highlight the unacceptability of the status quo. Anecdotal evidence suggests that some of the outstanding coaches have been transformational and charismatic, and thus, it would be important to empirically determine the extent to which these concepts are applicable to the athletic context (Chelladurai, 1993a).

Given the foregoing discussion, it becomes clear that there is a need to develop a more comprehensive list of leader behavior dimensions. These might be based on the criteria for classification proposed by Riemer and Chelladurai (1995); that is, adaptive (prescribed) and reactive (discretionary) behaviors. Further, Chelladurai and Riemer (1997) have recently classified facets of athlete satisfaction based on the criteria of (a) team versus individual level, (b) task versus social aspects, and (c) outcomes versus processes. The same set of criteria and any additional relevant criteria may be used to generate a list of leader behavior dimensions. Further, focus-groups procedures involving players and coaches may be employed to generate more meaningful categories of leader behavior born out of their experience and expertise. Such efforts to develop an exhaustive list of the dimensions/facets of athletic leadership would be consistent with the trend in organizational behavior research toward a greater number of dimensions to describe leader behavior (e.g., Yukl, 1981).

Actual Behavior

Actual behavior, central to the multidimensional model, has been operationalized as the average of the perceptions of members of a team (Chelladurai, 1978) (refer to the previous section for a discussion regarding the validity and reliability of the perception version of the LSS). There are two issues associated with this approach. First, to the extent player perceptions are likely to be influenced by their preferences and affective reactions, these perceptions may not reflect reality. For instance, Smith, Smoll, and associates (Smith et al., 1979; Smoll et al., 1978) have shown that player perceptions of leader behavior did not relate to observed leader behaviors. Thus, we may expect actual behaviors and player perceptions to deviate from each other. It is important that researchers be cognizant of these possibilities and be wary of making any categorical statements regarding findings associated with actual behavior when the latter have been operationalized as the mean of player perceptions.

The second issue relates to the debate over the homogeneity and heterogeneity of leader behavior. The question is whether the leader behaves the same way toward every member of the team. When one takes the average of the player perceptions to denote actual behavior, there is the implicit assumption of homogeneity of perceived and/or actual leader behavior. There may be very sound reasons for the leader to be consistent in certain forms of leader behavior. For instance, a coach of a basketball team may treat all players in the same way when it comes to training and instruction and rewarding them based on performance. However, to extend that argument to all forms of behavior in all contexts does negate the notion of leader's discretion in reacting differentially to individual preferences and needs (Graen & Cashman, 1975; House, 1971; Osborn & Hunt, 1975). For example, it is arguable that differentiated treatment of athletes results from differences between players in terms of athletic skill and ability. For instance, a coach may spend more time providing training and instruction for those players who are unable to perform certain skills proficiently. Chelladurai (1978) suggested that coaches of individual sports may indeed vary their behavior in dealing with individual members. He also suggested that a coach of a team sport may be consistent in task-related behaviors (training and instruction, and positive feedback), and extend his or her social support differentially based on member preferences and needs. Chelladurai (1978), used the variance of player perceptions from each of 10 basketball teams, 4 wrestling teams, and 6 track and field teams as a measure of homogeneity/heterogeneity of leader behavior. Although he did not find any support for the above hypotheses, the use of variance as a measure of homogeneity of leader behavior would prove useful in future research. Moreover, if it can be demonstrated that the variance in player perceptions is minimal (i.e., the coach is perceived to behave uniformly toward all players), the use of the average perception as a measure of actual behavior would be legitimate. However, if the variance is substantial, the use of average of perceptions becomes suspect. At the least, researchers should verify the extent to which player perceptions are homogeneous and report the results thereof to alert the readers.

Required Leader Behavior

One important component of the model that has not been investigated sufficiently is required behavior. There has only been one attempt to operationalize this variable (i.e., Chelladurai, 1978). He used the average of the preferences of all subjects from a sport (i.e., basketball) as the measure of required behavior. Chelladurai (1978) argued that when the mean score was computed, the influence of individual differences on preferred leadership would cancel out. The resulting score would then represent the influences of the macrovariables. Chelladurai (1993a) suggested that an extension of this argument would be to use the average of the self-reported behaviors of a significant number of successful coaches in a sport.

It must be noted that Chelladurai (1978) was concerned with required behavior in one homogeneous set of teams: Canadian intercollegiate basketball teams. Therefore, the use of the average preferences of all players in all teams as an estimate of the required behavior might have been legitimate. However, such an argument must be weighed carefully with other factors. The organizational contexts of various teams in one sport may be vastly different from each other, and therefore, use of a single estimate of required behavior for all teams may not be appropriate. For instance, much has been said about the differences in the climate and culture of the teams from former Eastern Bloc countries and the United States. These differences were presumed to be a function of the macrovariables of ideologies and forms of

government. Averaging the preferences of members of all teams in this case would cancel out not only the influences of individual differences but also the influences of the macrovariables associated with the two groups of teams. Therefore, it may be necessary to develop measures of required behavior specific to a particular context. As another example, we may have to develop different measures of required behavior for the professional, collegiate, and high school levels in basketball.

Even within one context, the average preferences of all subjects from a particular sport may account for the influence of some of the macrovariables associated with the sport (e.g., task variability, task interdependence) or with the type of group based on age, maturity, ability, etc. However, the average of the preferences can never account for those macrovariables that may vary from team to team. For instance, professional teams may belong to (a) individuals and/or families (e.g., the former Cleveland Browns), (b) corporate entities (e.g., Anaheim Mighty Ducks — Disney Corporation), and (c) communities (e.g., Green Pay Packers). Such differences in ownership may impose certain demands and constraints on leadership. These influences specific to a particular team would not be captured by the average over all teams. Similar arguments can be advanced for the differences between private and public educational institutions. Therefore, it is incumbent on researchers to ensure that the teams and/or athletes are under the influence of the same set and at the same levels of macrovariables when using one estimate of required behavior. If there are differences in the macrovariables, then it would be necessary to estimate different sets of required behavior. This approach also implies that enough data need to be collected to ensure that the information being used to operationalize required behavior is representative of all athletes for a given sport, a competitive level, and an organizational context—an enormous task indeed.

Outcome Variables

One of the serious drawbacks associated with the multidimensional model of leadership has been the lack of valid and reliable measures of the outcome variables of performance and satisfaction. In fact, this lack of psychometrically sound outcome measures does constrain the testing of several other psychological models in sport psychology (Courneya & Chelladurai, 1991). Moreover, the establishment of criterion validity for the LSS requires that reliable and valid scales of the consequences of leadership behavior be developed. The specific issues with these outcome measures are explicated below.

Performance. Generally speaking, performance as a consequence has not been dealt with adequately in the study of leadership (Chelladurai, 1993a). In fact, very few empirical investigations have included performance as a dependent variable (e.g., Chelladurai, 1978; Gordon, 1986; Serpa et al., 1991; Summers, 1983; Weiss & Friedrichs, 1986). Further, when examined the observed relationships between leadership and performance have been quite weak. This may be attributable to either the deficiencies in the leadership scale (which have been addressed earlier) or the performance measures themselves. The traditional measures of win-loss percentage, point differential (i.e., the difference between points scored for and against the team), and ratio of final score (of the two teams in a contest)

Table 8
Definitions of the Proposed Facets

Category	Facet	Definition
Individual task outcomes	Absolute performance	Satisfaction with an individual's own absolute task performance.
	Personal goal attainment	Satisfaction with whether an individual has reached his or her own goals
	Performance improvement	Satisfaction with one's own improvement in task performance
	Task contribution/role	Satisfaction with the importance of the contribution an individual makes to the team
	Personal growth	Satisfaction with the psychological and mental growth related to understanding strategies, tactics, task skills betterment and developing psychological skills to aid task execution
	Personal immersion	Satisfaction with the aesthetic pleasure associated with task performance
Team task outcomes	Absolute performance	Satisfaction with the team's win/loss record
	Team goal attainment	Satisfaction with extent to which the team has reached its goals
	Performance improvement	Satisfaction with the improvement in the team's task performance
	Team growth/development	Satisfaction with how, over the course of the season, the team has matured in terms of skills, fitness, strategies, etc.
	Group integration	Satisfaction with the extent to which members of the group contribute and coordinate their efforts toward the accomplishment of the group's task
Individual Social Outcomes	Belongingness	Satisfaction with the extent an athlete feels he or she belongs and is accepted by the group
	Friendship	Satisfaction with the affinities developed with individual members of the team
	Role (Social)	Satisfaction with the social role an athlete plays on the team
Team social outcomes	Interpersonal harmony	Satisfaction with how members get along as a group
Individual task processes	Ability utilization	Satisfaction with how an individual's talents and abilities are used and employed
	Training & instruction	Satisfaction with how an individual's physical skills and mental strategies are developed
	Positive feedback	Satisfaction with the provision of reinforcements for successful performance
	Personal inputs	Satisfaction with the personal effort an athlete puts forth
	Team contribution	Satisfaction with how an athlete's efforts fit with the rest of the team's efforts/work; does the athlete receive positive feedback from others on the team
	Recognition	Satisfaction with the recognition received for what the athlete brings to the task processes
	Compensation	Satisfaction with how the athlete is compensated (paid)
	Family support	Satisfaction with the support from family received for athletic participation
Team task processes	Strategy selection	Satisfaction with the strategies selected by the coach; a seasonal perspective
	Mobilization	Satisfaction with the extent to which appropriate and necessary talent is recruited
	Deployment(Staffing)	Satisfaction with how the coach uses the available talent in a coordinated manner to achieve success
	Practice	Satisfaction with practices
	Competition tactics	Satisfaction with the specific tactics employed by a coach during the competition
	Equitable treatment	Satisfaction with how the coach comes to decisions; the equity of the decision making process
	Ethics	Satisfaction with the leader's ethics
	Team effort coordination	Satisfaction with whether the effort put forth by members of the team is coordinated (social loafing)
	Facilities	Satisfaction with the physical facilities
	Budget	Satisfaction with the budget available to the team, scholarships, etc.
	Ancillary support	Satisfaction with academic counseling, trainers, medical coverage, game management
	Community support	Satisfaction with support from the community, media, etc. for the team
Team social processes	Loyalty support	Satisfaction with the loyalty of the coach/management to the team without reference to performance
	Decision participation	Satisfaction with the extent to which the coach allows the team to participate in the decision-making processes
Individual social processes	Social support	Satisfaction with the interpersonal relationships (warmth, supportive, unrelated to task) with coaches and teammates
	Loyalty support	Satisfaction with the loyalty of the coach/management to the athlete without reference to performance

have their own drawbacks. As Courneya and Chelladurai (1991) noted, these measures are contaminated by such factors as random chance, opponent's outstanding performance, strategic choices made by the team/coach, and officials' wrong calls. Noting that these measures are not sensitive enough to capture the subtle effects of any psychological interventions including leadership, Courneya and Chelladurai classified performance measures in baseball into primary (e.g., batting average), secondary (e.g., runs batted in), and tertiary (e.g., run differential) measures based on their conceptual proximity to skill execution and task performance. That is, the primary measures are less contaminated by external factors than the other two and, therefore, more indicative of performance. Courneya and Chelladurai also suggested that similar relatively purer forms of performance measures need to be developed for other sports.

Recognizing the deficiencies of existing performance measures, some scholars have used player perceptions as a measure of performance (e.g., Chelladurai, 1984; Horne & Carron, 1985). Such perceptions may relate to perceived actual performance, performance improvements, and attainment of previously set goals. It must, however, be noted that such player perceptions of performance will be closely related to players' affective reactions to such perceptions. As athletes' affective reactions are usually measured as satisfaction, it becomes problematic to empirically separate the two measures—perceived performance and affective reactions (i.e., satisfaction). Therefore, it is preferable to rely more on third-party-generated performance measures than on player-generated performance measure. This does not deny the significance of player perceptions and their affective reactions.

Satisfaction. Satisfaction has also not been adequately operationalized; there has been no systematic effort to develop a reliable and valid measure of athlete satisfaction. The scales used to measure the construct have consisted of (a) a single item (e.g., Horne & Carron, 1985; Riemer & Chelladurai, 1995), or (b) multiple single items measuring multiple dimensions of satisfaction (e.g., Chelladurai, 1984; Schliesman, 1987; Schliesman et al, in press). Chelladurai et al. (1988) factor analyzed several items and derived two dimensions of satisfaction: satisfaction with leadership and satisfaction with personal outcome. This scale, labeled Scale of Athlete Satisfaction (SAS), has not been subsequently tested for its subscale structure. Further, athlete satisfaction cannot be described in just two dimensions. It is an extremely complex construct, and any scale designed to operationalize it must reflect that complexity.

Recognizing the need for the development of a multidimensional scale of athlete satisfaction (Chelladurai, 1993a; Granito & Carlton, 1993; Riemer & Chelladurai, 1995), Chelladurai and Riemer (1997) have recently defined and classified 29 different facets of athlete satisfaction (Table 8). Based on Chelladurai and Riemer's (1997) dimensional representation, Riemer and Chelladurai (1997) have developed the Athlete Satisfaction Questionnaire, a multifaceted scale that exhibited initial evidence of validity and reliability.

General Measurement Issues

Level of analyses. An important issue related to the measurement of the multidimensional model of leadership is the level of analyses in assessing the various components of leadership. Required leader behavior and the actual leadership behavior are team concepts. That is, whenever these measures are used, the teams become the units of analysis (e.g., Chelladurai, 1978; Weiss & Friedrichs, 1986). In his study of basketball teams, Chelladurai (1978) hypothesized that the degree of congruence between required behavior and actual behavior would be related to team performance. As all three measures are group-based concepts, it was only logical to use the team as the unit of analysis. However, the extremely low number of teams in the Chelladurai study (*n*=10) did not permit any extensive testing of the hypotheses. Thus, it becomes necessary to collect data from a large number of teams to test any hypotheses at the team level.

In contrast, when preferred leader behavior and perceived leader behavior are used, the individual athletes become the unit of analysis. Thus, it becomes more practical to rely on preferred and perceived leadership measures because this treats the members of a team as the unit of analysis, a process that results in a large number of observations (i.e., subjects). Such large numbers permit more extensive investigation of the hypotheses with more sophisticated statistical procedures. Several studies have taken this approach (e.g., Chelladurai, 1984; Chelladurai et al., 1988; Horne & Carron, 1985; Schliesman, 1987). It is appropriate to use these measures and the players as units of analyses insofar as one is concerned with players' affective reactions, such as satisfaction, which is a significant outcome variable in and of itself. However, it would be unwise to relate these measures to any team level outcomes.

Measures of congruence. As noted before, the most significant tenet of the multidimensional model is that the congruence among the three states of leader behavior influences performance and satisfaction. The congruence among the three states of leader behavior has generally been operationalized as the discrepancy between preferences and perceptions (e.g., Chelladurai, 1984; Horne & Carron, 1985; Schliesman, 1987). Chelladurai (1993a) cautioned against the indiscriminate use of discrepancy scores and advocated that "a minimally acceptable approach would be to identify and use that set of scores (preferred, perceived, or discrepancy scores) that account for the greatest amount of variance in the dependent variable(s)" (p. 655). Chelladurai (1984) reported that discrepancy scores best predicted satisfaction, whereas Chelladurai et al. (1988) reported that perceptions of leadership were better predictors. Other researchers have also investigated the impact of perceptions on satisfaction (e.g., Schliesman, 1987; Schliesman et al., in press; Weiss & Friedrichs, 1986).

However, Riemer and Chelladurai (1995) note that the use of a single measure, such as preferences or perceptions of leadership behavior, violates the notion of congruence, which implies the composite effects of more than one leadership variable. Therefore, one cannot rely on a single measure if one is interested in testing the congruence hypothesis. In general, scholars in various fields have tended to use a discrepancy score (i.e., subtracting one measure from another) as a measure of congruence. Although discrepancy scores are intuitively appealing and widely employed, many authors have pointed out the problems inherent in their use (Berger-Gross & Kraut,

1984; Cronbach, 1958; Ferguson, 1976; Gardner & Neufeld, 1987; Johns, 1981; Linn & Slinde, 1977; Peter, Churchill & Brown, 1993; Wall & Payne, 1973). These include (a) decreasing reliability of the difference scores as the correlation between the base scores increases (i.e., most of the variance will be due to error); (b) variance restriction (i.e., when one component score is consistently higher than the other), and (c) spurious relationships between discrepancy scores and variables because discrepancy scores are not unique from their component parts. Further, Peter et al. (1993) have noted, "The difference between two variables provides no additional information for predicting or explaining a criterion beyond that held in the components themselves" (p. 660). That is, operationally the discrepancy score will be strongly related to at least one of its parts and will, therefore, lack discriminant validity (Johns, 1981; Peter et al., 1993; Wall & Payne, 1973).

A possible solution would be to have athletes directly report their own estimates of the discrepancies that exist between what they prefer and what they perceive to be receiving (Johns, 1981). This would require that a questionnaire be developed that would reliably and validly operationalize such a construct, certainly, a labor-intensive approach. However, Rice, McFarlin, and Bennett (1989) suggested that such an operationalization would result in an artificial comparison process that athletes might not ordinarily make. These problems and solutions were also noted in the context of leadership in sports (Chelladurai, 1990, 1993a).

Perhaps the most reasonable solution involves the use of a statistical technique. Given that Cronbach (1958) demonstrated how the interaction of two component parts is equivalent to the difference, the use of regression analysis may be used to test the congruence hypothesis (Berger-Gross, 1982; Berger-Gross & Kraut, 1984; Cronbach, 1958; Johns, 1981; Rice et al., 1989). The preferred and perceived scores (main terms) would be entered first, followed by the interaction term (preferred x perceived). If the interaction significantly increases the variance explained by the main effects, then the congruence hypothesis would be accepted.[2] The exact nature of the interaction would then be interpreted by plotting the regression lines suggested by the interaction. That is, points would be plotted by entering hypothetical/actual values into the regression equation with the inter-

action term. The four points would be defined by low and high preference scores plotted against low and high perception scores (Cohen & Cohen, 1983; Rice et al., 1989).

Following the above logic, Riemer and Chelladurai (1995) have applied the interaction approach to study the effects of congruence between preferred and perceived leadership on satisfaction. They found that the congruence hypothesis was supported only with respect to social support behavior and that the perceptions of training and instruction and positive-feedback behaviors were better predictors of satisfaction with leadership than their congruence with player preferences in those dimensions. The use of regression analysis would also then be appropriate to test the overall congruence hypothesis (congruence of the three states of leader behavior) proposed by the multidimensional model of leadership. This would entail an examination of three two-way interactions and one three-way interaction instead of a single two-way interaction examined by Riemer and Chelladurai (1995). Certainly, this approach is more appropriate to evaluating the congruence hypothesis (which is central to the MML). An implication of the foregoing discussion is any results of research using discrepancy scores are not tenable.

Context of leader behavior. Chelladurai (1993a) pointed out one other issue concerning the LSS. The response categories for the items refer to the frequencies with which the coach engages in specific forms of behavior. Such an approach overlooks the context in which such behavior is exhibited. For

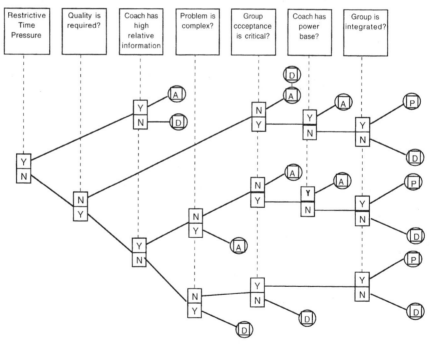

Figure 3. Normative Model of Decision Making (Chelladurai & Haggerty, 1978)
Key: A = Autocratic Style   D = Delegative Style   P = Participative Style
Note: From "A Normative Model of Decision Styles in Coaching" by P. Chelladuarai and T.R. Haggerty, 1978, *Athletic Administrator, 13,* p. 8. Copyright © 1977 by National Association of Collegiate Directors of Athletics. Reprinted with permission.

---

2 Berger-Gross (1982) and Berger-Gross & Kraut (1984) have demonstrated how this procedure overcomes the problems associated with difference scores. It is important to note that the critical issue is not how much variance is explained by the interaction, but whether it is statistically significant (McFarlin & Rice, 1991).

Table 9
Problem Attributes of the Normative Model of Decision Styles (Chelladurai & Haggerty, 1978)

Attribute	Description
Time pressure	This refers to the availability of time for participative decision making. That is, lack of time would preclude member participation.
Quality requirement	In some cases (e.g., selection of a play making guard in basketball), the coach has to ensure that an optimal decision is made. In some other cases (e.g., selection of a team manager), the coach may be satisfied with one of several acceptable candidates.
Coach's information	The selection of a particular style of decision making may also be affected by the information and knowledge possessed by the coach relative to the player's information and knowledge. This information may be related to the game, the players, and/or the problem situation.
Problem complexity	Some problems require the decision maker(s) to keep a number of factors in perspective and to think through a series of interlocking steps and procedures that link all the relevant factors (e.g., designing offensive and defensive strategies). According to the model, the coach or the individual with the best information is likely to solve complex problems better than the whole group.
Acceptance requirement	In some decision situations (e.g., to play full court press in basketball), the acceptance of the decision as practical and useful is critical for its effective implementation. In other cases (e.g., practicing foul shots), the acceptance may not be so critical because the execution can easily be monitored and controlled. Accordingly, the greater the need for acceptance, the greater the need for participation.
Coach's power	If the coach has the power to influence the members, then members are likely to accept his or her decisions. Therefore, the need for participation by members is lessened. Coach's power may stem from the control over rewards and punishments, the hierarchical authority, members' love and admiration for the coach, and/or coach's expertise and past performance.
Team integration	The quality of interpersonal relations among the group members (marked by warmth, concern, and respect for each other), and the relative homogeneity of the team in their orientations, tenure and ability would point to more participation by members. If these conditions are negative (i.e., presence of internal dissension and cliques), a participative style will only lead to inferior decisions and disrupt the already fragile solidarity of the team.

Note: From "A Normative Model of Decision Styles in Coaching" by P. Chelladuarai and T.R. Haggerty, 1978, *Athletic Administrator, 13*, p. 7-8. Copyright © 1977 by National Association of Collegiate Directors of Athletics. Modified with permission.

instance, the extent to which two coaches may be democratic may be the same, but they may be democratic in different sets of circumstances. It has been shown that the effectiveness of allowing members to participate in decision making may be dependent on the characteristics of the problem situation (Vroom & Jago, 1988; Vroom & Yetton, 1973). Researchers must realize that the LSS subscale of democratic behavior does not capture differences in problem situations, and they must also alert the readers to this significant issue.

Normative Model of Decision Styles in Coaching

Theoretical Overview

Using the works of Vroom and Jago (1974) and Vroom and Yetton (1973) as a foundation, Chelladurai and Haggerty (1978) proposed the normative model of decision styles in coaching (Figure 3). It assumes that the content and context of the problem are the key determinants of the extent to which a coach should allow his or her athletes to participate in decision making; that is, the nature of the problem and/or the situation must be taken into account.

The model included three types of decision-making styles based upon the criterion of who makes the decisions. The autocratic decision style refers to that style in which the coach makes the final decision. Originally conceived as including the consultative style in which the coach consults with team members prior to reaching the decision, Chelladurai and Arnott (1985) later treat the consultative style as separate and distinct. The participative decision style occurs when the "actual decision is made by the group, including the coach" (Chelladurai & Haggerty, 1978, p. 7). Finally, the delegative decision style is the one in which the leader allows other members of the organization to render the decision; the leader is not involved except perhaps to announce the decision.

According to the model, the appropriateness of a particular decision style to solve a problem is a function of its attributes. These include time pressure, quality requirement, coach's information, problem complexity, acceptance requirement, coach's power, and team integration (Table 9).

The model is presented in the form of a flow chart and/or decision tree (refer to Figure 3) where the decision maker begins on the left side and proceeds to the right based upon the "yes" or "no" response to questions posed at the top of the chart. At each end point, a decision style is specified as the most appropriate.

Primary Measurement Instrument

The primary instrument to test the normative model of decision styles has been the list of cases generated to outline the status of the problem attributes. A case (i.e., a short description of a

Table 10
Sample Case

Toward the end of the try-outs, a university coach is concerned about making the final cut. The available players are all newcomers, but the coach has seen them all in action during the previous year at their former high schools. The atmosphere during the try-outs has been very good and the players get along well with each other. The coach is faced with selecting the final team

	High	Low
Quality Requirement	✓	
Coach's Information	✓	
Problem Complexity	✓	
Acceptance Requirement		✓
Team Integration	✓	

Under the above circumstances, what decision style would you use in selecting the final team? (CHECK ONE RESPONSE ONLY)
❑ Autocratic I -   You solve the problem yourself using the information available at the time.
❑ Autocratic II -   You obtain the necessary information from relevant players, then decide yourself
❑ Consultive I -   You consult with your players individually, and then make the decision yourself.
❑ Consultive II -   You consult with your players as a group, then make the decision yourself.
❑ Group -   You and the players jointly make the decision.

hypothetical situation) is written in terms of the presence or absence (or high or low levels of) selected problem attributes. Such a case is developed for every possible configuration of two levels of the problem attributes included in the study. Following Hill and Schmitt (1977), a chart indicating the presence or absence (i.e., high or low levels) of each of the attributes included in the study follows the case description (e.g., Chelladurai & Arnott, 1985; Chelladurai, Haggerty, & Baxter, 1989; Chelladurai & Quek, 1995). After reading each case, the subjects are asked to select the most appropriate of the decision styles listed under each case. A sample case from Chelladurai et al. (1989) is shown in Table 10. If all seven attributes were to be employed with two levels in each, it would be necessary to generate 128 cases (2^7). Because reading and responding to 128 cases would be tedious to subjects, some of the following studies have restricted the number of attributes to four (i.e., 16 cases) or five (i.e., 32 cases). This general methodological approach has been used to measure (a) what coaches say they would do, (b) what players would prefer coaches to do, (c) what players perceive their coach would do, and (d) what players would do themselves.

One of two approaches has generally been used in analyzing the data. First, nonparametric analyses are used where the decision styles were the categories. The distribution of the frequencies of choices across the categories is compared with either the expected equal frequencies or the distribution in a comparable group. Although treating the various decisions styles as four or five levels of a categorical variable is straightforward and simple, it also restricts the analyses to nonparametric procedures. If one is interested in more sophisticated and robust analyses, it would be necessary to convert the decision-style choices as differing scores on a continuous variable. Following Vroom and Yetton (1973), Chelladurai and Arnott (1985), Chel-

ladurai et al. (1989), and Chelladurai and Quek (1995) employed this approach in their studies of the effects of situation and individual differences on decision-style choices as well as the main and interaction effects of the problem attributes. Because varying number and type of decision styles were used in these studies, researchers have used different metrics for the various decision styles. In assigning scale values to the attributes, two approaches have been undertaken. First, Chelladurai and Arnott (1985) asked a group of experts to place the four decision styles in their study (autocratic, consultative, group, and delegative) on a 10-point continuum in which autocratic style was placed at one end (1) and delegative style was placed on the other (10). The means of the scores assigned by these experts for the other two decision styles were used as continuous scores for the purposes of parametric analyses (Consultative style = 3.1; participative (group) style = 7.2). Chelladurai et al. (1989) and Chelladurai and Quek (1995) used the five decision styles proposed by Vroom and Yetton (1973) and, therefore, used the same scores as employed by Vroom and Yetton. These values were 0 for autocratic I; 0.625 for autocratic II; 5.00 for consultative I; 8.125 for consultative II; and 10 for group decisions.

Reliability

Test-retest reliability of the instrument has been addressed only by Chelladurai and Quek (1995). Twenty coaches responded to the decision-style cases a second time after a period of 8 weeks. Twenty-one of the 32 test-retest correlations involving individual cases were significant ($p<.05$). The correlations ranged from .39 to .82 (mean = .55). Nine of the nonsignificant correlations ranged from .20 to .37 (mean = .30), whereas the other two cases had very low values ($r=.05$ and .03). Some of these values are low and disturbing. That is, in at least 11 cases, coaches did not respond in a statistically signifi-cant similar manner after a span of 8 weeks. Moreover, the mean value of the 21 statistically significant correlations is also quite low; usually a value of at least .60 is desirable. Chelladu-rai and Quek (1995) also reported that the test-retest correlation of the total participation score (i.e., the mean of decision-style scores across all 32 cases) was .83. However, given the individ-ual case values, it is probable that this value is meaningless.

Estimating the internal consistency among the 32 cases is somewhat problematic because each case contained one of two levels of the five problem attributes. As each attribute is pur-ported to be independent of the other four attributes, attempting to derive one composite estimate would be inappropriate. How-ever, it is possible to assess the internal consistency related to each of the five attributes in the 32 cases. This was the approach taken by Chelladurai and Quek (1995), who divided the 32 cases into two subsets of 16 cases based on whether a given case was rated high or low on the particular attribute. This process yielded 10 subsets of cases (one subset for each of two levels of the five attributes). Internal consistency was then esti-mated by computing Cronbach's alpha and Spearman-Brown's equal length split-half reliability coefficient for each subset of cases. Cronbach's alpha across the 10 subsets ranged from .69 to .83 (mean = .77), and Spearman-Brown coefficients ranged from .68 to .88 (mean = .79).

Validity

Content/Face. Generally, the assessment of validity of the instrument has only involved a panel of experts. They were usu-ally asked to examine whether a given case description was clear and concise in correctly describing the level of the attrib-utes said to be associated with it (e.g., Chelladurai & Arnott, 1985; Chelladurai et al., 1989; Gordon, 1988). There has cer-tainly not been any concerted effort to evaluate the validity of the methodology beyond basic content validity.

Criterion. One method for establishing criterion validity of a particular instrument is the extent to which results from the various investigations have been consistent with theory and past research. Only four empirical investigations have em-ployed the model to verify the extent to which the respective subjects preferred or perceived participation in decision making (Chelladurai & Arnott, 1985; Chelladurai et al., 1989; Chel-ladurai & Quek, 1995; Gordon, 1988).

Chelladurai and Arnott (1985) assessed the decision-style preferences of Canadian male and female university basketball players in a given problem situation. They found that the del-egative style was almost totally rejected by their subjects. In ad-dition, players preferred group decision making in less than 50% of the times (46.9% for females and 34.1% for males). The percentage is calculated by dividing the number of times a par-ticular decision style was chosen by the total number of choices possible in a study (i.e., number of cases x number of subjects).

Gordon (1988) investigated the decision-style preferences of Canadian university soccer players (all males) for specific decision styles and their perceptions of what their coach's choices would be. In addition, Gordon also assessed coaches' choices of decision styles, and their perceptions of the choices of other coaches in their league. His results showed that the del-egative style was rejected by both players and coaches. The most interesting finding was that group decision style was iden-tified as viable in less than 20% of the times by both groups (in preferences as well as perceptions). Although the frequency of players' preferences for the autocratic style was 31.2%, their perceptions of their coaches' choices was 43%. Coaches them-selves said they would choose the autocratic style in 46.3% of the times and perceived that the other coaches would choose that style in 45.5% of the times.

Because the delegative style was rejected in the earlier studies, subsequent studies (Chelladurai et al., 1989; Chelladu-rai & Quek, 1995) employed the five decision styles proposed by Vroom and Yetton (1973) and shown in Table 11. Also, these two studies included five of the seven problem attributes pro-posed by Chelladurai and Haggerty (1978): quality require-ment, coach's information, problem complexity, acceptance re-quirement, and team integration. Chelladurai and colleagues' (1988) study of university basketball players (male and female) and coaches found that group decision making was chosen by all groups in less than 20% of the times. The most preferred style by all groups was Autocratic I followed by Consultative II and Autocratic II in that order. Interestingly, Consultative I in which the coach consults with a few selected players was the least chosen (less than 15%).

Chelladurai and Quek's (1995) study of high school bas-ketball coaches' choices of decision styles showed that the choices varied from 32.5% for Autocratic I, 15.4% for Auto-cratic II, 9.7% for Consultative I, 1.3% for Consultative II, and

---

Table 11
Decision Styles in Coaching

Autocratic I (AI)	The coach solves the problem him or herself, using the information available to him or her at the time
Autocratic II (AII)	The coach obtains the necessary information from relevant players, then decides him or herself. The coach may or may not tell the players what the problem is in getting the information. The role played by the players is clearly one of providing information to the coach, rather than generating or evaluating solutions
Consultative I (CI)	The coach consults with the players individually and then makes the decision him or herself. The coach's decision may or may not reflect the players' influence
Consultative II (CII)	The coach consults with the players as a group and then makes the decision him or herself. The coach's decision may or may not reflect the players' influence
Group (G)	The coach shares the problem with his or her players. Then, the coach and the players jointly make the decision.

21.% for Group decisions. In recent reviews of the foregoing studies, Chelladurai (1993a; 1993b) suggested that, because the preferences for and perceptions of group participation by both athletes and coaches were much less than expected, it is better to view the athletic situation as calling for relatively more autocratic decision making than considering the coaches themselves to be autocratic. When a famous football coach was questioned on his autocratic manner of coaching, he is reported to have said, "Hey, I was asked to run a football program, not a democracy" (Schwartz, 1973). The results of the above studies seem to substantiate his view.

The three studies employing the parametric analyses discussed earlier (i.e., Chelladurai & Arnott, 1985; Chelladurai et al., 1989; Chelladurai & Quek, 1995) reported that situational differences (i.e., the problem attributes) accounted for more variance (ranging from 24.1% to 52.3%) in decision-style choices than did individual differences (ranging from 6.6% to 22.4%). In general, the subjects preferred a relatively more autocratic style of decision making when the coach's information was high, and a more participative style when group acceptance was critical. An interesting finding in the three studies was that subjects preferred a more autocratic style when quality requirement and problem complexity were both high or were both low. That is, players preferred less participation in more serious as well as trivial decisions.

In general, the results from the four studies parallel each other and seem to be consistent with theory. For instance, the relative frequencies of choices of the various decision styles are similar across the four studies. In addition, the studies of Chelladurai and his associates show that, consistent with theory (Vroom & Yetton, 1973), the influence of the problem attributes is greater than the influence of individual differences. Further, the choice of a particular decision style was found to be related to the status of specific problem attributes. For instance, when coaches were deemed to have the information, subjects preferred a more autocratic style. Similarly, when group acceptance was critical more participative decisions were favored. When both quality requirement and problem complexity were high, athletes preferred the coach to make the decision. Insofar as these results are consistent with theory and past research, a certain degree of validity can be claimed for the instrument.

Other validity issues. It must be noted that the normative model of decision styles was based more on heuristics than on empirical findings. In this regard, subsequent studies have shown that the subjects rejected the delegative style although it was included as a viable option in the model. It was explained that delegating decision making to selected individuals in a team might be antithetical to the egalitarianism associated with team sports, and therefore, it could have been rejected by the subjects. In a subsequent review, Chelladurai (1993) noted that the notion of egalitarianism may not be relevant in sports where some players are placed in a superior position when compared to others (e.g., the quarterback in North American football). Moreover, an informal and socially derived pecking order may also exist that would permit the delegation of decision making to those at the top of the formal/informal hierarchy. Further, the delegative style may be eminently suitable in individual sports because (a) there is minimal coordination required among

members, (b) every member's task is independent of the tasks of other members, and (c) the issue of egalitarianism does not arise over task-related decisions.

Moreover, the individual cases were developed by the researchers. Although these cases were checked by experts for content validity, the generation of the cases was confined to a few individuals. These two issues indicate that both the model and the cases associated with it can be improved by employing focus groups, a panel of experts, in-depth interviews of coaches and athletes, and open-ended surveys to identify the significant attributes of problems in coaching and the varying forms of participation by athletes. Such focus groups and experts can also generate specific instances where involving athletes in decision making has been beneficial or detrimental. Such instances could be the substance from which cases can be formulated. These steps would address two important validity-related concerns, namely whether the model and its operationalization have really tapped all the relevant cues/attributes that impinge on the appropriateness of a decision style in a particular coaching situation, and whether the cases used reflect real-life problem situations in coaching (Chelladurai, 1993b).

Another concern relates to how coaches perceive a particular decision situation. That is, coaches may assess the presence or absence of the problem attributes differently than what is purported to be in a case (i.e., the researchers' perceptions). This is an important issue because the whole theory is based on the leader's assessment of the situation and the various attributes impinging on that situation. Two individuals (e.g., a coach and a researcher) may agree that given a certain configuration of the attributes, a specific decision style would be most appropriate and effective. However, the two individuals may perceive the attributes in a given situation differently. For instance, the coach may perceive his or her team to be quite integrated whereas an external observer may see the team to be split into conflicting cliques. These differential perceptions of the situation would elicit different decision styles, each consistent with the respective perception of the situation, and likely to undermine the validity of the instrument employed (i.e., the set of cases).

The foregoing issue of varying perceptions is analogous to the problem suggested by Smith et al. (1978) with reference to their mediational model. They suggested that coaches may have their own goals and that they may perceive some forms of their behavior to be more instrumental than other behaviors in achieving their goals. Smith et al. went on to suggest that it is important to assess the instrumentalities held by coaches for various forms of behaviors (importance of a goal x instrumentality of a behavior in achieving that goal). In a similar manner, Chelladurai (1993) also suggested that respondents may be asked to evaluate the cases presented to them in terms of specified attributes and relate these evaluations to the decision styles chosen by the respondents. Such an approach would permit evaluation of the extent to which coaches perceive a situation similarly, and whether their decision-style choices match theoretical expectations (given their own unique perceptions).

Summary

In the final analysis, the normative model of decision styles and the instrument have not been examined sufficiently to make any definitive judgments concerning their validity within the sport context. More work needs to be carried out to develop the measurement instrument and establish its psychometric properties. Research results from the management field may provide some insights regarding future directions. More specifically, Vroom and Jago (1988) summarize several shortcomings of their model.

The original model (i.e., Vroom & Yetton, 1973) presented only two levels (presence or absence/yes or no) of each of the problem attributes. Although Chelladurai and associates changed the wording to high and low, this change still represents only two levels of an attribute. This overlooks the varying degrees of a problem attribute across situations. In Vroom and Jago's (1988) newer version of the model, the respondents are expected to evaluate the attributes on a 5-point scale instead of two levels. Such an approach may be undertaken in sport-related research to allow for the description of a problem attribute on a 5-point continuum, and to tap into subjects' perceptions of the relative levels of the attributes in a situation.

Further, Vroom and Jago (1988) noted that the original seven attributes of a situation did not constitute an exhaustive list, and have proposed a newer list of 12 problem attributes. The questions defining the four attributes of *quality requirement, commitment requirement, motivation to minimize decision time, motivation to develop subordinates,* require estimates of the importance of the attribute (on a scale of 1 to 5 rather than yes-no responses). The questions defining the six attributes of *leader information, problem structure, goal congruence, subordinate conflict, subordinate information,* and *commitment probability* require probability estimates. Finally, the defining questions for *time constraints* and *geographical dispersion* permit the traditional dichotomous yes-no response.

Several of the attributes are equivalent to those in the original model except some of the names have been changed (e.g., commitment rather than acceptance). The notable addition is "motivation for subordinate development," which may indeed be a major goal of athletic endeavor (Chelladurai, Inglis, & Danylchuk, 1984). Thus, future revisions of the normative model of decision styles should consider including the opportunity for member development as a significant attribute of the problem situation. It is worth noting that the athletes in the studies conducted by Chelladurai and his associates did not prefer participation in trivial decisions. Perhaps they did not see any opportunity for their growth in such situations.

In summary, although the issue of autocratic style of decision making by coaches have been the subject of intense public debate, there has not been any systematic effort to study the issue in greater detail. Recent advances in organizational literature have focused on the situational imperatives of decision styles. Although the normative model and the studies associated with it represent a useful start, there is considerable room for improvement.

Conclusion

In conclusion, we have described and critiqued three different approaches to the measurement of leadership in sports: the mediational model of leadership, the multidimensional model of leadership, and the normative model of decision styles

in coaching. Although each of these approaches advances knowledge related to leadership in sports, it must be noted that each is unique to the extent that its application has been restricted to one set of participants or one aspect of leadership. That is, the research efforts of Smith, Smoll, and their associates (e.g., Smith and Smoll, 1990; Smith, Smoll, & Curtis, 1978; Smoll et al., 1993) have been restricted to the domain of youth sport whereas research on Chelladurai's multidimensional model (e.g., Chelladurai, 1984; Chelladurai et al., 1988; Dwyer & Fischer, 1988b; Gordon, 1986; Horn & Carron, 1985; Riemer & Chelladurai, 1995; Schliesman, 1987) has largely focused on adult and/or high-level sport. The normative model of decision styles is restricted to one aspect of leadership: the social processes of decision making. Despite the restrictive nature of past research, each approach has relevance to all levels of organized sport. It is conceivable that future efforts may attempt to incorporate the three approaches into a more comprehensive framework. Most critically, research should be undertaken to enhance the reliability and validity of the measures used to operationalize variables involved in each of the three approaches.

References

Bacharach, S.B. (1989). Organizational theories: Some criteria for evaluation. *Academy of Management Review, 14,* 496-515.

Bales, R.F., & Slater, P. (1955). Role differentiation in small decision-making groups. In P. Parsons and R.F. Bales (Eds.), *Family, socialization, and interaction process* (pp. 259-306). Glencoe, IL: Free Press.

Barnett, N.P., Smoll, F.L., & Smith, R.E. (1992). Effects of enhancing coach-athlete relationships on youth sport attrition. *The Sport Psychologist, 6,* 111-127.

Baron, R.M., & Kenny, D.A. (1986). The moderator-mediator variable distinction in social psychological research: Conceptual, strategic, and statistical considerations. *Journal of Personality and Social Psychology, 51,* 1173-1182.

Barrow, J.C. (1977). The variables of leadership: A review and coneptual framework. *Academy of Management Review, 2,* 231-251.

Bass, B.M. (1985). *Leadership and performance beyond expectations.* New York: Free Press.

Bentler, P.M. (1980). Multivariate analysis with latent variables: Causal modeling. *Annual Review of Psychology, 31,* 419-456.

Berger-Gross, V. (1982). Difference score measures of social perceptions revisited: A comparison of alternatives. *Organizational Behavior and Human Performance, 29,* 279-285.

Berger-Gross, V., & Kraut, A.I. (1984). "Great expectations": A no-conflict explanation of role conflict. *Journal of Applied Psychology, 69,* 261-271.

Bollen, K.A. (1989). *Structural equations with latent variables.* New York: Wiley.

Browne, M.W., & DuToit, S.H.C. (1991). Models for learning data. In L.M. Collins & J.L. Horn (Eds.), *Best methods for the analysis of change* (pp.47-68). Washington, DC: APA.

Chaumeton, N.R., & Duda, J.L. (1988). Is it how you play the game or whether you win or lose?: The effect of competitive level and situation on coaching behaviors. *Journal of Sport Behavior, 11: 3,* 157-174.

Chelladurai, P. (1978). *A contingency model of leadership in athletics.* Unpublished doctoral dissertation, Department of Management Sciences, University of Waterloo, Canada.

Chelladurai, P. (1981). The coach as motivator and chameleon of leadership styles. *Science periodical on research and technology in sport.* Ottawa, Canada: Coaching Association of Canada.

Chelladurai, P. (1984). Discrepancy between preferences and perceptions of leadership behavior and satisfaction of athletes in varying sports. *Journal of Sport Psychology, 6* (1), 27-41.

Chelladurai, P. (1986). Applicability of the Leadership Scale for Sports to the Indian context. *Proceedings of the VIII Commonwealth and International Conference on Sport, Physical Education, Dance, Recreation and Health,* Sports Science Section (pp. 291-296). Glasgow, Scotland: Management Committee.

Chelladurai, P. (1990). Leadership in sports: A review. *International Journal of Sport Psychology., 21,* 328-354.

Chelladurai, P. (1993a). Leadership. In R.N. Singer, M. Murphy, & L.K. Tennant (Eds.), *Handbook on research on sport psychology* (pp. 647-671). New York: McMillian.

Chelladurai, P. (1993b). Styles of decision making in coaching. In J.M. Williams (Ed.), *Applied sport psychology: Personal growth to peak performance* (2nd ed., pp. 99-109). Palo Alto, CA: Mayfield Publishing Company.

Chelladurai, P., & Arnott, M. (1985). Decision styles in coaching: Preferences of basketball players. *Research Quarterly for Exercise and Sport, 56* (1), 15-24.

Chelladurai, P., & Carron, A.V. (1978). *Leadership.* Ottawa: Canadian Association for Health, Physical Education and Recreation (Sociology of Sport Monograph Series).

Chelladurai, P., & Carron, A.V. (1981a). Applicability to youth sports of the leadership scale for sports. *Perceptual and Motor Skills, 53,* 361-362.

Chelladurai, P., & Carron, A.V. (1981b). Task characteristics and individual differences, and their relationship to preferred leadership in sports. *Psychology of Motor Behavior and Sport-1982* (p. 87). College Park, MD: North American Society for the Psychology of Sport and Physical Activity.

Chelladurai, P., & Carron, A.V. (1983). Athletic maturity and preferred leadership. *Journal of Sport Psychology, 5,* 371-380.

Chelladurai, P., & Haggerty, T.R. (1978). A normative model of decision styles in coaching. *Athletic Administrator, 13,* 6-9.

Chelladurai, P., Haggerty, T.R., & Baxter, P.R. (1989). Decision style choices of university basketball coaches and players. *Journal of Sport and Exercise Psychology, 11,* 201 215.

Chelladurai, P., Imamura, H., & Yamaguchi, Y. (1986). Sub-scale structure of the Leadership Scale for Sports in the Japanese context: A preliminary report. *Proceedings of the FISU/CESU Conference, Universiade '85* (pp. 372-377). Kobe, Japan: The International University Sports Federation (FISU).

Chelladurai, P., Imamura, H., Yamaguchi, Y., Oinuma, Y., Miyauchi, T. (1988). Sport leadership in a cross-national setting: The case of Japanese and Canadian university athletes. *Journal of Sport and Exercise Psychology, 10,* 374-389.

Chelladurai, P., Inglis, S. & Danlychuk, K. (1984). Priorities in intercollegiate athletics: Development of a scale. *Research Quarterly, 55 (1),* 74-79.

Chelladurai, P., Malloy, D., Imamura, H., & Yamaguchi, Y. (1987). A cross-cultural study of preferred leadership in sports. *Canadian Journal of Sport Sciences, 12,* 106-110.

Chelladurai, P., & Quek, C.B. (1995). Decision style choices of high school basketball coaches: The effects of situational and coach characteristics. *Journal of Sport Behavior, 18* (2), 91-108.

Chelladurai, P., & Riemer, H.A. (1997). A classification of facets of athlete satisfaction. *Journal of Sport Management, 11,* 133-159.

Chelladurai, P., & Saleh, S.D. (1978). Preferred leadership in sports. *Canadian Journal of Applied Sport Sciences, 3,* 85-92.

Chelladurai, P., & Saleh, S.D. (1980). Dimensions of leader behavior in sports: Development of a leadership scale. *Journal of Sport Psychology, 2,* 34-45.

Cohen, J. (1960). Coefficient of agreement for nominal scales. *Educational and Psychological Measures, 20,* 37-46.

Cohen, J. & Cohen, P. (1983). *Applied multiple regression/correlation analysis for the behavioral sciences* (2nd edition). Hillsdale, NJ: Erlbaum.

Conger, J.A., & Kanungo, R.N. (1988). *Charismatic leadership: The elusive factor in organizational research.* San Francisco, CA: Jossey-Bass.

Courneya, K.S., & Chelladurai, P. (1991). A model of performance measures in baseball. *Journal of Sport and Exercise Psychology, 13,* 16-25.

Cronbach, L. (1958). Proposals leading to analytic treatment of social perception scores. In R. Tagiuri & L. Petrullo (Eds.), *Person perception and interpersonal behavior* (pp. 353-359). Stanford: Stanford University Press.

Dwyer, J.M., & Fischer, D.G. (1988a). Psychometric properties of the coach's version of Leadership Scale for Sports. *Perceptual and Motor Skills, 67,* 795-798.

Dwyer, J.M., & Fischer, D.G. (1988b). Leadership style of wrestling coaches. *Perceptual and Motor Skills, 67,* 706.

Erle, F.J. (1981). *Leadership in competitive and recreational sport.* Unpublished master's thesis. University of Western Ontario. London, Canada.

Evans, M.G. (1970). Leadership and motivation: A core concept. *Academy of Management Journal, 13,* 91-102.

Ewing, M.E., & Seefeldt, V. (1989). *Participation and attrition patterns in American agency-sponsored and interscholastic sports: An executive summary* (Final Report). North Palm Beach, FL: Sporting Goods Manufacturer's Association.

Ferguson, G.A. (1976). *Statistical analysis in psychology and education.* New York: McGraw-Hill.

Fiedler, F.E. (1967). *A theory of leadership effectiveness.* New York: McGraw-Hill.

Fleishman, E.A. (1957a). A leader behavior description for industry. In R.M. Stogdill & A.E. Coons (Eds.), *Leader behavior: Its description and measurement* (pp. 103-119). Columbus, OH: The Ohio State University.

Fleishman, E.A (1957b). The leadership opinion questionnaire. In R.M. Stogdill & A.E. Coons (Eds.), *Leader behavior: Its description and measurement* (pp. 120-133). Columbus, OH: The Ohio State University

Gardner, R.C., & Neufeld, W.J. (1987). Use of the simple change score in correlational analysis. *Educational and Psychological Measurement, 47,* 849-864.

Garland, D.J., & Barry, J.R. (1988). The effects of personality and perceived leader behavior on performance in collegiate football. *The Psychological Record, 38,* 237-247.

George, T. (1993, September 8). Victory to Redskins, but credit to Petitbon. *The New York Times,* p. B18.

Gordon, S. (1986). *Behavioral correlates of coaching effectiveness.* Unpublished doctoral dissertation. University of Alberta, Canada.

Gordon, S. (1988). Decision styles and coaching effectiveness in university soccer. *Canadian Journal of Sport Sciences, 13* (1), 56-65.

Graen, G., & Cashman, J.F. (1975). A role-making model of leadership in formal organizations: A developmental approach. In J.G. Hunt & L.L. Larson (Eds.), *Leadership Frontiers* (pp. 181-185). Kent, OH: Kent State University.

Granito, V.J., & Carlton, E.B. (1993). Relationship between locus of control and satisfaction with intercollegiate volleyball teams at different levels of competition. *Journal of Sport Behavior, 16*:4, 221-228.

Hair, J.F., Anderson, R.E., Tatham, R.L., & Black, W.C. (1992). *Multivariate data analysis.* New York: Macmillian.

Halpin, A.W., & Winer, B.J. (1957). A factorial study of the leader behavior description. In R.M. Stogdill & A.E. Coons (Eds.), *Leader behavior: Its description and measurement* (pp. 39-51). Columbus: The Ohio State University.

Hill, T., & Schmitt, N. (1977). Individual difference in leadership decision-making. *Organizational Behavior and Human Performance, 19,* 353-362.

Horn, T.S. (1984). Expectancy effects in the interscholastic athletic setting: Methodological considerations. *Journal of Sport Psychology, 6,* 60-76

Horne, T., & Carron, A.V. (1985). Compatibility in coach-athlete relationships. *Journal of Sport Psychology, 7,* 137-149.

House, R.J. (1971). A path-goal theory of leader effectiveness. *Administrative Science Quarterly, 16,* 321-338.

House, R.J., & Dressler, G. (1974). A path-goal theory of leadership. In J.G. Hunt & L.L. Larson (Eds.), *Contingency approaches to leadership* (pp. 29-55). Carbondale, IL: Southern Illinois University Press.

Iordanoglou, D. (1990). *Perceived leadership in Greek soccer: A preliminary investigation.* Unpublished manuscript. University of Manchester, Department of Education.

Isberg, L., & Chelladurai, P. (1990). *The Leadership Scale for Sports: Its applicability to the Swedish context.* Unpublished manuscript, University College of Falun/Borlènge, Sweden.

Johns, G. (1981). Difference score measures of organizational behavior variables: A critique. *Organizational Behavior and Human Performance, 27,* 443-463.

Keehner, S.L. (1988). *A study of perceived leadership behavior and program adherence.* Unpublished doctoral dissertation, University of Maryland.

Kim, B-H., Lee, H-K., & Lee, J-Y. (1990). *A study on the coaches' leadership behavior in sports.* Unpublished manuscript, Korea Sport Science Institute, Seoul.

Komaki, J.L. (1986). Toward effective supervision: An operant analysis and comparison of managers at work. *Journal of Applied Psychology, 71,* 270-279.

Komaki, J.L., Zlotnick, S., & Jensen, M. (1986). Development of an operant based taxonomy and observational index of supervisory behavior. *Journal of Applied Psychology, 71,* 260-269.

Krane, V., Ecklund, R., & McDermott, M. (1991). Collaborative action research and behavioral coaching intervention: A case study. In W.K. Simpson, A. LeUnes, & J.S. Picou (Eds.), *The applied research in coaching and athletics annual 1991* (pp. 119-147). Boston, MA: American Press.

Lacoste, P.L., & Laurencelle, L. (1989). *The French validation of the Leadership Scale for Sports.* Unpublished abstract, Université du Québec à Trois-Rivières, Trois-Rivières,Canada.

Linn, R.L., & Slinde, J.A. (1977). The determination of the significance of change between pre- and posttesting periods. *Review of Educational Research, 47:1,* 121-150.

Liukkonen, J., & Salminen, S. (1989, Februrary). *Three coach-athlete relationship scales in relation to coaching climate.* Paper presented at the VIth International Congress on Sport Psychology, Lahti, Finland.

Liukkonen, J., & Salminen, S. (1990, June). *The athletes' perception of leader behavior of Finnish coaches.* Paper presented at the World Congress on Sport for All, Tampere, Finland.

McFarlin, D.B., & Rice, R.W. (1991). Determinants of satisfaction with specific job facets: A test of Locke's model. *Journal of Business and Psychology, 6,* 25-38.

McMillin, C.J. (1990). *The relationship of athlete self-perceptions and athlete perceptions of leader behaviors to athlete satisfaction.* Unpublished doctoral dissertation, University of Virginia.

Miller, M.L., & Thayer, J.F. (1988). On the nature of self-monitoring: Relationship with adjustment and identity. *Personality and Social Psychology Bulletin, 14,* 544-553.

Nesselroade, J.R. (1994). Exploratory factor analysis with latent variables and the study of processes of development and change. In A. von Eye & C. Clogg (Eds.), *Latent variables analysis* (pp. 131-154).

Thousand Oaks, CA: Sage.

Nunnally, J.C., & Bernstein, I.H. (1994). *Psychometric theory* (3rd ed.). New York: McGraw-Hill Book Company.

Osborn, R.N., & Hunt, J.G. (1975). An adaptive-reactive theory of leadership: The role of macro variables in leadership research. In J.G. Hunt & L.L. Larson (Eds.), *Leadership frontiers* (pp. 27-44). Kent,OH: Kent State University.

Parsons, T., & Bales, R.F. (1955). *Family, socialization and interaction process.* Glencoe, Il: The Free Press.

Patton, M.Q. (1990). *Qualitative Evaluation and Research Methods* (2nd ed.). Newbury Park, CA: Sage.

Peter, J.P., Churchill, Jr., G.A., & Brown, T.J. (1993). Caution in the use of difference scores in consumer research. *Journal of Consumer Research, 19,* 655-662.

Porter, L.W., & Lawler, E.E. (1968). *Managerial attitudes and performance.* Homewood, IL: Richard D. Irwin, Inc.

Rejeski, W., Darracott, C., & Hutslar, S. (1979). Pygmalion in youth sport: A field study. *Journal of Sport Psychology, 1,* 311-319.

Rice, R.W., McFarlin, D.E., & Bennett, D.E. (1989). Standards of comparison and job satisfaction. *Journal of Applied Psychology, 74,* 591-598.

Riemer, H.A., & Chelladurai, P. (1995). Leadership and satisfaction in athletics. *Journal of Sport and Exercise Psychology, 17,* 276-293.

Riemer, H. A., & Chelladurai, P. (1997). *Development of Athlete Satisfaction Questionnaire.* Manuscript submitted for publication.

Robinson, T.T., & Carron, A.V. (1982). Personal and situational factors associated with dropping out versus maintaining participation in competitive sport. *Journal of Sport Psychology, 4,* 364-378.

Salminen, S., Liukkonen, J., & Telama, R. (1990, July). *The differences in coaches' and athletes' perception of leader behavior of Finnish coaches.* Paper presented at the AIESEP Congress, Loughborough, England.

Schliesman, E.S. (1987). Relationship between the congruence of preferred and actual leader behavior and subordinate satisfaction with leadership. *Journal of Sport Behavior, 10* (3), 157-166.

Schliesman, E.S. Beitel, P.A. & DeSensi, J.T. (in press). Athlete and coach gender, leader behavior, and follower satisfaction in sport. *Journal of Sport and Social Issues.*

Schwartz, J.L. (1973). *Analysis of leadership styles of college level head football coaches from five Midwestern states.* Unpublished doctoral dissertation, University of Northern Colorado, Greeley, CO.

Serpa, S. (1990). *Research work on sport leadership in Portugal.* Unpublished manuscript. Lisbon Technical University.

Serpa, S., Pataco, V., & Santos, F. (1991). Leadership patterns in handball international competition. *International Journal of Sport Psychology, 22,* 78-89.

Sherman, M.A., & Hassan, J.S. (1986). Behavioral studies of youth sport coaches. In M. Pieron & G. Graham (Eds.), *The 1984 Olympic Scientific Congress proceedings: Vol. 6. Sport pedagogy* (pp. 103-108). Champaign, IL: Human Kinetics.

Smith, R.E., & Smoll, F.L. (1990). Self-esteem and children's reactions to youth sport coaching behaviors: A field study of self-enhancement processes. *Developmental Psychology, 26*(6), 987-993.

Smith, R.E., Smoll, F.L., & Curtis, B. (1978). Coaching behaviors in little league baseball. In F.L. Smoll & R.E. Smith (Eds.), *Psychological perspectives on youth sports* (pp. 173-201). Washington, DC: Hemisphere.

Smith, R.E., Smoll, F.L., & Curtis, B. (1979). Coach effectiveness training: A cognitive-behavioral approach to enhancing relationship skills in youth sport coaches. *Journal of Sport Psychology, 1,* 59-75.

Smith, R.E., Smoll, F.L., & Hunt, E.B. (1977a). A system for the behavioral assessment of athletic coaches. *Research Quarterly, 48,* 401-407.

Smith, R.E., Smoll, F.L., Hunt, E.B. (1977b). Training manual for the Coaching Behavior Assessment System. *Psychological Documents, 7.* (Ms. No. 1406)

Smith, R.E., Smoll, F.L., Hunt, E.B., Clarke, S.J. (1976). *CBAS audio visual training module* (Video). Seattle: University of Washington, 1976.

Smith, R.E., Zane, N.W.S., Smoll, F.L., Coppel, D.B. (1983). Behavioral assessment in youth sports: Coaching behaviors and children's attitudes. *Medicine and Science in Sport and Exercise, 15,* 208-214.

Smoll, F.L., & Smith, R.E. (1989). Leadership behaviors in sport: A theoretical model and research paradigm. *Journal of Applied Social Psychology, 19,* 1522-1551.

Smoll, F.L., Smith, R.E., Barnett, N.P., & Everett, J.J. (1993). Enhancement of children's self-esteem through social support training for youth sport coaches. *Journal of Applied Psychology, 78,* 602-610.

Smoll, F.L., Smith, R.E., Curtis, B., & Hunt, E. (1978). Toward a mediational model of coach-player relationships. *Research Quarterly, 49,* 528-541.

Speilberger, C.D. (1966). Theory and research on anxiety. In C.D. Speilberger (Ed.), *Anxiety and Behavior* (pp. 3-20). New York: Academic Press.

Steiger, J.H., & Lind, J.C. (1980, June). *Statisically based tests for the number of common factors.* Paper presented at the annual meeting of the Psychometric Society, Iowa City, IA.

Stogdill, R.M. (1963). *Manual for the Leader Behavior Description Questionnaire-Form XII.* Columbus, OH: The Ohio State University, Bureau of Business Research.

Summers, R.J. (1983). *A study of leadership in a sport setting.* Unpublished master's thesis. University of Waterloo, Canada.

Tabachnick, B.G. & Fidell, L.S. (1989) *Using multivariate statistics* (2nd ed.). Hillsdale, NJ: Erlbaum.

Terry, P.C. (1984). The coaching preferences of elite athletes competing at Universiade '83. *The Canadian Journal of Applied Sport Sciences, 9,* 201-208.

Terry, P.C., & Howe, B.L. (1984). The coaching preferences of athletes. *The Canadian Journal of Applied Sport Sciences, 9,* 188-193.

Toon, K. (1996). T*he relationship between the congruence of preferred and actual leadership behaviors and level of satisfaction among top ranked division I and division II ITA tennis teams.* Unpublished master's thesis. San Diego State University, CA.

Vroom, V.H., & Jago, A.G. (1974). On the validity of the Vroom-Yetton model. *Journal of Applied Psychology, 63,* 151-162.

Vroom, V.H., & Jago, A.G. (1988). *The new leadership: Managing participation in organizations.* Englewood Cliffs, NJ: Prentice Hall.

Vroom, V.H., & Yetton, R.N. (1973). *Leadership and decision-making.* Pittsburgh, PA: University of Pittsburgh Press.

Wall, T.D., & Payne, R. (1973). Are deficiency scores deficient? *Journal of Applied Psychology, 58,* 322-326.

Wandzilak, T., Ansorge, C.J., & Potter, G. (1988). Comparison between selected practice and game behaviors of youth sport soccer coaches. *Journal of Sport Behavior, 11:* 2, 79-88

Weiss, M.R., & Friedrichs, W.D. (1986). The influence of leader behaviors, coach attributes, and institutional variables on performance and satisfaction of collegiate basketball teams. *Journal of Sport Psychology, 8,* 332-346.

White, M.A. (1975). Natural rates of teacher approval and disapproval in the classroom. *Journal of Applied Behavior Analysis, 8,* 367-372.

White, M.C., Crino, M.D., & Hatfield, J.D. (1985). An empirical examination of the parsimony of perceptual congruence scores. *Academy of Management Journal, 28* (3), 732-737.

Yukl, G. (1971). Toward a behavioral theory of leadership. *Organizational Behavior and Human Performance, 6,* 414-440.

Yukl, G.A. (1981). *Leadership in organizations.* Englewood Cliffs, NJ: Prentice-Hall Inc.

Zeller, R.A., & Carmines, E.G. (1980). *Measurement in the social sciences.* New York: Cambridge University Press.

Part V

Aggression and Morality in Sport

PART V

Similar to concerns expressed about modern society, there is worry about the levels of violence exhibited in sport. Much work has been done on the causes and effects of aggressive behavior in the athletic context. However, according to Thirer (1993),

> aggression is one of the most frequently used, often misunderstood terms commonly selected to describe sport situations. On the one hand, it is used to describe performance in a positive, complimentary way, while on the other hand, it is utilized to demean or criticize sport participants and/or fans, or even the nature of sport itself. Seldom does one word have so many contradictory applications and definitions. (p. 365)

In Part V, the strengths and weaknesses of existent assessments of this misconstrued and misinterpreted construct are presented.

One more contemporary approach to the study of aggression has adopted a moral perspective (Shields & Bredemeier, 1995). Assessments and methodologies designed to measure moral functioning in the athletic context are also evaluated in this fifth section. Particular attention is given to assessments of moral content (such as values and attitudes toward sportspersonship), moral competencies and orientations, and moral behavior.

References

Shields, D., & Bredemeier, B. (1995). *Character development and physical activity*. Champaign, IL: Human Kinetics.

Thirer, J. (1993). Aggression. In R. N. Singer, M. Murphey, & L.K. Tennant (Eds.), *Handbook of research on sport psychology* (pp. 365-378). New York: Macmillan.

Chapter 14

MORAL ASSESSMENT IN SPORT PSYCHOLOGY

Brenda Jo Light Bredemeier
University of California, Berkeley
and
David Lyle Light Shields
John F. Kennedy University

In the past two decades, a body of theoretical and empirical literature has emerged on moral thought and action in sport and other physical activity contexts. Fortunately we have moved beyond the once common clash of cliches (for example, "sport builds character" vs. "sport builds characters") to a more careful analysis of the relations between sport experience and moral constructs. The study of morality in the context of sport is a field still in its infancy, however, and we have much to learn. To advance our theoretical and practical understanding, we must develop strong research programs, which in turn require valid and reliable methods and measures to assess moral constructs.

One critical issue that needs to be addressed in any field of inquiry is the parameters of the field itself. Unfortunately, there is little consensus on the definition of morality among philosophers or social scientists. Still, from a psychological standpoint, a serviceable definition is provided by Blasi (1987, 1990). According to Blasi (1987), a behavior or practice can be considered moral "if it is intentional, a response to some sense of obligation, and if the obligation is a response to an ideal, even if vaguely understood" (p. 86). Morality pertains to those prescriptive aspects of social relations that respond to images or ideals of right or good relationship. Promise keeping, for example, may be deemed a moral obligation because trust is essential to ideal human relationship. In the realm of sport, one relevant ideal is "the good sports contest" (Fraleigh, 1984, p. 30ff.). This ideal can give rise to felt obligations to abide by codes of fair play. To the extent that athletes embrace the ideal, they feel obligated to abide by the rules, or the "spirit" of the rules, and treat other contestants with respect.

We have sought to include in this chapter a discussion of measures and methods that draw from different theoretical standpoints. In fact, however, the vast majority of theoretically grounded research in this area stems from one of two classic paradigms: social learning and structural developmental. Theorists within the social learning tradition (e.g., Bandura, 1991)

typically define morality as behavior congruent with cultural moral norms. For these investigators, moral behavior is shaped through modeling and reinforcement in the same way as any other form of behavior. Because of these theoretical assumptions, most research within the social learning tradition focuses on overt behavior and its assumed environmental causes. Since morality entails reasons or motives in addition to overt behavior, most theorists use the term *prosocial behavior* when referring to the construct investigated by social learning researchers.

At the root of the structural developmental paradigm is the distinction between moral content and moral structure (e.g., Kohlberg, 1981; Piaget, 1932). To understand this distinction, consider the following analogy. Just as a person's overt speech relies on an underlying preconscious grasp of grammatical structure, so a person's moral content (for example, moral values, beliefs, attitudes, and judgments) reflects an underlying moral "grammar," or structure. The underlying structure of moral reasoning undergoes changes in its organizational pattern during the course of a person's development. These changes result from an interaction between the person's social experience and the person's developing ability to actively organize information gleaned from that experience. Research conducted from within the structural developmental paradigm often examines interactions between behavior and both intrapsychic meaning structures (such as moral stages) and environmental influences (as interpreted by the individual).

We have identified four clusters of measures and methods that researchers have created and/or adapted to assess moral functioning in the sport domain. These clusters form the scaffolding for our review of moral assessment in the sport literature. The first cluster is defined by its focus on moral content. It encompasses assessments of professed values, attitudes, beliefs, and judgments. This section also includes sportspersonship inventories because they typically operationalize sportspersonship in terms of a set of attitudes or beliefs. The second cluster concentrates on the personal competencies and orientations that underlie individuals' moral meaning constructions and moral negotiations. The third cluster centers on moral behavior, and this section focuses on methods of assessing observed and self-described behavior and action tendencies. The final cluster consists of hybrid measures designed to tap multiple dimensions of moral functioning. We conclude the chapter with a discussion of future directions in moral assessment.

Assessing Moral Content

The content of a person's moral perspective can be described in terms of the moral values, attitudes, or beliefs that one holds or the moral judgments that one makes. The definitions of each of these terms vary from theorist to theorist, and the concepts clearly overlap. In general, it can be said that attitudes reflect one's predisposition to evaluate people, objects and experiences in a favorable or unfavorable manner (Katz, 1960). Beliefs involve the acceptance of a "truth" on the basis of what one implicitly considers adequate grounds (English & English, 1958). The foundations of beliefs are often not examined, and beliefs are thought to be deeper and less subject to change than are attitudes. Values are personal conceptions of the desirable that are relevant to selective behavior (Smith, 1963). Like beliefs, values are seen as more basic and central than attitudes. Finally, a moral judgment may incorporate attitudes, beliefs, and/or values into a reasoned determination of whether a particular act or practice is right or appropriate.

The oldest form of moral research among sport psychologists involved administering a questionnaire designed to assess relevant beliefs or attitudes. The pioneering studies of Hartshorne and May (1928; Hartshorne, May, & Maller, 1929; Hartshorne, May, & Schuttleworth, 1930), who indiscriminately employed sport and physical activity tasks alongside other tasks, clearly stand out as the best of this period. Their primary objective was to analyze whether moral beliefs correlated with actual moral behavior. Unfortunately their research was largely descriptive, and they seldom addressed the validity and reliability of assessment measures.

By midcentury, moral researchers began implementing more sophisticated approaches to assess the content of people's moral perspective. One of the first and most important of these was developed by Rokeach (1973). His primary interest was in values, both moral and nonmoral. Although his values survey was not designed specifically for physical activity participants, it has become a popular measure among some sport psychologists.

The Rokeach Values Survey

Rokeach (1973) defines a value as "an enduring belief that a specific mode of conduct or end-state of existence is personally or socially preferable to an opposite or converse mode of conduct or end-state of existence" (p. 5). As implied in this definition, he divides values into two basic types: instrumental (modes of conduct) and terminal (end-states of existence). He further divides instrumental values into moral and competence values, and terminal values into the categories of personal and social. Illustrations of values included under each heading are included in Table 1.

Moral values, for Rokeach, pertain exclusively to modes of

behavior. Counter to the intuitions of many, he does not include in the moral domain concern for such terminal values as love, friendship, inner harmony, world peace, or equality. Also, for Rokeach (1973), moral values are those that "when violated, arouse pangs of conscience or feelings of guilt" (p. 8). Thus, Rokeach's understanding of morality is framed in terms of affect.

The Rokeach Value Survey (RVS) (Rokeach, 1973) represents Rokeach's primary contribution to the assessment literature, and the RVS has been used to investigate the values professed by athletes (Davis & Baskett, 1979; Lee, 1977, 1986; Symons, 1984; Wilcox, 1980). The survey contains two lists of 18 values, each printed on a gummed label, listed in alphabetical order. One list contains instrumental values; the other, terminal values. Each value is represented by a word or brief phrase, with a few words of explanation. The respondent is asked to arrange the values in order of priority.

The practical advantages of the RVS are numerous (Rokeach, 1973). It is simple in design, easy to administer to groups or individuals, takes only 10-20 minutes to complete, can be scored objectively, and is appropriate for a wide age range, beginning at about age 11. Also, it has been used extensively, so there is a significant body of literature that documents its psychometric attributes (Rokeach, 1973, 1979).

The primary limitations of the RVS are associated with Rokeach's conceptualization of values and value hierarchies. Rokeach assumes that respondents can order the values he has chosen for the two value lists into neat hierarchies and that this ranking process corresponds to the way those values actually function psychologically within the respondents. We would ask two sets of questions about these assumptions. First, are the values in each list really a coherent set? What logical sense does it make to rank order, for example, wisdom, friendship, national security, and a world of beauty? Is this not a list of the "apples and oranges" variety? Clearly, Rokeach's operational division of values into instrumental and terminal is too broad (Heath & Fogel, 1978). Why lump moral and nonmoral values into one indiscriminant list, for instance? Moreover, the means-ends dualism on which the instrumental-terminal distinction rests is itself problematic (Dewey, 1939; Shields, 1986).

Second, even if the values were all of a similar type, can we assume that one must always make choices from among them? For example, is it always necessary to prioritize or choose from among the values of wisdom, mature love, and true friendship? If interrelated values do not conflict with one another, or pull in different directions, then it is easy to imagine a person being

---

Table 1
Rokeach's (1973) Taxonomy of Values

Instrumental Values:
Moral values: e.g., honesty, love, politeness, responsibility
Competence values: e.g., ambition, capability, intellect, logic

Terminal Values:
Personal values: e.g., exciting life, sense of accomplishment, happiness, pleasure
Social values: e.g., world peace, a world of beauty, national security, equality

equally committed to those values simultaneously. Does the process of rank ordering a list of abstract, arbitrarily identified value terms create an artificial value hierarchy that bears little resemblance to the way values actually guide behavior?

Two other problems arise from the projective and ipsative nature of the RVS. The RVS presents lists of values identified by short labels. The precise meaning of each value, however, is open to interpretation, and each respondent must project her or his meaning onto the term. For example, would an 11-year-old interpret "mature love" in the same way as a 60-year-old? If individuals project different meanings onto the terms, then how useful can it be to compare their ordering of the values? People may even differ as to whether they perceive a particular value as moral or nonmoral (Turiel, 1983).

Rokeach (1973) acknowledges that his values survey is ipsative, meaning that it offers the respondent a limited, preset framework within which to reason and respond. The approach is warranted in his view because he believes the measure presents 36 values that are sufficiently diverse and inclusive, and he maintains that all people hold values in sufficiently parallel fashion. Both of these assumptions are questionable. There are serious omissions in Rokeach's lists of values, such as justice and truth. The range of values to which people commit themselves may be more expansive than Rokeach imagined (cf. Braithwaite & Law, 1985). Moreover, two people who rank "forgiving" equally high on their respective lists may still have quite different levels of commitment to that value. People are not endowed with equal "quantities" of value commitment that they then distribute among a set of potential value options. Thus, the RVS may lead to erroneous conclusions both about the content of people's values and their levels of commitment to those values (cf. Miethe, 1985; Ng, 1982; Rankin & Grube, 1980).

Rokeach's contributions have significantly shaped the study of human values, and the RVS remains the only theoretically sophisticated value-assessment instrument that has been used in published sport research.[1] The RVS, however, does not deal with values specific to sport, and the values motivating sport decisions may not be captured by such a broad-scope instrument. This problem is addressed by the next measure to be reviewed.

The Webb Scale and Its Variants

The Orientations Toward Play Scale (Webb, 1969)—often referred to simply as the Webb scale—is a sport-specific instrument that is familiar to most sport and exercise psychologists. Respondents are asked to rank order the values of winning, playing fair, and playing well. In some later studies, the value of having fun is also included. Webb's methodology was simple. He asked 1,200 children the following question: "What do you think is most important in playing a game: to play as well as you can, to beat the other player or team, or to play the game fairly?" Webb claimed that responses can be placed on a continuum bounded by two extremes. On one side is a *play orientation* in which fairness is of greatest concern and game outcome, least. On the other side is a *professional orientation* in which the values are reversed and winning is emphasized as

most important. A primary emphasis on skill mastery falls midway on the play-professional continuum.

The Webb scale has been used extensively by sport psychologists and sociologists (Blair, 1985; Card, 1981; Kidd & Woodman, 1975; Knoppers, Schuiteman, & Love, 1988; Loy, Birrell, & Rose, 1976; Maloney & Petrie, 1972; Mantel & Vander Velden, 1974; McElroy & Kirkendall, 1980; Nicholson, 1979; Nixon, 1980; Petrie, 1971a, 1971b; Sage, 1980; Snyder & Spreitzer, 1979; Theberge, Curtis, & Brown, 1982). Its popularity is no doubt related to its eloquent simplicity. It is easily understood by a wide age span, can be group administered, and takes no more than a couple of minutes to complete.

The Webb scale appears to have acceptable reliability. In his original study, Webb (1969) reported test-retest reliability coefficients above .90 for a sample of 920 public and 354 private school students. Though questions have been raised about scale format (Kidd & Woodman, 1975; Snyder & Spreitzer, 1979), data categorization (Knoppers, Shaw, & Love, 1984; Loy et al., 1976; Petrie, 1971a, 1971b; Sage, 1980; Theberge et al., 1982), and scale content (Knoppers, 1985; Knoppers et al., 1988; McElroy, 1981), no data have been reported that seriously undercut acceptance of the Webb scale's reliability.

The main drawbacks to the Webb scale parallel those of the Rokeach Value Survey. In her review of the relevant literature, Knoppers (1985) offered several insightful critiques. She pointed out that the rank ordering technique only determines each value's relative priority, but fails to reflect the magnitude of psychological investment that a person attaches to each value. Moreover, the Webb scale assumes the trio of values form a unitary variable that underlies a single continuum bounded by "play" and "professional" orientations at opposite ends. Knoppers suggested, however, that these value orientations are independent of one another. A person may highly value both winning and playing fair. Knoppers also claimed that key terms used in the Webb scale are left ambiguous. For example, some respondents may interpret *game* to mean a highly organized competitive sport event whereas others may have in mind a recreational backyard game.

To remedy some of the validity weaknesses inherent in the Webb scale, Knoppers, Schuiteman, and Love (1986) created the Game Orientation Scale (GOS). The GOS presents respondents with two specific scenarios: an informal sport game among friends (labelled the *recreational* scenario), and the state high school basketball championship (labelled the *competitive* scenario). In addition, rather than rank ordering the values of fairness, fun, playing well, and winning, GOS respondents rate the importance of each value on a 7-point Likert scale. Knoppers et al. (1986) reported alpha internal consistency coefficients of .77 for the recreational sport situation and .82 for the competitive sport situation. Test-retest reliability coefficients were .56 and .60 for the recreational and competitive sport situations, respectively.

The GOS is an improvement on the Webb scale, but more work needs to be done. Replacing the rank-order technique with Likert scales resolves some problems, but creates others.

---

1. Sport researchers interested in assessing values may wish to examine alternate theories and measures (e.g., Madhere, 1993; Mueller & Wornhoff, 1990; Schwartz 1994a, 1994b; cf. Schmitt, Schwartz, Steyer, & Schmitt, 1993).

Table 2

Sample Items From the Hahm-Beller Values Choice Inventory

1. Two rival basketball teams in a well-known conference played a basketball game on team A's court. During the game, team B's star player was consistently heckled whenever she missed a basket, pass, or rebound. In the return game on team B's home court, the home crowd took revenge by heckling team A's players. Such action is fair because both crowds have equal opportunity to heckle players. (Value=Justice; Answer=Strongly Disagree)

2. A gold medal track athlete was told to undergo drug testing during recent international competition. Because she played by the rules, competed on her merits, and did not use performance-enhancing drugs, she opposed the drug testing. She believed that athletic organizations had no moral authority to force her to be tested. Because she and other athletes are truthful and drug testing assumes they are untruthful, drug testing should not be mandatory. (Value=Honesty; Answer=Strongly Agree)

3. A tennis star is preparing to play a match. She complains of not feeling well during the warm-up. This star player finally lost a match. When discussing the game, she continually remarked that "I just did not play my best game." Because the player believed her best game was not played, her statement was acceptable. (Value=Responsibility; Answer=Strongly Disagree)

For example, when respondents give identical ratings to two or more values, they do not clarify which value is more important to them. The desire to win can, and often does, pull in a different direction from fairness. Perhaps both the rank-order and Likert scale approaches are needed. Also, an inductive, open-ended approach may be useful in some cases. For example, participants could identify and define the values that are most important to them and then prioritize the values according to their significance in the context of self-defined or investigator-defined sport scenarios.

The Webb scale and its variants are based on ranking or rating a small set of values that may motivate sport behaviors. Although responses to the Webb scale can offer insight into respondents' moral priorities, that is not its primary aim. The Webb scale values are not tethered to moral theory, and the scale was not designed to probe the moral psychology of respondents. This is, however, the aim of the next measure.

The Hahm-Beller Values Choice Inventory

The Hahm-Beller Values Choice Inventory (HBVCI) (Hahm, Beller, & Stoll, 1989) was designed to assess athletes' embrace of deontic sport ethics.[2] By intention, the *HBVCI* assesses moral content, namely, the embrace of a particular approach to sport ethics. It does not assess underlying moral structure. Thus, it is a measure of adherence to a set of moral principles, rather than a developmental measure of moral reasoning maturity.

The HBVCI consists of 21 brief sport scenarios, each featuring an action for which a moral rationale is offered. (Table 2 presents examples of HBVCI items.) The moral issues embedded in the scenarios involve honesty, responsibility, and justice. Respondents are asked to indicate on a 5-point Likert scale the extent to which they agree or disagree with the item. They are not free to respond separately to the action and the rationale presented in an item (for example, they cannot agree that the act is appropriate and disagree with the rationale offered to justify the act), nor can they offer their own independent rationale for why the behavior is or is not acceptable.

The authors report satisfactory validity and reliability data for the HBVCI. Face validity was established when several sport and philosophical ethicists concurred that the instrument measures deontological reasoning. Still, some of the items contain controversial issues and we would be surprised if all sport philosophers who embrace deontological ethics would agree with how each of the items is keyed. Beller (1990) determined concurrent validity by administering the HBVCI together with Rest's Defining Issues Test (discussed below) and found the two tests correlated at .82. Reported internal reliability coefficients for the HBVCI have been acceptable, ranging from .74 to .88 (Hahm, 1989; Hahm et al., 1989). There are no published reports of test-retest reliability.

The HBVCI was not designed as a measure of moral reasoning maturity. Its primary use, however, has been to test the effectiveness of intervention programs designed to improve moral reasoning (Beller & Stoll, 1992; Stoll & Beller, 1993) and to compare the moral reasoning adequacy of different populations (Stoll, Beller, Cole, & Burwell, 1995). These uses of the HBVCI raise two related questions. First, was the HBVCI designed to measure adherence to one ethical perspective among equally valid alternatives? If so, the HBVCI would not be an appropriate measure of reasoning adequacy. Second, are the authors making the much stronger (and more controversial) claim that those who score higher on the HBVCI are more "correct" in their moral thinking? If so, the authors need to offer more evidence that their keyed responses are philosophically "superior." If moral reasoning "adequacy" (as assessed by the HBVCI) is not equivalent to moral reasoning "maturity" (as assessed by a developmental measure), the authors need to elaborate on the justification for considering higher scores to be better scores.

An investigator's assessment tools, of course, should match her or his research goals. We believe that the HBVCI is best suited for comparing different groups' appreciation of deontic sport ethics. Based on the psychometric data currently available, its use in intervention studies is more questionable. Of particular importance, we need to know whether responses to the measure are associated with a social desirability response set and whether respondents can fake high scores after a brief introduction to deontic theory.

---

2. According to deontological theory, the rightness or morality of an act is determined by features intrinsic to the act rather than by the consequences of the act (Frankena, 1963).

Sportspersonship Inventories

Sportspersonship[3] has been a topic of considerable, but intermittent, interest to sport psychologists who have developed a large number of sportspersonship inventories over the years (Dawley, Troyer, & Shaw, 1951; Flory, 1958; Floyd, 1939; Haskins, 1960; Haskins & Hartman, 1960; Johnson, 1969; Kirkpatrick, 1940; Kistler, 1957; Lakie, 1964; McAfee, 1955; Vallerand, Brière, Blanchard, & Provencher, 1996; Wright & Rubin, 1989). It is beyond our scope to review each of these instruments separately, nor is there need to do so. Very few have been used beyond pilot investigations, and many share similar shortcomings. As noted by Kroll (1975), most authors did not offer an adequate definition of the domain of sportspersonship, nor did they adequately address problems associated with the scalability of sportspersonship items.

Sportspersonship is often linked to such concepts as fairness, respect for authority and opponents, politeness, honesty, self-control, integrity, sacrifice, loyalty, courage, a magnanimous spirit, and positive enthusiasm. Such a "bag of virtues" (Kohlberg, 1981, p. 2) does not necessarily define a coherent psychological domain. In the absence of definitional/theoretical clarity, most researchers have relied on a combination of personal intuition and the judgments of "experts" to operationally define sportspersonship, develop items for inventories, and specify "correct" responses. The measures constructed in this way tap only partial dimensions of sportspersonship and do so in a way that leaves the instrument "key" open to philosophical debate.

The first major effort to empirically root the concept of sportspersonship came when Crawford (1957) set out to systematically classify incidents of unethical actions in seven men's intercollegiate sports. He surveyed 300 colleges and universities, asking college presidents, athletic directors, officials, coaches, and athletic trainers (but not athletes!) to identify examples of unsportspersonlike behaviors. Crawford classified the 1,100 incidents that respondents identified into nine categories and specified the frequency of reported incidents for each: officiating (463), opponent relationships (156), rules of the game (152), player relationships (121), professional relationships (69), recruiting (66), public relations (47), eligibility rules (31), and scouting (10).

Johnson (1969) then constructed 152 inventory items designed to tap Crawford's categories of unsportspersonlike behaviors in football, basketball, and baseball. His refined Sportsmanship Attitude Scale (SAS) was pared down to a 21-item inventory in two equivalent forms. The coefficient of reproducibility for Form A was .812; for Form B, it was .863. The two forms correlated at .856. Correlation coefficients between the scale items and behavioral ratings varied widely, ranging from -.008 to .427. Unfortunately, additional studies utilizing the SAS have not been published, so independent confirmation of its validity and reliability is lacking.

The SAS was based on Crawford's (1957) data, so some of the problems inherent in the latter were transferred to the former. Three significant problems pertain to the range of athletic experiences addressed by Crawford. First, he limited his study to

male intercollegiate athletics in the late 1950s. Second, Crawford's list encompasses diverse behaviors, including many that may be appropriately labeled moral (e.g., fighting and cheating) and others that might be considered conventional or even matters of etiquette (e.g. protesting an official's call). Finally, some of the actions he categorized occur within the competitive process itself, whereas others lie outside the spatial and temporal boundaries of sport (e.g., recruiting incidents). This distinction is important because people tend to think about moral issues situated within the flow of sport competition differently than they reason about similar issues outside the competitive encounter (Bredemeier, 1985, 1995; Bredemeier & Shields, 1984).

One of the best among the first generation of sportspersonship questionnaires is the Competitive Attitude Scale (CAS) (Lakie, 1964). It consists of 22 items depicting unsportspersonlike behaviors. Respondents are asked to rate their approval of each of the behaviors using a 5-point Likert scale ranging from *strongly approve* to *strongly disapprove*. The CAS demonstrated a 3-month test-retest reliability of .64 and a KR reliability of .81.

While the original CAS data looked promising, the use of this instrument by subsequent researchers has raised questions about its adequacy. Duda, Olson, and Templin (1991) designed a basketball-specific version of the CAS and administered it to female and male interscholastic basketball players. Factor analyses revealed three CAS factors: Unsportsmanlike Play/Cheating, Strategic Play, and Sportsmanship. However, only the first factor, consisting of eight items, achieved an internal reliability coefficient above .70. Drawing from the work of Lakie (1964) and Duda et al. (1991), Stephens, Bredemeier, and Shields (in press) developed a nine-item soccer-specific version of the CAS and included it in a test battery administered to female youth soccer participants. The results from a principal components analysis indicated that the scale contained three factors (labeled "Bad Sport," "Good Sport," and "Strategic Play"). However, only the Bad Sport subscale, consisting of 4 items, achieved an internal reliability coefficient above .60.

Recently, Vallerand and his colleagues have undertaken a sophisticated research program to operationally define and measure sportspersonship. In the first phase of their investigation, they asked male and female athletes (n=60) to present their definition of the "sportsmanship" concept and to offer examples (Vallerand, Deshaies, Cuerrier, Brière, & Pelletier, 1996). From these definitions and examples, 21 situations were identified that potentially exemplified the meaning of sportspersonship. These 21 items were then presented to a sample of 1,056 French-Canadian athletes ranging in age from 10 to 18. The athletes, who were drawn from a variety of sport areas and levels, were asked to rate on a 4-point scale the extent to which each of the items dealt with sportspersonship. A factor analysis performed on these 21 items revealed the presence of five factors:

1. Respect and concern for one's full commitment toward sport participation
2. A negative approach toward sport; a "win at all costs" approach

---

3. We prefer the rather awkward term *sportspersonship* over the traditional *sportsmanship* because we believe it to be both more accurate and gender equitable in its connotation.

3. Respect and concern for the rules and officials
4. Respect for social conventions found in sport
5. Respect and concern for the opponent

Based on this preliminary investigation, Vallerand and his colleagues (Vallerand, Deshaies et al., 1996) have suggested that sportspersonship should be conceptualized as encompassing a number of related yet distinct dimensions. To operationalize their multidimensional definition of sportspersonship, they developed the Multidimensional Sportsmanship Orientations Scale (MSOS) (Vallerand, Brière et al., 1996). It was developed through several phases.

Initially, 20 items were prepared reflecting each of the five dimensions of sportspersonship identified above. Through efforts to establish content validity, these 20 items were pared down to 13 for each of the five dimensions. The 65-item MSOS was then administered to 132 male and female athletes reflecting various sport areas. An exploratory factor analysis revealed a five-factor solution, and a second factor analysis, retaining only the best 5 items for each factor, accounted for 53.3% of the variance. The internal consistency of the five subscales ranged from .60 to .85.

The MSOS was then administered to a new sample of 362 athletes. The athletes also completed a set of other psychological assessments, including the "Win" subscale of the Sport Orientation Questionnaire (Gill & Deeter, 1989), a three-item scale assessing the subjective importance of one's sport, and a 3-item variant of Crowne and Marlowe's (1960) Social Desirability Scale. A confirmatory factor analysis indicated that the five-factor model provided an acceptable fit for the data. Internal consistency was again checked and was found to be adequate (ranging from .71 to .86), except for an alpha value of .54 for the negative approach to sport subscale. Correlations with the other psychological measures generally supported the discriminant and content validity of the MSOS. Test-retest reliability over a 5-week interval was also assessed; correlations varied from .56 to .76, with a mean test-retest correlation of .67.

At this stage, the MSOS appears to be a valid and reliable instrument, apart from the negative approach to sport subscale. This subscale had the lowest internal consistency and test-retest reliability scores, and was found to correlate with a measure of social desirability. Its difficulties may derive from a lack of conceptual consistency among subscale items. The authors characterize the subscale as reflecting a "win at all costs" orientation, but the five items constituting the subscale seem to reflect neither this orientation nor any other coherent perspective.

Two other issues should be noted with regard to Vallerand's suggestion that his inductive methodology resolves the problem of defining sportspersonship. He believes that through repeated interactions in sport settings, athletes develop a consensus regarding the meaning of sportspersonship. This assumption should be tested. Perhaps individuals experience important developmental changes in their understanding of the concept. Perhaps cultural values and behavioral norms significantly influence the meaning athletes attach to the term. Moreover, even if all athletes do reach a general consensus about the meaning of sportspersonship, other groups for whom the concept may be important—coaches, fans, administrators, philosophers, and so

on—are not considered by Vallerand at all. Clearly, the suitability of the instrument for samples other than 10-to-20 year-old French-Canadian athletes needs to be scrutinized.

A second consideration is that the everyday language approach to definition, although useful, can also be problematic. One reason that every discipline develops a specialized vocabulary is the imprecision of everyday speech. If sportspersonship is to be a useful scientific concept, its definition must be both precise and coherent. This does not exclude multidimensional definition, but each distinct component must be given a precise and coherent definition, and the interrelations among components must be specified. Perhaps the best approach to definition involves an interactive process in which the language used by study participants to describe the meaning they attach to a particular construct is examined in light of scientific literature and philosophical reflection on the construct. Vallerand's work offers an important contribution to the former facet of this dialectic.

Prescriptive Judgment Methods

Sportspersonship inventories are designed to offer a comprehensive view of sport respondents' prescriptive beliefs or attitudes towards sport. Several recent instruments have been designed with a narrower scope, tapping respondents' judgments about the legitimacy of specific types of behaviors. Because people can form moral judgments about literally dozens of real or potential moral issues, these instruments tend to be highly content specific, and generalizations beyond the instrument content area can be made only with considerable caution. Sport psychologists have studied legitimacy judgments about athletic aggression and gender stratification in sport.

Bredemeier (1985) developed the Continuum of Injurious Acts (CIA) as an assessment technique designed to tap high school and college students' legitimacy judgments about athletic aggression in basketball. The CIA consists of a set of six 3x5 cards describing acts with intended consequences that become increasingly more serious. The CIA cards are presented in random sequence to the respondent, who sorts them into two piles: those viewed as legitimate and those viewed as illegitimate. The respondent is then given additional opportunities to classify acts as legitimate in response to a series of contingencies offering quasi-moral justifications for the acts. Bredemeier established face validity for the CIA through use of a panel of judges who ranked the cards in order of increasing severity, and content validity was supported when all responses fit the hierarchical model of increasingly serious aggression. Paper-and-pencil variants of the CIA have been used by other sport researchers (Duda et al., 1991; Hacker, 1992; Huston & Duda, 1992; Ryan, Williams, & Wimer, 1990), though none have supported their adaptations with additional psychometric data.

Silva (1983) also assessed legitimacy judgments about potential injurious sport acts among college students. His assessment method incorporated a set of eight slides depicting adult male athletes engaged in rule-violating and potentially injurious behavior. The slides were selected from a larger pool based on the clarity with which they depicted rule-violating behavior as determined by a set of expert judges. As a check of response validity, participants were requested to indicate the sport being played and the primary behavior or act portrayed on each slide. Only data from respondents who were able to accurately provide this information were used. Respondents then made judgments about the legitimacy of the viewed behaviors.

Bredemeier and her colleagues (Bredemeier, Weiss, Shields, & Cooper, 1987) conducted a follow-up study, examining the legitimacy judgments of fourth-through-seventh grade male and female students. Again, a series of slides was used as the stimulus material. A panel of judges was shown a set of 25 slides, including those used in the Silva (1983) study. Each slide depicted an adult male athlete engaging in potentially dangerous sport behavior. Based on the evaluations of the judges, 9 slides were selected for use in the study. There was 100% agreement among the judges that the 9 slides depicted behavior carrying high risk of injury. There also was unanimous agreement regarding the legality of 7 of the slides; for the remaining 2 slides, there was 93% agreement among the 15 judges.

The study participants first described the acts depicted in the slides in terms of whether a rule was being broken and whether someone was likely to get hurt. Agreement between the children and panel members regarding rule violations was 89%, and in 92% of the cases children thought the slides depicted potentially harmful activity. Following these evaluations, the children made legitimacy judgments about the actions of the adult male athletes depicted in the slides and about the same behaviors performed by children like themselves.

Solomon and her colleagues (Solomon, Bredemeier, & Shields, 1993) developed the Gender Stratification Interview (GSI) to assess children's beliefs and legitimacy judgments regarding gender stratification[4] in sport. The GSI consists of six brief sport scenarios, each depicting a situation of potential gender stratification. For example, one scenario reads, "Imagine that the adults who schedule the playing fields made a mistake. They scheduled the boys' baseball team and the girls' softball team to play a game on the same field at the same time." The respondent is then asked two questions: what would happen and what should happen. For example, the above scenario is followed by: "Which team do you think would get to use the field? Why? Which team do you think should get to use the field? Why?" Four additional questions enable respondents to elaborate on their answers. Coding for the GSI involves determining for each scenario the *response category* (male favored, female favored, neither gender favored) and the *thematic construct* (explanations based on ability, fairness, preference, responsibility, or social position) for both the interpretative (would) and legitimacy (should) judgments.

The GSI is administered orally and is coded through use of a user's guide. In preliminary investigations, evidence for the construct validity of the GSI was obtained as was high interrater reliability (91.5% agreement on codes), and the GSI scales were shown to have moderate but acceptable internal consistency. Still, sample sizes were relatively small, and an expected correlation between the GSI and Enright's (Enright, Franklin, & Manheim, 1980) Distributive Justice Scale (a measure of distributive justice reasoning) was not found. Further testing is needed before the GSI can be considered a valid and reliable instrument.

Taken as a whole, the measures that we have reviewed in this section—those that tap various aspects of moral content—demonstrate promise, yet more information about their validity and reliability is needed. Even at its best, however, the assessment of moral content has limited utility in developing a comprehensive understanding of sport morality. Take the case of measures assessing legitimacy judgments. Such measures can reveal aspects of an athlete's moral belief system that relate to a particular content area, such as aggression. But legitimacy judgments are inherently tethered to the specific focus of the instrument, and generalizing beyond that focus is problematic. Moreover, legitimacy judgments are highly responsive to situational details. For example, a respondent might state that it is wrong for a pitcher to "brush back" a batter but change that judgment if told that the batter had slid into second with spikes up on a previous at bat. Even relatively minor modifications of story detail can lead to changes in legitimacy judgments.

Though their intent is different, most sportspersonship inventories adopt the same basic method as the legitimacy judgment measures. Rather than focusing narrowly on one specific moral construct like cheating or aggression, however, they elicit legitimacy judgments about a host of loosely related sport acts. This gives them greater breadth in terms of their applicability across a diverse set of sport issues, but this expanded scope comes at some cost. Sportspersonship inventories have had difficulty establishing validity and adequate internal reliability. This is due in part to the fact that what counts as good sportspersonship often varies from one person to another, perhaps mediated by such variables as developmental stage, goal orientation, sport area, competitive level, cultural group, and historical period.

The challenge for sport researchers interested in moral phenomena in sport is to isolate central constructs that have explanatory depth—constructs that are likely related to a comprehensive range of moral phenomena. In the next section, we review research instruments that, like the sportspersonship inventories, are designed to tap a dimension of moral psychology that is broad and applicable across a diverse set of moral issues. Unlike the sportspersonship inventories, however, these instruments are designed to assess underlying moral structures rather than moral content. Rather than focusing on *what* a person believes to be right, these measures focus on the *reasons* a person believes what he or she does.

Assessing Moral Competencies and Orientations

Beginning in the mid-1980s, sport psychologists began to use the tools of structural developmental research to investigate moral competencies and how they related to other moral phenomena in the sport realm. This created a new set of complexities in terms of assessment. Establishing the validity and reliability of moral competency measures involves far more than determining test-retest correlations, internal consistency reliability scores, and similar psychometric calculations.

---

4. *Gender stratification* can be defined as the differential distribution of power, prestige, and privilege between males and females based on gender (Chafetz, 1984; Sage, 1990).

Figure 1. Story pair from the Piagetian Intentionality Measure

First, because these measures claim to be developmental, it is important to provide evidence that test scores change with age and that these changes are in the direction predicted by the theory. Longitudinal studies demonstrating that people progress in the predicted manner provide the most compelling evidence of an instrument's developmental validity.

Second, these instruments are designed to assess moral *competency*. Not only should higher test scores occur later in a chronological sequence, they also should represent more adequate moral thought processes. Higher scores should reflect thinking that is more complex and internally coherent, thinking that takes more morally-relevant factors into account and responds more adequately to a wider scope of moral concerns and issues. Thus, in addition to providing evidence that higher stages follow lower stages chronologically, the test developer needs to offer convincing justification for why a higher stage is a "better" stage (cf. Kohlberg, 1971a).

Additionally, moral competency measures are designed to assess *universal* competencies. Most structural developmentalists believe that beneath the evident diversity of moral belief systems lie a number of universal moral values and a relatively small number of developmentally tethered structural patterns that give coherence to, and establish priority among, those values. To determine whether an instrument taps only culture-spe-

cific moral norms or reveals more universal developmental patterns, evidence is needed from studies of both genders, as well as from people reflecting many cultures, religions, orientations, and traditions.

Finally, these instruments, if they are to be useful, must be shown to be relevant to moral behavior. Because moral reasoning competency is only one source of influence on moral behavior, correlations between moral stage scores and behavioral assessments need not be high, but they should be both statistically and practically significant.

The moral measures reviewed in this section are designed to identify a respondent's predominant stage or level of moral reasoning or fundamental moral orientation. Any measure of moral stages or levels should meet the demands suggested above. The instruments reviewed here do so with varying degrees of success. They draw from one of four major theorists—Piaget, Kohlberg, Haan, or Gilligan—and so we have organized our review accordingly.

Assessments Based on Piaget's Theory

Piaget (1932) pioneered the semistructured interview technique to probe the underlying structure of children's moral reasoning. For example, he would tell children a pair of stories that differed in some crucial aspect and then ask them about the differences. In one famous story pair, he first told about a girl who accidentally broke a whole tray of cups as she was carrying them to the dining room to set the table. That story was paired with another that described a girl who broke a single cup while climbing a kitchen counter in pursuit of a forbidden treat. After telling the stories, Piaget would query, "Which child do you think did the worse thing?" Depending on the response, he would follow up with additional questions to uncover more about the child's underlying structure of reasoning.

Piaget (1932) described two major phases of moral development: the heteronomous phase and the autonomous phase. One distinction between these two phases concerns how the developing child coordinates information about the actor's intent and the consequence that result from the actor's behavior. During the earlier phase, young children evaluate the morality of an act based on the *consequences* that result from it. Later, during the autonomous phase, children pay more attention to the *intent* of the actor. Correspondingly, theorists have used this consequences-intention relationship to design assessment instruments.

Bredemeier, Weiss, Shields, and Shewchuk (1986) designed the Piagetian Intentionality Task (PIT) to assess young children's moral reasoning maturity. The assessment technique involved telling five-to-seven year old children six stories about youngsters engaged in everyday life situations and six parallel sport-specific stories. For each daily-life and sport-specific story, a pair of drawings depicted one child who, though well-intentioned, caused considerable harm or damage, and another child whose ill-intentioned behavior caused little or no negative consequence. An illustration of these is provided in Figure 1.

Following each illustrated story pair, the child was asked to repeat the intent and consequence of the depicted acts and to identify which protagonist did the better or worse thing. The child's PIT score was simply the total percentage of autonomous (intent-based) responses; thus, it could range from 0 to 100. Unfortunately, psychometric properties of the measure were not reported in the Bredemeier et al. (1986) investigation.

Assessments Based on Kohlberg's Theory

Kohlberg's stage theory of moral development is well-known (see Shields & Bredemeier, 1995, for a review of its relevance to the sport setting), and it has spawned a number of distinct measures of moral stage development (Colby et al., 1987; Gibbs et al., 1984; Gibbs, Basinger, & Fuller, 1992; Gibbs & Widaman, 1982; Rest, 1979, 1986a). A comprehensive review of these instruments is beyond our scope, but three stand out as worthy of attention due to their use in sport research: Kohlberg's Moral Judgment Interview (Colby et al., 1987), Rest's Defining Issues Test (1979, 1986a), and Gibbs' Sociomoral Reflection Measure-Short Form (Gibbs et al., 1992).

Before discussing his measure, it is important to indicate just what Kohlberg's measure is designed to assess. Initially, Kohlberg described his work simply as an investigation of "moral development" (e.g., Kohlberg, 1969, 1971a, 1971b). By moral development, however, Kohlberg meant the ontogenetic changes that occur in the cognitive organization of moral understanding. His primary focus was not on such related topics as moral emotion, moral motivation, or moral behavior. In the final formulation of his theory, Kohlberg acknowledged that he had previously overstated the domain of his research and that his theory pertained exclusively to the development of justice reasoning (Kohlberg, 1984).[5] Still, for Kohlberg, justice defines the essential core of morality.

The Moral Judgment Interview. To assess moral stage development, Kohlberg relied on the semistructured clinical interview method. Kohlberg's moral stage measure underwent significant modification over the years, however, finally culminating in the Standard Issue Moral Judgment Interview and Scoring System, which was published in the massive two-volume set, *The Measurement of Moral Judgment* (Colby et al., 1987). The Moral Judgment Interview (MJI) comes in three parallel forms. Each form contains three hypothetical moral dilemmas featuring a conflict between two moral values. For example, in the most famous dilemma, a man is faced with a decision of whether to steal a drug to save his dying wife. The value of life is thus pitted against the values of law and property rights. After presenting each moral dilemma, the investigator asks a set of standardized probes designed to elicit from the respondent her or his rationale for advocated courses of action. Equally important, the interviewer adds spontaneously generated questions intended to help the respondent elaborate on her or his reasoning.

The MJI is most reliably administered as an oral, tape-recorded interview. Responses are then transcribed and scored. Considerable training is required both to conduct an interview that yields adequate information and to score the protocol. A typical interview lasts about 45 minutes, and scoring takes at least 30 minutes for a well-trained coder. The nature of the hypothetical dilemmas makes the MJI inappropriate for children below about age 10.

Scoring the MJI follows the hermeneutic approach upon which the manual is based. Hermeneutics, a common methodology in the humanities, concerns itself with the interpretation of texts and meaning systems. The goal is to understand the interviewee's point of view and, beyond that, to identify the organizational pattern or generative rules beneath the specific interview content. Obviously, efforts to identify the substrata of another's meaning constructions are fraught with possibilities for projection and misinterpretation. Consequently, the lengthy coding guide provides precise interpretive guidelines that must be followed rigorously. Thus, after responses to a dilemma have been meticulously broken down into component issues, norms, and elements, the scorer is ready to compare a distilled judgment against "criterion judgments" contained in the 900-plus pages of the *Standard Issue Scoring Manual*. Stage scores are initially established for each of the six issues in the MJI and then combined.

It took Kohlberg more than 15 years to develop the *Standard Issue Scoring Manual*, and the MJI remains the unchallenged leader in moral stage assessment techniques. The MJI has impressive test-retest (.96 to .99), interrater (.98) and alter-

---

5. Kohlberg (1984) defined justice as "the structure of conflict resolution for a dilemma of competing claims between or among persons. It is the parallel in the social world to the structure of logical thought in the physical world" (p. 245).

nate form reliability (.82 to .95), and internal consistency (.92 to .96). Construct validity for the measure is supported by a 20-year longitudinal study, and dozens of cross-cultural studies have generally supported Kohlberg's contention that (a) people follow an invariant developmental sequence[6] and (b) their moral reasoning reflects high internal consistency (Colby et al., 1987).

One controversial feature of the MJI has been its reliance on hypothetical dilemmas. Gilligan (1982), among others, has critiqued this feature, suggesting that real-life dilemmas might better capture the type of moral reasoning people actually employ when faced with moral decisions. The dispute, however, pertains more to research objectives than assessment methodology. Kohlberg was interested in assessing moral reasoning *competency* and developed a method to allow people to display their optimal reasoning. For that purpose, brief, standardized, hypothetical stories work well. The lack of context and detail not only minimizes the possibility for idiosyncratic response, it also enables the dilemmas to be used across diverse cultural worlds with minimal distortion. In contrast, other researchers have been less interested in defining competency than in understanding moral *performance*, that is, how people actually reason and behave. To understand the type of reasoning a person is likely to employ in real situations of moral choice, dilemmas designed to be more realistic and contextually relevant provide a better approach.

To date, the MJI, in its final form, has not been used in sport-related moral research. Hall (1981), however, used an earlier variant of the MJI in a study of male and female intercollegiate basketball players. She combined standard Kohlbergian hypothetical dilemmas with realistic sport-specific dilemmas. The sport dilemmas she constructed, however, did not portray moral choices that athletes face during competition. For example, one dilemma queries whether a basketball coach should ask the timekeeper to delay starting the clock at critical moments that would benefit the home team. Another focuses on whether an academically pressured athlete should ask the coach to exert influence to assure the athlete a good grade in a class. Such dilemmas, although related to sport, do not take place within the flow of sport competition and remain removed from the everyday experience of most athletes.

The primary drawbacks of the MJI are practical. Moral interviewing and scoring take considerable training, and use of the method is laborious and expensive. Due as much to these practical limitations as to theoretical concerns, researchers have developed alternative approaches to the assessment of moral reasoning competency.

The Defining Issues Test. Rest, an early research associate of Kohlberg's, recognized the need for an instrument that could be used more broadly than the MJI. Consequently, he developed the Defining Issues Test (DIT), which has now been used in well over a thousand studies (Rest, 1979, 1986b; Rest & Narváez, 1994), including a significant number of sport studies

(Beller & Stoll, 1992; Bredemeier & Shields, 1984; Brower, 1992; A. Brown, 1992; Case, Greer, & Lacourse, 1987; Hacker, 1992; Hahm, 1989; Henkel & Earls, 1985; Marczynski, 1989; Naples, 1987; Wandzilak, Carroll, & Ansorge, 1988). The DIT is a straightforward, objectively scored, paper-and-pencil measure. It presents the respondent with six hypothetical moral dilemmas, some identical to those in the MJI. Each dilemma is followed by a list of 12 items (short statements or questions) that the respondent is asked to rate in terms of their importance in deciding the dilemma. At the end of each dilemma, the respondent ranks the four most important items.

Most of the 72 items contained in the DIT represent bits of reasoning likely to appeal to a particular stage of moral thinking. Other items are designed to catch attempts to fake a high score, making the DIT resistant to social desirability responding. The primary moral reasoning maturity index is the P-Score, which is simply the percentage of principled (i.e., Stages 5A, 5B, and 6 combined) moral reasoning reflected in the 24 ranked items. Rest (1979, 1986a, 1986b; Rest & Narváez, 1994) has furnished ample and convincing evidence of the validity and reliability of the DIT. The test-retest correlations of the DIT average in the .80s, and internal reliability scores also average in the .80s. DIT scores correlate with age and educational experience, as one would expect. Cross-cultural investigations generally have supported the instrument's reliability, though some variability from study to study is also evident (Moon, 1986).

The ease with which the DIT is administered and scored is certainly one reason for its popularity. But it is important to emphasize that the DIT is not a direct substitute for the MJI. There are several important theoretical differences reflected in the two measures. The DIT, developed in the 1970s, was based on an early version of Kohlberg's moral stage definitions. Additionally, Rest does not hold to the Kohlbergian proposition of stage displacement. For Kohlberg, as each new stage of moral reasoning slowly evolves, previous stages gradually cease to exist because their constituent elements are restructured into the new stage. But Rest adopts a "layer-cake" approach to moral reasoning development. People are thought to retain access to all previous stages of development as they progress. This theoretical difference led Kohlberg and Rest to adopt different scoring schemes. The MJI leads to a stage score; a person is given a predominant and secondary stage designation. The P-score of the DIT simply locates a person on a developmental continuum without assigning a particular stage or set of adjacent stages.

Perhaps the most important difference between the DIT and the MJI stems from the type of task each measure presents to the respondent. Kohlberg's MJI requires respondents to spontaneously produce moral justifications, whereas Rest's DIT asks people to evaluate prefabricated reasoning.[7] Because it is easier to recognize high stage moral arguments than to produce them, respondents will often appear more "mature" on the DIT than on the MJI. Correlations between the DIT and the MJI

---

6. Evidence for the invariant sequence claim is strongest for the intermediate stages and weakest for the postconventional stages.

7. Both types of moral reasoning—production and recognition—are relevant to sport. For example, athletes frequently must make spontaneous moral decisions regarding novel situations as they arise. On the other hand, an athlete's coach may offer fragments of moral philosophy in the context of discussing game strategy. These bits of moral philosophy are likely to be accepted or rejected based on the athlete's competence in recognizing higher stage moral reasoning.

tend to be moderate (ranging between 0.6 and 0.7), suggesting that the two measures overlap but assess distinct moral-cognitive skills.

The distinction between production and recognition measures has a number of other theoretical and practical implications. The primary advantage of recognition measures is that they are easily administered and scored. Their chief liability is that they remain somewhat lengthy, require a significant attention span, and cannot be used with children lacking sound reading skills. The DIT, for example, cannot be used with those who have less than a 7th-grade reading ability. For production tasks, the demands placed on the respondent (in terms of reading and concentration) are lower, which may account for their better discriminant validity in distinguishing the moral judgment of delinquents from that of nondelinquents (Gibbs et al., 1992), but the demands placed on the researcher (to learn and utilize the interpretive scheme) are considerably higher.

The Sociomoral Reflection Measure—Short Form. Gibbs has developed another paper-and-pencil alternative to the MJI. Actually, he has developed several, but we will focus exclusively on the most recent and promising—the Sociomoral Reflection Measure—Short Form (SRM-SF) (Gibbs et al., 1992)—since it is the one that has been used by sport psychologists (Bredemeier, Shields, Carlton, & Miller, 1997; Carlton, Miller, & Bredemeier, 1997).

Like the DIT, the SRM-SF is premised on a moral development theory indebted to, but distinct from, Kohlberg's. Most importantly, Gibbs jettisons the upper end of Kohlberg's stage theory. According to Gibbs, full moral maturity is reached at Stages 3 and 4, and consequently, the SRM-SF leads to stage scores ranging from 1 to 4. What Kohlberg considers "postconventional" moral reasoning (Stages 5 and 6) is redefined by Gibbs as philosophical elaboration that does not represent any new developmental gain beyond what was present in Stages 3 and 4.

The unique feature of the SRM-SF is that it is a production measure of moral reasoning maturity that eliminates the use of moral dilemmas. The SRM-SF contains 11 brief questions in which respondents are first asked to make a moral judgment and then to justify it. For example, Question 4 asks, "In general, how important is it for people to tell the truth?" The respondent first circles "very important," "important," or "not important." She or he is then asked, "Why is that very important/important/not important (whichever one you circled)?" The respondent's answers are then matched to stage-specific criterion justifications in a manual.

The SRM-SF has demonstrated acceptable reliability and validity in populations ranging in age from fourth grade through adults (Gibbs et al., 1992). The test-retest correlation for the entire sample ($n = 384$) was .88, and item responses proved to be homogeneous (Cronbach's alpha = .92). Concurrent validity was shown between the SRM-SF and the MJI ($r = .69$), and convergent validity was demonstrated through positive correlations with the variables of age (.66), verbal intelligence (.49), and socioeconomic status (.20). All correlations were significant at the .001 level. Also, the SRM-SF evidenced discriminant validity by showing no correlation with a measure of social desirability. Construct validity was supported by showing that the SRM-SF successfully discriminated among

diverse age samples, and delinquent versus nondelinquent adolescents.

The SRM-SF requires approximately 25 minutes to administer and can be scored by a trained researcher in 20 to 30 minutes. By eliminating the use of moral dilemmas, Gibbs and his colleagues have developed an approach designed to tap moral competency with minimal interference from moral content issues. This strength is also a potential weakness. By totally decontextualizing moral reasoning, the SRM-SF runs the risk of tapping patterns of moral thought far removed from those that come to the fore in actual situations of moral conflict and choice.

Assessment Based on Haan's Theory

Haan (1977, 1978, 1985, 1986, 1991; Haan, Aerts & Cooper, 1985) has offered a revisionist approach to moral reasoning competency that is indebted to the work of Kohlberg but substantially departs from it. Rather than focusing on hypothetical moral reasoning competency, her focus was on the development of people's comprehension and practice of moral interdependency in everyday life contexts. Whereas Kohlberg was interested in defining a moral ideal toward which all development is thought to aim, Haan was interested in defining increasing levels of competency in dealing with moral ambiguity and negotiation. The significance of her theory for sport psychology researchers is discussed elsewhere (Shields & Bredemeier, 1995).

It might reasonably be argued that assessment is the weak link in Haan's contributions. Like Kohlberg, Haan used the moral-dilemma interview format to assess moral levels. Additionally, she coded instances of moral action displayed in simulation games according to her moral levels (Haan et al., 1985). Unlike Kohlberg, however, Haan did not produce a comprehensive scoring manual. She did write a brief scoring guide (Haan, 1977), but it was not designed to be a complete reference. The lack of such a manual arose, in part, from her own theoretical convictions. Haan was a clinical psychologist who objected on theoretical grounds to the use of standardized test construction procedures in the moral domain. She held more tenaciously than Kohlberg to the hermeneutic approach to assessment, an approach that relies on informed processes of interpretation. Learning to score involves working as an apprentice with a trained scorer, often in a group setting, to master the many interpretive nuances that cannot easily be replicated in a manual. The main form of reliability for such an approach is interrater reliability, and Haan and her colleagues were able to obtain quite satisfactory interrater reliability scores (ranging from .81 to .93). Correlations between Haan's "interactional morality" scores and scores on Kohlberg's moral interview run between .50 and .60.

Haan's approach to assessment may be theoretically sound, but its practical effect has been negative. With few people able or willing to engage in the arduous learning process required, the theory remains both underutilized and underdeveloped. These negative consequences have been augmented by the fact that most of the people who worked closely with Haan have gone on to other endeavors, and there are few trained scorers still working in the research field.

A number of sport psychology studies have been based on Haan's model and have featured her method of assessment (Bredemeier, 1985, 1994, 1995; Bredemeier & Shields, 1984,

1986a, 1986b; Bredemeier, Weiss, Shields, & Cooper, 1986, 1987; Frankl, 1991; Romance, Weiss, & Bockoven, 1986). In these studies, researchers have implemented a combination of standard hypothetical dilemmas and sport-specific ones encountered within the bounds of the competitive process. Where reported, interrater reliability has ranged from .85 to .91. Although these studies have added substantially to the literature, the future does not bode well for the Haanian model unless a more convenient and practical measure is developed.

Assessments Based on Gilligan's Theory

Gilligan (1982) has offered a highly influential critique of Kohlberg's theory, arguing that his reliance on the moral principle of justice was both too narrow and gender biased. She found that when women were asked to make "responsibility judgments"[8] in response to their own lived dilemmas, their decisions were more often guided by an ethic of care than justice. She contended that the principles of justice and care reflect differentially the experiences and commitments of males and females. Further, she claimed that women have their own, distinct path of moral development.

Despite the popularity of Gilligan's views, her theory is based on scanty empirical evidence. Rest and Narváez (1994) have made the point well:

> The main problem in empirically testing the 1982 claims of Gilligan is that no method for assessing stages of the Care orientation has been proposed. More than a decade has passed since Gilligan claimed that women follow a different path of moral development than men, but there is still no cross-sectional or longitudinal evidence that this is the case. Without a measure of developmental stages of Care, no studies can be done to test whether the later stages of Care are more advanced, or whether verbal expressions using care language predict to any behavior. ...Although there is research that gives the percent of "Care" language to "Justice" language for a subject on a given dilemma, this kind of analysis does not provide evidence for claiming there is a distinct *path of development* of the Care orientation. ...It is not clear that analyzing utterances into "Care" and "Justice" is anything more than attending to a style of verbal expressiveness (p. 12).

Though Gilligan has not produced a method to assess developmental changes within the Care orientation, her research group has published a sophisticated method for assessing the presence and relative salience of justice and care reasoning (L. Brown et al., 1988). Their method involves interviewing people regarding their real-life moral conflicts and choices and then submitting the narrative to carefully designed hermeneutic procedures. The scoring guide is not a coding manual; it is a reading guide.

In short, the interpretive procedure is as follows. First, the reader locates a description of a moral conflict within the larger interview text and then reads this story a total of four times. The first reading is designed simply to establish the narrative contours of the story (who, what, where, when, why, and so on). In addition, the reader is asked to reflect on his or her own relationship to the story, including one's feelings about it and thoughts about issues of commonality and difference. The second reading attends to how the interviewee situates the self in the narrative. The third reading attends to the use of the care voice, whereas the fourth reading attends to the use of the justice voice. The final step in the process can take several forms, depending on the nature of the research. Typically, narratives are classified as reflecting one of four categories: (a) neither care nor justice is present; (b) the care voice predominates; (c) the justice voice predominates; or (d) the care and justice voices are equally present.

Gilligan's group has offered a sophisticated model for conducting research rooted in qualitative and feminist methodology. Redefining the meaning of the terms in keeping with their theoretical perspective, Gilligan and her colleagues (L. Brown et al., 1988) report satisfactory validity and reliability for their measure, though reported interrater reliability ranges from .50 to .93. Construct validity for the measure was established by demonstrating that the justice orientation predominated among adolescent males and the care orientation predominated among adolescent females. Still, many scholars continue to doubt the basic claim of two distinct moral orientations linked to gender. In fact, the only two sport psychology studies that examined moral orientations in sport contexts (Crown & Heatherington, 1989[9]; Fisher & Bredemeier, 1996[10]) report findings that challenge Gilligan's contention that women tend to be more care oriented and men more justice oriented.

In summary, there are a variety of measures available to assess moral reasoning competency or moral orientation. Each has relative strengths and weaknesses. One important assessment issue that the researcher needs to consider is the level of content specificity desired. Some sport researchers (e.g., Bredemeier & Shields, 1986b; Hall, 1981; Romance et al., 1986) have written sport-specific dilemmas for use in their moral interviews. The more closely the content of dilemmas matches the moral action of interest to the researcher, the more likely assessed reasoning will relate to the corresponding behaviors (Bredemeier, 1985; Power, Higgins, & Kohlberg, 1989). On the other hand, the more content-specific a measure, the more open it becomes to idiosyncratic response and social desirability influence. To compensate for their respective weaknesses, the sport researcher may be interested in combining a general measure of moral reasoning competency like the MJI, DIT, SRM-SF, or Haanian interview with a measure more specifically tailored to a particular sport context, thereby tapping important dimensions of both moral structure and situationally relevant content.

---

8. *Responsibility judgments* are moral decisions about whether the actor is personally obligated to act or not act in a particular situation. They are distinct from deontic judgments, which are simply decisions about whether a particular contemplated action is morally right.

9. Crown and Heatherington (1989) used a scoring scheme based on one developed by Lyons (1982). That scheme classifies the considerations that people use in moral reasoning as reflecting either a morality of justice or a morality of care. Interrater reliability was reported as .88.

10. Fisher was the sole reader of the narratives, which were classified according to Gilligan's latest methodology.

Assessing Behavior

When we turn to moral behavior, an interesting paradox looms. Even more than attitudes, values, beliefs, or underlying reasoning structures, behavior is central to the concept of morality. Ultimately, it is moral action that matters. Despite the pivotal importance of behavior to moral researchers, however, there are no generally accepted instruments measuring it. The reason for this paradox is simple: Assessing moral behavior is one of the most challenging tasks confronting researchers interested in morality.

Effective behavioral assessments must meet philosophical, phenomenological, methodological, and ethical criteria, in addition to standard psychometric ones. Before moral behavior can be assessed, a philosophically defensible definition of what constitutes moral behavior must be put forth. Moreover, the behavior identified for study must not only fall within the moral domain as characterized by philosophers; it must also have clear moral import for the study participant. The participant must perceive the situation as one involving moral choice. Assessing moral behavior creates a new methodological problem as well, because moral action cannot be studied without some means of assessing the actor's intent. If one does not know the intent of the actor, then positive behavior that benefits another can be termed *prosocial,* but not moral. Finally, the assessment technique itself must be ethically sound. For example, is it justifiable to deceive study participants in order to investigate deception or cheating in sport? Though no methodology has yet been developed that completely satisfies all these criteria, a number of different approaches have been employed, including naturalistic studies, self-reports and evaluations by evaluative others, and field experiments.

Piaget's (1932) ground-breaking work on moral development originated with his own naturalistic study of children playing marbles. He observed how children understood, used, and manipulated the rules, and he engaged the children in conversation about the rules. Thus, Piaget got at the meaning of behavior through asking children to interpret their own actions. Although others have argued that game rules are not equivalent to moral rules (Turiel, 1983; Weiblen, 1972), Piaget's quasi-clinical methods have been widely imitated. In the sport realm, for example, Jantz (1975) employed a Piagetian observation-interview approach to demonstrate the applicability of Piagetian moral theory to children's understanding of basketball rules.

Piaget (1932) attempted to deal with the issue of validity through employing a triangulation methodology. Essentially, Piaget would check his interpretation through seeing if it fit multiple observations designed to elicit parallel responses. For example, he observed that young children thought the rules of marbles were fixed and handed down from adults. He interpreted this as reflecting a "heteronomous morality of restraint." To check this interpretation, he interviewed the children about other types of rules, and devised stories that would further reveal their reasoning about rules. Despite Piaget's sensitivity to issues of validity, later psychologists raised objections to Piagetian methods. Interestingly, as psychologists developed more psychometrically sound assessments, they moved from Piaget's engagement with real behavior to the use of brief descriptions of hypothetical behavior. Ecological validity was

sacrificed as other forms of validity and reliability became the center of focus.

Another naturalistic approach to the study of morally relevant behavior is the behavioral inventory. Horrocks (1979) developed the Prosocial Play Behavior Inventory (HPPBI) for use in the upper elementary school. The HPPBI contains 10 behavioral items on which students are rated. Behaviors include arguing, showing off, complaining, teasing, sharing, disobeying rules, and so on. The observer rates each child on each behavior using a 4-point Likert scale ranging from *not at all like the child* to *very much like the child.*

The HPPBI measures prosocial rather than moral behavior. Still, Horrocks believes with some justification that the two are overlapping. In fact, Horrocks found that ratings on the HPPBI correlated moderately with moral reasoning ($r = .55$), providing some evidence of the HPPBI's construct validity. Also, the checklist demonstrated high internal consistency reliability (.96 and .98 for two separate samples).

Like Piaget's methods, the HPPBI directly taps behavior. But, since the observed are not asked for their own interpretations of their behavior, the moral meaning of the rated behaviors remains unclear. In fact, the behaviors represented on the HPPBI are a somewhat arbitrary collection, and they may reflect qualitatively distinct domains of human interaction. Still, for those looking for a brief behavioral checklist of upper elementary children's prosocial play behaviors, the HPPBI would appear to be a sound choice.

A related method of behavioral assessment relies on reports of actual behavior or behavioral tendencies, either by oneself or by others in a position to offer an informed evaluation. Unlike the simple behavioral checklist, these approaches attempt to tap the knowledge of those in a position to evaluate the intentions of study participants as well as their actions. Bredemeier and Shields (1984), for example, used coaches as informed observers. The coaches were provided with a definition of aggression that required them to evaluate not only the outward behavior of their athletes, but also the motivation of that behavior.

The main drawback to using informed observers is that neutral observers are nonexistent. Observations are inevitably colored by a host of unacknowledged personal factors, such as level of interpersonal attraction, similarity of values, and so on. However, when multiple knowledgeable observers are used, this can be a powerful approach to recording behavioral tendencies in a valid and reliable way. Unfortunately, to date we have no good sport illustrations of this method.

Another approach to assessing morally relevant behaviors is the field experiment. In fact, this approach has been featured in such classic social psychology experiments as the Hartshorne and May (1928) character studies, the Milgrim "shock" experiments (Milgrim, 1974), Zimbardo's prison-and-guard simulation (Zimbardo, Haney, Banks, & Jaffe, 1975), and studies based on Prisoner's Dilemma (Luce & Raiffa, 1957; cf. Deutsch, 1985) and its group variant (Haan et al., 1985). An example of a morally relevant field experiment in the sport realm is provided by Kleiber and Roberts (1981). They used Knight and Kagen's (1977) Social Behavior Scale (SBS) to assess the effects of participation in a 2-week kick-soccer tournament on children's altruistic and rivalrous behavioral tendencies. The

SBS requires respondents to make choices among four possible distributions of poker chips, exchangeable for prizes. In all four options, the respondent receives three chips for him- or herself, but the number given to "the other" (e.g., an unnamed child in another school) varies from one to four.

The issue of motivation or intent is sidestepped in the field experiment paradigm. The idea is to contrive a situation that presents a clear and salient moral choice. The moral significance of action can then be inferred, it is assumed, from the participant's behavioral choice. Despite the effort of researchers to develop situations in which the moral issues are obvious, interpretation of field experiment results is still problematic. Even in seemingly straight forward situations, intent cannot be inferred from behavior. One reason is that people often enter social psychology experiments with a mindset to "figure out" what the experimenter wants or to "outwit" the experimenter. For example, in the Kleiber and Roberts (1981) experiment, a participant could have

decided to award four chips to the unknown other not out of altruism, but in hopes that doing so might shorten the experience. Even when well-intentioned, people often attach idiosyncratic meanings to their behavior. Because morality concerns motives and intentions as much as behavior, it does not easily lend itself to approaches that merely quantify behavioral responses.

Hybrid Measures

It is possible to assess multiple dimensions of moral functioning with a single instrument. One clear advantage of hybrid measures is the ability to tap a broader spectrum of morally-relevant personal attributes than is possible with any single unidimensional instrument. On the other hand, these measures are probably less adequate in their assessment of a particular construct than an instrument that has been designed to focus solely on that construct.

Stephens, Bredemeier, and Shields (in press) developed a

Table 3

One Scenario From the Judgments about Moral Behavior in Sport Questionnaire (JAMBYSQ)

Sally is a defender in front of the goal on a corner kick when the ball is volleyed toward Sally's position. Although she cannot get her foot to the ball to prevent the goal, she could deflect it outside the goalpost with one of her hands. Because the goal box is so packed with players, the referee will not see the illegal act. Sally must decide whether to use her hands.

As you can see, Sally is in a tough position. Imagine what it would be like to be in her situation. She might consider a number of things. She might think about her desire to win, what her coach or teammates would want, what would be fair, etc. Below you are asked to make decisions about what Sally *should do* and what you believe that other players actually *would do*. Try to be as honest as you can in answering these questions.

1. Ideally, what do you think Sally *should* do? (circle your answer)
    a. Sally *should* use her hands to deflect the ball.
    b. Sally *should not* use her hands to deflect the ball.

2. Realistically, how many girls on your team *would* use their hands to deflect the ball if they were in Sally's situation? (circle the number below)

1	2	3	4	5
none of the players	a few players	about half players	most of players	everyone players

3. Finally, imagine that *you* are in Sally's situation. Realistically, what do you think *you would do*?
    a. I *would* use my hands to deflect the ball.
    b. I *would not* use my hands to deflect the ball.

4. Listed below are a series of statements. Each statement changes the story in some way by adding detail. Some statements will present situations that are more tempting than others. First, read the statement and imagine that you were in that situation. Then, look at the numbers below stating how tempted you would be to *use your hands to deflect the ball*, and then write the number you have chosen on the line next to the situation.

1	2	3	4	5
not at all tempted	not very tempted	a little bit tempted	somewhat tempted	very tempted

_____ a. If the other team had gotten away with the same thing earlier in the game.
_____ b. If you had seen your coach praise one of your teammates for similar behavior in a previous game.
_____ c. If your team needed to have their spirits lifted.
_____ d. If the score was tied and this action was necessary to win the game.
_____ e. If you felt that your team trusted you to do all that you could to help the team.
_____ f. If the officials hadn't been calling a very tight game, so it would be easy to take advantage of the situation.

5. Which of the above situations (a, b, c, d, e, or f) did you find *most tempting*? _____

6. Imagine that you're actually in that situation. How likely would you be to use your hands to deflect the ball? (Circle your answer below.)

1	2	3	4	5
not at all likely	not very likely	a little bit likely	somewhat likely	very likely

---

Table 4
Coded Sample Items From the Gibbons et al. (1995) Measure of Moral Judgment, Reason, and Intention

1. While playing in PE class, you wonder what to do when classmates argue with you.
   a. Do you think it is OK to argue in PE class? (JUDGMENT)
      (1) It's OK to argue.
      (2) It's sometimes OK to argue.
      (3) It's not OK to argue.
   b. Which is the most important thing to consider when you decide whether it is OK to argue? (REASON)
      (1) whether or not I would get punished
      (2) whether I wanted to get even with a classmate
      (3) whether or not it is nice
      (4) whether it's against the rules
      (5) whether or not it's fair or right
   c. If classmates argue with you in future PE classes, what do you think you will do? (INTENTION)
      (3) never argue
      (2) sometimes argue
      (1) most of the time argue

---

hybrid instrument designed for use with upper elementary school girls participating in youth soccer. The Judgments About Moral Behavior in Sport Questionnaire (JAMBYSQ) was constructed to assess players' (a) self-described fair play action tendencies, (b) legitimacy judgments concerning unfair play, (c) developmentally influenced moral motives, as these relate to temptations to engage in unfair play, and (d) perceptions of team norms pertaining to unfair play behavior.

The JAMBYSQ consists of three soccer scenarios depicting hypothetical protagonists faced with choices about whether to engage in unfair but strategically advantageous behavior (lie to an official, hurt an opponent, and violate a game rule). Six items, parallel in format and content, follow each scenario. For an example of one of the scenarios and the items that follow it, see Table 3 (cheating scenario).

Item 1 was designed to tap the respondent's deontic judgment. In the cheating scenario, for example, the respondent is asked to judge whether the protagonist should or should not cheat. By estimating the number of teammates who actually would engage in the unfair behavior, Item 2 taps one dimension of moral atmosphere. Items 3 and 6 tap the respondent's self-described action tendencies. Finally, Items 4 and 5 assess dimensions of moral motivation. Item 4 presents six statements that reflect scenario modifications, each of which offers a possible motive for engaging in unfair behavior. Three of the six statements propose preconventional motives (a, d, and f) and three offer conventional motives (b, c, and e).

The JAMBYSQ appears to demonstrate good internal consistency and construct validity (Stephens, Bredemeier, & Shields, in press).[11] However, further testing is clearly needed. In particular, the question of whether the JAMBYSQ validly taps preconventional and conventional moral motivation has not yet been answered. A practical limitation is that the scenarios are soccer specific, though parallel scenarios have been developed for several other sports.

Another hybrid measure was developed by Gibbons, Ebbeck, and Weiss (1995) for an important study analyzing the effects of a fair-play program. The instrument was designed for use in conjunction with Horrocks' (1979) Prosocial Play Behavior Inventory. For each of the 10 behaviors observed in the HPPBI, three questions were written for the children to answer. The questions were designed to tap three critical moral constructs: moral judgment, moral reason, and moral intention. By these terms, Gibbons et al. are referring to three of the four moral processes identified by Rest (1984; cf. Shields & Bredemeier, 1995; see below). Table 4 presents the three questions that correspond to arguing.

Gibbons et al. (1995) report good internal-consistency reliabilities for their measure (Cronbach's alpha ranged from .80 to .92). Its validity, on the other hand, remains uncertain. For our purposes, it may prove instructive to examine these potential validity problems because they reflect common difficulties that can arise when single questions are used to assess highly complex psychological processes.

For each of the 10 behaviors represented on the Gibbons et al. (1995) measure, the first question is designed to assess moral judgment. It is implied that respondents who answer that it is not OK to argue, for example, are more advanced in their moral judgment than are those who answer otherwise. If the response options on the instrument do indeed reflect a developmental progression, however, then we would expect responses keyed higher to be more comprehensive and coherent. Are there really no cases, however, when arguing is justifiable? Doesn't a blanket prohibition of arguing reflect a less differentiated position than one recognizing the legitimacy of arguing in some circumstances? Moreover, is the implicit prohibition against argument even grounded in *moral* considerations, or does it stem more from concern about classroom or gymnasium management?

The second question pertaining to each behavior is designed to tap Kohlberg-related moral reasoning maturity. Supposedly,

---

11. The statistical procedures and results supporting this statement cannot easily be summarized, and the interested reader is referred to the original article.

the item responses as listed in Table 4 are in order of increasing moral stage. In each case, however, the moral stage designation of item responses is open to question. For example, according to the test key, the response reflecting the highest stage of moral reasoning is "whether or not it's fair or right." People at all developmental levels, however, have a conception of right and fairness, and so a person at any stage might select this item.

Gibbons et al. (1995) might reply that their measure, like all recognition measures of moral reasoning maturity, does not attempt to assess moral stage directly, but only indirectly. Moral reasoning development is assessed through probabilistic associations between moral stages and endorsement of particular moral content (in this case, one specific reason for why it is or is not OK to argue). For example, it is more likely that a person at Stage 5 will select an item that appeals to the conceptions of right and fairness than will someone at Stage 2. This is an acceptable strategy. Nonetheless, it must be remembered that a Stage 2 person will also think about what is right and fair. Everyone who has spent time with a three-year-old child knows that these words enter the vocabulary early. Although there are indeed probabilistic associations between a particular moral stage and the type of moral content that will be attractive, these associations are highly imperfect guides to identifying moral stages.

The only way to sidestep the problem is to incorporate in the measure a sufficiently large number of items with a sufficiently diverse range of stage-associated content. Thus, the respondent to Rest's (1979, 1986a) Defining Issues Test rates 72 distinct items, as opposed to the 5 items in the Gibbons et al. measure. Equally important, the DIT was designed to make it impossible to fake a high score, but the Gibbons et al. measure seems eminently teachable (that is, an intervention explicitly designed to enhance fair play could encourage the selection of item alternatives that present the term *fair*, regardless of the respondent's moral reasoning maturity).

Finally, the third question regarding each behavior reflected in the Gibbons et al. (1995) assessment seeks to operationalize "moral intention" by asking what the respondent intends to do. There are two potential problems with the question. First, because terms like "arguing" are loaded with social and moral connotations, answers may be skewed by a social desirability response set. This makes the question particularly problematic for assessing the effects of an intervention program since what may change from pretest to posttest, among other things, is the respondent's knowledge of what the experimenter wants. The validity of the question might also be suspect because of its abstract nature—its lack of context. In our lived experience, moral intention is forged through a complex process of weighing moral motivations against competing nonmoral motivations in the heat of conflict and choice (Rest, 1984). Simply asking someone whether they intend to argue in the future may provide little or no insight into what their actual intention will be when a real situation of conflict arises.

The above discussion of the measure developed by Gibbons and her colleagues highlights the need to carefully examine those issues of validity that we raised earlier. Measures that purport to be tethered to a developmental theory need to demonstrate clear age trends, hierarchical organization, and predictive validity. With all moral measures, the possibility of contamination due to people's desire to present themselves as moral also needs to be carefully considered. These comments point us to our final topic: future directions for moral research in the context of sport.

Future Directions

Researchers are beginning to develop a variety of measures and methods to assess the moral dimensions of sport experience. Still, a great deal of research in this emerging area of study relies on measures that have been subjected to little scrutiny. There is an urgent need to develop and employ valid and reliable measures that can shed light on such important questions as what aspects of organized sport enhance participants' moral development and what aspects are detrimental to it. Under what conditions does sport promote growth, and under what conditions does it retard growth? How can a commitment to fair and noninjurious play be nurtured? Does the moral atmosphere of youth sport influence participants' values and behaviors outside of the sport context?

Both qualitative and quantitative approaches are necessary to begin to answer some of these questions. We conclude this chapter with brief discussions of three important arenas in which future work might substantially aid our effort to better understand the moral dimensions of sport experience: the multidimensional nature of morality, the social dimension of morality, and the connection of morality to life history.

Most of the early work explicitly dealing with morality in sport focused on the relationship between a sport participant's level of moral reasoning maturity and some other variable of interest. Without doubt, moral stage analysis will continue to play a prominent role in sport morality research. In this connection, a valid and reliable measure of sport-specific moral reasoning is urgently needed. But moral psychology is much more extensive than moral reasoning development, and the field would profit from future research on other dimensions of moral psychology.

To help clarify the various psychological processes that moral action entails, Rest (1983, 1984) developed a four-component model of moral action, highlighting the processes of moral perception, reasoning and judgment, choice, and implementation (cf. Shields & Bredemeier, 1995). To date, only the process of moral reasoning and judgment has been adequately operationalized. We are in need of valid and reliable measures of moral perception, choice, and implementation.[12]

In addition to developing new measures to assess additional components of moral psychology, we need to recognize that morality is also a characteristic of groups. As groups evolve, they develop their own moral culture out of the synergistic interactions of the group's members. The term *moral atmosphere* has been coined to refer to the shared beliefs and values held by a group that have moral content (Power et al., 1989).

A couple of pilot investigations have been published that touch on the theme of moral atmosphere in the context of sport.

---

12. The authors and their colleagues currently are developing a sport-specific adaptation of Rest's (1979, 1986a) Defining Issues Test, and measures of moral identity and moral motivation, constructs related to the process of moral choice.

In the first, Shields, Bredemeier, Gardner, and Bostrom (1995) constructed a simple six-item Team Norm Questionnaire (TNQ). Designed to assess team norms regarding cheating and aggression, the TNQ asked respondents two questions that required them to estimate how many of their teammates would violate a rule if it would help their team win, and two questions that required them to estimate how many of their teammates would deliberately hurt an opponent if it would help their team win. Respondents also were asked about their coach's approval or disapproval of cheating and aggression. The authors assumed that a respondent's estimates of the number of teammates who would engage in a particular behavior would provide an indication of that individual's perceptions about collective norms for that behavior. Similarly, it was assumed that the coach plays a pivotal role in shaping collective norms. Stephens and Bredemeier (1996) employed a similar technique to assess the moral atmosphere of girls' soccer teams. These efforts are clearly first steps. Yet to be developed are valid and reliable measures that yield a comprehensive assessment of the interrelated components of moral atmosphere in sport contexts.

In addition to quantitative measures designed to assess the social and psychological aspects of morality, qualitative methods of investigation will also play a crucial role in future research. One area where these methods are particularly suitable is in the study of morality in the context of life history. For example, in-depth analyses of the life stories of sport moral exemplars may reveal information that more quantitative methods are likely to miss.

In short, the agenda for researchers who investigate sport morality is large and challenging. Most existing instruments in the area of sport and morality are in need of additional testing to ensure their validity and reliability. Moreover, there is a need to develop new measures and methods to assess the relations between morality and other constructs of theoretical and practical importance. If our understanding of the multidimensional nature of morality is to progress, we must not only pay increasing attention to the validity and reliability of our measures. We also must design research programs that coordinate the qualitative and quantitative assessment of morality in particular sport contexts and for groups and individuals with specific life experiences.

References

Bandura, A. (1991). Social cognitive theory of moral thought and action. In W. Kurtines & J. Gerwitz (Ed.), *Handbook of moral behavior and development: Vol. 1: Theory* (pp. 45-103). Hillsdale, NJ: Lawrence Erlbaum Associates.

Beller, J. (1990). A moral reasoning intervention program for Division I athletes—Can athletes learn not to cheat? (Doctoral dissertation, University of Idaho, 1990). *Dissertation Abstracts International, 52*, 01-A, 109.

Beller, J., & Stoll, S. (1992). A moral reasoning intervention program for student-athletes. *The Academic Athletic Journal*, Spring, 43-57.

Blair, S. (1985). Professionalization of attitude toward play in children and adults. *Research Quarterly in Exercise and Sport, 56*, 82-83.

Blasi, A. (1987). Comment: The psychological definitions of morality. In J. Kegan & S. Lamb (Eds.), *The emergence of morality in young children* (pp. 83-90). Chicago: The University of Chicago Press.

Blasi, A. (1990). How should psychologists define morality? or, The negative side effects of philosophy's influence on psychology. In

T. E. Wren (Ed.), *The moral domain: Essays in the ongoing discussion between philosophy and the social sciences* (pp. 38-70). Cambridge, MA: The Massachusetts Institute of Technology Press.

Braithwaite, V., & Law, H. (1985). Structure of human values: Testing the adequacy of the Rokeach Value Survey. *Journal of Personality & Social Psychology, 49*, 250-263.

Bredemeier, B. (1985). Moral reasoning and the perceived legitimacy of intentionally injurious sport acts. *Journal of Sport Psychology, 7*, 110-124.

Bredemeier, B. (1994). Children's moral reasoning and their assertive, aggressive, and submissive tendencies in sport and daily life. *Journal of Sport and Exercise Psychology, 16*, 1-14.

Bredemeier, B. (1995). Divergence in children's moral reasoning about issues in daily life and sport specific contexts. *The International Journal of Sport Psychology, 26*, 453-463.

Bredemeier, B., & Shields, D. (1984). The utility of moral stage analysis in the investigation of athletic aggression. *Sociology of Sport Journal, 1*, 138-149.

Bredemeier, B., & Shields, D. (1986a). Game reasoning and interactional morality. *Journal of Genetic Psychology, 147*, 257-275.

Bredemeier, B., & Shields, D. (1986b). Moral growth among athletes and nonathletes: A comparative analysis. *Journal of Genetic Psychology, 147*, 7-18.

Bredemeier, B., Weiss, M., Shields, D., & Cooper, B. (1986). The relationship of sport involvement with children's moral reasoning and aggression tendencies. *Journal of Sport Psychology, 8*, 304-318.

Bredemeier, B., Weiss, M., Shields, D., & Cooper, B. (1987). The relationship between children's legitimacy judgments and their moral reasoning, aggression tendencies and sport involvement. *Sociology of Sport Journal, 4*, 48-60.

Bredemeier, B., Weiss, M., Shields, D., & Shewchuk, R. (1986). Promoting moral growth in a summer sport camp: The implementation of theoretically grounded instructional strategies. *Journal of Moral Education, 15*, 212-220.

Bredemeier, B., Shields, D., Carlton, E., & Miller, S. (1997). *Temptation to violate game rules in three reward-structure conditions: Associations with moral reasoning, achievement orientation, and attitudes toward social interdependence*. Manuscript submitted for publication.

Brower, S. (1992). An assessment of the moral reasoning patterns of selected collegiate athletes (Doctoral dissertation, University of Northern Colorado). *Dissertation Abstracts International, 53*, 7-A, 2261.

Brown, A. (1992). Moral reasoning, motivational orientation, sport experience, and participant conduct in sport (Doctoral dissertation, University of Minnesota). *Dissertation Abstracts International, 53*, 11-A, 4081.

Brown, L., Argyris, D., Attanucci, J., Bardige, B., Gilligan, C., Johnston, K., Miller, B., Osborne, D., Tappan, M., Ward, J., Wiggins, G., & Wilcox, D. (1988). *A guide to reading narratives of moral conflict and choice for self and moral voice* (Monograph No. 1). Cambridge, MA: Harvard Graduate School of Education, Center for the Study of Gender, Education, and Human Development.

Card, A. (1981, April). *Orientation toward winning as a function of athletic participation, grade level, and gender*. Paper presented at the annual meeting of the AAHPERD, Detroit.

Carlton, E., Miller, S., & Bredemeier, B. (1997). *Promoting children's sociomoral development in a physical education context*. Manuscript submitted for publication.

Case, B., Greer, H., & Lacourse, M. (1987). Moral judgment development and perceived legitimacy of spectator behavior in sport. *Journal of Sport Behavior, 10*, 147-156.

Chafetz, J. (1984). *Sex and advantage: A comparative macrostructural theory of sex stratification*. Totowa, NJ: Roman & Allanheld.

Colby, A., Kohlberg, L., Speicher, B., Hewer, A., Candee, D., Gibbs, J., & Power, C. (1987). *The measurement of moral judgment*.

Cambridge, MA: Cambridge University Press.

Crawford, M. (1957). Critical incidents in intercollegiate athletics and derived standards for professional ethics (Doctoral dissertation, University of Texas, Austin). *Dissertation Abstracts International, 18,* 02, 489.

Crown, J., & Heatherington, L., (1989). The costs of winning? The role of gender in moral reasoning and judgments about competitive athletic encounters. *Journal of Sport and Exercise Psychology, 11,* 281-289.

Crowne, D., & Marlowe, D. (1960). A new scale of social desirability independent of psychopathology. *Journal of Consulting Psychology, 24,* 349-354.

Davis, H., & Baskett, G. (1979). Do athletes and nonathletes have different values? *Athletic Administration, 13,* 17-19.

Dawley, D., Troyer, M., & Shaw, J. (1951). Relationship between observed behavior in elementary school physical education and test responses. *Research Quarterly, 222,* 71-76.

Deutsch, M. (1985). *Distributive justice: A social-psychological perspective.* New Haven: Yale University Press.

Dewey, J. (1939). *Theory of valuation.* Chicago: University of Chicago Press.

Duda, J., Olson, L., & Templin, T. (1991). The relationship of task and ego orientation to sportsmanship attitudes and the perceived legitimacy of injurious acts. *Research Quarterly for Exercise and Sport, 62,* 79-87.

English, H., & English, A. (1958). *A comprehensive dictionary of psychological and psychoanalystic terms.* Essex, England: Longman.

Enright, R., Franklin, C., & Manheim, L. (1980). Children's distributive justice reasoning: A standardized and objective scale. *Developmental Psychology, 16,* 193-202.

Fisher, L., & Bredemeier, B. (1996). *Caring about injustice: The moral orientations of professional women bodybuilders.* Unpublished manuscript.

Flory, C. (1958). Sportsmanship attitudes of college students toward situations in competitive athletics (Doctoral dissertation, The University of Texas, Austin). *Dissertation Abstracts Internation, 19,* 06, 1269.

Floyd, V. (1939). *The relationship of information to practice in sportsmanship.* Unpublished Master's Thesis, University of Texas at Austin.

Fraleigh, W. (1984). *Right actions in sport: Ethics for contestants.* Champaign, IL: Human Kinetics.

Frankena, W. (1963). *Ethics.* Englewood Cliffs, N.J.: Prentice Hall.

Frankl, D. (1991). Sport participation and moral reasoning: Relationships among aspects of hostility, altruism, and sport involvement (Doctoral dissertation, Southern Illinois University at Carbondale). *Dissertation Abstracts International, 51,* 7-A, 2311-2312).

Gibbons, S., Ebbeck, V., & Weiss, M. (1995). Fair play for kids: Effects on the moral development of children in physical education. *Research Quarterly for Exercise and Sport, 66,* 247-255.

Gibbs, J., Arnold, K., Morgan, R., Schwartz, E., Gavaghan, M., & Tappan, M. (1984). Construction and validation of a multiple-choice measure of moral reasoning. *Child Development, 55,* 527-536.

Gibbs, J., Basinger, K., & Fuller, D. (1992). *Moral maturity: Measuring the development of sociomoral reflection.* Hillsdale, NJ: Lawrence Erlbaum.

Gibbs, J., & Widaman, K. (1982). *Social intelligence: Measuring the development of sociomoral reflection.* Englewood Cliffs, NJ: Prentice Hall.

Gill, D., & Deeter, T. (1989). Development of the Sport Orientation Questionnaire. *Research Quarterly for Sport and Exercise, 59,* 191-202.

Gilligan, C. (1982). *In a different voice: Psychological theory and women's development.* Cambridge: Harvard University.

Haan, N. (1977). *A manual for interactional morality.* Unpublished manuscript. Berkeley: Institute of Human Development, University of California at Berkeley.

Haan, N. (1978). Two moralities in action contexts: Relationship to thought, ego regulation, and development. *Journal of Personality and Social Psychology, 36,* 286-305.

Haan, N. (1985). Processes of moral development: Cognitive or social disequilibrium? *Developmental Psychology, 21,* 996-1006.

Haan, N. (1986). Systematic variability in the quality of moral action as defined by two formulations. *Journal of Personality and Social Psychology, 50,* 1271-1284.

Haan, N. (1991). Moral development and action from a social constructivist perspective. In W. Kurtines & J. Gewirtz (Eds.), *Handbook of moral behavior and development: Vol. 1: Theory* (pp. 251-273). Hillsdale, NJ: Lawrence Erlbaum Associates, Inc.

Haan, N., Aerts, E., & Cooper, B. (1985). *On moral grounds: The search for a practical morality.* New York: New York University.

Hacker, C. (1992). Moral judgment and the perceived legitimacy of injurious acts among collegiate athletes (Doctoral dissertation, University of Oregon). *Dissertation Abstracts International, 54,* 1-A, 124.

Hahm, C. (1989). Moral reasoning and development among general students, physical education majors, and student athletes (Korea, United States) (Doctoral dissertation, University of Idaho). *Dissertation Abstracts International, 50,* 08-A, 2422.

Hahm, C., Beller, J., & Stoll, S. (1989, March). *A new moral values inventory.* Paper presented at the annual convention of the Northwest District of the American Alliance for Health, Physical Education, Recreation, and Dance, Boise, ID.

Hall, E. (1981). Moral development levels of athletes in sport specific and general social situations (Doctoral dissertation, Texas Women's University). *Dissertation Abstracts International, 42,* 08-A, 3498.

Hartshorne, H., & May, M. (1928). *Studies in the nature of character: Vol. 1. Studies in deceit.* New York: Macmillan.

Hartshorne, H., May, M., & Maller, J. (1929). *Studies in the nature of character: Vol. 2. Studies in self control.* New York: Macmillan.

Hartshorne, H., May, M., & Schuttleworth, F. (1930). *Studies in the nature of character: Vol. 3. Studies in the organization of character.* New York: Macmillan.

Haskins, M. (1960). Problem solving test of sportsmanship. *Research Quarterly, 31,* 601-606.

Haskins, M., & Hartman, B. (1960). Action-choice tests for competitive sports situations. Copyright 1960.

Heath, R., & Fogel, D. (1978). Terminal and instrumental? An inquiry into Rokeach's value survey. *Psychological Reports, 42,* 1147-1154.

Henkel, S., & Earls, N. (1985). The moral judgment of physical education teachers. *Journal of Teaching in Physical Education, 4,* 178-189.

Horrocks, R. (1979). The relationship of selected prosocial play behaviors in children to moral reasoning, youth sports, participation, and perception of sportsmanship (Doctoral dissertation, University of North Carolina, Greensboro). *Dissertation Abstracts International, 40,* 04-A, 1949.

Huston, L., & Duda, J. (1992). *The relationship of goal orientation and competitive level to the endorsement of aggressive acts in football.* Unpublished manuscript.

Jantz, R. (1975). Moral thinking in male elementary pupils as reflected by perception of basketball rules. *Research Quarterly, 46,* 414-421.

Johnson, M. (1969). Construction of sportsmanship attitude scales. *Research Quarterly, 40,* 312-316.

Katz, A. (1960). The functional approach to the study of attitude. *Public Opinion Quarterly, 24,* 163-203.

Kidd, T., & Woodman, W. (1975). Sex and orientation toward winning in sport. *Research Quarterly, 46,* 476-483.

Kirkpatrick, J. (1940, September). Sportsmanship: What do you mean? *The School*, pp. 50-54.

Kistler, J. (1957). Attitudes expressed about behavior demonstrated in specific situations occurring in sports. *Annual Proceedings of the National College Physical Education Association for Men*, *60*, 55-58.

Kleiber, D., & Roberts, G. (1981). The effects of sport experience in the development of social character: An exploratory investigation. *Journal of Sport Psychology*, *3*, 114-122.

Knight, G., & Kagen, S. (1977). Development of prosocial and competitive behaviors in Anglo-American and Mexican-American children. *Child Development*, *48*, 1385-1394.

Knoppers, A. (1985). Professionalization of attitudes: A review and critique. *Quest*, *37*, 92-102.

Knoppers, A., Schuiteman, J., & Love, B. (1986). Winning is not the only thing. *Sociology of Sport Journal*, *3*, 43-56.

Knoppers, A., Schuiteman, J., & Love, B. (1988). Professional orientation of junior tennis players. *International Review for the Sociology of Sport*, *23*, 243-254.

Knoppers, A., Shaw, L., & Love, B. (1984, July). *Professionalism of attitudes in junior tennis players*. Paper presented at the Olympic Scientific Congress, Eugene, OR.

Kohlberg, L. (1969). Stage and sequence: The cognitive-developmental approach to socialization. In D. A. Goslin (Ed.), *Handbook of socialization theory and research* (pp. 347-480). Chicago: Rand McNally.

Kohlberg, L. (1971a). From is to ought: How to commit the naturalistic fallacy and get away with it in the study of moral development. In T. Mischel (Ed.), *Cognitive development and epistemology* (pp. 151-235). New York: Academic Press.

Kohlberg, L. (1971b). Stages of moral development as a basis for moral education. In C. Beck, B. Crittenden, & E. Sullivan (Eds.), *Moral education: Interdisciplinary approaches* (pp. 23-92). Toronto: University of Toronto Press.

Kohlberg, L. (1981). *Essays on moral development: Vol. 1. The philosophy of moral development*. San Francisco: Harper & Row.

Kohlberg, L. (1984). *Essays on moral development: Vol. 2. The psychology of moral development*. San Francisco: Harper & Row.

Kroll, W. (1975, March). *Psychology of sportsmanship*. Paper presented at the sports psychology meeting, National Association for Sport and Physical Education, Atlantic City, NJ.

Lakie, W. (1964). Expressed attitudes of various groups of athletes toward athletic competition. *Research Quarterly*, *35*, 497-503.

Lee, M. (1977). *Expressed values of varsity football players, intramural football players, and non-football players*. Eugene, OR: Microform Publications.

Lee, M. (1986). Moral and social growth through sport: The coach's role. In G. Gleeson, (Ed.), *The growing child in competitive sport* (pp. 248-255). London: Hodder and Stoughton.

Loy, J., Birrell, S., & Rose, D. (1976). Attitudes held toward agonetic activities as a function of selected social identities. *Quest*, *26*, 81-93.

Luce, R., & Raiffa, H. (1957). *Games and decision: Introduction and critical survey*. New York: John Wiley and Sons.

Lyons, N. (1982). *Conceptions of self and morality and modes of moral choice: Identifying justice and care in judgments of actual moral dilemmas*. Unpublished doctoral dissertation, Harvard University.

Madhere, S. (1993). The development and validation of the Current Life Orientation Scale. *Psychological Reports*, *72*, 467-472.

Maloney, T., & Petrie, B. (1972). Professionalization of attitude toward play among Canadian school pupils as a function of sex, grade, and athletic participation. *Journal of Leisure Research*, *4*, 184-195.

Mantel, R., & Vander Velden, L. (1974). The relationship between the professionalization of attitude toward play of preadolescent boys and participation in organized sport. In G. Sage (Ed.), *Sport and American society* (2nd ed.) (pp. 172-178). Reading, MA: Addison-Wellesley.

Marczynski, G. (1989). The effect of a moral dilemma discussion group on the social behavior of male college athletes (Doctoral dissertation, University of South Dakota, Vermillion). *Dissertation Abstracts International*, *50*, 07-A, 1946.

McAfee, R. (1955). Sportsmanship attitudes of sixth, seventh, and eighth grade boys. *Research Quarterly*, *26*, 120-121.

McElroy, M. (1981, April). *Parent-child relations and orientations toward sport*. Paper presented at the annual meeting of the AAHPERD, Detroit.

McElroy, M., & Kirkendall, D. (1980). Significant others and professionalized sport attitudes. *Research Quarterly for Exercise and Sport*, *51*, 645-667.

Miethe, T. (1985). The validity and reliability of value measurements. *Journal of Psychology*, *119*, 441-453.

Milgrim, S. (1974). *Obedience to authority: An experimental view*. New York: Harper & Row.

Moon, Y. (1986). A review of cross-cultural studies on moral judgment development using the Defining Issues Test. *Behavior Science Research*, *20*, 147-177.

Mueller, D., & Wornhoff, S. (1990). Distinguishing personal and social values. *Educational & Psychological Measurement*, *50*, 691-699.

Naples, R. (1987). The discussion of sport-specific dilemmas to enhance the moral development of club sport participation (Doctoral dissertation, Temple University). *Dissertation Abstracts International*, *49*, 01-A, 57.

Ng, S. (1982). Choosing between the ranking and rating procedures for the comparison of values across cultures. *European Journal of Social Psychology*, *12*, 169-172.

Nicholson, C. (1979). Some attitudes associated with sports participation among junior high school females. *Research Quarterly*, *50*, 661-667.

Nixon, H. (1980). Orientation toward sports participation among college students. *Journal of Sport Behavior*, *3*, 29-45.

Petrie, B. (1971a). Achievement orientations in adolescent attitudes toward play. *International Review of Sport Sociology*, *6*, 89-99.

Petrie, B. (1971b). Achievement orientations in the motivation of Canadian university students toward physical activity. *Journal of the Canadian Association of Health, Physical Education, and Recreation*, *37*, 7-13.

Piaget, J. (1965). *Moral judgment of the child* (M. Gabain, Trans.). New York: Free Press. (Original work published in 1932)

Power, C., Higgins, A., & Kohlberg, L. (1989). *Lawrence Kohlberg's approach to moral education*. New York: Columbia University Press.

Rankin, W., & Grube, J. (1980). A comparison of ranking and rating procedures for value system measurement. *European Journal of Social Psychology*, *10*, 233-246.

Rest, J. (1979). *Development in judging moral issues*. Minneapolis: University of Minnesota Press.

Rest, J. (1983). Morality. In P. Mussen (Series Ed.), J. Flavell & E. Markman (Vol. Eds), *Manual of child psychology: Vol. 3. Cognitive development* (4th ed.) (pp. 556-629). New York: John Wiley & Sons.

Rest, J. (1984). The major components of morality. In W. Kurtines & J. Gewirtz (Eds.), *Morality, moral behavior, and moral development* (pp. 356-629). New York: John Wiley & Sons.

Rest, J. (1986a). *Manual for the Defining Issues Test*. Minneapolis: Center for the Study of Ethical Development, University of Minnesota.

Rest, J. (1986b). *Moral development: Advances in research and theory*. New York: Praeger Press.

Rest, J., & Narváez, D. (Eds.) (1994). *Moral development in the professions: Psychology and applied ethics*. Hillsdale, NJ: Lawrence Erlbaum.

Rokeach, M. (1968). *Beliefs, attitudes, and values*. San Francisco: Jossey-Bass.

Rokeach, M. (1973). *The nature of human values*. New York: Free Press.

Rokeach, M. (1979). *Understanding human values: Individual and societal*. New York: Free Press.

Romance, T., Weiss, M., & Bockoven, J. (1986). A program to promote moral development through elementary school physical education. *Journal of Teaching in Physical Education, 5*, 126-136.

Ryan, K., Williams, J., & Wimer, B. (1990). Athletic aggression: Perceived legitimacy and behavioral intentions in girls' high school basketball. *Journal of Sport and Exercise Psychology, 12*, 48-55.

Sage, G. (1980). Orientation toward sport of male and female intercollegiate athletes. *Journal of Sport Psychology, 2*, 355-362.

Sage, G. (1990). *Power and ideology in American sport*. Champaign, IL: Human Kinetics.

Schmitt, M., Schwartz, S., Steyer, R., & Schmitt, T. (1993). Measurement models for the Schwartz values. *European Journal of Psychological Assessment, 9*, 107-121.

Schwartz, S. (1994a). Are there universal aspects in the structure and contents of human values? *Journal of Social Issues, 50*, 19-45.

Schwartz, S. (1994b). Studying human values. In A.M. Bouvy, F.J.R. van de Vijver, P. Boski, & P.G. Schmitz (Eds.), *Journeys into cross-cultural psychology* (pp. 239-254). Amsterdam, Netherlands: Swets & Zeitlinger.

Shields, D. (1986). *Growing beyond prejudices*. Mystic, CT: Twenty-Third Publications.

Shields, D., & Bredemeier, B. (1995). *Character development and physical activity*. Champaign, IL: Human Kinetics.

Shields, D., Bredemeier, B., Gardner, D., & Bostrom, A. (1995). Leadership, cohesion, and team norms regarding cheating and aggression. *Sociology of Sport Journal, 12*, 324-336.

Silva, J. (1983). The perceived legitimacy of rule violating behavior in sport. *Journal of Sport Psychology, 5*, 438-448.

Smith, M. (1963). Personal values in the study of lives. In R.W. White (Ed.), *The study of lives* (p. 332). Englewood Cliffs, NJ: Prentice-Hall.

Snyder, E., & Spreitzer, E. (1979). Orientations toward sport: Intrinsic, normative, and extrinsic. *Journal of Sport Psychology, 1*, 170-175.

Solomon, G., Bredemeier, B., & Shields, D. (1993). *Manual for the Gender Stratification Interview*. Unpublished manuscript, University of California at Berkeley.

Stephens, D., & Bredemeier, B. (1996). Moral atmosphere and judgments about aggression in girls' soccer: Relationships among moral and motivational variables. *Journal of Sport and Exercise Psychology, 18*, 158-173.

Stephens, D., Bredemeier, B., & Shields, D. (In press). Construction of a measure designed to assess players' descriptions and prescriptions for moral behavior in youth sport soccer. *International Journal of Sport Psychology*.

Stoll, S., & Beller, J. (1993). The effects of a longitudinal teaching methodology and classroom environment on both cognitive and behavioral moral development [Abstract]. *Research Quarterly for Exercise and Sport* (Suppl.), *64*, A-112.

Stoll, S., Beller, J., Cole, J., & Burwell, B. (1995). The relationship of competition and religious training on moral reasoning of college student athletes. *Research Quarterly for Exercise and Sport* (Suppl.), *66*, A-78.

Symons, C. (1984). *An assessment of the perceived value systems of former high school athletes and non-athletes*. Unpublished master's thesis, Pennsylvania State University.

Theberge, N., Curtis, J., & Brown, B. (1982). Sex differences in orientation toward games: Tests of the sport involvement hypothesis. In A. Dunleavy, A. Miracle, & O.R. Rees (Eds.), *Studies in the sociology of sport* (pp. 285-308). Fort Worth: Texas Christian University Press.

Turiel, E. (1983). *The development of social knowledge: Morality and convention*. New York: Cambridge University Press.

Vallerand, R., Brière, N., Blanchard, C., & Provencher, P. (1996). *Development and validation of the Multidimensional Sportsmanship Orientations Scale (MSOS)*. Manuscript submitted for publication.

Vallerand, R., Deshaies, P., Cuerrier, J., Brière, N., & Pelletier, L. (1996). Toward a multidimensional definition of sportsmanship. *Journal of Applied Sport Psychology, 8*, 123-135.

Wandzilak, T., Carroll, T., & Ansorge, C. (1988). Values development through physical activity: Promoting sportsmanlike behaviors, perceptions, and moral reasoning. *Journal of Teaching in Physical Education, 8*(1), 13-22.

Webb, H. (1969). Professionalization of attitudes toward play among adolescents. In G. Kenyon (Ed.), *Aspects of contemporrary sport sociology*. Chicago: The Athletic Institute.

Weiblen, J. (1972). Game rules and morality (Doctoral dissertation, University of North Carolina, Greensboro). *Dissertation Abstracts International, 33*, 04-A, 1498.

Wilcox. R. (1980). *Expressed values of college varsity athletes in England and the United States of America: A cross-national analysis*. Eugene, OR: Microform Publications.

Wright, W., & Rubin, S. (1989). The development of sportsmanship [Abstract]. *Proceedings of the 7th World Congress in Sport Psychology, 155*. Singapore.

Zimbardo, P., Haney, C., Banks, W., & Jaffe, D. (1975). The psychology of imprisonment: Privation, power, and pathology. In D. Rosenham and P. London (Eds.), *Theory and research in abnormal psychology* (2nd ed.) (pp. 270-287). New York: Holt, Rinehart and Winston.

Chapter 15

AGGRESSION

Dawn E. Stephens
University of Iowa

Few would argue that aggression is currently a problematic issue in society in general and sport in particular. Although society attempts to suppress aggressive acts in daily life contexts though the legal and penal systems, sport is a context in which aggressive play is many times rewarded and aggressive players can be seen as exemplifying the true spirit of the sporting context. As Russell (1993) states,

> Outside of wartime, sports is perhaps the only setting in which acts of interpersonal aggression are not only tolerated but enthusiastically applauded by large segments of society. It is interesting to consider that if the mayhem of the ring or gridiron were to erupt in a shopping mall, criminal charges would inevitably follow. However, under the umbrella of "sport," social norms and the laws specifying what constitutes acceptable conduct in society are temporarily suspended....[The official rules of sport] dictate the forms of aggression that are illegal (e.g., a low blow) and the conditions under which aggression is unacceptable (e.g., the late hit). (p. 181)

A substantial amount of research exists that examines aggression in sport; however, major conclusions resulting from this research have been limited due to differences in definitions, theoretical approaches, and measures. The purpose of this chapter is fourfold: (a) to examine the definitions of aggression and aggressive behavior that have been utilized in sport research, (b) to briefly present the theoretical frameworks that have been utilized in examining aggression in sport, (c) to present descriptions and psychometric properties of sport aggression measures, and (d) to provide future directions for sport aggression research, including brief descriptions and references for nonsport aggression measures that might prove fruitful in the development of new assessments in the field.

Definitions of Aggression

One of the primary problems with aggression research is the lack of consensus in its definition. Also adding to the confusion surrounding the investigation of aggression in sport is the interchangeable use of the terms aggression, violence, hostility, and assertiveness. A complete delineation of these terms is beyond the scope of this chapter; however, interested readers can find insightful discussions of these distinctions in Thirer (1992).

Aggression has been defined by Baron (1977) as "any form of behavior directed toward the goal of harming or injuring another living being who is motivated to avoid such treatment" (p. 7). Such behavior can be physical or nonphysical, such as psychological intimidation; however, the *intent* to cause harm must be present. Further distinctions in types of aggression have focused on the goal of the aggressor. Buss (1961) originally proposed a distinction between two types of aggression, namely hostile and instrumental. *Hostile aggression* refers to the aggressive response toward another who has angered or provoked the individual; others have labeled this type of aggressive response as *reactive* or *goal reactive aggression* (Anshel, 1994; Bredemeier, 1978; Thirer, 1992). *Instrumental aggression* serves as means to a particular goal, such as winning, in which injury to the opponent is involved. This type of injury is impersonal and designed to limit the effectiveness of the opponent (Russell, 1993). When this type of goal-oriented activity does not involve injury (and injury is not intended), the term *proactive assertion* has been used (Husman & Silva, 1984; Silva & Conroy, 1995). Cox (1990) emphasizes the point that assertive behavior that results in *accidental* injury is often misclassified as instrumental aggression. For the purposes of this chapter, aggression will be defined as an overt act (verbal or physical) that has the capacity to cause psychological or physical injury to another. The act must be purposeful (nonaccidental) and chosen with the *intent* of causing injury (Husman & Silva, 1984).

Russell (1993) suggests that sport presents a unique situation with respect to Baron's (1977) definition of aggression, in that in some sporting contexts (e.g., boxing), competitors willingly subject themselves to physical assault from their opponents. For other sports (e.g., football and rugby), injury or physical harm is usually viewed as an unfortunate or accidental by-product of the nature of the sport itself, not as the principal intent of the participants. It can be generally assumed that the rules of sport regulate against such intentional harm of another player (Zillman, 1979).

Operational Definitions

It is the "intentional" aspect of the definition of aggression, both hostile and instrumental, that presents one of the greatest difficulties in measuring aggression. Often the judgment as to the player's intentions is left to the officials to determine. Thus, some researchers use the criterion of aggressive rule violations as the operational definition (e.g., McCarthy & Kelly, 1978a, b; McGuire, Courneya, Widmeyer, & Carron, 1992; Russell, 1981; Russell & Russell, 1984; Vokey & Russell, 1992; Widmeyer & Birch, 1984). Such violations include penalized actions that occur during the course of the game that are intended to inflict harm and are in violation of the agreed-upon rules of the game (Russell & Russell, 1984). Other researchers have utilized interview techniques to directly query the participant as to her or his underlying intentions (Bredemeier & Shields, 1986). Paper and pencil measures also have been utilized to assess sport participants' assessments of (a) the legitimacy of injurious acts and rule-violating behavior (e.g. Duda, Olson, & Templin, 1991); (b) the likelihood of their aggressive actions in relation to assertive or submissive actions (Bredemeier, 1994); and (c) their self-reported likelihood to aggress in a game situation and their attitudes concerning aggression in that situation (Stephens & Bredemeier, 1996). Other operational definitions have utilized the rating of aggressiveness of participants by their coaches or peers (Bredemeier & Shields, 1984). The main section of this chapter examines the psychometric properties of selected aggression measures and is organized around these differing operational definitions.

Theoretical Frameworks

Four major theoretical frameworks have been utilized in the study of aggressive behavior: instinctual, frustration-aggression, social learning, and moral reasoning. These theoretical positions have attempted to understand the probable causes of aggression in order to explain, predict, and, potentially, channel or modify aggressive behavior (Anshel, 1994). Excellent reviews of these theories exist (Anshel, 1994; Russell, 1993; Shields & Bredemeier, 1995; Silva & Husman, 1995); however, in order to lay a theoretical foundation for the assessment of aggression, a brief summary of each of these approaches follows.

Instinctual theories. Originally proposed by Freud (1925), instinctual, or biological, theories of aggression assume that aggressive behavior is an innate, natural response in all individuals and has evolved to its present state through a struggle for survival, especially for territory (Ardrey, 1966; Lorenz, 1966). This theoretical stance is not without its opposition (Montagu, 1968; Morris, 1967); however, relatively recent research on twins at the Minnesota Center for Twin and Adoption Research and the University of Southern California has shown that aggressive tendencies may have a strong genetic component (Anshel, 1994).

According to this theoretical position, aggression builds up naturally in humans and requires release. This release, or catharsis, can be sought through unacceptable (criminal behavior) or acceptable (sport) channels (Lorenz, 1966). This viewpoint has been labeled the *catharsis hypothesis*. Thirer (1992) provides an excellent review of the sport literature supporting and challenging this hypothesis.

Frustration-aggression hypothesis. The concept of frustration leading to a display of aggression was further refined and elaborated on by a group of Yale psychologists (Dollard, Doob, Miller, Mowrer, & Sears, 1939). In its original state, the hypothesis stated that any thwarting of goal-directed behavior would result in frustration, with the inevitable outcome being an aggressive response. This hypothesis was first modified by Miller (1941) to include nonaggressive responses to frustration, and later by Berkowitz (1969, 1978; Berkowitz & Alioto, 1973), who, building on Miller's modification, added two conditions for frustration to lead to aggression: the opportunity for aggressive action and the presence of appropriate stimulus cues, such as anger. To apply this to a sport setting, Russell (1993) proposes that it is the absence of negative feelings (e.g., anger) that allows participants to dissociate the aggressive response from the frustration following the thwarting of their goal attainment. Although anecdotal evidence in support of this hypothesis abounds, empirical research is equivocal (see Anshel, 1994; Russell, 1993; Thirer, 1992).

Social learning theory. Bandura (1973) has provided considerable support for the social learning position that views aggression as a learned response pattern, influenced by reinforcement and modeling. In particular, the observer learns what level of success the model's aggression met with in achieving her or his goal and whether the model's aggressive behavior was rewarded or punished. Thus, the observer has learned not only the aggressive act but also under what circumstances the act might be praised or penalized.

In many sport settings, athletes are encouraged to exhibit aggressive behavior toward opponents in order to achieve their goal. Rewards for such actions are significant, including praise and recognition from teammates, coaches, fans, and media personnel, and punishment is either nonsignificant or minimal (Silva & Husman, 1995). Therefore, players learn through a socialization process the actual skills involved in aggressive behavior, and they learn that such behavior is often desired, expected, and considered normatively legitimate (Silva, 1984).

Much of the research addressing aggression and sport has been based upon social learning theory and has included as subjects sport participants, spectators, and television audiences (see Shields & Bredemeier, 1995, and Thirer, 1992, for reviews of this empirical literature). Although this theoretical approach has garnered empirical support, much of the research testing the tenets of social learning theory has operationally defined aggression as an overt, observable act. This operationalization overlooks the basic concept of *intent*. One difficulty with direct behavioral observation is that the meaning of specific behavior is never transparent and must be interpreted by the observer (Shields & Bredemeier, 1995). Moreover, assessing behavior through self-reports can also be problematic due to the potential socially desirable response (Stephens, Bredemeier, & Shields, in press).

Moral reasoning theory. Bredemeier, Shields, and colleagues (e.g,. Bredemeier & Shields, 1984; Bredemeier, Shields, Weiss, & Cooper, 1986, 1987; Stephens & Bredemeier, 1996; Stephens, Bredemeier, & Shields, in press) have utilized a moral reasoning framework for examining aggression in sport. This structural-developmental approach examines the reasoning, or meaning, associated with aggressive behavior (see Shields & Bredemeier, 1995, for a complete summary). Bredemeier (1983) proposes that one value of viewing aggression from a moral perspective is to clarify the distinction between hostile aggression, instrumental aggression, and proactive assertion through identifying the intent of the player. Rather than focusing on overt behavior, structural-developmentalists study the way the individual defines the situation and her or his choices in that situation. Utilizing a developmental framework, research on athletes' aggressive acts considers how athletes' actions and goals are mediated by their moral interpretation of the context and their level of moral reasoning. A few measures have been proposed to explore aggression from a moral perspective; due to the complexity of the underlying moral theory, those measures are discussed within a moral context in the chapter by Bredemeier and Shields (this volume).

Measures of Aggression

The purpose of this section is to present and critique the extant measures of aggression in sport and physical activity contexts. The following discussion is organized around categories of operational definitions utilized in sport-specific measures of aggression: (a) penalties incurred during the course of game/season, (b) perceptions of the legitimacy of injurious acts and rule-violating behavior, (c) perceptions of the likelihood of displaying aggressive actions in relation to assertive or submissive actions, and (d) aggressive behavior characteristics and tendencies.

Penalties. One category of aggression measurement that has been pursued, particularly in the sport of ice hockey, utilizes the number of certain penalties that have been assessed during the course of a game or season. The penalties utilized in this regard have included those that involve acts of body or stick that were in violation of formal written rules (Cullen & Cullen, 1971) and that were identified by trained judges, the officials. In collision sports, such as ice hockey, many aggressive acts are sanctioned by sport; thus, this type of measurement addresses only those aggressive acts that are in violation of formal norms. Inherent within this approach are several problematic issues. Using this type of measure overlooks one of the underlying aspects of defining aggression, that of intent to injure. Although this intent *may* be present, quantifying the number of observed or called fouls, even when the opponent does sustain injury, does not assess the intention of the actor. With regard to this issue, Widmeyer and Birch (1984) attempted to remedy this situation by questioning NHL officials and players and semiprofessional players as to their reasons for committing the acts for which certain penalties (slashing, spearing, high-sticking, butt-ending, cross-checking, charging, boarding, kneeing, elbowing, roughing, and fighting) were assessed. Findings suggested that these acts were committed with the intent to do harm or to intimidate. Based on these interviews, Widmeyer and Birch then excluded the penalties of tripping and interference from the list of aggressive penalties. It is important to note, however, that their findings were anecdotal, as neither quantification nor statistical analyses were presented.

Other problems with this operational definition, as identified by Widmeyer and Birch (1984), include the exclusion of aggressive actions that may be within either the official or norma-

tive rules of the sport, and the accuracy or bias of the observer, either researcher or referee, in identifying whether a foul was committed. With regard to the latter limitation, it can be assumed that such unnoticed aggressive acts would be equally distributed across teams (Widmeyer & Birch, 1984). Many studies have addressed the penalty-related operational definition of aggression. The distinctions raised in this work include type of penalty, number of penalties or minutes penalized, and season or game statistics (see McGuire et al., 1992); however, few such investigations have examined issues of validity and reliability.

McCarthy and Kelly (1978a, b) attempted to distinguish instrumental aggression from hostile aggression by differentiating hockey penalties that slow down play, an accepted strategy that sometimes draws penalties, from aggressive penalties involving an excessive level of bodily contact. Hostile aggression penalties included elbowing, slashing, boarding, roughing, cross-checking, high-sticking, butt-ending, fighting, misconduct, spearing, kneeing, and disqualifications. Instrumental aggression was defined as the norm-violating penalties of tripping, hooking, holding, interference, leaving feet, pushing, and illegal use of hands. In the first investigation, players with the highest numbers of overall penalties in their 4-year college careers received significantly more hostile aggression penalties and norm-violating penalties than did those players with the lowest number of overall penalties (McCarthy & Kelly, 1978b). A follow-up study (McCarthy & Kelly, 1978a) confirmed these findings in terms of number of penalties classified as aggressive. However, in terms of construct validity, the two groups (i.e., players with highest vs. lowest numbers of overall penalties) did not significantly differ on a self-report measure of aggression, defined as the physical expression of anger (The Anger Self-Report: Zelin, Adler, & Myerson, 1972).

Much of the research establishing the psychometric properties of aggressive penalty assessment has been done by Russell (Vokey & Russell, 1984). Defining physical aggression as the penalties of slashing, hooking, and fighting, Russell (1981) analyzed the archival records of Canadian ice hockey players ($N = 203$ members of the Western Hockey League). Results indicated that players' physical aggression scores were significantly related to their teams' staff ratings of "how hostile and hot tempered" they were (on an 11-point scale) ($r = .19$, $p<.005$). However, with less than 4% of the variance in aggression explained by these ratings, this finding adds little psychometric support in establishing either predictive or concurrent validity. Russell and Russell (1984), utilizing official records of 432 Western Hockey League (WHL) games, attempted to evaluate the dimensionality underlying aggressive penalties as recorded by game officials. Aggression was operationalized as total number of penalty minutes awarded for each of the 19 aggressive infractions. Results of a principal components analysis with a varimax rotation indicated an eight-dimensional solution, which accounted for 59.2% of total variance. The eight dimensions were

1. *Attack* (charging, slashing, and cross-checking): initiation of an altercation with an opponent;
2. *Fighting* (game misconduct and fighting): involvement in a bare-knuckle fight that persists despite efforts of game officials to intervene;

3. *Fractious* (high-sticking, roughing, misconduct, and elbowing): exchange of blows with opponent; however, players remain in possession of gloves and sticks;

4. *Obstruction* (tripping, holding, and unsportsmanlike conduct): attempts to impede or disrupt play of opposition;

5. *Boarding* (boarding and match misconduct): includes the fairly common occurrence of boarding and the ensuing match misconduct penalty for retaliation;

6. *Interference A* (interference, spearing, and unsportsmanlike conduct): includes meddlesome and provocative behaviors, sometimes aimed at game officials;

7. *Interference B* (gross misconduct, hooking, and holding): attempts to adversely affect play of those assigned to cover;

8. *Covert Aggression* (butt-ending and elbowing): the two most easily disguised acts of physical aggression. The authors concluded that aggression is multiply determined; that is, each penalty is an independent act and arises in response to a different set of motives and circumstances. Given this interpretation and that, with few exceptions, all penalties individually showed substantial loadings on only one factor, the authors conclude that the general practice of combining penalties for an overall measure of aggression is defensible (Russell & Russell, 1984).

Vokey and Russell (1992) replicated this earlier study. Results of a principle components analysis (varimax rotation) resulted in an eight-dimension solution that accounted for 58.2% of the variance; internal reliability coefficients were not reported. Although the two principle component solutions appeared similar at a superficial level, few of the dimensions were consistent across solutions. The one exception was the dimension of fighting, which included penalties of fighting and game misconduct; this factor appeared as the first component in this study, and the second component in Russell and Russell (1984) (accounting for 13% and 9% of the variance, respectively). The results of the Vokey and Russell study suggest caution in generalizations concerning aggression, as measured by penalties, across seasons. Recent research by Vokey and Russell, utilizing National Hockey League statistics, has failed to replicate the multidimensional structure of penalties but has provided support for a single "fighting" dimension. Rather than drawing previous research with the WHL into question, Russell suggests that the dimensional structures might be league specific (Russell, personal communication).

Vokey and Russell (1992) suggest establishing reliability through the examination of degree of consensus among multiple referees, especially for judgment calls (minor penalties, such as tripping and roughing) that may be used more to control the contest than to enforce official rules of play. The authors also suggest utilization of penalty indices as a behavioral measure of aggression to provide criterion validity for existing paper-and-pencil inventories. Real-life player aggression, as measured by penalty indices in a game context, is suggested as qualitatively different from aggression observed in lab settings. In the former case, aggressive behavior is met with "enthusiastic approval and encouragement from teammates, coaches and partisan spectators alike" (Vokey & Russell, 1992, p. 224).

Bredemeier and Shields (1984) also employed penalties as a behavioral measure along with evaluations by skilled others to assess aggression in collegiate basketball players. Athletes were rated and ranked among teammates by their coaches as to their level of aggressiveness. Coaches received instruction by the researchers as to the specific definition of aggression utilized in the study: an act motivated by the intent to physically or psychologically harm. As multiple coaches per team were asked to evaluate their players, interrater reliability was assessed and found to be satisfactory, with coefficients ranging from .51 to .80. The behavioral measure of aggression consisted of players' average fouls per minute played per season game. Coaches' ratings and rankings were highly correlated ($r=-.89$, $p<.001$); rankings and fouls committed were significantly related ($r=-.46$, $p<.01$), as were, albeit to a lesser extent, ratings and fouls ($r=.37$, $p<.05$).

Summary. Utilization of penalties as a behavioral measure of aggression is problematic on several levels: the inability to observe underlying intent, the potential lack of accuracy and freedom from bias of the official or observer, and the inability to distinguish hostile from instrumental types of aggression. Future research should examine the relationship between penalty indices and other qualitative and quantitative measurement of players' perceptions of aggressive actions, including legitimacy judgments, to provide construct validation of this type of observational measurement. Specific directions for validation include qualitative inquiry into players' intentions behind aggressive actions, both penalized and unpenalized, and inquiry into a stable dimensional structure of penalty violations across contexts (e.g., games, leagues) and even sports. Assessment of interrater reliability of referees' calls, with particular attention to judgment calls, will provide both construct validity by addressing the true purpose of the call (aggression or game control) and reliability of measurement through triangulation, particularly when utilizing separate raters in addition to game referees.

Perceptions as to the Legitimacy of Injurious Acts and Rule-Violating Behavior

Each sport consists of formal, or constitutive, rules and informal, or normative, rules. Constitutive rules govern behavior during a game and are agreed upon by teams, officials, and governing bodies before the contest; normative rules reflect informal, unwritten rules that define what is considered acceptable, or legitimate, behavior to players or coaches (Silva & Conroy, 1995). Although the employment of penalties to assess aggression may be useful when formal rules are breached, measures that address perceptions of the legitimacy of injurious acts and rule-violating behavior assess normative rules.

Certain constitutive rules exist to limit aggression, both physical (e.g., clipping in football) and psychological (e.g., taunting the opponent); however, injury can, and does, occur within these formal rules. Conversely, normative rules can involve behavior, such as fighting in hockey, that violates the formal rules. It would be problematic to label all physical contact in football as aggressive, in that some contact, such as tackling, is required and legitimate by the formal rules (Silva & Conroy, 1995). Again, it is the intent to do harm that classifies such activity as aggressive. Legitimacy measures operationally define aggression as the acceptance, as legitimate, of an act with the intent of, or indifference to, physical or psychological injury to another. Assessment of legitimacy judgments is accomplished through providing the subject with a scenario in which a potentially injurious act is described, followed by a series of questions as to the legitimacy, or acceptability, of such an action. Thus, in this way it is possible to address intention of harm or injury.

Silva (1983), using slides depicting rule-violating behavior that involved injury, addressed the perceived legitimacy of such aggressive behaviors. Using a social learning framework, Silva proposed that involvement in sport provided a process of unlearning internal prohibitions against rule-violating behavior and a learning of normative rules that legitimized such actions. Twelve slides that illustrated professional or collegiate male athletes in sports with varying levels of contact (baseball, basketball, football, ice hockey, and soccer) were initially selected; face validity was established through rating of the slides (4-point scale: 1 = *very ambiguous* to 4 = *extremely clear*) by college coaches and professors in physical education. Seven slides received a rating of 3.3 or above; interrater reliability was acceptable (r's > .8). The seven slides, plus one depicting acceptable behavior, included (a) two ice hockey players fighting, (b) a brushback pitch in baseball, (c) a trip on a driving basketball player, (d) an elbow to the upper body-neck area of a soccer player moving in on a goal, (e) two players going up for a rebound in basketball (acceptable behavior), (f) spearing in football, (g) slashing in ice hockey, and (h) a high arm tackle in football (clotheslining).

Subjects (N=203 college students) were shown each slide for 10 seconds, followed by a period in which they were asked to indicate (a) the sport being played, (b) the primary act or behavior portrayed, (c) the acceptability or legitimacy for the subject her- or himself to exhibit the behavior shown at some point during a game (4-point scale: 1 = *totally unacceptable* to 4 = *totally acceptable*). Each slide was reshown at the end of the series for a period of 5 seconds. Seventeen percent (n=36) of the subjects' responses were discarded due to their inability to identify the sport or action depicted in at least one of the slides (n=167: 89 males, 78 females). Scores represented the sum of legitimacy ratings for the seven rule-violating slides. Unfortunately, no statistics on the factor structure for the seven items to assess dimensionality of the construct nor any assessment of reliability, in terms of test-retest, were provided.

Results of linear and polynomial regression analyses supported the construct validity of the measure: Males perceived the behaviors as more legitimate than did females, with gender accounting for 57% of the variability in legitimacy scores. For males, level of contact in sport experience indicated a significant, positive linear response, as did years of participation in organized sport and highest level of organized sport played. These findings suggest that, for male athletes, involvement in sport may involve the learning of normative rules involving the acceptance of aggressive rule-violating behavior as legitimate. For females, lack of opportunity to participate in contact and collision sports may provide a possible explanation for lower levels of legitimacy ratings in this early study (Silva, 1983). In addition, socialization of females toward nonaggressive means

in nonsport situations might transfer into behavior in the sport arena, regardless of level of contact allowed within the constitutive rules of the sport. These findings support construct validity, as gender differences in aggression (nonsport) are well established in the psychological literature (Eagly & Steffen, 1986; Hyde, 1984, 1986).

Building on Silva's work, Bredemeier and colleagues (Bredemeier et al., 1987) developed a series of slides, the Injurious Sport Acts Series (ISAS), to assess children's legitimacy judgments regarding potentially injurious sport acts. The ISAS slides were selected from a collection of 25 slides (including those used in Silva's 1983 study); all slides showed male athletes participating in medium- or high-contact sports at the collegiate or professional level. Face validity was established by a panel of 15 coaches and physical educators who determined whether the act depicted was in violation of a rule and whether someone in the slide was likely to be injured. Unanimous agreement for potential harm existed between raters for nine slides and for the legality of the actions shown in seven of those slides, with 93% agreement for the remaining two slides. All nine slides chosen for the ISAS depicted high potential for injury; five slides contained depictions of rule-violating behavior, and four slides presented acts within the rules. The final series included five of Silva's (1983) original slides. Similar to Silva's method, with adjustments for age, slides were presented for 20 seconds; following each slide, subjects (N = 78, 4th through 7th graders; 32 girls and 46 boys) were instructed to indicate (a) the sport depicted in that slide, (b) whether the action depicted was against the rules, and (c) whether someone was likely to get hurt. Following the first series of slides, each slide was again displayed, and children were asked to indicate (a) whether the act depicted was okay and (b) whether the act would be okay if children their age rather than adults were involved.

In all cases, children correctly identified the sport; agreement between children and panel members as to rule violation was 89%, with agreement for individual slides ranging from 69% to 100%. In terms of harmful activity, children thought the slides depicted harmful activity (92%; individual slides ranged from 77% to 100%). Scoring of the ISAS consisted of adding the number of times the child approved of the act depicted in the slide. However, only acts that had been identified by the subject as either against the rules or likely to result in injury were counted; as a result, 2.5% of the judgments were excluded from the data analysis.

Results supported the construct and concurrent validity of the ISAS. The number of acts judged to be legitimate for adults was significantly greater than those judged legitimate for children. Boys were found to accept more acts as legitimate than were girls; older subjects accepted more acts as legitimate than did younger subjects. However, these findings could be confounded by the older male athletes depicted in the slides as engaging in the injurious action. According to social learning theory, the similarity of the model to the subject pool (older male subjects) might provide information as to the legitimacy of the act being portrayed, thus influencing these subjects' legitimacy ratings to a greater extent. Both of these findings provide some support as to the measure's discriminant validity, as both gender-related (Eagly & Steffen, 1986; Hyde, 1984, 1986) and age-related (Parke & Slaby, 1983) differences in nonsport aggression are supported in the literature. Legitimacy judgments for boys correlated significantly with perceptions of physical ($r=.31$, $p<.05$) and nonphysical ($r=.53$, $p<.001$) aggression levels in daily life settings (as measured by Deluty's (1979) Children's Action Tendency Scale: CATS) and physical ($r=.39$, $p<.01$) and nonphysical ($r=.48$, $p<.001$) aggression in sport-specific settings (as measured by Bredemeier et al.'s (1987) Scale of Children's Action Tendencies in Sport: SCATS), and participation ($r=.27$, $p<.05$) and interest ($r=.39$, $p<.05$) in high-contact sports. Legitimacy judgments for girls were significantly related to physical ($r=.40$, $p<.01$) and nonphysical ($r=.33$, $p<.05$) aggression in daily-life settings (CATS); correlations for physical ($r=.28$, $p<.06$) and nonphysical ($r=.28$, $p<.07$) aggression in sport settings with legitimacy judgments approached significance. No attempts to examine dimensionality or to establish reliability of the ISAS were reported.

The findings of greater correlations for boys between non-physical aggression (both daily life and sport) and legitimacy judgments for aggressive sport acts suggest less support for the criterion validity of the ISAS than is claimed by the authors. The lack of significant correlations for girls' legitimacy judgments and sport aggression tendencies may reflect the lesser role of sport in female socialization or, alternately, it may simply reflect a lack of identification of the female subjects with male athletes depicted in the slides (Bredemeier et al., 1986). Future validation of the ISAS should include comparison with direct observational measures to establish thought/action consistency and to support the validity of utilizing a cognitive measure to investigate aggressive actions. Additionally, a longitudinal design would allow investigation of cause-effect relationships and developmental patterns (Bredemeier et al., 1987).

Further work in this direction was undertaken by Bredemeier (1985) with the creation of the Continuum of Injurious Acts (CIA) to assess athletes' judgments of the legitimacy of selected injurious acts intentionally inflicted in a sport context. The CIA consists of a set of six 3" by 5" cards depicting sport acts with intended consequences that become increasingly more serious: (a) nonphysical intimidation, (b) physical intimidation, (c) making an opponent miss several minutes of play, (d) eliminating an opponent from the game, (e) injuring the opponent so that the opponent will miss the entire season, and (f) permanently disabling the opponent. Face validity was established through the ranking of the six cards according to severity of the act by five social scientists who served as judges. The ordering of the cards by each judge was consistent with the order proposed above.

Subjects, male and female high school and college basketball players ($N=40$), were asked to sort the cards into two piles, legitimate and not legitimate, on two occasions. The first card-sort followed a hypothetical sport setting described by the researcher (hypothetical setting) in which "Tom," a professional football player, had the opportunity to enhance his team's chances to play in the Super Bowl. The second card-sort occurred 3 weeks later, immediately following a basketball game in which the athlete had participated and which provided the context (engaged setting). Following the card sort, the researcher removed the legitimate cards and asked the subject if she or he would judge any of the remaining act(s) to be legiti-

mate if (a) it was necessary in order to win, (b) an opponent did it first, (c) the coach demanded it, or (d) the rules allowed it.

Responses to the CIA were scored by identifying each subject's "ceiling card," the card that represented the most serious act perceived as legitimate by the subject. The "continuum" aspect of the CIA was supported: No subject "skipped" an act by indicating an act as not legitimate that was less serious than her or his ceiling card. Subjects perceived a significantly higher number of CIA acts as legitimate in the engaged basketball context than in the hypothetical football context. Bredemeier interpreted this as indicative of the influence of self-involvement on legitimacy judgments. Males judged as legitimate more CIA acts in both contexts than did females, thus providing a measure of discriminant validity. Legitimacy judgments in the engaged context were differentiated by school level: College athletes indicated a greater number of CIA acts as legitimate. Further assessment of the concurrent validity of the CIA is necessary, especially employing behavioral measures to determine the relationship between legitimacy judgments about injurious acts and aggressive behavior.

The CIA, which originally employed an interviewer, has been modified by three sets of researchers to be administered as a paper-pencil inventory (Duda et al., 1991; Duda & Huston, 1995; Ryan, Williams, & Wimer, 1990); two of these research teams created basketball-specific versions, and one, football-specific. Duda et al.'s (1991) revision consisted of six written scenarios that depicted increasingly serious aggressive acts in basketball, ranging from nonphysical intimidation to permanent disability. Four judges, experienced in high school level basketball, developed the scenarios to be typical illustrations of acts that occur within the context of interscholastic basketball. Scenarios were presented to subjects (56 male and 67 female high school basketball players) in random order. Following each scenario, subjects were asked to indicate responses to the following questions: "In general, is this O.K. (legitimate) to do?" and "Is this O.K. (legitimate) to do if it was necessary to win the game?" Responses to both questions were indicated on a 5-point Likert-type scale (1 = *strongly approve*, 5 = *strongly disapprove*); results indicated that the responses to the two questions were highly correlated; thus, only the data concerning responses to the latter question were used in further analyses.

Results indicated support for the "continuum" aspect of this modification of the CIA, with the exception that physical intimidation was seen as more legitimate than nonphysical intimidation; follow-up interviews ($n = 13$) indicated that although "muscling under the boards" (physical intimidation) was seen as good strategy, "staring down" an opponent was viewed as unnecessary and unsportsmanlike (Duda et al., 1991). Males and females significantly differed in their judgments of legitimacy for all scenarios but permanent disability. This result provides further support for the discriminant validity of the CIA. Subjects who emphasized ego-oriented goals (as assessed by the TEOSQ: Duda, 1989; Duda & Whitehead, this volume) and, thus, were concerned with demonstrating superior ability, viewed physical intimidation and injury to cause an opponent to miss a game or be out for the entire season as more legitimate. Ego orientation was also related to a greater disapproval of nonphysical intimidation. Based on Nicholls' (1989) proposal that ego-oriented individuals should be more likely to go to any lengths to win, these findings support the concurrent validity of this modification of the CIA.

Ryan and her colleagues (1990) also developed a self-administered version of the CIA to minimize distortion due to social desirability and perceived interviewer expectations. This modification of the CIA included questions as to (a) the legitimacy of the act (legitimacy judgment) and (b) whether the subject would perform the depicted act (behavioral intention). Subjects ($N = 49$ female high school basketball players) responded to these questions in a yes or no format. These initial responses were followed by subsequent yes or no questions to assess whether particular situations would provoke a different response. Situations included (a) if it were necessary to win, (b) if your opponent did it first, (c) if the rules allowed it, (d) if it broke the rules, yet you knew you would not be caught, (e) if a teammate told you to do it, and (f) if your coach told you to do it. Contingency questions to a "yes" response to the situation involving the coach attempted to identify the appropriate reason: (a) "You trust the coach's judgment"; (b) "If you didn't, the coach would bench you"; if (c) "If neither, explain."

Scoring involved multiplying the percentage of affirmative responses at each level of the continuum by the operationally defined severity of the action (1 = *nonphysical intimidation* to 6 = *permanent disability*). Final scores were then calculated by summing these products for each category of judgments (legitimacy and behavioral intention), yielding a range of 0 to 21. Data were obtained twice, following practice sessions prior to the first game of the season and during the last 2 weeks of the season.

As a measure of actual aggressive behavior, subjects were queried during the latter data-collection session as to the number of times they had committed actions over the course of the season with the intent depicted in each of the six CIA scenarios. The number of committed acts was multiplied by the severity of the action and then summed to provide a score of aggressive action. Stepwise regression analyses determined preseason legitimacy judgments to be a significant predictor of actual aggression, alone accounting for 29.5% of the total variance; preseason behavioral intention did not enter the prediction equation. The authors concluded that perceptions regarding legitimacy of aggressive actions may provide an effective means of predicting future aggressive behavior. However, the "continuum" aspect of the CIA was not supported, as some subjects indicated that they might perform more severe acts without indicating an affirmative response for less severe acts. The authors propose that the athletes may have been eager to leave following practice and thus not have accurately interpreted the questions. Therefore, the results of this study and evidence concerning the psychometric properties of this self-administered version of the CIA should be cautiously interpreted. Future research might include comparison of these self-administered versions of the CIA with the original interview format to address possible implications of each methodology. Future directions in developing these types of measures might include differentiating between hostile and instrumental motives for aggression to further assist in understanding this issue.

Duda and Huston (1995) modified the CIA to be football specific, creating the Continuum of Injurious Acts in Football (CIAF). Scenarios for the CIAF were provided by 19 experts in football at the high school and college level, who were asked to provide typical situations in football that reflect the six categories of injurious acts. From these original situations, eight judges chose two for each category that best exemplified each type of injurious act, resulting in 12 scenarios for the CIAF. Each scenario was followed by a series of three questions:

1. Is this OK to do in order to win?
2. Would *you* do this if it was necessary in order to win?, and
3. Would *you* do this if the coach asked you to?

Responses were indicated on a 5-point Likert-type scale (1 = *strongly approve*, 5 = *strongly disapprove*). Findings supported the continuum aspect of the CIA for both high school ($n = 124$) and collegiate ($n = 142$) football players across the three probe questions. Results also supported Duda et al.'s (1991) findings of the relationship between ego orientation and perceived legitimacy, thus providing support for the CIAF's construct validity.

The Sport Aggression Justification Questionnaire (SAJQ: Thompson, Cook, & Tollefson, 1996) was developed to assess perceptions of the legitimacy of aggressive acts with regard to both the reasons for performing the act and the severity of resulting injury. Although the various versions of the CIA assess legitimacy of aggressive acts based on level of injurious outcome, the SAJQ provides a means to address the relationships between legitimacy judgments and (a) the purpose for the aggressive action, (b) the outcome of action in terms of injury, and (c) the interaction between purpose and outcome. The SAJQ includes six scenarios, each of which presents a different motivation for the same aggressive act, that of an elbow to the face of an opponent. The scenarios differ as to the motivation or reason for the aggressive act: retaliation for (a) self and (b) teammate, (c) as a tactic to win, (d) due to frustration, (e) unprovoked, and (f) accidental. It appears that the SAJQ provides an assessment of instrumental and hostile aggression; however, this aspect does not appear to have been pursued by the SAJQ's authors. Reasons 1 and 2 (retaliation) and 4 (frustration) might be classified as examples of hostile aggression, whereas Reason 3 (to win) could be viewed as instrumental. Reason 5 (unprovoked) is unclear as to this delineation as no purpose for the aggression is given, and Reason 6 would not be considered aggression as it does not include an intent to cause harm. Further development of this measure should include attempts to clarify these distinctions.

Three levels of injury severity followed each scenario: loss of concentration, forcing opponent to leave the game temporarily, or forcing opponent to leave for the rest of the game. For each level, subjects were asked to indicate how legitimate they perceived the aggressive act to be. Responses were indicated on a 5-point Likert-type scale (1 = *very justified* and 5 = *very unjustified*).

Initial testing of the SAJQ indicated one-week test-retest reliability of .84 ($N = 60$; 32 males and 28 females), and supported the measure's construct validity in that athletes ($N = 48$; 24 high school males, 24 college females) who were rated as high on aggression by their coaches scored significantly higher on the SAJQ than did athletes rated low in aggression (Thompson et al., 1996). No assessment of the measure's internal consistency has been reported.

Research by Thompson and Cook (1992) found a significant interaction between injury severity and the situation in which the aggression occurred. Subjects' ($N = 181$) responses followed a "stairstep pattern," which indicated the highest legitimacy score for the least severe outcome, a lower score for the moderately injurious outcome, and the lowest score for the most injurious outcome, providing support for the SAJQ's content validity. This pattern held across gender and situation. Legitimacy scores for situations ranged from a low for the unprovoked scenario to a high for the retaliation-for-self scenario (Thompson, 1991). Gender differences were not found when legitimacy judgments were averaged across situation and injury severity (Thompson, 1993). However, a gender by situation interaction proved significant, and a gender by situation interaction approached significance (p=08). Future research with the SAJQ should attempt to delineate these gender differences with regard to both injury severity and situation.

The SAJQ provides an initial attempt at understanding perceptions of legitimacy of injurious acts based on the consequences of that act in conjunction with the causes, or motivations, for the act. Although holding the aggressive action (an elbow to the face) constant does provide a standardized condition to assess various levels of injury and reasons for provocation, it becomes problematic in assessing general aggression in sport. Future research with the SAJQ might vary the aggressive act depicted in order to address a more generalized construct of aggression. In addition, further examination of its psychometric properties in a variety of sports and competitive levels is required.

A recent entry into this category of assessment tools, which uses legitimacy of potentially injurious acts as its operational definition, is the Carolina Sport Behavior Inventory (CSBI) (Conroy, Silva, Newcomer, Walker, & Johnson, 1996). The CSBI, a self-administered questionnaire, includes 10 scenarios that portray clearly aggressive, rule-violating behavior. When the type of sport depicted allowed it, male and female protagonists in the scenarios were balanced. Each scenario was accompanied by 12 questions regarding the legitimacy of the behavior described. Subjects ($N = 1018$: 475 females, 529 males; mean age = 13.3 years) were asked to respond on an 8-point Likert-type scale (1-2 = *Never OK*, 3-4 = *Seldom OK*, 5-6 = *Often OK*, and 7-8 = *Always OK*). Although not indicated to the subjects, the midpoint (4.5) was assumed to be the legitimacy threshold.

Three sections of questioning followed each scenario as to whether the behavior depicted was legitimate (OK). The first section asked if this action was OK for the subject to do when playing this sport; this question assesses the subjects's perception of legitimacy performing the aggression action her- or himself. The second section of questions included chronologically ordered competitive levels and asked the subject to respond as to the legitimacy of the action for a player at each of the levels ranging from elementary school to professional. This aspect of the CSBI assesses whether aggressive behavior is viewed as more legitimate as the level of competition increases, drawing a parallel to the "professionalization of attitude" literature (Blair, 1985; Knoppers, 1985; Webb, 1969), which suggests that athletes involved in higher levels of competitive sport tend to place a decreased emphasis on sportspersonlike values, including the importance of playing fair. Previous research has linked higher

levels of competition to increased legitimacy rating for aggressive actions (Bredemeier, 1985; Silva, 1983), suggesting that players who are involved in a higher level of competitive sport are more likely to approve of the intentional injury of an opponent than are players competing at lower levels. This second section of questions in the CSBI can address whether individuals' *perceptions* pertaining to legitimacy of aggressive acts for players participating at higher levels of competition are comparable to the perceptions of the players themselves.

The third section of questions for each scenario includes assessments of perceptions of legitimacy of these actions in each of five situations: (a) if the player wouldn't be caught, (b) if it is late in a close game and it will help the player's team to win, (c) if it will help their team win the championship game, (d) if someone from the other team has done it first, and (e) if the action results in the opponent's being seriously injured. Similar to the SAJQ, the CSBI has the capacity to assess differences in hostile (d: retaliation) and instrumental (b, c: means to win) aggression. Because the scenarios describe a *potentially* injurious act, the final question for each scenario assesses whether the action would still be considered legitimate if the opponent were *seriously* injured. Although this question provides an avenue to assess serious injury outcomes, it does little to assist in understanding and differentiating perceptions of legitimacy for various levels of injury.

Face validity for the CSBI was established through the use of a panel of experts who reviewed each situation for aggressive intent, and corresponding questions were evaluated as to the degree to which subjects' legitimacy judgments were assessed. Changes to the measure were based on the experts' recommendations.

Factor analysis, employed to assess the CSBI's dimensionality, resulted in a three-factor solution. However, factor loadings for every item were higher on the first factor than on either of the other two, suggesting that the CSBI might be unidimensional. Subsequent rotations confirmed the single-factor structure. Finally, a quartimax (orthogonal) rotation identified a single factor, which accounted for 82.6% of the variance in participants' scores. Internal consistency was high (Cronbach's alpha = .99); therefore, all 120 items were averaged to create an overall perceived legitimacy score.

Results indicated that males perceived aggressive sport behaviors as significantly more acceptable than did females, thus supporting the CSBI's discriminant validity. Results indicated partial support for social learning theory, revealing a statistically nonsignificant trend in increased levels of legitimacy with higher levels of competition. Responses to the third section of questioning indicated that aggressive sport behavior was considered least legitimate when injury would result and most legitimate when it would assist in winning the championship. However, it is important to note that in no situation did mean scores cross the level of legitimacy (4.5).

Stepwise regression analyses indicated that both collision-sport experience and age were significant, yet weak, predictors of legitimacy judgments, accounting for only 5% of the variance. Though the variance explained by these variables is minimal, this finding does support previous findings of greater levels of legitimacy for individuals with experience in collision and contact sports (Bredemeier et al., 1987; Silva, 1983).

Future directions in establishing the validity of the CSBI include separating the first question concerning legitimacy judgments for the player her- or himself from the other sections, in order to assess gender differences and any grouping of scenarios by severity or relevance/familiarity to the subject pool. The procedure utilized by Conroy et al. (1996) may be conflating issues of perceptions of legitimacy for the self with issues of legitimacy for other levels of sport. These distinctions are important ones and should be examined separately.

Summary. Assessment of legitimacy judgments provides an operational definition that is consistent with the "intent to harm" aspect of the conceptual definition. Research utilizing the "continuum" aspect of increasingly serious aggressive acts allows insight into level of severity of the consequences of aggressive behavior. Measures that do not specifically state this outcome rely on subjects perceiving similar levels of consequences. Additionally, provision of more than one scenario per level of injury, such as employed in the Duda and Huston (1995) study, allows a broader view of the level of consequence, rather than exacerbating the potential bias of subjects' responses due to the particular context or act depicted.

Both the SAJQ and the CSBI differentiate between hostile and instrumental aggression, whereas the variations of the CIA do not. By providing various reasons for an aggressive action, these two former measures include legitimacy assessments for injurious acts for both retaliation purposes (hostile) and as a means to win (instrumental). Unfortunately, neither the CSBI's nor the SAJQ's authors take advantage of utilizing this distinction in their data analysis. Future directions include establishing support for the validity and reliability of these measures through (a) qualitative inquiry into types of aggressive actions that occur in sport to provide content validity, (b) additional support of age- and gender-related differences in perceptions of the legitimacy of injurious acts in establishing discriminant validity, (c) further assessment of dimensionality and the internal consistency of dimensions, (d) comparison with observational measures and related constructs to establish criterion validity, and (e) multiple administrations to establish test-retest reliability.

Perceptions as to the Likelihood of Displaying Aggressive Actions

Whereas the previous section examined individuals' perceptions of the legitimacy of an aggressive act, the measures in this section address the reported *likelihood* that an individual will choose to act in an aggressive manner. Deluty's (1979) Children's Action Tendency Scale (CATS) is designed to assess children's self-reported aggressive tendencies in everyday situations, and included 10 scenarios involving provocation, frustration, and loss or conflict at home or at school. Each of these scenarios was followed by three response alternatives: aggressive (a hostile act involving self-expression at the expense of others), assertive (self-expression of one's thoughts and feelings, in a nonhostile manner, while not violating the rights of others), and submissive (a nonhostile act that considered others' feelings and rights over one's own). Responses were offered in three, forced-choice pairs, thus providing three responses for each situation. Scoring involved summing the number of times assertive, aggressive, and submissive alterna-

tives were chosen. The aggressive score could be further divided into physical and nonphysical aggression.

Using three separate public school samples, Deluty (1979) assessed the validity of the CATS. CATS aggressiveness score correlated significantly for all three samples with peer reports of physical aggression (r's ranged from .48 to .68, $p<.001$), although only one sample's aggression score correlated significantly with teachers' reports of physical aggression ($r=.31$, $p<.05$). However, when subjects were rated as to being among the five most or five least aggressive children in the class, CATS aggressiveness score was highly correlated with both peer ($r=.45$, $p<.001$) and teacher rankings ($r=.39$, $p<.01$) of high aggression and low aggression ($r=-.31$, $p<.05$ and $r=-.38$, $p<.01$, respectively). The CATS was found to possess moderate split-half (.77) and 4-month test-retest ($r=.48$, $p<.001$) reliability and internal consistency (.80: K-R 20 formula for dichotomous responses) (Bredemeier, 1994; Deluty, 1979). Boys had significantly higher scores on both the CATS aggression subscale and behavioral observations than did girls, thus supporting the scale's discriminant validity. However, the aggressive subscale of the CATS correlated significantly with behavioral observations for boys ($r=.46$, $p<.05$) but not for girls (Deluty, 1984), which suggests that the concurrent validity of the CATS aggression component is much stronger for boys than girls. In fact, the aggression scores for girls were much more highly correlated with the absence of submissive behavior ($r=-.54$, $p<.01$) than with the presence of aggressive behavior ($r=.14$, ns) (Deluty, 1984). Age-related differences in aggression scores were found (Deluty, 1984), thus providing support for the scale's concurrent validity based on research confirming age-related changes in aggression (Parke & Slaby, 1983). Further examination of the CATS aggression subscale is needed to establish its validity with female populations; longitudinal studies will also assist in establishing the developmental aspects of reported aggression as assessed via this instrument.

Bredemeier and her colleagues (Bredemeier et al., 1986) adapted the CATS to a sport setting. The Sport Children's Action Tendency Scale (SCATS) is identical to the CATS, with the exception that the SCATS scenarios involve game or sport contexts. As with the CATS, the SCATS aggression scores can be divided into physical and nonphysical subscales: Six of the 10 stories present physical aggression alternatives; four present nonphysical. Whereas the CATS aggressive responses represent reactive, or hostile, aggression, the SCATS included five instrumental aggression responses based on research establishing the prominence of this type of aggressive act in the sport realm (Bredemeier, 1978).

Face validity of the SCATS was established through the feedback of eight judges, four psychologists and four physical educators, concerning the types of behavior each SCATS item was designed to portray; judgments were accurate in all instances. The psychometric properties of the SCATS reviewed here focus on the aggression subscale. Using 4th through 7th graders as subjects ($N=106$), concurrent validity was established in two ways: The aggression subscales scores of the CATS and the SCATS were highly correlated for both physical ($r=.74$, $p<.001$) and nonphysical aggression ($r=.68$, $p<.001$), and SCATS aggression scores were significantly correlated to teacher behavioral ratings of observed physical ($r=.33$, $p<.001$) and verbal ($r=.22$, $p<.05$) aggression. Internal consistency was adequate (.85). For boys, legitimacy judgments (ISAS) were significantly correlated with physical ($r=.39$, $p<.01$) and non-physical ($r=.48$, $p<.001$) aggression; for girls, these correlations only approached significance (r's=.28, ns) (Bredemeier, 1994).

Males scored significantly higher than females in aggression, thus adding to the measure's discriminant validity. Older children indicated a greater tendency to choose aggressive responses, a finding that is aligned with other research reporting age-related changes in aggression. Unfortunately, the correlations between the CATS and SCATS subscales for boys and girls separately have not been provided in the literature; thus, analysis of the validity of the SCATS for girls has not been established, given the questionable concurrent validity of the CATS aggression subscale for females. Further research is called for which utilizes a developmental approach (Bredemeier, 1994).

Stephens, Bredemeier, and Shields (in press) developed another measure, Judgments About Moral Behavior in Youth Sport Questionnaire (JAMBYSQ), which contains a measure of likelihood to aggress against an opponent in a sport context. Due to its grounding in the moral literature, the JAMBYSQ will be discussed with regard to its moral dimension in the chapter on the measurement of moral issues (Bredemeier & Shields, this volume). However, several aspects of the JAMBYSQ are particularly germane to this discussion in that this instrument addresses individual perceptions of the appropriateness of the aggressive behavior for self and other, team norms for aggressive behavior, contextual situations under which aggression is more tempting, and likelihood of aggressive action.

Results of three youth sport samples (girls' soccer: $n=209$; coed soccer: $n=325$; ice hockey: $n=322$) utilizing the JAMBYSQ have indicated that subjects' likelihood to aggress was positively correlated with their perceptions of their teams' norm to aggress (r's>.54) and their coaches' ego orientation (r's >.19), providing support for the JAMBYSQ's construct validity (Stephens, 1995; Stephens & Bredemeier, 1996; Stephens & Kavanagh, 1996). In addition, subjects who indicated that the protagonist should aggress indicated a higher mean likelihood to aggress than did those who stated that the protagonist should not aggress (Stephens et al., in press). Results from the coed soccer sample indicated that males' likelihood to aggress was significantly greater than that for females, thus supporting the JAMBYSQ's discriminant validity (Stephens, 1995). Recent research (Shields, Gardner, Bredemeier, & Bostrum, 1995) has added to this line of inquiry by assessing subjects' perceptions of coaches' expectations in regard to aggressive behavior. Future research with the JAMBYSQ should utilize multiple scenarios to more accurately assess the complex nature of aggression and should administer other types of aggression measures, such as the CIA, to further establish the measure's construct validity. Currently the JAMBYSQ is being modified for use with adult populations in several different sports.

Summary. Both the SCATS and the JAMBYSQ provide tools for examining individual's self-described likelihood to perform an aggressive act, adding another dimension to understanding and predicting aggressive behavior. Psychometric data

has been presented that supports the utilization of the SCATS as a valid measurement of aggression in children; further study of its validity and reliability with other populations of various age and socioeconomic groups is both warranted and necessary. Further tests of concurrent validity utilizing behavioral observations for both the SCATS and the JAMBYSQ are needed, as well qualitative inquiry to more directly address the issue of normative rules in sport.

Measures of Aggressive Motivations

Although the two preceding categories of aggression measures have assessed perceptions concerning aggressive actions in specific hypothetical contexts, the measures addressed in this section assess more trait-like tendencies for aggressive actions. Bredemeier (1978) developed a measure designed to assess self-described motives, reactive or instrumental, for aggression in sport contexts. This measure, the Bredemeier Athletic Aggression Inventory (BAAGI), contains 100 items, divided equally into two scales: reactive ("At times I am surprised at my anger toward an opponent") and instrumental ("A winner is someone whose performance is completely detached from emotional responses to other people"). Each item is scored on a 4-point Likert-type scale (1 = *strong agreement*, 4 = *strong disagreement*). High scores indicate low levels of aggression whereas low scores indicate high levels of aggression. Initial testing of the instrument with female college athletes ($N= 166$) provided support for the BAAGI's concurrent and construct validity. Subscales were found to be highly and negatively correlated ($r=-.69$, $p<.01$); additional research has supported this finding (Sachs, 1978). The reactive scale of the BAAGI was found to be significantly correlated to the Buss-Durkee (1957) assault ($r=-.36$, $p<.01$), verbal ($r=-.32$, $p<.01$), and total ($r=-.54$, $p<.01$) hostility subscales, with high levels of reactive aggression associated with high levels of assault and hostility. High scores on the instrumental scale correlated with low scores on the verbal ($r=.27$, $p<.01$) and total ($r=.33$, $p<.01$) hostility subscales, but not the assault subscale ($r=.12$, ns). Significant correlations between scores of social desirability (as measured by the Crowne & Marlowe scale, 1960) and reactive ($r=.34$, $p<01$) and instrumental aggression ($r=-.46$, $p<.01$) indicated that reactive aggression was socially undesirable, whereas instrumental aggression was seen as more socially desirable by subjects. This should be expected, however, because aggression, even in an athletic context, is not socially desirable behavior for females (Bredemeier, 1978). BAAGI reactive scores correlated significantly with coaches' evaluations of the athletes' reactive aggression ($r=-.26$, $p<.01$). Thus, initial testing of the BAAGI supported its construct and concurrent validity.

However, Worrell and Harris (1986), in a season-long study of male ice hockey players, compared instrumental subscale scores to aggressive behavior (operationalized as penalties) and found negative correlations between perceived and observed aggression (actual r's not reported); players perceived themselves to be less aggressive than their observed play suggested. These findings call into question the concurrent validity of the BAAGI.

Further developments resulted in the BAAGI-short form (BAAGI-S) (Wall & Gruber, 1986), which contains 28 items, equally divided between the reactive and instrumental subscales. Items utilized for the BAAGI-S were those with the highest factor loadings for each subscale, and represented the elements of anger, hostility, and frustration dispositions toward aggression. Scoring of the BAAGI-S was reversed from that of the BAAGI: A high score indicated a high level of aggression. Subjects (*n*=21 female intercollegiate basketball players) were administered the BAAGI-S multiple times, i.e., pre- and postgame, for three easy and three crucial contests. Intraclass correlations between the subscales over these multiple administrations were significant (*p*<.05), ranging from .62 to .93 for instrumental and from .73 to .95 for reactive aggression. Mean levels for both subscales remained constant over time and did not appear to fluctuate.

In general, results have provided support for the concurrent and construct validity of the BAAGI and the BAAGI-S. However, examination of the items of the BAAGI-S shows it to be measuring constructs other than aggressive intent, thus confounding the measure. For example, one item states: Performing well is more important to me than the satisfaction I get from beating somebody. Agreement with this item can reflect a focus on task orientation, as measured by the TEOSQ (Duda, 1989). The existence of other, more valid measures of aggression preclude the further use of this measure. Other appropriate measures of aggression, used in conjunction with sound measures of other constructs, such as motivation-related variables, will result in a greater contribution of knowledge to the field.

Butt's (1979) Sport Motivation Scales (SMS) is based on her theoretical model that identifies three sources of sports motivation: aggression, conflict, and competence. Based on work by Lorenz (1966), Freud (1923), and White (1963), Butt examines sport motivation from four levels, which include the biological, psychological, social, and secondary reinforcement levels. She posits that the basic life energy of the biological level may be channelled into aggression, conflict, and competence at the psychological level and that these motivations are present in varying degrees in all individuals. Butt sees the highly aggressive individual as being very energetic and appearing to be active, eager, and impulsive. This type of athlete is quick to find fault with others and may attack them verbally or physically (Butt, 1995). This conceptual definition has been operationalized in the aggression subscale of the SMS. Based on her theoretical model, Butt has developed the SMS to assess the three previously mentioned psychological motivations and two social motivations, those of competition and cooperation. Both a short form (5 items per subscale) and a long form (10 items per subscale) have undergone testing. With regard to the aggression component of the SMS, the items are as follows: full of energy, impulsive, powerful, telling someone off, let someone have it if in your way, angry, excited, impatient, enraged, and vicious; the short form included the first five items listed. Items were generated based on accounts of athletes representing high levels of each motivational component. Subjects were instructed to respond as to the degree to which they felt each of the following behavioral descriptions; subjects were asked to provide their sport (anchoring item) prior to responding to the scale as a whole. Responses to each item utilize a true/false format; however, factor analysis testing utilized a 1-5 rating scale for responses (Butt, 1995).

Internal consistency of the aggression subscale (short form), based on results of 188 subjects (57 males, 121 females), was low (.43) for females, but higher for males (.51) (Butt, 1995). Two-week test-retest reliability was moderate (coefficients for all scales ranged from .50 to .80; individual scale statistics not provided). In terms of construct validity, aggression was found to be positively related to negative affect, as measured by the Bradburn and Caplovitz' affect scales (Bradburn, 1969), for both men (*r*=.34, *p*<.05) and women (*r*=.22, *p*<.05) and positive affect in men (*r*=.32, *p*<.05). Based on the results of six studies that examined males and females separately (Butt, 1987), aggression was found to correlate more highly with competition (males: *r*'s ranged from .14 [ns] to .45 [*p*<.001]; females: *r*'s ranged from .29 ([*p*<.001] to .44 [*p*<.001]) than with cooperation (males: *r*'s ranged from .01 [ns] to .33 [*p*<.001]; females: *r*'s ranged from -.20 [*p*<.001] to .26 [*p*<.001]). In a study of tennis players (Butt & Cox, 1992), elite athletes scored significantly higher in aggression than did university athletes or recreational players. No gender differences in aggression scores were found (Butt, 1995).

Initial psychometric data on the SMS-Long Form has indicated an increase in internal consistency for the 10- item aggression subscale over the 5-item form for both males (.76) and females (.56). The SMS-Long Form also revealed larger differences in aggression scores for males (*M*=4.6, *SD*=2.4) and females (*M*=3.9, *SD*=1.8); however, statistical significance was not indicated (Butt, 1995).

The SMS approaches aggression from a personality perspective, rather than from an examination of aggressive behavior or legitimacy of aggressive actions. Although a few of the items contained in the SMS do address the issue of intent (telling someone off and letting someone have it if in your way), it is a more general measure of affect (angry, impatient, impulsive, excited) that, according to Butt (1995), is typical of an aggressive athlete. The SMS may provide a useful tool for researchers wishing to measure aggression in this manner; however, internal consistency remains low, especially for females. Construct validity may be questioned due to lack of gender differences in the aggression subscale of the SMS-Short Form, however. It is important to note that the experimental samples utilized in Butt's work contained primarily noncontact sport athletes (e.g., tennis players, swimmers, figure skaters, and gymnasts).

Summary. The BAAGI and SMS both address aggression as a general trait-like disposition. However, the items of the BAAGI contain items that address constructs other than aggression; thus, it is suggested that more recent measures that utilize more valid operational definitions be utilized. The SMS, theoretically grounded in a biological / instinctual framework, has weak-to-moderate psychometric support for its dimensionality, construct validity, and reliability. Once the psychometric properties of the SMS have more substantial support, future directions in aggression research could address the relationship between this aggressive personality construct and other judgments and perceptions of aggressive behavior.

Overall Summary

Research has utilized a number of theoretical foundations and operational definitions in assessing aggression in sport contexts. The majority of this work has emanated from the social learning perspective, whereas recently a program of research examining sport aggression as a moral issue has emerged. The most enduring of the operational definitions has been the use of penalties to provide a measure of observed behavior. This method of defining aggression, however, is plagued by a lack of certainty concerning the intent of the aggressor, the inability to distinguish the motive of the aggressor, and reservations as to the accuracy and freedom from bias of the observer.

Research that utilizes perceptions of the legitimacy of injurious acts provides, along with the aggressive act, the aggressor's intent and the consequences of the act, rather than rely on subjects' correct interpretation of the intent and outcome. Different examples of this measurement style employ a "continuum" approach that queries the subject about the legitimacy of increasingly serious aggressive actions. Some of these measures include follow-up questions concerning the legitimacy of the act at various levels of competition and for a variety of motives. The measures of the perceived legitimacy of injurious acts allow researchers to further their understanding of perceptions of normative rules that exist at many levels of competi-

tion. The Continuum of Injurious Acts (CIA), in particular, has found support for its construct and concurrent validity and has been successfully adapted to different contexts; further developments of the Carolina Sport Behavior Inventory (CSBI) and Sport Aggression Justification Questionnaire (SAJQ) may establish their utility.

Initial psychometric support has been found for the Scale of Children's Action Tendencies in Sport (SCATS), which assesses children's choices of aggressive, assertive, and submissive actions in game or sport settings. Although this measure takes a step toward measuring actual behavior through assessing the likelihood that the child will act in an aggressive manner, further evidence for its validity and reliability is needed. The Judgments About Moral Behavior in Youth Sport Questionnaire (JAMBYSQ) provides a tool to examine individuals' likelihood to aggress in a sport situation. Two measures of aggressive motivations, the Bredemeier Athletic Aggression Inventory (BAAGI) and the Sports Motivation Scales (SMS), show limited support in understanding sport aggression; construct validity has yet to be established, and neither measure maintains a consistent focus with respect to "intent to harm."

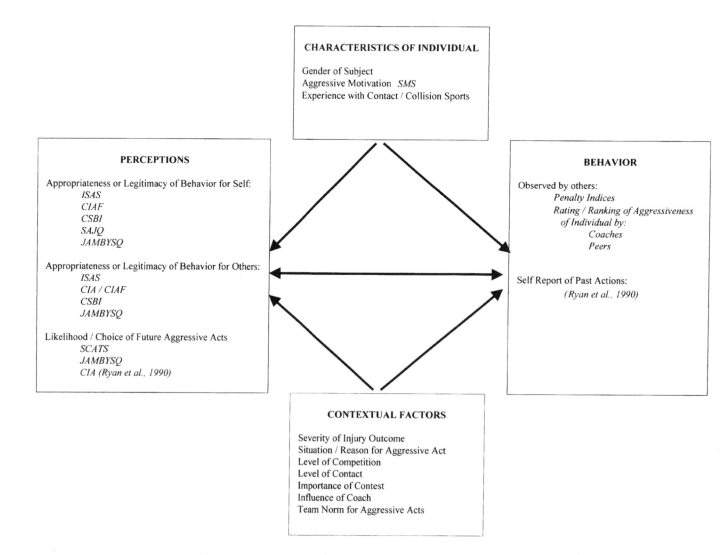

Figure 1. Interrelationships between various aspects of the aggression construct.

In general, the psychometric properties of existing aggression measures have not been thoroughly and extensively examined. This is especially apparent when the measures addressing this construct are compared to measures of other sport-related constructs, such as goal perspectives and state/trait anxiety. For example, although exploratory factor analysis has been utilized in some cases (penalty indices, CSBI, SMS), no evidence of confirmatory factor analysis has been provided for any of the measures reviewed. In addition, one important limitation of current aggression measurements is the general lack of an underlying conceptual framework to guide instrument development. Exceptions to this observation include the JAMBYSQ, the SMS, and the CSBI.

Future Directions

The measurement of aggression in sport contexts has suffered from a lack of consistency in operational definitions. Although the use of various definitions has limited the amount of research support for any one aggression measure, it does provide an opportunity to examine sport aggression from a number of distinct, yet related viewpoints (see Figure 1). Future directions in sport-aggression research should focus on creating programs of research to provide substantial psychometric support for measures utilizing a consistent operational definition, followed by examining the relationships between different aspects of the aggression construct. For example, several measures (i.e., the CSBI, SAJQ, CIA, JAMBYSQ) include contextual factors that have been found to impact perceptions of legitimacy of aggressive acts. Further investigation into the interaction between individual characteristics, contextual factors, perceptions, and behavior is necessary. These relationships should then be investigated across contexts and populations.

Aggression measures should be based on operational definitions that clearly include the intentional aspect of the aggression. Provision of a clear-cut outcome or consequence to the action would increase the validity and reliability of the measure. Further inquiry into understanding perceptions of normative rules is needed to provide a deeper understanding of the roles teammates and coaches play in athletes' aggression. Aggressive behavior in sport is poorly understood; thus, a call for qualitative inquiry into perceptions of aggression among individuals of different ages and competitive levels is imperative if we are committed to understanding this complex phenomenon.

Recently, a number of general, nonsport measures of aggression have been developed. Brief descriptions are included in the next section to guide sport researchers in instrument development and to provide measures that may be utilized in establishing criterion and concurrent validity of present and future sport-specific aggression measures. However, caution should be exercised with regard to utilizing measures of aggression in nonsport (daily-life) settings in order to provide validation for sport measures, in that aggression may be perceived substantially differently in the two contexts.

Nonsport aggression measures. The first part of this section will introduce self-report inventories of general, nonsport aggression. The last part will include behavioral and observational tools that show promise for adaptation for sport contexts.

Recently, Buss and Perry (1992) have constructed the Aggression Questionnaire (AQ). Some items of the AQ were borrowed intact from the Buss-Durkee Hostility Inventory (BDHI; Buss & Durkee, 1957), which was developed to measure trait aggression along seven components. Citing numerous problems with the older measure, Buss and Perry developed the AQ stating that "it retains the major virtue of the older inventory - analysis of aggression into several components - but...meets current psychometric standards" (p. 452). Initial testing reduced from 75 to 29 the number of items that address self-reports of behavior and feelings. Responses are made on a 5-point Likert-type rating scale (1 = *extremely uncharacteristic of me*, 5 = *extremely characteristic of me*). Four factors emerged from the principal axis factoring and oblimin rotation: physical aggression, verbal aggression, anger, and hostility. This factor structure was replicated across three samples (total $n=1,253$). Confirmatory factor analysis (LISREL IV) provided support for a model consisting of four factors of aggression, linked by a higher order of general aggression. All factors were significantly intercorrelated (r's ranged from .25 to .48). Internal consistency was adequate (alphas>.72) as was 9-week test-retest reliability (r's>.72; $n=372$). Males ($n=612$) scored significantly higher on all scales ($p<.005$), except for anger, than did females ($n=641$). These findings were substantiated by Archer, Kilpatrick, and Bramwell (1995). Factor scores also significantly correlated (r's>.20, $p<.05$) with peer nominations for behaviors that were representative of the factor items in a sample of 98 male college students, providing a modest support for the concurrent validity to the AQ. Based on these results, the AQ offers a multicomponent measure that shows promise for assessing general aggression. The AQ has recently been used in assessing aggression in ice hockey spectators (Russell & Arms, 1995).

Gladue (1991) created the Aggression Inventory (AI), a self-report measure designed to assess trait aggressive behavioral characteristics (Olweus, 1986; Olweus, Mattsson, Schalling, & Low, 1980). The AI contains 28 items scored using a 5-point Likert-type scale (1 = *does not apply at all to me*, 5 = *applies exactly to me*). Exploratory factor analyses (varimax rotation), performed separately for male ($n=517$) and female ($n=443$) subjects, each resulted in four factors containing identical items: physical (32.6% variance explained for males, 5.6% for females); verbal (12.7% males, 33.9% females); impulsive/impatient (8.4% males, 15.2% females); and avoid (4.9% males, 5.3% females). Measures of internal consistency were adequate (alphas>.70, except the avoidance factor for men, .65). In terms of mean factor scores, males were more physically and verbally aggressive, impatient/impulsive, and less likely to avoid confrontations than were females, thus supporting the measure's construct validity based on the literature (Eagly & Steffen, 1986; Hyde, 1984, 1986). Overall, the AI appears to be a useful self-report measure of aggressive behavior characteristics. It has already been utilized in a study of fighting behavior in a sample of males that included rugby and soccer players (Archer, Holloway, & McLoughlin, 1995).

In summary, two recently proposed measures, the Aggression Questionnaire (Buss & Perry, 1992) and the Aggression Inventory (Gladue, 1991), seem to provide psychometrically sound measures of trait aggression. However, test-retest support for reliability has been published only for the Aggression

Questionnaire (Buss & Perry, 1992). These measures show potential for providing sport researchers with assessment tools for trait aggression in nonsport contexts.

Rating and ranking scales. Researchers interested in developing checklists for aggression in the sport domain are referred to the work arising out of the development of the Teacher Checklist by Coie and Dodge (Coie, 1990; Coie & Dodge, 1988; Hudley & Graham, 1993; Price & Dodge, 1989), which was developed to assess aspects of aggressive and prosocial behavior, social sensitivity, and classroom task performance. Also, work by Epkins and Meyers (1994) and Skelton, Glynn, and Berta (1991) might be of interest in creating parental and teacher/coach checklists.

Behavior observation coding systems, again based on Coie and Dodge's work (Coie & Kupersmidt, 1983; Dodge, 1983; Dodge, Coie, Pettit, & Price, 1990; Price & Dodge, 1989) might prove useful for researchers interested in devising similar systems in sport and/or physical education settings. For research utilizing peer nominations, see the contributions of Epkins and Meyers (1994), Hudley and Graham (1993), and Walder, Abelson, Eron, Banta, and Laulich (1961).

References

Anshel, M. (1994). *Sport psychology: From theory to practice.* Scottsdale, AZ: Gorsuch Scarisbrick.

Archer, J., Holloway, R., & McLoughlin, K. (1995). Self-reported physical aggression among young men. *Aggressive Behavior, 21*, 325-342.

Archer, J., Kilpatrick, G., & Bramwell, R. (1995). Comparison of two aggression inventories. *Aggressive Behavior, 21*, 371-380.

Ardrey, R. (1966). *The territorial imperative.* New York: Atheneum.

Bandura, A. (1973). *Aggression: A social learning analysis.* Englewood Cliffs, NJ: Prentice-Hall.

Baron, R. (1977). *Human aggression.* New York: Plenum.

Berkowitz, L. (Ed.). (1969). *Roots of aggression.* New York: Atheneton.

Berkowitz, L. (1978). Whatever happened to the frustration-aggression hypothesis? *American Behavioral Sciences, 21*, 691-708.

Berkowitz, L., & Alioto, J. (1973). The meaning of an observed event as a determinant of its aggressive consequences. *Journal of Personality and Social Psychology, 28*, 206-217.

Blair, S. (1985). Professionalization of attitude toward play in children and adults. *Research Quarterly for Exercise and Sport, 56*, 82-83.

Bradburn, B. (1969). *The structure of psychological well-being.* Chicago, IL: Aldine- Atherton.

Bredemeier, B. (1978). The assessment of reactive and instrumental aggression. In *Proceedings of the International Symposium of Psychological Assessment in Sport* (pp. 136-145). Netanya, Israel: Wingate Institute for Physical Education and Sport.

Bredemeier, B. (1983). Athletic aggression: A moral concern. In J. Goldstein (Ed.), *Sports violence* (pp. 42-81). New York: Springer-Verlag.

Bredemeier, B. (1985). Moral reasoning and the perceived legitimacy of intentionally injurious sport acts. *Journal of Sport Psychology, 7*, 110-124.

Bredemeier, B. (1994). Children's moral reasoning and their assertive, aggressive, and submissive tendencies in sport and daily life. *Journal of Sport and Exercise Psychology, 16*, 1-14.

Bredemeier, B., & Shields, D. (1984). The utility of moral stage analysis in the investigation of athletic aggression. *Sociology of Sport Journal, 1*, 138-149.

Bredemeier, B., & Shields, D. (1986). Game reasoning and interactional morality. *The Journal of Genetic Psychology, 147*, 257-275.

Bredemeier, B., Shields, D., Weiss, M., & Cooper, B. (1986). The relationship of sport involvement with children's moral reasoning and aggression tendencies. *Journal of Sport Psychology, 8*, 304-318.

Bredemeier, B., Shields, D., Weiss, M., & Cooper, B. (1987). The relationship between children's legitimacy judgments and their moral reasoning, aggression tendencies, and sport involvement. *Sociology of Sport Journal, 4*, 48-60.

Buss, A. (1961). *The psychology of aggression.* New York: Wiley.

Buss, A., & Durkee, A. (1957). An inventory for assessing different kinds of hostility. *Journal of Consulting Psychology, 21*, 343-349.

Buss, A., & Perry, A. (1992). The aggression questionnaire. *Journal of Personality and Social Psychology, 63*, 452-459.

Butt, D. (1979). Short scales for the measurement of sport motivations. *International Journal of Sport Psychology, 10*, 203-216.

Butt, D. (1987). *Psychology of sport: The behavior, motivation, personality, and performance of athletes* (2nd ed.). New York: Van Nostrand Reinhold.

Butt, D. (1995). On the measurement of competence motivation. In P. Shout & S. Fiske (Eds.), *Personality research, methods, and theory* (pp. 313-331). Hillsdale, NJ: Lawrence Erlbaum.

Butt, D., & Cox, D. (1992). Motivational patterns in Davis Cup, university and recreational tennis players. *International Journal of Sport Psychology, 23*, 1-13.

Coie, J. (1990). *The Teacher Checklist.* Unpublished manuscript.

Coie, J., & Dodge, K. (1988). Multiple sources of data on social behavior and social status in the school: A cross-age comparison. *Child Development, 59*, 815-829.

Coie, J., & Kupersmidt, J. (1983). A behavioral analysis of emerging social status in boys' groups. *Child Development, 54*, 1386-1399.

Conroy, D., Silva, J., Newcomer, R., Walker, B., & Johnson., M. (1996). *The role of socialization in the perceived legitimacy of aggressive sport behavior.* Manuscript submitted for publication.

Cox, R. (1990). *Sport psychology: Concepts and applications.* Dubuque, IA: Brown.

Crowne, D., & Marlowe, D. (1960). A new scale of social desirability independent of psychopathology. *Journal of Consulting Psychology, 24*, 349-354.

Cullen, J., & Cullen, F. (1971). The structural and contextual conditions of group norm violation: Some implications form the game of ice hockey. *International Review of Sport Sociology, 11*, 69-77.

Deluty, R. (1979). Children's Action Tendency Scale: A self-report measure of aggressiveness, assertiveness, and submissiveness in children. *Journal of Consulting and Clinical Psychology, 47*, 1061-1071.

Deluty, R. (1984). Behavioral validation of the children's action tendency scale. *Journal of Behavioral Assessment, 6*, 115-130.

Dodge, K. (1983). Behavioral antecedents of peer social rejection and isolation. *Child Development, 54*, 1386-1399.

Dodge, K., Coie, J., Pettit, G., & Price, J. (1990). Peer status and aggression in boys' groups: Developmental and contextual analyses. *Child Development, 61*, 1289-1309.

Dollard, J., Doob, L., Miller, N., Mowrer, O., & Sears, R. (1939). *Frustration and aggression.* New Haven, CT: Yale University Press.

Duda, J. (1989). The relationship between task and ego orientation and the perceived purpose of sport among high school athletes. *Journal of Sport and Exercise Psychology, 11*, 318- 335.

Duda, J., & Huston, L. (1995). The relationship of goal orientation and degree of competitive sport participation to the endorsement of aggressive acts in American football. In R. Vanfraechem-Raway & Y. VandenAudweele (Eds.), *IXth European Congress on Sport Psychology Proceedings* (pp. 655-662). Brussels, Belgium.

Duda, J., Olson, L., & Templin, T. (1991). The relationship of task and ego orientation to sportsmanship attitudes and the perceived legitimacy of injurious acts. *Research Quarterly for Exercise and Sport, 62*, 79-87.

Eagly, A., & Steffen, V. (1986). Gender and aggressive behaviour: A meta-analytic review of the social psychological literature. *Psychological Bulletin, 100*, 309-330.

Epkins, C., & Meyers, A. (1994). Assessment of childhood depression, anxiety, and aggression: Convergent and discriminant validity of self-, parent-, teacher-, and peer-report measures. *Journal of Personality Assessment, 62*, 364-381.

Freud, S. (1925). *Collected papers*. London: Hogarth.

Freud, S. (1961). The ego and the id. In J. Strachey (Ed. and Trans.), *The standard edition of the complete psychological works of Sigmund Freud* (Vol. 19). London: Hogarth Press. (Original work published in 1923)

Gladue, R. (1991). Qualitative and quantitative sex differences in self-reported aggressive behavioral characteristics. *Psychological Reports, 68*, 675-684.

Hudley, C., & Graham, S. (1993). An attributional intervention to reduce peer-directed aggression among African American boys. *Child Development, 64*, 124-138.

Husman, B., & Silva, J. (1984). Aggression in sport: Definitional and theoretical considerations. In J. Silva & R. Weinberg (Eds.), *Psychological foundations in sport* (pp. 246-260). Champaign, IL: Human Kinetics.

Hyde, J. (1984). How large are gender differences in aggression? A developmental meta-analysis. *Developmental Psychology, 20*, 722-736.

Hyde, J. (1986). Gender differences in aggression. In J. Hyde & M. Linn (Eds.), *The psychology of gender: Advances through meta-analysis* (pp. 51-66). Baltimore, MD: Johns Hopkins University Press.

Knoppers, A. (1985). Professionalization of attitudes: A review and critique. *Quest, 37*, 92-102.

Lorenz, K. (1966). *On aggression*. New York: Harcourt, Brace & World.

McCarthy, J., & Kelly, B. (1978a). Aggression, performance variables, and anger self-report in ice hockey players. *Journal of Psychology, 99*, 97-101.

McCarthy, J., & Kelly, B. (1978b). Aggressive behavior and its effect on performance over time in ice hockey athletes: An archival study. *International Journal of Sport Psychology, 9*, 90-96.

McGuire, E., Courneya, K., Widmeyer, W., & Carron, A. (1992). Aggression as a potential mediator of the home advantage in professional ice hockey. *Journal of Sport and Exercise Psychology, 14*, 148-158.

Miller, N. (1941). The frustration-aggression hypothesis. *Psychological Review, 48*, 337-342.

Montagu, M. (1968). The new litany of "innate depravity," or original sin revisited. In M. Montagu (Ed.), *Man and aggression* (pp. 3-17). New York, Oxford University Press.

Morris, D. (1967). *The naked ape*. New York: McGraw-Hill.

Nicholls, J. (1989). *The competitive ethos and democratic education*. Cambridge, MA: Harvard University Press.

Olweus, D. (1986). Aggression and hormones: Behavioral relationship with testosterone and adrenaline. In D. Olweus, J. Block, & M Radke-Yarrow (Eds.), *Development of anti-social and prosocial behavior* (pp. 51-72). New York: Academic Press.

Olweus, D, Mattsson, A., Schalling, D., & Low, H. (1980). Testosterone, aggression, physical and personality measures in normal adolescent males. *Psychosomatic Medicine, 42*, 253-269.

Parke, R., & Slaby, R. (1983). The development of aggression. In P. Mussen (Ed.), *Handbook of child psychology: Vol 3. Socialization, personality, and social development* (pp. 547-641). New York: Wiley.

Price, J., & Dodge, K. (1989). Reactive and proactive aggression in childhood: Relations to peer status and social context dimensions. *Journal of Abnormal Child Psychology, 17*, 455-471.

Russell, G. (1981). Conservatism, birth order, leadership, and the aggression of Canadian ice hockey players. *Perceptual and Motor Skills, 53*, 3-7.

Russell, G. (1993). *The social psychology of sport*. New York: Springer-Verlag.

Russell, G., & Arms, R. (1995). False consensus effect, physical aggression, anger, and a willingness to escalate a disturbance. *Aggressive Behavior, 21*, 381-386.

Russell, G., & Russell, A. (1984). Sports penalties: An alternative means of measuring aggression. *Social Behavior and Personality, 12*, 69-74.

Ryan, K., Williams, J., & Wimer, B. (1990). Athletic aggression: Perceived legitimacy and behavioral intentions in girls' high school basketball. *Journal of Sport and Exercise Psychology, 12*, 48-55.

Sachs, M. (1978). An analysis of aggression in female softball players. *Review of Sports and Leisure, 3*, 85-97.

Shields, D., & Bredemeier, B. (1995). *Character development and physical activity*. Champaign, IL: Human Kinetics.

Shields, D., Gardner, D., Bredemeier, B., & Bostrum, A. (1995). Leadership, cohesion, and team norms regarding cheating and aggression. *Sociology of Sport Journal, 12*, 324-336.

Silva, J. (1983). The perceived legitimacy of rule violating behavior in sport. *Journal of Sport Psychology, 5*, 438-448.

Silva, J. (1984). Factors related to the acquisition and exhibition of aggressive sport behavior. In J. Silva & R. Weinberg (Eds.), *Psychological foundations of sport* (pp. 261-273). Champaign, IL: Human Kinetics.

Silva, J., & Conroy, D. (1995). Understand aggressive behavior and its effects upon athletic performance. In K. Henschen & W. Straub (Eds.) *Sport psychology: An analysis of athlete behavior* (pp. 149-159). Ithaca, NY: Mouvement Publications.

Silva, J., & Husman, B. (1995). Aggression: An historical perspective. In K. Henschen & W. Straub (Eds.) *Sport psychology: An analysis of athlete behavior* (pp. 149-159). Ithaca, NY: Mouvement Publications.

Skelton, D., Glynn, M., & Berta, S. (1991). Aggressive behavior as a function of taekwondo ranking. *Perceptual and Motor Skills, 72*, 179-182.

Stephens, D. (1995, Sept.). *Judgments about lying, hurting, and cheating in youth sport: Variations in patterns of predictors for female and male soccer players*. Paper presented at the Association for the Advancement of Applied Sport Psychology Conference, New Orleans, LA.

Stephens, D., & Bredemeier, B. (1996). Moral atmosphere and judgments about aggression in girls' soccer: Relationships among moral and motivational variables. *Journal of Sport and Exercise Psychology, 18*, 158-173.

Stephens, D., Bredemeier, B., & Shields, D. (in press). Construction of a measure designed to assess players' descriptions and prescriptions for moral behavior in youth sport soccer. *International Journal of Sport Psychology*.

Stephens, D., & Kavanagh, B. (1996). Aggression in youth sport: An examination of Canadian ice hockey. Manuscript in preparation.

Thirer, J. (1992). Aggression. In R. Singer, M. Murphey, & L. Tennant (Eds.), *Handbook of research in sport psychology* (pp. 365-387). New York: Macmillan.

Thompson, M. (1991). *Situation: An integral factor in the justification of sport aggression by NCAA Division 1-A varsity basketball players*. Paper presented at the Association for the Advancement of Applied Sport Psychology Conference, Savannah, GA.

Thompson, M. (1993). *Gender and aggression in sport: A stereotype is challenged*. Paper presented at the Association for the Advancement of Applied Sport Psychology Conference, Montreal, Quebec.

Thompson, M., & Cook, D. (1992). *Injury severity as a factor in the justification of sport aggression by NCAA Division 1-A varsity bas-*

ketball players (abstract). Paper presented at the Association for the Advancement of Applied Sport Psychology Conference, Colorado Springs, CO.

Thompson, M., Cook, D., & Tollefson, N. (1996). *Development of the Sport Aggression Justification Questionnaire.* Manuscript submitted for publication.

Vokey, J., & Russell, G. (1992). On penalties in sport as measures of aggression. *Social Behavior and Personality, 20*(3), 219-226.

Walder L., Abelson, R., Eron, L., Banta, T., and Laulich, J. (1961). Development of a peer rating measure of aggression. *Psychological Reports, 9*, 497-556.

Wall B., & Gruber, J. (1986). Relevancy of athletic aggression inventory for use in women's intercollegiate basketball: A pilot investigation. *International Journal of Sport Psychology, 17*, 23-33.

Webb, H. (1969). Professionalization of attitudes toward play among adolescents. In G. Kenyon (Ed.), *Aspects of contemporary sport sociology* (pp. 161-178). Chicago: The Athletic Institute.

White, R. (1963). Ego and reality in psychoanalytic theory: A proposal regarding independent ego energies. *Psychological Issues, 3*, 297-333.

Widmeyer, W., & Birch, J. (1984). Aggression in professional ice hockey: A strategy for success or a reaction to failure? *The Journal of Psychology, 117*, 77-84.

Worrell, G., & Harris, D. (1986). The relationship of perceived and observed aggression of ice hockey players. *International Journal of Sport Psychology, 17*, 34-40.

Zelin, M., Adler, G., & Myerson, P. (1972). The anger self-report: An objective questionnaire for the measurement of expression. *Journal of Consulting Psychology, 39*, 340.

Zillman, D. (1979). *Hostility and aggression.* Hillsdale, NJ: Erlbaum.

Part VI

Self Concept
and Body Image

PART VI

In more individualistic societies, it is assumed that self-perceptions (such as self-concept and self-esteem) are fundamental to the very quality and nature of people's lives. Numerous assessments of the overall self have been developed and are discussed in Part VI. However, specific attention is given to measures of self-perceptions concerning the physical being and their relationship to the more general assessments. Measurement in this area has taken both unidimensional (e.g., Coopersmith's [1967] Self-Esteem Inventory) and multidimensional approaches (e.g., Marsh and colleagues' Self-Description Questionnaires I-III; Marsh, 1997) and has generally been conceptually based.

Contemporary society seems to place particular import on physical appearance or attractiveness. Given the behavioral and health-related implications of societally fueled apprehensions concerning the body (or particular body parts), a number of measures of body estimation, satisfaction, and disturbance have been developed. Established perceptual, cognitive, affective, and behavioral assessments of body image are distinguished and reviewed in this section of the book.

References

Coopersmith, S. (1967). *The antecedents of self-esteem.* San Francisco: Freeman.

Marsh, H.W. (1997). The measurement of physical self-concept: A construct validation approach. In K. R. Fox (Ed.), *The physical self: From motivation to well-being.* Champaign, IL: Human Kinetics.

Chapter 16

ADVANCES IN THE MEASUREMENT OF THE PHYSICAL SELF

Kenneth R. Fox
University of Exeter

Introduction

In the Western world, the self has become the central feature of individual existence. Such is our need to establish and project a unique and individualized identity that it can dominate most of our waking lives. In much the same way that an executive director organizes and directs the interests and functions of the company, we evaluate, manage, and modify our ongoing interactions with the environment with a view to producing personally satisfying outcomes for ourselves. To this extent, many have regarded self-esteem as *the* critical indicator of life adjustment and emotional well-being. We *enjoy* feeling good about ourselves and avoid, defend against, and rationalize experiences that make us feel inadequate or bad about ourselves. So strong is this need that often we devote inordinate amounts of time seeking material, social, intellectual or professional indicators of our worth. We may even be prepared to risk our health through overwork or engaging in high-risk behaviors (e.g., excessive dieting) and frequently we will ignore or distort information about ourselves in order to see ourselves in the best possible light.

Given the complexity of the self and its importance to human functioning, it seems impertinent to suggest that we can access an individual's inner sanctum through simple paper-and-pencil research techniques. However, as indicated throughout this chapter, considerable progress has been made with instrument development over recent years. The conceptual underpinnings and psychometric attributes of the predominant measures of physical self-perceptions are described later in this chapter. This progression has enabled increasing enlightenment regarding the nature of the physical self. Moreover, substantial areas where further investigation is required will be highlighted throughout this chapter which concludes with potential direction for future inquiry concerning the physical self.

The Need for Assessment of Physical Self-Perceptions

The body provides the vehicle through which we interface with life. Through embodiment, we explore, learn, present ourselves, and express our sexuality; and through its state of health, its capabilities, and its appearance, the physical self becomes a central element of the whole self. Our perceptions of our physical selves therefore provide a key to understanding the constitution of our identities, the basis of our self-esteem, and many of our behavior patterns.

It is therefore not surprising that many motivational theories have been constructed around self-perceptions, and these have increasingly been applied to the physical domain. Theories based on effectance motivation (White, 1959), competence motivation (Harter, 1978), achievement motivation (Nicholls, 1989), personal investment (Maehr & Braskamp, 1986), self-schema (Kendzierski, 1994), self-presentation (Leary, 1992), and self-efficacy theory (Bandura, 1977) have perceptions of the self and its attributes as central components. These frameworks have provided insight into differences in the behavioral patterns related to physical appearance and expression of achievement in sport and exercise settings.

At the same time, the physical self has consistently emerged as a key component of identity and self-esteem, particularly in cultures that attach importance and status to physical attractiveness and prowess. The recognition of self-esteem as a primary element of mental well-being indicates that understanding the functioning of a person will be difficult in isolation of the physical aspects of self. This is substantiated by recent evidence (Sonstroem & Potts, 1996) that physical self-perceptions not only contribute to self-esteem but are also *directly* related to a range of mental adjustment variables independently of self-esteem. In essence, if we are to fully understand the human being and its functioning across the lifespan, we are dependent on research tools that allow us to document (a) the critical physical self-perceptions that characterize individuals and groups, (b) the influence of physical self-perceptions on physical activity and health behaviors, (c) the nature of physical self-perception change as a result of these behaviors, (d) the mechanisms by which such changes influence self-esteem and other global indicators of mental well-being.

Valid and practical measures that provide this information would not only satisfy theorists but would also help exercise, sport, and health professionals improve program design and provide critical psychological outcome measures that establish intervention effectiveness.

Developments in Self-Perception Measurement

Within the disciplines of psychology, sociology, and philosophy, vast amounts have been written on the self, and terminology has been confused. However, a consensus is emerging across the psychology literature. *Self-esteem* is generally viewed as a global and relatively stable evaluative construct reflecting the degree to which an individual feels positive about him- or herself. Campbell (1984) defines it as "the awareness of good possessed by the self." *Good* in this case does not necessarily carry moral connotations but reflects the criteria that are central to the value system of the individual. These may be in line or at odds with the normative values or morals of the rest of society. *Self-worth* has essentially the same meaning as self-esteem. Often *self-concept* has been confounded with these terms. However, self-concept is best seen as a self-description rather than a self-evaluation and refers to the multitude of attributes and roles through which individuals evaluate themselves to establish self-esteem judgments. As such, it provides a framework that is akin to *identity,* a term that is more frequently used in the sociology literature. Evaluative statements such as *athletic competence* (Harter, 1985a, 1988) or *sport competence* (Fox & Corbin, 1989) may then be attached to related elements such as *athletic identity* (Brewer, Van Raalte, & Linder, 1993) that make up this framework.

From unidimensionality to multidimensionality

Although there had been several attempts throughout the '60s and '70s to produce conceptual models of the self, these were rarely adopted in empirical research. The result was that instrumentation was simplistic and the findings from hundreds of studies were rather limited in value. Commonly used instruments, such as the Coopersmith Self-Esteem Inventory (Coopersmith, 1967) and the Piers-Harris Children's Self-Concept Scale (Piers, 1984), required participants to rate themselves on a range of items about their features or abilities. Item responses in such scales, which were sometimes simple yes-no dichotomies, were then simply summed to produce a single self-esteem score. This *unidimensional* approach was essentially a frequency count of positive and negative self-statements. It assumed that equal weighting was given by the individual to all the specific elements of the self that happened to be mentioned in the questionnaire. There were no systematic attempts to measure self-perceptions in different domains of life, and informa-

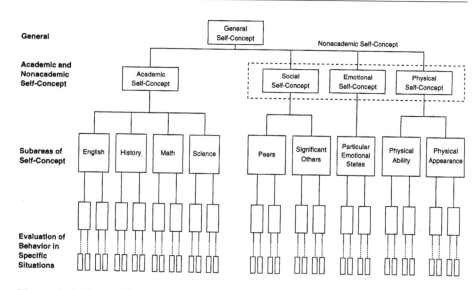

Figure 1. A hierarchical structure of self-concept.
Note: From G.R. Shavelson, J.J. Hubner, and G.C. Stanton, 1976. "Self-concept: Validation of Construct Interpretations." *Review of Educational Research, 46,* p. 413. Copyright © by the American Educational Research Association. Reprinted with permission.

tion that might have provided some insight into mechanisms of self-esteem change was lost. There has been for some time a consensus (Wylie, 1979) that such an approach to self-esteem assessment and related instrumentation is limited.

Most critical to the purposes of this chapter, unidimensionality precluded the recognition of the physical self as a distinct and measurable element of the whole self-concept. Some researchers had been interested for some time in isolated and specific aspects of the physical self. For example, Secord and Jourard (1953), through the Body Cathexis Scale, had attempted to assess self-perceptions of appearance of separate body parts. Sonstroem (1976) developed the Physical Estimation Scale, an assessment of perceived sport and physical ability, to accompany his psychological model of physical activity participation. However, there were no concerted efforts to simultaneously measure the physical self as a self-contained but essential element of the total self-concept until the late '70s - early '80s.

Harter (1982) originally developed the Perceived Competence Scale for Children to test her competence-based model of motivation. This instrument adopted a *multidimensional* profile approach to assess general self-worth alongside several elements of competence or adequacy in different life domains, which included athletic competence and physical appearance. Later, this instrument was extended and renamed The Self-Perception Profile for Children (Harter, 1985a) and led to the development of similar profiles for adolescents (Harter, 1988), college students (Neemann & Harter, 1986), and adults (Messer & Harter, 1986). A much richer source of information is provided by self-perception profiles as they allow the independent assessment of several elements of the self, and thus interrelationships among elements and their contribution to global self-esteem can be investigated. Self-perception profiles also provide the documentation of more discerning patterns of differences among individuals and populations that are more sensitive to change. The multidimensional profile approach to self-perception assessment, therefore, provided a much needed impetus to self-esteem research.

Self-Concept Models

The emergence of multidimensionality raised questions about the organizational structure of the different dimensions. In 1976, Shavelson, Hubner, and Stanton published a paper that detailed a model casting the multidimensionality of self within a hierarchical structure. This model, which was conceived for application to the educational setting, has provided the basis for the design of several self-concept instruments and has been well documented in the sport and exercise psychology literature (Fox, 1988; Sonstroem, 1984). The authors were careful to provide extensive direction on the model's properties and suggested testable hypotheses. The model is dendritic (rootlike) in form with a global self construct at the apex or trunk and the dimensionality represented by increasingly branching sublevels of self-perceptions of competence and adequacy. As lower levels in the branching are reached, then perceptions become more task or situation specific (see Figure 1).

This model was not systematically researched until the early to mid-80s when Marsh and colleagues (Marsh, Barnes, Cairnes, & Tidman, 1984) developed the Self-Description Questionnaire (SDQ-I) for pre-adolescents, the SDQ-II for adolescents (Marsh, Parker, & Barnes, 1985), and the SDQ-III for late adolescents/young adults (Marsh & O'Neill, 1984). Adopting the profile approach, the SDQ series measures specific elements of self-concept across the academic, social, physical, and emotional domains. During this period, advances in multivariate statistical techniques and computer capability have allowed much more sophisticated tests of the functioning of such models and their accompanying instrumentation, a topic that has absorbed the attention of Marsh and colleagues throughout the 80s and 90s (Marsh, 1997). Furthermore, several hybrids of multifaceted self-concept models have been carefully outlined and discussed (Byrne, 1996; Marsh & Hattie, 1996).

Multidimensionality and the Physical Self

With the establishment of multidimensionality, the physical self became systematically measurable as part of comprehensive models alongside perceived competence or adequacy in other life domains. In the self-perception or self-description profiles already mentioned, the physical self was represented by two short subdomain subscales, one to assess perceived physical appearance and the other to assess aspects of perceived physical ability or athletic competence. In both sets of instruments, a mixture of item content is used to summarize perceptions within each of the subdomains. For example, the SDQ Physical Ability subscale (Marsh, Parker, & Barnes, 1985) includes items as diverse as "running fast," "liking sport and games," "having good muscles," and "being good at throwing a ball." Harter's Physical Appearance subscale for children (1985a) features items referring to hair, face, and body.

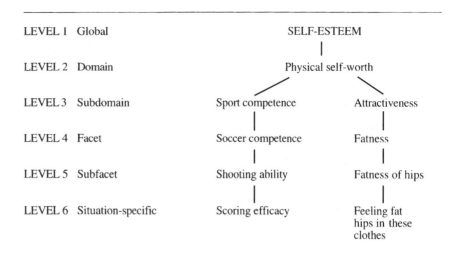

Figure 2. Levels of specificity of self-perceptions within the physical domain.

Although short subscales summarising two elements of the physical self are convenient for comparisons across other areas of self-concept, the content within subscales is confounded and may provide insufficient detail for research questions that need a closer focus on the physical domain. Furthermore, in the development of Harter's instruments and the SDQ series, there had been no concerted effort to establish whether or not two subscales adequately represented the content of the physical self-concept.

The increasingly heavy reliance by exercise and sport psychologists on aspects of physical self-perception warranted much more comprehensive and systematic study. In response to this need, and prompted by suggestions from Sonstroem (1984) and research with the Physical Estimation Scale (Fox, Corbin, & Couldry, 1985), Fox and Corbin launched a series of studies. Initially with a college population, these were directed at (a) the identification of salient self-perception content in the physical domain, (b) the development of a profile that could adequately reflect such content, and (c) the provision of initial evidence of the value of such assessment in understanding self-concept structure and behaviors in the physical domain. The resulting instrumentation was the 30-item Physical Self-Perception Profile (PSPP)(Fox, 1990; Fox & Corbin, 1989). This incorporates four 6-item subdomain subscales to assess sport competence, physical strength, physical conditioning, and bodily attractiveness. A fifth subscale, assessing physical self-worth, was also included and hypothesized to represent a combination of the subdomain physical self-perceptions at a higher level in a hierarchical self-concept structure.

Other multidimensional measures have also been developed to address the range of self-perception content in the physical domain. Ryckman, Robbins, Thornton, and Cantrell (1982) through principal components factor analysis, developed the Physical Self-Efficacy Scale. Lintunen (1987) developed the Perceived Physical Competence Scale for Children and, through exploratory and confirmatory factor analysis, derived subscales to assess perceived "physical performance capacity" (more recently termed "physical fitness") and "perceived ap-

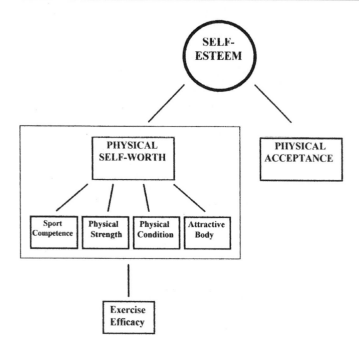

Figure 3. A four-level modification of the EXSEM model using the Physical Self-Perception Profile [Sonstroem, Harlow and Josephs (1994)].

pearance." Richards (1988) developed a seven-subscale Physical Self-Concept Scale (PSCS). However, the PSCS was only reported in a conference abstract and has been recently superseded by the 70-item Physical Self-Description Questionnaire (PSDQ), designed for individuals 12 years and older (Marsh, Richards, Johnson, Roche, & Tremayne, 1994). This instrument contains eight subscales to measure specific aspects of physical self-perceptions, along with general physical self-concept and general self-concept subscales. Further descriptions of a selection of these instruments, including information about their psychometric integrity and validity, are presented in a subsequent section of this chapter.

Specificity of Physical Self-Perceptions

Consistent with hierarchical modeling of the elements of self-concept, authors of some physical self-perception instruments (e.g. Fox & Corbin, 1989) have also proposed the existence of several measurable *levels* of self-perceptions within the physical self. These levels are determined by the degree of specificity of their content, with lower levels becoming increasingly task- or time/state-focused (see Figure 2).

It is theoretically important to identify the level of specificity of self-perception at which any scale or subscale is intended to operate. For example, self-efficacy measures are, by theoretical definition, situation-specific self-referent predictions about success at a task (see chapters by Feltz & Chase and McAuley & Mihalko, this volume) and are clearly at the lower level of any hierarchical classification. Assessments such as the PSPP Physical Self-Worth subscale or the General Physical Self-Concept subscale in the PSDQ are much more all-inclusive and are intended to provide a global estimate of the physical self at the highest level in the physical domain. Other assessments, such as body

image or sport competence, fall at an intermediate level. It is only through theoretically driven prediction of the placement, by level of specificity, of measures in hierarchical structures that we can logically relate instruments to one another and adequately test the robustness of the structures on which they are based.

Sonstroem and Morgan (1989) developed the Exercise and Self-Esteem Model (EXSEM) to indicate the utility of simultaneous assessment of self-perceptions at three levels of specificity. These are self-efficacy statements at the base, estimates of perceived physical ability and physical acceptance at the intermediate level, and global self-esteem at the highest level. This structure has been tested through structural equation modeling using the Physical Estimation Scale as the intermediary variable (Sonstroem, Harlow, Gemma, & Osborne, 1991). More recently, the PSPP subdomains and the physical self-worth subscale provide two intermediate levels of perceived physical competence in a four level EXSEM model (Sonstroem, Harlow, & Josephs, 1994). (See Figure 3.) This usage of multiple levels of self-perception measurement and analysis has much greater potential to assist in the detection of routes and mechanisms of change in the self-concept structure. For example, Sonstroem, Harlow, and Salisbury (1993) used a similar approach to investigate the direction of influence across a season between specific perceptions of performance efficacy and self-esteem. Sonstroem and his colleagues concluded that level of self-esteem had a greater influence on subsequent performance than the performance changes impacting on self-esteem.

To summarise, the development of measurement of the physical self has advanced rapidly and extensively in the past 15 years. From atheoretical studies using unidimensional measures, we have moved towards the use of multidimensional profiles that are compatible with testable hierarchical models featuring several levels of the self-system. Besides stimulating the development of two comprehensive physical self-concept instruments, such models have provided an important reference framework for locating the degree of specificity of other instruments measuring single aspects of the physical self. This allows researchers and practitioners more opportunity to (a) make sense of the array of self-perception instrumentation and (b) select the appropriate set of instruments, in terms of content and specificity, for addressing the question(s) at hand.

Considerations in Self-Perception Instrument Development

As a result of this substantial progress, we are now in a stronger position to outline a more sophisticated set of guidelines for facilitating the development of reliable and effective self-perception instrumentation.

Theory and Measurement Partnership

The development of theory and measurement form an integrated and inseparable partnership. This allows an iterative process to take place whereby instruments, initially designed around theoretical tenets, are in turn used to verify or question hypotheses based on their theoretical underpinnings. Subsequently, through this process, theory is modified and instruments further fine-tuned. Self-concept measurement instruments not based on an explicit theory or model may produce useful information for comparisons among individuals or groups, but have limited potential for advancing knowledge of mechanisms associated with self-concept, self-esteem, and behavior change.

Only two comprehensive physical self-concept instruments have been developed in line with theoretical frameworks. The PSPP and the PSDQ have both leaned heavily on the Shavelson et al. (1976) self-concept model. Each instrument is multidimensional in design, and has subscales that allow assessment of perception at two levels of specificity. The PSDQ also includes a general self-esteem scale to provide a third level. Fox (1990) recommends that the 10-item Rosenberg Self-Esteem Scale be used alongside the PSPP to provide a global measure. Thus, the instruments can be used to assess dimensionality and hierarchical and specificity elements of the theoretical model and provide opportunities to investigate links with a range of behaviors and attributes.

Item Development

One of the important functions of self-perception instruments is their ability to reflect content that is central to the lives and thoughts of the people they address. The *salience* of the content of the instrument has therefore to be first established. Without this centrality, we cannot expect instruments to reveal critical relationships with constructs such as self-esteem, mental well-being or exercise, sport, and health-related behaviors. Therefore, the initial phase is perhaps one of the most crucial in self-perception instrument development. This phase provides the access point or "gateway" to the thoughts of participants and is achieved through the identification of salient self-perception content and its establishment through the appropriate wording of items. Authors of high-quality instruments will have first searched the existing literature for similar instruments with established reliability and validity and appropriate theoretical derivation. These may

have provided guidance for determining the content and the structure of the new instrumentation. Attempts will then have been made to establish the pervasive and popular values and experiences of the population. Where hierarchical models of the self are concerned, particular emphasis will have been placed on content elements in the physical domain that have potential to contribute to global feelings of worth or esteem.

Furthermore, care will have been taken to select words and phrases that locate the theoretical construct through the everyday language of the population being addressed. These subtle elements of instrument design are best achieved through close contact with the population using techniques such as open-ended interviews and questionnaires, focus groups, and content analysis of conversation topics, magazines, and other popular media. Without attention to this early stage of instrument design, there is a danger that the final product will lack content validity and predictive power as the more critical self-perception content may not be included. Although statistical techniques can help *locate* ineffective and poor items and subscales at a later stage, they cannot substitute for important missing content.

Item Format

Several item formats have been used in physical self-perception research, three of which are featured in Table 1. Marsh and colleagues (Marsh, 1992a) have favored the use of a Likert-type format for the Self-Description Questionnaire series. In the PSDQ, for example, respondents are asked to rate themselves on simple statements such as "I am too fat" somewhere on the following range of stems: 1=false, 2=mostly false, 3=more false than true, 4=more true than false, 5=mostly true, and 6=true.

Harter (1985a), in comparison, has developed the structured-alternative format. This offers two alternative statements on the same topic that represent the response of two different types of people to the variable in question. The participant is

---

Table 1
Three Item Formats for Physical Self-Concept Instruments

The Perceived Physical Competence Scale (Lintunen, 1987)
Choose the point which is best suited to you and is true for you.

I am strong   ( )   ( )   ( )   ( )   ( )   I am weak

The Physical Self-Perception Profile (Fox & Corbin, 1989)

Really True for me	Sort of True for me			Sort of True for me	Really True for me
❑	❑	Some people feel that they are very strong and have well-developed muscles compared to most people	BUT Others feel that they are not so strong and their muscles are not very well developed	❑	❑

The Physical Self-Description Questionnaire (Marsh et al., 1994)

	MOSTLY FALSE	MORE FALSE THAN FALSE	MORE TRUE THAN TRUE	MOSTLY FALSE	TRUE	TRUE
I am a physically strong person	1	2	3	4	5	6

first asked to decide *which* kind of person he or she is most similar to. The participant is then asked to distinguish the *extent* to which this is true. This produces a range of possible scores from 1 to 4. The same format was adopted by Fox and Corbin (1989) for the PSPP.

An example of a third item format that takes some middle ground is provided by the Perceived Physical Competence Scale for Children (Lintunen, 1987). This presents two contrasting item-ends in a form similar to semantic differentials. Participants are asked to locate the appropriate stem on a scale from 1 to 5. No stem descriptors seem to be provided in this case, but participants are asked to rate themselves in comparison with others of the same age and sex.

Currently, it is not easy to determine which of these formats produces the best results. It would require the same content to be written in each of the formats and administered to the same population on a single occasion. This has not been done. Furthermore, some formats may have a higher reliability with some age groups and subpopulations than do others, or some formats may be more sensitive at different levels of content specificity than are others.

One advantage of the Likert-type format is that it is typical of many instruments, and therefore, more familiar to participants and compatible when used alongside other inventories. The format used by Marsh and colleagues, for example, is compatible across the PSDQ and the SDQ scales, making them easier to administer simultaneously. Difficulties with the structured-alternative format, featured in Harter's self-perception profiles and the PSPP, have been reported with children (Eiser, Eiser, & Haversmans, 1995) and adults (Marsh et al. 1994). The method is slower, and in the latter study, Marsh et al. found around 7% of the sample were confused by the instructions. In work with the PSPP, we have also found that around 5% of children and adults do not initially follow the instructions. However, this problem can be virtually eliminated by the use of instruction cards and one-to-one help where necessary in the first few minutes of administration. It can also be avoided in computerised administration which offers each item in two stages. An advantage of the structured-alternative format is that it appears to eliminate socially desirable responses and so may be best used in scales that tap more global constructs. Likert or semantic differential formats may be more suitable for subscales that are more anchored in specific competencies or adequacies that provide less opportunity for social emotivity.

Subscale Content

The purpose of self-perceptions instruments is to tap content that is central to the sense of self of the population for which they are designed. Traditionally, the subscale content of psychological instruments has been derived through ex post facto methods. This involves the development, usually by a panel of expert researchers, of a large bank of items around hypothetical constructs. These items are administered to the population and the responses subjected to exploratory principal component or principal axes factor analysis. Constructs are confirmed if strong factors emerge, and scales of items are then extracted to represent each factor.

This form of subscale derivation was used in the develop-

ment of the Physical Self-Efficacy Scale (Ryckman et al., 1982), and a reliance on this approach has been heavily criticized (Wylie, 1989). The emergence of a strong factor is in part due to the number of items with similar content appearing in the item bank. Insufficient numbers of items written around a particular competence or attribute can produce an insignificant factor, resulting in its omission from the final instrument, even though that attribute may be highly salient to the population. This makes the approach somewhat "hit and miss" as it is not guided by a coherent theoretical base and has proved to be less effective in self-perception research (Marsh, 1997).

Increasingly, in line with a theory-measurement partnership, content of subscales has been determined using an a priori framework. For example, Harter (1982) in the development of the Perceived Competence Scale for Children first identified critical self-perception content through open-ended research techniques and then designed and tested specific subscales with items built around emergent themes. Fox and Corbin (1989) used a similar approach to identify the content of the four subdomain subscales of the PSPP.

Another a priori approach is to base instrumentation on hypothesized and testable models of the self. Marsh (1992a, 1992b, 1992c) developed the Self-Description Questionnaire series, which contain several subscales, to explicitly test the elements hypothesized by the self-concept model of Shavelson, Hubner and Stanton (1976). Item content of the Perceived Physical Competence Scale for Children was also guided by a model by Pitkänen et al. (1979). Although, this is an improvement over exploratory principal components derivation, there remains a danger that the original untested model omitted important content or included irrelevant content so that the eventual predictive validity of the instrument is reduced. Sound instruments will be based on subdomains that feature in a theoretical model, contain item and subscale content that has been derived from the population itself, and be written in accessible language.

Subscale Specificity

More recently, with the development of hierarchical self-concept modeling, the *level of specificity* of self-perception subscales has also become a point for consideration. This will, in practice, be set during item generation. Similar to the ex post facto versus a priori approaches, a choice of two strategies is available. Taking perceived sport competence as an example, it is possible to pose single competence items on each of the popular sports, such as basketball, soccer, and volleyball, and simply add up the scores to represent the construct. This method is used in the physical self subscales of the self-perceptions profiles of Harter (1985a), in the SDQ series developed by Marsh (1992a,1992b,1992c) and in the subscales used by Lintunen (1987). In the sport example, this carries the assumptions that (a) all individuals have had the same exposure to each sport, (b) all individuals establish their sense of sports ability on the same reference group of sports, and (c) that it is meaningful to total the scores across these different sports. Clearly sports exposure and experiences vary considerably both within and between cultures, sex, schools, and geographical regions, and although this approach taps a range of content, this mix can eventually pose a threat to the external validity of the subscale.

An alternative strategy that is more compatible with the conception of levels of self-perceptions in hierarchical self-concept models is to produce items that allow the respondents to judge their sport ability *on their own terms of reference.* Rosenberg (1965) first recognised this need. Unlike the unidimensional approach discussed earlier where items of diverse content are summed, the items in the Rosenberg Self-Esteem Scale are nonspecific and reflect feelings of pride in self, self-respect, and general competence. Others have followed this approach in the design of self-esteem or self-worth scales (for example Harter, 1985a; Marsh & O'Neill, 1984) and also with global or general physical self-worth scales (for example, Fox & Corbin, 1989; Marsh et al., 1994).

This essentially phenomenological strategy can also be adopted for more specific subscales. Using the sport competence example, general items that refer to sport ability, confidence, and achievement in sport *settings* rather than in specific sports are developed. If the research question requires, extra subscales can be created at a lower level in the hierarchy for addressing a range of competencies in specific sports so that a *soccer competence* scale or a *basketball competence* scale, for example, might be of particular interest in a comparative study on soccer/basketball enjoyment or participation.

The same principle applies to the assessment of perceived appearance or body image (see Bain and McAuley, this volume). Content contributing to this construct could be as diverse as height, muscularity, slimness/fatness, or facial characteristics or hair. A global perceived appearance scale best avoids reference to this specific content. On the other hand, such a scale could be accompanied by short subscales to assess single aspects of appearance. This approach has been used to provide greater insight into the contribution of key elements of appearance to global perceived attractiveness and self-esteem in adolescents (Fox, Page, Armstrong, & Kirby, 1994).

Subscale Refinements and Reliability

Subscales built around theoretically determined constructs, incorporating item content that is salient and comprehensible, are more likely to be valid. However, they will still require fine-tuning through several administrations and analyses. Item descriptive statistics are important for modifications to wording. For example, means based around the midpoint of the scale will combat against ceiling or flooring effects. The full range of possible scores should be represented within the population to provide adequate variance, and these should approximate a normal distribution. Internal consistency (alpha reliability), item to subscale total correlations, and factor loadings can all be used in partnership to make informed decisions on which items to include, exclude, or modify.

Statistical techniques produce valuable summary data regarding the need for item and subscale refinements. However, this information must be viewed in partnership with the theoretical underpinnings of the instrument. A clean statistical solution that has a high degree of internal consistency may lack depth and eventually have restricted predictive validity. Repetition of similarly worded items around similar content, for example, is likely to produce very high alpha coefficients (>0.92),

to the extent that they are measuring almost identical content and are producing unnecessary redundancy. Where self-perception is concerned, it may be more critical to understanding the functioning of the self to have a range of perspectives on content within a subdomain scale such as sport confidence, sense of sport identity, and satisfaction, rather than rely totally on comparative competence ratings. The latter, however, may produce higher subscale reliabilities.

Decisions about the internal reliability (alpha) of self-perception scales are relatively simple compared with establishing a scale's reliability over time. The degree to which the construct is viewed as a stable entity is a theoretical issue. In the context of hierarchical models that hypothesize more global and stable constructs towards the apex, it would be important to establish the degree of stability of measures such as physical self-worth over a range of time periods. More specific elements that feature lower in the hierarchy such as self-efficacy statements or perceptions of specific physical abilities or features such as perceived fatness or fitness, may be viewed as more changeable. If test-retest reliability were attempted on such measures, it would not be easy to determine the degree to which measurement error and actual change contributed to low correlations.

Social Desirability

Instruments designed to measure attributes such as honesty, morality, self-esteem, and other attributes that are highly valued in a culture, are particularly susceptible to positively biased responses (Wylie, 1979). In the development and validation of self-perception instruments, therefore, it is important to concurrently apply scales of conformity and social desirability so that the degree of relationship can be estimated. Harter (1982) utilized the structured-alternative item format described earlier in order to overcome this problem. It was designed to transmit the feeling to the participant that the whole range of responses was acceptable in the population. Support for this strategy using the PSPP has been found with a sample of 76 college students (Fox & Corbin, 1989).

Sonstroem has paid most attention to social desirability in the context of exercise (Sonstroem, 1984). He outlined self-presentation strategies, defensiveness, deliberate deception, and social desirability as potential contributors to improvements in self-esteem scores reported in some exercise intervention studies. He has also systematically used social desirability measures alongside self-esteem and self-perception scales with the intent of partialling out its effect so that relationships with mental adjustment variables could be more clearly established. For instance, using the Physical Estimation Scale (Sonstroem, 1976), he demonstrated a negative association with neuroticism, maladjustment, and personality disorder, when social desirability and defensiveness were controlled. More recently, Sonstroem and Potts (1996) showed significant relationships between subscales of the PSPP and several mental adjustment variables when statistically controlling for scores on two measures of social desirability.

Construct Validation

Each stage of instrument development is critical, but construct validation remains the ultimate test of the value of the final product. As models of the self have become multifaceted, and instruments have become increasingly multidimensional, the need has arisen to simultaneously establish the validity of the whole instrument as well as its individual parts. This has meant that attention has to be paid to the validity of the internal structure of instruments as well as the more traditional aspects of their external construct validity.

Internal construct validation. To some extent the validity of self-perceptions profiles is determined by the degree to which they support the hypothesized structure of the framework in which they are conceived. Marsh (1997) has termed this *within-network validity*, and it is essentially determined by the nature and degree of the relationships among the constructs (subscales) making up the network. For example, Shavelson et al. (1976) explicitly define their model as both multidimensional and hierarchical. The degree of independence among the underlying elements (low correlations) at any particular level in the network indicates the extent of multidimensionality. If all elements are highly correlated, then the existence of multidimensionality is challenged. Conversely, if there is little or no relationship among the elements, then the likelihood that they form part of a strong hierarchical structure held together by superordinate or umbrella constructs is lessened. Confirmatory factor analysis (CFA) is now the appropriate method for testing the multidimensionality of instruments within these structures. This has been conducted on contemporary instruments such as the PSPP (Fox & Corbin, 1989; Sonstroem et al., 1994) the SDQ series (Marsh, 1987a,1989), and the PSDQ (Marsh et al., 1994).

Where an instrument has been developed to simultaneously measure more than one level of specificity in a hierarchical structure, then the functioning of scales hypothesized to represent superordinate constructs needs to be assessed. The two-level hierarchical ordering of subscales in the PSPP, for example, was initially established (Fox, 1990) using partial correlation analysis to compare the relationships among subdomain subscales and between them and self-esteem when the effect of physical self-worth (PSW) was either included or partialled out of the analysis.

These techniques have now been superseded by more sophisticated methods, and the two-level PSPP structure has since been confirmed using structural equation modeling (Sonstroem et al., 1994). Marsh (1987b) has described how hierarchical CFA can be applied to test the within-network validity of full models such as the Shavelson et al. model (1976). Furthermore, Marsh (1987a) has described how CFA can offer a more complete test of factorial invariance of instruments such as the SDQ across groups. This new set of statistical techniques has allowed opportunity for more rigorous scrutiny of the internal functioning of multidimensional self-concept instruments.

External construct validation. Traditionally with single scales, construct validation has been relatively straightforward. The new instrument is administered alongside established instruments and comparisons made to see if convergent or divergent relationships emerge along the lines of theoretical predictions. Multiple subscale instruments such as self-perception profiles, on the other hand, offer opportunities to investigate *patterns* of relationships between the subscales and external criteria. For example, following the tenets of competence motivation theory, Fox and Corbin (1989), through discriminant func-

tion analysis, determined that the PSPP subscales were able to correctly classify over 70% of a sample of college males and females into physically active and inactive groups. The Physical Condition subscale (which has reference to exercise in the items) loaded most strongly on the canonical function, with the Attractive Body subscale contributing little. In order to determine the extent to which the profile was associated with *choice* of physical activity mode, canonical correlation techniques, with self-perception subscale scores as one set of variables and categories of physical activity involvement as the other set, were used. Two significant canonical functions emerged that indicate logical activity-perception associations.

Other forms of construct validation have included examination for logical patterns of relationships between each subscale score and external criteria. For example, both the PSDQ subscales (Marsh & Roche, 1996) and the PSPP (Fox & Dirkin, 1992) and have been related to body-satisfaction measures and silhouettes depicting various levels of body fatness. Consistent with predictions, appearance subscales in both instruments were more closely related to perceived degree of fatness (as measured by the silhouettes) than were subscales measuring other physical abilities, such as sport competence or strength.

A further technique that can shed light on construct validity is to compare scores on the instrument across two population who contrast on relevant criteria. For example, Marsh, Perry, Horsely, and Roche (1995) compared responses on the SDQ-III between a population of 83 elite athletes and a normative sample of 2,436 nonathletes. Differences between the two groups were evident only on the physical ability subscale and some social subscales, but not academic or appearance subscales. Similarly, the PSPP mean subscale scores for a population of obese males and females have been compared with the full range of college-age males and females (Fox, 1990). As predicted, the obese population emerged with significantly lower scores on sport competence, body attractiveness, physical condition, and physical self-worth, but higher scores on perceived physical strength.

Marsh and Redmayne (1994) have used a *between-network validation* approach where correlation matrices assess relationships between the subscales of an early version of the PSDQ and sets of external criteria including items on an Australian national battery of fitness tests. Results indicated that the matrix of correlations was generally in line with a priori predictions establishing that the perception constructs (such as perceived strength) were more closely associated with the relevant fitness variable (strength) than other perception or fitness variables.

Marsh and colleagues (1994) have also applied the multitrait-multimethod (MTMM) technique to the PSPP, PSDQ, and PSC physical self-perception instruments. This provides the most comprehensive approach to between-network validation available, and is essentially a large correlation matrix that simultaneously allows an estimate of the convergent and divergent validity of each instrument. MTMM can also provide indications of potential instrument overlap, can help identify scales with different labels that measure similar constructs, or scales with similar labels that do not measure the same construct. It is therefore a very useful tool for progressing with instrumentation design, especially where there are comparable profiles available.

In summary, contemporary self-perception instrument development has become a complex and lengthy process. The developmental sequence involves the initial phase to identify critical self-perception content in the chosen population, followed by the construction and refinement of items and subscales, and tests of their internal reliability and stability. In order to adequately deal with multidimensionality and hierarchical structuring, the traditional methods of construct validation of single-scale instruments have now been supplemented with a range of multivariate and confirmatory factor techniques to assess the function of the instruments both within and between structures.

Contemporary Physical
Self-Perception Instrumentation

Given the demands of the lengthy and rigorous process of self-perception instrument development, and the fact that the recognition of the independence of the physical self is only relatively recent, it is not surprising that few comprehensive physical self-perception measures have emerged. This is particularly the case if, as recommended, the instrument should be accompanied by a sound theoretical model. Three types of instrument are available for consideration. These are (a) self-perception profiles that include subscales to measure aspects of the physical self, alongside other life domains; (b) self-perception profiles that focus solely on the physical domain, and (c) single scale instruments that focus on a specific element of physical self-perceptions. Those instruments that demonstrate a multidimensional design based on a model of self-concept and that have undergone some degree of reliability and validity analysis have been selected for brief review.

Multidimensional Measures Incorporating
Physical Self Subscales

Several multidimensional instruments include subscales that allow the assessment of aspects of the physical self alongside other important self-perception domains such as the social or academic self. Most prominent of these are Harter's self-perception profiles and the self-description questionnaires of Marsh and colleagues. Additionally, the Tennessee Self-Concept Scale (TSCS) (Fitts, 1965) has been widely used in the past, and recently Bracken (1992) has developed the Multiple Self-Concept Scale (MSCS) for children and adolescents. Although these instruments do not provide a comprehensive documentation of physical self-perceptions, they are mentioned here as they are worthy of consideration where an estimate of perceptions across several salient life domains is required.

Harter's self-perception profiles. Harter first developed the Perceived Competence Scale for children in 1982 to assess elements of her developmental model of effectance (1978). The instrument was superseded by the Self-Perception Profile for Children in 1985 (Harter, 1985a). This latter instrument is suitable for children 8 to 13 years of age and incorporates five 6-item subscales to assess perceptions of behavioral conduct, social acceptance, scholastic competence, alongside athletic competence, physical appearance, and also a global self-worth subscale. Harter and colleagues have also developed related instruments that include a pictorial version for children aged 4 to 7 (Harter & Pike, 1984), and self-perception profiles for ado-

lescents (Harter, 1988), for college students (Neemann & Harter, 1986), and for adults (Messer & Harter, 1986). Each of these profiles includes more subscales to reflect increasing multidimensionality with age, although the physical domain remains restricted to the original appearance and athletic competence subscales. Profiles are accompanied by importance profiles to assess the relative importance to self of each of the subdomains. These have been used to calculate competence-importance discrepancy scores with a view to test the hypothesis that perceived shortfalls in aspirations in a domain will contribute to lower self-worth.

Manuals are available for these instruments, but evidence of their psychometric properties and validity is surprisingly limited given their widespread use. Alpha reliabilities have been reported as acceptable to high (.70-.90) for the final versions of all subscales in each instrument. Factor structures are unambiguous although tests have been limited to principal components rather than confirmatory factor analysis. However, the children and adolescent profiles, in particular, have proved to be very useful for testing a range of hypotheses concerning the processes and determinants of self-concept and self-worth (Harter, 1986, 1990, 1996) and are worthy of serious consideration.

Marsh's Self-Description Questionnaires (SDQs). The Self-Description Questionnaires were developed to provide a test of the hierarchical model of Shavelson et al. (1976) and its modification (Marsh & Shavelson, 1985). Three versions are available, which include the SDQ-I (Marsh, 1992a) for preadolescent primary school children, the SDQ-II (Marsh, 1992b) for adolescent high school students, and the SDQ-III (Marsh, 1992c) for late adolescents and young adults. The SDQ-I incorporates 76 items in a 5-point Likert format in 8 subscales to assess physical ability; physical appearance; peer relations; parent relations; reading; math, and general school competence; and also general self-concept. The SDQ-II follows the same structure, and has 11 subscales with 102 items in a 6-point Likert format. The SDQ-III adds two further subscales resulting in 136 items presented in an 8-point Likert format.

Marsh (1992a, 1992b, & 1992c) has reported subscale alpha reliabilities ranging from .76 to .96 across the instruments with mean subscale alphas generally in the high 80s to low 90s. Test-retest reliabilities for the SDQ-I over a 6-month period range between .54 and .74 for 5th and 6th graders; for the SDQ-II with girls (Marsh & Peart, 1988), between .73 and .88 over 7 weeks, and a median of .74 over an 18-month period with the SDQ-III.

The instruments have been extensively used in research, particularly with regard to model testing using newer covariance analysis techniques. Confirmatory factor analysis has been used to establish the internal structure of each instrument; and construct-validation studies, including MTMM analysis with the SDQ-I, have been conducted with a range of related constructs and variables (Marsh, Richards, & Barnes, 1986). Certainly, this is the most rigorously tested set of self-concept instruments available. They provide simple and reliable estimates of a range of self-evaluative content that concurrently covers academic, social, emotional, and physical domains alongside global self-concept.

The Tennessee Self-Concept Scale (TSCS). The original TSCS (Fitts, 1965), which was intended for adolescents and adults, was the instrument of choice in the majority of studies, throughout the 70s and early 80s, that were concerned with the physical self. It carried a general popularity in self-concept research and was also one of the first instruments to explicitly incorporate multidimensionality into its design. It has recently been substantially revised, and an extensive manual documenting theoretical underpinnings and psychometric properties is now available (Roid & Fitts, 1994). A physical self subscale, tapping items such as appearance, health, skill, body build, and sexuality, is included with four other subscales to assess moral, personal, family, and social self-concepts. Additionally, a three-dimensional internal structure is built into the subscales that tap identity ("who I am"), self-satisfaction ("how satisfied I am"), and behavioral ("what I do") aspects of each domain.

Roid and Fitts (1994) report alphas for subscales ranging from the low 70s to 90s. Confirmatory factor analysis (McGuire & Tinsley, 1981) supported the five external and three internal factor structure of the instrument. However, further analyses using CFA and MTMM alongside the SDQ-II (Marsh & Richards, 1988) provided consistent support for the Family, Physical, and Social Self factors only.

Recently, in the clinical and research form, subscales to address adjustment, self-actualisation, and physical harmony have been added. Although less psychometrically sound than some instruments, the TSCS offers a broader and more clinical orientation to self-concept assessment than do those already mentioned, which focus quite heavily on statements of one's competence. For this reason, elements of the TSCS may be of particularly interest to researchers wishing to unravel the processes involved in self-esteem formation or document mental well-being change accompanying interventions.

The Multidimensional Self-Concept Scale (MSDS). Although well developed, the use of this relatively new multidimensional instrument (Bracken, 1992) has not been reported in the exercise and sport psychology literature. It has been designed and tested for children and adolescents and is based on many characteristics inherent in the Shavelson et al. model (1976). Life domains are addressed through six 25-item subscales to address social, competence, affect, academic, family, and physical (physical attractiveness and prowess) subdomains. However, an additional theoretical perspective is incorporated that has been ignored in other instruments. Bracken takes the view that evaluative information can be derived from two sources, namely, personal experience and interaction with others; and these orientations are built into the items. This may have particular relevance for those interested in researching links between self-concept and achievement orientations.

Reported subscale alpha reliabilities ranged between .85 and .97 and the mean test-retest reliability coefficient over a 4-week period was .74. Initial concurrent validity has been established through a number of studies, but the factor structure has not yet been tested through CFA. The rigour with which this new instrument has been developed, along with its additional theoretical considerations, make it worthy of testing among younger populations. Unfortunately, however, the MSDS approach to assessing self-concept in the physical domain is unidimensional as only a single total score is calculated.

Multidimensional Physical Self-Perception Measures

There are two key multidimensional instruments in this category that have recently featured frequently in the exercise and sport psychology literature. These are the Physical Self-Perception Profile and the Physical Self-Description Questionnaire.

The Physical Self-Perception Profile (PSPP). This instrument was developed in the mid 1980s by Fox and Corbin (1989) to reflect theoretical advances made by Harter (1985b), and Shavelson et al. (1976), and also to incorporate suggestions for instrument development made by Sonstroem (1984) in the context of exercise and self-esteem relationships. As this was the first attempt to comprehensively document the physical self-perceptions for a specific population, considerable effort was put into initial groundwork to ensure that the full range of normative perceptions had been identified. Preceding instruments and literature were examined, and content analyses of open-ended questionnaire and interviews were conducted to determine the number and scope of subscales necessary for adequate assessment of the physical domain.

Several pilot administrations led to the final 30-item profile featuring 6-item subscales to assess perception in the subdomains of sport competence, body attractiveness, physical strength, and physical conditioning. Subscales were designed to cover a range of perceptions concerning acquisition/maintenance (process items), competence/adequacy (product items), and self-presentation (confidence items). In line with the Shavelson et al. model, a two-tier structure within the physical domain was hypothesized, and a global physical self-worth subscale was modelled upon items from the Rosenberg Self-Esteem Scale (Rosenberg, 1965) to represent a higher order construct than the subdomains. The instrument was therefore developed to allow tests of the multidimensionality and hierarchical structuring within the physical domain.

The PSPP was also accompanied by the Perceived Importance Profile, which includes 2-item subscales designed to assess the relative centrality to the self of each subdomain content. This allows competence-importance discrepancies to be calculated in line with the hypotheses presented by Harter (1985a) regarding actual and aspired levels of adequacy (discrepancy) and their relationship with self-esteem.

A PSPP manual is available (Fox, 1990) providing the theoretical underpinnings, descriptive statistics, and evidence of psychometric integrity of the profile, including internal consistency, test-retest reliability, and social desirability, initial evidence of construct validity, and administration and scoring instructions. Initial development was based on four separate samples of college males and females (total $n = 1,191$). Analyses throughout were conducted separately for each sex. Subscale alpha reliabilities have consistently scored in the range .80 to .95 with the initial samples (Fox, 1990), a sample of middle-aged adults (Sonstroem, Speliotis, & Fava, 1992), a sample of British college students (Page, Ashford, Fox, & Biddle, 1993), and 578 overweight adults (Fox & Dirkin, 1992). Test-retest reliability was established with college students over 16- and 23-day periods with a range of reliability coefficients between .74 and .89 (Fox, 1990).

The items are presented in the structured-alternative format in order to be compatible with the Harter profiles and to reduce socially desirable responding. The profile was simultaneously administered with the short form of the Marlowe-Crowne Social Desirability Scale (Reynolds, 1982) with only two items producing significant but weak correlations, at the $p<.05$ level. Sonstroem and Potts (1996) have recently conducted one of the most rigorous tests of social desirability in the self-concept field using the Balanced Inventory of Desirable Responding (Paulhus, 1984) and the PSPP. Only one significant correlation emerged between the PSPP subscales and impression management ($p<.05$), but several were weakly correlated with the self-deception enhancement subscale.

The PSPP has been subjected to exploratory and confirmatory factor analysis (Fox & Corbin, 1989; Sonstroem et al., 1994) and a clear four-factor subdomain structure has been well supported across several samples and age groups. The hierarchical structure featuring physical self-worth as a superordinate global construct has been confirmed through partial correlation analyses (Fox, 1990) and more recently through structural equation modeling (Sonstroem et al., 1994).

Predictive validity has been addressed (Fox & Corbin, 1989) using discriminant and canonical correlation analyses with the subdomains of the PSPP and degree and choice of activity involvement. A similar study conducted by Sonstroem et al. (1994) with 216 aerobic dancers (mean age = 38 years) also provided strong evidence of logical links between various exercise behaviors and PSPP subscales, providing further support for the instrument's convergent validity.

Using regression analysis, Sonstroem and Potts (1996) established important links between PSPP subscales and mental adjustment variables, such as positive and negative affect, depression, and health complaints. These associations were independent of global self-esteem relationships or social desirability effects, and thus substantiated the construct validity of the PSPP.

Less attention has been paid to the Perceived Importance Profile. Test-retest reliabilities have ranged from .68 to .83 and nonsignificant correlations have been recorded for social desirability. Using principal components analysis, for males at least, the factor structure contained several cross-loadings. However, discrepancy scores have discriminated between levels of self-esteem and physical self-worth in line with Harter's (1985b) hypotheses. Furthermore, patterns of importance-competence correlations within each subdomain have indicated that low physical self-worth or self-esteem individuals are less able to discount their inadequacies. Although, the psychometric properties of the PIP are weak, these findings provide initial evidence of the potential of an importance profile approach.

A children's version of the PSPP and PIP, aimed at a junior high population (C-PSPP and C-PIP) has recently been published (Whitehead, 1995). Alpha reliabilities have ranged between 0.8 and 0.9; intraclass stability over 2 weeks ranged from .79 to .94; and there was no evidence of socially desirable responding. The factor structure and hierarchical structure have been confirmed using structural equation modeling (Whitehead, Eklund, & Welk, 1995). Subscales discriminate significantly and substantively between groups identified by their teachers as low or high competence. Subscales were generally logically related to tests of physical fitness supporting the instrument's concurrent validity. Further application of the scale

has been conducted with 760 athletic youngsters (Welk, Corbin & Lewis, 1995) and British children (Biddle et al., 1993) indicating that although the reliability of the instrument generally remains, the factor structure may vary across populations.

A version for older adults has also been developed (PSPP-A) (Chase, 1991; Chase & Corbin, 1995). Initial open-ended questionnaire content analysis revealed the need for alternative subscale content for a population of adults aged 65 and above. The final instrument contained subscales to assess sport competence, body attractiveness, health, and physical functioning. Although initial results show that the instrument is reliable and the structure is sound, further work is required.

In summary, the PSPP can now be regarded as a well-established, reliable and well-validated instrument. It has been translated into several languages, has featured in many published studies, and has been used effectively with a range of populations from college age through to middle-aged males and females. Further validation work is required, extending its validity to other populations, and establishing its concurrent and predictive validity with a range of mental well-being and behavioral variables. The establishment of versions with other age groups is also needed.

Physical Self-Description Profile (PSDQ). The PSDQ was developed by Marsh and colleagues (Marsh et al., 1994) to provide a more complete assessment of self-perceptions in the physical domain than could be offered by the two SDQ physical self subscales. Similar to the PSPP, the instrument encapsulated within the physical domain, the multidimensionality and hierarchical postulates of the Shavelson et al. model (1976). The content of these scales was based on the two SDQ physical scales, research with the Physical Self-Concept Scale (Richards, 1988), a previous version developed by Marsh and Redmayne (1994), and an attempt to parallel components of physical fitness derived from a confirmatory factor analysis of fitness items in an Australian Health and Fitness Survey. The final result is a 70-item instrument that measures nine elements of the physical domain, which are strength, body fat, activity, endurance/fitness, sports competence, coordination, appearance, flexibility, and health. There are also subscales to assess overall physical self-concept and global self-concept. Items are presented in a 6-point Likert-type format, similar to the SDQs.

Instrument reliability for the final version of the PSDQ was established on two samples of male and female adolescents: (a) Australian Outward Bound participants ($n=316$) and (b) high school students ($n=395$). Coefficient alphas ranged between .82 and .96. No information is yet available on test-retest reliability or the susceptibility to social desirability of the PSDQ.

In a short time, Marsh and colleagues (Marsh, 1997) have completed a comprehensive sequence of validation studies on the internal structure and external validity of this instrument. Using the preliminary version, with a sample of 105 high school girls, Marsh and Redmayne (1994) conducted CFA and hierarchical CFA to confirm the internal structure of the instrument. At the same time, between-network validation was addressed through correlation analysis with four tests of physical fitness (static strength, balance, a shuttle run, and sit-and-reach flexibility). Logical relationships between self-perceptions and fitness elements emerged, with appearance perceptions being unrelated. Also factorial variance across gender for the final version of the instrument was tested using CFA by Marsh et al. (1994). In addition, in a subsample in this study, the PSDQ subscales were related to physical activity participation, body silhouettes, and physical fitness scores. With a couple of exceptions, relationships between external criteria and PSDQ subscales were consistent with a priori predictions, providing initial support for the concurrent validity of the instrument.

In the same study, a multitrait-multimethod analysis was conducted to concurrently compare responses on the PSDQ, with established instrumentation (in this case the PSPP and the PSC). An initial CFA confirmed that all three instruments were functioning well, according to their hypothesized structures, with PSDQ items loaded highest on their latent factor (median loading = 0.88). The MTMM also supported the convergent and divergent validities of the PSDQ (Marsh, 1997; Marsh et al., 1994). Recently, test-retest reliability, over 4 occasions during a 14-month period, has been established (Marsh, 1996).

The PSDQ is a welcome addition to measurement instruments in the physical domain. Indications are that it provides a comprehensive assessment of self-perceptions covering a wide range of subdomains of the physical self. Initial psychometrics indicate, in line with the SDQs, that the PSDQ is showing excellent reliability, sound internal structure, and good evidence of construct validity. Marsh has not only brought a very useful and promising instrument to the domain but the field has also benefitted greatly from his expertise in the application of advanced statistical techniques to self-concept instrument development.

However, the PSDQ needs to be applied to a more diverse set of samples, as much of the validation work has been conducted on the same groups of Australian adolescents. Social desirability issues need to be addressed. Also, if the instrument is to help us shed light on the contribution of the physical self to aspects of self-esteem and mental well-being, then attention needs to be paid to validation alongside measures of psychological functioning.

Specific Physical Self-Perception Measures

The discussion so far has focused on comprehensive multidimensional measures. However, there are many other well-developed instruments available that measure more specific aspects of physical self-perception. In general they fall into three categories. These are measures to assess (a) physical ability, physical or movement competence (see Feltz & Chase, this volume; (b) body image, body esteem, social physique anxiety, and self-presentation (see Bane & McAuley, this volume); and (c) self-efficacy for physical tasks, and aspects of exercise and sport (see McAuley & Mihalko, this volume). Some of these instruments carry a degree of multidimensionality, usually derived through principal components factor analysis. Several are worthy of consideration where more complete coverage of an aspect of physical self is needed. For example, Lintunen (1987) developed the 10-item Perceived Physical Competence Scale for Children. This instrument contains 7 items related to physical performance and 3 items related to appearance. It has demonstrated good reliability and validity and has been used to document differences in physical self-perceptions between adolescents with and without disability (Lintunen, Heikinaro-Johansson, & Sherrill, 1995), and also the stability of children's self-perceptions over a four-year period (Lintunen, Lesksinen, Oinonen, Salinto, & Rahkila, 1995). Instruments that tap multiple dimensions of body image such as the Body Esteem Scale (Franzoi & Shields, 1984) could also be considered.

Guidance in Instrument Choice

The previous section has demonstrated that there is now an array of good quality instrumentation on offer to tap self-perception content in the physical domain. Valid profiles are available that allow the measurement of aspects of physical self-perceptions alongside those in other life domains. Furthermore, we are particularly fortunate to have two well-developed multidimensional profiles, the PSPP and PSDQ, that are capable of simultaneous assessment of a range of subdomains in the physical domain. Both instruments received high acclaim in a recent review of the leading self-concept measures (Byrne, 1996, pp.140, 188). Additionally, a range of good quality instruments that provide a greater focus on unitary aspects of the physical self are on offer to accompany these profiles.

Choice will clearly be determined by the demands of the research or evaluation question *and* evidence of the qualities of the instruments. Self-concept models, such as that presented by Shavelson et al. (1976), also present us with a framework on which to anchor the relative location of the range of available instruments. Three factors should be considered in instrument choice: (a) degree of focus required, (b) nature of the content to be addressed, and (c) levels of specificity of self-perception required.

The *degree of focus* is determined by the range of self-perception content needed to address the research question. If there is a need to investigate the physical self in the context of the whole person, then it may be important to measure self-perception across life domains. This would point towards the use of a comprehensive profile such as the SDQ. On the other hand, an interest in the relationship between self-perceptions and a specific behavior, such as resistance training, requires much greater focus on specific elements of the physical domain, such as perceived strength, or body image.

The *nature of the content* of interest is critical to the choice of instrumentation. Research questions concerned with dietary issues, for example, may require instruments that provide a rich source of information about elements such as body image, body satisfaction, body centrality, and perceived attractiveness. In contrast, a study into sport participation is likely to need more information on perceived-competence elements of the self. In some instances, it may be necessary to develop new subscales to assess specific subdomain content. For example, a study that adopts a competence motivation stance may require the construction of a *soccer* competence subscale, to accompany a more general measure of sport competence.

The *degree of specificity* required of instrumentation has received least attention in the past, yet this provides the key to intelligent instrument selection. In Figure 2, a range is available from global self-esteem as an outcome measure of self-evaluations across the whole self-concept, down to the more state- or task-specific assessments akin to self-efficacy statements. Where links between the physical self-concept and mental well-being are of particular interest, as in the study of Sonstroem and Potts (1996), then more global assessments of the physical self will be more important. Where relationships with specific physical behaviors or physical attributes such as fitness are of interest, then self-perceptions that are logically closely related are best included.

Inevitably, the majority of research questions would benefit from the assessment of self-perceptions at several levels of specificity, similar to the work conducted by Sonstroem and colleagues with the EXSEM model (Sonstroem et al., 1993; Sonstroem et al., 1994). For those projects devoted to comparison of self-perceptions across individuals and groups, this would provide a more complete map of differences. Where mechanisms of self-perception change are of interest, as in exercise, health or education intervention research, the paths and degree of change will be more discernible.

Future Instrument Development

There is little doubt that self-perception measurement within the physical domain has progressed dramatically in the last decade, and there is some cause for celebration. Despite this advancement, our research largely remained at the descriptive level. In our preoccupation with instrument development, we have neglected the mission that really underpins our need for sound measurement, that is, the need to further our understanding of the functioning of self-concept in people's lives. There has been limited advancement in knowledge of the mechanisms and interplay between self-perceptions, self-esteem , well-being, and behavioral patterns. Harter (1996) comments, "For investigators to merely describe the self-theory or the self-concept as a function of age, gender, ethnicity, social group etc. is to miss the very processes through which it comes to be constructed" (p. 7). A further phase of physical self-perception research is required that will build on the solid empirical and theoretical foundation of the more descriptive phase. The focus of this further phase needs to involve a closer look at the role of the self-perceptions in the dynamics, mechanisms, and agencies of self-esteem and behavior change. Progress will require more subtle attention to instrument design. There are a number of issues for readers to consider with respect to future directions in physical self-assessment. Several of these points are discussed at greater length elsewhere (Fox, 1997).

Recent instrumentation has been heavily dominated by self-assessments of competence. This is the case for Harter's profiles, which were originally developed in the operationalization of her competence motivation model. It is also true of Shavelson's model, which was directed at the educational setting and focused on academic attainment. In general, although physical competencies relate well to achievement behavior in sport and exercise, they do not exhibit strong associations with self-esteem, with typical correlation coefficients ranging between .1 and .4. The body has a more global significance as a vehicle for self-presentation, to the extent that it has been labelled the *public self*. In Western cultures at least, physical appearance has become a more powerful determinant of self-esteem than physical competence, particularly for females. Future measurement needs to pay greater attention to the subtleties and interaction involved in constructs such as body image, body satisfaction, body centrality, self-presentation confidence, and social physique anxiety.

The impact of competence measurement may be improved if consideration is paid to recent achievement goal theory (Duda, 1993; Duda & Whitehead, this volume). It is now clear that a sense of competence can be achieved through favorable self-referent perceptions about personal improvements and task fulfillment. In contrast, many of the contemporary instruments are dominated by external frames of reference, calling for comparisons with peers of similar age and sex. Recent theorizing by Deci and Ryan (1995) suggests that it is *self-determination* of competence that is critical to self-esteem development and that competence perceived to be the result of extrinsic, uncontrolled forces (e.g., possessing natural talents) can be less potent. This suggests that competence per se as well as the *sources* of competence (see Horn & Amorose, this volume) need to be assessed conjointly with the degree to which personal responsibility or empowerment for competence is experienced.

There has been some debate as to the validity of attempts to assess the relative importance attached to elements of self-concept by individuals. This technique is based on the assumption that value systems vary across subcultures and individuals. Processes are in operation whereby individuals use importance weightings to discount their inadequacies, boost their successes, and personalize the content of their self-system, in order to maximize self-esteem. Two sets of conflicting data are available on these hypotheses. On the one hand, independent sets of data indicate that individuals with low self-esteem appear less able to manipulate their competence information in this way to support their sense of self (Baumeister, 1993; Blaine & Crocker, 1993; Fox, 1990; Harter, 1990; Whitehead, 1995). On the other hand, importance weightings used in models of self-concept have not indicated that they can add to the prediction of self-esteem, beyond self-evaluations (Marsh, 1993; 1994; Marsh & Sonstroem, 1995). It seems that this contradiction may well arise from inadequate measurement techniques. It is an issue that it is clearly critical to understanding self-esteem processes and one that poses a serious challenge for future instrument development.

There remain fundamental questions to be answered regarding the nature and measurement of global self-esteem. Strategies such as self-serving bias in attributions may lead to a tendency towards self-deception and inflated scores when completing self-worth inventories. Many theorists would regard such efforts to present the self in the best possible light as healthy and normal if they are restrained to reasonable levels (Baumeister, 1993). Conversely, individuals who have a higher true regard for themselves may have the freedom to answer more critically and reflectively. Currently, the difference between such types of individuals would not be discernible and would emerge as error in our self-esteem instruments. Further, Deci and Ryan (1995) distinguish between *contingent* or *conditional* self-esteem and *true* or *unconditional* self-esteem. An individual who has conditional self-worth is reliant on regular feedback from indicators of success in the range of attributes and qualities typically assessed by contemporary self-concept measures. An individual with true self-esteem would find such feedback largely irrelevant to his or her sense of worth as it is derived from the individual's sense of autonomy and self-determination. Instruments are not currently available that allow us to identify individual differences on these important foundations to the self.

Paper and pencil instrumentation can at best provide a limited window into the complexities of the self-system. A range of research paradigms and qualitative techniques need to be considered in parallel with the quantitative approach. A particular focus is required that allows a richer documentation of the complexities of individual change. Cases where there has been an accelerated call for identity and self-esteem change, such as those initiated by serious illness or injury, provide interesting opportunities for study (Sparkes, 1994; 1997).

Finally, recent instrumentation involving the measurement of self-concept has relied almost exclusively on the multidimensional competence/adequacy-based models of Shavelson et al., (1976) and theoretical tenets developed by Harter (1985b). This theoretical consistency has contributed to the considerable progress that has been made. However, a reliance on a very limited range of theoretical and disciplinary origins for instrumentation to assess arguably the most critical and complex of psychological constructs is likely to be counterproductive in the long term.

In self-concept measurement, we are attempting to access probably the most critical, controversial, and complex of human qualities. Although we have travelled some distance, our instrumentation remains relatively simplistic, descriptive, and narrowly based. A combination of approaches is ultimately required that set nomological instrument techniques alongside a range of theoretical orientations and methods that allow more incisive access to processes of change in the self-system.

References

Bandura, A. (1977). Self-efficacy: Toward a unifying theory of behavioral change. *Psychological Review, 84*, 191-215.

Baumeister, R.F. (1993). Understanding the inner nature of self-esteem. In R.F. Baumeister (Ed.), *Self-esteem: The puzzle of low self-regard* (pp. 201-218). New York: Plenum.

Biddle, S.J.H., Page, A., Ashford, B., Jennings, D., Brooke, R., & Fox, K.R. (1993). Assessment of children's physical self-perception. *International Journal of Adolescence and Youth, 4*, 93-109.

Blaine, B., & Crocker, J. (1993). Self-esteem and self-serving biases in reactions to positive and negative events: An integrative review. In R.F. Baumeister (Ed.), *Self-esteem: The puzzle of low self-regard* (pp. 55-86). New York: Plenum.

Bracken, B.A. (1992). *Multidimensional Self-Concept Scale.* Austin, TX: Pro-ed.

Brewer, B.W., Van Raalte, J.L., & Linder, D.E. (1993). Athletic identity: Hercules' muscles or Achilles heel? *International Journal of Sport Psychology, 24*, 237-254.

Byrne, B.M. (1996). *Measuring self-concept across the lifespan: Issues and instrumentation.* Washington, DC: American Psychological Association.

Campbell, R.N. (1984). *The new science: Self-esteem psychology.* Lanham, MD: University Press of America.

Chase, L. (1991). *Physical self-perceptions and activity involvement in the older population.* Unpublished doctoral dissertation. Arizona State University, Tempe, AZ.

Chase, L.A., & Corbin, C.B. (1995). Development of the Physical Self-Perception Profile for older adults and prediction of activity involvement. *Medicine and Science in Sport and Exercise, 27*, (Suppl.), S42.

Coopersmith, S. (1967). *The antecedents of self-esteem.* San Francisco: Freeman.

Deci, E.L., & Ryan, R.M. (1995). Human autonomy: The basis for true self-esteem. In M. Kernis (Ed.), *Agency, efficacy, and self-esteem* (pp 31-49). New York: Plenum.

Duda, J.L. (1993). Goals: A social-cognitive approach to the study of achievement motivation in sport. In R.N. Singer, M. Murphey & L.K. Tennant (Eds.), *Handbook of research on sport psychology* (pp. 421-436). New York: Macmillan.

Eiser, C., Eiser, J. R. & Haversmans, T. (1995).The measurement of self-esteem: Practical and theoretical considerations. *Personality and Individual Differences, 18*, 429-432.

Fitts, W. H. (1965). *Tennessee Self-Concept Scale: Manual.* Los Angeles: Western Psychological Services.

Fox, K.R. (1988). The self-esteem complex and youth fitness. *Quest, 40*, 230-246.

Fox, K. R. (1990). *The Physical Self-Perception Profile Manual.* DeKalb, IL: Office for Health Promotion, Northern Illinois University.

Fox, K.R. (1997). The physical self and processes in self-esteem development. In K.R. Fox (Ed.). *The physical self: From motivation to well-being* (pp. 111-139). Champaign, IL: Human Kinetics.

Fox, K. R., & Corbin, C. B. (1989). The Physical Self-Perception Profile: Development and preliminary validation. *Journal of Sport and Exercise Psychology, 11*, 408-430

Fox, K. R., Corbin, C. B., & Couldry, W. H. (1985). Female physical estimation and attraction to physical activity. *Journal of Sport Psychology, 7*, 125-136.

Fox, K.R., & Dirkin, G.R. (1992). Psychosocial predictors and outcomes of exercise in patients attending multidisciplinary obesity treatment. *International Journal of Obesity, 16*, (Suppl. 1), 84.

Fox, K.R., Page, A., Armstrong, N., & Kirby, B. (1994). Dietary restraint and self-perceptions in early adolescence. *Personality and Individual Differences, 17*, 87-96.

Franzoi, S. L., & Shields, S. A. (1984). The Body Esteem Scale: Multidimensional structure and sex differences in a college population. *Journal of Personality Assessment, 49*, 173-178.

Harter, S. (1978). Effectance motivation reconsidered: Toward a developmental model. *Human Development, 21*, 34-64.

Harter, S. (1982). The Perceived Competence Scale for Children. *Child Development, 53*, 87-97.

Harter, S. (1985a). *Manual for the Self-Perception Profile for Children.* Denver, CO: University of Denver.

Harter, S. (1985b). Competence as a dimension of self-evaluation: Toward a comprehensive model of self-worth. In R. H. Leahy (Ed.), *The development of the self* (pp. 55-121). New York: Academic Press.

Harter, S. (1986). Processes underlying the construction, maintenance and enhancement of self-concept in children. In J. Suls & A. Greenwald (Eds.), *Psychological perspective on the self: Vol. 3* (pp. 136-182). Hillsdale, NJ: Erlbaum.

Harter, S. (1988). *Manual for the Self-Perception Profile for Adolescents.* Denver, CO: University of Denver.

Harter, S. (1990). Causes, correlates, and the functional role of global self-worth: A life-span perspective. In R. J. Sternberg & J. Kolligian, Jr. (Eds.), *Competence considered* (pp. 67-97). New Haven, CT: Yale University.

Harter, S. (1996). Historical roots of contemporary issues involving self-concept. In B.A. Bracken (Ed.), *Handbook of self-concept* (pp. 1-37). New York: Wiley.

Harter, S., & Pike, R. (1984). The Perceived Competence Scale for Young Children. *Child Development, 55*, 1969-1982

Kendzierski, D. (1994). Schema theory: An information processing focus. In R.K. Dishman (Ed), *Advances in exercise adherence* (pp.

137-159). Champaign, IL: Human Kinetics.

Leary, M.R. (1992). Self-presentational processes in exercise and sport. *Journal of Sport and Exercise Psychology, 14,* 339-351.

Lintunen, T. (1987). Perceived physical competence scale for children. *Scandinavian Journal of Sports Science, 9,* 57-64.

Lintunen, T., Heikinaro-Johansson, P., & Sherrill, C. (1995). Use of the perceived physical competence scale for adolescents with disabilities. *Perceptual and Motor Skills, 80,* 571-577.

Lintunen, T., Leskinen, E., Oinonen, M., Salinto, M., & Rahkila, P. (1995). Change, reliability, and stability in self-perceptions in early adolescence: A four-year follow-up study. *International Journal of Behavioral Development, 18,* 351-364.

Maehr, M.L., & Braskamp, L.A. (1986). *The motivation factor: A theory of personal investment.* Lexington, MA: Lexington Books.

Marsh, H.W., (1987a). The factorial invariance of responses by males and females to a multidimensional self-concept instrument: Substantive and methodological issues. *Multivariate Behavioral Research, 22,* 457-480.

Marsh, H. W. (1987b). The hierarchical structure of self-concept and the application of hierarchical confirmatory factor analysis. *Journal of Educational Measurement, 24,* 17-19.

Marsh, H. W. (1989). Age and sex effects in multiple dimensions of self-concept: Preadolescence to adulthood. *Journal of Educational Psychology, 81,* 417-430.

Marsh, H. W. (1992a). *Self-Description Questionnaire (SDQ) I: A theoretical and empirical basis for the measurement of multiple dimensions of preadolescent self-concept. A test manual and research monograph.* Macarthur, New South Wales, Australia: University of Western Sydney, Faculty of Education.

Marsh, H. W. (1992b). *Self-Description Questionnaire (SDQ) II: A theoretical and empirical basis for the measurement of multiple dimensions of adolescent self-concept. An interim test manual and research monograph.* Macarthur, New South Wales, Australia: University of Western Sydney, Faculty of Education.

Marsh, H. W. (1992c). *Self-Description Questionnaire (SDQ) III: A theoretical and empirical basis for the measurement of multiple dimensions of late adolescent self-concept. An interim test manual and research monograph.* Macarthur, New South Wales, Australia: University of Western Sydney, Faculty of Education.

Marsh, H. W. (1993). Relations between global and specific domains of self: The importance of individual importance, certainty, and ideals. *Journal of Personality & Social Psychology, 65,* 975-992.

Marsh, H. W. (1994). The importance of being important: Theoretical models of relations between specific and global components of physical self-concept. *Journal of Sport & Exercise Psychology, 16,* 306-325.

Marsh, H.W. (1996). Physical Self-Description Questionnaire: Stability and discriminant validity. *Research Quarterly for Exercise and Sport, 67,* 249-264.

Marsh, H.W. (1997). The measurement of physical self-concept: A construct validation approach. In K.R.Fox (Ed.) *The physical self: From motivation to well-being* (pp. 27-58). Champaign, IL: Human Kinetics.

Marsh, H.W., Barnes, J., Cairnes, L., & Tidman, M. (1984). The Self-Description Questionnaire (SDQ): Age and sex effects in the structure and level of self-concept for preadolescent children. *Journal of Educational Psychology, 76,* 940-956.

Marsh, H.W., & Hattie, J. (1996). Theoretical perspectives on the structure of self-concept. In B. A. Bracken (Ed.), *Handbook of self-concept.* New York, NY: Wiley.

Marsh, H.W., Parker, J., & Barnes, J. (1985). Multidimensional adolescent self-concept: The relationship to age, sex, and academic measures. *American Educational Research Journal, 22,* 422-444.

Marsh, H. W. & Peart, N. (1988). Competitive and cooperative physical fitness training programs for girls: Effects on physical fitness and on multidimensional self-concepts. *Journal of Sport and Exercise Psychology, 10,* 390-407.

Marsh, H.W., Perry, C., Horsely, C., & Roche, L. (1995). Multidimensional self-concepts of elite athletes: How do they differ from the general population? *Journal of Sport and Exercise Psychology, 17,* 70-83.

Marsh, H.W., & Redmayne, R. S. (1994) A multidimensional physical self-concept and its relation to multiple components of physical fitness. *Journal of Sport and Exercise Psychology, 16,* 45-55.

Marsh, H.W., & Richards, G. E. (1988). The Tennessee Self-Concept Scales: Reliability, internal structure, and construct validity. *Journal of Personality and Social Psychology, 55,* 612-624.

Marsh, H. W., Richards, G., & Barnes, J. (1986). Multidimensional self-concepts: A long-term follow-up of the effect of participation in an Outward Bound program. *Personality and Social Psychology Bulletin, 12,* 475-492.

Marsh, H.W., Richards, G., Johnson, S., Roche, L., & Tremayne, P. (1994). Physical Self Description Questionnaire: Psychometric properties and a multitrait-multimethod analysis of relations to existing instruments. *Journal of Sport and Exercise Psychology, 16,* 270-305.

Marsh, H.W., & Roche, L.A., (1996). Predicting self-esteem from perceptions of actual and ideal ratings of body fatness: Is there only on eideal supermodel? *Research Quarterly for Exercise and Sport, 67,* 13-23.

Marsh, H. W., & Shavelson, R. J. (1985). Self-concept: Its multifaceted, hierarchical structure. *Educational Psychologist, 20,* 107-125.

Marsh, H. W., & Sonstroem, R. J. (1995). Importance ratings and specific components of physical self-concept: Relevance to predicting global components of self-concept and exercise. *Journal of Sport and Exercise Psychology, 17,* 84-104.

McGuire, B., & Tinsley, H.E.A. (1981). A contribution to the construct validity of the Tennessee Self-Concept Scale: A confirmatory factor analysis. *Applied Psychological Measurement, 5,* 449-457.

Messer, B., & Harter, S. (1986). *Manual for the Adult Self-Perception Profile.* Denver, CO: University of Denver.

Neemann, J., & Harter, S. (1986). *Manual for the Self-Perception Profile for College Students.* Denver, CO: University of Denver.

Nicholls, J.G. (1989). *The competitive ethos and democratic education.* Cambridge, MA: Harvard University Press.

Page, A., Ashford, B., Fox, K.R., & Biddle, S.J.H. (1993). Evidence of cross-cultural validity of the Physical Self-Perception Profile. *Personality and Individual Differences, 14,* 585-590.

Paulhus, D.L. (1984). Two-component models of socially desirable responding. *Journal of Personality and Social Psychology, 46,* 598-609.

Piers, E.V. (1984). *Piers-Harris Children's Self-Concept Scale: Revise manual.* Los Angeles: Western Psychological Services.

Pitkänen, P., Komi, P.V., Nupponen, H., Rusko, H., Telama, R., & Tiainen, J. (1979). Evaluating the product of physical education. In T. Tammivuori (Ed.), *Evaluation in the development of physical education* (pp. 119-125). Somero, Finland: Liikuntatieteellinen seura.

Reynolds, W. M. (1982). Development of reliable and short forms of the Marlowe-Crowne Social Desirability Scale. *Journal of Clinical Psychology, 38,* 119-125.

Richards, G. E. (1988). *Physical Self-Concept Scale.* Sydney, Australia: Australian Outward Bound Foundation.

Roid, G.H., & Fitts, W.H. (1994). *Tennessee Self-Concept Scale* [Revised manual]. Los Angeles: Western Psychological Services.

Rosenberg, M. (1965). *Society and the adolescent self-image.* Princeton, NJ: University Press.

Ryckman, R.M., Robbins, M.A., Thornton, B., & Cantrell, P. (1982). Development and validation of a physical self-efficacy scale. *Journal of Personality and Social Psychology, 42,* 891-900.

Secord, P. F., & Jourard, S. M. (1953). The appraisal of body-cathexis: Body cathexis and the self. *Journal of Consulting Psychology, 17,* 343-347.

Shavelson, R. J., Hubner, J. J., & Stanton, G. C. (1976). Self-concept: Validation of construct interpretations. *Review of Educational Research, 46*, 407-411.

Sonstroem, R.J. (1976). The validity of self-perceptions regarding physical and athletic ability. *Medicine and Science in Sports, 8*, 126-132.

Sonstroem, R. J. (1984). Exercise and self-esteem. *Exercise and Sports Sciences Reviews, 12*, 123-155.

Sonstroem, R. J., Harlow, L. L., Gemma, L. M., & Osborne, S. (1991). Test of structural relationships within a proposed exercise and self-esteem model. *Journal of Personality Assessment, 56*, 348-364.

Sonstroem, R. J., Harlow, L. L., & Josephs, L. (1994). Exercise and self-esteem: Validity of model expansion and exercise associations. *Journal of Sport & Exercise Psychology, 16*, 29-42.

Sonstroem, R. J., Harlow, L. L., & Salisbury, K. S. (1993). Path analysis of a self-esteem model across a competitive swim season. *Research Quarterly for Exercise and Sport, 64*, 335-342.

Sonstroem, R. J., & Morgan, W. P. (1989). Exercise and self-esteem: Rationale and model. *Medicine and Science in Sports and Exercise, 21*, 329-337.

Sonstroem, R. J., & Potts, S.A. (1996). Life adjustment correlates of physical self-concepts. *Medicine and Science in Sports and Exercise, 28*, 619-625.

Sonstroem, R. J., Speliotis, E. D., & Fava, J. L. (1992). Perceived physical competence in adults: An examination of the Physical Self-Perception Profile. *Journal of Sport and Exercise Psychology, 14*, 207-221.

Sparkes, A. (1994). Life histories and the issue of voice: Reflections on an emerging relationship. *International Journal of Qualitative Studies in Education, 7*(2), 165-183.

Sparkes, A. (1997). Reflections on the socially constructed physical self. In K.R. Fox (Ed.), *The physical self: From motivation to well-being* (pp. 83-110). Champaign, IL: Human Kinetics.

Welk, G.J., Corbin, C.B., Lewis, L. (1995). Physical self-perceptions of high school athletes. *Pediatric Exercise Science, 7*, 152-161.

White, R.W. (1959). Motivation reconsidered: The concept of competence. *Psychological Review, 66*, 297-333.

Whitehead, J.R. (1995). A study of children's physical self-perceptions using an adapted physical self-perception questionnaire. *Pediatric Exercise Science, 7*, 133-152.

Whitehead, J.R., Eklund, R.C., & Welk, G.J. (1995, June). *Validity of the Children's Self-Perception Profile: A confirmatory factor analysis*. Paper presented at the American College of Sports Medicine Annual Conference, Minneapolis, MN.

Wylie, R. C. (1979). *The self-concept: Vol. 2*. Lincoln, NE: University of Nebraska Press.

Wylie, R. C. (1989). *Measures of self-concept*. Lincoln, NE: University of Nebraska Press.

Chapter 17

BODY IMAGE AND EXERCISE

Susan Bane
East Carolina University
and
Edward McAuley
University of Illinois

Introduction

Contemporary society exerts tremendous pressure on individuals to present their appearance in a positive manner. For women, a lean and fit body represents the ideal physique, whereas the expectation for men is a body that is lean and muscular. Given the advantages of being physically attractive, it is not surprising that men and women are enthusiastically responding to society's pressure to mold their physiques into the perfect body. For example, Steiner-Adair (1987) reported slim individuals were thought to be physically fit, attractive, successful, smart, and in control of their lives, in contrast to the overweight, who were viewed as lazy, sloppy, unattractive, and unable to control themselves. Attractive individuals have also been shown to be treated differently. Langlios (1986) reported that the amount of nurturing infants receive is directly related to how cute they are thought to be, and teachers have been found to react more positively to attractive children (Martinek, 1981). In the workplace, when unattractive and attractive persons with equal qualifications apply for the same job, the attractive person is more likely to be hired (Cash & Kilcullen, 1985).

The combination of anticipated rewards for appearing attractive and society's unyielding pressure to attain the ideal body may well drive individuals' attempts to "change" their physiques to fit the current standard of physical attractiveness. Altering one's physique, however, is not easy to do. Genetics play a major role in individual size and shape, and even exercise and dietary restraint may not result in the desired physique change (Brownell, 1991). This widespread inability to obtain the perfect body has led to the prevalence of body image disturbance in our society, with body image being broadly defined as self-attitudes towards one's body and particularly physical appearance (Cash & Pruzinsky, 1990).

Perhaps the most comprehensive and representative surveys in the literature examining body-image disturbance in the general population were conducted by *Psychology Today* magazine (Berscheid, Walster, & Bohrnstedt, 1973; Cash, Winstead, & Janda, 1986) and by a door-to-door survey of women living in five regions throughout the United States (Cash & Henry, 1995). Bersheid et al. (1973) measured the degree of satisfaction with various body parts. Fifteen percent of the men and 25% of the women stated they were dissatisfied with their overall appearance, with males being especially dissatisfied with their abdomen and weight and females with their abdomen, hips, thighs, and weight. Over a decade later, Cash et al. (1986) found that 34% of the men and 38% of the women were dissatisfied with their overall appearance. Once again, the body areas resulting in the greatest number of people being dissatisfied were the midtorso and weight for men and midtorso, lower torso, and weight for women. Thus, it appears dissatisfaction with overall appearance and with specific body areas intensified for males and females from 1973 to 1986.

In the most recent national survey, Cash and Henry (1995) surveyed a sample of women, aged 18-70. Relative to the 1985 sample, in which 30% of the women evaluated their appearance negatively, this recent study revealed a significant increase in the women (48%) who negatively evaluated their appearance. Body areas with which the greatest percentage of women were dissatisfied remained the same in both surveys, with the midtorso, lower torso, and weight being the aspects of the body with which the greatest number of women reported being most dissatisfied.

The findings of these surveys are typical of the burgeoning body-image literature demonstrating increasing body-image concerns in men and, particularly, women in our society (Adame, Frank, Serdula, Cole, & Abbas, 1990; Cash, Counts, & Huffine, 1990; Cash & Hicks, 1990; Fallon & Rozin, 1985; Cash, Counts, & Huffine, 1990; Hesse-Biber, Clayton-Matthews, & Downey, 1987; Keeton, Cash, & Brown, 1990; Cash, Counts, & Huffine, 1990). From a health perspective, the most alarming aspect of body-image disturbance is its association with several negative health consequences. For example, Cash and Hicks (1990) reported more frequent binge eating and dietary restraint to lose weight in self-classified overweight females relative to self-classified normal weight participants. Moreover, a negative body image is a core feature of such eating disorders as anorexia and bulimia nervosa (Thompson, 1996). Concerns about one's body may also lead to avoidance of exercise participation because the traditional exercise setting can be threatening due to the high potential of evaluation of one's body by others (Leary, 1992). For example, overweight women participating in an exercise program stated that the social situation of the program (visibility, embarrassment with their physical appearance and judgment by others) was the most powerful influence of how comfortable they felt while exercising (Bain, Wilson, & Chaikind, 1989). Similarly, Crawford and Eklund (1994) reported that subjects with higher levels of physique anxiety (or anxiety experienced when others evaluated their physiques) expressed preference for exercise settings that de-emphasized the physique (i.e., in which shorts and t-shirts could be worn), whereas those individuals low in physique anxiety preferred settings in which attire that emphasized the physique was worn (i.e., leotards and thongs).

Whereas concerns about the evaluation of one's body may lead some individuals to avoid exercise participation, for many, exercise is a strategy adopted to attenuate body-image disturbance. Indeed, several studies have examined the relationship between exercise and body image (Bane & McAuley, 1996; Bane & McAuley, 1996; Fisher & Thompson, 1994; Kennedy, Reis, Bane, & Stang, 1995; McAuley, Bane, & Mihalko, 1995; McAuley, Bane, Rudolph, & Lox, 1995). Whether or not changes in physical appearance due to exercise (e.g., weight loss, reduced body fat) are accompanied by reductions in body-image disturbance is equivocal, however. Although several studies reveal no difference or greater body-image disturbance in exercisers compared to nonexercisers (Davis & Cowles, 1991; Davis, Fox, Cowles, Hastings, & Schwass, 1990; Kennedy et al., 1995), other studies have shown reductions in body-image disturbance as a result of exercise participation (Bane & McAuley, 1996; Fisher & Thompson, 1994; McAuley, Bane, & Mihalko, 1995; McAuley, Bane, Rudolph, & Lox, 1995).

Perhaps the most important reason for this equivocality is the operational definition and measurement of body image employed. Constructs assessed under the rubric body image include perceptions of body size, evaluation of appearance, anxiety about one's physique, and avoidant behaviors related to appearance (Davis, 1990; Davis & Cowles, 1991; Kennedy et al., 1995; Fisher &Thompson, 1994; Pasman & Thompson, 1988). Because of the casual use of the term body image, caution must be taken when comparing studies that claim to assess body image because one study may examine perceptions of appearance whereas the other measures attitudes about appearance. We recommend, as have others, that body image be viewed and measured as a multidimensional construct and that the authors clearly define which aspect(s) of body image they are assessing (Cash & Brown, 1987; Thompson, Penner, & Altabe, 1990). Therefore, a useful way to conceptualize body

image is as an umbrella term that encompasses perceptions, cognitions, affect, and behaviors related to body image. Body image consists of: (a) a *perceptual component* of appearance that represents the accuracy of perceptions regarding body size; (b) a *cognitive component,* such as thoughts about the body, body satisfaction, and evaluation of appearance; (c) an *affective component* that represents feelings and anxiety related to appearance; and (d) a *behavioral component* that embodies behaviors related to appearance (i.e., eating, exercise, etc.).

To this end, we have organized the chapter in a manner that allows each component of body image to be discussed separately. We first review instruments that have frequently been used to assess the perceptual, cognitive, affective, and behavioral components of body image, respectively. Specifically, we provide a description of each instrument followed by a discussion of the psychometric properties of the measures and recommendations for the use of the instruments in exercise-related research. In order to clarify this section for the reader, we also provide a table listing each instrument, its reliability, and citations for development and validation (see Table 1). Incorporated in each section are findings from the exercise literature, with a focus on scales that have been used to determine the role of exercise in improving body image. The chapter concludes with a summary of recommendations for future research.

Measurement of Body Image

Perceptual Measures

Perceptual measures of body image assess the accuracy of perceptions regarding body size. There are two basic categories of instruments used to assess perception of size: body-part procedures and whole-body instruments. Body-part or site procedures require individuals to match the width of the distance between two points to their own estimation of the width of a certain body part, whereas whole-body techniques require individuals to select a single image that matches their body size.

Body-Part procedures. One of the first instruments developed to assess perception of size was the movable caliper technique (MCT) by Slade and Russell (1973), which consists of a horizontal bar with two lights mounted on a track. The participant is asked to adjust the width between the two lights to match his or her estimate of the width of a certain body part. The MCT was employed to assess perceptions of body parts in women with and without anorexia. The internal consistency in the 14 female anorexics was .72-.93, whereas internal consistency ranged from .37-.79 in 20 female controls. In a subsequent study, Slade (1985) reported a more acceptable internal consistency in anorexics (.72) than controls (.63).

The development of the MCT led to the generation of similar instruments used to assess body size, with the most frequently used measures being the Image Marking Procedure (IMP; Askevold, 1975), Body Image Detection Device (BIDD; Ruff & Barrios, 1986), Adjustable Light Beam Apparatus (ALBA;Thompson & Thompson, 1986), Body-Size Estimation Method (Kreitler & Kreitler, 1988), and Kinesthetic Size Estimation Apparatus (KSEA; Gleghorn, Penner, Powers, & Schulman, 1987). The IMP simply requires participants to mark their body widths on a sheet of paper attached to the wall, whereas the ODT asks participants to open a door to the width believed

Table 1
Measure of Body Image: Reliabilty and Study Details

Perceptual Measures

Measure	Authors	Initial Sample	Reliability	Validation Studies
Movable Caliper Technique (MCT)	Slade & Russell (1973)	14 females with anorexia 20 female controls	α = .72-.93 α = .37-.79	Gleghorn et al. (1987) Slade (1985)
Image Marking Procedure (IMP)	Askevold (1975)	Female patients with various illnesses	none given	Barrios, Ruff, & York (1989) Gleghorn et al. (1987)
Body Image Detection Device (BIDD)	Ruff & Barrios (1986)	20 women with bulimia 20 female controls	α = .91 α = .93 test-retest immediate .82-.87 1 week .72-.85	Barrios et al. (1989) Butters & Cash (1987) Cash & Green (1986) Keeton et al. (1990)
Adjustable Light Beam Apparatus (ALBA)	Thompson & Spana (1988)	159 college females	α = .83 test-retest immediate .83-.92 1 week .56-.86	Fisher & Thompson (1994) Pasman & Thompson (1988) Thompon & Spana (1988)
Body Size Estimation Method	Kreitler & Kreitler (1988)	240 males and females aged 4-30 y/o	α = .75-.88 Test-retest: .93-.97	
Kinesthetic Size Estimation Apparatus (KSEA)	Gleghorn et al. (1987)	55 females aged 17-45 with and w/o eating disorders	test-retest: .45-.65	

(continued on next page)

to allow passage through the door sideways. The BIDD projects a light beam onto a wall and asks the individual to adjust the width of the light to match the size of various body parts, whereas the ALBA simultaneously projects four light beams onto a wall and asks participants to adjust the light beams to match the width of their cheeks, waist, hips, and thighs. The Body Size Estimation Method requires participants to close their eyes and use the distance between their hands to indicate perceived size, whereas the KSEA assesses perceived size by having blindfolded participants adjust the distance between two calipers to match their size. With all of these instruments, once the individual has estimated his or her perceived size, an actual width is taken, and an over- or underestimation of body-part size is computed by examining the ratio of actual width to perceived width. As can be seen in Table 1, the initial psychometric properties for these instruments reveal a wide variety of internal consistencies and test-retest reliabilities. Additionally,

many of the devices have been developed in select populations, and thus the external validity is questionable. For example, with the exception of the Body-Size Estimation Method, all of the measures were developed with young women or women with eating disorders, resulting in the inability to use the instruments with other groups (e.g., men, older individuals) without further validation studies.

Whole-Body instruments. The second category of perceptual instruments consists of whole-image adjustment methods, which typically require individuals to confront a real-life photographic or videotaped image that has been modified to appear larger or smaller than actual body size. The individuals are then asked to select the image that matches their body size. Instruments included in this category are the distorting photograph technique (Glucksman & Hirsch, 1969) and the video distortion procedure (Touyz, Beaumont, Collins, & Cowie, 1985). With each of these instruments, a distorted image is presented to the individual (via a mirror, slide, or video camera), and the individual is asked to choose the image that best represents his or her actual body size. The Open Door Test (Simonson, 1978) is another whole-body device that simply requires the individual to adjust the width of a door to a distance that would allow the person to pass. Just as with the body-part devices, reliability estimates vary dramatically for the whole-body measures, and the data are again limited to young women and women with eating disorders (Table 1). Interestingly, the Open Door test, which is perhaps the most cost effective and easiest to perform, shows the highest reliability and has been tested in the broadest sample.

Psychometric data focusing on concurrent validity among perceptual measures have been somewhat limited, but those studies that do exist report similar findings. Gleghorn et al. (1987) examined relationships between two whole-body techniques, the Open Door Technique and Distorting Photograph Technique, and three single-site devices, the IMP, MCT, and KSEA (face, shoulder, waist, and hips). In a sample of 110 females with and without bulimia, the correlation between the two whole-body techniques was not significant (r=.03), whereas convergence occurred between the three single-site devices (r= .43-.52). However, different sites (e.g., waist and

Table 1 (cont)
Measure of Body Image: Reliabilty and Study Details

Distorting Photograph Technique	Glucksman & Hirsch (1969)	3 obese males 3 obese females	α: not applicable	Garner & Garfinkel (1981)
Video Distorting Technique	Touyz & Beaumont (1987)	Females with anorexia and bulimia	α: not applicable test-retest: 1 day: .63 8 weeks: .61	
Open Door Technique	Simonson (1978)	110 females	α: not applicable test-retest: immediate:.72-.92	
COGNITIVE MEASURES				
Body Cathexis Scale	Secord & Jourard (1953)	45 male and 43 female college students	α = .78-.83	Davis, Durnin, Dionne, & Gurevich (1994) Dworkin & Kerr (1987) Tucker (1983) Tucker & Maxwell (1992)
Body Esteem Scale	Franzoi & Shields (1984)	366 female and 257 male college students	α = .78-.87	Davis et al. (1993)
Body Dissatisfaction Scale of the EDI	Garner et al. (1983)	113 females with anorexia and 577 female controls	α = .90-.91	Bailey, Goldberg, Swap, Chomitz, & Housen (1990) Davis (1990) Fisher & Thompson (1994) McDonald & Thompson (1992)

(continued on next page)

hips) measured by the same device correlated more highly than did the same site measured by two different devices. Thus, simply using different body-part devices may lead to different estimates of size. Similarly, little convergence has been found between whole-body and body part devices. Gleghorn et al. reported minimal relationship occurring between the whole-body devices (ODT and DPT) and site-specific measures (IMP, MCT, and KSEA), whereas Keeton et al. reported no relationship between the BIDD and BIAP-R. The apparent lack of convergence between whole-body and body-part devices suggests that overestimation of body size may be site specific and is not necessarily related to whole-body overestimation.

Research recommendations. Whereas devices that assess

the perceptual aspect of body image dominated early research, recent research efforts have focused more on other components of body image because of several methodological concerns with perceptual measures. First, several theories exist that attempt to explain perceptual distortions of body size (i.e., cortical deficits, adaptive failure, perceptual artifacts), yet none of the perceptual instruments emanate from theory, and thus hypotheses can not be tested. Second, several factors associated with the research environment, such as type of clothing worn, lighting, and food consumption prior to testing, have been found to influence size estimation and thus impact internal validity (Thompson, 1996). Additionally, the instructional content given to the participants has been shown to influence ratings of size. For example, Thompson and Dolce (1989) found that individuals perceived themselves as larger if they were asked to rate how they felt versus how they rationally viewed their body. From clinical experience, we have found that sedentary women who begin an exercise program often state they "feel thinner" when they exercise, even though they may not have changed their percent body fat. Assessment of body size using the question "how do you feel?" may reveal that women do perceive specific body parts and/or their whole body as thinner as a result of exercise, whereas asking how individuals rationally view their bodies may not capture the change in perception that has occurred. This approach to questioning could also help determine whether individuals who lift weights perceive their muscle mass to be larger, even though significant hypertrophy may not have occurred.

Another factor to consider when using perceptual measures is that many individuals, and particularly women, become anxious when they are confronted with a whole-body image that is larger than their actual size (Thompson et al., 1990). Thus, whole-body techniques that present a large distorted image may lead to unnecessary discomfort for the participants. Lastly, the cost of the assessment must be considered. Body-part devices are typically inexpensive, whereas whole-body devices, other than the ODT, require video or camera equipment that is more costly.

Table 1 (cont)
Measure of Body Image: Reliabilty and Study Details

Body Parts Satisfaction Questionnaire (BPSQ)	Bersheid et al. (1973)			Keeton et al. (1990)
Figure Ratings/ Silhouettes	1. Fallon & Rozin (1985) 2. Powers & Erickson (1986)	1. 475 college students 2. 164 female college students	1. none given 2. none given	Crawford & Eklund (1994) Furnham, Titman, & Sleeman (1994) Hallinan & Schuler (1993) Rozin & Fallon (1988) Thompson & Psaltis (1988)
Body Image Automatic Thoughts Questionnaire (BIATQ)	Cash, Lewis, & Keeton (1987)	33 females with bulimia and 79 female controls	$\alpha = .90$	Rucker & Cash (1990)
Physical Attractiveness Self-Efficacy Scale (PASE)	Bane & McAuley (in review)	60 college females	$\alpha = .90$	Bane & McAuley (1995) Bane & McAuley (1996)
Multidimensional Body Self Relations Questionnaire (MBSRQ)	Cash et al. (1986)	2,000 adults	$\alpha = .79-.90$ test-retest: 2 week: .78-.94	Brown, Cash, & Mikulka (1990) Brown et al. (1988) Cash & Henry (1995) Cash, Wood, Phelps, & Boyd (1991) Keeton et al. (1990)
AFFECTIVE MEASURES				
Body Shape Questionnaire (BSQ)	Cooper et al. (1987)	Young women with and w/o bulimia	$\alpha = .93$	Rosen, Orosan, & Reiter (1995) Rosen et al. (1991) Rosen et al. (1990))

(continued on next page)

Given these limitations, it is not surprising that perceptual measures are being used less frequently in the body-image literature. Still, we believe perceptual measures can play a role in exercise-related research and should not be discounted completely. For example, it is unknown how actual change in size of body parts correlates with perceptions of change after participation in an exercise program. For example, does a change in perception of the size of one's waist correlate with an objective value of change such as a skinfold measure? Unfortunately, the only study that assessed size perception of various body parts after participation in an exercise program did not measure objective changes in these body areas (i.e., skinfolds, circumference)

(Fisher & Thompson, 1994). Thus, although improvements in size perception of waist, hips, and thighs occurred at posttesting, it cannot be determined if actual changes also occurred at these specific sites. We recommend using perceptual instruments together with physiological measures (i.e., circumference, skinfolds) to examine correlations between actual change and perceptions of change before and after exercise participation.

Cognitive Measures

Numerous instruments have been developed to assess what we have termed the cognitive component of body image. These scales are typically paper-and-pencil measures that assess degree of satisfaction regarding one's body size and shape as well as attitudes and thoughts about one's body.

Body satisfaction. Satisfaction with one's body has been assessed with scales that focus on specific body areas as well as instruments that assess satisfaction with the whole body. The earliest scale designed to assess satisfaction with body areas was the Body Cathexis Scale (Secord & Jourard, 1953). The Body Cathexis Scale is a 46-item scale in which individuals rate their degrees of satisfaction with various body parts (chest, legs, etc.) and processes (energy level, sexual activity, etc.). The original scale was found to have adequate internal consistency, as has an abbreviated form of the scale that assesses satisfaction with various body parts (Body Esteem Scale; Franzoi & Shields, 1984). Similarly, the Body Dissatisfaction Scale of the Eating Disorders Inventory (Garner, Olmstead,& Polivy 1983) is a nine-item subscale that assesses weight-related dissatisfaction with various body parts (e.g., "my thighs are too large"; "my stomach is too big"), whereas the Body Parts Satisfaction Questionnaire (BPSQ; Berscheid et al., 1973) lists 24 body parts that are rated on a 6-point scale ranging from *extremely dissatisfied* to *extremely satisfied*. These ratings yield a factor score for satisfaction with various components of the body (e.g., weight/midtorso, upper torso, and face). Last, the Body Area Satisfaction Scale (BASS; Cash et al., 1986) of the Multidimensional Body-Self Relations Questionnaire (MBSRQ) is an nine-item subscale that also assesses satisfaction with various body parts.

Table 1 (cont)
Measure of Body Image: Reliabilty and Study Details

Physical Appearance State and Trait Anxiety Scale (PASTAS)	Reed et al. (1991)	College students	α=.90	Fisher & Thompson (1994)
Social Physique Anxiety Scale (SPAS)	Hart et al. (1989)	College males and females	α = .90 test-retest: 8-week: .82	Crawford & Eklund (1994) Davis, Brewer, & Weinstein (1993) McAuley, Bane, & Mihalko (1995) McAuley, Bane, Rudolph, & Lox (1995) McAuley & Burman (1993) Eklund & Crawford (1994) Eklund et al. (1996)
Mirror Focus Procedure	Butters & Cash (1987)	College students	α: not applicable test-retest: not given	Keeton et al. (1990)
BEHAVIORAL MEASURES				
Body Image Avoidance Questionnaire (BIAQ)	Rosen et al. (1991)	353 college females	α = .89 test-retest: .87	Fisher & Thompson (1994) Rucker & Cash (1992)
Body Image Behavior Questionnaire	Rosen et al. (1990)	145 female college students	α = .87 test-retest: 2 weeks: .89	
Reasons for Exercise Inventory (REI)	Silberstein et al. (1988)			Cash et al.(1994) Crawford & Eklund (1994) Davis et al. (1995) McDonald & Thompson (1992)

General satisfaction with appearance versus satisfaction with various body areas has primarily been assessed with schematic figures or silhouettes of different body sizes, ranging from ectomorphs to endomorphs (Fallon & Rozin, 1985; Keeton et al., 1990; Thompson & Psaltis, 1988). Although the design of the scales varies slightly, all are alike in that they require individuals to choose the figure they think best represents their current and ideal size. The discrepancy between the two figures is taken as an indication of body size dissatisfaction.

Thoughts and cognitions. Body-image-related thoughts and cognitions have been assessed by the Body Image Automatic Thoughts Questionnaire (BIATQ; Brown, Johnson, Bergeron, Keeton, & Cash, 1988), Physical Attractiveness Self-Efficacy Scale (PASE; Bane & McAuley, 1996), and

Multidimensional Body Self Relations Questionnaire (MBSRQ; Cash et al., 1986). With the BIATQ, subjects rate the frequency of 52 appearance-related cognitions on a 5-point scale. Thirty-seven of the items are negative, and 15 are positive body-related self-statements. The PASE is a newly developed scale that measures women's belief in their ability to self-present in a physically attractive manner (Bane & McAuley, 1996). Participants indicate their degree of confidence in their capability to appear attractive to others in situations in which their bodies might be evaluated. Responses are scored on a 100-point percentage scale composed of 10-point increments (100% = complete confidence, 0% = highly uncertain). Initial validity evidence suggests that females who are more efficacious about their ability to appear attractive are leaner ($r=-.29$), have greater aerobic capacity ($r=.17$), are less physique anxious ($r=-.73$) and more satisfied with their bodies ($r=.70$).

The Multidimensional Body Self-Relations Questionnaire (MBSRQ; Cash et al., 1986) is the most comprehensive and psychometrically studied cognitive assessment of body image. The 69-item MBSRQ consists of nine subscales that assess the following body image components: (a) *appearance evaluation*, which is represented by feelings of physical attractiveness or dissatisfaction with looks; (b) *appearance orientation*, which assesses the amount of time spent trying to improve one's appearance; (c) *fitness evaluation*, characterized by feelings of being physically fit; (d) *fitness orientation*, which assesses amount of time spent trying to be physically fit or athletically competent; (e) *health evaluation*, typified by perceptions of physical health and/or freedom from illness; (f) *health orientation*, or amount of time spent trying to lead a healthy lifestyle; (g) *illness orientation*, which represented by the extent of reactivity to being or becoming ill; (h) *body area satisfaction*, which determines satisfaction with discrete body areas; and (i) *weight preoccupation*, reflects concerns about gaining weight. Finally, the MBSRQ employs two items with which individuals categorize their body weight and others' perceptions of their weight on a 5-point Likert scale ranging from *very underweight* to *very overweight*.

The MBSRQ is differentiated from the other cognitive measures of body image in that it includes measures that are designed to determine the amount of time spent trying to improve various aspects of oneself (orientation). The inclusion and measurement of orientation is clearly advantageous in the exercise domain as these measures allow one to ascertain whether time spent in the improvement of fitness and appearance has any impact on one's self-evaluation. It should be noted, however, that the fitness evaluation and orientation subscales of the MBSRQ, although labeled as fitness related, contain items that predominantly reflect sport- and skill-related content rather than fitness. Thus, positive changes in fitness evaluation brought about by exercise participation may not be adequately assessed with these scales.

As seen in Table 1, all the scales assessing cognitive aspects of body image possess adequate internal consistency. Moreover, validity evidence suggests that the convergence among the cognitive measures and other measures of body image has been fairly consistent. For example, Thompson and Psaltis (1988) reported correlations greater than .50 between physical appearance evaluation and figure ratings, with larger figure ratings being associated with greater body dissatisfaction. Similarly, Gleghorn et al. (1987) reported the BDQ and BPSQ to be significantly correlated (r=.66) and Keeton et al. (1990) report a significant correlation between the appearance evaluation subscale of the MBSRQ and BPSQ (r=.61). Finally, Cash (1989) found that overall appearance evaluation could be predicted from the sum of satisfaction with various body parts, unlike the whole-body and body-part perceptual devices, which were unrelated. Additionally, it is important to note that unlike the perceptual measures that have used females as participants, several of these measures (Body Cathexis Scale, Body Esteem Scale, Figure Ratings, and MBSRQ) have been validated with males and thus have greater external validity.

Research recommendations. Unlike the perceptual measures that have rarely been utilized in the exercise and body image literature, cognitive instruments have dominated the literature. Although our current understanding of the relationship between exercise and body image is based primarily on findings utilizing these scales, there are several limitations to these studies. First, several theories have been postulated to explain the prevalence of cognitive body-image disturbance in our society, with the most dominant theories examining the influence of cultural ideals and beliefs regarding physical beauty (Heinberg, 1996). Only recently, however, has there been the development of measures to test theories of body-image disturbance, with most of the advances occurring in the eating disorders literature (Thompson, 1996). Of the cognitive instruments cited above, only the PASE (Bane & McAuley, 1996) has been derived from a theoretical model (i.e., social cognitive theory; Bandura, 1986) and as such is one of the few scales that allows testing of theoretical hypotheses.

The second limitation focuses on the need to improve methods of data collection of physiological measures that are correlated with measures of body image. The exercise literature is dominated by studies that attempt to compare body image between exercisers and nonexercisers (Davis & Cowles, 1991; Davis et al., 1990; Kennedy et al., 1995; McDonald & Thompson, 1992). Exercise status is often determined by participants

self-classifying their exercise status, and thus underestimations or overestimations are quite likely. Exercise status may be determined by simply asking individuals if they participate in an exercise program. Those who answer yes are classified as exercisers, and those who answer no are nonexercisers. Additionally, one study may include all physical activity (e.g., housework, walking to class) as exercise whereas another may include only formal exercise (e.g., jogging, swimming laps). Therefore, not only is it unlikely that an accurate measure of exercise status is attained, but the relationships assessed also are actually between body image and self-reported exercise rather than between body image and physical fitness. Cardiovascular fitness should be assessed using standard testing protocols, such as cycle ergometry or treadmill testing. Similarly, improvement in the measurement of anthropometrics is needed. Far too often self-reported weight, height, or body mass index are utilized for an anthropometric measure. Actual measurements, such as weight, height, body mass index, circumferences, and/or skinfolds, should be taken such that changes in these values as a result of exercise participation can be assessed and correlated with perceptions and/or cognitive changes in body image. In support of these recommendations is research by McAuley and Bane (1996), who revealed that cardiovascular fitness and body composition, as measured by cycle ergometry and skinfolds respectively, were related to body dissatisfaction, physique anxiety, and physical attractiveness self-efficacy, whereas self-reported exercise frequency and duration were unrelated.

Finally, from a practical perspective, one must consider the length of the questionnaire used, particularly because the participants may be completing other scales in addition to those assessing the cognitive aspect of body and/or may be in an exercise environment where a lengthy scale is not appropriate. Silhouettes/figure drawings can be completed very quickly, as can the checklists of satisfaction with various body parts. The MBSRQ is a lengthy questionnaire (69 items), but can be divided into several scales used individually depending on the study objectives.

Affective Measures

Instruments that measure the affective component of body image attempt to tap into responses such as anxiety, discomfort, and negative feelings related to one's body. Unlike more traditional perceptual and cognitive measures, the generation of affective measures of body image has only begun to flourish in the last decade. The 34-item Body Shape Questionnaire (BSQ; Cooper, Taylor, Cooper, & Fairburn, 1987) is the only measure designed to assess concern and negative affect regarding body shape. Specifically, subjects rate how often (*never* to *always*) they worry or are concerned about their body (e.g., feeling fat after eating, crying because they dislike their body, etc.).

Three measures have been developed to assess anxiety related to body image. Hart, Leary, and Rejeski (1989) developed the Social Physique Anxiety Scale (SPAS) to measure the level of anxiety individuals experience when others evaluate their physique. The SPAS is a 12-item scale, with scores ranging from 12 to 60. Reed, Thompson, Brannick, and Sacco (1991) developed the Physical Appearance State and Trait Anxiety

Scale (PASTAS) to assess state and trait anxiety regarding weight- and non-weight-relevant body sites. The scale consists of two eight-item subscales that assess weight- and non-weight related items. The trait version of the scale requires individuals to rate their general level of anxiety regarding several body sites, whereas the state-anxiety version requires the participants to rate how they feel right now in the current situation. Specifically, state anxiety is assessed in three situations that are designed to produce low, medium, and high levels of appearance anxiety. Finally, Butters and Cash (1987) developed the mirror focus procedure that requires participants to examine their body in a full-length, tri-fold mirror for 30 seconds and then rate their comfort-discomfort level on a subjective units of distress scale from 0 (*absolute calm*) to 100 (*extreme discomfort*).

Although each of the measures tap anxiety related to body image, the BSQ, PASTAS, and mirror focus procedure highlight "private" anxiety characterized by anxiety about seeing oneself in the mirror or anxiety regarding various body parts. The SPAS, on the other hand, focuses on more "public" anxiety or anxiety resulting from a concern about how others are perceiving one's body. It is not known whether changes in levels of private anxiety that may be brought about by exercise participation lead to reductions in public anxiety.

The internal consistency for each of the affective measures described above is quite high (>.90). Examination of psychometric properties reveals adequate validity for each of the measures. The BSQ was developed and validated in a sample of young women with and without bulimia nervosa. The BSQ was significantly correlated with the Body Dissatisfaction Scale of the EDI ($r=.66$) and the Eating Attitudes Test ($r=.35-.61$) in both samples. Additionally, women who stated they were concerned about their weight and shape had significantly higher BSQ scores than did those who were not concerned. The PASTAS has been validated using three situations designed to invoke low, medium, and high anxiety (Reed et al., 1991) and unlike the BSQ has been utilized in the exercise setting by Fisher and Thompson (1994), who found the exercise participation was as effective as aerobic exercise participation in reducing state and trait anxiety. Keeton et al. (1990) reported that the females who reported greater anxiety while looking at themselves in the mirror (mirror focus procedure) reported feeling less attractive ($r=-.46$) and were more dissatisfied with their bodies ($r=-.50$) and weight ($r=-.50$).

The psychometric properties of the SPAS have been evaluated to the greatest extent and with the widest range of samples (male, female, young, and middle-aged). The SPAS has been shown to correlate moderately with several measures assessing concern with other's evaluation, physical efficacy, and anthropometrics (Bane & McAuley, 1994; Hart et al., 1989; McAuley & Burman, 1993). Hart et al. (1989) examined the construct validity of the SPAS by correlating it with a battery of scales including Interaction Anxiousness, Fear of Negative Evaluation, Body Cathexis, Body-Esteem, Self-Consciousness, and Social Desirability. In a sample of approximately 200 college males and females, the SPAS correlated moderately with measures assessing general evaluative concerns such as Interaction Anxiousness ($r=.33$), Body Cathexis ($r=-.51$), and Body Esteem ($r=-.36—.82$), but did not correlate with Private Self-Con-sciousness or Social Desirability. Thus, higher levels of physique anxiety were associated with increased concern about evaluation by others and lower perceived levels of physical attractiveness, suggesting the SPAS was closely related to concerns with aspects of physique.

Criterion validity was examined by comparing the reactions of self-reported high and low physique anxious college females during an actual evaluation of their physiques (body composition measurement using skinfolds). Support for the validity of the SPAS was obtained because higher scorers on the SPAS expressed greater apprehension and anxiety during the fitness evaluation than did low scorers. Further, females with higher body fat reported a greater perception of physique anxiety.

Using a sample of 236 adolescent competitive female gymnasts, McAuley and Burman (1993) utilized confirmatory factor analysis to demonstrate the unidimensional factor structure of the SPAS. However, they did find that Item 2 ("I would never worry about wearing clothing that might make me look too thin or overweight") had low intercorrelations with other scale items, the lowest standardized factor loadings across models, and low item-total correlations in all reliability analyses. Further analyses suggested the physique anxiety was inversely correlated with perceived physical ability and perceived physical efficacy. Specifically, individuals with lower levels of perceived physical efficacy had higher perceptions of physique anxiety. Similarly, Bane and McAuley (1994) provided further evidence for the construct validity of the SPAS in a sample of 69 college females. Greater perceptions of physique anxiety were associated with greater body fat as well as dissatisfaction with weight and areas of the body (e.g., lower torso, midtorso, etc.).

Most recently, Eklund, Mack, and Hart (1996) examined the factorial validity of the SPAS by conducting confirmatory factor analyses of three models using structural equation modeling. Similar to McAuley and Burman (1993), Item 2 of the SPAS was found to have low intercorrelations with other scale items, the lowest standardized factor loadings across models, and low item-total correlations in all reliability analyses. Additionally, these authors tested and were able to support a higher order factor structure of social physique anxiety, with the two underlying factors termed negative evaluation and physique presentation comfort. Eklund et al. argue for further examination of the factor structure of the SPAS suggesting that possible sampling variation might account for competing one- and two-factor models. Additionally, no validity evidence is presented to support the independence, conceptual or otherwise, of the two factors. We would endorse further examination of the factor structure of the SPAS, but caution that such endeavors be conceptually rather than data driven.

Research recommendations. Whereas the instruments to assess anxiety-related body image have been developed only in recent years, their role in understanding the relationship between exercise and body image is already evident, particularly with work conducted utilizing the SPAS (Bane & McAuley, 1996; McAuley, Bane, & Mihalko, 1995; McAuley, Bane, Rudolph, & Lox, 1995; Crawford & Eklund, 1994; Eklund & Crawford, 1994). The most probable reason for the recent advances in our understanding of the impact of exercise on body image (as assessed with the SPAS), is the strong conceptual background with which the SPAS was developed. The SPAS was developed from a self-presentational perspective, with self-presentation referring to processes by which people monitor and attempt to control how others perceive them (Schlenker, 1980). Basically, we try to make a good impression by what we do, what we say, or how we behave. Exercise is one such behavior in which individuals expect to gain self-presentational benefits, such as losing weight, looking trimmer, and appearing more attractive. With respect to physical appearance, self-presentational theory suggests that if one is motivated to present as physical attractive but doubts his or her capability to successfully do so, the outcome is physique anxiety (Hart et al., 1989). A social-cognitive perspective on the generation of physique anxiety would argue that such anxiety is a co-effect of self-efficacy that is the degree to which an individual believes he or she can successfully carry out a course of action (Bandura, 1977). Specifically, people should experience social anxiety when their self-presentational self-efficacy is low. Thus, individuals with lower perceptions of efficacy with respect to appearing physically fit and attractive and likely to be highly physique anxious, regardless of objective physical attractiveness.

These theoretical premises have been tested in several recent publications by McAuley and colleagues (Bane & McAuley, 1996; McAuley, Bane, & Mihalko, 1995; McAuley, Bane, Rudolph, & Lox, 1995) in which they utilized aerobic exercise participation as means to reduce physique anxiety. McAuley, Bane, and Mihalko (1995) and McAuley, Bane, Rudolph, and Lox (1995) demonstrated exercise participation to effectively reduce social physique anxiety (SPAS) in sedentary middle-aged males and females. Changes in hip circumference (R^2=.11, $p<0.001$) and self-efficacy (R^2=.12, $p<0.005$) were also shown to contribute to variation in physique anxiety. Thus, both actual changes in physical characteristics as well as changes in perceptions of one's physical self mediated changes in physique anxiety.

Bane and McAuley (1996) compared changes in body-image disturbance in 60 college females who were randomly assigned to either exercise-only or exercise plus a cognitive behavioral intervention, with a third group of sedentary women serving as controls. Both exercise groups showed significant improvements in cardiovascular fitness as a function of exercise program, whereas no change occurred in the control group. Similarly, greater improvements in the psychological variables occurred in the exercise groups, in particular the cognitive behavioral intervention. Although improvements in fitness (r=-.24) and body composition (r=-.32) were associated with reductions in physique anxiety, only increases in self-efficacy (R^2=.14, $p<0.002$) were statistically significant predictors of reduced physique anxiety in multiple regression analyses.

Although these findings somewhat contrast with those of McAuley, Bane, Rudolph, and Lox (1995), it is likely that the longer exercise program in the McAuley studies allowed for greater changes in anthropometrics than did the 8-week program employed by Bane and McAuley (1996). Whether physical fitness gains are necessary for reducing physique anxiety or whether participation, in and of itself, is a contributing factor to improved body image has yet to be consistently demonstrated, and further investigation is warranted.

A second avenue of research to continue examining is the mediating role of physique anxiety on exercise avoidance. Are individuals most in need of exercise (sedentary, overweight, etc.) avoiding traditional gym settings because of their intimidating nature (i.e., mirrors, fit individuals dressed in thongs, leotards, and tank tops)? As discussed earlier, anxiety about ones body may influence one's attitude about exercise settings and ultimately lead to avoidance (Bain et al., 1989; Eklund & Crawford, 1994; Leary, 1992). On these same lines, state-anxiety measures, such as the PASTAS and mirror focus procedure can be utilized to examine how the exercise environment can be manipulated to influence anxiety. For example, how does exercising in front of a mirror or an audience (as often is the case in gyms) influence one's state anxiety and thus future use of the facility?

Behavioral Measures

As with the affective component of body image, it has only been in recent years that scales assessing behaviors related to body image have been developed. The Body Image Avoidance Questionnaire (BIAQ; Rosen, Srebnik, Saltzberg, & Wendt, 1991) is a 19-item measure assessing self-reported frequency of avoidance behaviors related to body image and is typified by such behaviors as avoiding physical intimacy, wearing baggy clothes with the intention of hiding one's body, and avoiding social events. This contrasts with the content of the subsequent two scales, which examine lifestyle behaviors, such as eating and exercise habits, that may be related to body image disturbance. The Body Image Behavior Questionnaire (Rosen, Saltzberg, & Srebnik, 1990) requires subjects to rate 19 items with regard to the frequency with which they engage in behaviors that prompt concern with physical appearance. There are four subscales including clothing, social activities, eating restraint, and grooming and weighing. The Reasons for Exercise Inventory (REI; Silberstein, Streigel-Moore, Timko, & Rodin, 1988) is a 24-item inventory with seven separate subscales (exercising for weight control, attractiveness, tone, fitness, health, mood, and enjoyment). Responses are scored on a 7-point Likert scale (1 = *not at all important* and 7 = *extremely important*).

Body-image disturbance has been reported to be associated with avoidant behaviors, eating restraint, and exercising for weight control and physical appearance. Most research in this area has focused on the relationship between negative body image and eating disturbances, with consistent results showing eating dysfunction (restraint, eating disorders, etc.) being correlated with body image (Brown et al., 1988; Cash & Brown, 1987; Thompson & Psaltis, 1988). More recently, body-image disturbance has also been shown to be related to avoidant behaviors, with Rosen et al. (1991) reporting college females with more negative responses on the BIAQ to hold more negative attitudes toward their weight and shape (r=.78) and express greater overestimation of body size (r =.22). Individuals exercising for appearance-related reasons versus health-fitness-related reasons have also been found to have greater body image disturbance (Cash, Novy, & Grant, 1994; Davis & Cowles, 1991; McDonald & Thompson, 1992). Cash et al. (1994) used the REI with college females and found that exercising for appearance/weight management reasons (r=.40) was associated with greater body dissatisfaction than was exercising for fitness/health (r=.07), stress (r=-.08), or socialization (r=-.14).

Similarly, McDonald and Thompson (1992) reported that females exercise more for weight-related reasons than do males and that for both sexes, exercising for weight, tone, and physical attractiveness motives was associated with greater eating disturbance and body-image dissatisfaction than was exercising for health, enjoyment, and fitness.

Research recommendations. Exercise is a behavior in which individuals expect to gain appearance-related benefits, such as losing weight, gaining muscle size, and appearing more attractive. Indeed, appearance is a primary motive for exercise participation. Future research should build on the current findings discussed above suggesting that motives may moderate how body image is affected by exercise participation. Specifically, participating in exercise with motives that are unattainable (i.e., unrealistic body fat loss, "spot reducing", etc.) rather than attainable (i.e., reasonable fat loss, health benefits, etc.) may impact body image differently, with participation leading to greater body-image disturbance for those exercising with unrealistic goals. Indeed, several studies by Davis and colleagues suggest that exercise for some may be a behavior that actually leads to greater body-image concerns (Davis, 1990; Davis, Elliot, Dionne, & Mitchell, 1991; Davis, Fox, Brewer, & Ratusny, 1995; Davis, Shapiro, Elliot, & Dionne, 1993). Their work suggests that motives as well as personality factors such as neuroticism and extroversion may impact the effect of exercise on body image. Although such questions are intriguing, they are difficult to address without a theoretical basis and, as has been stated previously, the major limitation to this area is the lack of theoretically driven research.

Summary

A large number of measures exist to assess the various aspects of body-image disturbance. It is difficult to recommend the ideal battery of scales to use, given the multidimensional nature of body image and the wide variety of study objectives. However, if we are to further our understanding of the role of exercise in improving body image, the following general measurement recommendations for future research are provided:

1. Researchers must conceptualize body image as a multidimensional construct. We have chosen to operationalize body image as an umbrella term that encompasses perceptions, cognitions, affect, and behaviors related to body image. Studies should avoid using the global term body image and specify which aspect(s) of body image they are examining in order to allow comparison between studies.
2. Strong conceptual and theoretical frameworks should guide development of any new measures and study hypotheses.
3. Self-report of exercise status and anthropometrics should be avoided. Assessment of physiological measures such as cardiovascular fitness and skinfolds and/or circumferences should be made before and after exercise participation.

In summary, the combination of these recommendations along with a careful assessment of one's research purpose should result in well-designed studies that contribute to our understanding of the role of exercise in improving body image. The equivocality of the exercise and body image literature, coupled with the fact that physical appearance is a major motivator for individuals to exercise, highlights the importance of research in this field and the need for improving our approach to the assessment of body image.

References

Adame, D.A., Frank, R.E., Serdula, M.K., Cole, S.P., & Abbas, M.A. (1990). The relationship of self-perceived weight to actual weight, body image and health behaviors of college freshmen. *Wellness Perspectives: Research, Theory, and Practice, 7,* 31-40.

Askevold, R. (1975). Measuring body image: Preliminary report on a new method. *Psychotherapy and Psychosomatics, 26,*71-77.

Bailey, S.M., Goldberg, J.P., Swap, W.C., Chomitz, V.R., & Houser, R.F., Jr. (1990). Relationship between body dissatisfaction and physical measurement. *International Journal of Eating Disorders, 9,* 457-461.

Bain, L.L., Wilson, T., & Chaikind, E. (1989). Participant perceptions of exercise programs for overweight women. *Research Quarterly for Exercise and Sport, 60,* 134-143.

Bandura, A. (1977). Self-efficacy: Toward a unifying theory of behavioral change. *Psychological Review, 84,* 191-215.

Bandura, A. (1986). *Social foundations of thought and action.* Englewood Cliffs, NJ: Prentice Hall, Inc.

Bane, S.M., & McAuley, E. (1994). Physical attributes, body image, and social physique anxiety in college females: A self-presentational perspective. *Medicine and Science in Sport and Exercise, 26,* S198.

Bane, S.M., & McAuley, E. (1995). Reducing social physique anxiety in college females. *Medicine and Science in Sport and Exercise, 27,* S150.

Bane, S.M., & McAuley, E. (1996). The role of efficacy cognitions in reducing physique anxiety in college females. *Medicine and Science in Sport and Exercise, 28,* S85.

Bane, S.M., & McAuley, E. *The Physical Attractiveness Self-Efficacy Scale: Development and Preliminary Validation.* Manuscript submitted for publication.

Barrios, B.A., Ruff, G.A., & York, C.I. (1989). Bulimia and body image: Assessment and explication of a promising construct. In W.G. Johnson (Ed.), *Advances in eating disorders.* (pp. 67-89). New York: JAI Press.

Berscheid, E., Walster, E., & Bohrnstedt, G. (1973). The happy American body: A survey report. *Psychology Today, 7,* 119-131.

Brown, T.A., Cash, T.F., & Mikulka, P.J. (1990). Attitudinal body-image assessment: Factor analysis of the body-self relations questionnaire. *Journal of Personality Assessment, 55,* 135-144.

Brown, T.A., Johnson, W.G., Bergeron, K.C., Keeton, W.P., & Cash, T.F. (1988, November). *Assessment of body-related cognitions in bulimia: The Body Image Automatic Thoughts Questionnaire.* Paper presented at the Association for the Advancement of Behavior Therapy, New York.

Brownell, K.D. (1991). Personal responsibility and control over our bodies: When expectation exceeds reality. *Health Psychology, 10,* 303-310.

Butters, J.W., & Cash, T.F. (1987). Cognitive-behavioral treatment of women's body image dissatisfaction. *Journal of Consulting and Clinical Psychology, 55,* 889-897.

Cash, T.F. (1989). Body-image affect: Gestalt versus summing the parts. *Perceptual and Motor Skills, 69,* 17-18.

Cash, T.F., & Brown, T.A. (1987). Body image in anorexia nervosa and bulimia nervosa: A review of the literature. *Behavior Modification, 11,* 487-521.

Cash, T.F., Counts, B., & Huffine, C.E. (1990). Current and vestigial effects of overweight among women: Fear of fat, attitudinal body image, and eating behaviors. *Journal of Psychopathology and Behavioral Assessment, 12,* 157-167.

Cash, T.F., & Green, G.K. (1986). Body weight and body image among college women: Perception, cognition, and affect. *Journal of Personality Assessment, 50,* 290-301.

Cash, T.F., & Henry, P.E. (1995). Women's body images: The results of a national survey in the U.S.A. *Sex Roles, 33,* 19-28.

Cash, T.F., & Hicks, K.L. (1990). Being fat versus thinking fat: Relationships with body image, eating behaviors, and well-being. *Cognitive Therapy and Research, 14,* 327-241.

Cash, T.F., & Kilcullen, R. (1985). The eye of the beholder: Susceptibility to sexism and beautyism in evaluation of managerial applicants. *Journal of Applied Social Psychology, 15,* 591-605.

Cash, T.F., Lewis, R.J., & Keeton, P. (1987, March). *Development and validation of the Body-Image Automatic Thoughts Questionnaire: A measure of body-related cognitions.* Paper presented at the meeting of the Southeastern Psychological Association, Atlanta, GA.

Cash, T.F., Novy, P.L., & Grant, J.R. (1994). Why do women exercise? Factor analysis and further validation of the reasons for exercise inventory. *Perceptual and Motor Skills, 78,* 539-544.

Cash, T.F., & Pruzinsky, T. (1990). *Body images: development, deviance, and change.* New York: Guilford Press.

Cash, T.F., Winstead, B.A., Janda, L.H. (1986). The great American shape-up. *Psychology Today, 20*(4), 30-37.

Cash, T.F., Wood, K.C., Phelps, K.D., & Boyd, K. (1991). New assessments of weight-related body image derived from extant instruments. *Perceptual and Motor Skills, 73,* 235-241.

Cooper, P.J., Taylor, M.J., Cooper, Z., & Fairburn, C.G. (1987). The development and validation of the Body Shape Questionnaire. *International Journal of Eating Disorders, 6,* 485- 494.

Crawford, S., & Eklund, R.C. (1994). Social physique anxiety, reasons for exercise, and attitudes toward exercise settings. *Journal of Sport and Exercise Psychology, 16,* 70-82.

Davis, C., (1990). Weight and diet preoccupation and addictiveness: The role of exercise. *Personality and Individual Differences, 11,* 823-827.

Davis, C., Brewer, H., & Weinstein, M. (1993). A study of appearance anxiety in young men. *Social Behavior and Personality, 21,* 63-74.

Davis, C. & Cowles, M. (1991). Body image and exercise: A study of relationships and comparisons between physically active men and women. *Sex Roles, 25,* 33-44.

Davis, C., Elliot, S., Dionne, M., & Mitchell, I. (1991). The relationship of personality factors and physical activity to body satisfaction in men. *Personality and Individual Differences, 12,* 689-694.

Davis, C., Fox, J., Brewer, H., & Ratusny, D. (1995). Motivation to exercise as a function of personality characteristics, age, and gender. *Personality and Individual Differences, 19,* 165-174.

Davis, C., Fox, J., Cowles, M., Hastings, P., & Schwass, K. (1990). The functional role of exercise in the development of weight and diet concerns in women. *Journal of Psychosomatic Research, 34,* 563-574.

Davis, C., Durnin, J.V.G.A., Dionne, M., & Gurevich, M. (1994). The influence of body fat content and bone diameter measurements on body dissatisfaction in adult women. *International Journal of Eating Disorders, 15,* 257-263.

Davis, C., Shapiro, C.M., Elliot, S., & Dionne,M. (1993). Personality and other correlates of dietary restraint: An age by sex comparison. *Personality and Individual Differences, 14,* 297-305.

Dworkin, S.H., & Kerr, B.A. (1987). Comparison of interventions for women experiencing body image problems. *Journal of Counseling Psychology, 34,* 136-140.

Eklund, R.C., & Crawford, S. (1994). Active women, social physique anxiety, and exercise. *Journal of Sport and Exercise Psychology, 16,* 431-448.

Eklund, R.C., Mack, D., & Hart, E. (1996). Factorial validity of the Social Physique Anxiety Scale for females. *Journal of Sport and Exercise Psychology, 18,* 281-295.

Fallon, A., & Rozin, P. (1985). Sex differences in perceptions of desirable body shape. *Journal of Abnormal Psychology, 94,* 102-105.

Fisher, E., & Thompson, J.K. (1994). A comparative evaluation of cognitive behavior therapy (CBT) versus exercise therapy (ET) for the treatment of body image disturbance. *Behavior Modification, 18,* 171-185.

Franzoi, S.L., & Shields, S.A. (1984). The Body Esteem Scale: Multidimensional structure and sex differences in a college population. *Journal of Personality Assessment, 48,* 173-178.

Furnham, A., Titman, P., & Sleeman, E. (1994). Perception of female body shapes as a function of exercise. *Journal of Social Behavior and Personality, 9,* 335-352.

Garner, D.M. & Garfinkel, P.E. (1981). Body image in anorexia nervosa: Measurement, theory, and clinical applications. *International Journal of Psychiatry in Medicine, 11,* 263-284.

Garner, D.M., Olmstead, M.A., & Polivy H, (1983). Development and validation of a multidimensional eating disorder inventory for anorexia nervosa and bulimia. *International Journal of Eating Disorders, 2,* 15-34.

Gleghorn, A.A., Penner, L.A., Powers, P.S., & Schulman, R. (1987). The psychometric properties of several measures of body image. *Journal of Psychopathology and Behavioral Assessment, 9,* 203-218.

Glucksman, M., & Hirsch, J. (1969). The response of obese patients to weight reduction. III: The perception of body size. *Psychosomatic Medicine, 31,* 1-17.

Hallinan, C.J., & Schuler, P.B. (1993). Body-shape perceptions of elderly women exercisers and nonexercisers. *Perceptual and Motor Skills, 77,* 451-456.

Hart, E.A., Leary, M.R., & Rejeski, W.J. (1989). The measurement of social physique anxiety. *Journal of Sport and Exercise Psychology, 11,* 94-104.

Heinberg, L.J. (1996). Theories of body image disturbance: Perceptual, developmental, and sociocultural factors. In J.K. Thompson (Ed.), *Body image, eating disorders, and obesity: An integrative guide for assessment and treatment* (pp. 27-47). Washington, DC: American Psychological Association.

Hesse-Biber, S., Clayton-Matthews, A., and Downey, J. (1987). The differential importance of weight and body image among college men and women. *Genetic, Social, and General Psychological Monographs, 113,* 511-528.

Keeton, W.P., Cash, T.F., & Brown, T.A. (1990). Body image or body images? Comparative, multidimensional assessment among college students. *Journal of Personality Assessment, 54,* 213-230.

Kennedy, C., Reis, J., Bane, S.M, & Stang, J. (1995). A comparison of body image perceptions of exercising and nonexercising college students. *Wellness Perspectives, 11,* 3-15.

Klesges, R.C. (1983). An analysis of body-image distortions in a nonpatient population. *International Journal of Eating Disorders, 2,* 35-41.

Kreitler, S., & Kreitler, H. (1988). Body image: The dimension of size. *Genetics, Social, and General Psychology Monographs, 114,* 7-32.

Langlios, J.H. (1986). From the eye of the beholder to behavioral reality: Development of social behavior and social relations as a function of physical attractiveness. In C.P. Herman, M.P. Zanna, & E.T. Higgins (Eds.), *Physical appearance, stigmas, and social behavior: the Ontario symposium: Vol. 3* (pp. 23-51). Hillsdale, NJ: Erlbaum.

Leary, M.R. (1992). Self-presentational processes in exercise and sport. *Journal of Sport and Exercise Psychology, 14,* 339-351.

Martinek, T. (1981). Physical attractiveness: Effects on teacher expectations and dyadic interactions in elementary age children. *Journal of Sport Psychology, 3,* 196-205.

McAuley, E., & Bane, S.M. (1996). Exercise and body image in college females. *Medicine and Science in Sports and Exercise, 28,* S138.

McAuley, E., Bane, S.M., & Mihalko, S. (1995). Exercise in middle-aged adults: Self-Efficacy and self-presentational outcomes. *Preventive Medicine, 24,* 319-328.

McAuley, E., Bane, S.M., Rudolph, D., & Lox, C. (1995). Physique anxiety and exercise in middle-aged adults. *Journal of Gerontology, 50B,* 229-235.

McAuley, E., & Burman, G. (1993). The Social Physique Anxiety Scale: Construct validity in adolescent females. *Medicine and Science in Sport and Exercise, 25,* 1049-1053.

McDonald, K., & Thompson, J.K. (1992). Eating disturbance, body image dissatisfaction, and reasons for exercising: Gender differences and correlational findings. *International Journal of Eating Disorders, 11,* 289-292.

Pasman, L., & Thompson, J.K. (1988). Body image and eating disturbance in obligatory runners, obligatory weight-lifters, and sedentary individuals. *International Journal of Eating Disorders, 7,* 759-769.

Powers, P.D., & Erickson, M.T. (1986). Body-image in women and its relationship to self-image and body satisfaction. *The Journal of Obesity and Weight Regulation, 5,* 37-50.

Reed, D.L., Thompson, J.K., Brannick, M.T., & Sacco, W.P. (1991). Development and validation of the Physical Appearance State and Trait Anxiety Scale (PASTAS). *Journal of Anxiety Disorders, 5,* 323-332.

Rosen, J.C., Orosan, P., & Reiter, J. (1995). Cognitive behavior therapy for negative body image in obese women, *Behavior Therapy, 26,* 25-42.

Rosen, J.C., Saltzberg, E., & Srebnik, D. (1990). *Development of a body image behavior questionnaire.* Unpublished manuscript.

Rosen, J.C., Srebnik, D., Saltzberg, E., & Wendt, S. (1991). Development of a body image avoidance questionnaire. *Psychological Assessment, 8,* 32-37.

Rozin, P., & Fallon, A. (1988). Body image, attitudes to weight, and misperceptions of figure preference of the opposite sex: A comparison of men and women in two generations. *Journal of Abnormal Psychology, 97,* 342-345.

Rucker, C.E., & Cash, T.F. (1992). Body images, body-size perceptions, and eating behaviors among African-American and white college females. *International Journal of Eating Disorders, 12,* 291-299.

Ruff, G.A., & Barrios, B.A. (1986). Realistic assessment of body cathexia: Body cathexis and the self. *Journal of Consulting Psychology, 17,* 342-347.

Schlenker, B.R. (1980). *Impression management: The self-concept, social identity, and interpersonal relations.* Monterey, CA: Brooks/Cole Publishing Co.

Secord, P.F., & Jourard, S.M. (1953). The appraisal of body cathexia: Body cathexia and the self. *Journal of Consulting Psychology, 17,* 342-347.

Silberstein, L.R., Striegel-Moore, R.H., Timko, C., & Rodin, J. (1988). Behavioral and psychological implications of body dissatisfaction: Do men and women differ? *Sex Roles, 19,* 219-233.

Simonson, M. (1978, February). *The management of obesity.* Paper presented at the John Hopkins Medical Institution, Baltimore.

Slade, P.D. (1985). A review of body-image studies in anorexia nervosa and bulimia nervosa. *Journal of Psychiatric Research, 19,* 255-265.

Slade, P.D., & Russell, G.F.M. (1973). Awareness of body dimensions in anorexia nervosa: Cross-sectional and longitudinal studies. *Psychological Medicine, 3,* 188-199.

Steiner-Adair, C. (1987). Weightism: a new form of prejudice. *Newsletter of National Anorexic Aid Society Inc., 10,* 1-2.

Thompson, J.K. (1996). Assessing body image disturbance: Measures, methodology, and implementation. In J. K. Thompson (Ed.) *Body image, eating disorders, and obesity: An integrative guide for assessment and treatment* (pp. 27-47). Washington, DC: American Psychological Association.

Thompson, J.K., & Dolce, J.J. (1989). The discrepancy between emotional vs. rational estimates of body size, actual size, and ideal body ratings: Theoretical and clinical implications. *Journal of Clinical Psychology, 45,* 473-478.

Thompson, J.K., Penner, L.A., & Altabe, M.N. (1990). Procedures, problems, and progress in the assessment of body image. In T.F. Cash & T. Pruzinsky (Eds.), *Body images: Development, deviance, and change* (pp. 21-50). New York: Guilford Press.

Thompson, J.K. & Psaltis, K. (1988). Multiple aspects and correlates of body figure ratings: A replication and extension of Fallon & Rozin (1985). *International Journal of Eating Disorders, 7,* 813-817.

Thompson, J.K., & Spana, R.E. (1988). The adjustable light beam method for the assessment of size estimation accuracy: Description, psychometrics, and normative data. *International Journal of Eating Disorders, 7,* 521-526.

Thompson, J.K., & Thompson, C.M. (1986). Body size distortion and self-esteem in asymptomatic normal weight males and females. *International Journal of Eating Disorders, 5,* 1061-1068.

Touyz, S.W., & Beaumont, P.J.V. (1987). Body image and its disturbance. In P. J.V. Beaumont, G.D. Burrows, & R.C. Casper (Eds.), *Handbook of eating disorders* (pp. 171-187). New York: Elsevier Science Publishers.

Touyz, S.W., Beaumont, P.J.V., Collins, J.K., & Cowie, L. (1985). Body shape perception in bulimia and anorexia nervosa. *International Journal of Eating Disorders, 4,* 261- 265.

Tucker, L.A. (1983). The structure and dimensional satisfaction of the body cathexis construct of males: A factor analytic investigation. *Journal of Human Movement Studies, 9,* 189-194.

Tucker, L.A., & Maxwell, K. (1992). Effects of weight-training on the emotional well-being and body image of females: Predictors of greatest benefit. *American Journal of Health Promotion, 6,* 338-344.

Part VII

Exercise-Related Cognitions, Affect, and Motivation

PART VII

From both a scientific and practical perspective, there has been considerable interest in the interrelationships between exercise and the quality of life. As defined by Berger and McInman (1993), quality of life "emphasizes a state of excellence and/or an enhanced sense of well-being" (p. 751). The literature suggests that habitual exercise is linked to mental health, but there appear to be a number of factors influencing this association. To analyze and comprehend the complex interplay between physical activity and life quality, valid and reliable assessments of how individuals perceive the demands of exercise (with respect to one's ability, the exertion required) and emotionally respond to exercise are warranted. We also need accurate information about what motivates people to exercise in the first place and what prevents individuals from being physically active (Dishman, 1993). In Part VII, assessments of these relevant variables are described and evaluated.

References

Berger, B.G., & McInman, A. (1993). Exercise and the quality of life. In R.N. Singer, M. Murphey, and L.K. Tennant (Eds.), *Handbook of research on sport psychology* (pp. 729-760). New York: Macmillan.

Dishman, R.K. (1993). *Exercise adherence II*. Champaign, IL: Human Kinetics.

Chapter 18

MEASUREMENT OF EXERCISE-INDUCED CHANGES IN FEELING STATES, AFFECT, MOOD, AND EMOTIONS

Lise Gauvin
Université de Montréal
and
John C. Spence
University of Alberta

In recent years, there has been a growing recognition of the role of physical activity in the maintenance and promotion of mental health, psychological well-being, and health-related quality of life (Gauvin & Spence, 1996; Rejeski, Brawley, & Shumaker, 1996). In this regard, a focal point for researchers has been to study the outcomes of acute bouts of physical activity on transient psychological states. The literature shows that acute vigorous physical activity results in decreased state anxiety and depression (Byrne & Byrne, 1993; Landers & Petruzzello, 1994; North, McCullagh, & Tran, 1990) and improved feelings of energy, calmness, and hedonic tone (Gauvin & Rejeski, 1993; McAuley & Courneya, 1994; McAuley & Rudolf, 1995; Saklofske, Blomme, & Kelly, 1992; Thayer, 1989). Furthermore, other researchers (Blumenthal et al., 1991; Blumenthal, Emery, & Rejeski, 1988; Rejeski, Thompson, Brubaker, & Miller, 1992) have demonstrated that single bouts of physical activity can dampen the reactivity associated with psychosocial stressors that may contribute to the etiology of cardiovascular disease. More positive affective responses to exercise have been implicated in the process of exercise adherence (cf. Godin, 1994; Godin, Desharnais, Valois, & Bradet, 1995; Vlachopoulos, Biddle, & Fox, 1996). It is apparent that exercise-induced changes in psychological states, including but not limited to anxiety, depression, feelings of energy, and tranquility, constitute important outcome variables, moderator variables, and perhaps even mediator variables for the fields of exercise science, public health, and health psychology.

Given the relevance of studying exercise-induced changes in psychological states, the purpose of this chapter is to outline issues that render the measurement of exercise-induced changes in feeling states, affect, mood, and emotions, a unique challenge. The discussion will focus strictly on paper-and-pencil measurement technologies because an adequate discussion of physiological and behavioral indicators (e.g., facial expressions) of these phenomena would be too unwieldy to address in a single chapter. The interested reader is referred to other comprehensive treaties of these latter topics (cf. Cacioppo et al., 1992; Davidson, 1994; Ekman, 1993; LeDoux, 1994; Panksepp, 1994; Russell, 1994; Thayer, 1970). The first part of the chapter will define the concepts of feeling states, affect, mood, and emotions. In so doing, we will attempt to acquaint the reader with current controversies in the social psychological literature on affect and emotions as well as with potential pitfalls of incorrect use of terms. In furthering this discussion, we will outline boundaries between state-like and trait-like or individual-difference variables. Similarly, the role of personal, situational, and task variables in modulating exercise-induced changes in feeling states, affect, mood, and emotions will be discussed as will the relevance of different markers for gauging exercise-induced changes in psychological states. In the second part of the chapter, we will outline the consequences of these features for the psychometric validation of paper-and-pencil instruments assessing feeling states, affect, mood, and emotions. Specifically, we will comment on the value of different indicators of validity and reliability in the validation of state-like measures recognizing that these indicators were largely developed with trait-like variables in mind. Third, we will propose guidelines for developing a self-report measurement strategy for exercise-induced changes in psychological states. Finally, we will describe selected measurement instruments used in the study of exercise-induced changes in psychological states and comment on their relevance.

Feeling States, Affect, Mood, and Emotions: Deciphering Likenesses and Distinctive Features

Definitional Issues

One of the most daunting problems facing researchers interested in studying exercise-induced changes in psychological states is the difficulty associated with defining the concepts of feeling states, affect, mood, and emotions (cf. Ekman & Davidson, 1994b). Because a consensual definition has eluded researchers and because there exists no gold standard for knowing that an emotion has occurred (cf. Frijda, 1994; Kleinginna & Kleinginna, 1981; Scherer, 1994), leading theorists such as Ekman & Davidson (1994a) have proposed that developing an empirically supported definitional framework should be a priority for future research on affective phenomena. Recognizing the primacy of this caveat, we will nevertheless offer selected definitions of the terms feeling states, affect, mood, and emotions.

Averill (1994) suggests that the term *feeling* is inherently ambiguous because people use this word to refer to at least three categories of enmeshed human experiences. Specifically, individuals can experience *feelings of* something, *feelings about* something, or *feeling like* doing something. According to Averill, these feelings may occur simultaneously and cannot always be distinguished from one another at a given point in time. The *feelings of* category often refers to bodily reactions and experiences. In the realm of exercise, feelings of exertion or feelings of physical exhaustion would qualify as *feelings of*. The *feelings about* category refers to cognitive appraisals about the value ascribed to different objects or activities. Positive feelings about weight training or negative feelings about an ongoing exercise experience are examples of *feelings about* in the area of physical activity. Finally, the *feeling like* category refers to actual or potential instrumental responses. Feeling like working out or feeling like lying around are instances of potential instrumental responses. Given this broad sketch, we will use the expression *feeling states* to refer to those human experiences that include bodily reactions, cognitive appraisals, actual or potential instrumental responses, or some combination thereof.

The definitions of affect, mood, and emotions are complicated by yet another issue: No consensus exists about whether these phenomena are best described as discrete states or dimensions (Ekman & Davidson, 1994b; Gauvin & Brawley, 1993; Vallerand, 1983, 1984). On the one hand, categorical theorists (e.g., Frijda, 1987; Izard, 1977) have strived to define and study the determinants of a narrow group of discrete *emotional* experiences. In these conceptualizations, the feelings, physiology, behavioral expression, and antecedent conditions of specific

emotions have been examined. Current evidence suggests that there may be as few as four or five distinct discrete emotions (Ekman & Davidson, 1994a), namely, fear, anger, sadness, enjoyment, and disgust.

On the other hand, other conceptualizations (e.g., Diener & Emmons, 1985; Diener, Larsen, Levine, & Emmons, 1984; Russell, 1980; Watson & Tellegen, 1985) have focused on defining broad dimensions of affective experience (e.g., activation, hedonic tone), developing appropriate measurement technologies, and understanding their underlying determinants. In this regard, a functionally based definitional framework formulated by Batson, Shaw, and Oleson (1992) provides a useful illustration. These authors view affect as more general and primitive than mood and emotion. Affect is defined in terms of hedonic tone and intensity, and reveals preferences for certain feeling states over others. In their terms,

> change from a less valued to a more valued [feeling] state is accompanied by positive affect; change from a more valued to a less valued [feeling] state is accompanied by negative affect. Intensity of the affect reveals the magnitude of the value preference. (Batson et al., 1992, p. 298)

Thus, affect is the most fundamental expression of the value attached to a given feeling state. Furthermore, according to Batson et al., mood represents a more specific type of affective state that is also defined in terms of hedonic tone and activation. It can be distinguished from affect in that it is accompanied by a series of beliefs about impending pleasure or pain. (See Mayer, Salovey, & Gomberg-Kaufman, 1991 for a further discussion of this issue.) Positive moods are therefore indicative of the anticipation of positive affect whereas negative moods relate to anticipated negative affect. Finally, in this conceptualization, emotion is more specific and narrow than affect and mood, but also involves hedonic tone and intensity. Emotion "reflects the existence of a specific goal or of perceived change in one's relation to a specific goal in the present" (Batson et al., p. 301). For example, the emotion of grief could be experienced if a person strongly anticipated achieving a goal yet does not meet that goal. Similarly, the emotion of happiness might be experienced if a person perceives him-or herself moving toward attainment of the goal.

Yet another group of researchers has attempted to pioneer the idea of *emotion families* which refers to groups of affective states that share common expression, physiological activity, and prerequisite cognitive appraisals (Lazarus, 1991; Shaver, Schwartz, Kirson, & O'Connor, 1987). For example, the anger family of emotions might subsume the feeling states of irritation, annoyance, and rage whereas the fear family of emotions might include anxiety, panic, apprehension, and horror. Ekman and Davidson (1994b) suggest that this approach also constitutes a fruitful direction for future research.

In summary, although defining a construct always presents a challenge to the researcher, the concepts of feeling states, affect, mood, and emotions are particularly elusive. Therefore, the first challenge faced by the researcher interested in measuring exercise-induced changes in psychological states is to identify clearly what discrete emotion(s), what broad dimension(s) of affect, what specific feeling states, or alternatively, what mood(s) is(are) the focal point(s) of the investigation. To illustrate this challenge and its implications further, the tenets of selected approaches to the study of affective experience are presented in Table 1. (For a further description of alternative models, see Gauvin & Brawley, 1993.)

As can be seen, there are a great diversity and some overlap between the basic premises of each model. Accordingly, a researcher interested in the broad question of whether acute physical activity is associated with fluctuations in transient psychological states could therefore articulate the question in one of the following ways. Is acute physical activity associated with

- movement in two-dimensional affective space defined by hedonic tone and arousal?
- improvements in mood states as defined by the Profile of Mood States?
- decreases in state anxiety?
- changes in exercise-induced feeling states?
- exacerbation or alleviation of anger?

Thus, a finding that acute physical activity alleviates state anxiety offers only indirect evidence about the role of acute physical activity in improving hedonic tone and decreasing arousal. Similarly, findings that high-intensity physical activity heightens preexisting emotions of anger provide virtually no information about changes in specific exercise-induced feeling states. In sum, a careful consideration of alternative definitions and conceptual frameworks is required in the conceptualization of a project.

Additional Conceptual Concerns

The measurement of exercise-induced changes in feeling states, affect, mood, and emotions is unique for at least three other reasons beyond definitional challenges: (a) The boundaries between states and other concepts, such as temperament, emotional traits, or affective style, are difficult to delineate clearly; (b) state affect is particularly sensitive to a variety of personal, interpersonal, and environmental influences; and (c) the necessity of exercise-specific measures is still under debate.

Link to other affect-laden concepts. There is general agreement that feeling states, affect, mood, and emotions are transitory experiences (cf. Ekman & Davidson, 1994b; Thayer, 1989). By contrast, several stable individual-difference variables that are affect laden have been identified by researchers. For example, affect intensity has been defined as the general intensity of a person's affective reactions (Larsen & Diener, 1987). Similarly, temperamental traits have been defined as characteristic individual differences in the way basic emotions are experienced and expressed (Goldsmith, 1994). Presented in this way, this distinction is relatively straightforward. Consid-

---

Table 1
Selected Variables and Conceptual Definitions Adopted in the Study of Exercise-Related Affect.

Approach	*Concept*	*Conceptual Definition*	*Measurement Technology*
Circumplex Model of Affect (Russell, 1980)	Affect	Affective experience can be represented in two-dimensional space defined by hedonic tone and activation. Hedonic tone is anchored by pleasure-displeasure and activation by arousal-sleepiness.	Affect grid (Russell et al., 1989)
Mood states	Mood	Current, overall daily, or weekly averaged moods can be represented by six affective states including tension-anxiety, depression-dejection, anger-hostility, vigor, fatigue, and confusion-bewilderment.	POMS (Lorr et al., 1981)
Exercise-induced feelings	Feeling states	The stimulus properties of exercise can elicit feeling states including but not limited to positive engagement, revitalization, physical exhaustion, and tranquility.	EFI (Gauvin & Rejeski, 1993)
State anxiety	Emotion	Temporary feelings of apprehension and tensions that are accompanied by a general physiological activation; state anxiety is experienced in response to a perceived social or physical threat.	STAI (Spielberger et al., 1983)
State anger	Emotion	Temporary feelings of anger, irritability, and annoyance that are accompanied by a general physiological activitation.	STAS (Spielberger, 1980)

ered in light of its implications, the distinction becomes more intricate: Feeling states, affect, mood, and emotions vary between persons (i.e., individual-difference perspective) and within persons across time (i.e., transient mood perspective; see Nesselroade, 1991; Nesselroade & Hershberger, 1993 for a further discussion of this issue). Conceptually, and eventually operationally, the researcher must therefore decipher how the state and trait perspective will be meshed in order to gauge changes related to an acute bout of physical activity.

For example, some authors (e.g., Cohen et al., 1995) have suggested that the most appropriate method of casting state-like responses is to assess deviations from habitual level of responding (trait-like features). Accordingly, Cohen et al. had subjects in their study provide information about their typical negative affectivity (trait-like perspective) and their moods within the previous 24-hour period (state-like perspective). Both of these measures were then used as predictors of health/disease outcomes. Other authors (Diener & Emmons, 1985; Larsen, 1987) have sampled affect on many occasions and computed overall aggregate values of frequency and intensity or patterns of variability (i.e., indicators of typical status). Changes in state values could be interpreted in comparison to these typical patterns. Still other authors (Larsen, 1987; Larsen & Kasimatis, 1990, 1991) have applied time-series methods to harness how affect fluctuates across time and how it correlates with physical symptoms or weekly variations.

Another frequently adopted strategy for gauging the direction and magnitude of change is to obtain a baseline measurement and to compare post-intervention measurements with this baseline measure. Although this strategy has proved useful, it also espouses certain assumptions, the most important being that the baseline measure is a good indicator of the person's *average value* or *habitual level* on the target variable. Although this may be a reasonable assumption for many trait-like variables, it is a more tenuous assumption in the measurement of state-like variables because transient psychological states vary both between persons and within persons across time. Thus a pre-exercise measurement could represent a significant overestimation or underestimation of the person's habitual level.

This issue becomes even more critical in light of the very real possibility that baseline measures may moderate any effects of an exercise intervention. For example, several authors (Gauvin, Rejeski, & Norris, 1996; O'Connor & Davis, 1992; Rejeski, Gauvin, Hobson, & Norris, 1995) have observed that persons feeling the worst before exercise achieve the greatest mood benefits following acute exercise. The moderating role of pre-exercise affect/mood requires that the researcher either develop a method for rendering affect/mood similar across subjects (e.g., mood-induction procedure) before any physical activity intervention or alternatively employ statistical methods that account for treatment by baseline value interactions (Rejeski et al., 1995).

Any definitional framework must therefore provide information regarding the minimal length of time required to observe a change in feeling states, affect, mood, or emotions, to the extent of variation in a given time span and to typical patterns of response. In other words, the researcher should have some knowledge of the typical level, variability, and change-

ability of the states if he or she is to assess changes in states following acute exercise.

Sensitivity of state measures. A second issue pertains to the fact that feeling states, affect, mood, and emotions are sensitive to a host of intrapersonal, interpersonal, and environmental stimuli (Watson & Clark, 1994). For example, a sampling of recent research shows that positive affect displays diurnal and weekly patterns (e.g., Egloff, Tausch, Kohlman, & Krohne, 1995). Similarly, more severe cold symptoms—an intrapersonal biological event—are associated with greater reports of negative affect (Cohen et al., 1995; Salovey & Birnbaum, 1989). Also, interpersonal interactions that convey rejection elicit negative affect and low state self-esteem whereas social inclusion results in positive affect and high state self-esteem (Leary, Schreindorfer, & Haupt, 1995).

The conceptual framework should therefore include the identification of those stimuli to which the feeling states, affect, mood, or emotions are particularly sensitive or alternatively include a verification that the experimental setting does not modify the baseline values (cf. Petruzzello, 1995). That is, because it is impossible to imagine a naturalistic setting or to contrive an experimental setting that is completely without any personal, interpersonal, and environmental stimuli, careful consideration must be given to issues of experimenter bias, environmental influences, and demand characteristics. For example, all verbal and non verbal communications between experimenter and participant should be constructed so as to minimize subtle and overt expressions of (un)friendliness, (in)competence, acceptance(rejection), and the like. The environment within which people exercise must be as consistent as possible between individuals. The context and motives for having the subject complete a feeling state, affect, mood, or emotion inventory must be carefully construed such that the subject will be impelled to report on *actual* states rather than *normatively expected* states. The issue of reactivity to measurement is of particular concern. (See Ojanen, 1994 and Stone & Shiffman, 1992 for further discussions of this problem.) Indeed, having people report on current affective states may constitute a mood self-regulation strategy in and of itself as other researchers have shown (see Mayer & Salovey, 1995; Thayer, Newman, & McClain, 1994). In other words, the act of measuring feeling states, affect, mood, or emotions may augment, decrease, or change the phenomenon. In an effort to deal with this problem, researchers have tried to brief subjects in such a way as to stress honest and truthful responding and have strived to develop scales that are as short as possible (one item to several items) and require responses to one-word items (often adjectives that qualify an ongoing feeling).

Generic vs. exercise-specific measures. The third concern relates to a broader issue in the field of sport and exercise psychology, namely, the need and relevance for sport- or exercise-specific inventories (cf. Gauvin & Russell, 1993). In recent years, at least three new measures of exercise-induced changes in feeling states or affect have been developed (Gauvin & Rejeski, 1993; Hardy & Rejeski, 1989; McAuley & Courneya, 1994). As discussed later, the rationale for their development is founded on the position that exercise-specific measures can be more sensitive to the stimulus properties of exercise (e.g., profound physiological changes, whole body movement, perception of physical symptoms) than can measures that attempt to gauge movement along broader dimensions of human experience (Gauvin & Rejeski, 1993; Gauvin & Russell, 1993) because their content validity vis-à-vis exercise is of primary concern. This differential sensitivity may or may not be required for the purposes of a given investigation. Thus, from a conceptual standpoint, it is critical that the need for exercise-specific measures, or the lack thereof, be clearly articulated.

Consequences for Psychometric Validation

The above-mentioned features of feeling states, affect, mood, and emotions render the psychometric validation of measurement instruments particularly daunting. Indeed, many indicators of validity and reliability were developed to assess psychometric qualities of trait-like variables. Their value in establishing the validity and reliability of state-like measures requires careful consideration.[1]

One of the most frequently used indicators of reliability is test-retest reliability. In other words, the researcher administers the same test on two occasions with the expectation that the measures will be highly correlated (Anastasi, 1976). For the measurement of stable characteristics (i.e., trait like), this obviously represents a method of choice for establishing reliability. However, in the measurement of feeling states, affect, mood, and emotions as state variables, test-retest reliability is not particularly instructive. Indeed, two uncorrelated scores could be obtained not because the measurement is unreliable but because the state has changed. Alternatively, two highly correlated measures would not necessarily indicate good reliability as they could point to a measurement instrument that is insensitive to affective changes across time and situations. Thus, in gauging the value of an instrument, the researcher should carefully consider the conditions under which indices of test-retest reliability were obtained and evaluate the relevance of such indicators.

Another method of obtaining indices of reliability is to develop alternate forms of a measure (Anastasi, 1976). This strategy has not been extensively used in the area of psychological states perhaps because of the difficulty in developing several homogenous sets of affect-related items. However, it does represent a viable choice for future psychometric endeavours.

A third indicator of reliability is interitem consistency. Methods based on interitem consistency involve correlating different subsets of a test with one another and obtaining an overall index of relatedness within a measure. The main advantage of interitem consistency is that the issue of stability over time is not a concern because a given inventory is measured only once. For the measurement of a state-like variable, this obviously represents an important advantage. By the same token, the researcher must also be aware that high interitem consistency can be misleading. Indeed, more specific emotions, such as anger and fear, may co-occur in certain situations. Consequently, items representing these two qualitatively different emotions could correlate highly with one another because the stimulus properties of

the situation within which they are measured elicit both of these emotions. Thus, indicators of interitem consistency must be considered in parallel to indicators of validity.

Content validity, which is often the first type of validity to be considered, refers to whether the test content covers a representative sample of the domain of interest (Anastasi, 1976). It is achieved through consultation with "experts" as well as perusal of existing relevant materials. In the assessment of any concept, the prerequisite for determination of content validity of an instrument is an appropriate conceptual framework. The measurement of feeling states, affect, mood, and emotions is no exception in that content validity is a necessary and crucial indicator.

Another frequently used tool for establishing validity of affect-laden measures is exploratory and confirmatory factor analysis. Anastasi (1976) has noted that factorial validity is not a sufficient condition for establishing the validity of an instrument because it offers no information regarding the extent to which a test measures what it purports to measure. Rather, factor analysis allows the researcher to examine how a large number of items might be regrouped into a smaller set of factors, and in other words, it reveals the underlying dimensionality of a measure. Furthermore, factor analytic techniques, whether exploratory or confirmatory, are based on the analysis of covariance structures as are methods of interitem consistency. Thus, the same cautions raised earlier about interitem consistency in the measurement of state variables must also be considered in the context of factor analysis. Selected items on an inventory may have high loadings on the same factor on a factor analysis because they co-occur in the specific situation in which the state inventory was administered. There is a need to examine the factor structure of a measure across individuals and situations. The need for an interface between theory and data analysis in the use of factor analysis is thus rendered more pressing in the context of state measures, such as feeling states, affect, mood, and emotions.

Convergent and discriminant validities refer to the extent to which a specific measurement instrument correlates with those variables that it should theoretically correlate with (i.e., convergent) and does not correlate with those variables that it should not correlate with (i.e., discriminant). One method for establishing convergent and discriminant validities is referred to as the multitrait-multimethod matrix design. In such a design, two or more constructs are measured by two or more instruments. To establish convergent and discriminant validity, correlations within constructs should be greater than between constructs. For state-like variables, such as feeling states, affect, mood, and emotions, convergent and discriminant validity represent validity indicators of choice because they allow the researcher to establish uniqueness of constructs.

More recently, at least two one-item measurement instruments have been developed, namely, the affect grid, a measure of hedonic tone and activation (Russell, Weiss, & Mendelsohn, 1989), and the feeling scale, a measure of hedonic tone (Hardy

---

1. One reviewer suggested that generalizability theory (Shavelson & Webb, 1991) constitutes a more appropriate framework from within which to conceptualize the dependability of state-like measures. We believe that this suggestion constitutes a relevant direction for future research. To our knowledge, no applications exist in the affect literature. We therefore chose to focus our discussion on current as opposed to possible future applications.

& Rejeski, 1989). According to the developers of these scales, the validation of these scales rests greatly on demonstrating their sensitivity to selected stimuli (e.g., mood-induction procedures or exercise) and on showing their convergent and discriminant validities. There is clearly a need to establish the reliability of these measures, and as suggested previously, generalizability theory (Shavelson & Webb, 1991) may provide the needed statistical theory.

In sum, the unique nature of affective experience warrants that special consideration be given to the use and interpretation of common indicators of validity and reliability. For example, test-retest reliability may not be instructive for state measures whereas interitem consistency may be the most helpful indicator of reliability. Factorial validity, because it is based on correlations, must be given special attention. Theoretically confirmed convergent and discriminant relationships between affect variables and other variables may prove to be the most useful indicators of validity in the domain of feeling states, affect, mood, and emotions.

Developing a Strategy for Self-Report Assessment of Feeling States, Affect, Mood, and Emotions

At this point in the chapter it has, we hope, become apparent that the measurement of exercise-induced changes in feeling states, affect, mood, and emotions requires careful consideration of the psychometric qualities of the different instruments as well as to a series of issues pertinent to the context of measurement.

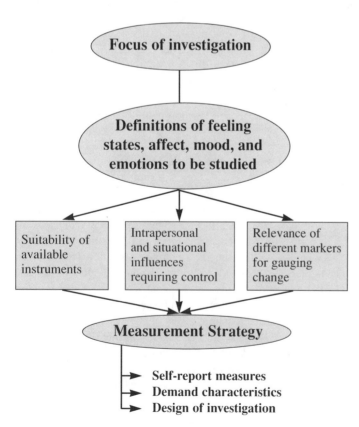

Figure 1. Components of a measurement strategy for the assessment of exercise-related affect.

In other words as illustrated in Figure 1, the measurement of exercise-induced changes in psychological states requires the *development of a measurement strategy*, in addition to the *selection of a measurement tool*.

The measurement strategy should be preceded by a definition of the specific concepts under investigation as well as the focus of the investigation. In this regard, a decision should be made as to what feeling states, affects, moods, or emotions constitute the main interest and whether or not there is a need to use exercise-specific measures. The resolution of these two conceptual issues will allow the researcher to identify available instruments, develop procedures to control for confounding intrapersonal and situational influences, and identify appropriate markers (e.g., baseline or average level of responding) against which any changes in feeling states, affect, mood, or emotions will be gauged. In enumerating relevant measurement tools, the researcher is encouraged to interface the listing of psychometric information with the actual purposes of the investigation. Finally, the investigator should list any other potential issues of concern, including but not limited to the age, gender, education level, exercise history, and mental health status of subjects as they may impose specific concerns for intrapersonal, interpersonal, or situational influences. Issues of diurnal variation as well as seasonal variation may also be listed here. With this information in hand, the researcher must then use critical thinking to make an informed decision toward formulation of an actual measurement strategy that should include at least the following items:

- selection of the specific instruments to be used
- description of the nature and purposes of the demand characteristics imposed upon the respondent
- statement regarding how the timing of measurements and potential reactivity to measurement are handled in the overall design of the investigation.

Selected Instruments in the Study of Exercise-Induced Changes

With the previous discussion as a backdrop, we will consider the appropriateness and psychometric qualities of selected instruments that have been frequently used in the study of exercise-induced changes in feeling states, affect, mood, and emotions. In approaching the discussion of the specific measurement instruments, our intention was *not* to categorically state whether an instrument was good or bad but rather to show how selected instruments are helpful in addressing some research questions although being decidedly limited in the study of others. Given this goal, our selection of instruments was more strategic than systematic. That is, we chose to discuss the Profile of Mood States (POMS; McNair, Lorr, & Droppleman, 1981) and the State-Trait Anxiety Inventory (STAI; Spielberger, Gorsuch, Lushene, Vagg, & Jacobs, 1983) because extant literature reviews on the psychological benefits of exercise (e.g., North et al., 1990; Petruzzello, Landers, Hatfield, Kubitz, & Salazar, 1991) indicate that these two instruments rank among the most frequently used.

On the other hand, at least three new measurement instruments of exercise-related feeling states or affect have been developed in recent years, namely, the Feeling Scale (FS; Hardy & Rejeski, 1989), the Exercise-Induced Feeling Inventory (EFI;

Gauvin & Rejeski, 1993), and the Subjective Exercise Experiences Scale (SEES; McAuley & Courneya, 1994). These instruments emerged as a result of an effort to overcome lacunae in the measurement of exercise-induced psychological states. We elected to discuss these measures because they will allow us to illustrate many of the issues raised above. It should not be concluded that these instruments should be preferentially used because they are exercise specific. Rather, our goal is to demonstrate that they offer complementary perspectives for our understanding of exercise-induced changes in feeling states, affect, mood, and emotions. Furthermore, to illustrate the process that the researcher may want to adopt in developing a measurement strategy and selecting an assessment tool, we have summarized much of the discussion in the form of a table that provides a grid for analyzing different measurement tools (see Table 2).

The Profile of Mood States

The POMS (McNair et al., 1981) is a 65-item paper-and-pencil instrument that assesses six discrete affective states, namely, tension-anxiety, depression-dejection, anger-hostility, vigor, fatigue, and confusion-bewilderment. The respondent is required to rate feelings in terms of a 5-point intensity scale ranging from "Not at all" to "Extremely." The instructions for responding can be varied to have subjects focus on current feelings, daily feelings, weekly feelings, or habitual feelings. The inventory can thus be adapted for measurement of state-like or trait-like concepts.

The impetus for developing the POMS came from the need to develop a convenient and economical method for assessing transient, fluctuating affective states in psychiatric populations and for gauging ongoing effects of psychotherapy in outpatients. A series of studies of psychotherapy outcomes as well as controlled drug trials have shown that the POMS adequately reflects changes in patient status. Subsequent studies have documented sensitivity to laboratory emotion-inducing conditions.

The psychometric qualities of the instrument are well docu-

Table 2
Consideration Grid Applied to Selected Measures of Affective States.

	POMS	STAI	EFI	SEES	FS
Considerations					
State vs trait	Both	Both	State	State	State
Sensitivity	Psychotherapy Laboratory manipulations	Perceived threat	Acute aerobic exercise Self-Efficacy	Acute aerobic exercise Self-Efficacy	Acute aerobic exercise Distress management training
Value of different markers for assessing change	Unknown	Baseline useful in non threatening situation	Baseline moderates responses to exercise	Unknown	Unknown
Exercise-sensitivity/ Relevance	Not directly tested	Questionable	Yes	Yes	Yes
Psychometric Qualities					
Test-Retest	High for shorter inter-test intervals	High for similar situations	Unknown	Unknown	Unknown
Alternate forms	Short form Bipolar form	Available	None	None	None
Interitem Consistencies	High	High	High	High	Not applicable
Content validity	Not documented	Available	Available	Available	Available
Factor analytic validity	Good	Good	Good	Good	Not applicable
Convergent validity	High	High	Good	Good	Unknown
Divergent validity	Unknown	High	Good	Good	Good
Influence of individual differences	Gender Age Treatment status	Gender Age	None documented	None documented	Sex-role orientation

mented and extensive. Specifically, McNair et al. (1981) have shown high interitem consistency across the different subscales and different samples ($\alpha > .84$), high test-retest reliability at short (e.g., around 20 days) intertest intervals ($r > .65$) and moderate test-retest reliability for longer (e.g., 6 weeks interspersed by psychotherapy) intertest intervals ($.42 < r > .55$). The content validity of the scale is high for assessing psychiatric outpatient treatment outcomes, the factor analytic structure has been consistent across patient and normal samples, the tension-anxiety scale has high concurrent validity with the Taylor Manifest Anxiety scale (Taylor, 1953), and the different subscales correlate highly with the Hopkins Symptom Check List (Derogatis, Lipman, Rickels, Uhlenhuth, & Covi, 1974) as well as other measures of psychotherapy outcome. Gender differences, age, and mental health-related differences have been observed such that separate norms are available for different samples. Although there are no alternative forms available, a bipolar form of the POMS exists (i.e., POMS-BI, Lorr & McNair, 1984). The POMS-BI was developed in an effort to document whether mood could be conceptualized as bipolar and to formulate a measure that tapped into positive, as opposed to only negative, dimensions of mood. Three studies aimed at establishing content and factor-analytic validity (see Lorr & McNair, 1984) support the viability of conceptualizing mood as a function of six bipolar states (i.e., composed-anxious, agreeable-hostile, elated-depressed, confident-unsure, energetic-tired, and clearheaded-confused). Furthermore, recent psychometric endeavors suggest that a bipolar approach may be more viable than a unipolar approach (Green, Goldman, & Salovey, 1993). However, as indicated previously, significant controversy exists as to how to define and operationalize moods (Ekman & Davidson, 1994b), and thus no firm conclusions on this issue can be drawn.

The POMS and the POMS-BI are not exercise specific in that they were not devised with the intent to be sensitive to the stimulus properties of exercise. To our knowledge, the POMS-BI has not been used in the exercise literature. However, the POMS has been successfully and extensively used by researchers to gauge the anxiolytic and antidepressant effects of acute exercise (see North et al., 1990; Petruzzello et al., 1991) and the effects of overtraining (see Morgan, Costill, Flynn, & Raglin, 1988; O'Connor, Morgan, & Raglin, 1991; O'Connor, Morgan, Raglin, & Barksdale, 1989).

For the study of exercise-induced changes in psychological states, the POMS does, however, have certain limitations. For example, many of the items on the POMS pertain to feelings experienced by psychiatric patients (e.g., bewildered, panicky, sorry for things done) that have little relevance to individuals with normal functioning who are involved in exercise settings. Furthermore, many of the questions of interest pertain to positive feeling states in persons with relatively low levels of anxiety and depression (cf. McAuley & Rudolph, 1995). The sensitivity of the vigor and fatigue scales to exercise stimuli has not been systematically examined, nor have researchers determined the practical significance of further reducing levels of anxiety and depression in persons already functioning within normal ranges. In regard to this latter issue, other authors (Gauvin & Brawley, 1993) have discussed the issue of ceiling and floor effects in the study of exercise-related affect. Further validation

studies are also required to examine issues of statistical significance versus theoretical significance of any changes in affective states in the normal range.

A more critical limitation pertains to the conceptual foundation underlying the POMS. As indicated previously, the POMS was developed for clinical purposes. It is not clear how the constructs measured by the POMS relate to broader conceptions of affective experience. Thus, although the POMS represents a measurement tool with good psychometric qualities, it does not systematically apply to the study of all phenomena pertinent to exercise-related feeling states, affect, mood, and emotions.

The State-Trait Anxiety Inventory

The STAI (Spielberger et al., 1983) is a 40-item inventory including 20 items that assess state anxiety (i.e., Form Y-1: feelings of apprehension and tension accompanied by physiological arousal) and 20 items that tap trait anxiety (i.e., Form Y-2: tendency to perceive a wide variety of situations as threatening and to respond to threat with state anxiety). A shorter 10-item version of the state measure has also been developed (Spielberger, 1979). Respondents are required to rate current feelings (in the case of state anxiety) according to a 4-point intensity scale ranging from Not at all to Very much so and general feelings (in the case of trait anxiety) according to a 4-point frequency scale ranging from "Almost never" to "Almost always."

The STAI was developed to meet the need for a valid and reliable tool to assess anxiety in basic research and has subsequently been suggested for use in clinical research and practice. Like the POMS, the STAI has strong psychometric qualities. Specifically, the test-retest reliability of the trait version is high ($r > .73$) whereas that of the state version is understandably much lower (r around .35). Interitem consistencies of both measures are also high ($\alpha > .82$). More importantly, the state measure has been shown to be sensitive to a wide variety of manipulations of threat whereas the trait scale has been found, as would be predicted theoretically, to correlate highly with state measures only when state anxiety data are collected in threatening situations. The scales have been found to have both convergent and divergent validities with other measures. Norms are available for adult men and women of various ages, college students, high school students, psychiatric patients, general medical and surgical patients, and prisoners.

The STAI is not exercise specific although other authors (Martens, 1977) have developed competition-specific versions of the instrument. Nevertheless, the STAI has been a measure of choice for researchers interested in the anxiolytic potential of acute exercise (see Petruzzello et al., 1991). Although the strong psychometric qualities of the STAI make it an attractive choice for the researcher, at least one study suggests that it is not always appropriate for research in the context of exercise. That is, Rejeski, Hardy, and Shaw (1991) showed that, during exercise, state anxiety scores increased. A closer inspection of items responsible for the apparent increases in state anxiety revealed that only items related to activation changed. Thus, whether or not the STAI assesses changes in physiological activation or actual changes in anxiety requires further empirical investigation as does the issue of the unidimensionality of the scale in exercise situations. Furthermore, the issue of ceiling and floor effects also requires attention.

In sum, the STAI has been extensively used in research on anxiety and exercise. Its psychometric qualities are sound when measured in relation to perceived threat. Its validity in relation to exercise is less well documented, thus imposing certain cautions for researchers interested in its use.

The Feeling Scale

The FS is a one-item measure represented by an 11-point bipolar scale ranging from -5 to +5. Odd integers are anchored by verbal descriptors (e.g., very good, very bad). Respondents are required to rate their current state by indicating the number that best describes their overall feelings. The FS provides a measure of the hedonic tone dimension (pleasure-displeasure) of affect. The measure was specifically designed to assess how bad-good a person feels while exercising and thus is an exercise-specific measure.

As discussed by other authors (Russell et al., 1989), the validation of one-item measures poses special problems because traditional indicators of reliability and validity, such as internal consistency, item analysis, and factor analysis, cannot be applied. When this notion is coupled with the limited relevance of test-retest reliability indicators, it becomes evident that the validation must rest on indicators of content, convergent, and discriminant validity.

Accordingly, Hardy and Rejeski (1989) conducted a series of three experiments to garner information on psychometric characteristics of the FS. In one study, Hardy and Rejeski provided evidence of content validity in showing that young adults draw upon different feeling states to operationalize feeling good and feeling bad during exercise. In a second experiment, Hardy and Rejeski demonstrated discriminant validity and sensitivity in that the FS was only moderately correlated with ratings of perceived exertion ($r = -.56$) and that FS varied substantially across persons for the same rating of perceived exertion. Finally, in a third experiment, Hardy and Rejeski demonstrated that the FS correlated progressively more strongly with ratings of perceived exertion as the intensity of the exercise increased. Yet, the correlations, even at the highest exercise intensities, were only moderate in size. These data further support the discriminant validity of the FS.

The FS has proven useful in a variety of exercise studies. For example, Rejeski, Best, Griffith, and Kenney (1987) observed that feminine-typed males reported lower scores on the FS for an identical rating of perceived exertion than did masculine-typed and androgenous males. Similarly, Kenney, Rejeski, and Messier (1987) showed that a distress management training program was effective in modifying FS responses to moderate intensity and high intensity exercise in women. Furthermore, Rejeski, Gauvin, Hobson, and Norris (1995) observed that higher FS scores during exercise were related to greater improvements in revitalization following acute aerobic exercise in women.

Although the FS has allowed researchers to uncover some interesting perspectives on exercise-induced changes in feeling states, affect, mood, and emotions, evidence of the convergent validity would obviously be desirable. For example, the extent to which the scale correlates with other measures of hedonic tone (e.g., the Affect Grid; Russell et al., 1989) would be instructive. Similarly, the convergent validity across persons and situations (exercise related or not) would be informative. In sum, the FS is one exercise-specific measure that has shown promise for the understanding of exercise-induced changes in feeling states, affect, mood, and emotions, particularly when the measurement of in-task responses was of interest either as a moderator or an outcome variable.

The Exercise-Induced Feeling Inventory

The EFI (Gauvin & Rejeski, 1993) is a 12-item adjective scale designed to measure four feeling states that are especially sensitive to the stimulus properties of exercise, namely, positive engagement, revitalization, physical exhaustion, and tranquility. Respondents are required to rate current feelings on a 5-point intensity scale ranging from "Do not feel" to "Feel very strongly." The development of the inventory was based on three assumptions: (a) that the stimulus properties of exercise could elicit unique feeling states including energy, calmness, enthusiasm, and fatigue; (b) that there was a need to better understand positive, as opposed to negative, feeling states that may arise from exercise involvement; and (c) that understanding exercise-induced feeling states could provide a window into our understanding of the link between physical activity and psychological well-being. However, initial psychometric efforts were focused on describing those feeling states that are particularly sensitive to the stimulus properties of exercise.

Initial psychometric data support the validity and reliability of the EFI. That is, interitem consistency of the different subscales is high ($\alpha = .80$), although the test-retest reliability is unknown. Special efforts were devoted to establishing the content validity of the scale for exercise research through the gathering of "expert" opinions. Factorial validity was strong and consistent across two samples of college students. Convergent and discriminant validities were also established. Finally, the scale has been shown to be sensitive to exercise manipulations across several studies and samples of adults (e.g., Spence, Gauvin, & Sellers, 1995; Vlachopoulos et al., 1996). Vlachopoulos et al. (1996) reported further support for the psychometric attributes of the EFI with a sample of adolescents aged 11 to 15 years.

The scale was developed in parallel to other psychometric efforts concerning exercise-related affect and feeling states (see McAuley & Courneya, 1994, below). Several recent studies (Bozoian, Rejeski, & McAuley, 1994; Gauvin et al., 1996; Rejeski et al., 1995) have documented that the EFI is useful in uncovering new perspectives on exercise-induced changes in psychological well-being.

However, the extant work on the EFI does have certain limitations. For example, the conceptual and empirical links between the specific feeling states measured by the EFI and broader conceptions of affective experience are virtually unchartered. Similarly, the inherent level and variability of positive engagement, revitalization, physical exhaustion, and tranquility between and within persons have not yet been described. Finally, the initial validation studies were conducted with college student populations. The suitability of the EFI with populations differing in age, health status, education level, and culture has not been extensively documented. Ongoing psychometric data will further advance our understanding of its utility.

Subjective Exercise Experiences Scale

The SEES (McAuley & Courneya, 1994) is a 12-item adjective scale requiring the subject to rate current feelings along a 7-point intensity scale ranging from "Not at all" to "Very much so." The instrument provides three subscale scores that are sensitive to the stimulus properties of exercise, namely, positive well-being, psychological distress, and fatigue.

Given the rationale for the development of the scale (i.e., the need to assess positive dimensions of affective responding that are sensitive to exercise stimuli), McAuley and Courneya (1994) also devoted significant attention to the issue of content validity. Their efforts led them to identify more global dimensions of affective responses to exercise than those that were identified by Gauvin and Rejeski (1993). The divergent paths explored by these researchers serve to illustrate how critical the process of content validation is to the development of a measurement instrument.

Like the EFI, the SEES has been shown to have high interitem consistency ($\alpha > .85$), good factorial validity, and appropriate convergent and divergent validity. Similarly, the SEES appears to be sensitive to exercise manipulations. Recent investigations have shown that the SEES is useful in understanding selected outcomes of exercise interventions (e.g., Lox, McAuley & Tucker, 1995; McAuley, Shaffer, & Rudolph, 1995; Mihalko & McAuley, 1996). However, currently, the SEES shares many of the shortcomings of the EFI, and its relevance should thus also be considered in light of the goals of a particular investigation. As mentioned by McAuley and Rudolph (1995), the empirical and conceptual links between the EFI and the SEES also merit further investigation.

Final Comments

At this point in the chapter, it seems appropriate to paraphrase Kerlinger (1979), who stated that "measurement can be the Achille's heel of the social sciences" (p. 141). Indeed, it was our intent to highlight the numerous and often unique challenges involved in measuring exercise-induced changes in feeling states, affect, mood, and emotions and to emphasize the need for a broad perspective to the quantification of these phenomena. In this regard, we hope that in some small way the current discussion has served to unravel some of the reasons that impelled Kerlinger to use such a compelling analogy.

References

Anastasi, A. (1976). *Psychological testing* (4th ed.). New York: Macmillan.

Averill, J. R. (1994). I feel, therefore I am — I think. In P. Ekman & R. J. Davidson (Eds.), *The nature of emotion: Fundamental questions* (pp. 379-385). New York: Oxford University Press.

Batson, C. D., Shaw, L. L., & Oleson, K. C. (1992). Differentiating affect, mood and emotion. *Review of Personality and Social Psychology, 13*, 294-326.

Blumenthal, J. A., Emery, C. F., Madden, D. J., Coleman, R.E., Riddle, M. W., Schiebolk, S., Cobb, F. R., Sullivan, M. J., & Higginbotham, M. D. (1991). Effects of exercise training on cardiorespiratory function in men and women >60 years of age. *American Journal of Cardiology, 67*, 633-639.

Blumenthal, J. A., Emery, C. F., & Rejeski, W. J. (1988). The effects of exercise training on psychosocial functioning after myocardial infarction. *Journal of Cardiopulmonary Rehabilitation, 8*, 183-193.

Bozoian, S., Rejeski, W. J., & McAuley, E. (1994). Self-efficacy influences feeling states associated with acute exercise. *Journal of Sport and Exercise Psychology, 16*, 326-333.

Byrne, A., & Byrne, D. G. (1993). The effect of exercise on depression, anxiety and other mood states: A review. *Journal of Psychosomatic Research, 37*, 565-574.

Cacioppo, J. T., Unchino, B. N., Crites, S. L., Snydersmith, M. A., Smith, G., & Berntson, G. G. (1992). Relationship between facial expressiveness and sympathetic activation in emotion: A critical review, with emphasis on modeling underlying mechanisms and individual differences. *Journal of Personality and Social Psychology, 62*, 110-128.

Cohen, S., Doyle, W. J., Skoner, D. P., Fireman, P., Gwaltney, J. M., & Newsom, J. T. (1995). State and trait negative affect as predictors of objective and subjective symptoms of respiratory viral infections. *Journal of Personality and Social Psychology, 68*, 159-169.

Davidson, R. J. (1994). Complexities in the search for emotion-specific physiology. In P. Ekman & R. J. Davidson (Eds.), *The nature of emotion: Fundamental questions* (pp. 237-242). New York: Oxford University Press.

Derogatis, L. R., Lipman, R. S., Rickels, K., Uhlenhuth, E. H., & Covi, L. (1974). The Hopkins Symptom Check List: A self-report symptom inventory. *Behavioral Science, 19*, 1-15.

Diener, E., & Emmons, R. A. (1985). The independence of positive and negative affect. *Journal of Personality and Social Psychology, 47*, 1105-1117.

Diener, E., Larsen, R. J., Levine, S., & Emmons, R. A. (1984). Frequency and intensity: The two dimensions underlying positive and negative affect. *Journal of Personality and Social Psychology, 48*, 1253-1264.

Egloff, B., Tausch, A., Kohlmann, C.-W., & Krohne, H. W. (1995). Relationships between time of day, day of the week, and positive mood: Exploring the role of the mood measure. *Motivation and Emotion, 19*, 99-110.

Ekman, P. (1993). Facial expression and emotion. *American Psychologist, 48*, 384-392.

Ekman, P., & Davidson, R. J. (1994a). Affective science: A research agenda. In P. Ekman, & R. J. Davidson (Eds.), *The nature of emotion: Fundamental questions* (pp. 411-430). New York: Oxford University Press.

Ekman, P., & Davidson, R. J. (Eds.) (1994b). *The nature of emotion: Fundamental questions*. New York: Oxford University Press.

Frijda, N. H. (1987). *The emotions*. New York: Cambridge University Press.

Frijda, N. H. (1994). Emotions require cognitions, even if simple ones. In P. Ekman & R. J. Davidson (Eds.), *The nature of emotion: Fundamental questions* (pp. 197-202). New York: Oxford University Press.

Gauvin, L., & Brawley, L. R. (1993). Alternative psychological concepts and methodologies for the study of exercise and affect. In P. Seraganian (Ed.), *Exercise psychology: The influence of physical exercise on psychological processes* (pp. 146-171). New York: Wiley & Sons.

Gauvin, L., & Rejeski, W. J. (1993). The Exercise-Induced Feeling Inventory: Development and initial validation. *Journal of Sport and Exercise Psychology, 15*, 403-423.

Gauvin, L., Rejeski, W. J., & Norris, J. L. (1996). A naturalistic study of the impact of acute physical activity on feeling states and affect of women. *Health Psychology, 15*, 391-397.

Gauvin, L., & Russell, S. J. (1993) Sport-specific and culturally-adapted measures in sport and exercise research: Issues and strategies. In R. N. Singer, K. Tennant, & M. Murphey (Eds.), *Handbook of research on sport psychology* (pp. 891-900). New York: Macmillan.

Gauvin, L., & Spence, J. C. (1996). Physical activity and psychological well-being: Knowledge base, current issues and caveats. *Nutri-*

tion Reviews, 54, S53-S65.

Godin, G. (1994). Social cognitive models. In R. K. Dishman (Ed.), *Advances in exercise adherence* (pp. 113-136). Champaign, IL: Human Kinetics Publ.

Godin, G., Desharnais, R., Valois, P., & Bradet, R. (1995). Combining behavioral and motivational dimensions to identify and characterize the stages in the process of adherence to exercise. *Psychology and Health, 10,* 333-344.

Goldsmith, H. H. (1994). Parsing the emotional domain from a developmental perspective. In P. Ekman & R. J. Davidson (Eds.), *The nature of emotion: Fundamental questions* (pp. 68-73). New York: Oxford University Press.

Green, D. P., Goldman, S. L., & Salovey, P. (1993). Measurement error masks bipolarity in affect ratings. *Journal of Personality and Social Psychology, 64,* 1029-1041.

Hardy, C. J., & Rejeski, W. J. (1989). Not what but how one feels: The measurement of affect during exercise. *Journal of Sport and Exercise Psychology, 11,* 304-317.

Izard, C. E. (1977). *Human emotions.* New York: Plenum.

Kenney, E. A., Rejeski, W. J., & Messier, S. P. (1987). Managing exercise distress: The effect of broad spectrum intervention on affect, RPE, and running efficiency. *Canadian Journal of Sport Sciences, 12,* 97-105.

Kerlinger, F. N. (1979). *Behavioral research: A conceptual approach.* New York: Holt, Rinehart & Winston.

Kleininna, P. R., & Kleininna, A. M. (1981). A categorized list of emotion definitions with suggestions for a consensual definition. *Motivation & Emotion, 5,* 345-379.

Landers, D. M., & Petruzzello, S. J. (1994). Physical activity, fitness and anxiety. In C. Bouchard, R. J. Shephard, & T. Stephens (Eds.), *Physical activity, fitness and health: International proceedings and consensus statement* (pp. 868-882). Champaign, IL: Human Kinetics.

Larsen, R. J. (1987). The stability of mood variability: A spectral analytic approach to daily mood assessments. *Journal of Personality and Social Psychology, 52,* 1195-1204.

Larsen, R. J., & Diener, E. (1987). Affect intensity as an individual difference characteristic: A review. *Journal of Personality and Social Psychology, 21,* 1-39.

Larsen, R. J., & Kasimatis, M. (1990). Individual differences in entrainment of mood to the weekly calendar. *Journal of Personality and Social Psychology, 58,* 164-171.

Larsen, R. J., & Kasimatis, M. (1991). Day-to-day physical symptoms: Individual differences in the occurrence, duration and emotional concomitants of minor daily illnesses. *Journal of Personality, 59,* 387-424.

Lazarus, R. S. (1991). Progress on a cognitive-motivational- relational theory of emotion. *American Psychologist, 46,* 819-834.

Leary, M. R., Schreindorfer, L. S., & Haupt, A. L. (1995). The role of low self-esteem in emotional and behavioral problems: Why is low self-esteem dysfunctional. *Journal of Social and Clinical Psychology, 14,* 297-314.

LeDoux, J. E. (1994). Emotion-specific physiological activity: Don't forget about CNS physiology. In P. Ekman & R. J. Davidson (Eds.), *The nature of emotion: Fundamental questions* (pp. 248- 251). New York: Oxford University Press.

Lorr, M., & McNair, D. M. (1984). *Profile of Mood States: Bi-Polar Form (POMS-BI).* San Diego, CA: Educational and Industrial Testing Service.

Lox, C. L., McAuley, E., & Tucker, R. S. (1995). Exercise as an intervention for enhancing subjective well-being in an HIV-1 population. *Journal of Sport and Exercise Psychology, 17,* 345-362.

Martens, R. (1977). *Sport Competition Anxiety Test.* Champaign, IL: Human Kinetics Publ.

Mayer, J. D., & Salovey, P. (1995). Emotional intelligence and the constructions and regulation of feelings. *Applied and Preventive Psychology, 4,* 197-209.

Mayer, J. D., Salovey, P., & Gomberg-Kaufman, S. (1991). A broader conception of mood experience. *Journal of Personality and Social Psychology, 60,* 100-111.

McAuley, E., & Courneya, K. S. (1994). The Subjective Exercise Experience Scale (SEES): Development and preliminary validation. *Journal of Sport and Exercise Psychology, 16,* 163-177.

McAuley, E., & Rudolph, D. (1995). Physical activity, aging and psychological well-being. *Journal of Aging and Physical Activity, 3,* 67-96.

McAuley, E., Shaffer, S. M., & Rudolph, D. (1995). Affective responses to acute exercise in elderly impaired males: The moderating effects of self-efficacy and age. *The International Journal of Aging and Human Development, 41,* 13-27.

McNair, D. M., Lorr, M., & Droppleman, L. F. (1981). *Manual for the Profile of Mood States.* San Diego, CA: Educational and Industrial Testing Service.

Mihalko, S. L., & McAuley, E. (1996). Strength training effects on subjective well-being and physical function in the elderly. *Journal of Aging and Physical Activity, 4,* 56-68.

Morgan, W. P., Costill, D. L., Flynn, M. G., & Raglin, J. S. (1988). Mood disturbances following increased training in swimmers. *Medicine and Science in Sports and Exercise, 20,* 408-414.

Nesselroade, J. R. (1991). Interindividual differences in intraindividual change. In L. M. Collins & J. L. Horn (Eds.), *Best methods for the analysis of change* (pp. 92-105). Washington, DC: American Psychological Association.

Nesselroade, J. R., & Hershberger, S. L. (1993). Intraindividual variability: Methodological issues for population health research. In K. Dean (Ed.), *Population health* (pp. 74-94). Beverly Hills, CA: Sage.

North, C. T., McCullagh, P., & Tran, W. (1990). Effects of exercise on depression. *Exercise and Sport Sciences Reviews, 18,* 379-414.

O'Connor, P. J., & Davis, J. (1992). Psychobiological response to exercise at different times of day. *Medicine and Science in Sports and Exercise, 24,* 714-719.

O'Connor, P. J., Morgan, W. P., & Raglin, J. S. (1991). Psychobiologic effects of 3 D of increased training in female and male swimmers. *Medicine and Science in Sports and Exercise, 23,* 1055-1061.

O'Connor, P. J., Morgan, W. P., Raglin, J. S., & Barksdale, C. M. (1989). Mood state and salivary cortisol levels following overtraining in female swimmers. *Psychneuroendocrinology, 14,* 303-310.

Ojanen, M. (1994). Can the true effects of exercise on psychological variables be separated from placebo effects? *International Journal of Sport Psychology, 25,* 63-80.

Panksepp, J. (1994). The clearest physiological distinctions between emotions will be found among the circuits of the brain. In P. Ekman & R. J. Davidson (Eds.), *The nature of emotion: Fundamental questions* (pp. 258-260). New York: Oxford University Press.

Petruzzello, S. J. (1995). Anxiety reduction following exercise: Methodological artifact or "real" phenomenon? *Journal of Sport and Exercise Psychology, 17,* 105-111.

Petruzzello, S. J., Landers, D. M., Hatfield, B. D., Kubitz, K. A., & Salazar, W. (1991). A meta-analysis on the anxiety-reducing effects of acute and chronic exercise: Outcomes and mechanisms. *Sports Medicine, 11,* 143-182.

Rejeski, W. J., Best, D. L., Griffith, P., & Kenney, E. A. (1987). Sex-role orientation and the response of men to exercise stress. *Research Quarterly for Exercise and Sport, 58,* 260- 264.

Rejeski, W. J., Brawley, L. R., & Shumaker, S. A. (1996). Physical activity and health-related quality of life. *Exercise and Sport Sciences Reviews, 24,* 71-108.

Rejeski, W. J., Gauvin, L., Hobson, M. L., & Norris, J. L. (1995). Effects of baseline responses, in-task feelings and duration of physical activity on exercise-induced feeling states in women. *Health Psychol-*

ogy, 14, 350-359.

Rejeski, W. J., Hardy, C. J., & Shaw, J. (1991). Psychometric confounds of assessing state anxiety in conjunction with acute bouts of vigorous exercise. *Journal of Sport and Exercise Psychology, 13*, 65-74.

Rejeski, W. J., Thompson, A., Brubaker, P. H., & Miller, H. S. (1992). Acute exercise: Buffering psychosocial stress responses in women. *Health Psychology, 11*, 355-362.

Russell, J. A. (1980). A circumplex model of affect. *Journal of Personality and Social Psychology, 39*, 1161-1178.

Russell, J. A. (1994). Is there universal recognition of emotion from facial expression? A review of cross-cultural studies. *Psychological Bulletin, 115*, 102-141.

Russell, J. A., Weiss, A., & Mendelsohn, G. A. (1989). Affect grid: a single item scale of pleasure and arousal. *Journal of Personality and Social Psychology, 57*, 491-502.

Saklofske, D. H., Blomme, G. C., & Kelly, I. W. (1992). The effect of exercise and relaxation on energetic and tense arousal. *Personality and Individual Differences, 13*, 623-625.

Salovey, P., & Birnbaum, D. (1989). Influence of mood on health-related cognitions. *Journal of Personality and Social Psychology, 57*, 539-551.

Scherer, K. R. (1994). An emotion's occurrence depends on the relevance of an event to the organism's goal/need hierarchy. In P. Ekman & R. J. Davidson (Eds.), *The nature of emotion: Fundamental questions* (pp. 227-231). New York: Oxford University Press.

Shavelson, R. J., & Webb, N. M. (1991). *Generalizability theory: A primer*. Newbury Park, CA: Sage.

Shaver, P., Schwartz, J., Kirson, D., & O'Connor, C. (1987). Emotional knowledge: Further exploration of a prototype approach. *Journal of Personality and Social Psychology, 52*, 1061-1086.

Spence, J. C., Gauvin, L., & Sellers, W. R. (1995, October). *The effects of moderately intense daily physical activity on the feeling states of healthy elderly persons*. Paper presented at the annual meeting of the Canadian Society for Psychomotor Learning and Sport Psychology, Vancouver, BC.

Spielberger, C. D. (1979). *Preliminary manual for the State-Trait Personality Inventory*. Tampa, FL: University of South Florida.

Spielberger, C. D. (1980). *Preliminary manual for the State-Trait Anger Scale (STAS)*. Tampa, FL: University of South Florida Human Resources Institute.

Spielberger, C. D., Gorsuch, R. L., Luschene, R., Vagg, P. R., & Jacobs, G. A. (1983). *Manual for the State-Trait Anxiety Inventory*. Palo Alto, CA: Consulting Psychologists.

Stone, A. A., & Shiffman, S. (1992). Reflections on the intensive measurement of stress, coping and mood, with an emphasis on daily measures. *Psychology and Health, 7*, 115-129.

Taylor, J. A. (1953). A personality scale of manifest anxiety. *Journal of Abnormal Psychology, 48*, 285-290.

Thayer, R. E. (1970). Activation states as assessed by verbal report and four psychophysiological variables. *Psychophysiology, 7*, 86-94.

Thayer, R. E. (1989). *The biopsychology of mood and arousal*. New York: Oxford University Press.

Thayer, R. E., Newman, J. R., & McClain, T. M. (1994). Self-regulation of mood: Strategies for changing a bad mood, raising energy, and reducing tension. *Journal of Personality and Social Psychology, 67*, 910-925.

Vallerand, R. J. (1983). On emotion in sports: Theoretical and social psychological perspectives. *Journal of Sport Psychology, 5*, 197-215.

Vallerand, R. J. (1984). Emotion in sport: Definitional, historical, and social psychological perspectives. In W. F. Straub & J. M. Williams (Eds.), *Cognitive sport psychology* (pp. 63-78). Lansing, NY: Sport Science Associates.

Vlachopoulos, S., Biddle, S., & Fox, K. (1996). A social- cognitive investigation into the mechanisms of affect generation in children's physical activity. *Journal of Sport and Exercise Psychology, 18*, 174-193.

Watson, D. A., & Clark, L. A. (1994). The vicissitudes of mood: A schematic model. In P. Ekman & R. J. Davidson (Eds.), *The nature of emotion: Fundamental questions* (pp. 400-405). New York: Oxford University Press.

Watson, D. A. & Tellegen, A. (1985). Toward a consensual structure of mood. *Psychological Bulletin, 98*, 219-235.

Chapter 19

PROBLEMS IN ASSESSING PERCEIVED BARRIERS TO EXERCISE: CONFUSING OBSTACLES WITH ATTRIBUTIONS AND EXCUSES

Lawrence R. Brawley
Kathleen A. Martin
and
Nancy C. Gyurcsik
University of Waterloo

"Personal change would be trivially easy if there were no impediments, or barriers to surmount" (Bandura, 1995, p. 3). Bandura's statement in his 1995 address to the Society of Behavioral Medicine identifies a variable given paramount attention in investigations that examine exercise adherence and a variety of health outcomes. Actual barriers to exercise/physical activity or the perception of barriers to involvement have been stressed as key variables for investigation in at least two recent, major consensus conferences on exercise, fitness, and health (i.e., 1988 International Conference on Exercise, Fitness, and Health; 1994 International Conference on Physical Activity, Fitness, and Health) and in well-known books that specifically focus on the study of exercise adherence (cf. Dishman, 1988, 1994). Perceived barriers also feature prominently in theories used to examine health behavior change and compliance, such as the health belief model (HBM: cf. Janz & Becker, 1984).

From Bandura's (1995) perspective, social cognitive theory distinguishes between various barriers. Some perceived barriers are of a type that slow or stop health behaviors, such as depression or fatigue (personal) or workload and poor weather (situational). A second class of barrier consists of factors that *physically* inhibit the behavior, such as unavailability of a resource (facilities, health educator, exercise leader). This second type of barrier usually prevents the individual from starting the behavior and is a service or system barrier. However, from the perspective of understanding exercise/physical activity adherence, which presumes at least initial involvement, the first class of barrier is more often examined. For the purposes of this chapter, we will focus on the first class of barrier and attempts to measure and interpret it relative to the adherence of physical activity.

In discussing perceived barriers to exercise, Dishman has argued that they can now be validly assessed in the population (cf. Dishman, 1994; Steinhardt & Dishman, 1989). However, Godin et al. (1994) have noted that the method of measuring perceived barriers has not been uniform across studies whereas Steinhardt and Dishman (1989) have also concluded that this problem has been an impediment to interpretation and use of past research findings. Godin and his colleagues (1994) suggest that the definition of perceived barriers should be cast within a theoretical framework—specifically, as part of the perceived behavioral control concept within Ajzen's (1985) theory of planned behavior. Godin et al. (1994) found that perceived barriers were related to exercise intentions in three different populations when they were assessed within the perceived behavioral control aspect of the theory of planned behavior. Other expectancy-value type theories used to examine health and exercise have also explicitly (i.e., health belief model) or implicitly (i.e., social-cognitive theory—self-efficacy) assessed barriers or impediments to action. For example, McAuley (1994) has reviewed numerous studies that have examined relationships between self-efficacy for overcoming perceived barriers/impediments to exercise (i.e., when tired, anxious, busy) and exercise behavior.

Although there is evidence that a theory-driven versus data-driven approach to investigating exercise adherence may be useful from both an understanding and an applied perspective, the results that focus upon perceived barriers may still be questioned. The use of the concept in a theoretical model is only as good as its measurement and interpretation. To gain some appreciation for why exercise investigators should still be wary of the measurement of perceived barriers to exercise research, we discuss a number of the concepts and methodologies used to measure perceived barriers and some of the inherent criticisms. These criticisms are not unique to exercise-related research but applied across domains of inquiry (e.g., physical activity, leisure, health promotion, and disease prevention). Although it is beyond the scope and purpose of this chapter to provide an extensive review, an illustration of the common problems found in the health, leisure, and exercise literature will serve to illustrate. We selectively sampled studies that exemplify the common characteristics of measures of perceived barriers. Further, we described these in tabular form so that the interested reader could have a perspective on how the measure was used. The common aspects of the measures and studies are summarized. To validate the subsequent conclusions drawn from our summaries, we sought reviews of the barriers/constraints literature where available. From these reviews, we compared their conclusions with those from our selective samples. The resulting commonalities, strengths, and limitations are provided. Suggestions for future research on barrier assessment are advanced for the reader's consideration.

The Conceptual Definition of Barriers

The incidence of nonparticipation in (leisure and physical activity), as well as high rates of nonadherence to and dropout from, programs of exercise and health behavior focused scientists and practitioners on barriers as the probable cause (cf. Dishman, 1988; Godin et al., 1994; Sallis, Hovell, Hofstetter, Faucher, Elder et al., 1989; Wankel, 1988). The notion of barriers to action has an attractive, intuitive appeal as an explanation for behavioral variability and complete nonadherence. However, just as the definitions of adherence vary widely (cf. Perkins & Epstein, 1988), so do the definitions of barriers.

In the leisure literature, Jackson (1988) argues that the word *barriers* is inadequate to capture the entire range of explanations for leisure nonparticipation and dropout. Instead, he suggests use of the word *constraints* in order to capture a wider range of explanations. Jackson's 1988 review summarizes the various classifications/definitions of constraints. For example, investigators have classified constraints as internal or external to the individual; intrapersonal (preferential) or interpersonal (participation); intervening and antecedent; blocking (precluding) and inhibiting (slowing or making situationally variable); permanent and temporary; and so on (Jackson, 1988).

The health literature has been strongly influenced by the health belief model (HBM: cf. Janz & Becker, 1984; Rosenstock, 1974). Thus the approach to conceptualizing perceived barriers has had a belief-oriented flavor. This conceptualization has often been assessed as an antecedent index of the likelihood of action where an index of perceived barriers to preventative action is subtracted from an index of the perceived benefits of preventative action. A key focus of this approach for the present article is what constitutes the perceived-barriers index. The

health literature discusses barriers in relation to classifications of barrier types, not unlike the leisure domain (cf. Jackson, 1988). However, the barrier index combines, for example, precluding barriers such as cost of health services with intrapersonal barriers such as feelings of embarrassment, fear of pain, and worry about a health procedure. Quite often this conceptual index is thought to be representative of potential barriers to a behavior, but little thought appears to be given to whether the barrier is relevant to the complex behavior being assessed. In many cases, the behavior is a specific health action such as obtaining a mammogram. Some of the barriers included in the index are not barriers per se although they may facilitate taking the health action. Conceptually they do not represent the construct assessed although they may be determinants of the construct. Thus an item about "having another person accompany you to the screening" is not a barrier per se, but may reflect on the determinant of social support. Confusing the measurement of a construct with its antecedents and consequences is not a problem unique to the barriers literature, but it is nonetheless problematic for the assessment of barriers.

A similar belief-based strategy for examining the impact of perceived barriers has been proposed when using the theory of planned behavior (TPB: cf. Ajzen, 1991) to examine health behaviors. In this model, perceived barriers form a part of an antecedent, belief-based index of perceived control. Furthermore, the index of beliefs about the absence of requisite resources and opportunities is usually combined, in multiplicative fashion, with an index of the individual's beliefs about his or her power to control factors that facilitate or inhibit desired health behaviors (cf. Godin et al., 1994).

Another social-cognitive approach (i.e., belief/expectation-based) to examining health behavior that implicitly includes the notion of barriers is Bandura's (1977, 1986) conceptualization of self-efficacy. Judgements of self-efficacy in the face of impediments often are used to form one type of index of self-efficacy. Respondents indicate how sure/certain they are about completing a health behavior when, for example, they feel tired or under pressure at work; when they have personal problems or are feeling depressed; when they have discomfort or have other more attractive things to do (cf. Bandura, 1995). However, concepts that implicitly incorporate barriers do not clarify what a barrier is (e.g., a perceived obstacle or perceived challenge). Interestingly, some health educators have raised the possibility that lack of self-efficacy is a "barrier" to making responsible health choices (cf. DeVellis, Alfierei, & Ahluwalia, 1995). Although self-efficacy for barriers may indeed moderate or mediate the choices individuals make about health behavior, self-efficacy becomes a personal barrier only when perceived as such by the individual. Unfortunately its discussion as a "barrier" from the perspective of the researcher or educator may tend to be a reason that self efficacy could be considered in the large inventory of barriers presumed to affect health actions. We return to this general point later in the chapter.

Finally, much attention has recently been given to the transtheoretical model of change (cf. Prochaska et al., 1994) in describing health behaviors. A key premise of the model is that people go through various stages of change in adopting and maintaining a health behavior. According to Prochaska et al.

(also see Prochaska & Marcus, 1994), constructs such as decision-balance (cf. Janis & Mann, 1977) and self-efficacy (cf. Bandura, 1986) can be integrated into the transtheoretical model, and Prochaska et al.'s (1994) studies reflect their use of these concepts. When the notion of barriers is considered, it can be argued that both these models implicitly incorporate perceived barriers. We have already discussed how self-efficacy does this. The constructs of the decision-balance model include instrumental costs to self and to others. These costs, such as taking too much of one's time (cost to self) or interfering with family activities or work (cost to others), are quite similar to the perceived barriers described in the health-behavior determinants literature and those discussed as perceived barriers in other decision-making, expectancy-value models (e.g., HBM, TPB).

The approach to examining barriers in the exercise-related literature is highly similar to that in the other two domains. Studies are often descriptive where barriers become predictors within large data-driven models or are identified as determinants in surveys of involvement in physical activity (cf. Dishman, 1994; Grilo, Brownell, & Stunkard, 1993; Steinhardt & Dishman, 1989; Stephens & Craig, 1990).

Recently, there has been evidence of a clear parallel with health through the implicit and explicit examination of exercise barriers when (a) examining the theories of reasoned action and planned behavior, (b) using self-efficacy theory (e.g., Dzewaltowski, Noble, & Shaw, 1990; Godin et al., 1994; McAuley, 1992; Sallis, Pinski, Grossman, Patterson, & Nader, 1988), and (c) employing the transtheoretical model (Marcus, Rakowski, & Rossi, 1992). In most of these theoretically-based studies, perceived barriers tend to be conceptualized as part of the larger concept of perceived behavioral control. For those studies that were not prospective in design, measures were obtained either at baseline/early program or were obtained at the end of the study through recall procedures. Because of the design and the measurement procedure, respondents' views of perceived barriers must then be generalized across a period of time and personal action. Such a generalized response tends to limit the estimation of a perceived behavioral control that changes as a function of the exercise experience.

For the prospective studies and for studies focussing on stages of behavior change, the perceived control concept is viewed as changeable and assessed as such. Respondents are typically asked about their exercise behavior during a specific time frame (e.g., a week) for a specific duration (e.g., a month, 6 months). For instance, self-efficacy for exercise when confronted with a perceived barrier (e.g., inclement weather or pressures from work) in the next 2 months would be a common item.

For the descriptive studies, respondents are typically asked to provide a generalized response without a focus on a specific time frame. For example, "the major reason when I do not exercise is *(perceived barrier)*" would be a common statement often scaled on a 1 *(strongly disagree)* to 5 *(strongly agree)* Likert-type scale (e.g., Steinhardt & Dishman, 1989).

The Measurement
of Perceived Barriers Methods

A wide variety of methods have been used to assess perceived barriers. Many examples of these methods have been summarized in Table 1. This table illustrates selected study characteristics of investigations drawn from each of the three domains that we sampled to obtain barrier methodologies. Regardless of the domain (i.e., leisure, health, exercise), one of the most common methods is to ask individuals who have previously been engaged in the target behavior what limited or hindered them from completing the behavior. Respondents typically provide barriers via an elicitation procedure or answer questions with respect to an investigator-provided list. Investigators then conduct a frequency analysis to determine the percentage of people most commonly indicating the existence of a specific, perceived barrier. Typically, no information is collected regarding the extent to which a given barrier was perceived to limit behavior (i.e., measure of the strength of the limitation imposed by the barrier) or the frequency with which the respondent experienced the barrier (i.e., number of times he or she experienced the barrier in a given time frame such as a week or month). This approach is characteristic of the descriptive studies in each of the domains we examined where the purpose was to identify barriers. These characteristic approaches were highly similar to the findings reported by Brawley (1991) after a search of the 17,000 citation Sport and Leisure Database where 21 leisure and physical activity barrier studies were identified as having many common barrier types and similar retrospective recall methodologies.

A second descriptive method often associated with both data-driven and theoretically driven studies consists of providing a list of previously elicited or previously reported barriers and asking respondents to respond about the influence of barriers with respect to, for example, (a) degree of agreement about influence or hindrance, (b) ease or difficulty of an action in the presence of the barrier, (c) degree of limitation to following a prescription or action, (d) likelihood that the barrier would hamper or limit, (e) degree of concern about the potential barrier, and (f) degree of agreement the barrier existed.

In the case of this second method, the extent of quantitative response is often used as a predictor of action. This is common in the health and exercise domains. For example, the likelihood of perceived barriers hindering an action is used as one estimate of perceived behavioral control (PBC). PBC is then used as a predictor of intention in the examination of models such as the Theory of Planned Behavior.

A third method, used recently to examine leisure constraints, was that described by Mannell and Zuzanek (1991). They were interested in examining the nature and variability of constraints over time. They used a methodology called experience sampling (ESM, e.g., Larson & Csikszentmihalyi, 1983), which allows the investigator to randomly or systematically sample constraints/reasons inhibiting participation or action within a dynamic situation. Respondents typically carry electronic pagers and are signalled when to respond to key questions regarding their immediate behavior. They carry a small booklet (pocket size) with a series of specific questions to which subjects respond about their immediate interest in their physical activity and also respond about factors/constraints that limit their participation.

This method allows the investigator to use a prospectively oriented methodology to sample constraints and compare them

Table 1
Summary of Perceived Barrier Studies in Three Domains

STUDY	PURPOSE	PERCEIVED BARRIER DEPENDENT MEASURE	STIMULUS ITEMS	SCALE	IS THE M LOWER THAN THE CONCEPTUAL MIDPOINT?*	OUTCOME
EXERCISE						
Johnson, Corrigan, Dubbert, & Gramling (1990)	To identify PBs to exercising and dieting of women who indicated they would like to exercise more, start exercising, or stopped exercising.	Applicability of barriers to self.	11 barriers to exercise and 9 barriers to dieting	Dichotomy: Applicable/Not Applicable	Exercise: Yes* with the exception of lack of time due to school/work for women who wanted to exercise more or who wanted to start excercising. Dieting: Yes*	Lack of time most significant PB to exercise. Willpower and time constraints most significant PBs to dieting.
Sallis, Hovell, Hofstetter, Elder, Faucher, et al. (1990)	To identify reasons for exercise relapse.	Reasons for stopping exercise the most recent time.	15 barriers to exercise	Not stated	Yes*	Injury most common reason for exercise relapse.
Verhoef & Love (1994)	To compare PBs to exercise between women with and without children.	Applicability of barriers to self.	21 PBs to exercise	Dichotomy: Applicable/Not Applicable	Mothers - Yes* with the exception of lack of time due to family obligations. Women without children - Yes*	Mothers perceived more barriers to exercise than women without children.
Godin et al. (1994)	To identify PBs to exercise for 3 groups: General Population (GP), Coronary Heart Disease (CHD), and Pregnant Women (PW).	Probability that the PBs would hamper regular exercise.	5 (GP), 9 (CHD), and 6 (PW) barriers to regular exercise	7-point Likert: (-3) unlikely to (+3) likely	Yes	PBs and their salience differed among the three groups.
Godin & Gionet (1991)	To identify variables predictive of exercise intentions.	Ease/difficulty of exercising despite listed barriers.	Not stated	7-point Likert: (1) easy to (7) difficult	Not determined	PBs, attitude toward physical activity, and exercise history accounted for slightly over 40% of the variance in exercise intention.
LEISURE						
Mannell & Zuzanek (1991)	To identify PBs to participating in physical activity.	Reasons for not wanting to participate in physical activity.	Open ended		Yes*	Lack of time was most frequently reported PB for not participating in physical activity.
Shaw, Bonen, & McCabe (1991)	To examine the relationship between PBs and physical activity participation.	Applicability of barriers to self.	11 barriers to increasing physical activity.	Dichotomy: Applicable/Not Applicable	Yes* with the exception of lack of time due to work.	Overall, PBs were not associated with low levels of physical activity participation. Three most frequently reported PBs were associated with increased participation levels.
Steinhardt & Dishman (1989)	To determine the reliability and validity of self-report scales for outcome expectancy and PBs to regular physical activity in a college sample (Study 1) and in a work site sample (Study 2).	Agreement with listed PBs.	Study 1: 14 PBs to regular physical activity. Study 2: 15 PBs to regular physical activity.	5-point Likert: (1) strongly disagree to (5) strongly agree	Study 1: Yes for 10 of 14 PBs. Study 2: Yes for 9 of 15 PBs.	Study 1: Three factors accounted for 48% of the variance in PBs to physical activity. Study 2: Four factors accounted for 57% of the variance in PBs to physical activity.

(Continued on next page)

Table 1 (cont)
Summary of Perceived Barrier Studies in Three Domains

STUDY	PURPOSE	PERCEIVED BARRIER DEPENDENT MEASURE	STIMULUS ITEMS	SCALE	IS THE M LOWER THAN THE CONCEPTUAL MIDPOINT?*	OUTCOME
HEALTH						
Hoogewerf, Hislop, Morrison, Burns, & Sizto (1990)	To identify PBs to compliance with a fecal occult blood test using hemoccult (HOII).	Reasons for not completing a HOII test.	Open ended		Yes*	PBs to a HOII varied across age groups; however "too busy" was a PB for all age groups.
Glasgow et al. (1989)	To identify PBs to adherence to 4 diabetes regimen behaviors.	Not stated.	Not stated.	7-point Likert: 1 to 7**	Yes	Exercise and diet have strongest barriers to adherence. Medication has fewest.
Zapka, Harris, Stoddard, & Costanza (1991)	To explore the construct validity of survey items including PBs to obtaining a mammogram and a clinical breast examination (CBE).	Degree of concern.	4 PBs to obtaining a mammogram and 3 PBs to obtaining a CBE.	4-point Likert: (1) extremely concerned to (4) not at all concerned	Unclear	Four PBs were related to obtaining a mammogram and three PBs were related to obtaining a CBE.
Champion (1995)	To develop and validate a PBs to mammography scale.	Agreement with PBs to obtaining a mammogram.	5 barriers to obtaining a mammogram	5-point Likert (strongly agree to disagree)**	Unable to determine	Preliminary evidence for the reliability and validity of a PBs to mammography scale.
Stein, Fox, Murata, & Morisky (1992)	To identify the influence of HBM constructs on prior mammography and mammogram intentions.	Not stated.	3 barriers to obtaining a mammogram	Not stated	Unable to determine	PBs to mammography were negatively related to prior mammography and future intentions.

Note. *Less than 50% of participants indicated that the stimulus items were indeed barriers. **Scale anchor values were not provided.

to previously reported perceived constraints/barriers. One obvious advantage of this comparison is the determination of whether the constraint is stable or variable. This contrasts with descriptive approaches that use a list of previously identified perceived barriers to obtain responses. In this methodology, there is an implicit assumption that perceived barriers are stable in an individual's life and will be observed every time the individual is assessed. However, Mannell and Zuzanek (1991) have clearly shown that a number of factors inhibiting participation are variable and temporary in their perceived influence. They argue that perceived influence may vary as a function of social context (e.g., distance and lack of transportation are problems only until car pools are established or bus schedules are obtained). If the survey question asks only for barrier identification and degree of limitation without a time and/or situation frame, individuals could respond that they experienced a barrier and it was limiting to some degree. However, if these individuals have learned to eliminate/manage the barrier and it is no longer a problem, then the data gathered through the investigator-provided list are misleading and probably overestimate the effect of the barrier. The ESM is one approach that can provide

additional information about barriers and thus reduce this type of problem because it provides multiple data samples over time. For example, Mannell and Zuzanek (1991) found that many of the perceived "barriers" typically reported for reducing participation in physical activity, such as tiredness, lack of energy, and lack of interest, were transient conditions and that time of day could be associated with the variation in their influence.

Common Problems

The majority of atheoretical descriptive studies use the survey technique. On these surveys, numerous questions about perceived barriers require recall of their influence and/or incidence. As the time between the occurrence of actions (i.e., health, leisure, exercise behaviors) and the response to the survey questions increases (i.e., 1 week, 1 month, 6 months), an individual's response relies more and more on memory. The accuracy of identifying a true barrier or a perceived barrier that existed when the action took place may be reduced because (a) individuals must retrieve the situation from memory and (b) from the information retrieved, the individual must be able to recognize the constraint and label it as a perceived barrier—

their reason for reducing participation or dropping out (cf. Mannell & Zuzanek, 1991).

This recall may be influenced by psychological processes common to situations where individuals are forced to judge ambiguous stimuli. For example, subjects are asked to recall barriers without reference to a time frame, a situational context, or a specific action. Under such ambiguous conditions, respondents rely on internal frames of reference, such as expectations, attitudes, or stereotypic reasons, to assist their response (cf. Sherif & Sherif, 1969). Although this "assisted" recall enables the generation of a response, the investigator would be in error in interpreting these responses as perceived barriers influencing the respondents' past actions. Leisure investigators such as Jackson (1988) and Mannell and Zuzanek (1991) have referred to such responses as "stereotypic" where previous experiences of reduced or nonparticipation elicit a generalized common excuse as an explanation (e.g., "not enough time", "too many conflicting activities").

Another common problem is the lack of consistency across studies in the principles used to develop scaled barrier indexes. In the cases where indexes have been developed, the purpose of a barrier index/measure is to provide a quantitative response. This value represents an estimate of the magnitude/strength of influence that a series of perceived barriers had on a respondent's participation at some earlier point in time. Although the scale and its endpoints might differ (i.e., because of specificity) between studies according to the domain of inquiry (i.e., leisure, health, exercise), common method principles could be the foundation for a perceived barrier index (e.g., such as the common set of principles/methods used to elicit and develop self-efficacy scales *or* theory of planned behavior scales).

This commonality is not evident, however, when various indexes of barrier "strength" are examined. If one looks at Table 1 and examines the scale endpoints and length of scale, many inconsistencies are evident. For example, some measures examine the *probability* that barriers will hamper an action yet use a scale that the lay respondent does not associate with the concept of probability (e.g., using a -3 to +3 scale vs. the percent chance or likelihood that something will occur). Others ask the respondent about *reasons* for not being involved in a broad class of behaviors (e.g., the major reason I do not exercise.......) without specific reference to a time frame or to a specific type of action even though the sample is from individuals engaged in a *specific* activity (e.g., the major reason I did not jog this past month was..........). Respondents answer this nonspecific question on a 1 (*strongly disagree*) to 5 (*strongly agree*) scale. An important question to raise with this approach to the assessment of barriers is whether investigators are encouraging respondents to (a) give excuses (i.e., attributions or reasons) versus thinking about a barrier; (b) give a generalized or normative agreement when no specific action or time frame is queried; and (c) give an opinion (i.e., agree or disagree) rather than elicit the degree to which the barrier limits, hampers or constrains (e.g., Steinhardt & Dishman, 1989). For other examples of the diversity of scale endpoints used to elicit a quantitative response, see Table 1 and our previous discussion of common methods.

Other problems that are common to the barriers literature are

1. The sheer diversity of types of barriers/constraints (e.g., behavioral, cognitive, environmental) selected for analyses

which makes between-study comparisons difficult even within a given domain of inquiry (e.g., exercise, health, leisure).

2. Differences in the number and content of barrier items.

3. Variation in methods to develop the list of barriers for response (e.g., past literature, investigator assumptions, elicitation from subjects).

4. Assignment of barriers to data-driven (e.g., environmental, socioeconomic) versus theoretically driven dimensions

5. Inconsistency in the way that barriers are conceptualized (e.g., actual versus perceived, antecedents or consequences of barriers versus the intervening barrier, barriers that can be behaviorally validated versus excuses, reasons, or attributions).

6. Variations in the demographics of the samples investigated.

However, as Jackson (1988) argues, not all of these common problems need detract from the literature. For example, descriptive studies that compare different types of behaviors within a domain may help to determine common categories of barriers. Studies of moderator variable influences (e.g., gender, age) on the reporting of constraints may also help to clarify some of the ambiguities among categories of barriers in the literature (e.g., Did the categories apply equally to men and women?), thus advancing descriptive study.

Clearly, the key problems for the perceived barriers literature are linked. The first problem is the conceptualization of the construct and the second, its measurement. The health, leisure, and exercise domains that we have discussed all reflect common problems. The remainder of this chapter focuses exclusively on exercise in order to examine some of its specific barrier-related characteristics.

Exercise Barriers: Strength of Influence

In studying perceived barriers, investigators have tried to provide evidence of their influence by illustrating their relationship to adherence. For example, exercise adherers and nonadherers have been asked about the combined strength of influence of several perceived barriers. The total influence on each group is then compared, and differences between adherers and nonadherers have been observed. Results have indicated that the influence (i.e., strength of limitation) of perceived barriers is greater for those who fail to adhere. However, upon closer inspection, these findings are perplexing.

For example, Steinhardt and Dishman (1989) conducted two different studies, one with a college sample and a second with a work site sample. In the former study, 14 barriers were examined and in the latter, 15 barriers. Respondents were asked if they agreed or disagreed whether each barrier was a major reason that they did not exercise (1 = *strongly disagree* to 5 = *strongly agree*). In the first study, none of the barrier means exceeded the middle value (3) of the scale, and values for all barriers were 3 or less (mean scores for each of 10 of 14 barriers were less than 3). For the second study, only two of the means for the 15 barriers exceeded 3, the middle value of the scale, with nine of the means being less than that value. In other words, respondents *disagreed* that the majority of barriers were their major reason for not exercising. Although it could be argued that a midpoint value of 2.5 is the true numerical middle

Table 2
Percent of Time Obstacles were Anticipated as Interfering with Exercise Attendance

	Onset	*Mid*	*End*
Adherers	3.28	3.08	2.23
	(192)	(132)	(99)
Dropouts	2.49	2.89	3.08
	(56)	(35)	(23)

Note: Scale of percent time obstacles were anticipated to interfere with attendance was 1 = 0%, 4 = 50%, 7 = 100%. Onset program was assessed at 3 weeks; Mid was assessed at 6 weeks; End was assessed at 9 weeks. No significant differences were observed. *n* in parentheses.

of the scale, respondents generally use the scale frame of reference that is provided and make their judgments relative to the adjectival endpoints of a numerical scale. Relative to this reference, investigators must be careful to interpret responses relative to the way subjects read and answered the scale. In so doing, researchers accurately summarize the respondent's appraisal versus the investigator's bias.

Recently, Godin, Desharnais, Valois, and Bradet (1995) used a likelihood scale [(-3) = *unlikely* to (+3) = *likely*] to investigate perceived barriers. They asked individuals whose activity was categorized in stages from sedentary through to very active about the probability that perceived barriers would hamper their exercising regularly three times per week for the next 6 months. The mean likelihood values for individuals classified within each stage of exercise was negative and less than the scale midpoint, indicating that the barriers were either neutral or unlikely agents in hampering regular exercise. This was also the case when Godin et al. (1994) examined differences in perceived barriers between respondents high and low in their intentions to exercise in three different samples (i.e., general population, individuals with coronary heart disease, and pregnant women).

Perceived barriers were identified via an elicitation procedure. Those barriers most frequently identified within each sample were used by respondents where they considered the likelihood that each of these barriers would hamper them from exercising regularly. Again the -3 *unlikely* to +3 *likely* scale was used. Individual scores for each barrier for each sample were reported. Although intention-related barrier differences were detected for the general population and the CHD samples, none was observed for pregnant women. What is more interesting, however, is that the mean scores for the vast majority of perceived barriers for low to moderate intenders *were negative*. Thus, the scores for most barriers fell on the "unlikely" side of the scale, suggesting that they did not hamper the low intenders' participation in regular, free-time physical activity.

Several questions arise from the results of these studies and others like them. Are individuals skewing their responses and somehow reflecting an optimistic bias? Are low-intention respondents suggesting there may be some influence of barriers, but not a strong one? Is there some aspect of the method and measurement that is inhibiting the respondent's admission that salient barriers hamper participation? Any one or a combination of these explanations seems possible.

In our own research on this topic, we have tried other methods and designs. Prospective studies with experienced exercisers should offer the opportunity to detect the influence of barriers that are based on actual immediate experience as opposed to the typical practice of asking respondents to recall experiences of the past. For example, Brawley and Horne (as reported in Brawley & Rodgers, 1993) conducted a prospective study of 250 experienced, intermediate-level exercisers, aged 20 to 65 years, who were exercising in community-based fitness programs of 3-month duration. Classes were offered at scheduled intervals three times weekly. As part of a larger study that examined attitude-behavior relationships, a list of the most common obstacles to exercise was developed by an elicitation procedure. Each obstacle was scaled as to the percent of time respondents forecast that it would interfere with attending their exercise classes (where 1 = 0%, 4 = 50%, and 7 = 100%). Assessments occurred at 3, 6, and 9 weeks. The relative influence of perceived obstacles can be observed in Table 2. There was no significant difference between exercise adherers and dropouts at any of the assessment points with respect to the mean amount of time they believed perceived obstacles would hinder their next 3 weeks of attendance. Both adherers and dropouts forecast that

Table 3
Measures of Barriers to Exercise for the Elderly

	Early Program	*Later Program*
	FREQUENCY	
Active	16.15*	14.61
	(14.54)	(17.65)
Nonactive	20.99*	21.22
	(16.16)	(13.63)
	EXTENT	
Active	2.18	2.06
	(.84)	(1.04)
Nonactive	2.63	2.57
	(.94)	(.92)
	WEIGHTED	
Active	38.29*	46.74
	(49.57)	(89.16)
Nonactive	72.92*	61.82
	(75.92)	(52.82)

Note: Frequency = From 0 to 100 % of the time, the barrier affected participation. Extent was where 1 = not all limiting to 7 = completely. Weighted barriers reflect the multiplicative combination of (frequency x extent). Weighted range = 0 to 700.
* *p*<.05 early program effect only

perceived obstacles would interfere with attendance between 30 and 40% of the time. Although both adherers and dropouts were experienced exercisers and thus had some basis for their forecasts about the influence of barriers, neither group anticipated a strong impact on their attendance and there was no apparent relationship to adherence.

Robinson and Brawley (as reported in Brawley, 1991) conducted a prospective study concerning the attitude-physical activity relationships of the elderly aged 55-80 years, who were engaged in regular, organized physical activity programs of 10-week duration. As part of the study, factors that the active elderly ($n = 60$) forecast as limiting or preventing their participation were explored. The comparison group comprised inactive elderly ($n = 42$). Factors such as muscle/joint pain, lack of motivation, heart/circulation problems, injuries, lack of transportation, and having no participant friends were examples of perceived barriers. These barriers were scaled first as to the strength of their limitation (*not at all* = 1 to *completely* = 7) and second as to what percent of the time a given barrier would limit participation. Some barriers may be very limiting but occur very infrequently, whereas others may not be a strong limitation, but occur quite often. Thus, a measure weighted by the influence of both limitation and frequency may be more reflective of how perceived barriers actually influence activity.

As can be observed in Table 3, scores for the strength of limitation, the frequency of limitation, and the weighted measure were low for both the active and the nonactive controls at both onset and midprogram. When the weighted barrier effects were examined, actives had lower weighted scores than did nonactives but this effect was only evident at the onset of programs.

Weighted measures may attenuate an overestimation bias stemming from the use of a unidimensional barriers measure and, when coupled with specific questions about immediate future behavior, reflect a more accurate estimate (vs. post hoc recall) of the influence of perceived barriers. Nevertheless, as was the case in other studies, we observed that perceived barriers were *not* considered to be strongly influential on the exercise and physical activity behavior of the elderly and did not discriminate active from nonactive groups. If barriers do not have a strongly reported impact in descriptive studies, does this have any implication for theoretically driven studies?

Perceived Barriers and Self-Efficacy

DuCharme and Brawley (1995) recently used self-efficacy theory to examine (among several questions) the indirect influence of barriers to exercise. When barriers are considered as obstacles to overcome, self-efficacy to perform a behavior in the face of those barriers becomes an important predictor of future behavior (cf. Bandura, 1995). In their prospective investigation, DuCharme and Brawley questioned whether novice exercisers (adult women) had sufficient experience with various barriers to enable the development of skills to overcome these challenges. A measure of barrier efficacy among novice exercisers might be an under-or overestimate of confidence in dealing with barriers in order to exercise. Are such potentially biased efficacy judgments capable of predicting exercise behavior? This question seems particularly important in studying novice exercisers, given Bandura's (1986) argument that cognitive control is more influential

when *acquiring* skills and abilities. To examine this question, barriers salient to this novice sample of women were elicited and used to develop efficacy items concerning an individual's ability to attend self-planned exercise sessions when confronted with each of the barriers (i.e., a fairly common measure in exercise research; cf. McAuley & Mihalko, this volume). A variation specific to this study, however, was that the efficacy measure only included those barriers that the individual anticipated encountering more than one time per week (i.e., on the basis of their experience with their daily schedules). To obtain this efficacy measure, each subject anticipated the frequency of encountering the salient barriers during the next month (i.e., target time interval for behavior) and estimated their efficacy for overcoming each barrier. An index of barrier efficacy was then computed that excluded infrequently experienced barriers (e.g., exclusion of childcare barrier for women without children). In addition, other measures of efficacy concerning strategies/scheduling to enable attendance were obtained. These measures were used to predict validated attendance.

Whereas efficacy for daily and weekly strategies/scheduling predicted attendance for the second 2 months of the program, no effects were observed for barrier efficacy. The investigators also tested whether past behavior would be a better predictor of future behavior than would both measures of efficacy. Only scheduling efficacy added significant, unique variance to the prediction of attendance independent of that accounted for by past behavior. In addition, barrier efficacy scores did not change significantly over time whereas a scheduling/strategy efficacy change was observed that paralleled the significant change in attendance. Apparently, exercisers adjusted their efficacy expectations on the basis of their experience at scheduling their exercise but did not adjust these expectations when they concerned the individual's trying to exercise when she felt tired, was pressed for time, or had family commitments. Perhaps the lack of change was due to lack of experience with obstacles.

The question of whether efficacy to overcome barriers to exercise is a reasonable predictor of behavior cannot be answered by a single study, but the previous study does raise a question about the type of efficacy being measured. A second study by Poag-DuCharme and Brawley (1993) also raised questions about the contribution of barriers efficacy to the prediction of attendance. Experienced exercisers ($n = 207$) were prospectively studied as they engaged in 12-week, structured exercise programs. A protocol similar to that described in the study of novices just discussed (DuCharme & Brawley, 1995) was used to test social cognitive predictors of attendance. Barriers efficacy did not predict attendance, but strategies/scheduling efficacy was an effective predictor. In this study, however, the authors reasoned that barriers efficacy might predict the attendance of a subsample of adherers who had experienced a frequently reported and limiting barrier. The subsample consisted of 97 mothers who reported day care as a frequent and limiting exercise barrier and, because they adhered, also had experience overcoming these barriers. Efficacy for exercising in the face of the day care obstacle should have developed due to successful mastery of the problem. Interestingly, barrier efficacy did *not* predict attendance although the barrier content of the measure was highly salient to exercising mothers. Instead, efficacy for scheduling/strategies accounted for a significant proportion of the unique variance in attendance in the second 6 weeks of the exercise programs.

Again, this study suggests that the influence of perceived barriers on social cognitions about exercise must be questioned. Specifically, we must ask whether the notion of perceived barriers, when coupled with self-efficacy, truly measures a social cognition based upon actual mastery experiences. At a more basic level, we must also ask if we currently have a clear conceptualization of perceived barriers. This is not to say that an individual cannot be efficacious about perceived (vs. actual) barriers and thus be motivated to act. However, we wonder about the reliable motivational influence of such efficacy estimates when individuals confront real barriers. A strategy that at least allows individuals the opportunity to experience barriers when they are initiating or restarting their exercise patterns is one used by McAuley and his colleagues (cf. McAuley & Mihalko, this volume). Their protocol for the administration of efficacy measures involves allowing a participation time period to elapse (i.e., specific to sample, design, and research question considerations) so that respondents might have direct experience with any of the skills and abilities required to participate regularly—including confronting and overcoming (or not) participation barriers. This could help to reduce some of the bias in barriers efficacy measures when respondents do not have various forms of experience in overcoming obstacles at the outset of their participation. The protocol we have recommended for validating the frequency and extent of limitation of a barrier should help to validate this direct experience and differentiate efficacy for overcoming an experienced obstacle from efficacy for overcoming a barrier stated as an excuse or reason for limited participation.

Perceived Barriers as Excuses and Reasons

Another conceptual question is whether perceived barriers might be conceptualized more accurately as attributions or excuses. Indeed, in their investigation of exercise adherence and its relationship to attributions and affect, McAuley, Poag, Gleason, and Wraith (1990) suggested that barriers may be attributed excuses rather than real obstacles. It should be recognized that conceptually, reasons have been viewed as a special case of excuses. Reasons are typically justifications that appear to be at least logical and often evidence based. For the purposes of the present discussion, it is important that the reader understand that there are psychological differences between "brands" of excuses (e.g., reasons, blaming others, minimizing the impact of transgression) but we will use excuses/reasons together, a use that serves to make our contrast with actual obstacles/barriers. The reader is referred to the excellent discussion about the conceptualization and function of excuses by Snyder, Higgins, and Stucky (1983) for further detail.

One clue as to whether investigators actually encourage subjects to provide reasons or attributions for inconsistent involvement or dropout from exercise is found in their methodology. As discussed earlier in the chapter, researchers ask individuals to provide retrospective views of why they stopped adhering or why they are completely inactive. As pointed out by Meichenbaum and Fong (1993), this open-ended task gives in-

dividuals the opportunity to relate reasons and other excuses for their behavior. Similarly, if we ask experienced exercisers who are somewhat inconsistent in their adherence to forecast barriers, they may provide us with recalled reasons or excuses. Why do individuals provide reasons or excuses for inactivity or poor adherence instead of real causes/barriers?

Meichenbaum and Fong (1993) argue that several psychological functions may be served when individuals provide reasons for nonadherence. These functions have been discussed in other literatures concerning attribution theory, coping with stress, and self-presentation. Essentially, the provision of reasons and/or excuses allows us to (a) control distressing feelings (e.g., depression, anxiety), (b) protect our view of ourselves and our world (e.g., self-esteem protection or maintenance), and (c) influence others in personal interactions (e.g., impression management). The reader is also referred to discussions of attributional perspectives of excuses (eg., Snyder, 1989; Weiner, Amirkhan, Folkes, & Verette, 1987; Weiner, Figueroa-Munoz, & Kakihara, 1991).

For example, consider "lack of time," one of the most commonly cited barriers for exercise nonparticipation. This response may represent a legitimate lack of time for an individual who desires to exercise (i.e., a barrier), an admitted unwillingness to sacrifice time spent doing something else (relaxing or participating in other leisure activities) in order to exercise (i.e., a reason; Jackson, 1988), or a socially acceptable excuse that masks the true reason for nonparticipation ("I'm too lazy," "I don't want to make the effort") and allows the individual's private and social esteem to be upheld. We contend that when "lack of time" is used as an *excuse* for not exercising, the individual may have little or no intention or desire to exercise. Because excuses may intimate that one does indeed have an intention to exercise, they may be misconstrued as perceived barriers. Conversely, when an individual actually wants or intends to exercise, but is prevented by time constraints (i.e., poor time- management skills and corresponding low self-efficacy for these skills), "lack of time" becomes a barrier to participation.

Kendzierski and Johnson (1993) have developed the Exercise Thoughts Questionnaire (ETQ), an instrument that assesses the "frequency with which individuals have thoughts involving reasons or excuses for not exercising at the present time" (p. 207). Several of the ETQ's 25 items are similar to items typically found on perceived barrier scales (e.g., "I'm too busy," "I'm too tired to exercise," "I'm just not motivated enough to exercise"). We administered the ETQ to a sample of 80 members of a university exercise program. Overall, the most experienced exercisers had fewer thoughts about reasons/excuses for not exercising than did beginner exercisers (Martin, Paskevich, & Brawley, 1995). For both groups, the most common reasons/excuses for considering whether or not to exercise over the previous week were lack of time and fatigue—probably the two most cited constraints in the perceived barrier literature. However, for these people, thoughts about time constraints and fatigue *did not prevent them from actually participating* in their aerobics classes that week. Nonetheless, in a barrier study, these people may have indicated such factors as constraints to their participation.

Like money, time and energy may be things of which we can never have enough. People may tend to identify such factors as limits to their participation, regardless of their actual level of participation and their availability of time and energy. This point highlights the importance of determining an individual's intentions to exercise (i.e., frequency intensity, time) and the frequency with which an impediment actually prevents exercise, before labeling that impediment as a barrier and targeting it for intervention. The distinction between real barriers, reasons, and excuses appears to be important for the measurement of actual impediments to participation for those who desire to be more active, and for the prediction of participation.

The Constructive Narrative Perspective

In the preceding section, it was argued that individuals' communicated reasons for not exercising do not necessarily represent legitimate barriers to physical activity. However, it should not be assumed that individuals are deliberately deceitful in their attempts to explain their own behavior. Although researchers may be able to recognize when a reason or excuse does not accurately reflect the reality of a situation, individuals frequently perceive their reasons and excuses to be legitimate. These perceptions are often rooted in deeply entrenched belief systems or are the consequence of faulty or irrational reasoning (e.g., the man with no history of cardiac arrhythmia who avoids exercising because he is afraid of having a heart attack). Meichenbaum and Fong (1993) have proposed that examination of these reasons, excuses, and rationalizations may lead to a greater understanding of the mechanisms that underlie and maintain nonadherence to health behaviors. Within the framework of a constructive narrative perspective, they have developed a strategy for categorizing and studying reasons for nonadherence. This approach may be useful for the measurement and evaluation of perceived barriers to exercise.

The constructive narrative perspective acknowledges that individuals actively construct their personal realities and create their own representational models of the world (Meichenbaum & Fong, 1993). Narrative psychology is the study of the stories we tell about ourselves and about our behavior to others, as well as to ourselves (cf. Bruner 1986, 1990; Howard, 1989, 1991). Meichenbaum and Fong (1993) have developed a three-level coding system for classifying the reasons that individuals offer for their noncompliant health behaviors. Level I reasons are *evidence-based* reasons whereby individuals question the validity of the theory or evidence relating to health-related advice. Often, however, when individuals try to apply logical reasoning, their reasoning is flawed (see Kahneman, Slovic, & Tversky, 1982). For example, flawed Level I reasons for not exercising may be "I know a woman who exercised four times a week and she still died young," or "I know plenty of healthy people who never exercise."

The Level II category consists of *self-relevant reasons* that describe the individual's perceived costs and benefits of compliance with the health-related advice. Level II reasons are generally factors that explain why the individual cannot change the behavior, such as perceived barriers, concerns about negative consequences, or low self-efficacy for implementing the recommended treatment regimen. Examples of Level II reasons for not exercising are "Exercise is too painful," "If I don't join a gym then I can save the money for a vacation," or "I don't have time."

Finally, Level III reasons consist of *affective-schema related* reasons that reflect deeply rooted, often highly affectively charged, schema-related beliefs and feelings that influence nonadherence decisions. In Meichenbaum and Fong's (1993) classification, these reasons include (a) expressions of dysphoric feelings (e.g., depression, fear), (b) negative models of the world and the self as victim (e.g., helplessness, fatalism—"We are all going to die anyway"), (c) denial and avoidance (e.g., "I'm not at risk"), and (d) arguments of free will (e.g., "No doctor is going to tell me how I should spend my free time"). Commensurate with cognitive-behavioral theorists' views of these cognitive-affective schemas (Mahoney, 1974), beliefs associated with such schemata are strongly held, highly resistant to change, and selectively organize and guide the narratives we construct and the reasons we offer for our actions. Such beliefs preclude thoughtful assessments of relevant evidence (e.g., exercise benefits), strategies (e.g., how to plan for or do exercise), or the support offered by others (e.g., spousal support).

Meichenbaum and Fong (1993) have suggested that an assessment of reasons for noncompliance provides information for predicting relapse and for formulating individually tailored interventions. Intervention strategies could be geared towards directly addressing the true nature of the nonadherence. For example, what value are educational programs designed to teach people the benefits of exercise (a Level I target for intervention), or strategies for starting and maintaining an exercise program (a Level II target), if the real reason for nonadherence stems from emotionally charged (Level III) reasons? Interventions that target specific belief processes and rationalizations are probably more effective than nonspecific generic, broad-based programs.

Level I, II, and III type reasons may be differentially related to exercise-related variables such as intentions, attitudes, and beliefs. Categorization of reasons may delineate underlying belief systems that moderate these social-cognitive variables, thus aiding in the prediction of exercise behavior and relapse.

An interesting upshot of applying the constructive narrative perspective to understand barriers to exercise is that the importance of cognition becomes clearly relevant to the conceptualization and study of perceived barriers. That is, there appears to be an assumption in some aspects of the literature that the barriers-physical activity relationship is a simple case of stimulus-response (barriers —> no activity; removal of barriers —> increased activity). Such an assumption ignores the psychology of the individuals and their active, cognitive role in motivating themselves to generate reasons for not exercising, in being concerned about self-presentation, and in developing their personal belief systems and cognitive schemata. Perhaps researchers should invest more time in understanding the social-cognitive processes related to perceiving and generating barriers/reasons/excuses for not exercising, rather than simply identifying the impediments.

Implications for Measuring and Understanding Perceived Barriers

There are several implications for measurement that can be suggested after considering the foregoing discussions about perceived barriers. These implications are associated with (a) the conceptual views of barriers, (b) the focus of the research question, and (c) eventual links to intervention research or application.

Detecting Barriers

As discussed earlier, a conceptual difference exists between a barrier and an excuse/reason. Jackson (1988) provided the argument that with absence of interest in an activity, it is difficult to argue that a person is constrained by a barrier. Thus, in the motivated samples studied by exercise researchers, it is important that the design of a study provide the opportunity to detect barriers. We believe the designs most likely to facilitate the detection of barriers will be prospective. In a prospective design, the participant is obviously not influenced by the recall of events as is the case with a retrospective design. Thus, participants who have had previous experience can be asked to forecast barriers. However, this alone is not sufficient. With this forecast, the respondent should be asked the frequency with which the anticipated barrier will occur and the degree to which it is thought to pose a limitation. Thus, investigators can determine the extent to which a barrier poses a problem that needs to be solved (e.g., ranging from high-frequency barrier but minimal limitation, thus no problem *to* low-frequency barrier but severe limitation, thus infrequent problem).

With the use of a prospective design, investigators can then use a validation technique called third-party validation. For example, when exercise attendance is the dependent measure, the barrier stated as responsible for the decline in a given week's attendance could be validated through an exercise partner, a family member, or an exercise leader. The barrier could then be matched with or added to the list of potential barriers in order to verify the barrier's influence/frequency for the duration of the study. Obviously, there are some practical difficulties with third-party validation that would need to be solved (e.g., agreement of use by the respondent and the third party). It may also be argued that this validation is impractical for every participant, but in a prospective study, random versus weekly, third-party validation may be more practical (i.e., fewer validation assessments required of the subject and the third party, thus less response burden for both). Randomization of validity assessments might occur every 3 weeks (vs. every week) according to a preset schedule. Random assignment of weeks to subjects allows for an unbiased third-party estimate of the occurrence of a subject-reported barrier. Thus, over the duration of the investigation, the true frequency of a barrier and its type could be obtained without a bias toward any time phase in the prospective study. Each subject and third party would follow the randomized schedule particular to their dyad. The third party would necessarily be a friend, co-worker, or family member who observed or was knowledgeable about the presence/absence of a barrier to exercise in a targeted week.

Other techniques that could be used to more accurately identify and examine barriers would be a weekly recall of barriers that stop or make participation difficult. In this approach, there is less chance of a recall bias being measured, and validation of the obstacle close to its occurrence is possible.

If the research question also concerned the reliability of the encounter and struggle that a person has with a barrier, the experience sampling method (ESM) mentioned earlier in the chapter could be useful. It allows the investigator to randomly sample days/weeks of participation and avoid selection and recall biases. The investigator can then examine the consistency or inconsistency with which barriers impact on a given individual and whether there is some commonality among respondents within a sample.

Once barriers are detected as reliable influences on exercise-related behavior, they can be examined for their moderating effects on behavior. For example, different classes of barriers (e.g., environmental versus interpersonal) could be examined for their differential effects on adherers and dropouts or for the relative impact they have on adherence variability (e.g., high frequency/minor limitation and low frequency/great limitation on rate of exercise adherence).

Detecting Excuses/Reasons

Using the earlier chapter discussion as a foundation for understanding the excuse/reasons/attributions for nonadherence to exercise (or their struggle with adherence), we advocate (a) use of the constructive narrative approach (CNA), (b) use of already developed instruments (e.g., Kendzierski & Johnson's ETQ, 1993: reasons/excuses for not exercising), and (c) use of existing theories of attribution (e.g., Weiner et al., 1991) in future research on perceived barriers.

Within the CNA, Meichenbaum and Fong's (1993) three-level coding system for classifying reasons for nonadherence to healthy behavior may prove to be a useful means of (a) classifying reasons/excuses and (b) identifying groups amenable to change on the basis of their beliefs. To illustrate, the three authors of this chapter independently coded the various excuses/reasons/barriers from the studies we reviewed to determine the most common level reported and the degree of intercoder agreement. We found that the vast majority of published "barriers" could be classified as self-relevant or Level II reasons for not carrying out health, leisure, and exercise actions (i.e., 85-90% agreement on classification). Although our post hoc classification is obviously not the way in which Meichenbaum and Fong's coding of reasons would normally be conducted, it does give a perspective on some of the published literature. More specifically, because the exercise-related research tends to be concerned with people struggling with adherence to a health behavior—that is, already motivated people—these individuals may offer primarily self-relevant Level II reasons to account for nonadherence and thus to protect their self-esteem.

An additional consideration for the prevalence of Level II reasons to explain problems with exercise adherence is that exercising is a complex behavior, having more potential for difficulties than other health behaviors, such as making a diagnostic appointment, taking medication, or wearing seatbelts. As well, when exercise is coupled with other lifestyle-change behaviors in order to manage complex health problems (e.g., obesity/weight control, diabetes, cardiac rehabilitation), the probability for making excuses also increases compared to simpler behaviors. Exercise alone has this higher probability for excuse making if the individual views exercise as a behavior requiring lengthy periods of time, coordination, effort, repeated weekly occurrences that require time management, *and* is tied to a self-relevant health outcome (e.g., reduced CHD risk) or self-presentational health outcome (e.g., weight loss).

Of what use is this narrative coding system to the study of exercise barriers? First, it may help uncover different levels of reasons that characterize adaptive (e.g., self-esteem protection) and maladaptive (i.e., increasing health risk) approaches to justifying nonadherence. Second, this system could be used to examine different groups of people, such as (a) individuals who are chronically inactive, (b) postcardiac patients who refuse to exercise or lose weight, or (c) struggling exercisers and adherent exercisers, in order to see if their reasons differ (i.e., Levels I, II, or III). If we currently can identify only Level II reasons in exercise research, it may suggest that we are sampling too narrowly. If clear differences between groups emerge, it may give intervention researchers clues as to how to target efforts toward change. For example, Meichenbaum and Fong (1993) argue that affectively laden Level III reasons, which are characterized by considerable distortions of reality, will be most resistant to persuasion to change.

Some may argue that investigations have already shown similarities in barriers (reasons?) between groups of exercisers and nonexercisers. However, we believe that previous observations of barriers/reasons have been confounded by moderating factors, such as (a) risk associated with exercise or with the reason for exercise (thereby eliciting increased excuses), (b) number of previous exercise attempts and failures (thereby provoking often used excuses), (c) complexity of exercise as an independent leisure activity or as part of a complex lifestyle-change package advocated for reduced disease risk (thereby increasing the probability for lapses and increased excuse making), and (d) demand characteristics/biases of barriers assessment. Use of the CNA with the Levels-of-Reasons coding system may help to clarify (given appropriate sampling and design) whether groups vary in their reasons for noninvolvement and nonadherence to exercise by offering respondents opportunity to expand upon their explanations—a feature not offered by current response methods—thus providing more data to aid with identification of reasons (i.e., to Levels).

Use of Kendzierski and Johnson's (1993) Exercise Thoughts Questionnaire (ETQ) may also prove to be useful in the study of excuses/reasons for not exercising; however, more research is required. The interesting feature of this scale is that it focuses on the frequency of thoughts that may influence exercise intentions. It may be hypothesized that individuals who express their reasons/excuses more frequently may be less motivated to exercise; that is, they *intend* to exercise less, although our initial data with motivated exercisers (those self-selected to enroll in programs) do not support reduced participation. Nonetheless, the ETQ focuses the researcher on tying together *the processes* involved in social-cognitive decision making with intentions and behavior, a needed research direction if we are to understand barriers/reasons from more than a descriptive perspective.

Finally, consideration of the psychological functions served by making excuses/giving reasons suggests that we must understand how they contribute to beliefs about, for example, competence in managing exercise, enjoyment of exercise, desirability of achieving disease prevention (i.e., must do activity) versus participating for health promotion (i.e., want to do activity). Measurement from an attributional perspective may pro-

vide insight into motives for giving reasons. For example, if such motives are not consistent with future intentions to exercise (i.e., protect self-esteem versus taking responsibility for nonadherence), measuring the casual dimensionality of attributions (i.e., focus, stability, control) may reflect the direction of the beliefs behind motives (e.g., adaptive, "I can do this" beliefs versus maladaptive, guilt-ridden "I can't" beliefs). Understanding the functions (i.e., self-protective, self-presentation) served by beliefs about nonadherence may aid the attempt to develop accurate measures (i.e., valid in what is being measured) and appropriate interventions (e.g., a change in beliefs versus an environmental intervention).

In conclusion, it is clear that many challenges lie ahead for the conceptualization and measurement of barriers to exercise adherence and physical activity participation. These challenges will not be remedied by solutions as simple as the development of a generic "gold standard" measure. Given the active psychological involvement of participants in making sense of their own nonadherence, efforts must be made to understand the psychology of perceived barriers if we expect to make advances toward facilitating greater involvement in physical activity. In writing this chapter, the complexity of these challenges has become clear to the authors. We hope this complexity stimulates an interest among investigators that spurs them toward alternative ways of investigating and measuring perceived barriers.

References

Ajzen, I. (1985). From intentions to actions: A theory of planned behavior. In J. Kuhl & J. Beckmann (Eds.), *Action control: From cognition to behavior* (pp. 11-40). Berlin: Springer-Verlag.

Ajzen, I. (1991). The theory of planned behavior. *Organizational Behavior and Human Decision Processes, 50*, 179-211.

Bandura, A. (1977). Self-efficacy: Toward a unifying theory of behavioral change. *Psychological Review, 84*, 191-215.

Bandura, A. (1986). *Social foundations of thought and action.* New York: Prentice-Hall.

Bandura, A. (1995, March). *Moving into forward gear in health promotion and disease prevention.* Keynote address presented at the Annual Meeting of the Society of Behavioral Medicine, San Diego.

Bouchard, C., Shephard, R.J., & Stephens, T. (Eds.) (1994). *Physical activity, fitness and health.* Champaign, Illinois: Human Kinetics Publishers.

Brawley, L.R. (1991, October). *The measurement of barriers to exercise: Problems and a possible solution.* Paper presented at the annual meeting of the Association for the Advancement of Applied Sport Psychology, Savannah, GA.

Brawley, L.R., & Rodgers, W.M. (1993). Social psychological aspects of fitness promotion. In P. Seraganian (Ed.), *Exercise psychology: The influence of physical exercise on psychological processes* (pp. 254-298). New York: Wiley.

Bruner, J.S. (1986). *Actual minds: Possible worlds.* Cambridge: Harvard University Press

Bruner, J.S. (1990). *Acts of meaning.* Cambridge: Harvard University Press.

Champion, V. (1995). Development of a benefits and barriers scale for mammography utilization. *Cancer Nursing, 18*, 53-59.

Crawford, D.W., & Godbey, G. (1987). Reconceptualizing barriers to family leisure. *Leisure Sciences, 9*, 119-127.

DeVellis, R.F., Alfierei, W.S., & Ahluwalia, I.B. (1995). The importance of careful measurement in health education research and practice. *Health Education Research, 10*, i-vi.

Dishman, R.K. (Ed.) (1988). *Exercise adherence: It's impact on public health.* Champaign, IL: Human Kinetics.

Dishman, R.K. (Ed.) (1994). *Advances in exercise adherence.* Champaign, Illinois: Human Kinetics.

Ducharme, K.A., & Brawley, L.R. (1995). Predicting the intentions and behavior of exercise initiates using two forms of self-efficacy. *Journal of Behavioral Medicine, 18,* 479-497.

Dzewaltowski, D.A., Noble, J.M., & Shaw, J.M. (1990). Physical activity participation: Social cognitive theory versus the theory of reasoned action and planned behavior. *Journal of Sport and Exercise Psychology, 12,* 388-405.

Glasgow, R.E., Toobert, D.J., Riddle, M., Donnelly, J., Mitchell, D.L., & Calder, D. (1989). Diabetes-specific social learning variables and self-care behaviors among persons with type II diabetes. *Health Psychology, 8,* 285-303.

Godin, G., Desharnais, R., Valois, P., Lepage, L., Jobin, J., & Bradet, R. (1994). Differences in perceived barriers to exercise between high and low intenders: Observations among different populations. *American Journal of Health Promotion, 8,* 279-285.

Godin, G., Desharnais, R., Valois, P., and Bradet, R. (1995). Combining behavioral and motivational dimensions to identify and characterize the stages in the process of adherence to exercise. *Psychology and Health, 10,* 333-344.

Godin, G., & Gionet, N.J. (1991). Determinants of an intention to exercise of an electric power commission's employees. *Ergonomics, 34,* 1221-1230.

Grilo, C.M., Brownell, K.D., & Stunkard, A.J. (1993). The metabolic and physiological importance of exercise in weight control. In A.J. Stunkard & T. Wadden (Eds.), *Obesity: Theory and therapy* (2nd ed.) (pp. 253-273). New York: Raven Press.

Hoogewerf, P.E., Hislop, T.G., Morrison, B.J., Burns, S.D., & Sizto, R. (1990). Health belief and compliance with screening for fecal occult blood. *Social Science and Medicine, 30,* 721- 726.

Howard, G.S. (1989). *A tale of two stories: Excursions into a narrative approach to psychology.* Notre Dame, IN: Academic Publications.

Howard, G.S. (1991). Culture tales: A narrative approach to thinking, cross cultural psychology and psychotherapy. *American Psychologist, 46,* 187-197.

Jackson, E.L. (1988). Leisure constraints: A survey of past research. *Leisure Sciences, 10,* 203-215.

Janis, I.L., & Mann, L. (1977). *Decision making: A psychological analysis of conflict, choice, and commitment.* New York: Collier Macmillan.

Janz, N.K., & Becker, M.H. (1984). The health belief model: A decade later. *Health Education Quarterly, 11,* 1-47.

Johnson, C.A., Corrigan, S.A., Dubbert, P.M., & Gramling, S.E. (1990). Perceived barriers to exercise and weight control practices in community women. *Women & Health, 16,* 177-191.

Kahneman, D., Slovic, P., & Tversky, A. (Eds.). (1982). *Judgment under uncertainty: Heuristics and biases.* Cambridge, England: Cambridge University Press.

Kendzierski, D., & Johnson, W. (1993). Excuses, excuses, excuses: A cognitive behavioral approach to exercise implementation. *Journal of Sport and Exercise Psychology, 15,* 207-219.

Larson, R., & Csikszentmihalyi, M. (1983). The experience sampling method. In H.T. Reis (Ed.), *Naturalistic approaches to studying social interaction* (pp. 41-56). San Francisco: Jossey- Bass.

Mahoney, M. (1994). *Cognition and behavior modification.* Cambridge, MA: Ballinger

Mannell, R.C., & Zuzanek, J. (1991). The nature and variability of leisure constraints in daily life: The case of the physically active leisure of older adults. *Leisure Sciences, 13,* 337-351.

Marcus, B.H., Rakowski, W., & Rossi, J.T. (1992). Assessing motivational readiness and decision-making for exercise. *Health Psychol-ogy, 11,* 257-261.

Martin, K.A., Paskevich, D.M., & Brawley, L.R. (1995, October). *Cognitive self-schemata and exercise-related thoughts, intentions, and behaviors.* Paper presented at the meeting of the Canadian Society for Psychomotor Learning and Sport Psychology, Vancouver, B.C.

McAuley, E. (1992). The role of efficacy cognitions in the prediction of exercise behavior in middle aged adults. *Journal of Behavioral Medicine, 15,* 65-88.

McAuley, E. (1994). Physical activity and psychosocial outcomes. In C.B. Bouchard, R.J. Shephard, & T. Stephens (Eds.), *Physical activity, fitness, and health* (pp. 551-568). Champaign, IL: Human Kinetics.

McAuley, E., Poag, K., Gleason, A., & Wraith, S. (1990). Attrition from exercise programs: Attributional and affective perspectives. *Journal of Social Behavior and Personality, 5,* 591-602.

Meichenbaum, D., & Fong, G.T. (1993). How individuals control their own minds: A constructive narrative perspective. In D.M. Wegner & J. W. Pennabaker (Eds.). *Handbook of mental control* (pp. 473-490). Englewood Cliffs, NJ: Prentice-Hall.

Poag-DuCharme, K.A., & Brawley, L.R. (1993). Self-efficacy theory: Use in the prediction of exercise behavior in the community setting. *Journal of Applied Sport Psychology, 5,* 178-194.

Prochaska, J.O., & Marcus, B.H. (1994). The transtheoretical model: Applications to exercise. In R. K. Dishman (Ed.), *Advances in exercise adherence* (pp. 161-180). Champaign, IL: Human Kinetics.

Prochaska, J.O., Velicer, W.F., Rossi, J.S., Goldstein, M.G., Marcus, B.H., Rakowski, W., Fiore, C., Harlow, L.L., Redding, L.A., Rosenbloom, D., & Rossi, S.R. (1994). Stages of change and decisional balance for twelve problem health behaviors. *Health Psychology, 13,* 39-46.

Rosenstock, I.M. (1974). The health belief model and preventive health behaivor. *Health Education Monographs, 2,* 354-386.

Sallis, J.F., Hovell, M.F., Hofstetter, C.R., Elder, J.P., Faucher, P., Spry, V.M., Barrington, E., & Hackley, M. (1990). Lifetime history of relapse from exercise. *Addictive Behaviors, 15,* 573- 579.

Sallis, J.F., Hovell, M.F., Hofstetter, C.R., Faucher, P., Elder, J.P., Blanchard, J., Casperson, C.J., Powell, K.E., & Christenson, G.H. (1989). A multivariate study of determinants of vigorous exercise in a community sample. *Preventive Medicine, 18,* 20-34.

Sallis, J. F., Pinski, R.B., Grossman, P.M., Patterson, T.L., & Nader, P.R. (1988). The development of self-efficacy scales for health-related diet and exercise behaviors. *Health Education Research, 3,* 283-292.

Shaw, S.M., Bonen, A., & McCabe, J.F. (1991). Do more constraints mean less leisure? Examining the relationship between constraints and participation. *Journal of Leisure Research, 23,* 286-300.

Sherif, M., & Sherif, C.W. (1969). *Social psychology.* New York, NY: Harper & Row.

Snyder, C.R. (1989). Reality negotiation: From excuses to hope and beyond. *Journal of Social and Clinical Psychology, 8,* 130-157.

Snyder, C.R., Higgins, R.L., & Stucky, R.J. (1983). *Excuses: Masquerades in search of grace.* New York: Wiley-Interscience.

Stein, J.A., Fox, S.A., Murata, P.J., & Morisky, D.E. (1992). Mammography usage and the health belief model. *Health Education Quarterly, 19,* 447-462.

Steinhardt, M.A., & Dishman, R.K. (1989). Reliability and validity of expected outcomes and barriers for habitual physical activity. *Journal of Occupational Medicine, 31,* 536-546.

Stephens, T., & Craig, C. (1990). *The well-being of Canadians.* Ottawa, ON: Canadian Fitness and Lifestyle Research Institute.

Verhoef, M.J., & Love, E.J. (1994). Women and exercise participation: The mixed blessings of motherhood. *Health Care for Women International, 15,* 297-306.

Wankel, L. (1988). Exercise adherence and leisure activity: Patterns of involvement and interventions to facilitate regular activity. In

R.K. Dishman, (Ed.), *Exercise adherence: Its impact on public health* (pp. 369-396). Champaign, IL: Human Kinetics.

Weiner, B., Amirkhan, J., Folkes, V.S., & Verette, J.A. (1987). An attributional analysis of excuse giving: Studies of a naive theory of emotion. *Journal of Personality and Social Psychology, 52,* 316-324.

Weiner, B., Figueroa-Munoz, A., & Kakihara, C. (1991). The goals of excuses and communication strategies related to causal perceptions. *Personality and Social Psychology Bulletin, 17,* 4-13.

Zapka, J.G., Harris, D.R., Stoddard, A.M., & Costanza, M.E. (1991). Validity and reliability of psychosocial factors related to breast cancer screening. *Evaluation & the Health Professions, 14,* 356-367.

Acknowledgement

The authors gratefully acknowledge the helpful comments of Dr. Jack Rejeski, Dr. Ed McAuley, Dr. Joan Duda, and an anonymous reviewer on an earlier version of this chapter. We also acknowledge that the preparation of this chapter was supported in part by a Canadian Fitness and Lifestyle Research Grant to Dr. Brawley and a Social Sciences and Humanities Research Council (SSHRC) Fellowship to Kathleen Martin.

Author Note

At the time of the writing of this chapter, Dr. Kathleen Martin and Nancy Gyurcsik were senior doctoral students in the Department of Kinesiology, University of Waterloo, Waterloo, Ontario. Dr. Lawrence Brawley is a professor in the same department. Dr. Martin is currently an SSHRC post-doctoral fellow at Wake Forest University, Winston-Salem, North Carolina.

Chapter 20

Perceived Exertion: The Measurement

Bruce J. Noble
and
John M. Noble
University of Nebraska at Omaha

Since its introduction in the 1960s, perceived exertion has become a dependable tool in the vast array of measurement possibilities available to exercise scientists, including sport and exercise psychologists. The absence of a perceived exertion scale is a rarity in practical exercise settings. Popularity of the construct is evidenced by its utility, and both ease of application and understanding. The purposes of this chapter will be to explore the scientific development of the construct, explicate its psychophysical origins, examine the reliability and validity of perceived exertion measurements, review measurement standards, and suggest fruitful avenues for future research.

Perceived exertion has been defined as the act of detecting and interpreting sensations arising from the body during physical exercise (B. J. Noble & Robertson, 1996). An equally appropriate definition describes the construct as one's subjective rating of the intensity of work being performed (Morgan, 1973). The father of perceived exertion is the Swedish psychologist, Gunnar Borg. Borg first discussed the construct and presented an early form of the perceived exertion (RPE) scale in 1961 (Borg, 1961a). Not until the late 1960s, following a visit by Borg to the United States, was significant scientific interest invested in the further elaboration of this construct. Such examination acknowledges that human adaptation to exercise is not merely a matter of uncovering physiological costs or biomechanical strains but involves understanding the nature of the subjective experience. That is to say, successful processing of perceptual information is critical to making appropriate energy expenditure choices in the context of exercise and sport. Currently, more than 450 journal articles have been devoted solely to issues related to perception of exertion during physical activity (B. J. Noble & Robertson, 1996). Thus, exercise science has answered Morgan's early challenge to unravel questions that go beyond "what the individual is doing" during exercise to "what he *thinks* he is doing" (Morgan, 1973).

Psychophysical Background

The foundation for Borg's work with perception is located squarely in psychophysics. Psychophysics is the branch of psychology that is concerned with the study of human perception. Classically, psychophysics has attempted to discover the laws that govern human perceptual response within a variety of sensory dimensions (B. J. Noble & Robertson, 1996). Psychophysical methods have worked well for basic sense modalities: visual, auditory, etc. It seems clear that humans are aware of changes in sensation as exercise increases in intensity, but what they sense when they perceive exertion is not so apparent. Important information is received from the basic senses; however, physical effort is dimensionally unique. The question of an "effort sense" or whether such a sense exists has been of theoretical interest for most of the 20th century. Sherrington, in 1900, rejected the notion of an "effort sense" because it requires a knowledge of events without the use of sense organs. In this limited interpretation, if a sense organ is not identifiable, bodily responses cannot be called "sensation." However, Merton (1964) provided evidence for an effort sense when he found that subjects knew how far they had moved a pointer even though their awareness of position had been removed. Moreover, Bartley (1970) identified what he called homeostatic and comfort perceptual systems, essentially negating Sherrington's argument that the presence of a sense organ is necessary to define human sensation.

It seems propitious to digress for a moment so that psychophysical measurement from Weber to Borg and beyond can be brought into historical perspective. Classical psychophysicist E. H. Weber (1795-1878) concerned himself with the relation between the presentation of known physical stimuli and the psychological experience of those stimuli. Classical methods were largely concerned with the measurement of thresholds. Identification of a so-called *stimulus threshold* establishes a zero point at which a stimulus can be sensed. *Terminal thresh-*

olds recognize the point at which a sensation is extinguished. Stimulus and terminal thresholds serve as the outer limits of the scale of human perception. Another threshold that interested Weber and his colleagues was the *difference threshold* or, as it is sometimes called, the "just noticeable difference" (jnd). The determination of a "jnd" enables the identification of the extent to which a stimulus must vary for detection of change to be possible. Without regard for interindividual differences or direct measurement of perception classical methods indirectly assessed stimulus-response relationships (Kling & Riggs, 1972).

Weber's law (Kling & Riggs, 1972) postulates that the ratio of a given physical stimulus (S) to a "just noticeable difference" in that stimulus (ΔS) is a constant fraction (K)

$$\frac{\Delta S}{S} = K$$

Even though we may not be interested in such methods today, it might be helpful to place Weber's work in a modern context using treadmill exercise. As an example, treadmill speed can be arbitrarily set at 4 mph (S). ΔS represents the speed necessary for an individual to identify a "just noticeable difference" in speed, that is a threshold for the detection of speed change. Hypothetically, a ΔS of 1 mph can be set. Thus, K = 0.25. Because Weber's law predicts a linear relationship between the stimulus and the change in sensory response, one would predict that K would equal 0.25 across the entire range of treadmill speeds.

A contemporary of Weber, G. T. Fechner (1801-1887), could not confirm Weber's law (Kring & Riggs, 1972). Fechner's law, S = K log R, postulates that the ratio is not constant, that is not linear, but increases with the logarithm of the stimulus. As the stimulus increases, the "just noticeable difference" (R) becomes larger and larger.

Modern psychophysics has been marked by the development of new methods to study perception. By the late-19th century direct scaling methods, in which the subject directly assigns numbers to the stimulus presented, began to appear. Scales with an absolute zero were preferred so that ratio responses could be made. One of the important ratio methods is called *magnitude estimation.* In this method, the subject is presented with a stimulus and asked to assign a numerical value relative to the perceived magnitude of that stimulus (B. J. Noble & Robertson, 1996). Free magnitude estimation allows a subject to assign a number to a perception without restriction. In a variation, a standard stimulus (SS) is presented to the subject and assigned an arbitrary numerical value by the experimenter. The subject then assesses the magnitude of each presented comparative stimulus (CS) relative to the SS. Using an exercise example, comparative stimuli, such as exercise intensities, could be presented in random order with subjects allocating numbers on the basis of perceived magnitude (intensity). If a SS, such as 150 kpm/min, was set at 10, any exercise intensity that felt as if it was 4 times the standard would be assigned the number 40 by the subject, etc. This latter ratio scaling method became the "gold standard" of modern psychophysical methodology.

Stevens (1957), the father of modern psychophysics, rejected Fechner's law by showing that sensation grows with the power of the stimulus and that each stimulus dimension (loud-ness, warmth, taste, handgrip, etc.) has its own power function. Stevens' Power Law is written $R = kS^n$, where R is the magnitude of the sensation, k is a constant specifically associated with the sensory dimension, S is the intensity of the physical stimulus, and n is the exponent of the power function (B.J. Noble & Robertson, 1996). From Stevens' work, a general psychophysical law was proposed. The law states that sensation (response) rises exponentially as a power function of the stimulus (Stevens, 1957).

Development of the Borg Scale

Borg's perceptual perspective is clear. He was trained in modern psychophysics. However, the heart of Borg's interest has been the desire to apply psychophysical methods to clinical settings. Borg wanted methods that would allow perceptual comparisons between individual subjects. Ratio methods, particularly free magnitude estimation, do not allow a practitioner to make the necessary comparisons that serve as the basis for making clinical judgments. Even though Stevens (1971) condemned the use of less powerful scaling methods, such as category scales with only ordinal and interval properties, Borg (1973b) favored these scales because, unlike magnitude estimation, they permit comparisons between subjects.

In the early 1960s, Borg introduced an effort scale, currently referred to as the Borg or RPE (Rating of Perceived Exertion) Scale (Borg, 1961a) In his seminal paper, "Interindividual Scaling and Perception of Muscular Force," Borg clearly makes his arguments in support of a category scale as a method of choice. Foremost among the assumptions underlying his method is that the perceptive range is set equally for all individuals. Borg posits a hypothetical weightlifting comparison of two individuals with differing capacities. The point is made that although the physical range of the two subjects differs, the perceptual range, from minimal to maximal effort, can be assumed to be equal. One may progress more quickly or slowly through the perceptual range compared to another, but the intersubjective range itself remains equal.

Borg's first scale, unlike the one in current use, was 21 graded, ranging from 0 to 20 (see Figure 1; Borg, 1961b). A valid scale was considered one in which the perceptual ratings would grow linearly with physiological strain. Because physiological strain could be roughly assessed through heart rate, Borg believed heart rate was an ideal criterion variable for evaluating perceptual validity. Borg also theorized that a linear relationship with heart rate substantiated the contention that the category scale was an equal interval scale (Gamberale, 1985). However, Borg's early research showed the 21 graded scale not to be linear with heart rate (Borg, 1961b). Thus, a 15 graded scale (6 to 20) was developed (see Figure 2). This scale was designed so that it directly paralleled the heart rate range of a normal, healthy male, that is 60 to 200 beats per minute. According to the theory, if the scale ratings were multiplied by 10, heart rate could be calculated: HR = RPE x 10 (Borg, 1961b). Although this scale's *linearity* with heart rate has been established many times (e.g. Ekblom & Goldbarg, 1971; B. J. Noble, Borg, Jacobs, Ceci, & Kaiser, 1983), the heart rate prediction has not proven accurate (B. J. Noble & Robertson, 1996), that is the prediction was developed from theory as a "rule of thumb"

```
0 –
1 –
2 –
3 – Extremely Light
4 –
5 – Very Light
6 –
7 – Light
8
9 – Rather Light
10 –
11 – Neither Light Nor Laborious
12 –
13 – Rather Laborious
14 –
15 – Laborious
16 –
17 – Very Laborious
18 –
19 – Extremely Laborious
20 –
```

Figure 1 – Borg 21 graded category scale (Borg, 1961a)

rather than from a regression equation. Therefore, preciseness is lacking.

Development of a scale that is linear with heart rate is a complex process. Linearity was manipulated by the careful placement of the adjective/adverb expressions (Gamberale, 1985). In order to develop a scale that was valid across the entire range of exercise intensities, Borg (1978) placed adjectives and adverbs according to the relative meaning of the expressions. This technique is referred to as *quantitative semantics.* Borg selected well-defined terms with a comparatively good intersubjective, constant meaning (Borg & Dahlstrom, 1962). Words were selected that were not only rank ordered, but the semantic intensity between expressions was also fairly constant (Borg & Lindblad, 1976); that is the semantic intensity between expressions like "very light" and "very, very light" and between "very hard" and "very, very hard" are about equal.

It is important to reiterate that the scale we refer to as the Borg (RPE) Scale is the 15 graded scale and *not* the 21 graded scale. From time to time, one can find this latter scale still used without realization of its measurement liabilities, for example, the lack of linearity with heart rate. Validity and reliability have been established with the 15 graded scale only.

Validity and Reliability of the Borg Scale and Other Measures of RPE

Assessment of validity and reliability of the Borg Scale has been of interest to investigators since perceived exertion research began. There was concern that progressive exercise protocols, standard in many experiments, forced increased perceptual ratings because it was obvious to the subject that physical work was increasing. Of course, it is important that subjects rate effort associated with changes in exercise sensation rather than simply sense the progressive change in work intensity. Skinner, Hustler, Bergsteinova, and Buskirk (1973) evaluated

validity of the 15 graded scale by comparing an exercise protocol in which intensity was presented in progressive order (low to high as in a graded exercise test) with a protocol in which intensities were presented in random order. The comparison paradigm utilized in this investigation required that perceptual measures be recorded under equal conditions. By recording perceptual intensity after physiological measures achieved steady state a mere transitional response is prevented. Analysis revealed that there were no significant differences in RPE between the two protocols, indicating a valid assessment of perceptual intensity. Obviously, subjects were able to appropriately order perceptual intensity even when physical intensity was presented out of order. In the same experiment, reliability was determined using a test-retest protocol. Reliability coefficients were .80 and .78, respectively, for the progressive and random presentations. The authors concluded that assessing perceived exertion with the 15 graded scale was both a reliable and valid method.

Stamford (1976) assessed validity using a similar experimental paradigm, that is progressive and random physical intensity presentations. However, validity was evaluated relative to plotted RPE/HR coordinates. The author asserted that linearity in the plotted data indicates validity. That is to say, if the Borg assumption of linearity between perception and the criterion measure (heart rate) is achieved, validity has been accomplished. Linearity was observed in both protocols. Utilizing a similar RPE/HR model, Gamberale (1972) reported a validity coefficient of .94. Test-retest reliability in the Stamford paper was calculated from terminal ratings for each protocol. Correlations were .90 for the progressive protocol and .71 for the random protocol. Although the reliability of each protocol was confirmed, the progressive presentation procedure accounted for considerably more of the variance (30%).

Most of the perceived exertion literature has utilized adult males as subjects. One exception to that practice is the work of Eston and Williams (1986) which found the Borg 15 graded scale to be valid in a group of male adolescents. RPE correlations during bicycle ergometry were .78 and .74 with power output and heart rate, respectively.

```
6 –
7 – Very, Very Light
8 –
9 – Very Light
10 –
11 – Fairly Light
12 –
13 – Somewhat Hard
14 –
15 – Hard
16 –
17 – Very Hard
18 –
19 – Very, Very Hard
20 –
```

Figure 2 – Borg 15 graded category scale (Borg, 1971)

```
1 –
2 – Not At All Stressful
3 –
4 –
5 –
6 –
7 –
8 – Very, Very Stressful
9 –
```

Figure 3 – Pittsburgh 9 graded category scale (Stamford & Noble, 1974)

Borg's 15 graded instrument has not been the only category scale developed to study perception of effort. During the early 1970s, a 9 graded scale was developed, validated, and found reliable by a group at the University of Pittsburgh (Stamford & Noble, 1974). This scale has several advantages: It contains fewer categories, has fewer adjective/adverb expressions, and has end anchors at 2 and 8 to protect against end-effects (see Figure 3). "End-effects" refers to the tendency for subjects to refrain from using extreme numbers on a scale.

Hogan, Ogden, Gebhardt, and Fleishman (1980) constructed a similar category scale with seven grades for use in studying perception in manual materials-handling tasks (see Figure 4). Interclass correlations revealed a coefficient of .83 indicating acceptable reliability. Validity was assessed utilizing energy expenditure during the tasks as the criterion variable. The resulting coefficient, .88, established the validity of the scale. A confirming validity study, in which perceived exertion was correlated with the energy expenditure of recreational activities, found a coefficient of .83 (Hogan & Fleishman, 1979).

The test-retest reliability of category scales has proven to be satisfactory with correlations ranging from .71 to .90. Likewise, these scales have been shown to be valid, using objective metabolic indicators as criterion measures (r=.83 to .94). Thus, category scales with 7, 9, or 15 grades can be considered efficacious measures of effort perception.

In the 1980s, Borg developed a new measure he called a category-ratio scale (CR10) (Borg, 1982). This scale has 10 grades with an option to select "maximum" intensity beyond 10 using free magnitude estimation, that is any number (see Figure 5). The purpose of the scale was to accommodate assessment of exertion when criterion physiological measures showed curvilinear increases with exercise intensity. Lactate accumulation and pulmonary ventilation are examples of such variables. B. J. Noble et al. (1983) examined the relationship of the CR10 scale

```
1 – Very, Very Light
2 –
3 –
4 – Somewhat Hard
5 –
6 –
7 – Very, Very Hard
```

Figure 4 – 7 graded category scale (Hogan & Fleishman, 1979)

ratings to blood lactate production during cycle ergometry. Scale ratings and lactate showed similar growth exponents, 1.6 and 2.0, respectively. This result supports the validity of the CR10 scale using lactate as the criterion measure. To the authors' knowledge, this study has not been duplicated for pulmonary ventilation. Likewise, test-retest reliability has not been reported for the CR10 scale.

Beginning in the early 1970s, scientific interest was shown in ratings that went beyond a single, gestalt measurement of exertion referred to as an *overall* or *undifferentiated rating*. Ekblom and Goldbarg (1971) developed a two-factor model of perceived exertion that identified differentiated sources for effort sensations. One source was called the *central factor* in reference to cues that arise from cardiopulmonary stimuli. A second factor referred to a cluster of cues arising from local musculature and joints at the site of contraction, the so-called *local factor*. These differentiated factors have been widely studied over the years; however, more recent literature refers to these sources of sensation as *respiratory-metabolic* (central) and *peripheral* (local) *mediators* (B. J. Noble & Robertson, 1996).

Within the limits of our search, we were unable to locate specific mention or empirical data to support the validity and reliability of differentiated ratings, respiratory-metabolic and peripheral. The assumption can be made that because plots of differentiated ratings invariably run parallel with the undifferentiated, overall rating, validity of the former need not be an issue. That may be true for validity of respiratory-metabolic ratings because many studies have substantiated linearity between scale ratings and heart rate. However, perhaps a better criterion variable could be found for peripheral ratings, for example, electromyographic records. Additionally, there is no reason that test-retest reliability of these measures cannot be easily obtained.

Administration of the Borg Scale

Assumptions of reliability and validity for the Borg scale are dependent on the degree to which researchers and practitioners comply with recommended administrative standards. Borg himself (personal communication, 1994) has become concerned in recent years that scale administration and interpretation have often been far from optimal. The ease in understanding the concept of category scales has often resulted in in-

```
0 – Nothing At All
0.5 – Extremely Weak (Just Noticeable)
1 – Very Weak
2 – Weak (Light)
3 – Moderate
4 – Somewhat Strong
5 – Strong (Heavy)
6 –
7 – Very Strong
8 –
9 –
10 – Extremely Strong (Almost Max)
0 – Maximal
```

Figure 5 – Borg category–ratio scale (Borg, 1982)

appropriate brevity in providing scale instructions. Instructions for Borg scale use should be undertaken with the same care as with any psychological measure. Maresh and Noble (1984) have discussed administrative requirements in detail. Following are six points that, based on over 30 years of experience with the measurement of perceived exertion, have proven useful and should be included in a comprehensive set of instructions.

Defining Perceived Exertion

Instructions should begin with a practical definition of the construct. It is helpful to place the definition within the context of the exercise mode. For instance, in a staged test, the subject is told what is to be expected relative to changes in physical intensity (load, speed, grade, etc.). Moreover, the subject should be alerted to expected changes in physiological responses that might be used as symptom cues, for example heart rate, pulmonary ventilation, and sweat rate. For the purpose of measuring perceived *exertion,* it is generally a good idea to instruct subjects to monitor sensation, that is syptomatology, as opposed to physical effort per se. Monitoring physical effort would focus on the physical stimulus rather than on the exertion experience in response to the physical stimulus.

Instructions need to be tailored to the purpose of the scale. Clients who will be rating exertion during graded exercise testing with a diagnostic purpose will require explanations that target the objectives of that setting. Likewise, instructions in an experimental setting may be fashioned differently from those used to instruct joggers in a health club who simply want to maintain a target heart rate.

Anchoring the Perceptual Range

Earlier it was mentioned that perceived exertion measurement assumes that interindividual perceptual ranges are equal. The extreme adjective/adverb expressions (perceptual range) for the 15 graded scale are *very, very light* (7) and *very, very strong* (19). It is helpful to the subject/client to put these anchors into context. A simple method to accomplish this goal would be to ask the subject/client to remember the least effortful bicycle ride (9) she could remember and, in contrast, the most difficult bicycle experience (19). The 19 anchor can also be defined as the "greatest effort imaginable" taking the explanation out of the realm of actual experience and placing it within the sphere of imagined experience. It is usually a good idea to make the explanation relative to the type of exercise used in the test.

A more direct approach to the anchoring question is to ask the subject to directly experience the scale extremes. For example, subjects can experience a maximal treadmill test during which the investigator can assign 7 and 19. The low anchor (7) could either be set as rest prior to exercise and labeled *No exertion at all* or as a very easy walk stage with no grade. "Maximal" or 19 can be assigned to the termination point of the test when the subject cannot continue any longer. The numbers 6 and 20 on all scales of this type add flexibility to the contruct. For instance, they allow subjects to identify feelings more or less effortful than the prescribed extremes.

Explaining the Use of the Scale

The subject/client should know that each number on the scale represents a category of sensation, hence the term *category scale,* ordered according to intensity. They should also know that the expressions attached to every other number are to be viewed as an aid to the selection of numbers. The subject should be instructed to select a single number or half number (optional) when a perception is requested.

Using Differentiated Ratings

Often test protocols will necessitate collecting perceptual information from a site or class other than, or in addition to, the holistic undifferentiated rating often referred to as the "overall" rating. These so-called differentiated ratings may include, for example, ratings from the muscles and joints in use, usually called the peripheral or local rating. In addition, the experimenter/clinician may want the subject/client to separate out those sensations associated with the cardiopulmonary system, usually called the respiratory-metabolic or central rating. "The goal is to have the subject provide sensation quantities from such consciously perceived qualities like ventilatory volume and respiratory rate as distinct from those cues arising from the working muscles themselves" (B. J. Noble & Robertson, 1996, p. 79). Of course, one would not be limited to these sites or classes of rating. In swimming for example, two peripheral ratings, arm and leg, would be appropriate in addition to respiratory-metabolic and overall ratings. It should be obvious that clear instructions should be given relative to what the subject is to monitor at each site.

Assessing Correctness of Perceptual Responses

Subjects/clients should know that there are no "right" or "wrong" perceptions. Some tend to doubt their ability to select perceptual intensities because such selections require more abstract rather than concrete estimates. In fact, subjective estimates are made every day throughout life mostly with superb success. Likewise, humans seem to have the ability to quite accurately assign numerical ratings to their feelings. Nonetheless, it is important to assure each user that he or she need not worry about some elusive perfection in the responses. In some cases, it might be advisable to provide a rating practice session for the purpose of giving the subject confidence or to assure the investigator that the subject can rate effectively. This could be a short session on an ergometer demonstrating several different loads where the subject should appropriately use the bottom, middle, and top of the scale. Another technique to assure the investigator of the subject's ability to rate involves the use of an unrelated measure, such as a line-length estimation task. A standard line length is shown followed by comparison lengths that the subject would have to successfully place in rank order or scale in a suitable manner. It has been the authors' experience that, in rare cases, a subject rates exertion to be "very light" throughout an entire graded exercise test. Such a subject either does not understand the concept of rating or, more likely, is revealing a character trait that would make his or her participation suspect. This exception aside, when it comes to feeling, by definition there are no "right" or "wrong" answers.

Asking for Questions

The process of providing detailed instructions in the use of the Borg Scale will often invoke questions from the subject. Therefore, it is imperative that the participant be asked for questions prior to the initiation of testing and, depending on the experimental or clinical protocol, during the test itself.

The Future

Alternative Perceptual Measures

Over the last 15 years perhaps the most frequently asked question about perceived exertion has been "What scale should I use?" On one level, this question implies the existence of multiple scales with differing characteristics, one being more suitable in one setting than another. The assumption is correct. Two or three alternatives exist from which investigators can choose. Usually the individual asking the question is looking for advice as to how to make the link between an experimental question and the scale characteristics. The most common confusion surrounds whether to use the 15 graded scale or the CR10 scale. In most cases, the answer is simple. The 15 graded Borg Scale should be used. This scale has been well validated, represents a reliable measure of perceptual intensity, and has proven to be robust in its usefulness.

However, on another level, this question speaks to an inherent flaw in the study of perceived exertion that was mentioned at the outset. Few exercise scientists study perception as a primary research topic. Some just want a reliable scale to add "feeling" responses as a secondary dimension of an experimental protocol. Others look for a well-documented scale so that they can quickly dispose of the measurement question in a perceptual study. The 15 graded scale has been so widely used that it is easier to ask a question that works with this scale than to develop a scale that works with the question.

In the minds of these authors, the study of perception should be dominated by questions. The scholar should be so well steeped in psychophysical measurement that quantification techniques can be developed as needed rather than asking questions that assume the use of the Borg Scale. Emphasis should be placed on understanding perception not on studying the results of the Borg Scale. Until that is done, the study of perceptual response during physical activity will reflect only what the Borg Scale measures. No one feels more indebted to, and humbled by, Professor Borg than the authors of this paper. We would not be where we are today if it had not been for his magnificent and far sighted work. Just as medicine has moved beyond the stethoscope to CAT scans and botany has moved from being exclusively a plant identification science to one in which satellite-imaging can monitor earth plant life, exercise scientists need to move on to new and more sophisticated measurements. Many theoretical questions about human effort perception do not require a scale that identifies interindividual differences, for example if the goal is to determine perceptual response equations. In such cases, modern psychophysical techniques, such as magnitude estimation, whereby each subject is free to use any numbers, might be more appropriate.

As noted above, perceptual scales other than the Borg Scale have been developed. Both a 9 graded (Pittsburgh) scale (Stamford & Noble, 1974) and a 7 graded scale (Hogan & Fleishman,

1979) have been constructed and validated. Measurement theory indicates that 7 to 10 categories in a scale are sufficient for successfully rating any dimension. Essentially, the Hogan and Fleishman scale is a 50% reduction of the Borg Scale. The Pittsburgh Scale (see Figure 3) uses adjective-adverb expressions only at 2 ("Not at all stressful") and 8 ("Very, very stressful"). Not anchoring the extreme numbers (1 and 9) on a scale protects against end effects, the tendency to use the middle of the scale rather than the terminal expressions or numbers. This 9 graded scale proved to be both reliable and valid (Stamford and Noble, 1974; Robertson, McCarthy, & Gillespie, 1976).

Borg (1973b) compared several category scales during two types of maximal tests. Although correlations with heart rate proved to be a little higher for the 15 graded scale compared to the 9 graded scale they both were high and significant. Borg concluded, without testing for significance, that the 15 graded scale should be used in most cases. If data generated by the two scales are not significantly different, then the two scales can be used interchangeably but this conclusion awaits verification. This would be a fruitful area for future research.

Borg himself saw certain limitations in the 15 graded scale. He realized that not all physiological variables that reflect changes in exercise intensity grow in a linear fashion. Therefore, a scale based on heart rate linearity would not be adequate. Examples of physiological measures that grow exponentially with exercise intensity are lactate accumulation and pulmonary ventilation. Lactate remains close to basal levels until exercise intensities approximating 50% of maximal oxygen consumption (VO2Max). After this lactate "inflection point," which varies with aerobic fitness, lactic acid rises precipitously. At roughly the same point, increases in pulmonary ventilation leave linearity with exercise intensity and grow in a positively accelerating fashion. Thus, Borg constructed the so-called category-ratio scale (CR10) that grew in a manner similar to lactate accumulation and pulmonary ventilation (Borg, 1982). It was a difficult task to develop a scale that had *ratio* properties to accommodate the positive acceleration of physiological variables as well as enable interindividual comparisons, a characteristic of *category* scales. In justification of his approach Borg (1973a) explained, "Knowledge of the physical intensities 'behind' the various verbal expressions has been used together with the knowledge of the general psychophysical function to identify the perceptual intensities for the expressions in question". By "general psychophysical function," he was referring to the fact that muscular effort is known to increase with an exponent of 1.6 according to Stevens' Power Law. In the CR10 scale, light effort is scaled over the first 20% of the scale whereas the final 80% of the scale goes from "Moderate" to "Extremely Strong". That is to say, when perception reaches moderate levels, the point at which subjects exert approximately 50% of physiological effort, the numbers begin to rise more rapidly. Empirical data have substantiated that the ratings did increase with an exponent of 1.6. (Borg, 1982)

Borg (1973a) found a correlation coefficient of .88 between ratings on the CR10 scale and heart rate. Although this is an interesting finding it seems irrelevant based on the designed purpose of the scale. More relevant is the calculation of RPE relationships with variables like lactate accumulation that increase exponentially with power output. B. J. Noble et al. (1983) examined power functions using the CR-10 scale. CR10 ratings and lactate both rose with a similar quadratic (square) trend. Thus, the new scale was found to be valid using lactate accumulation as the criterion variable. The nonlinearity of the CR10 scale

> does not invalidate the scale by any means but it does make the data less useful in most practical settings. On the other hand, the category-ratio scale can be very useful in certain experimental projects where 'ratio' data are required or where the goal is to assess sensations related to pulmonary ventilation or lactate accumulation. (B. J. Noble & Robertson, 1996, p.77)

Descriptive vs. Theoretical Research

It has already been pointed out that few researchers devote a substantial portion of their careers to the study of perception of physical effort. This fact is masked by the wide use of perception as a dependent variable in research projects. Explanation of this paradox can be found in the fact that RPE has been used frequently as a convenient clinical marker in studies that have assessed the physiological status of athletes or patients during graded exercise tests (Lollgen, Ulmer, & von Nieding, 1977; B. J. Noble, Kraemer, & Clark, 1982). This use of perceptual ratings as a descriptive variable usually results only in a perfunctory discussion of RPE significance.

Another frequent use of perceptual ratings has focused on comparative descriptions of various groups and conditions. Description can be looked at perjoratively as having little value to the development of theory. To the contrary, our view is that descriptive studies represent an early developmental stage in the maturation of a field of study, broadly defining pertinent parameters. However, after 25 years, the time has come for core attention to be more definitively focused on theoretical concerns. A dearth of theoretical models concerning the setting of perceptual ratings has been developed both on the physiological (B. J. Noble, 1977; B. J. Noble, 1986; Robertson, 1982) and psychological sides (Kinsman and Weiser, 1976; Rejeski, 1981) of this critical psychobiological construct. Our purpose is not to discuss the details of current theory in this paper, but we would be remiss if we did not emphasize the relative neglect by exercise scientists regarding keystone theoretical questions concerning human perception of physical effort. We emphasize the phrase "relative neglect" because there certainly have been significant contributions made on both the physiological and psychological sides, but much remains unanswered. The neglect of which we speak is partly due to a limited view of measurement, that is the tendency to ask questions that can be answered by existing measurement devices. The "cart" has definitely "pulled the horse" here.

Future Research

It must be obvious at this point that these authors feel that future research emphasis should be placed on theory building. B. J. Noble and Robertson (1996) have proposed a theoretical model that hypothesizes the initial stage of perception as involving the encoding of exercise-stimulated sensory cues into neural signals. Further, these signals are said to be amplified or dampened by certain psychological dispositional factors. These factors are undoubtedly integrated preconsciously. Situational factors additionally affect the neural signals but both consciously and preconsciously. Moreover, Rejeski (1981) posited an integrative model in which psychological factors are more salient at light and moderate exercise intensities than at high intensities. Although some experimental substantiation of the Rejeski model has been accomplished, there is some confusion in the literature. For example, Rejeski and Ribisl (1980) found an expected exercise duration effect at 85% of VO2max which they labeled "moderate" work. On the other hand, Hardy, Hall, and Prestholdt (1986) found coactor effects only at 25% and 50% but not at 75%, with the latter referred to as "heavy." The assumptions underlying these theoretical models need further experimental substantiation.

Again, the authors' biases about measurement in future research have already been made transparent. We support greater eclecticism in the measurement of exercise perceptions. It should not be concluded that the 15 graded Borg Scale or the CR10 scale lack merit. We do, however, urge greater emphasis on the research question as the primary determinant of measurement choice rather than letting the instrument dictate questions. Perceptual studies of a more general nature should consider psychophysical ratio techniques, such as magnitude estimation. Investigations of exercise intensity discrimination, a vastly understudied area, would do well to utilize classical techniques that establish difference thresholds. Category scales, such as those recommended by Hogan and Fleishman (1979) and Robertson et al. (1976), are viable alternatives to the 15 graded scale for studies in which interindividual comparisons are critical. Additionally, we concur with Hardy and Rejeski (1989), who have suggested that an affect (feeling) scale can often be a beneficial companion to ratings of perceived exertion. An affect scale qualifies the quantity of the sensation with an assessment of how the intensity is experienced, i.e., good or bad. For example, J. M. Noble, McCullagh, and Byrnes (1993) successfully used a feeling scale in conjunction with the RPE scale while studying the effects of training.

Of course, in order to advance theory, it is important to ensure validity and reliability of the perceptual measure. The 15 graded scale has been primarily studied with exercise administered in a graded format. Replication studies are needed in nongraded exercise, such as extended steady-state situations or game environments where production of physical intensity is relatively random.

To the authors' knowledge, no publication has addressed the reliability of the CR10 scale. Such a study would make a great contribution to the literature and could easily be designed. Likewise, we have found no reports of either reliability or validity assessments for the differentiated ratings (peripheral and respiratory-metabolic). Such studies would be valuable to continued study of exercise and sport perceptions.

Still another area where future research is needed involves the development of an appropriate criterion measure for establishing validity of peripheral ratings. Variables that adequately assess the status of muscle and joint tissue are often too physically invasive to easily measure, for example, muscle lactate. We would suggest the use of electromyography as a fruitful candidate for establishing validity. Although blood lactate only estimates the state of the muscle cell, it is easy to measure and could also be used as a criterion measure.

The past 25 years have been marked by exponential increases in the body of knowledge concerning perceived exertion. This advancement has been dominated by scale deveopment and construct description. We look forward to greater emphasis on theory development and measurement eclecticism in the next quarter century.

Summary

The purpose of this chapter was to assess the measurement status of the construct known as perceived exertion. This construct has been defined as the act of detecting and interpreting sensations arising from the body during physical exercise. The measurement of perceived exertion is based in psychophysics, the study of human perception. Classical psychophysics utilized indirect methods (comparison of perceptual responses rather than direct assessment of intensity) to discover the relation between physical stimuli and human perceptual response. Both Weber and Fechner postulated laws that purported to describe this relationship. Modern psychophysicist Stevens, using techniques that directly assessed perceptual intensity, rejected earlier laws showing that sensation grows with the power of stimulus. For example, Stevens (1957) utilized a ratio method called magnitude estimation to determine that the perception of grip effort grows as a power function (1.6) of the force applied.

Borg, although supporting the value of modern ratio scaling techniques for establishing general perceptual relations, has encouraged the use of interval or category scales because they permit interindividual comparisons valued in clinical and many experimental settings. Borg developed a category scale with 15 grades, from 6 to 20, that paralleled the increase in heart rate. This was achieved via a method known as quantitative semantics whereby adjective/adverb expressions are carefully placed along a numbered scale to achieve linearity. A number of studies have established the validity and reliability of this scale. Borg also developed a category-ratio scale (CR10) that grows linearly with exercise intensity at low levels but as a power function after moderate levels are attained. Such a scale enables correspondence with physiological variables like lactic acid and pulmonary ventilation that grow with the power of exercise intensity. Validity has been established for this scale, but reliability has not been reported.

Because validity and reliability studies of the 15 graded Borg Scale have been conducted with appropriate adherence to certain administrative standards, it would be wise for future investigators to follow these standards. The six basic administrative standards are presented in this chapter: defining the construct, anchoring the perceptual range, explaining scale use, explaining differentiated ratings (when appropriate), cautioning against the assumption that there are right and wrong perceptions, and asking for questions. Several alternative perceptual measures are discussed. In addition to the often used 15 graded Borg Scale, other category scales and the category-ratio scale are offered as options when the experimental question deems such a choice appropriate. Seven- and nine-graded scales have been shown to be equally valid and reliable alternatives.

Since 1960, over 450 articles have been published with perceived exertion in the title (B. J. Noble & Robertson, 1996). Most of these reports have been descriptive in nature. Future researchers are urged to focus their attention on theory building and developing new psychophysical techniques that match experimental questions.

References

Bartley, S. H. (1970). The homeostatic and comfort perceptual systems. *Journal of Psychology, 75,* 157-162.

Borg, G. (1961a). Interindividual scaling and perception of muscular force. *Kungliga Fysiografiska Sallskapets i Lund Forhandlingar, 31,* 117-125.

Borg, G. (1961b). Perceived exertion in relation to physical work load and pulse-rate. *Kungliga Fysiografiska Sallskapets i Lund Forhandlingar, 31,* 105-115.

Borg, G. (1971). The perception of physical performance. In R. J. Shephard (Ed.), *Frontiers of fitness* (pp. 280-294). Springfield, IL: Charles C. Thomas.

Borg, G. (1973a). A note on a category scale with "ratio properties" for estimating perceived exertion. *Internal Reports from the Institute of Applied Psychology. 36,* U. of Stockholm, 6P.

Borg, G. (1973b). Perceived exertion: A note on "history" and methods. *Medicine and Science of Sports, 5,* 90-93.

Borg, G. (1978). Psychological assessment of physical effort. *Proceedings of the 1978 International Symposium on Psychological Assessment in Sport,* Netanya, Israel, 49-57.

Borg, G. (1982). A category scale with ratio properties for intermodal and interindividual comparison. In H. Geissler & P. Petzold (Eds.), *Psychophysical judgment and the process of perception* (pp. 25-34). Berlin: VEB Deutscher Verlag der Wissenschaften.

Borg, G., & Dahlstrom, H. (1962). A pilot study of perceived exertion and physical working capacity. *Acta Soc. Med. Upsal., 67,* 21-27.

Borg, G. & Lindblad, I. (1976). The determination of subjective intensities in verbal descriptions of symptoms. *Internal Report from the Institute of Applied Psychology, 75,* U. of Stockholm.

Ekblom, B., & Goldbarg, A. N. (1971). The influence of physical training and other factors on the subjective rating of perceived exertion. *Acta Physiologica Scandinavica, 83,* 399-406.

Eston, R., & Williams, J. (1986). Exercise intensity and perceived exertion in adolescent boys. *British Journal of Sports Medicine, 20,* 27-30.

Gamberale, F. (1972). Perceived exertion, heart rate, oxygen uptake and blood lactate in different work operations. *Ergonomics, 15,* 545-554.

Gamberale, F. (1985). The perception of exertion. *Ergonomics, 26,* 299-308.

Hardy, C., Hall, E., & Prestholdt, P. (1986). The mediational role of social influence in the perception of exertion. *Journal of Sport Psychology, 8,* 88-104.

Hardy, C., & Rejeski, W. (1989). Not what, but how one feels: The measurement of affect during exercise. *Journal of Sport and Exercise Psychology, 11,* 304-317.

Hogan, J. C., & Fleishman, E. A. (1979). An index of the physical effort required in human task performance. *Journal of Applied Psychology, 64,* 197-204.

Hogan, J. C., Ogden, G. D., Gebhardt, D. L. & Fleishman, E. A. (1980). Reliability and validity of methods for evaluating perceived physical effort. *Journal of Applied Psychology, 65,* 672-679.

Kinsman, R. A., & Weiser, P. C. (1976). Subjective symptomatology during work and fatigue. In E. Simonson & P. C. Weiser (Eds.), *Psychological aspects of fatigue* (pp. 336-405). Springfield, IL: Charles C. Thomas.

Kling, J. W., & Riggs, L. A. (1972). *Experimental psychology:*

Sensation and perception. New York: Holt, Rinehart and Winston, Inc.

Lollgen, H., Ulmer, H. V., & von Nieding, G. (1977). Heart rate and perceptual response to exercise with different pedalling speed in normal subjects and patients. *European Journal of Applied Physiology, 37,* 297-304.

Maresh, C., & Noble, B. J. (1984). Utilization of perceived exertion ratings during exercise testing and training. In L. K. Hall (Ed.), *Cardiac Rehabilitation: Exercise Testing and Prescription* (pp. 155-173). Great Neck, NY: Spectrum Publications, Inc.

Merton, P. A. (1964). Human position sense and sense of effort. *Symposium of the Society for Experimental Biology, 18,* 387-400.

Morgan, W. P. (1973). Psychological factors influencing perceived exertion. *Medicine and Science of Sports, 5,* 97-103.

Noble, B. J. (1977, April). *Physiological basis of perceived exertion: A tentative explanatory model.* Paper presented at the Annual Meeting of the American Alliance of Health, Physical Education, Recreation, and Dance, Seattle, WA.

Noble, B. J., Borg, G., Jacobs, I., Ceci, R., & Kaiser, P. (1983). A category-ratio perceived exertion scale: Relationship to blood and muscle lactates and heart rate. *Medicine and Science of Sports and Exercise, 15,* 523-528.

Noble, B. J., Kraemer, W. J., & Clark, M. (1982). Response of selected physiological variables and perceived exertion to high intensity weight training in highly trained and beginning weight trainers. *National Strength and Conditioning Association Journal, 4,* 10-12.

Noble, B. J., Kraemer, W., Allen, J., Plank, J. & Woodard, L. (1986). The integration of physiological cues in effort perceptions: Stimulus strength vs. relative contribution. In G. Borg & D. Ottoson (Eds.), *The Perception of Exertion in Physical Work* (pp. 83-96). London: MacMillan Press Ltd.

Noble, B. J., & Robertson, R. J. (1996). *Perceived exertion.* Champaign, IL: Human Kinetics.

Noble, J. M., McCullagh, P., & Byrnes, W. C. (1993). Perceived exertion and feeling scale ratings before and after six months of aerobic exercise training. *Journal of Sport and Exercise Psychology, 15,* (Suppl.), S59.

Rejeski, W. J., & Ribisl, P. M. (1980). Expected task duration and perceived effort: An attributional analysis. *Journal of Sports Psychology, 2,* 227-236.

Rejeski, W. J. (1981). Perception of exertion: A social psychophysiological integration. *Journal of Sports Psychology, 3,* 305-320.

Robertson, R. J. (1982). Central signals of perceived exertion during dynamic exercise. *Medicine and Science of Sports and Exercise, 14,* 390-396.

Robertson, R. J., McCarthy, J., & Gillespie, R. (1976). Contribution of regional to overall perceived exertion during cycle ergometer exercise. *Medicine and Science of Sports, 8,* 64-65.

Robertson, R. J., Gillespie, R. L., McCarthy, J., & Rose, K. D. (1979). Differentiated perceptions of exertion: Part 1. Mode of integration of regional signals. *Perceptual and Motor Skills, 49,* 683-689.

Sherrington, C. S. (1900). The muscular sense. In E. A. Schafer (Ed.), *Textbook of physiology.* London: Pentland.

Skinner, J. S., Hustler, R., Bergsteinova, V., & Buskirk, E. R. (1973). The validity and reliability of a rating scale of perceived exertion. *Medicine and Science of Sports, 5,* 97-103.

Stamford, B. A. (1976). Validity and reliability of subjective ratings of perceived exertion during work. *Ergonomics, 19,* 53-60.

Stamford, B. A., & Noble, B. J. (1974). Metabolic cost and perception of effort during bicycle ergometer work performance. *Medicine and Science of Sports, 6,* 226-231.

Stevens, S. S. (1957). On the psychophysical law. *Psychological Review, 64,* 153-181.

Stevens, S. S. (1971). Issues in psychophysical measurement. *Psychological Review, 78,* 425-450.

Chapter 21

MEASURES OF INCENTIVES TO EXERCISE

Penny McCullagh
University of Colorado at Boulder
and
John M. Noble
University of Nebraska at Omaha

What motivates individuals to exercise? Why do some individuals choose to exercise excessively, whereas others choose either moderation or complete avoidance of exercise? Why does someone begin an exercise program and then suddenly cease to participate? Examining the perceived reasons that make exercise an attractive behavioral choice is one way of gaining insight into such motivational processes.

A critical component to the research and application of exercise motivation principles is the individual's perceived incentive to participate in exercise behavior. Once the incentives, or reasons, to exercise are fully understood, they may be applied to predictive models of future participation. A crucial aspect necessary for furthering the research base examining the role of exercise incentives in the decision to initiate and maintain exercise behaviors is the development of reliable, valid, and theoretically driven assessment tools. The primary purpose of this chapter is to examine the psychometric properties of exercise incentive measures. We will primarily focus on personal investment theory because incentives are a central construct of this theory. In addition, issues related to scale development and measurement characteristics of inventories will be covered.

Because exercise incentives are composed of personal thoughts pertaining to the exercise environment, the incentive approach falls under the rubric of cognitive approaches to exercise motivation. Cognitive approaches propose that internal processes such as thoughts and feelings act to direct, initiate, and energize observable behavior. Such observable exercise behaviors are manifested as behavioral choice (approach/avoidance), effort (intensity), and persistence (continued participation) of behavior. In other words, it is assumed that cognition guides our motivated behaviors. A number of empirical investigations have examined general reasons for exercising. However, incentives, per se, may not have been central to the theoretical framework employed.

For example, some research has employed measures that have attempted to assess reasons for discontinuing exercise (McAuley, Poag, Gleason, & Wraith, 1990) or reasons for be-

ginning an exercise program (Marcus, Rakowski, & Rossi, 1992). However, incentives were not central to the theme of these studies. Questioning the lack of theoretical investigations assessing the power of incentives to *predict* future exercise participation, Rodgers and Brawley (1991) stated:

> The cumulative nature of these problems does not encourage systematic research because no firm theoretical bases have been established. This may be part of the reason why prediction of participation intention and behavior from various participation motives has not been forthcoming. (p.411)

A Personal Investment Approach to Exercise Incentives

A notable exception to the preceding argument is the work of Duda, Tappe and their colleagues (1987, 1988, 1989a, 1989b, Tappe & Duda, 1988) stemming from Maehr and Braskamp's (1986) personal investment theory. Whereas other conceptual approaches may include some type of "incentive" measure, this theory specifically incorporates perceived incentives as a central construct. Historically, when examining issues of motivation, researchers have chosen to take a personal, situational, or interactional approach. A personal approach focuses on motivation as an individual trait that is rather enduring. Assessing individual psychological characteristics such as self-motivation (Dishman & Ickes, 1981), locus of control (McCready & Long, 1985), or goal orientation (Pemberton, 1986) to predict motivation for, and adherence to, exercise would exemplify this approach. In opposition, a situational approach would suggest that environmental factors are the major determinants of motivation. Using this framework, researchers have examined the influence of such manipulations as contracts (Wysocki, Hall, Iawata, & Riordan, 1979) and rewards (Keefe & Blumenthal, 1980) on motivation in exercise settings. Using an interaction approach emphasizes the importance of both personal and situational factors.

The theory of personal investment (Maehr & Braskamp,

1986) is clearly an attempt to employ an interactional framework to motivation. Based on 25 years of research, personal investment theory is really an integration of numerous theoretical perspectives. The theory is guided by five propositions that suggest how motivation is examined and assessed (see Maehr & Braskamp, 1986, pp. 45-46). The authors state that in order to study motivation, one must study behavior, and they refer to the patterns of behavior associated with motivation as personal investment. Because direction of behavior is important, the theory emphasizes the *choices* made by individuals. It is also recognized that the meaning of the situation determines personal investment and that this meaning can be assessed.

Finally, the theory approaches motivation as a process. Maehr and Braskamp (1986) view the determinants of motivated behavior to be quite complex. For example, they recognize that there are numerous junctions or decision points that influence whether a person will choose to continue with an activity, start a new activity, revise a current activity and so forth. From the perspective of the researchers, it is important to focus on these critical decision points and examine the behavior that is chosen.

Personal investment theory proposes that a person's individual characteristics and situational factors influence the individual to determine the *meaning* of the presented activity, and it is this interpretation of meaning that influences personal investment. Simply stated, the meaning of the situation determines what a person will chose to do or not to do. Given the same external situation, different individuals may have very different interpretations of the context at hand and may, therefore, choose very different courses of action. It is the subjective interpretation of the situation that influences behavior. According to the personal investment theory, meaning is composed of three different factors: sense of self, perceived options, and personal incentives. Personal incentives and perceived options are considered to be cognitive in nature, whereas thoughts about self are considered to be more dispositional. It is assumed that all the components can be assessed through the use of questionnaires or interviews. Because the primary focus of this chapter is on exercise incentives, we will only briefly describe the other two components of personal investment theory to provide a reference by which to understand the incentive construct. Subsequently, the personal-incentives construct will be thoroughly defined and the assessment tools reviewed.

Sense of self is defined as the "organized collection of perceptions, beliefs and feelings about who one is" (Maehr & Braskamp, 1986, p. 59) and is identified by four facets of self. The first component, identity, refers to an individual's perception that he or she belongs or is associated with certain reference groups (e.g., activity level of significant others). The second component, self-reliance, refers to the notion that an individual determines and is in control of his or her own destiny (e.g., perceived control). Goal directedness is the third component necessary for the conceptualization of a sense of self and refers to an individual's ability to set goals as well as the ability to delay gratification. The final aspect of selfhood is sense of competence. The notion here is that a person's sense of competence will guide his or her choices of activity.

A second component of personal investment theory is *perceived options*, which are defined as "the behavioral alternatives or action possibilities that a person perceives to be available to him or her in any given situation" (Maehr & Braskamp, 1986, p. 61). Perceived options concern not only those options perceived as possible, but also those perceived as acceptable. Tappe and Duda (1988) have operationalized this variable as a congruency index wherein the difference between the incentive and the opportunity to meet the incentive is calculated.

Maehr and Braskamp (1986) carefully chose the word *incentives* to describe the first construct within their theory and explained how this term is different from constructs proposed by others. For example, in the early literature a distinction had been made between needs (considered to be internal, such as satisfaction) and incentives (considered to be external, such as rewards). Maehr and Braskamp label this distinction as meaningless in a cognitive theory because it is the individual's perception of how the external factors may influence him or her that is important to determining motivation, not just the event itself. The fact that they refer to *personal* incentives recognizes this distinction because it is the individual interpretation of the situation that determines incentive. They also make a distinction between personal incentives and personal goals (see Duda & Whitehead, this volume) that they used in earlier work (Maehr, 1983; Maehr & Kleiber, 1980) because goals seem to be highly associated with the performance level an individual achieves as opposed to what an individual chooses to do.

Maehr and Braskamp (1986) were interested in motivation across a variety of domains, but were particularly interested in motivation in work settings. Because it was recognized that an individual may be motivated by a variety of personal incentives, personal incentives were organized into intrinsic (task and ego) and extrinsic (social and reward) categories to help interpret this wide range of possible factors. It was also recognized that individuals may be motivated by aspects inherent to the task itself, and Maehr and Braskamp (1986) provided further conceptual organization by suggesting two facets for this task involvement: task absorption and demonstration of competence.

When discussing task absorption, the example of children at play comes readily to mind. Children can spend countless hours devoted to simple activities, sometimes in solitude for long periods of time. Examples of adults involved in physical activity or exercise environments might also reflect intrinsic motivation driven by pure task involvement. The second intrinsic task motive an individual may have is to demonstrate competence, a construct central to most motivational theories. From a theoretical standpoint, it is predicted that if task personal incentives are highly salient for an individual, then the person will choose tasks that clearly challenge his or her ability and competence. Alternatively, if ego-involved personal incentives are salient, people prefer to engage in a social comparison process where outperforming another individual is of primary importance. Thus, a competitive environment may differentially affect an individual depending on his or her self perceptions of competence. These notions may therefore influence the type of physical activity or exercise setting a person would choose. For example, if a person is primarily engaging in an activity to fulfill task incentives, he or she may choose to exercise alone. On the other hand, if ego incentives are salient, individuals may choose to exercise with others so their performances could be compared.

Extrinsic personal incentives could be either related to social approval or rewards. In the work setting, it would be predicted that good interpersonal relations would lead to enhanced productivity, whereas conflict would lead to reduced productivity. If a person is primarily motivated by social incentives, demonstrating effort would be of prime importance. The notion of interpersonal relations or cohesion has received recent attention in the exercise psychology literature (e.g., Carron, Brawley, & Widmeyer, this volume; Carron, Widmeyer, & Brawley, 1988) and may well be related to this notion of social approval. Finally, the role of external rewards has received a tremendous amount of attention over the last 20 years (see, for example, Deci, 1975; Lepper & Greene, 1975).

Incentives have been interpreted with respect to a number of theories. In some cases, incentives have been a central construct in the theory; in other situations, incentives were assessed in a particular study, and an attempt was made to connect incentives with the theoretical framework employed. Whether or not research is conducted within a specific theoretical framework, it is essential that constructs are properly assessed. The following section will discuss measurement considerations inherent to incentive-based research followed by specific examples of incentive measurements.

Considerations in Scale Development

According to the American Psychological Association (APA, 1985), "psychological testing represents one of the most important contributions of behavioral science to our society" (p. 1). Psychological testing has also been heavily criticized, and in response to these criticisms, the APA, the American Educational Research Association, and the National Council on Measurement in Education have set up a panel to continuously review standards for educational and psychological testing. The following comments are derived from these standards and focus primarily on issues related to validity and reliability.

It is of course important to establish validity and reliability in measures, but the correct procedures for doing so are not always followed. According to the APA, there are three types of validity that we need to be concerned with in test development: construct, content, and criterion-related validity. To display construct validity, a measure must clearly assess the construct it purports to measure. In the case of personal incentives, it is necessary to ask whether any of the inventories demonstrate construct validity. That is, do they really measure exercise incentives? Accordingly, the construct should be imbedded in a conceptual or theoretical framework. "The conceptual framework specifies the meaning of the construct, distinguishes it from other constructs, and indicates how measures of the construct should relate to other variables" (APA, 1985, p. 10).

A second type of validity that is important is content validity. This type of validity, often called face validity, is generally determined by having judges or experts in the field rate whether the items seem to reflect or are representative of the content domain being measured.

Finally, there are two types of criterion-related validity: concurrent and predictive. If one is attempting to establish concurrent validity, the inventory is correlated with other validated inventories that measure a similar construct (positive correlation expected) or a dissimilar construct (negative correlation expected) at the same point in time. Predictive validity is established when a measure can predict some behavior in the future. According to the APA (1985), predictive validity studies are preferable to concurrent validity studies when selection tests for some future behavior are being generated whereas concurrent tests are preferable for "achievement tests, tests for certification, diagnostic tests or tests used as measures of a specified construct" (p.11).

Reliability or repeatability of measurement is another important consideration in test development. Reliability refers to the degree the test is free from measurement error. If a test is expected to measure a relatively stable or trait measure of behavior, it would be appropriate to determine its reliability by examining test-retest correlations as well as internal consistencies. If responses to a test are expected to change over time, then some sort of internal consistency measure such as Cronbach's alpha would be most appropriate. Although it might be anticipated that exercise incentives would change over time, it is probably reasonable to expect changes could take a relatively long time.

Measures of Incentives to Exercise

Inventory of Personal Investment (IPI)

Maehr and Braskamp (1986) developed an inventory of personal investment (IPI) designed to be a trait measure of personal investment as well as an inventory of work investment (IWI) designed to assess situational factors, meanings, and personal investment in work settings. Because these measures served as the basis for subsequent measures used in exercise environments, they will be briefly described. The IPI was designed to assess the two categories of meaning within personal investment theory: personal incentives as well as sense-of-self components. Based on item and factor analyses of responses from 744 individuals, Maeher and Braskamp identified eight relatively independent personal incentives that could be linked to the four theoretical categories of personal incentives previously described. The eight incentives were task involvement, striving for excellence, competition, power, affiliation, social concern, financial rewards, and recognition for accomplishment. The three sense-of-self factors derived from the analysis included goal directedness, self-reliance, and competence. The IWI is a more overall measure of motivation designed to assess not only personal incentives and sense of self but also options available within a particular work context. The IWI is a shortened version of the IPI but also includes perceived options. Two subscales of perceived options assess marketability, which deals with general career options and organizational advancement and the options the person feels he or she has within a current organization. Addressing the concept of construct validity, Maehr and Braskamp developed their measures of personal incentives with the theoretical framework of personal investment theory as their guiding conceptual framework. As such, they developed eight subscales of incentives that corresponded to four categories of personal incentives (intrinsic - task and ego; extrinsic - social solidarity and extrinsic rewards). Such a procedure is a good start on helping to establish construct validity, and the authors made clear predictions as to how personal investment or motivation should be influenced by each of the four personal incentive categories.

Personal Incentives for Exercise

Kimiecik, Jackson, and Giannini (1990) provide one example of application of the work of Maehr and Braskamp (1986) to the exercise domain. Kimiecik and his colleagues developed an inventory titled the Exercise Activity Inventory (EAI) designed for members of one specific health club by adapting the personal incentive items of Maehr and Braskamp for this population. The EAI comprises 16 items designed to assess four subscales of incentives related to exercise (mastery, competition, affiliation, and recognition). Cronbach alpha reliabilities of the items within each subscale were deemed satisfactory, ranging from .78 to .87. The authors noted, however, that a large interscale correlation between affiliation and recognition might indicate lack of independence between the subscales.

With the exception of the Kimiecik et al. (1990) study noted above, the majority of published work applying personal investment theory to the physical activity domain has been conducted by Duda and her associates. Duda, Smart, and Tappe (1989) conducted one study specifically designed to test the predictive validity of the three components of personal investment theory in a rehabilitation setting. Based on Maehr and Braskamp's (1986) work, they assessed five personal incentives: task involvement, ego involvement, power, recognition, and affiliation. The 25 items (5 for each incentive) were borrowed from the IPI described above and reworded to be specific for sport. Alpha reliabilities for the subscales ranged from .78 to .85. Of the five incentives, task involvement, which focuses on personal mastery and effort, was the best predictor of attendance of the rehabilitation sessions, exercise completion, exercise intensity, and adherence. The personal incentive variables were not as predictive as the other components of personal investment theory in predicting adherence behaviors in rehabilitation. However, as noted by Duda et al. (1989), the personal incentives assessed were related to sport and were not situation specific to the rehabilitation process.

Personal Incentives for Exercise Questionnaire (PIEQ)

To correct for the lack of an exercise-specific personal incentive measure, over a period of several years Duda and her colleagues developed four different versions of the Personal Incentives for Exercise Questionnaire (PIEQ) (see Duda & Tappe, 1987; 1988, 1989a, 1989b, Tappe & Duda, 1988). The initial item development (Duda & Tappe, 1987) was based on their review of the exercise psychology literature, the reliance on Maehr and Braskamp's (1986) theoretical framework of personal investment theory and their administration of an open-ended questionnaire to 165 male and female exercise participants. For the original scale, 85 items were developed, and 525 college students were administered the inventory. Factor analysis procedures were conducted to yield the nine factors within the inventory. Results from additional analyses reduced the scale to 48 items (PIEQ, Version 1) and factor analyses on data generated from an additional 352 college students yielded a stable factor structure across the two samples. (J.L. Duda, personal communication, September, 1989). Alpha reliabilities on subscales ranged from .74 to .94, and test-retest correlations ranged from .58 to .86. The 10 to 14 days allowed between test and retest provided a sufficient duration to assess repeatability. No

validity data were reported in the initial published studies. The only published paper that spoke to the scale development of the PIEQ was a short one-page report (Duda & Tappe, 1989a). The report mentioned that four versions of the scale had been developed. The items on the PIEQ are ranked on a 5-point scale ranging from 1(*strongly disagree*) to 5 (*strongly agree*). Sample items include "I exercise to look better," "Through exercise I can be physically strong," and "I find exercise fun, especially when competition is involved."

An early study published by Duda and Tappe (1988) used Version 1 of the PIEQ to investigate the relationship between personal investment theory constructs and exercise participation in 47 male and female adults ranging in age from 50 to 81. This 49-item inventory used a 5-point Likert scale and assessed personal incentives across seven categories: mastery, competition, social affiliation, recognition, health benefits, coping with stress, and physical fitness. The only psychometric data reported in this paper were the internal consistency of the subscales, determined by using Cronbach's alpha reliability coefficients. These ranged from .68 to .91, which were considered acceptable. In addition to incentives, sense of self and perceived options were also assessed. Incentives were more predictive than either of these other categories of variables in predicting present and future involvement in exercise.

Utilizing the second version of the PIEQ, Duda and Tappe (1989b) assessed personal investment in exercise among 145 middle-aged and older aged adults involved in an organized exercise program. Version 2 of the inventory contained 48 items and the same seven categories of incentives as Version 1. No additional psychometric data were reported beyond the alpha reliability coefficients that had been previously reported (Duda & Tappe, 1987).

Tappe and Duda (1988) employed Version 2 in examining the relationship between personal investment theory variables and life satisfaction among 85 adults, ranging in age from 50 to 81 years, who were participating in a community exercise program. No psychometric data were reported, but four of the seven incentives were found to be related to life satisfaction. A subsequent study (Tappe, Duda, & Menges-Ehrnwald, 1990) reported using a slightly revised Version 2 inventory (appropriately worded for adolescents), which had 49 items and 11 subscales (competition, appearance, affiliation, recognition, mental benefits, flexibility, mastery, health, weight management, strength, and solitude). It is not clear from this study why the Version 2 used in the 1989 study and the Version 2 used here had a different number of items and different subscales. Alpha reliabilities were reported to range from .74 to .88. In this study the personal incentives of strength, affiliation, and health discriminated high- from low-activity individuals.

We could find no published papers that reported using Version 3 of the inventory and one published paper that employed Version 4 (Finkenburg, DiNucci, McCune, & McCune, 1994). This study examined the relationship between personal incentives, gender, and activity level of 206 female and 88 male college students. In this study, the 48-item, 5-point Likert scale assessed 10 categories of personal incentives (affiliation, appearance, competition, fitness, flexibility/agility, health benefits, mastery, mental benefits, social recognition, and weight management). No psychometric information was reported in the published report but Finkenburg (personal communication, November 4, 1996) did report that a factor analysis was conducted on the data and that the factors were the same as had been reported by Duda and Tappe (1989a).

A doctoral dissertation by Kimiecik (1990) also utilized Version 4 of the PIEQ. Kimiecik reassessed the factor structure of the PIEQ with his sample of 332 corporate employees. Instead of the 10 distinct factors identified by Duda and Tappe (1989b), the factor analysis by Kimiecik identified 9 factors (Flexibility, Agility, Weight Control, Mastery, Competition, Appearance, Physical Fitness, Solitude, Affiliation, Social Recognition). These 9 factors accounted for 83.7% of the variance in his study, with Cronbach's alpha reliability values ranging from .75 to .94. The factor labeled Solitude included many of the items from the PIEQ's mental benefits factors. No health benefits factor emerged, and, in fact, the items from the health benefits factors did not appear to load on any of the other factors because they were not included in the item loadings reported by Kimiecik.

An examination of conference programs for both the Association for the Advancement of Applied Sport Psychology and the North American Society for the Psychology of Sport and Physical Activity indicated that a number of research studies have used some version of the PIEQ to examine exercise incentives. For example, Matzkanin (1991) used Version 4 of the PIEQ to examine the exercise adherence of 71 participants, ranging in age from 17 to 41, who were enrolled in a university aerobics program. Cronbach's alphas for the 10 personal incentive categories ranged from .72 to .93. In support of previous work by Duda and Tappe (1989b), personal incentives did vary as a function of age.

In a subsequent study, McCullagh, Matzkanin, and Figge (1996) examined the personal incentives of 66 male and 58 females, ranging in age from 21 to 77, who were masters swim participants. Version 4 of the PIEQ was employed, and to determine scale reliability, Cronbach's alphas were calculated on the 10 personal incentives. Values ranged from .77 to .91, so all factors were considered internally consistent.

Raedeke and Burton (1996) took a personal investment theory approach when they assessed the incentives of 292 participants in university wellness programs. Their primary purpose was to determine if individuals of differing activity levels varied on incentives for exercise as well as on other components of personal investment theory. To develop their initial pool of 208 items (rated on a 4-point Likert scale), the authors borrowed items from the PIEQ, modified some items from goal orientation inventories, and generated items from the exercise research and notions implicit in personal investment theory. Based on judges' ratings for clarity and face validity, items were eliminated and reworded leaving 156 items. The scale underwent three revisions based on factor analysis, item analysis, and item-to-subscale correlations; and a final 62-item inventory was used in data analysis. The final nine incentives that were identified from this test development procedure were Performance, Outcome, Social, Recognition, Mental Health, Involvement, Solitude, Feel Good, and Health/Fitness. Some of these categories overlap with categories on the PIEQ whereas others are new categories.

When Duda and Tappe (1987) developed the PIEQ, they stated that it was based on the exercise psychology literature and personal investment theory. However, it is not clear how the subscales fit into this conceptual framework, and thus construct validity may be questioned. For example, it is not clear how the subscales of the PIEQ relate to the four personal incentive categories within personal investment. Also, no predictions are made as to how the subscales should vary as a function of other variables. Although the authors stated that they surveyed the exercise psychology literature to generate items for the PIEQ, it is not evident that outside experts in the field reviewed any of the versions of their instrument to help establish content validity.

Exercise Motivations Inventory (EMI)

Markland and Hardy (1993) questioned the value of the 48-item, 10-subscale version of the PIEQ (we assume they are referring to Version 4) because it "appears to suffer from a number of problems which may influence its suitability for addressing research questions" (p. 290) related to personal investment theory. One problem that they identified was that the role of enjoyment as an exercise goal had been overlooked in the PIEQ. They noted that the original version of the PIEQ had a subscale called Involvement that included items related to enjoyment, such as ("It is fun, and I enjoy being active") but noted that this factor was dropped in further developments of the scale. They further argued that many items on the PIEQ do not reflect incentives to exercise but are rather general beliefs. They take issue with items such as "Winning at physical activities is important to me" and "I try to exercise with others whenever I can," suggesting that these items might reflect *how* people exercises but not *why* they exercise. Based on these two primary arguments, these authors deemed it worthwhile to develop a new instrument. Their inventory, the Exercise Motivations Inventory (EMI), was designed to be a "psychometrically derived multidimensional instrument which measures a wide range of possible reasons for exercising " (p. 290).

To develop the EMI, Markland and Hardy (1993) administered an open-ended questionnaire to 100 individuals who were all involved in regular exercise. They then classified responses into 9 categories of related reasons for exercising based on factors from the PIEQ or because "they reflected enjoyment-related reasons" (Markland & Hardy, 1993, p. 291). It is not clear why the current authors tried to force their open-ended responses into only 9 categories based on this reasoning. In the introduction of their paper, they clearly list the 10 subscales of the Duda and Tappe Version 4 (1987) inventory (see Table 1). If their primary argument was that an additional enjoyment factor needed to be added to the already existing 10 categories, they should have had 11 categories. Also, it was not discussed how the items on the EMI relate to the subscales of the PIEQ. We have attempted to align the factors from the EMI with the factors from the PIEQ, and they are not in complete agreement. A thorough discussion of this discrepancy was not provided by Markland and Hardy.

Based on the responses to the open-ended questionnaire and the PIEQ, Markland and Hardy (1993) formed an initial pool of 76 items. The items were examined by a panel of judges for clarity, lack of ambiguity, ease of understanding,

Table 1
Subscales reported by Duda and Tappe (1989b) and by Markland and Hardy (1993).

Duda and Tappe (Version 4)	Markland and Hardy Initial Open-Ended response categories	Markland and Hardy 6-Point Likert EMI
Appearance		Appearance
Competition	Competition	Competition
Mental Benefits	Stress Management	
Affiliation	Social/Affiliation	Affiliation
Mastery	Personal Skills	Personal Development
Fitness (Strength/Endurance)	Fitness	Fitness
Flexibility/Agility		
Social Recognition		Social Recognition
Health Benefits	Health	Health Pressures
Weight Management	Weight Management	Weight Management
	Improve Sporting Skills	
	Enjoyment	Enjoyment
		Re-creation
		Ill-Health Avoidance
		Stress Management

and content validity. This procedure reduced the original 76 items to 71 items to form Version 1 of the EMI. All responses on the inventory started with "Personally, I exercise...." and were rated on a 6-point Likert scale. This wording was used to tap into why individuals exercise and not why people in general might exercise (analogous to efficacy and outcome expectations). Based on a principal components analysis, 15 factors emerged. Of these, 11 were distinct factors. "The remaining factors were indeterminate in nature and there were a number of ambiguously loading items" (Markland & Hardy, 1993, p. 291). Therefore, the ambiguous items were eliminated, and the remaining 56 items were subjected to another principal components analysis. From this analysis, 12 factors emerged and are listed In Table 1. Six ambiguous or low-loading items were removed, thus reducing the scale to 50 items. After applying Cronbach's alpha, 6 more items were removed, and the authors considered the internal consistency of 10 of the 12 subscales to be adequate because they ranged from .63 to .92. The Fitness (.70) and Health Pressures (.63) scales scored lower on alpha reliabilities than did the other subscales. To determine test-retest reliability, the original sample of subjects retook the original EMI four to five weeks after the initial administration, and the observed values ranged from .59 to .88. The authors considered these quite acceptable considering that it was the original, and not the more psychometrically sound revised version of the scale that had been administered.

In an attempt to establish construct validity, Markland and Hardy (1993) determined if the EMI could discriminate between males and females. Within Maehr and Braskamp's (1986) personal investment theory, both gender and age differences are expected in terms of personal incentives. Although some evidence is cited that age and gender differences have been found in exercise participants, the direct application of theoretical constructs developed for work settings may be brought into question when considering exercise incentives. Based on previous findings in

the literature (Biddle & Bailey, 1985; Duda & Tappe, 1989b), it was predicted that women would exercise more for affiliation and weight management than would men and that men would exercise more for competition than women did. The results revealed that males exercised more for competition and recognition and less for weight management than did females. However, no differences on the Affiliation subscale were found. Although the predictions were partially upheld, it should be noted that hypotheses were made for only 3 of the 12 subscales.

To establish content or face validity, an early version of the EMI was reviewed by a panel of five expert judges, and the items were reworded in an attempt to reflect personal reasons for exercise. In an attempt to establish concurrent validity, two subscales from the EMI (Re-creation and Enjoyment) were correlated with a previously established interest/enjoyment measure of intrinsic motivation (Intrinsic Motivation Inventory, Ryan, 1982). Because the correlations ranged from .50 to .55 and were higher than the other EMI subscales, the authors were confident with the validity of the measure. They had also administered a social desirability scale, and because correlations between the EMI sub-scales and the social desirability scores were low (.01 to .23), they felt the EMI was not subject to social desirability. The authors concluded their paper suggesting the need to improve the Fitness and Health Pressure subscales of the EMI and further test the instrument's concurrent validity as well as determine the predictive validity of the inventory.

Outcome Expectancy

Another method to assess incentives or reasons for participation was described by Rodgers and Brawley (1991). They reviewed the literature and found that a great deal of work had been done on participation motives of children in youth sport. They noted, however, that little work had examined motivations for physical activity in adults. To determine motives, they began by pilot testing a group of university students using an open-ended format. All the items on this comprehensive list of possible reasons for participating in physical activity were then presented to the main study participants to provide respondents with a wide range of response alternatives. Consistent with the researchers' theoretically driven expectancy-value approach, main-study participants then rated each alternative with regards to its importance (3-point Likert scale), personal value to them (9-point Likert scale), and the likelihood of achieving the outcome (0% to 100%). Rodgers and Brawley (1991) argue that this method is superior to the majority of participation motivation literature, which asks participants only to rate response alternatives for their importance on 3 to 5-point scales. They argue that such short scales "limit respondents' use of a continuum to represent a range of perceptions" (Rodgers & Brawley, 1991, p. 417). They also derived a fourth measure of outcome expectancy (OE) that was a product of the likelihood and value measures. Because the OE measure showed a greater range of scores, the authors argued that these measures were better discriminators of reasons for exercise participation. Furthermore, because the correlations between the OE measure and the more typically used importance measure (.49) were interpreted as moderate, the authors argued that a measure that reflects two concepts and that has greater response variation is better than a measure that reflects only one concept (importance). It could be said OE has face validity because the original items were generated by the study participants and some degree of construct validity because it was theoretically derived. Further research will need to determine the criterion validity of this outcome expectancy measure. No other psychometric data were reported by Rodgers and Brawley (1991).

A subsequent study by Rodgers and Brawley (1996) also used the likelihood-by-value measure to assess incentives for exercise in individuals who enrolled for a weight-training class. Based on pilot testing, the investigators presented participants with 13 primary and 12 secondary outcomes. The primary outcomes were grouped into physical health, mental health, and appearance categories; and the secondary outcomes were related to mental health and appearance. The authors argued that the "primary outcomes should provide greater incentive to encourage future intentions to engage in weight training than the less valued secondary outcomes" (Rodgers & Brawley, 1996, p. 626). Regression analyses supported this prediction. Furthermore, the results suggested that outcomes, also labeled as incentives by the authors, would have a greater influence than self-efficacy on initial intentions, whereas self-efficacy had a greater influence on intentions once individuals had experience with the activity. Thus, Rodgers and Brawley (1996) were able to differentiate the influence of self-efficacy and incentives on intentions.

Reasons for Exercise Inventory

Another exercise-incentive measure, the Reasons for Exercise Inventory (REI), was developed by Silberstein and colleagues in an attempt to identify gender differences in body dissatisfaction (Silberstein, Striegel-Moore, Timko, & Rodin, 1988). The original derivation as well as how the items were grouped was not included in the written report. To generate this scale, 28 items were chosen to represent seven domains of reasons for pursuing exercise. These seven domains included weight control, fitness, health, body tone, physical attractiveness, mood, and enjoyment. Of the original 28 items, 4 were dropped due to a low item-total correlation leaving a total of 24 items with 3 to 4 items for each subscale. Reliability coefficients (Cronbach alpha) for each subscale ranged from .67 to .81. No other information concerning the factor structure of the instrument was reported, and none of the mainstream exercise psychology literature was reviewed to develop the subscales. It is not clear how the items were generated because it was merely reported that the inventory "was developed for the study" (Silberstein et al., 1988, p.223). Thus it appears that no attempt was made to establish content validity.

McDonald and Thompson (1992) employed the REI when they examined sex differences in reasons for exercise and the relationship of these reasons to eating disturbance, body dissatisfaction, and self-esteem among 199 male and 91 female undergraduates. No psychometric data for the REI were reported, but the authors did indicate that females scored higher on the weight and tone subscales than males did.

In an attempt to provide validation for the Reasons for Exercise Inventory, Cash, Novy, and Grant (1994) administered the inventory to 101 exercising women. The authors expressed surprise at the lack of research generated by the Reasons for Exercise Inventory as well as the lack of an established factor structure and its predictive validity for exercise behaviors. The factor structure produced by Cash et al. resulted in four factors labeled Fitness/Health Management, Appearance/Weight Management, Stress/Mood Management, and Socializing. Two of the original items were dropped because of insufficient loading (less than .50) on any single factor. Cronbach alphas on the four factors ranged from .73 to .91. The authors concluded that all of the factors and the resultant composite score had acceptable internal consistency. Significant relationships were also found between the exercise motives of appearance/weight management and measures of exercise frequency, body satisfaction, and body image, indicating an attempt to establish criterion-related validity. The authors called for further research before generalizing the findings to men.

Crawford and Eklund (1994) employed the REI to examine the relationship between reasons for exercise and social physique anxiety among 104 college-aged females. The Fitness, Health and Body Tone subscales revealed alpha coefficients ranging from .73 to .80. However, the alpha coefficients for the Weight Control, Mood, Physical Attractiveness and Enjoyment subscales were not considered sufficient until an item was deleted from each. The authors suggested that the small number of items on each subscale (3 to 4) may have contributed to the instability of the measure. In line with their hypotheses, body tone and weight control and physical attractiveness were all related to social physique anxiety. However, social physique anxiety was not significantly related to fitness, mood enhancement, health, or enjoyment.

Finally, Davis, Fox, Brewer and Ratusny (1995) employed the REI in their investigation of the influence of age, gender, physical activity level, and personality factors on reasons for participation in leisure-time physical activity among 106 male and 105 female exercisers. The 24 items on the REI were subjected to a confirmatory factor analysis using the data from the 211 individuals in this study as well as 155 participants from a previous study. In addition, the factor analysis model was fitted by weighted least squares using the LISREL program. Because the Fitness and Health factors were strongly correlated, they were combined. Some of the items loaded on different factors than on the original REI, and two items were dropped because they loaded on two factors. The final scale employed included 22 items, and the scales were named Sexual Attractiveness, General Appearance, Weight Control, Fitness and Health, Mood Improvement, and Enjoyment. Cronbach alpha coefficients for the six subscales ranged from .76 to .87.

Conclusions

The Personal Incentives for Exercise Questionnaire and the recent modifications and attempts at validation of the Exercise Motivations Inventory and Reasons for Exercise Inventory, as well as the outcome-expectancy measure, are a good start at scale development. Different authors have taken on the difficult task of developing inventories and then subjecting them to the rigors of validity and reliability. The Personal Incentives for Exercise Questionnaire appears to have received the most research attention. Various versions have been subjected to factor analyses, and many of these factors appear to maintain themselves across various samples. For the most part, the internal consistencies of the subscales are quite good in a wide variety of populations ranging from college students to corporate employees as well as older exercisers and masters swimmers. Although reliability has been fairly well established, validity measures, especially criterion-related validity, have not been well documented. Thus, if researchers are interested in measuring incentives using the PIEQ, additional research should be aimed at establishing validity.

The Exercise Motivations Inventory (Markland & Hardy, 1993) has received initial attempts at establishing both reliability and validity, but the limited amount of research does not speak clearly to the concurrent or predictive validity of the measure. The authors who developed the EMI criticized the PIEQ and its categories, but did not include a thorough discussion of the category comparisons between the two inventories. Also, it is not clear what theoretical orientation is being used to guide this research. The likelihood measure (OE) assessing reasons for participation is framed within an expectancy-value approach to behavior. Further research will be needed to determine the psychometric stability of this measure. Finally, the REI measure has been used most extensively in research that has also attempted to assess some aspect of body dissatisfaction or physique anxiety. Because the only known attempt at establishing a factor structure was conducted with women, more research on the REI employing males is needed for generalization purposes.

This chapter has reviewed the research that has attempted to assess exercise incentives. Only personal investment theory employs the term incentive as a central construct, whereas other theoretical or conceptual approaches use different terms to allude to this motivational construct. Different theoretical or conceptual approaches will obviously yield different measurement tools. However, it seems imperative that we continue to strive to develop reliable measures that can provide a valid assessment of exercise incentives within a theoretical framework.

References

American Psychological Association (1985). *Standards for educational and psychological testing.* Washington, D.C.: Author.

Biddle, S.J.H., & Bailey, C.I.A. (1985). Motives for participation and attitudes toward physical activity of adult participants in fitness programs. *Perceptual and Motor Skills, 61,* 831-834.

Carron, A.V., Widmeyer, W.N., & Brawley, L.R. (1988). Group cohesion and individual adherence to physical activity. *Journal of Sport and Exercise Psychology, 10,* 119-126.

Cash, T.E., Novy, P.L., & Grant, J.R. (1994). Why do women exercise? Factor analysis and further validation of the reasons for exercise inventory. *Perceptual and Motor Skills, 78,* 539-544.

Crawford, S., & Eklund, R.C. (1994). Social physique anxiety, reasons for exercise, and attitudes toward exercise settings. *Journal of Sport & Exercise Psychology, 16,* 70-82.

Davis, C., Fox, J., Brewer, H., & Ratusny, D. (1995). Motivations to exercise as a function of personality characteristics, age and gender. *Personality and Individual Differences, 19,* 165-174.

Deci, E.L. (1975). *Intrinsic motivation.* New York: Plenum.

Dishman, R.K., & Ickes, W. (1981). Self-motivation and adherence to therapeutic exercise. *Journal of Behavioral Medicine, 4,* 421-438.

Duda, J.L., Smart, A.E., & Tappe, M.K. (1989). Predictors of adherence in the rehabilitation of athletic injuries: An application of personal investment theory. *Journal of Sport and Exercise Psychology, 11,* 367-381.

Duda, J.L., & Tappe, M.K. (1987, September). *Personal investment in exercise: The development of the Personal Incentives for Exercise Questionnaire.* Paper presented at the Association for the Advancement of Applied Sport Psychology, Newport Beach, CA.

Duda, J.L., & Tappe, M.K. (1988). Predictors of personal investment in physical activity among middle-aged and older adults. *Perceptual and Motor Skills, 66,* 543-549.

Duda, J.L., & Tappe, M.K. (1989a). The Personal Incentives for Exercise Questionnaire: Preliminary development. *Perceptual and Motor Skills, 68,* 1122.

Duda, J.L., & Tappe, M.K. (1989b). Personal investment in exercise among adults: The examination of age and gender-related differences in motivational orientation. In A.C. Ostrow, (Ed.), *Aging and motor behavior* (pp. 239-256). Indianapolis: Benchmark Press.

Finkenburg, M.E., DiNucci, J.M., McCune, S.L., & McCune, E.D. (1994). Analysis of course type, gender, and personal incentives to exercise. *Perceptual and Motor Skills, 78,* 155-159.

Keefe, F.J., & Blumenthal, J.A. (1980). The life fitness program: A behavioral approach to making exercise a habit. *Journal of Behavioral Therapy and Exercise Psychiatry, 11,* 31-34.

Kimiecik, J.C. (1990). *The motivational determinants of exercise involvement: A social psychological process/stage approach.* Unpublished doctoral dissertation, University of Illinois.

Kimiecik, J.C., Jackson, S.A., & Giannini, J.M. (1990). Striving for exercise goals: An examination of the motivational orientations and exercise behavior of unsupervised joggers, swimmers, and cyclists. In L.V. Veldon & J.H. Humphrey (Eds.), *Psychology and sociology of sport: Current selected research: Vol. 2,* (pp. 17-32). New York: AMS Press.

Lepper, M., & Greene, D. (1975). Turning play into work: Effects of adult surveillance and extrinsic rewards on children's intrinsic motivation. *Journal of Personality and Social Psychology, 31,* 479-486.

Maehr, M.L. (1983). On doing well in science: Why Johnny no longer excels; why Sarah never did. In S. Paris, G. Olson, & H. Stevenson (Eds.), *Learning and motivation in the classroom* (pp. 179-210). Hillsdale, NJ.: Erlbaum.

Maehr, M.L., & Braskamp, L.A. (1986). *The motivation factor: A theory of personal investment.* Lexington, MA; Lexington Press.

Maehr, M.L., & Kleiber, D.A. (1980). The graying of America: Implications for achievement motivation theory and research. In L.J. Fyans, Jr. (Ed.), *Achievement motivation* (pp. 171-189). New York: Plenum Press.

Marcus, B.H., Rakowski, W., & Rossi, J.S. (1992). Assessing motivational readiness and decision making for exercise. *Health Psychology, 11,* 257-261.

Markland, D., & Hardy, L. (1993). The Exercise Motivations Inventory: Preliminary development and validity of a measure of individuals' reasons for participation in regular physical activity. *Personality and Individual Differences, 15,* 289-296.

Matzkanin, K.T. (1991). *An investigation of personal investment theory and adherence to an aerobic exercise program.* Unpublished master's thesis. University of Colorado, Boulder.

McAuley, E., Poag, K., Gleason, A., & Wraith, S. (1990). Attrition from exercise programs: Attributional and affective perspectives. *Journal of Social Behavior and Personality, 5*, 591-602.

McCready, M.L., & Long, B.C. (1985). Locus of control, attitudes toward physical activity and exercise adherence. *Journal of Sport Psychology, 7*, 346-359.

McCullagh, P., Matzkanin, K.T., & Figge, J. (1996). *Motivation for exercise in masters' swimmers: A personal investment approach.* Unpublished manuscript, University of Colorado, Boulder.

McDonald, K., & Thompson, J.K. (1992). Eating disturbance, body image dissatisfaction, and reasons for exercising: Gender differences and correlational findings. *International Journal of Eating Disorders, 11*, 289-292.

Pemberton, C. (1986). *Motivational aspects of exercise adherence.* Unpublished doctoral dissertation, University of Illinois.

Raedeke, T.D., & Burton, D. (1996). *Applying personal investment theory to the physical activity setting: Incentives and perceived options of wellness program participants.* Unpublished manuscript, University of Colorado, Boulder.

Rodgers, W.M., & Brawley, L.R. (1991). The role of outcome expectancies in participation motivation. *Journal of Sport and Exercise Psychology, 13*, 411-427.

Rodgers, W.M., & Brawley, L.R. (1996). The influence of outcome expectancy and self-efficacy on the behavioral intentions of novice exercisers. *Journal of Applied Social Psychology, 26*, 618-634.

Ryan, R.M. (1982). Control and information in the intrapersonal sphere: An extension of cognitive evaluation theory. *Journal of Personality and Social Psychology, 43*, 450-461.

Silberstein, L.R., Striegel-Moore, R.H., Timko, C., & Rodin, J. (1988). Behavioral and psychological implications of body dissatisfaction: Do men and women differ? *Sex Roles, 19*, 219-232.

Tappe, M.K., & Duda, J.L. (1988). Personal investment predictors of life satisfaction among physically active middle-aged and older adults. *The Journal of Psychology, 122*, 557-566.

Tappe, M.K., Duda, J.L., Menges-Ehrnwald, P. (1990). Personal investment predictors of adolescent motivational orientation toward exercise. *Canadian Journal of Sport Sciences, 15*, 185-192.

Wysocki, T., Hall, G., Iwata, B., & Riordan, M. (1979). Behavioral management of exercise: Contracting for aerobic points. *Journal of Applied Behavior Analysis, 12*, 55-64.

Chapter 22

Measuring Exercise-Related Self-Efficacy

Edward McAuley
University of Illinois at Urbana-Champaign
and
Shannon L. Mihalko
Pennsylvania State University

Introduction

In the past two decades the United States Public Health Service (U.S. Department of Health and Human Services, 1990) has developed a preventive orientation in public health policies, promoting regular participation by children and adults in exercise and physical fitness as a major health objective for the nation. Moreover, such participation has been identified as a behavioral orientation expected to reduce morbidity and mortality. A considerable literature exists to suggest that habitual physical activity can positively influence a broad range of health conditions, both physiological and psychological. Physical activity and fitness have been linked to risk or symptom reduction in coronary heart disease, cancer, and osteoporosis (Bouchard, Shephard, & Stephens, 1993); all-cause mortality (Blair, Kohl, Paffenbarger, Clark, & Cooper, 1989); and depression (Camacho, Roberts, Lazarus, Kaplan, & Cohen, 1991), as well as enhanced cognitive (Dustman, Emmerson, & Shearer, 1994) and psychosocial function (McAuley & Rudolph, 1995).

Best epidemiological estimates report that less than 20% of the 18 to 65 year-old population exercise at sufficient levels of intensity, frequency, and duration to accrue positive health and fitness benefits (Centers for Disease Control, 1987). Furthermore, between 30% and 59% of the adult population is estimated to lead a sedentary lifestyle (Casperson, Christianson, & Pollard, 1986). More important, many individuals who engage in organized fitness or exercise programs withdraw before any health benefits have been realized. Indeed, the statistics are well documented regarding the alarming attrition rate in exercise programs, which approximates 50% within the first 6 months for those initiating a program (Dishman, 1982).

One of the most frequently identified psychosocial determinants of adherence to physical activity is the individual's perceptions of personal capabilities or self-efficacy (Bandura, 1986, 1997). Efficacy expectations are the individual's beliefs in his or her capabilities to execute necessary courses of action to satisfy situational demands and are theorized to influence the activities that individuals choose to approach, the effort expended on such activities, and the degree of persistence demonstrated in the face of failure or aversive stimuli (Bandura, 1986). More recently, Bandura (1995, 1997) has refined the definition of self-efficacy to encompass those beliefs regarding individuals' capabilities to produce performances that will lead to anticipated outcomes. The term *self-regulatory efficacy* is now employed, and both the term and definition encompass a social cognitive stance that is representative of the role cognitive skills play in behavioral performance above and beyond simply behavioral or skill beliefs. Maddux (1995) suggests that this definitional development has led to the distinction between task self-efficacy, where simple motor skills or capabilities are assessed (e.g., walking a certain distance), and self-regulatory or coping efficacy, where efficacy is assessed relative to impediments or challenges to successful behavioral performance (e.g., carrying out one's walking regimen when tired or stressed, or during foul weather, etc).

Research in the exercise domain has demonstrated self-efficacy to be implicated in exercise adherence in diseased (Ewart et al., 1986; Toshima, Kaplan, & Ries, 1990; Ries, Kaplan, Limberg, & Prewitt, 1995) and asymptomatic populations (Dzewaltowski, 1989), large-scale community studies (Sallis, Haskell, Fortmann, Vranizan, Taylor, & Solomon, 1986), and in training studies (McAuley, 1992; McAuley, Courneya, Rudolph, & Lox, 1994). Moreover, it appears that the role played by efficacy cognitions in exercise participation is more potent in those circumstances where physical activity presents the greatest challenge such as in the initial stages of adoption (McAuley, 1992) and long-term maintenance of activity

(McAuley, Lox, & Duncan, 1993), as well as exercise prescribed for secondary prevention of disease (Ewart, Taylor, Reese, & DeBusk, 1983).

As well as being a determinant of physical activity, self-efficacy expectations are also influenced by the exercise experience. Exercise effects on self-efficacy cognitions would appear particularly important given the broad constellation of physiological, behavioral, cognitive, and biochemical outcomes that self-efficacy is theorized to influence (Bandura, 1986, 1992). For example, McAuley and his colleagues (McAuley, Courneya, & Lettunich, 1991; McAuley et al., 1993) demonstrated in a series of studies that both long-term exercise participation and acute bouts of exercise were capable of enhancing perceptions of physical self-efficacy in middle-aged males and females. Additionally, Bandura and Cervone (1983, 1986) present evidence to suggest that self-efficacy operates as a motivator during acute exercise whereby greater efficacy leads to enhanced effort regardless of whether exercise performance exceeds or fails to meet set goals. Moreover, there is ample evidence to suggest that self-efficacy plays an important role in determining exercise behaviors, is influenced by exercise participation, and is also linked to affective responses associated with both acute and chronic exercise behavior (e.g., McAuley, 1991; McAuley, Bane, & Mihalko, 1995).

In spite of this, consideration of the measurement of self-efficacy has largely been ignored in the exercise and health psychology literature and, as we shall see, the theoretical rationale behind the operationalization of the exercise self-efficacy construct and ultimately the construction of efficacy measures is often questionable. In this chapter, we begin with a brief theoretical overview of the efficacy construct (see Feltz & Chase, this volume) and strive to emphasize the conceptual differentiation between self-efficacy and other self-related constructs (e.g., self-esteem; see Fox, this volume) with which self-efficacy is sometimes confused. We then proceed to the heart of the chapter in which we classify and critique the extant measures employed in the literature. In so doing, we address the manner in which classes of measures (e.g., barriers efficacy) are typically developed and examine their psychometric properties. We conclude the chapter with some recommendations for future considerations in the measurement of self-efficacy.

Theoretical Backdrop and Relevance of Self-Efficacy to Exercise Behavior

Self-efficacy refers to the individual's beliefs in his or her capabilities to successfully carry out a course of action to meet particularized task demands and, as such, self-efficacy is the primary construct of interest within Bandura's (1986) more comprehensive social cognitive theory. As noted, it is possible to differentiate between task and self-regulatory efficacy, and the reader is directed to Maddux (1995) for a fuller discussion of this differentiation. These judgments of personal efficacy are by definition situation-specific, and efficacy measures are therefore specific to domains of functioning rather than generalized in nature. Efficacy expectations influence human behavior through a variety of processes. Individuals with a strong sense of personal efficacy approach more challenging tasks, expend greater efforts in these tasks, and persist longer in the face of aversive stimuli.

Efficacy beliefs also act as motivational regulators in that they contribute to the formulation of desires and aspirations, as well as to one's degree of commitment to these aspirations (Bandura, 1995). In short, self-efficacy beliefs are theorized to influence motivation, affect, and behavior (Bandura, 1986).

The decision to embark on an exercise program and the subsequent maintenance of this health behavior are fraught with challenges especially when individuals are sedentary, older, or recovering from a life-threatening disease. Inherent in any successful behavioral attempt at changing exercise behavior is the ability to exert appropriate amounts of effort to accrue the requisite physiological and health effects and to persist in the face of the naturally occuring aversive stimuli associated with initial exercise exposure. Contrary to the images presented in the fitness media, exercise is not always fun and enjoyable. Early exposures are associated with muscle stiffness and soreness, early onset of fatigue, possible injury, and potential embarrassing moments as sedentary bodies are exposed in exercise attire for perhaps the first time in many years. Individuals with a robust sense of physical/exercise efficacy are likely to address such challenge and be more successful in the maintenance of that exercise behavior than are their less efficacious counterparts (McAuley, 1992, 1993). More efficacious individuals are likely to expend greater amounts of effort in attaining heath-promoting levels of physical activity (Ewart et al., 1983), and when faced with setbacks, these individuals are likely to persist in their pursuits and redouble their efforts (McAuley et al., 1993). Exercise has for many years been inexorably linked to various aspects of positive mental health such as reduced anxiety (Landers & Petruzello, 1994) and depression (Camacho et al, 1991). Although the underlying mechanisms that may be operating to bring about these positive emotional changes are unclear, greater self-efficacy has consistently been linked to lower levels of anxiety and depression (Bandura, 1986, 1992). Additionally, several recent studies have shown self-efficacy to mediate exercise effects on affective responses (e.g., Bozoian, Rejeski, & McAuley, 1994; McAuley & Courneya, 1992). Given the importance of choice, effort, persistence, and emotional dimensions of exercise behavior, it appears clear that self-efficacy expectations represent a crucial social cognitive element of this behavioral domain.

Self-Efficacy and Related Constructs

A brief glance at the contents of this volume (e.g., chapters by Feltz & Chase, and Fox) is enough to suggest to the reader that self-related constructs are abundantly present in the exercise and sport psychology literature. Lest there be any confusion in differentiating self-efficacy from some of these other constructs, we now take a brief opportunity to outline how self-efficacy should be considered conceptually distinct from self-esteem/worth, general self-confidence (efficacy), intentions and outcome expectations.

Self-esteem or self-worth (see Fox, this volume) can broadly be defined as encompassing the favorable view that one holds regarding oneself. It is considered a focal aspect of psychological health and well-being, and is relatively stable (Rosenberg, 1979). Self-efficacy, on the other hand, is concerned with individuals' beliefs in their capabilities in varying behavioral domains and is a dynamic construct that can be influenced by cognitive, physiological, behavioral, and social information. Although some overtures have been made with respect to the underlying role that self-efficacy may play in the development of self-esteem, few empirical efforts have been made in this area (for exceptions, see McAuley, Mihalko, & Bane, 1997, and Sonstroem, Harlow, & Josephs, 1994).

A generalized sense of self-confidence or efficacy can be conceptualized as a dispositional quality to be optimistic about one's abilities to be successful across a broad array of unrelated domains. This is clearly distinct from self-efficacy, which is concerned with beliefs about capabilities in specific domains or situations. In those cases where omnibus measures of confidence have been compared to more specific efficacy measures, the latter have uniformly been more predictive of behavioral outcomes. Efficacy cognitions are composed of several dimensions. *Level* of efficacy is concerned with individuals' beliefs in their capability to accomplish a specific task or element of a task. *Strength* of efficacy is concerned with the degree of conviction that a task can be successfully carried out. Therefore, I may indicate that I can walk a block in 3 minutes (level) but only be 50% confident in successfully carrying out this task (strength). The final dimension of efficacy is *generality,* which is concerned with the facility of efficacy expectations to predict behavior in related tasks or domains that require parallel skills. Whether some authors are confusing general efficacy/confidence with the generality dimension of self-efficacy or not is unclear. Efficacy measures that tap individuals' capabilities to engage in strenuous aerobic activity, although developed specifically to predict walking or jogging, may also be useful in the prediction of aerobic dance or exercise cycling.

Two other constructs are sometimes unwittingly confused with self-efficacy. These are intentions and perceived behavioral control. The belief that one can successfully execute behaviors that bring about certain outcomes (i.e., self-efficacy) is clearly differentiated from what one plans or intends to do (i.e., intention). Unfortunately, if efficacy is measured as the degree to which one believes that one *will* carry out a course of action, as opposed to the degree to which one believes one *can* carry out those actions, then the two constructs become conceptually blurred, and intention, rather than efficacy, is measured. The case for differentiating perceived behavioral control and self-efficacy is less clear-cut. Perceived behavioral control is a pivotal construct in Ajzen's (1985) expansion of the theory of reasoned action, the theory of planned behavior. Ajzen conceptualizes perceived behavioral control as the perceived ease or difficulty of performing a behavior (Ajzen, 1991). Although often measured differently from self-efficacy, perceived behavioral control is, in effect, a measure of self-efficacy and is, therefore, accorded some consideration later in the chapter.

There is an important distinction to be made between outcome expectations and efficacy expectations. The former are concerned with beliefs regarding the outcomes that behavioral repertoires will bring about. The latter, however, are concerned with one's belief in one's capabilities to successfully carry out the behavior in question. Thus, belief that a regular regimen of exercise for a prolonged period of time will bring about decreases in one's weight is an outcome expectation,[1] whereas the belief that one can actually exercise at the prescribed frequency, duration, and intensity over time is an efficacy expectation.

The Measurement of Self-Efficacy in Exercise-Related Studies

We review 85 published empirical studies spanning 13 years (1983-1995) that have employed the self-efficacy construct as either a determinant or an outcome of exercise behavior. Studies reported at scientific meetings but not published in final form are not included. In an effort to be comprehensive, we provide the reader with details of the specific studies employing the measures, a detailed description of the nature of the efficacy measure, and the source of the original measure if other than the study being reported. We also classify each measure into one of several broad categories, provide information pertinent to the reliability of each measure, and briefly report the extent of the efficacy-exercise relationship. This information can be found in Table 1 (see Appendix).

In order to make some sense of the content of these efficacy measures (N=100), we elected to classify them into six general categories that capture the intent of the measures. *Exercise efficacy* (34%) refers to measures directed at the assessment of beliefs regarding subjects' capabilities to successfully engage in incremental bouts of physical activity. In essence, these measures capture the traditional behavioral or task efficacy construct. Such measures range from tapping frequency and duration at some level of intensity (e.g., Courneya & McAuley, 1994) through exercising over periods of time (e.g., Biddle, Goudas, & Page, 1994), to the assessment of particularized activities such as walking successive numbers of blocks in incremental periods of time (e.g., Ewart et al., 1983). The next major category of efficacy measures was *barriers efficacy (30%)* which typically assess beliefs in capabilities to overcome social, personal, and environmental barriers to exercising. Barriers efficacy clearly represents what has been more recently referred to by Bandura (1995, 1997) as self-regulatory efficacy. Such barriers typically encompass time-management, fatigue, weather, family and social demands, and inaccessibility of facilities (e.g., Marcus, Eaton, Rossi, & Harlow, 1994; McAuley, 1992). Because self-efficacy is argued to be particularly useful in predicting behavior in challenging situations, it is not surprising that a number of measures (16%) can be categorized under *disease-specific/health behavior efficacy.* This rather cumbersome title encompasses exercise-related efficacy measures that have been used in populations that are engaged in secondary prevention of disease via exercise rehabilitation e.g., arthritis (Buckelew, Murray, Hewett, Johnson, & Huyser, 1995), diabetes (Kavanagh, Gooley, & Wilson, 1993), and chronic obstructive pulmonary disease (Toshima, et al., 1990) or measures that have an exercise component incorporated with

---

1. A typical Bandurian perspective would hold that losing weight is not an outcome but a marker of performance. We would agree with Maddux (1995) that viewing weight loss as an outcome of weight-loss strategies such as exercising is quite logical and practical. Although looking healthier and appearing attractive are also important outcomes of losing pounds, this does not relegate weight loss to the level of simply a performance marker. It merely suggests that outcomes do lead to other outcomes and, as Maddux argues, outcomes evolve at differing levels.

subjects' beliefs in their capabilities to engage in health-promoting behaviors (e.g., Grembowski et al., 1993). Although there is some overlap with the measures of exercise efficacy, we believe it more useful to classify these measures related to health/disease separately. In this way, readers interested in applications of self-efficacy to exercise aspects of rehabilitation can more easily identify those studies of interest.

Within the framework of the theory of planned behavior (Ajzen, 1985), a construct of importance in the prediction of behavioral intention, and by extension behavior itself, is *perceived behavioral control*. This construct has been identified as being conceptually similar to self- efficacy (Ajzen, 1991), and several authors have attempted to measure perceived behavioral control as the self-efficacy construct. For these reasons, we include it as a category of efficacy measurement, although we would agree that good arguments could be made to distinguish between the constructs. This latter statement is particularly true from the perspective that appropriate measurement of exercise-related efficacy may be more specific than the recommended approach to the measurement of perceived behavioral control (Ajzen & Madden, 1986). For example, Courneya (1995) employs a three-question format to assess perceived behavioral control. A sample item reads, "How much control do you have over whether you engage in regular physical activity?" with the reponse ranging from -3 (*no control at all*) to +3 (*complete control*). At any rate, several studies (5%) in the exercise literature reviewed employ the perceived behavioral control construct.

In spite of the strong emphasis placed by Bandura (1986) on the relevance of efficacy measurement to the behavioral domain of interest and the consistent superiority of specific measures over omnibus assessments of global confidence, the use of these latter measures still persists in the exercise literature. Measures of *general efficacy* (11%) vary in their content assessing such beliefs as "generalized efficacy" (Tipton & Worthington, 1984), trait self-efficacy (Long, 1985), and physical self-efficacy (Kavussanu & McAuley, 1995). The latter measure is typically assessed by the Physical Self-Efficacy scale (PSE) (Ryckman, Robbins, Thornton, & Cantrell, 1982). Of the more general measures of the efficacy construct, the PSE would appear more relevant to the exercise domain than more general measures of overall confidence in the self due to its generalizing to physical activity. This may be particularly true if the PSE subscale of Perceived Physical Ability is employed to predict physical activity behavior. However, such measures are less likely to be predictive of more specific behaviors (e.g., exercise adherence) and are unlikely to be changed as a function of exposure to acute bouts of exercise, as are more specific measures of efficacy (e.g., McAuley et al., 1993; Taylor, Bandura, Ewart, Miller, & DeBusk, 1985).

Our final category of exercise-related self-efficacy measures is simply titled *Other* (4%) due to the diverse nature of measures included. These include such constructs as goal-efficacy (Poag & McAuley, 1992), physical fitness efficacy (Bezjak & Lee, 1990), and scheduling efficacy (DuCharme & Brawley, 1995). It could be reasonably argued that these measures may well be better suited to inclusion in other categories. For example, the fitness efficacy might be included under general efficacy or exercise efficacy, whereas scheduling efficacy may

be categorized under barriers efficacy. However, as we shall subsequently argue, there *may* be reason to consider the latter measure separately from barriers efficacy.

Psychometric Properties of Exercise Efficacy Measures

In the following section we review each of the above categories of efficacy measurement in terms of its development and their psychometric properties. In discussing the latter, it should be pointed out that the traditional discussion of reliability and validity of the measures is limited almost exclusively to the reporting of internal consistency. Construct validity of most measures has to be inferred from their ability to systematically predict those aspects of behavior that social cognitive theory (Bandura, 1986) proposes self-efficacy to influence or be influenced by. In those instances where particular measures are employed across different studies or at multiple time points in a study, it is possible for the industrious reader to assemble sufficient validity information to determine the usefulness of a particular measure. However, in large part, the notion of demonstrating validity appears to be implicit in many studies rather than explicit.

In Table 1, we also present a brief synopsis of the major exercise-efficacy relationships that have been demonstrated in the studies reviewed. These findings are, in general, testimony to the theorized relationships between exercise and elements of human behavior, and thereby demonstrate to a greater or lesser extent the validity of the measures used. The elements of behavior that one would theoretically expect to be influenced by self-efficacy include choice of behavior (e.g., adopting an exercise program), effort and persistence (e.g., ratings of perceived exertion and exercise adherence), thought patterns (e.g., causal attributions), and emotional responses (e.g., affective responses to acute or long-term exercise). Additionally, social cognitive theory would predict that successful exposure to exercise would bring about positive changes in exercise self-efficacy.

Efficacy and Choice of Behavior

From the perspective of *choice of behavior* there are a number of studies that consistently report self-efficacy to be related to intention to exercise (e.g., Biddle et al., 1994; DuCharme & Brawley, 1995) and adoption of exercise behavior (Marcus & Owen, 1992; McAuley, 1992). By far the most popular method of determining the validity of the measures employed has been in the prediction of exercise adherence. Other than general measures of efficacy, most of the types of measures employed in the reviewed studies show significant but often not greater than moderate relationships (R^2 range = .04 to .26) with exercise adherence patterns (e.g., Dzewaltowski, 1989; McAuley, 1993; Rodgers & Brawley, 1993; Kavanagh et al., 1993; Taylor et al., 1985). The necessity of employing measures specific to the domain of functioning is clearly highlighted when one contrasts the adherence findings using specific measures with those employing more general measures. For example, Long and Haney (1988a,b) employed a measure of general efficacy in an effort to examine the effects of aerobic activity and relaxation on anxiety and efficacy in chronically stressed adults. Although self-efficacy was influenced by the interventions, this general measure was found to be unrelated to exercise adherence, a finding that is at odds with the majority of the efficacy adherence studies. However, the consensus across studies is that the specific measures employed were valid in terms of their relationship to exercise adherence.

Efficacy and Thought Patterns

Fewer studies have attempted to examine relationships between exercise self-efficacy and *thought patterns,* but those that have done so support social cognitive predictions. Bandura (1986) has argued that personal efficacy can shape the type of explanations that we give for behavioral outcomes. McAuley (1991) and McAuley and Courneya (1993a) provided support for this argument by demonstrating a significant relationship between self-efficacy and the personal control and stability dimensions of causal attributions for exercise behavior (βs= .22 - .34). In turn, these measures were related to affective responses to the exercise stimuli thus demonstrating an indirect influence of efficacy on affect via attributions. Still other constructs have been demonstrated to be influenced by exercise-related self-efficacy including intrinsic motivation (McAuley, Wraith & Duncan, 1991), optimism (Kavussanu & McAuley, 1995), and self-esteem (Sonstroem et al., 1994).

Efficacy, Effort and Physiological Responses

Important data exist to indicate that *effort expenditure,* as evidenced by such measures as peak heart rate, self-reported intensity, and ratings of perceived exertion, is predicted by measures of exercise self-efficacy (e.g., Ewart et al., 1983; Ewart et al., 1986; McAuley et al., 1991; Poag & McAuley, 1992). Typical correlational values in this area are moderate, ranging from .30 to .53. Self-efficacy has also been demonstrated to be related to physiological responses and some of the more consistent patterns show up in clinical samples and training studies. For example, self-efficacy has been reported to be positively correlated with peak treadmill heart rate and performance and workload in coronary heart disease patients (e.g., Ewart et al., 1983; Ewart et al., 1986; Taylor et al., 1985), as well as vital capacity and expiratory volume in chronic obstructive pulmonary disease patients (Toshima et al., 1990). In healthy samples, self-efficacy has been shown to be related to estimated aerobic capacity and time to reach 70% maximal heart rate (McAuley et al., 1991). More important, perhaps, is the finding reported by Kaplan, Ries, Prewitt, and Eakin (1994) that exercise efficacy was a significant predictor of 5-year survival in pulmonary disease patients.

Exercise Influences on Self-Efficacy

Much of the literature supports the construct validity of the efficacy measures used by demonstrating relationships with theoretically relevant constructs such as effort, persistence, and affect. However, there is another aspect of efficacy theory that has been examined in the exercise literature. That is, social cognitive theory would predict that mastery exposures should lead to enhanced self-efficacy. Several authors have been able to demonstrate this in both acute and long-term settings. For example, acute bouts of exercise training, typically graded exercise tests, have been shown to boost efficacy expectation pre- to posttest (e.g., Ewart et al., 1983; Ewart et al., 1986; McAuley et al.,

1991; McAuley et al., 1993; Taylor et al., 1985). Similarly longer term exercise programs have been shown to influence both specific exercise self-efficacy (e.g., Brown, Welsh, Labbe, Vitulli, & Kulkarni, 1992; Carroll, 1995; Oldridge & Rogowski, 1990) and more general efficacy (e.g., Long, 1984, 1985).

Internal Consistency of Measures

The most frequently documented psychometric evidence in the measurement of self-efficacy is the reliability of the instruments. However, this varies depending upon the category of instrument. With respect to *barriers efficacy*, two thirds (66.7%) of the instruments used had documented reliability information, primarily internal consistency (coefficient alpha). In most cases, the barriers identified are internally consistent at conventional levels although the constitution of the measures differs somewhat across studies.

Approximately 52% of the measures of *exercise efficacy* report reliability information and, in large part, the items contained in these scales hold together quite well. Only 31% of the *disease- and health-related efficacy* measures report reliability information, and slightly better than 46% of the *general efficacy* measures provide such information. Once again, as can be seen in Table 1, where reported, values are generally acceptable. The case for internal consistency with measures of *perceived behavioral control* is less clear. Whereas 60% of the measures used have documented values for internal consistency these vary from the acceptable ranges of .81 and .71 (Biddle et al., 1994; Courneya, 1995) to the suspect value of .46 as reported by Wankel, Mummery, Stephens, and Craig (1994). Finally, of the four measures in the *Other* category, three (75%) reported internal consistencies in the acceptable range.

The Development of Exercise Self-Efficacy Measures

The next stage in this review considers the methods employed to construct self-efficacy measures. Examination of the studies reviewed indicates that the majority of the efficacy measures (87%) employed in these studies report no information relative to scale development other than to indicate that the measure was developed along the lines suggested by Bandura (1977). Such guidelines for the development of task or behavioral self-efficacy measures is relatively straightforward and consist, in large part, of constructing a scale that is comprised of hierarchical items leading to some target behavior and assessed along the dimensions of level (whether or not one has the capabilities to execute an individual item) and strength (the degree of confidence one has in one's capability to successfully execute the item), and, depending upon the level of domain specificity, perhaps generality. Respondents are asked to indicate whether or not they can execute increasingly more difficult behavioral tasks and the extent to which they are confident of successfully doing so. The traditional method of such assessment is to simply check the response "yes" or "no" for each task to determine level and then to detail confidence assessments at each level on a scale of 10 to 100 in gradations of 10. A response of "no" at the level dimension is obviously a confidence rating of 0. Strength of efficacy is then determined by summing all confidence ratings and dividing by the total number of levels. An alternative and perhaps more easily understood format is to provide confidence ratings of 0-100 with the descriptor ranges of "no confidence at all" (0) to "completely confident" (100). Therein, a zero rating would indicate that the subject could not complete that level.

What constitutes the items on a behavioral self-efficacy scale for exercise (or "exercise efficacy," to adopt the nomenclature of this chapter)? A simple example will serve to answer this question. Consider that the goal of an exercise program for sedentary overweight adults was to have participants walk for 30 minutes at a moderately challenging pace without stopping. This would be the final item on our scale and, at program onset, one that most individuals in our sample would be unable to achieve. If this were the only item, we would have a completely inefficacious lot to deal with, a point that should be noted when researchers employ single-item scales! To master 30 minutes of activity without stopping requires, of course, a gradual tolerance of the body to the physiological stress placed upon the body, that is, the build up of endurance. Therefore, in our hierarchy we may wish to begin with tapping efficacy for 5 minutes of continuous activity and increase each item in the hierarchy by 5 minutes until the target is reached. This time-based measure is clearly more closely related to our target behavior (exercise duration) than is a measure of exercise barriers or perceptions of strength and agility. The items are also likely to be highly internally consistent. Moreover, it would be hypothesized that if subjects' confidence in their capabilities to exercise for longer durations is high, then we would expect to observe subjects exercising longer. We might also reasonably expect to see significant correlations between efficacy and other indicants of exercise duration such as heart rate, ratings of perceived exertion, and so forth, thereby demonstrating further validity for the measure. We provide an example of such a measure in Appendix 2.

The development of scales to measure self-regulatory efficacy, as represented by barriers efficacy in the exercise domain, is more complex. Indeed, in such assessment the notion of hierarchy is difficult to attain, as some barriers may appear more difficult to some individuals than to others (see Brawley, Martin, & Gyurcsik, this volume, for a detailed discussion of perceived barriers to exercise). Several investigators have focused upon barriers and demonstrated this form of efficacy to be relatively consistent in the prediction of exercise behavior. In particular, Marcus and her colleagues (Marcus et al., 1994; Marcus, Pinto, Simkin, Audrain, & Taylor, 1994; Marcus, Selby, Niaura, & Rossi, 1992) and our own research group (e.g., Duncan & McAuley, 1993; Duncan, McAuley, Stoolmiller, & Duncan, 1993; McAuley, 1992; McAuley, 1993; McAuley et al., 1994) have invested considerable energy in this line of inquiry. But how are these measures developed? Marcus and her colleagues have typically employed a five-item self-efficacy measure assessing subjects' beliefs in their capabilities to "participate in regular exercise" in the face of the following barriers: being tired; being in a bad mood, not having time; being on vacation; when it is raining or snowing. These items were selected on the basis that they had been shown to be important by exercise and smoking researchers and were loosely extracted from a 2-factor 12-item scale developed by Sallis, Pinski, Grossman,

Patterson, and Nader (1988), which was validated on a single-item self-report measure of activity level.

Whereas we endorse the strategy of employing measures of barriers to exercise efficacy, we suggest that this scale contains a minimal number of barriers. Because Marcus and her colleagues have used the efficacy construct in the context of validating a transtheoretical model of behavior change, we believe the conceptualization and measurement of self-efficacy have received less careful attention than warranted. For example, in the only study examining the role of efficacy in the prediction of physical activity that employed longitudinal data (Marcus, Eaton et al., 1994) only three of the items were retained for subsequent analyses. However, because the five items have been listed in published form (Marcus et al., 1992), other researchers have somewhat arbitrarily employed this measure in their own work (e.g., Gorely & Gordon, 1995; Wyse, Mercer, Ashford, Buxton, & Gleeson, 1995).

An alternative approach to the development of barriers has been employed by our own research group (e.g., Duncan & McAuley, 1993; Duncan et al., 1993; McAuley, 1992; 1993; McAuley et al., 1994). Adopting the perspective that the individual should be an active agent in the process of identifying barriers to physical activity participation, we have conducted attributional analyses (e.g., McAuley, Poag, Gleason, & Wraith, 1990) in which we have had subjects a priori identify those circumstances that have caused them to dropout of previous exercise programs or contributed to infrequent attendance. In turn, we have used the most frequently-cited barriers or impediments as the items for efficacy measures. Our group has now conducted such analyses on three different samples from different regions of the United States and in one case (Minnifee & McAuley, in press) using a large (N=189) African-American sample. The similarity of the findings across the samples is remarkable. That is, there appear to be a number of barriers that adults identify as being problematic for successful maintenance of exercise behavior. These typically encompass barriers that include bad weather, time management, lack of interest/boredom, pain and discomfort, location accessibility, personal stress, and exercising alone. The manner in which these are presented as efficacy items is shown in Appendix 2.

There are several advantages and drawbacks with respect to the employment of this mode of barrier measurement. First, as stated above, it is an advantage to have the subjects play an active role in the identification of potential barriers. Second, this approach allows for a richer compendium of barriers than does the simple selection of a few barriers identified in the literature (cf. Marcus et al., 1992). This method can be further enhanced by asking subjects to identify the likelihood that a barrier might occur in the future (frequency) and the degree to which it might forestall exercise behavior (severity) (see Glasgow, McCaul, & Schafer, 1986). This allows for items that are not particularly frequent or difficult to overcome to be eliminated. One potential problem that has been identified with the use of barriers efficacy is that participants may not have previously experienced such barriers and therefore may be subject to over- or underestimation of efficacy (DuCharme & Brawley, 1995). Several steps can be taken to prevent the occurrence of such overestimation. An initial step is to assess barriers *within* the sample of interest before exercise or assessment takes place (e.g., DuCharme & Brawley, 1995; Dzewaltowski, 1989; McAuley, 1992), although it does appear that many of these barriers are consistent across samples. This approach allows one to eliminate barriers that are infrequently identified or are of little utility when subjected to conventional statistical procedures (e.g., exploratory and confirmatory factor analyses, reliability analyses). A second approach is to allow sufficient participation time for subjects to gain exercise experience in which barriers may emerge (e.g., McAuley, 1992). The downside of this latter strategy is that there is considerable potential for major attrition in the early stages of the exercise program (McAuley et al., 1994). Therefore, we strongly endorse the assessment of other aspects of efficacy (e.g., behavioral or exercise efficacy) in concert with barriers efficacy.

Several authors have broached this topic before and taken steps to more accurately predict efficacy-exercise behavior by their use of several efficacy measures. Recently, DuCharme and Brawley (1995) and Poag-DuCharme and Brawley (1993) have reported data wherein they employed barriers efficacy and scheduling efficacy (defined as subjects' ability to schedule or plan strategies for carrying out exercise). A sample item from the latter form of measure reads, "I am confident that I have the ability to get to my planned exercise session on time." Although Poag-DuCharme and Brawley (1993) argue that scheduling well is not synonomous with overcoming barriers, it could be reasonably argued that the correlation between scheduling efficacy and aspects of barriers efficacy may be substantial. However, this is an empirical question that remains to be appropriately tested. Regardless of their association, these authors have been able to demonstrate that the two measures may have independent contributions to exercise intention and behavior.

Other authors have also employed multiple measures of efficacy but treated them in slightly different ways when used as predictor variables. McAuley (1993) employed barriers efficacy and exercise efficacy in concert with past exercise behavior and aerobic capacity in an effort to predict exercise maintenance at 4-month follow-up in middle-aged adults who had participated in a 5-month exercise program. McAuley reported the measures to be highly correlated ($r=.88$) and therefore combined them in subsequent analyses. In retrospect, it may have been more illustrative to examine how each of these measures contributed to behavior. It should be noted that Dzewaltowski, Noble, and Shaw (1990) reported similarly high correlations between exercise and barriers efficacy ($r=.79$) and also elected to combine the measures. Further, Dzewaltowski, et al. (1990) measured barriers in an open-ended fashion by allowing subjects to identify any barriers that interfered with exercise participation and then rating their confidence to overcome these impediments to exercise.

A more sophisticated approach to examine the contributions of exercise and barriers efficacy was taken by Duncan and McAuley (1993) and Duncan and Stoolmiller (1993) in which these constructs were employed as manifest variables underlying the latent construct of self-efficacy in a structural equation analysis. McAuley, Mihalko, and Rosengren (in press) have recently noted that even though measures of efficacy may be highly correlated, the decision to assess only one element of ef-

ficacy may result in the failure to predict further small but perhaps, in a public health sense, meaningful variation. Clearly, the approach of choice is to think in terms of self-efficacy as an important latent construct and to measure it using multiple indicators of efficacy that are known to be related to the outcome variable of interest. Such indicators might capture, for example, scheduling, cardiovascular, exercise, and barriers efficacy.

Another approach to determination of items necessary to develop appropriate measures of exercise-related efficacy is the employment of focus or elicitation groups. In such an approach a subgroup of the population is interviewed with respect to potential efficacy items of importance. This would appear to be unnecessary in the case of efficacy measures that are amenable to hierarchical gradations (e.g., incremental duration of activity). However, in the case of measures for which no apparent hierarchy exists, and barriers would most certainly be one, interviews with individuals from the targeted group may be particularly useful.

A final point regarding the development of exercise-related efficacy measures (both behavioral and self-regulatory) concerns the need for appropriate levels of correspondence between the measures of self-efficacy and the measurement of behavior. In many of the cases reviewed, authors are interested in whether gradations in perceived capability to exercise at some prescribed level and/or whether subjects' beliefs in their capability to carry out a specified exercise regimen in the face of barriers or impediments reliably predict exercise adherence. Thus, some correspondence is attained. However, when authors veer away from these more specific methods of exercise efficacy, problems with correspondence occur. For example, in a recent study of leisure-time physical activity (LTPA) in the African-American population, Broman (1995) measured "efficacy of preventive health behavior" to predict a dichotomous (yes/no) assessment of LTPA. The efficacy measure comprised a series of statements regarding subjects' beliefs that AIDS, cancer, heart disease, dental problems, hypertension, and emotional problems can be prevented through their own efforts. A weak but statistically significant association was demonstrated in logistic regression analyses, and from these findings the author concluded that general preventive health efficacy is a significant predictor of LPTA. Whereas a mild association has been shown here, the true efficacy test of comparison of the general with specific measure has not been made. Moreover, as LTPA was measured as whether or not the subject ever engaged in exercise, one must question whether this is a true measure of LTPA and whether the associations are merely demonstrating a relationship among preventive health behavior tendencies.

Similarly, Clark, Patrick, Grembowski, and Durham (1995) examined relationships among socioeconomic status indicators, self-efficacy, and exercise behavior in a larger sample of older HMO participants. Their measure of self-efficacy was a single item reflecting subjects' surety with respect to whether they would exercise in the coming year. As the authors cautiously point out, single-item general measures are indeed problematic, and this one may be even more so, given that it reflects behavioral intention rather than self-efficacy beliefs.

In an effort to underscore the importance of measures of efficacy truly reflecting the behavior that we are interested in predicting, consider data from McAuley (1992). In this study, several assessments of self-efficacy and exercise behavior, as well as physiological variables, were made in a sample of previously sedentary middle-aged adults. Both general efficacy (perceived physical ability) and specific efficacy (barriers) were employed to predict frequency of exercise behavior. As social cognitive theory (Bandura, 1986) would predict, barriers efficacy was a significant predictor of exercise whereas general efficacy was nonsignificant. Thus, the conceptual thinking that guides the operational definition of exercise efficacy must also guide the definition of the behavior in question, exercise. At issue here is the degree of correspondence that exists between the predictor variable, in this case efficacy, and the behavior, an issue that has received considerable attention in the exercise-attitudinal research (see Courneya & McAuley, 1993b). General measures are likely to be useful in the prediction of general behaviors. However, the prediction of specific behaviors requires measures that are equally specific.

Why Are There So Many Measures of Exercise-Related Self-Efficacy?

The above question is a reasonable one to ask, as are questions regarding the variable content of the measures. The logical extension of this question is, of course, why can't we have one reliable and valid measure of self-efficacy to employ across physical activity domains or, better still, all health domains? The very nature of the self-efficacy construct opposes the notion of a single trans-situational measure of self-efficacy and argues for the consistent superiority of domain-specific measures over general, trait-like, omnibus measures. But is it parsimonious to have multiple measures of exercise or barriers efficacy? The fact that the relationship between exercise-related self-efficacy and exercise behavior has been remarkably consistent in spite of the broad array of measures used to assess efficacy is testimony to the robustness of the association. We are in agreement with Maibach and Murphy (1995) who, in commenting on the state of efficacy measurement in the field of health promotion, noted that researchers often sacrifice good measurement for the sake of brevity. This is abundantly clear in some of the exercise literature. Numerous studies have chosen to assess exercise efficacy using single-item scales such as "How confident are you that you can exercise three times per week for the next 6 months?" Such an approach embraces neither the hierarchical gradations of the continued exercise process nor the myriad impediments and barriers that may prevent one from carrying out the targeted behavior. In many respects, individuals may be perceiving such a question in terms of an intention. Indeed, signing up for an exercise program is indicative of good intention, but such intentions can go awry with time.

The single- or few-item approach to efficacy measurement is oftentimes not an a priori decision on the part of the authors, thereby leading to more frequent occurrences than are optimal. For example, several studies reviewed herein employ secondary data analysis of large survey databases. These databases include marginal measures of self-reported exercise and items that, while employed to represent the efficacy construct, were probably designed to measure something else. As noted earlier, Bro-

man (1995) assesses efficacy for preventive health behavior from the perspective of one's beliefs in disease prevention through one's own efforts. The attempt is then made to link such beliefs with physical activity. Several problems are evident here. First, the efficacy measure is composed of items reflecting different domains of functioning, albeit health-related. Second, the outcome behavior of interest, physical activity, lacks congruence with the predictor variable. In essence, these problems are indicative of those associated with secondary data analysis.

Clark et al. (1995) reporting data from a large sample of seniors enrolled in the Group Health Cooperative of Puget Sound, Washington, elected to interpret a single-item measure reflecting aspects of intention over a prolonged period of time ("How sure are you that you will exercise regularly in the coming year?") as self-efficacy. Although the authors were conscious of the conceptual blurring of the constructs, Grembowski et al. (1993) employ the same data set with a lesser degree of circumspection when drawing conclusions regarding relationships between their efficacy measure and exercise behavior. In sharp contrast, measures of disease and health-related efficacy that embrace gradations of difficulty in physical tasks (e.g., walking, lifting, stair-climbing) are quite successful at predicting such outcomes as treadmill time, exercise heart rate, and perceived exertion (e.g., Ries et al., 1995; Taylor et al., 1985). Although space and number of studies in this chapter do not permit an in-depth analysis of each of the measures relative to item sufficiency and representation, readers should be able to effectively judge from Table 1 the quality of these measures.

In essence, we believe that it may not be necessary to develop more measures than currently exist, if one is interested in predicting exercise adherence in the face of barriers, although we would recommend that the assessment of barriers efficacy be more comprehensive than reliance on four or five items which have been used elsewhere in the literature. Clearly, different populations may perceive different barriers as more salient and greater or lesser impediments to exercise participation. For example, the study of women's health has begun to attract the level of interest that it should have long ago been accorded. Inability to find satisfactory child care during scheduled exercise times may pose a barrier for some segments of the female population, whereas it would be of no consequence to others. Older individuals may also face barriers to exercise that are unique to them and are not tapped by measures of a few generic barriers.

However, we do believe that future studies of exercise behavior that employ the efficacy construct as a predictor of exercise behavior (adherence) would do well to assess beliefs in ability to exercise at some prescribed frequency, duration, and intensity over ascending periods of time (e.g., months), in addition to barriers to exercise. In other words, both task or behavioral self-efficacy that assesses gradations of the motoric act of exercise and self-regulatory efficacy which assesses beliefs relative to carrying out the motoric act in the face of impediments to doing so. Although the likelihood that these measures may be strongly correlated is high, it is unlikely that there will be perfect correspondence between them and that the two measures (or more) together would account for additional variation in behavior over that accounted for by the measures independently.

Summary and Concluding Remarks

We have reviewed a large number of studies and measures of exercise-related self-efficacy. In large part, these have been reliable and have demonstrated appropriate theoretical relations with elements of exercise behavior suggesting some evidence of construct validity. The most commonly employed measures are those assessing barriers or impediments to participation and those assessing beliefs in capabilities to carry out elements of exercise regimens (e.g., frequency, duration) over varying periods of time. Closely aligned to the latter are measures of exercise efficacy developed largely for clinical populations, although some of these have been adapted for use in nonclinical populations. It would appear at the very least that exercise performance measures and barriers efficacy should be employed in studies that attempt to predict long-term exercise behavior. Additionally, there is some preliminary evidence to suggest that measures assessing facets such as scheduling (DuCharme & Brawley, 1995) may provide additional predictive utility. However, such measures need to be more broadly tested before any definitive statements can be made. Indeed, it is recommended that continual attention be paid to the construct validity and to the reliability of efficacy measures employed in the exercise domain. As was noted earlier, internal consistency is infrequently reported. Additionally, test-retest reliability of efficacy measures may be useful in the case of comparing relations over time for specific versus more global (i.e., trait-like) measures of efficacy. Additionally, it is becoming increasingly necessary for researchers in the exercise domain to take a developmental perspective to the prediction of exercise behavior and the examination of its antecedents and consequences. By this we mean that the process of change over time needs to be studied. Self-efficacy has been thoroughly documented as contributing to change in all manner of behaviors. To study the ways in which efficacy contributes to changes in exercise over time and the role efficacy plays in mediating exercise effects on psychological health, approaches such as latent growth curve models (cf. Duncan & McAuley, 1993) need to be adopted. These techniques will further allow us to examine the measurement properties of efficacy measures. In closing, there can be little doubt that self-efficacy plays an important role in the development and maintenance of exercise behavior and, if recent work by Kaplan et al. (1994) is any indication, may be instrumental in actual survival. Regardless of the importance of this construct, we must be vigilant in our attention to appropriate and accurate conceptualization and measurement of self-efficacy, if we are to adequately determine its contribution to human functioning.

References

Ajzen, I. (1985). From intentions to actions: A theory of planned behavior. In J. Kuhl & J. Beckman (Eds.), *Action-control: From cognition to behavior* (pp. 11-39). Heidelberg: Springer.

Ajzen, I. (1991). The theory of planned behavior. *Organizational Behavior and Human Decision Processing, 50,* 179-211.

Ajzen, I., & Fishbein, M. (1977). Attitude-behavior relations: a theoretical analysis and review of empirical research. *Psychological Bulletin, 84,* 888-918.

Ajzen, I., & Madden, T.J. (1986). Prediction of goal-directed behavior: Attitudes, intentions, and perceived behavioral control. *Journal of Experimental Social Psychology, 22,* 453-474.

Armstrong, C.A., Sallis, J.F., Hovell, M.F., & Hofstetter, C.R. (1993). Stages of change, self-efficacy, and the adoption of vigorous exercise: A prospective analysis. *Journal of Sport and Exercise Psychology, 15,* 390-402.

Bandura, A. (1977). Self-efficacy: Toward a unifying theory of behavioral change. *Psychological Review, 84,* 191-215.

Bandura, A. (1986). *Social Foundations of Thought and Action. A Social Cognitive Theory.* Englewood Cliffs, NJ: Prentice Hall.

Bandura, A. (1992). Exercise of personal agency through the self-efficacy mechanism. In R. Schwarzer (Ed.), *Self-efficacy: Thought control and action* (pp. 3-38). Washington, DC: Hemisphere Publishing Corporation.

Bandura, A (1995). On rectifying conceptual ecumenism. In J. Maddux (Ed.), *Self- efficacy, adaptation, and adjustment: Theory, research, and application* (pp. 347-375). New York: Plenum Press.

Bandura, A. (1997). *Self-efficacy: The exercise of control.* New York: Freeman.

Bandura, A., & Cervone, D. (1983). Self-evaluative and self-efficacy mechanisms governing motivational effects of goal systems. *Journal of Personality and Social Psychology, 45,* 1017-1028.

Bandura, A., & Cervone, D. (1986). Differential engagement of self-reactive influences in cognitive motivation. *Organizational Behavior and Human Decision Processes, 38,* 98-113.

Bezjak, J.E., & Lee, J.W. (1990). Relationship of self-efficacy and locus of control constructs in predicting college students' physical fitness behaviors. *Perceptual and Motor Skills, 71,* 499-508.

Biddle, S., Goudas, M., & Page, A. (1994). Social-psychological predictors of self-reported actual and intended physical activity in a university workforce sample. *British Journal of Sport Medicine, 28,* 160-163.

Blair, S.N., Kohl, H.W., Paffenbarger, R.S., Jr, Clark, D.G., & Cooper, K.H. (1989). Physical fitness and all-cause mortality: A prospective study of healthy men and women. *Journal of the American Medical Association, 262,* 2395-2401.

Bouchard, C., Shephard, R.J., & Stephens, T. (Eds). (1994). *Physical activity, fitness and health: International proceedings and consensus statement.* Champaign, IL: Human Kinetics Publishers, Inc.

Bozoian, S., Rejeski, W.J., & McAuley, E. (1994). Self-efficacy influences feeling states associated with acute exercise. *Journal of Sport and Exercise Psychology, 16,* 326-333.

Brawley, L.R,. & Horne, T. (1989). *Refining attitude-behavior models to predict adherence in normal and socially supportive conditions.* Ottawa: Canadian Fitness and Lifestyle Research Institute.

Broman, C.L. (1995). Leisure-time physical activity in an African-American population. *Journal of Behavioral Medicine, 18,* 341-353.

Brown, S.W., Welsh, M.C., Labbe, E.E., Vitulli, W.F., & Kulkarni, P. (1992). Aerobic exercise in the psychological treatment of adolescents. *Perceptual and Motor Skills, 74,* 555-560.

Buckelew, S.P., Murray, S.E., Hewett, J.E., Johnson, J., & Huyser, B. (1995). Self-efficacy, pain, and physical activity among fibromyalgia subjects. *American College of Rheumatology, 8,* 43-50.

Camacho, T.C., Roberts, R.E., Lazarus, N.B., Kaplan, G.A., & Cohen, R.D. (1991). Physical activity and depression: Evidence from the Alameda County Study. *American Journal of Epidemiology, 134,* 220-231.

Carroll, D.L. (1995). The importance of self-efficacy expectations in elderly patients recovering from coronary artery bypass surgery. *Heart & Lung, 24,* 50-59.

Casperson, C.J., Christianson, G., & Pollard, R.A. (1986). Status of the 1990 physical fitness and exercise objectives: Evidence from NHIS 1985. *Public Health Reports, 101,* 587-592.

Centers for Disease Control. (1987). Sex-, age-, and region-specific prevalence for sedentary lifestyle in selected states in 1985: The behavioral risk factor surveillance system. *Morbidity and Mortality Weekly Reports, 36,* 195-198, 203-204.

Clark, D.O., Patrick, D.L., Grembowski, D., & Durham, M.L. (1995). Socioeconomic status and exercise self-efficacy in late life. *Journal of Behavioral Medicine, 18,* 355-376.

Condiotte, M.M., & Lichenstein, E. (1981). Self-efficacy and relapse in smoking cessation programs. *Journal of Consulting and Clinical Psychology, 49,* 648-658.

Coppel, D.B. (1980). *The relationship of perceived social support and self-efficacy to major and minor stressors.* Unpublished doctoral dissertation, University of Washington.

Corbin, C.B., Laurie, D.R., Gruger, C., & Smiley, B. (1984). Vicarious success experience as a factor influencing self-confidence, attitudes, and physical activity of adult women. *Journal of Teaching in Physical Education, 4,* 17-23.

Courneya, K.S. (1995). Understanding readiness for regular physical activity in older individuals: An application of the theory of planned behavior. *Health Psychology, 14,* 80-87.

Courneya, K.S., & McAuley, E. (1993a). Efficacy , attributional, and affective responses of older adults following an acute bout of exercise. *Journal of Social Behavior and Personality, 8,* 729-742.

Courneya, K.S., & McAuley, E. (1993b). Predicting physical activity from intention: Conceptual and methodological issues. *Journal of Sport and Exercise Psychology, 15,* 50-62.

Courneya, K.S. & McAuley, E. (1994). Are there different determinants of the frequency, intensity, and duration of physical activity. *Behavioral Medicine, 20,* 84-90.

Desharnais, R., Bouillon, J., & Godin, G. (1986). Self-efficacy and outcome expectations as determinants of exercise adherence. *Psychological Reports, 59,* 1155-1159.

Dishman, R.K., (1982). Compliance/adherence in health-related exercise. *Health Psychology, 1,* 237-267.

DuCharme, K.A,. & Brawley, L.R. (1995). Predicting the intentions and behavior of exercise initiates using two forms of self-efficacy. *Journal of Behavioral Medicine, 18,* 479-497.

Duncan, T.E,. & McAuley, E. (1993). Social support and efficacy cognitions in exercise adherence: A latent growth curve analysis. *Journal of Behavioral Medicine, 16,* 199-218.

Duncan, T.E., McAuley, E., Stoolmiller, M., & Duncan, S.C. (1993). Serial fluctuation in exercise behavior as a function of social support and efficacy cognitions. *Journal of Applied Social Psychology, 23,* 1498-1522.

Duncan, T.E,. & Stoolmiller, M. (1993). Modeling social and psychological determinants of exercise behaviors via structural equation systems. *Research Quarterly for Exercise and Sport, 64,* 1-16.

Dustman, R.E., Emmerson, R., & Shearer, D. (1994). Physical activity, age, and cognitive-neuropsychological function. *Journal of Aging and Physical Activity, 2,* 143-181.

Dzewaltowski, D.A. (1989). Toward a model of exercise motivation. *Journal of Sport & Exercise Psychology, 11,* 251-269.

Dzewaltowski, D.A., Noble, J.M., & Shaw, J.M. (1990). Physical activity participation: Social cognitive theory versus the theories of reasoned action and planned behavior. *Journal of Sport & Exercise Psychology, 12,* 388-405.

Ewart, C.K., Stewart, K.J., Gillilan, R.E., Kelemen, M.H., Valenti, S.A., Manley, J.D., & Kelemen, M.D. (1986). Usefulness of self-efficacy in predicting overexertion during programmed exercise in coronary artery disease. *American Journal of Cardiology, 57,* 557-561.

Ewart, C.K., Taylor, B., Reese, L.B., & DeBusk, R.F. (1983). Effects of early postmyocardial infarction exercise testing on self-perception and subsequent physical activity. *American Journal of Cardi-*

ology, 51, 1076-1080.

Fruin, D.J., Pratt,C., & Owen, N. (1991). Protection motivation theory and adolescents' perceptions of exercise. *Journal of Applied Social Psychology, 22,* 55-69.

Garcia, A.W., & King, A.C. (1991). Predicting long-term adherence to aerobic exercise: A comparison of two models. *Journal of Sport & Exercise Psychology, 13,* 394-410.

Glasgow, R.E., McCaul, K.D., & Schafer, L.C. (1986). Barriers to regimen adherence among persons with insulin-dependent diabetes. *Journal of Behavioral Medicine, 9,* 65-77.

Goldsmith-Cwikel, J., Dielman, T.E., Kirscht, J.P., & Israil, B.A. (1988). Mechanisms of psychosocial effects on health: The role of social integration, coping style and health behavior. *Health Education Quarterly, 15,* 151-173.

Gorely, T., & Gordon, S. (1995). An examination of the transtheoretical model and exercise behavior in older adults. *Journal of Sport & Exercise Psychology, 17,* 312-324.

Gortner, S.R., & Jenkins, L.S. (1990). Self-efficacy and activity level following cardiac surgery. *Journal of Advanced Nursing, 15,* 1132-1138.

Grembowski, D., Patrick, D., Diehr, P., Durham, M., Beresford, S., Kay, E., & Hecht, J. (1993). Self-efficacy and health behavior among older adults. *Journal of Health and Social Behavior, 34,* 89-104.

Gulanick, M. (1991). Is phase 2 cardiac rehabilitation necessary for early recovery of patients with cardiac disease? A randomized, controlled study. *Heart Lung, 20,* 9-15.

Harrison, D.A., & Liska, L.Z. (1994). Promoting regular exercise in organizational fitness programs: Health-related differences in motivational building blocks. *Personnel Psychology, 47,* 47-71.

Hickey, M.L., Owen, S.V., & Froman, R.D. (1992). Instrument development: Cardiac diet and exercise self-efficacy. *Nursing Research, 41,* 347-351.

Hofstetter, C.R., Hovell, M.F., & Sallis, J.F. (1990). Social learning correlates of exercise self-efficacy: Early experiences with physical activity. *Social Science and Medicine, 31,* 1169-1176.

Hogan, P.I., & Santomier, J.P. (1984). Effect of mastering swim skills on older adults' self-efficacy. *Research Quarterly, 55,* 294-296.

Holloway, J.B., Beuter, A., & Duda, J.L. (1988). Self-efficacy and training for strength in adolescent girls. *Journal of Applied Social Psychology, 18,* 699-719.

Horne, T.E. (1994). Predictors of physical activity intentions and behaviour for rural homemakers. *Canadian Journal of Public Health, 85,* 132-135.

Hovell, M., Sallis, J., Hofstetter, R., Barrington, E., Hackley, M., Elder, J., Castro, F., & Kilbourne, K. (1991). Identification of correlates of physical activity among Latino adults. *Journal of Community Health, 16,* 23-36.

Hovell, M.F., Sallis, J.F., Hofstetter, C.R., Spry, V.M., Faucher, P., & Casperson, C.J. (1989). Identifying correlates of walking for exercise: An epidemiologic prerequisite for physical activity promotion. *Preventive Medicine, 18,* 856-866.

Jenkins, L.S. (1985). *Self-efficacy in recovery from myocardial infarction.* No.DA8603203. University Microfilm, Ann Arbor, Michigan.

Kaplan, R.M., Atkins, C., & Reinsch, S. (1984). Specific efficacy expectations mediate exercise compliance in patients with COPD. *Health Psychology, 3,* 223-242.

Kaplan, R.M., Ries, A.L., Prewitt, L.M., & Eakin, E. (1994). Self-efficacy expectations predict survival for patients with chronic obstructive pulmonary disease. *Health Psychology, 13,* 366-368.

Kavanagh, D.J., Gooley, S., & Wilson, P.H. (1993). Prediction of adherence and control in diabetes. *Journal of Behavioral Medicine, 16,* 509-522.

Kavussanu, M., & McAuley, E. (1995). Exercise and optimism: Are highly active individuals more optimistic? *Journal of Sport and*

Exercise Psychology, 17, 246-258.

Kelly, R.B., Zyzanski, S.J., & Alemagno, S.A. (1991). Prediction of motivation and behavior change following health promotion: Role of health beliefs, social support, and self-efficacy. *Social Science and Medicine, 32,* 311-320.

Kingery, P.M. (1990). Self-efficacy and the self-monitoring of selected exercise and eating behaviors of college students. *Health Education, 21,* 26-29.

Labbe, E.E. & Welsh, C. (1993). Children and running: Changes in physical fitness, self-efficacy, and health locus of control. *Journal of Sport Behavior, 16,* 85-97.

Landers, D.M. & Petruzzello, S.J. (1994). Physical activity, fitness, and anxiety. In C. Bouchard, R.J. Shephard, & T. Stephens, (Eds.), *Physical activity, fitness and health: international proceedings and consensus statement* (pp. 868-882). Champaign, IL: Human Kinetics Publishers, Inc.

Long, B.C. (1984). Aerobic conditioning and stress inoculation: A comparison of stress-management interventions. *Cognitive Therapy and Research, 8,* 517-542.

Long, B.C. (1985). Stress-management interventions: A 15-month follow-up of aerobic conditioning and stress inoculation training. *Cognitive Therapy and Research, 9,* 471-478.

Long, B.C., & Haney, C.J. (1988a). Coping strategies for working women: Aerobic exercise and relaxation interventions. *Behavior Therapy, 19,* 75-83.

Long, B.C., & Haney, C.J. (1988b). Long-term follow-up of stressed working women: A comparison of aerobic exercise and progressive relaxation. *Journal of Sport & Exercise Psychology, 10,* 461-470.

Lorig, K., Chastain, R.L., Ung, E., Shoor, S., Holman, H. (1989). Development and evaluation of a scale to measure perceived self-efficacy in people with arthritis. *Arthritis and Rheumatology, 32,* 37-44.

Maddux, J. (1995). Looking for common ground: A comment on Bandura and Kirsch. In J. Maddux (Ed.) *Self-efficacy, adaptation, and adjustment: Theory, research, and application* (pp. 377-385). New York: Plenum Press.

Maibach E., & Murphy, D.A. (1995). Self-efficacy in health promotion research and practice: Conceptualization and measurement. *Health Education Research, 10,* 37-50.

Marcus, B.H., Eaton, C.A., Rossi, J.S., & Harlow, L.L. (1994). Self-efficacy, decision-making, and stages of change: An integrative model of physical exercise. *Journal of Applied Social Psychology, 24,* 489-508.

Marcus, B.H., & Owen, N. (1992). Motivational readiness, self-efficacy and decision-making for exercise. *Journal of Applied Social Psychology, 22,* 3-16.

Marcus, B.H., Pinto, B.M., Simkin, L.R., Audrain, J.E., & Taylor, E.R. (1994). Application of theoretical models to exercise behavior among employed women. *American Journal of Health Promotion, 9,* 49-55.

Marcus, B.H., Selby, V.C., Niaura, R.S., & Rossi, J.S. (1992). Self-efficacy and the stages of exercise behavior change. *Research Quarterly for Exercise and Sport, 63,* 60-66.

McAuley, E. (1991). Efficacy, attributional, and affective responses to exercise participation. *Journal of Sport & Exercise Psychology, 13,* 382-393.

McAuley, E. (1992). The role of efficacy cognitions in the prediction of exercise behavior in middle-aged adults. *Journal of Behavioral Medicine, 15,* 65-88.

McAuley, E. (1993). Self-efficacy and the maintenance of exercise participation in older adults. *Journal of Behavioral Medicine, 16,* 103-113.

McAuley, E., Bane, S.M., & Mihalko, S.L. (1995). Exercise in middle-aged adults: Self-efficacy and self-presentational outcomes. *Preventive Medicine, 24,* 319-328.

McAuley, E., & Courneya, K.S. (1992). Self-efficacy relationships with affective and exertion responses to exercise. *Journal of Applied Social Psychology, 22,* 312-326.

McAuley, E., Courneya, K.S., & Lettunich, J. (1991). Effects of acute and long-term exercise on self-efficacy responses in sedentary, middle-aged males and females. *The Gerontologist, 31,* 534-542.

McAuley, E., Courneya, K.S., Rudolph, D.L., & Lox, C.L. (1994). Enhancing exercise adherence in middle-aged males and females. *Preventive Medicine, 23,* 498-506.

McAuley, E., & Jacobson, L. (1991). Self-efficacy and exercise participation in sedentary adult females. *American Journal of Health Promotion, 5,* 185-191.

McAuley, E., Lox, C. & Duncan, T.E. (1993). Long-term maintenance of exercise, self-efficacy, and physiological change in older adults. *Journal of Gerontology, 48,* P218-P224.

McAuley, E., Lox, L., Rudolph, D., & Travis, A. (1994). Self-efficacy and intrinsic motivation in exercising middle-aged adults. *The Journal of Applied Gerontology, 13,* 355-370.

McAuley, E., Mihalko, S.L., & Bane, S.M. (1997). Exercise and self-esteem in middle-aged adults: Multidimensional relationships and physical fitness and self-efficacy influences. *Journal of Behavioral Medicine, 20,* 67-83.

McAuley, E., Mihalko, S.L., & Rosengren, K. (in press). Self-efficacy and balance correlates of fear of falling in the elderly. *Journal of Aging and Physical Activity.*

McAuley, E., Poag, K., Gleason, A., & Wraith, S. (1990). Attrition from exercise programs: Attributional and affective perspectives. *Journal of Social Behavior and Personality, 5,* 591-602.

McAuley, E. & Rowney, T. (1990). Exercise behavior and intentions: The mediating role of self-efficacy cognitions. In L.V. Velden & J.H. Humphrey (Eds.), *Psychology and sociology of sport* (pp. 3-15). New York: AMS Press, Inc.

McAuley, E., & Rudolph, D.L (1995). Physical activity, aging, and psychological well-being. *Journal of Aging and Physical Activity, 3,* 67-96.

McAuley, E., Shaffer, S.M., & Rudolph, D. (1995). Affective responses to acute exercise in elderly impaired males: The moderating effects of self-efficacy and age. *International Journal of Aging and Human Development, 41,* 13-27.

McAuley, E., Wraith, S., & Duncan, T.E. (1991). Self-efficacy, perceptions of success, and intrinsic motivation for exercise. *Journal of Applied Social Psychology, 21,* 139-155.

Minifee, M.A. & McAuley, E. (in press). An attributional perspective on African American adults' exercise behavior. *Journal of Applied Social Psychology.*

Oldridge, N.B., & Rogowski, B.L. (1990). Self-efficacy and inpatient cardiac rehabilitation. *The American Journal of Cardiology, 66,* 362-365.

Poag, K., & McAuley, E. (1992). Goal setting, self-efficacy, and exercise behavior. *Journal of Sport & Exercise Psychology, 14,* 352-360.

Poag-DuCharme, K.A., & Brawley, L.R. (1993). Self-efficacy theory: Use in the prediction of exercise behavior in the community setting. *Journal of Applied Sport Psychology, 5,* 178-194.

Rabinowitz, S., Melamed, S., Weisberg, E., Tal, S., & Ribak, J. (1992). Personal determinants of leisure-time exercise activities. *Perceptual and Motor Skills, 75,* 779-784.

Robertson, D. & Keller, C. (1992). Relationships among health beliefs, self-efficacy, and exercise adherence in patients with coronary artery disease. *Heart Lung, 21,* 56-63.

Rodgers, W.M., & Brawley, L.R. (1993). Using both self-efficacy theory and the theory of planned behavior to discriminate adheres and dropouts from structured programs. *Journal of Applied Sport Psychology, 5,* 195-206.

Ries, A.L., Kaplan, R.M., Limberg, T.M., & Prewitt, L.M. (1995). Effects of pulmonary rehabilitation on physiologic and psychologic outcomes in patients with chronic obstructive pulmonary disease. *Annals of Internal Medicine, 122*, 823-832.

Rodin, J. (1986). Aging and health: Effects of the sense of control. *Science, 233*, 1271-1276.

Rosenberg, M. (1979). *Conceiving the self.* New York: Basic Books.

Rudolph, D.L. & McAuley, E. (1995). Self-efficacy and salivary cortisol responses to acute exercise in physically active and less active adults. *Journal of Sport and Exercise Psychology, 17*, 206-213.

Ryckman, R.M., Robbins, M.A., Thornton, B., & Cantrell, P. (1982). Development and validation of a physical self-efficacy scale. *Journal of Personality and Social Psychology, 42*, 891-900.

Sallis, J.F., Haskell, W.L., Fortman, S.P., Vranizan, K.M., Taylor, C.B., & Solomon, D.S. (1986). Predictors of adoption and maintenance of physical activity in a community sample. *Preventive Medicine, 15*, 331-341.

Sallis, J.F., Hovell, M.F., Hofstetter, C.R., & Barrington, E. (1992). Explanation of vigorous physical activity during two years using social learning variables. *Social Science and Medicine, 34*, 25-32.

Sallis, J.F., Pinski, R.B., Grossman, R.M., Patterson, T.L., & Nader, P.R. (1988). The development of self-efficacy scales for health-related diet and exercise behaviors. *Health Education Research, 3*, 283-292.

Sharpe, P.A. & Connell, C.M. (1992). Exercise beliefs and behaviors among older employees: A health promotion trial. *The Gerontologist, 32*, 444-449.

Sherer, M., Maddux, J.E., Mercandante, B., Prentice-Dunn, S., Jacobs, B., & Rogers, R.W. (1982). The Self-Efficacy Scale: Construction and validation. *Psychological Reports, 51*, 663-671.

Sonstroem, R.J., Harlow, L.L., & Josephs, L. (1994). Exercise and self-esteem: Validity of model expansion and exercise associations. *Journal of Sport and Exercise Psychology, 16*, 29-42.

Taylor, C.B., Bandura, A., Ewart, C.K., Miller, N.H., & DeBusk, R.F. (1985). Exercise testing to enhance wives' confidence in their husbands' cardiac capability soon after clinically uncomplicated acute myocardial infarction. *American Journal of Cardiology, 55*, 635-638.

Tipton, R.M., Harrison, B.M., & Mahoney, J. (1980). Faith and locus of control. *Psychological Reports, 46*, 1151-1154.

Tipton, R.M. & Worthington, E.L. (1984). The measurement of generalized self-efficacy: A study of construct validity. *Journal of Personality Assessment, 48*, 545-548.

Toshima, M.T., Kaplan, R.M., & Ries, A.L. (1990). Experimental evaluation of rehabilitation in chronic obstructive pulmonary disease: Short-term effects on exercise endurance and health status. *Health Psychology, 9*, 237-252.

United States Department of Health and Human Services. (1990). *Healthy people 2000: National health promotion and disease prevention objectives.* Washington, DC:US Government Printing Office.

Vroom, V.H. (1964). *Work motivation.* New York: Wiley.

Wankel, L.M., Mummery, W.K., Stephens, T., & Craig, C.L. (1994). Prediction of physical activity intention from social psychological variables: Results form the Campbell's Survey of Well-Being. *Journal of Sport and Exercise Psychology, 16*, 56-69.

Wyse, J., Mercer, T., Ashford, B., Buxton, K., & Gleeson, N. (1995). Evidence for the validity and utility of the Stages of Exercise Behaviour Change scale in young adults. *Health Education Research, 10*, 365-377.

Yordy, G.A. & Lent, R.W. (1993). Predicting aerobic exercise participation: Social cognitive, reasoned action, and planned behavior models. *Journal of Sport and Exercise Psychology, 15*, 363-374.

Acknowledgements

The preparation of this chapter was funded in part by a grant from the National Institute on Aging (#1 RO1-AG12113-01). The authors appreciate the insightful comments of David Dzewaltowski on an earlier draft of this manuscript.

Appendix 1

Table 1
Exercise-Related Self-Efficacy Scales: Classification and Psychometric Properties

STUDY	ORIGINAL SCALE AUTHOR	SCALE CLASSIFICATION	RELIABILITY	EXERCISE-EFFICACY RELATIONSHIP
Broman, C.L. (1995).	Based upon measure by: Goldsmith-Cwikel, Dielman, Kirscht, & Israil (1988).	Disease/health-related efficacy	None given	Efficacy for preventive health behavior weakly related to leisure-time physical activity.
Buckelew, S.P., Murray, S.E., Hewett, J.E., Johnson, J., & Huyser, B. (1995).	Arthritis Self-Efficacy Scale: Lorig, Chastain, Ung, Shoor, Holman (1989).	Disease/health-related efficacy	Reference to Lorig et al. (1989).	Higher efficacy associated with less pain and less impaired activity in arthritis patients.
Carroll, D.L. (1995).	Jenkins Self-Efficacy Expectation Scales: Jenkins, Unpublished data, 1987.	Disease/health-related efficacy	$\propto$'s = .76 to .96	Efficacy increased over time during coronary by-pass recovery. Self-efficacy predictive of self-care activities.
Clark, D.O., Patrick, D.L., Grembowski, D., & Durham, M.L. (1995).	Developed by authors, adapted from Grembowski et al. (1993).	Exercise efficacy	None given	Self-efficacy weakly related to age and education and strongly predicted by outcome expectations.
Courneya, K.S. (1995).	Ajzen & Madden (1986).	Perceived behavioral control	$\propto$ = .71	Perceived behavioral control influences stage of physical activity directly and indirectly through intention.
DuCharme, K.A., & Brawley, L.R. (1995).	Developed by authors	1) Other 2) Barrier efficacy	$\propto$ = .60 to .90	Barriers and scheduling efficacy predicted intention and scheduling efficacy predicted exercise frequency.

STUDY	ORIGINAL SCALE AUTHOR	SCALE CLASSIFICATION	RELIABILITY	EXERCISE-EFFICACY RELATIONSHIP
Gorely, T., & Gordon, S. (1995).	Self-Efficacy Questionnaire (SEQ): Marcus, Selby, Niaura, & Rossi (1992).	Barriers efficacy	Reference to: Marcus et al.(1992): $\underline{r}$ = .90; & Marcus & Owen (1992): $\propto$ = .85, .80	Efficacy increases across stages of exercise behavior.
Kavussanu, M., & McAuley, E. (1995).	The Physical Self-Efficacy scale (PSE) Ryckman et al. (1982).	General efficacy	$\propto$ = .84	Physical self-efficacy positively related to optimism.
McAuley, E., Bane, S.M., & Mihalko, S.L. (1995).	1) McAuley, Courneya, & Lettunich (1991). 2) PSE: Ryckman et al. (1982).	1) Exercise efficacy 2) General efficacy	All $\propto$ > .90	Acute and long-term exercise significantly enhances self-efficacy. Enhanced efficacy resulted in significant reductions in physique anxiety over 5-month exercise program.
McAuley, E., Shaffer, S.M., & Rudolph, D. (1995).	Developed by authors based on premise set by Bandura, A. (1986).	Exercise efficacy	None given	More efficacious individuals reported more positive and less negative affect following acute exercise bout.
Ries, A.L., Kaplan, R.M., Limberg, T.M., & Prewitt, L.M. (1995).	Adapted from Kaplan, Atkins, Reinsch (1984).	Exercise efficacy	None given	Pulmonary rehabilitation intervention significantly enhanced self-efficacy when compared to an education group.
Rudolph, D.L., & McAuley, E. (1995).	Developed by authors based on premise set by Bandura (1986).	Exercise efficacy	None given	More physically active individuals were more efficacious. Self-efficacy predictive of cortisol responses during activity.

Table 1 (cont.)

Exercise-Related Self-Efficacy Scales: Classification and Psychometric Properties

STUDY	ORIGINAL SCALE AUTHOR	SCALE CLASSIFICATION	RELIABILITY	EXERCISE-EFFICACY RELATIONSHIP
Wyse, J., Mercer, T., Ashford, B., Buxton, K., & Gleeson, N. (1995).	Marcus et al. (1992).	Barriers efficacy	None given	Self-efficacy increased across stages of exercise behavior.
Biddle, S., Goudas, M., & Page, A. (1994).	1) Ajzen & Fishbein (1977). 2) Developed by authors.	1) Perceived behavioral control 2) Exercise efficacy	$\propto$ = .81, .91	Self-efficacy significantly related to intention and self-reported strenuous physical activity.
Bozoian, S., Rejeski, W.J., & McAuley, E. (1994).	Developed by authors based on premise set by Bandura (1986).	Exercise efficacy	None given	More efficacious females reported more positive affective responses post-acute exercise.
Courneya, K.S., & McAuley, E. (1994).	Developed by authors.	Exercise efficacy	$\propto$ = .87 to .93	Self-efficacy predictive of frequency and intensity of self-reported physical activity.
Harrison, D.A., & Liska, L.Z. (1994).	1) Vroom (1964). 2) Ajzen & Madden (1986).	Perceived behavioral control	None given	Exercise and barrier self-efficacy significantly related to exercise goal attractiveness and goal commitment.
Horne, T.E. (1994).	1) Ajzen & Madden (1986). 2) Brawley & Horne (1989).	1) Perceived behavioral control 2) Barriers Efficacy	None given	Self-efficacy significantly discriminated between active and inactive Canadian homemakers and related to future intention for activity.
Kaplan, R.M., Ries, A.L., Prewitt, L.M., & Eakin, E. (1994).	Adapted from: Ewart, Taylor, Reese, & DeBusk (1986).	Disease/health-related efficacy	None given	Exercise self-efficacy significant predictor of 5-year survival in chronic obstructive pulmonary patients.

STUDY	ORIGINAL SCALE AUTHOR	SCALE CLASSIFICATION	RELIABILITY	EXERCISE-EFFICACY RELATIONSHIP
Marcus, B.H., Eaton, C.A., Rossi, J.S., & Harlow, L.L. (1994).	Marcus, Selby, Niaura, & Rossi (1992).	Barriers efficacy	Reference to Marcus et al. (1992): $\propto$ = .82	Self-efficacy indirectly related to self-reported physical activity through stages of change.
Marcus, B.H., Pinto, B.M., Simkin, L.R., Audrain, J.E., & Taylor, E.R. (1994).	Marcus et al. (1992).	Barriers efficacy	$\propto$ = .84	Self-efficacy increased through stages of self-reported exercise behavior.
McAuley, E., Courneya, K.S., Rudolph, D.L., & Lox, C.L. (1994).	Developed by authors.	Exercise efficacy	$\propto$ = .92	Efficacy-based intervention increases adherence by 12% over attention-control group. Self-efficacy predicted adherence at 2 and 4 months.
McAuley, E., Lox, L., Rudolph, D., & Travis, A. (1994).	McAuley, Poag, Gleason, & Wraith (1990).	Barriers efficacy	$\propto$ = .92	Reciprocally determining relationship demonstrated between barriers self-efficacy and intrinsic motivation.
Sonstroem, R.J., Harlow, L.L., & Josephs, L. (1994).	Developed by authors based upon premise set by Bandura (1977).	Exercise efficacy	$\propto$ = .70	Authors demonstrate significant relationships between exercise efficacy and domain specific elements of self-esteem (sport, physical condition, attractive body, and strength).
Wankel, L.M., Mummery, W.K., Stephens, T., & Craig, C.L. (1994).	Ajzen & Madden (1986).	Perceived behavioral control	$\propto$ = .46	Perceived behavioral control related to exercise intention in a large probability sample.
Armstrong, C.A., Sallis, J.F., Hovell, M.F., Hofstetter, C.R. (1993).	Developed by authors.	Barriers efficacy	None given	Contemplators had greater efficacy than precontemplators. Self-efficacy predictive of 6-month self-reported (one item) exercise.

Table 1 (cont.)

Exercise-Related Self-Efficacy Scales: Classification and Psychometric Properties

STUDY	ORIGINAL SCALE AUTHOR	SCALE CLASSIFICATION	RELIABILITY	EXERCISE-EFFICACY RELATIONSHIP
Courneya, K.S. & McAuley, E. (1993).	McAuley, Courneya, & Lettunich (1991).	Exercise efficacy	$\propto = .90$	Exercise efficacy influenced causal attributions and had an indirect effect on affect following an acute bout of exercise.
Duncan, T.E. & McAuley, E. (1993).	1)Developed by authors based on premise set by Bandura (1977). 2)McAuley, Poag, Gleason, & Wraith (1990).	1) Exercise efficacy 2) Barriers efficacy	$\propto = .93$	Latent growth modeling techniques revealed social support effects on exercise behavior to be mediated by self-efficacy (barriers and exercise).
Duncan, T.E., McAuley, E., Stoolmiller, M., & Duncan, S.C. (1993).	McAuley, et al. (1990).	Barriers efficacy	$\propto = .82$ to $.96$	Self-efficacy cognitions not predictive of intra-individual change in exercise adherence over time.
Duncan, T.E. & Stoolmiller, M. (1993).	1)Developed by authors based on premise set by Bandura (1977). 2)McAuley et al. (1990).	1) Exercise efficacy 2) Barriers efficacy	$\propto = .94, .93$	Changes in social support over time influenced exercise behavior through the mediation of changes in self-efficacy over time.
Grembowski, D., Patrick, D., Diehr, P., Durham, M., Beresford, S., Kay, E., & Hecht, J. (1993).	Developed by authors based on Rodin (1986).	Disease/health-related efficacy	None given	Exercise efficacy in combination with other health-related efficacy measures positively related to health status in older adults.

STUDY	ORIGINAL SCALE AUTHOR	SCALE CLASSIFICATION	RELIABILITY	EXERCISE-EFFICACY RELATIONSHIP
Kavanagh, D.J., Gooley, S., & Wilson, P.H. (1993).	Developed by authors.	Disease/health-related efficacy	$r > .60$	Exercise efficacy predicted adherence to diabetes management.
Labbe, E.E., & Welsh, C. (1993).	Adapted from Kaplan et al. (1984).	Exercise efficacy	$r = .76$ to $.86$	Exercise efficacy increased in aerobic exercise group versus a physical education control group of elementary school children.
McAuley, E. (1993).	1)McAuley, et al. (1990). 2)Developed by authors.	1) Barriers efficacy 2) Exercise efficacy	$\propto > .90$	Combined exercise and barriers efficacy predicted maintenance of physical activity and energy expenditure at 4-month follow-up.
McAuley, E., Lox, C. & Duncan, T.E. (1993).	Developed by authors based on premise set by Bandura (1977, 1986).	1) Exercise efficacy 2) Exercise efficacy	All $\propto > .85$	Acute exercise bout increased exercise efficacy. Exercise efficacy associated with long-term exercise maintenance.
Poag-DuCharme, K.A. & Brawley, L.R. (1993).	Developed by authors based on premise set by Bandura (1977).	1) Barriers efficacy 2) Other 3) Exercise efficacy.	$\propto = .72$ to $.92$	Barriers, in-class, and scheduling efficacy related to intention. Scheduling efficacy better predictor of exercise attendance in beginning and for experienced exercisers.
Rodgers, W.M., & Brawley, L.R. (1993).	Developed by authors.	Disease/health-related efficacy	$\propto = .75$ to $.95$	Self-efficacy predicts exercise adherence in self-help intervention in community hospital.
Yordy, G.A., & Lent, R.W. (1993).	Adapted from Dzewaltowski (1989).	Barriers efficacy	$\propto = .83$ $r = .76$	Barriers efficacy related to intentions and self-reported physical activity.

Table 1 (cont.)
Exercise-Related Self-Efficacy Scales: Classification and Psychometric Properties

STUDY	ORIGINAL SCALE AUTHOR	SCALE CLASSIFICATION	RELIABILITY	EXERCISE-EFFICACY RELATIONSHIP
Brown, S.W., Welsh, M.C., Labbe, E.E., Vitulli, W.F., & Kulkarni, P. (1992).	The Self-Efficacy Questionnaire: devised for this study.	General efficacy	None given	Efficacy enhanced by physical activity participation in adolescent psychiatric patients.
Hickey, M.L., Owen, S.V., & Froman, R.D. (1992).	Cardiac diet and Cardiac exercise self-efficacy instruments developed by authors.	Disease/health-related efficacy	α = .90 both scales r = .86, .87	Males demonstrated significantly higher cardiac exercise efficacy than females and marathon runners more efficacious than cardiac rehabilitation patients.
Marcus, B.H. & Owen, N. (1992).	Adapted from: Condiotte & Lichenstein (1981).	Barriers efficacy	α = .85	Barriers self-efficacy successfully differentiated individuals at different stages of the exercise process.
Marcus, B.H., Selby, V.C., Niaura, R.S., & Rossi, J.S. (1992).	Developed by authors.	Barriers efficacy	α = .82 & .76	Self-efficacy (barriers) differentiated individuals at different stages of exercise.
McAuley, E. (1992).	PSE, Ryckman et al. (1982). 2)Based upon McAuley et al. (1990).	1) General efficacy 2) Barriers efficacy	α = .89, .88	General physical efficacy predicted intensity of exercise while barriers efficacy significantly related to exercise frequency in first 3-months of program.
McAuley, E. & Courneya, K.S. (1992).	Adapted from Ewart, Taylor, Reese, & DeBusk (1983).	Exercise efficacy	α = .96	More efficacious subjects reported lower effort expenditure and more positive affect during acute activity. Affective responses in turn predicted post-exercise efficacy.

STUDY	ORIGINAL SCALE AUTHOR	SCALE CLASSIFICATION	RELIABILITY	EXERCISE-EFFICACY RELATIONSHIP
Poag, K., & McAuley, E. (1992).	Developed by authors.	1) Other 2) Barriers efficacy	1) None given 2) α = .89	Exercise efficacy related to exercise intensity but no frequency. Goal efficacy significantly related to perceived goal achievement.
Rabinowitz, S., Melamed, S., Weisberg, E., Tal, S., & Ribak, J. (1992).	Based on premise set by Bandura (1982).	Exercise efficacy	None given	Single-item exercise efficacy measure correlated with single-item report of leisure-time exercise and correct dietary practices.
Robertson, D. & Keller, C. (1992).	The Self-Efficacy Scale: Jenkins (Unpublished manuscript, 1987).	Exercise efficacy	Reference to Jenkins: α = .87 to .94	Exercise adherence influenced by exercise self-efficacy in patients with coronary artery disease.
Sallis, J.F., Hovell, M.F., Hofstetter, C.R., & Barrington, E. (1992).	No reference given. Within text mention of Bandura (1986).	Barriers efficacy	Reference to test-retest: Hovell et al. 1989	Barriers self-efficacy significant predictor of change in exercise over 24 months in a large community sample.
Sharpe, P.A. & Connell, C.M. (1992).	No reference given.	1) Barriers efficacy 2) Exercise efficacy	None given	Single-item exercise efficacy measure predictive of intention to exercise.
Fruin, D.J., Pratt,C., & Owen, N. (1991).	No reference given.	Exercise efficacy	None given	Subjects presented with high efficacy information reported stronger efficacy for exercising. Efficacy was significantly related to exercise intention.
Garcia, A.W. & King, A.C. (1991).	No specific reference given-developed by authors.	Barriers efficacy	α = .90 r = .67	Self-efficacy associated with exercise adherence of community adults at 6 and 12 months.

Table 1

Exercise-Related Self-Efficacy Scales: Classification and Psychometric Properties

STUDY	ORIGINAL SCALE AUTHOR	SCALE CLASSIFICATION	RELIABILITY	EXERCISE-EFFICACY RELATIONSHIP
Gulanick, M. (1991).	Developed by authors.	Disease/health-related efficacy	None given	Self-efficacy increased over time for patients involved in phase 1 cardiac rehabilitation. No effect of differential treatments (including exercise) on efficacy.
Hovell, M., Sallis, J., Hofstetter, R., Barrington, E., Hackley, M., Elder, J., Castro, F., & Kilbourne, K. (1991).	No reference given. Within survey designed by authors.	Barriers efficacy	None given	Self-efficacy significant correlate of vigorous physical activity in Hispanic adults.
Kelly, R.B., Zyzanski, S.J., & Alemagno, S.A. (1991).	No reference given- developed by authors.	Exercise efficacy	None given	Motivation to change lifestyle (including exercise) linked to efficacy which also predicted exercise behavior change.
McAuley, E. (1991).	McAuley, et al. (1990).	Barriers efficacy	$\propto = .85$	Barriers self-efficacy influenced attributions and affective responses in sample of middle-aged adults.
McAuley, E., Courneya, K.S., & Lettunich, J. (1991).	Developed by authors based on premise set by Bandura (1977, 1982).	Exercise efficacy	All $\propto$'s > .80	Acute bout of efficacy enhanced exercise efficacy . Efficacy correlated with estimated VO2 max and time to reach 70% maximal heart rate.
McAuley, E., & Jacobson, L. (1991).	Developed by authors based on premise set by Bandura (1977).	Barriers efficacy	All $\propto$'s > .70	Barriers efficacy related to both formal exercise and self-reported free-living exercise in a sample of adult females.

STUDY	ORIGINAL SCALE AUTHOR	SCALE CLASSIFICATION	RELIABILITY	EXERCISE-EFFICACY RELATIONSHIP
McAuley, E., Wraith, S., & Duncan, T.E. (1991).	Developed by authors based on premise set by Bandura (1977).	Exercise efficacy	None given	More efficacious individuals enjoyed exercise more, put forth greater effort, and felt more competent than less efficacious peers.
Bezjak, J.E., & Lee, J.W. (1990).	Developed by authors.	Other	$\propto = .84$	Physical fitness efficacy related to musculo-skeletal flexibility, endurance, and self-reported activity.
Dzewaltowski, D.A., Noble, J.M., & Shaw, J.M. (1990).	1) Mention of Bandura (1986). 2) Adapted from Dzewaltowski (1989).	1) Exercise efficacy 2) Barriers efficacy	Combined $\propto = .97$	Combined barriers and exercise efficacy successfully predicted physical activity even when controlling for past behavior and behavior intention in a large sample of college undergraduates.
Gortner, S.R. & Jenkins, L.S. (1990).	Jenkins (1985).	Disease/health-related efficacy	$\propto$'s = .67 to .99 from baseline to 24 weeks	Self-efficacy correlated with several self-reported exercise behaviors post-cardiac surgery. Efficacy also related to mood states and exercise at 24 weeks.
Hofstetter, C.R., Hovell, M.F., & Sallis, J.F. (1990).	No reference given.	Barriers efficacy	$\propto = .82$	Perceived barriers, social modeling, and self-rated coordination identified as determinants of self-efficacy. Efficacy strong correlate of self-reported vigorous exercise and walking for exercise.
Kingery, P.M. (1990).	Developed by authors.	Exercise efficacy	$r = .65$	Self-efficacy correlated more strongly with retrospectively than prospectively assessed exercise behavior.

Table 1 (cont.)

Exercise-Related Self-Efficacy Scales: Classification and Psychometric Properties

STUDY	ORIGINAL SCALE AUTHOR	SCALE CLASSIFICATION	RELIABILITY	EXERCISE-EFFICACY RELATIONSHIP
McAuley, E., & Rowney, T. (1990).	Developed by authors based upon premise set by Bandura (1977).	Exercise efficacy	None given	Exercise self-efficacy related to exercise attendance and perceptions of performance. The latter variables influenced postprogram efficacy which was significantly related to behavioral intention to continue exercising.
Oldridge, N.B. & Rogowski, B.L. (1990).	Reference to Ewart et al. (1983) & Taylor et al., (1985).	Disease/health-related efficacy	None given	Cardiac rehabilitation patients randomly assigned to an exercise plus counseling group or ward ambulation plus counseling group improved efficacy over treatment course. Efficacy in exercise group for walking and exertion was significantly higher than controls.
Toshima, M.T., Kaplan, R.M., & Ries, A.L. (1990).	Kaplan et al. (1984).	Disease/health-related efficacy	None given	Rehabilitation intervention for chronic obstructive pulmonary disease patients significantly enhanced self-efficacy over an education control group. Increased self-efficacy correlated with exercise endurance.
Dzewaltowski, D.A. (1989).	Developed by author.	Barriers efficacy	α's = .80 to .97	Self-efficacy predictive of number of days of exercise over 8 weeks in undergraduate sample.
Hovell, M.F., Sallis, J.F., Hofstetter, C.R., Spry, V.M., Faucher, P., & Casperson, C.J. (1989).	No reference given.	Barriers efficacy	r = .92	Walking for exercise in sedentary sample related to barriers efficacy

STUDY	ORIGINAL SCALE AUTHOR	SCALE CLASSIFICATION	RELIABILITY	EXERCISE-EFFICACY RELATIONSHIP
Holloway, J.B., Beuter, A., & Duda, J.L. (1988).	1) The Physical Self-Efficacy Scale: Ryckman et al. (1982). 2) The Physical Strength and Self-Efficacy Test: Developed by authors.	1) General efficacy 2) Exercise efficacy	1) None given 2) r = .75, .90	Strength training influenced physical, weight training, and confrontation self-efficacy in adolescent females.
Long, B.C., & Haney, C.J. (1988a).	The General Self-Efficacy Scale: Sherer et al. (1982).	General efficacy	Reference to Sherer & Adams (1983): α = .86	Exercise and relaxation both increased general self-efficacy. Self-efficacy unrelated to adherence to exercise.
Long, B.C., & Haney, C.J. (1988b).	The General Self-Efficacy Scale: Sherer et al. (1982).	General efficacy	None given	At 14 month follow-up exercise and relaxation interventions had enhanced self-efficacy.
Sallis, J.F., Pinski, R.B., Grossman, R.M., Patterson, T.L., & Nader, P.R. (1988).	Self-Efficacy for Exercise Behaviors Scale: Developed by authors.	Barriers efficacy	α's = .83-.85 r = .68	Barriers efficacy significantly correlated with self-reported vigorous activity.
Bandura, A., & Cervone D. (1986).	Developed by authors.	Exercise efficacy	none given	Stronger sense of efficacy positively related to difficulty of goals
Desharnais, R., Bouillon, J., & Godin, G. (1986).	No reference given.	Exercise efficacy	None given	Single-item efficacy measure discriminated between "adherers" and "dropouts" in university fitness program.

Table 1 (Cont.)
Exercise-Related Self-Efficacy Scales: Classification and Psychometric Properties

STUDY	ORIGINAL SCALE AUTHOR	SCALE CLASSIFICATION	RELIABILITY	EXERCISE-EFFICACY RELATIONSHIP
Ewart, C.K., Stewart, K.J., Gillilan, R.E., Kelemen, M.H., Valenti, S.A., Manley, J.D., & Kelemen, M.D. (1986).	Developed by authors.	Disease/health-related efficacy	None given	Self-efficacy related to number of minutes coronary heart disease patients exercise above or below prescribed intensity levels. Baseline efficacy correlated with treadmill test performance and heart rate responses to exercise.
Sallis, J.F., Haskell, W.L., Fortman, S.P., Vranizan, K.M., Taylor, C.B., & Solomon, D.S. (1986).	Developed by authors.	Exercise efficacy	None given	Self-efficacy predicted adoption of vigorous physical activity and maintenance of moderate physical activity in a community sample. Efficacy also predicted increases in activity level for men but not for women.
Long, B.C. (1985).	Trait self-efficacy: Coppel (1980).	General efficacy	None given	Jogging and stress-inoculation training shown to increase 'trait' self-efficacy at 15-month follow-up in chronically anxious adults.
Taylor, C.B., Bandura, A., Ewart, C.K., Miller, N.H., & DeBusk, R.F. (1985).	Developed by authors.	Disease/health-related efficacy	$r = .94, .85$	Exposure to treadmill walking enhanced wives' efficacy in husbands' physical and cardiac efficacy. Spouse and patient efficacy were correlated with treadmill heart rate and workload.
Corbin, C.B., Laurie, D.R., Gruger, C., & Smiley, B. (1984).	Developed by authors.	General efficacy	None given	General efficacy/confidence for exercise was enhanced by vicarious success experiences.
Hogan, P.I., & Santomier, J.P. (1984).	Swim Self-Efficacy Scale (SSES): Developed by authors, based upon premise set by Bandura (1977; 1981).	Exercise efficacy	$r = .99$	Mastery experience focused program increased swimming efficacy for older adults.

STUDY	ORIGINAL SCALE AUTHOR	SCALE CLASSIFICATION	RELIABILITY	EXERCISE-EFFICACY RELATIONSHIP
Kaplan, R.M., Atkins, C., & Reinsch, S. (1984).	Adapted from Ewart et al. (1983).	Disease/health-related efficacy	None given	Experimental manipulations involving behavior modification led to changes in self-efficacy. Exercise efficacy correlated with exercise tolerance, vital capacity, and expiratory volume in chronic obstructive pulmonary disease patients.
Long, B.C. (1984).	Self-Efficacy Scale: Coppel (1980).	General efficacy	None given	Aerobic activity and stress inoculation successfully increased general self-efficacy in chronically anxious adults.
Tipton, R.M., & Worthington, E.L. (1984).	General Self-Efficacy Scale (GSE): Adapted from Tipton, Harrison, & Mahoney (1980).	General efficacy	None given	General self-efficacy related to muscular endurance.
Bandura, A., & Cervone D. (1983).	Developed by authors.	Exercise efficacy	none given	Greater self-dissatisfaction and stronger self-efficacy resulted in intensified effort.
Ewart, C.K., Taylor, B., Reese, L.B., & DeBusk, R.F. (1983).	Developed by authors, based upon premise set by Bandura (1977).	Disease/health-related efficacy	None given	Intensity and duration of home physical activity of post-myocardial infarction patients strongly correlated with exercise efficacy, which was also moderately correlated with treadmill performance and peak treadmill heart rate. Treadmill performance enhanced efficacy with further increases resulting from cardiac counseling.

Appendix 2

Examples of Self-Regulatory and Behavioral or Task Self-Efficacy Scales
for Exercise Self-Regulatory Efficacy: Barriers Efficacy Scale

The items below reflect common reasons preventing people from participating in exercise sessions or, in some cases, dropping out or quitting exercise altogether. Using the scale below, please indicate how confident you are that you could exercise in the event that any of the following circumstances were to occur.

0%	10%	20%	30%	40%	50%	60%	70%	80%	90%	100%

No Confidence At all   Somewhat Confident   Completely Confident

For example, if you have *complete confidence* that you can continue to exercise, even if you are bored by the activity, you would circle 100%. However, if you are absolutely sure that you could not exercise if you failed to make or continue to make progress you would circle 0% (*No Confidence at all*).[2]

I believe that I can exercise 3 times per week if:
1. The weather is very bad (hot, humid, rainy, snow, cold).
2. I was bored by the program or activity.
3. I was on vacation.
4. I felt pain or discomfort when exercising.
5. I had to exercise alone.
6. Exercise was not enjoyable or fun.
7. It became difficult to get to the exercise location.
8. I didn't like the particular activity program that I was involved in..
9. My work schedule conflicted with my exercise session.
10. I felt self-conscious about my appearance when I exercised.
11. The instructor did not offer me any encouragement.
13. I was under personal stress of some kind.

Behavioral or Task Self-Efficacy for Treadmill Walking

Please indicate below how confident you are that you can successfully carry out each of the activities listed below using the following scale.

0%	10%	20%	30%	40%	50%	60%	70%	80%	90%	100%

No Confidence At all   Somewhat Confident   Completely Confident

For example, if you have *complete confidence* that you can walk on the treadmill for 5 minutes at a moderately fast pace, you would circle 100%. However, if you are not very confident that you could walk for 20 minutes without stopping, you would circle a number closer to the zero end of the scale.

I BELIEVE THAT I CAN WALK ON THE TREADMILL:
1. For **5 minutes at a moderately fast pace** without stopping.
2. For **10 minutes at a moderately fast pace** without stopping.
3. For **15 minutes at a moderately fast pace** without stopping.
4. For **20 minutes at a moderately fast pace** without stopping.
5. For **25 minutes at a moderately fast pace** without stopping.
6. For **30 minutes at a moderately fast pace** without stopping.

---

2. The confidence scales would appear under each item. Strength of efficacy is calculated by summing the confidence scales and dividing by total number of items used.

Part VIII

Special Considerations and Alternative Approaches

PART VIII

In this final section, new or not typically considered methods of assessing the validity and reliability of sport and exercise psychology inventories are presented. Also discussed are the ethical standards and principles significant to measurement development, administration, and interpretation. When we look at the current knowledge base, most of the work on the psychometric attributes of sport and exercise measures is biased toward older youth and adult mainstream participants. This body of information should be expanded to include more culturally diverse samples. It is also essential that the assessments employed be developmentally appropriate; specifically, more child-based instruments are needed in the field. The rationale and methodological strategies for fostering such expansion are described in two subsequent chapters. Finally, in Part VIII, we examine the adequacy of existing sport and exercise psychology measures in regard to their use in applied settings.

Chapter 23

ASSESSING THE STABILITY OF PSYCHOLOGICAL TRAITS AND MEASURES

Robert W. Schutz
University of British Columbia

Introduction

Researchers are frequently interested in obtaining answers to questions such as "How consistent, over time, are people with respect to ...(some trait)?" For example, Finn (1986) examined the stability of personality self-ratings over a 30-year period, Marsh has conducted a number of studies on the stability of self-esteem (e.g., Marsh, 1993a), and Long and Schutz (1995) tested the stability of stress and coping measured eight times over 2 years. To answer these and other questions involving repeated assessments over time, the researcher needs to compute statistics that represent both the longitudinal reliability of the measure and the stability of the trait. Traditionally, a correlation coefficient, usually the Pearson product-moment correlation coefficient (PPMC), has been used to quantify both, and in fact these two constructs, reliability and stability, are usually considered as synonyms, and a single statistic is calculated to represent the longitudinal consistency of a set of observed scores. However, recent developments in psychometric theory have led to the development of much more sophisticated procedures for quantifying stability and reliability. Heise's 1969 paper, "Separating Reliability and Stability in Test-Retest Correlation," should have alerted us to the problems with using simple correlations to infer both reliability and stability, but unfortunately we paid little heed to this and other similar papers (Blalock, 1970; Wiley & Wiley, 1970) at that time—probably because of the unavailability of suitable computer software to perform the rather complex calculations. The rapid growth of the theory of longitudinal covariance structural analysis (or structural equation modeling) and the development of associated computer programs, however, have led to a proliferation of methodological and applied papers on the appropriate statistical techniques for the measurement and quantification of stability

and reliability. These techniques, although being available in the current periodical literature, do not yet appear in measurement textbooks, nor are they being utilized by many researchers in sport psychology. Therefore, the purpose of this chapter is to give an overview of the theory underlying these relatively new measures of stability and reliability and to provide some examples of its application.

An acceptance of the existence of psychological traits is foundational to the study of stability in psychological research. If a trait is defined as "the relatively stable behavior of a certain kind over an ecologically representative sample of situation - occasions" (Epstein, 1990, p. 99), then we require a measurement/statistical methodology to assess the degree of stability of that trait. Although some would argue that the assumption that behavior is stable over occasions and situations is false (e.g., Steyer & Schmitt, 1990), there appears to be general agreement that attributes such as self-concept, extroversion, anxiety and intelligence can be considered traits, and the study of their temporal stability is a worthwhile endeavor (this agreement usually is based upon the assumption that the trait must be measured by more than a single item). Schuerger, Zarrella, and Hotz's (1989) study in which they examined the temporal stability of "personality by questionnaire" in 89 published studies reflects the interest in this type of research.

Given that the measurement of stability is a necessary component of empirical research, it would seem appropriate to have an agreed-upon definition of stability and a common method for quantifying it. Unfortunately, this is not the case. The terms, reliability (PPMC, Cronbach's alpha, intraclass r, Hoyt's r, G-coefficients), stability (mean stability, differential stability, structural stability, covariance stability, temporal stability, individual stability), and consistency (temporal constancy) are defined differently by different authors, and/or are used synonymously by others. In a following section, I attempt to define and explain the stability terms that are gradually gaining acceptance in the periodical literature. Because the true meaning of these terms is determined by the mathematical derivation of the equation used to compute a stability coefficient, I have also described the statistical method(s) associated with each term (but have avoided any mathematical derivations). First, however, because these terms and coefficients have their roots in classical test theory, or are confused with a classical test theory interpretation of "reliability," a brief review of reliability theory is provided.

Reliability in the Framework of Classical Test Theory and Generalizability Theory

According to the true-score model in classical test theory, an observed score is viewed as a composite of two components—a theoretical score (true score) and an error score, that is, x = t + e, where, x is the observed score; t is the true score; and e is random error. Fundamental assumptions imposed by classical test theory are (a) the true scores are stable over time; (b) the expected error score is zero: E(e)=0; and (c) the correlation between error score and true score is zero: $r_{te} = 0$ (Ghiselli, Campbell, & Zedeck, 1981). Consequently, the variance of observed scores is simply the sum of the true and error score variances, $\sigma^2_x = \sigma^2_t + \sigma^2_e$. Given this, the ratio of the true score variance to observed variance is called the reliability of measure x and can be expressed as, $r_x = \sigma^2_t / \sigma^2_x$. This ratio can be shown to be equal to the squared correlation between observed and true scores and indicates the degree to which test scores are free from errors of measurement.

Since the true-score model includes an unobservable element (true score), in practice the reliability of a measure is assessed by correlating parallel measurements. By definition (Ghiselli et al., 1981), two measurements are said to be parallel if they have identical true scores and equal variances. It can be shown that the correlation between parallel measures is an estimate of the reliability of either one of them, and one can estimate reliability of a measure by administering two parallel measures. However, parallel measures (and the similar alternative-form method) are difficult to construct in psychological research, and thus the most common methods for ascertaining reliability have been the test-retest method and the internal consistency method.

Test-Retest Reliability

The test-retest method is used when a test user is interested in how consistently examinees respond to the same measure at different times. The same measure is readministered to the same group, under the same conditions, within a certain time period, and the correlation coefficient between the two sets of scores, traditionally called the coefficient of stability, is taken as an estimate of the test reliability. However, the use of the correlation coefficient in the test-retest method as a measure of reliability has been criticized by many researchers (e.g., Heise, 1969; Marsh & Grayson, 1994). The correlation between the test and retest scores of the same measure will inevitably be less than perfect because of the temporal instability of measures taken at multiple points in time and the measurement error. It is

also possible that an obtained low test-retest correlation may not indicate that the reliability of the test is low but may, instead, signify that the underlying theoretical concept itself (true score) has changed. As a result, a simple test-retest correlation is inappropriate to estimate a variable's true reliability, as well as the variable's temporal stability, unless one can assume that either the underlying variable remains perfectly stable, or the variable is measured with perfect reliability.

It is common practice by some researchers to "correct" a test-retest reliability coefficient for the unreliability of the measure itself, where the internal consistency coefficient is used as the reliability of the measure. It has been claimed that such a "reliability corrected for attenuation" coefficient is a valid estimator of the reliability of the true scores of the test and retest, as it has removed the negative effect of random measurement error. But as Marsh and Grayson (1994) and others point out, although removing the negative bias caused by the unreliability of the measure does remove the random error influence, the disattenuated correlation may now be positively biased due to the existence of a positive correlation among the specific error variances. More recent techniques (structural equation modeling) provide methods for accounting for this component of error variance.

Internal Consistency

For multi-indicator trait measures (computed by summing a number of items to obtain a single trait score), a measure of internal consistency is often reported as the "reliability" of the scale. Several approaches to the estimation of the internal-consistency have been formulated based on the assumption that all items are measures of the same underlying attribute, and a general form for this approach is known as Cronbach's alpha (Cronbach, 1951), which can be computed by the formula:

$$\alpha = \frac{k}{k-1} \left[1 - \frac{\sum \sigma^2_i}{\sum \sigma^2_i + 2(\sum \sigma_{ij})} \right]$$

where k is the number of items in the measure, and σ^2_i and σ_{ij} are the variance of item i and the covariance of any pair of items i and j (where, $i > j$), respectively. Cronbach's alpha is a general form of the Kuder-Richardson 20 or KR-20 coefficient, and it yields identical results with the KR-20 when items are scored dichotomously. In addition, when all items are standardized, having a mean of zero and a variance of one, it is reduced to the Spearman-Brown formula. Thus, Cronbach's alpha is equivalent to the mean of all possible split-half coefficients of a given measure and is approximately equal to the average of all k(k-1) between-item correlations for a k-item scale. It must be noted however that a high internal consistency does not tell us anything about temporal stability, but only about the degree to which all items measure the same latent construct.

Intraclass Correlations

The intraclass correlation method can be used to estimate reliability coefficients in situations where a number of subjects are measured once on a number of items, or repeatedly on a single item, or, most importantly, repeatedly on a number of items. ANOVA procedures are then utilized to calculate variances (mean squares) to estimate the various sources of variance. Depending on what assumptions the researcher wishes to make about error variances and true-score variances, different intraclass reliability coefficients can be calculated (e.g., see Shrout & Fleiss, 1979).

One of the first attempts to use the intraclass correlation as an estimate of reliability appears in Hoyt (1941). Hoyt derived this equation as a means of estimating reliability in a Persons by Items design. Hoyt related this formula to the theoretical definition of the reliability by noting that the MS_p represents the observed score variance, and the MS_e represents the error variance in the theoretical reliability expression [i.e., $(\sigma^2_x - \sigma^2_e) / \sigma^2_x$]. Hoyt noted that these ANOVA procedures do not depend on any particular choice in subdividing the items, and they approximate an average of all the possible correlations that might have been obtained by different ways of assigning items to alternative forms. Therefore, this method of estimating the reliability of a test gives a better estimate than does any method based on an arbitrary division of the test into halves or into any other fractional parts. Although Hoyt drew attention to its application only to the case where items are scored dichotomously, the equation for the reliability of the mean test score yields identical results with Cronbach's alpha, as well as with KR-20. Hoyt's equation, for a persons (n) by items (k) factorial design, for the intraclass correlation coefficient for a single item score is

$$r_1 = \frac{MS_p - MS_e}{MS_p + (k-1)\, MS_e},$$

and that for the mean test score over all items is

$$r = \frac{MS_p - MS_e}{MS_p},$$

where MS_p is the mean square due to persons, and MS_e is the mean square due to error (the Persons x Items interaction effect). This formulation completely ignores the variance due to items, assuming it to be zero and not part of the true variance or the total variance. In some situations it may be desirable to account for any systematic variance among items.

Generalizability Theory

To overcome some of the measurement problems underlying classical test theory, Cronbach and his colleagues proposed generalizability theory (G theory) as an alternative to classical test theory (Cronbach, Rajaratnam, & Gleser, 1963). Based on the variance component estimates, they derived a formula for calculating an intraclass correlation coefficient for a composite score in a one-facet design (i.e., a two-way, persons (n) by items (k), random effects ANOVA model), which is identical to the reliability coefficient from the Hoyt ANOVA procedure. Further theoretical work (e.g., Brennan & Kane, 1977; Cardinet, Tourneur, & Allal, 1976) led to the development of a very useful method (generalizability theory) for estimating variance components and G-coefficients for a large number of designs under a variety of assumptions. Although most often applied in educational research, it has been used in the evaluation of motor behavior and sport performances (Godbout & Schutz, 1983; Looney & Heimerdinger, 1991), and occasionally in the assessment of personality (Violato & Travis, 1988).

The G coefficient, like the reliability coefficient, reflects the proportion of variability in individuals' scores (i.e., the object of measurement) that is systematic. The population G coefficient for the one-facet design, expressed in terms of variance components, is

$$G_1 = \frac{\sigma^2 p}{\sigma^2 p + \sigma^2 e / k},$$

and expressing the estimate of G_1, $^\wedge G_1$, in terms of the estimated mean squares yields

$$^\wedge G_1 = \frac{MS_p - MS_e}{MS_p}.$$

This formula is exactly identical to Hoyt's formula for a reliability coefficient presented in the previous section, which in turn gives the same results as the Cronbach's alpha for any metric, and as the KR-20 when items are scored dichotomously.

So What Is the "Real" Reliability Coefficient?

It is apparent from the above discussion that the term "reliability" can take on many different meanings. Different reliability coefficients (e.g., Cronbach's alpha, Hoyt's r, G-coefficient for a one-facet design) may actually be identical in meaning and magnitude, and a single reliability coefficient (e.g., G-coefficients, intraclass correlations) could assume a number of different meanings and different magnitudes depending on what variances are considered error or true. It is essential that we be very explicit in describing the type of reliability we are reporting and the assumptions we made about the nature of the error variances. It should also be apparent that most of these traditional measures of reliability have serious shortcomings in that they try to combine all the components of reliability/stability into a single coefficient. If we accept the concept of traits, then we need to examine the reliabilities of the trait itself (the "true" score), of the measurement errors associated with measuring that trait, and of any systematic variances associated with the measurements but not reflected in the traits. Traditional reliability coefficients cannot separate these variances and consequently tend to underestimate the reliability of the trait itself and ignore the reliabilities of random measurement errors and systematic error variance. Gottman and Rushe (1993) point out the fallacies in many of the long-held myths about change and stability analyses and summarize some of the possible new approaches for examining stability.

A "New" Method for Assessing Reliability and Stability

It has long been acknowledged that valid estimates of traits, and consequently of trait stability, require more than one measure of the trait, and therefore most traits are assessed through a multi-item scale of some type. Psychometric theory is based on the assumption that this trait can be conceptualized as an unobserved "latent" variable that gives rise to the observed "manifest" responses on the measurement scale. Variability in the observed scores, over repeated assessments with the same measurement scale, may be a result of changes in the level of the trait, random variability in the latent trait itself (lack of stability), variability in the random measurement error associated with the manifest variables (unreliability of the measure), and variability in the systematic error variance associated with the manifest variables. Although some early work was done on developing mathematical methods to quantify these various sources of variance (e.g., Blalock, 1970), the major advances in this area have come about quite recently.

In the 1980s, numerous textbooks and journal articles were published to explain and apply the theory of structural equation modeling—a method of testing models of relationships among variables that included both latent and manifest variables. The terms used to define this procedure of model testing are many, for example, structural equation modeling, covariance structure analysis, latent modeling, structural modeling, causal analysis, and even LISREL (which is actually a computer program). For consistency, I will use structural equation modeling (SEM) throughout the remainder of this chapter. The large number of empirical studies using this new technique was probably a direct result of the availability of computer software capable of performing the very complex calculations, most notably LISREL (Joreskog & Sorbom, 1976) and EQS (Bentler, 1983). This was a great step forward in psychometrics as up to this point we had been restricted to dealing only with observed variables (we would compute a weighted sum of a number of items and refer to this sum as anxiety, flexibility, etc.). It is only recently, however, that SEM has been applied to longitudinal data analyses (Hertzog & Nesselroade, 1987; Marsh & Grayson, 1994; McArdle & Epstein, 1987, Willet & Sayer, 1994).

The use of SEM has three major advantages over traditional approaches: (a) It allows for direct tests of construct stability (factorial invariance) over time (Kenny & Campbell, 1989; Marsh, 1993b): (b) it provides an optimal method for estimating the stability of latent variables, which are free from any errors of measurement in the observed (manifest) variables (Reddy, 1992; Usala & Hertzog, 1991): and (c) it provides a method to quantify the temporal stability of the unexplained (error) variances, thus separating out the random and systematic components of error variance. A limitation, however, of using SEM to assess stability is that at least three time periods are required in order to obtain valid estimates of the stability coefficients, and with fewer than four assessments it is necessary to make some assumptions about the equality of the stability coefficients and/or the equality of the measurement errors (Kenny & Campbell, 1989). The two examples presented in the latter part of this chapter provide examples of how SEM can be used to assess the reliability and stability of both a multi-indicator trait and a single-indicator trait. I do not present any of the theory or definitions of longitudinal SEM at this point, but rather incorporate it into the examples. First, it is necessary to provide some definitions of relevant terms.

Mean Stability

This term is self-defining, and refers to the equality of the group means over repeated assessments. Marsh (1993b), and

Long and Schutz (1995) use this label, whereas Caspi and Bem (1990) call it "absolute stability." It is usually tested with ANOVA or MANOVA. Mean stability permits inferences about individual stability only if the between-time correlations are equal to 1.0. Then if the means are unchanged from time t to time $t+1$, we know that the scores for all individuals were unchanged over that time period. If the correlations are substantially less than perfect, then it is quite possible to have large intraindividual variabilities that cancel each other out, resulting in no changes in the group means. Also, a high reliability as indicated by a high test-retest correlation does not indicate anything about mean stability. If all subjects increase or decrease by approximately the same amount, the reliability will be high even though the group mean could change significantly. For these reasons all reliability studies should also test for mean stability, and all studies focusing on mean change over time should examine the between-time variances and covariances.

Differential Stability

This is a fairly new term used to define an old construct, the stability or consistency of individual differences over time (Caspi & Bem, 1990; Long & Schutz, 1995, Usala & Hertzog, 1991). Marsh (1993b) originally just referred to it as the stability of individual differences, but now he uses the term "covariance stability" (Marsh & Grayson, 1994, p. 319). It is a *relative* measure of intraindividual stability: that is, it is a measure of the extent to which individuals maintain the same relative position in the group over time. If all individuals vary over time in the same direction and to the same extent, the differential stability will be high. Thus Asendorpf (1992) refers to it as the "absence of inter-individual differences in intra-individual change" (p.104).

Correlation coefficients of repeated measures are the most commonly used indicators of differential stability, and many studies (e.g., Finn, 1986; Schuerger et al., 1989) use such procedures to draw conclusions about "temporal stability" (a more general term). The usual PPMC coefficient used to indicate traditional reliability provides a measure of the differential stability of the observed scores, and if corrected for attenuation (unreliability), it supposedly provides a measure of the differential stability of the true scores (but could still be biased due to systematic error variance). Within a SEM framework, differential stability of the latent traits is indicated by the paths (beta coefficients) between the latent variables, and differential stability of measurement errors can be assessed with the correlations between the errors (the off-diagonal elements of the theta-delta or theta-epsilon matrices in LISREL).

Structural Stability

Structural stability applies only to multi-indicator variables and is a measure of the degree to which the observed measures are constant (over time) in their representation of the latent construct. Caspi and Bem (1990) and Long and Schutz (1995) use the term structural stability, Usala and Hertzog (1991) refer to it as "factorial invariance," and Marsh (1993b) uses the phrase "invariant factor loadings" (and includes it, along with differential stability, as a component of covariance stability). A more general term used occasionally is factor stability. It is empirically represented by the stability (equality) of the factor loadings over time. That is, if a latent construct is represented by p indicators each with a factor loading of λ_i, then if structural stability holds, the λ_1, λ_2, ...,λ_p, at time t_1 will be identical to λ_1, λ_2, ...,λ_p, at time t_2. A statistical test of the hypothesis of equal factor loadings at each time period can be conducted by testing a model with this restraint against a model in which the loadings are free to vary at each time period.

Structural stability is an important condition in studies examining change in traits brought about by interventions, aging, etc. If structural stability does not hold, then a comparison of the trait scores at time t and $t+1$ is difficult to interpret as the different factor loadings at the two time periods suggest that the measured items are not measuring the same construct at each time. Thus any study that uses a summed score (factor score) in a repeated measures design should test the assumption of structural stability before attempting to interpret any differences in mean levels.

Temporal Stability

This is not a well-defined term. Some researchers (e.g., Tanaka & Huba, 1987) have used it as a rather general descriptor to reflect either (or both) differential and structural stability. Others (e.g., Schuerger et al., 1989) use the term to represent test-retest reliability as measured by correlation coefficients. According to Marsh (1993b), temporal stability has been frequently assessed by computing the within-subject standard deviation of the repeated measures separately for each subject, with a low standard deviation indicating strong temporal stability. The problem with this approach is that a systematic trend over time will inflate these standard deviations. Additionally, there is no direct statistical test of the hypothesis of stability — as there is with the SEM approach. *Temporal stability* is used in this chapter as a general term to reflect all of the above types of stability: mean, differential and structural.

Consistency

Like temporal stability, the term consistency is used rather loosely and is often used as a synonym for stability (primarily differential). Epstein (1990) does make a useful distinction between consistency and stability in the context of defining a trait as something that is consistent across occasions and situations. He uses *consistency* to indicate the equality of observed behavior over different situations, and *stability* to indicate the equality of observed behavior over repeated time periods. As the focus of this chapter, and of the definitions provided, is on replicability over time and not over situations, Epstein's use of the term stability is consistent with that used in this chapter.

Example 1: Engagement Coping - A Single-Indicator Construct

Overview of the Study

The data for this first example are from a study by Long and Schutz (1995) in which structural equation modeling was used to test the month-to-month stability of a model of managerial women's work-related stress. The subjects in the study were women who were employed as managers in nontraditional occupations (occupations in which less than 35% of Canadian employees are women). Data were collected monthly for 6 months (Time 1 to 6), 6 months later (Time 7), and finally 13 months after the start of the study (Time 8). The measure used in this example, engagement coping (E-COP) was assessed at six of these eight time periods (T2 to T6, and T8), but for the present purpose, these time periods are referred to as T1 to T6.

Our model of stress was based on Lazarus and Folkman's (1984) psychosocial stress theory, and we used a retrospective assessment strategy that took into account the actual appraisal and coping processes of managerial women. The model was based on the expectation that the way a person copes with a specific event reflects, to some degree, their coping in general. We deviated from the way Lazarus and Folkman operationalized coping (e.g., problem- and emotion-focused functions) and instead assessed coping as engagement (i.e., stood ground, planning and scheduling, found silver lining) and disengagement (i.e., avoiding people and problems, wishful thinking, self criticizing, leaving work). Because E-COP was used as a single-indicator variable in the model, it was necessary to treat it as such when assessing its longitudinal stability. Although E-COP was assessed through a multi-itemed questionnaire, the summed-score was used in the model stability study because of the already large number of measured and latent variables in the model (26 and 10, respectively). The E-COP score is a sum of 14 items scored on a 0 to 3 scale; thus the total score can range from 0 to 42.

Results: General

Table 1 provides the descriptive statistics for the six E-COP scores. Skewness and kurtosis indices are low (all less than 1.0), and therefore the data can be considered to be approx-

Table 1
Distribution Statistics and Correlations for Engagement Coping

	E-COP1	E-COP2	E-COP3	E-COP4	E-COP5	E-COP6
Mean	21.19	19.71	19.20	18.36	18.95	20.61
St. dev.	7.83	7.38	7.37	7.43	7.60	8.26
Skewness	-0.08	0.01	-0.04	0.07	0.01	-0.00
Kurtosis	-0.64	-0.43	-0.73	-0.19	-0.51	-0.71
Correlations						
E-COP1	1.000					
E-COP2	.560	1.000				
E-COP3	.448	.539	1.000			
E-COP4	.387	.538	.495	1.000		
E-COP5	.326	.438	.451	.492	1.000	
E-COP6	.367	.474	.489	.460	.465	1.000

imately normally distributed. Deviations from normality, especially nonsymmetric distributions as indicated by skewness values of 2.0 or greater (or skewness greater than 1.0 and differential skewness across the measures), may result in biased chi-square tests and parameter estimates in SEM procedures (West, Finch, & Curran, 1995). Although earlier publications in SEM suggested the use of asymptotically distribution-free methods in the presence of any nonnormality, recent work suggests that both generalized least squares and maximum likelihood estimation procedures are quite robust to violations of the assumption of multivariate normality (e.g., Chou & Bentler, 1995). Regardless, these data appear to have met the assumptions.

The correlation matrix presented in Table 1 indicates that the data follow a simplex pattern; that is, the correlations gradually decrease from the diagonal. Adjacent time periods are most highly correlated, and the strength of the relationship decreases as a function of the time between the measures (T6 for some reason does not follow this pattern). The presence of this simplex pattern suggests that a simplex model (Joreskog, 1970) will be appropriate for testing the longitudinal stability of E-COP.

Mean Stability

Mean stability was tested with MANOVA using the multivariate model (treating the repeated measures as multiple dependent variables) and Hotelling's T^2 test statistic to examine the equality of the mean E-COP over time. This approach was employed rather than a repeated measures ANOVA because it is less sensitive to violations of assumptions, noncircularity or sphericity in particular. As a point of interest, with these data it would have been equally valid to use a repeated measures ANOVA procedure as there was no violation of assumptions of circularity (the Huynh-Feldt epsilon is .96). The results, $T^2(5,207)=6.59$, $p<.001$, indicated that, as a group, the subjects did not maintain the same level of coping strategies over the six time periods. Examination of the means shows that, on average, the subjects decreased their level of E-COP from T1 through to T4 and then increased at T5 and T6 (T6 can be explained by the one-year delay, but we had no explanation for the T5 increase). It should be noted that the T^2 and F tests are very powerful for a repeated measures design with over 200 subjects and between-time correlations of approximately .50, and thus it is useful to also examine effect sizes. Only 5 of the 15 possible pairwise differences have more than a "small" effect size ($d>.20$), and all but one (T2-T5) are less than .30. Looking at the total effect rather than pairwise differences, Cohen's f has a value of .17, which lies between his small ($f=.10$) and medium ($f=.25$) effect sizes (Cohen, 1988). This would convert to an eta-squared of approximately .03, indicating that the variance in the six means accounts for approximately 3% of the total variance. A reasonable conclusion would be that E-COP does not exhibit mean stability, with the group mean showing a decline in level from T1 to T4, a slight rise at T5, and a larger increase at T6. These differences, however, are substantively rather small.

Traditional Reliability Indicators

The adjacent trial correlations, all about .50, form one possible set of estimators of the one-month test-retest stability of coping. With more than two repeated measures, it is often sug-

gested that the intraclass correlation be computed, and in this case that yields:

$$\frac{MSs - MSsxt}{MSs + (k-1)MSsxt} = \frac{193.14 - 31.66}{193.14 + 5(31.66)} = .460,$$

which, as noted above, is approximately equal to the average of all 15 pairwise correlation coefficients (equal to .462 with these data). This value of .460 is precisely the value one would get if the same data were analyzed to obtain Cronbach's alpha (and is the same formulae as Hoyt's r). It tells us that there exists some stability in the interindividual differences of the observed E-COP scores; that is, these managerial women had true interindividual differences in their responses to the coping questionnaire, and these differences were maintained with some degree of consistency (I would call it a "weak-to-moderate" stability) over the six assessment periods. However, we do not know to what extent this stability, or lack of stability, was a function of response bias or some other systematic measurement error, or of random measurement error. Alternative analyses are required to estimate the true stability of the construct of E-COP and the unreliability of the measurement itself. Often the MSsxt effect is omitted from the denominator, thus giving an estimate of the reliability of a mean of six trials. In this case that value works out to be .836, but it has no practical utility in this situation as it is highly unlikely that we would be interested in taking a mean of six measures (taken over a one-year period) and averaging them to obtain a score for prediction or further analyses.

Structural Equation Modeling Methods

General procedures. LISREL 8 (Joreskog & Sorbom, 1993), using maximum likelihood estimation procedures with a covariance matrix as data input, was used for the assessment of differential and structural stability. I prefer LISREL only because it is the program with which I am most familiar; any other computer program (e.g., AMOS, CALIS, EQS, EzPATH, LIS-COMP, Mx) could be used for this purpose as well. It was necessary to analyze the covariance matrix rather than the correlation matrix because LISREL may produce incorrect chi-squares and standard errors when a correlation matrix is fitted to a model with equality constraints (Joreskog & Sorbom, 1993). Equality constraints are rarely imposed in many applications of SEM (e.g., confirmatory factor analysis), but they are necessary in the stability models tested in this example.

Assessing the fit. The fit of all models was evaluated with five goodness-of-fit indices (from the more than 20 such indices produced in LISREL 8). The decision as to which fit indices should be used is an ongoing issue (e.g., see Marsh, Balla, & Hau, 1996; Yadama & Padey, 1995), but it is generally acknowledged that different indices provide different types of information, and thus it is necessary to report a number of these measures. The following indices were selected as they each provide some useful and unique information: the χ^2 statistic and its associated p-value, Steiger's (1990) Root Mean Square Error of Approximation (RMSEA), the standardized Root Mean Square Residual (RMRs), and two "incremental" or "comparative" goodness-of-fit indices; Mulaik et al.'s (1989) parsimony goodness-of-fit index (PGFI), and Bentler's (1990) comparative fit index (CFI).

The chi-square test of a model is a test of the null hypothesis that the model fits the data, and therefore a nonsignificant result is usually the desired outcome. That is, we can conclude that there is insufficient evidence to reject the hypothesis that our model is a reasonable representation of reality. Note that a nonsignificant result does not confirm our model, but rather merely does not provide evidence to reject it. The RMSEA is a fit index that provides information as to how well the model may hold in the population (the other indices are based solely on sample-model discrepancies) and takes into account the number of parameters being estimated (actually, the degrees of freedom). An RMSEA of .05 or less indicates that the model based on the sample data represents a "close fit" to the population, and values less than .08 a "reasonable" fit (Browne & Cudek, 1993). The RMRs was chosen over the more commonly used root mean square residual (RMR) because the latter is not a standardized index and thus is difficult to interpret when a covariance matrix is analyzed. However, Version 8 of LISREL includes a "standardized RMR" that may overcome the disadvantage of the RMR index, and thus it has been included here. The two incremental fit indices, the PGFI and CFI, indicate how much better the model fits than a null model (a model in which all the observed variables are uncorrelated). The PGFI, which takes into account model size (a function of the ratio of the degrees of freedom to the number of observed variables), was selected because of its utility in comparing competing but nested models (the larger the PGFI, the more parsimonious the model). The CFI, a function of the ratio of the fit model to the null model, was selected over some other normed fit indices because it is contained in the 0-1 interval (unlike some other normed indices, which can yield computed values of greater than 1.0). CFI values in the .90s are deemed to indicate an adequate fit of the model to the data, even with a PGFI as low as .50 (Mulaik et al., 1989).

The sample size of 212 used in this study is considered to be sufficiently large for valid model testing. Recent work has shown that stable and unbiased goodness-of-fit indices (Chou, Bentler, & Satorra, 1991) and parameter estimates (Henly, 1993) are obtained with maximum likelihood estimation using data that is distributed approximately multivariate normal with sample sizes of 200 or greater.

The Single-Indicator Simplex Model

Stability parameters were estimated through the fitting of simplex models under a number of different constraints. Actually, quasi-simplex rather than perfect simplex models were assumed as the former allows for sizable measurement errors, whereas the latter assumes that the observed variables contain no measurement error (Joreskog, 1970). The simplex model is commonly used to assess the stability of individual differences in studies where the same construct is measured repeatedly over time. The model is based on the assumptions that (a) change over time occurs, (b) there are true individual differences in the amount of change, and (c) the true score at any point in time is primarily a result of the true score at the immediately preceding time period. This last assumption is essentially the assumption

underlying any autoregressive type model (a model in which status at time t is primarily a function of status at time t-1), and forms the basis for linear panel analyses, path analyses, etc. It should be noted that autoregressive models have come under considerable criticism in the last few years, primarily when they are used to detect correlates of change. These criticisms, and alternative methods for analyzing change, are discussed under the caveat section later in this chapter.

Following the suggestion of Marsh (1993b), the simplex model was compared to an alternative plausible stability model, a higher-order (general factor) model. The general factor model makes no assumptions about the temporal nature of the data and assumes that correlations among the repeated measures of the construct are due to some general underlying common trait (the general factor). A comparison of the fits of these two models may assist in determining if a trait is stochastic, that is, if the strength of the trait at time t+1 is a function of the strength at time t (and the dependency weakens over time) or if it is time independent.

Figure 1 provides a schematic representation of the simplex model for the trait E-COP measured at each of the six time periods by a single measure. The circles, labeled eta (η_i), represent the unobserved latent constructs (the engagement coping trait), and the squares (Y_i) the observed manifest measures, E-COP. The beta coefficients (β_i) represent the differential stability of the latent construct, the zeta values (ζ_i) represent the random disturbance terms (random errors) that directly affect the latent constructs at each point in time; and the epsilon values (ε_i) are the measurement errors associated with the observed measures (unreliability of the measure itself, not of the trait). The variances of Y, η, ζ and ε, are estimated by the LISREL program, and by computing a ratio of true-score variance to total variance, it is possible to calculate "reliability" coefficients for both the manifest and latent variables. Formulae for performing these calculations are given in the Results section of this example.

Marsh suggests that "a one-factor model provides a viable alternative to the simplex model in fitting one-variable multiwave data" (Marsh, 1993b, p. 162). This model, diagrammed in Figure 2, is essentially a confirmatory factor analysis model for a single factor, where the indicators are the repeated assessments of the same construct. In classical test theory, it is a congeneric measurement model (Fleishman & Benson, 1987). The essential difference between the one-factor model and simplex model is that the latter contains a number of latent constructs and the former only one. If the strength of a construct at time t is solely a function of the strength of that construct at time t-1 plus some random disturbance, then the simplex model will provide the best fit to the data. On the other hand, if all factor loadings (λ_i) are equal in the one-factor model, then this provides support for the one-factor model as such equalities would not be commensurate if the data exhibited a simplex pattern. If the one-factor model is supported with the data, this suggests that there exists a fairly stable latent trait and that observed behaviors (the measures) are a direct result of this trait (plus random measurement error and/or situation-specific events). The strength of a trait at time t has no direct influence on the strength of the trait a time t+1.

Single-indicator simplex and general-factor models are tested under the assumption that the ε_i are uncorrelated; that is, the measurement error of Y_1 is uncorrelated with the measurement error of Y_2. This is often an unreasonable assumption with longitudinal designs in which the repeated observations are measured in the same manner with the same instrument at each time period. In these situations any systematic measurement errors (such as response bias) that are part of the error variance at t_1 will probably also be present at t_2, and failure to account for this in the model tends to result in a positive bias in the beta coefficients (Kenny & Campbell, 1989). With multi-indicator constructs the presence of correlated errors can be tested and, if present, incorporated into the model. However, this is not possible with single-indicator model, and thus one must be aware of the possibility of an overestimation of these stability (differential) coefficients.

Testing the Model

Differential stability, the stability of individual differences in "true" scores across different occasions, was assessed through a series of analyses. The methodologies used here have been developed through the combined efforts of many individuals, but the procedures presented in the publications of Joreskog and Sorbom (1993) and Marsh (1993b) were followed. Following their recommendations, the single-item construct E-COP was tested with a simplex model in the following sequence:

Model 1 (M1). Two pairs of error variances (ε_1 and ε_2, and

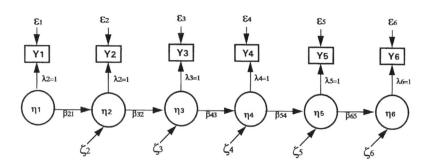

Figure 1. The Single-Indicator Simplex Model

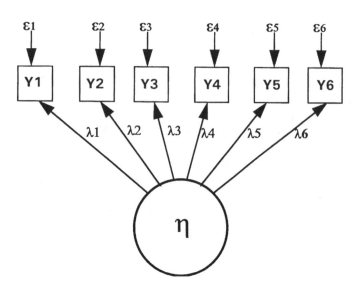

Figure 2. The General Factor Model for Longitudinal Data

ε_5 and ε_6) were set equal in order to eliminate the indeterminacies in the model. Factor loadings were fixed at 1.0, and the stability coefficients (betas) were freed for adjacent time periods only. No other equalities or constraints were imposed.

Model 2 (M2). The above model was retested with the constraint that all beta paths were equal, thus testing the hypothesis of constant differential stability over time.

Model 3 (M3). The initial model was retested with the constraint that all error variances were equal, thus testing the hypothesis that measurement errors are constant over repeated testing.

Model 4 (M4). If both equalities (2 and 3 above) were tenable, the final model included both sets of constraints. This model, if acceptable, would be the most parsimonious simplex model available and thus the model of choice.

The general factor model was tested in a similar fashion, the only differences being that the equality of the factor loadings instead of the beta paths was tested in M2 and M4.

Because all the constrained models are nested within a higher level model, equality constraints were tested with the chi-square difference test (change in chi-square relative to change in degrees of freedom). A model with some equalities imposed among the parameters will have fewer parameters to estimate and thus have more degrees of freedom (i.e., it is a more parsimonious model). The chi-square test of the adequacy of the model fit for a constrained model will always be as large as or larger than the chi-square for the less constrained (and therefore fewer degrees of freedom) model. However, if the increase in the chi-square, using the increase in the degrees of freedom to test its significance, is not significant, then one can conclude that the constrained model is not any worse than the model with no (or fewer) constraints. Given that it is not any worse, and because it is more parsimonious than the less constrained model, it is accepted as the preferred model.

Results

Simplex model. Table 2 contains information on the adequacy of the model fitting for both the simplex and the general factor models. For the simplex model, the basic model (M1) provided a good fit to the data as indicated by virtually all of the fit indices. The chi-square was small (ratio of χ^2 to df is less than 1.0) and nonsignificant ($p=.77$), the CFI is at its maximum and the RMSEA at its minimum. A caution is warranted, however. Because we estimated so many parameters, relatively speaking, it is not unlikely to get such a "good fit". With six measures there are 21 ((6*7)/2) elements in the variance-covariance matrix, that is, 21 "data points" to be used in the analysis. In M1 there were no equality constraints imposed (other than setting two pairs of error terms to be equal in order to identify the model), and thus the model had to estimate 15 parameters: 5 beta, 4 epsilon (not 6, because of the two equalities imposed), and 6 psi, thus leaving only 21-15=6 degrees of freedom. This is somewhat analogous to fitting a regression equation with 15 predictors and only 21 subjects—it is quite possible to get a good fit, just by chance. The low parsimony index of 0.28 reflects the fact that the model has very few degrees of freedom, given the number of measures, and thus is not a very desirable model.

M2 included the constraint that all beta paths are equal, thus allowing for a test of this interesting hypothesis as well as providing a more parsimonious model (four more df, as now we estimate only one beta rather than five). A test of the difference between M1 and M2 resulted in a χ^2 difference of 9.18 with a df difference of 4. This could be considered a nonsignificant increase in χ^2 ($p \approx .06$), and thus M2 is to be preferred over M1 because it is more parsimonious and not any worse as far as fit is concerned. This is not a strong conclusion, however, because with a $p \approx .06$ there is considerable evidence to suggest that M2 may result in a worse fit than M1. Nevertheless, M2 still provides a very good fit to the data, with a nonsignificant χ^2 ($p=.26$) and all fit indices indicating support for the model. Additionally, the PGFI has now risen to .49 (a reasonable value with so few df).

Next, M3, with the constraint that all error variances would be equal, was tested. As can be seen in Table 2, the χ^2 showed virtually no decrease from M2 to M3, despite the decrease in the df. Chi-square difference tests indicate that M3 is not significantly better than M2 (and therefore we retain M2 as it is more parsimonious), and that M3 is significantly ($p<.05$) worse than M1 (and therefore we do not want to reject M1, the more parsimonious model, in favor of M3). Clearly the assumption of equal error variances is not tenable. My conclusion is that these results suggest that M2 provides a good model of the data, and thus it is the model to be retained. Others may conclude that the test of equality of beta paths was not very strong and that M1 is more reasonable. Such are the ambiguities of model testing—it is not a "cut-and-dried" procedure.

General factor model. The results for the general factor models' tests of goodness-of-fit were similar to those for the simplex models, only much clearer. M2 was definitely superior to M1 as indicated by the small and nonsignificant increase in χ^2 ($p>.60$). Additionally, all the fit indices were indicative of a good model fit. M3 did not provide a good fit to the data ($p<.01$) and was significantly worse than both M1 and M2 ($p<.01$). Thus M2 is the model of choice here.

Which model is best: Simplex or general factor? There is not a clear answer to this question. The simplex model is suitable for data that produce a correlation matrix that conforms to a simplex pattern (the magnitudes of the coefficients are smaller as they become further away from the diagonal). Looking at the correlation matrix for E-COP in Table 1, we see that this condition holds quite well for T1 through to T5, but breaks down at T6. Assuming that we accept M2 as the best model in both cases, the choice between the simplex and the general factor is difficult. The χ^2 and p-values are similar (slightly favoring the simplex); the CFIs are the same; the general factor model does a slightly better job of reproducing the observed correlations (lower RMRs) and is more parsimonious (higher PGFI), but the simplex fits the model better on a "per degree of freedom" basis (i.e., lower RMSEA). A decision as to which model is most suitable, if such a decision had to be made, would need to be based on theoretical grounds. The statistical evidence does not reject either model. For the purposes of this chapter, we are primarily interested in looking at measures of reliability and stability. Thus, using the simplex model as the example, we now turn to those results.

Note that the general factor model is a more parsimonious model than the simplex model in this case, having 9 df in contrast to the 6 df in the simplex. The simplex requires 15 parameters to be estimated: 5 beta paths, 6 variances, and 4 error variances (4, not 6, because of the equality constraints, $\varepsilon_1=\varepsilon_2$ and $\varepsilon_5=\varepsilon_6$). Given that there are 21 pieces of data (the $6(6+1)/2$ variances and covariances formed by the 6 measures), this leaves 21-15=6 df. The general factor model estimates only 12 parameters: 5 factor loadings (one is set to 1.0 to fix the scale), 1 variance, and 6 error variances, resulting in 21-12=9 df. If all else was equal, theoretically and statistically, then the general factor model might be preferred over the simplex model because of its greater parsimony.

Stabilities. The standardized beta coefficients for the simplex model reported in Table 3 can be perceived as the stabilities of the latent construct (or true scores) of engagement coping. They are very high, all above .85, and the estimate of the common unstandardized path coefficient was equal to .91 (the common unstandardized beta coefficient is provided when a model includes the constraint of equal beta paths — note that the standardized beta paths will still differ). This suggests two things. First, the trait itself is a robust trait, and although it exhibits quite large interindividual variability in the population (a coefficient of variation of approximately .38 in the observed scores), the interindividual differences are constant over the six measurement periods. That is, there exists strong differential stability of individual differences over time. Second, these coefficients are most likely overestimates of the true stability values. As noted earlier, if the measurement errors are correlated over time, as they most likely are in a repeated measures designs such as this one, failure to incorporate this into the model will probably lead to overestimates of the beta coefficients. The single-indicator simplex model cannot be identified if correlated

Table 2
Model Fit Statistics for Simplex and General Factor Models

	χ^2	df	p	CFI	PGFI	RMSEA	RMRs
Simplex Models							
M1: basic model	3.29	6	.77	1.00	.28	.000	.014
M2: equal β	12.47	10	.26	.99	.49	.034	.054
M3: equal ε	12.25	9	.42	.99	.42	.041	.031
General Factor Models							
M1: basic model	15.89	9	.07	.98	.42	.060	.034
M2: equal λ	18.13	13	.15	.99	.60	.043	.046
M3: equal ε	32.81	14	<.01	.95	.86	.080	.055

Note. CFI = comparative fit index, PGFI = parsimony goodness-of-fit index, RMSEA = root mean square error of approximation, RMRs = standardaized root mean square residual.

Table 3
Stability of the Latent Construct Engagement Coping

Standardized Beta Coefficients for Simplex Model					*Standardized Lambda Coefficients for General Factor Model*					
T1-2	T2-3	T3-4	T4-5	T5-6	T1	T2	T3	T4	T5	T6
.89	.92	.93	.94	.86	.61	.74	.72	.71	.67	.65

T=Time (1 month separates each Time, except for 6 months from T5 to T6).

errors are included, and thus there is no solution to this problem. In an ideal situation, what is needed is to use multi-indicators of engagement coping and then test its stability with a multi-indicator simplex model, which permits correlated errors. This actually could be done, as the original data for the Long and Schutz (1995) study did use a number of items to assess engagement coping, but because it was modeled as a single-indicator variable (using the sum of the items) in the larger longitudinal model, it seems more valid to test the stability of that form of the construct. Nevertheless, despite the likelihood of some inflation in the stability coefficients, the results do indicate that the construct engagement coping is quite stable, considerably more so than the observed measure of E-COP test-retest r's of approximately .46.

The statistics provided by the LISREL program permit the calculation of other interesting reliability coefficients, where reliability is interpreted in the classical test theory manner as the ratio of true score variance to total variance. The results of M1 for the simplex model are used as an example (when equality constraints are included in the model, as in M2, the variance components are not additive, and thus the reliability calculations would be slightly biased). I use the variable E-COP at T3 as an example, and Table 4 gives the elements contained in the LISREL output that can be used to calculate the reliability coefficients for E-COP3 (or to help in the understanding of the calculations, as LISREL actually does the calculations).

To calculate the reliability of the observed score, recall that the variance in the observed score (Y) is the sum of the true score variance and error variance, thus B = A+C, in raw score units (see Table 4). The reliability of E-COP3 is the ratio of true score variance to observed variance, or C/B = 29.50/54.36 = .54. If we want to use standardized units we need to compute the true score variance as total minus error, or 1-.46 = .54. Then the reliability is the ratio true/observed, or .54/1.00 = .54. This value is given directly in the LISREL output as the SMC (squared multiple correlation) for the Y variables, in this case for E-COP3.

The reliability of a latent construct can be determined in a number of ways: (1) by calculating the ratio of true (observed - error) variance to observed variance, that is, (C-D)/D = (29.50-6.86)/29.50 = .77; (2) doing the same thing with the standardized units, (1.00-.23)/1.00 = .77; (3) reading it directly from the LISREL output as the E-COP3 value of the "SMC for the structural equations" (F); or (4) squaring the standardized beta path leading to the latent construct at time 3, that is, $E^2 = .88^2 = .77$.

Conclusion. A large number of "reliability" or "stability" coefficients have been presented in the last few pages. Which ones should be used? It depends on what data are available and with what sort of stability we are interested. If only two observations existed, say T2 and T3, then we would have no choice but to calculate the test-retest reliability of the observed scores (.539, Table 1). With more than two repeated observations, and preferably four or more, there are other options. The intraclass correlation (or Cronbach's alpha) provides an estimate of the average between-occasion test-retest reliabilities of the observed scores (equal to .460 here). The problem with this measure is that it confounds random and systematic error variance with the reliability of the true score (the latent trait). Fitting a simplex model to the data resulted in a stability coefficient for the unobserved trait of engagement coping at T3 of .88 for M1 (Table 4), or .92 for M2 (Table 3), yielding reliability coefficients of $.88^2 = .77$ and $.92^2 = .84$, respectively. Thus it is concluded that engagement coping is a fairly stable trait, with a differential stability of approximately .90 (or a reliability of approximately .80). However, we must acknowledge the fact that this is probably an overestimate because the single-indicator simplex model was not able to account for the presence of correlated measurement errors.

Table 4
LISREL Elements for the Modeling of E-COP at T3

Element of the model	*LISREL label*	*Raw score[b]*	*Standardized score[c]*
A. ε (error in Y)[a]	TE(3,3)	24.86	0.46
B. Y (observed score)	E-COP3	54.36	1.00
C. η (latent construct)	ETA(3,3)	29.50	1.00
D. ζ (error in η)	PSI(3,3)	6.86	0.23
E. ß (path from η to η)	BETA(3,2)	0.76	0.88
F. Reliability of η	SMC for structural eq's.	0.77	0.77
G. Reliability of Y	SMC for Y variables	0.54	0.54

[a] "Error in Y" and "error in " should be interpreted as error associated with Y and, respectively.
[b] The raw score metric is variances and covariances, as those are the data being analyzed.
[c] Standardized scores refers to both the LISREL "standardized" and "completely standardized" scores, as they are identical in this example.

Example 2: Baseball Offensive Production, a Multi-indicator Construct

Methodology

An example of examining the longitudinal stability of a multi-indicator construct is now given, thus providing an opportunity to look at structural stability as well as differential stability. Also, with a multi-indicator measure we can test for the presence of correlated errors, an important aspect of modeling stability with simplex models. In this example mean stability is not examined, nor is the general factor model compared to the simplex model. Both these procedures may be necessary in a research study, but their application has already been shown in the engagement coping example, and therefore it seems unnecessary to repeat it here. The only differences with a multi-indicator variable would be that the test of mean stability would require a doubly multivariate MANOVA (Schutz & Gessaroli, 1987), and the tests of the general factor model would be a little more complex (but very similar in method and interpretation).

The example presented here comes from a paper presented at the Statistics in Sports Section of last year's annual meeting of the American Statistical Association (Schutz, 1995). In that paper, simplex models were used to assess the 5-year stability over four time sequences (1928-32, 1948-1952, 1968-1972, and 1988-1992) of Major League Baseball players' performances in seven offensive skills: home runs (HR), runs batted-in (RBI), slugging percentage (SLP), on-base percentage (OBP), batting average (BA), runs scored (RUNS), and walks (WALKS), and one defensive skill, fielding average (FA). Only the three measures that represented the construct POWER—HR, SLP, and RBI—are presented and expanded upon here. The purpose of the study was to examine the stability of individual performance of Major League Baseball players over a 5-year period, and to test if this stability has changed from the 1930s to the 1990s. It was speculated that the stability of performance has declined over the last 40 years - perhaps due to increased travel and night games.

A baseball encyclopedia (Thorn & Palmer, 1993) was used to provide individual statistics for all players who had at least 100 official at bats each year for any one of four 5-year periods: 1928-32 (N=74), 1948-1952 (N=75), 1968-1972 (N=108), and 1988-1992 (N=129). Thirteen performance measures were recorded for each player, and from those measures a number of derived measures were calculated. For example, the SLP, a commonly used baseball statistic, was computed from the individual data by dividing the total number of bases (i.e., singles=1, doubles=2, triples=3, home runs=4) by the total number of at-bats. Complete data were available for all players. Comparisons between players and between years for the same player are not directly comparable due to the different number of at bats per year, which ranged from 100 to 698. Consequently, all statistics were transformed into ratio variables by dividing by the number of at bats for a given year.

As the purpose was to ascertain the stability of the general underlying abilities (latent constructs) rather than for each individual performance measure, exploratory factor analyses were conducted to establish a factor structure. Actually, principal component analyses rather than common factor analyses were utilized (most researchers include principal components under the general label of exploratory factor analysis). Some measures, such as 2B and 3B hits, are reflected in SLP and thus were redundant. Two measures, Fielding Average and Stolen Base Percent exhibited such extreme skewness (>|2|) and/or kurtosis (>5) that they were not included in further analyses. Preliminary principal components analysis with oblique rotation performed on both the 1988 and 1989 data sets suggested that two factors could represent offensive baseball performance. These were POWER, consisting of HR, SLP, and RBI, and AVERAGE, consisting of BA, OBP, and Runs. Subsequent confirmatory factor analyses on the remaining 18 years of data confirmed the validity of this factor structure. The stability of the POWER construct is presented here.

Testing the Model

Stability parameters were estimated through the fitting of quasi-simplex models for the latent construct POWER, a skill that is assumed to be measured by the three indicators; HR, SLP and RBI. The stability of this multi-indicator construct was assessed with the following sequence of models:

M1. A basic model with no equality constraints. Betas were free for adjacent time periods only, and all factor loadings were free (other than setting one loading to 1.0 at each time period to establish the scale).

M2. The above model with the constraint that all corresponding measurement errors were free to correlate; that is, the measurement error for a manifest variable was free to correlate with the measurement error for the same variable at all other time periods. Marsh (1993b), Reddy (1992), and others have pointed out the need to allow for correlated measurement errors as failure to do so leads to an overestimation of the stability estimates of the constructs.

M3. The above model with the additional constraint that the loadings for a variable were equal across all time periods for that same variable. This provides a test of the degree to which the construct is definitionally stable over time, that is, structural stability. If M2 was not accepted the equal loadings constraint was applied to M1.

M4. The above model with the additional constraint that all error variances were equal, thus testing the hypothesis that measurement errors are constant over repeated testing. If M3 was not accepted this constraint was applied to M2.

M5. The above model with the constraint that all beta paths were equal, thus testing the hypothesis of constant differential stability over time. As before, this constraint was applied to the best model to this stage (M4 or M3 or M2 or M1).

Results

General. Table 5 gives summary descriptive statistics for the variables under examination. There has been an increase in HR production over the 60-year period, but a decrease in SLP and RBI performances. Of interest to the stability analysis is the finding that the standard deviations have decreased quite markedly over this period of time. With a lower interindividual variability, it will be more difficult to obtain high intraindividual stability over the 1988-92 period than for the 1928-32 period. Table 6 gives the mean performance per year for the three

Table 5
Five-year Averages for POWER Measures: Means and Average Between-Player Standard Deviations

	1928 - 1932 (N = 74)	1948 - 52 (N = 75)	1968 - 72 (N = 108)	1988 - 92 (N = 129)
At-Bats	406 ± 138	443 ± 144	454 ± 132	450 ± 128
Home Runs	9.7 ± 10.9	11.4 ± 10.1	12.7 ± 10.5	12.1 ± 9.6
Slugging Percentage	.449 ± .096	.414 ± .076	.399 ± .079	.405 ± .070
Runs Batted-in	72.6 ± 35.8	61.4 ± 29.8	55.1 ± 27.0	57.4 ± 26.0
Games Scheduled	154	154	162	162

Table 6
Yearly Averages for Selected Statistics, Expressed as Ratios (per at bat), and Intraclass Correlations Coefficients for Each Five-Year Period

| | *Power Measures* . | | |
	HR	**SLP**	**RBI**
1928	.017	.442	.143
1929	.022	.462	.161
1930	.023	.482	.169
1931	.015	.432	.141
1932	.019	.429	.144
Mean	.019	.449	.152
Intraclass r	.813	.727	.725
1948	.022	.409	.135
1949	.024	.417	.141
1950	.029	.437	.145
1951	.026	.419	.135
1952	.022	.387	.129
Mean	.025	.414	.137
Intraclass r	.770	.626	.624
1968	.021	.370	.100
1969	.030	.414	.126
1970	.032	.423	.134
1971	.028	.403	.123
1972	.025	.378	.113
Mean	.027	.399	.119
Intraclass r	.755	.641	.676
1988	.026	.407	.123
1989	.026	.405	.125
1990	.028	.415	.131
1991	.028	.410	.130
1992	.023	.389	.120
Mean	.026	.405	.126
Intraclass r	.731	.515	.616

Note:
HR = home runs, SLP = slugging percentage, RBI = runs batted in.

POWER measures, expressed as averages per at bat. As is well known to any baseball fan, there are considerable year-to-year fluctuations in mean performance — some years the pitchers dominate and some years the batters dominate. For example, for the 1948-52 period, all variables had their highest scores in 1950, and from 1968 to 1969 there was a dramatic increase in offensive output (a 43% increase in HRs per at bat). However, these yearly averages do not provide any information about *individual* stability or change over time. The intraclass correlation coefficients (or Cronbach's alphas), which do reflect intraindividual variability, indicate that the observed scores for each of the three measures exhibited moderate to strong stabilities within each 5-year period and that these stabilities have declined somewhat over the last 60 years (see Table 6). Still, these statistics do not provide a measure of the stability of the general construct of POWER, but only of the separate measures. Additionally, they do not provide tests of the structural stability of the constructs or the equivalence of the year-to-year stability coefficients. Thus there is a need to model the data with simplex models using SEM.

Differential and structural stability. Table 7 gives the model-fitting results and goodness-of-fit statistics, using the 1988-92 POWER data as an example, and Figures 2a, 2b, and 2c portray Models 1, 2, and 5, respectively. Examination of Figure 3a shows that the three observed variables, HR, SLP and RBI, are well represented by the construct POWER, with all three factor loadings (λ s) being greater than .84 for each of the 5 years. The error (unexplained) variances of the observed measures are given for 1988 only, as they can be easily calculated from the factor loadings ($1-\lambda^2$). The standardized stability coefficients (βs) indicated strong differential stability, although the 1991-92 value of .76 is quite a bit lower than the other three values. The fact that these values are larger than the simple correlation coefficients for any single measure indicates that the POWER factor, a weighted sum of HR, SLP and RBI, is more stable than any of the single measures.

The base model (M1) obviously had something missing, as indicated by the large χ^2 and CFI value of .84, and therefore some modifications (theoretically justifiable ones) were necessary. With multi-indicator longitudinal models it makes sense to allow for correlated errors among repeated measures on the same variables, as has been noted previously in this chapter. In this example it could be that the variance in HR that is unexplained by the POWER factor may, in part, be accountable by some other factor (e.g., home park dimensions), and thus the

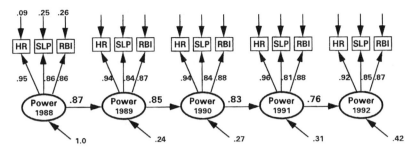

(a) Model 1 - Simplex model, no equalities

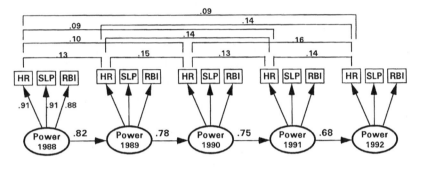

(b) Model 2 - Simplex model, correlated errors

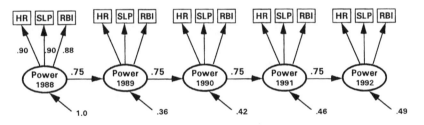

(c) Model 5 - Simplex model, correlated errors, equal factor loadings
equal error variances, equal stability coefficients

**Figure 3. Multi-Indicator Simplex Models M1, M2, and M5
for the Construct Power**

error variances for HR would be correlated. Figure 3b diagrams the 10 correlated errors only for HR (to include them for the other two variables would make the figure very cluttered), but the fully respecified model (M2) included correlated errors for all three variables. The magnitudes, although not large (.09 to .16), did account for a significant amount of the unexplained variance in the model. Additionally, and as was expected, the inclusion of correlated errors resulted in a decrease in the stability coefficients (from approximately .85 to about .75). Table 7 shows that the reduction in $\chi 2$ (290) relative to the reduction in degrees of freedom (30) was significant ($p<.001$), indicating the M2 is a preferred model to M1.

The next three models permitted tests of equal factor loadings (structural stability over time), equal error variances, and equal beta coefficients (differential stability of the construct POWER over time). Each successive model resulted in a slight increase in $\chi 2$, but in no case was this increase significant (see Table 7). Given that models M2 through M5 are not significantly different and that M5 is the most parsimonious model, it was retained as the model of choice. Note that the parsimony goodness-of-fit index (PGFI) is largest for M5, and the comparative fit index (CFI) is higher than or equal to any other model. Figure 3c (error variances and correlated errors not diagrammed) gives the parameter estimates for M5. The factor loadings were constant for all time periods, and the completely standardized stability coefficients decline from .80 to .72 (but are equal, all with values of .75, in the unstandardized form).

Of some concern is the observation that the RMRs values increased from M1 to M2. With a better fit for M2 (as indicated by the other fit indices), one would expect the estimated variances and covariances would be closer approximations to the observed values. Instead, they got worse.

An examination of the residuals revealed that the autocorrelations, especially for HR (e.g., the correlation between HR at time t and HR at time $t+i$), were underestimated in M1, and the inclusion of the correlated errors in M2 resulted in a further reduction. For example, the observed correlation between HR1 and HR2 was .79: M1 estimated it as .78, and M2 as .71. These differences increased as a function of i, such that for HR1 and HR5 the observed correla-

Table 7
Sequential Testing of Longitudinal Stability Models for POWER Factor, 1988 - 1992

Model	χ^2	df		RMSEA	CFI	PGFI	RMRs
M1. Base model	447	86		.18	.84	.47	.07
M2. Correl. errors	157	56		.12	.95	.40	.14
(M1-M2 difference	290	30	p<.001 significantly better)				
M3. Equal lambda	159.6	64		.11	.95	.46	.14
(M3-M1 difference	2.6	8	p>.50 not significantly worse)				
M4. Equal TE	167.7	76		.097	.96	.54	.14
(M4-M3 difference	8.1	12	p>.50 not significantly worse)				
M5. Equal BE	169.4	79		.095	.96	.56	.15
(M5-M4 difference	1.7	3	p>.50 not significantly worse)				

Note: RMSEA = root mean square error of approximation, RMRs = standardized root mean square residual, CFI = comparative fit index, PGFI = parsimony goodness-of fit-index.

Table 8
Factor Loadings and Stability Coefficients for the Construct "Power"

| *Constant Factor Loadings* | | | | *Stability Coefficients* | | | | |
5-year period	HR	SLP	RBI	T1-T2	T2-T3	T3-T4	T4-T5	*Constant stability coefficient*
1928-32	.92	.92	.85	.87	.88	.89	.88	.89
1948-52	.88	.89	.85	.77	.80	.76	.78	.79
1968-72	.93	.91	.90	.80	.84	.76	.76	.80
1988-92	.90	.90	.88	.80	.76	.73	.72	.75

tion was .61, M1 estimated .41 and M2 resulted in a further reduction to .31. It is not apparent why this happened, and further analyses may be warranted. Nevertheless, the overall model provided a good fit to the data and all other parameter estimates are reasonable.

The same sequential model-testing approach was used with the 1928-32, 1948-52 and 1968-72 data sets, and in each case similar results were obtained, with M5 yielding the best fit to the data. Table 8 presents the final parameter estimates for M5 for all four data sets. The structural stability holds up well across the 40-year time period with there being little change in the magnitudes of the factor loadings. The differential stability results support the hypothesis that there is a decrease in the stability of individual performance, especially from 1928-32 to 1948-52 and again from 1968-72 to 1988-92. We can conclude that there exists a high level of individual stability in the power component of baseball, but that today's players do not exhibit the same level of year-to-year stability as did the players of previous eras.

A Caveat

The methodology presented is this chapter is a useful and generally accepted technique for modeling reliability and stability in longitudinal data; however, it is not the only method, and it is not universally endorsed. Others have great difficulty in accepting any statistical model that involves unobserved variables — just as some mathematicians and statisticians did 50 years ago when factor analysis was becoming popular. For example, Ssemakula (1993) wrote the following about SEM:

> It illustrates some statistical fantasies that sometimes arise when data goes in search of theory. Remember those childhood games when you stared at the clouds and saw all kinds of beasties? The beasties were merely figments of your imagination — though sometimes they looked so real! The bottom line is that all this huffing and puffing about "structural models" in journals and conference proceedings may not be worth too much.

Such criticisms can be made of any methodology, and they are warranted if the methodology is inappropriately used. However, it is the misuse, not the technique itself, that should be criticized. Ssemakula and other critics are offended by the terms *causal* models and *confirmatory* factor analysis, and note that we cannot infer causality from correlational data and we can rarely confirm anything statistically. This is well recognized by most users

of SEM, and their results are interpreted accordingly. As George Box was purported to have said, "All models are wrong, but some are more useful than others." Our task is to try to find the most useful models to help interpret our data.

There exists a long-standing debate in the psychometric community over the suitability of using simplex and other SEM procedures to analyze change. Rogosa (Rogosa, 1987, 1993, 1995; Rogosa & Willett, 1985) has been one of the harshest critics and has provided empirical examples of how some SEM procedures can lead to parameter estimates that are completely uninterpretable. He has stated a number of "myths" regarding the analysis of longitudinal data in general: For example; (a) two observations are sufficient for longitudinal research; (b) difference scores are unreliable or unfair indicators of change; (c) analyses of correlation matrices will provide valid tests of whether or not the same thing is being measured over time and may provide valid information about change; and (d) stability coefficients tell us something about the consistency over time of individual differences. The last two myths could be perceived as being harsh criticisms of the methods proposed in this chapter, as I have analyzed a covariance matrix to estimate stability coefficients and interpreted these as reflecting the stability of intraindividual differences. How can it be that Joreskog and Sorbom (1993), Marsh (1993b) and others advocate the use of simplex models to assess stability, yet Rogosa and others (see Stoolmiller & Bank [1995] for a good overview of this issue) so oppose it? It seems that the criticisms, like so many criticisms of statistical methodologies, are primarily directed at the *misuse* of the methodology. If the purpose of the analysis is to detect changes in the level or the growth patterns of individuals, or identify correlates of change, then the simplex models may yield parameter estimates that are misleading. This is particularly true when there are nonlinear growth patterns (Rogosa, 1993). However, if the purpose is to examine stability in the absence of growth or learning, as was the case for the two examples presented in this chapter, then the simplex model is appropriate.

McArdle and Epstein (1987), Meredith and Tisak (1990), Rogosa (1993), Rogosa and Willett (1985), and others, have used "individual growth modeling" to examine individual differences in change over time. A regression-type model (linear or nonlinear) is used to fit the longitudinal data for each individual, with the data for each individual being assumed to follow the same functional form (perhaps with different parameters), and these individual parameters then become the unit of analysis in subsequent analyses. Recently, Duncan and Duncan (1995), Stoolmiller (1995), and Willett and Sayer (1994,1996) have written excellent methodological papers showing how individual growth modeling can incorporate the concept of latent variables into the models. Willett and Sayer describe the methodology as an integration of individual growth modeling and covariance structure approaches, and Duncan and Duncan refer to the methodology as a latent growth model. Individual growth modeling, either with or without the latent variable modeling component, is a well-established and useful statistical procedure. If a researcher wished to examine the stability of change in level, or the stability of intraindividual differences in the presence of change in levels over time, then perhaps the LGM approach would be preferable to the simplex model methods.

Traditional reliability methods, autoregressive or simplex models, and latent growth models are not the only methodologies currently being advocated as suitable procedures to examine stability and change. The topic of the analysis of change continues to be one of the most salient issues in psychometrics (e.g., see Gottman's [1995] excellent edited text on recent advances in assessing change). Embretson (1991) has combined latent trait modelling with item response theory to quantify learning and change; Cardinet (1994) uses generalizability theory to estimate individual reliabilities; Gardner (1995) explores methods to assess the reliability of ordinal sequential data; and Bryk and Raudenbush (1992) continue to develop their hierarchical linear model to accommodate missing data and unequally spaced time intervals. It is beyond the scope of this chapter (and the knowledge of this author) to try to explain and compare all these methods. All procedures, with the possible exception of Embretson's, have been well tested and adopted by numerous researchers. Each has its particular strength or weakness, and it is up to the individual researcher to select the method appropriate for his or her research design, data, and hypotheses.

Summary

It is clear that simple correlation coefficients based on test-retest data are not adequate statistical indicators of the stability of traits. More than two repeated assessments are required, and four or more are desirable. Procedures such as the intraclass correlation coefficient and Cronbach's alpha are suitable for these multiple repeated measures designs, but the resultant reliability coefficient is no more than an average of all possible pairwise correlations and does not reflect the reliability of the underlying trait or take into account the correlation among the measurement errors. Structural equation modeling procedures do not suffer from these weaknesses. They permit the testing of interesting hypotheses regarding the temporal dependencies of the repeated measures (simplex versus general factor models); they provide statistical indicators of the stability of the trait and of the reliability of the observed measures, and the extent to which there exist systematic measurement errors. The availability of computer software for conducting these analyses is such that all researchers should now be able to take advantage of this methodology when conducting a major study (large sample sizes are required). Researchers in sport and exercise psychology are urged to consider using SEM and/or other new methods to assess stability when planning their research projects.

References

Asendorpf, J.B. (1992). Beyond stability: Predicting inter-individual differences in intra-individual change. *European Journal of Personality, 6*, 103-117.

Bentler, P.M. (1983). *Theory and implementation of EQS, a structural equations program.* Los Angeles: BMDP Statistical Software.

Bentler, P.M. (1990). Comparative fit indexes in structural models. *Psychological Bulletin, 107*, 238-246.

Blalock, H.M. (1970). Estimating measurement error using multiple indicators and several points in time. *American Sociological Reviews, 35*, 101-111.

Brennan, R.L., & Kane, M.T. (1977). An index of dependability for mastery tests. *Journal of Educational Measurement, 14*, 277-289.

Browne, M.W., & Cudek, R. (1993). Alternative ways of assessing model fit. In K. A. Bollen & J. S. Long (Eds.), *Testing structural equation models* (pp.136-162). Newbury Park, CA: Sage Publications.

Bryk, A. S., & Raudenbush, S. W. (1992). *Hierarchical linear models.* Newbury Park, CA: Sage Publications.

Cardinet, J. (1994). Control of the value of an intra-subject measurement design. In D. Laveault, B. Zumbo, M. Gessaroli, & M. Boss (Eds.), *Modern theories of measurement: Problems and issues* (pp. 181-212). Ottawa: University of Ottawa.

Cardinet, J., Tourneur, Y., & Allal, L. (1981). Extension of generalizability theory and its applications in educational measurement. *Journal of Educational Measurement, 18*, 183-204.

Caspi, A., & Bem, D. J. (1990). Personality continuity and change across the life course. In L. A. Pervin (Ed.), *Handbook of personality: Theory and research* (pp. 549-575). New York: Guilford.

Chou, C., & Bentler, P.M. (1995). Estimates and tests in structural equation modeling. In R. H. Hoyle (Ed.), *Structural equation modeling: Concepts, issues, and applications* (pp. 37-55). Thousand Oaks, CA: Sage.

Chou, C., Bentler, P.M., & Satorra, A. (1991). Scaled test statistics and robust standard errors for non-normal data in covariance structure analysis: A Monte Carlo study. *British Journal of Mathematical and Statistical Psychology, 44*, 347-357.

Cohen, J. (1988). *Statistical power analysis for the behavioral sciences.* Hillsdale, N.J.: Lawrence Erlbaum.

Cronbach, L.J. (1951). Coefficient alpha and the internal structure of tests. *Psychometrika, 16*, 297-334.

Cronbach, L.J., Rajaratnam, N., & Gleser, G.C. (1963). The theory of generalizability: A liberalization of reliability theory. *British Journal of Statistical Psychology, 16*, 137-163.

Duncan, T.E., & Duncan, S.C. (1995). Modeling the processes of development via latent variable growth curve methodology. *Structural Equation Modeling, 2*, 187-213.

Embretson, S. E. (1991). A multidimensional latent trait model for measuring learning and change. *Psychometrika, 56*, 495-515.

Epstein, S. (1990). Comment on the effects of aggregation across and within occasions on consistency, specificity, and reliability. *Methodika, 4*, 95-100.

Finn, S.E. (1986). Stability of personality self-ratings over 30 years: Evidence for an age/cohort interaction. *Journal of Personality and Social Psychology, 50*, 813-818.

Fleishman, J., & Benson, J. (1987). Using LISREL to evaluate measurement models and scale reliability. *Educational and Psychological Measurement, 47*, 925-939.

Ghiselli, E.E., Campbell, J.P., & Zedeck, S. (1981). *Measurement theory for the behavioral sciences.* New York: W.H. Freeman and Company.

Godbout, P., & Schutz, R.W. (1983). Generalizability of ratings of motor performances with references to various observational designs. *Research Quarterly for Exercise and Sport, 54*, 20-27.

Gottman, J. M. (Ed.). (1995). *The analysis of change.* Mahwah, NJ: L. Erblaum.

Gottman, J. M., & Rushe, R. H. (1993). The analysis of change: Issues, fallacies, and new ideas. *Journal of Consulting and Clinical Psychology, 61*, 907-910.

Heise, D.D. (1969). Separating reliability and stability in test-retest correlation. *American Sociological Review, 34*, 93-101.

Henly, S.J. (1993). Robustness of some estimators for the analysis of covariance structures. *British Journal of Mathematical and Statistical Psychology, 46,* 313-338.

Hertzog, C., & Nesselroade, J.R. (1987). Beyond autoregressive models: Some implications of the state-trait distinction for the structural modeling of developmental change. *Child Development, 58,* 93-109.

Hoyt, C.J. (1941). Test reliability estimated by analysis of variance. *Psychometrika, 6,* 153-160.

Joreskog, K. G. (1970). Estimation and testing of simplex models. *British Journal of Mathematical and Statistical Psychology, 23,* 121-145.

Joreskog, K. G., & Sorbom, D. (1976). *LISREL III: Estimation of linear structural equation systems by maximum likelihood methods.* Chicago: National Educational Resources, Inc.

Joreskog, K. G., & Sorbom, D. (1993). *LISREL 8: User's reference guide.* Chicago: Scientific Software.

Kenny, D. A., & Campbell, D. T. (1989). On the measurement of stability in over-time data. *Journal of Personality, 57,* 445-481.

Lazarus, R. S., & Folkman, S. (1984). *Stress, appraisal, and coping.* New York: Springer.

Long, B.C., & Schutz, R.W. (1995). Temporal stability and replicability of a workplace stress and coping model for managerial women: A multiwave panel study. *Journal of Counseling Psychology, 42,* 266-278.

Looney, M.A., & Heimerdinger, B.M. (1991). Validity and generalizability of social dance performance ratings. *Research Quarterly for Exercise and Sport, 62,* 399-405.

Marsh, H.W. (1993a). Self-esteem stability and responses to the stability of self scale. *Journal of Research in Personality, 27,* 253-269.

Marsh, H.W. (1993b). Stability of individual differences in multiwave panel studies: Comparison of simplex models and one-factor models. *Journal of Educational Measurement, 30,* 157-183.

Marsh, H.W., Balla, J.R. & Hau, K. (1996). An evaluation of incremental fit indices: A clarification of mathematical and empirical properties. In G. A. Marcoulides & R. E. Schumacker (Eds.), *Advanced structural equation modeling: Issues and techniques* (pp. 315-353). Mahwah, NJ: L. Erlbaum.

Marsh, H.W., & Grayson, D. (1994). Longitudinal stability of latent means and individual differences: A unified approach. *Structural Equation Modeling, 1,* 317-359.

McArdle, J.J., & Epstein, D. (1987). Latent growth curves within developmental structural equation models. *Developmental Psychology, 58,* 110-133.

Meredith, W. & Tisak, J. (1990). Latent curve analysis. *Psychometrika, 55,* 107-122.

Mulaik, S.A., James, L.R., Van Alstine, J., Bennett, N., Lind, S., & Stilwell, C.D. (1989). Evaluation of goodness-of-fit indices for structural models. *Psychological Bulletin, 105,* 430-445.

Reddy, S. K. (1992). Effects of ignoring correlated measurement error in structural equation models. *Educational and Psychological Measurement, 52,* 549-570.

Rogosa, D. (1987). Causal models do not support scientific conclusions: A comment in support of Freedman. *Journal of Educational Statistics, 12,* 185-195.

Rogosa, D. (1993). Individual unit models versus structural equations: Growth curve examples. In K. Haagen, D.J. Bartholomew, & M. Deistler (Eds.), *Statistical modelling and latent variables* (pp. 259-281). Amsterdam: North-Holland.

Rogosa, D. (1995). Myths and methods: "Myths about longitudinal research" plus supplemental questions. In J. M. Gottman (Ed.), *The analysis of change* (pp. 3-66). Mahwah, NJ: L. Erlbaum.

Rogosa, D., & Willet, J.B. (1985) Understanding correlates of change by modeling individual differences in growth. *Psychometrika, 50,* 203-228.

Schuerger, J.M., Zarrella, K.L, & Hotz, A.N. (1989). Factors that influence the temporal stability of personality by questionnaire. *Journal of Personality and Social Psychology, 56,* 777-783.

Schutz, R. W. (1995, August). *The stability of individual performance in baseball: An examination of four 5-year periods, 1928-32, 1948-52, 1968-72, 1988-92.* Paper presented at the Annual Meeting of the American Statistical Association, Orlando, FL.

Schutz, R.W., & Gessaroli, M.E. (1987). The analysis of repeated measures designs involving multiple dependent variables. *Research Quarterly for Exercise and Sport, 58,* 132-149.

Shrout, P.E., & Fleiss, J.L. (1979). Intraclass correlations: Uses in assessing rater reliability. *Psychological Bulletin, 86,* 420-428.

Steiger, J.H. (1990). Structural model evaluation and modification: An interval estimation approach. *Multivariate Behavioral Research, 25,* 173-180.

Steyer, R., & Schmitt, M.J. (1990). The effects of aggregation across and within occasions on consistency, specificity and reliability. *Methodika, 4,* 58-94.

Ssemakula, J. (1993, June 8). Structural equations and causal analysis: A critique. E-mail posted on the edstat-l listserve, Edstat-l@jse.stat.ncsu.edu, June 8.

Stoolmiller, M. (1995). Using latent growth curve models to study developmental process. In J. M. Gottman (Ed.), *The analysis of change* (pp. 103-138). Mahwah, NJ: L. Erlbaum.

Stoolmiller, M., & Bank, L. (1995). Autoregressive effects in structural equation models: We see some problems. In J. M. Gottman (Ed.), *The Analysis of Change* (pp. 261-276). Mahwah, NJ: L. Erlbaum.

Tanaka, J.S., & Huba, G.J. (1987). Assessing the stability of depression in college students. *Multivariate Behavioral Research, 22,* 5-19.

Thorn, J., & Palmer, P. (Eds), (1993). *Total baseball: The ultimate encyclopedia of baseball.* New York: Harper Collins.

Usala, P.D., & Hertzog, C. (1991). Evidence of differential stability of state and trait anxiety in adults. *Journal of Personality and Social Psychology, 60,* 471-479.

Violato, C., & Travis, L.D. (1988). An application of generalizability theory to the consistency-specificity problem: The transitutional consistency of behavioral persistence. *The Journal of Psychology, 122,* 389-407.

West, S.G., Finch, J.F., & Curran, P.J. (1995). Structural equation models with nonnormal variables: Problems and remedies. In R.H. Hoyle (Ed.), *Structural equation modeling: Concepts, issues, and applications* (pp. 56-75). Thousand Oaks, CA: Sage.

Wiley, D.E., & Wiley, J.A. (1970). The estimation of measurement error in panel data. *American Sociological Reviews, 35,* 112-117.

Willett, J.B., & Sayer, A.G. (1994). Using covariance structure analysis to detect correlates and predictors of individual change over time. *Psychological Bulletin, 116,* 363-381.

Willett, J.B., & Sayer, A.G. (1996). Cross-domain analyses of change over time: Combining growth modeling and covariate structure analysis. In G. A. Marcoulides & R. E. Schumacker (Eds.), *Advanced structural equation modeling: Issues and techniques* (pp. 125-157). Mahwah, NJ: L. Erlbaum.

Yadama, G.N., & Padey, S. (1995). Effect of sample size on goodness-of-fit indices in structural equation models. *Journal of Social Service Research, 20,* 49-70.

Chapter 24

APPLICATION OF THE RASCH ANALYSIS TO SPORT AND EXERCISE PSYCHOLOGY MEASUREMENT

Gershon Tenenbaum
and
Gerard Fogarty
University of Southern Queensland

AN INTRODUCTION TO RASCH ANALYSIS

The Basic Requirements of Measurement

Quantitative measures such as length, weight, or volume make sense to almost every person who is acquainted with them. In these cases, we know what it is that we are measuring, and we accept the standards that have been developed to make the measurements. However, measures of psychological constructs such as opinions, attitudes, and personality are still somewhat ambiguous. It is simply not possible to show precisely what it is that is being assessed, and the measuring devices themselves tend to be "introspective." Introspective measures, unlike measures of a physical nature, consist of items intended to represent an abstract variable. The items constitute an operational definition of the abstract variable for measurement purposes. The essential prerequisites for constructing such a measure constitute (a) a consistent definition of the domain of investigation (Thurstone, 1928), (b) selection of items that best represent the domain and share a common content classified under a single heading (Guttman, 1944), and (c) administration of the resulting scale to a sample of the relevant population in order to examine the response patterns. This last requirement has led to the development of a wide range of techniques designed to evaluate these introspective measures. In this chapter we will compare two approaches to test validation, one based on what is called classical test theory (CTT), the other a variant of the item response theory (IRT) approach called Rasch analysis. We will argue that Rasch analysis solves some of the more subtle (and often unrecognized) problems in measurement.

Recently, Schutz (1994) placed measurement methods among the most important topics that should be addressed in order to advance the domain of sport and exercise psychology. The main concerns are that (a) measures in this domain rely heavily upon the use of introspective techniques and (b) even when proper care is taken in the construction of items in a scale, there can be no guarantee that the items map the full range of the underlying dimension. It would be rather common, for example, to end up with a scale that sampled some parts of the dimension better than it did others. In most cases, we would not even know that this is happening; we would simply carry on as though the scale were measuring a linear continuum. This is a problem that needs to be addressed. How can scores on scales be interpreted and how can intervention effects (i.e., pre-post change) be considered meaningful when the measures themselves are not considered to be linear in nature? This concern and others have been addressed in recent years by the IRT models (see Hambleton, Swaminathan, & Rogers, 1991, for an overview). The basic assumption underlying the IRT concept is that introspective measures can share fundamental characteristics of physical measurement requirements. These requirements are outlined below.

Origin, Unit of Measurement, and Linearity

As early as 1928, Thurstone stated that scales are not sufficient if they do not satisfy the requirement of having an "origin" or a defined "zero-point" with units of measurement that extend from the origin in a linear fashion. To achieve this, Thurstone (1928) stipulated that there should be a systematic attempt to select items that in fact do elicit a linear response from "low" to "high." The requirement for a zero origin poses some difficulties for the classical measurement model. What does it mean to have a score of zero on a test in the classical measurement approach? It is difficult to say. Any other score would provide more information. A score of 2, for example, contains information about what the examinee can and cannot do. A score of zero tells us little because it does not indicate that the individual has zero ability; it simply indicates that the individual did not answer any of the items in the test correctly. These are not the same thing. Nor can we easily make interpretations about the intervals between different total scores. Classical measurement processes do not satisfy the requirement for a zero origin and equal units of measurement in the way stipulated by Thurstone.

Sample-Free Measurement: Item Calibration and Item Fit

"Item calibration" and "item fit" are concepts that help to avoid the problem of developing measures with psychometric characteristics that are overly influenced by the particular samples used in their development. In principle, the linear continuum is supposed to remain consistent across samples with the location of valid items on the linear measurement continuum unchanged. Thus, the calibration of items on a linear continuum should be independent of the sample of subjects responding to the items, in the same way that a yardstick is unchanged by the objects that it measures. This does not happen in the CCT approach, where it is quite possible for item difficulty and item discrimination indices to change markedly depending on the sample to which the items were administered.

Wright and Stone (1979) have termed this requisite fit, meaning that an efficient and sufficient measurement process should produce items that elicit expected responses from persons responding to them. IRT achieves this by actually calculating the fit of each item. For example, an item might change its position on the linear continuum: to some people it appears easy relative to other items; to other people, it appears difficult relative to these same items. It would be almost impossible to develop an expectation of how people might respond to such an item, and we could say that it has poor fit. Although such an item might well be discarded in a CTT approach, it has a greater chance of being detected using IRT. It is this emphasis on the information provided by properly calibrated and "good fitting" items that makes IRT such a powerful measurement technique. The statistical characteristics of the items answered, either correctly or incorrectly, determine the person's score. They do not have to be the same items, and the item sets do not have to be equal in number.

Sample-free Measurement: Reliability and Validity

Validity and reliability are concepts that are fundamental to the measurement process. The two requirements should be inherent in the measurement of opinions and attitudes. Scale values must be as free as possible from actual opinions of individuals and groups. In order for a scale to be valid, the values for its items should remain within a given range of error regardless of the characteristics of the people rating the items. For example, when two responders with opposing attitudes make similar ratings for an item, this requirement is met because the calibration of the item *stays constant* and free of individuals and groups. Only such items may establish a scale. A valid item is one that causes minimal ambiguity to responders. Many such items construct a valid scale.

The concept of reliability has always been a problem for CTT. The nature of the problem is well described by Weiss and Yoes (1991) when they comment that because reliability involves the total score variance, both the estimate of the individual's true score and its standard error of measurement (SEM) are dependent on the sample. In IRT, on the other hand, computation of SEM is not necessary in order to compute the reliability. Furthermore, in IRT, it is possible to compute SEMs that can differ for different individuals. (p.71).

The Rasch Model

When these fundamental requirements of measurement are met, the resulting instruments can be generalizable and objective. By way of example, one should imagine a yardstick with which persons are measured. A yardstick is considered sufficient and adequate for measurement when it is sample-free and contains absolute origin (zero) and equal units of measurement across all its range. The measures produced by such a yardstick are objective and generalizable. The IRT models have all these properties. One pertinent model within the IRT family of models is the Rasch model (1960) which has been applied to dichotomous scales (Wright & Stone, 1979) and rating scales (Andrich, 1981; Wright & Masters, 1982). The Rasch model is one of the simplest of the IRT models and is well-suited to the present task of illustrating the use of IRT in the validation of a psychological test.

Andrich (1981) argued that the requirements outlined by Thurstone (1959) and Guttman (1944, 1950) which define the concept of psychological scaling, are solved by the Rasch model. In Andrich's (1981) words,

> The most important distinguishing feature of Rasch's models is that, when they hold within some specified frame of reference, they provide explicit comparisons of person parameters which are independent of other persons to be compared and also independent of the parameters of the questions or items used to obtain the required responses. In achievement testing these parameters are the abilities of persons and the difficulty of items, while in attitude measurement they may be termed respectively attitudes and, following Thurstone, affective values. The explicit separation distinguishes these models from other psychometric models, generally called latent trait models, within which framework the Rasch models are often placed. (p.2)

The Rasch method yields person measures and item values

that are independent of each other. Both represent points on linear continuums. The model is probabilistic in nature and provides a test of response validity through a "fit" statistic, and therefore yields objective and reliable estimates for both items and persons. How it does this will become clearer as we introduce the main concepts inherent in Rasch analysis and then apply the model to some specific measures from the sport and exercise psychology field.

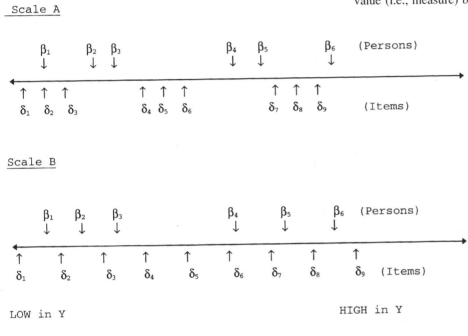

Scale A

Scale B

LOW in Y   HIGH in Y

Figure 1. Calibration of persons and items on a linear continuum

The Rasch Model: Basic Mathematical Considerations

Measurement is designed to discriminate among persons who differ in some property that is represented by scale items. The items differ each from the other in their "ease" or "difficulty' to "endorse" or "reject" (in dichotomous-type of response)[1] or in choosing a "step" in a Likert-type scale. Therefore, a person v with attitude β_v is expected to endorse or chose high categories on items located on a linear continuum as far as his or her attitude enables him or her to do so. From a certain point on the continuum, this person is expected to "reject", "disagree", or chose the lower categories on the remaining items. This is an essential process in order to meet the basic assumptions of linearity, unit of measurement, and "fit" (validity) of responses. Thus, the simplest representation of the person v taking item i responding X_{vi} is governed by his or her attitude β_v and the item's "difficulty or ease to endorse," δi. To measure a subject, estimation of β_v is re-

quired; to calibrate an item, estimation of δ_i is required. In other words, the difference between ($\beta_v - \delta_i$) governs the probability of endorsement or rejection of a dichotomously scored item.

To illustrate the concept, let's assume that we designed two scales that contain nine items each and measure the same variable Y. This illustration is presented in Figure 1.

As one can see, Scale A consists of nine items that are spread unequally along the abstract continuum that represents variable Y. Persons β_2 and β_3 who differ on Y will actually have the same value (i.e., measure) because they happen to fall in the interval covered by items 3 and 4. So will persons β_4 and β_5 on Scale A. This is an undesirable result and is an outcome of the way in which the items in this scale tap the underlying dimension. However, the nine items on Scale B are ordered equally along the linear continuum and enable efficient discrimination in measures of persons β_2 and β_3 as well as between persons β_4 and β_5. As far as this property is concerned, Scale B is therefore considered a desirable scale.

The response X_{vi} of person v to item i governed by the subject's attitude β_v and item value ("difficulty /ease to endorse") δ_i is shown in Figure 2.

As previously mentioned, the difference ($\beta_v - \delta_i$) governs the response X_{vi}. This difference can vary from $-\infty$ to $+\infty$, whereas the probability of a successful response should always remain within the 0 - 1 limits. Therefore, the difference ($\beta_v - \delta_i$) is treated as an exponent of the natural constant e = 2.71828 so that $e^{(\beta_v - \delta_i)} = \exp(\beta_v - \delta_i)$. This expression has

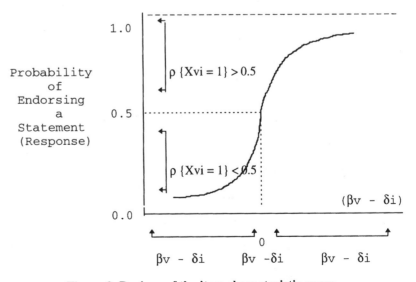

Figure 2. Regions of the item characteristic curve

---

1. The vocabulary used here will pertain to the simpler dichotomous response. However, the Rasch model applies to other kinds of scaled responses that will be addressed later.

limits between $-\infty$ to $+\infty$; so, to bring the probability within the boundaries 0 to 1, the expression is transformed into a ratio:

$$\exp(\beta_v - \delta_i) / [1 + \exp(\beta_v - \delta_i)]$$

This expression has an ogive shape and is used to define the Rasch Model (equation 1)

$$P\{X_{vi} = 1 \mid \beta_v - \delta_i\} = \exp(\beta_v - \delta_i) / [1 + \exp(\beta_v - \delta_i)] \qquad (1)$$

a logistic function that makes both linearity and generality of measure possible (Wright & Stone, 1979). The mathematical formulation to estimate β_v and δ_i independently from each other was suggested by Rasch (1961, 1967), Anderson (1973, 1977), and Barndorff-Nielsen (1978).

> When the estimators for β_v and item's value δ_i are derived by maximizing a conditional likelihood, they are unbiased, consistent, efficient, and sufficient. Simple approximation for these conditional maximum likelihood estimators, which are accurate enough for almost all practical purposes, are described in Wright and Panchapakesan (1969), Wright and Douglas (1975a, 1975b, 1977a, 1977b), and Wright and Mead (1976). (Wright & Stone, 1979, pp.15-16)

A person's measure β_v and item's value δ_i are defined "logits" in the Rasch Model. A "logit" is defined by Wright and Stone (1979) accordingly: "A person's ability in logits is their natural log odds for succeeding on items of the kind chosen to define the "zero" point on the scale. And an item's difficulty in logits is its natural log odds for eliciting failure from persons with "zero ability" (p. 17). Logits must not be confused with standard errors of estimation. A logit reflects the amount of information in one item. The standard error (SE) reflects the amount of information in a test or a scale containing several items. Regardless of what the items are like, the SE can be made as small as we like by using more items, whereas the information in each item can only be increased by improving the items (Mead, 1981).

The Rasch model includes additional mathematical properties that enable a goodness of fit test between the predicted values and the actual data observed. Following the estimation of β_v and δ_i, the residuals of the model are calculated by estimating the value expected for each X_{vi} from β_v and δ_i, and subtracting this expectation from the observed X_{vi}. The fit statistics are essential features of the way in which the Rasch model contributes to improved reliability and validity because they help to detect individual persons whose pattern of response differs from that of the rest of the sample and also individual items that attract odd response patterns. A person with an odd response pattern in an achievement test would be someone who got difficult items right and easy items wrong. A poorly fitting item in this same achievement test would attract unusual patterns of response from students of differing ability levels, with perhaps the more able students giving wrong answers. The Rasch technique identifies such persons and items.

Techniques for calibrating items, measuring persons and estimating fit by Rasch analysis are described in detail in Wright and Stone (1979) and Wright and Masters (1982). It is not our aim to present here the mathematical formulation of these estimates and the error terms associated with them. Instead, key issues in this concept are addressed to clarify the analyses applied to the sport psychology scales later in this chapter.

Rasch Model Applications in Rating Scales

Early work with Rasch models concentrated mostly on dichotomous item response data, where the items were scored as *correct* or *incorrect*. There are also nondichotomous Rasch models that can be used with rating scales (e.g., Likert scales). A rating scale consists of a series of ordered categories connected to each other by "steps". The steps can be ordered in relation to several criteria that are presented in Figure 3.

"Steps" can be ranked by various

Criterion	"Steps"					
Frequency	(1) almost always		(2) once in a while		(3) hardly ever	
Amount	(1) all	(2) a bit	(3) quite a bit	(4) some	(5) hardly any	(6) none
Degree (Quantity)	(1) extremely entirely completely	(2) very very much strongly		(3) somewhat	(4) a little lightly weakly	
Judgment	(1) very good	(2) slightly good	(3) ?	(4) slightly bad	(5) very bad	

Nature	"Steps	
Belief	true / false	(may be modified with adjectives like "strongly agree", "agree", etc.)
Opinion	agree / disagree	
Preference	like / dislike	
Loyalty	for / against	
Value	good / bad	
Potency	strong / weak	
Activity	intense / release	

Figure 3. Steps in typical rating scales

formats, such as

Format 1:	1	2	3	4	5
Format 2:	- 2	- 1	0	+ 1	+ 2
Format 3:	- 5	- 4	- 3	- 2	1
Format 4:	0	1	2	3	4

The number of steps is the number of response activities minus 1. For example, in the case of five categories, four steps result as shown in Figure 4.

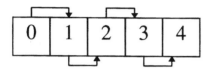

Figure 4. Steps in a five-category rating scale

The main concerns associated with steps are (a) whether all the steps are perceived similarly by respondents, and (b) what the probability is of choosing a given step, skipping those "beneath" and avoiding those "above". Rasch (1960; cited in Wright & Masters, 1982) thus breaks each item down into a series of steps, without any *a priori* assumption of response distribution. The steps are graphically shown in Figure 5.

Introducing the dichotomous model as

$$\beta_{vil} = \exp(\beta_v - \delta_{i1}) / [1 + \exp(\beta_v - \delta_{i1})]$$

in which β_{vil} is the probability of person v endorsing category 1 of item i rather than rejecting it, given the person's attitude β_v and item δi's "ease/difficulty to endorse" (δ_1) of one step. When more steps are required, a position, β_v, is established for

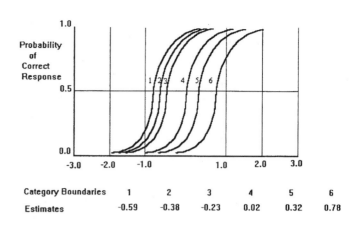

Category Boundaries	1	2	3	4	5	6
Estimates	-0.59	-0.38	-0.23	0.02	0.32	0.78

Figure 6. Item characteristic curves for different threshold values

each subject, a scale value (δ_i) is estimated for each item i, and response "thresholds," $r_1, r_2, r_3.., r_m$, are estimated for m + 1 rating categories (see Wright & Masters, 1982).

The probability of choosing a category for each item is adjusted to the different scoring formats (dichotomous, partial credit, rating scale, binomial trials, and Poisson counts). The mathematical and statistical techniques for separating item estimations from person measures and establishing reliability and validity estimates of the scale through "fit" statistics are further discussed in Wright and Masters (1982, pp. 57-58, 90-115). For illustration, let's assume that item i of a given scale contains seven possible categories (i.e., 6 steps). The conditional thresholds provide the probability of "moving" from one category to the other (steps) as a function of the difference between the person's attitude and how much of the attitude the item elicits ($\beta_v - \delta_i$). Additional analysis gives the category boundary estimates as a function of the difference. Figure 6 provides an illustration of the information provided by this analysis.

The category boundaries of the items are at the point where the probability of moving from one category to the other (making a step) is 0.50. This procedure enables one to decide whether a step can be deleted (i.e., to confine the number of response alternatives). In Figure 6, the boundaries are increasing gradually from the first step to the sixth step. The distance between Steps 2 and 3 is quite small, but gives no strong indication that Steps 2 and 3 should be combined, thus condensing the number of steps into five instead of six. Categories boundaries do not always line up in such a neat fashion, and there is an excellent example in Fogarty and Bramston (1996) where an analysis of this kind led to a decision to collapse two response categories into one.

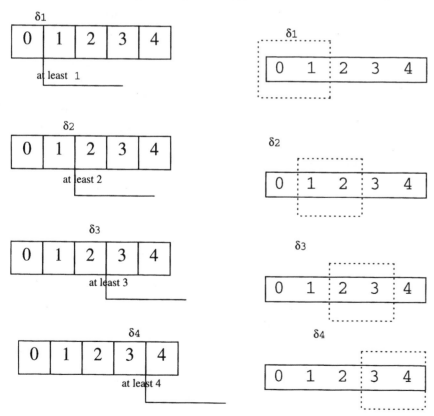

Figure 5. Endorsement regions for different steps

Rasch Measurement and Classical Test Theory

The measurement properties of opinions and attitudes are quite problematic as they do not share deterministic properties of a physical character. It is for this reason that classical test theory has striven for internal and external types of validity by developing various indices of measurement error (all types of reliability), seeking objectivity in scoring formats and judging protocols, developing techniques of score interpretation (criterion and norm referenced), and refining methods for analyzing individual items and the structure of scales from which they are drawn. The achievements of classical test theory are substantial and represent an enormous contribution to the field of psychological measurement. We do not wish — for even one moment — to belittle the achievements in this field. Rather, we would argue that Rasch analysis can complement the traditional approach by adding new assumptions and requirements and developing better mathematical formulations to meet and satisfy them. The assumptions of sample-free measurement, linearity,

A COMPARISON OF SOME DIFFERENT METHODS OF ANALYZING TESTS

Description of Test

The scale chosen for these analyses was Duda and Nicholls' (see Duda, 1989) Task and Ego Orientation in Sport Questionnaire (TEOSQ). It has 13 items, 6 of which form an Ego subscale; the remaining 7 items form a Task subscale. For the purpose of these illustrations, data were collected on 1,591 adolescents (837 males) as part of a survey on youth participation in sport and fitness activities in Australia, New Zealand, and the United States. We will commence with an item analysis that is based on classical test theory techniques.

Analyzing Items and Tests Using Conventional Procedures

Reliability Analysis Using the SPSS Package

As far as item analysis is concerned, most researchers do not go past the scale analysis procedures found in the SPSS package. The default procedure for reliability analysis in this package is Cronbach's alpha, which can be very useful for detecting misfit items and for gaining some overall estimate of the internal consistency of the scale. A typical SPSS reliability analysis of the two subscales of the TEOSQ using SPSS produced the output shown in Table 1.

SPSS is a versatile package, and it is possible to obtain output that might look a bit different from what is seen above by requesting different options, but this output is based on a fairly standard set of options and produces the main statistics of interest to test developers. The two columns on the right-hand side are what most people will check first. The corrected item-total correlations tell us whether or not a particular item correlates with the total test score. A low correlation suggests that the item is not contributing to test performance and could be deleted. Crocker and Algina (1986) discuss various ways of estimating cut-off points for these corrected item-total correlations. The right-hand column gives an indication of the effect of the item on the overall internal consistency (alpha) of the test. We can see from these analyses that both scales have acceptable internal consistency reliability and that all items make some contribution to the reliability. In terms of a conventional analysis of this kind, there are really no, what might be called, "poor" performing items. Analysis with SPSS is usually limited to an inspection of these item-total correlations

Table 1
Reliability Analyses of the Ego and Task Subscales

	Scale Mean If Item Deleted	Scale Variance If Item Deleted	Corrected Item-Total Correlation	Alpha if Item Deleted
Ego Subscale				
Ego1	15.53	23.07	0.63	0.85
Ego2	15.41	22.67	0.71	0.84
Ego3	15.52	22.10	0.72	0.83
Ego4	15.90	22.61	0.64	0.85
Ego5	15.38	22.70	0.64	0.85
Ego6	15.74	21.21	0.66	0.85
				Alpha = .87
Task Subscale				
Task1	24.80	18.94	0.67	0.87
Task2	24.69	19.27	0.61	0.88
Task3	24.60	18.22	0.73	0.86
Task4	24.60	18.20	0.70	0.87
Task5	24.79	18.04	0.73	0.86
Task6	24.73	18.55	0.69	0.87
Task7	24.40	18.96	0.63	0.88
				Alpha = .89

origin, unit of measurement, and fit of items and persons are all new and share probabilistic (stochastic) properties. When these properties remain consistent across samples and situations, the measures of persons are reliable so that differences and "rate of change" are equal across the whole linear continuum, just like a yardstick measuring the height of subjects.

The differences between the methods of classical test theory and Rasch analysis can best be exemplified by looking at the processes and the outputs of a traditional test analysis and comparing those with what happens in a typical Rasch analysis. These analyses are presented in the next section.

Table 2
Factor Pattern Matrix for TEOSQ

Variable	Factor 1	Factor 2
Task3	0.79	0.00
Task5	0.78	0.02
Task4	0.75	-0.01
Task6	0.71	0.11
Task1	0.71	0.05
Task7	0.69	-0.10
Task2	0.65	-0.03
Ego3	-0.02	0.81
Ego2	0.04	0.77
Ego6	-0.06	0.73
Ego4	-0.06	0.71
Ego1	0.07	0.68
Ego5	0.06	0.67

Note: The correlation between these factors was 0.196.

and attempts to improve reliability by deleting some items.

It is possible to do some quite sophisticated test analyses using traditional techniques. The ITEMAN routines from the MicroCAT testing software (Assessment Systems Corporation, 1989), for example, allow the user to compute the classical index of discrimination for each item in the scales. This index measures how well the item can differentiate between high- and low-scoring examinees. The index is the difference between the proportion correct in the high-ability group (say, top 27%) and the low-ability group (Crocker & Algina, 1986). With Likert-style items, however, ITEMAN yields much the same information as SPSS, and we will not include the analyses here.

Using Exploratory Factor Analysis to Clarify the Structure of a Test

At this stage of the test validation process, researchers will often employ factor analysis to check the dimensionality of the test. In many situations, the factor analysis will actually precede the reliability checks, especially if there is not a strong *a priori* basis for forming subscales. In the present case, we can assume that the subscale structure was known beforehand and that the reliability checks occurred first. Obtaining good internal consistency estimates for the subscales, however, does not tell us much about the structure of the overall test. It is possible that both the Task and Ego subscales are tapping one dimension in a population. If they do, it would be pointless leaving them as two separate subscales, each with good internal consistency, but basically measuring the same underlying trait.

Factor analysis (FA) and principal components analysis (PCA) are the techniques most often used in the classical test tradition to determine the number of dimensions underlying the items in a test. In the following analysis, a type of exploratory factor analysis known as principal axis factoring (PAF) has been used to explore the structure of the TEOSQ. Using the root one criterion, two factors were extracted accounting for approximately 60.8% of the variance. The eigenvalue for the first factor

was 4.72 (36.3%), and for the second factor, 3.12 (24.5%). The next factor to be extracted accounted for just 5.8% of the variance, leaving no room for doubt that a two-factor solution was most appropriate. Rotating the axes to oblique positions, the solution shown in Table 2 was obtained.

In a test validation exercise, this output would considerably strengthen our confidence in the underlying structure of the test. We now know that there is a clear two-factor structure underlying the TEOSQ and that, in this sample at least, the factors are virtually uncorrelated. Furthermore, we know from the reliability analyses that the two subscales defined by these factors demonstrate good internal consistency.

There is no doubt that exploratory factor analysis is a useful tool in test-content validation. The problem with the exploratory factor analysis, however, is that the solution obtained is just one of many possible patterns. We have control over the number of factors that emerge, but no control over the pattern itself. This is a limitation of all exploratory factor analytic or principal component routines: Failure to obtain the pattern we expect indicates that other patterns provide a better "fit" between the reproduced and original correlation matrices, but we do not know by how much our preferred pattern misses the mark — or, indeed, if it misses the mark at all. In the case of the TEOSQ, it so happens that the structure is very clear, and it has

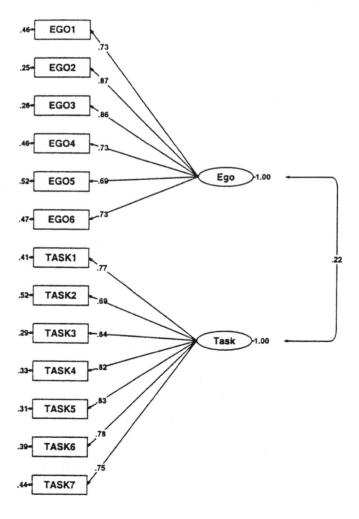

Figure 7. Lisrel model for TEOSQ

emerged nicely in the exploratory analyses. Things do not always turn out this way, and to test whether a particular structure does underlie a test, it may be necessary to resort to confirmatory factor analytic techniques. In the present situation, where we are dealing with an established test that has two subscales, we might choose to use confirmatory rather than exploratory factor analysis.

Using Confirmatory Factor Analysis to Clarify the Structure of a Test

The pattern expected to underlie the TEOSQ is quite straightforward: Using the terminology of confirmatory factor analysis, six of the items are intended to serve as indicator variables for the Ego factor and seven other items were included in the test to define the Task factor. The LISREL 8.12a input file needs only to specify that there are two factors in this model and that items 1 (ego1), 3 (ego2), 6 (ego3), 7 (ego4), 9 (ego5) and 11 (ego6) define the first factor and the remaining items the second factor. The model should also allow the factors to be correlated, unless the theoretical model clearly specifies that the underlying dimensions are orthogonal. The advantage of allowing the factors to be correlated is that orthogonal solutions are among the permissible outcomes. It was this same line of reasoning that led us to choose oblique rotation in the exploratory analysis. The model itself and the estimates for the various parameters are shown in Figure 7.

This model is similar to the one obtained with exploratory factor analysis. In CFA, the researcher posits an *a priori* structure and tests the ability of a solution based on this structure to fit the data by demonstrating that: (a) the solution is well defined; (b) the parameter estimates are consistent with theory and *a priori* predictions; and (c) the χ^2 likelihood ratio and subjective indices of fit are reasonable (McDonald & Marsh, 1990). For present purposes, the Non-Normed Fit Index (NNFI) recommended by McDonald and Marsh (1990) and the Root Mean Square Error of Approximation (RMSEA) recommended by Browne and Cudeck (1993) were considered as well as the usual χ^2 measure of goodness of fit. The NNFI varies along a 0-1 continuum in which values greater than .9 are taken to reflect an acceptable fit. Browne and Cudeck (1993) suggest that an RMSEA value of .05 indicates a close fit and that values up to .08 are still acceptable.

It is apparent that the solution in Figure 7 meets the first two of these criteria. There is no doubt that the pattern of loadings is clear and in line with predictions. With regard to the third criterion, however, the outcome may be regarded as somewhat less than desirable. The most widely-used of these indices of fit is the chi-square test of goodness of fit. If the chi-square value is too high relative to the number of degrees of freedom employed in the analysis, we have to reject the hypothesis that there is a good fit. In the present case, chi-square with 64 degrees of freedom was 1246.32 ($p < .01$), indicating that the fit is rather poor. The NNFI was .89, very close to the .90 recommended level (McDonald & Marsh, 1990). The RMSEA was .11, again indicating some degree of misfit. This is not uncommon when working at the item rather than the scale level.

When the fit is less than what might be considered desirable, it is usual to search for other structural models that result in

a better fit. In most cases, this search is made on substantive theoretical grounds. In the present case, we are using the TEOSQ as a vehicle to compare various test validation methods, and we really have no theoretical grounds for altering the above structure, so we can request the LISREL program to display what are called *modification indices*. These indices suggest changes to the structural model that will substantially improve the fit. Without going into details here, it turned out to be rather easy to achieve a good fit with the TEOSQ. One modification suggested by the programme was that Items 5 and 6 in the Ego scale be allowed to share some unique variance. When this was permitted, the chi-square value decreased to 987.05, the RMSEA to .096, and the NNFI increased to .91. Allowing some Task items to have minor loadings on the Ego factor brought the fit indices within acceptable limits. There is nothing alarming about this; it simply means that if we wish to explain all the correlations between the items, we have to abandon the unrealistic notion that they are factorially pure and that Task items can have minor loadings on the Ego factor. Apart from this structural information, at the item level, the LISREL analyses have confirmed that the various items do indeed serve as indicator variables for their respective latent constructs. The question of factorial complexity might warrant further consideration, but at least the items are serving the purpose for which they were intended.

Summary of Conventional Techniques

LISREL might seem a step above the other procedures used in this section, but it is essentially a conventional technique that provides information about how well individual items define underlying latent constructs. In this sense, we are justified in including it with these other techniques, all of which either provide information about how well items group together or how well the groups represent underlying constructs the test was designed to measure. We can see that the conventional techniques have the capacity to offer a lot of information about the performance of individual items and the scales of which they are a part. They should always be used in the initial stages of test validation where they can serve the additional purpose of testing assumptions required by Rasch analysis. Some of these assumptions will be described in the next section where we describe the procedures and discuss the output generated by a Rasch analysis.

RASCH ANALYSIS OF THE TEOSQ

The analysis of the TEOSQ questionnaire through the traditional psychometric techniques has indicated that the Task and Ego orientations should be perceived as somewhat independent psychological entities. Each orientation type has high internal consistency, indicating high shared variance among the items within each orientation type and relatively low shared variance across the orientations. This is important because one of the assumptions of the Rasch model is that the data are unidimensional. We know from the factor analyses that the TEOSQ questionnaire can be divided into two almost unidimensional scales, so we can say that this assumption is tenable. A second assumption is that the test items are not speeded. This is clearly true. Because the Rasch model is a one-parameter model (that is, only one parameter — ability or attitude — is es-

Table 3
Item Locations (in logits) for Ego and Task Orientation Scales for Female, Male, and Combined Samples

Item	Abbreviated Description	Females			Males			All		
		Location	SE	Fit	Location	SE	Fit	Location	SE	Fit
EGO										
3	Can do better than friends	-0.17	0.078	4.84	-0.45	0.078	3.02	-0.34	0.074	1.37
9	I score the most points	-0.45	0.072	0.82	-0.12	0.068	2.21	-0.34	0.070	2.51
4	Others can't do as well as me	-0.06	0.074	0.91	-0.17	0.075	5.92	-0.16	0.073	3.03
1	I am the only one who can play	-0.13	0.072	1.76	0.06	0.067	0.16	0.01	0.068	0.07
11	I am the best	0.23	0.065	0.13	0.20	0.059	1.69	0.12	0.062	1.49
6	Others mess up and I don't	0.58	0.073	0.19	0.49	0.067	0.14	0.69	0.068	0.07
TASK										
7	Learn new skills - trying hard	-0.20	0.093	4.36	-0.59	0.092	2.71	-0.44	0.097	5.17
13	I do my very best	-0.09	0.088	0.79	-0.24	0.084	0.93	-0.22	0.087	0.58
8	I work really hard	0.00	0.088	4.90	-0.09	0.083	1.36	-0.22	0.089	7.52
2	A skill learned...want to practise more	0.03	0.098	2.42	0.13	0.093	0.24	0.18	0.096	3.69
12	A skill learned...feels right	0.21	0.090	0.26	0.37	0.086	1.16	0.19	0.094	1.03
5	I learn something...keen to do	-0.31	0.096	4.15	0.20	0.082	2.42	0.23	0.087	4.53
10	Something I learned..practise more	0.36	0.087	2.42	0.22	0.089	0.53	0.27	0.096	0.02

timated), a third assumption is that all item-discrimination indices are equal. As mentioned earlier, the item-total correlations of the SPSS Reliability analyses are usually regarded as approximations to item-discrimination indices. We know from the SPSS output that for both scales these correlations were all positive and, although not equal, reasonably similar, so we can say that this assumption is also tenable. The third assumption has to do with guessing, and that is clearly not a problem in this rating scale. With these assumptions met, the Rasch analysis can proceed. The software package used to conduct these analyses was *Ascore2c* (Andrich, Sheridan, & Lyne, 1991), a package that handles both dichotomous and rating scale data.

In order to examine whether the items of each of the TEOSQ subscales share a desired linear continuum with equal units, we have calculated the locations of the items ("difficulty" estimates) and their standard errors for females, males, and the entire sample, separately. The relevant sections of output are summarized in Table 3.

The order of the items on the linear continuum was determined by the location of the items in the entire sample in both the Task and the Ego scales. For example, Item 3 of the Ego scale ("I can do better than my friends") with an overall location of -0.34 logits, is the easiest item to rate highly, whereas Item 6 on this scale ("Others mess up and I don't"), with a location of

0.69 logits, is the hardest to rate highly. In simple terms, it means that only people with a very strong Ego orientation should rate Item 6 highly. In the Task orientation scale, the easiest item to rate highly was 7 ("I learn a new skill by trying hard") because its value was -0.44 logits, whereas Item 10 ("Something I learn makes me want to go and practise more") was the hardest to rate highly. In both scales, the rest of the items are located on a linear continuum between the two extremes.

At this point, it is worth checking whether the items are spaced equally along the continuum, as in the second example shown in Figure 1. This is usually best accomplished by constructing a graphic representation. With such a small number of items, however, we can see just by looking at the output that the Ego scale is too narrow (-0.34 to 0.69) and that the units are not equally spaced. The Task scale is also very narrow (-0.44 to 0.27) and the items somewhat unequally spread over section of the attitudinal continuum that the scale covers. The narrow ranges indicate the ratings given to the items by the participants were not spread sufficiently over the five alternatives for each item. It may also be a function of the young sample used for these analyses. Under normal circumstances, the narrow range would be taken as an indication that additional items should be included in the scales. The particular items needed are those that will extend the range of the scales and fill in some of the gaps between items.

The fit values shown in Table 3 are actually chi-square goodness of fit estimates. They indicate whether items elicit acceptable response patterns from the subjects. That is to say, whether subjects are endorsing items with a high value and then failing to endorse "easy" items. The values were all acceptable for the Ego subscale but were a little higher than we might wish for items 5, 7, and 8 in the Task subscale. The separate estimates for males and females indicates that the misfit for these items is occurring in the female sample. A check of the scale and item statistics using SPSS revealed that the

Table 4
Section of ASCORE Output for a Particular Subject

Item Number	Expected Score	Observed Score	Standardized Residual
Task1	3.213	3	-.350
Task2	3.260	1	-3.322
Task3	3.633	4	.674
Task4	3.686	4	.566
Task5	3.184	4	1.265
Task6	3.306	4	1.167
Task7	3.718	4	.529
		Ability = 1.968	

Figure 8a: Scatter of Points for Ego

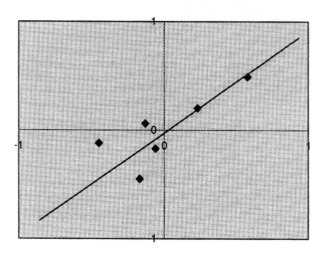

Figure 8b: Scatter of Points for Task

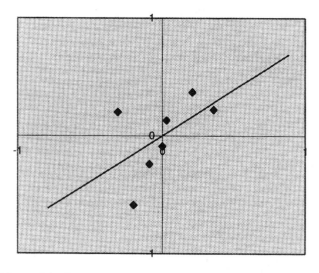

Figure 8 (a & b). Scatterplot comparing location values for males and females on Ego (a) and Task (b) scales

below what one would expect, and this person has been identified by *Ascore2c* as a poorly fitting subject.

Separate analyses were conducted on the female ($n = 300$) and male ($n = 300$) sections of the sample. As previously stated, items should be independent of the sample responding to them. Thus, it was expected that the item locations would be equal for males and females on both the Ego and Task scales. The correspondence is most easily observed if item locations for both genders are arranged in a scatterplot. This is shown in Figure 8.

It can be seen that the order of the items, as well as the range between the lowest and the highest values, is reasonably similar for both genders. Similar patterns should be obtained if the sample were to be split in other ways.

Finally, it is possible with a Rasch analysis to measure persons on the ability/attitudinal continuum. In classical test theory, a total score is used to represent a person's "ability" or "attitude." In Rasch analysis, that estimate takes the form of a location value on the linear continuum previously described. The location estimates and associated standard errors for each possible total score are shown in Table 5. Note that the five response options have been rescaled from 1-5 to 0-4 for the purposes of the analysis meaning that the lowest possible score on both scales was 0, and the maximum possible score was 24 for the Ego scale (6 x 4), and 28 for the Task scale (7 x 4). Extreme minimum and maximum scores were deleted because the response patterns for these people could not yield any information about individual item difficulties. This meant that the minimum scores on both scales was 1, and the maximum 23 for Ego and 27 for Task.

In order to measure persons on a linear continuum, these attitudinal or "dispositional" estimates in logits should be considered. The higher the score, the higher the Ego or Task orientation. This is true of total scores in classical test theory as well. The advantage of the logits, however, is that they enable us to tell by how much people differ from one another. The logits are a true interval scale, so a difference of a certain magnitude in one section of the continuum means the same as the corresponding difference elsewhere. For researchers and practitioners, this is of the utmost importance, and it constitutes one of the main reasons for translating subject measures into logits.

Summary

We began this chapter with a discussion of the basic requirements of measurement and argued that procedures based on classical test theory (CTT) do not meet all these requirements, whereas those based on item response theory (IRT) do. Readers familiar with the psychometric literature will realize that the situation is not quite so clear-cut, and it would be remiss to conclude this chapter without acknowledging the substantial overlap between the CTT and IRT approaches. Rasch analysis is not the only way of meeting the basic requirements of measurement. As Kline (1993) points out, both Thorndike (1919) and Thurstone (1925) developed their own procedures for overcoming the problem of item parameters changing with different samples (item invariance). Englehard (1984) showed that the Thorndike, Thurstonian, and Rasch methods all yielded similar results. The success of the Rasch model is undoubtedly due to the very large technical literature on item characteristic curves

Task scale in this sample is very negatively skewed ($z = 18.4$) and that these items in particular show high levels of negative skewness, especially for the female subsample. The particular software package used for these analyses (*Ascore2c*) also allows the user to identify people with particularly unusual response patterns. The user thus has the opportunity of deleting some of these individuals, including people with extreme scores. To illustrate what we mean, a section of the output from the above run is shown in Table 4.

We can see that this section of the output describes how well subject 291's responses to the seven Task items fits with the expected pattern for that subject. The ability estimate for the subject is 1.968, which means that he or she has a reasonably high level of Task orientation. The response to Item 2 is clearly

Table 5
Goal Orientation Estimates Corresponding to Scores on Ego and Task Scales

		EGO				*TASK*	
Raw Score	Freq.	Goal Estimate (In logits)	S.E	Raw Score	Freq.	Goal Estimate (In logits)	S.E
1	2	- 3.31	1.03	1	0	- 2.86	.92
2	0	- 2.56	.74	2	0	- 2.27	.64
3	6	- 2.10	.62	3	1	- 1.94	.52
4	2	- 1.76	.55	4	0	- 1.70	.46
5	5	- 1.48	.51	5	0	- 1.50	.42
6	6	- 1.24	.48	6	0	- 1.34	.39
7	9	- 1.02	.46	7	0	- 1.19	.38
8	14	- .82	.45	8	0	- 1.06	.36
9	11	- .62	.44	9	1	- .93	.36
10	16	- .43	.43	10	1	- .80	.35
11	21	- .25	.43	11	1	- .68	.35
12	28	- .06	.43	12	0	- .55	.35
13	22	.13	.44	13	2	- .43	.36
14	20	.32	.45	14	7	- .29	.37
15	21	.52	.44	15	3	- .15	.44
16	11	.73	.47	16	1	.54	.38
17	23	.96	.49	17	9	.16	.41
18	25	1.20	.51	18	10	.34	.43
19	12	1.48	.54	19	14	.54	.46
20	14	1.80	.59	20	20	.76	.48
21	7	2.19	.66	21	30	1.01	.51
22	6	2.70	.78	22	28	1.29	.55
23	4	3.50	1.05	23	16	1.62	.59
				24	26	1.99	.64
Mean		0.32		25	26	2.44	.70
S.D.		1.10		26	36	3.01	.82
				27	19	3.87	1.08
				Mean		1.62	
				S.D.		1.18	

(e.g., Lord, 1974, 1980) and the advent of computer software that has made the technique available to many researchers.

In this chapter, we have used some of this software to compare the Rasch method of analysis with an approach that was based on the classical test approach to test validation. To illustrate the two approaches, we administered the TEOSQ to a sample of 1,591 subjects. The classical approach indicated that the two scales had good internal consistency and also that they were measuring separate dimensions. Had we employed data-screening procedures, some problems that emerged in the Rasch analysis would have become apparent and could have been dealt with before attempting reliability or structural analyses. The point of the chapter, however, is not to show how the test validation process should proceed with either the CTT or IRT approach, but to draw attention to the *types* of information that are obtained in both. At the end of the traditional analysis, we knew that scores were fairly high on both subscales but that they were internally consistent, not highly correlated, and easily recovered in factor analysis. All in all, most test developers would be reasonably happy with the outcome of these analyses.

The Rasch analysis also indicated that the two scales had

good internal consistency and that most items "fitted" into their respective scales quite well. On further analysis, the items with poor fit were shown to have high levels of negative skewness in this sample. This problem could also have been detected using traditional procedures, but it is made much more evident in the Rasch analysis where the notion of fit is fundamental. The Rasch analysis also indicated people whose patterns of response were aberrant. What to do with these people remains the researcher's problem, but their routine detection in IRT applications is a strong reminder of the sophistication of these models for test development research.

In addition, the Rasch analysis indicated that both scales covered a rather narrow "attitudinal" range. We are not prepared to make much of this finding because the sample consists of adolescents who may not exhibit the full range of Ego and Task orientation scores, but it does highlight one of the major advantages of the Rasch analysis over the traditional approach. Difficulty indices for scales and individual items can be obtained in the CTT model where they are based on proportion correct. However, the calculation of the location estimates for the various items in IRT gives much more direct information about the properties of a scale and yields more stable estimates than those based on proportion correct. We can see at a glance whether the scale covers a broad or a narrow range and whether there are gaps in the coverage of the attitudinal continuum. The Rasch analysis is capable of providing this information not only because of its particular mathematical formulations, but also because of its ability to satisfy the basic measurement requirements outlined earlier in this paper: (a) It is sample free (although that property is not well illustrated in the data set employed here); (b) measurement is on a linear continuum; (c) there is a defined origin; (d) there is a measure of fit for each of the items in the scales; and (e) one can also obtain a measure of fit for each person.

That is not to say that the application of Rasch modelling is problem free. A major problem for Rasch analysis is that it assumes unidimensionality, and if this is not present, the findings are unreliable. Difficulty parameters will still be estimated, but the item characteristic curves would not refer to any latent trait. A factor analysis will detect this but it is a limitation of the one-dimensional models. The more complex two- and three-parameter models do allow infringements of unidimensionality to be detected. Some of the more recent multidimensional IRT models (e.g., McDonald, 1989) will handle these data sets quite well. The one-parameter model is also bound by the assumption that items are equally discriminating. Some theorists (e.g., Waller & Reise, 1989) have argued that this restricts use of the one-parameter model to ability and achievement tests and that the two-parameter model, which estimates item discrimination indices for individual items, may be better in personality and attitude measurement.

This last point is important when considering the type of model to use for test validation purposes. The one-dimensional model proved quite suitable for our purposes here when working with a test about which quite a lot is already known. However, it would have to be used in conjunction with classical test theory techniques, such as factor analysis, in the early stages of scale development. The main obstacles to immediate application of the Rasch model in this situation would be the unknown dimensionality of the test and uncertainty about the equality of item-discrimination indices. One-dimensional factor analysis — perhaps employing a method developed especially for IRT (e.g., Bock, Gibbons, & Muraki, 1988) — will help to resolve the question of number of factors; checking for homogeneity of biserial or point-biserial correlations in a traditional item analysis will give some indication whether the assumption of equal item discrimination may be viable (Hambleton et al., 1991). Another alternative, as pointed out above, is to use one of the more sophisticated latent trait models that have emerged over recent years.

In summary, there is a strong case for more widespread use of latent-trait models —such as the Rasch model — in sport and exercise psychology. Until recently, researchers may have argued that the latent-trait models were too difficult for the average researcher to use. That argument can scarcely be used any longer. There are now at least 12 commercially-available programs (see Hambleton, et al., 1991) some of which come with complete test development, administration, and assessment sections. These packages differ in terms of the models used —

some are based on a one-parameter models, others on two- or three-parameter models — and also in terms of the types of data they handle. Hambleton et al. (1991) reported that "Research on IRT models and their applications is being conducted at a phenomenal rate" (p.153) with interesting developments in the areas of polytomous unidimensional response models and polytomous multidimensional response models. The package we used in our demonstrations (*Ascore2c*) is one of five that we use in our laboratory (others include NOHARM, RASCAL, BILOG, PARSCALE — see Hambleton et al., 1991 for descriptions) and is particularly suited to sports applications because it handles the Likert-style response format so prevalent in our field of study. PARSCALE also does this and allows estimation of two-parameter models. More widespread use of this software would lead to the development of better tests and better internal validity for the large number of research projects in our area that rely on test data (Fogarty, 1995). The adoption of latent-trait techniques would also help to address the measurement concerns raised by Schutz (1994).

References

Andersen, E.B. (1973). *Conditional inference and models for measuring*. Copenhagen: Mental-hygiejnisk.

Andersen, E.B. (1977). Sufficient statistics and latent trait models. *Psychometrika*, *42*, 69-81.

Andrich, D. (1981). *Rasch's models and Guttman's principles for scaling attitudes*. Paper presented at the International Conference on Objective Measurement. Chicago: The University of Chicago, Department of Education.

Andrich, D, Sheridan, B., & Lyne, A. (1991). *ASCORE: Manual of procedures*. Perth: Faculty of Education, University of Western Australia.

Assessment Systems Corporation (1989). *User's manual for the ITEMAN conventional item analysis program*. (Version 3.50). St. Paul, MN: Author.

Barndorff-Nielsen, O. (1978). *Information and exponential families in statistical theory*. NY: John Wiley.

Bock, R.D., Gibbons, R., & Muraki, E. (1988). Full information factor analysis. *Applied Psychological Measurement*, *12*(3), 261-280.

Browne, M.W., & Cudeck, R. (1993). Alternative ways of assessing model fit. In K.A. Bollen & J.S. Long (Eds.), *Testing structural equation models*. Newbury Park, Ca: Sage.

Crocker, L., & Algina, J. (1986). *Introduction to classical and modern test theory*. New York: Holt, Rhinehart & Winston.

Duda, J.L. (1989). Relationship between task and ego orientation and the perceived purpose of sport among high school athletes. *Journal of Sport and Exercise Psychology*, *11*, 318-335.

Englehard, G. (1984). Thorndike, Thurstone and Rasch: A comparison of their methods of scaling psychological traits. *Applied Psychological Measurement*, *8*, 21-38.

Fogarty, G. (1995). Some comments on the use of tests in sport settings. *International Journal of Sport Psychology*, *26*, 161-170.

Fogarty, G., & Bramston, P. (in press). Validation of the Lifestress Inventory for people with mild intellectual handicap. *Research in Developmental Disabilities*.

Guttman, L. (1944). A basis for scaling quantitative ideas. *American Sociological Review*, *9*, 139-150.

Guttman, L. (1950). Problems of attitude and opinion measurement. In Stouffer et al. (Eds.). *Measurement and prediction*. NY: John Wiley.

Hambleton, R. K., Swaminathan, H., & Rogers, H.J. (1991). *Fundamentals of item response theory*. Newbury Park, Ca: Sage.

Joreskog, K.G., & Sorbom, D. (1993). *New Features in LISREL 8*. Chicago: Scientific Software.

Kline, P. (1993). *The handbook of psychological testing*. London: Routledge.

Lord, F.M. (1974). *Individualized testing and item characteristic curve theory*. Princeton: ETS.

Lord, F.M. (1980). *Applications of item response theory to practical testing problems*. Hillsdale, NJ: Erlbaum.

McDonald, R.P. (1989). Future directions for item response theory. *International Journal of Educational Research*, 13(2), 127-143.

McDonald, R.P., & Marsh, H.W. (1990). Choosing a multivariate model: Noncentrality and goodness-of-fit. *Psychological Bulletin*, *107*, 247-255.

Mead, R.J. (1981). *Straight lines, units of measurement, and psychometrics*. Paper presented at International Conference on Objective Measurement. Chicago: The University of Chicago, Department of Education.

Rasch, G. (1960). *Probabilistic models for some intelligence and attainment tests*. Copenhagen: Danish Institute for Education Research.

Rasch, G. (1961). On general laws and the meaning of measurement in psychology. In *Proceedings of the Fourth Berkeley Symposium on Mathematical Statistics and Probability*, IV (p. 321-334). Berkeley: University of California Press.

Rasch, G. (1967). An informal report on the state of a theory of objectivity in comparisons. In L.J. Van der Kamp and C.A.J. Viek (Eds.), *Proceedings of the NUFFIC International Symposium Summer Session in Science at "Het Oude Hof"*. Leiden.

Schutz, R.W. (1994). Methodological issues and measurement problems in sport psychology. In S. Serpa, J. Alves, & V. Pataco (Eds.), *International perspectives on sport and exercise psychology* (pp. 35-56). Morgantown, WV: Fitness Information Technology.

Thorndike, E.L. (1919). *An introduction to the theory of mental and social measurements*. New York: Teachers' College, Columbia.

Thurstone, L.L. (1925). A method of scaling psychological and educational tests. *Journal of Educational Psychology*, *16*, 433-451.

Thurstone, L.L. (1928). The measurement of opinion. *Journal of Abnormal and Social Psychology*, *22*, 415-430.

Thurstone, L.L. (1959). *The measurement of values*. Chicago: University of Chicago Press.

Waller, N.G., & Reise, S.P. (1989). Computerised adaptive personality assessment. *Journal of Personality and Social Psychology*, *57*, 1051-1056.

Weiss, D.J., & Yoes, M.E. (1991). Item response theory. In R.K. Hambleton & J.N. Zaal (Eds.), *Advances in educational and psychological testing* (pp. 69-95). Boston: Kluwer Academic Publishers.

West, S.G., Finch, J.F., & Curran, P.J. (1995). Structural equation models with nonnormal variables: problems and remedies. In Bollen, K.A., Long, J.S. (Eds.), *Testing Structural Equation Models* (pp.56-75). Newbury Park, California: Sage.

Wright, B.D. (1973). Solving measurement problems with the Rasch model. *Journal of Educational Measurement*, *14*, 97-116.

Wright, B.D., & Douglas, G.A. (1975a). Best test design and self-tailored testing. *Research Memorandum No. 19*, Statistical Laboratory, Department of Education, University of Chicago.

Wright, B.D., & Douglas, G.A. (1975b). Best test design and self-tailored testing. *Research Memorandum No. 20*, Statistical Laboratory, Department of Education, University of Chicago.

Wright, B.D., & Douglas, G.A. (1977a). Best procedures for sample-free analysis. *Applied Psychological Measurement*, *1*, 281-294.

Wright, B.D., & Douglas, G.A. (1977b). Conditional versus unconditional procedures for sample-free item analysis. *Educational and Psychological Measurement*, *37*, 573-586.

Wright, B.D., & Masters, G.N. (1982). *Rating scale analysis*.

Chicago: University of Chicago Press.

Wright, B.D., & Panchapakesan, N. (1969). A procedure for sample-free item analysis. *Educational and Psychological Measurement*, *29*, 23-48.

Wright, B.D., & Stone, M.N. (1979). *Best test design*. Chicago: Mesa Press.

Chapter 25

ETHICS IN ASSESSMENT AND TESTING IN SPORT AND EXERCISE PSYCHOLOGY

Edward Etzel
Michael T. Yura
and
Frank Perna
West Virginia University

Johnnie came home one afternoon as asked to speak to his father. He said: "Dad, my teacher was telling us about a new word today in school that I really had a hard time understanding. What does the word 'ethical' mean?" His dad thought for a moment and replied. "Johnnie, you know that your uncle Sammie and I run a grocery store. If a customer came in and gave us $20.00 for $10.00 worth of goods, ethical would mean that I would have to split the extra $10.00 with your uncle Sammie."

— (Jones, 1993)

Ethics means different things to different people. What do we mean by "ethics" within the context of sport and exercise psychology? In general, ethics can be thought of as a set of moral ideals or principles that serve as guidelines for our thoughts and behaviors associated with our professional work. Ethics are those principles that influence the acquisition and use of knowledge and related skills offered to others who seek that knowledge or skills from those who are members of a particular profession.

Zeigler (1987) described six necessary features of occupations considered to be "professions"; one is "establishing a creed or code of ethics" (p. 139). In fact, the Association for the Advancement of Applied Sport Psychology (AAASP) Ethics Committee recently contacted more than 50 professions and noted that all of them possessed some form of ethical guidelines (Whelan, 1994).

Those who belong to a profession claim by virtue of their unique education, training, and experience to possess knowledge, skills, and abilities that allow them the privilege to "profess" their ability to assist people in ways that nonprofessionals are not qualified to assist. With the privilege to profess and practice a profession comes the implicit, personal responsibility

to serve others in a conscientious manner—a manner that does not jeopardize the public's well-being. By assuming this privilege and the obligations associated with it, professionals agree to serve people in ways that do not abuse or exploit them or put them at risk for harm (Whelan, 1993). Professional ethics, then, are intended to advance and maintain consumer trust in professions and their members. Ethics also suggest reasonable limits on work-related behavior. These guidelines also help regulate the use of influence or power associated with professional status and the special relationships professionals have with those they serve.

The purpose of this chapter is to discuss ethics regarding assessment and testing when one is involved in teaching, consulting, or conducting sport and exercise psychology research. A brief discussion follows concerning the general topics of ethical principles and standards, who must follow such guidelines, an historical overview of ethics in sport and exercise psychology, and certain controversial issues. Further, specifically related to ethics and testing in sport and exercise psychology, information will be presented on test and assessment instrument use, competence, test-user qualifications, use of obsolete instruments, computer interpretations, test-taker welfare, confidentiality and informed consent, and cultural and gender issues as well as psychometric and normative properties of assessment devices.

Principles And Standards

Professional ethical guidelines may take two general forms: (a) principles or (b) standards. First, we can think of ethical *principles* as codified, overarching assumptions that underlie professional values (e.g., competence, integrity, responsibility) that should be used to shape our professional judgments and behaviors. In contrast, ethical *standards* are codified guidelines that specify prescribed and proscribed behaviors in the various circumstances associated with the applied sport psychology workplace. The latter provide specific guidance concerning professional "should's and shouldn'ts." Furthermore, standards can help applied sport psychology professionals deal with the numerous "gray" areas associated with carrying out their various professional roles and obligations.

Who Must Follow Ethical Guidelines?

Any persons accepting membership in a professional organization must adhere to the organization's ethics code. Persons who are not members of an organization are not required to adhere to an organization's principles or standards. For example, a member of AAASP who is not a member of the American Psychological Association (APA) need not adhere to APA ethical standards.

Ethical principles and standards may be valuable to sport and exercise psychology professionals in a variety of life situations that require responsible decision making. However, ethical guidelines are intended to direct professional behavior only in professional settings, not in other contexts. The usefulness of ethical principles is limited only to the extent that those who choose to adopt them abide by the ideals contained in those principles.

Ethics Codes: Historical Perspectives

Interestingly, despite recent discussion about ethics in sport and exercise psychology (Petitpas, Brewer, Rivera, & Van Raalte, 1994; Whelan, Elkin, Etzel, & Meyers, 1995; Whelan, Elkin, & Myers, 1996) and in other professions (Bersoff, 1995; Canter, Bennett, Jones, & Nagy, 1994; Windt, Appleby, Battin, Francis, & Landesman, 1989), rather little can be found on the topic in the literature (and even less on ethics and assesment). Nearly 20 years ago, Ogilvie (1977, 1979) discussed practical ethical considerations for consultants working with professional sport organizations, emphasizing that ethical behavior was critical to their effective functioning. Subsequently, the importance of ethics relative to the conduct of research was emphasized by the International Society of Sport Psychology (Salmela, 1981). At the same time, Nideffer (1981) published the first book devoted to the ethics and practice of applied sport psychology. He then argued that applied sport psychology professionals should possess and follow a set of standardized ethical guidelines. His position, the position of psychologists in general, was that the ethical code of the APA should be adopted by applied sport psychology specialists.

The North American Society for the Psychology of Sport and Physical Activity (NASPSPA) and Canadian Society for Psychomotor Learning and Sport Psychology (CSPLSP) considered creating unique ethical standards during the late 1970s and early 1980s. Those organizations ultimately decided to adopt modified versions of APA ethical guidelines (Canadian Society for Psychomotor Learning and Sport Psychology, 1982; "Ethical Standards," 1982; Nideffer, 1987). The American Alliance for Health, Physical Education Recreation and Dance (AAHPERD) has not established ethical principles or standards (Singer, 1993). In the fall of 1994, AAASP adopted a set of ethical principles. AAASP continued to work toward developing and refining standards of ethical service provision (Williams,

1995) and adopted a code of ethical standards in the fall of 1996 that has direct applicability for the ethical use of tests and assessment instruments. Furthermore, AAASP leadership publishes a column entitled "Considering Ethics" in its newsletter.

The Current Ethics Debate

Today, there are few more controversial issues within the applied sport psychology community than those surrounding what (if any) ethical principles and standards should govern professional behavior. To say the least, a wide range of opinion exists (Coppel, Hanson, Hart, Gould, & Rotella, 1993; Singer, 1993; Zeigler, 1987).

On one hand, some people believe that ethical guidelines of other allied professions (e.g., counseling or psychology) are to varying degrees not appropriate or specific enough to be applicable across sport and exercise psychology functions (Sachs, 1993). Some holding this perspective maintain that the practice of applied sport psychology and many applied sport psychology activities, particularly those considered "educational" in nature (e.g., assessment of psychological skills, psychological skill training programs), should not be considered the practice of professional psychology (Singer, 1993). Accordingly, applied sport psychology consultants are primarily seen as teachers of mental skills or as mental training "coaches" (Dodson, 1995; Rotella, 1992). Similarly, the administration of sport-performance-related instruments for professional practice and research purposes does not need to be guided by an agreed-upon code of ethical principles or standards. Rather, a set of personal beliefs is seen as sufficient. Additionally, some professionals maintain that the unique settings applied sport psychology consultants work in and the populations they serve (e.g., athletes, coaches, sports medicine professionals) should shape and define the ethics of professionals (Silva, 1989).

A contrasting view holds that the behaviors in which the professional engages (e.g., assessment and intervention) and not the context (e.g., the population or level of psychopathology) should be the basis for a determination of the appropriateness of a given set of ethical guidelines. Furthermore, it is believed that the assessment and intervention practices that applied sport psychology professionals engage in are in many respects identical to those of the psychotherapeutic professions. Therefore, an ethics code like those developed and followed by similar professions (e.g., counseling, psychology, or social work) should be adopted and used by the sport psychology field.

Curiously, many people in the field may be apathetic or bored with the topic of ethics. Indeed, Whelan (1994) reported a less than one percent response rate from the entire membership of AAASP to a call for their views on the adoption of APA ethical principles by the AAASP membership. Similarly, only 28% of the 508 AAASP members (113 professionals) responded to a survey on ethical beliefs and behaviors in applied sport psychology initiated by the AAASP Executive Board (Petitpas, et al., 1994).

Why the Split View?

How is it possible to have such a divergence of opinion? A reason for this schism seems to be what Taylor (1994) referred to as the "divergent educational paths" of sport science professionals and those of other professional backgrounds (e.g., psychology, medicine). In fact, approximately half of AAASP members have professional "roots" in the sport and exercise sciences or physical education, whereas approximately half come from psychology or counseling backgrounds (AAASP, 1990). Members of these related professions often view and value ethics differently. Accordingly, some academic programs may emphasize professional ethics differently or more effectively incorporate into their curricula how to integrate ethical principles into work-related activities (Sachs, 1993). Beyond exposure to the ethics associated with the conduct of scientific research (Thomas & Nelson, 1996), course work concerning ethics may not be an integral part of sport and exercise science or physical education graduate curricula (L. Housner, personal communication, October 19, 1994).

In comparison to professional psychology programs, in which training in ethical issues is considered indispensable, such course work may not be included or emphasized in applied sport psychology graduate curricula that are not standardized (Silva, 1996). For example, Wilson and Ranft (1993) discovered that 94% of counseling psychology graduate programs require such course work.

Unfortunately, despite the view that issues associated with professional ethics may be the most critical to the future of applied sport psychology as we know it (Hardy, 1993), some professionals may have become disenchanted with the difficulty of the debate because: (a) they may be resistant to the prospect of having psychology-based ethics guidelines regulate their professional activities, (b) they may want to follow more sport-and exercise-specific guidelines, or (c) the adoption of specific ethical standards may represent an unwanted restriction of professional practice activities they may have been interested in, involved in, and profited from for many years.

Ethics in Assessment and Testing

The use of various psychometric instruments has historically distinguished psychologists from other helping professionals (e.g., counselors, social workers, psychiatrists). "Testing" is frequently employed by professionals across the broad range of sport and exercise psychology settings and clientele. Within sport and exercise psychology settings, such instruments are often used for assessment purposes in four areas: (a) clinical/counseling (e.g., evaluation of psychopathology or career-related interests), (b) health and exercise (e.g., mood changes as a function of participation in aerobic activity or self-reported behaviors in the physical domain), (c) performance enhancement (e.g., sport-related imagery capabilities), and (d) for special purposes (e.g., talent identification, neuropsychological testing) (Heil & Henschen, 1996).

Although some sport and exercise professionals have viewed testing as controversial (Heil, Henschen, & Nideffer, 1996; Silva, 1984) and may eschew testing (Orlick, 1989), many make systematic assessments, and many integrate testing as regular elements of their professional functions (Ostrow, 1996). Those who use tests and other assessment devices, do so for four basic reasons: (a) to efficiently and accurately assess the psychological characteristics and concerns of test takers, (b) to create hypotheses about appropriate intervention methods

(Kanfer & Goldstein, 1986), (c) to measure the progress of behavioral change in their clients' functioning, (d) to be accountable for their professional work, and (e) to gather information for teaching and research purposes.

Whatever one's academic background, professional position, or views on ethics in applied sport psychology, it is imperative that all professionals and "professionals in the making" be acutely aware of the many ethical and legal issues associated with the development and use of assessment devices (e.g., questionnaires and inventories) and the information they provide. Further, sport and exercise psychology educators, researchers, and clinicians must also adhere to the ethical principles and/or standards governing the assessment and testing processes in their profession.

Testing and Assessment

Before proceeding much further, it seems useful to define some key concepts for the reader. Specifically, what do we mean when we use the terms *test* and *assessment* in the following discussion? Anastasi (1982) defined a psychological *test* as "an objective and standardized measure of a sample of behavior" (p.22). Tests are "standardized" because the test content, administration, scoring, and interpretation procedures are consistent and comparable. Standardized tests are essential to the process of psychological assessment, which can be thought of as "the set of processes used...for developing impressions and images, making decisions and checking hypotheses about another person's pattern of characteristics that determines his or her behavior in interaction with the environment" (Sundberg, 1977, p. 21).

Testing Concerns

As noted earlier, psychological tests are regularly used in an ethical manner by numerous sport and exercise psychology professionals. Unfortunately, tests have been misused in the past, and they likely will continue to be misused by some in the future. For example, Nideffer (1981) reported several, avoidable improprieties, such as (a) not informing athletes about the purposes of testing, (b) compelling them to complete tests, (c) not informing test takers of the results, (d) not revealing how the results were to be used and by whom, (e) unqualified people's (e.g., coaches, management) using tests, (f) using tests for screening and team selection purposes that likely overextended the predictive validity limits of the instruments, and (g) inappropriate test selection and administration (e.g., Minnesota Multiphasic Personality Inventory to those who did not present with any psychopathological symptoms). All these behaviors are generally considered to be unethical and should be avoided.

In view of the above, and other related phenomena (e.g., repeated requests to test athletes and teams, breaches in confidentiality, high costs), it is no wonder that many athletes, coaches, and other organizations are often wary about testing. For example, controversies surrounding test misuse led the National Football League's Player's Association to halt the administration of personality tests to their athletes several years ago (Nideffer, 1981).

As an aside, this anti-testing bias does not appear to be as strong today as in years past (C. Carr, personal communication, March 6, 1996), as a few organizations use psychological tests for screening of draft prospects. Heil (1993) pointed out that astute sport psychologists should be alert to "strong preconceptions" about psychological testing that may exist in consultation environments, which may adversely influence their professional credibility and possibly jeopardize the effectiveness of their work with others.

Professional Test and Assessment Instrument Use

As noted earlier, no ethical standards governing the professional use of tests in sport and exercise settings have been universally embraced across disciplines. In the absence of such guidelines, which it is hoped will be developed, the most recent APA ethical code's guidelines concerning evaluation and assessment will be relied upon in this chapter to provide some useful parameters for these functions (APA, 1992). Due to the space constraints, only the most relevant of the APA guidelines relative to evaluation, assessment, and testing will be reviewed.

Testing in Professional Relationships

According to APA ethical standard 2.01, assessment and testing should be undertaken only within the context of a clearly defined professional or scientific relationship (e.g., when one is conducting a research project, providing counseling or consulting services, teaching sport psychology). Because a potential for harm exists, it is inappropriate to administer tests without a clear professional or scientific purpose. Psychological tests are not to be frivolously administered to friends, family members, partners, students, team members, or others. The public may be harmed by misinterpretation of results, making people aware of things about themselves they may not want to know or formulating a diagnosis based upon limited information.

Testing is a serious undertaking. Matarazzo (1995) tells us:

> The testing by one individual of another human's intellectual, personality and related characteristics is an invasion of privacy to an extent no less intimate than that involved in an examination carried our on that same individual's person or resources by a physician, attorney, or agent of the Internal Revenue Service. (p.295)

Therefore, testing should be used only when there is a specific research question(s), referral question(s), or instructive reason.

Test Use by Unqualified People

APA Standard 2.06 cautions professionals not to allow the use of assessment techniques by unqualified people. Untrained people (e.g., students, coaches, or inexperienced professionals) should be allowed to use such techniques only under the direct supervision of a qualified professional. When an applied sport psychology professional does agree to supervise the use of assessment devices, she or he is ultimately responsible for the actions of those she or he oversees (Canter et al. 1994). Professionals who choose to oversee the use of tests by unqualified others must be clear about the competencies of subordinates, monitor their work closely, and appreciate the implications of their decision to supervise them.

Relatedly, APA Standard 2.02 points out that it is unethical to release "raw" psychological data (e.g., numerical scores, written reports, notes about the testing situation, specific test-taker responses) and findings to those who are not qualified to interpret them (Tranel, 1995). The intent here is to prevent the misuse of data that may cause harm in some way(s) to test takers. Therefore, applied sport psychology professionals should refrain from releasing such information to coaches, management, teams, students, or other parties. Rather, they should provide carefully constructed, sensitive interpretations of the data within the context of the reason(s) for having administered testing in the first place (e.g., to understand an athlete's emotional response to injury, aspects of personality, or leadership potential).

Test Security

APA ethical Standard 2.10 advises professionals to maintain the security and integrity of tests and other assessment procedures they may use. They do not release test items, test manuals, or protocols because doing so may jeopardize the validity and reliability of an instrument when administered to those familiar with its content (i.e., test takers would no longer be naive). Test security is particularly important to protect for those instruments that are copywritten or intended for restricted use vis-à-vis legal regulations. For example, an applied sport psychology professional would not share a copy of the *Profile of Mood States* (McNair, Lorr, & Droppleman, 1971), a copywritten, restricted-use test, with an athletic team she or he is working with to educate them about their potential responses to injury that may occur in the future.

Clearly, test takers need to be informed about the general nature of instruments and the findings obtained from testing; students need to be trained in their specific makeup, administration, and interpretation; and professionals need to be able to consult about the interpretation of test data (Anastasi, 1982). However, professionals should be very careful not to reveal specific information about test purposes or content, especially those that involve the use of copywritten instruments that involve "contractual obligations" with publishers (APA, 1992).

Competence

Across allied professions, a fundamental shared principle centers on assumptions associated with "competence." The principle of competence presupposes that professionals provide services of the highest standard possible. They assume the responsibility to have acquired a broad range of understanding and skill, based on extensive training and experience in a variety of functional areas, assessment and testing being one of those areas.

Competence in assessment and testing implies that professionals develop and clarify personal and professional areas of expertise. Expertise is obtained not only from past education and training experiences but also from regular continuing education and training to maintain and/or enhance expertise. In fact, professionals *must* remain knowledgeable about the process of assessment and psychometrics in general. Further, APA ethical standards (i.e., 2.04, "Use of Assessment in General and With Special Populations") indicate that to be considered competent, it is the responsibility of test users, or supervi-

Table 1
Levels of Test Use and Their Qualifications

Level Symbol	User Qualifications
A	Nonpsychologists who understand the instrument they administer and the general reasons for testing
B	Knowledge of psychometrics, statistics, test construction, and appropriate psychology course work
C	Advanced degree in an appropriate profession or membership in state professional associations, professional state licensure, or professional national certification

sors of test users, to stay current with any developments surrounding the applicability, psychometric properties (i.e., validity and reliability), and normative information concerning any instruments or methodologies they use.

When specific training in these areas was not seen as necessary or was not possible during one's initial education and training, one must obtain appropriate training and supervision from another qualified professional before the lesser qualified individual administers these unfamiliar instruments. Moreover, it is crucial that untrained students or other less qualified professionals obtain such supervision on an ongoing basis for two reasons: (a) to better ensure the provision of high-quality services and thereby avoid potential test misemployment of existing instruments, and (b) to obtain training and guidance from qualified supervisors in the use of certain unfamiliar or new assessment devices.

Applied sport psychology professionals must also provide appropriate supervision to others (e.g., students, trainees, lesser qualified professionals seeking supervision) in the proper use of particular assessment instruments. Professionals are responsible for (a) obtaining permission to use and administer psychological instruments, (b) maintaining confidentiality and privilege associated with the results provided by instruments, and (c) overseeing the nature and quality of the interpretation of these results provided by supervisees to those tested.

Lastly, because they have the ethical obligation to maintain the highest level of psychological practice within their discipline, persons who have knowledge of the misuse of tests by unqualified persons are ultimately responsible for such misuse. Notifying an individual(s) about potential or apparent test misuse would be the first step a professional should take to attempt to intervene in such matters.

Test User Qualifications

Who is "qualified" to administer and interpret tests? Anastasi (1982) observed several years ago that "...with the diversification of the field and the consequent specialization of training, no psychologist is equally qualified in all areas" (p.47). However, for those who wish to be well-informed about, or claim to be competent in, the ethical practice of assessment and the use of psychological tests in sport and exercise settings, useful information can be found in the *Standards for Educational and Psychological Testing* (American Educational Research Association [AERA], American Psychological Association, and National Council on Measurement in Education [NCME], 1985). Specifically, the above-mentioned publication provides information for users on central issues such as (a) methods of evaluating the quality and applicability of tests and (b) the prac-

tice of testing, as well as (c) the consequences of test administration and interpretation. The knowledge contained in the *Standards* is indispensable to competent test users and students who wish to become proficient in this area.

Some general user qualification standards also exist for the employment of certain types of tests, questionnaires, and other assessment instruments. These standards date from the early APA system of test complexity classification (APA, 1954). Three basic levels of tests, were identified and are still in use today, in particular, by commercial test publishers (e.g., Consulting Psychologists Press) (See Table 1).

As Table 1 shows, "A"-level tests can be administered, scored, and interpreted by the least trained people. Examples of "A"-level instruments are achievement tests (e.g., California Achievement Test [CAT/5], McGraw-Hill, 1993) and sport-oriented instruments like the "Sport Imagery Questionnaire" (Vealey, 1993).

In comparison, "B"-and "C"-level instrument use requires greater knowledge and specialized training experiences (i.e., master's or doctoral level training in psychology or comparable areas). Examples of "B"- level tests are the Myers-Briggs Type Indicator (Briggs & Myers, 1962), the Strong Interest Inventory (Consulting Psychologists Press, 1994). In the realm of sport and exercise science, an instrument like the Profile of Mood States (McNair et al., 1971) would be considered a "B"-level instrument.

"C"-level tests are individually administered instruments that should be used by only the most highly trained people (APA, 1954). As seen in Table 1, users of such sophisticated instruments that typically are used to assess personality characteristics (e.g., Minnesota Multiphasic Personality Inventory-2) (Butcher, Dahlstrom, Graham, Telegren, & Kaemmer, (1989) or intelligence (e.g., Wechlser Adult Intelligence Scale-Revised) (Wechsler, 1981) must be licensed professionals, state or nationally certified, or at very least members of a state professional organization (Walsh & Betz, 1995). These guidelines would also be applicable in the realm of applied sport psychology when tests like the "Test of Attentional and Interpersonal Style" (Nideffer, 1976) are administered. As the reader might surmise, this tripartite system of restricting the use of a psychological instrument has its shortcomings. It has not been universally adopted by test publishers for sales control, or incorporated into the ethical standards of professional organizations.

Use of Obsolete Instruments

Although many tests undergo few modifications over time, many are revised on a regular basis (Ostrow, 1996). From an ethical perspective, APA standard 2.07 ("Obsolete Tests and

Outdated Test Results") directs test users to avoid developing hypotheses or making recommendations from (a) old data and/or (b) from outdated instruments. In the first instance, professionals should not utilize information on test takers that is probably not characteristic of them presently, unless one is comparing past data with current data for some purpose. Second, the basic purpose of a test is to validly and reliably measure the construct(s) or behavior(s) it is supposed to measure. If one chooses to use an instrument that is obsolete (i.e., an older form), it may not be as effective a measure as a newer form, unless there is evidence supporting the use of older versions with special populations (Canter et al., 1994).

Computer Interpretations

With the advent of sophisticated computer-assisted assessment programs for instruments like the Myers-Briggs Type Indicator, Strong Interest Inventory, and Minnesota Multiphasic Personality Inventory-2, use of detailed interpretations of test-taker responses can raise the quality of feedback when provided by individuals trained in their use and application. However, with the advent of computer-assisted assessment, it is also possible that people who have neither the academic training nor the practical experience to employ these instruments may cause harm to test takers. Putting complex as well as sensitive personal analyses in the hands of untrained or undertrained individuals can have both negative emotional as well as legal and ethical implications. For example, if an untrained person merely provides an athlete, team, or organization with "automated" interpretation printouts, without taking into consideration information about the person's reasons for seeking assistance, the purpose for having taken the test(s), various contextual/life factors, personality characteristics, attitudes toward the testing experience, and other special considerations (e.g., age, gender, ethnicity), the potential exists for misinterpretation of results and harm. Those who are less well trained will likely overlook useful background information and miss important data provided in a computerized interpretation. It is crucial that computer-generated reports be used and monitored with the same scrutiny as if they were scored and interpreted by the professional administering the instrument(s).

Client Welfare, Confidentiality, and Informed Consent

Respect for people's rights and dignity is seen as the primary goal of psychological ethics codes (Whelan, Elkin, & Meyers, 1996). To protect the welfare of consumers, the most recent AAASP statement of ethical ethical principles (1995) indicates that members should "do no harm...to ensure the dignity and welfare of individuals we serve and the public" (p.1). (Meyers, 1995). This respect is directly related to applied sport psychologists' responsibility to protect the right to privacy and confidentiality of those they serve in professional capacities.

Confidentiality is an ethical concept, and in some professional relationships, states, and institutions it is a legal right. It refers to the agreement by professionals not to reveal any information about the clients, students, research participants, or others they work with without the permission of those being served, or in some extreme legal instances (noted below) without their permission.

Within the context of assessment and testing, the nature of any information surrounding the reason(s) for testing or information obtained from testing must not be disclosed to anyone (e.g., coaches, parents, management) except in the following three legal circumstances: (a) if the test taker provides written permission to do so, or the permission of a parent or guardian is obtained in the case of a minor or someone who is somehow incapable of making decisions for him or herself; (b) if information obtained indicates that the test taker is dangerous to her or himself (i.e., suicidal) or to others (i.e., homicidal); or (c) if test information is subpoenaed by the court.

In advance of any assessment activities, this information must be clearly communicated to, understood by, and agreed upon by test takers as part of the act of providing *informed consent*. Informed consent must be provided by all test takers in all sport and exercise settings (e.g., research projects, performance enhancement consultations, clinical relationships). It is unethical to require or compel athletes, teams, or other clientele to participate in testing.

In every situation in which a professional agrees to conduct assessments, one must be clear about who the "real client" is (Ogilvie, 1979). One can ethically serve only one party and may share information about assessment and testing activities and findings only with that person. To avoid problems with credibility and trust, as well as ethical binds associated with so-called "dual relationships," professionals must set and adhere to specific boundaries.

Consistent with current AAASP and APA ethical guidelines, the applied sport psychology consultant's primary responsibility must be to serve the individual(s) whom the professional is evaluating or studying. It is crucial that the roles and responsibilities of the professional are outlined and agreed upon for the athlete client(s), research participant(s), and/or third parties (e.g., coaches, management, sports medicine staff) at the onset. Although a referral for testing may have been made by a third party (e.g., management, parents, coaches), it is imperative that the nature of the assessment consultation and its limitations relative to the boundaries of confidentiality be clearly stated and agreed upon by all involved parties during the initial consultation at and before the onset of any professional activity. Failure to secure this contract is unethical. Further, breaching a confidentiality contract by revealing confidential test-related information is grounds for malpractice.

An ethical/legal exception to the foregoing is important to note. Confidentiality is *not* guaranteed when the sport psychologist is testing a person under the age of 18. Because the young athlete client is legally considered a minor, privilege is held by the parent(s) or legal guardian(s) of that athlete. Privilege cannot be waived by an adolescent; it may be waived only by the parent or guardian of the young person. It is imperative that privilege be understood by all parties prior to any data-gathering interactions between a professional and an athlete. Any limits on the information gathered during assessments must be agreed upon with parent(s) prior to testing and understood by the young athlete if the young client and the sport psychology professional are to establish and engage in an open, trusting relationship.

It is important for professionals who are involved in assessment and testing, in either a research or consulting capacity, to be careful not to reveal the identities of person(s) or organizations associated with testing consultations and/or the data obtained from these activities (Sachs, 1993). When discussing or reporting any type of information dealing with evaluations (e.g., in scholarly writings or for educational purposes), the identities of test takers must be disguised. The focus should be on the results, not on individual client or team identities.

In addition to respecting others' rights to privacy and confidentiality, professionals must work to safeguard test takers rights of self-determination and autonomy. Test administrators need to insure that test takers are aware of these rights. Whether they are being asked to take various psychological measures to enhance sport performance or to participate in a research project, test takers have basic rights. They have the right to know why they are being asked to complete an instrument, how it might be useful to the professional consultation, and any other pertinent questions involved with their voluntary agreement to participate in the assessment process.

Test takers should provide written evidence of their understanding of the conditions surrounding assessments by signing an informed consent document. This is a contract that serves as a clear and fair agreement between the testing professional and the test taker. This agreement assumes that the athlete has the right to know whatever conclusions or results are drawn from the assessment data. Moreover, test takers should know that the information obtained from testing is their "property" and, therefore, is the subject of privilege and confidentiality issues.

Test takers also need to be informed about the limits of test results. Indeed, depending on the purpose for assessment, such data are intended to provide information on the psychological attributes of clients, to test research hypotheses, and/or to acquire information that may be useful to behavior change.

Test Feedback

Test takers have the right to know about the results of testing and related information. Feedback must be provided to test takers in clearly understandable language. Professionals should avoid using labels and technical jargon that may not be understandable to laypersons. They should also be sensitive to the language they use, the backgrounds of test takers, and adjust their interpretations with respect to test takers' "gender, age, race, ethnicity, national origin, religion, sexual orientation, disability, language, or socioeconomic status" (APA, 1992, p. 1604).

All test takers have the legal and ethical right to receive feedback related to (a) their performance on assessment devices and (b) the ways in which test results could be personally useful or possibly useful to third parties, (if written permission was granted by the test taker for others to know about assessment information). This is true even if the purpose of testing involves analyzing group attributes or behavior (e.g., motivation, attitudes toward sport, performance anxiety). Group assessment does not preclude the sport psychology professional from providing individual interpretations to each test taker. That is, it is appropriate to offer a follow-up appointment to interested athletes who want to obtain an individual interpretation of their test results.

It is also the ethical responsibility of researchers to provide individual interpretations to research participants, particularly to those whose test results reveal a potential problem. For example, if a test administrator discovers the anxiety level of the particular athlete is high enough to hamper normal functioning, it is the administrator's responsibility to contact that participant and offer to assist him or her to develop an appropriate strategy for dealing with that anxiety or to offer a referral.

Releases of Information

All test takers should be made aware of their rights concerning the dissemination of assessment data gathered by the sports psychology professional prior to any assessments. Because trust is one of the most crucial factors in the relationship between a sport psychology consultant and a client, it is important that athletes know that their test results will not be used in decisions associated with their athletic performance, team status, or other aspects of their sport participation without their permission or the permission of parents or guardians.

For persons less than 18 years of age, parents or guardians of minors own the privilege of access to all assessment data. In contrast, that right belongs to the athlete for people 18 years of age or older. Therefore, it will be necessary for those who have reached the age of 18 to sign a release of information for anyone else to have access to specific assessment data. Regardless of test-taker age, it is imperative that athletes be made aware that, even when a release is signed giving permission to share assessment data with others deemed appropriate by the test taker, permission is limited to the information specified in the release and must not include any other information in the athlete's records or any personal information shared with the sport psychology consultant. Coaches, parents, or other interested third parties do *not* have an inherent right to information obtained from an athlete's assessment.

It should be noted, however, that certain unique situations may exist that preclude the provision of feedback to test takers (e.g., when they waive the right to see information obtained from testing). These exceptions are based upon written agreements made by test takers (e.g., prospective professional athletes) before testing with organizations (e.g., sport teams), or in the case of forensic evaluations (See APA Standard 2.08, "Test Scoring and Interpretation Services").

Assessment Contracts

A practice that minimizes ethical problems is the use of contracts between the athlete/client and the sport psychologist professional. Contracts specify the responsibilities and policies concerning privilege and confidentiality. Such agreements set clear boundaries that demonstrate to those being assessed that their welfare is of paramount importance to the sport psychology professional.

Cultural and Gender Issues

Cultural Considerations

Cultural issues are important and pertinent to assessment and testing in sport and exercise psychology. Unfortunately, limited attention has been paid to cross-cultural differences in applied sport psychology (Duda & Allison, 1990). Nevertheless, these concerns are critical to the development, administration, and interpretation of assessment devices with sport-and exercise-related populations. (See Duda & Hayashi, this volume.)

Professionals' backgrounds and skills in these areas as applied to assessment and treatment is essential to effective and ethical professional practice (Parham, 1996). Assessment of culturally diverse populations can be effective if the tester displays both cultural sensitivity and competence when working with diverse sport and exercise populations. It is crucial to develop this sensitivity and skills when teaching assessment to others (e.g., students, supervisees) who will be working with diverse populations. The ethical person should not engage in evaluating persons with special characteristics that have not been included in their training or experience.

Because sport psychology professionals employ various instruments when working with diverse populations, using instruments appropriate for a particular group of people is paramount. Unfortunately, efforts to develop "culture-fair" or "culture-reduced" tests have generally been unsuccessful; there are no "culture-free" tests. Therefore, it is the responsibility of the sport psychology professional to (a) use instruments that minimize potential cultural bias, (b) take into consideration the background of the population that an instrument was designed for and normed on vis-à-vis the general nature of the population one is testing, as well as (c) weigh any limitations of certainty that may be associated with the use of a test(s) with people from diverse backgrounds (APA, 1992; Sachs, 1993).

Paniagua (1994) provided some guidelines that can be used to minimize bias in assessment with multicultural groups:

1. Professionals should examine any of their own biases and prejudices before evaluating people who are from different racial or ethnic backgrounds than their own;
2. Professionals should evaluate any socioeconomic variables and culturally related syndromes that may affect test use;
3. Professionals should ask culturally relevant questions; and
4. Professionals should attempt to use the least potentially biased instruments available. (p. 106)

Sport psychology professionals also must take into account issues such as family, education, disability status, and cultural background when interpreting test results. These factors may affect test scores and assessment outcomes.

Gender Issues

Gill (1995) contends that the consideration of gender issues and their professional implications are not commonplace in exercise and sport psychology practice. Nevertheless, they probably influence everything we do. APA Standard 2.03 indicates that test users need to be sensitive to gender considerations when selecting, administering, scoring, and interpreting any assessment techniques (APA, 1992).

An example of an assessment area many applied sport psychology professionals are likely to be involved in with female athletes is that of interest testing (i.e., relative to various transitions, such as major selection, occupational choice, and retirement). Betz and Fitzgerald (1987) discuss the problem of attempting to integrate interest-inventory results in a society of gender-role socialization and occupational gender segregation.

The process involves the socialization of women into traditional occupations and roles, as well as personality traits, interests, and skills. These phenomena may also affect male response styles on various instruments. Although some changes have been made in the construction of certain instruments (e.g., Strong Interest Inventory), careful consideration needs to be made to develop sensitivity to response patterns of women who are more similar to their male counterparts (and vice versa), rather than making the false assumption that all women or men respond similarly. Walsh and Betz (1995) suggested that these patterns may lead to interpreting test results that perpetuate female overrepresentation in traditional roles.

Walsh and Betz (1995) provided two useful suggestions relative to the minimization of unethical gender bias in testing. First, test users must regularly consult test reviews to see that language bias and test-item content insensitive to bias has been addressed and minimized. Second, testing consumers need to be sensitive to gender-role socialization for males and females that may adversely affect test-response patterns. Professionals also need to regularly self-assess any gender biases or prejudices that may undesirably impact their work with test takers and take efforts to minimize their effects.

Psychometric and Normative Properties of Assessment Devices

Psychometric Issues

As noted earlier, there are some applied sport psychologists who refrain from using any type of psychological assessment devices or inventories in their normal practice. However, many do regularly rely on the use of such instruments to teach or to do research, to understand presenting psychological concerns, and to develop interventions.

For those sport psychology professionals who use instrumentation, it is crucial that they clearly understand the unique psychometric properties of the test(s) they administer and interpret. It is essential that test properties such as validity and reliability be fully understood and examined before the administration and interpretation of any instrument to an athlete or other test taker.

Validity issues need to be reviewed to assure not only that a selected test measures what it reports to measure, but also that the purpose of the testing will be consistent with the purpose of the instrument being employed. Knowledge of content- and criterion-related validities is particularly relevant to the ethical use and application of tests in general, as well as of the specific instruments used by applied sport psychologists (Thomas & Nelson, 1996).

One additional psychometric component that applied sport psychologists need to understand is that of the "standard error of measurement" (SEM). They need incorporate this concept attempting to interpret specific scores associated with any instrument being administered. Further, helping test takers understand SEM is crucial when feedback is provided to them or to other third parties to whom test takers have provided a release for the professional communicate the test findings. The SEM helps the client who has been tested to recognize the potential variety in his or her scores and to appreciate that a score produced on a test may or may not remain stable over time. Without considering the SEM, the likelihood of unethically misinterpreting test results for individual athletes or groups of athletes is highly possible.

Test Norm Issues

Another issue concerning the ethical use of psychometrically sound instruments involves normative data associated with the instrument. Although a sport psychology professional may use a measure in a manner consistent with the intent of the test developer, the use of outdated norms and test use with populations different from those the tests were normed on is unethical. In contrast, it is advisable to develop local norms and establish the instruments' criterion validity for a previously undersampled groups (e.g., athletes, ethnic minorities, women).

Common Interpretation Issues

Assessment anxiety. Conditions affecting the athlete at the time of an evaluation (e.g., test setting, test-taker characteristics) must be considered with sensitivity if we are to understand the scores test takers produce. Indeed, it probably is equally important to attend to the client's test-taking behavior to understand how a person takes a test as it is to know what test she or he took (Sundberg, 1977).

To illustrate, ethical professionals need to be attentive to a common, natural artifact of the evaluative process (i.e., test anxiety). Just as performance anxiety may affect performance on the field, on the court, or in the pool, conditions such as test anxiety can adversely affect test-takers' performance when completing an instrument. APA Standard 2.05 suggests that if test takers are observed to have been test anxious or report having felt so, ethical professionals must take into account the potential impact of such experiences and factor in its potential impact into their interpretation of test data.

Response styles. Another common factor that may influence the validity or reliability of test data in sport and exercise settings concerns response styles to test questions (Nideffer, 1981). Issues such as "faking good" (minimization) or "faking bad" (exaggeration) impact the accuracy and usefulness of test scores. For example, athletes may not want to reveal certain things about themselves for fear that such revelations may have an impact on their team status or "draftability," in the case of professional prospects. If a sport psychology professional has chosen an appropriate and sound instrument for use with a particular athlete or group of athletes, and if the circumstances or goals associated with the assessment appear consistent with the purpose of the instrument, it seems logical that the results could be used in a valid manner. However, if a test taker responded to this instrument with a unique response style (e.g., responding consistently indifferently on a 5-point Likert scale), this may technically invalidate the results for that particular athlete. Such response patterns must be noted by the sport psychology professional when conducting any evaluation.

Conclusion

The issues surrounding the ethical use of tests and other assessment methods are critical to many applied sport and exercise psychology consultants in their functioning across professional roles. Within the limits of this chapter, we have tried to provide an overview of general ethical guidelines relevant to professionals involved in psychological assessment and testing in sport and exercise settings. Such a task is a formidable one. Clearly, this chapter is not in any way an all-encompassing reference. Therefore, we would hope that the reader would look at the foregoing as an ambitious attempt to provide some useful information on the subject at hand and consult one or more of the many references that follow to assist in thinking about ethics in testing and general professional practices.

References

American Educational Research Association, American Psychological Association, & National Council on Measurement in Education (1985). *Standards for educational and psychological testing.* Washington, DC: American Psychological Association.

American Psychological Association (1954). *Technical recommendations for psychological tests and diagnostic techniques.* Washington, DC: Author.

American Psychological Association (1992). Ethical principles and code of conduct. *American Psychologist, 47,* 1597-1611.

Anastasi, A. (1982). Psychological testing (5th ed.). New York: Macmillan.

Bersoff, D. (1995). *Ethical conflicts in psychology.* Washington, DC: American Psychological Association.

Betz, N., & Fitzgerald, L. (1987). *The career psychology of women.* New York: Academic Press.

Briggs, K., & Myers, I., (1962). *Myers-Briggs Type Indicator.* Princeton, NJ: Educational Testing Service.

Butcher, J., Dahlstrom, W., Graham, J., Telegren, A., & Kaemmer, B. (1989). *Minnesota Multiphasic Personality Inventory: Manual for administration and scoring.* Minneapolis, MN: University of Minnesota Press.

Canadian Society for Psychomotor Learning and Sport Psychology (1982). *Ethical standards for sport psychology educators, researchers, and practitioners.* Unpublished manuscript.

Canter, M., Bennett, B., Jones, S., & Nagy, T. (1994). *Ethics for psychologists: A commentary on the APA ethics code.* Washington, DC: American Psychological Association.

Coppel, D., Hanson, T., Hart, E., Gould, D., & Rotella, R. (1993). Professional issues influencing ethical behavioral choices. In *Proceedings of the Association for the Advancement of Applied Sport Psychology Conference* (p. 30). Montreal, Quebec: Association for the Advancement of Applied Sport Psychology.

Dodson, J. (May, 1995). The brain game. *Golf Magazine,* pp. 20, 24, 33.

Duda, J., & Allison, M. (1990). Cross-cultural analysis in exercise and sport psychology: A void in the field. *Journal of Sport & Exercise Psychology, 12,* 114-131.

Ethical standards for provision of services by NASPSPA members (1982, Fall). *NASPSPA Newsletter,* pp. ii-vi.

Gill, D. (1995). Gender issues: A social-educational perspective. In S. Murphy (Ed.), *Sport psychology interventions* (pp. 205-234). Champaign, IL: Human Kinetics.

Hardy, C. (1993, Winter). President's message. *AAASP Newsletter,* pp. 1, 3.

Heil, J. (1993). Diagnostic methods and measures. In J. Heil (Ed.), *Psychology of sport injury* (pp. 89- 112). Champaign, IL: Human Kinetics.

Heil, J., & Henschen, K. (1996). Assessment in sport and exercise psychology. In J. Van Raalte & B. Brewer (Eds.), *Exploring sport and exercise psychology* (pp. 229-255). Washington, DC: American Psychological Association.

Heil, J., Henschen, K., & Nideffer, R. (1996). Psychological assessmentin applied sport psychology. *Journal of Applied Sport Psychology, 8* (Suppl.), S32.

Jones, S. (1993, April). *Revised ethical standards for the American Psychological Association.* Paper presented at the meeting of the West Virginia Psychological Association, Canaan Valley, WV.

Kanfer, F., & Goldstein, A. (Eds.) (1986). *Helping people change: A textbook of methods* (3rd ed.). New York: Pergamon.

Mattarazzo, J. (1995). Computerized clinical psychological test interpretations: Unvalidated plus all mean and no sigma. In D. Bersoff (Ed.), *Ethical conflicts in psychology* (pp. 295-297). Washington, DC: American Psychological Association.

McNair, D., Lorr, M., & Dropplemen, L. (1971). *Profile of Mood States.* San Diego: Educational and Industrial Testing Services.

Meyers. A. (1995, Winter). Ethical principles of AAASP. *AAASP Newsletter,* pp.15, 21.

Nideffer, R. (1981). *The ethics and practice of applied sport psychology.* Ithaca, NY: Mouvement Publications.

Nideffer, R. (1987). Applied sport psychology. In J. May & M. Asken (Eds.), *Sport psychology: The psychological health of the athlete* (pp. 1-18). New York: PMA.

Ogilvie, B. (1977). Walking the perilous path of the team psychologist. *The Physician and Sports Medicine, 5,* 62-68.

Ogilvie, B. (1979). The sport psychologist and his professional credibility. In P. Klavora & J. Daniel (Eds.), *Coach, athlete, and the sport psychologist* (pp. 44-55). Toronto: University of Toronto.

Orlick, T. (1989). Reflections of sportpsych consulting with individual team sport athletes at summer and winter Olympic games. *The Sport Psychologist, 3,* 358-365.

Ostrow, A. (Ed.) (1996). *Directory of psychological tests in the sport and exercise sciences* (2nd ed.). Morgantown, WV: Fitness Information Technology.

Paniagua, F. (1994). *Assessing and testing culturally diverse clients.* Thousand Oaks, CA: Sage.

Parham, W. (1996). Diversity within intercollegiate athletics: Current profile and welcomed opportunities. In E. Etzel, A. Ferrante, & J. Pinkney (Eds.), *Counseling college student-athletes: Issues and interventions* (2nd ed.) (pp. 27-53). Morgantown, WV: Fitness Information Technology.

Petitpas, A., Brewer, B., Rivera, P., & Van Raalte, J. (1994). Ethical beliefs and behaviors in applied sport psychology: The AAASP ethics survey. *Journal of Applied Sport Psychology, 6,* 135-151.

Rotella, R. (1992, Fall). Sport psychology: Staying focused on a common and shared mission for a bright future. *AAASP Newsletter,* pp. 8-9.

Sachs, M. (1993). Professional ethics in sport psychology. In R. Singer, M. Murphy, & L. Tennant (Eds.), *Handbook of research in sport psychology* (pp. 921-932). New York: MacMillan.

Salmela, J. (1981). *The world sport psychology sourcebook.* Ithaca, NY: Mouvement Publications.

Silva, J. (1984). Personality and sport performance: Controversy and challenge. In J. Silva & R. Weinberg (Eds.), *Psychological foundations of sport* (pp.59-69). Champaign, IL: Human Kinetics.

Silva, J. (1989). Toward the professionalization of sport psychology. *The Sport Psychologist, 3,* 265- 273.

Silva, J. (1996). A second move: Confronting persistent issues that challenge the advancement of applied sport psychology. *Journal of Applied Sport Psychology, 8* (Suppl.), S52.

Singer, R. (1993). Ethical issues in clinical services. *Quest, 45,* 88-105.

Sundberg, N. (1977). *Assessment of persons.* New York: Prentice-Hall.

Taylor, J. (1994). Examining the boundaries of sport science and psychology trained practitioners in applied sport psychology: Title usage and area of competence. *Journal of Applied Sport Psychology, 6,* 185-195.

Thomas, J., & Nelson, J. (1996). *Research methods in physical activity* (3rd ed.). Champaign, IL: Human Kinetics.

Tranel, D. (1995). The release of psychological data to nonexperts: Ethical and legal considerations. In D. Bersoff (Ed.), *Ethical conflicts in psychology* (pp. 274-280). Washington, DC: American Psychological Association.

Vealey, R. (1993). Imagery training for performance enhancement and personal development. In J. Williams, (Ed.), *Applied sport psychology: Personal growth to peak performance* (pp. 201-224). Mountain View, CA: Mayfield.

Walsh, B., & Betz, N. (1995). *Tests and assessment* (3rd ed.). Englewood Cliffs, NJ: Prentice Hall.

Wechsler, D. (1981). *Manual for the Wechsler Adult Intelligence Scale-Revised.* New York: Psychological Corporation.

Whelan, J. (1994, Summer). Considering ethics. *AAASP Newsletter,* pp. 24, 27.

Whelan, J., Elkin, T., Etzel, E., & Meyers, A. (1995, September). *Ethics in exercise and sport psychology: Consideration of specific guidelines.* Workshop conducted at the annual meeting of the Association for the Advancement of Applied Sport Psychology, New Orleans, LA.

Whelan, J. Elkin, T., & Meyers, A. (1996). Ethics in sport and exercise psychology. In J. Van Raalte & B. Brewer (Eds), *Exploring sport and exercise psychology* (pp. 431-447). Washington, DC: American Psychological Association.

Williams, J. (1995). Applied sport psychology: Goals, issues and challenges. *Journal of Applied Sport Psychology, 7,* 81-91.

Wilson, L., & Ranft, V. (1993). The state of ethical training for counseling psychology doctoral students. *The Counseling Psychologist, 21,* 445-456.

Windt, P., Appleby, P., Battin, M., Francis, L., & Landesman, B. (Eds.). (1989). *Ethical issues in the professions.* Englewood Cliffs, NJ: Prentice-Hall.

Zeigler, E. (1987). Rationale and suggested dimensions for a code of ethics for sport psychologists. *The Sport Psychologist, 1,* 138-150.

Chapter 26

APPLIED SPORT PSYCHOLOGY: MEASUREMENT ISSUES

Robin S. Vealey
and
Megan Garner-Holman
Miami University

Because human thought, emotion, and behavior are not easily quantifiable, measurement in sport psychology has remained a dominant issue throughout the evolution of the field. Early personality research in the 1960s was deemed largely inconclusive due to controversy surrounding the measurement of broad personality traits. Debate arose in the 1970s as to the external validity and relevance of measuring psychological phenomena of interest to sport psychologists within laboratory settings (Martens, 1979). In the 1980s, the emphasis on cognitive psychology spurred a shift in the dominant psychobehavioral measures in sport psychology from traits or motives towards cognitions or self-perceptions. The 1980s were also marked by a rise in the use of psychophysiological measures (Hatfield & Landers, 1983) to understand and predict human behavior in sport. Thus, questions surrounding *what* should be measured as well as *how*, *where*, *when*, and *why* phenomena should be measured have remained dominant issues in sport psychology.

Measurement issues such as what, how, where, when, and why have particular relevance to applied sport psychology. In the context of this chapter, *applied sport psychology* is defined as the application of psychological knowledge to enhance the personal development and performance of individuals in sport. Measurement in applied sport psychology involves specialized validity and ethical concerns regarding the assessment of psychobehavioral change processes that occur in sport psychology interventions with athletes. Thus, the purpose of this chapter is to examine the status of measurement in sport psychology in relation to applied intervention in the field.

The chapter is divided into four sections. First, a framework from which to examine measurement issues in applied sport psychology is presented. Second, a brief overview of assessment methods in applied sport psychology is presented to ensure a common understanding of *how* phenomena are measured. Third,

the main objectives for measurement in both professional practice and applied research in sport psychology are identified to understand *what* phenomena related to intervention in sport psychology are measured and *why* it is important to measure them. Finally, a critical analysis of measurement issues in applied sport psychology is provided, and future directions for measurement consideration in applied sport psychology are suggested.

Interspersed throughout the chapter are data representing the results of a survey conducted by the authors for this chapter. The survey was conducted to examine applied measurement practices and perceptions of various assessment issues from the perspective of active applied sport psychology consultants. A purposive or criterion-based sampling technique (Goetz & LeCompte, 1984) was used as the authors selected consultants for inclusion in the survey if they were Certified Consultants of the Association for the Advancement of Applied Sport Psychology (AAASP) or if they were well-known practicing sport psychology consultants in their country. One hundred questionnaires were mailed to consultants in North America, Europe, and Australia. The questionnaire contained 12 open-ended questions that assessed demographic information and consultants' uses of various assessment techniques in their intervention with athletes. The response rate was 68% ($N = 68$), and consultants returned the anonymous questionnaires in stamped envelopes provided by the authors. Seventy-seven percent of the sample were primarily employed as academicians, with 18% primarily employed as clinicians. The highest academic degree earned by 97% of the sample was a doctorate, whereas the remaining 3% had earned master's degrees. Fifty-six percent of the sample earned their degrees in the field of psychology as opposed to 41% who earned their degrees in kinesiology-related fields. The results are presented throughout the chapter to provide relevant evidence as to the current uses of various assessment techniques in applied sport psychology.

A Framework for Assessment in Applied Sport Psychology

The field of applied sport psychology is extremely diverse with professionals trained in such fields as counseling psychology, social psychology, clinical psychology, kinesiology, and education. This diversity in training is logically followed by differences in competencies, approaches to assessment and intervention, philosophies, and style. Regarding measurement or assessment, many models or approaches have been established for applied sport psychology that focus the assessment and resulting intervention based on the training and background of the author (e.g., Davies & West, 1991; Murphy, 1995; Nideffer, 1981). Although there is room in the field for the rich diversity of assessment approaches, several contentious issues have arisen, such as professional boundary maintenance, perceptions of assessment effectiveness, and even the very use of the term *sport psychologist*.

Basically, issues regarding measurement or assessment in applied sport psychology may be divided into two broad categories. Although these two categories of issues are related, they are differentiated here based on their resultant consequences. The first category includes *practical issues*, such as what approaches to or methods of assessment are most effective at what times for which athletes. For the most part, practical issues focus on the effectiveness or quality of assessment, and the most extreme negative consequence within this category for athletes would be less than accurate or useful assessment.

The second category of assessment issues in applied sport psychology includes *ethical issues* (see previous chapter by Etzel, Yura, and Perna in this volume), such as who is qualified to use which assessments as well as how these assessments should or should not be used (such as for team selection or retention). The ethical issues frame problems in the field with much direr consequences for athletes and the integrity of sport psychology. That is, if consultants use assessment techniques or methods beyond their boundaries of competence or if they allow these techniques to be used inappropriately, then athletes are exploited, and the field of applied sport psychology is misrepresented and undermined.

Throughout the remainder of the chapter, examples from these two categories of assessment issues are examined. To provide a generic organizational scheme for issues surrounding measurement in applied sport psychology, a framework is presented in Fig-

ure 1 that depicts four broad domains that serve as the basis for assessment and subsequent intervention and evaluation with athletes.

The first, and most obvious, domain includes the individual characteristics of the athlete, such as age, level, goals, and personality characteristics. Although unidimensional approaches to assessment might focus totally on athlete characteristics as the basis for subsequent intervention strategies, effective assessment in applied sport psychology should account for other domains within the framework. The second domain relevant to sport psychology assessment includes contextual characteristics, such as coaches, teammates, family, and time of competitive season. Although the actual assessment of contextual factors varies widely based on consultant training and philosophy, most emerging approaches emphasize the importance of considering this domain in sport psychology assessment (e.g., Danish, Petitpas, & Hale, 1995; Hellstedt, 1995; Whelen, Meyers, & Donovan, 1995). The third factor, organizational culture of sport, may be considered another contextual domain, but it is depicted separately to emphasize its significance. Sport, as a subculture of

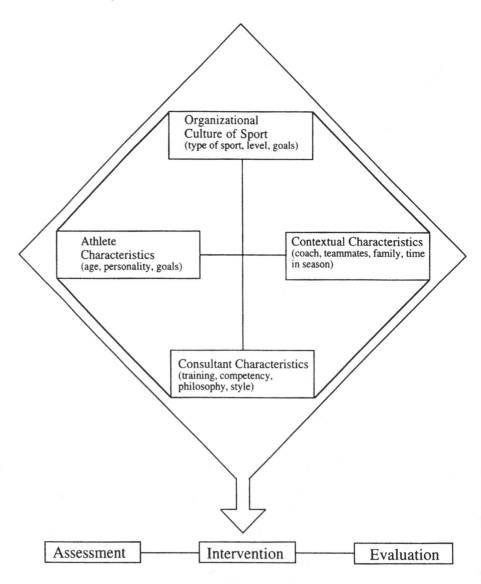

Figure 1. Multidomain assessment framework for applied sport psychology.

larger society, has an organizational culture of its own based on the type and level of sport and goals of the organization. Clearly, effective assessment in applied sport psychology must account for whether the athlete is a scholarship football player at a Division I university, a recreational bowler, or a professional ice hockey player for the Detroit Red Wings. The final domain to be considered in the assessment process includes the characteristics of the consultant, such as training, competency, philosophy, and style. This domain is included to emphasize that assessment can take many forms and follow several models based on the unique approach and training of the consultant.

Despite the diversity in assessment approaches, the point of the framework is to demonstrate that all assessment should take into account these four domains. Practical and ethical issues arise when one domain is ignored, such as when a consultant misperceives his or her expertise, fails to consider the organizational culture of a particular sport, or ignores a crucial contextual factor such as coaches' feedback or parental overinvolvement. Practical and ethical issues also arise when incongruency occurs between these domains, such as when an organizational culture's goals for assessment are antithetical to the philosophy of the consultant (e.g., personality testing for team selection) or when a consultant attempts to force a style or method that is not effective within the unique context and individual characteristics of the athlete. Overall, then, major assessment issues in applied sport psychology may be addressed and perhaps resolved via clear conceptualization of the assessment process within this framework. In the next two sections, types and uses of assessment in applied sport psychology are overviewed to examine issues that arise within the framework.

HOW Phenomenon Are Measured in Applied Sport Psychology

Although this chapter is certainly not a primer on research methods, it seems important to briefly identify the various assessments methods used in applied sport psychology. Interestingly, the major methods of psychological assessment in the ancient world were astrology, physiognomy, and humorology (McReynolds, 1986). Although it may seem absurd to assume that human behavior can be understood by examining the stars, the physical features of individuals, or the bodily fluids of individuals, these ancient methods of assessment pioneered the important idea that psychological makeups of individual persons can be systematically described.

The beginning of a more scientific approach to assessment occurred in the 17th century when Thomasius (1692) developed the first system of psychological rating scales, which he published in an article titled "New Discovery of a Well-Grounded and for the Community Most Necessary Science to Know the Secrets of the Hearts of Other Men [sic] From Daily Conversation, Even Against Their Will." Although Thomasius' intent may be amusing to us now, his work is significant in that it established that psychological characteristics may be conceptualized in quantitative terms. The historical and sociocultural bases of psychological measurement provide important perspectives on the assumptions and issues regarding the efficacy of assessment in applied sport psychology. For example, certain sport psychologists disagree with Thomasius' contention that

personality characteristics can be quantified via questionnaires in a way that is useful in their applied work with athletes (e.g., Halliwell, 1990; Rotella, 1990). Also, Thomasius' orthodox science approach, which empowers the investigator as knowing more than the individuals being assessed ("even against their will"), has been challenged in both research and practice in sport psychology (e.g., Dewar & Horn, 1992; Gill, 1994; Krane, 1994; Martens, 1987).

Along with historical perspective, another important aspect to consider is that psychological assessment is integrally related to the theoretical perspective of the consultant. This theoretical perspective is included in the consultant characteristics domain in the assessment framework shown in Figure 1. Nideffer (1981) states that the selection of a theoretical perspective is imperative for the practicing sport psychologist because this theoretical perspective should then determine the assessment focus. Thus, theory provides a conceptual model for the assessment process and for the subsequent intervention with athletes. From an epistemological standpoint, assessment is never completely standardized because the kinds of information sought are heavily influenced by the consultants' theoretical emphasis. Phares (1992) emphasizes that assessment should not assume to target reality or truth because there are different theoretical realities (e.g., trait reality, cognitive reality, behavioral reality). According to Phares, the purpose of assessment is simply to describe in a useful way. Therefore, assessment in applied sport psychology is not seeking truth, but rather useful ways of describing and understanding athletes in an attempt to enhance their sport participation.

Typically, practitioners in sport psychology utilize five types of methods to systematically assess the thoughts, feelings, and behaviors of athletes. These common methods include the psychological inventory, survey questionnaire, interview, behavioral observation, and psychophysiological measures. Although there are other assessment methods used in psychology (e.g., projective techniques, archival or case histories), the five methods presented here are the most typical and widely used in applied sport psychology. Because many issues and misunderstandings surround the use of assessment methods in sport psychology, it is important to establish a common understanding and definition of these methods.

The first type of method, the *psychological inventory*, is a standardized measure of a specific sample of behavior (Anastasi, 1988). Standardization implies uniformity of procedures in developing, administering, and scoring these inventories based on accumulated evidence for the validity and reliability of the measures. In applied sport psychology, two types of psychological inventories are used. The first category of inventories includes general inventories that assess psychological dimensions stemming from a particular theoretical orientation, such as the Minnesota Multiphasic Personality Inventory (MMPI; Hathaway & McKinley, 1943), the 16 Personality Factor Questionnaire (16PF; Cattell, 1946), the Test of Attentional and Interpersonal Style (TAIS: Nideffer, 1976), and the Profile of Mood States (McNair, Lorr, & Droppleman, 1981). The second category of psychological inventories is sport-specific measures that have been developed to assess the thoughts, feelings, and behaviors of athletes within the context of their sport participation. Examples of these types of inventories include the Athletic Motivation Inventory (AMI; Tutko, Lyon, & Ogilvie, 1969), the Competitive State Anxiety Inventory-2 (CSAI-2; Martens, Vealey, & Burton, 1990), and the Psychological Skills Inventory for Sports (PSIS; Mahoney, Gabriel, & Perkins, 1987).

It is important to consider that psychological inventories are standardized and validated for use *by* certain types of individuals *with* certain types of individuals *for* certain types of situations. Inventories developed for licensed psychologists to use in clinical assessment are inappropriate for consultants to use outside of that area of expertise (American Psychological Association, 1985). Any inventory used in assessment should be completely understood by the consultant and clearly within that consultant's boundaries of training and practice. Misuse of inventories based on a lack of competence and/or training is one of the main ethical issues in applied sport psychology, and the results of this misuse include exploitation of athletes and a breach of professional integrity. In our consultant survey, eight main ethical concerns regarding the use of psychological inventories in applied sport psychology were voiced. The top concern listed by consultants was a lack of training or competence by the person administering the inventory. In descending order as cited by consultants, other concerns were confidentiality, use of instruments that lack established psychometric properties, failure to give athletes feedback on results, inappropriate use of inventories, use of inventories for selection or recruiting, misinterpretation of results, and too much emphasis on inventory results. These concerns all echo one important theme: Choosing assessment techniques in applied sport psychology involves thorough knowledge and training related to that type of assessment and careful and deliberate planning as to how the assessment is conducted, interpreted, and used within the total intervention program.

In conjunction with this ethical issue, the practical issue as to the value of using psychological inventories in sport psychology intervention has been debated extensively in the literature. Unfortunately, this debate is often typified by polarized views that fail to consider that using or not using inventories is dependent upon consultant style and training as well as the influence of the other domains represented in the chapter framework. Certain consultants feel the use of inventories is unnecessary and even detrimental to their style of intervention work (Dorfman, 1990; Halliwell, 1990; Orlick, 1989; Ravizza, 1990;

Rotella, 1990), yet other consultants indicate that psychological inventories are facilitative when used in conjunction with other methods (Gardner, 1995; Gordin & Henschen, 1989; May & Brown, 1989; Nideffer, 1981, 1989; Perna, Neyer, Murphy, Ogilvie, & Murphy, 1995). This debate seems to be a pseudo-issue as deciding whether or not to use psychological inventories in interventions is simply a choice made by consultants based on their unique philosophies and experience. Some consultants evidently feel that interviews and observation facilitate their assessment of athletes more so than do psychological inventories. The framework presented in this chapter as the basis for assessment in applied sport psychology advocates the importance of considering multiple domains in applied sport psychology, yet allows for individual differences in the exact methods used for assessment in each domain.

The second type of assessment method used in applied sport psychology is *survey questionnaires* that measure self-reports of behavior, thoughts, or feelings of athletes. These types of questionnaires differ from psychological inventories in that they are less standardized, typically use an open-ended as opposed to Likert format, and are usually developed to gain practical information rather than to attempt measurement of a particular psychological construct, such as a trait, mood, or motive. Examples of these questionnaires used in applied sport psychology include Orlick's (1986) Competition Reflections, the Performance Feedback Sheet developed by Ravizza (1993), and other types of forms that consultants design themselves to assess a variety of items, such as type and frequency of self-talk, type and amount of imagery practice, or progress in a goal-setting program. This method of assessment often continually assesses athletes' progress through systematic self-monitoring with checklists, rating scales, and feedback sheets.

In the survey conducted by the authors for this chapter, 75% of the consultants indicated that they utilize some type of psychological inventories or survey questionnaires in their applied work with athletes. This is similar to a previous finding by Gould, Tammen, Murphy, and May (1989), who found that 63% of the sport psychology consultants in their sample regularly used inventories and/or questionnaires in their intervention work with athletes. In the survey for this chaper, consultants identified 94 separate inventories and questionnaires that they used in sport psychology interventions with athletes. This finding indicates that sport psychology consultants use a wide range of inventories and/or questionnaires in their applied work with athletes. Table 1 lists the eight most widely used inventories/questionnaires reported by consultants in the survey. The POMS and the TAIS were used most frequently, followed by Orlick's (1986) Competition Reflections, the CSAI-2, the Sport Competition Anxiety Test (Martens et al., 1990), the Trait and State Sport-Confidence Inventories (Vealey, 1986), feedback logs and questionnaires designed by the consultants, and the MMPI. These findings are similar to the previous research by Gould and colleagues (1989), which showed the POMS to be the most popular inventory/questionnaire used in consult-

Table 1
Psychological Inventories/Questionnaires Used by Consultants in Survey

Inventory/Questionnaire*	% of consultants
Profile of Mood States	26%
Test of Attentional and Interpersonal Style	20%
Competition Reflections	17%
Competitive State Anxiety Inventory-2	14%
Sport Competition Anxiety Test	14%
Trait and State Sport-Confidence Inventories	09%
Self-designed questionnaire for specific use	09%
Minnesota Multiphasic Personality Inventory	07%

*Eighty-six other inventories/questionnaires were listed by 1 to 3 consultants

ing, followed by the SCAT, the TAIS, the CSAI-2, and the Psychological Skills Inventory for Sport (PSIS; Mahoney et al., 1987). Also, Gould and colleagues (1989) found that 19% of the consultants in their study had constructed instruments specific to the sports and athletes with whom they were working.

The third assessment method used in applied sport psychology is *interview*, which is defined as a carefully planned and deliberately executed interaction between at least two persons designed to achieve a consciously selected purpose or gathering of information (Phares, 1992). An important distinction of the interview method is that each participant contributes to the process, and each influences the responses of the other. This emphasizes the individualized approach of interviews, which is effective in an idiographic sense of understanding the whole person. As previously noted, the theoretical orientation of the interviewer will inevitably color the specific techniques used within the interview process as well as the kind of information that is sought from athletes. Phares emphasizes that it is a mistake to take interviewing for granted or believe that it involves no special skills, as the usefulness of the interview as an assessment technique is totally dependent upon the skill and sensitivity of the interviewer.

The fourth type of assessment method used in applied sport psychology is *behavioral observation*. Obviously, the consultant may observe the behavior of athletes to assess typical responses in various situations, yet behavioral observation also includes self-monitoring by the athlete, which is simply deliberately attending to one's own behavior. Obviously, these techniques are related to the underlying theoretical orientation of behavioral psychology with an emphasis on sampling behavior and its determinants in context so that appropriate interventions can be targeted and implemented (Nelson & Hayes, 1986). This differs from the more psychodynamic approaches in which athletes' underlying traits and personality structures are assessed. Behavioral observation has been used systematically in sport psychology research with checklists or coding systems designed to ensure that the behavior is being observed within a particular set of parameters. Two observers are typically used to code behavior, and their results are checked against each other to ensure a consistent reliable assessment of behavior in a situation. However, in consulting with athletes in applied settings, most behavioral observation is more informal and is used to augment other types of assessment used by the consultant, such as feedback questionnaires and interview discussions with the athlete.

The consultants surveyed for this chapter were asked to designate a percentage for how much of their assessment of athletes involved the use of inventories/questionnaires, interviews, and observations. The results showed that consultants used interview methods the greatest amount of time (57.2%) followed by behavioral observation (21.2%) and inventories/questionnaires (17.3%). Thus, although the survey found that 75% of all consultants use psychological inventories or survey questionnaires, these instruments are used sparingly and not as often as interview and observation. A *t*-test analysis showed that consultants trained in psychology (*M*=20.29%) used inventories/questionnaires more frequently in assessment than did consultants trained in kinesiology (*M*=14.80%), *t* (62) = 2.75, *p* < .005. Overall, although consultants vary in their emphasis on different

methods, most tend to use a multimodal approach that utilizes several assessment methods when intervening with athletes. Gardner (1995) advocates the multiple use of psychological inventories, survey questionnaires, interview, and behavioral observation to develop a full understanding of interpersonal dynamics, individual personality structure, and mental skills development of athletes.

The final method of assessment in applied sport psychology includes *psychophysiological measures*, which assess physiological responses in relation to environmental, psychological, or behavioral events (Kallmann & Feuerstein, 1977). These measures are based on the premise that "nothing is more certain than that our behavior is a product of our nervous systems" (Bower & Hilgard, 1981, p. 745). For example, sport psychologists might use electromyography to measure the amount of tension in muscles to assess how well athletes can learn to physically relax through mental training. Electroencephalography and cardiac deceleration have been studied in relation to attentional focus related to rifle shooting (Landers, Christina, Hatfield, Doyle, & Daniels, 1980), archery shooting (Wang & Landers, 1988), and golf putting (Boutcher & Zinsser, 1990). The measurement of autonomic responses by psychophysiological assessment seems especially relevant to sport due to the stressors inherent in this evaluative and competitive environment.

WHAT Phenomenona Are Measured in Applied Sport Psychology and WHY

Moving beyond a basic understanding of *how* phenomena are measured in applied sport psychology, more complex questions arise as to the reasons for engaging in measurement in the field. What are the objectives of assessment in applied sport psychology? What should be measured in applied sport psychology, and why is it important to measure these things? The American Psychological Association (1985) defines assessment as a method used to measure various characteristics of people. In applied sport psychology, many characteristics are measured to provide useful insight into the practice of sport psychology. In this section, several objectives or uses of assessment in applied sport psychology are overviewed that include both professional practice and applied intervention research.

Pre-Intervention Assessment or Problem Identification

Assessment prior to intervention implementation with athletes is a fundamental component of applied sport psychology. The term *diagnosis* has been disparaged in the applied sport psychology literature due largely to its clinical overtones and ethical concerns over testing and sharing results with athletes. However, all pre-intervention assessment serves as a careful examination and analysis of the athlete in an attempt to understand the athlete's thoughts, feelings, and behaviors within his or her specific sport context. As stated by Whelen et al. (1995), creating significant and lasting behavior change requires a clear picture of what needs to be changed, some ideas of how to precipitate that change, and the foresight to predict possible hindrances to the change process.

Whelen et al. (1995), in their focus on personal enhancement of athletes, identify two important strategies or techniques to be used in the initial assessment, or diagnosis, of athletes.

First, they advocate the method of "pinpointing" (Patterson, 1974) as a way to gain clear statements from the athlete about the nature of the problem. This is similar to a functional analysis (Fisch, Weakland, & Segal, 1982; Nelson & Hayes, 1986) in which performance problems are identified within a specific temporal context. This involves specifying antecedent conditions and triggers that spawn these performance problems as well as the behavioral, emotional, and cognitive consequences resulting from the problem. Functional analysis is concerned with gaining information from athletes that is clearly explicit and in behavioral terms (what individuals say and do in performing the problem and their attempts to deal with it) rather than vague or general statements or explanatory interpretations.

Whelen et al. (1995) also advocate the assessment of multiple contexts and systems within the athlete's life similar to the multiple domains depicted in the assessment framework (see Figure 1). Specifically, Whelan and colleagues suggest that five primary contexts of athletes should be assessed, including individual, family, sport, work, and social functioning. Importantly, these authors indicate that this cross-contextual assessment is not to search for psychopathology, but rather to more wholistically understand how the athlete functions in various contexts and how behavioral responses may be interrelated across contexts. From this initial contextual assessment, additional assessment within each system can occur depending upon the athlete and his or her unique situation. For example, Hellstedt (1995) has developed an assessment framework within which to examine athletes' family contexts. This framework involves four assessment areas: the level and sources of stress in the family, the degree of cohesiveness in the family, the ability of the family to adapt to change, and the interaction patterns in the family. Hellstedt suggests considering family assessment in relation to such sport-related problems as burnout and overtraining, coach-athlete-parent relationship issues, parental overinvolvement, and rehabilitation from injury.

A multimodal pre-intervention assessment approach termed BASIC-ID (Lazarus, 1976) has been applied in sport by Davies and West (1991) as well as Perna et al. (1995) to identify key mental skills, reasons for performance blocks, and potential intervention targets. The modalities assessed in this approach are represented by the acronym BASIC-ID: behavior, affect, sensations, imagery, cognitions, interpersonal relations, and biological functioning (drugs/diet). Assessment of each modality can take many forms such as use of inventories, questionnaires and self-monitoring, interviews, and observations. For example, Perna et al. use a variety of methods within the BASIC-ID approach including the psychological inventories POMS, CSAI-2, Sport Anxiety Scale (SAS; Smith, Smoll, & Shutz, 1990), and Sports Inventory of Mental Skills (SIMS; Murphy, Hardy, Thomas, & Bond, 1993).

From the initial assessment, a modality firing order (Lazarus, 1976) can be identified that is the athlete's chaining or sequencing of the modalities. Thus, a gymnast who initiates a loss of focus by a negative thought about performance, which then triggers tension in her muscles, poor performance, negative feedback from her coach, and lack of support from her family, demonstrates a firing order of C-S-B-I. Once this sequencing has been identified, interventions may be designed in an attempt to break the chain, preferably at the onset. Lazarus' BASIC-ID assessment approach appears quite useful for sport psychology in that it assesses thoughts, feelings, and behavior within a specific context and could be used by consultants with various approaches and styles in measuring each component.

One of the domains in the assessment framework (Figure 1) that is often overlooked in applied sport psychology intervention is the organizational culture of the sport. Importantly, many consultants advocate that initial assessment should include an analysis of the particular sport requirements and environment. For example, Boutcher and Rotella (1987), in their psychological skills education program for closed skills, advocate two phases of assessment. The first phase involves an analysis of the particular skill from a biomechanical and physiological perspective prior to the second phase, which is the psychological assessment of the athletes. Boutcher and Rotella's rationale is that a basic understanding of the sport skill is needed so that all problems encountered by athletes are not automatically assumed to be psychological in origin. This concept has been applied in professional baseball consulting by training and supervising an individual with specialized baseball technical knowledge to provide psychological services within the organization (Smith & Johnson, 1990). Termed *organizational empowerment*, this approach is an excellent example of focusing psychological assessment and intervention within the specific subculture of the athletes.

Ravizza (1988) states that significant barriers to effective sport psychology consulting include a lack of sport-specific knowledge on the part of the consultant as well as inadequate knowledge regarding the organizational politics of the specific sport subculture. Ravizza emphasizes that effective assessment in sport psychology consulting must involve gaining knowledge about specific team and organizational dynamics to understand such factors as the flow of decision-making and specific situational demands for certain teams.

Overall, initial assessment prior to intervention initiation is critical to identify specific behaviors, emotions, cognitions, and organizational factors related to the performance and well-being of the athlete. This initial assessment then leads to the selection of intervention targets and also serves as the basis for evaluating intervention effects. Significant productive psychobehavioral change begins with effective assessments of the constellation of factors in athletes' lives that influence their sport participation.

Athlete Self-Awareness and Feedback

A second objective of psychological assessment in applied sport psychology is to provide feedback to athletes regarding their specific thoughts, feelings, and behaviors and also to encourage them to engage in critical self-reflection and self-assessment. It is an arbitrary distinction to designate this section on athlete self-awareness and feedback as separate from the previous section on pre-intervention assessment and problem identification. Clearly, most sport psychology consultants view the assessment process as a method to provide continuous feedback to athletes to enable them to engage in the critical self-reflection and self-monitoring that is a necessary precursor of psychobehavioral change. In fact, Nideffer (1981) states that, from an ethical perspective, consultants are required to explain to athletes why they are being assessed, what conclusions are drawn on the basis of the assessment, and how the assessment information will be used. Various assessment methods, such as psychological inventories and survey questionnaires, serve to enhance athletes' self-awareness by providing evaluations from which they can assist in the planning and implementation of specific interventions.

Self-assessment has its roots in social-cognitive perspectives in which self-regulated learning is viewed as the key to motivation and achievement behavior (Bandura, 1986). Self-regulated learning comprises three subprocesses: self-observation, self-judgment, and self-reaction. Basically, it is assumed that athletes deliberately monitor their own behavior via some type of self-recording and then assess their progress in relation to previous performance or goals. Weiss (1995) provides an excellent example of using this approach to enhance the psychosocial development of children in sport by teaching them to be self-regulated learners.

Assessment targeted for athlete self-awareness and feedback often utilizes survey questionnaires designed specifically for consulting purposes. Ravizza's (1993) Performance Feedback Sheet and Botterill's (1990) Mental Skills Checklist serve as open-ended self-monitoring tools for athletes. Orlick (1986) has developed several self-monitoring questionnaires for athletes. Orlick's Competition Reflections questionnaire is targeted to help athletes develop awareness of their thoughts and feelings prior to and during competition and is widely used by applied sport psychology consultants. Orlick (1986) also provides other examples of self-monitoring techniques with questionnaires and log sheets designed for goal setting, focus plans, imagery, and competition evaluation. Halliwell (1989) states that these questionnaires served three purposes in his work with the Canadian sailing team at the 1988 Summer Olympic Games: (a) Athletes obtained a better understanding of their psychological/emotional/social needs; (b) the information was used to develop individual competition focus plans; and (c) the information was used to develop an effective social support system within the team.

As found in the consultant survey conducted for this chapter, many consultants personalize survey questionnaires for use in specific sports. Similarly, Orlick (1990) has designed a set of self-directed interview questions designed for athletes to use for self-assessment and identification of their needed foci for positive change. From this interview, Orlick presents various self-growth strategies that athletes may use in their personal pursuit of psychobehavioral change. Gipson, McKenzie, and Lowe (1989) designed questionnaires to gather feedback from the 1988 U.S. Olympic volleyball team on team issues such as satisfaction with coach behavior, roommates, travel schedule, and practice content. Gipson and colleagues also utilized systematic behavioral observation to assess skill development, verbal interactions between players, and coach interactions with players. These observational data along with video feedback were used by the consultants to facilitate players' skill development and refinement, enhance coaches' feedback behaviors, and enhance motivation and confidence through the use of personal highlight films with players.

One emerging technique that seems useful to enhance athlete self-awareness and feedback is the performance profile (Butler & Hardy, 1992; Jones, 1993). Performance profiling applies Kelly's (1955) personal construct theory to assessment by helping athletes "construe" targeted behaviors. Personal construct theory emphasizes the uniqueness of construing in that each individual differs in how situations are perceived and interpreted, what is considered important, and what is implied by his or her particular construing of the event. First, athletes identify constructs or qualities that they feel are fundamental to elite performance in their sport (e.g., confidence, focus, balance, strength). Then, athletes assess their own status in relation to these constructs. These constructs are labeled on a grid or graph so that athletes have a visual depiction of their current mental and physical functioning in relation to their desired goals. What makes performance profiling unique is the use of the athletes' own labels for the qualities they wish to pursue, a process that enhances the personal meaning and perceived ownership of the assessment and subsequent intervention. For example, Jones (1993) used performance profiling in conjunction with the Sport-Related Psychological Skills Questionnaire (SPSQ) developed by Nelson and Hardy (1990) at regular intervals during an athlete-intervention program to monitor the athlete's progress and effectiveness of the intervention.

As part of the survey conducted for this chapter, consultants were asked to designate percentages for how much of their work used inventories/questionnaires (a) for their own diagnosis, (b) for helping athletes engage in self-awareness and self-assessment, and (c) for both purposes. The mean percentages indicated that consultants used these methods 47% of the time for athlete self-awareness/assessment, 30% of the time for both objectives, and only 13% of the time for diagnosis. However, the sample of consultants indicated that they share the results of inventories/questionnaires with athletes 85% of the time in their applied work. The most frequently cited reasons for using inventories/questionnaires in applied work were (in order) (a) making an initial assessment, (b) evaluating and monitoring intervention, (c) increasing coach awareness, (d) establishing treatment plans and goals, (e) quickly facilitating an open and honest dialogue, and (f) confirming consultant's observations. Overall, these survey results support the contention that assessment may serve many purposes within applied sport psychology.

Predicting Outcomes of Importance

Thus far, this chapter has largely focused on intervention or mental training with athletes. However, measurement or assessment issues in applied sport psychology must consider applied research that is an integral part of any profession (Smith, 1989). A major area of applied research in sport psychology has examined the measurement of psychological constructs in an attempt to predict an outcome of importance (e.g., performance, flow, success, injury vulnerability).

Since the early sport personality research of the 1960s, sport psychologists have been intrigued by the possibility of finding a measure that can predict future success in sport. However, to date, no measure has been developed that can predict who will succeed in sport, despite many claims to the contrary (e.g., Tutko et al., 1969). However, many in the lay public cling to this belief as evidenced by the use of the Athletic Motivation Inventory (Tutko et al., 1969) by the National Hockey League as a screening device to assess the psychological traits of prospective draft choices. As Singer (1988) states, the ethical use of psychological inventories for team selection/retention assumes that we know (a) which psychological characteristics are relevant to success, (b) what the ideal level of that characteristic is, (c) how much athletes can compensate in some characteristics for the lack of others, and (d) that the particular inventory being used provides a valid and reliable measure of these attributes. In short, we do not know these things, and selection decisions based on psychological inventories are questionable in validity. Gardner (1995) emphasizes the need to view these measures as valid predictors of certain facets of human behavioral characteristics, which is very different from viewing them as predictors of success.

The search for a psychological inventory that can predict important sport outcomes has continued with the development of instruments such as the PSIS (Mahoney et al., 1987), which assesses the cognitive components of anxiety control, concentration, confidence, mental preparation, motivation, and team focus. Despite the intuitive appeal of these constructs as important characteristics of successful athletes, psychometric research has not supported the PSIS (Chartrand, Jowdy, & Danish, 1992; chapter by Murphy & Tammen, this volume). The most recent assessment measure of psychological skills is the Athletic Coping Skills Inventory (ACSI; Smith, Smoll, Schutz, & Ptacek, 1995), which assesses coping with adversity, peaking under pressure, goal setting/mental preparation, concentration, freedom from worry, confidence and achievement motivation, and coachability. Although initial research is promising based on an emerging interest in cognitive *coping* skills (as opposed to the measure of enduring traits or dispositions in previous research), Smith and Christensen (1995) emphasize that the ACSI should not be used for selection purposes as response distortion inherent in this type of self-report inventory masks the relationship between these psychological skills and subsequent outcome variables such as performance and success.

Several research studies have examined the effects of various sport psychology interventions on the subsequent performance of athletes. Reviews by Greenspan and Feltz (1989) as well as Vealey (1994) have identified several measurement issues related to this research, including the need for controls, manipulation checks, maintenance data, more specific treatment descriptions, and ecologically valid research settings. However, these authors also lament the breach between research and practice that occurs in measuring intervention effects within traditional experimental designs. This breach that is so often discussed in the sport psychology literature (Dewar & Horn, 1992; Martens, 1987; Nideffer, 1981; Smith, 1989; Vealey, 1988, 1994) is fundamentally a measurement or assessment issue and, on a grander scale, even an epistemological issue. It seems that we have attempted to predict important outcomes such as success or performance within positivistic nomothetic research designs that may mask the more subtle complex intraindividual responses and changes that occur in sport psychology interventions. Almost all sport psychology

consultants have at certain times observed the positive effects of psychological interventions, yet these effects are far more complicated to quantify or measure in a systematic way based on the current accepted scientific method. Advances in applied sport psychology measurement that will lead to significant advances in applied sport psychology knowledge await more enlightening philosophies of science that more effectively capture subtle intra-individual psychobehavioral change.

Additional Applied Research Assessment Objectives

Although the prediction of sport performance and success has long been a popular measurement objective in applied sport psychology, assessment in the field is also targeted toward several other important objectives. Applied researchers as well as professional practitioners are interested in assessing psychological change over time, evaluating the effectiveness of their interventions, and assessing athletes' and coaches' perceptions of consultant effectiveness and mental training programs. As eloquently argued by Smith (1989), effective professional development in applied sport psychology requires accountability for our actions, and evaluation research is imperative to provide critical feedback about our interventions.

Assessing psychological change. One effective method of evaluating psychological interventions is to assess psychological change over time. This design typically involves establishing a baseline measure of a particular psychological construct and then assessing its change over time in response to some type of treatment, such as a mental skills training program. Interestingly, most of these types of studies have focused on anxiety as the dependent variable of interest (e.g., Crocker, Alderman, & Smith, 1988; Dewitt, 1980; Elko & Ostrow, 1991; Maynard & Cotton, 1993; Maynard, Warwick-Evans, & Smith, 1995; Prapavessis, Grove, McNair, & Cable, 1992) with varying results. Often, these types of studies fail to indicate changes in psychological processes over time, even though social validation via reports from participants indicates that they felt the intervention was helpful.

Although one could scoff that these reports are biased, it may also be that psychobehavioral changes resulting from sport psychology interventions are not easily detected using measurement instruments developed for research purposes. For example, several studies have utilized the CSAI-2 (Martens et al., 1990) to assess changes in cognitive and somatic state anxiety over the course of an intervention. The CSAI-2 was developed via nomothetic research principles that used large samples of subjects to validate an instrument to operationalize the cognitive and somatic state anxiety in competitive situations based on multidimensional anxiety theory. Like most inventories developed this way, several items representing different expressions of cognitive and somatic anxiety (e.g., "I am concerned about performing poorly," and "My body feels tense") were developed and included in the inventory. Yet how well does the CSAI-2, developed nomothetically, measure the idiographic nature of a state anxiety response in an athlete? Consider a gymnast who scores low on all of the CSAI-2 items except for the item "My body feels tense." Does this mean that she is not anxious? Her CSAI-2 score would indicate, related to group norms, that she is not. However, she could be extremely anxious based on her individualized anxiety response of tension, which, of course, would be very disruptive to the performance of a gymnast. Lacey, Bateman, and Van Lehn (1953) term this "autonomic response stereotypy" and indicate that averaging different physiological (as well as psychological) predictors across groups of subjects may mask individuals' typical responses. For example, the results of a cognitive-affective stress-management program indicated that negative thoughts decreased as a result of the intervention, but there was no concurrent reduction in cognitive anxiety as measured by the CSAI-2 (Crocker et al., 1988). This again raises the question as to the efficacy of using nomothetically developed assessment instruments to assess the complex intra-individual changes in psychological functioning that may occur during an intervention.

Evaluating interventions. Any sport psychology intervention should have an evaluation component that may take many forms, such as a formal research analysis, informal feedback given to consultants, and consultant self-evaluations. Smith and Johnson (1990) provide results from a survey questionnaire mailed to players in the Houston Astros' minor-league development program asking them to evaluate the effectiveness of the psychological intervention program implemented with their teams. The players rated how helpful each program component had been to them personally, and they also were invited to make written comments and to suggest ways the program could be improved in the future. This type of evaluation not only provided meaningful feedback to enhance further mental training within the organization, but also provided important social validation for the efficacy of mental training for the consultants as well as club management. In addition, this type of evaluation serves to provide credibility for the consultants in the eyes of the players as their views about mental training are seen as useful and important.

Gould, Petlichkoff, Hodge, and Simons (1990) used survey questionnaires with rating scales to evaluate the results from elite-athlete mental training programs with respect to athletes' perceived usefulness and knowledge of the material as well as their planned and actual use of the mental training effects. A follow-up study by Brewer and Shillinglaw (1992) replicated Gould et al.'s (1990) findings using an experimental design as an attempt to provide better control from which to infer causality in the evaluation process. Brewer and Shillinglaw are to be commended for using an innovative interrupted time-series design so that all members of an intact lacrosse team could receive the benefits of the psychological intervention. However, their attempts at gaining control call into question the true ecological validity of their results within the brief treatment phases. Is it more favorable to conduct evaluation research with tight controls or to use a simple survey approach (e.g., Smith & Johnson, 1990) to gain athletes' perspectives on psychological interventions? The answer to this question seems related to our objectives as applied sport psychology professionals. Once again, issues such as this in applied sport psychology beg further discussion and fresh perspectives as to how best to evaluate our interventions.

A significant development in intervention assessment was the development of the Sport Psychology Consultant Evaluation Form (CEF) by Partington and Orlick (1987a). The CEF was developed based on the authors' insights gained from extensive interviews about consultant effectiveness with Olympic athletes and coaches. The CEF combines a rating scale with the opportunity for open-ended suggestions regarding consultant characteristics and effectiveness, and initial psychometric properties and usefulness were established (Partington & Orlick, 1987a). The authors offer useful suggestions to practitioners as to how the CEF may be used and admit that the form was designed for use with elite athletes so that additional modification for use with other populations may be warranted. Gould, Murphy, Tammen, and May (1991) used the CEF along with additional survey questions to evaluate the effectiveness of U.S. Olympic sport psychology consultants and to identify future consultant and program needs. Their evaluation research was unique in that athletes, coaches, administrators, and the consultants themselves were all assessed and that survey results were congruent across the four subsamples in the study. In addition to questionnaires such as the CEF, interviews with athletes have also provided important evaluation information as to effective consultant characteristics (Orlick & Partington, 1987b). Similarly, survey questionnaires (Gould et al., 1989; Partington & Orlick, 1991) have also been used to assess sport psychology consultants' evaluations of their own services and perceptions of consultant effectiveness.

Overall, measurement and evaluation in applied sport psychology range from tightly controlled experimental designs to informal interviews and open-ended questionnaires. Again, this points to broader epistemological questions in sport psychology about how knowledge should be generated and who should benefit from this knowledge. These broader issues are discussed in the next section.

Critical Issues and Future Directions in Applied Sport Psychology Measurement

From the previous information presented in the chapter, several basic conclusions may be stated to serve as a reference point for the framing of critical issues and future directions for applied sport psychology measurement:

1. Challenges and advances in measurement have served as precursors for significant professional development in sport psychology.
2. All measurement (and science) is (are) influenced by historical and sociocultural factors that ultimately shape the knowledge that is produced.
3. Assessment in applied sport psychology is seeking not truth or reality, but rather useful ways of describing and understanding athletes in an attempt to enhance their sport participation.
4. The goal of applied sport psychology is to enhance the personal development and performance of individuals in sport.
5. Although there is great diversity in approaches to assessment in applied sport psychology, multiple domains (e.g., athlete characteristics, consultant characteristics, contextual characteristics, and organizational culture of sport) and multiple methods should be considered for effective assessment and intervention.

6. An important measurement objective for applied sport psychology is the evaluation of intervention effectiveness, yet a breach exists between what may be thought of as research and practical measures of intervention effectiveness.

These conclusions can be alternatively stated as questions to frame important future directions for measurement in applied sport psychology. What measurement advances should we now embrace to enhance our work in applied sport psychology? What historical and sociocultural factors are currently influencing our assessment and interventions in applied sport psychology? What is the most useful way to understand and describe athletes based on the goal of applied sport psychology? How can consultants stay within their boundaries of training, competence, and philosophies while engaging in multidomain and multimethod assessment techniques with athletes? Finally, are positivistic nomothetic psychometric assessment instruments and approaches applicable to sport psychology interventions in professional practice settings? It is important for the field of sport psychology to begin addressing these questions although their somewhat rhetorical nature precludes definitive answers at this time.

Three future directions are suggested in this section to initiate needed professional discourse related to these questions. First, the applied sport psychology goals of wanting to help athletes and wanting to gain scientific credibility must be clarified, admitted, and made to coexist as opposed to the current situation in which these goals are juxtaposed, which creates tension and perpetuates the science-practice rift. Second, applied sport psychology, with its emphasis on humanistic individual development, must embrace alternative and emerging epistemologies and methodologies to develop more practical measurement instruments to enhance our assessments with athletes. Third, clarifying competence and training boundaries may be better achieved via focusing on assessment and intervention *possibilities* within *inclusive frameworks* for practice, as opposed to focusing on assessment and intervention *limitations* within *exclusive models* for practice.

Clarifying the Dual Goals of Applied Sport Psychology

Although the stated intention of applied sport psychology is to help people (enhance the personal development and performance of athletes and coaches), the other less stated goal of the field is to gain scientific and professional credibility. Measurement, or assessment, in applied sport psychology is especially affected by these goals that in theory are the same, but that in reality are quite disparate. Our quest for scientific credibility spawned previous measurement issues in sport psychology, including the adoption of the experimental social psychology paradigm for research in the 1970s and then the flood to descriptive field research in response to Martens' (1979) plea for more "jocks" and fewer "smocks." We embraced cognitive measurement techniques in the 1980s in response to the zeitgeists of attribution, cognitive evaluation, and competence motivation theories in the parent discipline of social psychology. With the rise in applied sport psychology interventions in the 1980s, we rushed to repel criticism about our professional ac-

tivities by designing evaluation research to support the efficacy of our interventions. However, it seems that our quest for scientific credibility and professional respect often is pursued at the expense of practicality and usefulness.

The development, use, and criticism of the TAIS (Nideffer, 1976) provides a pertinent example of this dilemma. The TAIS has been one of the most widely used psychological inventories in sport psychology in both research and professional practice settings (e.g., Botterill, 1990; Gordin & Henschen, 1989; Gould et al., 1989; Nideffer, 1976, 1981, 1987, 1989, 1990; Salmela, 1989) because of its potential relevance to sport performance. A theoretical framework incorporating two attentional dimensions was developed to conceptualize four attentional styles and serve as the conceptual basis for the TAIS (Nideffer, 1976). Nideffer admits that the TAIS was designed to serve as a research tool to investigate the relationship between attentional processes and performance as well as a feedback device to be used in psychological interventions. Previous research has supported its internal consistency, test-retest reliability, and construct and predictive validity; and sport-specific modifications of the TAIS have been developed for tennis (Van Schoyck & Grasha, 1981), baseball/softball (Albrecht & Feltz, 1987), and basketball (Bergandi, Shryock, & Titus, 1990; Vallerand, 1983).

Despite its popularity, the TAIS has been subjected to intense statistical scrutiny and criticisms based on what Nideffer (1990) feels is a lack of understanding about the conceptualization of attentional processes and the practical utility of the inventory. Specifically, the reliability and validity of the TAIS have been challenged based on questions surrounding the factor structure of the attentional dimensions and what are perceived to be inappropriate intercorrelations between dimensions (Bergandi et al., 1990; Dewey, Brawley, & Allard, 1989; Van Schoyk & Grasha, 1981). However, Nideffer (1990) convincingly argues that statistical independence of the attentional subscales is pragmatically irrelevant and as well as counterintuitive. He contends that the call for reducing several practically useful independent attentional constructs into one or more global dimensions just so they are neatly and cleanly represented by factor analysis would totally reduce the practical utility of the TAIS. Nideffer (1990) challenges the assumption by others that certain positive attentional processes should be negatively correlated (as some theorists argue based on their statistical preoccupation with the two-dimensional model of attention) and rightly asserts that few theorists would predict that athletes good at external environmental assessment would then by nature be bad at internal analysis. He states,

> From a theoretical standpoint the complete independence of attentional and interpersonal constructs [measured in the TAIS] might be highly desirable. Independent scales would make prediction much easier. From a practical standpoint, however, scales that were completely independent would not reflect what we know to be true about human behavior (e.g., that various attentional and interpersonal styles are interrelated).
> —(Nideffer, 1990, p. 290).

Similar criticisms were leveled at the CSAI-2 (Martens et al., 1990) during its development. Reviewers indicated that moderate correlations between cognitive and somatic anxiety disputed the predicted theoretical independence of these constructs within multidimensional anxiety theory. Clearly, cognitive and somatic anxiety represent separate manifestations of anxiety and are elicited by different antecedents, but of course these psychological responses are interrelated within competitive contexts. Multidimensional anxiety theory spawned important practical implications for matching stress-management programs according to specific anxiety responses, and validation of this "matching hypothesis" has supported the theoretical independence (and practical significance) of cognitive and somatic anxiety. However, it should be remembered that the CSAI-2 was developed as a research tool, in contrast to the TAIS, which was developed to serve dual purposes.

Professional discourse over the validity of the TAIS and CSAI-2 represents the often incompatible nature of the dual goals of applied sport psychology. This rigidity and incompatibility between the goals of helping athletes and gaining scientific prestige must be addressed by examining the epistemological assumptions of our professional work. This means we must critically examine the ways in which we justify our beliefs or legitimize rigid types of knowledge development. Any young sport psychology professor working towards tenure at a university can quickly tell you that empirical research that may or may not be relevant to practice is essential for scientific credibility in the field. As noted by Nideffer (1987), the current reward system and publishing guidelines in sport psychology devalue contributions that examine the usefulness of measurement in applied settings. Frankly, what drives our epistemology (or approach to science) is the fact that careers are made via approval of members of our disciplinary community, not that of the target population affected by our work.

Obviously, the two goals in applied sport psychology of helping athletes and gaining academic respect from attempting to do so should not be disparate. This disparity is largely the result of a scientific status hierarchy that has valued and rewarded empiricism over humanism, research over practice, and traditional psychometrics over insightful assessment aimed at significant human development. Sherif (1987) states that the most underdeveloped question in psychology is how people feel and experience themselves and why, when, and how these self-experiences affect their action. In the next section, some specific methodological and epistemological extensions in measurement in applied sport psychology are offered to begin to address this question.

Toward Practical Measurement in Applied Sport Psychology

Any field wants to be seen as valid or having sound evidence upon which to base its practices. Nideffer (1987) argues for more inclusive ways to validate principles in the field. For example, he lauds the technique of consensual validation as a way in which sport psychology practitioners can glean evidence from multiple sources (coach's observations, psychological inventories, athlete's perceptions of responses to the psychological inventories, etc.) to develop sound assessment evidence upon which to develop individualized intervention programs. Importantly, the validity of a measure should be as-

sessed in relation to how the measure is used. As defined previously in this chapter, assessment simply means to describe in a useful way and should not be assumed to target reality, but rather to provide a useful way of describing athletes in an attempt to enhance their sport participation (Phares, 1992). Thus, it is conceivable that measurement instruments could be developed specifically for professional practice and validated based upon their effectiveness in this context. Consensual validation reports based on an accumulation of interventions with athletes would support the validity of these measures.

Traditional nomothetic psychometric research to develop valid research instrumentation should be coupled with more idiographic psychometric approaches for assessment in intervention work with athletes. Often, psychological inventories are "misused" in practical settings as consultants discuss athletes' responses to various items in an attempt to gain more specific information. For example, Savoy (1993) describes her use of Kroll's (1979) Competitive Athletic Stress Scale (CASS) as an interview technique to assess specific elements of competition that cause anxiety for individual athletes. An important future direction for the field might be to develop companion measurement instruments: one based on nomothetic principles of measuring universally applicable constructs related to a theoretical perspective and the other based on idiographic principles of assessing the unique manner in which the construct of interest is manifested in one particular athlete. For example, the Trait Sport-Confidence Inventory (Vealey, 1986) was developed as a research tool to test conceptual predictions about self-confidence in sport. However, this instrument could be modified in format or even instructions so that practitioners could use it (within a multiple assessment approach and engaging in consensual validation) to provide insights into situations that trigger low confidence or important sources of confidence. These approaches may even provide a fresh perspective on theory development as the accumulation of idiographic evidence assessed by practitioners evolves into more broadly conceptualized theoretical frameworks. This practice-theory relationship is represented by this misquote of Lewin (1931) that "there is nothing so theoretical as a good practice."

A move toward a more idiographic approach to measurement in applied sport psychology could also be implemented by accounting for such moderators as trait relevance or self-schema in assessment with athletes. The concept of trait relevance (Paunonen, 1988) means that not all psychological dimensions apply equally well to all people. This has also been discussed in terms of self-schema (Markus, 1983), which represents the ways in which individuals organize and process information about themselves and the world. In helping athletes make significant psychobehavioral change, applied sport psychology consultants must be able to assess which characteristics are most salient in terms of influencing behavior and then focus the intervention on that salient aspect of the athlete. Using a predetermined battery of inventories or questionnaires may not be relevant for certain athletes if the characteristics measured are not as relevant to their psychobehavioral functioning. This concept is typically assessed in sport psychology interventions by "focusing" the assessment or pinpointing the exact construct that is creating problem behaviors or hampering performance (e.g., cognitive anxiety related to peer evaluation or attentional dsyfunction following a performance error). Overall, strategies to enhance idiographic measurement in applied sport psychology are needed because "as long as psychology deals only with universals and not with particulars, it won't deal with much" (Allport, 1960, p. 146.).

For the field of applied sport psychology to significantly and innovatively advance in measurement, a patient broadmindedness is needed. Significant changes in measurement based on idiographic objectives will result in psychometric work that is complex and stretches the limits of conventionally approved scientific methods. In short, it will be messy. However, as argued by Nideffer (1987), limited short-sighted measurement development that is cleanly designed should not be valued more than significant yet less neat attempts to extend our epistemological and methodological limits to develop useful and sound assessment tools in applied sport psychology. Koch (1981) warns against "epistemopathology" or the entrenchment of methods that ultimately limit vision and the development of useful knowledge. A broader, more inclusive, more utilitarian acceptance of measurement development targeted to achieving the stated goal of applied sport psychology is needed to avoid this epistemopathology.

Developing Inclusive Frameworks for Assessment and Intervention

A framework representing four broad domains that all consultants should consider in assessment and intervention with athletes was presented at the beginning of the chapter (see Figure 1). Assessment within the framework is dependent upon the characteristics and interrelatedness of the domains as clearly not all types of consultants should engage in all types of assessment techniques with all types of athletes in all types of contexts. However, the purpose of the framework is to attempt to provide a common articulation of assessment considerations in applied sport psychology. Much of the literature on measurement and assessment focuses on exclusion, boundaries, and limiting models for practice. Obviously, this dialogue and these models are useful in professional training and continuing education, especially with regard to ethics. However, simply because sport psychology is diverse does not mean that we cannot (or should not) find any common ground with regard to assessment and intervention techniques. Two excellent examples of inclusionary approaches to applied sport psychology are the books by Nideffer (1981) and Murphy (1995). These texts more than adequately cover exclusionary issues that our diverse field should always consider, but their focus is on the practice of applied sport psychology for all individuals irrespective of their training.

By focusing more on inclusionary frameworks for assessment and practice, the diversity in applied sport psychology will become enriching as opposed to divisive. By broadening our definitions of science, method, and legitimate knowledge, our field can create congruency between the goals of helping athletes and attaining scientific credibility. By focusing on the development of practical assessment instruments and methods, theory and research in sport psychology will be extended through more idiographic knowledge pursuits. By focusing on the possibilities, rather than the limitations, of assessing psy-

chobehavioral characteristics of athletes, our professional practice should more effectively pursue our stated goal to enhance the personal development and performance of athletes.

References

Albrecht, R.R., & Feltz, D.L. (1987). Generality and specificity of attention related to competitive anxiety and sport performance. *Journal of Sport Psychology, 9*, 231-248.

Allport, G.W. (1960). *Personality and social encounter*. Boston: Beacon Press.

American Psychological Association. (1985). *Standards for educational and psychological testing*. Washington, D.C.: American Psychological Association.

Anastasi, A. (1988). *Psychological testing*. New York: Macmillan.

Bandura, A. (1986). *Social foundations of thought and action: A social cognitive theory*. Englewood Cliffs, NJ: Prentice-Hall.

Bergandi, T.A., Shryock, M.G., & Titus, T.G. (1990). The Basketball Concentration Survey: Preliminary development and validation. *The Sport Psychologist, 4*, 119-129.

Botterill, C. (1990). Sport psychology and professional hockey. *The Sport Psychologist, 4*, 358-368.

Boutcher, S.H., & Rotella, R.J. (1987). A psychological skills educational program for closed-skill performance enhancement. *The Sport Psychologist, 1*, 127-137.

Boutcher, S.H., & Zinsser, N. (1990). Cardiac deceleration of elite and beginning golfers during putting. *Journal of Sport and Exercise Psychology, 12*, 37-47.

Bower, G.H., & Hilgard, E.R. (1981). *Theories of learning*. Englewood Cliffs, NJ: Prentice-Hall.

Brewer, B.W., & Shillinglaw, R. (1992). Evaluation of a psychological skills training workshop for male intercollegiate lacrosse players. *The Sport Psychologist, 6*, 139-147.

Butler, R.J., & Hardy, L. (1992). The performance profile: Theory and application. *The Sport Psychologist, 6*, 253-264.

Cattell, R.B. (1946). *Description and measurement of personality*. Yonkers-on-Hudson, NY: World.

Chartrand, J., Jowdy, D.P., & Danish, S.J. (1992). The Psychological Skills Inventory for Sports: Psychometric characteristics and applied implications. *Journal of Sport and Exercise Psychology, 14*, 405-413.

Crocker, P.R.E., Alderman, R.B., & Smith, F.M.R. (1988). Cognitive-affective stress management training with high performance youth volleyball players: Effects on affect, cognition, and performance. *Journal of Sport and Exercise Psychology, 10*, 448-460.

Danish, S.J., Petitpas, A., & Hale, B.D. (1995). Psychological interventions: A life development model. In S.M. Murphy (Ed.), *Sport psychology interventions* (pp. 19-38). Champaign, IL: Human Kinetics.

Davies, S., & West, J.D. (1991). A theoretical paradigm for performance enhancement: The multimodal approach. *The Sport Psychologist, 5*, 167-174.

Dewar, A., & Horn, T.S. (1992). A critical analysis of knowledge construction in sport psychology. In T.S. Horn (Ed.), *Advances in sport psychology* (pp. 13-22). Champaign, IL: Human Kinetics.

Dewey, D., Brawley, L., & Allard, F. (1989). Do the TAIS attentional-style scales predict how information is processed? *Journal of Sport and Exercise Psychology, 11*, 171-186.

DeWitt, D.J. (1980). Cognitive and biofeedback training for stress reduction with university athletes. *Journal of Sport Psychology, 2*, 288-294.

Dorfman, H.A. (1990). Reflections on providing personal and performance enhancement consulting services in professional baseball. *The Sport Psychologist, 4*, 341-346.

Elko, P.K., & Ostrow, A.C. (1991). Effects of a rational-emotive education program on heightened anxiety levels of female collegiate gymnasts. *The Sport Psychologist, 5*, 235-255.

Fisch, R., Weakland, J.H., & Segal, L. (1982). *The tactics of change*. San Francisco, CA: Jossey-Bass.

Gardner, F. (1995). The coach and team psychologist: An integrated organizational model. In S.M. Murphy (Ed.), *Sport psychology interventions* (pp. 147-175). Champaign, IL: Human Kinetics.

Gill, D.L. (1994). A feminist perspective on sport psychology practice. *The Sport Psychologist, 8*, 411-426.

Gipson, M., McKenzie, T., & Lowe, S. (1989). The sport psychology program of the USA women's national volleyball team. *The Sport Psychologist, 3*, 330-339.

Goetz, J.P., & LeCompte, M.D. (1984). *Ethnography and qualitative design in educational research*. Orlando, FL: Academic Press.

Gordin, R.D., & Henschen, K.P. (1989). Preparing the USA women's artistic gymnastics team for the 1988 Olympics: A multimodal approach. *The Sport Psychologist, 3*, 366-373.

Gould, D., Murphy, S., Tammen, V., & May, J. (1991). An evaluation of U.S. Olympic sport psychology consultant effectiveness. *The Sport Psychologist, 5*, 111-127.

Gould, D., Petlichkoff, L., Hodge, K., & Simons, J. (1990). Evaluating the effectiveness of a psychological skills educational workshop. *The Sport Psychologist, 4*, 249-260.

Gould, D., Tammen, V., Murphy, S., & May, J. (1989). An examination of U.S. Olympic sport psychology consultants and the services they provide. *The Sport Psychologist, 3*, 300-312.

Greenspan, M.J., & Feltz, D.L. (1989). Psychological interventions with athletes in competitive situations: A review. *The Sport Psychologist, 3*, 219-236.

Halliwell, W. (1989). Delivering sport psychology services to the Canadian sailing team at the 1988 Summer Olympic Games. *The Sport Psychologist, 3*, 313-319.

Halliwell, W. (1990). Providing sport psychology consulting services in professional hockey. *The Sport Psychologist, 4*, 369-377.

Hatfield, B.D., & Landers, D.M. (1983). Psychophysiology - A new direction for sport psychology. *Journal of Sport Psychology, 5*, 243-259.

Hathaway, S.R., & McKinley, J.C. (1943). *MMPI manual*. New York: Psychological Corporation.

Hellstedt, J.C. (1995). Invisible players: A family systems model. In S.M. Murphy (Ed.), *Sport psychology interventions* (pp. 117-146). Champaign, IL: Human Kinetics.

Jones, G. (1993). The role of performance profiling in cognitive behavioral interventions in sport. *The Sport Psychologist, 7*, 160-172.

Kallman, W.M., & Feuerstein, M. (1977). Psychophysiological procedures. In A.R. Ciminero, K.S. Calhoun, & H.E. Adams (Eds.), *Handbook of behavioral assessment* (pp. 329-364). New York: Wiley.

Kelly, G.A. (1955). *The psychology of personal constructs*. New York: Norton.

Koch, S. (1981). The nature and limits of psychological knowledge: Lessons of a century qua "science." *American Psychologist, 36*, 257-269.

Krane, V. (1994). A feminist perspective on contemporary sport psychology research. *The Sport Psychologist, 8*, 393-410.

Kroll, W. (1979). The stress of high performance athletics. In P. Klavora & J. Daniel (Eds.), *Coach, athlete, and the sport psychologist* (pp. 211-219). Champaign, IL: Human Kinetics.

Lacey, J.I., Bateman, D.E., & Van Lehn, R. (1953). Autonomic response specificity: An experimental study. *Psychosomatic Medicine, 15*, 8-21.

Landers, D.M., Christina, B.D., Hatfield, L.A., Doyle, L.A., & Daniels, F.S. (1980). Moving competitive shooting into the scientists' lab. *American Rifleman, 128*, 36-37, 76-77.

Lazarus, A.A. (1976). *Multimodal behavior therapy*. New York: Springer.

Lewin, K. (1931). The conflict between Aristotelian and Galilean modes of thought in contemporary psychology. *Journal of General Psychology, 5*, 141-177.

Mahoney, M.J., Gabriel, T.J., & Perkins, T.S. (1987). Psychological skills and exceptional athletic performance. *The Sport Psychologist, 1*, 181-199.

Markus, H. (1983). Self-knowledge: An expanded view. *Journal of Personality, 51*, 543-565.

Martens, R. (1979). About smocks and jocks. *Journal of Sport Psychology, 1*, 94-99.

Martens, R. (1987). Science, knowledge, and sport psychology. *The Sport Psychologist, 1*, 94-99.

Martens, R., Vealey, R.S., & Burton, D. (1990). *Competitive anxiety in sport*. Champaign, IL: Human Kinetics.

May, J.R., & Brown, L. (1989). Delivery of psychological services to the U.S. alpine ski team prior to and during the Olympics in Calgary. *The Sport Psychologist, 3*, 320-329.

Maynard, I.W., & Cotton, P.C.J. (1993). An investigation of two stress-management techniques in a field setting. *The Sport Psychologist, 7*, 375-387.

Maynard, I.W., Warwick-Evans, L., & Smith, M.J. (1995). The effects of a cognitive intervention strategy on competitive state anxiety and performance in semiprofessional soccer players. *Journal of Sport and Exercise Psychology, 17*, 428-446.

McNair, D.M., Lorr, M., & Droppleman, L.F. (1981). *Profile of Mood States*. San Diego: Educational and Industrial Testing Service.

McReynolds, P. (1986). History of assessment in clinical and educational settings. In R.O. Nelson & S.C. Hayes (Eds.), *Conceptual foundations of behavioral assessment* (pp. 42-80). New York: Guilford.

Murphy, S.M. (Ed.). (1995). *Sport psychology interventions*. Champaign, IL: Human Kinetics.

Murphy, S.M., Hardy, L., Thomas, P., & Bond, J. (1993). *The Sports Inventory of Mental Skills*. Unpublished manuscript, U.S. Olympic Committee, Colorado Springs.

Nelson, D., & Hardy, L. (1990). The development of an empirically validated tool for measuring psypchological skill in sport. *Journal of Sports Sciences, 8*, 71.

Nelson, R.O., & Hayes, S.C. (1986). The nature of behavioral assessment. In R.O. Nelson & S.C. Hayes (Eds.), *Conceptual foundations of behavioral assessment* (pp. 3-41). New York: Guilford.

Nideffer, R.M. (1976). Test of Attentional and Interpersonal Style. *Journal of Personality and Social Psychology, 34*, 394-404.

Nideffer, R.M. (1981). *The ethics and practice of applied sport psychology*. Ithaca, NY: Mouvement Publications.

Nideffer, R.M. (1987). Issues in the use of psychological tests in applied settings. *The Sport Psychologist, 1*, 18-28.

Nideffer, R.M. (1989). Psychological services for the U.S. track and field team. *The Sport Psychologist, 3*, 350-357.

Nideffer, R.M. (1990). Use of the Test of Attentional and Interpersonal Style (TAIS) in sport. *The Sport Psychologist, 4*, 285-300.

Orlick T. (1986). *Psyching for sport: Mental training for athletes*. Champaign, IL: Human Kinetics.

Orlick, T. (1989). Reflections on sportpsych consulting with individual and team sport athletes at summer and winter Olympic games. *The Sport Psychologist, 3*, 358-365.

Orlick, T. (1990). *In pursuit of excellence*. Champaign, IL: Human Kinetics.

Orlick, T., & Partington, J. (1987). The sport psychology consultant: Analysis of critical components as viewed by Canadian Olympic athletes. *The Sport Psychologist, 1*, 4-17.

Partington, J., & Orlick, T. (1987a). The Sport Psychology Consultant Evaluation Form. *The Sport Psychologist, 1*, 309-317.

Partington, J., & Orlick T. (1987b). The sport psychology consultant: Olympic coaches' views. *The Sport Psychologist, 1*, 95-102.

Partington, J., & Orlick, T. (1991). An analysis of Olympic sport psychology consultants' best-ever consulting experiences. *The Sport Psychologist, 5*, 183-193.

Patterson, G.R. (1974). Interventions for boys with conduct problems: Multiple settings, treatments, and criteria. *Journal of Clinical and Consulting Psychology, 42*, 471-481.

Paunonen, S.V. (1988). Trait relevance and the differential predictability of behavior. *Journal of Personality, 56*, 599-619.

Perna, F., Neyer, M., Murphy, S.M., Ogilvie, B.C., & Murphy, A. (1995). Consultations with sport organizations: A cognitive-behavioral model. In S.M. Murphy (Ed.), *Sport psychology interventions* (pp. 235-252). Champaign, IL: Human Kinetics.

Phares, E.J. (1992). *Clinical psychology: Concepts, methods and profession* (4th ed.). Belmont, CA: Brooks/Cole.

Prapavessis, H., Grove, J.R., McNair, P.J., & Cable, N.T. (1992). Self-regulation training, state anxiety, and sport performance: A psychophysiological case study. *The Sport Psychologist, 6*, 213-229.

Ravizza, K. (1988). Gaining entry with athletic personnel for season-long consulting. *The Sport Psychologist, 2*, 243-254.

Ravizza, K. (1990). Sportpsych consultation issues in professional baseball. *The Sport Psychologist, 4*, 330-340.

Ravizza, K. (1993). Increasing awareness for sport performance. In J.M. Williams (Ed.), *Applied sport psychology: Personal growth to peak performance* (pp. 148-157). Mountain View, CA: Mayfield.

Rotella, R.J. (1990). Providing sport psychology consulting services to professional athletes. *The Sport Psychologist, 4*, 409-417.

Salmela, J.H. (1989). Long-term intervention with the Canadian men's Olympic gymnastics team. *The Sport Psychologist, 3*, 340-349.

Savoy, C. (1993). A yearly mental training program for a college basketball player. *The Sport Psychologist, 7*, 173-190.

Sherif, C.W. (1987). Bias in psychology. In S. Harding (Ed.), Feminism and methodology (pp. 37-56). Bloomington, IN: Indiana University Press.

Singer, R.N. (1988). Psychological testing: What value to coaches and athletes? *International Journal of Sport Psychology, 19*, 87-106.

Smith, R.E. (1989). Applied sport psychology in an age of accountability. *Journal of Applied Sport Psychology, 1*, 166-180.

Smith, R.E., & Christensen, D.S. (1995). Psychological skills as predictors of performance and survival in professional baseball. *Journal of Sport and Exercise Psychology, 17*, 399-415.

Smith, R.E., & Johnson, J. (1990). An organizational empowerment approach to consultation in professional baseball. *The Sport Psychologist, 4*, 346-357.

Smith, R.E., Smoll, F.L., & Schutz, R.W. (1990). Measurement and correlates of sport-specific cognitive and somatic trait anxiety: The sport anxiety scale. *Anxiety Research, 2*, 263-280.

Smith, R.E., Smoll, F.L., Schutz, R.W., & Ptacek, J.T. (1995). Development and validation of a multidimensional measure of sport-specific psychological skills: The Athletic Coping Skills Inventory - 28. *Journal of Sport and Exercise Psychology, 17*, 379-398. Thomasius, C. (1692). *Das verborgene des herzens anderer menschen auch wider ihren willen laus der taglichen conversation zuerkennen.* Halle, Germany: Christoph Salfeld.

Tutko, T.A., Lyon, L.P., & Ogilvie, B.C. (1969). *Athletic Motivation Inventory.* San Jose, CA: Institute for the Study of Athletic Motivation.

Vallerand, R.J. (1983). Attention and decision making: A test of the predictive validity of the Test of Attentional and Interpersonal Style (TAIS) in a sport setting. *Journal of Sport Psychology, 5*, 449-459.

Van Schoyck, R.S., & Grasha, A.F. (1981). Attentional style variations and athletic ability: The advantages of a sport-specific test. *Journal of Sport Psychology, 3*, 149-165.

Vealey, R.S. (1986). Conceptualization of sport-confidence and competitive orientation: Preliminary investigation and instrument development. *Journal of Sport Psychology, 8*, 221-246.

Vealey, R.S. (1988). Future directions for psychological skill training. *The Sport Psychologist, 2*, 318-336.

Vealey, R.S. (1994). Current status and prominent issues in sport psychology interventions. *Medicine and Science in Sports and Exercise, 26*, 495-502.

Wang, M.Q., & Landers, D.M. (1988). *Cardiac responses and hemispheric differentiation during archery performance: A psychophysiological investigation of attention.* Unpublished manuscript, Arizona State University, Tempe, AZ.

Weiss, M.R. (1995). Children in sport: An educational model. In S.M. Murphy (Ed.), *Sport psychology interventions* (pp. 39-69). Champaign, IL: Human Kinetics.

Whelan, J.P., Meyers, A.W., & Donovan, C. (1995). Competitive recreational athletes: A multisystematic model. In S.M. Murphy (Ed.), *Sport psychology interventions* (pp. 71-116). Champaign, IL: Human Kinetics.

Chapter 27

APPLIED EXERCISE PSYCHOLOGY: MEASUREMENT ISSUES

Jay C. Kimiecik
and
Bryan Blissmer
Miami University

Many measurement issues exist in applied exercise psychology. This chapter cannot hope to address them all, and thus, we focus on the measurement issues that appear to us to be most important, but keep in mind that ours is only one perspective. The focus in other chapters of this book has been on the development of state-of-the art measurement instruments to assess such psychological constructs as social physique anxiety, perceived barriers to exercise, and exercise-related self-efficacy. The primary focus of this chapter is on measurement issues pertaining to the application and use of some of these instruments.

Before we can present and discuss some of the measurement issues, a definition of applied exercise psychology needs to be presented. To our knowledge there is no consensus definition of applied exercise psychology. It may help, then, first to examine a definition of applied psychology as provided by Gifford (1991): "...the part of psychology that, while retaining the goal of advancing knowledge through a scientific approach to human behavior, is dedicated to research and practice that ameliorate the immediate and developing problems of individuals and organizations" (p. 2). This definition would suggest that applied exercise psychology could be the part of exercise psychology that, while retaining the goal of advancing knowledge through a scientific approach to exercise behavior, is dedicated to research *and* practice that aids individuals in making positive changes in their exercise behavior and enhances the quality of their exercise experiences.

In this chapter, the focus is primarily on the measurement issues pertaining to helping people change their exercise behavior in both *research* and *practice* settings. Within applied psychology, a distinction is typically made between applied and applicable research (Belbin, 1979; Davies, Spurgeon, & Chapman, 1994). *Applied research* is mainly oriented toward the accumulation of knowledge within a particular area. In contrast, *applicable research* is directed at the solution of a particular practical problem, for example, increasing the physical activity behavior of employees in a worksite setting through an incentive program (e.g., Blake et al., 1996). In essence, applicable research is considered to be exercise interventions designed and evaluated by scientific researchers and implemented in practice settings (e.g., Physician-Based Assessment and Counseling for Exercise (PACE); Pender, Sallis, Long, & Calfas, 1994). There has been a recent upsurge of these kinds of interventions designed to increase people's physical activity, and this chapter will examine some of the measurement issues associated with developing and implementing applicable research in exercise contexts. Issues of professional practice applications will also be discussed.

Practice refers to any environment in which health-promotion professionals (e.g., worksite health and fitness staff) attempt to help clients (e.g., employees) change their exercise behavior without necessarily using a scientifically accepted research design. It is important to keep in mind that, ultimately, health professionals in practice settings are the group primarily responsible for developing and implementing exercise behavior change programs. They may use instruments and findings obtained from both applied and applicable exercise research studies to guide their exercise programming attempts, or they may not. Hence, it makes sense to examine the applicability of exercise psychology measurement instruments developed and used in scientific research studies for use in practice settings. By making a distinction between researchers and practitioners, we do not mean to reinforce age-old stereotypes. However, although there is presently some applicable research that is the result of collaboration between the researcher and the practitioner, this separation does exist, and it has major implications for a discussion of measurement issues in applied exercise psychology.

In sum, we make a distinction between applied and applicable exercise psychology research and practitioner-oriented exercise programming. In this chapter, we focus primarily on measurement issues pertaining to applicable exercise psychology research, some of which relate to how applied exercise psychology research is typically conducted. We should point out that our primary emphasis in this chapter is *not* on evaluating the effectiveness of exercise behavior interventions. There are many excellent reviews of these kinds of interventions (e.g., Dishman & Buckworth, 1996). Rather, our approach is to address the critical measurement issues within applicable research interventions and as they pertain to exercise programming developed by practice-oriented health professionals. Specifically, the purposes of this chapter are to (a) briefly discuss the measurement issue pertaining to the assessment of exercise behavior, (b) examine some of the critical measurement issues related to the use of psychological-oriented instruments in typical exercise behavior intervention studies conducted by researchers (i.e., applicable research), (c) examine some of the measurement issues related to practitioners' use of psychological-oriented instruments when helping people change exercise behavior, and (d) present some suggestions for future applied exercise psychology measurement in research and practice.

Measurement Issues Pertaining to the Assessment of Exercise Behavior

As Dishman (1994a) points out, measuring exercise behavior is, in fact, a conundrum, and space constraints as well as the primary focus of this chapter prohibit a lengthy discussion of the myriad measurement issues associated with its assessment. We do present two issues to keep in mind pertaining to this difficult, and important, measurement challenge. First, nearly all exercise behavior interventions, whether they be guided by cognitive-behavior modification techniques (e.g., contracting) or social cognitive theory (e.g., planned behavior), utilize self-report of exercise behavior. According to Dishman and Buckworth (1996), relatively few interventions "verified self-reported physical activity by measuring increases in fitness expected to result from increased physical activity or by concomitantly using an objective measure of activity such as a motion sensor or observation" (p. 713). The lack of concurrent validity established for self-report of physical activity is significant, especially in light of work that shows that social-cognitive variables are related to self-reports of physical activity but not to objective estimates of physical activity (Dishman, Darracott, & Lambert, 1992). Hence, what is known about the strength of the relationship between some social psychological determinants (e.g., self-efficacy) and exercise behavior may be quite tenuous and a direct result of the inaccurate assessment of the dependent variable. Only more rigorous evaluations by journal reviewers and editors and standardization of physical activity measurement will serve as catalysts to develop concurrent validity for self-reported physical activity measures.

A second issue is that the recent findings on the relationship of physical activity, fitness, and health (see Blair & Connelly, 1996) make it extremely difficult for intervention-oriented researchers to determine what kind of physical activity behavior to focus on, change, and measure: daily light-to-moderate physical activity or vigorous physical activity performed at least 3 days per week (i.e., exercise). Many of the psychologically oriented interventions in this area have focused on exercise as the dependent variable, but the public health data sug-

gest that light-to-moderate physical activity may be just as important for reducing risk from certain chronic degenerative diseases. Of course, both light-to-moderate physical activity and exercise can be measured. The measurement issue for the applied exercise psychology researcher is one of selecting the dependent behavior of interest and then determining the best way to measure it. This is not an easy task. Researchers interested in conducting physical activity interventions from a social psychological perspective need to spend as much conceptual and measurement time with the dependent measure as they do with the independent measures. In addition, the interventionist needs to be very clear about which kind of physical activity she or he is interested in changing because studies have found different determinants for light-to-moderate and vigorous physical activity (Sallis et al., 1986). It should be clear that anyone interested in conducting applied or applicable exercise psychology research will need to address the conundrum of measuring physical activity (see Ainsworth, Montoye, & Leon, 1994; Montoye, Kemper, Saris, & Washburn, 1996, for some of the more current physical activity measurement methods).

In sum, corroborating self-report physical activity or exercise data with more objective measures is essential. In addition, the targeted behavior needs to be precisely defined so that the psychosocial determinants of different kinds of physical activity (i.e., light, moderate, or vigorous) can be better understood (see King, 1994, for a similar recommendation).

Measurement Issues Pertaining to the Assessment of Psychological Constructs in Applicable Exercise Behavior Research

As stated earlier, it is not our objective here to review the effectiveness of exercise behavior interventions that have utilized a social psychological framework. This has been done very well by others (see U.S Department of Health and Human Services, 1996, and a review by Dishman & Buckworth, 1996). In addition, it is a difficult task to critique the measurement of the myriad psychological constructs that have been utilized within these interventions. In many interventions, exercise or physical activity is only one of several health behaviors targeted, and psychological constructs are usually embedded in a comprehensive approach to health-behavior change (see the CATCH intervention on school-age children as an example; McGraw et al., 1994). Keeping this in mind, the major goal of this section is to present an analysis of how psychological constructs have been used and measured in typical interventions focused on changing exercise behavior.

A major measurement issue pertaining to applicable exercise psychology research (i.e., exercise behavior interventions grounded in a social psychological orientation) is that psychological constructs are *not* typically measured. This may, at first, seem surprising, but a closer look at some of the typical social psychological-oriented exercise behavior interventions indicates this to be true. This is particularly evident for interventions that could be categorized within the individual or personal level (see excellent reviews by King, 1994, and U.S. Department of Health and Human Services, 1996). Many of these personal interventions use cognitive/behavioral modification strategies, such as self-monitoring, contracting, and goal setting. For example, self-monitoring has typically involved individuals keeping written records or logs of their physical activity frequency, duration, and intensity. Studies generally find that self-monitoring enhances adherence or attendance to exercise classes, but the effects have been small, and it is not clear under what circumstances behavioral management approaches work best (U.S Department of Health and Human Services, 1996).

What is missing with most of these kinds of studies is any measurement or assessment of the social psychological *change process* underlying the targeted outcome (i.e., attendance or increased physical activity). Strategies to increase physical activity may be implemented and tested based on social learning, relapse prevention, or behavioral management theory, but without measuring psychological process or change variables within the intervention, the potential for developing an applied exercise psychology knowledge base will be limited. A number of exercise researchers have recommended a more dynamic, process approach to studying exercise and conducting interventions (Prochaska & Marcus, 1994; Sallis & Hovell, 1990).

Findings from a study by McAuley (1992) point to the importance of examining and measuring psychological processes. Self-efficacy, which was assessed at Week 3 and Week 12 of a 5-month exercise program, was significantly related to exercise behavior in the early stages of the program (adoption) but not later (maintenance). This kind of dynamic measurement and assessment approach provides a much more in-depth understanding of the ongoing process of exercise behavior change than does a static intervention approach that either does not measure psychological variables or only includes a pre-post assessment of such variables. Another study (King, Taylor, Haskell, & De-Busk, 1989), although not directed at changing exercise behavior per se, found that a process approach was crucial for examining changes in psychological well-being during an exercise program. Psychological well-being was assessed every 2 weeks over the course of the 6-month intervention. Results indicate that changes in perceptions of the body occurred primarily during the first month of the program and then leveled off for the remainder of the program. If a typical pre-post approach to changes in psychological well-being had been adopted by the researchers, this important change data would have been missed.

Pulling from the health-education evaluation literature, exercise behavior interventions adopting a social psychological approach need to include more systematic *impact evaluation*, which is designed to assess a program's effectiveness in achieving desired changes in targeted mediators, such as knowledge, attitudes, beliefs, and behavior of the target group (Israel et al., 1995). If the assumption is that personal change in relevant social and psychological variables precedes changes in exercise behavior, then it makes sense to measure these variables over time within interventions to better understand the how, why, and when of the process of change. Many of the psychological constructs that are the focus of chapters in this book would serve as excellent process-type variables to measure and assess within exercise behavior intervention studies.

A similar measurement observation can be made pertaining to larger scale health-behavior interventions focusing on communities and/or schools. For instance, an intervention study by Marcus, Banspach et al. (1992) used the stages-of-change model to tailor a different set of self-help materials for individuals categorized into contemplation, preparation, and action stages of exercise behavior, respectively. The findings showed a significant increase in physical activity after 6 weeks. This type of study is certainly a positive step towards a process-oriented approach to exercise behavior interventions, but without including the measurement of process-type psychological constructs before, during, and after the intervention, we still do not really know the underlying mechanisms of that change. Did this tailoring approach help to enhance people's exercise-related self-efficacy? Did it help increase the enjoyment of the behavior? Did it increase exercise-related positive affect? These are not criticisms of such cutting-edge work. We use it to point out that understanding the process of change within exercise behavior interventions can be done only by including and measuring psychological variables that are likely to undergird behavior change.

The development of the Exercise Processes of Change Questionnaire (EPCQ; see Marcus, Rossi, Selby, Niaura, & Abrams, 1992) may begin to facilitate an understanding of the process underlying exercise behavior change. The EPCQ is divided into experiential and behavioral components. A recent study by Marcus, Simkin, Rossi, and Pinto (1996) showed that behavioral processes, rather than cognitive processes, decreased for employees who relapsed from one exercise stage to another in a negative direction. The implications of this finding are that the behavioral skills associated with maintaining exercise behavior may be more critical than the cognitive processes related to the behavior. This kind of process-oriented analysis is a critical next step in the development, implementation, and evaluation of exercise behavior interventions adopting a social psychological orientation.

School-based health-behavior interventions also tend not to assess the process of change from a psychosocial perspective. The Sports, Play, and Active Recreation for Kids (SPARK) study and the Child and Adolescent Trial for Cardiovascular Health (CATCH) study are excellent examples of large-scale interventions designed to examine the effects of combining health-related physical education curriculum, family involvement, and/or in-service programs on children's physical activity. Both studies (Luepker et al., 1996; McKenzie, Sallis, Faucette, Roby, & Kolody, 1993) showed significant increases in children's vigorous physical activity during their participation in physical education classes. However, although the SPARK intervention demonstrated behavior change on the part of children, we know very little about the psychosocial process underlying that change. Did children also change their perceptions of physical competence? Self-efficacy pertaining to physical activity? Enjoyment associated with the physical activity? Measuring changes in these psychological process variables is critical if it is believed that certain psychosocial factors influence exercise behavior in the long term. Changing children's physical activity behavior via a health-related physical education curriculum is one thing; understanding the psychosocial process underlying that change is quite another.

Interestingly, findings related to the effects of the CATCH intervention on psychosocial determinants of children's physical activity have been recently reported (Edmundson et al., 1996). As reviewed in the Surgeon General's Report on Physical Activity and Health (U.S. Department of Health and Human Services, 1996), although the intervention students showed significant increases in their perceptions of positive social reinforcement and self-efficacy for exercise from baseline, these psychosocial determinants were not significantly more prevalent than those observed among the control groups at follow-up. In essence, results for the physical activity determinants were weak. Hence, as with SPARK, children's physical activity was increased, but the psychosocial mechanisms underlying the how or why of the increase in children's physical activity remain unclear.

The significance of the above analysis is to demonstrate that a large gap exists between what psychosocial-oriented interventions have accomplished from a behavioral perspective and what is known about the psychosocial process underlying those effects. Perhaps this is a primary reason as to why in most exercise behavior intervention studies the "increases in physical activity or fitness associated with the interventions were diminished as time passed after the intervention ended" (Dishman & Buckworth, 1996, p. 713). This is both an evaluation and a measurement issue. The gap exists because impact evaluation has not been emphasized enough on the part of the interventionists, and when it has, the psychosocial process variables that are most likely involved in the change process either have not been assessed or have been measured in static (i.e., pre-post), rather than dynamic (i.e., before, during, after), ways.

Measurement Issues Pertaining to the Use of Exercise Psychology Instruments in Practice

Ultimately, a goal of applied exercise psychology is to help health and fitness professionals utilize measurement and assessment tools that will enable them to facilitate exercise behavior change for their clients. This is a major challenge. Applicable exercise psychology interventions conducted by scientific researchers is typically not the same approach taken by health and fitness practitioners who develop products, programs, and services designed to increase the physical activity of their clients. Hence, there are a whole host of measurement issues when examining the relationship between applicable exercise psychology research and practitioners' approaches to exercise behavior change, but we focus on two. First, any discussion of measurement issues in the context of practice must include an analysis of the *scientific paradigm* within which typical exercise psychology instruments are developed. A second, related measurement issue pertains to an analysis of the psychological constructs and their corresponding measurement that may be most *useful* to practitioners' attempts in facilitating people's exercise behavior change.

The Issue of Scientific Paradigms

In essence, most of the applied exercise psychology measurement instruments have been developed and used by researchers within a positivistic, basic research paradigm. As suggested by Christina (1987), the major goal of basic research is the development of theory-based knowledge. Solving practical problems, such as helping people change exercise behavior, is not the immediate concern. The assumption is that the theory-based knowledge will at some point guide practitioners in solving their practice problems. Hence, much of the present exercise psychology measurement orientation is focused on developing instruments that meet the requirements of positivistic, basic research science.

Because the research orientation and subsequent instrumentation has been quite theoretical, it is difficult for health and fitness professionals to utilize measurement and assessment instruments in practice settings. This is because "the vast majority of practitioners do not think like researchers" (Lawson, 1990, p. 172). Newell (1990) suggests that researchers typically focus on theoretical knowledge, which "relates directly to broad networks of ideas and observations that provide the basis for description, prediction, and explanation..." (p. 249). Professionals focus more on practitioner knowledge, which Newell says pertains primarily to the development of practical competence. The important point here is that researchers and practitioners work in different worlds and, as Lawson (1990) states, "think and act differently because of their respective socialization experiences, work organizations, career commitments, and work demands" (p. 167).

It is important to spend some time with this macromeasurement issue because the dominant paradigm—a positivistic, basic research orientation—has been guiding much of the work in applied exercise psychology. The outcome of this emphasis has been a fixation on method and the development of valid and reliable measurement instruments. This is not atypical as Strong (1991) has made a similar observation about the field of counseling psychology. Exercise psychology has become method and instrument-development bound. This is a logical step for this discipline because only through rigorous method and the development of valid and reliable instruments can exercise psychology progress according to the criteria of the dominant paradigm. The upside to this emphasis is that it has the potential to build a theoretical knowledge base; the downside is that it may take the discipline of applied exercise psychology farther and farther away from the world of practice. The researchers' argument is that once the discipline of exercise psychology has strengthened its theoretical knowledge and measurement instruments, practitioners will be better able to understand the importance of such psychological constructs for practice and to use the information in practical ways. However, there are some who would argue that this approach to research and practice is not optimal for helping the practitioner (e.g., Garner, 1972).

Another critical, and related, issue to consider within this paradigm-oriented discussion about measurement is that typical applied exercise psychology research is conducted within a nomothetic orientation. Allport (1962) used the word nomothetic to characterize the search for general laws. As Runyan (1983) explains, "According to the classic nomothetic view, the search for broad generalizations about all human beings will enable us to adequately explain and predict behavior at the group *and* individual level" (p. 417; emphasis added). Within this research approach, subjects are typically divided into low and high self-efficacy or low and high social physique anxiety groups and then compared using inferential statistics as to how they might differ in their exercise behavior patterns. There are numerous criticisms of the nomothetic approach (Allport, 1962; Lincoln & Guba, 1985; Runyan, 1983), and they are very relevant to a discipline such as applied exercise psychology. As Runyan (1983) explains:

> ...explanation and prediction often depend crucially upon knowledge available only at the particular level of analysis. Anyone who attempts to interpret a life solely in terms of universal generalizations soon becomes aware of the limitations of this approach. Rather, explanation at the individual level often occurs, not through the deductive application of universal generalizations, but rather through processes such as searching for the individual's reasons for acting in a particular way, through collecting as much information as possible about the individual and looking for idiographic patterns within it, and through organizing information about the case into an intelligible narrative. (p. 418)

This issue becomes critical when we begin to apply exercise psychology constructs, such as social physique anxiety (Bain & McAuley, this volume), exercise-related affect (Gauvin & Spence, this volume), and exercise-related self-efficacy (McAuley & Mihalko, this volume), to help people change exercise behavior. The knowledge base pertaining to these constructs was developed primarily through nomothetic methods for the purpose of contributing to theoretical knowledge in exercise psychology. We do not know, nor can we say, how such constructs influence each unique individual's exercise behavior change attempts. We can not even say how relevant any of the constructs are to the reality of behavior-change attempts for each individual. Vealey and Garner-Holman (this volume) present similar cautions when applying a specific measurement instrument, such as the CSAI-2, developed within nomothetic research approaches to specific athletes in applied sport psychology interventions.

The potential for similar application problems exists when helping people change exercise behavior. For example, consider the 12-item Social Physique Anxiety Scale (Bain & McAuley, this volume). Evidence has been presented by a number of researchers that demonstrates the validity and reliability of the SPAS (Crawford & Eklund, 1994; Hart, Leary, & Rejeski, 1989; McAuley & Burman, 1993). How well does the SPAS explain the exercise behavior of a sedentary, older female who has joined an exercise program for the first time? When she completes the SPAS, she scores low on all of the items on the scale except one, which in total indicates a low degree of social physique anxiety. The one item she scored high on was "Unattractive features of my physique/figure make me nervous in certain social settings." Now, can we conclude that this woman is really low on social physique anxiety? No. Within group data, this one item is evened out by her responses to the other 11 items. For this particular individual, however, it may be that this one item is most relevant to her social physique anxiety. In addition, we do not really know how relevant social physique anxiety is to this woman's exercise behavior. The point is that extreme caution must be used when we begin to apply nomothetically developed exercise psychology instruments to assess a specific individual's psychosocial orientation towards exercise and then use that information to guide behavior-change programming in professional practice contexts.

In sum, most of the exercise psychology measurement instruments have been developed within a positivistic, nomothetic, basic research paradigm for the primary purpose of advancing theoretical knowledge. In addition, almost all of the applicable exercise psychology research (i.e., interventions) has been conducted within a group-comparative, experimental design. As Knapp (1995) points out, "group comparative studies are harder to realize in practice than on paper, and the logic often breaks down" (p. 14). Finally, much of this research and instrument development has been conducted outside the realm of professional practice settings. That is, practitioner knowledge has had very little influence on the exercise psychology research and instrument-development process. Hence, the way in which measurement instruments are developed by exercise psychology researchers makes it quite unlikely that they can and will be used by many health/fitness practitioners interested in helping the vast majority of their clients develop physically active lifestyles. This is due to the fact that the researcher and practitioner reside in different work worlds and usually have different goals and ideas about what motivates people's behavior.

Although there are limitations in the application of typical exercise psychology instruments for facilitating people's exercise behavior change attempts in practice contexts, this does not mean that exercise psychology has no application in these settings. The next section provides a discussion on the potential application of psychological constructs in health and fitness practice settings.

The Issue of Application of Exercise Psychology Constructs in Practice Settings

In this section, an analysis of the practicality of select psychological constructs to guide practitioner-based programs focused on helping people adopt and maintain more physically active lives is presented. In addition, five questions and answers are presented as a way of discussing some of the measurement and application issues pertaining to the relationship between research and practice.

Practicality of Psychological Constructs in Practice Settings

The psychological constructs included in this section have been found in applied exercise psychology work to be significantly related to exercise behavior; the ones we have selected to critique certainly do not constitute an exhaustive list. Separate psychological constructs and their accompanying measurement are analyzed, rather than the complete theories in which some are embedded, which parallels the approach taken by this book. The following exercise psychology constructs and measurement are examined as to their practicality and usefulness: physical self perceptions, exercise self efficacy, locus of control and perceived control, exercise-related affect, social physique anxiety, enjoyment, and stages of change. We provide a table that summarizes our assessment of each psychological construct measurement instrument's *application potential in practice settings*. This rating scheme is designed to be a rough assessment of the practicality of each construct *and* its accompanying measurement tool for use by practitioners in health and fitness settings.

Certainly evidence is moderately strong that physical self perceptions are relevant to people's exercise behavior (see Fox, this volume). With respect to physical self-perceptions, three scales have been developed that seem relevant to exercise behavior: the Physical Self-Perception Profile (PSPP; Fox, 1990), the Physical Self-Concept (PSC) scale (Richards, 1988), and the Physical Self-Description Questionnaire (PSDQ; Marsh, Richards, Johnson, Roche, & Tremayne, 1994). All of these physical self-perception instruments are based on a hierarchical, multidimensional model of self-concept. In essence, this model orientation assumes that we all have a global self-esteem, which is dependent upon our perceptions of ourselves in various life domains, such as academic, social, and physical. These life domains can then be further subdivided into various components. This is where these physical self-perception instruments come into the picture as they assess the various components of an individual's physical life domain. As Fox points out (this volume), there are data to support the validity and reliability of these physical self-perception dimensions as well as data to suggest that specific components of physical self-perception are related to exercise activity (Marsh & Sonstroem, 1995).

Although the conceptualization of physical self-perceptions and the rigor of its measurement are quite strong, the practicality of physical self-perceptions and the accompanying measurement, as it relates to facilitating behavior change, seem minimal. The PSDQ, for example, could serve as more of a research tool to determine changes in physical self-perceptions based on participation in a regular exercise program. For example, does a person's perception of appearance change as a result of going from sedentary to a regular exerciser? In addition, many of the subscales pertain to sport, which becomes somewhat problematic in more traditional exercise settings. Certainly a person's perceptions of his or her physical self are involved in exercise motivation, but it may be difficult for health/fitness practitioners to utilize the construct in concrete ways to facilitate behavior change.

Exercise-related self efficacy (see McAuley & Mihalko, this volume) could be categorized as a physical self-perception in the sense that it is a belief a person has pertaining to his or her confidence in performing regular vigorous physical activity. Self-efficacy is a component of social cognitive theory (Bandura, 1986), which incorporates efficacy and outcome expectations as well as four primary sources of efficacy: performance attainment, imitation and modeling, verbal and social persuasion, and judgments of physiological states. Certainly, exercise-related self-efficacy has received much attention as to its relevance in influencing whether or not people are sedentary or exercise regularly. In general, the data show that those high in self-efficacy are more likely to exercise regularly than are those low in their efficacy beliefs. The measurement recommendation by Bandura is that self-efficacy be assessed at a micro, situation-specific level. In exercise contexts, self-efficacy has typically been assessed by examining people's confidence to overcome perceived barriers (see Brawley, Martin, and Gyurscik, this volume) to regular exercise. The list of barriers generally ranges from 5 to 10 items in which the respondent must determine his or her confidence to overcome each barrier to exercise on the list.

Self-efficacy seems to have strong application potential for helping people change behavior. By assessing an individual's confidence in changing exercise behavior, the practitioner can identify those who may need more support and assistance to exercise regularly. As an example, the practitioner can help the individual enhance efficacy expectations through setting realistic goals and achieving success through mastery experiences. From a practical perspective, it also makes sense to tap into an individual's perceived barriers to exercise and then ascertain his or her confidence to overcome each barrier to exercise. This not only helps the client become more aware of barriers but also gives the practitioner some valuable information about the kind of barriers each individual is dealing with in his or her attempts to exercise.

Locus of control and perceived control are two psychological constructs that have received considerable attention by exercise behavior researchers. The locus-of-control construct has

Table 1

Exercise Psychology Constructs, Measurement Instruments, and Potential for Application in Exercise Practice Settings

Exercise Psychology Constructs	Measurement Instrument	Application Potential
Physical self-perceptions	PSDQ (strong)	Minimal
Self-efficacy	Situation specific	Strong
Locus of control		
General	I-E scale (strong)	Minimal
Health	MHLC (strong)	Minimal
Exercise	EXLOC (weak)	Minimal
	EOLOC (weak)	Minimal
	FITLOC (weak)	Minimal
Perceived control	Recommended to use self-efficacy measurement protocol	
Exercise-related affect	EFI (strong)	Moderate
Social physique anxiety	SPAS (strong)	Strong
Enjoyment	PACES (weak)	Moderate
Stages of change	Stages-of-change instrument (strong)	Strong

a long history and is a central part of Rotter's (1954) social learning theory but plays less of a role in K. Wallston's (1992) modified social learning theory. Locus of control has an interesting history when applied to health behaviors such as exercise. It started with Rotter's internal-external (I-E) scale. In order to increase the predictability of locus of control in health-related situations, the health locus of control (HLC) scale was developed (B. Wallston, Wallston, Kaplan, & Maides, 1976). K. Wallston, Wallston, and DeVellis (1978) then developed the psychometrically superior multidimensional HLC (MHLC) scale, which included "chance" and "powerful others" as external beliefs. With respect to health behaviors, K. Wallston (1992) argues that the internal dimension (IHLC) is and should be the most frequently studied of the three health locus-of-control dimensions because the internal dimension typically predicts health behaviors the best and because the external dimensions are rarely correlated with health behaviors. The MHLC scale contains 18 items, using 6 items each to assess internal, powerful others, and chance dimensions.

Taking the notion of specificity even further, some exercise researchers felt the predictability of locus of control could be enhanced by developing exercise-specific locus-of-control scales (McCready & Long, 1985; Noland & Feldman, 1984; Whitehead & Corbin, 1988). Noland and Feldman developed the Exercise Locus of Control Scale (EXLOC); McCready and Long developed the Exercise Objectives Locus of Control scale (EOLOC); and Whitehead and Corbin devised a locus-of-control scale for physical fitness behaviors (FITLOC). Although the intent behind the development of these scales is a scientifically valid one and a worthy endeavor, the locus-of-control construct has not lived up to its promise (K. Wallston, 1992). The argument could be made, of course, that this is due to inappropriate methodology, inadequate instrumentation, or incorrect application of social learning theory (e.g., not examining the interaction between locus expectancies *and* value). Wallston believes that at this time, generalized expectancy does not seem to be as critical to people's behavior, especially in health contexts, as was once thought. Wallston summarizes his modified social learning theory:

...SLT states that the potential for an individual's engaging in a set of health-promoting behaviors is a function of the interaction of HV [health value] and perceived control over health. People must value health as an outcome, believe that their health actions influence their health status, *and concurrently* believe that they are capable of carrying out the necessary behaviors in order to have a high likelihood of engaging in a health-directed action. (p. 195)

In essence, Wallston is suggesting that perceived control—more or less operationalized as self-efficacy—is more important than locus of control and is now more congruent with Bandura's (1986) social cognitive theory and Ajzen's (1987) theory of planned behavior in which perceived control plays a central role. Because perceived control and self-efficacy are conceptually similar and because the measurement protocol set out by Bandura (1986) is more clear up to this point, it makes sense to use self-efficacy, rather than perceived control, as the primary construct. Brawley (1993) also points out that the measurement protocol of self-efficacy is better developed than that of perceived control at this time.

Hence, locus of control probably has weak potential for use in practice settings unless new data come out suggesting otherwise. K. Wallston (1992) has argued recently that locus of control "constitutes a relatively small portion of the larger and more important construct, perceived control over health" (p. 186). In addition, most studies examining locus of control in exercise contexts have found respondents to score high on internal locus of control. The homogeneity of the construct as it relates to exercise behavior is quite common (i.e., people tend to score high on internal locus of control), which reduces the ability of the construct to predict behavior. This also reduces its significance in practice settings. If people who drop out of exercise programs score as high as the people who stay in them, obtaining information on locus of control will not be of much help to the practitioner.

It is reasonable to assume that exercise-related affect (see Gauvin & Spence, this volume) is certainly relevant to people's exercise behavior. Most would argue that how people feel before, during, and after exercise must impact their motivation to participate in the behavior. However, as Gauvin and Brawley (1993) have pointed out:

Little is known about the actual magnitude and pervasiveness of exercise-related mood benefits, and few, if any, practical applications for mental health or exercise adherence have been drawn because the affective experience that accompanies exercise has not been thoroughly described (p. 147).

There is some interesting work beginning to emerge related to the study of exercise-related affect and exercise behavior (e.g., Gauvin, Rejeski, & Norris, 1996). Gauvin and Rejeski (1993) have developed the 12-item Exercise-Induced Feeling Inventory (EFI), which consists of four distinct feeling states: revitalization, tranquillity, positive engagement, and physical exhaustion.

Exercise-related affect has moderate application potential at this time, but once more is learned about the role of affect in exercise motivation, it could have strong implications for exercise behavior change. Understanding the feelings that people tie to their exercise experiences could be very beneficial to practitioners. If health/fitness practitioners better understood the unique exercise-related affective experiences of each of their clients, they could help clients choose the kinds of activities that would optimize positive affect and minimize negative affect.

A construct that falls within the conceptualization of affect is social physique anxiety (see Bain & McAuley, this volume). In essence, this construct refers to the anxiety that people experience in response to others' evaluations of their physiques (Hart et al., 1989). Social physique anxiety has been shown to be related to certain aspects of exercise behavior (Eklund & Crawford, 1994; Hart et al., 1989). The practical implication of social physique anxiety is that if a person is high in physique anxiety he or she may avoid exercise settings (e.g., an aerobics class) because of a concern with how others may view or evaluate his or her body (Leary, Tchividjian, & Kraxberger, 1994). The construct of social physique anxiety emerged from Leary et al.'s self-presentation perspective, which "refers to the processes by which people control how they are perceived and evaluated by others" (p. 461). Hart and colleagues (1989) developed the 12-item Social Physique Anxiety Scale (SPAS) and established satisfactory psychometric properties. Eklund and Crawford (1994) rephrased one item of the SPAS to clear up confusion on the part of the respondents.

Social physique anxiety has strong application potential. Knowing the physique anxiety of individuals within exercise settings, practitioners could do a number of things. First, they would know that individuals high in social physique anxiety may need an exercise environment that minimizes social evaluation. Second, with this information, the fitness professional becomes more aware about how typical exercise classes may be having negative influences on participation of high social-physique-anxiety individuals. Third, this knowledge could serve as a catalyst for discussion between fitness professional and client pertaining to the role that physique anxiety plays in a client's motivation and participation in exercise behavior. It is possible that this approach may serve to begin to decrease physique anxiety for some individuals and subsequently enhance exercise behavior.

Another construct that has been considered by some researchers to be within the affective domain is enjoyment (Scanlan & Simons, 1992; Wankel, 1993). Although there is some disagreement as to whether enjoyment is really positive emotion (Kimiecik & Harris, 1996), Wankel (1993) is probably correct when he asserts that "enjoyment is an essential consideration for enhancing exercise adherence so that the anticipated physical and psychological benefits might be realized" (p. 152). Kendzierski and DeCarlo (1991) have developed the 18-item Physical Activity Enjoyment Scale (PACES) in which the respondent is asked to rate how she or he feels at the moment immediately following an acute bout of physical activity. In this sense the PACES is very similar to the EFI described earlier. Both of these instruments assess various aspects of physical activity-related affect. Recent psychometric work on the PACES by Crocker, Bouffard, and Gessaroli (1995) found that the PACES may be tapping more than one dimension of enjoyment. In addition, caution is warranted in using this scale because it is not embedded in any precise operationalization of enjoyment in regard to theory. Rotter (1990) is critical of this approach to measurement and argues that the "heuristic value of a construct is considerably enhanced if it is imbedded in a broader theory of behavior" (p. 490).

An understanding of enjoyment is crucial to enhancing people's maintenance of exercise (Wankel, 1985). However, the way in which the exercise psychology research has operationalized and measured the enjoyment construct up to this point makes it difficult for practitioners to use enjoyment in any systematic way to help people change exercise behavior. In addition, most people do not have the same view on enjoyment. For example, Heck and Kimiecik (1993) asked regular exercisers to define enjoyment with respect to their exercise experiences. The results indicated that the participants' definitions were diverse and multidimensional. This makes the construct of enjoyment problematic when using it as a process variable for behavior change.

The final construct to be considered in this section is stages of change, a core construct within the transtheoretical model of behavior change (Prochaska & Marcus, 1994). Prochaska and Marcus clearly define their concept of stages:

> The concept of stages falls somewhere between traits and states. Traits are typically constructed as stable and not open to change. States, on the other hand, are readily changed and typically lack stability. Stages can be both stable and dynamic in nature. That is, although stages may last for considerable periods of time, they are open to change. This is the nature of most high risk behaviors—stable over time yet open to change. (p. 162)

The stages have been labeled as precontemplation, contemplation, preparation, action, maintenance, and termination. Recent work has begun to apply this stages-of-change construct within exercise settings with positive results (Marcus, Banspach et al., 1992; Marcus, Selby, Niaura, & Rossi, 1992). From a measurement perspective, Marcus, Rossi, et al. (1992) developed a scale to measure stages of change for exercise. A number of studies have examined the reliability and validity of this stages-of-change scale, and it has been shown to be psychometrically strong. For example, Marcus and Simkin (1993) found that the stages-of-change scale compared favorably with the well-established Seven Day Physical Activity Recall Questionnaire (Blair, 1984). An appealing feature of the stages-of-change construct is that it takes into account the dynamic nature of exercise behavior (Prochaska & Marcus, 1991). In addition, this construct takes into account an individual's readiness for change. Finally, another strong asset of this approach is that, based on an individual's present stage of change, different processes can be utilized to promote transitions from one stage to the next. The study by Marcus, Banspach, et al. (1992) found preliminary evidence of the effectiveness of this approach in a community-wide exercise-behavior intervention.

Stages of change has strong application potential because the construct is very easy to understand, it can be assessed by most practitioners very easily, and it is very concrete (i.e., places people into certain stages of exercise-behavior change). The difficult part is for the fitness professional to determine what to do next once he or she has a better idea of an individual's stage of change. At the very least, assessing stages of change gives the practitioner an idea of where his or her clients are with respect to exercise behavior. This provides baseline information and allows the practitioner and the client to monitor change over time.

In sum, a variety of exercise psychological constructs have a range of application potential in practice settings, and we could not discuss all of them in this chapter. Of course, future work with any of these constructs may change the way in which they are utilized by health/fitness practitioners. The following section discusses some critical issues of application via a question-and-answer format.

Question #1: Should practitioners select a specific theoretical orientation and then work with the constructs from that theory alone? No. This is unrealistic and impractical. A study conducted by Burdine and McLeroy (1992) in a health-education context support this. The authors conducted semistructured interviews with a group of health education practitioners and asked them, "How do you use theory in your practice?" One of the themes to emerge was that theory is not well enough developed to be of much practical use. One of the practitioners had this to say (Burdine & McLeroy, 1992): "I haven't found any single theory with enough utility to be of much practical value—I use elements of many theories, and theory applies to the average—what I do is work at the fringe—so little theory applies" (p. 335). The point is that practitioners do not and will not use a specific theory, such as planned behavior or social cognitive, when working with individual exercise behavior change. Even the most parsimonious psychology theories are quite complex in spelling out relationships and how the theory really works to understand and change behavior.

Question #2: Is it appropriate for practitioners to work with psychological constructs from various theories? Yes. In fact, if practitioners are going to apply exercise psychology at all, it is likely that they will do so in the form of applying select psychological constructs removed from their parent theory. Pure exercise psychology theorists may look askance at this orientation because the opposite is true in the research world. That is, applying one theory to understand and predict exercise behavior in a quality way is amply rewarded in the scientific research community. The world of the practitioner is chaotic and messy, and he or she needs to use a variety of psychological constructs in combination with his or her experiential or tacit knowledge (Martens, 1987) to motivate behavior change.

Question #3: How should practitioners select which psychological constructs to focus on for which clients? Let the practitioner decide. Referring to Table 1 presented earlier, it makes sense from a motivational perspective for practitioners to know as much as possible about a beginning exerciser's perceptions of confidence pertaining to his or her ability to overcome personal barriers to exercise, his or her notions about physique anxiety and how they may be impeding or facilitating exercise in certain environments, and his or her present stage of change to get a better idea about readiness to change and to track stage changes every 6 months. In addition, it would certainly help if practitioners understood each individual's emotional experience (positive or negative) related to his or her exercise and if they helped all of their clients better understand their own feelings regarding exercise and how those feelings might be impeding or facilitating exercise behavior. Finally, helping each client learn to enjoy the exercise experience and become intrinsically motivated is critical for long-term maintenance of exercise.

Question #4: Should the practitioner use the identical measurement instruments for assessment purposes developed by exercise psychology researchers? Probably not. The problem is that if the practitioner wants to conduct a motivational assessment incorporating a variety of measurement instruments tapping various psychological constructs, the number of items would be too unwieldy. The measurement instruments developed by exercise psychology researchers are not practical for this reason, nor were they designed for this purpose. For example, the PSDQ contains 70 items; the PACES, 18 items. In addition, the items are typically so repetitive (for research reliability purposes) that prospective exercisers come to believe they may be wasting their time completing these questionnaires and this can serve as an initial turnoff to the exercise behavior change process.

For practitioners to be better able to incorporate exercise psychology construct measurement tools into practice, two things may be done. First, perhaps the instrumentation described in this and other chapters in this volume could be used in practice settings if the number of items in certain exercise psychology measurement instruments were significantly reduced. Much time is spent developing items that are similar, yet different, to obtain adequate reliability. When helping people change exercise behavior, could practitioners get the same information from 1 item as 12 items? For instance, the SPAS measures social physique anxiety with 12 items. In scanning the scale, is there one item that could tell a practitioner if a client is probably high or low on social physique anxiety? It is probably not the item "When in a bathing suit, I often feel nervous about the shape of my body." How many times do we exercise in our bathing suits? How many people could truthfully answer no to that question? How about "In the presence of others, I feel apprehensive about my physique/figure?" This item seems to be a realistic one and could pertain to exercising situations that may involve other people. If someone strongly agrees with this item, would there not be a good chance that he or she might experience social physique anxiety in a group exercise setting? Would this not be useful information for the practitioner to obtain? With fewer items per scale, the chances of practitioners' utilizing exercise psychology constructs to guide behavior change efforts would increase. Selecting individual items from established scales may not be ideal or easy to do, and every measurement instrument may not be amenable to this strategy. If the items composing these instruments are not pared down, practitioners and their clients are certainly not going to use the cumbersome ones that presently exist.

Second, instead of using paper-and-pencil type instruments, or in addition to them, it should be possible to develop interview questions directed at assessing a variety of psychological constructs involved in the exercise behavior change process. People are much better at talking about these motivational issues than they are at completing questionnaires and scales. This approach is similar to qualitative interviewing, a research evaluation technique advocated by Patton (1990), except the goal in this case is for the practitioner to help a client begin the process of exercise behavior change. Qualitative interviewing can be a powerful tool for helping practitioners enter and understand the world of their clients.

Assessing certain psychological constructs via a questioning process could be very helpful in obtaining a "motivational starting point" for each client. The practitioner could incorporate any or all of these questions in a semistructured consultation/interview with each beginning exerciser. Table 2 includes a sample list of questions with their accompanying psychological construct(s). Some of these constructs have been discussed in this chapter; some have not. The questions serve solely as examples of how a practitioner could tap into a variety of psychological constructs that are known to influence people's exercise motivation and the resultant behavior. These questions could be one part of a practitioner/client initial consultation in which other aspects of a person's life as it pertains to physical activity would be addressed.

In sum, the practicality of exercise psychology constructs

Table 2
Questions Assessing Corresponding Psychological Constructs That Could Be Used in a Practitioner/Client Exercise Behavior Consultation

Psychological Construct	*Question*
Perceived behavioral history	Can you tell me a little about your past exercising attempts?
Personal goals	What do you want to do?
Personal readiness	What are you ready to do?
Exercise incentives	Why do you want to do it?
Perceived barriers	What might be the barriers preventing you from doing what you want to do?
Self-efficacy	How confident are you that you can control or overcome each of these barriers to do what you want to do?
Perceived benefits	What do you think will be the benefits of achieving your goal or exercising regularly?
Social physique anxiety	Which kind of physical activities do you feel you will be the most comfortable participating in?
Affect	How does exercising typically make you feel? How does not exercising make you feel?
Social support	Do you need support from family and friends to achieve your goal? If you do, how will you obtain their support?
Enjoyment	What kinds of physical activities do you enjoy participating in the most? What is it specifically about these activities that you enjoy? How can you find ways to participate regularly in these actitivies?

could be brought to life when helping people change exercise behavior by (a) paring down the actual instrumentation developed by researchers and/or (b) ascertaining a person's motivation to exercise through a variety of questions asked by the practitioner in a semistructured interview. The effectiveness of this approach could be tested through evaluation research conducted by practitioners in collaboration with applied-oriented exercise psychology researchers.

Question #5: If exercise psychology measurement instruments have been developed within a nomothetic research orientation, can the practitioner ethically use them when working with individual clients? Yes. If practitioners and their clients can use assessment tools and instruments provided in self-help books with absolutely no sound measurement development approach underlying them, why cannot the instruments developed under more rigorous conditions be used as well? For example, an applied book called the *Exercise Habit* by Gavin (1992) includes a section on psychological motives and how to use them. The author describes these psychological motives as the "keys to your personal fulfillment through exercise" (Gavin, p. 59). He includes 5-item scales for six motives: self-esteem, achievement, moods/tension, stress, meaning, and playfulness. The reader can self-score each scale and create a personal profile. Nowhere in the book does the author present validity and reliability for these scales. Are there data to support the notion that these psychological motives function in the way the author says they do? Is this ethical? Do these scales really help? There are many examples of these kind of books on the market, and there is nothing inherently wrong with them. However, is it not as likely that exercise psychology instruments grounded in some theoretical and measurement substance, even if they were not designed for individuals, can be just as helpful? This may not be easy to do, but it can be done.

Suggestions for Future Measurement and Assessment in Applied Exercise Psychology

Based on some of the measurement issues presented in this chapter, the following suggestions may improve the practicality of measurement instruments in applied exercise psychology. These suggestions are not in any order of importance. These suggestions are really designed to help make research in exercise psychology more applicable to the practice contexts of health and fitness.

Researcher/Practitioner Partnerships Should Be Established

Earlier in the chapter, it was suggested that the worlds of the researcher and the practitioner are quite different, which makes it very difficult for theory to influence practice or vice versa. As Phillips (1989) points out, "One of the problems of applying science to practice, therefore, is to overcome attitudes that tend to justify and reinforce the isolation of the scientific community, on the one hand, and the practitioner community, on the other" (p. 4). Most exercise psychology measurement instruments are developed in isolation from the health/fitness practitioners who most need these kinds of tools. Practitioners would use these instruments more if they were more understandable and practical. One solution to this measurement conundrum is for researchers and practitioners to enter into dialogue and partnerships to reduce the isolationism that presently exists between the exercise psychology scientific community and the health/fitness practitioner community. As stated by Garner almost 25 years ago (1972):

...the quality of the basic research is improved by communication between the basic research scientist and the people who have problems to solve. Thus, for the scientists to engage in goal-oriented research, research aimed at solving problems already known to exist, is both to perform a service to society and to improve the quality of the basic research itself. (p. 945)

Collaboration and partnership will make exercise psychology measurement and assessment instruments better, but this is also a difficult process. The first author is presently collaborating with health/fitness practitioners at Bethesda Preventive Health Systems in Cincinnati on a health-behavior intervention project with high health risk employees. It took numerous meetings and discussions before we came to agreement about the theoretical orientation to guide the intervention and the measurement instruments that would be used. This collaborative process can be successful only if both the scientist and the practitioner keep very open minds.

There are ways to formalize the partnering process. Hooper-Briar and Lawson (1994) advocate interprofessional education and collaboration and service integration as ways to address problems associated with children, youth, and families. These approaches could be ways to address some of the scientist-practitioner issues outlined in this chapter. In essence, interprofessional education and collaboration provide the scientist and the practitioner with a common denominator of knowledge, language, values, sensitivities, and skills (Lawson, 1994). Not only do scientists conduct educational seminars for the practitioners, but the practitioners may also co-teach an exercise behavior or exercise psychology course. The point behind these kinds of activities is to foster a dynamic, symbiotic relationship between the scientist and the practitioner, which would ultimately help to make the research in exercise psychology more usable by practitioners.

Adopt a MultiDisciplinary Approach to Measurement and Assessment

One of the reasons for the impracticality of present exercise psychology research and accompanying instrumentation is its narrow, disciplinary focus. Exercise behavior change is a complex, multicause, multieffect process that involves relations among the individual, his or her culture, and the physical environment (Kimiecik & Lawson, 1996). Within this contextual orientation (Ford & Lerner, 1992), an individual's perceptions, thoughts, and beliefs are only one part of the exercise behavior change process. Exercise psychology researchers typically study this part of behavior although ignoring contextual influences. Hence, Dishman (1994b) points out that typical interventions with a psychological emphasis have "shown potential efficacy (they can work) for increasing exercise and physical activity, but their effectiveness (do they work?) for increasing exercise, physical activity, fitness, or health in the population remains unclear" (p. 99). Interventions that continue to be solely psychologically based may have limited practical utility because for practitioners to be effective in helping people change behavior in the long term, they must address the multicause, multieffect processes that go along with it. Ford and Lerner (1992) address this issue quite well:

Interventions that include only one source of influence (i.e., univariate/unilevel interventions) are more

likely to provide only short-lived benefits and to produce relatively little change due to a lack of attention to altering concurrently relevant variables from other levels of analysis. (p. 225)

A biopsychosocial model (Schwartz, 1982) of measurement and assessment would enhance the ultimate effectiveness of practitioner-oriented interventions in applied exercise settings. Following Schwartz's assumptions for applying the biopsychosocial model for medical diagnosis, an assessment for helping an individual change exercise behavior should include biological, psychological, and social factors. This perspective does not suggest that exercise psychology and its measurement tools are ineffective. It does suggest that future work in exercise psychology must become more integrated with biological and social factors to provide comprehensive assessments of individuals, which should lead to more effective interventions. Of course, this is an empirical question, and it remains to be tested.

Create, Implement, and Evaluate Innovative Measurement and Assessment Approaches

Based on the first two suggestions, new and alternative approaches to exercise psychology measurement and to individual assessments within applied exercise contexts are needed. To make measurement and assessment more practical, researchers are needed who can move back and forth between the study of group-specific generalizations and implementation and evaluation of exercise-behavior interventions for specific individuals. This work should be done in collaboration with practitioners because they will keep us honest in keeping an eye toward the idiographic use of instruments we have developed and will develop in the future. Runyan (1983) outlines a number of idiographic approaches that could facilitate more useful measurement and application of exercise psychology. The essence of these suggestions is how to make the general specific.

For instance, Runyan (1983) suggests that subjects be allowed to determine which standard rating scales are relevant to them. The ipsative method is another possibility whereby an individual's scores on a certain measure are considered in relation to his or her scores in other areas, rather than in relation to group scores or averages on this single test (Broverman, 1962). Inverse factor analysis (Nunnally, 1955) can be conducted where items of relevance to a single subject can be factor analyzed. Runyan also describes other idiographic possibilities: data collection on an individual at a number of points over time and single-case experimental designs, in which variables are manipulated and causal relations investigated within single cases. This approach has become more popular in sport psychology research, but there has been very little of it in exercise psychology. Finally, a case-study method could be adopted whereby the relevancy of select psychological constructs to an individual's exercise life could be studied over time.

This suggestion is somewhat mixing measurement recommendations with research method, but the two are inseparable. The point to this final section is to demonstrate that there are exciting measurement and assessment possibilities that await the creative and innovative exercise psychology researcher who is willing to go beyond the boundary of the dominant research paradigm. It is through researcher/practitioner partnership collaboratives, multidisciplinary approaches, and idiographic-oriented interventions that exercise psychology will have the greatest chance of making an impact in the world of practice. This will not be easy, but it is necessary.

Both science and practice should shape and influence the theories and measurement instruments developed in applied exercise psychology. This has not been the case. The scale has been tipped in favor of positivistic, nomothetic science for a long time. The danger is that this kind of work takes us farther and farther away from the needs of the health/fitness practitioner and has the potential for disregarding the unique elements of behavior change for each individual. It should not be assumed that the answer to applying exercise psychology is the development of scientifically rigorous measurement instruments. This alone is not enough. To end, a story about Abraham Lincoln's appraisal of a church sermon, as told by Phillips (1989) seems appropriate:

> Abraham Lincoln often attended the New York Avenue Presbyterian Church on Wednesday evenings...On a particular Wednesday, while walking home, his aide asked Mr. Lincoln his appraisal of the sermon. The President, thoughtful in his reply, said "The content was excellent...he delivered with eloquence...he had put work into the message...." (pp. 7-8)
>
> "Then you thought it was a great sermon?" questioned the aide.
>
> "No," replied Mr. Lincoln.
>
> "But you said the content was excellent...it was delivered with eloquence...it showed much work."
>
> "That's true," Mr. Lincoln said, "but Dr. Gurley forgot the most important thing. He forgot to ask us to do something great."

There is no doubt that the content of many of the measurement instruments developed within exercise psychology are excellent, that they are explained with eloquence by the developers, that much work has been put into their development, but the greatest challenge—and achievement—lies ahead. To have the greatest impact on people's exercise behavior change, exercise psychology measurement instruments must be developed, applied, and tested in the world of health/fitness practitioners and their clients.

References

Ainsworth, B., Montoye, H., & Leon, A. (1994). Methods of assessing physical activity during leisure and work. In C. Bouchard, R. Shephard, & T. Stephens (Eds.), *Physical activity, fitness, and health: International proceedings and consensus statement* (pp. 146-159). Champaign, IL: Human Kinetics.

Ajzen, I. (1987). Attitudes, traits, and actions: Dispositional prediction of behavior in personality and social psychology. In L. Berkowitz (Ed.), *Advances in experimental social psychology* (pp. 1-63). New York: Academic Press.

Allport, G.W. (1962). The general and the unique in psychological science. *Journal of Personality, 30*, 405-422.

Bandura A. (1986). *Social foundations of thought and action: A social cognitive theory*. Englewood Cliffs, NJ: Prentice-Hall.

Belbin, E. (1979). Applicable psychology and some natural problems: A synopsis of the 1978 Myers lecture. *Bulletin of British Psychological Society, 32*, 241-244.

Blair, S. (1984). How to assess exercise habits and physical fitness. In J. Matarazzo, S. Weiss, J. Herd, & N. Miller (Eds.), *Behavioral health: A handbook of health enhancement and disease prevention* (pp. 424-447). New York: Wiley.

Blair, S., & Connelly, J. (1996). How much physical activity should we do: The case for moderate amounts and intensities of physical activity. *Research Quarterly for Exercise and Sport, 67*, 193-205.

Blake, S., Caspersen, C., Finnegan, J., Crow, R., Mittlemark, M., & Ringhofer, K. (1996). The shape up challenge: A community-based worksite exercise competition. *American Journal of Health Promotion, 11*, 23-34.

Brawley, L.R. (1993). The practicality of of using social psychological theories for exercise and health research and intervention. *Journal of Applied Sport Psychology, 5*, 99-115.

Broverman, D. (1962). Normative and ipsative measurement in psychology. *Psychological Review, 69*, 295-305.

Burdine, J.N., & McLeroy, K.R. (1992). Practitioners' use of theory: Examples from a workgroup. *Health Education Quarterly, 19*, 331-340.

Christina, R.W. (1987). Motor learning: Future lines of research. In M.J. Safrit & H.M. Eckert (Eds.), *The cutting edge in physical education and exercise science research* (pp. 26-41). Champaign, IL: Human Kinetics.

Crawford, S., & Ecklund, R.C. (1994). Social physique anxiety, reasons for exercise, and attitudes toward exercise settings. *Journal of Sport and Exercise Psychology, 16*, 70-82.

Crocker, P., Bouffard, M., & Gessaroli, M. (1995). Measuring enjoyment in youth sport settings: A confirmatory factor analysis of the Physical Activity Enjoyment Scale. *Journal of Sport and Exercise Psychology, 17*, 200-205.

Davies, D., Spurgeon, P., & Chapman, A. (1994). *Elements of applied psychology*. Chur, Switzerland: Harwood Academic Publishers.

Dishman, R. (1994a). Introduction, consensus, problems, and prospects. In R. Dishman (Ed.), *Advances in exercise adherence* (pp. 1-27). Champaign, IL: Human Kinetics.

Dishman, R. (1994b). Predicting and changing exercise and physical activity: What's practical and what's not. In H. Quinney, L. Gauvin, & A. Wall (Eds.), *Toward active living* (pp. 97-106). Champaign, IL: Human Kinetics.

Dishman, R., & Buckworth, J. (1996). Increasing physical activity: A quantitative synthesis. *Medicine and Science in Sports and Exercise, 28*, 706-719.

Dishman, R., Darracott, C., & Lambert, L. (1992). Failure to generalize determinants of self-reported physical activity to a motion sensor. *Medicine and Science in Sports and Exercise, 24*, 904-910.

Edmundson, E., Parcel, G., Perry, C., Feldman, H., Smyth, M., Johnson, C., Layman, A., Bachman, K., Perkins, T., Smith, K., & Stone, E. (1996). The effects of Child and Adolescent Trial for Cardiovascular Health Intervention on psychosocial determinants of cardiovascular disease risk behavior among third-grade students. *American Journal of Health Promotion, 10*, 217-225.

Eklund, R.C., & Crawford, S. (1994). Active women, social physique anxiety, and exercise. *Journal of Sport and Exercise Psychology, 16*, 431-448.

Ford, D., & Lerner, R. (1992). *Developmental systems theory*. Newbury Park, CA: Sage.

Fox, K. (1990). *The Physical Self-Perception Profile Manual*. DeKalb, IL: Office for Health Promotion, Northern Illinois University.

Garner, W.R. (1972). The acquisition and application of knowledge: A symbiotic relationship. *American Psychologist, 27*, 941-946.

Gauvin, L., & Brawley, L.R. (1993). Alternative psychological models and methodologies for the study of exercise and affect. In P. Seraganian (Ed.), *Exercise psychology: The influence of physical exercise on psychological processes* (pp. 146-171). New York: Wiley.

Gauvin, L., & Rejeski, W.J. (1993). The Exercise-Induced Feeling Inventory: Development and initial validation. *Journal of Sport and Exercise Psychology, 15*, 403-423.

Gauvin, J., Rejeski, W., & Norris, T. (1996). A naturalistic study of the impact of acute physical activity on feeling states and affect in women. *Health Psychology, 15*, 391-397.

Gavin, J. (1992). *The exercise habit.* Champaign, IL: Human Kinetics.

Gifford, R. (1991). *Applied psychology: Variety and opportunity.* Needham Heights, MA: Allyn and Bacon.

Hart, E., Leary, M., & Rejeski, W.J. (1989). The measurement of social physique anxiety. *Journal of Sport and Exercise Psychology, 11*, 94-104.

Heck, T., & Kimiecik, J. (1993). What is exercise enjoyment?: A qualitative investigation of adult exercise maintainers. *Wellness Perspectives, 10*, 3-21.

Hooper-Briar, K., & Lawson, H. (1994). *Serving children, youth and families through interprofessinal collaboration and service integration: A framework for action.* Oxford, OH: The Institute for Educational Renewal at Miami University & The Danforth Foundation.

Israel, B., Cummings, K., Dignan, M., Heaney, C., Perales, D., Simons-Morton, B., & Zimmerman, M. (1995). Evaluation of health education programs: Current assessment and future directions, *Health Education Quarterly, 22*, 364-389.

Kendzierski, D., & DeCarlo, K. (1991). Physical activity enjoyment scale: Two validation studies. *Journal of Sport and Exercise Psychology, 13*, 50-64.

Kimiecik, J., & Harris. A. (1996). What is enjoyment?: A conceptual/definitional analysis with implications for sport and exercise psychology. *Journal of Sport and Exercise Psychology, 18*, 247-263.

Kimiecik, J.C., & Lawson, H.A. (1996). Toward new approaches for exercise behavior change and health promotion. *Quest, 48*, 102-125.

King, A. (1994). Clinical and community interventions to promote and support physical activity participation. In R. Dishman (Ed.), *Advances in exercise adherence* (pp. 183-212). Champaign, IL: Human Kinetics.

King, A., Taylor, C., Haskell, W., & DeBusk, R. (1989). Influence of regular aerobic exercise on psychological health: A randomized, controlled trial of healthy middle-aged adults, *Health Psychology, 8*, 305-324.

Knapp, M. (1995). How shall we study comprehensive, collaborative services for children and families. *Educational Researcher, 24*, 5-16.

Lawson, H. (1990). Beyond positivism: Research, practice, and undergraduate professional education. *Quest, 42*, 161-183.

Lawson, H. (1994, July). *Economic, political and cultural changes: Their import for new models for practice.* Keynote address presented at the AIESEP World Congress, Berlin, Germany.

Leary, M., Tchividjian, L., & Kraxberger, B. (1994). Self-presentation can be hazardous to your health: Impression management and health risk. *Health Psychology, 13*, 461-470.

Lincoln, Y., & Guba, E. (1985). *Naturalistic inquiry.* Newbury Park: Sage.

Luepker, R., Perry, C., McKinlay, S., Nader, P., Parcel, G., & Stone, J. (1996). Outcomes of a field trial to improve children's dietary patterns and physical activity: The Child and Adolescent Trial for Cardiovascular Health (CATCH). *Journal of the American Medical Association, 275*, 768-776.

Marcus, B., Banspach, S., Lefebrve, R., Rossi, J., Carleton, R., & Abrams, D. (1992). Using the stages of change model to increase the adoption of physical activity among community participants. *American Journal of Health Promotion, 6*, 424-429.

Marcus, B., Rossi, J., Selby, V., Niaura, R., & Abrams, D. (1992). The stages and process of exercise adoption and maintenance in a worksite sample. *Health Psychology, 11*, 386-395.

Marcus, B., Selby, V., Niaura, R., & Rossi, J. (1992). Self-efficacy and the stages of exercise behavior change. *Research Quarterly for Exercise and Sport, 63*, 60-66.

Marcus, B., & Simkin, L. (1993). The stages of exercise behavior. *Journal of Sports Medicine and Physical Fitness, 33*, 83-88.

Marcus, B., Simkin, L., Rossi, J., & Pinto, B. (1996). Longitudinal shifts in employees' stages and processes of exercise behavior change. *American Journal of Health Promotion, 10,* 195-200.

Marsh, H., Richards, G., Johnson, S., Roche, L., & Tremayne, P. (1994). Physical Self-Description Questionnaire: Psychometric properties and a multitrait-multimethod analysis of relations to existing instruments. *Journal of Sport and Exercise Psychology, 16*, 270-305.

Marsh, H., & Sonstroem, R. (1995). Importance ratings and specific components of physical self-concept: Relevance to predicting global components of self-concept and exercise. *Journal of Sport and Exercise Psychology, 17*, 84-104.

Martens, R. (1987). Science, knowledge, and sport psychology. *The Sport Psychologist, 1*, 29-55.

McAuley, E. (1992). The role of efficacy cognitions in the prediction of exercise behavior of middle-aged adults. *Journal of Behavioral Medicine, 15*, 65-88.

McAuley, E., & Burman, G. (1993). This social physique anxiety scale: Construct validity in adolescent females. *Medicine and Science in Sports and Exercise, 25*, 1049-1053.

McCready, M., & Long, B. (1985). Locus of control, attitudes toward physical activity, and exercise adherence. *Journal of Sport Psychology, 7*, 346-359.

McGraw, S. Stone, E., Osganian, S., Elder, J., Perry, C., Johnson, C., Parcel, G., Webber, L., & Luepker, R. (1994). Design of process evaluation within the Child and Adolescent Trial for Cardiovascular Health (CATCH). *Health Education Quarterly, 21 (*Suppl. 2), S5-S26.

McKenzie, T., Sallis, J., Faucette, N., Roby, J., & Kolody, B. (1993). Effects of a curriculum and inservice program on the quantity and quality of elementary physical education classes. *Research Quarterly for Exercise and Sport, 64*, 178-187.

Montoye, H., Kemper, H., Saris, W., & Washburn, R. (1996). *Measuring physical activity and energy expenditure.* Champaign, IL: Human Kinetics.

Newell, K. (1990). Physical activity, knowledge types, and degree programs. *Quest, 42*, 243-268.

Noland, M., & Feldman, R. (1984). Factors related to the leisure exercise behavior of "returning" women college students. *Health Education, 15*(2), 32-36.

Nunnally, J. (1955). An investigation of some propositions of self-conception: The case of Miss Sun. *Journal of Abnormal and Social Psychology, 50*, 87-92.

Patton, M. (1990). *Qualitative evaluation and research methods* (2nd ed.). Newbury Park, CA: Sage.

Pender, N., Sallis, J., Long, B., & Calfas, K. (1994). Health-care provider counseling to promote physical activity. In R. Dishman (Ed.), *Advances in exercise adherence* (pp. 213-235). Champaign, IL: Human Kinetics.

Phillips, B.N. (1989). Role of the practitioner in applying science to practice. *Professional Psychology: Research and Practice, 20*, 3-8.

Prochaska, J., & Marcus, B. (1994). The transtheoretical model: Applications to exercise. In R. Dishman (Ed.), *Advances in exercise adherence* (pp. 161-180). Champaign, IL: Human Kinetics.

Richards, G. (1988). *Physical Self-Concept Scale.* Sydney: Australian Outward Bound Foundation.

Rotter, J. (1954). *Social learning and clinical psychology.* Englewood Cliffs, NJ: Prentice-Hall.

Rotter, J. (1990). Internal versus external control of reinforcement: A case history of a variable. *American Psychologist, 45*, 489-493.

Runyan, W.M. (1983). Idiographic goals and methods in the study of lives. *Journal of Personality, 51*, 413-437.

Sallis, J., Haskell, W., Fortmann, S., Vranizan, K., Taylor, C., & Solomon, D. (1986). Predictors of adoption and maintenance of physical activity in a community sample. *Preventive Medicine, 15*, 331-341.

Sallis, J., & Hovell, M. (1990). Determinants of exercise behavior. In J. Pondolf & J. Holloszy (Eds.), *Exercise and sports science reviews: Vol. 18* (pp. 307-330). Baltimore, MD: Williams & Wilkins.

Scanlan, T., & Simons, J. (1992). The construct of sport enjoyment. In G. Roberts (Ed.), *Motivation in sport and exercise* (pp. 199-215). Champaign, IL: Human Kinetics.

Schwartz, G. (1982). Testing the biopsychosocial model: The ultimate challenge facing behavioral medicine? *Journal of Consulting and Clinical Psychology, 50*, 1040-1053.

Strong, S.R. (1991). Theory-driven science and naive empiricism in counseling psychology. *Journal of Counseling Psychology, 38*, 204-210.

Surgeon General's Office (1996). Surgeon General's Report on Physical Activity and Health. Washington, DC: U.S. Government Printing Office.

Wallston, K. (1992). Hocus-pocus, the focus isn't strictly on locus: Rotter's social learning theory modified for health. *Cognitive Therapy and Research, 16*, 183-199.

Wallston, K., Wallston, B., & DeVellis, R. (1978). Development of the multidimensional health locus of control (MHLC) scales. *Health Education Monographs, 6*, 160-170.

Wallston, B., Wallston, K., Kaplan, G., & Maides, S. (1976). The development and validation of the health related locus of control (HLC) scale. *Journal of Consulting and Clinical Psychology, 44*, 580-585.

Wankel, L. (1985). Personal and situational factors affecting exercise involvment: The importance of enjoyment. *Research Quarterly for Exercise and Sport, 56*, 275-282.

Wankel, L. (1993). The importance of enjoyment to adherence and psychological benefits from physical activity. *International Journal of Sport Psychology, 24*, 151-169.

Whitehead, J., & Corbin, C. (1988). Multidimensional scales for the measurement of locus of control of reinforcements for physical fitness behaviors. *Research Quarterly for Exercise and Sport, 59*, 108-117.

Chapter 28

DEVELOPMENTAL CONSIDERATIONS IN SPORT AND EXERCISE PSYCHOLOGY MEASUREMENT

Robert J. Brustad
University of Northern Colorado

Opportunities for sport and exercise involvement are present throughout the lifespan. However, the purpose and quality of this involvement may vary considerably among individuals according to developmental status (Brodkin & Weiss, 1990). In particular, cognitive-developmental influences can affect the means by which individuals appraise their physical activity involvement (Weiss & Bredemeier, 1983). An appreciation for the nature of developmental change is thus essential for researchers interested in understanding the characteristics of sport and exercise participation across the lifespan. The purpose of this chapter is to address developmental considerations that affect our efforts to measure and understand the psychological dimensions of participation.

The need for a developmental perspective is particularly apparent when studying children and adolescents in sport (Weiss & Bredemeier, 1983). Child and adolescent athletes constitute a large proportion of organized sports participants in the United States (Ewing & Seefeldt, 1996). However, the childhood and adolescent years also correspond with a period of tremendous change that extends to the cognitive, physical, emotional, social, and ethical dimensions of development. It is imperative that researchers recognize that "the young athlete is not a miniature adult" (Gould, 1996, p. 413) but rather a youngster who perceives sport experiences in a manner that is consistent with his or her developmental level.

Development refers to a sequence of change that results in an increasingly organized and specialized functional capacity for an individual (Timiras, 1972). Development is thus distinct from *growth*, which merely refers to those changes in size that accompany maturation (Malina, 1996). Evidence of developmental differences in functioning between children and adults exists in relation to a number of physiological, psychological, and mechanical characteristics of movement and performance. For example, children progress through qualitatively different

phases of motor skill patterning (e.g., throwing technique) that contribute to the enhancement of motor skill performance over and above incremental size and strength changes (Haywood, 1986). Similarly, notable physiological differences in thermal regulation capacity (Bailey & Rasmussen, 1996; Rowland, 1993) and anaerobic energy production (Reybrouck, 1989) exist between children and adults and reflect developmental differences in underlying physiological processes.

Just as growth and development are differentiated, so must age and development remain conceptually distinct. Typically, developmental advancement occurs with age. However, large individual differences also exist among individuals of the same chronological age in the rate and timing of development (e.g., physical maturation). Thus, the developmental process can be regarded as age related but not age dependent.

This chapter will focus primarily on patterns of cognitive-developmental change as such change influences our efforts to understand the psychological characteristics of sport and exercise involvement. A cognitive-developmental focus is highly relevant to our purposes for at least two reasons. First, due to developmental differences, individuals evaluate their physical activity participation differently at various phases of their lifetime. For example, differences exist among children, adolescents, and adults in their understanding of the causes of achievement outcomes (Nicholls, 1978); information-processing patterns (Thomas, Thomas, & Gallagher, 1993); and capacities for abstract reasoning (Piaget, 1952; Selman, 1971). A second reason for adhering to a cognitive-developmental perspective is to remain consistent with the strong cognitive emphases that underlie currently prominent theories in our field. In contrast to previous eras, in which personality and learning perspectives were predominant, current theories emphasize the role of cognitive variables, such as self-efficacy (Bandura, 1977), perceived competence and control (Harter, 1978, 1981a) and achievement goal orientations (Duda, 1989a) to explain behavioral variation among individuals. Thus, a cognitive-developmental perspective is compatible with prevailing theoretical views regarding the importance of cognitive processes although also remaining sensitive to developmental considerations.

Far too often, research in our field has neglected developmental considerations in the design of studies. Much of this research has examined age-related differences in psychological processes but has failed to select age groups for research on the basis of known cognitive-developmental criteria (Weiss & Bredemeier, 1983). In the words of Weiss and Bredemeier (1983), "we must stop objectifying children as subjects for research and instead focus on the changes in cognitive structures and abilities that will help us understand maturational differences in psychological behaviors" (p. 217).

In order to more fully understand the physical activity experiences of individuals differing in cognitive maturational status, we must be concerned with the creation and use of developmentally appropriate measures. Developmentally appropriate measures share at least three common characteristics. First, such measures are created with some consideration for known qualitative differences that exist among individuals in relation to cognitive-developmental status (Weiss & Bredemeier, 1983). As a consequence of these qualitative differences in cognitions, research measures used with children and youth should reflect the underlying cognitive structure of youngsters at a given developmental stage. For example, children proceed through various developmental stages in their understanding of competition (Coakley, 1986). Thus, developmentally appropriate research measures are those that take into account these maturational differences.

A second dimension of developmentally appropriate measures is that they are understandable and readily comprehensible by individuals of the intended age range. Measures need to be written using a language and format that are suitable for the age group studied. Frequently, measures generated with adults may need to be revised for use with children so that the complexity of the scale and terminology are appropriate.

Third, developmentally appropriate measures address salient and meaningful concerns for the age group studied. For example, we can modify the language of adult-based measures for use with children, but doing so does not guarantee that the constructs assessed are necessarily important to children. Thus, we may need to review the developmental literature to ensure that we are addressing issues relevant to our study populations.

The importance of developmentally sensitive measures in sport and exercise psychology research is highlighted by two considerations. First, sport and physical activity involvement can extend throughout the lifespan, and developmentally appropriate research measures can help us to understand the psychological dimensions of this involvement over time. Second, a great deal of concern exists relative to the effects of sport and physical activity involvement upon the cognitive, social, and ethical development of individuals (see Shields & Bredemeier, 1995). Developmentally appropriate measures are needed if we are to assess the effects of such participation upon individual maturational processes and patterns of change. To design appropriate measures, developmental concepts and principles must be addressed.

Cognitive-Developmental Considerations in the Design of Research Measures

Developmental differences in cognitive functioning can have a profound influence upon how individuals of different ages appraise their sport and exercise involvement. Recognizing the nature of key cognitive-developmental differences among children, adolescents, and adults should impact the design of our research measures. Three cognitive-developmental considerations are highly relevant to this concern. These relate to developmental differences in abstract reasoning abilities, information-processing capacity, and the structure of the self-concept.

Abstract reasoning capacities. Developmental differences exist among children, adolescents, and adults in the ability to engage in abstract reasoning processes. Prior to about age seven, children adopt an "egocentric" worldview (Piaget, 1952), in which they base decisions and plan behavioral strategies on the basis of direct personal experience. However, because of their reliance on personal experience, children of this age have difficulty in taking the perspective of an outside, or third. person (Selman, 1971). Furthermore, they have difficulty in understanding complex and hypothetical relationships (Piaget, 1952). The egocentric nature of younger children's cognitive development is exemplified by their behavior in sports such as soccer or basketball when players swarm to the ball "like bees to honey" while neglecting their positional duties on the field and failing to effectively anticipate what is likely to occur. Coaches have tremendous difficulty in presenting plays and strategies to younger children because children of this age are not yet capable of adopting an outside, objective perspective on team play.

During later childhood (roughly ages 8 to 11 years), children demonstrate an increasing capacity for abstract thought and reasoning. However, children of this age are typically not fully capable of dealing with complex relationships but require a concrete (tangible or visible) representation of relationships in order to effectively solve problems. It is only during the early adolescent years (roughly 11 to 14 years), a phase corresponding to Piaget's formal operational period, that individuals demonstrate an adult-like capacity for abstract thought.

Developmental differences in abstract reasoning processes affect both theoretical and measurement issues. Due to limitations in children's abstract reasoning processes, many adult-generated theoretical perspectives, and their accompanying research measures, are inappropriate for use with children. As Gould (1996) stated, "Too often we erroneously assume that psychological processes and theories that have been based on research with adults automatically transfer to younger age groups" (p. 412). For example, several prominent theories used in the study of physical activity, such as as the theory of planned behavior (Ajzen, 1985) and the theory of reasoned action (Fishbein & Ajzen, 1975), were developed to explain the cognitive processes underlying adult behavioral change processes. Because these theories rely upon the assumption that individuals can, and do, engage in complex, hypothetical reasoning processes, the developmental appropriateness of their use with children can be questioned. Similarly, much of the current health and exercise psychology research is generated from the-

Table 1
Measures Recommended for Use with Children and Adolescents.
(All measures have shown evidence of internal reliability and construct validity.)

Measure	Recommended age range
Children's Physical Self-Perception Profile (Whitehead, 1995)	12-14 years
Perceived Competence Scale for Children (Harter, 1982)	8-12 years
Perceived Athletic Competence Scale (Harter, 1985a)	8-12 years
Physical Self-Description Questionnaire (Marsh et al., 1994)	13-18 years
Physical Competence Information Scale (Horn, et al., 1993)	14-18 years
Motivational Orientation in Sport Scale (Weiss, et al., 1985)	8-12 years
Task and Ego Orientation in Sport Questionnaire (Duda, 1992)	8 years to adulthood
Perceptions of Success Questionnaire (Treasure & Roberts, 1994)	10-16 years
Scale of Children's Action Tendencies (Bredemeier, 1994)	10-13 years
Sport Anxiety Scale (Smith, et al., 1990)	8 years to adulthood
Children's Attraction to Physical Activity Scale (Brustad, 1993b)	8-12 years

ories that were designed to explain the processes by which adults choose to adopt physical activity in response to some perceived health risk. This class of theories, including the Health Belief Model (Rosenstock, 1974) and the Transtheoretical Model (Prochaska & DiClemente, 1983), would intuitively seem to be inappropriate for use with children and adolescents because youngsters do not necessarily appraise health risks in the same manner as do adults.

In addition to the limitations of using adult-based theories with children, measurement issues also arise. As a consequence of limitations in abstract reasoning capacities, measures that require children to engage in complex and hypothetical reasoning processes are simply not warranted with children. Just as youth coaches should not expect children to be able to fully handle complex strategies and interrelationships on the field, neither should researchers expect children to be able to generate hypothetical or complex behavioral plans in an adult-like manner. Developmentally appropriate research measures take into account these differences in the capacity for abstract thought.

Information-Processing characteristics. A second relevant consideration in the design of developmentally appropriate research measures pertains to differences in the information-processing characteristics of individuals at various cognitive-developmental levels. Overall, children are less adept at information processing than are adolescents and adults (Thomas, et al., 1993). In particular, children are unable to fully process various sources of information simultaneously. Once again, these considerations would encourage the use of measures of limited complexity in research with children.

Children's inability to process discrete forms of information concurrently is reflected in their inability to fully differentiate among the concepts of ability, effort, and task difficulty as causes of specific achievement outcomes (Nicholls, 1978; Nicholls & Miller, 1984). Research (Nicholls, 1978) indicates that between the ages of 7 and 9 years, children typically believe that effort is the cause of all performance outcomes, thus implicitly discounting the importance of ability. At about 9 or 10 years of age, children begin to partially differentiate the influences of effort and ability in contributing to performance outcomes but fail to consistently apply this logic (Nicholls, 1978). Finally, around 11 or 12 years of age, effort and ability are fully differentiated, and youngsters realize that a person who has to try hard to succeed probably has less ability than one who can succeed without trying hard.

The line of research related to developmental changes in the ability to understand the causes of performance outcomes prior to later childhood and adolescence is logically linked to the investigation of attributional and motivational processes (Duda, 1987; Nicholls & Miller, 1984). However, attributional research measures generated from adults, such as the Causal Dimension Inventory (Russell, 1982), would obviously not be appropriate for use with children due to qualitative differences between children and adults in understanding the causes of achievement outcomes. However, attributional measures designed for a specific cognitive-developmental level could help us to understand variability in behavior among individuals of the same maturational status.

In sum, because of limitations in various information processing-capacities, it is essential that measures used with children do not require high levels of these information-processing abilities. This concern for complexity should be considered with regard to both the format and content of instruments.

Structure of the self system. A substantial amount of theory and research in sport and exercise psychology addresses the role of various self-concept dimensions in contributing to variability among individuals in motivational and behavioral patterns. In this line of investigation, extensive attention is given to a variety of self variables including self-efficacy, self-esteem, and self-perceptions of competence. However, an essential consideration that should precede the design of research studies in this area is that the content and structure of the self-concept is, itself, developmentally based (Demo, 1992). Specifically, the nature and number of dimensions that compose the self-concept are dependent upon the cognitive maturational status of the individual (Harter, 1983). With development, an increasing number of self-concept dimensions are differentiated, and the relative importance of various dimensions to overall feelings of self-worth changes as well (Harter, 1985b). Consequently, it is not possible to theorize about, or describe, the self system in the same way across the lifespan.

Harter's research indicates that individuals identify and articulate an increasing number of competency dimensions with development (Harter, 1988). Her findings (Harter, 1983; Harter & Pike, 1984) indicate that between the ages of four and seven years, children begin to make differentiations relative to cognitive competence, physical competence, social acceptance, and behavioral conduct. However, these appraisals are still rather crude as children in this age range do not completely differentiate the cognitive from the physical domains nor the social from the behavioral areas. During the middle childhood years, children begin to differentiate among five domains, including academic competence, physical competence, peer acceptance, behavioral conduct, and physical appearance. Furthermore, a global sense of self-worth emerges during this period that is independent of judgments in the specific achievement domains. Further refinement and elaboration of the self-concept occurs throughout adolescence and adulthood. For example, adults may differentiate among as many as 14 different self-concept areas (Harter, 1988).

With development, individuals also become increasingly accurate in their assessments of their personal capacities. In part, this increasing accuracy is related to a developmental shift in the sources of competence information used. During childhood, children rely heavily upon task accomplishment as an indication of ability (Nicholls, 1978). However, with development, children show an increasing capacity to use social comparison processes and tend to rely more upon such comparative information in making judgments (Ruble, 1983). Older children and adolescents demonstrate greater reliance upon information provided by peers, as well as upon personal judgments, in evaluating their abilities (Horn & Hasbrook, 1987; Horn & Weiss, 1991).

From a measurement standpoint, two implications for the design of research measures arise from this knowledge base. First, given changes in the structure of the self system with development, it is not appropriate to utilize a singular or universal approach for assessing the self system across the lifespan. Instead, measures should be designed in ways that tap the structure of the self at a specific developmental level. Second, developmental changes occur in the sources of information used by individuals to assess their competence. Measures designed to assess the nature of socialization influences upon motivation and behavior should thus include consideration for differences in the salience of varied information sources (self, peers, parents) at differing developmental levels.

Developmental Perspectives on Measurement: A Review

Within sport and exercise psychology, systematic and widespread attention has yet to be devoted to the design of developmentally appropriate research measures. This shortcoming can be attributed to a common tendency for researchers in our field to generalize findings across age groups and thereby disregard developmental considerations (Weiss & Bredemeier, 1983). Furthermore, many investigators have relied heavily upon adult-generated theories and measures to conduct research with children and adolescents in both sport and exercise settings (Brustad, 1991; Weiss & Bredemeier, 1983).

The limitations of adult-based measures, specifically the ap-

plication of adult-generated constructs for use with children, can be evidenced by problems encountered with the use of the Children's Attitudes Toward Physical Activity (CATPA) scale (Simon & Smoll, 1974). CATPA was used to assess individual differences among children in their interest in physical activity and was patterned after the Attitudes Toward Physical Activity (ATPA) scale developed by Kenyon (1968b) for use with adult participants. The ATPA scale emanated from research (Kenyon, 1968a) that indicated that adults' interest in physical activity involvement was dependent upon attitudes toward six specific aspects of physical activity. These dimensions included social characteristics, health and fitness aspects, vertigo (feelings of risk and physical excitement), catharsis (release of tension), aesthetic dimensions relating to graceful movement, and ascetic elements, reflecting feelings about hard and strenuous training. The strength of the ATPA and CATPA scales derived from their multifaceted conception of physical activity interest.

CATPA was not a developmentally based research measure, however, because the content of the instrument had been generated with adults. In fact, only the wording of the scale had been modified to make the measure more appropriate for children. In addition, the hypothesized six-factor structure of this scale was never established as a valid representation of children's perceptions of physical activity. Intuitively, the ascetic dimension, involving hard physical training, does not seem to represent an attractive aspect of physical activity for children. Due to other psychometric limitations, primarily involving low test-retest reliability (Schutz, Smoll, & Wood, 1981), the recommendation was made that CATPA not be used for the study of attitude-behavior relationships over time, or for research involving the study of individual differences in physical activity attitudes (Schutz et al., 1981).

The discussion of problems with the CATPA scale is intended only to illustrate common issues associated with the use of adult-based measures with children. In many cases, adult-generated scales simply do not reflect children's perspectives on the behavior in question. An alternate approach is to attempt to design measures that are specific to the cognitive-developmental status of targeted groups rather than to try to generate measures that might be applicable across all age ranges. The developmentally-specific focus has been Harter's approach to measurement, and a discussion of her work should be beneficial to this discussion.

Harter's Conceptual and Methodological Approach to Measurement

Harter's measurement efforts have contributed substantially to questionnaire development in sport and exercise psychology research. Her research focus has been upon the constitution of the self system at various developmental phases, as well upon the identification of contributors to intrinsic and extrinsic motivational orientations during childhood and adolescence (Harter, 1981a, 1983, 1988). Central to her work has been a focus upon generating a set of measures designed specifically for younger and older children, adolescents, and adult populations. Her theoretical and measurement approaches have been frequently emulated by researchers interested in developmental issues in sport (e.g., Horn & Weiss, 1991; Klint & Weiss, 1987).

Harter has concentrated her efforts in three areas. First, her measures have been designed to reflect a multidimensional view of the self, in contrast with previously used self-concept measures, such as the Coopersmith (1967) self-esteem inventory for children and the Piers-Harris (1969) scale, which maintained a unidimensional perspective. The multidimensional view is essential because research indicates that individuals differentiate between many aspects of the self and that these different dimensions are not of equal value to the individual (Harter, 1988). The nature and number of dimensions also change developmentally (Harter, 1983).

Harter's measurement approach has also attempted to avoid the social desirability bias that is prevalent in measures used with children. Her examination (Harter, 1982) of previously used measures, particularly those using a true-false format, indicated that such scales are significantly correlated with "lie-item" scores and overall scores on the Children's Social Desirability Scale (Crandall, Crandall, & Katkovsky, 1965). This finding led her to conclude that these measures tend to reflect a developmental tendency for children to present an "ideal self," as opposed to an "actual self," when responding to research measures. In order to reduce these social desirability tendencies among children, Harter's scales utilize a "structured-alternative" format. In this format, a child is presented with a description of two children who differ in an important way. Scale items are worded so as to imply that many children in the child's reference group view themselves in one way whereas many others perceive themselves in a contrasting manner. The child is then asked to select which of the two children he or she is more like, and then to respond as to whether this description is just "sort of true" or "really true" for the participant. An example of an item assessing perceived physical competence is, "Some kids do very well at all kinds of sports, but others don't feel that they are very good when it comes to sports."

The third developmentally related goal in the design of Harter's measures has been to generate measures that accurately represent the thought processes and word choice of the population of interest. In developing her first measure, the Perceived Competence Scale for Children (Harter, 1982), Harter utilized large samples of third- through sixth-grade children, and the measure underwent extensive pilot testing. In the initial stages of scale development, the questionnaire was always individually administered, and each item was read out loud to the child. Upon making a choice, the child was then asked to explain why he or she had responded in this particular manner. One goal of this procedure was to enhance the face validity of the items included, as well as to identify items that were likely to be misunderstood or misinterpreted. Similar procedures were followed in the construction of self-concept measures for adolescents (Harter, 1988).

Harter's scales have also undergone thorough psychometric scrutiny. Internal consistency values for each of the four subscales have been good with Kuder-Richardson values of .73-.83 obtained (Harter, 1982). The structured-alternative approach produces a good distribution of scores, with means typically just above each scale's midpoint. Factor analysis has been used to establish that the hypothesized structure of the scale is supported by relatively clean patterns of factor loadings. Additional evidence of the validity of the scale has been attained through the use of convergent, construct, and discriminant procedures (Harter, 1982).

Assessing the Developmental Appropriateness of Commonly Used Measures

Harter's approach provides an exemplary model for the design of developmentally appropriate measures. Ideally, researchers will develop scales with similar concern for differences in cognitive processes, social desirability effects, and levels of comprehension. Additional, and complementary, suggestions for the construction of developmentally appropriate measures will be provided.

It is recommended that researchers initially consider conducting a content analysis of any developmental research on the topic area of interest (e.g., differences in self-perception patterns, moral development characteristics). The purpose of a content analysis is to determine whether known developmental differences exist that need to be accounted for in the design of measures. If developmental differences have been identified in the literature, then the researcher should attempt to develop measures that reflect the cognitive processes of individuals within a specific developmental range. For example, the knowledge that qualitative differences exist in individuals' understanding of the role of effort and ability as contributors to performance outcomes (Nicholls, 1978) might affect the design of research measures used in the areas of motivation and attributional patterns. Because these underlying cognitive differences represent fundamentally different patterns of comprehension among groups of individuals differing in developmental status, rather than incremental or quantitative differences, a "one-size-fits-all" measure would not be appropriate across age groups. If no known developmental differences are found on the variables of interest, the researcher might still assess whether differences exist on mean scores or factor loadings as such information might reflect underlying differential patterns. If some age-related differences are identified, the researcher might wish to restrict the age range within which a particular measure is used.

Consistent with Harter's approach, pilot testing and follow-up interview procedures can be very beneficial in determining the comprehensibility of measures. In order to avoid social desirability bias, a social desirability scale can be administered along with the questionnaire to determine if response bias may be present. A number of psychometric concerns also should be addressed after a measure is developed. The internal consistency of the measure should be examined because poor internal consistency may also indicate problems with comprehension and interpretation of items and concepts. Concurrent validity should be assessed by examining whether scores on the measure of interest correlate as anticipated with other instruments that measure similar constructs. The construct validity of a measure can be assessed in terms of whether the instrument predicts actual behavior, or group membership, in the manner that has been anticipated. Finally, it is very important to examine the factor structure of measures to determine if a stable factor structure exists across groups differing by developmental status. For example, if a measure comprises a number of subscales, it is essential to establish that when this measure is used with differing populations (e.g., younger children, older adults), the hypothesized subscale factors emerge as reflected by an anticipated pattern of factor loadings. This goal can be best accomplished through confirmatory factor analytic procedures.

Chi and Duda's (1995) multiple-group assessment of the Task and Ego Orientation in Sport Questionnaire (TEOSQ) is a useful example of the benefits of confirmatory factor analysis to address the developmental appropriateness of research measures. In their study, three athletic samples (junior high school sport participants, high school athletes, and intercollegiate skiers) and one nonathletic sample of college students completed the TEOSQ measure. The findings from the study indicated that an invariant two-factor structure relating to task and ego orientations in sport was not identified across the four groups. In other words, some differences existed in the conceptualization of the task and ego constructs among the four groups. However, a reasonable index of fit for the TEOSQ was obtained within each of the three athletic groups, supporting the merits of the TEOSQ for use across groups of athletes differing in age and ability.

Few scales in sport and exercise psychology have been subjected to the demanding psychometric procedures that have been suggested, in large part because developmental issues are not typically the principal focus of our research (Weiss & Bredemeier, 1983). However, some measures have been developed with a concern for patterns of developmental change, and the merits of a number of other measures have been examined among groups differing in age. The developmental appropriateness of commonly used measures in seven content areas will be evaluated.

Self-concept measures. Measures of self-concept are integral to the study of psychological processes in sport and exercise. Currently used self-concept measures include those developed by Harter (1982, 1985a), Fox and Corbin (1989), and Marsh (Marsh & Redmayne, 1994; Marsh, Richards, Johnson, Roche, & Tremayne, 1994). In addition, Whitehead (1995) has recently published a modified version of Fox and Corbin's scale for use with children. For a thorough review of self-concept measures refer to the chapter by Fox in this volume.

Harter's perceived physical competence (1982) and perceived athletic competence scales (1985a) have been used extensively in youth sport research (e.g., Feltz & Brown, 1984; Horn & Weiss, 1991; Klint & Weiss, 1987; Williams & Gill, 1995). In many cases (e.g., Black & Weiss, 1992; Williams & Gill, 1995), researchers have modified the scales to present a sport-specific assessment of ability judgments. Because Harter's intent was to estimate children's feelings of perceived physical competence across a variety of physical activities, her original scales are more appropriate when assessing overall feelings of physical competence or when establishing a profile of children's competence perceptions across the physical, social, and academic domains (Harter, 1985a). However, when situation-specific perceptions of competence are desired, a modified and sport-specific version that retains the same structured-alternative format of the scale should be more beneficial. The perceived competence measures have been used in sports with individuals ages 7 to 18 years and have demonstrated reasonably good internal consistency, with Cronbach alpha levels generally in the .69 (Black & Weiss, 1992) to .76 (Williams & Gill, 1995) range. Construct validity for the measure is supported by research that

indicates that perceived and actual levels of sport competence are reasonably well correlated (Feltz & Brown, 1984) and by research that supports theoretical predictions about the role of perceived competence in contributing to motivational processes (Brustad, 1993b; Williams & Gill, 1995).

The Physical Self-Perception Profile (PSPP), developed by Fox and Corbin (1989), is grounded in Harter's conceptualization of a multidimensional, hierarchical self-concept. However, the PSPP provides a more specific assessment of physical self-concept as it measures physical self-perception characteristics across four subdomains. These four subdomains relate to perceptions of bodily attractiveness, sports competence, physical strength, and physical conditioning/exercise capacity. The hierarchical conception of the self proposed by Fox and Corbin, is reflected by the view that self-perceptions across these four subdomains contribute to an overall sense of physical self-worth that, in turn, is one component of self-esteem. Furthermore, dimensions of competence that are viewed as more important to the individual are anticipated to have greater impact upon an individual's self-esteem. Through both exploratory and confirmatory factor analysis (Fox, 1990, cited in Marsh & Redmayne, 1994), this multidimensional and hierarchical model of the self has been supported with a population of young adults.

A modified version of the PSPP was recently developed by Whitehead (1995) for use with younger individuals. This measure was tested with a group of seventh- and eighth-grade students, and reliability and validity assessments were conducted. The factorial validity of the Children's PSPP (C-PSPP) was evaluated through principal components analysis that yielded a four-factor solution that generally reflected the four dimensions identified in the adult-generated measure. Internal reliability and intraclass stability of the measure over a 2-week time period was supported by reliability (coefficient alpha) levels generally in the .75-.90 range. Concurrent validity was demonstrated by the presence of conceptually congruent patterns of correlations among the C-PSPP scale and physical fitness test scores. Conversely, a separate measure of importance, the Perceived Importance Scale, was not well supported through assessments of factorial validity. In general, the C-PSPP scale appears to be a promising tool for measuring the physical self-perception characteristics of youngsters. However, its utility with youngsters of a broader age range will need to be demonstrated.

The Physical Self-Description Questionnaire (Marsh & Redmayne, 1994; Marsh et al., 1994) assesses six components of physical self-concept, including physical appearance and sport competence, in addition to five dimensions of physical fitness, including strength, body composition, and endurance. Research to date has assessed the construct validity of the measure in regard to the similarity of individuals' perceived and actual abilities. In an investigation using adolescent girls, ages 13 and 14 years, Marsh and Redmayne (1994) found acceptable correlations between perceived and actual abilities on five of the six fitness measures ($r = .21 - .64$). The measure of balance self-concept, however, was weakly correlated with the balance test ($r = .10$). Additional research will be needed to confirm the presence of a stable factor structure across age groups.

Anxiety measures. Understanding the sources, extent, and consequences of anxiety in youth sport has been a heavily researched topic area (for a review see Brustad, 1993a; Smoll & Smith, 1996). Research measures used in this area have undergone considerable change in the past 10 years.

To assess competitive trait anxiety, which represents an individual's "tendency to perceive competitive situations as threatening," Martens (1977) developed the Sport Competition Anxiety Test (SCAT, p. 36). The children's version of this scale has demonstrated desirable psychometric properties and has been used extensively in youth sport research. The scale contains 15 items, of which 5 items are "dummy questions" that are not scored. The 10 remaining items are summed to create a composite anxiety score. The SCAT has demonstrated good predictive validity in that research using this measure has supported hypothesized relationships linking higher levels of competitive trait anxiety with greater precompetitive state anxiety (Gould, Eklund, Petlichkoff, Peterson, & Bump, 1991; Scanlan & Lewthwaite, 1984); greater concern for negative evaluation by others (Brustad, 1988; Lewthwaite & Scanlan, 1989; Passer, 1983); and lower self-esteem in young athletes (Brustad, 1988). Lewthwaite and Scanlan noted that the SCAT contains a preponderance of items related to somatic anxiety and relatively few items assessing cognitive anxiety levels. Given current perspectives on the multidimensional nature of anxiety (Martens, Vealey, & Burton, 1990), the SCAT may not be the most appropriate measure for assessing children's competitive trait anxiety.

The Sport Anxiety Scale (SAS) was developed by Smith, Smoll, and Schutz (1990) to provide a multidimensional assessment of trait anxiety in sport. The SAS contains three subscales assessing somatic anxiety, cognitive disruption, and worry and contains 21 items overall. SAS has demonstrated favorable psychometric properties in research with high school and college athletes (Smith et al., 1990). However, its use with younger individuals has been limited to a single study (Weiss, Ebbeck, & Horn, in press). These researchers modified 6 items to make them more appropriate for the 8- to 13-year old children in their sample, and deleted 3 additional items. Weiss et al. obtained Cronbach internal reliability estimates of .73 - .80 for the three modified subscales. Predictive validity for the measure was supported by an anticipated pattern of relationships that linked high competitive trait anxiety with low sport competence and self-esteem.

The measurement of state anxiety has also been an important dimension of sport psychology research (see chapter by Burton, this volume). State anxiety levels in young athletes have primarily been assessed through the Competitive State Anxiety Scale for Children, or CSAI-C (Martens, Burton, Rivkin, & Simon, 1980). The CSAI-C has been employed to assess the immediate precompetition anxiety state experienced by young athletes in numerous studies (e.g., Gould et al., 1991; Weiss, Weise, & Klint, 1989). Similar to the SCAT measure, this inventory generates an overall score for precompetitive state anxiety rather than distinguish among cognitive and somatic components. Martens, Vealey, and Burton (1990) advanced the measurement process in this area through their construction of the Competitive State Anxiety Inventory-2 (CSAI-2). This measure reflects a multidimensional view of anxiety and contains somatic anxiety, cognitive anxiety, and state self-confidence subscales. The psychometric properties of the CSAI-2 for use with children are not established because

published research using this scale with individuals younger than high school age has not been reported in the literature.

Sources-of-competence information measure. Spurred by an interest in the nature of developmental shifts in individuals' reliance upon varied sources of information to form perceptions of competence, Horn and Hasbrook (1986) developed the Physical Competence Information Scale (PCIS). More recently, an improved scale was generated through further testing and content analysis of the developmental literature (Horn, Glenn, & Wentzell, 1993). Included in the measure are a total of 10 possible information sources, tapping such diverse areas as teacher or coach feedback, peer feedback, peer comparison, parental feedback, self-comparison and degree of skill improvement over time, and ease of learning new skills. Internal consistency levels for the 10 subscales have been high, with Cronbach (1951) alpha levels ranging from .74 to .90 (Horn et al., 1993). Horn and Amorose (this volume) review this measure in greater detail.

Intrinsic/extrinsic motivational orientation measure. Weiss, Bredemeier, and Shewchuk (1985) developed a measure of motivational orientation patterned after Harter's (1981b) scale. The merits of Harter's five-factor scale for use in the sport setting were assessed, and through confirmatory factor analysis, it was concluded that these dimensions did not adequately represent data obtained from youngsters (mean age = 10.2 years) participating in a summer sports camp. Weiss et al. used exploratory factor analysis to develop a six-factor model that is included in the Motivational Orientation in Sport Scale. Typically, youth sport researchers have utilized selected subscales from this measure. Adequate internal reliability levels (alpha = .74-.79) have been obtained when this measure has been used with children (Brustad, 1988) and adolescents (Black & Weiss, 1992). The construct validity of this measure is supported by research that indicates that, in accordance with theoretical predictions, motivational orientation is positively related to coaching behaviors (Black & Weiss) and sport enjoyment (Brustad, 1988).

Achievement goal orientation measures. Achievement goal orientations have commonly been assessed through the Task and Ego Orientation in Sport Questionnaire (Duda, 1992). The TEOSQ appears to be a developmentally sound instrument in that it has demonstrated good psychometric properties in research with older children (Duda, Fox, Biddle, & Armstrong, 1992; Duda & Hom, 1993), younger adolescents (Chi & Duda, 1995; Newton & Duda, 1993), older adolescents (Duda, 1989b), and adults (Duda & White, 1992). The construct validity of this scale is supported by research that indicates that task and ego goal orientations are significantly related, in predicted ways, to views on the purpose of sport (Duda, 1989b) and beliefs about the roles of cooperation, ability, and effort in contributing to successful sport outcomes (Duda et al, 1992).

A similar scale, the Perceptions of Success Questionnaire (POSQ), has been devised by Treasure and Roberts (1994) and also assesses goal orientations in sport contexts. The factor structure of this 12-item scale, as assessed through exploratory factor analysis, has been found to be relatively similar across three age groups with mean ages of 11.3, 13.4, and 15.5 years of age (Treasure & Roberts, 1994). Measures of achievement goal orientations are thoroughly reviewed elsewhere in this book (see Duda & Whitehead, this volume).

Moral reasoning and behavior measure. Bredemeier's (1994) Scale of Children's Action Tendencies in Sport (SCATS) was designed to assess children's assertive, aggressive, and submissive action tendencies in sport settings. The measure was patterned after the Children's Action Tendency Scale (CATS) developed by Deluty (1979). The content of the scale was generated though open-ended questioning of fourth-through seventh-grade children regarding conflict situations experienced within sport contexts. The construct validity of SCATS has been supported by research showing significant relationships between children's moral reasoning levels, as assessed through interview techniques, and their scores on SCATS (Bredemeier, 1994). This measure is also more thoroughly described in this text (Stephens, this volume).

Measures of exercise and physical activity interest. Three measures have assessed interest in exercise and physical activity participation among children and adolescents. The limitations of the CATPA scale (Simon & Smoll, 1974) for use with children have been previously discussed. Similarly, the adult-generated Physical Activity Enjoyment Scale (Kendzierski & DeCarlo, 1991), which is designed to measure affective response to physical activity, has been found to be less appropriate for use with children and adolescents than with adults (Crocker, Bouffard, & Gessaroli, 1995). Through confirmatory factor analysis, Crocker et al. found that the unidimensional factor structure obtained with adults did not hold for younger individuals.

The Children's Attraction to Physical Activity (CAPA) scale (Brustad, 1993b) represents a third attempt to measure children's interest in exercise and physical activity. The CAPA scale was designed for children in grades three through seven. The content of the scale was child generated in that open-ended discussions were held with elementary school children to identify aspects of physical activity that they found to be attractive or unattractive. Through repeated pilot testing, five dimensions of attraction to physical activity were identified (Brustad, 1993b). These dimensions reflect children's liking of vigorous exercise, extent of peer acceptance in games and sports, liking of games and sports, interest in exercise for health reasons, and perceptions of the fun of physical exertion. CAPA is thus conceptually similar to CATPA in that a multidimensional perspective is taken toward physical activity, and considerable individual variability is assumed. To date, acceptable internal reliability has been shown for the CAPA subscales (Cronbach alphas averaging about .70), and the construct validity of the measure has been supported by research that has shown relatively strong relationships between perceived physical competence and attraction to physical activity in fourth- through seventh-grade children (Brustad, 1993b; Brustad, 1996). Minimal cross-loading of items between factors has been evident although confirmatory factor analysis would be beneficial to provide further evidence of the existence of a stable factor structure.

Summary

In order to appropriately study the physical activity involvement of children, adolescents, and adults, a cognitive-developmental perspective is warranted. This perspective should be comprehensive in nature and extend to the theoretical and conceptual foundations of our research, to the research mea-sures that are employed, and to the means by which the findings of research studies are interpreted.

The major concepts and principles that guide the design of other research measures in sport and exercise psychology (e.g., reliability and validity concerns) apply to the construction of developmentally appropriate inventories. However, one very fundamental additional consideration that must be addressed relates to the fact that children, adolescents, and adults frequently view the world from qualitatively different frameworks due to differences in maturation and experience.

In order to effectively study the psychological dimensions of sport and physical activity involvement across the lifespan, recognition of the nature of cognitive-developmental differences must exist. Recognition of developmental change processes should be used to help construct appropriate measurement tools and thereby advance our knowledge of the psychological dimensions of sport and physical activity involvement.

References

Ajzen, I. (1985). From intentions to actions: A theory of planned behavior. In J. Kuhl & J. Beckman (Eds.), *Action control: From cognition to behavior* (pp. 11-39). Heidelberg: Springer.

Bailey, D.A., & Rasmussen, R.L. (1996). Sport and the child: Physiological and skeletal issues. In F.L. Smoll & R.E. Smith (Eds.), *Children and youth in sport: A biopsychosocial perspective* (pp. 187-199). Dubuque, IA: Brown & Benchmark.

Bandura, A. (1977). Self-efficacy: Toward a unifying theory of behavioral change. *Psychological Review, 84,* 191-215.

Black, S.J., & Weiss, M.R. (1992). The relationship among perceived coaching behaviors, perceptions of ability, and motivation in competitive age-group swimmers. *Journal of Sport and Exercise Psychology, 14,* 309-325.

Bredemeier, B.J.L. (1994). Children's moral reasoning and their assertive, aggressive, and submissive tendencies in sport and daily life. *Journal of Sport and Exercise Psychology, 16,* 1-14.

Brodkin, P., & Weiss, M.R. (1990). Developmental differences in motivation for participating in competitive swimming. *Journal of Sport and Exercise Psychology, 12,* 248-263.

Brustad, R.J. (1988). Affective outcomes in competitive youth sport: The influence of intrapersonal and socialization variables. *Journal of Sport and Exercise Psychology, 10,* 307-321.

Brustad, R.J. (1991). Children's perspectives on exercise and physical activity: Measurement issues and concerns. *Journal of School Health, 61,* 228-230.

Brustad, R.J. (1993a). Youth in sport: Psychological considerations. In R.N. Singer, M. Murphey, & L.K. Tennant (Eds.), *Handbook of research on sport psychology* (pp. 695-717). New York: Macmillan.

Brustad, R.J. (1993b). Who will go out and play? Parental and psychological influences on children's attraction to physical activity. *Pediatric Exercise Science, 5,* 210-223.

Brustad, R.J. (1996). Attraction to physical activity in urban schoolchildren: Parental socialization and gender influences. *Research Quarterly for Exercise and Sport, 67,* 316-323.

Chi, L., & Duda, J.L. (1995). Multi-sample confirmatory factor analysis of the Task and Ego Orientation in Sport Questionnaire. *Research Quarterly for Exercise and Sport, 66,* 91-98.

Coakley, J. (1986). When should children begin competing? A sociological perspective. In M.R. Weiss & D. Gould (Eds.), *Sport for children and youths* (pp. 59-63). Champaign, IL: Human Kinetics.

Coopersmith, S. (1967). *The antecedents of self-esteem.* San Francisco: Freeman.

Crandall, V.C., Crandall, V.J., & Katkovsky, W.A. (1965). A children's social desirability questionnaire. *Journal of Consulting Psychology, 29*, 27-36.

Crocker, P.R.E., Bouffard, M., & Gessaroli, M.E. (1995). Measuring enjoyment in youth sport settings: A confirmatory factor analysis of the Physical Activity Enjoyment Scale. *Journal of Sport and Exercise Psychology, 17*, 200-205.

Cronbach L.J. (1951). Coefficient alpha and internal structure of tests. *Psychometrika, 16*, 297-333.

Deluty, R.H. (1979). Children's Action Tendency Scale: A self-report measure of aggressiveness, assertiveness, and submissiveness in children. *Journal of Consulting and Clinical Psychology, 47*, 1061-1071.

Demo, D.H. (1992). The self-concept over time: Research issues and directions. *Annual Review of Sociology, 18*, 303-326.

Duda, J.L. (1987). Toward a developmental theory of children's motivation in sport. *Journal of Sport Psychology, 9*, 130-145.

Duda, J.L. (1989a). Goal perspectives and behavior in sport and exercise settings. In C. Ames & M. Maehr (Eds.), *Advances in motivation and achievement: Vol. 6* (pp. 81-115). Greenwich, CT: JAI Press.

Duda, J.L. (1989b). The relationship between task and ego orientation and the perceived purpose of sport among male and female high school athletes. *Journal of Sport and Exercise Psychology, 11*, 318-335.

Duda, J.L. (1992). Motivation in sport and exercise settings: A goal perspective approach. In G. Roberts (Ed.), *Motivation in sport and exercise* (pp. 57-92). Champaign, IL: Human Kinetics.

Duda, J.L., Fox, K.R., Biddle, S.J.H., & Armstrong, N. (1992). Children's achievement goals and beliefs about success in sport. *British Journal of Educational Psychology, 62*, 313-323.

Duda, J.L., & Hom, H. (1993). Interdependencies between the perceived and self-reported goal orientations of young athletes and their parents. *Pediatric Exercise Science, 5*, 234-241.

Duda, J.L., & White, S.A. (1992). Goal orientations and beliefs about the causes of sport success among elite skiers. *The Sport Psychologist, 6*, 334-343.

Ewing, M.E., & Seefeldt, V. (1996). Patterns of participation and attrition in American agency-sponsored youth sports. In F.L. Smoll & R.E. Smith (Eds.), *Children and youth in sport: A biopsychosocial perspective* (pp. 31-45). Dubuque, IA: Brown & Benchmark.

Feltz, D., & Brown, E. (1984). Perceived competence in soccer skills among young soccer players. *Journal of Sport Psychology, 6*, 385-394.

Fishbein, M., & Ajzen, I. (1975). *Belief, attitude, intention, and behavior: An introduction to theory and research.* Reading, MA: Addison-Wesley.

Fox, K.R., & Corbin, C.B. (1989). The Physical Self-Perception Profile: Development and preliminary validation. *Journal of Sport and Exercise Psychology, 11*, 408-430.

Gould, D. (1996). Sport psychology: Future directions in youth sport research. In F.L. Smoll & R.E. Smith (Eds.), *Children and youth in sport: A biopsychosocial perspective* (pp. 405-422). Dubuque, IA: Brown & Benchmark.

Gould, D., Eklund, R.C., Petlichkoff, L., Peterson, K., & Bump, L. (1991). Psychological predictors of state anxiety and performance in age-group wrestlers. *Pediatric Exercise Science, 3*, 198-208.

Harter, S. (1978). Effectance motivation reconsidered: Toward a developmental model. *Human Development, 21*, 34-64.

Harter, S. (1981a). A model of intrinsic mastery motivation in children: Individual differences and developmental change. In W.A. Collins (Ed.), *Minnesota Symposium on Child Psychology: Vol. 14* (pp. 215-255). Hillsdale, NJ: Erlbaum.

Harter, S. (1981b). A new self-report scale of intrinsic versus extrinsic orientation in the classroom: Motivational and informational components. *Developmental Psychology, 17*, 300-312.

Harter, S. (1982). The Perceived Competence Scale for Children. *Child Development, 53*, 87-97.

Harter, S. (1983). Developmental perspectives on the self-system. In E.M. Hetherington (Ed.), *Handbook of child psychology, socialization, personality, and social development* (pp. 275-385). New York: Wiley.

Harter, S. (1985a). *Manual for the Self-Perception Profile for Children.* Denver: University of Denver.

Harter, S. (1985b). Processes underlying the construction, maintenance, and enhancement of the self-concept in children. In J. Suls & A. Greenwald (Eds.), *Psychological perspectives on the self: Vol. 3* (pp. 137-181). Hillsdale, NJ: Erlbaum.

Harter, S. (1988). Causes, correlates, and the functional role of global self-worth: A life-span perspective. In J. Kolligan & R. Sternberg (Eds.), *Perceptions of competence and incompetence across the life-span* (pp. 67-98). New Haven, CT: Yale University Press.

Harter, S., & Pike, R. (1984). The Pictorial Perceived Competence Scale for young children. *Child Development, 55*, 1962-1982.

Haywood, K.M. (1986). *Lifespan motor development.* Champaign, IL: Human Kinetics.

Horn, T.S., Glenn, S.D., & Wentzell, A.B. (1993). Sources of information underlying personal ability judgments in high school athletes. *Pediatric Exercise Science, 5*, 263-274.

Horn, T.S., & Hasbrook, C.A. (1986). Informational components underlying children's perceptions of their physical competence. In M.R. Weiss & D. Gould (Eds.), *Sport for children and youths* (pp. 81-88). Champaign, IL: Human Kinetics.

Horn, T.S., & Hasbrook, C.A. (1987). Psychological characteristics and the criteria children use for self-evaluation. *Journal of Sport and Exercise Psychology, 9*, 208-221.

Horn, T.S., & Weiss, M.R. (1991). A developmental analysis of children's self-ability judgments in the physical domain. *Pediatric Exercise Science, 3*, 310-326.

Kendzierski, D., & DeCarlo, K.J. (1991). Physical Activity Enjoyment Scale: Two validation studies. *Journal of Sport and Exercise Psychology, 13*, 50-64.

Kenyon, G.S. (1968a). A conceptual model for characterizing physical activity. *Research Quarterly, 39*, 96-104.

Kenyon, G.S. (1968b). Six scales for assessing attitude toward physical activity. *Research Quarterly, 39*, 566-574.

Klint, K.A., & Weiss, M.R. (1987). Perceived competence and motives for participating in youth sports: A test of Harter's competence motivation theory. *Journal of Sport Psychology, 9*, 55-65.

Lewthwaite, R. & Scanlan, T.K. (1989). Predictors of competitive trait anxiety in male youth sport participants. *Medicine and Science in Sports and Exercise, 21*, 221-229.

Malina, R.M. (1996). The young athlete: Biological growth and maturation in a biocultural context. In F.L. Smoll & R.E. Smith (Eds.), *Children and youth in sport: A biopsychosocial perspective* (pp. 161-186). Dubuque, IA: Brown & Benchmark.

Marsh, H.W., & Redmayne, R.S. (1994). A multidimensional physical self-concept and its relations to multiple components of physical fitness. *Journal of Sport and Exercise Psychology, 16*, 43-55.

Marsh, H.W., Richards, G.E., Johnson, S., Roche, L., & Tremayne, P. (1994). Physical Self-Description Questionnaire: Psychometric properties and a multitrait-multimethod analysis of relations to existing instruments. *Journal of Sport and Exercise Psychology, 16*, 270-305.

Martens, R. (1977). *Sport Competition Anxiety Test.* Champaign, IL: Human Kinetics.

Martens, R., Burton, D., Rivkin, F., & Simon, J. (1980). Reliability and validity of the Competitive State Anxiety Inventory (CSAI). In C.H. Nadeau, W.C. Halliwell, K.M. Newell, & G.C. Roberts (Eds.), *Psychology of motor behavior and sport- 1979* (pp. 91-99). Champaign, IL: Human Kinetics.

Martens, R, Vealey, R.S., & Burton, D. (1990). *Competitive anxiety in sport.* Champaign, IL: Human Kinetics.

Newton, M., & Duda, J.L. (1993). Elite adolescent athletes' achievement goals and beliefs concerning success in tennis. *Journal of Sport and Exercise Psychology*, *15*, 437-448.

Nicholls, J.G. (1978). The development of the concepts of effort and ability, perception of own attainment, and the understanding that difficult tasks require more ability. *Child Development*, *49*, 800-814.

Nicholls, J.G., & Miller, A.T. (1984). Development and its discontents: The differentiation of the concept of ability. In J. Nicholls (Ed.), *Advances in motivation and achievement: Vol. 3. The development of achievement motivation* (pp. 185-218). Greenwich, CT: JAI Press.

Passer, M.W. (1983). Fear of failure, fear of evaluation, perceived competence and self-esteem in competitive trait anxious children. *Journal of Sport Psychology*, *5*, 172-188.

Piaget, J. (1952). *The origins of intelligence in children*. New York: International Universities Press.

Piers, E., & Harris, D. (1969). *The Piers-Harris Children's Self-Concept Scale*. Nashville, TN: Counselor Recordings and Tests.

Prochaska, J.O., & DiClemente, C. (1983). Stages and processes of self-change of smoking: Toward an integrative model of change. *Journal of Consulting and Clinical Psychology*, *51*, 390-395.

Reybrouck, T.M. (1989). The use of anaerobic threshold in pediatric exercise testing. In O. Bar-Or (Ed.), *Advances in pediatric sport sciences* (pp. 131-149). Champaign, IL: Human Kinetics.

Rosenstock, I. M. (1974). The Health Belief Model and preventive health behavior. *Health Education Monographs*, *2*, 354-386.

Rowland, T. W. (1993). The physiological impact of intensive training on the prepubertal athlete. In B.R. Cahill & A.J. Pearl (Eds.), *Intensive participation in children's sports* (pp. 167-193). Champaign, IL: Human Kinetics.

Ruble, D. N. (1983). The role of social comparison processes in achievement-related self-socialization. In E.T. Higgins, D.N. Ruble, & W.W. Hartup (Eds.), *Social cognition and social development: A sociocultural perspective* (pp. 134-157). New York: Cambridge University Press.

Russell, D. (1982). The Causal Dimension Scale: A measure of how individuals perceive causes. *Journal of Personality and Social Psychology*, *42*, 1137-1145.

Scanlan, T.K. & Lewthwaite, R. (1984). Social psychological aspects of competition for male youth sport participants: I: Predictors of competitive stress. *Journal of Sport Psychology*, *6*, 208-226.

Schutz, R.W., Smoll, F.L., & Wood, T.M. (1981). A psychometric analysis of an inventory for assessing children's attitudes toward physical activity. *Journal of Sport Psychology*, *3*, 321-344.

Selman, R.L. (1971). Taking another's perspective: Role-taking development in early childhood. *Child Development*, *42*, 1721-1734.

Shields, D.L.L., & Bredemeier, B.J.L. (1995). *Character development and physical activity*. Champaign, IL: Human Kinetics.

Simon, J.A., & Smoll, F.L. (1974). An instrument for assessing children's attitudes toward physical activity. *Research Quarterly*, *45*, 407-415.

Smith, R.E., Smoll, F.L., & Schutz, R.W. (1990). Measurement correlates of sport-specific cognitive and somatic trait anxiety: The Sport Anxiety Scale. *Anxiety Research*, *2*, 263-280.

Smoll, F.L., & Smith, R.E. (1996). Competitive anxiety: Sources, consequences, and intervention strategies. In F.L. Smoll & R.E. Smith (Eds.), *Children and youth in sport: A biopsychosocial perspective* (pp. 359-380). Dubuque, IA: Brown & Benchmark.

Thomas, J.R., Thomas, K.T., & Gallagher, J.D. (1993). Developmental considerations in skill acquisition. In R.N. Singer, M. Murphey, & L.K. Tennant (Eds.), *Handbook of research on sport psychology* (pp. 73-105). New York: Macmillan.

Timiras, P.S. (1972). *Developmental physiology and aging*. New York: Macmillan.

Treasure, D.C., & Roberts, G.C. (1994). Cognitive and affective concomitants of task and ego goal orientations during the middle school years. *Journal of Sport and Exercise Psychology*, *16*, 15-28.

Weiss, M.R., & Bredemeier, B.J. (1983). Developmental sport psychology: A theoretical perspective for studying children in sport. *Journal of Sport Psychology*, *5*, 216-230.

Weiss, M.R., Bredemeier, B.J., & Shewchuk, R.M. (1985). An intrinsic/extrinsic motivation scale for the youth sport setting: A confirmatory factor analysis. *Journal of Sport Psychology*, *7*, 75-91.

Weiss, M.R., Ebbeck, V., & Horn, T.S. (1997). Childeen's self-perceptions and sources of competence information: A cluster analysis. *Journal of Sport and Exercise Psychology, 19,* 52-70.

Weiss, M.R., Weise, D.M., & Klint, K.A. (1989). Head over heels with success: The relationship between self-efficacy and performance in competitive youth gymnastics. *Journal of Sport and Exercise Psychology*, *11*, 444-451.

Whitehead, J.R. (1995). A study of children's physical self-perceptions using an adapted Physical Self-Perception Profile questionnaire. *Pediatric Exercise Science*, *7*, 132-151.

Williams, L., & Gill, D.L. (1995). The role of perceived competence in the motivation of physical activity. *Journal of Sport and Exercise Psychology*, *17*, 363-378.

Chapter 29

MEASUREMENT ISSUES IN CROSS-CULTURAL RESEARCH WITHIN SPORT AND EXERCISE PSYCHOLOGY

Joan L. Duda
Purdue University
and
Carl T. Hayashi
Texas Tech University

The majority of research in sport and exercise psychology has examined a stereotypical mainstream population comprised of white, college-aged, middle-class, and mostly male individuals (Dewar & Horn, 1992; Duda & Allison, 1990; Weiss & Chaumeton, 1992). The use of such exclusive sample characteristics fails to consider individuals of the opposite gender and of other racial, cultural, and socioeconomic groups. As a result, conclusions and recommendations stemming from this research may not be applicable to all individuals and, in fact, may be inappropriate.

Within their report on liberal education, the American Psychological Association (APA) has acknowledged the importance of cross-cultural study to psychology (McGovern, Furumoto, Halpern, Kimble, & McKeachie, 1991). Unfortunately, however, cross-cultural psychology is often viewed as reflecting attempts to replicate North American-based findings in some remote part of the world or, within the United States specifically, equated to research on ethnic minorities (Betancourt & Lopez, 1993). Moreover, in the general field of psychology, a number of writers have pointed to a gap between mainstream investigators and cross-cultural researchers (Betancourt & Lopez, 1993; Clark, 1987; Lee, 1994).

Betancourt and Lopez (1993) suggested "our main concern is that whereas mainstream investigators do not consider culture in their research and theories, cross-cultural researchers who study cultural differences frequently fail to identify the specific aspects of culture and related variables that are thought to influence behavior" (p. 629). In Clark's view (1987), "it is a rare investigator who integrates cross-cultural findings into research hypotheses or who uses a cross- cultural approach as one of many tools in a broad program of research" (p. 461). She goes on to state that this breach between mainstream psychologists and those involved in cross-cultural work is "artificial and unneccessary." From a theoretical standpoint, these two groups of researchers vary in terms of the significance they put on culture as a determinant of human behavior. Mainstream psychologists tend to deem intrapsychic processes or characteristics specific to the individual as more relevant. Cross-cultural researchers "view cultural factors as essential to a psychological understanding of human beings, not as nuisance variables to be controlled or ignored" (Clark, 1987, p. 462). In principle, however, the methodological and measurement-related challenges that cross-cultural psychologists face should be (although sometimes they are not) also confronted by researchers in mainstream psychology. For example, issues of conceptual equivalence (Are two assessments measuring the same construct?) and metric equivalence (Do two inventories that measure the same construct have the same scale properties?) need to be grappled with by both research traditions. It is just a question of degree and what price is paid if such factors are dismissed.

Lee (1994) posits a stronger and harsher position concerning the cause of the schism between mainstream and cross-cultural psychologists and, in particular, the failure for mainstream psychology to consider cultural variation. He feels that this neglect is due to primarily American psychologists' individuocentrism. In Lee's view, such an individual-orientedness means that this collectivity of researchers are concerned more with individual processes than groups, overemphasize controlled experimental studies (with little concern for external validity), tend to be reductionistic, and are often ethnocentric.

What about the field of sport and exercise psychology? Is there a gap within this discipline in terms of cross-cultural research? Although there is still a striking paucity of information, it appears that interest in the examination of individuals from various cultural perspectives appears to be slowly gaining in popularity in *mainstream* sport and exercise psychology. Specifically, researchers are attempting to fill the "void in the field" through the inclusion of subjects from outside the mainstream (Duda & Allison, 1990, p. 14). For example, cross-cultural investigations by Duda and associates (e.g., Duda, 1985, 1986a,b; Duda & Allison, 1982; Gano-Overway & Duda, 1996) and Hayashi and colleague (e.g., Hayashi, 1996; Hayashi & Weiss, 1994) have examined differences in goal perspectives among Anglo-American, African-Americans, Mexican-American, Navajo, Hawaiian, and Japanese athletes. Most critically, this work promotes a relativistic approach (different, but equal) rather than the previously accepted universalistic approach (apparently different, but really the same) that allows researchers to recognize and acknowledge the cultural diversity among individuals.

According to Hughes and colleagues (Hughes, Seidman & Willliams, 1993), "culture intersects various phases of the research process, and therefore influences what and how we ...observe, measure, analyze, and interpret data" (p. 688). In this chapter, we will present evidence concerning the state of research employing cross-cultural analyses in sport and exercise psychology. We will then argue for why comparative studies are paramount to the field's theoretical and empirical growth. The bulk of the chapter will focus on measurement issues facing the cross-cultural investigator (Berry, 1969, 1980; Gauvin & Russell, 1993). In particular, we raise a number of considerations that should be kept in mind when conducting comparative studies in sport and exercise psychology and provide some strategies for overcoming the methodological trials inherent to cross-cultural inquiry. This chapter will not provide a comprehensive review of what has been done to date in terms of cross-cultural study in sport and exercise psychology. Rather, where possible, we will pull from the existent literature to illustrate the points we are making. The goal of this work is to promote more and better cross-cultural measurement within the discipline.

The Void

A number of years ago, Duda and Allison (1990) argued for the methodical consideration of race and ethnicity in sport and exercise psychology research and practice. Acknowledging the attention given to the concepts of race and ethnicity within the fields of sport sociology and the anthropology of play, they were interested in determining the extent to which cross-cul-

tural concerns had been incorporated in the field of sport and exercise psychology. To do so, they examined 36 issues of the *Journal of Sport and Exercise Psychology* between the years of 1979 and 1987. Only empirical ($n = 186$) and theoretical ($n = 13$) articles were analyzed. Their findings indicated that: (a) none of the articles utilized race/ethnicity as an independent variable and focused on these concepts at a conceptual level with respect to the research questions addressed, (b) one article considered race/ethnicity as an independent (albeit categorical) variable in the analyses conducted, (c) in approximately 3% of the articles, race/ethnicity was considered in the description and/or randomization of the subjects although analyses were not conducted nor were results discussed in terms of the subjects' racial/ethnic background, (d) in 96% of the articles, the race/ethnic composition of the sample was not reported, and (e) only one theoretical article mentioned the potential impact of race in regard to the conceptual issues being presented. Duda and Allison (1990) concluded that "not only have (race and ethnicity) not been used as simple descriptors of sampling frames, but there has been no systematic attempt to deal with race and ethnicity as conceptual and meaningful categories of human experience" (p. 117). In explicating these disappointing findings and attempting to encourage more research on the influence of culture, Duda and Allison pointed to the demands associated with cross-cultural work and outlined a number of methodological strategies. They strongly suggested that these challenges presented a barrier that needed to be overcome.

Duda and Kim (1995) updated the Duda and Allison (1990) analysis to determine whether comparative work and cross-cultural analyses had become more prevalent in sport and exercise psychology. Two hundred and seven manuscripts that were published in the *Journal of Sport and Exercise Psychology* between 1988 and mid-1994 were examined in regard to the classification developed in the former work. Additionally, Duda and Kim categorized articles with reference to whether the sample was not North American as well as to whether cross-cultural issues (in terms of the question(s) at hand) were employed to explicate the results. They found a slight increase (from approximately 3 to 10%) in work in which ethnicity/race was utilized as an independent variable and/or criterion for describing and/or randomizing subjects. However, a large number of articles (76%) still did not describe the racial/ethnic breakdown of the subject pool, and no papers considered race/ethnicity at a conceptual level. As was the case in the Duda and Allison (1990) paper, Duda and Kim went on to describe methodological issues and measurement considerations in an attempt to promote subsequent cross-cultural research in the field.

Why Is Cross-Cultural Analysis Important?

Duda and Allison (1990) made a number of arguments for why more research is needed within sport and exercise psychology that incorporates cross-cultural analyses. Citing participation statistics (and especially patterns of minority overrepresentation and underrepresentation in certain sports), they pointed out that sport and exercise involvement is not exclusive to the white mainstream. Pulling from the existent sport sociology and anthropological literatures (e.g., Allison, 1979, 1982), they also argued that considerable evidence exists concerning variation in the styles expressed in and meaning of sport. Duda and Allison (1990) also indicated that, if research on the psychological dimensions of sport and exercise behavior is delimited to the mainstream group only, such studies are running contrary to the very essence of scientific inquiry. They proposed that a lack of comparative investigations in sport and exercise psychology will result in theoretical frameworks that are particularistic or even misleading in their presumed generalizability. Moreover, it was suggested that culture and ethnicity will most likely be important explanatory variables in psychological models of sport/exercise-related cognitions, affect, and behavior. That is, through the inclusion of cross-cultural analyses, they argued that investigators will make important contributions to theory development and the knowledge base in the field.

Duda and Allison (1990) emphasized that cross-cultural study allows us to learn more about the mainstream as well as other cultural groups because "culture is made more visible by cultural shock" (p. 122). In essence, we become more aware of psychological processes, their antecedents, and their consequences by observing variation in these processes.

Further, Duda and Allison (1990) reminded us that the cross-cultural psychology literature clearly demonstrates the marked impact of culture on people's cognitions, values, and emotional responses. The work of Markus and Kitayama (1991, 1994), which contrasts the Eastern and Western cultural perspectives on self-perceptions and achievement motivation, exemplifies this influence. As stated by Taft (1977),

> culture...shapes the individual's way of dealing with his perceptual world and provides such cognitive structures as schemata, concepts, categories, stereotypes, expectations, attributions, subjective probabilities, associations and images. At a more molar level the culture provides rules, systems of logic, collective memories, beliefs, ideologies, connotation networks for understanding social roles, and verbal and non-verbal language systems. (p. 130)

Finally, Duda and Allison (1990) call for more cross-cultural study because research within the helping professions underscores the importance of cross-cultural variation to the perspective on, nature of, and responses to therapeutic and clinical interventions and assistance (Sue & Sue, 1987). This literature has obvious implications for our efforts in applied sport and exercise psychology. According to Westwood and Borgen (1988), "...space, time, roles, and role relationships as they are perceived and constituted in the counseling context may differ vastly from culture to culture. These differences provide fertile ground for misunderstanding and conflict" (p. 120). Clearly, a consideration of cultural diversity should impact how we implement sport psychology interventions and the tools we use to evaluate the effectiveness of these interventions.

Measurement Issues

According to Gauvin and Russell (1993), "cross-cultural measurement issues have not received a great deal of attention in the sport and exercise psychology testing literature" (p. 891-892). These authors were surprised with this state of affairs "given that sport and exercise transcend so many geographical and cultural boundaries, and that is it widely acknowledged that such cultural factors can potentially produce major distortions and inaccuracies in test interpretation" (p. 892). In their chapter on this topic, Gauvin and Russell provide an excellent introduction to several cross-cultural considerations pertinent to test development and usage. In the present chapter, we are not attempting to replicate their effort. Rather, we will briefly highlight their major points and then raise other measurement issues. Our aim is to update and expand the discussion with examples from the recent sport and exercise psychology literature. The present chapter also points to additional strategies that can enhance comparative research.

Within sport and exercise psychology measurement, we want to avoid cultural bias. This occurs when we compare the test scores from different racial/ethnic groups that do not stem from comparable assessments. As pointed out by Hughes et al. (1993), culture impacts "the meanings and interpretations respondents attach to the research setting, constructs and instruments" (p. 689). Cultural bias is also evidenced when the results of such testing lead to an inaccurate appraisal (e.g., quickly assuming that the observed cultural variability is based on some biological difference or "cultural deprivation") or disparate treatment of the groups being examined (Helms, 1992; Sue & Sue, 1987). To combat cultural bias in our work, cross-cultural investigations must incorporate an accurate conceptualization of culture. We must be cognizant that culturally dependent values, norms, and attitudes may impact whether the constructs of interest have the same meaning (or even have meaning at all) across different cultural groups. In addition, cultural sport and exercise psychology researchers must resolve problems related to assessment among individuals who speak different languages. Finally, we must be sensitive to the point that culture differences "can have implications for the way in which the test is administered, the style of questioning, as well as the context in which the questions are framed" (Gauvin & Russell, 1993, p. 896). In sum, cultural bias is attenuated when our methods and measures have cultural equivalence.

Conceptualization of Culture

The first issue that cross-cultural investigation in sport and exercise psychology must address relates to the concept of culture employed (Rohner, 1984). According to Clark (1987), "a distinguishing feature of cross-cultural psychology is the prominence it gives to culture as a causal variable...culture is the independent variable, so it would seem important to define it precisely and to specify the unit of analysis" (p. 461). Although there is "no single definition of culture that is universally accepted by social scientists" (Hughes et al., 1993, p. 688), culture is typically viewed as a social construct equated to "shared attitudes, beliefs, categorizations, expectations, norms, roles, self-determinations, values, and other such elements of subjective culture found among individuals whose interactions are facilitated by shared language, historical period, and geographic region" (Triandis, 1972, p. 3). In his most recent work (e.g., Triandis, 1996), Triandis refers to the elements presumed to underly culture as "cultural syndromes" and suggests that they consist of "shared attitudes, beliefs, norms role and self definitions, and values of members of each culture that are organized around a theme" (p. 407).

This definition of culture has important implications for sport and exercise psychology research and practice. First, when culture is conceptualized in terms of particular psychological dimensions (e.g., such as individualism-collectivism), the construct is then more readily measurable. Second, this conceptualization of culture implies that a particular culture may be comprise individuals from different racial and ethnic backgrounds who possess similar socialization experiences. Helms (1992) echoes this caveat by stating that

> culture ...is not a static entity. Nor is it uniform. Therefore, a person does not either have culture or not have culture. Rather, acculturation, or the learning of culture, is a dynamic process that individuals undoubtedly accomplish at different rates, even within the same ostenible environment. (p. 1091)

Finally, culture as defined, may play a role in a research design as an antecedent or moderating variable, a set of mediating psychological variables, or a collection of response variables (Triandis et al., 1980).

It is important to note that the cultural dimension approach to defining culture is not without its critics. For example, Misra and Gergen (1993) challenge the operationalization of culture in terms of quantifiable dimensions. They ask:

> If cultures are made up of complex webs of interdependence, lodged within mixtures of interwoven traditions, and sustained by dynamic multiplicity of intellegibilities at the psychological level, how much understanding of culture will result if this vast and intricately woven composite is translated into the language of linear dimensions? (p. 230)

Providing an example from research examining cultural variation in achievement motivation between American and Eastern Indian subjects (Agarwal & Misra, 1986), Misra and Gergen (1993) argue that the "researcher (should) be a co-participant in the joint construction of reality" and advocate the use of interpretive modes of knowing (p. 237). In essence, Misra and Gergen question solely quantatitive approaches to measuring culture.

As pointed out by Betancourt and Lopez (1993), "scholars often use the concept of culture interchangeably with race, ethnicity, or nationality which limits our understanding of the specific factors that contribute to group differences, but it also leads to interpretations of findings that stimulate or reinforce racist conceptions of human behavior" (p. 630-631). An ethnic group is a group "characterized in terms of a common nationality, culture, or language" (Betancourt & Lopez, 1993, p. 631). Thus, a shared subjective culture can determine one's ethnic identity, but other determinants are possible as well. Moreover, ethnicity provides a mechanism for sharing elements of the subjective culture. Ethnicity also encompasses race (Phinney, 1996) and refers "to broad groupings of Americans (or other nationalities, for that matter) on the basis of both race and culture of origin" (p. 919). It should be emphasized, however, that even within an ethnic group, there is often great heterogeneity in terms of cultural or racial attributes (Betancourt & Lopez, 1993; Jackson, 1989; Phinney, 1996).

Race is considered a biological characteristic (Thomas,

1986). It would be most questionable if we operationalize cultural variability in terms of racial group membership. Research has indicated that individuals within a racial group vary more, in terms of the characteristics deemed to distinguish the races, than do individuals who are from different racial groups (Betancourt & Lopez, 1993). Helms (1992) cautions us that "knowledge of a person's racial group membership reveals nothing about the amount or type of culture the person has absorbed" (p. 1091).

In his study of variations in achievement motivation among a diverse sample of active males, Hayashi (1996) attempted to tease apart the influence of culture, race, and ethnicity. His findings suggested the presence of cultural, rather than racial or ethnic differences. Specifically, both Hawaiian and Anglo-American male weight lifters who resided in Hawaii (i.e., Hawaiian culture) perceived the environment of their weight room from an interdependent perspective that promoted positive relationships with others through not standing out, showing off, or "acting." Conversely, the perceptions of the weight room climate by Anglo-American males who resided in the mainland United States (i.e., Anglo-American culture) were not found to de-emphasize standing out or showing off. These results were reflective of the shared attitudes and norms found among individuals belonging to the Hawaiian ethnic group and Mongoloid race, and the Anglo-American ethnic group and Caucasoid race who shared a common language and lived in the same geographic location.

In terms of operationalizing ethnic variation in sport and exercise psychology work, we might think of turning toward measures of acculturation (such as language usage, common practices, place of birth). *Acculturation* refers to the degree to which minority groups adhere to traditional versus mainstream cultural practices. However, as pointed out by Betancourt and Lopez (1993), such criteria are only "indirect measures of cultural values and beliefs" (p. 634). Moreover, these indicators may be confounded by the "acculturative stress" often acccompanying attempts to assimilate into a second cultural group.

Besides including assessments of subjects' adherence to particular cultural values and attitudes (or cultural syndromes; Triandis, 1996), Phinney (1996) reminds us to consider as well that "individuals differ in their strength of identification with their ethnic group, that is their *ethnic identity*" (p. 922). A number of dimensions, such as self-labeling, a sense of belonging, positive evaluation, preference for the group, ethnic interest and knowledge, and involvement in activities associated with the group comprise this concept of ethnic identity (Phinney, 1990). The Multigroup Ethnic Identity Measure (MEIM) was developed to assess an individual's sense of belongingness to and identification with a particular ethnic group (Phinney, 1992).

In a study of Anglo- and African-American high school track athletes, Gano-Overway and Duda (1996) examined the effect of race, sex, and ethnic identity differences on goal orientations, beliefs about the causes of success, enjoyment of one's sport, and coping strategies. The athletes' sense of ethnic identity was assessed via the MEIM. Results indicated that 74% of the African-American athletes could be classified as possessing a strong ethnic identity whereas only 38% of the white athletes were classified in this group. This finding is consistent with the work of Deaux (1992) which suggests that ethnic identity is more pronounced when people's presumed ethnic identity is more obvious and they are not part of the majority culture (e.g., because of the color of their skin). Gano-Overway and Duda also observed a mean effect for ethnic identity for each of the dependent variables. Moreover, in a regression analysis in which race, sex, and ethnic identity were entered as independent variables, the latter characteristic emerged overall as the best predictor of the motivational indices of interest in this study.

All of this suggests that we need to do more than just describe our samples in sport and exercise psychology studies in terms of their race, cultural background, and ethnicity. The use of such descriptors makes these rich and complex characteristics sound like discreet categories. These demographic markers assume that boundaries between groups are fixed, and they also gloss over within-group variability. Contemporary thought in cross-cultural psychology, on the other hand, regards culture, race, and ethnic group membership as dynamic, multidimensional, psychological variables that need to be *measured* before we move forward with comparative investigations.

Cultural Equivalence in Measurement

Sue and Sue (1987) indicate that the most frequently employed approach to comparative research is *point research*. This "involves the use of an instrument derived in one culture with members of another culture. In many cases, the scores on the instruments are compared between the different cultures and are interpreted from the norms developed from one culture" (p. 484). Sue and Sue (1987) cogently argue that there are serious limitations resulting when we employ an emic (i.e., culturally specific) assessment tool and use it as though it were etic (i.e., applicable cross-culturally). Unfortunately, even a perusal of the limited cross-cultural work in North American sport and exercise psychology investigations suggests a preponderance of point research (e.g., Guivernau & Duda, 1994; Kang, Gill, Acevedo, & Deeter, 1990; Theodorlakis & Anderson, 1996; Xiang, Lee, & Solmon, in press). In general, it appears we tend to take an established instrument (such as the Leadership Scale for Sports; Chelladurai, Malloy, Imamura, & Yamaguchi, 1987), translate it, and then compare scores across cultural groups on this particular measure.

As pointed out by Helms (1992), there are numerous types of equivalence that lay the bases for culturally comparable measurement across cultural groups: (a) *functional equivalence* or the degree to which assessment scores hold the same meaning and reflect psychological or behavioral characteristics that occur with the same frequency within different cultural groups, (b) *conceptual equivalence* or the degree to which cultural groups are similarly familiar with the test items and interpret them in the same way, (c) *linguistic equivalence* or the degree to which the language used in the assessment reflects an equivalent meaning across translated versions of the instrument at hand, (d) *psychometric equivalence* or the degree to which assessments are tapping the same constructs at the same levels across cultural groups, (e) *testing condition equivalence* or the degree to which the testing procedures and context are similarly familiar and comfortable to the cultural groups, and (f) *sampling equivalence* or the degree to which the "samples representing each racial or ethnic group are comparable at the test development, validation,

and interpretation stages" (p. 1092). When we do not carefully insure these different but related forms of equivalence, sport and exercise psychology researchers and practitioners will likely commit the cultural equivalence fallacy (Helms, 1992).

Functional and conceptual equivalence. In regard to sound measurement, one challenge that cross-cultural researchers in sport and exercise psychology must meet is the acquisition of dimensional identity. Berry (1969, 1980) suggested that dimensional identity exists when a phenomenon was equivalent across cultures; that is, we have conceptual and functional equivalence in terms of the construct at hand. He also warned that the attainment of dimensional identity was essential in order for accurate cross-cultural comparisons to take place in our work.

According to Berry (1969, 1980), the development of dimensional identity creates a contradiction within cross-cultural research. That is, cross-cultural research must reflect both emic and etic approaches in order for dimensional identity to be evidenced. The emic approach is characterized by (a) an interest in one culture, (b) an interest in differences among cultural perspectives, and (c) an insider's perspective of reality. Characteristics of the etic approach include (a) an interest in culture-free aspects of the world, (b) an interest in similarities among cultural perspectives, and (c) an outsider's perspective of reality. The resultant contradiction in cross-cultural research that promotes the identification of unique characteristics of a cultural perspective (emic approach) and the comparison of that culture with other perspectives (etic approach) is termed the *emic-etic problem* (Berry, 1969).

Berry (1980) proposes that the resolution to the emic-etic problem is the imposed etic approach. Specifically, this approach begins with the researcher's entering each cultural perspective with a predetermined expectation of individuals' behavior based on a theoretical or conceptual framework that is flexible to contrary kinds of data variation (imposed etic approach). Next, modifications to the researcher's perception of the phenomenon (i.e., insider's perspective) will occur based on experiences and observations within the culture (emic approach). Subsequently, valid comparisons of the phenomenon among various cultures (etic approach) and the particular cultural perspective (emic approach) are now possible. Finally, valid interpretations of these comparisons can be made by expressing similarities and differences among cultural perspectives.

Clark (1987) provides a nice example of addressing the emic-etic challenge in her work on the cross-cultural generalizability of positive and negative affect mood dimensions observed in research on Americans. She and her colleagues first developed a set of mood adjectives that parallel the American set but also capture the Japanese emotional repertoire. To allow for comparability and address the issue of conceptual equivalence, one half of the terms were identical between the two sets. The other half, which were specific to the Japanese culture, represented the emic component of the investigation. Clark found evidence of the two affective dimensions in both cultural groups. The distribution of scores for both dimensions was similar across the Japanese and U.S. subjects, thus providing evidence for metric equivalence. One difference was found, namely that the adjective "sleepiness" was negatively related to "energy" and "alertness" among the Americans but unrelated in the case of the Japanese. The anthropological literature on Japanese culture and subjects' daily diaries (which were kept in combination with the mood ratings) were consulted to carefully explicate this difference. According to Clark (1987), this study did "illustrate that, with careful attention to both individual and cultural variables and with the use of appropriate procedures for assuring comparability, solid findings with implications for both mainstream and cross-cultural research are possible" (p. 470).

In their work on achievement motivation, Maehr and Nicholls (1980) have proffered an emic/etic approach to understanding cultural variability in achievement goals. Specifically, they proposed that we should identify diverse interpretations of success/failure particular to various cultural groups. It was also suggested, in terms of an etic perspective, that there would most likely be classes of achievement behavior that are universal (such as ability-oriented motivation, task-oriented motivation, and social approval-oriented motivation). In her work on the assessment of achievement goals in the United Kingdom, Whitehead (1992, 1993) employed open-ended and subsequent factor analytic techniques to provide support for the three universal orientations as well as culture-specific perspectives on achievement (see Duda & Whitehead, this volume, for more details).

The fixed-choice response format of measurement instruments, which is quite popular in sport and exercise psychology assessment, may also produce inequivalencies in interpretation among individuals of different cultures. For example, the fixed responses developed from the mainstream cultural perspective may not be representative of the actual response(s) of the cultural group in question and/or vary in their familiarity. In this case, the subjects are forced to limit their responses to the available choices, a restriction that prevents the researcher from obtaining individuals' true interpretation of the constructs at hand.

A possible resolution to this issue is the implementation of methods (e.g., open-ended response format) that enable subjects to respond in their own words and from their perspective. An illustration of this strategy in sport and exercise psychology research would be the employment of the Russell's Causal Dimension Scale (Russell, 1982). Rather than presenting subjects with fixed alternatives in terms of causal attributions, the CDS requests the individual to provide (in an open-ended manner) the most significant reason for his or her performance and then rate this attribution according to the dimensions of controllability, causality, and stability. In their study of the effects of gender, experience and ethnicity on causal dimensions scores (as assessed by the CDS), Morgan, Griffin and Heyward (1996) found differences in dimensional ratings among African-American, Anglo, Hispanic and Native American track athletes. Unfortunately, as described above, the concept of ethnicity employed in this research reflected a categorical approach to cultural group membership. Further, as recommended by Duda and Allison (1989), this cross-cultural investigation did not establish that the three causal dimensions hold an equivalent meaning and psychometric and test condition equivalence across the targeted groups.

Other possible resolutions to the problem of having forced-choice assessment items that are not culturally pertinent are reflected in the work of Kawano and Ewing (1994) and Gano-

Overway and Duda (1996). In the former study, an open-ended instrument was employed to solicit the perceived antecedents and consequences of athletic success and failure among U.S. and Japanese college students. Specifically, utilizing Triandis' (1977) antecedent-consequent method, the students were requested to fill in the blanks to items such as "If you have _____, then you have success/failure in school/sports" and "If you have success/failure in school/sports, then you have _____." The responses provided in the solicitation phase of the research were used to develop a second, fixed-item questionnaire, and then potential gender and cultural differences in definitions of sport achievement were explored among new samples of U.S. and Japanese undergraduates.

With respect to the Gano-Overway and Duda (1996) research, both open-ended responses and a review of the anthropological literature on African-Americans laid the bases for the formation of a scale to assess a new goal perspective, that is, expressive individualism. For both African- and Anglo-American high school track athletes, the nature and motivational significance of this alternative achievement goal were determined by examining its relationship to the established goals of task and ego orientation as well as various motivational indices such as reported enjoyment of and satisfaction in sport.

With the aim of promoting conceptual and functional equivalence, the use of an interview format would allow researchers to follow up on the fixed alternative responses of their subjects and result in the acquisition of detailed and high-quality information. For example, Hayashi (1996) was able to identify and define the slang word "acting" used by members of the Hawaiian culture in their responses via a poststudy interview. Duda (1986a) also used an interview to clarify the fixed-choice responses of her sample of Navajo interscholastic athletes in terms of whether they preferred ability- or effort-based achievement in sport and the classroom. In sum, the adoption of methods that enable the subject to respond from his or her own perspective (before, during, and/or subsequent to the assessment per se) may alleviate some of the difficulties associated with inequivalencies of the responses of individuals from different cultures.

Linguistic equivalence. When the content and grammar of survey items and questions have an equivalent meaning across cultural groups, the instrument has linguistic equivalence. Almost all the measures within North American sport and exercise psychology have been developed based on the values and norms of the mainstream perspective (see Vallerand & Fortier, this volume, for some exceptions involving French Canadians). As a result, inequivalent interpretations of the items of instruments may be produced from differences in (a) language, (b) translation and interpretation of words, c) slang terminology, and (d) socialization experiences. As argued by Helms (1992), "it should be obvious that equivalence cannot exist unless the percepts of a construct are communicated in a language that is equally comprehensible to both groups" (p. 1092).

It is critical to note that the mere translation of an established instrument in North American sport and exercise psychology to a second language (by a bilingual individual) can cause problems. Back translation (which entails one individual's translating a questionnaire from one language to a second language, a second individual's then translating the same instrument from this second language back to the first language, and then a comparison between this re-translated version and the original inventory) certainly is a necessary step to insuring linguistic equivalence (Brislin, 1980). Although quite popular in cross-cultural sport and exercise psychology research (e.g., Chelladurai et al., 1987; Kim, Williams & Gill, 1995; Xiang et al., in press), this procedure may also not be sufficient to eliminate cultural bias. We need to remember that the translation procedure is a process that continues (i.e., translating and independently back translating) until semantic equivalence is achieved. Moreover, it is paramount that the translators involved not only be bilingual but also understand the theoretical underpinning of the concepts being assessed. The translators also need to be well familiar with the "sport lingo" within the cultures in question. As pointed out by Dunnigan, McNall, and Mortimer (1993), a major difficulty that needs to be overcome when establishing linguistic equivalence is the effective translation of figurative expressions. That is, we must be weary of producing a literal translation of items from one language to the next that does not capture the metaphoric meanings attached to the words in question. This issue is especially relevant to slang expressions. For example, Hayashi and Weiss (1994) found the slang English term *mess up* in one item of the Task and Ego Orientation in Sport Questionnaire (see Duda & Whitehead, this volume) to be confusing to their subjects, despite an accurate translation into the Japanese language by the first researcher.

The cross-cultural psychology literature suggests that a team approach (utilizing more than one bilingual person in the translation process) strengthens the search for linguistic equivalence as does the employment of a blind back translation. The latter requires that the individuals doing the back translation not be familiar with the original instrument.

Finally, decentering (Werner & Campbell, 1970) is another approach to questionnaire translation that entails constructing items or interview questions simultaneously in the languages of the targeted cultural groups. These procedure leads to two different but related assessment tools. To our knowledge, the decentering strategy has not been utilized in North American sport and exercise psychology comparative research.

Psychometric equivalence. As pointed out by Helms (1992), "cultural bias is generally examined through psychometric statistical analyses of measures and selection procedures" (p. 1089). For example, typically the same measure is administered to two cultural groups, and then average scores and/or patterns of responses are compared via statistical indicators (e.g., internal reliability analysis, regression lines, factor patterns). If responses to this instrument lead to culturally similar coefficients of internal reliability, equivalent factor patterns (as discerned via exploratory factor analysis or confirmatory factor analysis) or the observed regression lines do not significantly differ between groups (when relating this variable to another variable), then it is assumed that cultural bias has been overcome. Equivalence is also suggested when the associations between the measurement instrument and theoretically related constructs are similar across cultural groups (Hughes et al., 1993).

An examination of the existent cross-cultural research in sport and exercise psychology exemplifies each of these path-

ways to providing evidence concerning psychometric equivalence. Studies have examined the internal reliabilities of mainstream questionnaires (such as the Leadership Scale for Sports, the Intrinsic Motivation Inventory, the Physical Self-Perception Profile, the Sport Orientation Questionnaire, and the Sport Competition Anxiety Test) when employed in different cultural contexts (e.g., Chelladurai, Imamura, Yamaguchi, Oinuma, & Miyauchi, 1988; Kang, Gill, & Acevedo, & Deeter, 1990; Page, Ashford, Fox, & Biddle, 1993). Other research has utilized exploratory factor analysis to test the factorial dimensionality of sport/exercise psychology assessments cross-culturally (e.g., Balaguer, Castillo, & Tomas, 1996; Duda, Fox, Biddle, & Armstrong, 1992; Kim et al., 1995; Shi & Ewing, 1994). Comparative investigations in sport and exercise psychology have also looked toward theoretically consistent associations between translated inventory scores and other variables to suggest psychometric equivalence for the former measures (Duda et al., 1992; Guivernau & Duda, 1995; Kim, 1995; Kim, Gill, & Chang, 1996; Lu & Gill, 1996; Theodorulakis & Anderson, 1996; Xiang et al., in press).

Recently, researchers have considered more stringent statistical treatments when examining the psychometric integrity of sport and exercise psychology measures cross-culturally. In particular, confirmatory factor analytic procedures are being employed to test factorial equivalence and structured latent mean differences in measures among diverse cultural groups. The research of Li and his colleagues (Li, Harmer, Chi, & Vongjaturapat, 1996; Li, Harmer, Acock, Vongjaturapat, & Boonverabut, in press) on the cultural validity of the Task and Ego Orientation in Sport Questionnaire provides an excellent example of this approach.

Surely, such psychometric determinations are a step in the right direction in the development of cross-culturally valid and reliable sport and exercise psychology instruments. However, Helms (1992) warns us that "none of these statistical strategies necessarily demonstrates the presence of cultural equivalence" (p. 1089). In fact, the statistics we typically use to examine the psychometric characteristics of questionnaires assume that the cultural groups in question are independent. Further, we must keep in mind that the significant correlations between measure items or a predictor and criterion variable across cultures may be an artifact of an "overlap on a third unmeasured factor resulting from cross-group exposure" (e.g., exposure to racist attitudes) and not evidence for cross-cultural generalizability (Helms, 1992, p. 1089).

Testing condition equivalence. The cross-cultural investigator in sport and exercise psychology has a variety of methods to draw upon including interview, paper-and-pencil assessments, and observation. When the investigator decides upon a certain way of ascertaining information from certain person(s) on certain topics, it is paramount that he or she understand the appropriateness of the topic and the method within the cultural groups in question. For example, cultural variation in preferences for testing in a group or individual setting and the comfort associated with private versus public assessment can affect the results of a study. Within some cultural groups, asking questions about internal states may be considered intrusive (Gauvin & Russell, 1993). Research has shown that cultural differences in response style also exist. Clark (1987) reinforces these concerns by stating that:

> Tasks or methodological techniques presented to respondents may be unfamiliar or confusing leading to problems of scale equivalence. Some respondents may have difficulty with Likert scales, or forced-choice questions. It cannot be assumed that all respondents will understand different scale formats or that they will result in valid indicators of behavior. (In fact)...for some cultural and ethnic groups, the entire survey and interviewing processing may constitute an uncomfortable and unfamiliar social situation. (p. 466)

Sue and Sue (1987) concur and argue that reported ethnic differences in the psychology literature may be a result of the measure and/or methodology utilized. To support this position, they review research revealing a difference between Asian-Americans and Anglo-Americans when social anxiety and assertiveness are assessed with paper-and-pencil measures but not when these attributes are assessed behaviorally during role-playing situations.

Further, in terms of the potential effect of testing conditions, we need to be concerned with *scale equivalence,* or the degree to which response choices are equatable across cultural groups. For example, research has indicated that certain cultural groups, when compared to the white mainstream, tend to use extreme response categories on Likert-type scales (Bachman & O'Malley, 1984; Hui & Triandis, 1989). It is difficult to discern, however, whether such response styles stem from cultural differences in responding to such stimuli or cultural variability in the ability "to map subjectively held internal states onto the rating categories researchers provide" (Hughes et al., 1993, p. 693). Cultural groups have also been found to vary in their tendency to alter responses based on social desirability concerns and, of course, would most likely differ in what is deemed socially desirable or not (Crittenden, Fugita, Bae, Lamug, & Lin, 1992).

When faced with a research situation or testing condition, perceptions of what is expected or required can be distinguished as a function of culture. Thus, sport and exercise psychology researchers must also keep in mind the need to establish *task equivalence* or the "extent to which respondents' familiarity with, or interpretation of, the assessment situation and task demands are [sic] similar across cultural groups" (Hughes et al., 1993, p. 693).

Sampling equivalence. Clearly, the search for sampling equivalence is difficult to realize unless questionnaire developers in sport and exercise psychology begin describing the cultural, racial, and ethnic (and social class) characteristics of the samples involved (Duda & Allison, 1990; Duda & Kim, 1995). We need to do more, however, than merely characterize the convenience samples employed in psychometric studies. In all stages of test development, such as item generation, validation, and interpretation, the ethnic and racial diversity that exists in the athletic realm should be represented.

Future Directions in Sport and Exercise Psychology Measurement

In this section, strategies (psychometric, analytic, and conceptual) that emanate from the contemporary cross-cultural psychology literature will be briefly reviewed. We recommend that comparative investigators in sport and exercise psychology seriously contemplate the use of one or more of these strategies in their subsequent work.

Helms (1992) and Hughes and associates (1993) provide a number of considerations to assist in the movement toward cultural equivalence in assessment. First, it is suggested that measures for assessing interracial and interethnic group cultural dependence and the subjects' level of acculturation and degree of assimilation be developed relevant to the physical domain. If we are going to define a cultural group with one variable, it is critical that we are sure that this is a most representative and shared characteristic. In contrast, the stronger approach would be "to define the population with a rich nomological network of salient manifest indicators." A second proposal is that we modify the content of existing sport/exercise psychology measures to include items indicative of diversity in cultural content. When modifying current instruments or formulating new measures, the input of "multiple stakeholders" should be solicited. These stakeholders might be individuals who fulfill different roles within the culture(s) of interest as well as researchers representing different disciplines and areas of methodological expertise. It should be kept in mind that a between-group investigation should not be undertaken unless conceptual and measurement equivalence have been established. Third, we should utilize theoretical perspectives to investigate the "environmental" factors influencing the observed validity and reliability of our instruments. If we find that existing measurement tools do not readily generalize, we should generate and then employ separate cultural norms (perhaps based on different measures) in terms of the construct at hand. Finally, combinations of methods and measures appropriate to the research question(s) posed are encouraged.

Theoretically based work: Bottom up or top down. Besides employing culturally valid and reliable measures, sport and exercise psychology researchers need to conduct theoretically grounded comparative investigations. Specifically, we should avoid conducting analyses that primarily involve the categorical comparison of subjects from alternative racial/ethnic groups with the mainstream. Legitimate cross-cultural comparisons are based on theoretical or conceptual frameworks that attempt to explain and predict behavior among individuals from various cultures (e.g., Markus & Kitayama, 1991; Triandis, 1988). To this end, Betancourt and Lopez (1993) recommend:

> As a general approach, ...that both mainstream and cross-cultural investigators identify and measure directly what about the group variables (e.g., what cultural element) of interest to their research influences behavior. Then, hypothesized relationships between such variables and the psychological phenomenon of interest could be examined and such research could be incorporated within a theoretical framework. We believe that an adherence to this approach will serve to enhance our understanding of both group-specific and group-general (universal) processes as well as contribute to the integration of culture in theory development and the practice of psychology. (p. 630)

In a similar vein, Clark (1987) suggests that "conceptual progress in psychology requires a unified base for investigating psychological phenomena with culture-relevant variables included as part of the matrix" (p. 465). Congruent with the "cultural syndrome" perspective (Triandis, 1996), she reminds us that culture is "a complex and multidimensional structure." Leung (1989) also argues that "it is now commonly accepted in cross-cultural psychology the identification of cross-cultural differences alone is not sufficient. A more important goal is to explore the relationship between cultural differences and culture processes...and to render such differences interpretable" (p. 703).

Drawing from the work of Betancourt and Lopez (1993), two approaches are recommended to promote the study of culture within the field of sport and exercise psychology. First, we can adopt a "bottom-up" strategy and commence with a psychological process we observe in our culture and then examine this process cross-culturally in a test of a theory of human behavior. On the other hand, we can take a "top-down" approach and start with a conceptual framework (which most likely does not include the concept of cultural variation at the present time) and then integrate dimensions of culture to widen its theoretical applicability.

The work of Triandis et al. (1986) epitomizes the former approach. Identifying cultural elements via a review of the anthropological literature, they first developed valid and reliable measures of these dimensions (such as their assessment of individualism-collectivism). Then, various cultures were sampled and placed along the dimensional continuum. Finally, across cultures, the predicted relationships between these dimensional attributes and certain behavioral or psychological variables were examined.

This bottom-up approach is consonant with a culturalist perspective. According to Sue and Okazi (1990), a culturalist perspective entails that we specify the cultural dimensions predicted to characterize members of a cultural group, assess these dimensions in a valid and reliable manner, and indicate how the presence or absence of the dimension(s) in question impact the variables of interests across cultural groups.

The top-down approach is exemplified in the work of Betancourt and colleagues (Betancourt, 1985, 1990; Betancourt & Weiner, 1982) in their research grounded in attribution theory. In a first study involving samples of U.S. and Chilean college students, they examined the associations between the three attributional dimensions (i.e., stability, causality, and controllability) and the theoretically predicted psychological consequences. The results supported both cultural generality and cultural specificity. In regard to the former, the predicted relationship between the perceptions of the attribution's stability and subsequent performance expectations emerged for both cultural groups. Indicative of cultural specificity, the controllability dimension was not a strong predictor of affective and interpersonal reactions (e.g., liking the person) for the Chilean students as is theoretically hypothesized and was observed for the U.S. students. Betancourt and Weiner pulled from the tenets and concepts of attribution theory in an attempt to explicate these findings. Realizing that this strategy alone was not sufficient, Betancourt (1985) examined the cross-cultural psychology and anthropological literatures to identify potential cultural

dimensions that might explain cultural distinctions in attributional processes. He identified what is termed the "control over versus subjugation to nature" value orientation, developed an assessment of this orientation, and then determined the impact of the orientation on the relationship between the controllability dimension and helping behavior. This series of studies "progresses from mainstream social psychological research and theory to the study of cultural variables relevant to the theory and search for universals" (Betancourt & Lopez, 1993, p. 634).

Between/within-group quantitative and qualitative analyses. In our hope to conduct "culturally anchored research" in sport and exercise psychology, there might be mixed feelings about which research design is most beneficial; that is, between cultural group designs or studies within a particular cultural group. We agree with Hughes and colleagues (1993), who suggest that both approaches can contribute much to knowledge about social psychological processes as long as there is compatibility between the research question(s) posed and the design selected. Within-group designs are recommended if the phenomenon of interest appears to be emic or culturally specific, it is not possible to establish conceptual equivalence, and/or the challenges related to measurement equivalence cannot be overcome.

In general, the cross-cultural psychology literature calls for a combination of quantitative and qualitative methods (Hughes et al., 1993; Maton, 1993). According to Maton, qualitative or ethnographic methods allow "constructs and theory to be grounded in members' subcultural experience, and facilitates an in-depth understanding of context...(whereas quantitative approaches) allow systematic comparisons across subcultures or among individuals within a subculture." Employing both methods "constitutes a valuable bridge between the culture of the researcher and that of the subcultural population under study, a bridge whose cultural and scientific viability should be greater than the viability of its constituent parts" (Maton, 1993, p. 750).

Hines (1993) also argues for linking qualitative and quantitative methods in cross-cultural research but reminds us of the cost and time involved with the former. As another alternative, she suggests that we pull from strategies derived from cognitive science. Specifically, Hines proposes that techniques such as free listings, frames pile sorts, and rank-order tests can be utilized to tap "the underlying rules and categories of different cultural groups" (p. 737). Another cognitive technique that is recommended is protocol analysis. In this case, subjects are requested to "think aloud" as they do a task or respond to a questionnaire. Hines and Snowden (1993) indicate how this latter technique can provide valuable information in terms of how different cultural groups interpret questions and formulate their responses. With this insight, comparative researchers can construct items and scales that are less culturally biased.

With a focus on clinical and counseling-related assessment, Jones and Avril (1987) emphasize the significance of post-assessment narratives to quantitative assessments. These narrative accounts help to reconceptualize the data by providing access to subjects' impressions about what they believed the instrument was attempting to assess, what the items or questions meant to them, and what meaning the test-taking situation held for them; in short, what motives, expectations, and understandings they brought to the assessment situation (p. 493). Jones and Avril (1987) suggest that this narrative method can also provide evidence concerning the cross-validation of results; that is, when a second group of individuals from a particular culture who are different from the initial collection of subjects who completed the assessments are asked to interpret the measures and findings.

Individual vs. cultural level of analyses. Leung (1989) argues for the incorporation of both individual-level and culture-level analyses in comparative research. In terms of the former, cultural differences (within each culture to be sampled) are equated to individual differences. For example, we might have the case that Culture A is higher than Culture B in some construct X (e.g., competitive stress). It is assumed that this difference is due to the fact that Culture A is higher than Culture B in terms of another construct, Y (e.g., fear of failure) and that X and Y are associated within each culture. However, as pointed out by Helms (1992), this approach does not negate the possibility that a form of bias or other extraneous variable (Z) caused the culture differences in variables X and Y.

With respect to culture-level analyses, culture is the unit of analysis, and it is not assumed that culture- and individual-level relationships necessarily exist. This approach entails the comparison of mean scores on measures across cultures and may lead to empirically derived etics. In this case, cultural variability in variable Y is related to cultural differences in variable X across cultural groups. However, it is not expected that X and Y are associated within a particular cultural group. In fact, Leung (1989) proposes that the association between two variables may indeed change when this relationship is examined in the aggregate form. This is not a limitation but a challenge. It is up to the investigators to delineate what other variables might produce the difference in results from the two levels of analysis. If we observe a significant relationship at the culture level, pertinent dimensions of cultures should be examined as the probable perpetrators of this effect. It is suggested that culture-level analyses may push us toward a consideration of more sociological (or structural) explanatory variables rather than an overreliance on psychological factors.

Leung (1989) argues that there would be a lower probability of bias in a culture-level in contrast to individual-level analysis, but a combination of both approaches would be most fruitful. To date, comparative research in mainstream psychology has primarily adopted the individual-level perspective. One practical reason for this is that a large sample of cultures (approximately 30) is neccessary for a culture-level analysis to have validity and value.

To counter this sample size problem, Leung and Bond (1989) have proposed an "individual level multi-cultural factor analysis" procedure that can lead to etic dimensions at the individual level and attenuate variation due to response styles. This method entails that all scores on a questionnaire be standardized, first within subject and then across items. A factor analysis is then conducted on these doubly standardized scores, and it is suggested that the factors that emerge are independent of culture. These dimensions are assumed to be strong etics if they also are revealed in "pancultural" or "cross-cultural" factor analyses. If not, they are considered weak etics. Triandis et al. (1993) explains this factor analytic method as follows: "Sup-

pose one has 100 responses, to 20 attitude items, from 10 cultures. A "pancultural" factor analysis of the 20 items is based on the 20 by 20 matrix of correlations, based on 1,000 observations per variable" (p. 369). In contrast, we can conduct intracultural analyses. Pulling from the illustration above, this analysis would be based "on the 20 by 20 matrix, based on 100 observations per variable, (but) there would be 10 such analyses, because they are 10 cultures" (Triandis et al., 1993, p. 369). Dimensions that evolve from intracultural factor analysis that were not found in the Leung and Bond (1989) procedure are deemed to be emic or within-culture factors.

In a comparative study of individualism and collectivism, Triandis and his colleagues (1993) analyzed the responses of 1,614 subjects from 10 cultures utilizing the Leung-Bond method as well as via pancultural and intracultural factor analyses. Their results revealed both strong and weak etics. Moreover, enlightening culture-specific (emic) information about the cultural groups sampled emerged via the latter treatment of the data. It is suggested that the inclusion of these varied methods "allows a richer understanding of the meaning of the constructs" of interest (Triandis et al., 1993, p. 381).

Social learning analysis. Zane, Sue, Hu, and Kwon (1991) champion a social learning analysis of cultural influence. The premise here is that such an analysis may assist in the systematic identification of particular contextual and individual difference variables that account for cultural variability in assessments of behavior. They were interested in explicating observed differences in assertiveness between Asian- and Anglo Americans. By examining the link between social learning processes (e.g., past experience, outcome expectations, self-efficacy) and assertive behaviors, one purpose of this research was to test the cross-cultural vericity of social learning theory. Further, these investigators examined whether reported assertiveness among the two cultural groups in question would vary across a number of diverse situations. First, a survey method, interview, and observation were employed to identify a multitude of situations that may require assertiveness in the life of Asian- and Anglo American undergraduate students. Twenty-two situations were retained and then used in a following response enumeration phase. In this stage of the research, the students were asked to provide a large list of responses that are likely to emerge in each of the 22 situations. A team of experts then evaluated these responses in terms of whether or not they reflected effective psychosocial functioning. As a result of this phase, 9 situations were identified for the final version of the assertiveness questionnaire. The Asian- and Anglo American students who served as subjects in this study then: (a) rated the degree to which they have been in a situation similar to the one described, (b) indicated their most likely response from the list of responses provided, (c) provided a rating of self-efficacy in regard to their certainty to perform each of the listed responses, and (d) indicated the likely outcome for each of the behavioral options. Results indicated that the predictors of assertive behavior were comparable across the two cultural groups (i.e., self efficacy and outcome expectancies emerged as the strongest predictors for both the Asian- and Anglo American students). In the opinion of Zane and his colleagues (1991), their findings suggested that "the cultural differences in asssertiveness are not a matter of different social learning processes that underlie assertiveness. Rather, ethnic differences in assertion are situational" (p. 68).

Linear, multimethod and parallel strategies. In Sue and Sue's (1987) opinion, the popular point research approach to cross-cultural inquiry is severely limited. They describe three other alternatives, namely linear and multimethod models and parallel research, to comparative study. A linear research model involves conducting a series of investigations to test hypotheses that evolve from the construct or process of interest. As is the case in point research, the measures are developed in one culture and then employed across the comparative cultural groups. It is the search for the reproducability of findings stemming from these instruments, however, that makes the linear approach superior to point research.

The multimethod model requires the employment of more than one assessment tool, such as paper-and-pencil questionnaires and observation. If one is assessing possible cultural variability and there is consistency across methods and the differences/similarities assessed are congruent with theory, then the researcher can have greater confidence in his or her findings.

In contrast, the focus of parallel research is "to develop a means of conceptualizing the behavioral phenomena from both cultures in question" (Sue & Sue, 1987, p. 485). In essence, this model entails employing linear approaches that are specific to each cultural group. Both emic and etic strategies are employed as the construct or process targeted is assumed to be etic, but the assessment(s) are devised and validated in an emic fashion.

Concluding Comments

In conclusion, there are a number of key conceptual and measurement issues that are inherent to cross-cultural research and applied work. Sport psychology researchers must be able to grasp the true concept of culture and its dimensions as well as obtain an equivalent interpretation of the responses of their subjects in order for accurate and relevant conclusions to emerge. Most critically, they must establish whether the constructs they are assessing have the same conceptual meaning and psychometric features across cultural groups. Approaches to sport or exercise-specific measure development and usage that consider both emic and etic levels of analyses and quantitative and qualitative methods would be helpful in this regard. We need to avoid an imposed etic in which "a culture-specific schema (is) erroneously presumed to be universal" (Jones & Thorne, 1987, p. 489). In short, sport and exercise psychologists should develop and employ measures and methods which are relevant to the physical domain and "culturally sensitive, ecologically grounded, and empirically sophisticated" (Maton, 1993, p. 751).

To paraphrase the thoughts of Boneau with particular reference to our field (1992), we need to keep working toward the big picture that is "a science of humanity, a discipline concerned with understanding and explaining the human individual coping in a social-cultural-environmental context" within the physical domain (p. 1596). In terms of applied work, we are bound by both ethical and social responsibility considerations to ensure that our instruments and interventions are sensitive to cultural differences. The celebration and promotion of cultural diversity can occur only when researchers and consultants focus on the inclusion of subjects from outside the mainstream and conduct their work with an openness and flexibility to variation. The theory and practice of sport and exercise psychology will be strengthened because of this.

References

Agarwal, R., & Misra, G. (1986). A factor analytic study of achievement goals and means: An Indian view. *International Journal of Psychology*, *21*, 717-731.

Allison, M.T. (1979). On the ethnicity of ethnic minorities in sport. *International Review for Sociology Sport*, *14*, 89-96.

Allison, M.T. (1982). Sport, ethnicity, and assimilation. *Quest*, *34*, 165-175.

Bachman, J.G., & O'Malley, P.M. (1984). Yes-saying, nay-saying, and going to extremes: Black-white differences in response styles. *Public Opinion Quarterly*, *48*, 491-509.

Balaguer, I., Castillo, I., & Tomas, I. (1996). Analisis de las Questionario de Orientacion al Ego y a la Tarea en el Deported (TEOSQ) en su traduccion al castellano. *Psicologica*, *17*, 71-81.

Berry, J. W. (1969). On cross-cultural comparability. *International Journal of Psychology, 4*, 119-128.

Berry, J. W. (1980). Introduction to methodology. In H. C. Triandis & J. W. Berry (Eds.), *Handbook of cross-cultural psychology, Vol. 2* (pp. 1-28). Boston, MA: Allyn and Bacon.

Betancourt, H. (1990). An attribution-empathy model of helping behavior: Behavioral intentions and judgments of help-giving. *Personality and Social Psychology Bulletin*, *16*, 573- 591.

Betancourt, H., & Lopez, S. (1993). The study of culture, ethnicity, and race in American psychology. *American Psychologist*, *48*, 629-637.

Betancourt, H., & Weiner, B. (1982). Attributions for achievement-related events expectancy, and sentiments: A study of success and failure in Chile and the United States. *Journal of Cross-Cultural Psychology*, *13*, 362-374.

Boneau, C.A. (1992). Observations on psychology's past and future. *American Psychologist*, *47*, 1586-1696.

Brislin, R.W. (1980). Translation and content analysis of oral and written material. In H.C. Triandis & J.W. Berry (Eds.), *Handbook of cross-cultural psychology: Vol. 2. Methodology* (pp. 389-444). Boston: Allyn & Bacon.

Chelladurai, P., Imamura, H., Yamaguchi, Y., Oinuma, Y., & Miyauchi, T. (1988). Sport leadership in a cross-national setting: The case of Japanese and Canadian university athletes. *Journal of Sport and Exercise Psychology*, *10*, 374-389.

Chelladurai, P., Malloy, D., Imamura, H., & Yamaguchi, Y. (1987). A cross-cultural study of preferred leadership in sports. *Canadian Journal of Sport Sciences*, *12*, 106-110.

Clark, L.A. (1987). Mutual relevance of mainstream and cross-cultural psychology. *Journal of Consulting and Clinical Psychology*, *55*, 461-470.

Crittenden, K.S., Fugita, S.S., Bae, H., Lamug, C.B., & Lin, C. (1992). A cross-cultural study of self-report depressive symptoms among college students. *Journal of Cross-cultural Psychology*, *23*, 163-178.

Deaux, K. (1992). Personalizing identity and socializing self. In G. Breakwell (Ed.), *Social psychology of identity and the self concept* (pp. 9-33). San Diego, CA: Academic Press.

Dewar, A., & Horn, T. S. (1992). A critical analysis of knowledge construction in sport psychology. In T. S. Horn (Ed.), *Advances in sport psychology* (pp. 13-22). Champaign, IL: Human Kinetics.

Duda, J. L. (1985). Goals and achievement orientations of Anglo and Mexican-American adolescents in sport and the classroom. *International Journal of Intercultural Relations, 9*, 131-155.

Duda, J.L. (1986a). A cross-cultural analysis of achievement motivation in sport and the classroom. In L. VanderVelden & J. Humphrey (Eds.), *Current selected research in the psychology and sociology of sport* (pp. 115-132). New York: AMS Press.

Duda, J.L. (1986b). Perceptions of sport success and failure among white, black and Hispanic adolescents. In J. Watkins, T. Reilly, & L. Burwitz (Eds.), *Sport science* (pp. 214-222). London: E & F.N. Spon.

Duda, J. L., & Allison, M. T. (1982). The nature of sociocultural influences on achievement motivation: The case of the Navajo Indian. In J. W. Loy (Ed.), *Paradoxes of play* (pp. 188-197). New York: Leisure Press.

Duda, J.L., & Allison, M.T. (1989). The attributional theory of achievement motivation: Cross-cultural considerations. *International Journal of Intercultural Relations, 13*, 273-286.

Duda, J. L., & Allison, M. T. (1990). Cross-cultural analysis in exercise and sport psychology: A void in the field. *Journal of Sport and Exercise Psychology, 12*, 114-131.

Duda, J.L., Fox, K.R., Biddle, S.J.H., & Armstrong, N. (1992). Children's achievement goals and beliefs abut success in sport. *British Journal of Educational Psychology, 62*, 313-323.

Duda, J.L., & Kim, M. (1995). Cross-cultural analysis in North American exercise and sport psychology: The void continues. In the *Proceedings of the International Sports Science Congress.* Seoul, Korea: KAHPERD.

Dunnigan, T., McNall, M., & Mortimer, J.T. (1993). The problem of metaphorical nonequivalence in cross-cultural survey research. *Journal of Cross-Cultural Psychology, 24*, 344-365.

Gano-Overway, L., & Duda, J.L. (1996). Goal perspectives and their relationship to beliefs and affective responses among African and Anglo American athletes. *Journal of Applied Sport Psychology, 8* (Suppl.), S138.

Gauvin, L., & Russell, S. J. (1993). Sport-specific and culturally adapted measures in sport and exercise psychology research: Issues and strategies. In R. N. Singer, M. Murphey, & L. K. Tennant (Eds.), *Handbook of research on sport psychology* (pp. 891-900). New York: MacMillan.

Guivernau, M., & Duda, J.L. (1995). Psychometric properties of a Spanish version of the Task and Ego Orientation in Sport Questionnaire (TEOSQ) and Beliefs About the Causes of Success Inventory. *Revista de Psicologia del Deporte, 5*, 31-51.

Hayashi, C. T. (1996). Achievement motivation among Anglo-American and Hawaiian male physical activity participants: Individual differences and social contextual factors. *Journal of Sport and Exercise Psychology, 18*, 194-215.

Hayashi, C. T., & Weiss, M. R. (1994). A cross-cultural analysis of achievement motivation among Anglo-American and Japanese marathon runners. *International Journal of Sport Psychology, 25*, 187-202.

Helms, J.E. (1992). Why is there no study of cultural equivalence in standardized cognitive ability testing? *American Psychologist, 47*, 1083-1101.

Hines, A.M. (1993). Linking qualitative and quantitative methods in cross-cultural survey research: Techniques from cognitive science. *American Journal of Community Psychology, 21*, 729-746.

Hines, A.M., & Snowden, L.R. (1993). Survey and interviewing procedures: Cross-cultural validity and the use of protocol analysis. In J.E. Trimble, C.S. Bolek, & S. Niemcryk (Eds.), *Conducting cross-cultural substance abuse research: Emerging strategies and methods* (pp. 25-45). Newbury Park, CA: Sage.

Hughes, D., Seidman, E., & Williams, N. (1993). Cultural phenomena and the research enterprise: Toward a culturally anchored methodology. *American Journal of Community Psychology, 21*, 687-703.

Hui, C.H., & Triandis, H.C. (1989). Effects of culture and response format on extreme response style. *Journal of Cross-Cultural Psychology, 20*, 296-309.

Jackson, J. (1989). Race, ethnicity, and psychological theory and research. *Journal of Gerontology: Psychological Sciences, 44*, 1-2.

Jones, E. E. & Thorne, A. (1987). Rediscovery of the subject: Intercultural approaches to clinical assessment. *Journal of Consulting and Clinical Psychology, 55*, 488-495.

Kang, B., Gill, D.L., Acevedo, E.O., & Deeter, T.E. (1990). Competitive orientations of athletes and nonathletes in Taiwan. *International Journal of Sport Psychology, 21*, 146-157.

Kawano, R., & Ewing, M.E. (1994, September). *A cross-cultural view of Japanese and American students' definition of achievement in sport.* Paper presented at the meetings of the Association for the Advancement of Applied Sport Psychology, Lake Tahoe, NV.

Kim, B.J. (1995). Psychometric evaluation of the TEOSQ and the IMI in a Korean sport setting. *Journal of Sport and Exercise Psychology, 17* (Suppl.), S66.

Kim, B.J., Gill, D.L., & Chang, Y.I. (1996). *Goal orientation and reasons for participation in sports among Korean middle school athletes.* Paper presented at the meetings of the American Alliance for Health, Physical Education, Recreation and Dance, Atlanta, GA.

Kim, B.J., Williams, L., & Gill, D.L. (1995). *A cross-cultural study of achievement orientation and intrinsic motivation in young American and Korean athletes.* Manuscript submitted for publication.

Lee, Y-T. (1994). Why does American psychology have cultural limitations? *American Psychologist, 49*, 524.

Leung, K. (1989). Cross-cultural differences: Individual-level versus culture-level analysis. *International Journal of Psychology, 24*, 703-719.

Leung, K., & Bond, M.H. (1989). On the empirical identification of dimensions for cross-cultural comparison. *Journal of Cross-Cultural Psychology, 20*, 133-151.

Li, F., Harmer, P., Acock, A.C., Vongjaturapat, N., & Boonverabut, S. (in press). Testing the cross-cultural validity of the TEOSQ and its factor covariance and mean structure across gender. *International Journal of Sport Psychology.*

Li, F., Harmer, P., Chi, L., & Vongjaturapat, N. (1996). Cross-cultural validation of the Task and Ego Orientation in Sport Questionnaire. *Journal of Sport and Exercise Psychology, 18*, 392-407.

Lu, F.J-H, & Gill, D.L. (1996). *The participation motivation of Taiwanese athletes in sport.* Paper presented at the meetings of the American Alliance for Health, Physical Education, Recreation and Dance, Atlanta, GA.

Maehr, M.L., & Nicholls, J.G. (1980). Culture and achievement motivation: A second look. In N. Warren (Ed.), *Studies in cross-cultural psychology* (pp. 341-363). New York: Academic Press.

Markus, H. R., & Kitayama, S. (1991). Culture and the self: Implications for cognition, emotion, and motivation. *Psychological Review, 98*, 224-253.

Markus, H.R., & Kitayama, S. (1994). A collective fear of the collective: Implications for selves and theories of selves. *Personality and Social Psychology Bulletin, 20*, 568-579.

Maton, K.I. (1993). A bridge between cultures: Linked ethnographic-empirical methodology for culture anchored research. *American Journal of Community Psychology, 21*, 747-773.

McGovern, T.V., Furumoto, L., Halpern, D.F., Kimble, G.A., & McKeachie, W.J. (1991). Liberal education, study in depth, and the arts and sciences major - Psychology. *American Psychologist, 46*, 598-605.

Misra, G., & Gergen, K.J. (1993). On the place of culture in psychological science. *International Journal of Psychology, 28*, 225-243.

Morgan, L.K., Griffin, J., & Heyward, V.H. (1996). Ethnicity, gender, and experience effects on attributional dimensions. *The Sport Psychologist, 10*, 4-16.

Page, A., Ashford, B., Fox, K., & Biddle, S. (1993). Evidence of cross-cultural validity for the Physical Self-Perception Profile. *Person-*

ality and Individual Differences, 14, 585-590.

Phinney, J.S. (1990). Ethnic identity in adolescents and adults: A review of research. *Psychological Bulletin, 108*, 499-514.

Phinney, J.S. (1992). The Multigroup Ethnic Identity Measure: A new scale for use with diverse groups. *Journal of Adolescent Research, 7*, 156-176.

Phinney, J.S. (1996). When we talk about American ethnic groups, what do we mean? *American Psychologist, 51*, 918-927.

Rohner, R.P. (1984). Toward a conception of culture for cross-cultural psychology. *Journal of Cross-Cultural Psychology, 15*, 111-138.

Russell, D. (1982). The Causal Dimension Scale: A measure of how individuals perceive causes. *Journal of Personality and Social Psychology, 42*, 1137-1145.

Shi, J., & Ewing, M.E. (1994). A cross-cultural study of participation motivation in table tennis. *Journal of Sport and Exercise Psychology, 16* (Suppl.), S105.

Sue, S., & Okazi, S. (1990). Asian-American educational achievements: A phenomenon in search of an explanation. *American Psychologist, 45*, 913-920.

Sue, D., & Sue, S. (1987). Cultural factors in the clinical assessment of Asian Americans. *Journal of Consulting and Clinical Psychology, 55*, 479-489.

Taft, R. (1977). Coping with unfamiliar cultures. In N. Warren (Ed.), *Studies in cross-cultural psychology* (pp. 121-154). New York: Academic Press.

Theodorulakis, N.V., & Anderson, D.F. (1996, April). *Sport leadership in a cross-cultural context: Examination of Greek and American basketball camp participants.* Paper presented at the meetings of the American Alliance for Health, Physical Education, Recreation and Dance, Atlanta, GA.

Thomas, D.R. (1986). Culture and ethnicity: Maintaining the distinction. *Australian Journal of Psychology, 38*, 371-380.

Triandis, H. C. (1972). *The analysis of subjective culture.* New York: Wiley.

Triandis, H. C. (1988). Collectivism v. individualism: A reconceptualisation of a basic concept in cross-cultural social psychology. In G. K. Verma & C. Bagley (Eds.), *Cross-cultural studies of personality, attitudes, and cognition* (pp. 60-95). London: MacMillan.

Triandis, H.C. (1996). The psychological measurement of cultural syndromes. *American Psychologist, 51*, 407-415.

Triandis, H.C., Bontempo, R., Betancourt, H., Bond, M., Leung, K., Brenes, A., Georgas, J., Hui, C., Marin, G., Setiadi, B., Sinha, J.B.P., Verma, J., Spangenberg, J., Touzard, H., & de Montmollin, G. (1986). The measurement of the etic aspects of individualism and collectivism across cultures. *Australian Journal of Psychology, 38*, 257-267.

Triandis, H.C., Lambert, W., Berry, J., Lonner, W., Heron, A., Brislin, R., & Braguns, J. (Eds.). (1980). *Handbook of cross-cultural psychology: Vols 1-6.* Boston: Allyn & Bacon.

Triandis, H.C., McCusker, C., Betancourt, H., Iwao, S., Leung, K., Salazar, J.M., Setiadi, B., Sinha, J.B.P., Touzard, H., & Zaleski, Z. (1993). An etic-emic analysis of individualism and collectivism. *Journal of Cross-Cultural Psychology, 24*, 366-383.

Weiss, M. R., & Chaumeton, N. (1992). Motivational orientations in sport. In T. S. Horn (Ed.), *Advances in sport psychology* (pp. 61-100). Champaign, IL: Human Kinetics.

Werner, O., & Campbell, D.T. (1970). Translating, working through interpreters, and the problem of de-centering. In R. Naroll & R. Cohen (Eds.), *A handbook of method in cultural anthropology* (pp. 398-420). New York: American Museum of Natural History.

Westwood, M.J., & Borgen, W.A. (1988). A culturally embedded model for effective intercultural communication. *International Journal for the Advancement of Counseling, 11*, 115-125.

Whitehead, J. (1992). Toward the assessment of multiple goal perspectives in children's sports. *Abstracts of the Olympic Scientific Congress, Malaga, Spain, Abstracts Vol. 2*, PSY14.

Whitehead, J. (1993). Multiple goal perspectives and persistence in children's sport. *Psychological foundations and effects, Volume 1: Motivation, emotion and stress (pp. 51-56). Proceeding of the VIII European Congress on Sport Psychology*, Cologne, Germany.

Xiang, P., Lee, A., & Solmon, M. (in press). Achievement goals and their correlates among American and Chinese students in physical education: A cross-cultural analysis. *Journal of Cross-Cultural Psychology.*

Zane, N.W.S., Sue, S., Hu, L., & Kwon, J-H. (1991). Asian-American assertion: A social learning analysis of cultural differences. *Journal of Counseling Psychology, 38*, 63-70.

Author Index

C

H

I

J

L

SUBJECT INDEX